ORGANIZATION DEVELOPMENT

Theory, Practice, and Research

ORGANIZATION DEVELOPMENT

Theory, Practice, and Research

Edited by

Wendell L. French
Graduate School of Business Administration
University of Washington

Cecil H. Bell, Jr.
Graduate School of Business Administration
University of Washington

Robert A. Zawacki
Graduate School of Business Administration
University of Colorado,
Colorado Springs

1989   Third edition

BPI
IRWIN

Homewood, Illinois 60430

Sponsoring editor: William R. Bayer
Project editor: Ethel Shiell
Production manager: Carma W. Fazio
Cover Design: Image House Inc.
Compositor: Carlisle Communications, Ltd.
Typeface: 10/12 Times Roman
Printer: Malloy Lithographing, Inc.

LIBRARY OF CONGRESS
Library of Congress Cataloging-in-Publication Data

Organization development : theory, practice, and research / edited by
    Wendell L. French, Cecil H. Bell, Jr., Robert A. Zawacki.—3rd ed.
        p. cm.
    Includes bibliographies.
    ISBN 0-256-06077-0 (pbk.)
    1. Organizational change.   I. French, Wendell L., 1923–
II. Bell, Cecil, 1935–   III. Zawacki, Robert A., 1937–
                    HD58.8.O724 1989
                    658.4'06 —dc19   88–17785
                                    CIP

Printed in the United States of America

2 3 4 5 6 7 8 9 0 ML 5 4 3 2 1 0 9

From Wendell to Marjorie,
From Cecil to Dianne,
From Bob to three people who taught me the meaning of change:
Ray Bartley, Gordon Haffeman, and Joe Sestak

Preface

The field of organization development continues to gain followers and develop new technologies. It has been applied in a wide range of settings and has become a preferred strategy for facilitating change in organizations. What began as isolated experiments for improving organizational dynamics and managerial practices in the 1950s has now become a coherent discipline of applied behavioral science practices to promote increased individual and organizational effectiveness. Organization development (or OD as it is called) provides a generally correct view of how people *and* organizations and people *in* organizations function, and what is required to make them function better.

Organization development offers a prescription for improving the goodness of fit between an individual and the organization and between the organization and its environment. Ingredients of that prescription include a focus on the culture and processes of the organization; guidelines for designing and implementing action programs; conceptualizing the organization and its environment in system theory terms; and creating change processes that empower individuals through involvement, participation, and commitment.

OD is the applied domain of organizational psychology and sociology. It is the engineering side of the organizational sciences. Planned change involves common sense; hard work applied diligently over time; a systematic, goal-oriented approach; and valid knowledge about organizational dynamics and how to change them. The valid knowledge comes from basic and applied behavioral science. The total prescription comes from almost four decades of practice in discovering what works in organizations and why.

We think it is important to know how to help individuals and organizations function better in today's increasingly fettered world. But a good road map is needed to get one to the destination of improved effectiveness. We have assembled this book of readings on theory, practice, and research in organization development to serve as a road map for you.

We wish to acknowledge our debt to the authors whose writings we have included. In addition, we wish to thank Paul R. Hansen, Dean James T. Rothe, Barbara Finnegan, Kathy A. Abeyta, Kathy Claybaugh, Frank Prochaska, Les Gaskins, Robert W. Nordeman, and Jimmie L. Zawacki.

Wendell L. French
Cecil H. Bell, Jr.
Robert A. Zawacki

Contents

ORGANIZATION DEVELOPMENT

Theory, Practice, and Research

Introduction

Organization development (OD) is a powerful set of concepts and techniques for improving organizational effectiveness and individual well being that had its genesis in the behavioral sciences and was tested in the laboratory of real-world organizations. OD addresses the opportunities and problems involved in managing human dynamics in organizations. It offers solutions that have been shown to work. Organization development consists of intervention techniques, theories, principles, and values that show how to take charge of planned change efforts and achieve success.

Understanding what OD is and how it is practiced is important for several reasons. First, it works. Organization development programs can improve individual performance, create better morale, and increase organizational profitability. Many chronic problems of organizations can be cured by OD techniques.

Second, the use of organization development is growing. The approach and methods of OD are applied throughout the gamut of today's organizations and industries. Manufacturing and service companies, high-technology and low-technology organizations, and public- and private-sector institutions all have sponsored successful OD programs.

Third, it is now recognized that the most important assets of organizations are human assets—the men and women who produce the goods and make the decisions. Finding ways to protect, enhance, and mobilize human assets doesn't just make good human-relations sense, it makes good economic sense. OD offers a variety of methods to strengthen the human side of organizations to the benefit of both the individual and the organization.

Fourth, OD is becoming a critical managerial tool. We believe that the concepts and techniques of organization development will soon be as much a part of the well-trained manager's repertoire as knowledge of accounting, marketing, and finance. We predict that a significant period of transition lies just ahead in which the charter and boundaries of organization development will be expanded; specifically, the practice of OD will be incorporated within the art and science of management. Organization development offers a set of generic tools available to any managers and members of organizations who want to improve goal achievement. Today's managers manage change, and OD is a prescription for managing change. Managers need to know what OD is and how to use it. A good understanding of organization development has great practical value for present and future managers.

1

This collection of readings tells the story of OD's theory, practice, and research foundations. Articles by prominent authors in the field present a comprehensive portrait that we hope will be useful to managers, students of oranizational dynamics, and professionals in the fields of human resource management and organization development.

The field of organization development is fun and exciting. We hope this anthology will convey some of that sense of excitement.

AN OVERVIEW OF THE BOOK

This third edition is substantially different from its predecessors. The first edition contained 53 articles. The second edition contained 70 articles, including 44 new ones. The present edition contains 66 articles with 24 new ones. The field of organization development is evolving and this anthology evolves with it.

Part 1, "Mapping The Territory," lays the foundation by examining history, definitions, and descriptions of OD from several perspectives. This section gives an overview of the domain of interest and indicates that there are several different ways to view the field. Part 2, "The Foundations of OD: Theory and Practice on Change in Organizations," provides a background for understanding some of the theoretical underpinnings of OD. The nature of planned change and the nature of client systems are examined here. OD practitioners utilize implicit and explicit conceptual schemas regarding change, human behavior, and organizational dynamics as they operate in organizations. There is currently no comprehensive theory of organization development, but the field is based on partial theories and a variety of conceptual foundations.

Most of the actual work in OD consists of structuring sets of activities (interventions) so that learning or change takes place. These OD interventions form the technology available to OD practitioners and managers. Part 3 describes most of the mainstream OD interventions. Part 4 focuses on interventions that supplement or complement OD programs. The essays in Parts 3 and 4 describe interventions directed toward individuals, teams, groups in conflict, and total systems, showing the techniques available, how and when to use them, and the conditions that determine success or failure. The "Structural Interventions" described in Part 5 are additional proven methods for causing organizational improvement, such as sociotechnical systems, job enrichment, quality of work life, management by objectives, and the like. These are presented and then compared with organization development.

Part 6 addresses power and politics in organizations along with the role of the OD practitioner in a political arena. To be effective, OD consultants and organization members alike must understand political dynamics, the rules of the game, and the moves of the players. Part 7 deals with organizing and implementing OD programs. How to get started, establishing the contract, getting agreement on expectations, and ensuring healthy client-consultant relations are some of the issues that are explored—issues that can increase the likelihood of success. Part 8 presents examples of OD programs in the service and public sectors. These examples demonstrate that OD can be applied in a variety of settings with good results.

Part 9 examines research results and research issues in organization development. Does OD work, that is, does it cause improvements in performance? How do we know? What difficulties are involved in answering these questions? These topics are addressed in Part 9. Part 10 deals with the future of organization development. What are the major current and future trends? What are the unresolved issues facing the field? What will organization development be like in the 1990s?

These 10 sections present history, foundations, technologies, approaches, and concepts that show organization development to be a unique strategy for improving organizational functioning and employee well being. This book of readings is offered for those of you who want to know what OD is and, perhaps, to begin using its theory and practices to improve performance in your own organizations.

PART 1

Mapping the Territory

The subject matter of this book is organization development, a relatively specific kind of planned change effort aimed at helping members of organizations do the things they want to do—better. We have attempted to fashion a systematic examination of organization development to help the reader determine the applicabilty, utility, and viability of this particular approach as a means of organization improvement.

Organization development (OD) focuses primarily on the human and social aspects of organizations; it views organizational behavior as consisting essentially of the coordinated goal-directed activities of a number of people. Other possible approaches to understanding and intervening in organizations exist—one can focus on organization structure and design, technology and task design, or organization-environment congruence, for example. Organization development programs attend to these issues, but the principal emphasis is on the human aspects of the organization conceived as a social system.

In Part 1 we begin at the beginning—mapping the territory of organization development. What is OD? What characteristics differentiate OD from other improvement programs? What are some of the varieties of OD?

TOWARD A DEFINITION OF ORGANIZATION DEVELOPMENT

The words *organization development* refer to something about organizations and developing them. According to Edgar Schein, "An organization is the planned coordination of the activities of a number of people for the achievement of some common explicit purpose or goal, through division of labor and function, and through a hierarchy of authority and responsibility."[1] Organizations are social systems possessing characteristics described by Schein, and OD efforts are directed toward organizations or major subparts of them.

Development is the act, process, result, or state of being developed—which in turn means to advance, to promote the growth of, to evolve the possibilities of, to further, to improve, or to enhance *something*. Two elements of this definition seem important: first,

---

[1] Edgar H. Schein, *Organizational Psychology,* 3rd ed. (Englewood Cliffs, N.J.: Prentice-Hall, 1980), p. 15.

development may be an act, process, or end state; second, development refers to "bettering" something.

Combining these words suggests that organization development is the act, process, or result of furthering, advancing, or promoting the growth of an organization. According to these definitions, organization development is anything done to "better" an organization. But this definition is too broad and all-inclusive. It can refer to almost anything done in an organizational context that enhances the organization—hiring a person with needed skills, firing an incompetent, merging with another organization, installing a computer, removing a computer, buying a new plant, and so on. This definition serves neither to identify and specify nor to delimit (perhaps something done to "worsen" an organization would be ruled out). The term *organization development* must be given added meaning, must refer to something more specific, if productive discourse on the subject is desired.

Another way of defining organization development is to examine the following definitions which have been suggested in the literature:

> Organization development is an effort (1) *planned,* (2) *organizationwide,* and (3) *managed* from the *top,* to (4) *increase organization effectiveness* and *health* through (5) *planned interventions* in the organization's "processes," using *behavioral-science* knowledge.[2]
>
> *Organization development* (OD) is a response to change, a complex educational strategy intended to change the beliefs, attitudes, values, and structure of organizations so that they can better adapt to new technologies, markets, and challenges, and the dizzying rate of change itself.[3]
>
> *Organization development* is the strengthening of those human processes in organizations which improve the functioning of the organic system so as to achieve its objectives.[4]
>
> *Organization renewal* is the process of initiating, creating, and confronting needed changes so as to make it possible for organizations to become or remain viable, to adapt to new conditions, to solve problems, to learn from experiences, and to move toward greater organizational maturity.[5]
>
> OD can be defined as a planned and sustained effort to apply behavioral science for system improvement, using reflexive, self-analytic methods.[6]
>
> Organization development is a process of planned change—change of an organization's culture from one which avoids an examination of social processes (especially decision making, planning and communication) to one which institutionalizes and legitimizes this examination.[7]
>
> In the behavioral science, and perhaps ideal, sense of the term, *organization development is a long-range effort to improve an organization's problem-solving and renewal processes, particularly through a more effective and collaborative management of organization culture—with special emphasis on the culture of formal work teams—with the assistance of a change*

---

[2]Richard Beckhard, *Organization Development: Strategies and Models* (Reading, Mass.: Addison-Wesley Publishing, 1969), p. 9.

[3]Warren G. Bennis, *Organization Development: Its Nature, Origins, and Prospects* (Reading, Mass.: Addison-Wesley Publishing, 1969), p. 2.

[4]Gordon L. Lippitt, *Organization Renewal* (New York: Appleton-Century-Crofts, 1969), p. 1.

[5]Ibid., p. 4.

[6]Richard Schmuck and Matthew Miles, *Organization Development in Schools* (Palo Alto, Calif.: National Press Books, 1971), p. 2.

[7]Warner Burke and Harvey A. Hornstein, *The Social Technology of Organization Development* (Fairfax, Va.: Learning Resources Corp., 1972), p. xi.

agent, or catalyst, and the use of the theory and technology of applied behavioral science, including action research.[8] [Italics in the original.]

Analysis of these definitions suggests that organization development is *not* just "anything done to better an organization"; it is a particular kind of change process designed to bring about a particular kind of end result. In Figure 1 the definitions are dissected and put into an analytic framework to discover the particular kind of change processes and the particular kind of end results desired.

Examination of Figure 1 suggests the following conclusion. Organization development (OD) is a prescription for a process of planned change in organizations in which the key prescriptive elements relate to (1) the nature of the effort or program (it is a long-range, planned, systemwide process); (2) the nature of the change activities (they utilize behavioral science interventions of an educational, reflexive, self-examining, learn-to-do-it-yourself nature); (3) the targets of the change activities (it is directed toward the human and social processes of organizations, specifically individuals' beliefs, attitudes, and values, the culture and processes of work groups—viewed as basic building blocks of the organization—and the processes and culture of the total organization); and (4) the desired outcomes of the change activities (the goals are *needed changes* in the targets of the interventions that cause the organization to be better able to adapt, cope, solve its problems, and renew itself). Organization development thus represents a unique strategy for system change, a strategy largely based in the theory and research of the behavioral sciences, and a strategy having a substantial prescriptive character. Organization development is thus a normative discipline; it prescribes how planned change in organizations should be approached and carried out if organization improvement is to be obtained.

In summary, organization development is a process of planned system change that attempts to make organizations (viewed as social-technical systems) better able to attain their short- and long-term objectives. This is achieved by teaching the organization members to manage their organization processes and culture more effectively. Facts, concepts, and theory from the behavioral sciences are utilized to fashion both the process and the content of interventions. A basic belief of OD theorists and practitioners is that for effective, lasting change to take place, the system members must grow in the competence to master their own fates.

Let us examine in detail some of the distinguishing characteristics of OD. These characteristics may be useful as criteria for determining what is and is not OD.

DISTINGUISHING CHARACTERISTICS OF ORGANIZATION DEVELOPMENT

Perusal of the many descriptions and definitions of organization development in the literature leads to the conclusion that most authors believe that OD is a unique change strategy, but few of them go beyond listing the features of OD to the statement that programs and strategies not possessing these features are not OD. We believe OD programs possess the

---

[8]Wendell L. French and Cecil H. Bell, Jr., *Organization Development*, 2nd ed. (Englewood Cliffs, N.J.: Prentice-Hall, 1978), p. 14.

FIGURE 1 An Analysis of Selected Definitions of Organization Development

| Author | Components of the Organization Development Process | | | | Desired Goals, Outcomes, or End States of Organization Development Effort |
	Nature and Scope of the Effort	Nature of Activities/Interventions	Targets of Interaction/Activities	Knowledge Base	
Beckard	Planned. Organizationwide. Managed from the top.	Planned interventions in the organization's "processes."	Total organization. Organization's "processes."	Behavioral science knowledge.	Increased organization effectiveness and health.
Bennis	Complex educational strategy. A response to change.	Educational. Change-oriented.	Beliefs, attitudes, values, and structures of organizations.		Better ability to adapt to new technologies, markets, and challenges, and the dizzying rate of change itself.
Gordon Lippitt (on OD)		Designed to strengthen human processes in organizations.	Those human processes in organizations that improve the organic system.		Enable the organization to achieve its objectives (through improved functioning of the organic system).
Gordon Lippitt (on organization renewal)	A process.	A process of initiating, creating and confronting needed changes.	[Implied] total organization.		Enhance the ability of the organization to: Become or remain viable. Adapt to new conditions. Solve problems. Learn from experience. Move toward greater organizational maturity.
Schmuck and Miles	A planned and sustained effort.	Apply behavioral science for system improvement. Using reflexive, self-analytic methods.	Total system (organization).	Behavioral science.	System improvement. [implied] continued self-analysis and reflection.
Burke and Hornstein	A process of planned change.	Change-oriented and self-examining oriented; specifically change of an organization's culture from one which avoids an examination of social processes in organization . . . to one which institutionalizes and legitimizes this examination.	The organization's culture and the social processes in organization, especially decision making, planning, and communication.		[Self-examination] of social processes in organization, especially decision making, planning, and communication.
French and Bell	A long-range effort.	Designed to bring about a more effective and collaborative management of organization culture; using assistance of change agent, or catalyst.	Organization culture. Culture of formal work teams. Organization's problem-solving and renewal processes.	The theory and technology of applied behavioral science, including action research.	Improve an organization's problem-solving and renewal processes.

characteristics described in this section; we believe programs that do not possess these characteristics are not OD. They may be efficacious, they may be legitimate change strategies, and they may be powerful tools for organization improvement, but they are not OD.

Two of us (Wendell and Cecil) have been concerned with the issue of identifying and specifying the nature of organization development for some time now. In an earlier publication we stated:

> We see eight characteristics that we think differentiate organization development interventions from more traditional interventions:
>
> 1. An emphasis, although not exclusively so, on group and organizational processes in contrast to substantive content.
> 2. An emphasis on the work team as the key unit for learning more effective modes of organizational behavior.
> 3. An emphasis on the collaborative management of work-team culture.
> 4. An emphasis on the management of the culture of the total system.
> 5. Attention to the management of system ramifications.
> 6. The use of the action research model.
> 7. The use of a behavioral scientist-change agent, sometimes referred to as a "catalyst" or "facilitator."
> 8. A view of the change effort as an ongoing process.
>
> Another characteristic, number 9, a primary emphasis on human and social relationships, does not necessarily differentiate OD from other change efforts, but it is nevertheless an important feature.[9]

While we still believe these characteristics describe organization development efforts, let us add another means of identifying OD.

An Organization Development Program Is a Long-Range, Planned, and Sustained Effort that Unfolds According to a Strategy.

The key elements here are long range, planned and sustained, and strategy. There is a long-range time perspective on the part of both the client system and the consultant in OD programs. Both parties envision an ongoing relationship of one, two, or more years together if things go well in the program. A one-shot intervention into the system is thus not organization development according to this criterion even though the intervention may be one that is used in OD efforts. Thus the dozens of case studies reporting a three-day or week-long T-group (T for training) experience for system members do not constitute OD as we see it, if the T-group experience was the only intervention of the program.

The reasons for OD practitioners and theorists conceptualizing OD programs in long-range terms are several. First, changing a system's culture and processes is a difficult, complicated, and long-term matter if lasting change is to be effected. OD programs envision that the system members become better able to manage their culture and processes in problem-solving and self-renewing ways. Such complex new learning takes time.

---

[9]Ibid., p. 18.

Second, the assumption is made that organizational problems are multifaceted and complex. One-shot interventions probably cannot solve such problems, and they most assuredly cannot teach the client system to solve them in such a short time period.

OD programs are planned and sustained efforts. They are planned, not accidental—they represent a deliberate entry of either an OD consultant or OD activities into the client system. And they are sustained. The assumption is made that follow-up and sustained effort and energy are needed in order to solve organization problems. These points are fairly straightforward. There is, however, a related point that is a source of some confusion. When some good management practices are taking place in an organization without an OD program—for example, a manager has worked out effective ways to manage team and intergroup culture and processes—is that organization development? We do not think so. OD practitioners try to inculcate good management practices in organizations, that is, they try to help organization members learn to manage themselves and others better. But many managers and many organizations are competently managing their affairs without help from organization development consultants and OD programs; what they are doing would not be called OD even though they may be using some techniques found in the OD technology. OD practitioners did not invent good management practices; OD practitioners are not the sole source for learning good management practices; and finally, the term *organization development* is not synonymous with the term *good management*.

Organization development programs unfold according to a strategy. A part of the planned nature of OD programs almost always involves an overall strategy even though the strategy may be only dimly obvious and articulable, and even though the strategy may emerge and change shape over time. (From our experience, the more viable OD efforts have a fairly clear and openly articulated strategy.) Consultants and clients develop overall goals and paths to goals in organization development programs, and these guide the programmatic activities. It is preferable and usual for the strategy to be developed out of the diagnosed problems of the client system, the client system's desires and capabilities, and the consultant's capabilities and insights into client system needs.

The Organization Development Consultant Establishes a Unique Relationship with Client System Members

Probably the most fundamental differences between organization development programs and other organization improvement programs are found in the role and behavior of the consultant vis-à-vis the client system. In OD the consultant seeks and maintains a collaborative relationship of relative equality with the organization members. Collaboration means "to labor together"—essentially it implies that the consultant does not do all the work while the client system passively waits for solutions to its problems; and it means that the client system does not do all the work while the consultant is a disinterested observer. In organization development, consultant and client co-labor.

A second distinguishing feature of the consultant-client relationship is that it is one of relative equality—the two parties come together as relative equals, each possessing knowledge and skills different from but needed by the other. The client group is encouraged to critique the consultant's program and his or her effectiveness in terms of meeting client system needs and wants. In OD the consultant's role is generally that of a facilitator, not an expert on matters of content; the consultant acts primarily as a question-asker, and secondarily as an answer-giver.

The consultant's role is often described as nondirective and that is partially true, but the rationale behind this nondirective posture is less well understood. The OD consultant role rests on three beliefs. The first belief is simply an affirmation of the efficacy of division of labor and responsibility: let the consultant be responsible for doing what he or she does best (structuring activities designed to solve certain problems); and let the client system do what it does best (bring to bear its special knowledge and expertise on the problem and alternative solutions). The second belief is derived from the question: Where is the best solution to this problem likely to be found? In situations where the consultant is in an expert role, the answer to the question is that the best solution is in the consultant's head due to that person's education, experience, and expertise. Both clients and consultant believe this. In organization development situations where the consultant is playing an enabling and facilitating role, the answer is that the best solution is in the heads of the client members and the challenge is to structure situations to allow it to become known. The third belief is that the responsibility for changing something rests ultimately in the client system members, not in the consultant. Therefore the members of the client system must "own" the problem and the solution, and that is best done when they generate both the problems and the solutions. This belief no doubt rests on Lewin's conceptualization of "own" and "induced" forces. Lewin believed, and demonstrated, that an individual's own forces toward a particular behavior were more powerful in determining the behavior than forces/motives/pushes induced by some outside agent.

The consultant is both expert and directive on matters relating to the best ways to facilitate/enable the client group to approach, diagnose, and solve its problems. In organization development, it is this expertise that the clients expect from the consultant—the expertise to offer the clients effective *ways* to work on problems, not *answers* to problems.

The Nature of the Intervention Activities Differentiates OD from Other Improvement Strategies

OD consultants fashion, conduct, or cause to happen, interventions—structured sets of activities and events in the life of the organization designed to achieve certain outcomes. As indicated in Figure 1, the nature of these interventions is that they are reflective, self-analytical, self-examining, proactive, diagnostically oriented, and action oriented. Further, they focus on the organization culture and its human processes. OD consultants try to inculcate diagnostic skills, self-analytical skills, and reflexive skills in organization members, based on the belief that the organization's members must be able to diagnose situations accurately in order to arrive at successful solutions. But there are several additional beliefs hidden in this statement. Diagnosis and self-reflection are necessary skills to have for problem solution—that is a belief of OD consultants. But *who* should possess those skills? "The client system members," answer OD consultants; "me," answer expert consultants. This is a key difference in the OD prescription. Another belief involved here is the belief that both the problems and the solutions to the problems abound in the client system members. Teaching the client system to diagnose and solve problems and take corrective actions is the goal of the OD consultant. The overriding goal is that the client system members learn to do it themselves. This tenet derives from nondirective therapy notions suggesting that responsibility for improvement and change rests in the individual (organization) that needs to change, not some outside agent. This is supported by most discussions of normalcy and maturity in psychotherapy that include the patient's ability to solve problems, adapt effectively, and cope effectively as criteria for a healthy organism. Many authors, including Gordon Lippitt, speak of the organization ''learning from experience,'' and the OD literature suggests that ''learning how to learn'' is a desired outcome of OD interventions. This is what is being discussed: that the client system become expert in self-examination, diagnosis, and corrective action taking.

Planning, problem solving, and self-renewal are also mentioned as important processes for the client system to be reflexive about. The same overriding goal applies here: the client system members must learn to manage these processes effectively by themselves. There is thus a unique character to the nature of OD interventions: the intent that the client system becomes proficient in solving its own problems—present and future—*by itself*. The ancient Chinese proverb seems to describe the underlying rationale: ''Give a man a fish, and you have given him a meal; teach a man to fish, and you have given him a livelihood.''

The Targets of OD Interventions Differentiate OD from Other Improvement Strategies

The OD prescription calls for certain configurations of people as targets of OD interventions—intact work groups, two or more work-related groups, subsystems of organizations, and total organizations. Katz and Kahn speak of ''role sets,'' the offices (positions) and people an individual interacts with while performing role-relevant behavior in an organization. They state:

> Each member of an organization is directly associated with a relatively small number of others, usually the occupants of offices adjacent to his in the work-flow structure or in the hierarchy of authority. They constitute his role set and typically include his immediate supervisor (and perhaps his supervisor's immediate superior), his subordinates, and certain members of his own or other departments with whom he must work closely. These offices are defined into his role set by virtue of the work-flow, technology, and authority structure of the organization.[10]

Many of an individual's values, norms, and perceptions of organization reality are derived from contact with role-set members. Role-enactment problems derive from interaction with role-set members. A person's immediate work group, immediate superior, and immediate subordinates are immensely important factors for an individual's effectiveness in an organization. OD interventions concentrate on work-relevant constellations of people in the belief that these groups have inherent in them considerable power to determine

---

[10]Daniel Katz and Robert L. Kahn, *The Social Psychology of Organizations* (New York: John Wiley & Sons, 1966), p. 174.

individual and group behavior and also contain many of the sources of organizational problems.

What goes on *between* units is also of vital importance in organizational effectiveness. OD goes beyond intact work teams and also focuses on enhancing key interdependencies across units and levels. For example, data are typically collected about the degree of cooperation versus dysfunctional competition between the various units, and identified problems are then worked on with members of the relevant groups present. Thus, inter-group configurations are a second major target of OD interventions.

A third target of OD interventions is the organization's processes and culture. In a sense, OD is a comprehensive long-term effort to collaboratively manage the culture of an organization (since processes can be considered part of organization culture). As shown in Figure 1, some of the authors mention culture and some of the authors mention human and social processes as the targets of OD interventions. Problem-solving, planning, self-renewal, decision-making, and communications processes are identified as important processes. This focus on culture and processes is simply a part of the bet/hypothesis/belief system that OD consultants have: culture and processes are important strategic leverage points in an organization for bringing about organization improvement and change. Other consultants and practitioners make different bets on the best strategic leverage points—the technology of the organization, the structure of the organization, its design, and so forth. OD consultants, because they are working with a behavioral science knowledge base, focus on culture and processes. And the OD prescription suggests that these two targets are important ingredients in the process of planned organizational change.

OD Consultants Utilize a Behavioral Science Base

This is a characteristic of the practice of OD, but it is shared by many different improvement strategies. We will not discuss this point extensively. Perhaps it is sufficient to say that the behavioral science knowledge base of the practice of OD contributes to its distinctive gestalt. OD is an applied field in which theories, concepts, and practices from sociology, psychology, social psychology, education, economics, psychiatry, and management are brought to bear on real organizational problems.

The Desired Outcomes of OD Are Distinctive in Nature

The desired outcomes of OD efforts are both similar to other improvement strategies, and different from other improvement strategies. OD programs and efforts are designed to produce organizational effectiveness and health, better system functioning, greater ability to achieve objectives, and so forth, as shown in some of the definitions in Figure 1. But some of the definitions point to additional desired outcomes: outcomes relating to a changed organization culture, to changed processes (especially renewal and adaptation processes) and to the establishing of norms of continual self-study and proaction.

Michael Beer lists the aims of OD as: ''(1) enhancing congruence between organizational structure, processes, strategy, people, and culture; (2) developing new and creative organizational solutions; and (3) developing the organization's self-renewing capacity.''[11] It is these self-renewal outcomes that seem particularly distinctive in the OD process.

SUMMARY OF THE DISTINCTIVE FEATURES OF ORGANIZATION DEVELOPMENT

We believe that organization development is a particular kind of organization improvement strategy possessing distinguishing characteristics as follows:

1. An OD program is a long-range, planned, and sustained effort that is based on an overall strategy.
2. A consultant (one or more) is used, and that consultant establishes a unique relationship with the client system: the consultant seeks and maintains a collaborative relationship of relative equality with the organization members.
3. OD interventions are distinctive in their nature: they are reflexive, self-analytical, self-skill-building in nature. Another way of saying this is that a pervasive use of a collaborative action-research model underlies most OD interventions.
4. OD interventions assume that work-related groups of individuals and work-related intergroup configurations are more important leverage points for change than are other configurations, and also assume that organization culture and organizational processes are strategic leverage points for effecting organizational change.
5. OD utilizes a behavioral science base.
6. The desired outcomes of organizational effectiveness and health are supplemented in OD with the goal that organization culture and processes be changed in order that the organization continue to be reflexive and self-examining.

This overview provides a broad outline of the field. The rest of the book will expand on these themes, will add details and implications, and will make clearer what organization development is and what it can do.

---

[11]Michael Beer, *Organization Change and Development* (Santa Monica, Calif.: Goodyear Publishing, 1980), p. 10.

History, Definitions, and Characteristics of Organization Development

---

The roots, birth, and major milestones in the development of the field of organization development are described in the first of the five articles in this section. Wendell French has been intrigued with tracing the history of OD for many years. The first selection was written by him; it appears in a book on organization development by Wendell French and Cecil Bell.[1] French points to the importance of Kurt Lewin as a prime contributor to events leading up to the emergence of OD, and to three mainstreams of activities as precursors of OD—laboratory training, survey research and feedback, and action research. Early projects and the people involved in them are described, using as source materials both published accounts and extensive correspondence with the individuals who were in the forefront of the new applied behavioral science development at that time—Robert Blake, Herbert Shepard, Ronald Lippitt, Richard Beckhard, and others.

An article on the history of OD by Michael McGill, not included in this reader, gives a somewhat different view of early events.[2] McGill goes back to just after World War II to search for the beginnings of OD and, in so doing, finds reason to include the activities, writings, and conceptualizations of Leland Bradford and Neely Gardner as important foundations. Both Leland Bradford and Neely Gardner were engaged in training and development activities in large organizations and conceived the necessity to develop *both* the individual and the organization. Bradford has been intimately involved with most of the applied behavioral science developments in the United States because he was the director of the National Training Laboratory in Group Development (NTL) from its inception in 1947 to his retirement in 1970. NTL (now the NTL—Institute for Applied

---

[1]Wendell L. French and Cecil H. Bell, Jr., *Organization Development: Behavioral Science Interventions for Organizational Improvement,* 3rd ed. (Englewood Cliffs, N.J.: Prentice-Hall, 1984).

[2]Michael E. McGill, "The Evolution of Organization Development: 1947–1960," *Public Administration Review,* March–April 1974, pp. 98–105.

Behavioral Science) was both a source of support for the fledgling organization development movement and also a source of most of the OD practitioners.[3]

The next two selections focus on the characteristics of OD efforts. As we have stated, we believe that OD is a unique improvement strategy possessing characteristics that differentiate it from other improvement strategies, and in this section we map that domain. Richard Beckhard asks and answers the question: What is organization development? His operational definition, operational goals of OD, and characteristics of OD efforts combine to make his selection one of the best available statements of what OD is all about. He is pithy, to the point, and right on target. It is clear from his article that OD has several crucial distinguishing features that are not found in other organizational change efforts, and we have drawn on his ideas for our definition of OD.

Matthew Miles and Richard Schmuck likewise describe and define OD clearly and succinctly but their definition appears, on the surface, to be quite different from that of Beckhard. But this is more a difference between an operational definition and an abstract definition; they are in fact describing the same phenomenon. Key new words in the Miles and Schmuck definition relate to the methods used in the OD process—reflexive, self-analytic methods. Reflexive methods are methods that direct attention back on the organization, its processes, its norms and values, its culture. Self-analysis for self-improvement (with a little outside help) is a theme of organization development, and Miles and Schmuck make this point very well. Their section on "How OD Works" is helpful perhaps especially to readers not very familiar with the field. Their "OD Cube" is a useful and cogent device for understanding the content and method of the practice of OD. And their section on the "Effects of OD" suggests that OD is effective as an organizational improvement strategy.

There are literally dozens of organization improvement strategies and approaches. Frank Friedlander and Dave Brown perform the herculean task of making sense of and summarizing much of the OD and cognate literature. They describe most of the important change strategies on the contemporary scene that impact principally on the human-social dimensions of organizational systems. All of the strategies they describe are presumably included under the rubric, OD, although we tend to separate out some strategies Friedlander and Brown include, preferring instead to specify the conditions that must be met for some of the strategies to be considered as organization development as we are using the term in this book. But this selection by Friedlander and Brown, excerpted from a much larger essay, is excellent for mapping the domain of the most important "people" approaches to organizational change.

The selection by Michael Beer and Anna Elise Walton suggests that the theory and practice of organization development are no longer the sole province of OD practitioners; OD is becoming an integral part of general management and human resource management. The authors state: "Thus as a field, organization development will have to become concerned with the theory and practice of managing the continual adaptation of internal organizational arrangements to changes in the external environment. In this capacity, intervention methods become episodes in a long-term process, and [OD] consultants

---

[3]Leland P. Bradford, *National Training Laboratories—Its History: 1947–1970.* Copyright 1974 by Leland P. Bradford, Bethel, Maine.

become actors in a process orchestrated by general managers.'' They further say: ''As organizations have struggled in an increasingly competitive economy, superior human resources are increasingly seen as a competitive advantage. This has culminated in substantial interest in developing high-commitment work systems that will attract, motivate, and retain superior employees. Indeed the term human resources is coming to represent an integration of personnel administration, labor relations, and organization development, with OD the senior partner.''

If Beer and Walton are correct, and we think they are, the field of organization development is making a transition toward becoming a crucial general management tool. Present and future managers will be required to know about OD concepts, techniques, and practices.

Reading 1

A HISTORY OF ORGANIZATION DEVELOPMENT

Wendell L. French and Cecil H. Bell, Jr.

The history of organization development is rich with the contributions of behavioral scientists and practitioners, many of whom are well known, and the contributions of many people in client organizations. Even if we were aware of all the significant contributors, which we are not, we could not do justice to the richness of this history in a short essay. Therefore, all we can do is write about what we believe to be the central thrusts of that history based on our research to date and hope that the many people who are not mentioned will not be offended by our incompleteness.

Systematic organization development activities have a recent history and, to use the analogy of a mangrove tree, have at least three important trunk stems. One trunk stem of OD consists of innovations in the application of laboratory training insights to complex organizations. A second major stem is survey research and feedback methodology. Both stems are intertwined with a third stem, the emergence of action research. Paralleling these stems, and to some extent linked, was the emergence of the Tavistock sociotechnical and socioclinical approaches. The key actors focused upon in this account interacted with each other and were influenced by experiences and concepts from many fields, as we will see.

Source: Wendell L. French and Cecil H. Bell, Jr., *Organization Development: Behavioral Science Interventions for Organization Improvement*, 3rd ed., © 1984, pp. 24–44. (Englewood Cliffs, N.J.: Prentice-Hall.) Reprinted with permission of the publisher.

The Laboratory Training Stem

The T-Group

One stem of OD, laboratory training, essentially unstructured small-group situations in which participants learn from their own interactions and the evolving dynamics of the group, began to develop in about 1946 from various experiments in the use of discussion groups to achieve changes in behavior in back-home situations. In particular, an Inter-Group Relations workshop held at the State Teachers College in New Britain, Connecticut, in the summer of 1946 was important in the emergence of laboratory training. This workshop was sponsored by the Connecticut Interracial Commission and the Research Center for Group Dynamics, then at MIT.

The Research Center for Group Dynamics (RCGD) had been founded in 1945 under the direction of Kurt Lewin, a prolific theorist, researcher, and practitioner in interpersonal, group, intergroup, and community relationships.[1] Lewin had been recruited to MIT largely through the efforts of Douglas McGregor of the Sloan School of Management who had convinced MIT President Carl Compton of the wisdom of establishing a center for group dynamics. Lewin's original staff included Marian Radke, Leon Festinger, Ronald Lippitt, and Dorwin Cartwright.[2] Lewin's field theory and his conceptualizing about group dynamics, change processes, and action research were of profound influence on the people who were associated with the various stems of OD.

The staff for the New Britain Workshop of 1946 consisted of Kurt Lewin, Kenneth Benne, Leland

Bradford, and Ronald Lippitt. Feedback at the end of each day to groups, and to group leaders and members about their individual and group behavior, stimulated great interest and appeared to produce more insight and learning than did lectures and seminars. From this experience emerged the National Training Laboratory in Group Development, which was organized by Benne, Bradford, and Lippitt (Lewin died in early 1947) and which held a three-week session during the summer of 1947 at the Gould Academy in Bethel, Maine. Participants met with a trainer and an observer in Basic Skill Training Groups (later called T-groups) for a major part of each day. The 1947 laboratory was sponsored by the Research Center for Group Dynamics (MIT), the National Education Association (NEA), Teachers College of Columbia University, University of California at Los Angeles (UCLA), Springfield College, and Cornell University. The work of that summer was to evolve into the National Training Laboratory, later called NTL Institute for Applied Behavioral Science, and into contemporary T-group training. Out of the Bethel experiences and NTL grew a significant number of laboratory training centers sponsored by universities. One of the first was the Western Training Laboratory, headed by Paul Sheats and sponsored by UCLA. The Western Training Laboratory offered its first program in 1952.

In addition to Lewin and his work, influences on Bradford, Lippitt, and Benne relative to the invention of the T-group and the subsequent emergence of OD included extensive experience with role playing and Moreno's psychodrama.[3] Further, Bradford and Benne had been influenced by John Dewey's philosophy of education, including concepts about learning and change and about the transactional nature of humans and their environment.[4] In addition, Benne had been influenced by the works of Mary Follett, an early management theorist, including her ideas about integrative solutions to problems in organizations.[5]

As a footnote to the emergence of the T-group, the widespread use of flip-chart paper as a con-venient way to record, retrieve, and display data in OD activities and in training sessions was invented by Ronald Lippitt and Lee Bradford during the 1946 New Britain sessions. As Lippitt reports,

> The blackboards were very inadequate, and we needed to preserve a lot of the material we produced. So I went down to the local newspaper and got a donation of the end of press runs. The paper was still on the rollers. We had a "cutting bee" of Lee, Ken, myself and several others to roll the sheets out and cut them into standard sizes that we could put up in quantity with masking tape on the blackboards and walls of the classrooms. We took the practice back to MIT and I had the shop make some boards with clamps across the top. We hung them in our offices and the seminar room, and Lee did the same thing at the NEA in Washington. . . . The next summer at Bethel we had a large supply of cut newsprint and used some of the boards on easels, as well as using the walls.[6]

Bradford also reports that he and Ronald Lippitt used "strips of butcher paper" in their early work with organizations.[7]

Over the next decade, as trainers began to work with social systems of more permanency and complexity than T-groups, they began to experience considerable frustration in the transfer of laboratory behavioral skills and insights of individuals into the solution of problems in organizations. Personal skills learned in the "stranger" T-groups setting were very difficult to transfer to complex organizations. However, the training of "teams" from the same organization had emerged early at Bethel and undoubtedly was a link to the total organizational focus of Douglas McGregor, Herbert Shepard, and Robert Blake, and subsequently the focus of Richard Beckhard, Chris Argyris, Jack Gibb, Warren Bennis, and others.[8] All had been T-group trainers in NTL programs.

Robert Tannenbaum

Within our present awareness, some of the earliest sessions of what would now be called "team building" were conducted by Robert Tannenbaum in 1952 and 1953 at the U.S. Naval Ordnance Test Station at China Lake, California.[9] According to Tannenbaum, the term "vertically structured groups" was used, with groups dealing with "personal topics (such as departmental sociometrics, interpersonal relationships, communication, and self-analysis), and with organizational topics (such as deadlines, duties and responsibilities, policies and procedures, and—quite extensively—with interorganizational-group relations)."[10] These sessions, which stimulated a 1954 *Personnel* article by Tannenbaum, Kallejian, and Weschler, were conducted "with all managers of a given organizational unit present."[11] The more personally oriented dynamics of such sessions were described in a 1955 *Harvard Business Review* article by the same authors.[12]

Tannenbaum, along with Art Shedlin, also was the leader of what appears to be the first nondegree training program in OD, the Learning Community in Organizational Development at UCLA. This annual program was first offered as a full-time, 10-week, residential program, January–March 1967.[13]

Tannenbaum, who held a Ph.D. in Industrial Relations from the School of Business at the University of Chicago, had early been influenced by such authors as Mary Parker Follett in management theory, V. V. Anderson's *Psychiatry in Industry,* Roethlisberger and Dickson's *Management and the Worker,* and Burleigh Gardner's *Human Relations in Industry.* He was on the planning committee for the Western Training Laboratory (WTL) and a staff member for the first session (1952). During that first session he co-trained with a psychiatric social worker who had attended a Bethel program, and in subsequent sessions, in his words, "co-trained with a psychiatrist, an educator, a clinical psychologist . . . and I learned much from them."[14]

Douglas McGregor

Douglas McGregor, as a professor-consultant, working with Union Carbide, beginning about 1957, was also one of the first behavioral scientists to begin to solve the transfer problem and to talk systematically about and to help implement the ap-

plication of T-group skills to complex organizations.[15] John Paul Jones, who had come up through industrial relations at Union Carbide, in collaboration with McGregor and with the support of a corporate executive vice president and director, Birny Mason, Jr. (later president of the corporation), established a small internal consulting group that in large part used behavioral science knowledge in assisting line managers and their subordinates to learn how to be more effective in groups. McGregor's ideas were a dominant force in this consulting group; other behavioral scientists who had had an influence on Jones's thinking were Rensis Likert and Mason Haire. Jones's organization was later called an "organization development group."[16]

Herbert Shepard

During the same year, 1957, Herbert Shepard, through introductions by Douglas McGregor, joined the employee relations department of Esso Standard Oil (now Exxon) as a research associate. Shepard was to have a major impact on the emergence of OD. While we will focus mainly on Shepard's work at Esso, it should also be noted that Shepard was later involved in community development activities and, in 1960, at the Case Institute of Technology, founded the first doctoral program devoted to training OD specialists.

Before joining Esso, Shepard had completed his doctorate at MIT and had stayed for a time as a faculty member in the Industrial Relations Section. Among influences on Shepard were Roethlisberger and Dickson's *Management and the Worker* (1939) and a biography of Clarence Hicks. (As a consultant to Standard Oil, Hicks had helped to develop participative approaches to personnel management and labor relations.) Shepard was also influenced by Farrell Toombs, who had been a counselor at the Hawthorne plant and had trained under Carl Rogers, a leading theorist and practitioner in nondirective counseling. In addition, Shepard had been heavily influenced by the writings of Kurt Lewin. NTL influence was also an important part of Shepard's background; he attended an NTL lab in 1950 and subsequently was a staff member in many of its programs.[17]

In 1958 and 1959 Shepard launched three experiments in organization development at major Esso refineries: Bayonne, New Jersey; Baton Rouge, Louisiana; and Bayway, Texas. At Bayonne an interview survey and diagnosis were made and discussed with top management, followed by a series of three-day laboratories for all members of management.[18] Paul Buchanan, who had worked earlier at the Naval Ordnance Test Station and more recently had been using a somewhat similar approach in Republic Aviation, collaborated with Shepard at Bayonne and subsequently joined the Esso staff.

Blake and Shepard

At Baton Rouge, Robert Blake joined Shepard, and the two initiated a series of two-week laboratories attended by all members of "middle" management. At first, an effort was made to combine the case method with the laboratory method, but the designs soon emphasized T-groups, organizational exercises, and lectures. One innovation in this training program was an emphasis on intergroup as well as interpersonal relations. Although working on interpersonal problems affecting work performance was clearly an organizational effort, between-group problem solving had even greater organization development implications in that a broader and more complex segment of the organization was involved.

At Baton Rouge, efforts to involve top management failed, and as a result follow-up resources for implementing organization development were not made available. By the time the Bayway program started, two fundamental OD lessons had been learned: the requirement for active involvement in and leadership of the program by top management and the need for on-the-job application.

At Bayway, there were two significant innovations. First, Shepard, Blake, and Murray Horwitz utilized the instrumented laboratory, which Blake and Jane Mouton had been developing in social psychology classes at the University of Texas and which they later developed into the Managerial Grid approach to organization development.[19] (An essential dimension of the instrumented lab is the use of feedback based on scales and measurements of group and individual behavior during sessions.)[20] Second, at Bayway more resources were devoted to team development, consultation, intergroup conflict resolution, and so forth than were devoted to laboratory training of "cousins," that is, organization members from different departments. As Robert Blake stated, "It was learning to *reject* T-group stranger-type labs that permitted OD to come into focus," and it was intergroup projects, in particular, that "triggered real OD."[21]

Robert Blake

As in the case of Shepard and others, influences on Robert Blake up to that point were important in the emergence of OD. While at Berea College majoring in psychology and philosophy (later an M.A., University of Virginia, and a Ph.D., University of Texas), Blake had been strongly influenced by the works of Korzybski and the general semanticists and found that "seeing discrete things as representative of a continuous series was much more stimulating and rewarding than just seeing two things as 'opposites.'" This thinking contributed in later years to Blake's conceptualization of the Managerial Grid with Jane Mouton and to their intergroup research on win-lose dynamics. This intergroup research and the subsequent design of their intergroup conflict management workshops were also heavily influenced by Muzafer Sherif's fundamental research on intergroup dynamics.[22] Jane Mouton's influence on Blake's thinking and on the development of the Grid stemmed partly, in her words, "from my undergraduate work (at Texas) in pure mathematics and physics which emphasized the significance of measurement, experimental design, and a scientific approach to phenomena."[23] (Mouton later attained an M.A. from the University of Virginia and a Ph.D. from the University of Texas).

During World War II, Blake served in the Psychological Research Unit of the Army Air Force where he interacted with a large number of behavioral scientists, including sociologists. This contributed to his interest in "looking at the system rather the individuals within the system on an isolated one-by-one basis."[24] (This is probably one of many links between systems concepts or systems theory and OD.)

Another major influence on Blake had been the work of John Bowlby, a medical member of the Tavistock Clinic in London, who was working in family group therapy. Blake, after completing his Ph.D. work in clinical psychology, went to England for 16 months in 1948 and 1949 to study, observe, and do research at Tavistock. As Blake states it,

> Bowlby had the clear notion that treating mental illness of an individual out of context was an . . . ineffective way of aiding a person. . . . As a result, John was unprepared to see patients, particularly children, in isolation from their family settings. He would see the intact family: mother, father, siblings . . . . I am sure you can see from what I have said that if you substitute the word organization for family and substitute the concept of development for therapy, the natural next step in my mind was organization development.

Among others at Tavistock who influenced Blake were Wilfred Bion, Henry Ezriel, Eric Trist, and Elliott Jaques.[25]

After returning from Tavistock and taking an appointment at Harvard, Blake joined the staff for the summer NTL programs at Bethel. His first assignment was co-responsibility for a T-group with John R. P. French. Blake was a member of the Bethel staff from 1951 to 1957 and continued after that with NTL labs for managers at Harriman House, Harriman, New York. Among other influences on Blake were Jacob Moreno's action orientation to training through the use of psychodrama and sociodrama and E. C. Tolman's notions of purposive behavior in humans.[26]

Richard Beckhard

Richard Beckhard, another major figure in the emergence and extension of the OD field, came from a career in the theater. In his words,

I came out of a whole different world—the theatre—and went to NTL in 1950 as a result of some discussions with Lee Bradford and Ron Lippitt. At that time they were interested in improving the effectiveness of the communications in large meetings and I became involved as head of the general sessions program. But I also got hooked on the whole movement. I made a career change and set up the meetings organization, "Conference Counselors." My first major contact was the staging of the 1950 White House conference on children and youth. . . . I was brought in to stage the large general sessions with six thousand people . . . . I had been doing a lot of large convention participative discussion type things and had written on the subject. . . . At the same time I joined the NTL summer staff. . . . My mentors in the field were Lee Bradford, in the early days, and Ron Lippitt and later, Ren Likert, and very particularly, Doug McGregor, who became both mentor, friend, father figure . . . and in the later years, brother. Doug had left MIT and was at Antioch as president. . . . Doug and I began appearing on similar programs. One day coming back on the train from Cincinnati to Boston, Doug asked if I was interested in joining MIT. . . .

In the period 1958–63, I had worked with him (McGregor) on two or three projects. He brought me to Union Carbide, where I replaced him in working with John Paul Jones, and later, George Murray and the group. We (also) worked together at . . . Pennsylvania Bell and . . . at General Mills.[27]

Beckhard worked with McGregor at General Mills in 1959 or 1960, where McGregor was working with Dewey Balsch, vice president of personnel and industrial relations, in an attempt to facilitate "a total organizational culture change program which today might be called quality of work life or OD." Beckhard goes on to say, "The issues that were being worked were relationships between workers and supervision; roles of supervision and management at various levels; participative management for real. . . . This experience was one of the influences on Doug's original paper, 'The Human Side of Enterprise' . . . and from which the book emerged a year or so later."[28]

Beckhard developed one of the first major non-degree training programs in OD, NTL's Program for Specialists in Organizational Training and De-velopment (PSOTD). The first session was an in-tensive four-week session held in the summer of 1967 at Bethel, Maine, the same year as UCLA launched its Learning Community in OD. Core staff members the first year in the NTL program were Beckhard as dean, Warner Burke, and Fritz Steele. Additional resource persons the first year were Herbert Shepard, Sheldon Davis, and Chris Argyris. In addition, along with McGregor, Rensis Likert, Chris Argyris, Robert Blake, Lee Bradford, and Jack Gibb, Beckhard was a founder of NTL's Management Work Conferences that are essentially laboratory training experiences for middle man-agers. As an extension of this program, Beckhard was also active in the development and conducting of NTL's senior executive conferences and presi-dents' labs.[29]

The Term "Organization Development"

It is not entirely clear who coined the term *orga-nization development,* but it is likely that the term emerged more or less simultaneously in two or three places through the conceptualization of Rob-ert Blake, Herbert Shepard, Jane Mouton, Douglas McGregor, and Richard Beckhard.[30] The phrase *development group* had earlier been used by Blake and Mouton in connection with human relations training at the University of Texas and appeared in their 1956 document that was distributed for use in the Baton Rouge experiment.[31] (The same phrase appeared in a Mouton and Blake article first pub-lished in the journal *Group Psychotherapy* in 1957.)[32] The Baton Rouge T-groups run by Shep-ard and Blake were called *development groups,*[33] and this program of T-groups was called "orga-nization development" to distinguish it from the complementary management development pro-grams already underway.[34]

Referring to his consulting with McGregor at General Mills, Beckhard gives this account of the term emerging there:

> At that time we wanted to put a label on the program at General Mills. . . . We clearly didn't want to call it management development because it

was total organization-wide, nor was it human relations training although there was a component of that in it. We didn't want to call it organization improvement because that's a static term, so we labelled the program "Organization Development," meaning system-wide change effort.[35]

Thus, the term emerged as a way of distinguishing a different mode of working with organizations and as a way of highlighting its developmental, sys-temwide, dynamic thrust.

The Role of Personnel and Industrial Relations Executives

It is of considerable significance that the emer-gence of organization development efforts in three of the first corporations to be extensively involved, Union Carbide, Esso, and General Mills, included personnel and industrial relations people seeing themselves in new roles. At Union Carbide, John Paul Jones, in industrial relations, now saw him-self in the role of a behavioral science consultant to other managers.[36] At Esso, the headquarters human relations research division began to view itself as an internal consulting group offering ser-vices to field managers rather than as a research group developing reports for top management.[37] At General Mills, the vice president of personnel and industrial relations, Dewey Balsch, saw his role as including leadership in conceptualizing and coordinating changes in the culture of the total organization.[38] Thus, in the history of OD we see both external consultants and internal staff de-partments departing from their traditional roles and collaborating in a new approach to organi-zation improvement.

The Survey Research and Feedback Stem

Survey research and feedback,[39] a specialized form of action research . . . constitutes the second ma-jor stem in the history of organization develop-ment. The history of this stem, in particular, revolves around the techniques and approach de-veloped by staff members at the Survey Research Center of the University of Michigan over a period of years.

Rensis Likert

The SRC was founded in 1946 after Rensis Likert, director of the Division of Program Surveys of the Federal Bureau of Agricultural Economics, and other key members of the division, moved to Michigan. Likert held a Ph.D. in psychology from Columbia, and his dissertation, *A Technique for the Measurement of Attitudes,* was the classic study in which the widely used five-point "Likert scale" was developed. After a period of university teaching, Likert had been employed by the Life Insurance Agency Management Association where he conducted research on leadership, motivation, morale, and productivity. He had then moved to the U.S. Department of Agriculture, where his Division of Program Surveys furthered a more scientific approach to survey research in its work with various federal departments, including the Office of War Information.[40] After helping to develop and direct the Survey Research Center, following World War II, in 1948 Likert then became the director of a new Institute for Social Research, which included both the SRC and the Research Center for Group Dynamics, the latter moving to Michigan from MIT after Lewin's death.

Floyd Mann, Rensis Likert, and Others

Part of the emergence of survey research and feedback was based on the refinements made by SRC staff members in survey methodology. Another part was the evolution of the feedback methodology. As related by Rensis Likert,

> In 1947, I was able to interest the Detroit Edison Company in a company-wide study of employee perceptions, behavior, reactions and attitudes which was conducted in 1948. Floyd Mann, who had joined the SRC staff in 1947, was the study director on the project. I provided general direction. Three persons from D.E.: Blair Swartz, Sylvanus Leahy and Robert Schwab with Mann and me worked on the problem of how the company could best use the data from the survey to bring improvement in management and performance. This led to the development and use of the survey-feedback method. Floyd particularly played a key role in this

development. He found that when the survey data were reported to a manager (or supervisor) and he or she failed to discuss the results with subordinates and failed to plan with them what the manager and others should do to bring improvement, little change occurred. On the other hand, when the manager discussed the results with subordinates and planned with them what to do to bring improvement, substantial favorable changes occurred.[41]

Another aspect of the Detroit Edison study was the process of feeding back data from an attitude survey to the participating departments in what Mann calls an "interlocking chain of conferences."[42] Additional insights are provided by Baumgartel, who participated in the project and who drew the following conclusions from the Detroit Edison study:

> The results of this experimental study lend support to the idea that an intensive, group discussion procedure for utilizing the results of an employee questionnaire survey can be an effective tool for introducing positive change in a business organization. It may be that the effectiveness of this method, in comparison to traditional training courses, is that it deals with the system of human relationships as a whole (superior and subordinate can change together) and it deals with each manager, supervisor, and employee in the context of his own job, his own problems, and his own work relationships.[43]

Links between the Laboratory Training Stem and the Survey Feedback Stem

Links between people who were later to be key figures in the laboratory training stem of OD and people who were to be key figures in the survey feedback stem occurred as early as 1940 and continued over the years. These links were undoubtedly of significance in the evolution of both stems. Of particular interest are the links between Likert and Lewin and between Likert and key figures in the laboratory training stem of OD. As Likert states it, "I met Lewin at the APA annual meeting at State College, Pa., I believe in 1940. When he came to Washington during the War, I saw him several times and got to know him and his family quite well."[44] In 1944

Likert arranged a dinner at which Douglas Mc-Gregor and Kurt Lewin explored the feasibility of a group dynamics center at MIT.[45]

Likert further refers to McGregor: "I met McGregor during the war and came to know him very well after Lewin had set up the RCGD at MIT. After the War, Doug became very interested in the research on leadership and organizations that we were doing in the Institute for Social Research. He visited us frequently and I saw him often at Antioch and at MIT after he returned." Likert goes on to refer to the first NTL lab for managers that was held at Arden House in 1956: "Douglas McGregor and I helped Lee Bradford launch it. . . . Staff members in the 1956 lab were: Beckhard, Benne, Bradford, Gordon Lippitt, Malott, Shepard and I. Argyris, Blake and McGregor joined the staff for the 1957 Arden House lab."[46]

Links between group dynamics and survey feedback people were extensive, of course, after the RCGD moved to Michigan with the encouragement of Rensis Likert and members of the SRC. Among the top people in the RCGD who moved to Michigan were Leon Festinger, Dorwin Cartwright, Ronald Lippitt, and John R. P. French, Jr. Cartwright, who was selected by the group to be the director of the RCGD, was particularly knowledgeable about survey research, since he had been on the staff of the Division of Program Surveys with Rensis Likert and others during World War II.[47]

The Action Research Stem

Earlier we briefly described action research as a collaborative, client-consultant inquiry consisting of preliminary diagnosis, data gathering from the client group, data feedback to the client group, data exploration and action planning by the client group, and action. As we will describe later, there are at least four versions of action research, one of which, participant action research, is used with the most frequency in OD. The laboratory training stem in the history of OD has a heavy component of action research; the survey feedback stem is the history of a specialized form of action research; and Tavistock projects have had a strong action research thrust, as we will discuss shortly.

Because we will treat the history of action research in some detail later, we will mention only a few aspects here. For example William F. Whyte and Edith L. Hamilton were using action research in their work with Chicago's Tremont Hotel in 1945 and 1946; John Collier, commissioner of Indian Affairs, was describing action research in a publication in 1945; Kurt Lewin and his students conducted numerous action research projects in the mid-1940s and early 1950s. The work of these and other scholars and practitioners in the invention and utilization of action research was basic in the evolution of OD.

Sociotechnical and Socioclinical Parallels

Somewhat parallel to the work of the RCGD, the SRC, and NTL was the work of the Tavistock Clinic in England. The clinic had been founded in 1920 as an outpatient facility to provide psychotherapy based on psychoanalytic theory and insights from the treatment of battle neurosis in World War I. A group focus emerged early in the work of Tavistock in the context of family therapy in which the child and the parent received treatment simultaneously.[48] The action research mode also emerged at Tavistock in attempts to give practical help to families, organizations, and communities.

W. R. Bion, John Rickman, and Others

The staff of the Tavistock Clinic was extensively influenced by such innovations as World War II applications of social psychology to psychiatry, the work of W. R. Bion and John Rickman and others in group therapy, Lewin's notions about the "social field" in which a problem was occurring, and Lewin's theory and experience with action research. Bion, Rickman, and others had been involved with the six-week "Northfield Experiment" at a military hospital near Birmingham during World War II. In this experiment each soldier was required to join a group that both performed some task such as handicraft or map reading and discussed feelings, interpersonal relations, and administrative and managerial problems as well. Insights from this experiment were to carry over into Bion's theory of group behavior.[49]

Eric Trist

It is of significance that Tavistock's sociotechnical approach to restructuring work grew out of Eric Trist's visit to a coal mine and his insights as to the relevance of Lewin's work on group dynamics and Bion's work on leaderless groups to mining problems.[50] Trist was also influenced by the systems concepts of Von Bertalanffy and Andras Angyal.[51] Trist's subsequent experiments in work redesign and the use of semiautonomous work teams in coal mining were the forerunners of other work redesign experiments in various industries in Europe, India, and the United States. Thus, there is a clear historical link between the group dynamics field and sociotechnical approaches to assisting organizations.

Tavistock-U.S. Links

Tavistock leaders, including Trist and Bion, had frequent contact with Kurt Lewin, Rensis Likert, and others in the United States. One product of this collaboration was the decision to publish *Human Relations* as a joint publication between Tavistock and MIT's Research Center for Group Dynamics.[52] Some Americans prominent in the emergence and evolution of the OD field, for example, Robert Blake, as we noted earlier, and Warren Bennis,[53] studied at Tavistock.

Although the sociotechnical approach focused on the nonexecutive ranks of organizations and was therefore not a complete systemwide approach, many aspects were congruent with OD as we have characterized it. . . . The focus on teams and the use of action research and participation were certainly consistent with contemporary OD approaches. (As we will discuss . . . some contemporary quality of work life [QWL] programs are an amalgamation of OD, sociotechnical, and other approaches. Further, some OD efforts have been criticized as not involving rank-and-file employees; sociotechnical approaches are additions to the repertoire of improvement strategies that clearly focus on this level.)

Extent of Application

Applications emerging from one or more of the stems just described are evident in the organization development efforts now occurring in many countries, including England, Japan, Norway, Canada, Sweden, Finland, Australia, New Zealand, the Philippines, and Holland, as well as in the United States. The growing number of organizations in America that have embarked on organization development efforts include Union Carbide and Exxon (the first two companies), Connecticut General Insurance Company, Graphic Controls, Equitable Life Assurance Company, Digital Equipment Corporation, Procter & Gamble, Mountain Bell Telephone, Searle Laboratories, General Motors, Bankers Trust, Ford Motor Company, Heinz Foods, IBM, Polaroid, Sun Oil, and TRW Inc. A random sample of half of the *Fortune* 500 companies, yielding 71 respondents, found 46 percent (33) of the responding firms to be using organization development techniques.[54]

Applications at the TRW Systems Group, a large research and development organization in the aerospace field, commenced in the early 1960s, have been as extensive and innovative as those found anywhere in the world, and are of major significance in the emergence and history of OD. (Three organizations have now been created out of TRW Systems Group: Electronic Systems Group, Defense Systems Group, and Space and Technology Group.) Among the key figures in the emergence of the OD effort at TRW Systems were Jim Dunlap, director of industrial relations; Shel Davis, who was later promoted to that position; Ruben Mettler, president of TRW Systems; and Herb Shepard. T-group labs conducted by internal trainers, NTL, and UCLA staff members were also important in providing impetus to the effort in its early phases. Efforts at TRW Systems and in the total organization, TRW, have included team building, intergroup team building, interface laboratories between departments and between company and customers, laboratory training, career assessment workshops, sensing, and organization redesign and restructuring for improved productivity and quality of working life. OD activities at the previous TRW Systems Group and the newly formed Three Groups to a large extent are part of the management process, with personnel department managers extensively used as facilitators.[55]

In England, Europe, Japan, and the Philippines, illustrative of the growing interest in organization development is the involvement of such companies as Imperial Chemical Industries (United Kingdom and elsewhere), J. Lyons & Company (England), the Royal Dutch Shell Group, Business Consultants, Inc. (Tokyo), and the San Miguel Corporation headquartered in Manila. Projects at Imperial Chemical Industries, a large company headquartered in London, have included job enrichment, survey research, team building, and open systems planning.

Industrial organizations, however, are by no means the only kinds of institutions involved. There are applications, for example, in public school systems; colleges; medical schools; social welfare agencies; police departments; professional associations; governmental units at the local, county, state, and national levels; various health care delivery systems; churches; and American Indian tribes.

Applications have also occurred in the U.S. military. In 1980, it was reported that the Navy was using approximately 700 officers and noncommissioned officers full time in its Human Resource Management Program. Consultants are trained in a 12-week program and are then assigned to one of five HRM centers having detachments throughout the world. The thrust of the Navy effort seems to be based on a survey feedback process, but the depth to which the process and data are used appears to vary widely depending upon commanding officer (CO) interest. In some instances, questionnaire data go only to the CO; in other instances, the consulting team works with overlapping, intact teams and uses a variety of OD interventions.[56]

Much of the thrust of the Air Force behavioral science type of consulting activities appears to have been of a technostructural nature, such as job enrichment. However, a wide variety of OD efforts has also emerged. For example, team building, intergroup development, and third-party peacemak-

ing have been used in Air Force research laboratories, and team building and survey feedback have been used in logistics centers. Some of the OD efforts appear to involve all members of the hierarchy in a unit; others seem to have had little top-management involvement. In 1981, the Air Force's Management Consulting Program was manned by 44 consultants from lieutenant colonel to senior noncommissioned officer ranks who were part of a Leadership and Management Development Center at Maxwell Air Force Base, Alabama.[57]

The U.S. Army opened an Organizational Effectiveness Center and School at Fort Ord, California, in the mid-1970s, and between 1975 and late 1981, it had trained about 1,200 OD (OE) consultants. In 1981 there were 388 authorized OE positions at the officer rank and 100 newly created OE positions at the noncommissioned officer level. The OE Center and School also trains consultants for the National Guard and the Reserves; in 1981 there were 24 authorized OE positions in the Guard. OE consultants are assigned in the Army on the basis of two per division or installation or one per brigade. Officers are assigned to a consultancy role for 18 months to a maximum of three years, at which time they return to their other military specialties. Some may be reassigned to the OE effort later on.[58] The 82nd Airborne Division, one of the first Army organizations to be involved, had an extensive OE effort, including team building at the top ranks, by 1977.[59]

Some ''community development'' strategies have a number of elements in common with organization development, such as the use of action research, the use of a change agent, and an emphasis on facilitating decision-making and problem-solving processes.[60] Undoubtedly, some of the commonality stems from OD practitioners working in the community development field. For example, in 1961 Herbert Shepard conducted community development laboratories at China Lake, California, sponsored by the Naval Ordnance Test Station. These one-week labs involved military persons and civilians and people of all ages and socioeconomic levels. Outcomes included the resolution of some community and intercommunity issues.[61]

In addition to emphasizing the diversity of types of systems using OD consultants, we want to emphasize that intraorganization development efforts have not focused on just top-management teams, although the importance of top-management involvement will be discussed in later chapters. The wide range of occupational roles that have been involved in OD is almost limitless and has included production workers,[62] managers, soldiers, military officers, miners, scientists and engineers, ministers, psychologists, geologists, lawyers, accountants, nurses, physicians, teachers, computer specialists, foresters, technicians, secretaries, clerical employees, and board members.

Symptomatic of the widespread application of organization development concepts is the emergence and growth of the OD Network, which began in 1964 and in late 1981 had a membership of about 2,100. Most members either have major roles in the OD efforts of organization or are scholar-practitioners in the OD field. The Network began with discussions at the Case Institute of Technology between Herbert Shepard, Sheldon Davis of TRW Systems, and Floyd Mann of the University of Michigan,[63] and through the initiative of Leland Bradford and Jerry Harvey of NTL and a number of industrial people who had attended labs at Bethel. Among the industrial founders of the organization, originally called the Industrial Trainers Network, were Sheldon Davis of TRW Systems, George Murray of Union Carbide, John Vail of Dow Chemical, and Carl Albers of the Hotel Corporation of America. Other early members were from Procter & Gamble, Weyerhaeuser, Bankers Trust, West Virginia Pulp and Paper Company, the U.S. State Department, the U.S. National Security Agency, Pillsbury, Eli Lilly, Polaroid, Esso, Parker Pen, American Airlines, Goodrich-Gulf Chemicals, RCA, Sandia, National Association of Manufacturers, General Foods, Armour & Company, Heublein, and Dupont. Jerry Harvey was the first secretary/coordinator of the emerging organization, and Warner Burke assumed that role in 1967 shortly after joining NTL on a full-time basis. There were fewer than 50 members at that time; when

Warner Burke stepped aside as executive director in 1975, there were approximately 1,400 members.[64] That same year the OD Network became independent of NTL.

An OD Division of the American Society for Training and Development was established in 1968 and had more than 4,000 members by the summer of 1981. It is also significant that the Academy of Management, whose members are mostly professors in management and related areas, established a Division of Organization Development within its structure in 1971, and this unit had approximately 1,100 members in late 1983. The Division of Industrial and Organizational Psychology of the American Psychological Association has held workshops on organization development at the annual APA conventions; several annual conventions going back at least to 1965 have included papers or symposia on organization development or related topics.[65] In 1974 the *Annual Review of Psychology* for the first time devoted a chapter entirely to a review of research on organization development.[66] Other chapters on OD appeared in 1977[67] and 1982. The 1982 chapter was entitled "Organizational Development and Change" and was written by authors from the Netherlands and France.[68]

The first doctoral program devoted to training OD specialists was founded by Herbert Shepard in 1960 at the Case Institute of Technology. Originally called The Organizational Behavior Group, this program is now part of the Department of Organizational Behavior, School of Management, Case Western Reserve University. Masters degree programs in organization development or masters programs with concentrations in OD have been offered in recent years by several universities, including New York University, Brigham Young, Pepperdine, Loyola, Bowling Green, New Hampshire, Columbia, and Case Western Reserve and Sheffield Polytechnic in England. The American University and NTL Institute jointly offer a masters degree program in Human Resource Development. Many other major universities, if not most, now have graduate courses directly bearing on organization development, including UCLA, Stanford, Harvard, University of Southern California, Hawaii, Oklahoma, Colorado, Indiana, and Purdue, and in England, such courses are found at the University of Manchester Institute of Science and Technology and the University of Bath.[69]

This rapid growth in OD interest and attention has been given impetus by NTL's Program for Specialists in Organization Development (originally called PSOTD), discussed earlier in this chapter. PSOD started as an intensive, four-week session held in the summer at Bethel and was partly an outgrowth of an Organization Intern Program that had included some OD training. PSOD subsequently became a two-week program for experienced practitioners with required prerequisites of T-group attendance and consultation skills training. Other professional programs in OD have been or are now being offered in the United States, Canada, the United Kingdom, Australia, New Zealand, and elsewhere under the sponsorship of universities, foundations, professional associations, and other institutions.

Summary

Organization development has emerged largely from applied behavioral sciences and has three major stems: the invention of the T-group and innovations in the application of laboratory training insights to complex organizations, the invention of survey feedback technology, and the emergence of action research. Parallel and linked to these stems was the emergence of the Tavistock sociotechnical and socioclinical approaches.

Key figures in this early history interacted with each other and across these stems and were influenced by concepts and experiences from a wide variety of disciplines and settings. These disciplines and settings included clinical and social psychology, family group therapy, military psychology and psychiatry, the theater, general semantics, systems theory, mathematics and physics, philosophy, psychodrama, nondirective counseling, survey methodology, experimental and action research, personnel and industrial relations, and general management theory.

The history of OD is emergent in that a rapidly increasing number of behavioral scientists and practitioners in organizations are building on the research and insights of the past as well as discovering the utility of some of the earlier insights. These efforts are now expanding and include a wide range of organizations, types of institutions, occupational categories, and geographical locations around the world.

In the chapters that follow, the assumptions, theory, and techniques of organization development will be examined in substantial depth along with some speculation as to its future viability.

Notes

1. The phrase ''group dynamics'' was coined by Kurt Lewin in 1939. See Warren Bennis, address to the Academy of Management, San Diego, California, August 3, 1981.

2. This and the next paragraph are based on Kenneth D. Benne, Leland P. Bradford, Jack R. Gibb, and Ronald O. Lippitt, eds., *The Laboratory Method of Changing and Learning: Theory and Application* (Palo Alto, Calif.: Science and Behavior Books, 1975), pp. 1–6; and Alfred J. Marrow, *The Practical Theorist: The Life and Work of Kurt Lewin* (New York: Basic Books, 1969), pp. 210–214. For additional history, see Leland P. Bradford, ''Biography of an Institution,'' *Journal of Applied Behavioral Science*, 3 (April–June 1967), pp. 127–143; and Alvin Zander, ''The Study of Group Behavior During Four Decades,'' *The Journal of Applied Behavioral Science*, 15 (July–September 1979), pp. 272–282. We are indebted to Ronald Lippitt for his correspondence, which helped to clarify this and the following paragraph.

3. Peter B. Smith, ed., *Small Groups and Personal Change* (London: Methuen & Co. 1980), pp. 8–9.

4. Robert Chin and Kenneth D. Benne, ''General Strategies for Effecting Changes in Human Systems,'' in Warren G. Bennis, Kenneth D. Benne, and Robert Chin, eds., *The Planning of Change*, 2nd ed. (New York: Holt, Rinehardt and Winston, 1969), pp. 100–102.

5. Ibid., p. 102.

6. Correspondence with Ronald Lippitt.

7. Conversation with Lee Bradford, conference on current theory and practice in organization development, San Francisco, March 16, 1978.

8. Based largely on correspondence with Ronald Lippitt. According to Lippitt, as early as 1945 Bradford and Lippitt were conducting ''three-level training'' at Freedman's Hospital in Washington, D.C., in an effort ''to induce interdependent changes in all parts of the same system.'' Lippitt also reports that Leland Bradford very early was acting on a basic concept of ''multiple entry,'' that is, simultaneously training and working with several groups in the organization.

9. Correspondence with Robert Tannenbaum.

10. Tannenbaum correspondence; memorandum of May 12, 1952, U.S. Naval Ordnance Test Station from E. R. Toporeck to ''Office, Division and Branch Heads, Test Department,'' and '''Minutes, Test Department Management Seminar, 5 March 1953.''

11. Robert Tannenbaum, Verne Kallejian, and Irving R. Weschler, ''Training Managers for Leadership,'' *Personnel,* 30 (January 1954), p. 3.

12. Verne J. Kallejian, Irving R. Weschler, and Robert Tannenbaum, ''Managers in Transition,'' *Harvard Business Review,* 33 (July–August 1955), pp. 55–64.

13. Tannenbaum correspondence.

14. Ibid.

15. See Richard Beckhard, W. Warner Burke, and Fred I. Steele, ''The Program for Specialists in Organization Training and Development,'' p. ii, mimeographed paper (NTL Institute for Applied Behavioral Science, December 1967); and John Paul Jones, ''What's Wrong with Work?'' in *What's Wrong with Work?* (New York: National Association of Manufacturers, 1967), p. 8. According to correspondence with Rensis Likert, the link between McGregor and John Paul Jones occurred in the summer of 1957. Discussions took place between the two when Jones attended one of the annual two-week seminars at Aspen, Colorado, organized by Hollis Peter of the Foundation for Research on Human Behavior and conducted by Douglas McGregor, Mason Haire, and Rensis Likert.

16. Gilbert Burck, ''Union Carbide's Patient Schemers,'' *Fortune,* 72 (December 1965), pp. 147–149. For McGregor's account, see ''Team Building at Union Carbide,'' in Douglas McGregor, *The Professional Manager* (New York: McGraw-Hill, 1967), pp. 106–110.

17. This paragraph is based on interviews with Herbert Shepard, August 3, 1981. For a brief discussion of the career of Clarence Hicks, see Wendell French, *The Personnel Management Process,* 5th ed. (Boston: Houghton Mifflin, 1982), Chap. 2.

18. Much of the historical account in this paragraph and the following three paragraphs is based on correspondence and interviews with Herbert Shepard, with some information added from correspondence with Robert Blake.

19. Correspondence with Robert Blake and Herbert Shepard. For further reference to Murray Horwitz and Paul Buchanan, as well as to comments about the innovative contributions of Michael Blansfield, see Herbert A. Shepard, ''Explorations in Observant Participation,'' in Bradford, Gibb, and Benne, eds., *T-Group Theory,* pp. 382–383. See also Marshall Sashkin, ''Interview with Robert R. Blake and Jane Srygley Mouton,'' *Group and Organization Studies,* 3 (December 1978), pp. 401–407.

20. See Robert Blake and Jane Srygley Mouton, ''The Instrumented Training Laboratory,'' in Irving R. Weschler and Edgar M. Schein, eds., *Selected Readings Series Five: Issues in Training* (Washington, D.C., National Training Laboratories, 1962), pp. 61–85. In this chapter, Blake and Mouton credit Muzafer and Carolyn Sherif with important contributions to early intergroup experiments. Reference is also made to the contributions of Frank Cassens of Humble Oil and Refinery in the early phases of the Esso program. For a brief description of the development of the two-dimensional Managerial Grid, see Robert Blake and Jane Srygley Mouton, *Diary of an OD Man* (Houston: Gulf 1976), pp. 332–336.

21. Based on correspondence with Robert Blake. See also Robert R. Blake and Jane Srygley Mouton, ''Why the OD Movement Is 'Stuck' and How to Break It Loose,'' *Training and Development Journal,* 33 (September 1979), pp. 12–20.

22. Blake correspondence.

23. Mouton correspondence.

24. Blake correspondence.

25. Ibid.

26. Ibid.

27. Correspondence with Richard Beckhard.

28. Ibid.

29. Based on Beckhard correspondence and other sources.

30. Interpretations of Blake correspondence, Shepard interview, Beckhard correspondence, and Larry Porter, "OD: Some Questions, Some Answers—An Interview with Beckhard and Shepard," *OD Practitioner,* 6 (Autumn 1974), p. 1.

31. Blake correspondence.

32. Jane Srygley Mouton and Robert R. Blake, "University Training in Human Relations Skills," *Selected Readings Series Three: Forces in Learning* (Washington, D.C.: National Training Laboratories, 1961), pp. 88–96, reprinted from *Group Psychotherapy,* 10 (1957), pp. 342–345.

33. Shepard and Blake correspondence.

34. Interview with Herbert Shepard, San Diego, California, August 3, 1981.

35. Beckhard correspondence.

36. Burck, "Union Carbide's Patient Schemers," p. 149.

37. Harry D. Kolb, "Introduction" to *An Action Research Program for Organization Improvement* (Ann Arbor, Mich.: Foundation for Research on Human Behavior, 1960), p. i. The phrase *organization development* is used several times in this monograph based on a 1959 meeting about the Esso programs and written by Kolb, Shepard, Blake, and others.

38. Based on Beckhard correspondence.

39. This history is based largely on correspondence with Rensis Likert and partially on "The Career of Rensis Likert," *ISR Newsletter,* Winter 1971; and *A Quarter Century of Social Research,* Institute for Social Research, 1971.

40. "Rensis Likert," *ISR Newsletter,* p. 6.

41. Likert correspondence. Floyd Mann later became the first director of the Center for Research on the Utilization of Scientific Knowledge (CRUSK) when the center was established by ISR in 1964. See also Floyd C. Mann, "Studying and Creating Change," in Bennis, Benne, and Chin, eds., *Planning of Change,* pp. 605–613.

42. Mann, "Studying and Creating Change," p. 609.

43. Howard Baumgartel. "Using Employee Questionnaire Results for Improving Organizations: The Survey (Feedback) Experiment," *Kansas Business Review,* 12 (December 1959), pp. 2–6.

44. Likert correspondence.

45. Marrow, *The Practical Theorist,* p. 164. This book, about the life and work of Kurt Lewin, is rich with events that are important to the history of OD.

46. Likert correspondence.

47. Ibid.

48. H. V. Dicks, *Fifty Years of the Tavistock Clinic* (London: Routledge & Kegan Paul, 1970), pp. 1, 32.

49. Based on Ibid., pp. 5, 7, 133, 140; and Robert DeBoard, *The Psychoanalysis of Organizations* (London: Tavistock 1978), pp. 35–43.

50. Eric Trist and Marshall Sashkin, "Interview," *Group & Organization Studies,* 5 June 1980), pp. 150–151.

51. Ibid., p. 155.

52. The previous three paragraphs are based largely on ibid., pp. 144–151. The brief statement about action research is also partly based on Alfred J. Marrow, "Risks and Uncertainties in Action Research," *Journal of Social Issues* 20, No. 3, (1964), p. 17.

53. Bennis address, Academy of Management, August 3, 1981.

54. Stephen R. Michael, "Organizational Change Techniques: Their Present, Their Future," *Organizational Dynamics,* 11 (Summer 1982), p. 77.

55. Interview with Sam Shirley, February 4, 1982; correspondence with Sheldon A. Davis; Sheldon A. Davis, "An Organic Problem-Solving Method of Organizational Change," *Journal of Applied Behavioral Science,* 3 (November 1, 1967), pp. 3–21; and the case study of the TRW Systems Group in Gene Dalton, Paul Lawrence, and Larry Greiner, *Organizational Change and Development* (Homewood, Ill.: Irwin-Dorsey, 1970), pp. 4–153.

56. Denis M. Umstot, "Organization Development Technology and the Military: A Surprising Merger?" *Academy of Management Review,* (April 1980), pp. 193–194.

57. Ibid., pp. 196–197; and Steve Ferrier, "The U.S. Air Force Management Consulting Program: Implications for Army OE." *OE Communique,* 5, No. 3 (1981), pp. 29–35.

58. Interview with Lt. Col. Ronald Sheffield, U.S. Army Organizational Effectiveness Center and School, July 1981. See also the Army's publication, *OE Communique.*

59. Presentation by Lt. Col. Robert L. Phillips, Academy of Management Annual Meeting, Orlando, Florida, August 16, 1977.

60. See Eva Schindler-Rainman, "Community Development Through Laboratory Methods," in Benne, Bradford, Gibb, eds.; and Lippitt, *Laboratory Method of Changing and Learning,* pp. 445–463.

61. Shepard correspondence. Starting in 1967, Herbert Shepard was involved in the applications of OD to community problems in Middletown, Connecticut.

62. See Scott Myers, "Overcoming Union Opposition to Job Enrichment," *Harvard Business Review,* 49 (May–June 1971), pp. 37–49; and Robert Blake, Herbert Shepard, and Jane Mouton, *Managing Intergroup Conflict in Industry* (Houston: Gulf, 1964), pp. 122–138.

63. Shepard correspondence.

64. Correspondence with W. Warner Burke and memoranda and attendance lists pertaining to 1967–1969 Network meetings furnished by Burke.

65. For example, the following topics were included in the program of the 1965 convention: "Strategies for Organization Improvement: Research and Consultation," "Managerial Grid Organization Development," and "The Impact of Laboratory Training in Research and Development Environment," *American Psychologist,* 20 (July 1965), pp. 549, 562, 565.

66. Frank Friedlander and L. Dave Brown, "Organization Development," *Annual Review of Psychology,* 25 (1974), pp. 313–341.

67. Clay Alderfer, "Organization Development," *Annual Review of Psychology,* 28 (1977), pp. 197–223.

68. Claude Faucheux, Gilles Amada, and André Laurent, "Organizational Development and Change," *Annual Review of Psychology,* 33 (1982), pp. 343–370.

69. D. D. Warrick, ed., *OD Newsletter,* OD Division, Academy of Management, Spring 1979, p. 7.

Reading 2

WHAT IS ORGANIZATION DEVELOPMENT?

Richard Beckhard

Definition. Organization development is an effort (1) *planned,* (2) *organizationwide,* and (3) *managed* from the *top,* to (4) increase *organization effectiveness* and *health* through (5) *planned interventions in* the organization's "processes," using *behavioral-science* knowledge.

1. It is a *planned change* effort.

An OD program involves a systematic diagnosis of the organization, the development of a strategic plan for improvement, and the mobilization of resources to carry out the effort.

2. It involves the total *"system."*

An organization development effort is related to a total organization change such as a change in the culture or the reward systems or the total managerial strategy. There may be tactical efforts which work with subparts of the organization but the "system" to be changed is a total, relatively autonomous organization. This is not necessarily a total corporation, or an entire government, but refers to a system which is relatively free to determine its own plans and future within very *general* constraints from the environment.

3. *It is managed from the top.*

In an organization development effort, the top management of the system has a personal investment in the program and its outcomes. They actively participate in the *management* of the effort. This does not mean they must participate in the same *activities* as others, but it does mean that they must have both knowledge and *commitment* to the

Source: Richard Beckhard, *Organization Development: Strategies and Models* (Reading, Mass.: Addison-Wesley Publishing, 1969), pp. 9, 10, 14. Reprinted with permission.

goals of the program and must actively support the methods used to achieve the goals.

4. It is designed to *increase organization effectiveness* and *health.*

To understand the goals of organization development, it is necessary to have some picture of what an "ideal" effective, healthy organization would look like. What would be its characteristics? Numbers of writers and practitioners in the field have proposed definitions which, although they differ in detail, indicate a strong consensus of what a healthy operating organization is. Let me start with my own definition. An effective organization is one in which:

a. The total organization, the significant subparts, and individuals, manage their work against *goals* and *plans* for achievement of these goals.

b. Form follows function (the problem, or task, or project, determines how the human resources are organized).

c. Decisions are made by and near the sources of information regardless of where these sources are located on the organization chart.

d. The reward system is such that managers and supervisors are rewarded (and punished) comparably for:
Short-term profit or production performance.
Growth and development of their subordinates.
Creating a viable working group.

e. Communication laterally and vertically is *relatively* undistorted. People are generally open and confronting. They share all the relevant facts including feelings.

f. There is a minimum amount of inappropriate win/lose activities between individuals and groups. Constant effort exists at all levels to treat conflict, and conflict situations, as *problems* subject to problem-solving methods.

g. There is high "conflict" (clash of ideas) about tasks and projects, and relatively little energy spent in clashing over *interpersonal* difficulties because they have been generally worked through.

h. The organization and its parts see themselves as interacting with each other *and* with a *larger* environment. The organization is an "open system."

i. There is a shared value, and management strategy to support it, of trying to help each person (or unit) in the organization maintain his (or its) integrity and uniqueness in an interdependent environment.

j. The organization and its members operate in an "action-research" way. General practice is to build in *feedback mechanisms* so that individuals and groups can learn from their own experience.

Another definition is found in John Gardner's set of rules for an effective organization. He describes an effective organization as one which is *self-renewing* and then lists the rules:

The *first rule* is that the organization must have an effective program for the recruitment and development of talent.

The *second rule* for the organization capable of continuous renewal is that it must be a hospitable environment for the individual.

The *third rule* is that the organization must have built-in provisions for self-criticism.

The *fourth rule* is that there must be fluidity in the internal structure.

The *fifth rule* is that the organization must have some means of combating the process by which men become prisoners of their procedures.[1]

Edgar Schein defines organization effectiveness in relation to what he calls "the adaptive coping cycle," that is, an organization that can effectively adapt and cope with the changes in its environment. Specifically, he says:

The sequence of activities or processes which begins with some change in the internal or external environment and ends with a more adaptive, dynamic equilibrium for dealing with the change, is the organization's "adaptive coping cycle." If we identify the various stages or processes of this cycle, we shall also be able to identify the points where organizations typically may fail to cope adequately and where, therefore, consultants and researchers have been able in a variety of ways to help increase organization effectiveness.[2]

The organization conditions necessary for effective coping, according to Schein, are:

The ability to take in and communicate information reliably and validly.

Internal flexibility and creativity to make the changes which are demanded by the information obtained (including structural flexibility).

Integration and commitment to the goals of the organization from which comes the willingness to change.

An internal climate of support and freedom from threat, since being threatened undermines good communication, reduces flexibility, and stimulates self-protection rather than concern for the total system.

Miles et al. (1966) define the healthy organization in three broad areas—those concerned with task accomplishment, those concerned with internal integration, and those involving mutual adaptation of the organization and its environment. The following dimensional conditions are listed for each area:

In the task-accomplishment area, a healthy organization would be one with (1) reasonably clear, accepted, achievable and appropriate

---

[1]J. W. Gardner, "How to Prevent Organizational Dry Rot," *Harper's Magazine*, October 1965.

[2]E. H. Schein, *Organizational Psychology* (Englewood Cliffs, N.J.: Prentice-Hall 1965.

goals; (2) relatively understood communications flow; (3) optimal power equalization.

In the area of internal integration, a healthy organization would be one with (4) resource utilization and individuals' *good fit* between personal disposition and role demands; (5) a reasonable degree of cohesiveness and "organization identity," clear and attractive enough so that persons feel actively connected to it; (6) high morale. In order to have growth and active changefulness, a healthy organization would be one with innovativeness, autonomy, adaptation, and problem-solving adequacy.[3]

Lou Morse, in his recent thesis on organization development, writes that:

> The commonality of goals are cooperative group relations, consensus, integration, and commitment to the goals of the organization (task accomplishment), creativity, authentic behavior, freedom from threat, full utilization of a person's capabilities, and organizational flexibility.[4]

5. Organization development achieves its goals through *planned interventions* using behavioral science knowledge.

A strategy is developed of intervening or moving into the existing organization and helping it, in effect, "stop the music," examine its present ways of work, norms, and values, and look at alternative ways of working, or relating, or rewarding. . . . The interventions used draw on the knowledge and technology of the behavioral sciences about such processes as individual motivation, power, communications, perception, cultural norms, problem-solving, goal-setting, interpersonal relationships, intergroup relationships, and conflict management.

Some Operational Goals in an Organization-Development Effort

To move toward the kind of organization conditions described in the above definitions, OD efforts usually have some of the following operational goals:

1. To develop a self-renewing, *viable system* that can organize in a variety of ways depending on tasks. This means systematic efforts to change and loosen up the way the organization operates, so that it organizes differently depending on the nature of the task. There is movement toward a concept of "form follows function," rather than that *tasks* must *fit* into existing structures.

2. To optimize the effectiveness of both the stable (the basic organization chart) and the temporary systems (the many projects, committees, etc., through which much of the organization's work is accomplished) by built-in, *continuous improvement mechanisms*. This means the introduction of procedures for analyzing work tasks and resource distribution, and for building in continuous "feedback" regarding the way a system or subsystem is operating.

3. To move toward *high collaboration* and *low competition* between interdependent units. One of the major obstacles to effective organizations is the amount of dysfunctional energy spent in inappropriate competition—energy that is not, therefore, available for the accomplishment of tasks. If all of the energy that is used by, let's say, manufacturing people disliking or wanting to "get those sales people," or vice versa, were available to improve organization output, productivity would increase tremendously.

4. To create conditions where conflict is brought out and managed. One of the fundamental problems in unhealthy (or less than healthy) organizations is the amount of energy that is dysfunctionally used trying to work around, or avoid, or cover up, conflicts which are inevitable in a complex organization. The goal is to move the organization towards seeing conflict as an inevitable condition and as problems that need to be *worked* before adequate decisions can be made.

[3]M. B. Miles et al., "Data Feedback and Organization Change in a School System" (Paper given at a meeting of the American Sociological Association, August 27, 1966).

[4]L. H. Morse, "Task-Centered Organization Development." (Master's thesis, Sloan School of Management, MIT, June 1968).

5. To reach the point where decisions are made on the basis of information source rather than organizational role. This means the need to move toward a *norm* of the *authority of knowledge* as well as the authority of role. It does not only mean that decisions should be moved down in the organization; it means that the organization manager should determine which is the best source of information (or combination of sources of information) to work a particular problem, and it is there that the decision making should be located.

Reading 3

THE NATURE OF ORGANIZATION DEVELOPMENT

Matthew B. Miles and Richard A. Schmuck

Definition of OD

OD can be defined as a planned and sustained effort to apply behavioral science for system improvement, using reflexive, self-analytic methods. Let us examine each element of this definition in detail.

System Improvement

The emphasis of OD is on the system, rather than the individual, as the target of change. In this respect the approach differs from "sensitivity training" and "management development." "System" may mean either an entire organization or a subsystem such as an academic department or team of teachers. The emphasis, however, is always on improving both the ability of a *system* to cope and the relationships of the system with subsystems and with the environment. Individuals, of course, often gain insights and new attitudes during such improvement processes, but the primary concern of OD is with such matters as adequate organizational communication, the integration of individual and organizational goals, the development of a climate of trust in decision making, and the effect of the reward system on morale.

Reflexive, Self-Analytic Methods

OD involves system members themselves in the assessment, diagnosis, and transformation of their own organization. Rather than simply accepting diag-

Source: Reprinted from Richard A. Schmuck and Matthew B. Miles, eds., *Organization Development in Schools* (San Diego, Calif.: University Associates, 1976), pp. 2–3, 7–10. Used with permission.

nosis and prescription from an outside "technocratic" expert, organization members themselves, with the *aid* of outside consultants, examine current difficulties and their causes and participate actively in the reformulation of goals, the development of new group process skills, the redesign of structures and procedures for achieving the goals, the alteration of the working climate of the system, and the assessment of results.

Planned and Sustained Effort

OD involves deliberately planned change, as contrasted with system "drifts." Unlike an innovative project or program it is generally not limited to a specific period of time. To implement OD, an organizational subsystem (such as a Department of Organization Development) is created and charged with the specific responsibility for planning, managing, and evaluating the continuous process of organizational self-renewal. Members of such a subsystem act as inside change agents or OD development specialists . . . and usually link with outside consultants to carry out their mission. The essential concept is that some fraction of an organization's resources is devoted to continuous organizational maintenance, rebuilding, and expansion. Such a concept is familiar to managers in the field of plant equipment maintenance but is much less widely known and accepted in the maintenance of the human organization.

Organizations are not easily or quickly transformed. The available evidence (see, e.g., Buchanan, 1967 and 1969) suggests that in large organizations two to three years of OD effort is typical before the completion of serious and self-sustaining change. In addition, it must be borne in mind that an organization is never transformed permanently. Instead, institutionalized, built-in OD functions must continually be involved in facing the dilemmas and vicissitudes of organizational renewal.

Applied Behavioral Science

OD relies strongly on concepts from the behavioral sciences: primarily social psychology but also psychology and sociology. Such concepts are used to diagnose an organization's problems, to equip organization members with a conceptual language for talking about phenomena they are facing; to redesign unsatisfactory structures and procedures, and to provide a basis for evaluation of OD interventions and processes.

How OD Works

A typical sequence of events in the initiation and development of an OD program is as follows:

1. Middle or top management of an organization becomes interested in OD and feels that the organization has problems which can be met through training. Initial interest is often developed after a manager's personal attendance at a T-group laboratory.
2. Management invites an outside OD consultant to visit the organization.
3. After the consultant's entry and contact with a variety of organization roles and groups, the organization works out a contract with the consultant specifying the nature of the projected relationship and its goals and general procedures.
4. The consultant, working with insiders, collects data about the organization via interviews, questionnaires, and observations.
5. These data form the basis of a joint diagnosis of the points of difficulty in the organization and, if appropriate, between the organization and its environment. Goals for change are explicitly identified.
6. A first "intervention" (usually an intensive meeting involving several key roles, a group,

or more than one group) is planned. The data collected earlier are often fed back and discussed. Exercises for training in communication skills or group functioning are often used as constructive vehicles for discussing the data. (For a delineation of the range of interventions employed, see below.)
7. The intervention is evaluated following a new collection of data. Often the future success of the effort depends on the degree to which key figures have been "freed up" to be more open, concerned, and creative about organizational improvement.
8. Subsequent steps in intervention are planned on the basis of these data, and the process continues.

The usual primary effect of the early stages of an OD training program is to change the "culture" of the organization: it becomes more open, trusting, collaborative, self-analytical, and inclined to take risks. As a program proceeds, structural changes become more typical as outcomes; reorganizations, the development of new roles and groups, and new forms of work-flow are planned and set into motion. Typical additional steps in the OD program which occur at this later stage are as follows:

9. The OD function itself becomes institutionalized within the organization. An OD department or group is formed and takes central responsibility for continuing the OD process, drawing on outside resources as needed.
10. The internal OD specialists become increasingly professionalized and responsible for their own development via such bodies as NTL and networks of other professionals. They may at times serve as outside change agents to other organizations.

Technology of OD

The OD cube in Figure 1 displays the typical interventions employed in OD training. At the left are the *problems diagnosed* by the inside/outside change team; they may include difficulties in goal-setting and planning, communication, climate, and

FIGURE 1 The OD Cube: A Scheme for Classifying OD Interventions

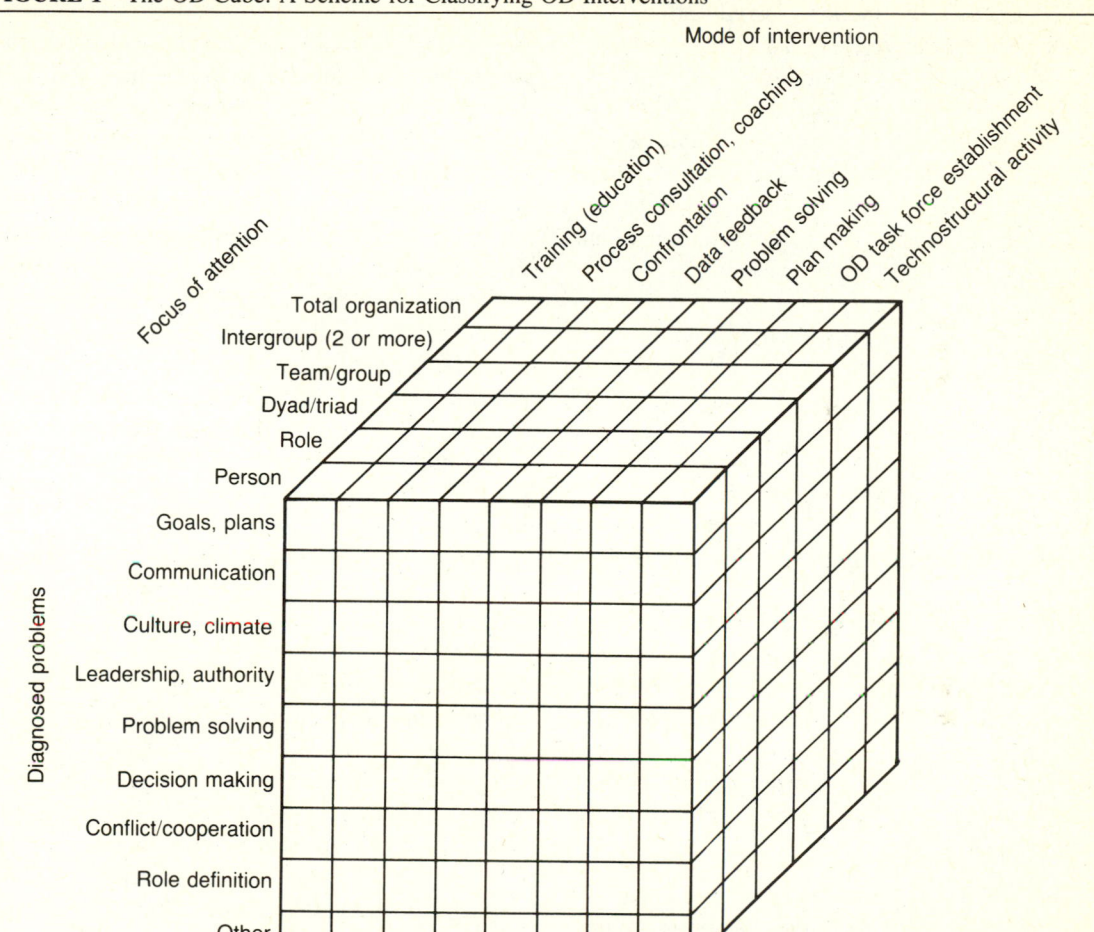

other matters. These problems may occur either in *existing* units, or in such *new* units as those created during the start-up phase of a new organization, those developed during the course of mergers with or acquisitions of other organizations, and those emerging during the course of the major reorganization of a firm. For clarity, the three additional "cubes" for start-ups, mergers and reorganizations are not shown here. The interventions used in such new systems often differ substantially from those used in existing systems.

The diagonal edge of the cube identifies the *focus of attention* of the forthcoming intervention. The intervention may be focused essentially on a change in persons (individuals), in roles, in dyads or triads (two-or three-person groups), in work teams, in the relations between two or more groups, or in the organization as a whole. OD training most frequently focuses on key roles, teams, relationships between groups, and the total organization.

The modes of intervention which can be employed are as follows:

1. Training or education: procedures involving direct teaching or experience-based learning. Such technologies as lectures, exercises, simulations, and T-groups are examples.
2. Process consultation: watching and aiding ongoing processes and coaching to improve them.
3. Confrontation: bringing together units of the organization (persons, roles, or groups) which have previously been in poor communication: usually accompanied by supporting data.
4. Data feedback: systematic collection of information, which is then reported back to appropriate organizational units as a base for diagnosis, problem solving, and planning.
5. Problem solving: meetings essentially focusing on problem identification, diagnosis, and solution invention and implementation.
6. Plan making: activity focused primarily on planning and goal setting to replot the organization's future.
7. OD task force establishment: setting up ad hoc problem-solving groups or internal teams of specialists to ensure that the organization solves problems and carries out plans continuously.
8. Technostructural activity: action which has as its prime focus the alteration of the organization's structure, work flow, and means of accomplishing tasks.

These intervention modes flow into each other and are not mutually exclusive. They range roughly from "soft" (person-changing) to "hard" (task-oriented or structure-changing) in emphasis. A strong OD program will typically involve all eight components at one time or another.

Any particular OD intervention can be classified according to problem, focus of attention, and mode of intervention. For example, an intervention might be aimed at increasing problem-solving and decision-making skills in an existing team—a plant manager and his seven subordinate division heads, for example. Its mode might be process consultation: the outside change agent watches the group work and provides feedback from time to time on their process (*how* they are proceeding, who is and is not listened to, whether the boss's word always holds sway, etc.). For another example, an intervention might focus on the entire faculty of a new junior high school to increase its ability to solve problems. The modes of the intervention could be training in communication skills, followed by training in problem solving and then process consultation during real-life problem solving at faculty meetings.

As the latter example shows, the OD process is further complicated by the fact that most training interventions sequence various modes in unique ways. As one considers the complexities of OD design, the number of combinations involving all three of these dimensions becomes very large. Research as yet tells us little about optimal sequencing of interventions directed toward specific targets and problems over a period of years, but such strategic planning is the central stock-in-trade of the OD specialist.

Reading 4

ORGANIZATION DEVELOPMENT

Frank Friedlander and L. Dave Brown

Introduction

Organization development (OD) has emerged both from the demands of a changing environment and from knowledge provided by the evolution of the applied behavioral sciences. Rapid changes within organizational environments have demanded organizational processes and structures which are far more flexible and responsive than traditional bureaucratic structures (22, 112). There have also been dramatic shifts in the social environment—in the life styles, needs, and values of the human working force. Increase in professionalization, educational level, and ease of mobility have decreased organizational loyalty and dependency. There have been efforts to challenge authority, a gradual shift from organizational relevance to personal relevance (66), and a trend toward preference for collaborative rather than hierarchical roles (131). Much of the alienation and disenchantment in our current society is attributed to the institution of work (139). Work is seen as an arena in which considerable leverage can be exerted to improve the quality of life.

Concurrent with and in partial response to these changes in the environment, a number of developments have occurred in the behavioral science disciplines. These include the realization that a variety of social and psychological factors affect work performance (127); the discovery that group decision making affects personal involvement, motivation, and commitment (118); findings that participation increases ownership of change (56); and the use of groups as agents of change in organizations (48). T-groups and sensitivity training began in the late 1940s as an educational method which focused upon group processes and group dynamics (37). Approaches to sociotechnical systems (162) and work motivation (98, 99) have more recently incorporated the organizational tasks and social structures as important dimensions of organizational change. With a few major exceptions (15, 112, 113), contemporary organization theory has not yet contributed heavily to the field of organization development. Its prime concern is in describing, analyzing, and theorizing about the status quo of the organization rather than the planned change processes which might improve its condition.

Today OD is emerging as a field of interdisciplinary academic study and as a recognized profession. Increasing numbers of practitioners are employed by organizations. There is an accrediting agency for OD practitioners[1] plus several professional organizations with OD divisions. Although research and theory have seriously lagged behind the practice of OD, a number of original books devoted primarily to OD have appeared in the past five years: Argyris (15, 16); Golembiewski (86); French & Bell (75); Beckhard (20); Bennis (23); Blake & Mouton (27); Lawrence & Lorsch (113); Schein (145); Walton (168); Fordyce & Weil (73); Lippitt (119). In addition, several edited collections on OD have appeared: Bennis, Benne & Chin (24); Hornstein et al. (101); Burke (41); Burke & Hornstein

Source: Frank Friedlander and L. Dave Brown, reprinted, with permission, from ''Organization Development,'' *Annual Review of Psychology,* vol. 25, pp. 313–16, 320–31, 336–41. Copyright © 1974 by Annual Reviews, Inc. All rights reserved.

This review was supported in part by the National Institute of Mental Health, U.S. Public Health Service (Research Grant 5 R01 MH 20719).

[1]The International Association for Applied Social Scientists.

(42); Margulies & Raia (124); Schmuck & Miles (147). Review chapters and papers are now in progress which attempt to review a number of studies and to suggest frameworks for understanding organizational change (5, 21, 84, 159).

The framework we shall use in reviewing OD views organizations as composed of people with different sets of values, styles, and skills; technologies with different characteristics; and processes and structures which reflect different kinds of relationships between people or between people and their work (114). Processes and structures are the integrating mechanisms for (*a*) applying human resources to technological processes for task accomplishment, and (*b*) facilitating the utilization of technological processes for human fulfillment. From this perspective OD is a method for facilitating change and development in people (e.g., styles, values, skills), in technology (e.g., greater simplicity, complexity), and in organizational processes and structures (e.g., relationships, roles) (80). The objectives of OD generally can be classified as those optimizing human and social improvement or as those optimizing task accomplishment or more likely as some (often confused) blend of the two.

Our concept of organization development calls for change in technology and structure (technostructural) or change in individuals and their interaction processes (human-processual), rather than efforts to change only the people, only the structure/process, or only the technology of the organization. The rationale behind this decision is twofold. First, the organizational processes and structures are the major linkage between the human and technological inputs into the organization; process and structure are thus core concepts of the organization as a system. Second, much of the literature on change indicates the relative impotence of efforts to change only technology (e.g., industrial engineering, operations research, and scientific management approaches), only people (e.g., selection methods, sensitivity groups, and most training), or only the structure (e.g., rearrangements and reorganizations based only on structural elements). For example, strong resistance or failure is often encountered in efforts to

change only the organization structure (59), only the technology of the organization (163), or only the individual (46, 47, 71, 81).

The framework for our discussion of OD is pictured in Figure 1. An organization includes people, technology, and process/structure. These components interact in the technostructural and human-processual systems on behalf of the objectives of human fulfillment and task accomplishment. Although we have not pictured it in Figure 1, the environment obviously interacts with all of these components in terms of input to and output from the organization.

As indicated in Figure 1, the human-processual and technostructural-change approaches converge at the interface of the organization process and structure. Both process and structure are concerned with authority, communication, decision making, goal setting, and conflict resolution. But process implies the implementation of these as dynamic behavioral events and interactions, whereas structure describes these as ongoing sets of durable roles and relationships. Attitudes and behavior are clearly affected by both process (130) and structure (137). Over time, structures can be changed by processes that are inconsistent with them and processes are constrained and facilitated by organizational structures. Since process and structure are embedded in each other, it is almost impossible to create lasting change in one without modification of the other. Yet there are those who focus on changing organizational structures with no involvement in the behavioral processes in which these structures are embedded, and those who are totally concerned with changing processes, oblivious of the ongoing structures which underlie these processes.

If organizations can be viewed as composed of three components (people, technologies, and structures), so also can OD itself be understood by this model. It is at once a set of personal values, a set of change technologies, and a set of processes or structures through which the change agent relates to the organizational system. Thus OD interventions can be described in terms of the degree to which they incorporate values of humanism, democracy, economics, and science; the degree to

FIGURE 1 Approaches to Organization Development

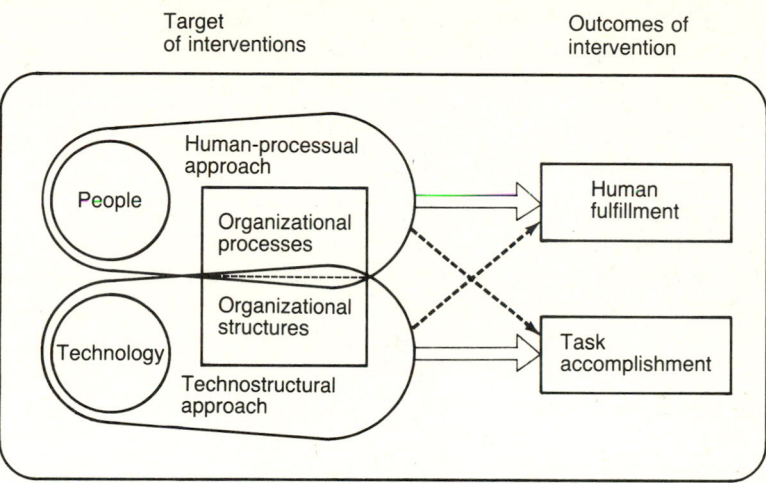

which they utilize such technologies as team building, job design, and survey feedback; the degree to which they incorporate collaborative or unilateral relationships between change agent and organization, and the degree to which they are intended to optimize human-social benefit or productivity/performance objectives.

The values of the more humanistic and democratic approaches to OD are stated rather explicitly in the literature. Many of these stem from the Theory Y assumptions of McGregor (128). Tannenbaum & Davis (160), for example, clearly state these as values in transition in society: toward a positive and confirming view of man as a whole person, in process; toward encouraging the effective expression of feelings, authenticity, risk, confrontation, and collaboration. These values are similar to the humanistic-democratic values expressed by others (22, 86, 124).

The objectives of OD are obviously colored by these values. They include creating an open problem-solving climate, supplementing the authority of role and status with the authority of knowledge and competence, locating decision making and problem solving as close to information sources as possible, building trust and collaboration, devel-

oping a reward system which recognizes the organizational mission and the growth of people, helping managers to manage according to relevant objectives rather than past practices, and increasing self-control and self-direction for people within the organization (42, 155). Others see OD objectives as increased problem-solving capacity (15, 155), cultural change (42), or reeducation (86, 174).

The relationships of OD practitioners to organizational systems vary from facilitative-collaborative to unilateral-directive. In the latter, the change agent gathers data, analyzes it, reports his findings to senior management, and recommends changes. In the more facilitative role, the change agent helps others engage in exploration, diagnosis, and development. Phases in the facilitative-collaborative process include helping the organization identify problems, set priorities, develop data, plan action strategy, test and implement alternatives, and evaluate the change effort (20, 109, 120, 124).

The main body of this review is divided into these two sections: technostructural and human-processual change approaches. We exclude studies and conceptualizations not encompassed in one of these two approaches. We omit studies which were not concerned with change per se, or which were not field studies in organizational settings. We have also not considered some approaches because of space limitations or inclusion in previous reviews: e.g., management by objectives, pay and incentive systems, staffing systems.

Technostructural Approaches

Technostructural approaches to OD refer to theories of and interventions into the technology (e.g., task methods and processes) and the structure (e.g., the relationships, roles, arrangements) of the organization. Technostructural approaches are rooted in the fields of engineering, sociology, psychology, economics, and open systems theory. Change interventions are intended to affect the work content and method and to affect the sets of relationships among workers. Within the broad heading of technostructural development are included sociotechnical systems perspectives, job design and enlargement, and job enrichment. These methods are easier to separate in theory than in practice, but the conceptual distinction among them has implications that are important enough to warrant their preservation in this discussion.

Sociotechnical systems and job design are, in part, a reaction to and an emergence from two earlier and still current perspectives of change: (*a*) scientific management and industrial engineering which focus upon the physical environment and physiological requirements of workers and (*b*) psychology and social psychology, which focus on the social relationships and personal needs of the workers. Proponents of sociotechnical systems and job design criticize the physical approach for treating social groups and individuals mechanistically, and criticize the psychological approach for ignoring the technology of the organization or treating it as unchangeable. Further criticism is that both approaches treat the organization as a closed system, dealing with intraorganizational issues in piecemeal fashion and ignoring the important linkages between the organization and its environment (60).

The concept of sociotechnical systems has been applied to the work initiated by England, particularly at the Tavistock Institute. Sociotechnical interventions are directed at the fit between the technological configurations and the social structure of work units. The term *job design* until recently has been applied to developments in the United States, particularly those initiated at the University of California at Berkeley. Job design studies have sought to manipulate the configuration of technology, as in task designs and assignments making up jobs, and to explore the effects of these changes on personal, social, and organizational phenomena (60). We have grouped job design studies together with job enlargement studies since the methodologies are similar. Job design and enlargement are concerned with increasing satisfaction and performance, although there seems to be greater concern in job design to enhance performance, and greater concern in job enlargement to enhance job satisfaction. Job enrichment is derived from theories of motivation, whereas job enlargement is based on industrial engineering principles. In job enrichment, work functions from a vertical slice of the unit are brought together into a single job to increase the challenge of that job (and therefore the motivation of the jobholder); in job enlargement, work functions from horizontal slices of the work unit are consolidated to provide greater variety and a sense of the whole task.

There are also differences in scope among these three approaches. Sociotechnical systems take into account the entire system, job design focuses upon sets of interrelated functions, and job enrichment is concerned primarily with single jobs. Successful job enrichment, for example, may enrich a single job at the expense of other jobs in that unit. Sociotechnical systems, on the other hand, frequently rearrange relationships among roles or tasks or the sequence of activities.

Sociotechnical Systems

In one of the earliest studies in sociotechnical systems, Trist & Bamforth (163) found that two different social systems in British coal mining were associated with very different levels of productivity, absenteeism, and accidents. Traditional coal mining utilized small, cohesive work groups working as autonomous teams, each establishing its own system of work with each worker performing a variety of tasks. Technological advances led to a change in which work groups of about 40 men in three shifts were formed, with their activities spread over a wide area. The task requirements prohibited close interpersonal relations and group identification; workers were assigned to narrow tasks and paid on an individual rather than a team basis. The longwall method resulted in lowered performance, higher absenteeism, feelings of passivity and indifference and emotional strain. When many of the social and group relationships were reintroduced into a "composite longwall method," productivity, attendance, safety, and morale were substantially improved (70, 164).

Rice (140), another member of the Tavistock group, applied similar concepts in an Indian weaving mill. Installation of automatic looms and task specialization led to a decline in the quantity and quality of woven products. Rice introduced a number of changes: the number of job levels was reduced from nine to three, tasks were made interchangeable, and semiautonomous work groups were created and placed in charge of a set of looms. During the following two years, productivity rose, wasted-cloth rate declined, and morale rose dramatically.

More recently, Tavistock group members have worked with the employee relations group of Shell UK Limited to develop and diffuse throughout the organization a philosophy of management that explicitly emphasizes the maintenance and development of human resources as well as productivity as corporate goals (100). Originally conceived as the initial step in a companywide effort to decrease worker alienation and apathy, the diffusion of the new philosophy and the subsequent changes in procedures and productivity bargains presage major changes in the quality of life and levels of productivity in the organization.

On a larger scale, the Tavistock group is now heavily involved in experiments in "industrial democracy" being carried out at the national level in Norway. In collaboration with workers, employers, and the Norwegian government, a number of field experiments in the effects of different work phi-

losophies and sociotechnical arrangements have been carried out. Though the results available are only preliminary, there is evidence (70a, 160a, 162a) that the changes do indeed have important effects on both productivity and alienation.

Job Design and Job Enlargement

Like the sociotechnical systems approach, job design and enlargement focus upon both the technical aspects of the job and the social structures which support it. They also attempt to increase satisfaction and performance by building in greater variety, discretion, feedback, identity, and responsibility for whole task completion.

In one of the earliest studies in job design, Marks (125), as reported in Davis & Canter (61), conducted an experiment on the shop floor to change the configuration of technology through task design and job assignments. For example, operations, inspection, and securing of materials were combined into one job and performed at individual work stations. This design resulted in improvements in output, quality, production flexibility, and job attitude. In a similar study (57) in which assembly jobs were changed over to more independent bench jobs, production time decreased and quality increased. Preference for self-pacing was found as the reason for preferring bench jobs, but social interaction and work interaction showed sharp reductions. Similar results have been found for enlargement of maintenance jobs (63). Job enlargement for supervisors has resulted in a greater orientation to the technical problems of production and to worker training. Although no changes were observed in production, costs, absenteeism, grievances, or transfers, there were significant increases in quality (62). In a summary of a number of job enlargement projects, Stewart (158) found that quality of product improved, labor costs decreased, operators generally preferred job enlargement in a short time, and problems inherent in paced groups largely disappeared.

Alderfer (3) concludes in a review that job enlargement results in increased overall job satisfaction and greater meaningfulness of work. Lawler (111) reviewed ten studies and found quality improvements in all, but productivity increases in only four. Davis (60) explains such improvements as a consequence of increased number and variety of tasks, self-determination of pacing, increased responsibility for quality, increased discretion of work methods, and sense of work completion. Alderfer (3) found that enlarged jobs are judged by non-jobholder experts as requiring more technical competence and opportunity for innovation, more variety of duties, and more need to deal with people. Incumbents of enlarged jobs reported increased satisfaction with opportunities to use their skills and abilities and decreased satisfaction with their relations with superiors. Friedman (82) reports a study in which interaction and communication between foremen and workers increased, resulting in increased prestige for workers. However, at least two studies report negative effects of job enlargement on interpersonal work relationships. Conant & Kilbridge (57) note that social interaction opportunities and work interaction showed sharp reductions in bench work. Alderfer (3) reports that job enlargement resulted in lower satisfaction with respect from superiors.

Alderfer (3) suggests that differing results of job enlargement on interpersonal relations is contingent upon the technology. In continuous process technology, where there is a high demand for interdependency among employees, job enlargement may place greater stress on these interdependencies, resulting in lowered satisfaction.

Job Enrichment

Job enrichment is the restructuring of the content of a set of jobs or functions which are vertically related to enhance the employee's opportunity for responsibility, achievement, challenge, and growth. It generally involves collapsing various vertical functions into a single more responsible function. Proponents of job enrichment are somewhat critical of job enlargement, claiming that job enlargement condenses the boredom and monotony of several jobs into one job. Job enrichment as an organizational process evolved from the two-factor motivation theory developed by Herzberg, Mausner & Snyderman (99); the theory stresses that man's needs at work are met essentially by the nature of his work. The major motivators that can be built into work are increased achievement, recognition, responsibility, advancement, task capability, and knowledge. Herzberg's research and theory (98, 99) have focused upon individual motivation rather than upon the implementation of organizational change processes which might increase motivation. It is essentially a theory of motivation rather than a theory of change.

The most widely known study in the implementation of job enrichment was done by Ford (72) at American Telephone. Underlying these efforts has been the assumption that increased motivation cannot result from training or other attempts to instill in workers greater energy and involvement. Rather, all one can do is provide the employee a task which offers greater challenge; he will then become intrinsically motivated. The initial target of change is job content, not the employee. Ford (72) studied a number of job enrichment programs at American Telephone in a variety of departments with different tasks, utilizing several different methods to introduce the job enrichment intervention. An effort was made to keep the environment of the job constant so that results could be attributed solely to change in the job content. Results indicated that turnover and absenteeism were reduced, quality of service was increased, and employee attitudes toward work improved in work units which received job enrichment.

There are a number of reviews of job enrichment applications (10, 122, 143) and several additional accounts of application findings (129, 135). Although the number of well-designed studies is too few to make broad generalizations, there are indications that job enrichment has positive effects on satisfaction and motivation (72). There is reason to believe that the quality of production increases more than the quantity (10, 111), although this applies to applications which combine job enrichment and enlargement. In much of the literature, the concept of "motivation" is used as a convenient device to explain increased performance or satisfaction. The direct effect on motivation of job enrichment programs is unexplored.

There are a number of questions regarding the relative impact of the process through which changes are introduced and implemented and the impact of the restructured job. In some studies employees participated in decisions, while in others only supervisors influenced the restructuring. The assumption which underlies directive implementation is that task-related experiences lead to changes in attitudes and needs (89, 121); changed work experience will result in attitude change, rather than vice versa. In connection with this, Hackman & Lawler (92) and Alderfer (3) suggest that experiencing higher order need satisfaction will result in the development of higher order needs.

Job enrichment and job enlargement generally ignore individual and technological differences; most proponents assume that job enrichment or enlargement are applicable and relevant regardless of the individual concerned and regardless of the technology of the organization. But Turner & Lawrence (165) found that enriched jobs resulted in greater satisfaction and less absenteeism for small-town workers but not for urban employees. Similarly, Hulin & Blood (103) and Blood & Hulin (33) found that workers who hold traditional values about work and achievement respond positively to complex jobs, but more alienated (urban, blue-collar) workers respond negatively to complex jobs. Hackman & Lawler (92) report positive correlations between job complexity (variety, autonomy, task identity, feedback) and motivation, satisfaction and performance *only* for employees with higher order need strength (e.g., for accomplishment, growth, challenge, variety, participation). Wanous (170) found that higher order need strength accounted for more of the relationships between job complexity and positive outcomes than either the blue-collar, urban distinction made by Hulin & Blood (103) or the Protestant ethic values distinction made by Blood (32). Standing (156) found that the degree of satisfaction within a single set of jobs varied as a function of the cognitive complexity of the em-

ployee. The degree of satisfaction with the work itself was an inverted U-shaped function of cognitive complexity. These studies suggest a contingency theory in which the probability of job enrichment and enlargement resulting in increased performance or satisfaction is contingent upon the needs of the employee, his cognitive complexity, and his cultural milieu.

Similarly, increases in performance and satisfaction resulting from these changes may be contingent upon the technology of the organization. Task identity, for example, may be difficult to establish in a continuous process technology, but autonomy and feedback seem easier to implement in an automated process technology than in heavy assembly work (31). Several organizations are finding job enrichment and enlargement simply impossible given their huge investments in stationary equipment. Other contingencies which the organization may face include lack of sufficient skills to take on more demanding work, short-term lowered performance which frequently accompanies organizational change, union resistance or disinterest (143).

The sociotechnical studies reviewed in this section consistently indicate increased performance and productivity—a finding that is less clear for job design/enlargement or job enrichment. The evidence on job enrichment is too sparse as yet to make unqualified claims as to its effectiveness; more research is needed. All three approaches seem to result in quality increases, lowered absenteeism, and lowered turnover. The evidence for production time decreases and cost savings is mixed for job enlargement and job enrichment. In terms of attitudinal change, job satisfaction tends to increase as a result of job enlargement and job enrichment. Job enlargement, however, tends to result in a more socially isolated role for the workers, which increases both the need and difficulty in relating to others with whom their tasks are interdependent. Sociotechnical systems avoid this issue by social restructuring of the work group, resulting in clear increases in group morale.

Changes in job design have typically incorporated many simultaneous changes in task variety, self-determination and discretion, responsibility, challenge, and wholeness; in the degree to which the task requires hierarchical, collaborative, or autonomous behavior; and in different technologies. Research has generally not attempted to isolate these as independent variables, nor has it explored relative changes in different kinds of motivation, satisfaction, and performance. We need to explore the relative effects of participative and non-participative change processes upon the implementation and success of job design changes. At this point, much of what we can say is: given these employees, this technology, this change process, and this job design structure, this happened in terms of satisfaction and performance. We need more specificity of the complex interactions of independent, dependent, moderator, and process variables to specify cause, effect, and contingency.

Human Processual Approaches

Human process intervention focuses on the human participants and the organization processes (e.g., communication, problem solving, decision making) through which they accomplish their own and the organization's goals. This orientation to OD is rooted in the academic fields of psychology, social psychology, and anthropology and in the applied disciplines of group dynamics and the human relations movement. Human process-orientation change agents tend to value human fulfillment highly and to expect improved organizational performance to follow on improved human functioning and processes (152). These two don't necessarily go hand in hand, even though it may be more comfortable to assume this.

Process-oriented consultants typically have been sensitive to the nature of the consultant role (145, 157). A good deal of thought has been given to some of the dilemmas experienced by consultants (11, 15), the problems of developing a valid organizational diagnosis (15), and the risks of alternative interventions (94).

Although practitioners have developed a number of alternative interventions concerned with human processes in organizations (cf., Beckhard 20, Fordyce & Weil 173, Burke & Hornstein 42, French

& Bell 75), most research efforts focus on three general areas of process-oriented intervention: survey feedback, group development, and intergroup development.

These three intervention strategies are founded on some common assumptions: sharing information can be valuable, particularly when it hitherto has remained unshared but has influenced organizational processes (like some covert feelings); confronting and working through differences among people who must work together can enhance collaboration; participation in decision making can lead to increased commitment. Survey feedback involves organizational groups in discussing diagnostic data and planning action steps. Group development activities emphasize improving group abilities to accomplish their tasks. Intergroup development interventions press for improved management of the interfaces between groups. These three forms of intervention are at least potentially compatible, and often are used in sequence, beginning with survey feedback and moving to group and intergroup development activities.

Survey Feedback

Survey feedback is a process in which data is systematically collected (usually by questionnaires) from members of an organization, analyzed in summary fashion, and fed back selectively to organization members. To varying degrees, outside staff and organization members collaboratively design the questions to be asked, jointly analyze and interpret the data, and feed back in meetings to organization units from which the data was collected for purposes of diagnosis and potential change. The intervention has developed from traditional attitude surveys which were administered to employees and fed back to management; in recent years findings have been presented to employee respondents as well, partly to gain their cooperation in future studies. Such feedback has now taken on clear organizational development purposes as well (36, 130), on the assumption that discrepancies between organizational ideals and actual responses to the survey will generate motivation for change (136).

Early participation of organization members in the design and collection of data is likely to increase the relevance of the feedback (123, 130, 132). Organization members may be asked to develop questions for the survey, or they may be interviewed to determine what issues are relevant (130). Early involvement in one study increased awareness of interpersonal problems between supervisors and subordinates (7).

The part played by organizational superiors in the feedback meetings is critical. Baumgartel (17) found that perception of supervisory behavior changed as a consequence of increased information flow and problem confrontation between hierarchical levels after feedback. Chase (49) reports that the feedback process tended to equalize power even in a highly threatening environment, and Klein, Kraut & Wolfson (108) report that use of line managers rather than personnel representatives to feed back data resulted in more satisfaction and greater perceived utilization of the data. Participation of superiors in discussion of the feedback may facilitate effective use of the information. On the other hand, a resistant or antagonistic superior can undermine the process; Alderfer & Ferriss (7) suggest that managers meet in peer groups to prepare for feedback of potentially threatening results before meeting with their subordinates in family groups.

External consultants can play an important role in the survey feedback process; they may design instruments, analyze, present and interpret the data, plan for action steps, and analyze the process of the feedback meetings (cf., Miles et al., 130). Alderfer & Ferriss (7) found that participants reacted more favorably to feedback by outsider-insider consultant teams than to insiders alone, and Chase (49) reports better problem-solving and meeting outputs with an outside consultant present.

Processes which occur during the feedback meetings also appear to influence the outcomes of those meetings. In the Detroit Edison studies, groups which had more intensive feedback sessions (aided by a consultant) showed more positive attitude change than groups with less intensive sessions (17). Brown (38) found evidence that participants were more receptive to feedback after the meetings,

and Klein, Kraut & Wolfson (108) found that face-to-face feedback meetings were more effective than written reports. Participation in feedback meetings can effect the group's perceptions of problems (49), its expectations of improvement (7), and the quality of its interaction (130).

It seems clear that survey feedback meetings can lead to attitudinal changes by participants. Miles et al. (130) report improved satisfaction with decisions (even though they were not implemented); Mann (123) found improvement in attitudes toward work, supervisors, progress, and group ability to get the job done; Bowers (35) reports improvement in organizational climate, managerial task and interpersonal leadership, and satisfaction; Brown (38) found increased participant involvement in the organization.

But the longer term changes in individual behavior or organizational performance appear to be contingent on more than just survey feedback. Despite highly successful meetings and increased satisfaction, Miles et al. (130) found that few action steps or structural changes emerged from the meeting and so little change occurred. Brown (38) notes that the higher involvement did not persist without follow-up, and Frohman (83) found that more change occurred with consultant follow-up than without it.

The research literature suggests that the effectiveness of survey feedback can be increased by collaborative involvement of the participants, participation of unit management, facilitation by an outside consultant, and specific decisions about follow-up and action steps. There is evidence that survey feedback can be an effective "bridge" between diagnostic activities (e.g., interviewing or questionnaire administration) and active intervention, since its primary effects seem to be on attitudes and perceptions of the situation. But there is little evidence that survey feedback alone leads to changes in individual behavior or organizational performance.

Group Development Intervention

OD practitioners have emphasized the importance of the work group rather than the individual (40,

102). Group development interventions like "team building," according to French & Bell, are "probably the most important single group of (OD) interventions" (75, p. 112).

Descriptions of different forms of team-buildings technology are easily obtained (e.g., Clark 53, 54; French & Bell 75; Fordyce & Weil 73; Golembiewski 86; Burke & Hornstein 42). Beer (21) classifies the different approaches to group development according to the primary issues they treat: (*a*) goal-setting activities (18, 20) that establish clear goals for the team to achieve; (*b*) interpersonal relations development (12, 13, 152) to improve the quality of interaction among team members; (*c*) role analysis work (65, 95) for increased clarity about each member's role and responsibilities; and (*d*) "Managerial Grid" group development (26) to prepare the group for later phases in the grid OD program.

The literature contains a number of case studies of group development activities from the vantage point of the consultant (69, 110). But these case studies offer little more than the flavor of the experience.

The impact of team-building activities has been explored systematically by several investigators. Argyris (12) and Harrison (93) report interview, observation, and questionnaire data from three groups of managers, two of which experienced T-group training and a comparison group. The study was frankly exploratory and suffers from methodological problems, but the data suggested changes in values and behavior of participants occurred. In a subsequent study, Argyris (13) trained an executive group to be more "interpersonally competent"; time series analysis of tape recordings suggested that the training affected executive meeting behavior, though only anecdotal evidence for the relationship between the changed behavior and increased effectiveness was available. In a larger study, Friedlander (76) found that four trained teams reported significantly higher levels of group effectiveness, mutual influence, and personal involvement and participation than did the eight control groups. Schmuck, Runkel & Langmeyer (148) trained the faculty of a junior high school and compared the experimental faculty with the faculties

of several similar schools. The experimental faculty reported more positive perceptions of the principal, the staff meetings, and the level of innovations in teaching, and they espoused more norms consistent with laboratory values than the controls; the authors also report anecdotal data about positive changes.

The critical elements of the team-building process remain only partially explored. Friedlander further analyzed the data from his field experiment (76) and found that the impact of the team building varied greatly across the four participant groups (77). Comparison of the most positively affected group with the two least positively affected led to the discovery that the context in which the team building took place was very important: ". . . the quality of integrated prework and postwork processes surrounding the laboratory is a far more potent determiner of developmental impact than are variations in trainer role and behavior or differences in climate and content of laboratory training session" (77, p. 395). Another analysis of the same data (79) revealed that the impact of team-building activities was also influenced by the level of intragroup trust at the outset. Initial intragroup trust was a better predictor of subsequent perceptions of group effectiveness and the worth of group meetings than the initial ratings on the same dimensions. But intragroup trust itself was not increased by the training except when pre- and postwork with the consultant occurred. Harvey & Boettger (96) found that a brief "experiment" involving member confrontation of the group leader led to behavior change. They also found that the four participants who confronted the leader during the "experiment" were significantly more positive about him a year later than the eight participants who did not. Since those who confronted the leader selected themselves, we cannot be sure that the confrontation alone accounted for the differing perceptions, but the finding is consistent with the theory that confrontation is a critical element of successful team building, even if it cannot be considered unambiguous.

There remains a dearth of evidence for the effects of team building external to the group developed. Harrison (93) noted that the changed interpersonal perceptions of Argyris' T-group participants did not generalize to the participants' subordinates. Bigelow (25), on the other hand, found that participation in group development activities affected teachers in the classroom, even though the group development activities were not designed to change classroom behavior. Analysis of tapes of teacher classroom behavior indicated that participants became more integrative and less dominative than controls, and that student perception of relationships with their peers improved in the classrooms with trained teachers. Fosmire, Keutzer & Diller (74) report the results of group development with the entire faculty of a new high school. Their intervention led to increased interpersonal openness and acceptance of conflict among the faculty and to increased perceptions by students of the faculty as responsive and themselves as responsible.

Though none of the research designs is flawless, there is convergent evidence that group development activities affect participant attitudes and sometimes their behavior as well. These effects may also "spill over" in some fashion to other organization members. It remains unclear, however, what mechanisms operate in successful team development activities, or what critical conditions must be satisfied for successful generalization of learnings outside the team, or what effects group development has on actual task performance.

Intergroup Relations Development

Problems at the interfaces between groups in an organization are endemic in modern organizations, and they are a matter of central concern to OD practitioners (23, 75). Lawrence & Lorsch (113) suggest that intergroup relations problems are an inevitable correlate of the differentiation of organizational subsystems to meet and deal with environmental complexity. Important conflict has been reported between different departments in business organizations (68, 151), between headquarters and field teams (30), between field and administrative officers of the State Department (23), between a management development program and other subsystems in a bank (4), between union and man-

agement representatives (29, 30), among different occupational specialities in coal mines (164), and between potential merger partners (34).

There is no shortage of ideas for managing intergroup conflict. Some theories have been developed in social psychological research (154), others from work with organizations (141). Neilsen (133) describes seven strategies for intervening in intergroup conflict that vary in the degree to which they deal with behavior alone or with both behavior and attitudes. Walton (167) has suggested four interventions for third parties to help manage intergroup conflict: (*a*) reduce the potential for conflict (e.g., change structure or personnel); (*b*) resolve substantive issues (e.g., make the decisions); (*c*) help manage manifest conflict (e.g., be a referee); and (*d*) facilitate a change in the relationships.

The first two alternatives require power over the combatants, an option that some technostructural consultants have used to great effect. Trist et al. (164), for example, eliminated counterproductive intergroup conflict among coal miners by changing the sociotechnical system. But most human process consultants have no such power or they decline to use it. They have preferred the latter two interventions: helping manage manifest conflict and facilitating relationship changes. Walton (168) offers some provocative insights into the complexities of the third-party role; his approach involves improving intergroup relations by improving relations between their representatives.

A more common approach has been to foster a general "problem-solving" approach to the relations between groups. Blake, Shepard & Mouton (30) argue for problem solving in the context of a nine-cell typology of intergroup conflicts based on the degree of inevitability of the conflict, the size of the stakes, and the possibility of agreement. Schmidt & Tannenbaum (146) suggest four different approaches, culminating with problem solving. "Problem solving" is the preferred outcome for both if the groups are interdependent.

Intergroup development interventions to change relationships and manage conflict in practice are based on information sharing, confrontation of differences, and working through to new understandings. The prototype design requires groups to develop lists of their perceptions of themselves, the other group, and their views of the other group's perceptions of them, and then to use the lists as input to developing better understanding of each other and to creating future action plans. This design was developed by Blake and his colleagues (29, 30), but it has been used and recommended by many others (e.g., Beckhard 20; French & Bell 75).

There is very little systematic research on the effectiveness of such interventions in the field. Case studies abound (e.g., Blake, Mouton & Sloma 29), but they leave many questions about the efficacy of the intervention unresolved. Golembiewski & Blumberg (87, 88) report attitudinal changes after a workshop that included confrontation among several groups from the same organization, but while participant attitudes changed in the ways predicted by the investigators, no data were collected on the consequences of the intervention for individual behavior or organizational performance. Further, effects of the intergroup intervention may have been confounded by a simultaneous confrontation between the participants and the consultants (who, after all, constituted an extraorganizational group that was potentially a unifying "external enemy" for all participants).

It is painfully evident that more research is needed before much can be said about the utility of the present process-oriented technology for managing intergroup relations. There is a good deal of activity going on, but relatively little in the way of unambiguous findings available. We simply do not know much about whether OD interventions lead to better management of intergroup relations or not.

A related area that demands further investigation is the role of the consultant in the management of intergroup relations. The consultant's impact as representative of a group—a group external to and possibly a threat to his client—is not often considered. Lewicki & Alderfer (116) have explored some of the dilemmas encountered by researcher/consultants to intergroup conflicts, but further investigation of this aspect of OD research/consultation is needed.

* * * * *

We are saying that current OD theory and practice may be a small part of a rich, broad, far-reaching, relevant field of planned change. As the wider field is legitimized and developed, and as broader technologies and theories are developed, these will feed back into and enrich the field of OD.

If the practice and theory of OD is to merge into a broader field of planned change, what role will research play in this transformation? We believe that research will either play a far more crucial role in the advancement of this field, or become an increasingly irrelevant appendage to it. Thus far it has utilized its techniques primarily for evaluation and validation, and its current techniques are well adapted to this. Thus far it has chosen to play a relatively uninvolved and distant role in the change-practice situation. Thus far it has focused on producing data for research needs rather than practice needs. As a result, we have theory from an external research perspective only. We have generally failed to produce a theory of change which emerges from the change process itself. We need a way of enriching our understanding and our action synergistically rather than at one or the other's expense—to become a science in which knowledge-getting and knowledge-giving are an integrated process, and one that is valuable to all parties involved. We believe that a theory of planned change must be a theory of practice, which emerges from practice data and is of the practice situation, not merely about it.

References

1. Alderfer, C. P. 1968. Comparison of questionnaire responses with and without preceding interviews, *J. Appl. Psychol.* 52:335–40.
2. Alderfer, C. P. 1968. Organizational diagnosis from initial client reactions to a researcher. *Hum. Organ.* 27:260–65.
3. Alderfer, C. P. 1969. Job enlargement and the organizational context. *Personnel Psychol.* 22: 418–26.
4. Alderfer, C. P. 1971. Effect of individual, group and intergroup relations on attitudes toward a man-

agement development program. *J. Appl. Psychol.* 55: 302–11.

5. Alderfer, C. P. 1974. Change processes in organizations. In *Handbook of Industrial and Organizational Psychology,* ed. M. D. Dunnette. Chicago: Rand McNally.

6. Alderfer, C. P., Brown, L. D. 1972. Designing an empathic questionnaire for organizational research. *J. Appl. Psychol.* 56:456–60.

7. Alderfer, C. P., Ferriss, R. 1972. Understanding the impact of survey feedback. See Ref. 42, 234–43.

8. Alinsky, S. D., 1972. *Rules for Radicals*. New York: Vintage.

9. Alschuler, A. 1972. Toward a self-renewing school. *J. Appl. Psychol.* 8:577–600.

10. Anderson, J. W. 1970. The impact of technology on job enrichment. *Personnel* 47:29–37.

11. Argyris, C. 1961. Explorations in consultant-client relationships. *Hum. Organ.* 20:121–33.

12. Argyris, C. 1962. *Interpersonal Competence and Organizational Effectiveness*. Homewood, Ill.: Dorsey.

13. Argyris, C. 1965. *Organization and Innovation*. Homewood, Ill.: Irwin-Dorsey.

14. Argyris, C. 1968. Unintended consequences of rigorous research. *Psychol. Bull.* 70:185–97.

15. Argyris, C. 1970. *Intervention Theory and Method*. Reading, Mass.: Addison-Wesley.

16. Argyris, C. 1971. *Management and Organizational Development: The Path from Xa to Yb*. New York: McGraw-Hill.

17. Baumgartel, H. 1959. Using employee questionnaire results for improving organizations. *Kans. Bus. Rev.* 2–6.

18. Beckhard, R. 1966. An organization improvement program in a decentralized organization. *J. Appl. Behav. Sci.* 2:3–25.

19. Beckhard, R. 1967. The confrontation meeting. *Harvard Bus. Rev.* 45:149–55.

20. Beckhard, R. 1969. *Strategies of Organizational Development*. Reading, Mass.: Addison-Wesley.

21. Beer, M. 1974. The technology of organization development. See Ref. 5.

22. Bennis, W. G. 1966. *Changing Organizations*. New York: McGraw-Hill.

23. Bennis, W. G. 1969. *The Nature of Organization Development*. Reading, Mass.: Addison-Wesley.

24. Bennis, W. G., Benne, K. D., Chin, R., Eds. 1969. *The Planning of Change*. New York: Holt, Rinehart & Winston, 2nd ed.

25. Bigelow, R. C. 1971. Changing classroom interaction through OD. See Ref. 147, 71–85.

26. Blake, R. R., Mouton, J. S. 1968. *Corporate Excellence Through Grid Organization Development*. Houston: Gulf Publ.

27. Blake, R. R., Mouton, J. S. 1969. *Building a Dynamic Organization Through Grid Organization Development*. Reading, Mass.: Addison-Wesley.

28. Blake, R. R., Mouton, J. S., Barnes, L. B., Greiner, L. E. 1964. Breakthrough in organizational development. *Harvard Bus. Rev.* 42:37–59.

29. Blake, R. R., Mouton, J. S., Sloma, R. L. 1965. The union-management intergroup laboratory: strategy for resolving intergroup conflict. *J. Appl. Behav. Sci.* 1:25–57.

30. Blake, R. R., Shepard, H. A., Mouton, J. S. 1964. *Managing Intergroup Conflict in Industry*. Ann Arbor: Found. Res. Hum. Behav.

31. Blauner, R. 1964. *Alienation and Freedom*. Univ. Chicago Press.

32. Blood, M. R. 1969. Work values and job satisfaction. *J. Appl. Psychol.* 53:456–59.

33. Blood, M. R., Hulin, C. L. 1969. Alienation, environmental characteristics, and worker responses. *J. Appl. Psychol.* 51:284–90.

34. Blumberg, A., Wiener, W. 1971. One from two: facilitating an organizational merger. *J. Appl. Behav. Sci.* 7:87–102.

35. Bowers, D. G. 1973. OD techniques and their results in 23 organizations: the Michigan ICL Study. *J. Appl. Behav. Sci.* 9:21–43.

36. Bowers, D. G., Franklin, J. F. 1972. Survey-guided development: using human resources measurement in organizational change. *J. Contemp. Bus.* 1:43–55.

37. Bradford, L. P., Gibb, J. R., Benne, K. D. 1964. *T-Group Theory and Laboratory Method*. New York: Wiley.

38. Brown, L. D. 1972. Research action: organizational feedback, understanding, and change. *J. Appl. Behav. Sci.* 8:697–74.

39. Buchanan, P. C. 1971. Crucial issues in OD. See Ref. 101, 386–400.

40. Burke, W. W. 1971. A comparison of management development and organization development. *J. Appl. Behav. Sci.* 7:569–79.

41. Burke, W. W. 1972, *Contemporary Organization Development: Conceptual Orientation and Interventions*. Washington: NTL/IABS.

42. Burke, W. W., Hornstein, H. A., Eds. 1972. *The Social Technology of Organization Development.* Fairfax, Va.: NTL Learning Resources Corp.

43. Campbell, D. T. 1969. Reforms as experiments. *Am. Psychol.* 24:409–29.

44. Campbell, D. T., Fiske, D. W. 1959. Convergent and discriminant validation by the multitrait-multimethod matrix. *Psychol. Bull.* 56:81–105.

45. Campbell, D. T., Stanley, J. C. 1963. *Experimental and Quasi-Experimental Designs for Research.* Chicago: Rand-McNally.

46. Campbell, J. P. 1971. Personnel training and development. *Ann. Rev. Psychol.* 22:291–306.

47. Campbell, J. P., Dunnette, M. D. 1968. Effectiveness of T-group experiences in managerial training and development. *Psychol. Bull.* 70:73–104.

48. Cartwright, D. 1951. Achieving change in people: some applications of group dynamics theory. *Hum. Relat.* 4:381–92.

49. Chase, P. 1968. A survey feedback approach to organization development. In *Proceedings of the Executive Study Conference.* Princeton: Educ. Test. Serv.

50. Chein, I., Cook, S. W., Harding, J. 1948. The field of action research. *Am. Psychol.* 3:43–50.

51. Chesler, M. A., Lohman, J. E. 1971. Changing schools through student advocacy. See Ref. 147, 185–211.

52. Clark, A. W. 1972. Sanction: a critical element in action research. *J. Appl. Behav. Sci.* 8:713–31.

53. Clark, J. V. 1970. Task group therapy 1: goals and the client system. *Hum. Relat.* 23:263–77.

54. Ibid. Task group therapy 2: intervention and problems of practice, 383–403.

55. Clark, J. V., Krone, C. G. 1972. Towards an overall view of organizational development in the early seventies. In *Management of Change and Conflict,* ed. J. M. Thomas, W. G. Bennis. Baltimore: Penguin Books.

56. Coch, L., French, J. R. P. 1948. Overcoming resistance to change. *Hum. Relat.* 1:512–32.

57. Conant, E. H., Kilbridge, M. D. 1965. An interdisciplinary analysis of job enlargement: technology, costs and behavioral implications. *Ind. Labor Relat. Rev.* 18:377–95.

58. Culbert, S. A. 1972. Using research to guide an OD project. *J. Appl. Behav. Sci.* 8:203–36.

59. Dalton, M. 1965. Managing the managers. *Hum. Organ.* 14:4–10.

60. Davis, L. E. 1966. The design of jobs. *Ind. Relat.* 6:21–45.

61. Davis, L. E., Canter, R. R. 1956. Job design research. *J. Ind. Eng.* 7:275.

62. Davis, L. E., Volfer, E. S. 1965. Intervening responses to changes in supervisor job designs. *Occup. Psychol.* 34:171.

63. Davis, L. E., Werling, R. 1960. Job design factors. *Occup. Psychol.* 34:109–32.

64. Davis, S. A. 1967. An organic problem-solving method of organizational change. *J. Appl. Behav. Sci.* 3:3–21.

65. Dayal, I., Thomas, J. M. 1968. Operation KPE: developing a new organization. *J. Appl. Behav. Sci.* 4:473–586.

66. DeSalvia, D. N., Gemmill, G. R. 1971. An exploratory study of the personal value system of college students and managers. *Acad. Manage. J.* 14:227–38.

67. Duhl, L. J., Steetle, N. J. 1969. Newark: community or chaos, a case study of the medical school controversy. *J. Appl. Behav. Sci.* 5:537–72.

68. Dutton, J. M., Walton, R. E. 1972. Interdepartmental conflict and cooperation: two contrasting studies. In *Managing Group and Intergroup Relations,* ed. J. W. Lorsch, P. R. Lawrence, 285–309. Homewood, Ill.: Irwin-Dorsey.

69. Dyer, W. G., Maddocks, R. F., Moffitt, J. W., Underwood, W. J. 1970. A laboratory-consultation model for organization change. *J. Appl. Behav. Sci.* 6:211–27.

70. Emery, F. E., Trist, E. L. 1960. Socio-technical systems. In *Management Sciences: Models and Techniques,* ed. C. W. Churchman, M. Verhulst. New York: Pergamon.

70a. Emery, F. E., Thorsrud, E. 1969. *Form and Content in Industrial Democracy.* London: Tavistock.

71. Fleishman, E. A. 1953. Leadership climate, human relations training, and supervisory behavior. *Personnel Psychol.* 6:205–22.

72. Ford, R. N. 1969. *Motivation Through Work Itself.* New York: American Manage. Assoc.

73. Fordyce, J. K., Weil, R. 1971. *Managing with People.* Reading, Mass.: Addison-Wesley.

74. Fosmire, F., Keutzer, C., Diller, R. 1971. Starting up a new senior high school. See Ref. 147, 87–112.

75. French, W. L., Bell, C. H. 1973. *Organization Development.* Englewood Cliffs, N.J.: Prentice-Hall.

76. Friedlander, F. 1967. The impact of organizational training laboratories upon effectiveness and intervention of ongoing work groups. *Personnel Psychol.* 20:289–308.

77. Friedlander, F. 1968. A comparative study of consulting processes and group development. *J. Appl. Behav. Sci.* 4:377–99.

77a. Friedlander, F. 1968. Behavioral research as a transactional process. *Hum. Organ.* 27:369–79.

78. Friedlander, F. 1970. Emerging blackness in a white research world. *Hum. Organ.* 29:239–50.

79. Friedlander, F. 1970. The primacy of trust as a facilitator of further group accomplishment. *J. Appl. Behav. Sci.* 6:387–400.

80. Friedlander, F. 1972. Congruence in organization development. *Proc. 31st Ann. Meet. Acad. Manage.* 1971, 153–60.

81. Friedlander, F., Greenberg, S. 1971. The effect of job attitudes, training and organization climate upon performance of the hard-core unemployed. *J. Appl. Psychol.* 55:287–95.

82. Friedman, G. 1961. *The Anatomy of Work.* Glencoe, Ill.: Free Press.

83. Frohman, M. A. 1970. *An empirical study of a model and strategies for planned organizational change.* Ph.D. dissertation. Univ. Michigan.

84. Frohman, M. A., Sashkin, M. 1970. *The practice of organization development: a selective review.* Unpublished data.

85. Gamson, W. 1968. *Power and Discontent.* Homewood, Ill.: Dorsey.

86. Golembiewski, R. T. 1972. *Renewing Organizations.* Itasca, Ill.: Peacock Publ.

87. Golembiewski, R. T., Blumberg, A. 1967. Confrontation as a training design in complex organizations: attitudinal changes in a diversified population of managers. *J. Appl. Behav. Sci.* 3:525–47.

88. Golembiewski, R. T., Blumberg, A. 1968. The laboratory approach to organization change: confrontation design. *Acad. Manage. J.* 11:199–210.

89. Goodman, P., Baloff, N. 1968. Task experience and attitudes toward decision making. *Organ. Behav. Hum. Perform.* 3:202–16.

90. Goodstein, L. D., Boyer, R. K. 1972. Crisis intervention in a municipal agency: a conceptual case history. *J. Appl. Behav. Sci.* 8:318–40.

91. Greiner, L. E. 1967. Patterns of organizational change. *Harvard Bus. Rev.* 45:119–28.

92. Hackman, J. R., Lawler, E. E. 1971. Employee reactions to job characteristics. *J. Appl. Psychol.* 55:259–86.

93. Harrison, R. 1962. Impact of the laboratory on perceptions of others by the experimental group. See Ref. 12, 261–71.

94. Harrison, R. 1970. Choosing the depth of organizational intervention. *J. Appl. Behav. Sci.* 6:181–202.

95. Harrison, R. 1972. Role negotiation: a tough minded approach to team development. See Ref. 42, 84–96.

96. Harvey, J. B., Boettger, C. R. 1971. Improving communication within a managerial workgroup. *J. Appl. Behav. Sci.* 7:164–74.

97. Heller, F. A. 1969. Group feedback analysis: a method of field research. *Psychol. Bull.* 72: 108–17.

98. Herzberg, F. 1966. *Work and the Nature of Man.* Cleveland: World Publ.

99. Herzberg, F., Mausner, B., Snyderman, B. B. 1959. *The Motivation to Work.* New York: Wiley.

100. Hill P. 1971, *Towards a New Philosophy of Management.* New York: Barnes and Noble.

101. Hornstein, H. A., Bunker, B. B., Burke, W. W., Gindes, M., Lewicki, R. J. 1971. *Social Intervention: A Behavioral Science Approach.* New York: Free Press.

102. Hornstein, H. A., Bunker, B. B., Hornstein, M. G. 1971. Some conceptual issues in individual and group oriented strategies of intervention into organizations. *J. Appl. Behav. Sci.* 7:557–67.

103. Hulin, C. L., Blood, M. R. 1968. Job enlargement, individual differences, and workers' responses. *Psychol. Bull.* 69:41–55.

104. Hunt, R. G., Lichtman, C. M. 1972. Pretest influences in evaluating the organizational effects of a supervisory counseling training program. *J. Appl. Behav. Sci.* 8:503–6.

105. Huse, E. F., Beer, M. 1971. Eclectic approach to OD. *Harvard Bus. Rev.* 49:103–12.

106. Jaques, E. 1952. *The Changing Culture of a Factory.* New York: Dayden.

107. Jenks, R. S. 1970. An action-research approach to organizational change. *J. Appl. Behav. Sci.* 6:131–50.

108. Klein, S. M., Kraut, A. I., Wolfson, A. 1971. Employee reactions to attitude survey feedback: study of the impact of structure and process. *Admin. Sci. Quart.* 16:497–514.

109. Kolb, D. A., Frohman, A. L. 1970. An organization development approach to consulting. *Sloan Manage. Rev.*

110. Kuriloff, A. H., Atkins, S. 1966. T-group for a work team. *J. Appl. Behav. Sci.* 2:63–93.

111. Lawler, E. E. 1969. Job design and employee motivation. *Personnel Psychol.* 22:426–35.

112. Lawrence, P. R., Lorsch, J. W. 1967. *Organization and Environment.* Boston: Div. Res., Harvard Bus. Sch.

113. Lawrence, P. R., Lorsch, J. W. 1969. *Developing Organizations: Diagnosis and Action.* Reading: Addison-Wesley.

114. Leavitt, H. J. 1965. Applied organizational change in industry: structural, technological, and humanistic approaches. In *Handbook of Organizations,* ed. J. G. March, Chicago: Rand McNally.

115. Levin, G., Stein, D. D. 1970. System intervention in a school community conflict. *J. Appl. Behav. Sci.* 6:337–52.

116. Lewicki, R. J., Alderfer, C. P. 1972. "Researchers" dilemmas in studying intergroup conflict. Yale Univ. working paper.

117. Lewin, K. 1946. Action research and minority problems. *J. Soc. Issues.* 2:34–46.

118. Lewin, K. 1947. Group decision and social change. In *Readings in Social Psychology,* ed. T. Newcomb, E. Hartley. New York: Holt. Rev. ed.

119. Lippitt, G. L. 1969. *Organization Renewal.* New York: Appleton-Century-Crofts.

120. Lippitt, R., Watson, J., Westley, B. 1958. *The Dynamics of Planned Change.* New York: Harcourt, Brace.

121. Locke, E. A. 1968. Toward a theory of task motivation and incentives. *Organ. Behav. Hum. Perform.* 3:157–89.

122. Maher, J. R. 1971. *New Perspectives in Job Enrichment.* New York: Van Nostrand-Reinhold.

123. Mann, F. C. 1961. Studying and creating change. See Ref. 24, 605–15. 1st ed.

124. Margulies, N., Raia, A. P. 1972. *Organization Development: Values, Process, and Technology.* New York: McGraw-Hill.

125. Marks, A. R. N. 1954. *An investigation of modifications of job design in an industrial situation and their effects on some measures of economic productivity.* Ph.D. dissertation. Univ. California, Berkeley.

126. Marrow, A. J., Bowers, D. G., Seashore, S. E. 1967. *Management by Participation.* New York: Harper and Row.

127. Mayo, E. 1933. *The Human Problems of an Industrial Civilization.* New York: Macmillan.

128. McGregor, D. 1960. *The Human Side of Enterprise.* New York: McGraw-Hill.

129. Meyers, S. M. 1964. Who are your motivated workers? *Harvard Bus. Rev.* 42:73–88.

130. Miles, M. G., Hornstein, H. A., Callahan, D. M., Calder, P. H., Schiavo, R. S. 1969. The consequences of survey feedback: theory and evaluation. See Ref. 24, 456–68.

131. Miner, J. B. 1971. Changes in student attitudes toward bueucratic role prescriptions during the 1960's. *Admin. Sci. Quart.* 16:227–38.

132. Neff, F. W. 1965. Survey research: a tool for problem diagnosis and improvement in organizations. In *Applied Sociology,* ed. S. M. Miller, A. W. Gouldner. New York: Free Press.

133. Neilsen, E. H. 1972. Understanding and managing intergroup conflict. See Ref. 68, 329–43.

134. Oppenheimer, M. 1969. *The Urban Guerilla.* Chicago: Quadrangle.

135. Paul, W. J., Robertson, K. B., Herzberg, F. 1969. Job enrichment pays off. *Harvard Bus. Rev.* 47:61–78.

136. Peak, H. 1955. Attitude and motivation. In *Nebraska Symposium on Motivation,* ed. M. R. Jones. Lincoln: Univ. Nebraska.

137. Porter, L. W., Lawler, E. E. 1965. Properties of organization structure in relation to job attitudes and job behavior. *Psychol. Bull.* 64:23–51.

138. Rapoport, R. N. 1970. Three dilemmas in action research. *Hum. Relat.* 23:499–513.

139. Report of a Special Task Force to the Secretary of Health, Education and Welfare, 1973. *Work in America.* Cambridge, Mass.: M.I.T. Press.

140. Rice, A. K. 1958. *Productivity and Social Organization: The Ahmedabad Experiment.* London: Tavistock.

141. Rice, A. K. 1969. Individual, group and intergroup processes. *Hum. Relat.* 22:565–84.

142. Ross, R. 1971. OD for whom. *J. Appl. Behav. Sci.* 7:58–85.

143. Rush, H. M. F. 1971. *Job Design for Motivation.* New York: Conf. Board Rep. 515.

144. Sanford, N. 1970. Whatever happened to action research? *J. Soc. Issues* 26:3–23.

145. Schein, E. H. 1969. *Process Consultation: Its Role in Organization Development.* Reading, Mass.: Addison-Wesley.

146. Schmidt, W. H., Tannenbaum, R. 1972. Management of differences. See Ref. 42, 127–40.

147. Schmuck, R. A., Miles, M. B., Eds. 1971. *OD in Schools.* Palo Alto: National Press.

148. Schmuck. R. A., Runkel, P. J., Langmeyer, D. 1969. Improving organizational problem solving in a school faculty. *J. Appl. Behav. Sci.* 5:455–90.

149. Seashore, S. E., Bowers, D. G. 1963. *Changing the structure and functioning of an organization.* Monogr. 33, Univ. Michigan Survey Res. Center.

150. Seashore, S. E., Bowers, D. G. 1970. Durability of organizational change. *Am. Psychol.* 25:227–33.

151. Seiler, J. A. 1963. Diagnosing interdepartmental conflict. *Harvard Bus. Rev.* 41:121–32.

152. Shepard, H. A. 1965. Changing interpersonal and intergroup relations in organizations. See Ref. 114, 115–43.

154. Sherif, M., Harvey, O. J., White, B. J., Hood, W. R., Sherif, C. 1961. *Conflict and Cooperation: the Robbers' Cave Experiment.* Norman, Okla.: Univ. Book Exch.

155. Sherwood, J. J. 1971. An introduction to organization development. *Exp. Publ. Syst. APA* 11.

156. Standing, T. E. 1973. Satisfaction with the work itself as a function of cognitive complexity. *Proc. 81st Ann. Conv. APA.*

157. Steele, F. I. 1969. Consultants and detectives. *J. Appl. Behav. Sci.* 5:187–202.

158. Stewart, P. A. 1967. *Job Enlargement.* Iowa City: Univ. Iowa Coll. Bus. Admin.

159. Strauss, G. 1973. Organization development. In *Handbook of Work Organization in Society,* ed. R. Dubin. Chicago: Rand McNally.

160. Tannenbaum, R., Davis, S. A. 1969. Values, man and organizations. *Ind. Manage. Rev.* 10: 67–86.

160a. Thorsrud, E. 1969. A strategy for research and social change in industry: a report on the industrial democracy project in Norway. *Soc. Sci. Inform.* 9 (5): 65–90.

161. Torezyner, J. 1972. The political conflict of social change: a case study of innovation in adversity in Jerusalem. *J. Appl. Behav. Sci.* 8:287–317.

162. Trist, E. L. 1969. On socio-technical systems. See Ref. 24, 269–82.

162a. Trist, E. 170. A socio-technical critique of scientific management. Presented at Edinburgh Conf. Impact Sci. Technol. Edinburgh Univ.

163. Trist, E. L., Bamforth, K. W. 1951. Some social and psychological consequences of the longwall method of coal getting. *Hum. Relat.* 4:3–38.

164. Trist, E. L., Higgin, G. W., Murray, H., Pollock, A. B. 1963. *Organizational Choice.* London: Tavistock.

165. Turner, A. N., Lawrence, P. R. 1968. *Industrial Jobs and the Worker.* Cambridge, Mass.: Harvard Univ. Grad. Sch. Bus. Admin.

166. Walton, R. E. 1965. Two strategies of social change and their dilemmas. *J. Appl. Behav. Sci,* 1:167–79.

167. Walton, R. E. 1967. Third party role in interdepartmental conflict. *Ind. Relat.* 7:29–43.

168. Walton, R. E. 1969. *Interpersonal Peacemaking: Confrontations and Third Party Consultation.* Reading, Mass.: Addison-Wesley.

169. Walton, R. E. 1970. A problem-solving workshop on border conflicts in Eastern Africa. *J. Appl. Behav. Sci.* 6:453–89.

170. Wanous, J. P. 1973. Individual differences and employee reactions to job characteristics. *Proc. 81st Ann. Conv. APA.*

171. Webb, E. J., Campbell, D. T., Schwartz, R. D., Sechrest, L. 1965. *Unobtrusive Measures: Nonreactive Research in the Social Sciences.* Chicago: Rand McNally.

172. Wedge, B. 1971. A psychiatric model for intercession in intergroup conflict. *J. Appl. Behav. Sci.* 7:733–61.

173. Whyte, W. F., Hamilton, E. L. 1964. *Action Research for Management.* Homewood, Ill.: Irwin-Dorsey.

174. Winn, A. 1969. The laboratory approach to organization development: a tentative model of planned change. *J. Manage. Stud.* 6:157.

175. Zand, D. E., Steele, F. I., Zalkind, S. S. 1969. The impact of an organizational development program on perceptions of interpersonal, group, and organizational functioning. *J. Appl. Behav. Sci.* 5:393–410.

Reading 5

ORGANIZATION CHANGE AND DEVELOPMENT

Michael Beer and Anna Elise Walton

Applying theory from psychology and organizational behavior, organization development (OD) comprises a set of actions undertaken to improve organizational effectiveness and employee well-being. These actions, or "interventions," are typically designed and sequenced by an OD consultant following his/her diagnosis of an organization's needs and shortcomings. The tool kit these practitioners draw on ranges broadly from organization-wide changes in structure and systems to psychotherapeutic counseling sessions with groups and individuals. OD, measured as something that professional OD consultants do, appears to be growing moderately.

The application of OD by managers rather than OD consultants has grown even further. In the past five years, general management literature and practice have absorbed many of the concepts, values, and methods OD propounds. This can be seen in the widespread application, and in some cases institutionalization, of innovative plant designs, participative management approaches, collaborative approaches to union–management relations, the use of task forces and other organizational overlays to identify and solve problems, and the frequent practice of off-site team-building or mission-building sessions (Beer & Spector 1985). We see OD concepts strongly emerging in the burgeoning general management literature, specifically via culture and leadership concepts. OD concepts can also be seen in the increasingly common view of organizations as open systems.

Source: Michael Beer and Anna Elise Walton, *Annual Review of Psychology* 38 (1987), pp. 339–67. Copyright © 1987 Annual Reviews Inc. Reproduced with permission. All rights reserved.

Major environmental changes have focused management attention on managing discontinuities in organizations' lives. Revitalization, turnaround, innovation, and the management of decline are becoming major topics in both general management and OD literature. Human-resource management has also absorbed many of OD's precepts, and organizations increasingly realize human resources can be critical strategic and competitive factors.

As the knowledge base of organizational behavior and psychology filters into general management literature, we believe OD must broaden itself. Theorists and practitioners must move away from programs in which the consultant orchestrates interventions to programs in which general managers, staff groups, and consultants work together to manage change, to redirect organizational efforts and performance. The OD practitioner may have specialized behavioral-science expertise but will also need expertise in understanding and interpreting environmental changes. The OD consultant will support changes initiated by general managers.

Thus as a field, organization development will have to become concerned with the theory and practice of managing the continual adaptation of internal organizational arrangements to changes in the external environment. In this capacity, intervention methods become episodes in a long-term process, and consultants become actors in a process orchestrated by general managers. This conception of the field has profound implications for research methodology, theory building, and practice. As its techniques have become staples of modern corporate management, the status of OD becomes more difficult to ascertain. This broader definition makes it impossible to state how widely OD is practiced, since the field no longer has professional boundaries.

Here we review: the status of OD as consultant-centered intervention, the traditional focus of OD; OD-related trends in general management literature; recent literature on organizational adaptation and realignment; trends in human-resource management and their OD implications; and finally, the implementation of change.

OD as Consultant-Centered Intervention

There have been no new breakthroughs in intervention methodologies. Rather, variations on the basic idea of surfacing information and feeding it back for discussion by organizational members continue to be developed. Survey and questionnaire methodologies appear to be growing in popularity. New surveys have been introduced (Kilmann 1984, Sashkin 1985) and established ones are still being utilized (Kleiner 1983, Levine 1983, Gavin 1984). Various forms of team building and the use of collateral organizations are also widely employed (Kanter 1983, Beer & Spector 1985). Process consultation appears in the literature less frequently than the above. We suspect it is a less bounded intervention and therefore more difficult to research with traditional methodologies.

Sashkin et al (1984) note that some types of OD, specifically structural interventions according to contingency theory, third-party consultation, and sociotechnical systems changes have not become as popular. They believe the popular approaches have clear goals and are highly structured. The client knows what the consultant will be doing at any given time.

We do not review new applications of traditional intervention methods because we do not regard extensions of intervention methodology as the frontier of progress in the practice or theory of OD. Moreover, as we discuss in the section on managing change, the manager and/or consultant, their assumptions about organizations and their skills in managing an organic change process, are probably more important than methodology in the final

analysis. It is probably because effective change managers or consultants are in such short supply that Sashkin finds more structured methods in greater use.

Recent Research and Evaluation of OD Efforts

In the past five years, several articles (Nicholas 1982, Roberts & Porras 1982, Vicars & Hartke 1984, Nicholas & Katz 1985, Guzzo et al 1985, Macy et al 1986) have reviewed the OD and organization change literature to assess the relative effectiveness of typical interventions. These researchers looked at studies of team building, laboratory training, survey feedback, technostructural interventions, and process consultation.

Vicars & Hartke (1984) evaluated 15 recent studies relative to an earlier study (Morrison 1978) and noted an increase in validity criteria and noticeably more controls. They also noted that OD evaluations often encountered several rival hypotheses: Change results from maturation, history, self selection, and so forth.

Nicholas (1982) reviewed 64 studies and assessed the comparative impact of the interventions on ''hard criteria,'' which ranged from costs and productivity to quality and absenteeism. He noted limitations in the research findings—e.g. outcomes could be the result of intervention duration or the time of posttest (immediately following the intervention or several years later). Nicholas concluded that ''The single most apparent finding of this research is that no one change technique or class of techniques works well in all situations'' (p. 540).

Katzell & Guzzo (1983) in a literature review of 207 psychologically based productivity experiments reported that 87% found evidence of some productivity improvement. Guzzo et al (1985) performed a meta-analysis of 98 of these experiments and found worker productivity increased by nearly one half standard deviation.

Macy et al (1986) meta-analyzed 56 empirical organization change and work innovation experiments and found an across-study positive and significant relationship with productivity. They found that reward system changes had no significant relationship with productivity and had significant negative relationships with leadership and work involvement measures. Autonomous and semiautonomous work groups, team building, and training related positively and significantly to productivity but were negatively associated with 11 dependent variables (including leadership, work involvement, general attitude, and satisfaction measures).

Both Guzzo et al (1985) and Macy et al (1986) note that most published reports lack the quantitative data necessary for meta-analysis. Both also qualify their findings by recognizing the bias toward publishing positive outcomes.

Measuring attitudinal change has proved tricky. A fair amount of research (Roberts & Porras 1982, Porras 1985, Van de Vliert et al 1985) is going into investigating the types of change: alpha (or "real" change, but no conceptual shift), beta ("scale recalibration," or shift due to changes in expectations), and gamma (a complete conceptual redefinition of the phenomena). These distinctions derive from a study (Golembiewski et al 1976) that observed rating declines after an intervention. The study argued that these declines occurred because participants had undergone a conceptual shift; their standards of evaluation had changed. Armenakis et al (1983) claimed that this is now the focus of OD research, displacing earlier concerns about experimental design and statistical methods.

In sum, investigators have felt the need for, and have begun to use, quantitative data, sophisticated research designs, and statistical procedures aimed at accurate measurement of change. Nicholas & Katz (1985) and Armenakis et al (1983) call for more longitudinal measures, and Armenakis et al (1983) add that more frequent measurements are needed. Seashore et al (1983) published a major text cataloging current methods and techniques. Researchers of this bent argue that in future lean times OD practitioners will need hard data to justify their projects to management by bottom-line criteria.

Despite more sophisticated research methods, OD research results are still inconclusive. One can find support for many different conclusions, among the results reported in the studies. Why should this be so?

Problems in Research on Intervention Methods

This research suffers from four problems. First, the research aims to isolate causation. By relying on normal science, this research tries to identify the results of a single intervention (though the intervention may combine technologies of team building, technostructural change, etc) and overlooks the systemic nature of organizations. Exogenous variables and intervening events will always prevent any powerful conclusions. For example, influential figures change (Roberts & King 1985), or management changes production methods or makes material changes (Passmore & Friedlander 1982, Fiedler et al 1984). Even worse, normal science methodology can damage the experiment itself. Blumberg & Pringle (1983) describe a sociotechnical intervention, including job redesign and worker participation in a unionized mine, in which the "control" group found out about the experimental group. The "control" miners so resented the experimental group's advantage that they voted to prevent further changes in the workplace.

Traditional research methods make assumptions that may be entirely inappropriate for field research. For example, the concept of control groups or uninformed subjects may diminish the value of the information (survey responses may be more "thoughtless") or halt the experiment altogether (via control-group hostility). Normal science rests on replication, something unquestionably impossible in field research. Finally, events may be multicausal, the constellation of causes being of significance. Thus, it would be impossible to identify the precise effect of a given action.

Second, much of the research overlooks time and is not sufficiently longitudinal. By assessing the events and their impact at only one nearly contemporaneous moment, the research cannot discuss how permanent the changes are. As noted above, different posttest times may support different experimental conclusions.

Third, the research is "flat." While being precise about methodology and instruments, it is often imprecise in depth and description of the intervention and situation. The nature and history of the occupational groups involved are often not explored. The environmental context is overlooked. Notably, one study compares two interventions eight years apart. The environmental context may have changed, thus affecting the intervention's effects. Quantitative description may not be the best method for understanding a multi-causal phenomenon.

Fourth, the research does not fit the needs of its user. This is surprising given the action research tradition of OD. Noting that research knowledge has been slow to transfer to practice, the "crisis in utilization" is increasingly coming under scrutiny (Lindblom & Cohen 1979, Legge 1984, Lawler et al 1985, Kilmann et al 1983). Good science may be antithetical to good action. More complex statistical techniques and more complex quasi-experimental designs, in attempts to achieve more precision and tighter scientific "proof," neglect the "social construction" of knowledge in the social sciences. The complexity of the subject material and the existence of nonrational responses to data will inhibit acceptance of even the most tightly controlled experiments. As Legge (1984) notes, the best predictor of utilized knowledge is the "personal factor," the interest the users have in the evaluation study. Beer (1980) argued that managers make decisions about OD based not on evaluation research but on suitability to their agenda. Rather than create increasingly esoteric designs and increasingly narrow inferences, OD might do better to aim research at needs identified by managers and utilize language managers can understand.

OD research seems to be at a turning point. As long as OD researchers emulate traditional science methodology, they will confine themselves to isolated episodes of change. By evaluating a specific intervention, they neglect the interrelatedness of elements in a system; and because the organization is a system, exogenous variables will prevent any powerful conclusions.

Rather than attempt to find the perfect quantitative methodology and "scientifically" prove its value, OD should attempt to build a different model of knowledge. Argyris et al (1985) proposed action science. Critiquing traditional science methods, they argued for the combination of action and thinking to achieve double-loop, or self-corrective learning. Schon (1983) called for similar methodology. The call for rejection of typical positivistic assumptions is growing (Carnall 1982, Morgan 1983, Legge 1984, Peters & Robinson 1984). This would require a new format of journal reporting as well. What we are recommending is a return to the action research traditions of OD with full participation of the client in the research but with much longer time frames and the inclusion of rich descriptions of context and system dynamics.

Pettigrew provided a persuasive critique and useful counterexample of mainstream OD research and literature. Reviewing the history of and research on OD, he concluded that "theory and practice of change in organizations would continue to remain as circumscribed and ill developed as long as change is studied and thought about as episodes and projects separate from the ongoing processes of continuity and change of which those change projects are a part" (p. 26). His book, *The Awakening Giant: Continuity and Change in ICI,* provides an in-depth look at the history from 1960 to 1983 of Imperial Chemical Industries and four OD groups operating in it. Pettigrew, too, concluded that more longitudinal studies must be conducted.

Our critique of OD research is, of course, also a critique of OD's preoccupation with consultant-centered intervention methods. If research designs that define change too narrowly can be misleading, defining change as a single intervention at a given point in time is too confining. We have therefore decided not to review new intervention methods in depth and instead turn now to the general manager's problem of developing organizations to improve competitiveness and employee well-being.

OD as General Management

Managers are learning that they must manage change. Increasing international competition, deregulation, the decline of manufacturing, the changing values of workers, and the growth of information technology have changed the concepts and approaches managers must use. As Beckhard (1969) and Bennis (1969) argued early on, these changes require adaptive, flexible organizations, and skilled managers to manage these changes.

Many OD concepts have filtered into the management literature, and OD techniques are being addressed to the manager (Dyer 1983, Kirkpatrick 1985). Specifically, OD's concept of explicitly intervening to manage norms and culture is emerging in management journals. OD's views on leadership and managing "soft" (style versus systems) change are emerging in the leadership literature. The systemic view of organizations has also received attention.

Culture

OD has long recognized the importance of culture and considered culture management to be within its purview, but it has never developed the concept. Almost completely separate from the OD literature, a group of writings on organizational culture has sprung up. Much of it asserts a positive correlation between type of organizational culture and organizational effectiveness (Ouchi 1981, Deal & Kennedy 1982, Denison 1984). Not surprisingly, these cultures look much like Beckhard's (1969) definition of a healthy organization. Delegating, results-oriented, information-sharing, developmental, egalitarian, employee-centered cultures are believed to enhance adaptiveness, productivity, innovation, and performance (Kanter 1983, Denison 1984, Walton 1985). This view was brought to the practicing public in Peters & Waterman's popular book, *In Search of Excellence* (1982). Reviewing the characteristics of excellent companies, Peters & Waterman cited the elements of these companies' shared values—achieving productivity through people, the importance of people as individuals,

tolerance of failure, and informality to promote communication. Performance is achieved via expectations and peer review rather than management direction and sophisticated control systems.

Surveying several companies, and relying on extensive field experience, Kanter (1983) found certain companies more adaptive and innovative. These companies engendered a culture of pride and encouraged their employees to take risks. Innovators were not separated from the mainstream organization (as some earlier literature had recommended) but integrated their ideas and proposals into the organization by involving the important stakeholders. The innovative organization promotes high levels of collaboration between functions.

In addition to type of culture, the strength of culture can be important. Wilkins & Ouchi (1983) suggested that strong cultures (clan mechanisms) may enhance organizational efficiency only under conditions of uncertainty and ambiguity (hence high "transactions" costs), stability of membership, and reasonably equitable and inescapable reward systems. If these conditions do not exist, markets or hierarchies may better meet the firm's need for internal integration.

A flood of literature on managing corporate culture resulted from the popularizing of culture as a competitive advantage. Current theory suggests that managers spread culture through stories, symbolic acts, and other "soft" techniques (Peters & Waterman 1982, Kanter 1983, Kilmann 1984, Sathe 1985, Schein 1985), much as Barnard (1938) and Selznick (1957) said long ago. The literature offers managers a "culture audit" (Wilkins 1983), which can identify problems and actionable areas for management. The Kilmann-Saxton Culture Gap Survey (Kilmann et al 1985) identifies differences between desired and actual culture and lays out a five-track program for redirecting the culture. Kilmann (1984) claims that any effort to manage change without such a comprehensive program is an ill-fated attempt at a quick fix.

Efforts directed at managing culture alert us to the problem of defining culture. Schein (1985) argued that popular notions of culture reflect culture rather than describe its essence (norms, observed behavioral regularities, dominant values, philosophy, climate, etc). He argued that culture is multi-layered: The essence of culture may be found in the organization's embedded, preconscious, basic assumptions and beliefs about human nature, the nature of the world, and so forth. On a second, observable level, culture manifests itself as values, which are testable only by social consensus. Values are about how things ought to be done, or what works. When a value is agreed upon by a group, the group begins the process of cognitive transformation, in which the value becomes a belief or assumption, taken for granted rather than debatable. On the surface layer are artifacts and creations, which include things like art, technology, and behavioral patterns; these have meaning but are often not decipherable.

But how manageable is culture? Can a five-track program like Kilmann's (1984) enable managers to gain control of corporate culture? Or, is culture more powerful than managers, so that "culture controls the manager more than the manager controls the culture" (Schein 1985, p. 315)? It has been argued that cultural change cannot be managed and that special events that trigger change require managers to be temporarily out of control (Deal 1985). Changing and managing are incompatible. We suspect (as we will argue below in more depth) that the idea of planned change, long advocated by OD, requires reexamination and reformation. Preprogrammed approaches such as the five-track Culture Gap Survey are not likely to accord with how managers think and act (Kotter 1982) any more than Grid OD did.

Research suggests that culture may be more resilient than implied by the exhortations to manage it. Researchers examining the "cultural relativity" of change programs have generally found that interventions and technology that suit the host culture are most effective. In their earlier OD review, Faucheux et al (1982) noted that different cultures (US, European, Latin American) have developed different change technologies and that cross-cultural transfers of change technology have proved diffi-

cult and slow. Established change techniques used to intervene in culture directly have failed to overcome cultural resistance, suggesting that culture may be a lag rather than a lead variable.

Schein pointed out that the role of culture tends to vary with an organization's life cycle stage. For the youthful company, culture is often seen as a competitive advantage to be nurtured. For the mature company, culture may be a barrier to innovation: it may diminish integration and be a phenomenon to be managed and turned around. Change methods differ in appropriateness depending on the organization's life-cycle stage. For example, revolutionary change through outsiders may help an organization move from early growth to midlife, planned change and organization development may be most useful during organizational midlife, while coercive persuasion may suit a mature organization facing destruction or a turnaround. We believe that a theory of OD relevant to the general manager will only achieve usefulness if change problems, strategy, and tactics are tied to a life-cycle framework.

Leadership

OD has long recognized the importance of leadership in managing change. A vision, a new model for managing (Beer 1980), a "picture of the future" (Beckhard & Harris 1977) have been considered powerful means by which leaders might motivate behavior change.

Management literature has focused recently on the role of leadership in managing major corporate transformations. In line with OD ideas, this research has found the envisioning skills of the executives to be critical in managing change. Anderson et al (1985) studied 17 companies that had undergone revitalization; each company had transformed itself from a substandard into a superior performer in a period of 5–10 years. A key factor in these change efforts was the existence of a "championing" leader. Such leaders fight persistently for their ideas, are more ideological than their business-as-usual counterparts, manage by symbols, set an example of championing leadership for potential leaders throughout the corporation, and use rewards and interchampion competition as motivators.

Bennis & Nanus (1985) interviewed 90 renowned figures in business, government, labor, academics, and the arts. They found little commonality in behavior, dress, or speech but identified four themes in action. First, leaders got their followers' attention through a vision, agenda, or focus; second, they gave meaning to events and actions through communication, thus developing "shared meanings" among their followers; they engendered trust through positioning, being reliable, and sticking to their goals; and they used their own optimism and positive self-regard to inspire others. Followers benefited through feelings of significance, competence, community, and enjoyment.

These formulations share several themes. First, the leaders articulate and propagate a vision or agenda. Second, the leader assigns meaning and significance to events, expectations, and the vision, and in so doing, structures a cognitive world. In this sense, the leader achieves results not through formal structure or formalized control systems but by creating an understanding of reality that then motivates behavior. Much as OD has argued, the manager creates a set of expectations that powerfully influence behavior in the organization.

Key to these formulations is the notion that leaders empower others, a value long held by OD (Kanter 1983, Burke 1985). Bennis & Nanus's leaders "empower others to translate intention into reality and sustain it" (p. 80). Sashkin (1985) noted that "research is consistent in suggesting that effective leaders involve subordinates rather than dominating and . . . give away power . . . leaders achieve goals through others, and unless others have the power to do what the leader wants done, such achievements are not likely" (p. 5).

The implication of this research is clear. Managers' leadership, not OD consultants', is central to managing major cultural transformations. Unfortunately, none of the research on leadership has specified the skills required of transformational leaders. This specification is required before managers can be helped to develop them, if indeed they are developable. A beginning has been made by Sashkin (1985) and Burke (1985) in profiling leadership style via a questionnaire. Research is also required on the role OD consultants can play in helping managers lead or in symbolically representing the leaders' desire for change.

Open Systems Analysis

OD maintains that the organization is an open system, that it interacts with its environment to maintain a state of fit between internal arrangements and the environment (Katz & Kahn 1966, Lawrence & Lorsch 1967, Beer 1980, Burke 1982). Based on this view, OD has asserted the organization's need for "environmental mapping" or "mapping the demand system" (Beckhard & Harris 1977). Here the organization looks at the transactions that occur across the organization/environment interface and assesses the importance of those transactions.

Popular management books are now arguing that organization effectiveness is a state of fit or congruence between business strategy and several internal organizational arrangements such as systems, structure, management style, skills, staff, and shared values (Pascale & Athos 1981, Peters & Waterman 1982).

The open-systems view receives even greater attention through stakeholder and network concepts. Recent writings have recognized the importance of stakeholder relationships to management strategy. Freeman (1984) explicitly described techniques for identifying important stakeholders and managing stakeholder relationships. He included specific OD programs as one tool for supporting stakeholder relationships (p. 130). Stakeholder input is achieved via the inclusion of "boundary spanners" in the strategic planning process (Freeman 1984, p. 79). Freeman considered proactive stakeholder management capability critical to managing organizational change. Others have argued for formal inclusion of stakeholders in the corporate governance processes (Auerbach 1984).

OD practitioners are expanding open-systems theory and applying stakeholder concepts in diagnosis and action planning (Roberts & King 1985, Porras 1985). Golembiewski (1985) has found it important to involve stakeholders in major public projects. Kilmann (1983) has used stakeholder analysis to formulate theories and test assumptions in research. The concept of networks has received greater attention. Mandrell (1984) found network analysis valuable in developing roles for managers in a public project.

Senge (1985) has used systems-dynamics thinking and computer technology, previously applied to the creation of a microeconomic model, to the development of a systems-dynamic model of organizations. Based on interviews with managers of innovative, adaptive organizations, he constructed a computer model that specifies system characteristics crucial for creating and maintaining an adaptive organization, one in which information for decision making is widely shared. This model supports much of OD's assumptions about adaptive organizations. With a computer model he plans to train executives in systems dynamics so that they can manage organizations more effectively. This line of research promises to make some breakthroughs in how general managers learn to develop organizations.

OD as Creating Adaptive Organizations

OD has long been concerned with fostering organizational adaptation to environmental changes. Management literature is increasingly interested in the organization environment interface as well. The literature has expanded its focus to deal with issues of revitalization and decline.

Designing Innovative Organizations

Stimulated by the competitive crisis, an emerging stream of research (Tushman & Katz 1980, Kanter 1983, Lawrence & Dyer 1983, Nord & Tucker 1986) on innovation and entrepreneurship speaks to the question of adaptation and revitalization. While this research notes the importance of cultural factors, it also considers the key dilemma of integration and differentiation in developing innovative organizations (Lawrence & Lorsch 1967, Lawrence & Dyer 1983).

Early ideas on innovation suggested that product-planning groups be separated and "protected" from the organization at large. Kanter (1983) suggested more recently that such segmentation may be counterproductive and create barriers to innovations. Innovators must sell ideas into the organization for them to be successful.

Rubenstein & Woodman (1984) accorded critical importance to the boundary-spanner role. Boundary-spanning roles, such as territorial sales person or public relations representative, are considered conducive to innovation since these employees bring environmental information into the firm. While the boundary spanner may be a useful source of information, innovation may be more successful if all members are boundary spanners (Tushman & Katz 1980).

Research on innovation has also focused on the introduction of new technology. Graham & Rosenthal (1986) studied the implementation of flexible machining centers (FMCs) in eight companies. They found those sites that built flexibility into their human systems to be satisfied with results. Specifically, organizations need human flexibility in the composition and organization of product teams; the relations between in-house and vendor teams; and the selection, compensation, and organization of the FMC workforce. Flexibility indicators included broad skill mixes, cross-training, cross-functional cooperation, team building, and so forth. Zuboff (1985) distinguished between technologies that "informate"—bring together information so as to enhance workers' ability to think and act—and technologies that automate—technologies that minimize required skills and remove the need for thinking workers. Informating technologies are said to enhance organizational flexibility. Thus, Zuboff alerts us to the opportunities provided by new information technology for extending decisions down the hierarchy (creating a healthy and adaptive organization).

Nord & Tucker (1986) examine the implementation of an "administrative innovation," the offering of NOW accounts both in large and small banks and in savings and loans. They find that successful implementations shared four characteristics: (*a*) flexibility with regard to roles, decision making, and communication routes; (*b*) power concentrated somewhere (high or low); (*c*) technical readiness and access to technical and social competence (talent for pulling together people to solve problems); and (*d*) attention to the views of those directly responsible for implementation. These characteristics of successful implementations, except perhaps for the findings about power, might easily have been OD prescriptions.

The above findings suggest that some OD technology may be on target, some not. For example, getting input from those involved in implementation sounds like OD, while a particular cultural style is not requisite for implementation. In fact, it may be that technology and technological readiness are lead variables, while style may be a lag variable. The value of this type of research is that it translates general principles from OD into situation-specific prescriptions while clarifying the role of power in managing change, an area neglected by OD. Much more of such research is needed.

In order to achieve faster, more flexible internal communication routes, some organizations are restructuring, becoming flatter. These organizations have fewer power differentials (fewer titles, levels, status distinctions, reward differentials, etc) and rely on teams to accomplish tasks. Autonomous work groups responsible for a whole task have become popular. This trend parallels OD's precepts that decision making should occur at the level closest to the information (Beckhard 1969). There is continuing interest in organizational overlays: matrix organizations, parallel organizations, and collateral organizations (Zand 1974). The overlaps enhance the permeability at the organization's boundaries and thus allow the corporation to become more adaptive.

Rubenstein & Woodman (1984) noted the advantages of the collateral organization for individuals in the form of fulfillment, heightened perceptions, and connections to senior management. The organization benefits from enhanced disaster preparedness, decision-making ability at lower levels, the receipt of better information, and transmission of the ethos of senior management down to lower levels of the organization.

Interorganizational Relations

In their efforts to adapt to competitive forces organizations are increasingly looking to joint ventures and other interorganizational arrangements. These arrangements are subject to problems of intergroup relationships that OD has been concerned with for a long time. Gray (1985) has begun investigating conditions that enhance interorganizational collaboration. Van de Ven & Walker (1984) have looked at the dynamics of interorganizational cooperation and found that increased communications promote positive feelings and resource exchanges but also increase resource dependence. Johnson et al (1983) have described the innovative linkage model used between university, government, and the criminal justice system.

Buono et al (1985) looked at the pre- and post-merger attitudes in two savings banks. Owing to changes in the industry, most employees recognized the need for the merger, though there was evidence for postmerger ethnocentrism and irrational resistance. They note that management ''managed'' the hard factors more than the soft factors. Though the merger was between equals, one culture eventually dominated. Buono found that attitudes towards hard factors (compensation, hours of work, training policies, etc) changed less than attitudes toward organizational commitment and top management style.

Sales & Mirvis (1984) analyzed the features of managing an acquisition. They identified phases of cultural adjustment: first, employees feel anger, grief, dread, or anxiety; second, cross-cultural contact promotes change; third, acculturation occurs when the two cultures come to terms with each others. Sales & Mirvis anticipated conflict due to power differences, a one-directional flow from the buyer, and resistance from the subdominant group.

Organizational Decline

The 1974–1975 and 1981–1982 recessions and the declining performance of major US industries have focused the attention of managers and consultants on the task of managing decline. Decline, too, is organization development, possibly as natural as growth or revitalization. Research and theory on decline have grown substantially, though some argue more needs to be done (Nicoll 1982).

Undoubtedly, decline creates high organizational stress, and management is likely to observe irrational responses (Sutton 1983; Krantz 1985). While hostility, denial, and anger may be part of the emotional climate, depression, sadness, fear, and embarrassment may be the more powerful factors. Sutton (1983) notes, too, that lack of acceptance may be rational if possibilities for saving the company exist. Managers face many dilemmas: how to handle blaming (place it on external environment, accept it themselves, scapegoat others); which activities to sustain and which to disband; what and how much advance information to give to customers and employees, offering hope or taking it away (Sutton 1983). The results of different strategies are still unclear, though some generalizations seem possible. Management will need to spend more time on employees' personal concerns. It may be hard to contain information and rumors. Management may be unable to divert all blame from itself. Performance can decline but may well improve, due to increased management effort to deal with the feelings and perceptions of employees.

Cummings et al (1983) identified transorganizational systems as one positive response to managing decline. Conditions likely to facilitate the development of transorganizational systems included environmental turbulence, interdependence, lack of exit options, altruism, or mandates. Cummings et al reviewed transorganizational systems between similar organizations (such as the Microelectronics and Computer Technology company formed by semiconductor companies) or between dissimilar organizations (such as the Jamestown Labor-Management-Government system). They outlined strategies for setting up and running transorganizational systems. Trist (1983) suggested that interorganizational collaboration may be required to handle some of the complex problems facing organizations today. Cummings (1984) has begun exploring the opportunities for transorganizational development.

This research could bear fruit if it helps managers and consultants guide organizations through business or industry changes. It follows our general predisposition toward the development of OD theory that can help general managers manage major transitions or transformations in the life cycles of their organizations.

OD as Human-Resource Management

As organizations have struggled in an increasingly competitive economy, superior human resources are increasingly seen as a competitive advantage. This has culminated in substantial interest in developing high-commitment work systems that will attract, motivate, and retain superior employees. Indeed the term human resources is coming to represent an integration of personnel administration, labor relations, and organization development, with OD the senior partner. The human-resource function and the practice of human-resources management (HRM) are absorbing the values and often the practices of OD (Beer & Spector 1984).

Human-resource managers have been struggling to define a new change-oriented function for their departments. There is an increasing tendency for human-resources personnel to be consultative, aiding with problem solving on key issues and helping management identify new trends (Finlay 1984, Harris & Harris 1983, Lippitt et al 1983). Many are noting that human-resource managers must model nondefensive behavior (Argyris 1985b) and implement change in the human-resource function to demonstrate that they, as part of the organization, must change.

Human-resource managers with an OD orientation have gained power as organizations attempt to change labor relations from adversarial to collaborative. OD technology has been applied in "relationship by objectives," or in third-party consultation directed at mediating grievance and arbitration disputes (Goldberg & Brett 1983). Solberg (1985) described GM's Black Lake experience, in which labor and management got together to sanction, discuss, and discover quality-of-work-life objectives. He described a deeply emotional and personal experience brought about by close interaction between union leaders and managers. This event had dramatic impact on the rest of the organization. Isolated experiments with job enrichment, sociotechnical designs, and quality of work life have given way to concerted efforts by corporations to change the nature of their relationship with employees and unions. Much of this work draws on OD values and technology.

Quality-of-work-life programs, reviewed extensively in the last *Annual Review* chapter, continue to flourish, although the name is not as much in vogue. Walton (1985) estimates that over 1000 plants in the United States may now be involved in major system redesign. These include special efforts to recruit, select, orient, and train employees so that they fit into an organization that requires higher levels of involvement, responsibility, and interpersonal competence. That requirement comes from the design of autonomous work groups and/or the use of special problem-solving groups. Skill-based compensation systems are also being designed to support the employee growth and development so critical for the functioning of work teams in which individuals rotate jobs and perform vertical tasks. In our view a false distinction has arisen between quality-of-work-life programs, as these plant innovations are sometimes called, and OD. Both the design of a high-commitment work system in a new plant and the transformantion of an older plant employ OD concepts, values, intervention methods, and practitioners. Both are organization development.

Through an examination of six cases in which he was a consultant Walton (1980) was able to identify the dynamics of developing innovative green field plants. He found that in the early stages these plants face a human-resource gap. The employees lack the technical or interpersonal skills demanded by the new work system. Training and stress reduction are the key organization development tasks. In later stages there is a human-resource surplus where maintaining challenge and excitement are the key organization development tasks. More research that specifies the dynamics of organization development is needed.

Compensation systems are increasingly being used by management to revitalize organizations.

Lawler (1981) has argued that changes in compensation systems can be a lead variable in OD. Scanlon plans and skill-based pay systems are used as examples. Beer et al (1984) argued that in most instances pay system redesign should not be used to lead change, that better management and leadership can often accomplish the same thing without incurring some of the problems that result from rising expectations.

Employee ownership through Employee Stock Ownership Plans (ESOPs) has been tried as a means of increasing employee commitment and of helping failing companies (Simmons & Mares 1983, Kuttner 1985). By making employees owners, ESOPs are expected to achieve greater productivity, greater interest in the business, and heightened flexibility on both management and union sides. (Some ESOPs have been undertaken merely for the tax advantage associated with them.) Research shows that ownership without a climate of participation is unlikely to have a dramatic impact on performance (Long 1982, Bradley 1983). Indeed only when employee ownership or gains sharing is preceded or accompanied by extensive organization development are basic relationships between management and labor likely to change. Much more research is needed on the role of pay, gains sharing, and ownership in organization development, an area of research pioneered by Lawler (1981) and Frost et al (1974) but not continued by others.

OD as Implementing Change

What does the research and practice tell us about managing change? What precursors can indicate change opportunities? The introduction of new business strategies, technology, and administrative practices in response to specific changes in the environment demand that general managers become more competent in these matters. Below, we consider what we have learned about managing change.

Where Does Change Start?

Argyris (1985a) argues it starts with the individual. He offers a five-phase model for bringing about individual changes. Organizations do not develop self-corrective learning because they do not distinguish between espoused theories and theories in use. Though managers may espouse new, adaptive dictates (take risks, communicate openly), their behavior gives contraindications (failure and honesty are punished). This creates mixed messages, which are undiscussable. Because they are undiscussable, they cannot be changed. Only by confronting individuals with their inconsistencies will organizations develop the ability to critique current practice and develop double-loop, or self-corrective learning. To do this, Argyris suggests consultants start small and at the top. Many others have focused on individual change, particularly on trying to change the behavior of leaders and managers, claiming that this is where OD change starts.

Others disagree, and suggest that organization change comes about from change in systems and structures (Greenbaum et al 1983, Macy et al 1986). The argument here is that systemic change is needed to support changes in individual behavior. For example, Tainio & Santalainen (1984) compared the results of Grid OD training and found that it was less successful in Finland, where it fit poorly with organization structure and culture, than in the United States. Even in the United States individual approaches to organization change, most notably the T group movement of the 1960s, have failed.

Yet even system-wide efforts have failed. Researchers note that sociotech and other interventions are often not institutionalized and fade out after two years (Walton 1978, Beer 1979, Goodman & Dean 1982). This has led some to argue that change needs to start at the industry level. For example, Sandeberg (1983) consulted to unions about technology introduction and noted the need for workers and unions alike to be better informed so as to approach industry-wide new technology implementation proactively, rather than have the circumstance defined by management. Related are the findings of Roggemma (1983), who concluded that despite intensive efforts to change practices in the shipping industry, inertia and existing industry structure and institutional forces made lasting change impossible.

Obviously change must occur at the individual, organizational, and industry level for it to be institutionalized. More research is needed, however, on the problems and opportunities created by starting at one or the other of these levels and the most effective sequencing of change once it starts at each of these levels.

Can Change Be Planned?

This question strikes at the very heart of OD assumptions. In increasing numbers, researchers and practitioners are expressing doubt (Lippitt et al 1985). Management literature parallels this emerging consensus. Quinn's (1980) study of strategic planning at 10 large companies led him to call the process "logical incrementalism." In this conception, managers make plans, which work imperfectly and attract a great deal of attention, disagreement, and support. The response of the system then affects and redirects the plan. Even managers have a hard time following grand plans (Pettigrew 1975) and must sometimes be out of control. Change is not brought about by following a grand master plan but by continually readjusting direction and goals. Research is needed on the structures and processes organizations must develop to allow an organic planning process to take place.

What Causes Change?

If change cannot be planned, then what causes change? While this question has no simple answer, it seems possible that OD has focused too narrowly on planned, internal efforts and neglected the role of environmental factors. Yet environmental factors may play a critical role in actual change. In a history of General Motors, Fox (1984) suggested that although Dupont placed several of GM's senior managers, had substantial equity in the firm, and continually pressed for changes, GM did not change until environmental contingencies forced change upon it. Dyer's (1985) research suggests that external events and crises precipitate changes far more than planned events. Precipitating events may often be anticipated but not controlled by managers.

Some (Anderson et al 1985, Fry & Killing 1985) are suggesting a taxonomy of change based on environmental factors. For example, a turnaround may occur after the organization has performed poorly over a long period. In this situation, where dissatisfaction and the perceived need to change are likely to be high and thus resistance lower, change may proceed quickly. In a revitalization situation, performance is mediocre and expected to decline. However, the perceived need to change is less acute; hence, slower change must be planned around likely resistance. In the case where mediocre performance has not yet occurred but is anticipated, change is likely to be even more difficult and must proceed at an even slower pace.

What Are the Roles in Change?

The faster pace of change is highlighting the centrality of the manager in managing change. Increasingly, OD practitioners are realizing the limitations on consultants' power and recognizing that it is best to have the manager center stage. Pettigrew (1985) noted that when consultants take greater control of process than management, or when the consultant has a highly visible role, the change process meets management resistance. Dyer (1983) argued that "Organization Development specialists (both internal and external) can assist in the process, but it should be managed by those who are ultimately responsible for all organizational consequences" (p. xiv). Cole (1982) pointed out that change has been better institutionalized in Japan and Sweden, countries in which managers drive the change with little assistance from external consultants.

Our view is that the manager must be central to change management and that OD must become a general management skill. The leader is more an architect than a director. He or she creates the environment (systems, strategy, models, symbols, etc) in which motivation for change will flourish. In this formulation, the leader/manager of an adaptive organization develops a vision of the future and attempts to infuse the organization with that vision, thereby motivating action and change. The manager must be flexible, willing to redraw plans and policies based on new information and system reactions. The manager needs a sense of timing, the ability to seize opportunities for change from the inevitable crises that occur in a firm's life. The leader must be able to pick consultants who will help him or her, particularly those who can provide strengths where he or she is weak. As yet, relatively little empirical research has been done on the leadership function in managing change. We also have focused on the titular head of the organization and neglected to investigate a broad set of leaders and the roles they play in change.

Role of "Change Targets"

The individuals to be affected by organizational change have been involved with some success in planning and implementing that change. Elden (1983) used a diagonal slice of the organization to assess internal relationships, and argued that those at the lower levels identify more system variables and describe more complex interrelationships between them than do employees higher in the organization. Levine (1983) described a self-developed quality-of-work-life (QWL) measure whose items reflected the most common statements by organization members about their work life. Levine demonstrated that this instrument had more criterion and convergent validity when compared with the Job Diagnostic Survey and saw distinct advantages to using the self-developed measure. This survey did not take job constructs as givens and was therefore less likely than the JDS to imply technological determinism.

Interventions are increasingly using teams for data gathering, analysis, and intervention. Friedlander & Schott (1981) described the use of groups as the intervention agent. In this model, the consultant's role is to help group members define tasks and roles, help with data collection, help develop team skills, and aid in understanding the larger organization in systems terms. Lundberg & Glassman (1983) used internal experts, relying on an informant panel for an organizational diagnosis. This is a promising approach to organization interventions, one that takes the consultant out of the limelight.

The Role of the Consultant

The consultant facilitates the managers' actions, providing them with data, skills, and suggestions. The consultant must be an expert in identifying opportunities for motivating change and clarifying visions. Consultants must help managers and staff learn. Naturally occurring events may be more educative and significant than the traditional interventions (laboratory, survey).

This suggests consultants must develop a better sense of what enables learning. In his study of how managers think, Isenberg (1984) found that acting and thinking may not be separable events. He argued that managers do not follow a classical rational problem-solving model but work on several problems at a time and may act on a problem before thinking about it. This again suggests that learning must be integrated with action. Certainly readiness is a key ingredient.

OD needs a new concept of the consultant's role. We believe it must become less purist, less programmed, and less value-laden. Current conceptions of consulting roles and plans are often too grandiose, developing research, knowledge, and practice that empower the consultant rather than the client.

Less Purist

OD practitioners often describe their role as neutral, as consulting to the entire "system," and as antithetical to the power politics that pervade organizations. Recent research is critiquing this concept of OD, noting vast differences between OD as written and as practiced (Lovelady 1984). Mendenhall & Oddou (1983) noted that many programs try to teach Theory-Y principles but use a Theory-X style themselves.

McLean et al (1982) noted that many reports of OD projects may be misrepresentative. Their study of OD consultants' practices identified numerous actions, ranging from overt "power plays" to unconsciously "acting like an expert," that directly contradicted consulting norms presented in the literature. They also concluded that change does not occur in the linear, planned phases of typical OD, and that the best consultants are able to take advantage of events, identifying opportunities to foster change. They identified two types of consultants: the centered consultant, who is opportunistic, takes a long-range view, has high tolerance for ambiguity, realizes organizations are messy, and is gratified with small successes; and the unintegrated consultant, who controls the client's definition of situations and events, is reluctant to exploit natural opportunities, and uses theory as a blueprint for truth.

Many (Carnall 1982, Pettigrew 1985) criticize OD's naiveté in the field of politics. Margulies & Raia (1984) argued that OD has neglected politics, yet politics are a key to success in consulting. Arguing that the consultant cannot be neutral, they outlined how consultants can help clients with the political aspects of problems. Jones (1984) cautioned consultants to look at politics skeptically and to question their clients' perceptions of organizational politics. Brown (1982) noted the difficulty of consulting to a group embroiled in internal conflict and described how politics can undermine the consultant's efforts.

Less Programmed

Research on change clearly argues that change does not obey the linear, phased plan of manager or consultant. Change does not occur in single episodes or interventions. Preprogrammed phase models may be unrealistic. McLean et al (1982) noted that the planned-change model is still used but often breaks down in four typical ways: The cycle (contracting, data collection, analysis, and feedback) results in insufficient data for action and cycles back to data collection; an educational program is set up as a precursor to change activities but detracts from objectives and becomes an end rather than a means; and a steering group may get bogged down analyzing its own process and neglect the problem it was formed to solve (p. 87–89). This raises questions about the more programmed (Blake & Mouton 1981, Kilmann 1984) approaches.

McLean et al (1982) pointed out that the opportunities for powerful interventions arise irregularly and unannounced. The skillful practitioner uses naturally occurring events to enhance the pressure for change. This suggests, too, that consultants need to be opportunistic and develop political skills.

Programs must consider the environment and the situation. In a fast-changing environment, managers learn primarily by doing (Boulden & Lawlor 1982, Eisenstat 1984). A flexible consultant working with managers to solve problems on the job might thus stimulate more of what Eisenstat has called behavioral learning (through doing) as opposed to representational learning (through language) typically delivered by standardized testing programs.

These findings suggest that managers and consultants must design interventions that are embedded in the work situation and tailored to it. Such interventions demand that consultants become effective in diagnosing problems and designing and managing experiences that permit inductive learning. The field will have to develop guidelines for designing and managing learning experiences. These would be the equivalent of a contingency theory of intervention.

Plans must also suit the readiness of the client system. Readiness refers to the social, technological, or systemic ability of a group or organization to change or try new things. Programs need to identify where change is possible, rather than attempt to impose change on a highly resistant, unready system. Schlesinger & Oshry (1984) and Jick & Ashkenas (1985) have argued that in order to effect long-term changes, planners must start small, exploit early successes, and seek to tie the elements of change to existing systems and structures.

In assessing a program's impact on a client system, OD consultants must also consider the magnitude of change. Organizations are constantly changing, adding new products, reorganizing, modifying strategy, in a sense fine tuning the existing organization. Tushman et al (in press) observed two basic types of organizational change: converging change, which consists of iterative improvements toward an essentially unchanged goal; and framebreaking change, in which the system drastically reorganizes and redirects itself. They argued that major redirections must be undertaken quickly and powerfully to avoid getting bogged down in politics. Converging change may be managed in a more consensual process.

Throughout our discussion, we have raised the question of lead versus lag variables. Change methods and organizational values appropriate for one organizational situation may be dysfunctional at another phase in the life cycle. Interventions effective in a stable environment may be inefficient in unstable environments. An organization with a powerful culture may use a technological change as a lead intervention, and follow with cultural change. This variability suggests a problem for advocates of a one-best-way approach.

Each consultant may need to specialize in what fits his or her style and experience. Schon (1983) maintained that the best professionals know more than they can put into words. To meet the challenges of their work, they rely less on graduate school theory than on their experience in responding to problems that arise in practice. This suggests that OD consultants, or for that matter managers concerned with knowing what they have learned, need to spend time in reflection to develop their own theory of change.

Less Value-Laden

Some practitioners believe that a return to the simple value of democratic management would create organizational effectiveness, yet evidence suggests that such management may be neither universally advantageous nor universally desired.

Even OD interventions designed to create more open and participative organizations may have negative outcomes for individuals. Walters (1984) points out that OD may reduce an individual's freedom, privacy, or self esteem. For example, consultants may not inform survey respondents of possible negative outcomes (a powerful manager may retaliate after receiving negative feedback); team building or confrontation may dragoon people into revealing private or interpersonal information, imposing on their freedom and privacy for the presumed advantage of improved team performance. These interventions may benefit the organization but harm the individual (Gavin 1984).

The evidence that certain organizational forms or styles foster organizational effectiveness is inconclusive. Though many advocate the open, participative organization, others have found that these attributes do not always correlate with success. Some situations simply may not allow integration of employee and organizational needs. The best organizational style and form is contingent on the organization's task, what it needs to do to succeed in its environment. Moreover, advocacy of values by OD practitioners has not worked well, as evidenced by the rise and decline of many corporate OD efforts. If corporations today are adopting OD values in their efforts to revitalize, they are doing so because environmental pressures are pushing them to do so.

In Conclusion

In the introduction we said our conception of the field involves a reconsideration of its research methodology, theory building, practice, and values. Here we return to a brief discussion of this conception.

Theory building in the field has always been weak. We believe this stems from the traditional focus of the field. Rather than cataloging the technology of organizational change, we need to catalog how external forces create the opportunities for change. Rather than assume that there is a single way to change organizations, a way consistent with our technology and values, we should develop a contingency theory of organization change. Such a theory would specify alternative change strategies appropriate to an organization's stage of development. It would highlight the skills required of the leader, OD consultant, and other supporting change agents as well as their relationship to each other and the task of change, with particular emphasis on what they must know about the business of the organization and its politics. The theory would deal

with time frames more explicitly than current theories, and it would specify how continuity of leadership and consultation relate to effective adaptation. In short, we need a theory of organizational adaptation that incorporates *all* types of interventions, applying them to the management of the numerous crises all organizations face. Such a theory could benefit from the general-management orientation of business policy and could contribute to the field ideas about leadership, organizational culture, and change.

The primary research methodology appropriate to this orientation would not be that of normal science, which attempts to answer little questions precisely. Instead we would be more concerned with broader longitudinal designs, creating knowledge that could be used. We suggest a return to the action research traditions of the field but with a longer time frame and a more thorough investigation of the context in which episodes occur. OD need not become lax in its search for knowledge, but we must recognize that our sphere of inquiry is fundamentally different from that of normal science. We cannot borrow the tools and techniques of another paradigm; we must develop our own.

The practice of OD must also change. We suggest the focus should move away from structured and preprogrammed consultant-centered interventions. The general manager is the central character in the drama of organization development. OD practitioners must therefore be more concerned with the selection and development of these leaders. They must also adopt the perspective of the general manager. This means knowledge of the business and task; understanding of the competitive environment and the opportunities for change and development it provides; and much more sophistication in diagnosis, politics, and intervention design suited to the situation. All of this raises serious questions about the source and development of OD consultants and their relationship to general managers and the human-resource function.

Tension has always existed in the field between a concern for effectiveness and a concern for the well-being of employees. Our review suggests that in some ways this tension has been eased by the natural evolution of organizations, pushed by competitive forces, toward the values of OD. But, we do not believe this evolution has come about because OD practitioners have been successful in imposing their values on organizations nor that future evolution toward the healthy organization will come from OD practitioners who advocate humanistic values. OD practitioners—general managers and consultants alike—would be well advised to retain a normative vision for long-term guidance while adopting a situational perspective in diagnosing organizational problems and taking action to improve them. As with many human endeavors, managing this paradox is the critical skill.

Literature Cited

Anderson, D. G., Phillips, J. R. Kaible, N. 1985. *Revitalizing Large Companies., Work. Pap.* Cambridge, MA: Mass. Inst. Technol. 35 pp.

Argyris, C. 1985a. *Strategy, Change and Defensive Routines*. Boston: Pitman. 368 pp.

Argyris, C. 1985b. *Reinforcing Defensive Routines: An Unintended Human Resources Activity.* Draft. 24 pp.

Argyris, C., Putnam, R., Smith, D. M. 1985. *Action Science.* San Francisco: London: Jossey-Bass. 480 pp.

Armenakis, A. A., Bedian, A. G., Pond, S. B. III. 1983. Research issues in OD evaluation: past, present and future. *Academy of Management, Rev.* 8:320–28.

Auerbach, J. 1984. *The Now and Future Business Corporation.* Work. pap. Boston: President & Fellows Harvard College.

Barnard, C. I. 1938. *The Functions of the Executive.* Cambridge, MA: Harvard Univ. Press. 334 pp.

Beckhard, R. 1969. *Organization Development: Strategies and Models.* Reading, MA: Addison-Wesley. 119 pp.

Beckhard, R., Harris, R. T. 1977. *Organizational Transitions: Managing Complex Change.* Reading, MA: Addison-Wesley, 110 pp.

Beer, M. 1979. The longevity of organization development. In *Organization Change Sourcebook I: Cases in Organization Development,* ed. B. Lubin, L. D. Goodstein. A. W. Lubin. pp. 62–65. La Jolla, CA: Univ. Assoc.

Beer, M. 1980. *Organization Change and Development: A Systems View.* Santa Monica: Goodyear. 367 pp.

Beer, M., Spector, B. 1984. Human resource management: the integration of industrial relations and organization development. In *Research in Personnel and Human Resources Management,* ed. K. M. Rowland, G. R. Ferris, pp. 261–97. San Francisco: JAI Press.

Beer, M. Spector, B. 1985. Corporate-wide transformations: In *HRM Trends and Challenges,* ed. R. Walton, P. Lawrence. Boston: Harvard Bus. Sch. Press.

Beer, M., Spector, B., Lawrence, P. R., Mills, D. Q., Walton, R. E. 1984. *Managing Human Assets.* New York: The Free Press. 209 pp.

Bennis, W. 1969. *Organization Development: Its Nature, Origins, and Prospects.* Reading, MA: Addison-Wesley, 87 pp.

Bennis, W., Nanus, B. 1985. *Leaders.* New York: Harper & Row. 244 pp.

Blake, R. R., Mouton, J. S. 1981. *The New Managerial Grid.* Houston: Gulf. 329 pp.

Blumberg, M., Pringle, C. D. 1983. How control groups can cause loss of control in action research: the case of Rushton Coal Mine. *J. Appl. Behav. Sci.* 19:409–25.

Boulden, G., Lawlor, A. 1982. Surviving in a changing world: the nature of change and its application. *Leadership Organ. Dev. J.* 3:3–9.

Bradley, K. 1983. *Worker Capitalism: The New Industrial Relations.* Boston: MIT Press. 192 pp.

Brown, C. M. 1982. Administrative succession and organizational performance: the succession effect. *Admin. Sci. Q.* 27:1–16.

Buono, A., Bowditch, J. L., Lewis, J. W. III. 1985. When cultures collide: the anatomy of a merger. *Hum. Relat.* 38:477–500.

Burke, W. W. 1982. *Organization Development, Principles and Practices.* Boston/Toronto: Little, Brown. 402 pp.

Burke, W. W. 1985. *Leadership as Empowering Others.* New York: W. Warner Burke Assoc. 31 pp.

Carnall, C. A. 1982. *The Evaluation of Organizational Change.* Brookfield, VT: Gower. 130 pp.

Cole, R. E. 1982. Diffusion of participatory work structures in Japan, Sweden, and the United States. In *Change in Organizations,* ed. P. Goodman and Associates, pp. 166–225. San Francisco/London: Jossey-Bass.

Cummings, T. G. 1984. Trans-organization development. *Res. Organ. Behav.* 6:

Cummings, T. G., Blumenthal, J., Greiner, L. 1983. Managing organizational decline: the case for transorganizational systems. *Hum. Resour. Manage.* 22(4):377–90.

Deal, T. E. 1985. Cultural change: opportunity, silent killer, or metamorphosis? In *Gaining Control of the Corporate Culture,* ed. R. H. Kilmann, M. J. Saxon, R. Serpa. pp. 292–331. San Francisco/London: Jossey-Bass.

Deal, T., Kennedy, A. 1982. *Corporate Cultures.* Reading, MA: Addison-Wesley. 232 pp.

Denison, D. R. 1984. Bringing corporate culture to the bottom line. *Organ. Dyn.* 13:4–22.

Dyer, W. G. 1983. *Contemporary Issues in Management and Organization Development.* Reading, MA: Addison-Wesley. 231 pp.

Dyer, W. G. 1985. The cycle of cultural evolution in organizations. See Kilmann et al 1985, pp. 200–29.

Eisenstat, R. A. 1984. *Organizational learning in the creation of an industrial setting.* PhD thesis. Yale Univ., New Haven, CT. 240 pp.

Elden, M. 1983. Democratization and participative research in developing local theory. *J. Occup. Behav.* 4:21–33.

Faucheux, C., Amado, G., Laurent, A. 1982. Organizational development and change. *Ann. Rev. Psychol.* 33:343–70.

Fiedler, F. E., Bell, C., Chemers, M., Patrick, D. 1984. Increasing mine productivity and safety through management training and organization development: a comparative study. *Basic Appl. Soc. Psychol.* 5:1–18.

Finlay, J. S. 1984. Diagnose your HRD problems away. *Train. Dev. J.* 38:50–52.

Fox, W. 1984. General Motors: Dupont's tough OD case. *Group Organ. Stud.* 9:71–80.

Freeman, R. E. 1984. *Strategic Management: A Stakeholder Approach.* Boston: Pitman. 276 pp.

Friedlander, F., Schott, B. 1981. The use of task groups and task forces in organizational change. In *Groups At Work,* ed. R. Payne, C. Cooper, pp. 191–218. New York: Wiley.

Frost, C. F., Wakeley, J. H., Ruh, R. A. 1974. *The Scanlon Plan for Organization Development: Identity, Participation, and Equity.* East Lansing, MI: Mich. State Univ. Press. 197 pp.

Fry, J. N., Killing, J. P. 1985. *Strategic Analysis and Action.* Englewood Cliffs, NJ: Prentice-Hall.

Gavin, J. F. 1984. Survey feedback: the perspectives of science and practice. *Group Organ. Stud.* 9(1):29–70.

Goldberg, S. B., Brett, J. M. 1983. An experiment in the mediation of grievance. *Monthly Labor Rev.* 106:23–29.

Golembiewski, R. T. 1983. Lessons from a fast-paced public project: perspectives on doing better the next time around. *Public Admin. Rev.* 43:547–56.

Golembiewski, R. T., Billingsley, K., Yeager, S. 1976. Measuring change and persistence in human affairs: types of change generated by OD designs. *J. Appl. Behav. Sci.* 12:133–57.

Goodman, P., Dean, J. W. 1982. Creating long term change in organizations. In *Change in Organizations,* ed. P. Goodman and Associates, pp. 226–79. San Francisco/London: Jossey-Bass.

Graham, M. B. W., Rosenthal, S. R. 1986. Flexible manufacturing systems require flexible people. In *Human Systems Management.* In press.

Gray, B. 1985. Conditions facilitating interorganization collaboration. *Hum. Relat.* 38(10):911–86.

Greenbaum, H. H., Holden, E. J. Jr., Spartaro, L. 1983. Organizational structure and communications processes: a study of change. *Group Organ. Stud.* 8(1):61–82.

Guzzo, R. A., Jette, R. D., Katzell, R. A. 1985. The effects of psychologically based intervention programs on worker productivity: a meta-analysis. *Personnel Psychol.* 38:275–92.

Hackman, R., Oldham, G. R. 1975. Development of the job diagnostic survey. *J. Appl. Psychol.* 60:159–170.

Harris, P. R., Harris, D. L. 1983. Twelve trends you and your CEO should be monitoring. *Train. Dev. J.* 37:62–69.

Isenberg, D. J. 1984. How senior managers think. *Harv. Bus. Rev.* 62:80–90.

Jick, T. D., Ashkenas, R. N. 1985. Involving employees in productivity and QWL improvements: what OD can learn from the manager's perspective. In *Contemporary Organization Development: Current Thinking and Applications,* ed. D. D. Warrick, pp. 218–30. Glenview, IL: Scott, Foresman.

Johnson, K. W., Frazier, W. D., Riddick, M. R. 1983. A change strategy for linking the worlds of academia and practice. *J. Appl. Behav. Sci.* 19:439–60.

Jones, S. 1984. The politics of problems: intersubjectivity in defining powerful others. *Hum. Relat.* 37:881–94.

Kanter, R. M. 1983. *The Change Masters: Innovation and Entrepreneurship in the American Corporation.* New York: Simon & Schuster. 432 pp.

Katz, D., Kahn, R. L. 1966. *The Social Psychology of Organizing.* New York: Wiley. 838 pp.

Katzell, R. A., Guzzo, R. A. 1983. Psychological approaches to productivity improvement. *Am. Psychol.* 38:468–72.

Kilmann, R. 1984. *Beyond the Quick Fix: Managing Five Tracks to Organizational Success.* San Francisco/London: Jossey-Bass. 300 pp.

Kilmann, R., Saxton, J. J., Serpa, R., eds. 1985. *Gaining Control of the Corporate Culture.* San Francisco/London: Jossey-Bass. 451 pp.

Kilmann, R. H. 1983. A dialectic approach to formulating and testing social science theories: assumptional analysis. *Hum. Relat.* 36(1):1–22.

Kilmann, R. H., Thomas, K. W., Slevin, D. P., Nath, R., Jerrell, L., eds. 1983. *Producing Useful Knowledge for Organizations.* New York: Praeger. 731 pp.

Kirkpatrick, D. 1985. *How to Manage Change Effectively.* San Francisco/London: Jossey-Bass. 280 pp.

Kleiner, B. 1983. The interrelationship of Jungian modes of mental functioning with organizational factors: implications for management development. *Hum. Relat.* 36(11):997–1012.

Kotter, J. P. 1982. *The General Managers.* New York/London: Free Press. 221 pp.

Krantz, J. 1985. Group process under conditions of organization decline. *J. Appl. Behav. Sci.* 21:1–18.

Kuttner, R. 1985. Sharing power at Eastern Air Lines. *Harv. Bus. Rev.* 6:91–101.

Lawler, E. E. 1981. *Pay and Organization Development.* Reading, MA: Addison-Wesley.

Lawler, E. E., Mohrman, A. M. Jr., Mohrman, S. A., Ledford, G. E. Jr., Cummings, T. G., eds. 1985.

Doing Research That Is Useful for Theory and Practice. San Francisco/London: Jossey-Bass. 371 pp.

Lawrence, P. R., Lorsch, J. W. 1967. *Organizations and Environment: Managing Differentiation and Integration.* Homewood, IL: Irwin. 279 pp.

Lawrence, P. R., Dyer, D. 1983. *Renewing American Industry.* New York: The Free Press. 384 pp.

Legge, K. 1984. *Evaluating Planned Organizational Change.* Orlando: Academic. 243 pp.

Levine, M. F. 1983. Self-developed QWL measures. *J. Occup. Behav.* 4:35–46.

Lindblom, C. E., Cohen, D. K. 1979. *Usable Knowledge: Social Science and Social Problem Solving.* New Haven: Yale Univ. Press. 129 pp.

Lippett, G., Lippett, R., Lafferty, C. 1983. Cutting edge trends in organizational development. *Train. Dev. J.* 38:59–62.

Lippitt, G. L., Langseth, P., Mossop, J. 1985. *Implementing Organizational Change.* San Francisco/London: Jossey-Bass. 185 pp.

Long, R. J. 1982. Worker ownership and job attitudes: a field study. *Ind. Relat.* 21:196–215.

Lovelady, L. 1984. Change strategies and the use of OD consultants to facilitate change. II. The role of the internal consultant in OD. *Leadership Organ. Dev. J.* 5:2–12.

Lundberg, C. C., Glassman, A. M. 1983. The informant panel: a retrospective methodology for guiding organizational change. *Group Organ. Stud.* 3(2):249–64.

Macy, B. A., Hurts, C. C. M., Izumi, H., Norton, L. W., Smith, R. R. 1986. Presented at Natl. Acad. Manage., 46th Ann. Meet., Chicago, IL. 101 pp. 52.

Mandrell, M. 1984. Application of network analysis to the implementation of a complex project. *Hum. Relat.* 37:659–79.

Margulies, N., Raia, A. P. 1984. The politics of OD. *Train Dev. J.* 38:20–23.

McLean, A. J., Sims, D. B. P., Mangan, I. L., Tuffield, D. 1982. *Organization Development in Transition: Evidence of an Evolving Profession.* New York: Wiley. 131 pp.

Mendenhall, M., Oddou, G. 1983. The integrative approach to OD: McGregor revisited. *Group Organ. Stud.* 8:291–301.

Morgan, G., ed. 1983. *Beyond Method: Strategies for Social Research.* Beverly Hills, CA: Sage. 424 pp.

Morrison, P. 1978. Evaluation in OD: A review and assessment. *Group Organ. Stud.* 3:42–70.

Nicholas, J. 1982. The comparative impact of organization development interventions on hard criteria measures. *Acad. Manage. Rev.* 9:531–43.

Nicholas, J., Katz, M. 1985. Research methods and reporting practices in organization development: a review and some guidelines. *Acad. Manage. Rev.* 10:737–49.

Nicoll, D. 1982. Organization declines as an OD issue. *Group. Organ. Stud.* 7:165–78.

Nord, W. R., Tucker, S. 1986. *Implementing Radical and Routine Innovation.* Lexington, MA: Lexington Books. 416 pp.

Ouchi, W. G. 1981. *Theory Z: How American Business Can Meet the Japanese Challenge.* Reading, MA: Addison-Wesley. 283 pp.

Pascale, R. T., Athos, A. G. 1981. *The Art of Japanese Management.* New York: Simon & Schuster. 221 pp.

Passmore, W., Friedlander, F. 1982. An action research program for increasing employee involvement in problem solving. *Admin. Sci. Q.* 27:343–62.

Peters, M., Robinson, V. 1984. The origins and status of action research. *J. Appl. Behav. Sci.* 20:113–24.

Peters, T., Waterman, R. H. 1982. *In Search of Excellence.* New York: Harper & Row. 360 pp.

Pettigrew, A. 1985. *The Awakening Giant: Continuity and Change in ICI.* Oxford/New York: Blackwell, 542 pp.

Porras, J. I. 1985. *OD Research Paper #802,* March.

Quinn, J. B. 1980. *Strategies for Change: Logical Incrementalism.* Homewood, IL: Irwin. 222 pp.

Roberts, N., King, P. 1985. *The Stakeholder Audit: A Key Political Tool in the Change Process.* Draft.

Roberts, N. C., Porras, J. I. 1982. Progress in OD research. *Group Organ. Stud.* 7(1):91–116.

Roggemma, J., Smith, M. H. 1983. Organizational change in the shipping industry: issues in the transformation of the basic assumptions. *Hum. Relat.* 8:765–90.

Rubenstein, D., Woodman, R. W. 1984. Spiderman and the Burma Raiders: collateral organization theory in action. *J. Appl. Behav. Sci.* 20:1–21.

Sales, A. L., Mirvis, P. H. 1984. When cultures collide: issues in acquisition. In *Managing Organizational Transitions,* ed. J. R. Kimberly, R. E. Quinn, pp. 107–33. Homewood, IL: Irwin.

Sandeberg, A. 1983. Trade union-orientated research for democratization of planning in work life—problems and pitfalls. *J. Occup. Behav.* 4:59–71.

Sashkin, M. 1985. *Visionary Leadership: A New Look at Executive Leadership.* Washington, DC: Off. Educ. Res. Improve. 9 pp.

Sashkin, M., Burke, R. J., Lawrence, P. R., Pasmore, W. A. 1984. Organization development approaches: analysis and application. In *Contemporary Organization Development, Current Thinking and Applications,* ed. D. D. Warrick. Glenview, IL: Scott, Foresman. 502 pp.

Sathe, V. 1985. *Culture and Related Corporate Realities.* Homewood, IL: Irwin. 579 pp.

Schein, E. 1985. *Organizational Culture and Leadership.* San Francisco: Jossey-Bass. 357 pp.

Schlesinger, L. A., Oshry, B. 1984. Quality of work life and the manager: muddle in the middle. *Organ. Dyn.* 13:4–19.

Schon, D. E. 1983. *The Reflective Practitioner: How Professionals Think in Action.* New York: Basic Books, 374 pp.

Seashore, S. E., Lawler, E. E., Mirvis, P. H., Camman, C., eds. 1983. *Assessing Organizational Change: A Guide to Methods, Measures and Practices.* New York: Wiley.

Selznick, P. 1957. *Leadership in Administration.* White Plains, NY: Row, Peterson. 162 pp.

Senge, P. M. 1985. *System dynamics, mental models and the development of management intuition.* Presented at the 1985 Int. Syst. Dyn. Conf., Keystone, CO.

Simmons, J., Mares, W. 1983. *Working Together.* New York: Knopf. 319 pp.

Solberg, S. L. 1985. Changing culture through ceremony: an example from GM. *Hum. Resour. Manage.* 24:329–40.

Sutton, R. I. 1983. Managing organizational death. *Hum. Resour. Manage.* 22:391–412.

Tainio, R., Santalainen, T. 1984. Some evidence for the cultural relativity of organization development programs. *J. Appl. Behav. Sci.* 20(2):93–111.

Terpstra, D. E. 1982. Evaluating selected OD interventions: the state of the art. *Group Organ. Stud.* 7(4):402–17.

Trist, E. 1983. Referent-organizations and the development of inter-organization domains. *Hum. Relat.* 36(3):269–84.

Tushman, M., Katz, R. 1980. External communication and project performance: an investigation into the role of gatekeepers. *Manage. Sci.* 26:1071–85.

Tushman, M., Newman, W. H., Romanelli, E. 1986. Convergence and upheavals: managing the unsteady pace of organizational evolution. *Calif. Manage. Rev.* 28: In press.

Van de Ven, A., Walker, G. 1984. The dynamics of interorganizational coordination. *Admin. Sci. Q.* 29:598–621.

Van de Vliert, E., Huismans, S. E., Stok, J. J. L. 1985. The criterion approach to unraveling beta and alpha change. *Acad. Manage. Rev.* 10:269–74.

Vicars, W. M., Hartke, D. D. 1984. Evaluating OD evaluations: a status report. *Group Organ. Stud.* 9(2):177–88.

Walters, G. A. 1984. Organizational development and individual rights. *J. Appl. Behav. Sci.* 20:423–39 (Special issue)

Walton, R. E. 1978. The Topeka story: part II. *Wharton Mag.* 3:36–41.

Walton, R. E. 1980. Establishing and maintaining high commitment work systems. In *The Organizational Life Cycle: Issues in the Creation, Transformation and Decline of Organizations,* ed. J. R. Kimberly, R. H. Miles, and Associates. San Francisco/London: Jossey-Bass.

Walton, R. E. 1985. From control to commitment in the workplace. *Harv. Bus. Rev.* 63:76–84.

Wilkins, A. L. 1983. The culture audit: a tool for understanding organizations. *Organ. Dyn.* 12:24–38.

Wilkins, A. L., Ouchi, W. G. 1983. Efficient cultures: exploring the relationship between culture and organizational performance. *Admin. Sci. Q.* 28:468–81.

Zand, D. E. 1974. Collateral organizations: a new change strategy. *J. Appl. Behav. Sci.* 10(1):63–89.

Zuboff, S. 1985. Technologies that informate: implications for human resource management in the computerized industrial workplace. In *HRM Trends and Challenges,* ed. R. E. Walton, P. R. Lawrence, pp. 103–40. Boston: Harv. Bus. Sch. Press.

PART 2

The Foundations of OD: Theory and Practice on Change in Organizations

The field of organization development came into being as advances were made in understanding the nature of change and the nature of organizational dynamics. We examine those topics in Part 2.

Organization development is an applied behavioral science discipline that attempts to translate knowledge from the basic and applied behavioral sciences into action programs intended to solve problems, correct deficiencies, and seize opportunities in ongoing organizations. In the broadest and most general sense, the objective of organization development programs is to increase short-term and long-term organizational effectiveness. Operationally this means the client system (organization) must be able to "sense" the current state of affairs, must be able to solve the current problems it faces—usually consisting of two major types, deficiencies to be corrected and opportunities to be exploited—and must build the capacity to be able to do this over time as conditions, demands, and exigencies change. To cope successfully with current events requires effective problem-solving and action-taking skills; to adjust successfully to future events requires the ability to sense environmental demands, the ability to respond to those demands, and the ability to maintain this adaptive flexibility over time. This latter skill is called organizational self-renewal. The role of the OD practitioner is to help the organization members solve current problems and develop the competence for self-renewal.

At least four kinds of knowledge are required of OD practitioners or managers who desire to create problem-solving, self-renewing organizations: knowledge of how organizations work; knowledge of how change occurs; knowledge of how to intervene in an organization to produce desired change; and knowledge of how to diagnose and solve problems.

The knowledge of how organizations work comes mainly from basic behavioral science research and theory. It entails an understanding of the dynamics of individuals, groups, and goal-oriented social systems. Knowledge of how change occurs involves understanding the processes of change and changing. Such knowledge is required in all applied disciplines. In the case of organization development, gaining this knowledge was made more difficult because the phenomena are so complex and are themselves changing as they are being studied. But it was progress in the theory and practice of change that helped launch the field of OD. Knowledge of how to intervene in an ongoing organization relates to change but goes beyond it to investigate the consultation or helping process. How does one intervene effectively? What are the ingredients of effective client-consultant relationships? When is help helpful? Other applied disciplines, such as education, psychotherapy, and social work, provided numerous insights about intervening in organizations. Knowledge of diagnosis and problem solving comes from many sources, but culminates in the ability to answer the questions: What is wrong?: What made it wrong?: What must be done to correct the situation? Competent problem solving and action taking require being able to do two things: classify problem situations accurately, and select appropriate remedies. This competence in turns rests on the prior existence of two bodies of knowledge: valid diagnostic categories (having a good classification scheme for different kinds of problems), and an efficacious set of remedial treatments (having an array of different solutions or actions that will solve different problems). In relatively advanced applied sciences, such as medicine, great progress has been made in refining diagnostic categories and in discovering appropriate treatments. Less progress has been made in OD, but advances have been substantial.

It is not possible to explore all the foundations of organization development in this section. Instead, we concentrate on the nature of change and the nature of organizational dynamics.

THE NATURE OF PLANNED CHANGE

The action arena of OD is organizations. The name of the game is planned change. Organization improvement requires an understanding of change processes and a knowledge of the nature of organizations.

Kurt Lewin was the great practical theorist whose action and research programs provided much of the early foundation for understanding change processes in social situations.[1] Lewin (1890–1947) was a personality theorist, a social psychologist, and a man who wanted to improve the lot of humankind through behavioral science knowledge and application. To improve things means to change them; to change them requires knowledge of the structure and dynamics of change. Lewin's work had a significant impact on group dynamics, intergroup relations, and applied social psychology. Lewin once said, "If you want to understand a phenomenon, try to change it." And he devoted a considerable part of his career trying to understand processes of change.

Two concepts proposed by Kurt Lewin are especially useful in thinking about change. The first idea suggests that what is occurring at any point in time is the result of a field of opposing forces. Thus, for example, the production level of a manufacturing plant or the level of morale in a work group should be thought of as *equilibrium points* in a field

---

[1]Alfred J. Marrow, *The Practical Theorist: The Life and Work of Kurt Lewin* (New York: Basic Books, 1969).

of forces, some forces pushing toward higher and some pushing toward lower levels of production or morale. In order to understand a problematic situation the investigator must know what major forces are operating in that particular instance. A technique called the Force Field Analysis diagrams the field of forces and shows how to develop actions plans for moving the equilibrium point in one direction or another. This is a useful model for understanding what is going on in complex situations.

The second idea proposed by Lewin analyzes what must occur for permanent change to take place. He conceptualized change as a three-stage process: *unfreezing* the old behavior, *moving* to a new level of behavior, and *freezing* the behavior at the new level. This is a useful model for knowing how to move an equilibrium point to a new, desired level and *keep it there*. These two simple ideas undergird the theories of change of most OD practitioners.

Ronald Lippitt, Jeanne Watson, and Bruce Westley later refined Lewin's three phases into a seven-phase model of the change process as follows:

Phase 1. The development of a need for change. This phase corresponds to Lewin's *unfreezing* phase.

Phase 2. The establishment of a change relationship. This is a crucial phase in which a client system in need of help and a "change agent" from outside the system establish a working relationship with each other.

Phase 3. The clarification or diagnosis of the client system's problem.

Phase 4. The examination of alternative routes and goals; establishing goals and intentions of action.

Phase 5. The transformation of intentions into actual change efforts. Phase 3, 4, and 5 correspond to Lewin's *moving* phase.

Phase 6. The generalization and stabilization of change. This corresponds to Lewin's *freezing* phase.

Phase 7. Achieving a terminal relationship.[2]

The models of change developed by Lewin and by Lippitt, Watson, and Westley have advanced both theory and practice in organization development. They are foundations of the discipline. Causing change in organizations presents additional challenges, however. In an article entitled "Change Does Not Need to be Haphazard," Kenneth Benne and Max Birnbaum suggest some principles that form a strategy for effecting organizational change. Their principles are as follows:

1. To change a subsystem or any part of a subsystem, relevant aspects of the environment must also be changed.

2. To change behavior on any one level of a hierarchical organization, it is necessary to achieve complementary and reinforcing changes in organization levels above and below that level.

3. The place to begin change is at those points in the system where some stress and strain exist. Stress may give rise to dissatisfaction with the status quo and thus become a motivating factor for change in the system.

---

[2]Ronald Lippitt, Jeanne Watson, and Bruce Westley, *The Dynamics of Planned Change* (New York: Harcourt Brace Jovanovich, 1958). See chapter 6 for a discussion of the phases of planned change.

4. If thoroughgoing changes in a hierarchical structure are desirable or necessary, change should ordinarily start with the policy making body.
5. Both the formal and the informal organization of an institution must be considered in planning any process of change.
6. The effectiveness of a planned change is often directly related to the degree to which members at all levels of an institutional heirarchy take part in the factfinding and the diagnosing of needed changes and in the formulating and reality testing of goals and programs of change.[3]

THE NATURE OF ORGANIZATIONAL DYNAMICS

Organization development efforts are directed toward deliberately established social systems called organizations. Organizations exist to accomplish specific purposes or goals—a mission, task, products, or services. In most organizations the decision to belong is a voluntary choice made by the individual. There is division of labor and responsibility in organizations with the consequence that a social structure of roles, duties, and offices is created. Individuals perform "role behaviors"; they are expected to do some things and not others by virtue of the positions they hold. One can not know how organizations function simply by knowing how individuals function and then "summing across" individuals, because organizations have unique characteristics of their own.

One characteristic of organizations is that much of the work gets done by teams consisting of bosses and subordinates. Work teams are the basic building blocks of organizations. If teams function well, it is more likely that the organization as a whole will function well. Advances in understanding the dynamics of groups served as a foundation for the development of OD. Insights, theories, and techniques concerning group processes formed a large part of the basic toolkit of early OD practitioners.

Relations between groups in organizations are often problematic and dysfunctional. Another characteristic of organizations is that these relations are very important for organizational performance. As knowledge about intergroup dynamics was developed, it was incorporated into organization development.

A fundamental tenet of OD is that organizations are open systems. Russell Ackoff defines a system as "a set of interrelated elements. Thus a system is an entity which is composed of at least two elements and a relation that holds between each of its elements and at least one other element in the set. Each of a system's elements is connected to every other element, directly or indirectly.[4] Systems (and organizations) must be treated from a holistic point of view because certain properties derive from the *relationships* between the parts of the system and cannot be discovered from an analysis of the components themselves. In addition, organizations are open systems—they are in interaction with and in exchange with their environments. Organizations are impacted by and have an impact on their environments. As Katz and Kahn state: "Organizations as a special

---

[3]Kenneth D. Benne and Max Birnbaum, "Change Does Not Need to be Haphazard," *Notebook for Summer Participants,* NTL Institute for Applied Behavioral Science.

[4]Russell L. Ackoff, "Toward a System of Systems Concepts," *Management Science,* July 1971, p. 662.

class of open systems have properties of their own, but they share other properties in common with all open systems. These include the importation of energy from the environment, the throughput or transformation of the imported energy into some product form that is characteristic of the system, the exporting of that product into the environment, and the reenergizing of the system from sources in the environment."[5]

The organization development practitioner must understand the nature of the client systems in which he or she works. That is a basic prerequisite. The selections in this section plus the suggested additional readings provide a start in that direction.

THEORY AND PRACTICE ON CHANGE IN ORGANIZATIONS

The readings in this section are classic statements that improve with age and with each rereading.

The first two selections are excerpts from Kurt Lewin's highly influential book, *Field Theory in Social Science.* Lewin's field theory approach, which postulates that any phenomenon is the resultant in a field of opposing forces, is presented first. His view of change as a three-stage process is next.

The third article, written by Robert Chin and Kenneth D. Benne, describes three broad general strategies for effecting changes in human systems—the empirical-rational strategy, the normative-reeducative strategy, and the power-coercive strategy. This elegant and erudite essay was written for the book, *The Planning of Change,* edited by Warren Bennis, Kenneth Benne, and Robert Chin. The historical development of the three strategies of change is traced in detail and examples of each strategy in operation are given. It is our opinion that the organization development approach to planned change rests primarily on a normative-reeducative strategy and secondarily on an empirical-rational strategy. For this reason, understanding the three general strategies for change is important for the OD practitioner as well as for managers who may be interested in OD efforts in their organizations.

OD practitioners intervene in ongoing organizations in order to help produce positive results. But the intervention process itself was mainly based on rules of thumb and principles derived from experience until Chris Argyris formulated a systematic statement of intervention theory and method. Argyris sees three primary tasks of the interventionist: to help the client system generate valid information; to help ensure that client system members act on the basis of free and informed choice; and to help ensure internal commitment to the choices made. What is the practitioner trying to do? What theory is available to guide behavior and give overall direction? The contribution by Argyris addresses these issues.

The group dynamics literature is one of the major sources of insights into effective team functioning. Dorwin Cartwright's article presenting some of the implications and applications of group dynamics theory was written in the late 40s and is still one of the best statements available. Cartwright was a member of the staff of the Research Center

---

[5]Daniel Katz and Robert L. Kahn, *The Social Psychology of Organizations,* 2nd ed. (New York: John Wiley & Sons, 1978), p. 33.

for Group Dynamics at Massachusetts Institute of Technology, and was the director of the center when it moved to the University of Michigan after Kurt Lewin's death. In this article he cites some of the insights from this "new" field of study—group dynamics. The theory and practice of OD rely heavily on knowledge from the study of group processes and structures.

A classic article by Kenneth Benne and Paul Sheats written in 1948 views group dynamics from a different perspective: the behaviors that must occur for a group to function effectively. Either the leader or the group's members may perform these behaviors, but they must be present for the group to maintain itself as a viable group and for the group to accomplish its tasks. Look around you at some of the meetings you attend. Are these behaviors being performed? If not, the meetings are probably not as productive as they might be.

Intergroup relations are especially important phenomena in organizations. Just as individuals may be interdependently related on a work team for task accomplishment, entire teams are interdependently related to other teams for task accomplishment. The ways groups work together can either help or hinder organizational performance. The selection by Edgar Schein summarizes much of the literature on cooperation and competition between groups. Schein has packaged a wealth of empirical research, much of it conducted by Muzafer Sherif and Robert Blake and Jane Syrgley Mouton, in such a way that the OD practitioner and the manager alike can gain insights into this important area.

The final selection is from Theodore Caplow's insightful and audacious little book, *Managing An Organization*. In just a few pages he cogently describes the nature of organizations and throws in some basic principles of management for good measure.

Reading 6

THE FIELD APPROACH: CULTURE AND GROUP LIFE AS QUASI–STATIONARY PROCESSES

Kurt Lewin

This question of planned change or of any "social engineering" is identical with the question: What "conditions" have to be changed to bring about a given result and how can one change these conditions with the means at hand?

One should view the present situation—the *status quo*—as being maintained by certain conditions or forces. A culture—for instance, the food habits of a certain group at a given time—is not a static affair but a live process like a river which moves but still keeps a recognizable form. In other words, we have to deal, in group life as in individual life, with what is known in physics as "quasi-stationary" processes.[1]

Food habits do not occur in empty space. They are part and parcel of the daily rhythm of being awake and asleep; of being alone and in a group; of earning a living and playing; of being a member of a town, a family, a social class, a religious group, a nation; of living in a hot or a cool climate, in a rural area or a city, in a district with good groceries and restaurants, or in an area of poor and irregular food supply. Somehow all of these factors affect food habits at any given time. They determine the food habits of a group every day anew just as the amount of water supply and the nature of the river bed determine from day to day the flow of the river, its constancy, or its change.[2]

Food habits of a group, as well as such phenomena as the speed of production in a factory, are the result of a multitude of forces. Some forces support each other, some oppose each other. Some are driving forces, others restraining forces. Like the velocity of a river, the actual conduct of a group depends upon the level (for instance, the speed of production) at which these conflicting forces reach a state of equilibrium. To speak of a certain culture pattern—for instance, the food habits of a group—implies that the constellation of these forces remains the same for a period or at least that they find their state of equilibrium at a constant level during that period.

Neither group "habits" nor individual "habits" can be understood sufficiently by a theory which limits its consideration to the processes themselves and conceives of the "habit" as a kind of frozen linkage, an "association' between these processes. Instead, habits will have to be conceived of as a result of forces in the organism *and* its life space, in the group *and* its setting. The structure of the organism, of the group, of the setting, or whatever name the field might have in the given case, has to be represented and the forces in the various parts of the field have to be analyzed if the processes (which might be either constant "habits" or changes) are to be understood scientifically. The process is but

Source: Kurt Lewin, *Field Theory In Social Science* (New York: Harper & Row, 1951), pp. 172–74.

[1] For the general characteristics of quasi-stationary processes see Wolfgang Koehler, *Dynamics in Psychology* (New York: Liveright Publishing, 1940).

[2] The type of forces, of course, is different; there is nothing equivalent to "cognitive structure" or "psychological past" or "psychological future" in the field determining the river.

the epiphenomenon, the real object of study is the constellation of forces.

Therefore, to predict which changes in conditions will have what result we have to conceive of the life of the group as the result of specific constellations of forces within a larger setting. In other words, scientific predictions or advice for methods of change should be based on an analysis of the "field as a whole," including both its psychological and nonpsychological aspects.

Reading 7

CHANGING AS THREE STEPS: UNFREEZING, MOVING, AND FREEZING OF GROUP STANDARDS

Kurt Lewin

A change toward a higher level of group performance is frequently short lived; after a "shot in the arm," group life soon returns to the previous level. This indicates that it does not suffice to define the objective of a planned change in group performance as the reaching of a different level. Permanency of the new level, or permanency for a desired period, should be included in the objective. A successful change includes therefore three aspects: unfreezing (if necessary) the present level L^1, moving to the new level L^2, and freezing group life on the new level. Since any level is determined by a force field, permanency implies that the new force field is made relatively secure against change.

The "unfreezing" of the present level may involve quite different problems in different cases. Allport has described the "catharsis" which seems to be necessary before prejudices can be removed. To break open the shell of complacency and self-righteousness it is sometimes necessary to bring about deliberately an emotional stir-up.

Source: Kurt Lewin, *Field Theory In Social Science* (New York: Harper & Row, 1951), pp. 228–29.

Reading 8

GENERAL STRATEGIES FOR EFFECTING CHANGES IN HUMAN SYSTEMS

Robert Chin and Kenneth D. Benne

Discussing general strategies and procedures for effecting change requires that we set limits to the discussion. For, under a liberal interpretation of the title, we would need to deal with much of the literature of contemporary social and behavioral science, basic and applied.

Therefore, we shall limit our discussion to those changes which are planned changes—in which attempts to bring about change are conscious, deliberate, and intended, at least on the part of one or more agents related to the change attempt. We shall also attempt to categorize strategies and procedures which have a few important elements in common but which, in fact, differ widely in other respects. And we shall neglect many of these differences. In addition, we shall look beyond the description of procedures in commonsense terms and seek some genotypic characteristics of change strategies. We shall seek the roots of the main strategies discussed, including their variants, in ideas and idea systems

prominent in contemporary and recent social and psychological thought.

One element in all approaches to planned change is the conscious utilization and application of knowledge as an instrument or tool for modifying patterns and institutions of practice. The knowledge or related technology to be applied may be knowledge of the nonhuman environment in which practice goes on or of some knowledge-based "thing technology" for controlling one or another feature of the practice environment. In educational practice, for example, technologies of communication and calculation, based upon new knowledge of electronics—audiovisual devices, television, computers, teaching machines—loom large among the knowledges and technologies that promise greater efficiency and economy in handling various practices in formal education. As attempts are made to introduce these new thing technologies into school situations, the change problem shifts to the human problems of dealing with the resistances, anxieties, threats to morale, conflicts, disrupted interpersonal communications, and so on, which prospective changes in patterns of practice evoke in the people affected by the change. So the change agent, even though focally and initially concerned with modifications in the thing technology of education, finds himself in need of more adequate knowledge of human behavior, individual and social, and in need of developed "people technologies," based on behavioral knowledge, for dealing effectively with the human aspects of deliberate change.

The knowledge which suggests improvements in educational practice may, on the other hand, be behavioral knowledge in the first instance—knowl-

Source: From *The Planning of Change,* 3rd ed., by Warren G. Bennis, Kenneth D. Benne, Robert Chin, and Kenneth E. Corey. Copyright © 1961, 1969 by Holt, Rinehart and Winston, Inc. © 1976 by Holt, Rinehart and Winston. Reprinted by permission of Holt, Rinehart and Winston. CBS College Publishing.

Prepared especially for this volume and used by permission. This paper is adapted from a paper by Robert Chin prepared for "Designing Education for the Future—An Eight State Project" (Denver, Colo., 1967). Kenneth D. Benne joined in revising and expanding sections of the original paper for inclusion in this volume. In the process of revision, what is in several respects a new paper emerged. The original focus on changing in education has been maintained. Historical roots of ideas and strategies have been explored. The first person style of the original has also been maintained. Citations have been modified to include articles contained in this volume, along with other references.

edge about participative learning, about attitude change, about family disruption in inner-city communities, about the cognitive and skill requirements of new careers, and so forth. Such knowledge may suggest changes in school grouping, in the relations between teachers and students, in the relations of teachers and principals to parents, and in counseling practices. Here change agents, initially focused on application of behavioral knowledge and the improvement of people technologies in school settings, must face the problems of using people technologies in planning, installing, and evaluating such changes in educational practice. The new people technologies must be experienced, understood, and accepted by teachers and administrators before they can be used effectively with students.

This line of reasoning suggests that, whether the focus of planned change is in the introduction of more effective thing technologies or people technologies into institutionalized practice, processes of introducing such changes must be based on behavioral knowledge of change and must utilize people technologies based on such knowledge.

Types of Strategies for Changing

Our further analysis is based on three types or groups of strategies. The first of these, and probably the most frequently employed by men of knowledge in America and Western Europe, are those we call empirical-rational strategies. One fundamental assumption underlying these strategies is that men are rational. Another assumption is that men will follow their rational self-interest once this is revealed to them. A change is proposed by some person or group which knows of a situation that is desirable, effective, and in line with the self-interest of the person, group, organization, or community which will be affected by the change. Because the person (or group) is assumed to be rational and moved by self-interest, it is assumed that he (or they) will adopt the proposed change if it can be rationally justified and if it can be shown by the proposer(s) that he (or they) will gain by the change.

A second group of strategies we call normative-reeducative. These strategies build upon assump-

tions about human motivation different from those underlying the first. The rationality and intelligence of men are not denied. Patterns of action and practice are supported by sociocultural norms and by commitments on the part of individuals to these norms. Sociocultural norms are supported by the attitude and value systems of individuals—normative outlooks which undergird their commitments. Change in a pattern of practice or action, according to this view, will occur only as the persons involved are brought to change their normative orientations to old patterns and develop commitments to new ones. And changes in normative orientations involve changes in attitudes, values, skills, and significant relationships, not just changes in knowledge, information, or intellectual rationales for action and practice.

The third group of strategies is based on the application of power in some form, political or otherwise. The influence process involved is basically that of compliance of those with less power to the plans, directions, and leadership of those with greater power. Often the power to be applied is legitimate power or authority. Thus the strategy may involve getting the authority of law or administrative policy behind the change to be effected. Some power strategies may appeal less to the use of authoritative power to effect change than to the massing of coercive power, legitimate or not, in support of the change sought.[1]

---

[1]Throughout our discussion of strategies and procedures, we will not differentiate these according to the size of the target of change. We assume that there are similarities in processes of changing, whether the change affects an individual, a small group, an organization, a community, or a culture. In addition, we are not attending to differences among the aspects of a system, let us say an educational system, which is being changed—curriculum, audiovisual methods, team teaching, pupil grouping, and so on. Furthermore, because many changes in communities or organizations start with an individual or some small membership group, our general focus will be upon those strategies which lead to and involve individual changes.

We will sidestep the issue of defining change in this paper. As further conceptual work progresses in the study of planned change, we shall eventually have to examine how different definitions of change relate to strategies and procedures for effecting change. But we are not dealing with these issues here.

Empirical-Rational Strategies

A variety of specific strategies are included in what we are calling the empirical-rational approach to effecting change. As we have already pointed out, the rationale underlying most of these is an assumption that men are guided by reason and that they will utilize some rational calculus of self-interest in determining needed changes in behavior.

It is difficult to point to any one person whose ideas express or articulate the orientation underlying commitment to empirical-rational strategies of changing. In Western Europe and America, this orientation might be better identified with the general social orientation of the enlightenment and of classical liberalism than with the ideas of any one man. On this view, the chief foes to human rationality and to change or progress based on rationality were ignorance and superstition. Scientific investigation and research represented the chief ways of extending knowledge and reducing the limitations of ignorance. A corollary of this optimistic view of man and his future was an advocacy of education as a way of disseminating scientific knowledge and of freeing men and women from the shackles of superstition. Although elitist notions played a part in the thinking of many classic liberals, the increasing trend during the 19th century was toward the universalization of educational opportunity. The common and universal school, open to all men and women, was the principal instrument by which knowledge would replace ignorance and superstition in the minds of people and become a principal agent in the spread of reason, knowledge, and knowledge-based action and practice (progress) in human society. In American experience, Jefferson may be taken as a principal, early advocate of research and of education as agencies of human progress. And Horace Mann may be taken as the prophet of progress through the institutionalization of universal education opportunity through the common school.[2]

Basic Research and Dissemination of Knowledge through General Education.

The strategy of encouraging basic knowledge building and of depending on general education to diffuse the results of research into the minds and thinking of men and women is still by far the most appealing strategy of change to most academic men of knowledge and to large segments of the American population as well. Basic researchers are quite likely to appeal for time for further research when confronted by some unmet need. And many people find this appeal convincing. Both of these facts are well illustrated by difficulties with diseases for which no adequate control measure or cures are available—poliomyelitis, for example. Medical researchers asked for more time and funds for research and people responded with funds for research, both through voluntary channels and through legislative appropriations. And the control measures were forthcoming. The educational problem then shifted to inducing people to comply with immunization procedures based on research findings.

This appeal to a combination of research and education of the public has worked in many areas of new knowledge-based thing technologies where almost universal readiness for accepting the new technology was already present in the population. Where such readiness is not available, as in the case of fluoridation technologies in the management of dental caries, general strategy of basic research plus educational (informational) campaigns to spread knowledge of the findings do not work well. The cases of its inadequacy as a single strategy of change have multiplied, especially where "engineering" problems, which involve a divided and conflicting public or deep resistances due to the threat by the new technology to traditional attitudes and values, have thwarted its effectiveness. But these cases, while they demand attention to

---

[2] We have indicated the main roots of ideas and idea systems underlying the principal strategies of changing and their subvariants on a chart which appears as Figure 1 at the end of this essay. It may be useful in seeing both the distinctions and the relationships between various strategies of changing in time perspective. We have emphasized developments of the past 25 years more than earlier developments. This makes for historical foreshortening. We hope this is a pardonable distortion, considering our present limited purpose.

other strategies of changing, do not disprove the importance of basic research and of general educational opportunity as elements in a progressive and self-renewing society.

We have noted that the strategy under discussion has worked best in grounding and diffusing generally acceptable thing technologies in society. Some have argued that the main reason the strategy has not worked in the area of people technologies is a relative lack of basic research on people and their behavior, relationships, and institutions and a corresponding lack of emphasis upon social and psychological knowledges in school and college curricula. It would follow in this view that increased basic research on human affairs and relationships and increased efforts to diffuse the results of such research through public education are the ways of making the general strategy work better. Auguste Comte, with his emphasis on positivistic sociology in the reorganization of society, and Lester F. Ward in America may be taken as late 19th-century representatives of this view. And the spirit of Comte and Ward is by no means dead in American academia or in influential segments of the American public.

Personnel Selection and Replacement. Difficulties in getting knowledge effectively into practice may be seen as lying primarily in the lack of fitness of persons occupying positions with job responsibilities for improving practice. The argument goes that we need the right person in the right position, if knowledge is to be optimally applied and if rationally based changes are to become the expectation in organizational and societal affairs. This fits with the liberal reformers' frequently voiced and enacted plea to drive the unfit from office and to replace them with those more fit as a condition of social progress.

That reformers' programs have so often failed has sobered but by no means destroyed the zeal of those who regard personnel selection, assessment, and replacement as a major key to program improvement in education or in other enterprises as well. This strategy was given a scientific boost by the development of scientific testing of potential-

ities and aptitudes. We will use Binet as a prototype of psychological testing and Moreno as a prototype in sociometric testing, while recognizing the extensive differentiation and elaboration which have occurred in psychometrics and sociometrics since their original work. We recognize too the elaborated modes of practice in personnel work which have been built around psychometric and sociometric tools and techniques. We do not discount their limited value as actual and potential tools for change, while making two observations on the way they have often been used. First, they have been used more often in the interest of system maintenance rather than of system change, since the job descriptions personnel workers seek to fill are defined in terms of system requirements as established. Second, by focusing on the role occupant as the principal barrier to improvement, personnel selection and replacement strategies have tended not to reveal the social and cultural system difficulties which may be in need of change if improvement is to take place.

Systems Analysts as Staff and Consultants. Personnel workers in government, industry, and education have typically worked in staff relations to line management, reflecting the bureaucratic, line-staff form of organization which has flourished in the large-scale organization of effort and enterprise in the 20th century. And other expert workers—systems analysts—more attuned to system difficulties than to the adequacies or inadequacies of persons as role occupants within the system, have found their way into the staff resources of line management in contemporary organizations.

There is no reason why the expert resources of personnel workers and systems analysts might not be used in nonbureaucratic organizations or in processes of moving bureaucratic organizations toward nonbureaucratic forms. But the fact remains that their use has been shaped, for the most part, in the image of the scientific management of bureaucratically organized enterprises. So we have placed the systems analysts in our chart under Frederick Taylor, the father of scientific management in America.

The line management of an enterprise seeks to organize human and technical effort toward the most efficient service of organizational goals. And these goals are defined in terms of the production of some mandated product, whether a tangible product or a less tangible good or service. In pursuing this quest for efficiency, line management employs experts in the analysis of sociotechnical systems and in the laying out of more efficient systems. The experts employed may work as external consultants or as an internal staff unit. Behavioral scientists have recently found their way, along with mathematicians and engineers, into systems analysis work.

It is interesting to note that the role of these experts is becoming embroiled in discussions of whether or not behavioral science research should be used to sensitize administrators to new organizational possibilities, to new goals, or primarily to implement efficient operation within perspectives and goals as currently defined. Jean Hills has raised the question of whether behavioral science when applied to organizational problems tends to perpetuate established ideology and system relations because of blinders imposed by their being "problem centered" and by their limited definition of what is "a problem."[3]

We see an emerging strategy, in the use of behavioral scientists as systems analysts and engineers, toward viewing the problem of organizational change and changing as a wide-angled problem, one in which all the input and output features and components of a large-scale system are considered. It is foreseeable that with the use of high-speed and high-capacity computers, and with the growth of substantial theories and hypotheses about how parts of an educational system operate, we shall find more and more applications for systems analysis and operations research in programs of educational change. In fact, it is precisely the quasi-mathematical character of these modes of research

that will make possible the rational analysis of qualitatively different aspects of educational work and will bring them into the range of rational planning—masses of students, massive problems of poverty and educational and cultural deprivation, and so on. We see no necessary incompatibility between an ideology which emphasizes the individuality of the student and the use of systems analysis and computers in strategizing the problems of the total system. The actual incompatibilities may lie in the limited uses to which existing organizers and administrators of educational efforts put these technical resources.

Applied Research and Linkage Systems for Diffusion of Research Results. The American development of applied research of a planned system for linking applied researchers with professional practitioners and both of these with centers for basic research and with organized consumers of applied research has been strongly influenced by two distinctive American inventions—the land-grant university and the agricultural extension system. We, therefore, have put the name of Justin Morrill, author of the land-grant college act and of the act which established the cooperative agricultural extension system, on our chart. The land-grant colleges or universities were dedicated to doing applied research in the service of agriculture and the mechanic arts. These colleges and universities developed research programs in basic sciences as well and experimental stations for the development and refinement of knowledge-based technologies for use in engineering and agriculture. As the extension services developed, county agents—practitioners—were attached to the state land-grant college or university that received financial support from both state and federal governments. The county agent and his staff developed local organizations of adult farm men and women and of farm youth to provide both a channel toward informing consumers concerning new and better agricultural practices and toward getting awareness of unmet consumer needs and unsolved problems back to centers of knowledge and research. Garth Jones has made one of the more comprehensive studies

---

[3]Jean Hills, "Social Science, Ideology and the Purposes of Educational Administration," *Education Administration Quarterly,* Autumn 1965, pp. 23–40.

of the strategies of changing involved in large-scale demonstration.[4]

All applied research has not occurred within a planned system for knowledge discovery, development, and utilization like the one briefly described above. The system has worked better in developing and diffusing thing technologies than in developing and diffusing people technologies, though the development of rural sociology and of agricultural economics shows that extension workers were by no means unaware of the behavioral dimensions of change problems. But the large-scale demonstration, through the land-grant university cooperative extension service, of the stupendous changes which can result from a planned approach to knowledge discovery, development, diffusion, and utilization is a part of the consciousness of all Americans concerned with planned change.[5]

Applied research and development is an honored part of the tradition of engineering approaches to problem identification and solution. The pioneering work of E. L. Thorndike in applied research in education should be noted on our chart. The processes and slow tempo of diffusion and utilization of research findings and inventions in public education is well illustrated in studies by Paul Mort and his students.[6] More recently, applied research, in its product development aspect, has been utilized in a massive way to contribute curriculum materials and designs for science instruction (as well as in other subjects). When we assess this situation to find reasons why such researches have not been more effective in producing changes in instruction, the answers seem to lie both in the plans of the studies which produced the materials and designs and in the potential users of the findings. Adequate linkage between consumers and researchers was frequently not established. Planned and evaluated demonstrations and experimentations connected with the use of materials were frequently slighted. And training of consumer teachers to use the new materials adaptively and creatively was frequently missing.

Such observations have led to a fresh spurt of interest in evaluation research addressed to educational programs. The fear persists that this too may lead to disappointment if it is not focused for two-way communication between researchers and teachers and if it does not involve collaboratively the ultimate consumers of the results of such research—the students. Evaluation researches conducted in the spirit of justifying a program developed by expert applied researchers will not help to guide teachers and students in their quest for improved practices of teaching and learning, if the concerns of the latter have not been taken centrally into account in the evaluation process.[7]

Recently, attempts have been made to link applied research activities in education with basic researchers on the one hand and with persons in action and practice settings on the other through some system of interlocking roles similar to those suggested in the description of the land-grant extension systems in agriculture or in other fields where applied and development researches have flourished.

The linking of research-development efforts with diffusion-innovation efforts has been gaining headway in the field of education with the emergence of federally supported research and development centers based in universities, regional laboratories connected with state departments of education, colleges and universities in a geographic area, and

[4]Garth Jones, ''Planned Organizational Change, a Set of Working Documents,'' Center for Research in Public Organization, School of Public Administration (Los Angeles: University of Southern California, 1964).

[5]For a review, see Ronald G. Havelock and Kenneth D. Benne, ''An Exploratory Study of Knowledge Utilization,'' in *The Planning of Change,* 2nd ed. Warren G. Bennis, Kenneth D. Benne, and Robert Chin (New York: Holt, Rinehart & Winston, 1969), chap. 3, p. 124.

[6]Paul R. Mort and Donald R. Ross, *Principles of School Administration* (New York: McGraw-Hill, 1957). Paul R. Mort and Francis G. Cornell, *American Schools in Transition: How Our Schools Adapt Their Practices to Changing Needs* (New York: Bureau of Publications, Teachers College, Columbia University Press, 1941).

[7]Robert Chin, ''Research Approaches to the Problem of Civic Training,'' in *The Adolescent Citizen,* ed. F. Patterson (New York: Free Press, 1980).

with various consortia and institutes confronting problems of educational change and changing. The strategy of change here usually includes a well-researched innovation which seems feasible to install in practice settings. Attention is directed to the question of whether or not the innovation will bring about a desired result, and with what it can accomplish, if given a trial in one or more practice settings. The questions of *how* to get a fair trial and *how* to install an innovation in an already going and crowded school system are ordinarily not built centrally into the strategy. The rationalistic assumption usually precludes research attention to these questions. For, if the invention can be rationally shown to have achieved desirable results in some situations, it is assumed that people in other situations will adopt it once they know these results and the rationale behind them. The neglect of the above questions has led to a wastage of much applied research effort in the past.

Attention has been given recently to the roles, communication mechanisms, and processes necessary for innovation and diffusion of improved education practices.[8] Clark and Guba have formulated very specific processes related to and necessary for change in educational practice following upon research. For them, the necessary processes are: *development,* including invention and design; *diffusion,* including dissemination and demonstration; *adoption,* including trial, installation, and institutionalization. Clark's earnest conviction is summed up in this statement: "In a sense, the educational research community will be the educational community, and the route to educational progress will self-evidently be research and development."[9]

The approach of Havelock and Benne is concerned with the intersystem relationships between basic researchers, applied researchers, practitioners, and consumers in an evolved and evolving organization for knowledge utilization. They are concerned especially with the communication difficulties and role conflicts that occur at points of intersystem exchange. These conflicts are important because they illuminate the normative issues at stake between basic researchers and applied researchers, between applied researchers and practioners (teachers and administrators), between practitioners and consumers (students). The lines of strategy suggested by their analysis for solving role conflicts and communication difficulties call for transactional and collaborative exchanges across the lines of varied organized interests and orientations within the process of utilization. This brings their analysis into the range of normative-reeducative strategies to be discussed later.

The concepts from the behavioral sciences upon which these strategies of diffusion rest come mainly from two traditions. The first is from studies of the diffusion of traits of culture from one cultural system to another, initiated by the American anthropologist, Franz Boas. This type of study has been carried on by Rogers in his work on innovation and diffusion of innovations in contemporary culture and is reflected in a number of recent writers such as Katz and Carlson.[10] The second scientific

---

[8]Matthew B. Miles, *Some Propositions in Research Utilization in Education* (March 1965), in press. Kenneth Wiles, paper for seminar on Strategies for Curriculum Change (Columbus: Ohio State University, 1965). Charles Jung and Ronald Lippitt, "Utilization of Scientific Knowledge for Change in Education," in *Concepts for Social Change* (Washington, D.C.: National Educational Association, National Training Laboratories, 1967). Havelock and Benne, "Exploratory Study of Knowledge Utilization," in Bennis et al., *Planning of Change,* chap. 3, p. 124. David Clark and Egon Guba, "An Examination of Potential Change Roles in Education," seminar on Innovation in Planning School Curricula (Columbus: Ohio State University, 1965).

[9]David Clark, "Educational Research and Development: The Next Decade," in *Implications for Education of Prospective Changes in Society,* a publication of "Designing Education for the Future—an Eight State Project" (Denver, Colo., 1967).

[10]Elihu Katz, "The Social Itinerary of Technical Change: Two Studies on the Diffusion of Innovation," in Bennis et al., *Planning of Change,* chap. 5, p. 230. Richard Carlson, "Some Needed Research on the Diffusion of Innovations" (paper at the Washington Conference on Educational Change, Columbus, Ohio, Ohio State University). Everett Rogers, "What Are Innovators Like?" in *Change Processes in the Public Schools,* Center for the Advanced Study of Educational Administration (Eugene: University of Oregon, 1965). Everett Rogers, *Diffusion of Innovations* (New York: Free Press, 1962).

tradition is in studies of influence in mass communication associated with Carl Hovland and his students.[11] Both traditions have assumed a *relatively passive recipient of input* in diffusion situations. And actions within the process of diffusion are interpreted from the standpoint of an observer of the process. Bauer has pointed out that scientific studies have exaggerated the effectiveness of mass persuasion since they have compared the total number in the audience to the communications with the much smaller proportion of the audience persuaded by the communication.[12] A clearer view of processes of diffusion must include the actions of the receiver as well as those of the transmitter in the transactional events which are the units of diffusion process. And strategies for making diffusion processes more effective must be transactional and collaborative by design.

Utopian Thinking as a Strategy of Changing. It may seem strange to include the projection of utopias as a rational-empirical strategy of changing. Yet inventing and designing the shape of the future by extrapolating what we know of in the present is to envision a direction for planning and action in the present. If the image of a potential future is convincing and rationally persuasive to men in the present, the image may become part of the dynamics and motivation of present action. The liberal tradition is not devoid of its utopias. When we think of utopias quickened by an effort to extrapolate from the sciences of man to a future vision of society, the utopia of B. F. Skinner comes to mind.[13] The title of the Eight State Project, "Designing Education for the Future," for which this paper was prepared, reveals a utopian intent and

aspiration and illustrates an attempt to employ utopian thinking for practical purposes.[14]

Yet it may be somewhat disheartening to others as it is to us to note the absence of rousing and beckoning normative statements of what both can and ought to be in man's future in most current liberal-democratic utopias, whether these be based on psychological, sociological, political, or philosophical findings and assumptions. The absence of utopias in current society, in this sense, and in the sense that Mannheim studied them in his now classical study,[15] tends to make the forecasting of future directions a problem of technical prediction, rather than equally a process of projecting value orientations and preferences into the shaping of a better future.

Perceptual and Conceptual Reorganization through the Clarification of Language. In classical liberalism, one perceived foe of rational change and progress was superstition. And superstitions are carried from man to man and from generation to generation through the agency of unclear and mythical language. British utilitarianism was one important strand of classical liberalism, and one of utilitarianism's important figures, Jeremy Bentham, sought to purify language of its dangerous mystique through his study of fictions.

More recently, Alfred Korzybski and S. I. Hayakawa, in the general semantics movement, have sought a way of clarifying and rectifying the names of things and processes.[16] While their main applied concern was with personal therapy, both, and especially Hayakawa, were also concerned with bringing about changes in social systems as well. People disciplined in general semantics, it was hoped, would see more correctly, communicate

[11]Carl Hovland, Irving Janis, and Harold Kelley, *Communication and Persuasion* (New Haven, Conn.: Yale University Press, 1953).

[12] Raymond Bauer, "The Obstinate Audience: The Influence Process from the Point of View of Social Communication," in Bennis et al., *Planning of Change,* chap. 9, p. 507.

[13]B. F. Skinner, *Walden Two* (New York: Crowell-Collier and Macmillan, 1948).

[14]"Designing Education for the Future—an Eight State Project" (Denver, Colo., 1967).

[15]Karl Mannheim, *Ideology and Utopia* (New York: Harcourt Brace Jovanovich, 1946).

[16]Alfred Korzybski, *Science and Sanity,* 3rd ed. (International Non-Aristotelian Library Publishing Company, 1948). S. I. Hayakawa, *Language in Thought and Action* (New York: Harcourt Brace Jovanovich, 1941).

more adequately, and reason more effectively and thus lay a realistic common basis for action and changing. The strategies of changing associated with general semantics overlap with our next family of strategies, the normative-reeducative, because of their emphasis upon the importance of interpersonal relationships and social contexts within the communication process.

Normative-Reeducative Strategies of Changing

We have already suggested that this family of strategies rests on assumptions and hypotheses about man and his motivation which contrast significantly at points with the assumptions and hypotheses of those committed to what we have called rational-empirical strategies. Men are seen as inherently active, in quest of impulsive and need satisfaction. The relation between man and his environment is essentially transactional, as Dewey[17] made clear in his famous article on "The Reflex-Arc Concept." Man, the organism, does not passively await given stimuli from his environment in order to respond. He takes stimuli as furthering or thwarting the goals of his ongoing action. Intelligence arises in the process of shaping organism-environmental relations toward more adequate fitting and joining of organismic demands and environmental resources.

Intelligence is social, rather than narrowly individual. Men are guided in their actions by socially funded and communicated meanings, norms, and institutions, in brief by a normative culture. At the personal level, men are guided by internalized meanings, habits, and values. Changes in patterns of action or practice are, therefore, changes, not alone in the rational informational equipment of men, but at the personal level, in habits and values as well and, at the sociocultural level, changes are alterations in normative structures and in institutionalized roles and relationships, as well as in cognitive and perceptual orientations.

For Dewey, the prototype of intelligence in action is the scientific method. And he saw a broadened and humanized scientific method as man's best hope for progress, if men could learn to utilize such a method in facing all of the problematic situations of their lives. *Intelligence,* so conceived, rather than *reason* as defined in classical liberalism, was the key to Dewey's hope for the invention, development, and testing of adequate strategies of changing in human affairs.

Lewin's contribution to normative-reeducative strategies of changing stemmed from his vision of required interrelations between research, training, and action (and, for him, this meant collaborative relationships, often now lacking, between researchers, educators, and activists) in the solution of human problems, in the identification of needs for change, and in the working out of improved knowledge, technology, and patterns of action in meeting these needs. Man must participate in his own reeducation if he is to be reeducated at all. And reeducation is a normative change as well as a cognitive and perceptual change. These convictions led Lewin[18] to emphasize action research as a strategy of changing, and participation in groups as a medium of reeducation.

Freud's main contributions to normative-reeducative strategies of changing are two. First, he sought to demonstrate the unconscious and preconscious bases of man's actions. Only as a man finds ways of becoming aware of these nonconscious wellsprings of his attitudes and actions will he be able to bring them into conscious self-control. And Freud devoted much of his magnificent genius to developing ways of helping men to become conscious of the main springs of their actions and so capable of freedom. Second, in developing therapeutic methods, he discovered and developed ways of utilizing the relationships between change agent (therapist) and client (patient) as a major tool in

---

[17]John Dewey, *Philosophy, Psychology and Social Practice,* ed. Joseph Ratner (New York: Capricorn Books, 1967).

[18]Kurt Lewin, *Resolving Social Conflicts* (New York: Harper & Row 1948). Kurt Lewin, *Field Theory in Social Science* (New York: Harper & Row, 1951).

reeducating the client toward expanded self-awareness, self-understanding, and self-control. Emphasis upon the collaborative relationship in therapeutic change was a major contribution by Freud and his students and colleagues to normative-reeducative strategies of changing in human affairs.[19]

Normative-reeducative approaches to effecting change bring direct interventions by change agents, interventions based on a consciously worked out theory of change and of changing, into the life of a client system, be that system a person, a small group, an organization, or a community. The theory of changing is still crude but it is probably as explicitly stated as possible, granted our present state of knowledge about planned change.[20]

Some of the common elements among variants within this family of change strategies are the following. First, all emphasize the client system and his (or its) involvement in working out programs of change and improvement for himself (or itself). The way the client sees himself and his problem must be brought into dialogic relationship with the way in which he and his problem are seen by the change agent, whether the latter is functioning as researcher, consultant, trainer, therapist, or friend in relation to the client. Second, the problem confronting the client is not assumed a priori to be one which can be met by more adequate technical information, though this possibility is not ruled out. The problem may lie rather in the attitudes, values, norms, and the external and internal relationships of the client system and may require alteration or reeducation of these as a condition of its solution. Third, the change agent must learn to intervene mutually and collaboratively along with the client into efforts to define and solve the client's problem(s). The here and now experience of the two provide an important basis for diagnosing the problem and for locating needs for reeducation in the interest of solving it. Fourth, nonconscious elements which impede problem solution must be brought into consciousness and publicly examined and reconstructed. Fifth, the methods and concepts of the behavioral sciences are resources which change agent and client learn to use selectively, relevantly, and appropriately in learning to deal with the confronting problem and with problems of a similar kind in the future.

These approaches center in the notion that people technology is just as necessary as thing technology in working out desirable changes in human affairs. Put in this bold fashion, it is obvious that for the normative-reeducative change agent, clarification and reconstruction of values is of pivotal importance in changing. By getting the values of various parts of the client system, along with his own, openly into the arena of change, and by working through value conflicts responsibly, the change agent seeks to avoid manipulation and indoctrination of the client, in the morally reprehensible meanings of these terms.

We may use the organization of the National Training Laboratories (NTL) in 1947 as a milestone in the development of normative-reeducative approaches to changing in America. The first summer laboratory program grew out of earlier collaborations among Kurt Lewin, Ronald Lippitt, Leland Bradford, and Kenneth Benne. The idea behind the laboratory was that participants, staff, and students would learn about themselves and their back-home problems by collaboratively building a laboratory in which participants would become both experimenters and subjects in the study of their own developing interpersonal and group behavior within the laboratory setting. It seems evident that the five conditions of a normative-reeducative approach to changing were met in the conception of the training laboratory. Kurt Lewin died before the 1947 session of the training laboratory opened. Ronald Lip-

---

[19]For Freud, an interesting summary is contained in Otto Fenichel, *Problems of Psychoanalytic Technique* (Albany: NT Psychoanalytic Quarterly, 1941).

[20]W. Bennis, K. Benne, and R. Chin, *The Planning of Change,* 1st ed. (New York: Holt, Rinehart & Winston, 1961). R. Lippitt, J. Watson, and B. Westley, *The Dynamics of Planned Change* (New York: Harcourt Brace Jovanovich, 1958). W. Bennis, *Changing Organizations* (New York: McGraw-Hill, 1966).

pitt was a student of Lewin's and carried many of Lewin's orientations with him into the laboratory staff. Leland Bradford and Kenneth Benne were both students of John Dewey's philosophy of education. Bradford had invented several technologies for participative learning and self-study in his work in WPA adult education programs and as training officer in several agencies of the federal government. Benne came out of a background in educational philosophy and had collaborated with colleagues prior to 1943 in developing a methodology for policy and decision making and for the reconstruction of normative orientations, a methodology which sought to fuse democratic and scientific values and to translate these into principles for resolving conflicting and problematic situations at personal and community levels of human organization.[21] Benne and his colleagues had been much influenced by the work of Mary Follett,[22] her studies of integrative solutions to conflicts in settings of public and business administration, and by the work of Karl Mannheim[23] on the ideology and methodology of planning changes in human affairs, as well as by the work of John Dewey and his colleagues.

The work of the National Training Laboratories has encompassed development and testing of various approaches to changing in institutional settings, in America and abroad, since its beginning. One parallel development in England which grew out of Freud's thinking should be noted. This work developed in efforts at Tavistock Clinic to apply therapeutic approaches to problems of change in industrial organizations and in communities. This work is reported in statements by Elliot Jaques[24] and in this volume by Eric Trist. Another parallel development is represented by the efforts of Roethlisberger and Dickson to use personal counseling in industry as a strategy of organizational change.[25] Roethlisberger and Dickson had been strongly influenced by the pioneer work of Elton Mayo in industrial sociology[26] as well as by the counseling theories and methodologies of Carl Rogers.

Various refinements of methodologies for changing have been developed and tested since the establishment of the National Training Laboratories in 1947, both under its auspices and under other auspices as well. For us, the modal developments are worthy of further discussion here. One set of approaches is oriented focally to the improvement of the problem-solving processes utilized by a client system. The other set focuses on helping members of client systems to become aware of their attitude and value orientations and relationship difficulties through a probing of feelings, manifest and latent, involved in the functioning and operation of the client system.[27] Both approaches use the development of "temporary systems" as a medium of reeducation of persons and of role occupants in various ongoing social systems.[28]

Improving the Problem-Solving Capabilities of a System. This family of approaches to changing rests on several assumptions about change in human systems. Changes in a system, when they are reality oriented, take the form of problem solving. A system to achieve optimum reality orientation in its adaptations to its changing internal and external environ-

[21]Raup, Benne, Smith, and Axtelle, *The Discipline of Practical Judgment in a Democratic Society,* Yearbook No. 28 of the National Society of College Teachers of Education (Chicago: University of Chicago Press, 1943).

[22]Mary Follett, *Creative Experience and Dynamic Administration* (New York: David McKay, 1924).

[23]Karl Mannheim, *Man and Society in an Age of Reconstruction* (New York: Harcourt Brace Jovanovich, 1940).

[24]Elliot Jaques, *The Changing Culture of a Factory* (New York: Holt, Rinehart & Winston, 1952).

[25]William J. Dickson and F. J. Roethlisberger, *Personal Counseling in an Organization: A Sequel to the Hawthorne Researches* (Boston: Harvard Business School, 1966).

[26]Elton Mayo, *The Social Problems of an Industrial Civilization* (Cambridge, Mass., Harvard University Press, 1945).

[27]Leland Bradford, Jack R. Gibb, and Kenneth D. Benne, *T-Group Theory and Laboratory Methods* (New York: John Wiley & Sons, 1964).

[28]Matthew B. Miles, "On Temporary Systems," in *Innovation in Education,* ed. M. B. Miles (New York: Bureau of Publications, Teachers College, Columbia University Press, 1964), pp. 437–92.

ments must develop and institutionalize its own problem-solving structures and processes. These structures and processes must be tuned both to human problems of relationship and morale and to technical problems of meeting the system's task requirements, set by its goals of production, distribution, and so on.[29] System problems are typically not social *or* technical but actually sociotechnical.[30] The problem-solving structures and processes of a human system must be developed to deal with a range of sociotechnical difficulties, converting them into problems and organizing the relevant processes of the data collection, planning, invention, and tryout of solutions, evaluation and feedback of results, replanning, and so forth, which are required for the solution of the problems.

The human parts of the system must learn to function collaboratively in these processes of problem identification and solution and the system must develop institutionalized support and mechanisms for maintaining and improving these processes. Actually, the model of changing in these approaches is a cooperative, action-research model. This model was suggested by Lewin and developed most elaborately for use in educational settings by Stephen M. Corey.[31]

The range of interventions by outside change agents in implementing this approach to changing is rather wide. It has been most fully elaborated in relation to organizational development programs. Within such programs, intervention methods have been most comprehensively tested in industrial settings. Some of these more or less tested intervention methods are listed below. A design for any organizational development program, of course, normally uses a number of these in succession or combination.

1. Collection of data about organizational functioning and feedback of data into processes of data interpretation and of planning ways of correcting revealed dysfunctions by system managers and data collectors in collaboration.[32]
2. Training of managers and working organizational units in methods of problem solving through self-examination of present ways of dealing with difficulties and through development and tryout of better ways with consultation by outside and/or inside change agents. Usually, the working unit leaves its working place for parts of its training. These laboratory sessions are ordinarily interspersed with on-the-job consultations.
3. Developing acceptance of feedback (research and development) roles and functions within the organization, training persons to fill these roles, and relating such roles strategically to the on-going management of the organization.
4. Training internal change agents to function within the organization in carrying on needed applied research, consultation, and training.[33]

Whatever specific strategies of intervention may be employed in developing the system's capabilities for problem solving, change efforts are designed to help the system in developing ways of scanning its operations to detect problems, of diagnosing these problems to determine relevant changeable factors in them, and of moving toward collaboratively determined solutions to the problems.

Releasing and Fostering Growth in the Persons Who Make Up the System to Be Changed. Those committed to this family of approaches to changing tend to see the person as the basic unit of social

---

[29]Robert R. Blake and Jane S. Mouton, *The Managerial Grid* (Houston: Gulf Publishing, 1961).

[30]Jay W. Lorsch and Paul Lawrence, "The Diagnosis of Organizational Problems," in Bennis et al., *Planning of Change*, chap. 8, p. 468.

[31]Stephen M. Corey, *Action Research to Improve School Practices* (New York: Bureau of Publications, Teachers College, Columbia University Press, 1953).

[32]See contributions by Miles et al., "Data Feedback and Organizational Change in a School System," in Bennis et al., *Planning of Change*, chap. 8, p. 457; and Lorsch and Lawrence, "Diagnosis of Organizational Problems," in Bennis, et al. *Planning of Change*, chap. 8, p. 468.

[33]C. Argyris, "Explorations in Consulting-Client Relationships," in Bennis et al., *Planning of Change*, chap. 8, p. 434. See also Richard Beckhard, "The Confrontation Meeting," in Bennis et al., *Planning of Change*, chap. 8, p. 478.

organization. Persons, it is believed, are capable of creative, life-affirming, self- and other-regarding and respecting responses, choices, and actions, if conditions which thwart these kinds of responses are removed and other supporting conditions developed. Rogers has formulated these latter conditions in his analysis of the therapist-client relationship—trustworthiness, empathy, caring, and others.[34] Maslow has worked out a similar idea in his analysis of the hierarchy of needs in persons.[35] If lower needs are met, higher need-meeting actions will take place. McGregor[36] has formulated the ways in which existing organizations operate to fixate persons in lower levels of motivation and has sought to envision an organization designed to release and support the growth of persons in fulfilling their higher motivations as they function within the organizations.

Various intervention methods have been designed to help people discover themselves as persons and commit themselves to continuing personal growth in the various relationships of their lives.

1. One early effort to install personal counseling widely and strategically in an organization has been reported by Roethlisberger and Dickson.[37]
2. Training groups designed to facilitate personal confrontation and growth of members in an open, trusting, and accepting atmosphere have been conducted for individuals from various back-home situations and for persons from the same back-home setting. The processes of these groups have sometimes been described as "therapy for normals."[38]

3. Groups and laboratories designed to stimulate and support personal growth have been designed to utilize the resources of nonverbal exchange and communication among members along with verbal dialogue in inducing personal confrontation, discovery, and commitment to continuing growth.
4. Many psychotherapists, building on the work of Freud and Adler, have come to use groups, as well as two-person situations, as media of personal reeducation and growth. Such efforts are prominent in mental health approaches to changing and have been conducted in educational, religious, community, industrial, and hospital settings. While these efforts focus primarily upon helping individuals to change themselves toward greater self-clarity and fuller self-actualization, they are frequently designed and conducted in the hope that personal changes will lead to changes in organizations, institutions, and communities as well.

We have presented the two variants of normative-reeducative approaches to changing in a way to emphasize their differences. Actually, there are many similarities between them as well, which justify placing both under the same general heading. We have already mentioned one of these similarities. Both frequently use temporary systems—a residential laboratory or workshop, a temporary group with special resources built in, an ongoing system which incorporates a change agent (trainer, consultant, counselor, or therapist) temporarily—as an aid to growth in the system and/or in its members.

More fundamentally, both approaches emphasize experience-based learning as an ingredient of all enduring changes in human systems. Yet both accept the principle that people must learn to learn from their experiences if self-directed change is to be maintained and continued. Frequently, people

---

[34]Carl Rogers, "The Characteristics of a Helping Relationship," in Bennis et al., *Planning of Change,* chap. 4, p. 153.

[35]Abraham Maslow, *Motivation and Personality* (New York: Harper & Row, 1954).

[36]Douglas M. McGregor, "The Human Side of Enterprise," in W. Bennis et al., *The Planning of Change,* 1st ed. (New York: Holt, Rinehart & Winston, 1961), pp. 422–31.

[37]Dickson and Roethlisberger, *Personal Counseling in an Organization.*

[38]James V. Clark "A Healthy Organization," in Bennis et al., *Planning of Change,* chap. 6, p. 282. Irving Weschler, Fred Massarik, and Robert Tannenbaum, "The Self in Process: A Sensitivity Training Emphasis," in *Issues in Training,* ed. I. R. Weschler and E. Schein. Selected Reading Series No. 5 (Washington, D.C.: National Training Laboratories).

have learned to defend against the potential lessons of experience when these threaten existing equilibria, whether in the person or in the social system. How can these defenses be lowered to let the data of experience get into processes of perceiving the situation, of constructing new and better ways to define it, of inventing new and more appropriate ways of responding to the situation as redefined, of becoming more fully aware of the consequences of actions, of rearticulating value orientations which sanction more responsible ways of managing the consequences of actions, and so forth? Learning to learn from ongoing experience is a major objective in both approaches to changing. Neither denies the relevance or importance of the non-cognitive determinants of behavior—feelings, attitudes, norms, and relationships—along with cognitive-perceptual determinants, in effecting behavioral change. The problem-solving approaches emphasize the cognitive determinants more than personal growth approaches do. But exponents of the former do not accept the rationalistic biases of the rational-empirical family of change strategies, already discussed. Since exponents of both problem-solving and personal growth approaches are committed to reeducation of persons as integral to effective change in human systems, both emphasize norms of openness of communication, trust between persons, lowering of status barriers between parts of the system, and mutuality between parts as necessary conditions of the reeducative process.

Great emphasis has been placed recently upon the releasing of creativity in persons, groups, and organizations as requisite to coping adaptively with accelerated changes in the conditions of modern living. We have already stressed the emphasis which personal growth approaches put upon the release of creative responses in persons being reeducated. Problem-solving approaches also value creativity, though they focus more upon the group and organizational conditions which increase the probability of creative responses by persons functioning within those conditions than upon persons directly. The approaches do differ in their strategies for releasing creative responses within human systems.

But both believe that creative adaptations to changing conditions may arise *within* human systems and do not have to be imported from *outside* them as in innovation-diffusion approaches already discussed and the power-compliance models still to be dealt with.

One developing variant of normative-reeducative approaches to changing, not already noted, focuses upon effective conflict management. It is, of course, common knowledge that differences within a society which demand interaccommodation often manifest themselves as conflicts. In the process of managing such conflicts, changes in the norms, policies, and relationships of the society occur. Can conflict management be brought into the ambit of planned change as defined in this volume? Stemming from the work of the Sherifs in creating intergroup conflict and seeking to resolve it in a field-laboratory situation,[39] training in intergroup conflict and conflict resolution found its way into training laboratories through the efforts of Blake and others. Since that time, laboratories for conflict management have been developed under NTL and other auspices and methodologies for conflict resolution and management, in keeping with the values of planned change, have been devised. Blake's and Walton's work represents some of the findings from these pioneering efforts.[40]

Thus, without denying their differences in assumption and strategy, we believe that the differing approaches discussed in this section can be seen together within the framework of normative-reeducative approaches to changing. Two efforts to conceptualize planned change in a way to reveal the similarities in assumptions about changing and in value orientations toward change underlying these

---

[39]Muzafer and Carolyn Sherif, *Groups in Harmony and Tension* (New York: Harper & Row, 1953).

[40]Robert Blake et al., "The Union Management Inter-Group Laboratory," in Bennis et al., *Planning of Change*, chap. 4, p. 176. Richard Walton, "Two Strategies of Social Change and Their Dilemmas," in Bennis et al., *Planning of Change*, chap. 4, p. 167.

variant approaches are those by Lippitt, Watson, and Westley and by Bennis, Benne, and Chin.[41]

Another aspect of changing in human organizations is represented by efforts to conceive human organization in forms that go beyond the bureaucratic form which captured the imagination and fixed the contours of thinking and practice of organizational theorists and practitioners from the latter part of the nineteenth through the early part of the twentieth century. The bureaucratic form of organization was conceptualized by Max Weber and carried into American thinking by such students of administration as Urwick.[42] On this view, effective organization of human effort followed the lines of effective division of labor and effective establishment of lines of reporting, control, and supervision from the mass base of the organization up through various levels of control to the top of the pyramidal organization from which legitimate authority and responsibility stemmed.

The work of industrial sociologists like Mayo threw doubt upon the adequacy of such a model of formal organization to deal with the realities of organizational life by revealing the informal organization which grows up within the formal structure to satisfy personal and interpersonal needs not encompassed by or integrated into the goals of the formal organization. Chester Barnard may be seen as a transitional figure who, in discussing the functions of the organizational executive, gave equal emphasis to his responsibilities for task effectiveness and organizational efficiency (optimally meeting the human needs of persons in the organization).[43] Much of the development of subsequent organizational theory and practice has centered on problems of integrating the actualities, criteria, and concepts of organizational effectiveness and of organizational efficiency.

A growing group of thinkers and researchers have sought to move beyond the bureaucratic model toward some new model of organization which might set directions and limits for change efforts in organizational life. Out of many thinkers, we choose four who have theorized out of an orientation consistent with what we have called a normative-reeducative approach to changing.

Rensis Likert has presented an intergroup model of organization. Each working unit strives to develop and function as a group. The group's efforts are linked to other units of the organization by the overlapping membership of supervisors or managers in vertically or horizontally adjacent groups. This view of organization throws problems of delegation, supervision, and internal communication into a new light and emphasizes the importance of linking persons as targets of change and reeducation in processes of organizational development.[44]

We have already stressed McGregor's efforts to conceive a form of organization more in keeping with new and more valid views of human nature and motivation (Theory Y) than the limited and false views of human nature and motivation (Theory X) upon which traditional bureaucratic organization has rested. In his work he sought to move thinking and practice relevant to organization and organizational change beyond the limits of traditional forms. "The essential task of management is to arrange organizational conditions and methods of operation so that people can achieve their own goals best by directing their own efforts toward organizational objectives."[45]

Bennis has consciously sought to move beyond bureaucracy in tracing the contours of the organizations of the future.[46] And Shephard has described an organizational form consistent with support for continual changing and self-renewal, rather than with a primary mission of maintenance and control.[47]

---

[41]Lippitt et al., *Dynamics of Planned Change.* Bennis et al., *Planning of Change,* 1st ed.

[42]Lyndall Urwick, *The Pattern of Management* (Minneapolis: University of Minnesota Press, 1956).

[43]Chester I. Barnard, *The Functions of the Executive* (Cambridge, Mass.: Harvard University Press, 1938).

[44]Rensis Likert, *New Patterns of Management* (New York: McGraw-Hill, 1961).

[45]McGregor, "Human Side of Enterprise," pp. 422–31.

[46]W. G. Bennis, "Changing Organizations," in Bennis et al., *Planning of Change,* chap. 10, p. 568.

[47]H. A. Shephard, "Innovation-Resisting and Innovation-Producing Organizations," in Bennis et al., *Planning of Change,* chap. 9, p. 519.

Power-Coercive Approaches to Effective Change

It is not the use of power, in the sense of influence by one person upon another or by one group upon another, which distinguishes this family of strategies from those already discussed. Power is an ingredient of all human action. The differences lie rather in the ingredients of power upon which the strategies of changing depend and the ways in which power is generated and applied in processes of effecting change. Thus, what we have called rational-empirical approaches depend on knowledge as a major ingredient of power. In this view, men of knowledge are legitimate sources of power and the desirable flow of influence or power is from men who know to men who don't know through processes of education and of dissemination of valid information.

Normative-reeducative strategies of changing do not deny the importance of knowledge as a source of power, especially in the form of knowledge-based technology. Exponents of this approach to changing are committed to redressing the imbalance between the limited use of behavioral knowledge and people technologies and the widespread use of physical-biological knowledge and related thing technologies in effecting changes in human affairs. In addition, exponents of normative-reeducative approaches recognize the importance of non-cognitive determinants of behavior as resistances or supports to changing—values, attitudes, and feelings at the personal level and norms and relationships at the social level. Influence must extend to these noncognitive determinants of behavior if voluntary commitments and reliance upon social intelligence are to be maintained and extended in our changing society. Influence of non-cognitive determinants of behavior must be exercised in mutual processes of persuasion within collaborative relationships. These strategies are oriented against coercive and nonreciprocal influence, both on moral and on pragmatic grounds.

What ingredients of power do power-coercive strategies emphasize? In general, emphasis is upon political and economic sanctions in the exercise of power. But other coercive strategies emphasize the utilization of moral power, playing upon sentiments of guilt and shame. Political power carries with it legitimacy and the sanctions which accrue to those who break the law. Thus getting a law passed against racial imbalance in the schools brings legitimate coercive power behind efforts to desegregate the schools, threatening those who resist with sanctions under the law and reducing the resistance of others who are morally oriented against breaking the law. Economic power exerts coercive influence over the decisions of those to whom it is applied. Thus federal appropriations granting funds to local schools for increased emphasis upon science instruction tend to exercise coercive influence over the decisions of local school officials concerning the emphasis of the school curriculum. In general, power-coercive strategies of changing seek to mass political and economic power behind the change goals which the strategists of change have decided are desirable. Those who oppose these goals, if they adopt the same strategy, seek to mass political and economic power in opposition. The strategy thus tends to divide the society when there is anything like a division of opinion and of power in that society.

When a person or group is entrenched in power in a social system, in command of political legitimacy and of political and economic sanctions, that person or group can use power-coercive strategies in effecting changes which they consider desirable, without much awareness on the part of those out of power in the system that such strategies are being employed. A power-coercive way of making decisions is accepted as in the nature of things. The use of such strategies by those in legitimate control of various social systems in our society is much more widespread than most of us might at first be willing or able to admit. This is true in educational systems as well as in other social systems.

When any part of a social system becomes aware that its interests are not being served by those in control of the system, the coercive power of those in control can be challenged. If the minority is committed to power-coercive strategies, or is aware of no alternatives to such strategies, how can they make headway against existing power relations within the system? They may organize discontent against the present controls of the system and achieve power outside the legitimate channels of authority in the system. Thus teachers' unions may develop power against coercive controls by the central administrative group and the school board in a school system. They may threaten concerted resistance to or disregard of administrative rulings and board policies or they may threaten work stoppage or a strike. Those in control may get legislation against teachers' strikes. If the political power of organized teachers grows, they may get legislation requiring collective bargaining between organized teachers and the school board on some range of educational issues. The power struggle then shifts to the negotiation table and compromise between competing interests may become the expected goal of the intergroup exchange. Whether the augmented power of new, relevant knowledge or the generation of common power through joint collaboration and deliberation are lost in the process will depend on the degree of commitment by all parties to the conflict and to a continuation and maintenance of power-coercive strategies for effecting change.

What general varieties of power-coercive strategies, to be exercised either by those in control as they seek to maintain their power or to be used by those now outside a position of control and seeking to enlarge their power, can be identified?

Strategies of Nonviolence. Mahatma Gandhi may be seen as the most prominent recent theorist and practitioner of nonviolent strategies for effecting change, although the strategies did not originate with him in the history of mankind, either in idea or in practice. Gandhi spoke of Thoreau's *Essay on Civil Disobedience* as one important influence in his own approach to nonviolent coercive action. Martin Luther King was perhaps America's most distinguished exponent of nonviolent coercion in effecting social change. A minority (or majority) confronted with what they see as an unfair, unjust, or cruel system of coercive social control may dramatize their rejection of the system by pub-

licly and nonviolently witnessing and demonstrating against it. Part of the ingredients of the power of the civilly disobedient is in the guilt which their demonstration of injustice, unfairness, or cruelty of the existing system of control arouses in those exercising control or in others previously committed to the present system of control. The opposition to the disobedient group may be demoralized and may waver in their exercise of control, if they profess the moral values to which the dissidents are appealing.

Weakening or dividing the opposition through moral coercion may be combined with economic sanctions—like Gandhi's refusal to buy salt and other British manufactured commodities in India or like the desegregationists' economic boycott of the products of racially discriminating factories and businesses.

The use of nonviolent strategies for opening up conflicts in values and demonstrating against injustices or inequities in existing patterns of social control has become familiar to educational leaders in the demonstrations and sit-ins of college students in various universities and in the demonstrations of desegregationists against de facto segregation of schools. And the widened use of such strategies may be confidently predicted. Whether such strategies will be used to extend collaborative ways of developing policies and normative-reeducative strategies of changing or whether they will be used to augment power struggles as the only practical way of settling conflicts, will depend in some large part upon the strategy commitments of those now in positions of power in education systems.

Use of Political Institutions to Achieve Change. Political power has traditionally played an important part in achieving changes in our institutional life. And political power will continue to play an important part in shaping and reshaping our institutions of education as well as other institutions. Changes enforced by political coercion need not be oppressive if the quality of our democratic processes can be maintained and improved.

Changes in policies with respect to education have come from various departments of government. By far the most of these have come through legislation on the state level. Under legislation, school administrators have various degrees of discretionary powers, and policy and program changes are frequently put into effect by administrative rulings. Judicial decisions have played an important part in shaping educational policies, none more dramatically than the Supreme Court decision declaring laws and policies supporting school segregation illegal. And the federal courts have played a central part in seeking to implement and enforce this decision.

Some of the difficulty with the use of political institutions to effect changes arises from an overestimation by change agents of the capability of political action to effect changes in practice. When the law is passed, the administrative ruling announced, or the judicial decision handed down legitimizing some new policy or program or illegitimizing some traditional practice, change agents who have worked hard for the law, ruling, or decision frequently assume that the desired change has been made.

Actually, all that has been done is to bring the force of legitimacy behind some envisioned change. The processes of reeducation of persons who are to conduct themselves in new ways still have to be carried out. And the new conduct often requires new knowledge, new skills, new attitudes, and new value orientations. And, on the social level, new conduct may require changes in the norms, the roles, and the relationship structures of the institutions involved. This is not to discount the importance of political actions in legitimizing changed policies and practices in educational institutions and in other institutions as well. It is rather to emphasize that normative-reeducative strategies must be combined with political coercion, both before and after the political action, if the public is to be adequately informed and desirable and commonly acceptable changes in practice are to be achieved.

Changing through the Recomposition and Manipulation of Power Elites. The idea or practice of a ruling class or of a power elite in social control was by no means original with Karl Marx. What

was original with him was his way of relating these concepts to a process and strategy of fundamental social change. The composition of the ruling class was, of course, for Marx those who owned and controlled the means and processes of production of goods and services in a society. Since, for Marx, the ideology of the ruling class set limits to the thinking of most intellectuals and of those in charge of educational processes and of communicating, rationales for the existing state of affairs, including its concentration of political and economic power, is provided and disseminated by intellectuals and educators and communicators within the system.

Since Marx was morally committed to a classless society in which political coercion would disappear because there would be no vested primate interests to rationalize and defend, he looked for a counterforce in society to challenge and eventually to overcome the power of the ruling class. And this he found in the economically dispossessed and aliented workers of hand and brain. As this new class gained consciousness of its historic mission and its power increased, the class struggle could be effectively joined. The outcome of this struggle was victory for those best able to organize and maximize the productive power of the instruments of production—for Marx this victory belonged to the now dispossessed workers.

Many of Marx's values would have put him behind what we have called normative-reeducative strategies of changing. And he recognized that such strategies would have to be used after the accession of the workers to state power in order to usher in the classless society. He doubted if the ruling class could be reeducated, since reeducation would mean loss of their privileges and coercive power in society. He recognized that the power elite could, within limits, accommodate new interests as these gained articulation and power. But these accommodations must fall short of a radical transfer of power to a class more capable of wielding it. Meanwhile, he remained committed to a power-coercive strategy of changing until the revolutionary transfer of power had been effected.

Marxian concepts have affected the thinking of contemporary men about social change both inside

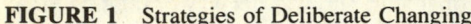

FIGURE 1   Strategies of Deliberate Changing

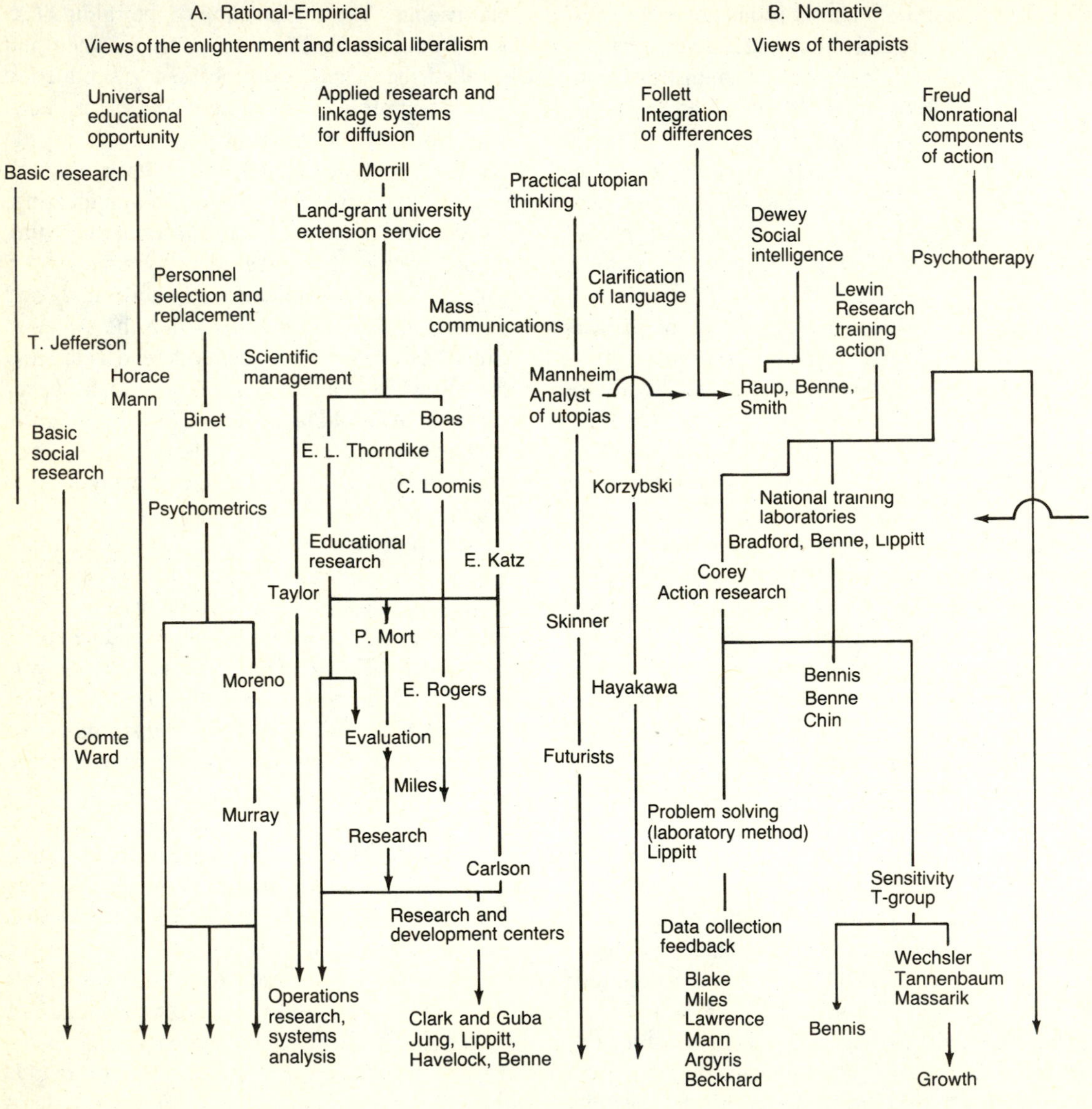

A. Rational-Empirical

Views of the enlightenment and classical liberalism

B. Normative

Views of therapists

Universal educational opportunity

Applied research and linkage systems for diffusion

Follett Integration of differences

Freud Nonrational components of action

Basic research

Morrill

Land-grant university extension service

Practical utopian thinking

Dewey Social intelligence

Psychotherapy

Personnel selection and replacement

Mass communications

Clarification of language

Lewin Research training action

T. Jefferson

Scientific management

Mannheim Analyst of utopias

Raup, Benne, Smith

Horace Mann

Binet

Boas

E. L. Thorndike

Basic social research

C. Loomis

Korzybski

National training laboratories Bradford, Benne, Lippitt

Psychometrics

Educational research

E. Katz

Taylor

Corey Action research

P. Mort

Skinner

Moreno

E. Rogers

Bennis Benne Chin

Evaluation

Hayakawa

Comte Ward

Miles

Murray

Research

Futurists

Carlson

Problem solving (laboratory method) Lippitt

Research and development centers

Sensitivity T-group

Data collection feedback

Operations research, systems analysis

Clark and Guba Jung, Lippitt, Havelock, Benne

Blake Miles Lawrence Mann Argyris Beckhard

Bennis

Wechsler Tannenbaum Massarik

Growth

and outside nations in which Marxism has become the official orientation. His concepts have tended to bolster assumptions of the necessity of power-coercive strategies in achieving fundamental redis-tributions of socio-economic power or in recom-posing or manipulating power elites in a society. Democratic, reeducative methods of changing have a place only after such changes in power allocation

FIGURE 1 *(concluded)*

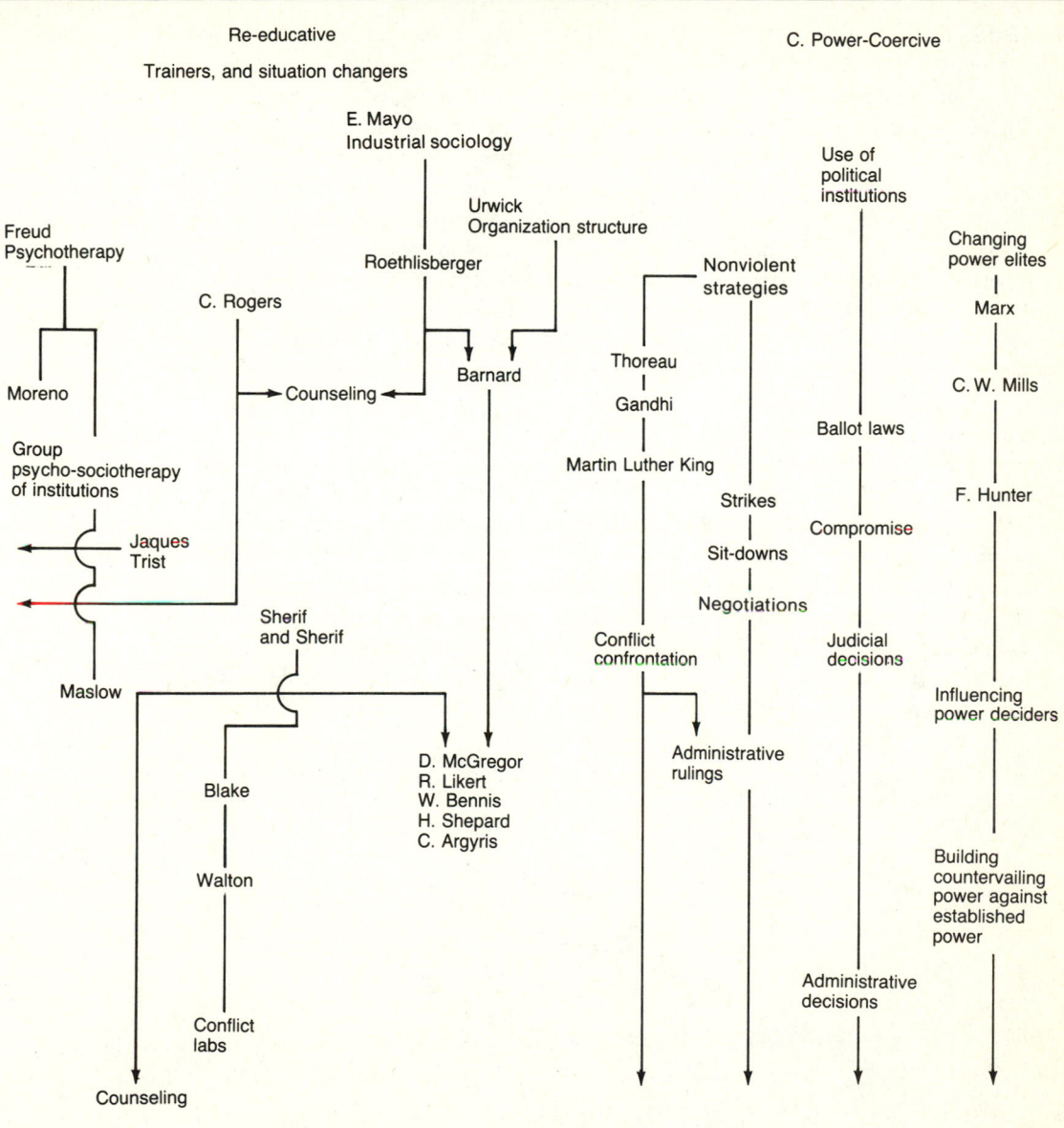

have been achieved by power-coercive methods. Non-Marxians as well as Marxians are often committed to this Marxian dictum.

In contemporary America, C. Wright Mills has identified a power elite, essentially composed of industrial, military, and governmental leaders, who direct and limit processes of social change and accommodation in our society. And President Eisenhower warned of the dangerous concentration of power in substantially the same groups in his farewell message to the American people. Educators committed to democratic values should not be blinded to the limitations to advancement of those values, which are set by the less than democratic ideology of our power elites. And normative-reeducative strategists of changing must include power elites among their targets of changing as they seek to diffuse their ways of progress within contemporary society. And they must take seriously Marx's questions about the reeducability of members of the power elites, as they deal with problems and projects of social change.

The operation of a power elite in social units smaller than a nation was revealed in Floyd Hunter's study of decision making in an American city. Hunter's small group of deciders, with their satellite groups of intellectuals, front men, and implementers, is in a real sense a power elite. The most common reaction of educational leaders to Hunter's "discovery" has been to seek ways in which to persuade and manipulate the deciders toward support of educational ends which educational leaders consider desirable—whether bond issues, building programs, or anything else. This is non-Marxian in its acceptance of power relations

in a city or community as fixed. It would be Marxian if it sought to build counter power to offset and reduce the power of the presently deciding group where this power interfered with the achievement of desirable educational goals. This latter strategy, though not usually Marxian inspired in the propaganda sense of that term, has been more characteristic of organized teacher effort in pressing for collective bargaining or of some student demonstrations and sit-ins. In the poverty program, the federal government in its insistence on participation of the poor in making policies for the program has at least played with a strategy of building countervailing power to offset the existing concentration of power in people not identified with the interests of the poor in reducing their poverty.

Those committed to the advancement of normative-reeducative strategies of changing must take account of present actual concentrations of power wherever they work. This does *not* mean that they must develop a commitment to power-coercive strategies to change the distribution of power except when these may be necessary to effect the spread of their own democratically and scientifically oriented methods of changing within society.

Reading 9

INTERVENTION THEORY AND METHOD

Chris Argyris

A Definition of Intervention

To intervene is to enter into an ongoing system of relationship, to come between or among persons, groups, or objects for the purpose of helping them. There is an important implicit assumption in the definition that should be made explicit: the system exists independently of the intervenor. There are many reasons one might wish to intervene. These reasons may range from helping the clients make their own decisions about the kind of help they need to coercing the clients to do what the intervenor wishes them to do.

Our view acknowledges interdependencies between the intervenor and the client system but focuses on how to maintain, or increase, the client system's autonomy; how to differentiate even more clearly the boundaries between the client system and the intervenor; and how to conceptualize and define the client system's health independently of the intervenor's. This view values the client system as an ongoing, self-responsible unity that has the obligation to be in control over its own destiny. An intervenor, in this view, assists a system to become more effective in problem solving, decision making, and decision implementation in such a way that the system can continue to be increasingly effective in these activities and have a decreasing need for the intervenor.

Source: Chris Argyris, *Intervention Theory and Methods: A Behavioral Science View* (Reading, Mass.: Addison-Wesley Publishing, 1970), pp. 15–20. © 1970, Addison-Wesley. Reprinted with permission.

Basic Requirements for Intervention Activity

Are there any basic or necessary processes that must be fulfilled regardless of the substantive issues involved, if intervention activity is to be helpful with any level of client (individual, group, or organizational)? One condition that seems so basic as to be defined axiomatic is the generation of *valid information*. Without valid information, it would be difficult for the client to learn and for the interventionist to help.

A second condition almost as basic flows from our assumption that intervention activity, no matter what its substantive interests and objectives, should be so designed and executed that the client system maintains its discreteness and autonomy. Thus *free, informed choice* is also a necessary process in effective intervention activity.

Finally, if the client system is assumed to be ongoing (that is, existing over time), the clients require strengthening to maintain their autonomy not only vis-à-vis the interventionist but also vis-à-vis other systems. This means that their commitment to learning and change has to be more than temporary. It has to be so strong that it can be transferred to relationships other than those with the interventionist and can do so (eventually) without the help of the interventionist. The third basic process for any intervention activity is therefore the client's *internal commitment* to the choices made.

In summary, valid information, free choice, and internal commitment are considered integral parts of any intervention activity, no matter what the substantive objectives are (for example, developing a management performance evaluation scheme, reducing intergroup rivalries, increasing the degree of trust among individuals, redesigning budgetary systems, or redesigning work). These three processes are called the primary intervention tasks.

Primary Tasks of an Interventionist

Why is it necessary to hypothesize that in order for an interventionist to behave effectively and in order that the integrity of the client system be maintained, the interventionist has to focus on three primary tasks, regardless of the substantive problems that the client system may be experiencing?

Valid and Useful Information

First, it has been accepted as axiomatic that valid and useful information is the foundation for effective intervention. Valid information is that which describes the factors, plus their interrelationships, that create the problem for the client system. There are several tests for checking the validity of the information. In increasing degrees of power they are public verifiability, valid prediction, and control over the phenomena. The first is having several independent diagnoses suggest the same picture. Second is generating predictions from the diagnosis that are subsequently confirmed (they occurred under the conditions that were specified). Third is altering the factors systematically and predicting the effects upon the system as a whole. All these tests, if they are to be valid, must be carried out in such a way that the participants cannot, at will, make them come true. This would be a self-fulfilling prophecy and not a confirmation of a prediction. The difficulty with a self-fulfilling prophecy is its indication of more about the degree of power an individual (or subset of individuals) can muster to alter the system than about the nature of the system when the participants are behaving without knowledge of the diagnosis. For example, if an executive learns that the interventionist predicts his subordinates will behave (a) if he behaves (b), he might alter (b) in order not lead to (a). Such an alteration indicates the executive's

power but does not test the validity of the diagnosis that if (a), then (b).

The tests for valid information have important implications for effective intervention activity. First, the interventionist's diagnoses must strive to represent the total client system and not the point of view of any subgroup or individual. Otherwise, the interventionist could not be seen only as being under the control of a particular individual or subgroup, but also his predictions would be based upon inaccurate information and thus might not be confirmed.

This does not mean that an interventionist may not begin with, or may not limit his relationship to, a subpart of the total system. It is totally possible, for example, for the interventionist to help management, blacks, trade union leaders, etc. With whatever subgroup he works he simply should not agree to limit his diagnosis to its wishes.

It is conceivable that a client system may be helped even though valid information is not generated. Sometimes changes occur in a positive direction without the interventionist having played any important role. These changes, although helpful in that specific instance, lack the attribute of helping the organization to learn to gain control over its problem-solving capability.

The importance of information that the clients can use to control their destiny points up the requirement that the information must not only be valid, it must be useful. Valid information that cannot be used by the clients to alter their system is equivalent to valid information about cancer that cannot be used to cure cancer eventually. An interventionist's diagnosis should include variables that are manipulable by the clients and are complete enough so that if they are manipulated effective change will follow.

Free Choice

In order to have free choice, the client has to have a cognitive map of what he wishes to do. The objectives of his action are known at the moment of decision. Free choice implies voluntary as opposed to automatic; proactive rather than reactive. The act of selection is rarely accomplished by maximizing or optimizing. Free and informed choice entails what Simon has called "satisficing," that is, selecting the alternative with the highest probability of succeeding, given some specified cost constraints. Free choice places the locus of decision making in the client system. Free choice makes it possible for the clients to remain responsible for their destiny. Through free choice the clients can maintain the autonomy of their system.

It may be possible that clients prefer to give up their responsibility and their autonomy, especially if they are feeling a sense of failure. They may prefer, as we shall see in several examples, to turn over their free choice to the interventionist. They may insist that he make recommendations and tell them what to do. The interventionist resists these pressures because if he does not, the clients will lose their free choice and he will lose his own free choice also. He will be controlled by the anxieties of the clients.

The requirement of free choice is especially important for those helping activities where the processes of help are as important as the actual help. For example, a medical doctor does not require that a patient with a bullet wound participate in the process by defining the kind of help he needs. However, the same doctor may have to pay much more attention to the processes he uses to help patients when he is attempting to diagnose blood pressure or cure a high cholesterol. If the doctor behaves in ways that upset the patient, the latter's blood pressure may well be distorted. Or, the patient can develop a dependent relationship if the doctor cuts down his cholesterol—increasing habits only under constant pressure from the doctor—and the moment the relationship is broken off, the count goes up.

Effective intervention in the human and social sphere requires that the processes of help be congruent with the outcome desired. Free choice is important because there are so many unknowns, and the interventionist wants the client to have as much willingness and motivation as possible to work on the problem. With high client motivation and commitment, several different methods for change can succeed.

A choice is free to the extent the members can make their selection for a course of action with minimal internal defensiveness; can define the path (or paths) by which the intended consequence is to be achieved; can relate the choice to their central needs; and can build into their choices a realistic and challenging level of aspiration. Free choice therefore implies that the members are able to explore as many alternatives as they consider significant and select those that are central to their needs.

Why must the choice be related to the central needs and why must the level of aspiration be realistic and challenging? May people not choose freely unrealistic or unchallenging objectives? Yes, they may do so in the short run, but not for long if they still want to have free and informed choice. A freely chosen course of action means that the action must be based on an accurate analysis of the situation and not on the biases or defenses of the decision makers. We know, from the level of aspiration studies, that choices which are too high or too low, which are too difficult or not difficult enough will tend to lead to psychological failure. Psychological failure will lead to increased defensiveness, increased failure, and decreased self-acceptance on the part of the members experiencing the failure. These conditions, in turn, will tend to lead to distorted perceptions by the members making the choices. Moreover, the defensive members may unintentionally create a climate where the members of surrounding and interrelated systems will tend to provide carefully censored information. Choices made under these conditions are neither informed nor free.

Turning to the question of centrality of needs, a similar logic applies. The degree of commitment to the processes of generating valid information, scanning, and choosing may significantly vary according to the centrality of the choice to the needs of the clients. The more central the choice, the more the system will strive to do its best in developing valid information and making free and informed choices. If the research from perceptual psychology is valid, the very perception of the clients is altered by the needs involved. Individuals tend to scan more, ask for more information, and be more careful in their choices when they are making decisions that are central to them. High involvement may produce perceptual distortions, as does low involvement. The interventionist, however, may have a greater probability of helping the clients explore possible distortion when the choice they are making is a critical one.

Internal Commitment

Internal commitment means that course of action or choice that has been internalized by each member so that he experiences a high degree of ownership and has a feeling of responsibility about the choice and its implications. Internal commitment means that the individual has reached the point where he is acting on the choice because it fulfills his own needs and sense of responsibility, as well as those of the system.

The individual who is internally committed is acting primarily under the influence of his own forces and not induced forces. The individual (or any unity) feels a minimal degree of dependence upon others for the action. It implies that he has obtained and processed valid information and that he has made an informed and free choice. Under these conditions, there is a high probability that the individual's commitment will remain strong over time (even with reduction of external rewards) or under stress, or when the course of action is challenged by others. It also implies that the individual is continually open to reexamination of his position because he believes in taking action based upon valid information.

Reading 10

ACHIEVING CHANGE IN PEOPLE:
SOME APPLICATIONS OF GROUP
DYNAMICS THEORY

Dorwin Cartwright

I

We hear all around us today the assertion that the problems of the 20th century are problems of human relations. The survival of civilization, it is said, will depend upon man's ability to create social inventions capable of harnessing, for society's constructive use, the vast physical energies now at man's disposal. Or, to put the matter more simply, we must learn how to change the way in which people behave toward one another. In broad outline, the specifications for a good society are clear, but a serious technical problem remains: How can we change people so that they neither restrict the freedom nor limit the potentialities for growth of others; so that they accept and respect people of different religion, nationality, color, or political opinion; so that nations can exist in a world without war, and so that the fruits of our technological advances can bring economic well-being and freedom from disease to all the people of the world? Although few people would disagree with these objectives when stated abstractly, when we become more specific, differences of opinion quickly arise. How is change to be produced? Who is to do it? Who is to be changed? These questions permit no ready answers.

Before we consider in detail these questions of social technology, let us clear away some semantic obstacles. The word "change" produces emotional reactions. It is not a neutral word. To many people it is threatening. It conjures up visions of a revo-

lutionary, a dissatisfied idealist, a troublemaker, a malcontent. Nicer words referring to the process of changing people are education, training, orientation, guidance, indoctrination, therapy. We are more ready to have others "educate" us than to have them "change" us. We, ourselves, feel less guilty in "training" others than in "changing" them. Why this emotional response? What makes the two kinds of words have such different meanings? I believe that a large part of the difference lies in the fact that the safer words (like education or therapy) carry the implicit assurance that the only changes produced will be good ones, acceptable within a currently held value system. The cold, unmodified word "change," on the contrary, promises no respect for values; it might even tamper with values themselves. Perhaps for this very reason it will foster straight thinking if we use the word "change" and thus force ourselves to struggle directly and self-consciously with the problems of value that are involved. Words like education, training, or therapy, by the very fact that they are not so disturbing, may close our eyes to the fact that they too inevitably involve values.

Another advantage of using the word "change" rather than other related words is that it does not restrict our thinking to a limited set of aspects of people that are legitimate targets of change. Anyone familiar with the history of education knows that there has been endless controversy over what it is about people that "education" properly attempts to modify. Some educators have viewed education simply as imparting knowledge, others mainly as providing skills for doing things, still others as producing healthy "attitudes," and some

Source: Dorwin Cartwright, *Human Relations* 4, no. 4 (1951), pp. 381–92.

have aspired to instill a way of life. Or if we choose to use a word like "therapy," we can hardly claim that we refer to a more clearly defined realm of change. Furthermore, one can become inextricably entangled in distinctions and vested interests by attempting to distinguish sharply between, let us say, the domain of education and that of therapy. If we are to try to take a broader view and to develop some basic principles that promise to apply to all types of modifications in people, we had better use a word like "change" to keep our thinking general enough.

The proposal that social technology may be employed to solve the problems of society suggests that social science may be applied in ways not different from those used in the physical sciences. Does social science, in fact, have any practically useful knowledge which may be brought to bear significantly on society's most urgent problems? What scientifically based principles are there for guiding programs of social change? In this paper we shall restrict our considerations to certain parts of a relatively new branch of social science known as "group dynamics." We shall examine some of the implications for social action which stem from research in this field of scientific investigation.

What is "group dynamics?" Perhaps it will be most useful to start by looking at the derivation of the word "dynamics." It comes from a Greek word meaning force. In careful usage of the phrase, "group dynamics" refers to the forces operating in groups. The investigation of group dynamics, then, consists of a study of these forces: what gives rise to them, what conditions modify them, what consequences they have, etc. The practical application of group dynamics (or the technology of group dynamics) consists of the utilization of knowledge about these forces for the achievement of some purpose. In keeping with this definition, then, it is clear that group dynamics, as a realm of investigation, is not particularly novel, nor is it the exclusive property of any person or institution. It goes back at least to the outstanding work of men like Simmel, Freud, and Cooley.

Although interest in groups has a long and respectable history, the past 15 years have witnessed a new flowering of activity in this field. Today, research centers in several countries are carrying out substantial programs of research designed to reveal the nature of groups and of their functioning. The phrase "group dynamics" has come into common usage during this time and intense efforts have been devoted to the development of the field, both as a branch of social science and as a form of social technology.

In this development the name of Kurt Lewin has been outstanding. As a consequence of his work in the field of individual psychology and from his analysis of the nature of the pressing problems of the contemporary world, Lewin became convinced of society's urgent need for a *scientific approach* to the understanding of the dynamics of groups. In 1945 he established the Research Center for Group Dynamics to meet this need. Since that date the center has been devoting its efforts to improving our scientific understanding of groups through laboratory experimentation, field studies, and the use of techniques of action research. It has also attempted in various ways to help get the findings of social science more widely used by social management. Much of what I have to say in this paper is drawn from the experiences of this center in its brief existence of a little more than five years (2).

II

For various reasons we have found that much of our work has been devoted to an attempt to gain a better understanding of the ways in which people change their behavior or resist efforts by others to have them do so. Whether we set for ourselves the practical goal of improving behavior or whether we take on the intellectual task of understanding why people do what they do, we have to investigate processes of communication, influence, social pressure—in short, problems of change.

In this work we have encountered great frustration. The problems have been most difficult to solve. Looking back over our experience, I have become convinced that no small part of the trouble has resulted from an irresistible tendency to conceive of our problems in terms of the individual. We live in an individualistic culture. We value the individual highly, and rightly so. But I am inclined to believe that our political and social concern for the individual has narrowed our thinking as social scientists so much that we have not been able to state our research problems properly. Perhaps we have taken the individual as the unit of observation and study when some larger unit would have been more appropriate. Let us look at a few examples.

Consider first some matters having to do with the mental health of an individual. We can all agree, I believe, that an important mark of a healthy personality is that the individual's self-esteem has not been undermined. But on what does self-esteem depend? From research on this problem we have discovered that, among other things, repeated experiences of failure or traumatic failures on matters of central importance serve to undermine one's self-esteem. We also know that whether a person experiences success or failure as a result of some undertaking depends upon the level of aspiration which he has set for himself. Now, if we try to discover how the level of aspiration gets set, we are immediately involved in the person's relationships to groups. The groups to which he belongs set standards for his behavior which he must accept if he is to remain in the group. If his capacities do not allow him to reach these standards, he experiences failure, he withdraws or is rejected by the group and his self-esteem suffers a shock.

Suppose, then, that we accept a task of therapy, of rebuilding his self-esteem. It would appear plausible from our analysis of the problem that we should attempt to work with variables of the same sort that produced the difficulty, that is to work with him either in the groups to which he now belongs or to introduce him into new groups which are selected for the purpose and to work upon his relationships to groups as such. From the point of view of preventive mental health, we might even attempt to train the groups in our communities— classes in schools, work groups in business, families, unions, religious and cultural groups—to make use of practices better designed to protect the self-esteem of their members.

Consider a second example. A teacher finds that in her class she has a number of troublemakers, full of aggression. She wants to know why these children are so aggressive and what can be done about it. A foreman in a factory has the same kind of problem with some of his workers. He wants the same kind of help. The solution most tempting to both the teacher and the foreman often is to transfer the worst troublemakers to someone else, or if facilities are available, to refer them for counselling. But is the problem really of such a nature that it can be solved by removing the troublemaker from the situation or by working on his individual motivations and emotional life? What leads does research give us? The evidence indicates, of course, that there are many causes of aggressiveness in people, but one aspect of the problem has become increasingly clear in recent years. If we observe carefully the amount of aggressive behavior and the number of troublemakers to be found in a large collection of groups, we find that these characteristics can vary tremendously from group to group even when the different groups are composed essentially of the same kinds of people. In the now classic experiments of Lewin, Lippitt, and White (7) on the effects of different styles of leadership, it was found that the same group of children displayed markedly different levels of aggressive behavior when under different styles of leadership. Moreover, when individual children were transferred from one group to another, their levels of aggressiveness shifted to conform to the atmosphere of the new group. Efforts to account for one child's aggressiveness under one style of leadership merely in terms of his personality traits could hardly succeed under these conditions. This is not to say that a person's behavior is entirely to be accounted for by the atmosphere and structure of the immediate group, but it is remarkable to what an extent a strong, cohesive group can control aspects of a member's behavior traditionally thought to be expressive of enduring personality traits. Recognition of this fact rephrases the problem of how to change such behavior. It directs us to a study of the sources of the influence of the group on its members.

Let us take an example from a different field. What can we learn from our efforts to change people by mass media and mass persuasion? In those rare instances when educators, propagandists, advertisers, and others who want to influence large numbers of people, have bothered to make an objective evaluation of the enduring changes produced by their efforts, they have been able to demonstrate only the most negligible effects (1). The inefficiency of attempts to influence the public by mass media would be scandalous if there were agreement that it was important or even desirable to have such influences strongly exerted. In fact, it is no exaggeration to say that all of the research and experience of generations has not improved the efficiency of lectures or other means of mass influence to any noticeable degree. Something must be wrong with our theories of learning, motivation, and social psychology.

Within very recent years some research data have been accumulating which may give us a clue to the solution of our problem. In one series of experiments directed by Lewin, it was found that a method of group decision, in which the group as a whole made a decision to have its members change their behavior, was from two to ten times as effective in producing actual change as was a lecture presenting exhortation to change (6). We have yet to learn precisely what produces these differences of effectiveness, but it is clear that by introducing group forces into the situation a whole new level of influence has been achieved.

The experience has been essentially the same when people have attempted to increase the productivity of individuals in work settings. Traditional conceptions of how to increase the output of workers have stressed the individual: select the right man for the job; simplify the job for him; train him in the skills required; motivate him by economic incentives; make it clear to whom he reports; keep the lines of authority and responsibility simple and straight. But even when all these conditions are fully met we are finding that productivity is far below full potential. There is even good reason to conclude that this individualistic conception of the determinants of productivity actually fosters negative consequences. The individual, now isolated and subjected to the demands of the organization through the commands of his boss, finds that he must create with his fellow employees informal groups, not shown on any table of organization, in order to protect himself from arbitrary control of his life, from the boredom produced by the endless repetition of mechanically sanitary and routine operations, and from the impoverishment of his emotional and social life brought about by the frustration of his basic needs for social interactions, participation, and acceptance in a stable group. Recent experiments have demonstrated clearly that the productivity of work groups can be greatly increased by methods of work organization and supervision which give more responsibility to work groups, which allow for fuller participation in important decisions, and which make stable groups the firm basis for support of the individual's social needs (3). I am convinced that future research will also demonstrate the people working under such conditions become more mature and creative individuals in their homes, in community life, and as citizens.

As a final example, let us examine the experience of efforts to train people in workshops, institutes, and special training courses. Such efforts are common in various areas of social welfare, intergroup relations, political affairs, industry, and adult education generally. It is an unfortunate fact that objective evaluation of the effects of such training efforts has only rarely been undertaken, but there is evidence for those who will look that the actual change in behavior produced is most disappointing. A workshop not infrequently develops keen interest among the participants, high morale and enthusiasm, and a firm resolve on the part of many to apply all the wonderful insights back home. But what happens back home? The trainee discovers that his colleagues don't share his enthusiasm. He learns that the task of changing others' expectations and ways of doing things is discouragingly difficult. He senses, perhaps not very clearly, that it would make all the difference in the world if only there were a few other people sharing his enthusiasm and insights with whom he could plan activities, evaluate consequences of efforts, and from whom he could gain emotional and motivational support. The approach to training which conceives of its task as being merely that of changing the individual probably produces frustration, demoralization, and disillusionment in as large a measure as it accomplishes more positive results.

A few years ago the Research Center for Group Dynamics undertook to shed light on this problem by investigating the operation of a workshop for training leaders in intercultural relations (8). In a project, directed by Lippitt, we set out to compare systematically the different effects of the workshop upon trainees who came as isolated individuals in contrast to those who came as teams. Since one of the problems in the field of intercultural relations is that of getting people of good will to be more active in community efforts to improve intergroup relations, one goal of the training workshop was to increase the activity of the trainees in such community affairs. We found that before the workshop there was no difference in the activity level of the people who were to be trained as isolates and of those who were to be trained as teams. Six months after the workshop, however, those who had been trained as isolates were only slightly more active than before the workshop whereas those who had been members of strong training teams were now much more active. We do not have clear evidence on the point, but we would be quite certain that the maintenance of heightened activity over a long period of time would also be much better for members of teams. For the isolates the effect of the workshop had the characteristic of a "shot in the arm" while for the team member it produced a more enduring change because the team provided continuous support and reinforcement for its members.

III

What conclusions may we draw from these examples? What principles of achieving change in people can we see emerging? To begin with the most general proposition, we may state that the behavior, attitudes, beliefs, and values of the individual are all firmly grounded in the groups to which he belongs. How aggressive or cooperative a person is, how much self-respect and self-confidence he has, how energetic and productive his work is, what he aspires to, what he believes to be true and good, whom he loves or hates, and what beliefs, and prejudices he holds—all these characteristics are highly determined by the individual's group memberships. In a real sense, they are properties of groups and of the relationships between people. Whether they change or resist change will, therefore, be greatly influenced by the nature of these groups. Attempts to change them must be concerned with the dynamics of groups.

In examining more specifically how groups enter into the process of change, we find it useful to view groups in at least three different ways. In the first view, the group is seen as a source of influence over its members. Efforts to change behavior can be supported or blocked by pressures on members stemming from the group. To make constructive use of these pressures the group must be used *as a medium of change*. In the second view, the group itself becomes the *target of change*. To change the behavior of individuals it may be necessary to change the standards of the group, its style of leadership, its emotional atmosphere, or its stratification into cliques and hierarchies. Even though the goal may be to change the behavior of *individuals,* the target of change becomes the group. In the third view, it is recognized that many changes of behavior can be brought about only by the organized efforts of groups *as agents of change*. A committee to combat intolerance, a labor union, an employers association, a citizens group to increase the pay of teachers—any action group will be more or less effective depending upon the way it is organized, the satisfactions it provides to its members, the degree to which its goals are clear, and a host of other properties of the group.

An adequate social technology of change, then, requires at the very least a scientific understanding of groups viewed in each of these ways. We shall consider here only the first two aspects of the problem: the group as a medium of change and as a target of change.

The Group as a Medium of Change

Principle No. 1. If the group is to be used effectively as a medium of change, those people who are to be changed and those who are to exert influence for change must have a strong sense of belonging to the same group.

Kurt Lewin described this principle well: "The normal gap between teacher and student, doctor and patient, social workers and public, can . . . be a real obstacle to acceptance of the advocated conduct." In other words, in spite of whatever status differences there might be between them, the teacher and the student have to feel as members of one group in matters involving their sense of values. The chances for reeducation seem to be increased whenever a strong we-feeling is created (5). Recent experiments by Preston and Heintz have demonstrated greater changes of opinions among members of discussion groups operating with participatory leadership than among those with supervisory leadership (12). The implications of this principle for classroom teaching are far-reaching. The same may be said of supervision in the factory, army, or hospital.

Principle No. 2. The more attractive the group is to its members the greater is the influence that the group can exert on its members.

This principle has been extensively documented by Festinger and his co-workers (4). They have been able to show in a variety of settings that in more cohesive groups there is a greater readiness of members to attempt to influence others, a greater readiness to be influenced by others, and stronger pressures toward conformity when conformity is a relevant matter for the group. Important for the practitioner wanting to make use of this principle is, of course, the question of how to increase the attractiveness of groups. This is a question with many answers. Suffice it to say that a group is more attractive the more it satisfies the needs of its members. We have been able to demonstrate ex-

perimentally an increase in group cohesiveness by increasing the liking of members for each other as persons, by increasing the perceived importance of the group goal, and by increasing the prestige of the group among other groups. Experienced group workers could add many other ways to this list.

Principle No. 3. In attempts to change attitudes, values, or behavior, the more relevant they are to the basis of attraction to the group, the greater will be the influence that the group can exert upon them.

I believe this principle gives a clue to some otherwise puzzling phenomena. How does it happen that a group, like a labor union, seems to be able to exert such strong discipline over its members in some matters (let us say in dealings with management), while it seems unable to exert nearly the same influence in other matters (let us say in political action)? If we examine why it is that members are attracted to the group, I believe we will find that a particular reason for belonging seems more related to some of the group's activities than to others. If a man joins a union mainly to keep his job and to improve his working conditions, he may be largely uninfluenced by the union's attempt to modify his attitudes toward national and international affairs. Groups differ tremendously in the range of matters that are relevant to them and hence over which they have influence. Much of the inefficiency of adult education could be reduced if more attention were paid to the need that influence attempts be appropriate to the groups in which they are made.

Principle No. 4. The greater the prestige of a group member in the eyes of the other members, the greater the influence he can exert.

Polansky, Lippitt, and Redl (11) have demonstrated this principle with great care and methodological ingenuity in a series of studies in children's summer camps. From a practical point of view it must be emphasized that the things giving prestige to a member may not be those characteristics most prized by the official management of the group. The most prestige-carrying member of a Sunday school class may not possess the characteristics most similar to the minister of the church. The teacher's pet may be a poor source of influence within a class. This principle is the basis for the common observation that the official leader and the actual leader of a group are often not the same individual.

> *Principle No. 5.* Efforts to change individuals or subparts of a group which, if successful, would have the result of making them deviate from the norms of the group will encounter strong resistance.

During the past few years a great deal of evidence has been accumulated showing the tremendous pressures which groups can exert upon members to conform to the group's norms. The price of deviation in most groups is rejection or even expulsion. If the member really wants to belong and be accepted, he cannot withstand this type of pressure. It is for this reason that efforts to change people by taking them from the group and giving them special training so often have disappointing results. This principle also accounts for the finding that people thus trained sometimes display increased tension, aggressiveness toward the group, or a tendency to form cults or cliques with others who have shared their training.

These five principles concerning the group as a medium of change would appear to have readiest application to groups created for the purpose of producing changes in people. They provide certain specifications for building effective training or therapy groups. They also point, however, to a difficulty in producing change in people in that they show how resistant an individual is to changing in any way contrary to group pressures and expectations. In order to achieve many kinds of changes in people, therefore, it is necessary to deal with the group as a target of change.

The Group as a Target of Change

> *Principle No. 6.* Strong pressure for changes in the group can be established by creating a shared perception by members of the need for

change, thus making the source of pressure for change lie within the group.

Marrow and French (9) report a dramatic case study which illustrates this principle quite well. A manufacturing concern had a policy against hiring women over 30 because it was believed that they were slower, more difficult to train, and more likely to be absent. The staff psychologist was able to present to management evidence that this belief was clearly unwarranted at least within their own company. The psychologist's facts, however, were rejected and ignored as a basis for action because they violated accepted beliefs. It was claimed that they went against the direct experience of the foremen. Then the psychologist hit upon a plan for achieving change which differed drastically from the usual one of argument, persuasion, and pressure. He proposed that management conduct its own analysis of the situation. With his help management collected all the facts which they believed were relevant to the problem. When the results were in they were now their own facts rather than those of some "outside" expert. Policy was immediately changed without further resistance. The important point here is that facts are not enough. The facts must be the accepted property of the group if they are to become an effective basis for change. There seems to be all the difference in the world in changes actually carried out between those cases in which a consulting firm is hired to do a study and present a report and those in which technical experts are asked to collaborate with the group in doing its own study.

> *Principle No. 7.* Information relating to the need for changes, plans for change, and consequences of change must be shared by all relevant people in the group.

Another way of stating this principle is to say that change of a group ordinarily requires the opening of communication channels. Newcomb (10) has shown how one of the first consequences of mistrust and hostility is the avoidance of communicating openly and freely about the things producing the tension. If you look closely at a pathological group (that is, one that has trouble making decisions or effecting coordinated efforts of its members), you will certainly find strong restraints in that group against communicating vital information among its members. Until these restraints are removed there can be little hope for any real and lasting changes in the group's functioning. In passing it should be pointed out that the removal of barriers to communication will ordinarily be accompanied by a sudden increase in the communication of hostility. The group may appear to be falling apart, and it will certainly be a painful experience to many of the members. This pain and the fear that things are getting out of hand often stop the process of change once begun.

> *Principle No. 8.* Changes in one part of a group produce strain in other related parts which can be reduced only by eliminating the change or by bringing about readjustments in the related parts.

It is a common practice to undertake improvements in group functioning by providing training programs for certain classes of people in the organization. A training program for foremen, for nurses, for teachers, or for group workers is established. If the content of the training is relevant for organizational change, it must of necessity deal with the relationships these people have with other subgroups. If nurses in a hospital change their behavior significantly, it will affect their relations both with the patients and with the doctors. It is unrealistic to assume that both these groups will remain indifferent to any significant changes in this respect. In hierarchical structures this process is most clear. Lippitt has proposed on the basis of research and experience that in such organizations attempts at change should always involve three levels, one being the major target of change and the other two being the one above and the one below.

IV

These eight principles represent a few of the basic propositions emerging from research in group dynamics. Since research is constantly going on and

since it is the very nature of research to revise and reformulate our conceptions, we may be sure that these principles will have to be modified and improved as time goes by. In the meantime they may serve as guides in our endeavors to develop a scientifically based technology of social management.

In social technology, just as in physical technology, invention plays a crucial role. In both fields progress consists of the creation of new mechanisms for the accomplishment of certain goals. In both fields inventions arise in response to practical needs and are to be evaluated by how effectively they satisfy these needs. The relation of invention to scientific development is indirect but important. Inventions cannot proceed too far ahead of basic scientific development, nor should they be allowed to fall too far behind. They will be more effective the more they make good use of known principles of science, and they often make new developments in science possible. On the other hand, they are in no sense logical derivations from scientific principles.

I have taken this brief excursion into the theory of invention in order to make a final point. To many people "group dynamics" is known only for the social inventions which have developed in recent years in work with groups. Group dynamics is often thought of as certain techniques to be used with groups. Role-playing, buzz groups, process observers, post-meeting reaction sheets, and feedback of group observations are devices popularly associated with the phrase "group dynamics." I trust that I have been able to show that group dynamics is more than a collection of gadgets. It certainly aspires to be a science as well as a technology.

This is not to underplay the importance of these inventions nor of the function of inventing. As inventions they are all mechanisms designed to help accomplish important goals. How effective they are will depend upon how skillfully they are used and how appropriate they are to the purposes to which they are put. Careful evaluative research must be the ultimate judge of their usefulness in comparison with alternative inventions. I believe that the principles enumerated in this paper indicate some of the specifications that social inventions in this field must meet.

References

Cartwright, D. ''Some Principles of Mass Persuasion: Selected Findings of Research on the Sale of United States War Bonds.'' *Human Relations* 2 (1949), pp. 253–67.

Cartwright, D. *The Research Center for Group Dynamics: A Report of Five Years' Activities and a View of Future Needs*. Ann Arbor, Mich.: Institute for Social Research, 1950.

Coch, L., and French, J. R. P., Jr. ''Overcoming Resistance to Change.'' *Human Relations* 1 (1948), pp. 512–32.

Festinger, L., et al. *Theory and Experiment in Social Communication*. Collected papers. Ann Arbor: Institute for Social Research, 1950.

Lewin, K. *Resolving Social Conflicts*. New York: Harper & Row, 1948.

Lewin, K. *Field Theory in Social Science*. New York: Harper & Row, 1951, pp. 229–36.

Lewin, K.; R. Lippitt; and R. K. White. ''Patterns of Aggressive Behavior in Experimentally Created 'Social Climates'.'' *Journal of Social Psychology* 10 (1939), pp. 271–99.

Lippitt, R. *Training in Community Relations*. New York: Harper & Row, 1949.

Marrow, A. J., and J. R. P. French, Jr. ''Changing a Stereotype in Industry.'' *Journal of Social Issues* 1, no. 3 (1945), pp. 33–37.

Newcomb, T. M. ''Autistic Hostility and Social Reality.'' *Human Relations* 1 (1947), pp. 69–86.

Polansky, N.; R. Lippitt; and F. Redl. ''An Investigation of Behavioral Contagion in Groups.'' *Human Relations* 3 (1950), pp. 319–48.

Preston, M. G., and R. K. Heintz. ''Effects of Participatory versus Supervisory Leadership on Group Judgment.'' *Journal of Abnormal and Social Psychology* 44 (1949), pp. 345–55.

Reading 11

FUNCTIONAL ROLES OF GROUP MEMBERS

Kenneth D. Benne and Paul Sheats

The Relative Neglect of Member Roles in Group Training

Efforts to improve group functioning through training have traditionally emphasized the training of group leadership. And frequently this training has been directed toward the improvement of the skills of the leader in transmitting information and in manipulating groups. Little direct attention seems to have been given to the training of group members in the membership roles required for effective group growth and production. The present discussion is based on the conviction that both effective group training and adequate research into the effectiveness of group training methods must give attention to the identification, analysis, and practice of leader *and* member roles, seen as co-relative aspects of over-all group growth and production.

Certain assumptions have undergirded the tendency to isolate the leadership role from membership roles and to neglect the latter in processes of group training. (1) "Leadership" has been identified with traits and qualities inherent within the "leader" personality. Such traits and qualities can be developed, it is assumed, in isolation from the functioning of members in a group setting. The present treatment sees the leadership role in terms of functions to be performed within a group in helping that group to grow and to work productively. No sharp distinction can be made between leadership and membership functions, between leader and member roles. Groups may operate with

Source: Kenneth D. Benne and Paul Sheats: Reprinted with permission of *The Journal of Social Issues,* Spring 1948, pp. 41–49.

various degrees of diffusion of "leadership" functions among group members or of concentration of such functions in one member or a few members. Ideally, of course, the concept of leadership emphasized here is that of a multilaterally shared responsibility. In any event, effectiveness in the leader role is a matter of leader-member relationship. And one side of a relationship cannot be effectively trained in isolation from the retraining of the other side of that relationship. (2) It has been assumed that the "leader" is uniquely responsible for the quality and amount of production by the group. The "leader" must see to it that the "right" group goals are set, that the group jobs get done, that members are "motivated" to participate. On this view, membership roles are of secondary importance. "Membership" is tacitly identified with "followership." The present discussion assumes that the quality and amount of group production is the "responsibility" of the group. The setting of goals and the marshalling of resources to move toward these goals is a group responsibility in which all members of a mature group come variously to share. The functions to be performed both in building and maintaining group-centered activity and in effective production by the group are primarily member roles. Leadership functions can be defined in terms of facilitating identification, acceptance, development and allocation of these group-required roles by the group. (3) There has frequently been a confusion between the roles which members enact within a group and the individual personalities of the group members. That there are relationships between the personality structures and needs of group members and the range and quality of group membership roles which members can learn to perform is not denied. On the contrary, the importance of studies designed to describe and explain and to increase our control of these relationships is affirmed. But, at the level of group functioning, member roles, relevant to group growth and accomplishment, must be clearly distinguished from the use of the group environment by individuals to satisfy individual and group-irrelevant needs, if clear diagnosis of member-roles required by the group and adequate training of members to perform group-required roles are to be advanced. Neglect of this distinction has been associated traditionally with the neglect of the analysis of member roles in group growth and production.

A Classification of Member Roles

The following analysis of functional member roles was developed in connection with the First National Training Laboratory in Group Development, 1947. It follows closely the analysis of participation functions used in coding the content of group records for research purposes. A similar analysis operated in faculty efforts to train group members in their functional roles during the course of the laboratory.[1]

The member-roles identified in this analysis are classified into three broad groupings.

1. Group task roles. Participant roles here are related to the task which the group is deciding to undertake or has undertaken. Their purpose is to facilitate and coordinate group effort in the selection and definition of a common problem and in the solution of that problem.

2. Group building and maintenance roles. The roles in this category are oriented toward the functioning of the group as a group. They are designed to alter or maintain the group way of working, to strengthen, regulate and perpetuate the group as a group.

3. Individual roles. This category does not classify member-roles as such, since the "participations" denoted here are directed toward the satisfaction of the "participant's" individual needs. Their purpose is some individual goal which is not relevant either to the group task or to the functioning of the group as a group. Such participants are, of course, highly relevant to the problem of group training, insofar as such training is directed toward improving group maturity or group task efficiency.

Group Task Roles

The following analysis assumes that the task of the discussion group is to select, define and solve common problems. The roles are identified in relation to functions of facilitation and coordination of group problem-solving activities. Each member may of course enact more than one role in any given unit of participation and a wide range of roles in successive participations. Any or all of these roles may be played at times by the group "leader" as well as by various members.

a. The *initiator-contributor* suggests or proposes to the group new ideas or a changed way of regarding the group problem or goal. The novelty proposed may take the form of suggestions of a new group goal or a new definition of the problem. It may take the form of a suggested solution or some way of handling a difficulty that the group has encountered. Or it may take the form of a proposed new procedure for the group, a new way of organizing the group for the task ahead.

b. The *information seeker* asks for clarification of suggestions made in terms of their factual adequacy, for authoritative information and facts pertinent to the problem being discussed.

c. The *opinion seeker* asks not primarily for the facts of the case but for a clarification of the values pertinent to what the group is undertaking or of values involved in a suggestion made or in alternative suggestions.

---

[1] A somewhat different analysis of member-participations, in terms of categories used by interaction observers in observation of group processes in the First National Training Laboratory, is described in the *Preliminary Report* of the laboratory, pages 122–32. The number of categories used by interaction observers was "directed primarily by limitations of observer load."

d. The *information giver* offers facts or generalizations which are "authoritative" or relates his own experience pertinently to the group problem.

e. The *opinion giver* states his belief or opinion pertinently to a suggestion made or to alternative suggestions. The emphasis is on his proposal of what should become the group's view of pertinent values, not primarily upon relevant facts or information.

f. The *elaborator* spells out suggestions in terms of examples or developed meanings, offers a rationale for suggestions previously made and tries to deduce how an idea or suggestion would work out if adopted by the group.

g. The *coordinator* shows or clarifies the relationships among various ideas and suggestions, tries to pull ideas and suggestions together or tries to coordinate the activities of various members or subgroups.

h. The *orienter* defines the position of the group with respect to its goals by summarizing what has occurred, points to departures from agreed upon directions or goals, or raises questions about the direction which the group discussion is taking.

i. The *evaluator-critic* subjects the accomplishment of the group to some standard or set of standards of group-functioning in the context of the group task. Thus, he may evaluate or question the "practicality", the "logic", the "facts" or the "procedure" of a suggestion or of some unit of group discussion.

j. The *energizer* prods the group to action or decision, attempts to stimulate or arouse the group to "greater" or "higher quality" activity.

k. The *procedural technician* expedites group movement by doing things for the group—performing routine tasks, e.g., distributing materials, or manipulating objects for the group, e.g., rearranging the seating or running the recording machine, etc.

l. The *recorder* writes down suggestions, makes a record of group decisions, or writes down the product of discussion. The recorder role is the "group memory."

Group Building and Maintenance Roles

Here the analysis of member-functions is oriented to those participations which have for their purpose the building of group-centered attitudes and orientation among the members of a group or the maintenance and perpetuation of such group-centered behavior. A given contribution may involve several roles and a member or the "leader" may perform various roles in successive contributions.

a. The *encourager* praises, agrees with and accepts the contribution of others. He indicates warmth and solidarity in his attitude toward other group members, offers commendation and praise and in various ways indicates understanding and acceptance of other points of view, ideas, and suggestions.

b. The *harmonizer* mediates the differences between other members, attempts to reconcile disagreements, relieves tension in conflict situations through jesting or pouring oil on the troubled waters, etc.

c. The *compromiser* operates from within a conflict in which his idea or position is involved. He may offer compromise by yielding status, admitting his error, by disciplining himself to maintain group harmony, or by "coming half-way" in moving along with the group.

d. The *gate-keeper and expediter* attempts to keep communication channels open by encouraging or facilitating the participation of others ("We haven't got the ideas of Mr. X yet," etc.) or by proposing regulation of the flow of communication ("Why don't we limit the length of our contributions so that everyone will have a chance to contribute?", etc.)

e. The *standard setter* or *ego ideal* expresses standards for the group to attempt to achieve in its functioning or applies standards in evaluating the quality of group processes.

f. The *group-observer* and *commentator* keeps records of various aspects of group process and feeds such data with proposed interpretations into the group's evaluation of its own procedures.

g. The *follower* goes along with the movement of the group, more or less passively accepting the ideas of others, serving as an audience in group discussion and decision.

"Individual" Roles

Attempts by "members" of a group to satisfy individual needs which are irrelevant to the group task and which are non-oriented or negatively oriented to group building and maintenance set problems of group and member training. A high incidence of "individual-centered" as opposed to "group-centered" participation in a group always calls for self-diagnosis of the group. The diagnosis may reveal one or several of a number of conditions—low level of skill-training among members, including the group leader; the prevalence of "authoritarian" and "laissez faire" points of view toward group functioning in the group; a low level of group maturity, discipline and morale; and inappropriately chosen and inadequately defined group task, etc. Whatever the diagnosis, it is in this setting that the training needs of the group are to be discovered and group training efforts to meet these needs are to be defined. The outright "suppression" of "individual roles" will deprive the group of data needed for really adequate self-diagnosis and therapy.

a. The *aggressor* may work in many ways—deflating the status of others, expressing disapproval of the values, acts or feelings of others, attacking the group or the problem it is working on, joking aggressively, showing envy toward another's contribution by trying to take credit for it, etc.

b. The *blocker* tends to be negativistic and stubbornly resistant, disagreeing and opposing without or beyond "reason" and attempting to maintain or bring back an issue after the group has rejected or by-passed it.

c. The *recognition-seeker* works in various ways to call attention to himself, whether through boasting, reporting on personal achievements, acting in unusual ways, struggling to prevent his being placed in an "inferior" position, etc.

d. The *self-confessor* uses the audience opportunity which the group setting provides to express personal, non-group oriented, "feeling", "insight", "ideology", etc.

e. The *playboy* makes a display of his lack of involvement in the group's processes. This may take the form of cynicism, nonchalance, horseplay and other more or less studied forms of "out of field" behavior.

f. The *dominator* tries to assert authority or superiority in manipulating the group or certain members of the group. This domination may take the form of flattery, of asserting a superior status or right to attention, giving directions authoritatively, interrupting the contribution of others, etc.

g. The *help-seeker* attempts to call forth "sympathy" response from other group members or from the whole group, whether through expressions of insecurity, personal confusion or depreciation of himself beyond "reason."

h. The *special interest pleader* speaks for the "small business man", the "grass roots" community, the "housewife", "labor", etc., usually cloaking his own prejudices or biases in the stereotype which best fits his individual need.

The Problem of Member Role Requiredness

Identification of group task roles and of group building and maintenance roles which do actually function in processes of group discussion raises but does not answer the further question of what roles are required for "optimum" group growth and productivity. Certainly the discovery and validation of answers to this question have a high priority in any advancing science of group training and development. No attempt will be made here to review the bearing of the analyzed data from the First National Training Laboratory in Group Development on this point.

It may be useful in this discussion, however, to comment on two conditions which effective work on the problem of role-requiredness must meet. First, an answer to the problem of optimum task role requirements must be projected against a scheme of the process of group production. Groups in different stages of an act of problem selection and solution will have different role requirements. For example, a group early in the stages of problem selection which is attempting to lay out a range of possible problems to be worked on, will probably have relatively less need for the roles of "evaluator-critic", "energizer" and "coordinator" than a group which has selected and discussed its problem and is shaping a decision. The combination and balance of task role requirements is a function of the group's stage of progress with respect to its task. Second, the group building role requirements of a group are a function of its stage of development—its level of group maturity. For example, a "young" group will probably require less of the role of the "standard setter" than a more mature group. Too high a level of aspiration may frustrate a "young" group where a more mature group will be able to take the same level of aspiration in its stride. Again the role of "group observer and commentator" must be carefully adapted to the level of maturity of the group. Probably the distinction between "group" and "individual" roles can be drawn much more sharply in a relatively mature than in a "young" group.

Meanwhile, group trainers cannot wait for a fully developed science of group training before they undertake to diagnose the role requirements of the groups with which they work and help these groups to share in such diagnosis. Each group which is attempting to improve the quality of its functioning as a group must be helped to diagnose its role requirements and must attempt to train members to fill the required roles effectively. This describes one of the principal objectives of training of group members.

The Problem of Role Flexibility

The previous group experience of members, where this experience has included little conscious attention to the variety of roles involved in effective group production and development, has frequently stereotyped the member into a limited range of roles. These he plays in all group discussions whether or not the group situation requires them. Some members see themselves primarily as "evaluator-critics" and play this role in and out of season. Others may play the roles of "encourager" or of "energizer" or of "information giver" with only small sensitivity to the role requirements of a given group situation. The development of skill and insight in diagnosing role requirements has already been mentioned as an objective of group member training. An equally important objective is the development of role flexibility, of skill and security in a wide range of member roles, on the part of all group members.

A science of group training, as it develops, must be concerned with the relationships between the personality structures of group members and the character and range of member roles which various personality structures support and permit. A science of group training must seek to discover and accept the limitations which group training per se encounters in altering personality structures in the service of greater role flexibility on the part of all members of a group. Even though we recognize the importance of this caution, the objective of developing role flexibility remains an important objective of group member training.

Methods of Group Member Training

The objectives in training group members have been identified. Some of the kinds of resistances encountered in training group members to diagnose the role requirements of a group situation and to acquire skill in a variety of member roles have been suggested. Before analyzing briefly the methods used for group member training in the First National Training Laboratory, a few additional comments on resistances to member training may be useful. The problem of group training is actually a problem of retraining. Members of a training group have had other group experiences. They bring to the training experience attitudes toward group work, more or less conscious skills for dealing with leaders and other members, and a more or less highly developed rationale of group processes.

These may or may not support processes of democratic operation in the training group. Where they do not, they function as resistances to retraining. Again, trainees are inclined to make little or no distinction between the roles they perform in a group and their personalities. Criticism of the role a group member plays is perceived as criticism of "himself." Methods must be found to reduce ego-defensiveness toward criticism of member roles. Finally, training groups must be helped to make a distinction between group feeling and group productivity. Groups which attain a state of good group feeling often perceive attempts to diagnose and criticize their level of productivity as threats to this feeling of group warmth and solidarity.

1. Each Basic Skill Training group in the Laboratory used self-observation and diagnosis of its own growth and development as a primary means of member training.

a. Sensitization to the variety of roles involved in and required by group functioning began during the introduction of members to the group. In one BST group, this early sensitization to member role variety and role requiredness began with the "leader's" summarizing, as part of his introduction of himself to the group, certain of the member roles in which he was usually cast by groups and other roles which he found it difficult to play, even when needed by the group. He asked the group's help in criticizing and improving his skill in those roles where he felt weakest. Other members followed suit. Various members showed widely different degrees of sensitivity to the operation of member roles in groups and to the degree of their own proficiency in different roles. This introduction procedure gave the group a partial listing of member roles for later use and supplementation, initial self-assessments of member strengths and weaknesses and diagnostic material concerning the degree of group self-sophistication among the members. The training job had come to be seen by most members as a retraining job.

b. A description of the use of training observers in group self-evaluation sessions is given in the next paper in this issue. At this point, only the central importance which self-evaluation sessions played in member training needs to be stressed. Research observers fed observational data concerning group functioning into periodic discussions by the group of its strengths and weaknesses as a group. Much of these data concerned role requirements for the job the group had been attempting, which roles had been present, which roles had probably been needed. "Individual" roles were identified and interpreted in an objective and nonblaming manner. Out of these discussions, group members came to identify various kinds of member roles, to relate role requiredness to stages in group production and in group growth and to assess the range of roles each was able to play well when required. Out of these discussions came group decisions concerning the supplying of needed roles in the next session. Member commitments concerning behavior in future sessions also came out of these evaluations. These took the form both of silent commitments and of public commitments in which the help of the group was requested.

c. Recordings of segments of the group's discussion were used by most Basic Skill Training groups. Groups listened to themselves, diagnosed the member and leader functions involved and assessed the adequacy of these.

2. Role-played sessions in each group, although they were pointed content-wise to the skills of the change-agent, offered important material for the diagnosis of member roles and of role-requiredness. These sessions offered an important supplement to group self-diagnosis and evaluation. It is easier for members to get perspective on their participation in a role-played episode of group process than it is on their own participation in a "real" group. The former is not perceived as "real". The role is more easily disengaged for purposes of analysis and evaluation from the person playing the role. Ego-defensiveness toward the role as enacted is reduced. Role-playing sessions also provided practice opportunity to members in a variety of roles.

3. Practice by group members of the role of *observer-commentator* is especially valuable in developing skill in diagnosing member roles and in

assessing the role requirements of a group situation. In several groups, each member in turn served as observer, supplementing the work of the research observers in evaluation sessions. Such members worked more or less closely with the anecdotal observer for the group on skill-problems encountered. Practice opportunity in the *observer-commentator* role was also provided in clinic group meetings in the afternoon.

Summary

Training in group membership roles requires the identification and analysis of various member roles actually enacted in group processes. It involves further the analysis of group situations in terms of roles required in relation both to a schema of group production and to a conception of group growth and development. A group's self-observation and self-evaluation of its own processes provides useful content and practice opportunity in member training. Practice in enacting a wider range of required roles and in role flexibility can come out of member commitment to such practice with help from the group in evaluating and improving the required skills. Member training is typically retraining and resistances to re-training can be reduced by creating a non-blaming and objective atmosphere in group self-evaluation and by using role-playing of group processes for diagnosis and practice. The training objectives of developing skill in the diagnosis of group role requirements and developing role flexibility among members also indicate important research areas for a science of group training.

Reading 12

INTERGROUP PROBLEMS IN ORGANIZATIONS

Edgar H. Schein

The first major problem of groups in organizations is how to make them effective in fulfilling both organizational goals and the needs of their members. The second major problem is how to establish conditions between groups which will enhance the productivity of each without destroying intergroup relations and coordination. This problem exists because as groups become more committed to their own goals and norms, they are likely to become competitive with one another and seek to undermine their rivals' activities, thereby becoming a liability to the organization as a whole. The overall problem, then, is how to establish collaborative intergroup relations *in those situations where task interdependence or the need for unity makes collaboration a necessary prerequisite for organizational effectiveness.*

Some Consequences of Intergroup Competition

The consequences of intergroup competition were first studied systematically by Sherif in an ingeniously designed setting (Sherif, Harvey, White, Hood, & Sherif, 1961). He organized a boys' camp in such a way that two groups would form and would gradually become competitive. Sherif then studied the effects of the competition and tried various devices for reestablishing collaborative relationships between the groups. Since his original experiments, there have been many replications with adult groups; the phenomena are so constant that it has been possible to make a demonstration ex-

Source: Edgar H. Schein, *Organizational Psychology*, 3rd ed., 1980, pp. 172–80. Reprinted by permission of Prentice-Hall, Inc., Englewood Cliffs, N.J.

ercise out of the experiment (Blake & Mouton, 1961). The effects can be described in terms of the following categories:

A. What happens *within* each competing group?

1. Each group becomes more closely knit and elicits greater loyalty from its members; members close ranks and bury some of their internal differences.
2. The group climate changes from informal, casual, playful to work and task oriented; concern for members' psychological needs declines while concern for task accomplishment increases.
3. Leadership patterns tend to change from more democratic toward more autocratic; the group becomes more willing to tolerate autocratic leadership.
4. Each group becomes more highly structured and organized.
5. Each group demands more loyalty and conformity from its members in order to be able to present a "solid front."

B. What happens *between* competing groups?

1. Each group begins to see the other group as the enemy, rather than merely a neutral object.
2. Each group begins to experience distortions of perception—it tends to perceive only the best parts of itself, denying its weaknesses, and tends to perceive only the worst parts of the other group, denying its strengths; each group is likely to develop a negative stereotype of the other ("they don't play fair like we do").
3. Hostility toward the other group increases while interaction and communication with the other group decreases; thus it becomes easier to maintain the negative stereotype and more difficult to correct perceptual distortions.
4. If the groups are forced into interaction—for example, if they are forced to listen to representatives

plead their own and the others' cause in reference to some task—each group is likely to listen more closely to their own representative and not to listen to the representative of the other group, except to find fault with his or her presentation; in other words, group members tend to listen only for that which supports their own position and stereotype.

Thus far, we have listed some consequences of the competition itself, without reference to the consequences if one group actually wins out over the other. Before listing those effects, I would like to draw attention to the generality of the above reactions. Whether one is talking about sports teams, interfraternity competition, labor-management disputes, or interdepartmental competition as between sales and production in an industrial organization—or about international relations and the competition between the Soviet Union and the United States—the same phenomena tend to occur. These responses can be very useful to the group, by making it more highly motivated in task accomplishment, but they also open the door to group think. Furthermore, the same factors which improve intragroup effectiveness may have negative consequences for intergroup effectiveness. For example, as we have often seen in labor-management disputes or international conflicts, if the groups perceive themselves as competitors, they find it more difficult to resolve their differences, and eventually both become losers in a long-term strike or even a war.

Let us next look at the consequences of winning and losing, as in a situation where several groups are bidding to have their proposal accepted for a contract or as a solution to some problem. Many intraorganizational situations become win-or-lose affairs, hence it is of particular importance to examine their consequences.

C. What happens to the *winner*?

1. Winner retains its cohesion and may become even more cohesive.
2. Winner tends to release tension, lose its fighting spirit, become complacent, casual, and playful (the condition of being "fat and happy").
3. Winner tends toward high intragroup cooperation and concern for members' needs, and low concern for work and task accomplishment.
4. Winner tends to be complacent and to feel that the positive outcome has confirmed its favorable stereotype of itself and the negative stereotype of the "enemy" group; there is little motivation for reevaluating perceptions or reexamining group operations in order to learn how to improve them, hence the winner does not learn much about itself.

D. What happens to the *loser*?

1. If the outcome is not entirely clear-cut and permits a degree of interpretation (say, if judges have rendered it or if the game was close), there is a strong tendency for the loser to *deny or distort the reality of losing;* instead, the loser will find psychological escapes like "the judges were biased," "the judges didn't really understand our solution," "the rules of the game were not clearly explained to us," "if luck had not been against us at the one key point, we would have won," and so on. In effect, the loser's first response is to say "we didn't really lose!"
2. If the loss is psychologically accepted, the losing group tends to seek someone or something to blame; strong forces toward scape-goating are set up; if no outsider can be blamed, the group turns on itself, splinters, surfaces previously unresolved conflicts, fights within itself, all in the effort to find a cause for the loss.
3. Loser is more tense, ready to work harder, and desperate (the condition of being "lean and hungry").
4. Loser tends toward low intragroup cooperation, low concern for members' needs, and high concern for recouping by working harder in order to win the next round of the competition.
5. Loser tends to learn a lot about itself as a group because its positive stereotype of itself and its negative stereotype of the other group are disconfirmed by the loss, forcing a reevaluation of perceptions; as a consequence, the loser is likely to reorganize and become more cohesive and effective once the loss has been accepted realistically.

The net effect of the win-lose situation is often that the losers refuse psychologically to accept their loss, and that intergroup tension is higher than before the competition began.

Intergroup problems of the sort we have just described arise not only out of direct competition between clearly defined groups, but are, to a degree, intrinsic in any complex society because of the many bases on which a society is stratified. Thus, we can have potential intergroup problems between men and women, between older and younger generations, between higher and lower ranking people, between blacks and whites, between people in power and people not in power, and so on (Alderfer, 1977). Any occupational or social group will develop "ingroup" feelings and define itself in terms of members of an "outgroup," toward whom intergroup feelings are likely to arise. Differences between nationalities or ethnic groups are especially strong, particularly if there has been any conflict between the groups in the past.

For intergroup feelings to arise we need not belong to a psychological group. It is enough to feel oneself a member of what has been called a "reference group," that is, a group with which one identifies and compares oneself or to which one aspires. Thus, aspirants to a higher socioeconomic level take that level as their reference group and attempt to behave according to the values they perceive in that group. Similarly, members of an occupational group uphold the values and standards they perceive that occupation to embody. It is only by positing the existence of reference groups that one can explain how some individuals can continue to behave in a deviant fashion in a group situation. If such individuals strongly identify with a group that has different norms they will behave in a way that attempts to uphold those norms. For example, in Communist prison camps some soldiers from elite military units resisted their captors much longer than draftees who had weak identification with their military units. In order for the Communists to elicit compliant behavior from these strongly identified prisoners, they had to first weaken the attachment to the elite unit—that is, destroy the reference group—by attacking the group's image or convincing the prisoner that it was not a group worth belonging to (Schein, 1961). Intergroup problems arise wherever there are any status differences and are, therefore, intrinsic to all organizations and to society itself.

Reducing the Negative Consequences of Intergroup Competition

The gains of intergroup competition may, under some conditions, outweigh the negative consequences. It may be desirable to have work groups pitted against one another or to have departments become cohesive loyal units, even if interdepartmental coordination suffers. Often, however, the negative consequences outweigh the gains, and management seeks ways of reducing intergroup tension. Many of the techniques proposed to accomplish this come from the basic researches of Sherif, Blake, Alderfer, and others; they have been tested and found to be successful. The chief stumbling block remains not so much being unable to think of ways for reducing intergroup conflict as being *unable to implement some of the most effective ways*.

Destructive intergroup competition results basically from a conflict of goals and the breakdown of interaction and communication between the groups. This breakdown in turn permits and stimulates perceptual distortion and mutual negative stereotyping. The basic strategy of reducing conflict, therefore, is to locate goals which the competing groups can agree on and to reestablish valid communication between the groups. Each of the tactical devices that follows can be used singly or in combination.

Locating a Common Enemy

For example, the competing teams in a league can compose an all-star team to play another league, or conflicts between sales and production can be reduced if both can harness their efforts to helping their company successfully compete against another company. The conflict here is merely shifted to a higher level.

Bringing Leaders or Subgroups of the Competing Groups into Interaction

An isolated group representative cannot abandon his or her group position, but a powerful leader or a subgroup that has been delegated power not only can permit itself to be influenced by its counterpart negotiation team, but also will have the strength to influence the remainder of its home group if negotiation produces common agreements. This is the basis for ''summit meetings'' in international relations.

Locating a Superordinate Goal

Such a goal can be a brand-new task which requires the cooperative effort of the previously competing groups, or it can be a task like analyzing and reducing the intergroup conflict itself. For example, the previously competing sales and production departments can be given the task of developing a new product line that will be both cheap to produce and in great customer demand; or, with the help of an outside consultant, the competing groups can be invited to examine their own behavior and reevaluate the gains and losses from competition (Walton, 1969).

Experiential Intergroup Training

The procedure of having the conflicting parties examine their own behavior has been tried by a number of psychologists, notably Blake and Mouton (1962), with considerable success. Assuming the organization recognizes that it has a problem, and assuming it is ready to expose this problem to an outside consultant, the experiential workshop approach to reducing conflict might proceed with the following steps:

1. The competing groups are both brought into a training setting and the common goals are stated to be an exploration of mutual perceptions and mutual relations.

2. The two groups are then separated and each group is invited to discuss and make a list of its perceptions of itself and the other group.

3. In the presence of both groups, representatives publicly share the perceptions of self and other which the groups have generated, while the groups are obligated to remain silent (the objective is simply to report to the other group as accurately as possible the images that each group has developed in private).

4. Before any exchange has taken place, the groups return to private sessions to digest and analyze what they have heard; there is a great likelihood that the representatives' reports have revealed discrepancies to each group between its self-image and the image that the other group holds of it; the private session is partly devoted to an analysis of the reasons for these discrepancies, which forces each group to review its actual behavior toward the other group and the possible consequences of that behavior, regardless of its intentions.

5. In public session, again working through representatives, each group shares with the other what discrepancies it has uncovered and the possible reasons for them, focusing on actual, observable behavior.

6. Following this mutual exposure, a more open exploration is then permitted between the two groups on the *now-shared goal* of identifying further reasons for perceptual distortions.

7. A joint exploration is then conducted of how to manage future relations in such a way as to minimize a recurrence of the conflict.

Interspersed with these steps are short lectures and reading assignments on the psychology of intergroup conflict, the bases for perceptual distortion, psychological defense mechanisms, and so on. The goal is to bring the psychological dynamics of the solution into conscious awareness and to refocus the groups on the common goal of exploring jointly the problem they share. In order to do this, they must have valid data about each other, which is provided through the artifice of the representative reports.

Blake's model deals with the entire group. Various other approaches begin by breaking down group prejudices on an individual basis. For example, groups A and B, each proposing an alternative product (idea), can be divided into pairs composed of an A and a B member. Each pair can be given the assignment of developing a joint product that combines the best ideas from the A product and the B product. Or, in each pair, members may be asked to argue for the product of the opposing group. It has been shown in a number of experiments that one way of changing attitudes is to ask a person to play the role of an advocate of the new attitude to be learned (Janis & King, 1954). The very act of arguing for another product, even if it is purely an exercise, makes the person aware of some of its virtues which he or she can now no longer deny. A practical application of these points might be to have some members of the sales department spend time in the production department and be asked to represent the production point of view to some third party, or to have some production people join sales teams to learn the sales point of view.

Most of the approaches cited depend on a *recognition* of some problem by the organization and a *willingness* on the part of the competing groups to participate in some program to reduce negative consequences. The reality, however, is that most organizations neither recognize the problem nor are willing to invest time and energy in resolving it. Some of the unwillingness also arises from each competing group's recognition that in becoming more cooperative it may lose some of its own identity and integrity as a group. Rather than risk this loss, the group may prefer to continue the competition. This may well be the reason why, in international relations, nations refuse to engage in what may seem like perfectly simple ways of resolving their differences. They resist partly in order to protect their integrity—that is, save face. For all these reasons, the *implementation* of strategies and tactics for reducing the negative consequences of intergroup competition is often a greater problem than the initial development of such strategies and tactics.

Preventing Intergroup Conflict

Because of the great difficulties of reducing intergroup conflict once it has developed, it may be desirable to prevent its occurrence in the first place. How can this be done? Paradoxically, a strategy of prevention challenges the fundamental premise upon which organization through division of labor rests. Once it has been decided by a superordinate authority to divide up functions among different departments or groups, a bias has already been introduced toward intergroup competition; for in doing its own job well, each group must, to some degree, compete for scarce resources and rewards from the superordinate authority. The very concept of division of labor implies a reduction of communication and interaction between groups, thus making it possible for perceptual distortions to occur.

The organization planner who wishes to avoid intergroup competition need not abandon the concept of division of labor, but should follow some of the steps listed below in creating and handling the different functional groups.

1. Relatively greater *emphasis should be given to total organizational effectiveness* and the role of departments in contributing to it; departments should be measured and rewarded on the basis of their contribution to the total effort rather than their individual effectiveness.
2. *High interaction and frequent communication* should be stimulated between groups to work on problems of intergroup coordination and help; organization rewards should be given partly on the basis of help rendered to other groups.
3. *Frequent rotation of members* among groups or departments should be encouraged to stimulate a high degree of mutual understanding and empathy for one another's problems.
4. *Win-lose situations should be avoided* and groups should never be put into the position of competing for some scarce organizational reward; emphasis should always be placed on pooling resources to maximize organizational effectiveness; rewards should be shared equally with all the groups or departments.

Most managers find the fourth point particularly difficult to accept because of the strong belief that performance can be improved by pitting people or groups against one another in a competitive situation. This may indeed be true in the short run, and may even on occasion work in the long run, but the negative consequences described above are undeniably the product of the win-lose situation. Thus, if managers wish to prevent such consequences, they must face the possibility that they may have to abandon competitive relationships altogether and seek to substitute intergroup collaboration toward organizational goals. The more *interdependent* the various units are, the more important it is to stimulate collaborative problem solving.

Implementing a preventing strategy is often more difficult, partly because most people are inexperienced in stimulating and managing collaborative relationships. Yet observations of organizations using the Scanlon Plan not only reveal that it is possible to establish collaborative relationships, even between labor and management, but also that when this has been done, organizational and group effectiveness have been as high as or higher than under competitive conditions. Training in how to set up collaborative relations may be a prerequisite for any such program to succeed, especially for those managers who have themselves grown up in a highly competitive environment.

Reading 13

WHAT AN ORGANIZATION IS

Theodore Caplow

What an Organization Is

An organization is a social system deliberately established to carry out some definite purpose. It consists of a number of people in a pattern of relationships. The pattern is not entirely dependent on the particular persons who belong to the organization at a given time. The organization assigns a *position* to each of its members, and the incumbent of a position has a set part to play in the organization's collective *program*. Every organization has a program—a set of planned activities that can go well or badly. If they consistently go well, the organization thrives. If they go badly, it disappears or is restructured for another try. The manager of an organization is the person who has the primary responsibility for making its activities go well.

An organizational program always involves considerably more than one central activity. Whether the central activity is a production process, a game, a fight, or a ceremony, the organization must also maintain its internal structure, keep its members happy, and adapt to changes in the external environment. In addition, the manager of any organization has the peculiar and personal problem of establishing authority. In discussing problems, we will take that one up first, since unless the manager can keep the right to manage, the other parts of the managerial assignment quickly become irrelevant. The first chapter of this manual is about "Authority."

It does the organization little good, however, for the manager to establish authority unless that au-

Source: "What an Organization Is" from *Managing an Organization* by Theodore Caplow, copyright © 1983 by Holt, Rinehart and Winston, reprinted by permission of the publisher.

thority is used to hold the organization together and achieve its purposes. Holding the organization together does not imply that all members of the organization will have identical goals and agree about how to achieve them, but it does require them to agree sufficiently for the organization to pursue its collective goals in a unified way. This limited agreement results from continuous communication up, down, and sideways within the organization. Most of this communication flows through established channels, formal or informal, and is modified in predictable ways by these channels. All this is discussed in the second chapter, "Communication."

But communication is not an end in itself. It is a means of getting the organization's job done, which is, of course, what management is all about. A manager is someone who supervises the work of others and can, by his or her own actions, increase or diminish their productivity. In practice, there are two quite different modes of supervision—direct and indirect—and they call for somewhat different strategies. In addition to the problems of routine supervision, there are all sorts of special problems that appear in any division of labor and interfere with the efficiency or the effectiveness of a work group. These matters are considered in chapter three, "Productivity."

The belief that productivity and morale are necessarily correlated is part of the folklore of organization. Like most folklore, it contains a grain of truth. Sudden increases in productivity are likely to stimulate short-term improvements of morale, and vice versa. But the general relationship between productivity and morale is more complex. As empirical studies in diverse types of organization have shown, high morale often accompanies low productivity, and crises of morale may be brought about by rising productivity. There is always some significant relationship between the output of an organization and the emotions of its members, but the relationship is far too intricate to suggest that productivity and morale are interchangeable. The managerial policies that sustain morale are described in "Morale," the fourth chapter.

No organization, however limited its goals, can safely ignore the larger social systems from which it draws its people and its resources. Every organization attempts to control the external environment, but no matter how large, rich, or sacred it becomes, it cannot develop any real immunity to changes in the external environment. Some of these external changes are attributable to the organization's own activities; some result from long-term trends and can be anticipated in a general way; some are so surprising that they cannot be imagined until they have actually occurred. In a complex, modern society, this last category is nearly inexhaustible. The unanticipated effects of legislation, technology, political upheavals, moral fashions, migration and other forms of mobility; innovations in transportation, communication, and entertainment; the movement of prices, and the fluctuation of scarcities now guarantee a fairly adventurous history to even the most insulated and reclusive organizations, such as craft unions and boarding schools. The problem of adapting an organization to external change is particularly challenging because external changes not only affect the conditions under which the organization pursues its goals but may also transform the goals. The problems that arise in this way cannot be as neatly resolved as some of those discussed under other headings, but they are not hopelessly difficult, as we shall see in the final chapter, "Change."

These five topics—authority, communication, productivity, morale, and change—are the substance of this manual. We shall take them up in order, but before turning to the first topic I would like to draw your attention to some basic principles of management.

Basic Principles of Management

1. All human organizations resemble each other so closely that much of what is learned by managing one organization can be applied to managing any other organization. Every organization, for example, has a collective identity; a roster of members, friends, and antagonists; a program of activity and a time schedule to go with it; a table of organization; a set of formal rules partly contradicted by informal rules; procedures for adding and removing members; utilitarian objects used for organizational tasks; symbolic objects used in organizational rituals; a history; a special vocabulary; some elements of folklore; a territory; and a method of placing members within that territory according to their relative importance. Every organization has a division of labor that allocates specialized tasks to its members and a status order that awards them unequal shares of authority, honor, and influence.

2. Every organization—except the very smallest—is a cluster of suborganizations of varying sizes, which are organizations in their own right and have all of the features described above. Some suborganizations are departments of the parent organization; some are illegitimate factions of it; some are formally independent of it, like a union local in a factory, or attached to it temporarily, like an orchestra hired for a club dance. The important thing to remember about suborganizations is that their goals are never completely compatible with the goals of the parent organization. It is seldom possible to reform a suborganization for the benefit of the parent organization without encountering resistance. On the other hand, it is quite impossible to manage a large organization without occasionally offending, damaging, or destroying some of its suborganizations.

3. The problems of managing a large organization are similar to the problems of managing a small or medium-sized organization, if only because every large organization is run by a managerial oligarchy which is itself a small organization—there is no other way to do it. Problems of communication, data retrieval, and public relations are necessarily more complex in a large organization, but there are more people to help with them too. Running a large organization should not require more of your time and effort than running a small organization. If it does, something is probably wrong with the way your job is set up or with your personal style.

4. During any given interval in an organization's history, it will be growing, stable, or declining. Some organizations, such as business corporations, normally strive for growth but do not always achieve it. Some, such as exclusive clubs, attempt to avoid either growth or decline. Others, such as legislatures and baseball teams, have a fixed number of members, although the number of assistants and supernumeraries can vary. Still others, such as social movements past their peak, continue to operate for long periods of time while declining in size. The task of management is easiest in a growing organization because growth itself—whatever its real cause—is usually viewed as a sign of managerial success and because the input of new resources occasioned by growth can be used to pay for mistakes. Managing a stable organization is a more difficult task and calls for a finer adjustment of means and ends, careful decision-making, and alertness to the external environment. The management of a declining organization may be easy or hard, depending upon whether the decline is regarded as inevitable. In the face of an inevitable decline, standards of managerial performance may be low. In the case of a decline that is regarded as reversible, the task of the manager is always difficult and sometimes impossible.

5. Most organizations find it harder to satisfy one of their goals than others, for reasons beyond their control. When this is the case, the manager's success with the critical goal is the thing that matters, while the achievement of other goals is overlooked or taken for granted. Maintaining authority is critical, for example, in a prison or penitentiary; maintaining membership is what counts in a civic association; as director of a summer camp you are judged almost exclusively by whether you can keep up morale; as coach of a football team that can win all its games you need not worry about much else.[1] Thus, every type of organization tends to develop managers who are overspecialized in the accomplishment of one assignment and who minimize their other responsibilities until this neglect catches up with them in the shape of rebellion, schism, bankruptcy, or reform by outsiders.

6. Many organizations develop crises from time to time. An organizational crisis is a situation in which the priorities of management are forcibly rearranged by some unforeseen combination of circumstances. The qualities that you, as manager, are called upon to display in a crisis may be quite different from those routinely required. College presidents are called on for personal courage, prison wardens are asked to show Christian charity, long-term planners are compelled to make snap decisions. Skill and luck play equal parts in the management of crises. The skill can be practiced, but not the luck, so that while a few well-handled major crises may strengthen an organization and its leadership, a long series of crises will almost certainly ruin it. If you, as a manager, perceive your role as "putting out fires," then you are a poor manager and ought to be replaced by someone who attaches more importance to fire prevention. The fundamental procedures for preventing organizational crises are early detection and the rehearsal of drills that transform crises into routine problems.

---

[1] Some interesting evidence for the point made here is presented by David R. James and Michael Sorel, "Managerial Theory: Unmaking of the Corporation President," *American Sociological Review* 46, no. 1 (February 1981), pp. 1–18.

OD Interventions: An Overview

Part 3 is central to this volume because it includes fairly detailed descriptions of the OD interventions that tend to be the most used in contemporary OD practice. Team building, intergroup activities, survey feedback, and other interventions are described. Although diagnostic activities underlie all of these interventions, diagnosis is so fundamental that additional attention is paid to it.

The introduction to Part 3 first defines intervention, then looks at different ways of classifying interventions, and then looks at diagnosis as a special, but pervasive, kind of intervention in OD. A discussion of the essays in the Part 3 sections then follows.

A DEFINITION OF "INTERVENTION"

Argyris defines "intervention" as follows: "To intervene is to enter into an ongoing system of relationships, to come between or among persons, groups, or objects for the purpose of helping them."[1] More specifically related to OD, the term *OD interventions* refers to the range of planned, programmatic activities clients and consultants participate in during the course of an organization development program. Largely these are diagnostic and problem-solving activities that ordinarily occur with the assistance of a consultant who is not a regular member of the particular system or subsystem culture. However, many of the activities become absorbed by the client system as the process unfolds.

CLASSIFICATIONS OF OD INTERVENTIONS

There are a number of ways of classifying OD interventions, depending upon the dimensions one wishes to emphasize.[2] One classification method is based on the *type of*

---

[1]Chris Argyris, *Intervention Theory and Method: A Behavioral Science View* (Reading, Mass.: Addison-Wesley Publishing, 1970), p. 15.

[2]For a more detailed discussion of several of these dimensions, see Wendell French and Cecil Bell, *Organization Development: Behavioral Science Interventions for Organization Improvement,* 3rd ed. (Englewood Cliffs, N.J.: Prentice-Hall, 1984), chap. 9.

causal mechanism hypothesized to underlie the particular technique used. For example, feedback, which refers to receiving new data about oneself, others, or group dynamics, is assumed to have potential for constructive change if it is not too threatening. Techniques for providing more *awareness of changing organizational norms* are assumed to result in modification of behavior, attitudes, and values. *Increased interaction* and communication may effect changes in attitudes and behavior. Homans, for example, suggests that increased interaction leads to positive sentiments,[3] and Murphy refers to "tunnel vision" or "autism," which develops in individuals and groups in isolation.[4] *Confrontation,* a surfacing and addressing of differences in perceptions, values, attitudes, feelings, or norms, is assumed to help remove obstacles to effective interaction if handled in constructive ways. *Education* is designed to upgrade (1) knowledge and concepts, (2) outmoded beliefs and attitudes, and/or (3) skills, and has long been accepted as a change mechanism.

Depth of intervention is another useful dimension for classifying interventions. In an essay by Roger Harrison that appears in Part 7, interventions can be distinguished in terms of the accessibility of the data and the degree of individuality or self exposure involved. For example, we see a family T-group involving a work group and formal leader ("family" group) as a deeper intervention than a task-oriented team-building (problem-solving) workshop with such a group. The use of a collage may be a deeper intervention than an interview that includes general questions about how things are going in a unit.

A different approach to classifying OD interventions is provided by Robert Blake and Jane Mouton when they list the major interventions in terms of their *underlying themes.*[5] They describe the following kinds of interventions: (1) a *discrepancy intervention,* which calls attention to a contradiction in action or attitudes that then leads to exploration; (2) a *theory intervention,* in which behavioral science knowledge and theory are used to explain present behavior and assumptions underlying the behavior; (3) a *procedural intervention,* which represents a critiquing of how something is being done to determine whether the best methods are being used; (4) a *relationship intervention,* which focuses attention on interpersonal relationships (particularly ones where there are strong negative feelings) and surfaces the issues for exploration and possible resolution; (5) an *experimentation intervention,* in which two different action plans are tested for their consequences before a final decision on one is made; (6) a *dilemma intervention,* in which an imposed or emergent dilemma is used to force close examination of the possible choices involved and the assumptions underlying them; (7) a *perspective intervention,* which draws attention away from immediate actions and demands and allows a look at historical background, context, and future objectives in order to assess whether or not the actions are still on target; (8) an *organization structure intervention,* which calls for examination and evaluation of structural causes for organizational ineffectiveness; and (9) a *cultural intervention,* which examines traditions, precedents, and practices—the fabric of the

[3]George C. Homans, *The Human Group* (New York: Harcourt Brace Jovanovich, 1950).

[4]G. Murphy, "The Freeing of Intelligence," *Psychological Bulletin* 42 (1945), pp. 1–19.

[5]Robert R. Blake and Jane Srygley Mouton, *The Managerial Grid* (Houston: Gulf Publishing, 1964), pp. 282–83.

organization's culture—in a direct, focused approach. These are largely process consultation interventions and they tend to occur within the context of a broader intervention, such as team building or in intergroup activities.

The *time and comprehensiveness* involved in the intervention can be another way of distinguishing between interventions. Some interventions, such as the use of a simple questionnaire, may take only minutes; others, such as the Role Analysis Technique may take two hours relative to one job incumbent. Team building of different varieties may be an intervention taking place over one to three or more days, and will include within it a variety of brief interventions. It should be added that successful interventions will probably always have a broader context; even the simplest of interventions needs to occur in the setting of some prework which serves to make the intervention acceptable to the client, and needs follow-up to maximize the odds of success.

Another way of classifying OD interventions, although somewhat spurious, might be in terms of the emphasis on *task* versus *process*. Some team-building activities, for example, may have a high focus on interpersonal and group processes such as the quality of communications or the dynamics of informal leadership and influence processes occurring in the group. Other activities might have a more task-related orientation such as goal setting or the reallocating of responsibilities. This dichotomy of task and process can be somewhat misleading, however, because they are highly interrelated.

Finally, another way of classifying OD interventions, and a way we will use, is in terms of the *size and complexity of the client group*. For example, the client group may consist of *(a) individuals, (b) dyads or triads, (c) intact work teams,* including the formal leader, *(d) intergroup configurations* (two or more interfacing units), or *(e) total organizations*. As we move from interventions with individuals, to dyads, to group, to intergroups and then to the total organization; the interdependencies and the number of dimensions to be concerned about obviously increases. For example, an intervention which is successful in dealing with two groups that are in conflict must also successfully deal with the intragroup communications problems and conflict that become manifest. That is one reason why assistance to teams in helping them with internal problems and in increasing their interpersonal and group skills is usually a wise step before intergroup activities are undertaken.

A simple classification scheme based on the size and complexity of the client group is shown in Figure 1. Some interventions appear in more than one category because they have utility with more than one type of client group. What the table does not show, of course, are the many "mini" interventions used by the OD consultant within the context of broader interventions like team building, or even within techniques used in team building, e.g., the Role Analysis Technique—that is, there are interventions within interventions. For example, this table says nothing about the consultant's ability to point out a discrepancy, or to provide support, or to clarify, or to use subgroups, or to have data made visible on newsprint, or, for that matter, to know when to use their interventions. (A number of these professional skills are discussed in Part 7.)

This classification scheme generally underlies the organization of Parts 3 and 4 of this book. However, we start with team interventions instead of with interventions focusing on individuals because we see team interventions as central and fundamental to OD. We then move on to intergroup activities, and then to comprehensive strategies. Individual interventions appear later and are viewed as largely supplemental to the OD process.

FIGURE 1   Typology of Interventions Based on the Size and Complexity of the Client Group

Client Group	Types of Interventions
Interventions designed to improve the effectiveness of *individuals*.	Life and career-planning activities. Role analysis technique. Coaching and counseling. T-group (sensitivity training). Education and training to increase technical skills, relationship skills, group process skills, or decision-making, problem-solving, planning, goal-setting skills. Grid OD phase1.* Transactional analysis.
Interventions designed to improve the effectiveness of *dyads/triads*.	Interviews or questionnaires. Process consultation. Third-party peacemaking. Grid OD phases 1, 2. Gestalt OD. Transactional analysis.
Interventions designed to improve the effectiveness of *teams and groups*.	Interviews or questionnaires. Team building. Family T-group. Survey feedback. Process consultation. Role negotiation subgrouping. Role analysis technique. Collages. "Start-up" team-building activities. Education in decision making, problem solving, planning, goal setting in group settings. Subgrouping.
Interventions designed to improve the effectiveness of *intergroup relations*.	Interviews or questionnaires. Intergroup activities. Organizational mirroring (three or more groups). Process consultation. Subgrouping. Third-party peacemaking at group level. Grid OD phase 3. Survey feedback.
Interventions designed to improve the effectiveness of the *total organization*.	Interviews or questionnaires. Sensing. "Confrontation" meetings (Beckhard). Subgrouping. Team building at all levels. Strategic planning activities. Grid OD phases 4, 5, 6. Survey feedback. OD strategy planning.

*For a discussion of the Managerial Grid® approach to OD, see Robert R. Blake and Jane Srygley Mouton, *Consultation* (Reading, Mass.: Addison-Wesley Publishing, 1976), chapter 27.

Source: Modified from Wendell L. French and Cecil H. Bell, Jr., *Organization Development: Behaviorial Science Interventions for Organization Improvement,* 3rd ed. (Englewood Cliffs, N.J.: Prentice-Hall, 1984), p. 131.

NOTES ON DIAGNOSIS

As is evident throughout this book, diagnostic activities are pervasive aspects of the collaborative action research model that underlies organization development. Basically, to diagnose is to identify the underlying forces or conditions giving rise to the present state of affairs. Diagnosis may pertain broadly to the present state of a system, including the many positive forces giving rise to desirable outcomes, or may be narrower in the sense of focusing on the dysfunctional forces that are producing undesirable outcomes, or may focus on changes in the state of the system over time.

Three Types of Theories

As Ronald Lippitt has stated, "Every consultant has a cluster of ideas, or a set of concepts, which guide his perception of 'what exists' and 'what is going on' when he comes in contact with a particular group or organization . . ." this *descriptive-analytic theory*, to whatever degree of refinement, assists the consultant in understanding and interpreting the complexities of group or organization functioning. Lippitt goes on to say that every consultant has, in addition, some form of *diagnostic theory* that assists in identifying symptoms of disturbances in the system and what some of the probable causes might be. A diagnostic theory, to Lippitt then, is a set of notions that relate more to the dysfunctional or anomalous aspects of organizational life than does descriptive analytic theory.[6] We might add that OD consultants also need some form of *change theory* that assists in understanding the consequences of the interaction of various forces over time. This would be congruent with Lippitt's ideas. Thus, organizational diagnosis stems from some theoretical base, however partially or completely formulated.

An illustration of a descriptive analytic theory (perhaps combined with a diagnostic theory) is the theory underlying the "Survey of Organizations" questionnaire developed by the Institute for Social Research at the University of Michigan. The Survey is based, as Taylor and Bowers describe, on a "metatheory of organizational system functioning" as presented by Rensis Likert and others in various writings. Part of the theory is represented by a model which includes the notions of causal variables, intervening variables, and end-result variables. Questionnaire categories and items are related to these broader concepts and to the underlying theory.[7]

Other Diagnostic Models

Other diagnostic models (partial representations of broader theories) that should be mentioned are John Seiler's "Elementary Framework for Diagnosing Human Behavior in

---

[6]Ronald Lippitt, "Dimensions of the Consultant's Job," in *The Planning of Change,* 1st ed., ed. Warren G. Bennis, Kenneth D. Benne, and Robert Chin (New York: Holt, Rinehart & Winston, 1961), p. 157.

[7]James C. Taylor and David G. Bowers, *Survey of Organizations* (Ann Arbor: Institute for Social Research, University of Michigan, 1972), pp. 1–6.

Organization''; Paul Lawrence and Jay Lorsch's ''differentiation and integration'' model; and Chris Argyris's model of Organizational Dynamics. Seiler's model[8] is somewhat similar to Likert's model and focuses on the interdependency of inputs (human, technological, social, and organizational), actual behavior (activities, sentiments, and interactions), and outputs (productivity, satisfaction, and development), and the notion of functional and dysfunctional patterns of behavior. In various works, Lawrence and Lorsch elaborate on the concepts of differentiation and integration and show how they can be related to creating more effective structural designs of organizations.[9]

The model by Argyris suggests that traditional organizational values tend to decrease authentic behavior and increase nonauthentic behavior. Nonauthentic behavior—including ''giving evaluation feedback about self and others,'' and ''projecting or denying one's attitudes, values, and feelings''—are seen as leading to a decrease in interpersonal competence, to conformity, mistrust, and dependence, and in turn, to decreased organizational effectiveness.[10] This model underlies a more detailed system of categories, such as ''owning up to behavior'' and ''openness'' which the consultant can use in collaboration with the client to observe and record behaviors that add to or detract from interpersonal competence and thus organizational effectiveness. While the use of these categories underlies much of Argyris's consultation and research with top executive teams,[11] Argyris also recommends that the consultant obtain a much broader range of data about the total system. Some of these categories include ''the present level of self-awareness,'' ''the existence of informal activities such as absenteeism turnover, trade unionism, apathy . . . ,'' etc.[12]

Dimensions to Consider in Diagnosis

In addition to the importance of the consultant having descriptive, analytic, and diagnostic theories, a number of other dimensions of diagnosis are important for the consultant to consider. A description of eight such dimensions follows.

Timing of the diagnostic activities is a significant dimension. To give an example from an area that is not strictly OD (in Part 5 we will discuss some dimensions that we believe useful in differentiating OD interventions from non-OD interventions), it is one thing to collect and analyze data about repetitiveness in jobs after it has been decided to launch a job enrichment effort, but quite another to collect and analyze data about job repeti-

---

[8]John A. Seiler, *Systems Analysis in Organizational Behavior* (Homewood, Ill.: Richard D. Irwin, 1967).

[9]P. R. Lawrence and J. W. Lorsch, *Organization and Environment: Managing Differentiation and Integration* (Boston: Division of Research, Harvard Graduate School of Business Administration, 1967); and Gene W. Dalton, Paul R. Lawrence, and Jay W. Lorsch, *Organizational Structure and Design* (Homewood, Ill.: Richard D. Irwin, 1970).

[10]Chris Argyris, *Interpersonal Competence and Organizational Effectiveness* (Homewood, Ill.: Dorsey Press, 1962), p. 43.

[11]See Chris Argyris, *Management and Organizational Development: The Path From XA to YB* (New York: McGraw-Hill, 1971); and Chris Argyris, *Behind the Front Page* (San Francisco: Jossey-Bass, 1974).

[12]Chris Argyris, *Intervention Theory and Method: A Behavioral Science View* (Reading, Mass.: Addison-Wesley Publishing, 1970), pp. 284–91.

tiveness and other factors *before* a job enrichment program is prescribed. In the latter instance, it might develop that job enrichment was not the appropriate prescription for the situation. The field of OD is not, of course, immune from the possibility of inadequate early diagnosis. To illustrate, while early and periodic diagnosis is a fundamental aspect of OD, it is quite possible to begin systematic data gathering with insufficient preliminary diagnosis of the relevancy of OD. It is unlikely that extensive data gathering as to the state of the system would do much harm; a case can be made for the wisdom of periodically taking a reading on the state of organizational health. On the other hand, much time (and therefore resources) can be wasted if organizational participants are not prepared to work with the data. It is also important for diagnostic activities to reoccur periodically during an improvement program in order to assess what changes are occurring in the system.

Extent of participation is a key aspect of diagnosis. Who, in a preliminary way, decided that diagnosis should take place? Who decided how it should be done? Which people were systematically involved in supplying data, and further, in analyzing and describing the dynamics revealed by the data? One person? Two people? The top team? The top team plus others? One or more people in conjunction with a consultant? All of the members of the system or subsystem? Customers of the system? One of the underlying assumptions in OD is the efficacy of participative problem identification and diagnosis in contrast to unilateral problem identification and diagnosis.

The dimension of *confidentiality,* or individual-anonymous versus group surfacing of data, has important facets. In the early stages of an OD effort, when trust between group members may be low and their feedback skills inadequate, the situation may call for individual interviews with responses kept anonymous and only reported to the group in terms of themes. As trust is earned and grows, people can become more open in terms of surfacing attitudes, feelings, and perceptions about organizational dynamics in group settings.

The degree to which there was *preselection of variables versus an emergent selection of variables* to be considered is another important dimension. The University of Michigan version of survey feedback utilizes the questionnaire, "Survey of Organizations," which taps some 19 dimensions subsumed under three broad categories: leadership, organizational climate, and satisfaction. Another approach, Grid OD, depends heavily in early phases on an analysis of leadership style using a questionnaire called the "Managerial Grid." This analysis focuses on two dimensions: concern for people, and concern for production. On the other hand, data gathering can be more emergent with less structuring of questions. Some OD consultants will use interviews which are structured only to the extent that two or three general questions are asked at the outset such as: What things are going well in the organization? What problems do you see? Follow-up probes are then used to pursue important issues uncovered.

The extent to which data gathering and analysis are isolated events in contrast to being part of a long-range strategy is also important. One usual assumption in OD efforts is that diagnostic activities should be part of an overall plan. Diagnostic activities lead to action programs that in turn call for diagnostic activities—this is the action research model. Diagnostic activities that are not part of any such plan or that are prompted by someone's whim to know "what they are thinking" may produce resentment and resistance and can seriously hinder attempts to get valid data from system members.

The nature of the target population in both preliminary and later systematic data gathering and analysis is also a key dimension. The size and nature of the target group can affect the acceptability of the diagnostic process, what kinds of interdependencies can be examined, and what kinds of issues can be worked successfully. The data-providing group can be different from the data-analyzing group, of course, but in OD, suppliers of the information usually work with their own data in intact work teams.

The type of technique used obviously has a number of important ramifications. By type we mean questionnaire-versus-interview techniques, individual-versus-group surfacing of data, or other categories of techniques that can be differentiated in major ways. We have already discussed how the type of instrument, such as the Survey of Organizations, can structure the responses. As another example of the importance of technique selection, an interview can be used for trust building as well as collecting data; a face-to-face conversation is a better vehicle for building a relationship than sending someone a questionnaire. Concerns can be expressed and responded to, questions can be answered, assurances can be provided as to how the data will be used, etc. As another example of the importance of the type of technique selected, giving diagnostic assignments to subgroups in a workshop setting can be a powerful diagnostic technique. But the way these groups are constituted—for example, heterogeneous versus homogeneous in terms of rank, position, or aggressiveness-reticence—can be crucial to the amount and candor of the data generated.

Finally, the *depth of the diagnostic intervention* is a dimension of major importance to constructive diagnosis. Gathering data can be a powerful intervention in itself, and professional judgment must be exercised as to the depth of the data gathering in terms of its proximity to self and the accessibility of the data. Since an essay by Roger Harrison in Part 7 will treat this dimension in detail, we will not elaborate here.

A. Diagnostic Activities: Data Gathering and Data Analysis

The first selection, by Jack Fordyce and Raymond Weil, briefly describes a number of methods for data collection, ranging from questionnaires to more projective methods such as drawings and physical representations of organizations. Some limitations and operating hints of each method are included. While we will not analyze this essay in detail in terms of the depth of intervention represented by particular techniques, the reader will be aware that collages, drawings, and physical representations are, to some extent, projective devices and must be used with caution and great care. They are, Fordyce and Weil say, "highly confronting."

The second essay in this section, by Richard Beckhard, focuses on a much broader area than diagnosis, but was selected because of its overall excellence and because it illustrates a number of the dimensions of diagnosis described above. In Beckhard's selection we see the involvement of several levels of the total management group in data gathering in a one-day workshop setting. Heterogeneous subgroups generate data which are reported as a group product on newsprint to the total group; and grouping by functional work teams occurs later in the day. By and large, the diagnosis is emergent in that the first task of the subgroups in quite open-ended; e.g., "What different conditions, if any, would make the organization more effective and make life in the organization better?"

The essay by Marvin Weisbord presents a model for use in organizational diagnosis. Six categories of phenomena are presented which consultants can use in looking for potential sources of trouble in organizational functioning. Weisbord diagrams these as interrelated boxes on a chart and stresses that sources of trouble can occur both within and between these categories.

A diagnostic technique not included in this book because of space limitations is "Force Field Analysis." This is a diagnostic technique stemming from Kurt Lewin's works that is highly congruent with the notions about systems and change which underlie organization development.[1] Basically, the technique involves identifying the forces driving toward a

---

[1] Kurt Lewin, *Field Theory in Social Science: Selected Theoretical Papers* (New York: Harper & Row, 1951), chap. VIII ("Psychological Ecology," written in 1943).

desired condition and the forces restraining movement in that direction.[2] Force Field Analysis, while not a complete problem-solving model, has considerable utility in some team building/group problem-solving sessions. If used when relevant to the particular problem under review and in a group having present the key people who are most closely related to the problem or to its solution, it can be a highly useful tool. It also highlights a way of thinking or frame of reference for organizational analysis.

---

[2]David H. Jenkins, "Social Engineering in Educational Change: An Outline of Method," *Progressive Education,* May 1949, pp. 193–97.

Reading 14

METHODS FOR FINDING OUT
WHAT'S GOING ON

Jack K. Fordyce and Raymond Weil

This section contains seven basic methods for collecting information. They include:

- Questionnaires and Instruments
- Interviewing
- Sensing
- Polling
- Collages
- Drawings
- Physical Representation of Organizations

The methods are ranked in order of degree of confrontation. Thus Questionnaires are generally relatively impersonal because the source of the information is not publicly revealed, while Physical Representations (in which, for example, participants literally position themselves according to degree of influence) are highly confronting.

As a rule of thumb, the more confronting the method, the richer the response and the stronger the impulse to change. But groups vary considerably in their readiness to work with intimate methods.

Another important method for collecting information is Subgrouping. However, Subgrouping has more general uses and consequently it is described in the section on Methods for Better Meetings.

1. Questionnaires and Instruments

Questionnaires are an old standby for detecting opinion and sentiment. We send out questionnaires to customers, production workers, the professional staff, constituents, television and movie viewers,

Source: Jack K. Fordyce and Raymond Weil, *Managing with People*, 2nd ed. (Reading, Mass.: Addison-Wesley Publishing, 1979), pp. 143–58. Reprinted with permission.

lower levels of management, people who sojourn at motels and ride in planes, and others.

Unfortunately, traditional questionnaires have often been disappointing as a means of bringing about significant change within organizations. They do not create the kind of personal involvement and discussion that is so valuable in changing hearts and minds. The information garnered by questionnaires tends to be canned, anonymous, ambiguous, and detached—cool data rather than hot. The replies may be interesting but they lack punch. It is too easy to hold them at arm's length, put them off until another day, or take token action. And the questionnaire asks the person only what *we* want to know, not what he or she thinks we should know. You might say a filled-out questionnaire amounts to half a conversation. The employee opinion questionnaire is regarded by many as a device that some managements use to avoid coming to grips with strong opinions and sentiments.

Nevertheless, to our mind the questionnaire can be useful when it is developed jointly by the manager and representatives of the population to be canvassed.

The *instrument* as used in organization development is similar to the questionnaire, with the important addition that it is constructed around a theory of management in such manner as to help the respondent understand the theory and rate himself or herself or the organization in terms of that theory. Thus in ''Grid Organization Development,'' the manager answers questions which help to place himself or herself in the grid model of management styles. Others in the group rate the manager too. In this manner, instruments are a means by which a group can collect information from itself about itself. This information then provides the starting point for feedback and confrontation within the group.

Uses

As a primary vehicle for learning in one complete system of organization development (Grid Organization Development).

To collect information as part of a specific, planned strategy of change, preferably jointly managed.

Instruments may be used by a group to collect information quickly about itself, as part of a diagnostic or team-building meeting. In this use, the instrument is the same as Polling except that the instrument is predesigned and may incorporate criteria for evaluation.

Benefits

Questionnaires and instruments are economical means for gathering information from a large population.

They lend themselves readily to legitimate statistical use.

Instruments are valuable for self-confrontation, for learning, and as stepping stones to interpersonal confrontations.

You can more readily afford to spend time and money on the quality of the questionnaires or instruments because the unit cost is low.

There is wide acceptance of these methods.

They reduce reliance on expert third parties.

Anonymity may bring to light previously undisclosed strong sentiment.

Limitations

Questionnaries and instruments produce findings which seem canned, a quality which is mitigated if they are used, as in Grid Organization Development, as a steppingstone to confrontation. The hazard is that the parties involved may merely imitate the motions of engaging with one another—shadowbox, so to speak.

One becomes too readily dependent on the questionnaire, pressing upon it (and thrusting away from oneself) a load it can't carry: direct human communication.

Operating Hints

Unless the objective is purely personal learning, be sure the questionnaire or instrument leads to real engagement among people. Make sure that those involved are really hearing one another well enough—both heart-to-heart and head-to-head—so that their communication may have consequences in constructive action.

2.   Interviewing

Before a team-building or similar meeting, it is common practice to interview the participants. The interviewer is generally a third party. The purpose of the interview is to explore ways in which the group can be more effective. The interviews uncover both positive and negative opinions and sentiments about a wide range of subjects—for example, clarify of individual and group goals, impact of the manager's style, and personal concerns that have never been aired.

The question should help the interviewee to express whatever is on his or her mind about life in the organization. Examples of general opening questions:

"How are things going around here?"

"What changes would you like to see?"

"How do you think this organization could be more effective? What do you feel it does best? Does poorly?"

The interviewer may also ask about management:

"How would you describe the management style of X? How do you think he or she could be more effective?"

Questions may also be asked about relationships within the organization:

"Whom do you like to work with most? Least?"

"Who is most influential in your organization?"

"Are you kept informed of what goes on?"

And about relationships with other organizations:

"When there are problems with other organizations, what can you do about them?"

"Can you give examples of unresolved issues with other organizations?"

"Do you think you could give them advice that would help them do a better job?"

Information from the interviews is fed back to the total group, usually at the beginning of the meeting.

Uses

Interviewing is a way to get private views and feelings out on the table. The information collected often furnishes the principal basis for the meeting agenda.

Benefits

The interview is an excellent way to probe for the problems and opportunities of the organization. Interviewing has the virtue of facilitating private expression. A sensitive interviewer can also invite ideas and emotions that the subject has not previously formulated in any conscious way. Interviewing also furnishes an occasion to develop trust between the third party and members of the organization; such trust is valuable in later work.

Limitations

A good interview often takes one to two hours. For a large organization, interviewing can therefore consume a lot of time.

Skillful interviewing runs the risk of turning up more information of a personal and perhaps threatening nature than the group is ready to

deal with. When confronted with the interview findings, the group may close up, reject the information, and attack the interviewers.

If the interviewer is clumsy or is not trusted as impartial, interviewing may worsen matters. Under these circumstances, it is best to gather information by open group process. (See methods 3–7 in this section.)

Operating Hints

There should be an understanding between the interviewer, the manager, and members of the team as to how the information will be used, especially with respect to protecting the privacy of sources. Normally, interviewees are promised that the information will be presented anonymously. The interviewer must keep that promise.

The information can be presented verbatim or thematically. The former has greater impact but does not protect privacy as well, and some data may be too hot for the group to handle. Thematically presented material has the opposite virtues: it's cooler, protects privacy better, has a softer impact. It is usually easily summarized, and hence easier to grasp.

One variation in reporting is to present themes and to back them up with supporting verbatim quotes.

If the findings are highly critical of the manager or another member of the group, it is advisable for the interviewer to disclose enough of the information to the manager in advance of the group meeting so that he or she will not feel ambushed.

Interviews may be carried out on an individual or subgroup basis, the latter having the obvious advantage of saving time. Interviewing of subgroups does not confer the same advantages of privacy and sensitivity, but the information disclosed tends to be of a character that the group is ready and willing to deal with. Moreover, the person who volunteers data in a subgroup interview normally feels committed to confirm it in a larger meeting.

A way to disseminate the interview findings is to type and distribute copies to all members of the group. Summary statements and corroborative information can then be posted on chart pads.

3. Sensing

Sensing is an organized method by which a manager can learn about the issues, concerns, needs, and resources of persons in any suborganization with which he or she has limited personal contact. It takes the form of an unstructured group interview and is usually tape-recorded. The recording may be then used to educate others.

Example

The general manager of an organization which employs 2000 wants to make an annual report to employees highly pertinent to their interests. To discover what subjects most concern them, the personnel manager schedules a series of meetings with a sampling of employees.

The personnel manager schedules four meetings, each two hours in length and each with a different group of 12 employees. To aid the general manager get a "feel" for people in all parts of the organization, the personnel manager selects the attendees as follows:

Group I—Nonsupervisory, shop and service, and technical and office employees.

Group II—Professional employees and staff specialists.

Group III—Supervisors.

Group IV—A diagonal cross section (i.e., one person from each organizational level; no one of the persons selected reports to any other).

Before scheduling the meetings, the personnel manager contacts the supervisor of each prospective participant. He or she explains the purpose of the meeting and the intention that no direct actions will ensue which might affect the supervisor or people who report to the supervisor.

Each meeting begins with a statement from the personnel manager who says that the general manager will arrive in half an hour. The personnel manager explains the general manager's purpose for the meeting and the hope that the conversation will be open and informal. The personnel manager suggests: "Suppose you board an airplane to Europe and you happen to find yourself sitting next to the general manager. What would you say?" The personnel manager also tells the group that, unless they object, to ease the burden of notetaking, the meeting will be tape-recorded. The general manager may also later use the tape as an aid to memory or to present illustrative excerpts to the division's top staff. If any member of the group prefers, the recorder will be promptly turned off now or at any time during the conversation.

During the meeting, the general manager spends most of the time listening, sometimes asking clarifying questions. The general manager also expresses his or her own thoughts and intentions regarding the various topics introduced.

Another Example

A manager has been hearing from outsiders that recently hired engineers in the organization are dissatisfied. To better understand the nature of their complaints, the manager asks the personnel manager to rearrange sensing sessions with several groups of engineers and a group of engineering supervisors.

Another Example

A third party uses the sensing procedure to make a quick assessment of the health of a company. He or she meets with four representative small groups from different parts of the organization, asking each group to discuss what is going well in the company and what needs to be changed. To avoid inhibiting the discussion, the third party does not record it but periodically stops the conversation and, in front of the group, dictates into the tape recorder a digest of what they have said. Then, with the recorder still running, he or she asks if they have been heard correctly and records their response. In a day's time, a 15-minute tape can summarize the four discussions. This tape is given to the top management group of the company.

If the consultant were collecting information for a team-building meeting, he or she might use a different question, such as: "The general manager and the division directors are going to hold an off-site meeting to work on improving their performance as a management team. What issues do you think they should take up?"

Uses

To collect information as part of a general diagnosis of the organization.

To learn the desires and agonies of a group that seems to be dissatisfied.

To learn how organization objectives are understood by diverse people within an organization.

To test a proposed course of action for its effect on various groups of people.

To collect information for a team-building meeting.

Benefits

The interaction of the group often produces rich information and ideas.

More economical than individual interviews.

May provide a quick glimpse of what's going on.

Allows for communication of impressions and feelings as well as opinions and ideas.

Provides a check on conventional and more formal communication channels.

Admits the rumble of humanity into the ivory tower.

Tapes from sensing sessions communicate more vividly to later listeners than second-hand transmission, written reports, or questionnaires.

Limitations

Won't work well unless the relations at various levels in the organization are basically trusting.

Is not as statistically rigorous or as economical as a questionnaire.

May be suspected as "snooping."

Success of the meeting is highly dependent on the manager's ability to listen effectively and on a willingness to engage with the members of the group in a personal way.

The meeting may fail to get at the attendees' real concerns because for one reason or another they are not willing to reveal them.

Operating Hints

Make sure that all intermediate supervisors understand the objectives and possible outcomes of the meeting so that they will not feel "spied upon." Be clear and explicit about the objectives of the meeting and what is to become of the information.

Notetaking may interfere with easy, informal discussion while the tape recorder is less likely to. But tape-record the session only if the group is willing. Be explicit about how the tape will be used and make a commitment to control its use.

Don't try to use sensing as a substitute for maintaining effective communication channels throughout the organization, or to "get the boss's message across," or to reprimand or judge.

Allow about two hours (enough time for a comfortable discussion).

Provide some warm-up time with a third party, especially for people who have never seen the big boss.

Convene the session in a comfortable setting and one that is not strange or intimidating to the group. (Don't meet in the boss's office.)

Establish a single and limited objective for a given sensing session. Don't try to cover too much at once. Start the meeting in an open-ended way. This will permit individuals to express their viewpoints (e.g., ''How does it feel to work around here?'' or ''I'm interested in how things are going,'' rather than, ''Do you like the company benefits plan?'').

If the manager doing the sensing is a poor listener, include a third party who, by prearrangement, can intervene if the manager seems to be blocking the group's efforts to express itself.

Don't do a lot of sensing unless the groups sensed can see positive results coming from it. Overuse of sensing can be as bad as overuse of questionnaires. Sensing may be conducted by persons other than a key manager; for example, by a third party or someone from the personnel department.

4. Polling

Sometimes a group becomes uneasy with itself. The members may feel anxious, bored, or in some way out of tune with one another. Such conduct is a common symptom of a buried issue. The way out is to move the discussion to the unspoken agenda item. Polling is a way to reveal it. Or, in a more positive way, a group may wish to evaluate its current state as a prelude to action.

One approach is to poll the group on a question that calls attention to its present condition. The third party might float a tentative question and, with the help of the group, modify the question so that it becomes one that the group wants to deal with. The participants must also decide upon the procedure for conducting the poll.

Example

The group has been planning goals for improvement. At this time, the discussion is agreeable but lethargic. The third party suggests polling the group members on their optimism about whether they can agree upon and later achieve a goal involving significant change. The group consents. He or she suggests a procedure and draws on the chalkboard a scale of optimism:

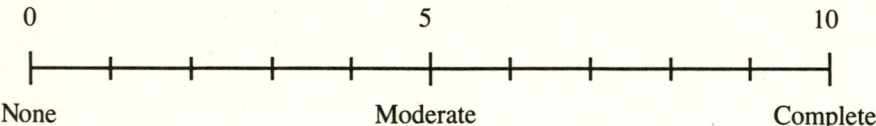

Each member is asked to assign a number to his or her degree of optimism. The third party will mark each response on the scale.

The responses cluster around 2½. Now the group members begin to comment on their pessimism, on their history of past failures at meeting their goals. They begin to analyze weaknesses in their methods of planning and execution of change. More than one member acknowledges a feeling of guilt at not having been able to subscribe to the manager's wishes, having done instead what seemed fitting and necessary.

The truth begins to sink in. As a group, they have a way to travel before they can plan realistic goals to which they will feel strongly committed.

Another Example

One person remarks that participation in the meeting has been uneven. Some have said little or nothing. Others have made important comments to which there was no response; perhaps they have not been heard. One or two have dominated the conversation.

The group determines to poll itself on this concern. The members will score one another (from 1 to 5) on two questions:

- Amount of participation?
- Quality of participation?

Each member writes a self-rating and a rating of the others with respect to the two questions. The

FIGURE 1

Raters

	John	Betty	Ted	Sam	Francis	Fred
John	②	1	1	1	2	1
Betty	5	⑤	5	5	5	5
Ted	4	5	③	4	4	5
Sam	2	1	2	①	2	2
Frances	1	2	1	1	③	1
Fred	1	1	1	1	1	②

Subjects

Circled numbers are self-ratings

results are presented to the group on grids, one grid for each question (See Figure 1). Following the poll, the group members agree on the need to police themselves better. They also decide to rotate responsibility for calling attention to weaknesses in future meetings.

Another Example

One member wonders aloud about how effective the group is as a team. The third party suggests that the members first decide upon the attributes of an effective team (in their situation) and then rate themselves on each attribute. The group now *develops its own* questionnaire, which is posted. Each member now marks his or her ratings (see Figure 2). Now the group members reflect on why the ratings came out as they did. They become specific about what they do well and what they do poorly as a team.

Another Example

The third party asks on what questions would the members like to know the position of the others. The group arrives at a set of questions:

- Should we do something about our relationship with organization X?
- Am I able to influence what goes on in this organization?
- Do I plan to leave this organization in the next two years?

Each member jots down a yes or no reply to each question, and then predicts the number of yes and no answers for the total group. The results are tabulated and posted on the wall (see Figure 3). The range of the *predictions* is an indicator of common understanding. The *actual count* starts the group working on some real problems.

FIGURE 2

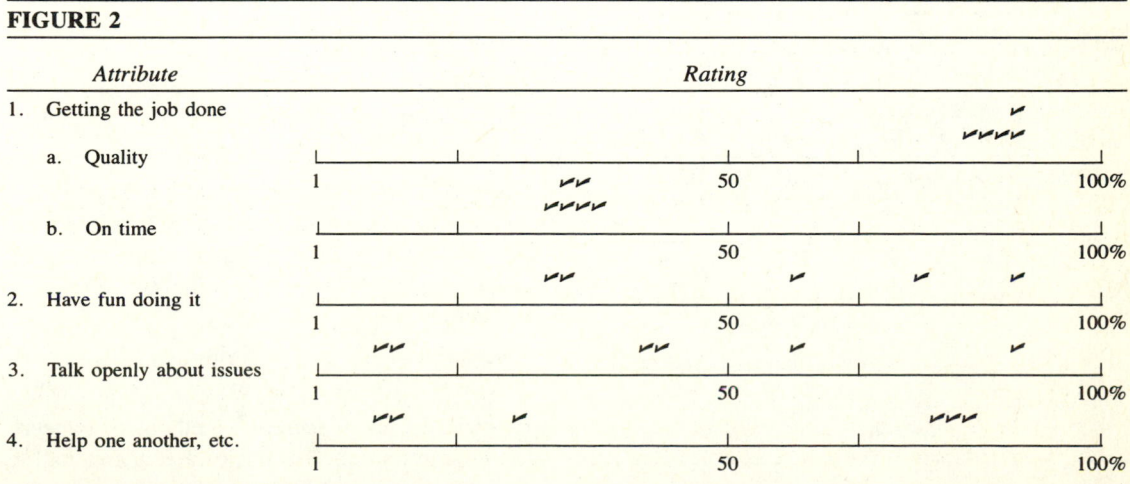

| Attribute | Rating |

FIGURE 3

	Actual Count		Predicted Count (range)	
Question	Yes	No	Yes	No
1. Organization X	5	5	3-8	2-7
2. Influence	3	7	1-4	6-9
3. Leaving, etc.	4	6	2-5	5-8

Another Example

After an effort lasting some period of time, the group has reached a fairly high level of trust and mutual helpfulness. However, one member is troubled by certain relationships among members, and feels the group has been avoiding the subject.

The third party invites each group member to pursue two questions:

- Which two persons in the group do I *like* working with the *most*?
- Which two persons in the group do I *like* working with the *least*?

The responses are collected on signed slips of paper and tabulated on a grid (see Figure 4). In the ensuing discussion, the group deals with the intensity of the choices, the reasons for them, and perhaps what sort of conduct can improve the relationships.

FIGURE 4

		Choosers				
	Jane	Frank	Nan	Mary	Ken	Mark
Jane		✔		X	X	X
Frank	✔		✔			✔
Nan	✔	✔		✔	✔	✔
Mary	X		✔		✔	
Ken		X	X	✔		X
Mark	X	X	X	X	X	

✔ = most   X = least

(left margin label: Chosen)

Uses

Polling is a quick way of bringing buried issues to light. Such issues may be of two types:

- Those which are interfering with the progress of a meeting.
- Chronic problems in the organization.

Benefits

Polling is fast, interesting, and simple. Anyone can devise his or her own questions and polling procedure.

The whole group takes part in the process and feels greater commitment to the results. It is an easy way to get issues out into the open, and a good way to move from general, inconclusive discussions to specifics that can be dealt with. It is a highly flexible method that can be improvised to suit the needs of the moment.

Limitations

The questions aren't as carefully thought out as those on professionally developed questionnaires, and they don't lend themselves to large groups. They are most useful in groups of 5 to 30.

Operating Hints

Don't rush into polling at your next meeting to suit *your* interests. The questions and the procedure must make sense to the group. If not, the responses won't be very useful, and other members will start wondering about *you*.

Group involvement is important for another reason. As the examples show, polls can touch people where they are quite sensitive. The group's OK to go ahead is the only evidence that they feel up to it.

If sensitive relationships are to be taken up, it's wise to have a competent third party present.

Be cautious about secretive methods of collecting information. An occasional secret ballot may be all right, but beware of raising issues which the group is unwilling to confront openly.

Once the questions have been answered, move the discussion to specifics as soon as possible. General discussions leave a lot of fog in the atmosphere.

5. Collages

Individuals, subgroups, or groups may be asked to prepare collages around a theme (e.g., "How do you feel about this team?", "How do you feel about yourself in this organization, and this organization in the company?", "What is happening to this organization and the team?"). Materials for the collage include large sheets of paper, magazines from which pictures and words may be clipped, crayons, felt pens, glue, scissors, etc. Each finished collage is then described for the total group by the individual or subgroup preparing it. If a single, large collage is prepared by the total group, it becomes the focal point for a total group discussion.

Uses

As an instrument for tracing the cultural and emotional topography of a group. The collage allows the members to express themselves to one another on a fairly deep, personal level. Common themes from collages tend to find their way onto group agendas.

Benefits

Collages can be quite effective in breaking the ice. Afterwards, the group may be more willing to deal with personal and interpersonal issues. Besides, they are fun to do.

When the group produces a large single collage, the members are apt to be proud of their accomplishment. The experience is unifying.

Limitations

Groups that are formal in behavior may resist what first appears to be a children's game.

As noted, collages are highly expressive. On the other hand, they may reveal little that is hard and specific.

Operating Hints

Lead boldly into the assignment to help the group overcome its resistance to this "child's play."

If they want, let the participants suggest the theme for the collage. Provide plenty of magazines and ample space, and be prepared to wind up with a cluttered room.

Suggest to the participants that they cut out any pictures or words which "ring a bell" without giving much thought to why they do so.

The time for preparing the collages should be approximately one-half hour to an hour and a half. Judge the time by whether the participants seem productively employed, but apply deadline pressure to discourage excessive deliberation.

Don't let the responses to the presentation turn into a game of interpretation. The object is to understand the presenter without putting words into his or her mouth and without awakening defensiveness.

The boss's collage should be presented last so as not to set the tone for others.

6. Drawings

One member of the group (or some, or all members) is asked to make a drawing about an aspect of the individual's life, or something about the nature of the organization. The drawings are made on large sheets of paper posted on the walls. The authors are then asked to discuss their drawings in the presence of the group. Members of the group may ask questions to clarify the author's intent. Common themes and problems, or significant differences of opinion, are then culled from the drawings and posted on chart pads. Here is an example of an instruction given to all members of a group:

Draw a circle for each person in the group, including your boss and your boss's boss. Make the circle proportionately larger for those individuals who seem to have greater influence over the way the group does its work.

Place the circles near or far apart, depending on how closely you feel those individuals must work together to get their job done. Label the circles with the names of the people.

With a blue line, connect those people who are personally close to one another. Connect with a red line those people who are far apart (i.e., individuals who communicate very little with one another or between whom you feel there is friction).

Other Examples

Draw a picture of how it feels to be in your organization.

Draw a picture of your organization today and another picture of what you would like it to be in five years.

The drawings may vary in style from conventional organization charts to imaginative symbolic representations.

Uses

Drawings of the sort suggested can be a powerful way of unearthing for the group issues that have been buried alive—for example, the presence of cliques, inappropriate competition, or personal influence contrary to organizational goals. While they may be used to describe a current situation, drawings can also display what people want and hope for in place of what they have now.

Drawings can be used for building an agenda for team-building or similar meetings.

Benefits

Pictures are often rich compressions of meaning. Moreover, they are inherently stimulating to work

with. Drawings may also afford an easy entry into discussion of tender subjects.

Limitations

Drawings are an expressive medium. But they are difficult for some to enter into unless the directions are quite literal and easy to follow.

Operating Hints

Don't attempt to cover too many subjects in a single drawing or it will become difficult to understand.

Spend enough time on the instructions so that the members understand the *objectives* of the activity. Don't discourage people from departing from your rules; they may do better in their own fashion.

When a person presents a drawing to the group, encourage clarifying questions. *Discourage* general discussion, debate, or clever interpretation of the drawing by other members of the group.

Keep in readiness large sheets of paper, colored markers, and tape.

Some groups need more guidance than others. A group that is esthetically inclined is apt to respond swiftly to the assignment. Others may want more specific instruction.

7.   Physical Representation of Organization

Members of a group are asked to arrange themselves physically in the room according to some group characteristic they are troubled about. For example, if the participants are apparently concerned about cliques, they may be asked to position themselves in the room so that each stands nearest to those he or she feels warmest about and farthest from those he or she feels coolest about. Or, if inappropriate influence is an issue, they may be asked to arrange themselves closer or farther from the boss according to the amount of influence they feel they have. Usually, the manager takes a position in the middle of the room as a starting point.

Members are asked to call attention to any aspect of the deployment which they believe to be inaccurate. Usually no further instructions are given. Discussion normally occurs spontaneously.

Uses

For bringing into the open relationship issues which are bothering the group. These may include cliques, feelings about being ''in'' or ''out'' of the group, influence, competitiveness, communication channels, etc.

Benefits

A good, rapid, and dramatic diagnostic tool for disclosing interpersonal issues that are hindering a group.

Creates strong motivation to improve the situation.

Limitations

Many groups find this sort of thing too ''far out,'' so the method isn't useful to them and may do more harm than good.

Operating Hints

You will need a qualified third party.

Reading 15

THE CONFRONTATION MEETING

Richard Beckhard

One of the continuing problems facing the top management team of any organization in times of stress or major change is how to assess accurately the state of the organization's health. How are people reacting to the change? How committed are subordinate managers to the new conditions? Where are the most pressing organization problems?

In the period following a major change—such as that brought about by a change in leadership or organization structure, a merger, or the introduction of a new technology—there tends to be much confusion and an expenditure of dysfunctional energy that negatively affects both productivity and morale.

At such times, the top management group usually spends many hours together working on the business problems and finding ways of coping with the new conditions. Frequently, the process of working together under this pressure also has the effect of making the top team more cohesive.

Concurrently, these same managers tend to spend less and less time with their subordinates and with the rest of the organization. Communications decrease between the top and middle levels of management. People at the lower levels often complain that they are less in touch with what is going on than they were before the change. They feel left out. They report having less influence than before, being more unsure of their own decision-making authority, and feeling less sense of ownership in the organization. As a result of this, they tend to

Source: Richard Beckhard, "The Confrontation Meeting," *Harvard Business Review,* 45 March–April 1967, pp. 159–55.

make fewer decisions, take fewer risks, and wait until the "smoke clears."

When this unrest comes to the attention of top management, the response is usually to take some action such as:

Having each member of the top team hold team meetings with his subordinates to communicate the state of affairs, and following this procedure down through the organization.

Holding some general communication improvement meetings.

Conducting an attitude survey to determine priority problems.

Any of these actions will probably be helpful, but each requires a considerable investment of time which is competitive with the time needed to work on the change problem itself.

Action Plans

Recently I have experimented with an activity that allows a total management group, drawn from all levels of the organization, to take a quick reading on its own health, and—*within a matter of hours*—to set action plans for improving it. I call this a "confrontation meeting."

The activity is based on my previous experience with an action-oriented method of planned change in which information on problems and attitudes is collected and fed back to those who produced it, and steps are taken to start action plans for improvement of the condition.

Sometimes, following situations of organizational stress, the elapsed time in moving from identification of the problem to collaborative action planning must be extremely brief. The confrontation meeting can be carried out in $4\frac{1}{2}$ to 5 hours' working time, and it is designed to include the entire management of a large system in a joint action planning program.

I have found this approach to be particularly practical in organization situations where there are large numbers in the management group and/or where it is difficult to take the entire group off the job for any length of time. The activity has been conducted several times with a one evening and one morning session—taking only $2\frac{1}{2}$ hours out of a regular working day.

The confrontation meeting discussed in this article has been used in a number of different organization situations. Experience shows that it is appropriate where:

There is a need for the total management group to examine its own workings.

Very limited time is available for the activity.

Top management wishes to improve the conditions quickly.

There is enough cohesion in the top team to ensure follow-up.

There is real commitment to resolving the issues on the part of top management.

The organization is experiencing, or has recently experienced, some major change.

In order to show how this technique can speed the process of getting the information and acting on it, let us first look at three actual company situations where this approach has been successfully applied. Then we will examine both the positive results and the possible problems that could occur through the use and misuse of this technique. Finally, after a brief summary there are appendixes for the reader interested in a more elaborate description of the phasing and scheduling of such a meeting.

Case Example A

The initial application of the confrontation meeting technique occurred in 1965 in a large food products company. Into this long-time family-owned and closely controlled company, there was introduced for the first time a non-family professional general manager. He had been promoted from the ranks of the group that had previously reported to the family-member general manager.

This change in the "management culture," which had been carefully and thoroughly prepared by the family executives, was carried out with a minimum number of problems. The new general manager and his operating heads spent many hours together and developed a quite open problem-solving climate and an effective, cohesive team. Day-to-day operations were left pretty much in the hands of their immediate subordinates, while the top group focused on planning.

A few months after the change, however, the general manager began getting some information that indicated all was not well further down in the organization. On investigation, he discovered that many middle-level managers were feeling isolated from what was going on. Many were unclear about the authority and functions of the "management committee" (his top team); some were finding it very difficult to see and consult with their bosses (his operating heads); others were not being informed of decisions made at his management committee meetings; still others were apprehensive that a new power elite was developing which in many ways was much worse than the former family managers.

In discussing this feedback information with his operating heads, the general manager found one or two who felt these issues required immediate management committee attention. But most of the members of the top team tended to minimize the information as "the usual gripping," or "people needing too many decisions made for them," or "everybody always wanting to be in on everything."

The general manager then began searching for some way to:

Bring the whole matter into the open.

Determine the magnitude and potency of the total problem.

Give his management committee and himself a true picture of the state of the organization's attitudes and concerns.

Collect information on employee needs, problems, and frustrations in some organized way so that corrective actions could be taken in priority order.

Get his management committee members in better tune with their subordinates' feelings and attitudes, and put some pressure on the team members for continued two-way communication within their own special areas.

Make clear to the total organization that he—the top manager—was personally concerned.

Set up mechanisms by which all members of the total management group could feel that their individual needs were noticed.

Provide additional mechanisms for supervisors to influence the whole organization.

The confrontation meeting was created to satisfy these objectives and to minimize the time in which a large number of people would have to be away from the job.

Some 70 managers, representing the total management group, were brought together for a confrontation meeting starting at 9:00 in the morning and ending at 4:30 in the afternoon. The specific "design" for the day, which is broken down into a more detailed description in Appendix A, had the following components:

1. Climate setting—establishing willingness to participate.
2. Information collecting—getting the attitudes and feelings out in the open.
3. Information sharing—making total information available to all.
4. Priority setting and group action planning—holding work-unit sessions to set priority actions and to make timetable commitments.
5. Organization action planning—getting commitment by top management to the working of these priorities.

6. Immediate follow-up by the top management committee—planning first actions and commitments.

During the daylong affair, the group identified some 80 problems that were of concern to people throughout the organization; they selected priorities from among them; they began working on these priority issues in functional work units, and each unit produced action recommendations with timetables and targets; and they got a commitment from top management of actions on priorities that would be attended to. The top management team met immediately after the confrontation meeting to pin down the action steps and commitments.

(In subsequent applications of this confrontation meeting approach, a seventh component—a progress review—has been added, since experience has shown that it is important to reconvene the total group four to six weeks later for a progress review both from the functional units and from the top management team.)

Case Example B

A small company which makes products for the military had been operating at a stable sales volume of $3 million to $4 million. The invention of a new process and the advent of the war in Vietnam suddenly produced an explosion of business. Volume rose to the level of $6 million within six months and promised to redouble within another year.

Top management was desperately trying to (a) keep raw materials flowing through the line, (b) get material processed, (c) find people to hire, (d) discover quicker ways of job training, and (e) maintain quality under the enormously increased pressure.

There was constant interaction among the five members of the top-management team. They were aware of the tension and fatigue that existed on the production line, but they were only vaguely aware of the unrest, fatigue, concern, and loneliness of the middle manager and foreman groups. However, enough signals *had* filtered up to the top team to cause concern and a decision that something needed to be done right away. But, because of the pressures of work, finding the time to tackle the problems was as difficult as the issues themselves.

The entire management group agreed to give up one night and one morning; the confrontation meeting was conducted according to the six component phases described earlier, with phases 1, 2, and 3 being held in the evening and phases 4, 5, and 6 taking place the following morning.

Case Example C

A management organization took over the operation of a hotel which was in a sorry state of affairs. Under previous absentee ownership, the property had been allowed to run down; individual departments were independent empires; many people in management positions were nonprofessional hotel people (i.e., friends of the owners); and there was very low competence in the top management team.

The general manager saw as his priority missions the need to:

Stop the downhill trend.

Overcome a poor public image.

Clean up the property.

Weed out the low-potential (old friends) management.

Bring in professional managers in key spots.

Build a management team.

Build effective operating teams, with the members of the top-management team as links.

He followed his plan with considerable success. In a period of one year he had significantly cleaned up the property, improved the service, built a new dining room, produced an enviable food quality, and begun to build confidence in key buyers, such as convention managers. He had acquired and developed a very fine, professional, young management team that was both competent and highly motivated. This group had been working as a cohesive team on all the hotel's improvement goals;

differences between them and their areas seemed to have been largely worked through.

At the level below the top group, the department and section heads, many of whom were also new, had been working under tremendous pressure for over a year to bring about improvements in the property and in the hotel's services. They felt very unappreciated by the top managers, who were described as "always being in meetings and unavailable," or "never rewarding us for good work," or "requiring approval on all decisions but we can't get to see them," or "developing a fine top management club but keeping the pressure on us and we're doing the work."

The problem finally was brought to the attention of the top managers by some of the department heads. Immediate action was indicated, and a confrontation meeting was decided on. It took place in two periods, an afternoon and the following morning. There was an immediate follow-up by the top management team in which many of the issues between departments and functions were identified as stemming back to the modus operandi of the top team. These issues were openly discussed and were worked through. Also in this application, a follow-up report and review session was scheduled for five weeks after the confrontation meeting.

Positive Results

The experience of the foregoing case examples, as well as that of other organizations in which the confrontation meeting technique has been applied, demonstrates that positive results—particularly, improved operational procedures and improved organization health—frequently occur.

Operational Advantages

One of the outstanding plus factors is that procedures which have been confused are clarified. In addition, practices which have been non-existent are initiated. Typical of these kinds of operational improvement, for example, are the reporting of financial information of operating units, the handling of the reservation system at a hotel, and the inspection procedures and responsibilities in a changing manufacturing process.

Another advantage is that task forces, and/or temporary systems, are set up as needed. These may be in the form of special teams to study the overlap in responsibilities between two departments and to write new statements and descriptions, or to work out a new system for handling order processing from sales to production planning, or to examine the kinds of information that should flow regularly from the management committee to middle management.

Still another improvement is in providing guidance to top management as to specific areas needing priority attention. For example, "the overtime policy set under other conditions is really impeding the achievement of organization requirements," or "the food in the employee's cafeteria is really creating morale problems," or "the lack of understanding of where the organization is going and what top management's goals are is producing apathy," or "what goes on in top management meetings does not get communicated to the middle managers."

Organization Health

In reviewing the experiences of companies where the confrontation meeting approach has been instituted, I have perceived a number of positive results in the area of organization health:

A high degree of open communication between various departments and organization levels is achieved very quickly. Because people are assigned to functional units and produce data together, it is possible to express the real feeling of one level or group toward another, particularly if the middle echelon believes the top wants to hear it.

The information collected is current, correct, and "checkable."

A real dialogue can exist between the top management team and the rest of the management organization, which personalizes the top manager to the total group.

Larger numbers of people get "ownership" of the problem, since everyone has some influence through his unit's guidance to the top-management team; thus people feel they have made a real contribution. Even more, the requirement that each functional unit take personal responsibility for resolving some of the issues broadens the base of ownership.

Collaborative goal setting at several levels is demonstrated and practiced. The mechanism provides requirements for joint goal setting within each functional unit and between top and middle managers. People report that this helps them to understand "management by objectives" more clearly than before.

The top team can take corrective actions based on valid information. By making real commitments and establishing check or review points, there is a quick building of trust in management's intentions on the part of lower level managers.

There tends to be an increase in trust and confidence both toward the top-management team and toward colleagues. A frequently appearing agenda item is the "need for better understanding of the job problems of other departments," and the output of these meetings is often the commitment to some "mechanism for systematic interdepartmental communication." People also report a change in their stereotypes of people in other areas.

This activity tends to be a "success experience" and thus increases total morale. The process itself, which requires interaction, contribution, and joint work on the problems and which rewards constructive criticism, tends to produce a high degree of enthusiasm and commitment. Because of this, the follow-up activities are crucial in ensuring continuation of this enthusiasm.

Potential Problems

The confrontation meeting technique produces, in a very short time, a great deal of commitment and desire for results on the part of a lot of people. Feelings tend to be more intense than in some other settings because of the concentration of time and manpower. As a result, problems can develop through misuse of the techniques.

If the top management team does not really use the information from its subordinates, or if there are great promises and little follow-up action, more harm can be caused to the organization's health than if the events were never held.

If the confrontation meeting is used as a manipulative device to give people the "feeling of participation," the act can boomerang. They will soon figure out management's intentions, and the reaction can be severe.

Another possible difficulty is that the functional units, full of enthusiasm at the meeting, set unrealistic or impractical goals and commitments. The behavior of the keyman in each unit—usually a department manager or division head—is crucial in keeping suggestions in balance.

One more possible problem may appear when the functional units select a few priority issues to report out. While these issues may be the most *urgent,* they are not necessarily the most *important.* Mechanisms for working *all* of the information need to be developed within each functional unit. In one of the case examples cited earlier, the groups worked the few problems they identified very thoroughly and never touched the others. This necessitated a "replay" six months later.

In Summary

In periods of stress following major organization changes, there tends to be much confusion and energy expended that negatively affects productivity and organization health.

The top-management team needs quick, efficient ways of sensing the state of the organization's attitudes and feelings in order to plan appropriate actions and to devote its energy to the most important problems.

The usual methods of attitude surveys, extended staff meetings, and so forth demand extensive time and require a delay between getting the information and acting on it.

A short micromechanism called a confrontation meeting can provide the total management group with:

An accurate reading on the organization's health.

The opportunity for work units to set priorities for improvement.

The opportunity for top management to make appropriate action decisions based on appropriate information from the organization.

An increased involvement in the organization's goals.

A real commitment to action on the part of subgroups.

A basis for determining other mechanisms for communication between levels and groups, appropriate location of decisions, problem solving within subunits, as well as the machinery for upward influence.

Appendix A: Confrontation Meeting

Here is a detailed description of the seven components which make up the specific "design" for the day-long confrontation meeting.

Phase 1. Climate Setting (45 minutes to one hour)

At the outset, the top manager needs to communicate to the total management group his goals for the meeting, and his concern for and interest in free discussion and issue facing. He also has to assure his people that there is no punishment for open confrontation.

It is also helpful to have some form of information session or lecture by the top manager or a consultant. Appropriate subjects might deal with the problems of communication, the need for understanding, the assumptions and the goals of the total organization, the concept of shared responsibility for the future of the organization, and the opportunity for and responsibility of influencing the organization.

Phase 2. Information Collecting (one hour)

The total group is divided into small heterogeneous units of seven or eight people. If there is a top management team that has been holding sessions regularly, it meets as a separate unit. The rest of the participants are assigned to units with a "diagonal slice" of the organization used as a basis for composition—that is, no boss and subordinate are together, and each unit contains members from every functional area.

The assignment given to each of these units is along these lines:

Think of yourself as an individual with needs and goals. Also think as a person concerned about the total organization. What are the obstacles, ''demotivators,'' poor procedures or policies, unclear goals, or poor attitudes that exist today? What different conditions, if any, would make the organization more effective and make life in the organization better?

Each unit is instructed to select a reporter to present its results at a general information-collecting session to be held one hour later.

Phase 3. Information Sharing (one hour)

Each reporter writes his unit's complete findings on newsprint, which is tacked up around the room.

The meeting leader suggests some categories under which all the data from all the sheets can be located. In other words, if there are 75 items, the likelihood is that these can be grouped into six or seven major categories—say, by type of problem, such as ''communications difficulties''; or by type of relationship, such as ''problems with top management''; or by type of area involved, such as ''problems in the mechanical department.''

Then the meeting breaks, either for lunch or, if it happens to be an evening session, until the next morning.

During the break all the data sheets are duplicated for general distribution.

Phase 4. Priority Setting and Group Action Planning (one hour and 15 minutes)

The total group reconvenes for a 15-minute general session. With the meeting leader, they go through the raw data on the duplicated sheets and put category numbers by each piece of data.

People are now assigned to their functional, natural work units for a one-hour session. Manufacturing people at all levels go to one unit, everybody in sales to another, and so forth. These units are headed by a department manager or division head

of that function. This means that some units may have as few as 3 people and some as many as 25. Each unit is charged to perform three specific tasks:

1. Discuss the problems and issues which affect its area. Decide on the priorities and early actions to which the group is prepared to commit itself. (They should be prepared to share this commitment with their colleagues at the general session.)
2. Identify the issues and/or problems to which the top management team should give its priority attention.
3. Decide how to communicate the results of the session to their subordinates.

Phase 5. Organization Action Planning (one to two hours)

The total management group reconvenes in a general session, where:

1. Each functional unit reports its commitment and plans to the total group.
2. Each unit reports and lists the items that its members believe the management team should deal with first.
3. The top manager reacts to this list and makes commitments (through setting targets or assigning task forces or timetables, and so on) for action where required.
4. Each unit shares briefly its plans for communicating the results of the confrontation meeting to all subordinates.

Phase 6. Immediate Follow-Up by Top Team (one to three hours)

The top-management team meets immediately after the confrontation meeting ends to plan first follow-up actions, which should then be reported back to the total management group within a few days.

Phase 7. Progress Review (two hours)

Follow-up with total management group four to six weeks later.

Appendix B: Sample Schedule

9:00 A.M. Opening Remarks, by general manager
  Background, goals, outcomes.
  Norms of openness and ''leveling.''
  Personal commitment to follow-up.
9:10 General Session
  Communications Problems in Organizations, by
    general manager (or consultant).
  The communications process.
  Communications breakdowns in organizations
    and individuals.
  Dilemmas to be resolved.
  Conditions for more openness.
10:00 Coffee
10:15 Data Production Unit Session
  Sharing feelings and attitudes.
  Identifying problems and concerns.
  Collecting data.

11:15 General Session
  Sharing findings from each unit (on newsprint).
  Developing categories on problem issues.
12:15 P.M. Lunch
 2:00 General Session
  Reviewing list of items in categories.
  Instructing functional units.
 2:15 Functional Unit Session
  Listing priority actions to be taken.
  Preparing recommendations for top team.
  Planning for presentation of results at general
    meeting.
 3:15 General Session
  Sharing recommendations of functional units.
  Listing priorities for top team action.
  Planning for communicating results of meeting
    to others.
 4:15 Closing Remarks, by general manager
 4:30 Adjournment

ORGANIZATIONAL DIAGNOSIS: SIX PLACES TO LOOK FOR TROUBLE WITH OR WITHOUT A THEORY

Marvin R. Weisbord

No single model or conceptual scheme embraces the whole breadth and complexity of reality, even though each in turn may be useful in particular instances. This is why management remains an art, for the practitioner must go beyond the limits of theoretical knowledge if he is to be effective. (Tilles, 1963, pp. 73–81).

For several years I have been experimenting with "cognitive maps" of organizations. These are labels that would help me better describe what I saw and heard, and understand the relationships among various bits of data. I started this endeavor when I realized that though I knew many organization theories, most were either (1) too narrow to include everything I wished to understand or (2) too broadly abstract to give much guidance about what to do.

This article represents a progress report on my efforts to combine bits of data, theories, research, and hunches into a working tool that anyone can use. It is one example of a process I believe goes on among practitioners that is neither well documented nor well understood (Weisbord, 1974a). The process does not take place in a mode consistent with the protocols of social science research. It is not tied to any particular theory, nor is it subject to easy translation into research instruments. It is not intended to prove or disprove hypotheses. Rather, it represents what Vaill (1975; Friedlander & Brown, 1974) calls a "practice theory"—a synthesis of knowledge and experience into a concept that bears "some relation to public, objective the-

ories about organizational situations, but in no sense (is) identical to them."

I think this accurately describes what I have been calling, for want of a more elegant name, the "Six—Box Model." This model (Figure 1) has helped me rapidly expand my diagnostic framework from interpersonal and group issues to the more complicated contexts in which organizations are managed. It provides six labels, under which can be sorted much of the activity, formal and informal, that takes place in organizations. The labels allow consultants to apply whatever theories they know when doing a diagnosis and to discover new connections between apparently unrelated events.

We can visualize Figure 1 as a radar screen. Just as air controllers use radar to chart the course of aircraft—height, speed, distance apart, and weather—those seeking to improve an organization must observe relationships among the boxes and not focus on any particular blip.

Organizational "process" issues, for example, will show up as blips in one or more boxes, signaling the blockage of work on important organizational tasks. (Process issues relate to *how* and *whether* work gets done, rather than *what* is to be done.)

Unfortunately, such issues too often are seen as the result of someone's personality. For example, the failure of a group to confront its differences may be diagnosed as the inability of one or two people to assert themselves. Yet, if the consultant were to look closely, he might find that no one in the organization confronts, independent of the assertion skills they may have. Those who do confront may be considered deviant and may be tolerated only to the extent that they have power.

Source: Marvin R. Weisbord, reprinted from *Group & Organization Studies*, December 1976, pp. 430–47.

FIGURE 1   The Six-Box Organizational Model

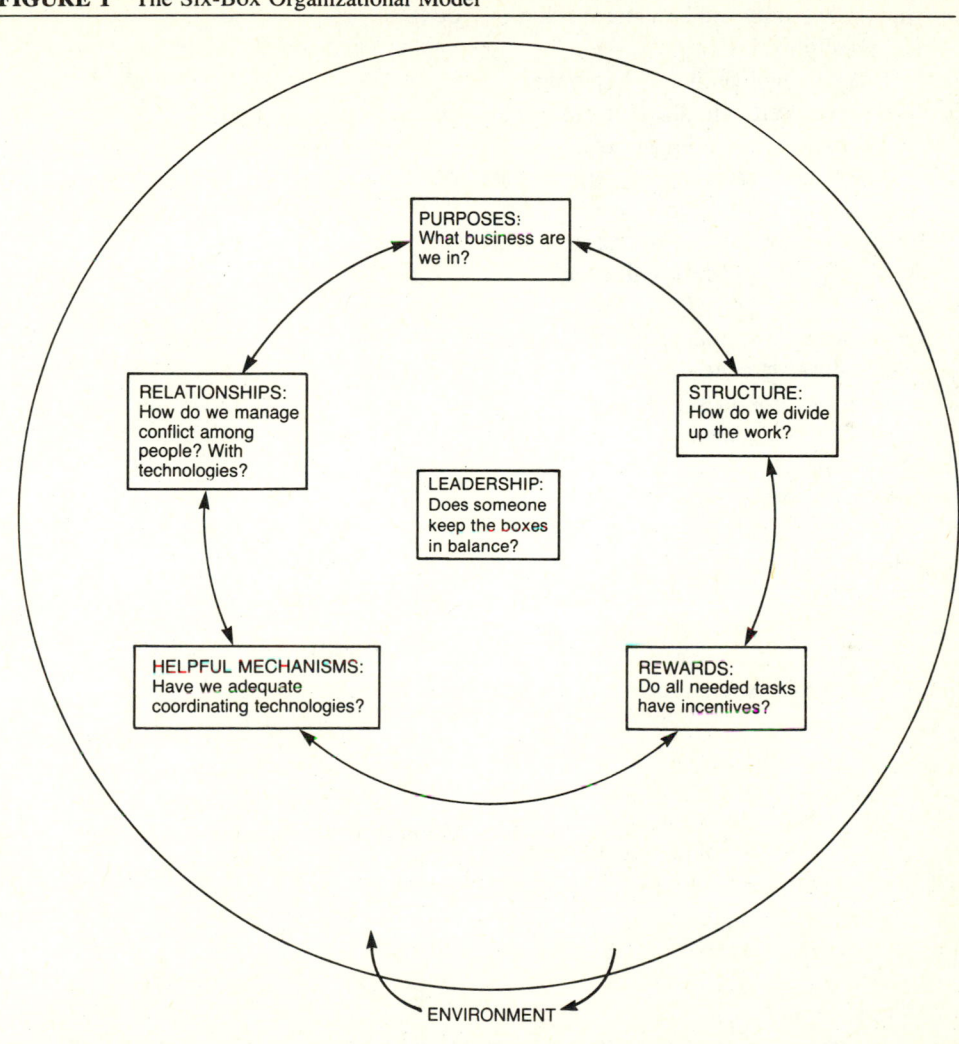

From a management standpoint, it is probably more useful to think of process issues as systemic, that is, as part of the organization's management culture. This culture can be described as:

1. "Fit" between *organization* and *environment*—the extent to which purposes and structure support high performance and ability to change with conditions; and/or

2. "Fit" between *individual* and *organization*—the extent to which people support or subvert

formal mechanisms intended to carry out an organization's purposes.

The relationship between individual and organization is the basis for many important books in the organizational literature. McGregor (1960) argued that a better fit might be attained under Theory Y assumptions (people like to work, achieve, and be responsible) than Theory X assumptions (people are passive, dependent, and need to be controlled). Blake and Mouton (1964) devised elaborate change strategies (variations of "Grid" theory) based on the notion that productivity and human satisfaction need not be mutually exclusive.

Maslow (1971) struggled in his last years to reconcile employee self-actualization—personal growth and creativity—with an organization's needs for structure, order, and predictability. Argyris has written extensively on the potential incompatibilities of individuals and organizations and the threat that bureaucratic structures pose to self-esteem (Argyris, 1957).

In the last 10 years, both managers and consultants have become much more conscious of organizations as open systems in which structure and behavior are heavily influenced by environment. Lawrence and Lorsch (1967) compared high- and low-performance businesses in terms of structural requirements—based largely on rate of change in business technology and environment—and came up with a contingency theory: the way subunits of an organization are structured depends not only on their functions but on environmental factors, which results in different policies and procedures for different organizations.

Sociotechnical theorists such as Trist (1969) have tried to reconcile structured technologies and work systems with people's individual and social needs, theorizing that high performance equals an optimum balance between technology ("task") and people ("process").

Each of the possible frameworks highlights important organizational issues; each has been the basis for useful interventions in the organization development repertoire. Yet, none is an adequate tool for the management of an entire organization without an expansion of concepts.

Management needs a view simple enough, and complete enough, to improve the quality of its decisions. What follows is a description of how the Six-Box Organizational Model can be used to put into perspective *whatever* theories and concepts a consultant already knows along with *whatever* problems present themselves in diagnosing an organization's problems.

The circle in Figure 1 describes the boundaries of an organization to be diagnosed. *Environment* means forces difficult to control from inside that demand a response—customers, government, unions, students, families, friends, etc. It is not always clear where the boundaries are or should be. Although such a system can be characterized accurately as "open," its rationality depends on partially closing off infinite choices. Deciding where the boundary lies is an act of reason wed to values, for there are no absolutes (Vickers, 1965).

The consultant may find it necessary to set boundaries arbitrarily so that a diagnosis can proceed. I do this by picking a unit name (i.e., XYZ Company, ABC Department, QUR Team) and listing groups or individuals inside the boundary by virtue of dollar commitments, contract, or formal membership. Within the boundaries, the boxes interact to create what is sometimes called an input-output system, whose function is to transform resources into goods or services. Figure 2 illustrates the Six-Box organization/environment using input-output terms. Given that organizations function or do not function depending on what is going on in and between each of the six boxes, a consultant has a basis for doing an organizational diagnosis.

Formal and Informal Systems

Within each box are two potential trouble sources— the formal system that exists on paper and the informal system—or what people actually do. Neither system is necessarily better, but both exist. In doing a diagnosis, it helps to identify blips in each system and to attempt to define the relationships among them.

Diagnosing the formal system requires some informed guessing, based on knowledge of what the organization *says*—in its statements, reports, charts, and speeches—about how it is organized. The guessing comes after comparing its rhetoric with its environment and making a judgment about whether everything fits—whether society will value and underwrite an organization with such a purpose and such a means of organizing itself. Much expert consultation is aimed at bringing organizational rhetoric into better harmony with the outside world.

FIGURE 2 The Six-Box Organizational Model Using Input-Output Terms

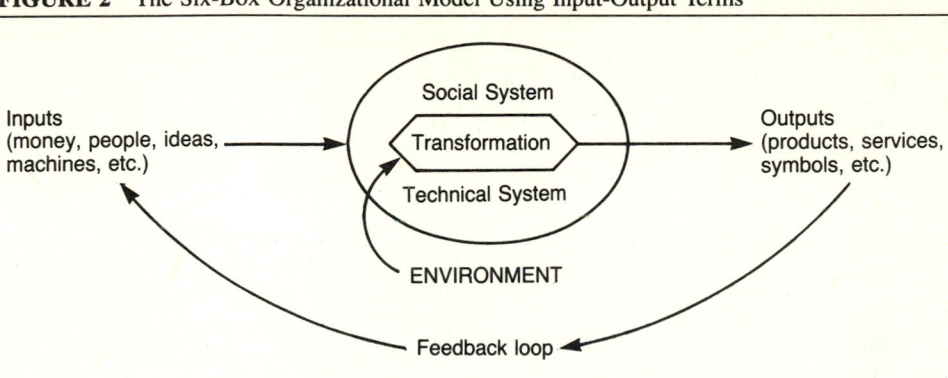

However, in every organization there is another level of behavior—what people actually do. Diagnosing these informal systems is sometimes called "normative" diagnosis (Clapp, 1974). It focuses on the frequency with which people take certain actions in relation to how impoortant these actions are for organizational performance. Normative behavior usually determines whether otherwise technically excellent systems succeed or fail, because normative behavior indicates the degree to which the system as designed meets the needs of the people who have to operate it. Sometimes norms cannot be changed informally, so there is a need to study relationships *between* the two levels of analysis. By persisting in such an inquiry, a consultant discovers some of the reasons why the input-transformation-output stream is not flowing as smoothly as it could.

How to Collect Data

Collecting data on which to base a diagnosis can be as simple as brainstorming or as complex as a "grand design" research methodology involving hypotheses, instruments, and computer analysis. Complexity aside, there are four ways to collect data:

1. *Observation*. Watch what people do in meetings, on the job, on the phone, etc.
2. *Reading*. Follow the written record—speeches, reports, charts, graphs, etc.

3. *Interviews*. Question everyone involved with a particular project.
4. *Survey*. Use standard questionnaires or design your own. Surveys are most useful when they ask for information not readily obtainable in any other way, such as attitudes, perceptions, opinions, preferences, beliefs, etc.

All four methods of data collection can be used to isolate the two major kinds of discrepancy—between what people say (formal) and what they do (informal) and between what is (organization as it exists) and what ought to be (appropriate environmental fit). The trick is not to use any particular methods, but to sort the evidence of one's senses into some categories that encourage sensible decisions.

Where to Start

There are two main reasons why one might want to diagnose an organization: to find out systematically what its strengths and weaknesses are or to uncover reasons why either the producers or consumers of a particular output are dissatisfied. Because the latter reason is most often the trigger for corrective actions, I suggest starting a diagnosis by considering one major output. Tracing its relationship to the whole system will result in an understanding of the gaps in the organization between "what is" and "what ought to be."

Let us look at one output—say a single product or service—and determine how satisfied the *consumers* are and how satisfied the *producers* are. The central assumption behind this activity is that consumer acceptance, more than any other factor, determines whether an organization prospers or fades. Satisfied consumers generally indicate a good fit with the environment at one major contact point. Without satisfied consumers, producer satisfaction is likely to be unstable.

A consultant must watch for two situations in particular when diagnosing helpful mechanisms. One is the lack of any rational planning, budgeting, control, or measurement systems. In this case, no amount of interpersonal or group process work will ''improve'' an organization. Second, and worse, is the organization that has budgeting and controls, but no goals that the people doing the work agree are *organizationally* relevant (for them). The latter describes some universities and medical centers, for example, in which financial control systems provide an illusion of rationality that, like beauty, is only skin deep (Drucker, 1974b).

OD in such situations is not an *organization* development process at all. The best that a consultant can do is help members make more rational decisions about their own careers, thereby contributing to their personal growth. Certainly there is no interdependency to be negotiated in the absence of agreement about the ends toward which the organization is being managed (Weisbord, 1976).

The Six-Box Organization Model is a useful ''early-warning system'' for a consultant who is trying to decide where and whether to take corrective action. There are three levels of diagnosis that provide clues to appropriate interventions:

1. Does the organization fit its environment? If not, it cannot be developed until the fit can be rationalized and supported.
2. Is the organization structured to carry out its purposes? If not, work on structure is required before an examination of interpersonal and group processes can take on meaning other than personal growth.

3. Are the organization's norms out of phase with its intent? How much discrepancy exists between formal and informal systems? If this is the main problem (as it often is in otherwise successful businesses) most of the management and organization development interventions will apply.

Any diagnostic questions a consultant asks about any of the boxes will yield useful data. Figure 3 summarizes the important questions about both formal and informal systems. There are as many ways to use these ideas as there are managers. I have offered this practice theory as the basis for starting new teams, task forces, and committees or for helping existing teams decide what they need to do next. Others have adapted the Six-Box Model to screen prospective employers, evaluate the management literature in terms of which issues it illuminates, write job descriptions, and organize research findings. It is also a useful teaching tool in comparing various types of organizations.

Finally, the Six-Box Organization Model provides an easy way of testing the extent to which an intervention seems right. I have used it both to explain and to anticipate my failures and have found that more anticipating means less explaining. In my experience, all interventions that ''fail'' eventually do so for one of three reasons (Bowers, Franklin, & Pecorella, 1975):

1. The intervention is inappropriate to the problem or organization. (A T-group may improve relationships without surfacing serious deficiencies of purpose, structure, or technology.)

2. The intervention deals with the wrong (less salient) blip on the radar screen. (When the pressing problem is ineffective leadership, a new reward system, no matter how desirable, may not make a difference.)

3. The intervention solves the identified problem, thus heightening issues in other boxes it was *not* designed to solve. An organization can be restructured to better fit its environment without changing norms and relationships that require other interventions.

FIGURE 3 Matrix for Survey Design or Data Analysis

	Formal System (work to be done)	*Informal System* (process working)
1. Purposes	Goal clarity	Goal agreement
2. Structure	Functional, program, or matrix?	How work is actually done or not done.
3. Relationships	Who should deal with whom on what? Which technologies should be used?	How well do they do it? Quality of relations? Modes of conflict management?
4. Rewards (incentives)	Explicit System What is it?	Implicit, psychic rewards. What do people *feel* about payoffs?
5. Leadership	What do top people manage? What systems in use?	How? Normative "style" of administration?
6. Helpful Mechanisms	Budget system Management information (measures?) Planning Control	What are they actually used for? How function in practice? How are systems subverted?

Note: Diagnostic questions may be asked on two levels:
1. How big a gap is there between formal and informal systems? (This speaks to the fit between individual and organization.)
2. How much discrepancy is there between "what is" and "what ought to be"? (This highlights the fit between organization and environment.)

References

Argyris, C., *Personality and organization: The conflict between system and the individual*. New York: Harper & Row, 1957.

Blake, R.R., & Mouton, J.S. *The managerial grid*. Houston, Tex.: Gulf Publishing, 1964.

Bowers, D.G., Franklin, J.L., & Pecorella, P.A. Matching problems, precursors, and interventions in OD: A systemic approach. *Journal of Applied Behavioral Science*, 1975, *11*(4), 391–409.

Clapp, N.W. Work group norms: Leverage for organizational change, I–theory, II–application. *Organization development reading series* (No. 2). Plainfield, N.J.: Block Petrella Associates, 1974.

Drucker, P.F. The dimensions of management. In P.F. Drucker, *Management: Tasks, responsibilities, practices*. New York: Harper & Row, 1974.(a)

Drucker, P.F. Why service institutions do not perform. In P.F. Drucker, *Management: Tasks, responsibilities, practices*. New York: Harper & Row, 1974.(b).

Fiedler, F.E. *A theory of leadership effectiveness*. New York: McGraw–Hill, 1967.

Friedlander, F., & Brown, L.D. Organization development. *Annual Review of Psychology*, 1974, 25, 319.

Gulick, L. Notes on the theory of organizations. In L. Gulick & L.F. Urwick (Eds.), *Papers on the science of administration*. Columbia University, Institute of Public Administration, 1937.

Herzberg, F., Mausner, B., & Snyderman, B. *The motivation to work*. New York: John Wiley & Sons, 1959.

Kast, F.E., & Rosenzweig, J.E. *Organization and management: A systems approach*. New York: McGraw-Hill, 1970.

Kingdon, D.R. *Matrix organization: Managing information technologies*. London: Tavistock, 1973.

Lawrence, P.R., & Lorsch, J.W. *Organization and environment*. Boston: Harvard University, Graduate School of Business Administration, 1967.

Lawrence, P.R., Weisbord, M.R., & Charns, M.P. *Academic medical center self-study guide*. Washington, D.C.: Report of Physicians' Assistance Branch, Bureau of Health, Manpower Education, National Institute of Health, 1973.

Likert, R. *The human organization: Its management and value*. New York: McGraw–hill, 1967.

Maslow, A.H. *Motivation and personality*. New York: Harper & Row, 1954.

Maslow, A.H. Synergy in the society and in the individual. In A.H. Maslow, *The farther reaches of human nature*. New York: Viking Press, 1971.

McGregor, D. *The human side of enterprise*. New York: McGraw-Hill, 1960.

Meyer, H. H. The pay-for-performance dilemma. *Organizational Dynamics*, 1975, *3*(3), 39–50.

Selznick, P. *Leadership in administration*. New York: Harper & Row, 1957.

Steers, R.M., & Porter, L.W. *The role of task goal attributes in employee performance* (Report No. TR–24). Washington, D.C.: Office of Naval Research, April, 1974.

Tilles, S. The manager's job: A systems approach. *Harvard Businesss Review*, 1963, *41*(1), 73–81.

Trist, E.L. On socio-technical systems. In W.G. Bennis, K.D. Benne, & R. Chin, *The planning of change* (2nd ed.). New York: Holt, Rinehart & Winston, 1969.

Vaill, P.B. Practice theories in organization development. In J.D. Adams (Ed.), *New technologies in organization development: 2*. La Jolla, Calif.: University Associates, 1975.

Vickers, G. *The art of judgment*. New York: Basic Books. 1965.

Weisbord, M.R. The gap between OD practice and theory—and publication. *Journal of Applied Behavioral Science*, 1974, *10*(4), 476–484.(a).

Weisbord, M.R. A mixed model for medical centers: Changing structure and behavior. In J. Adams (Ed.), *Theory and method in organization development: An evolutionary process*. Arlington, Va.: NTL Institute for Applied Behavioral Science, 1974.(b).

Weisbord, M.R. Why organization development hasn't worked (so far) in medical centers. *Health Care Management Review*, April 1976, 17–28.

Whyte, W.F. & Miller, F.B. Industrial sociology. In J.B. Gittler (Ed.), *Review of sociology: Analysis of a decade*. New York: John Wiley & Sons, 1957.

B. Team Building and Team Interventions

Team building and interventions with an intact work team are at the heart of organization development, in our opinion. By team building we mean problem diagnosis and problem-solving workshops involving the use of a facilitator, data gathering about relevant problems and issues to be addressed, feedback of the data, problem prioritization, problem diagnosis, and action planning. The label "team building" probably emerged because the consequences are usually enhanced team capability and an enhanced spirit of teamness. Beckhard's article "The Confrontation Meeting" which appears in Section A, Part 3, can be considered team building using these criteria.

Section B of Part 3 includes both general articles on team building and articles that describe specific techniques that are appropriate under certain team-building circumstances. William Dyer's selection is a practical overview; Richard Beckhard looks at the importance of clarifying the purposes of team-building efforts. In particular, Beckhard expresses the point of view that the central purpose of a team-building session should be defined by the client, not by the facilitator. He then goes on to provide suggestions for enhancing team-building outcomes.

In the third essay in this section, Stanley Herman discusses the application of gestalt approaches to team building. While the gestalt mode is generally congruent with other forms of team building and with process consultation, the gestalt-oriented facilitator will press for a deeper exploration of a problem between two or more people. As Herman states it,

> Most importantly we emphasize *staying with* the transaction until both partites have *completed* their business with each other. The individual or contesting parties are encouraged to dramatize and even exaggerate their behavior—to become fully aware of what they are doing and how they are doing it (not why).

In this process, negative feelings are fully aired to completion in contrast to what Herman calls "a premature objectivity or problem-solving approach." Managers and subordinates alike are encouraged to take risks with power and aggression as well as "truth and love."[1]

The gestalt approach would appear to assume a "contract," with a willingness on the part of the client system for the consultant to press for these deeper resolutions of interpersonal and group problems. This approach would appear to assume sufficient continuity in the relationship between consultant and client system to ensure that problems are worked through and new equilibria supported for a reasonable period of time. To state the case negatively, the gestalt approach does not appear to be the kind of team building that readily lends itself to a one-shot, in-and-out approach. Of course, no team building will be very effective with a transitory, casual approach, but the less deep versions will probably leave the client system in less turmoil if the effort is short-lived.

Beyond these general articles, Section B includes several selections which present specific techniques that can be used in team-building settings when appropriate. The Rogers article presents guidance for working with client systems in strategic planning. The Dayal and Thomas, Beckhard and Harris, and Harrison selections all present techniques that have a common thread of role negotiation and clarification based on shared perceptions. Each approach presented can be a powerful tool when used properly; each provides a vehicle for careful exploration of relationships under controlled conditions.

Care must be taken, however, that these interventions are on target and are not too threatening. For example, for RAT to be effective, the role incumbent must be willing to undergo the process and be reasonably comfortable with it. This the consultant must assess ahead of time. Part of the power of these techniques lies in the dimension of group interdependency—the solution to many problems lies in simultaneously altering several aspects of a complex web of forces.

---

[1]For a description of the history and goals of gestalt therapy, from which gestalt approaches to OD have emerged, see Robert L. Harman, "Goals of Gestalt Therapy," *Professional Psychology*, May 1974, pp. 178–84.

Reading 17

BASIC PROGRAMS AND PLANS

William G. Dyer

Team development is an intervention conducted in a work unit as an action to deal with a condition (or conditions) seen as needing improvement. It is vital to the success of the program that it be the result of a good diagnosis of the needs of the work team; depending on the need, different team-development designs may be appropriate. It would, for example, make little sense to conduct a team-development program designed to improve trust and communications if the problem is a lack of clarity of job assignments or one of general apathy and lack of innovation and energy.

Since diagnosis is dependent on clear and accurate information about the conditions to be improved, the first step is to gather data about the conditions in the system. There may already be certain indications that something is not going well in the work group. Records may show that work output is down, grievances are up, loss time is increasing, quality of work is suffering, or the number of people requesting transfer or quitting is on the increase. Or, the manager may simply become aware that more and more of his or her time is being spent in dealing with people problems.

These initial evidences prompt the manager, executive, or administrator to ponder the questions: Why are these negative trends occurring? What should I begin to do about them?

One underlying assumption regarding teams in organizations is that resources are available in the individuals in the work unit. They have the capability to address and deal with the above questions, and the problems behind these questions, if given

Source: William G. Dyer, *Team Building: Issues and Alternatives* (Reading, Mass.: Addison-Wesley Publishing Co., 1977), pp. 41–44 and 46–49. Reprinted with permission.

the time, encouragement, and freedom needed to work honestly toward solutions. Team development in its best sense is creating the opportunity for people to come together to share their concerns, their ideas, and their experiences, and to begin to work together to solve their mutual problems and achieve common goals.

Team Development as a Data-Gathering, Diagnostic, Action-Planning Process

An important perspective in planning the team-development program is to envision the activity as the beginning of a process of getting work-unit members together and involving them in a total problem solving and development. Data-gathering, diagnosis, and action-planning activities are the initial steps in a team-development program, with action taking and evaluation as follow-up activities. In this context, the preparations for the team-development program are very simple. The manager communicates either verbally or in written form the following: "I find certain indications that we are not achieving the kinds of personal or collective results that we would like." (Here the manager may be wise to identify such indicators.) "I think we should come together and spend some time examining our own activities and begin to plan for our own improvement. I would like to start with a two-day development program. Let us all come prepared to deal with the following questions: (1) What keeps us from being as effective a unit as we could be? (2) What problems do you experience that we should work on? (3) What changes do you feel we need to make to be more effective?"

With this introduction, the group members begin to make the necessary psychological and informational preparations. Generally, a team development process is going to be more effective if the following conditions are present.

Cognitive Understanding. People are usually more willing to commit themselves to expending their time and energy on an activity if they clearly understand what they are doing and why they are doing it. Prior to beginning the team-development program, it would be well to spend time with the staff discussing the rationale behind team development, clarifying the activities that will be involved, agreeing on the time demands, and arriving at a commitment of all group members to participate. Since it is difficult to build a team if certain members are absent, every person who is an integral member of the team should be involved. This means they should be committed psychologically to participate and the program scheduled at times when all can be present.

Membership Attendance. Ordinarily a team-development program involves a complete working unit—those people who report to a common superior; whose work connects them with each other; and who must have at least a minimal degree of coordination, common planning, shared goals, and shared decision making in order for them to get work done. Should secretaries or office assistants be included? This depends on the role of that person in the work of the unit. Some secretaries are pure functionaries; they do only work that is assigned. Others are an extension of their bosses and are involved in setting schedules, making decisions, and carrying out action. If everyone recognizes the person as a member whose absence would affect the results of the team effort, that person should be included.

Usually the team represents only one level of an organization—a manager and his or her subordinates. However, organizations vary greatly in their organization structures and operations and, in some systems, mixed levels more accurately represent the working-team compositions.

The number of people is also a factor to consider. A group of 25–30 might be difficult to manage in

a design that calls for each person to clarify his or her job and expectations. However, in a design centered around identifying problems and working out solutions in subgroups, that many people could be handled without major difficulty.

A general rule of thumb about whom to include and how many to have would be: When in doubt—include them. It's far better to have a few more in the program than to leave someone out who feels he or she should belong or be included in the department plans.

Length and Location of Program

Team development should be thought of as an ongoing process, not as a single event. People who want to get away for a couple of days and "do team building" with the idea that they will then return to doing business as usual have an incorrect notion of the purpose of team building. The whole program is designed to alter the way an integrated unit functions together. This change is *started* at an initial meeting and continues through the next several months or years until the group really learns to function as a team.

The team-development process often starts with a block of time devoted to helping the group look at its current level of team functioning, and devising more effective ways of working together. This initial data-sharing, diagnosis, and action-planning sequence takes time and should not be crammed into a couple of hours. Ideally, the members of the work group could plan to meet for at least one full day, and preferably two days, for the initial program. A common format is to meet for dinner, have an evening session, and then meet all the next day or for however long a time has been set aside.

Most team-building facilitators would prefer to have a longer block of time (up to three days) to begin a team-development program. This may not be practical in some situations and modifications must be made. Since we are thinking of team development as an ongoing process, it is possible to start with shorter amounts of time regularly scheduled over a period of several weeks. Some units have successfully conducted a program that opened with an evening meeting, followed by a two- to four-hour meeting each week for the next several weeks. Commitment to the process, regular attendance, high involvement, and good use of time are all more important than length of time.

It is customary to hold the initial team-development program away from the work site. The argument given is that, if people meet at the work location, they will find it difficult to "turn off" their day-to-day concerns in order to concentrate fully on the goals of the program. This argument is compelling, even though there is little research evidence regarding the effect of the location on learning and change. Most practitioners do prefer to have development programs at a location where they can have people's full time and attention.

The Team-Building Cycle

Ordinarily a team-building program will follow a cycle similar to that depicted in the accompanying diagram. The whole program begins because someone recognizes a problem or problems. Either before or during the team-building effort, data are gathered to determine the causes of the problem. The data are then analyzed and a diagnosis is made of what is wrong and what is causing the problem. Following the diagnosis, the work unit engages in appropriate planning and problem solving. Actions are planned and assignments made. The plans are then put into action and the results honestly evaluated.

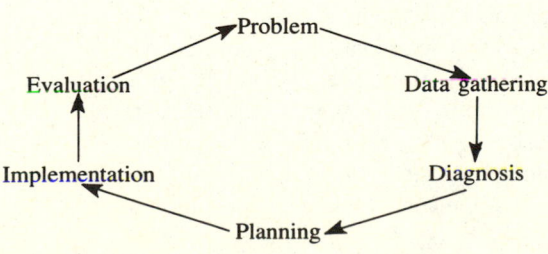

The manager and the consultant will work together in carrying through the program, from the time the program has been identified through some form of evaluation.

Data Gathering

Since team development is essentially a program for training a staff to do its own problem solving, and since a critical condition for effective problem solving is accurate data, a major concern of the manager-consultant team is to gather clear data as to the "causes" behind the symptoms or problems originally identified. The consultant may initially assist in the data gathering, but eventually a team should develop the skill, so it can collect its own data as a basis for working on its own problems. Following are some common data-gathering devices.

Interviews. At times, the consultant can perform a useful service by interviewing the members of the staff or unit. The consultant is trying to determine the factors behind the problem(s) in order to pinpoint those conditions that may need to be changed or improved. In these interviews, the consultant will often explore the following areas: (a) Why is this unit having the kinds of problems it has? (b) What keeps you personally from being as effective as you would like to be? (c) What things do you like best about this department or unit—things you want to continue? (d) What changes would make you and this unit more effective? (e) How could this unit begin to work more effectively together as a productive team?

Following the interviews, a common practice is to have the consultant do a content analysis of the interviews, identify and major "themes" or suggestions that emerge, and prepare a summary presentation. At the team-building meeting the consultant would then present this summary and the unit, under the manager's direction, would engage in analyzing the data and in action planning to deal with the major concerns.

Some consultants prefer *not* to conduct interviews prior to the team-building meeting and do not want to present a data summary. They have found that information shared in a private interview with a consultant is not as readily discussed in the open with all other team members present, especially if some of those members have been the object of some of the interview information. Consultants have painfully discovered that people will often deny their own interviews, fight the data, and refuse to use it as a basis of discussion and planning. An alternative form of data gathering to interviewing is open data sharing.

Open Data Sharing. This method asks each person in the unit to share data publicly with the other group members. The data shared may not be as inclusive as that revealed in an interview, but each person feels responsible to "own up" to the information he or she presents to the group and to deal with the issues raised. To prevent forced disclosure, one good ground rule is to tell people that they should raise only those issues they feel they can honestly discuss with the others. People will generally present only the information they feel comfortable discussing; thus, the open sharing of data may result in less information, but more willingness to "work the data."

The kinds of questions suggested above for the interview format are the same ones that people share openly at the beginning of the team-building session. Each presents his or her views on what keeps the unit from being as effective as it could be or suggests reasons for a particular problem. Each person also describes the things he or she likes about the unit, those things that hinder personal effectiveness, and the changes he or she feels would be helpful. All of the data are compiled on a flip chart or chalk board. Following this, the group moves on to the next stage of the team-building cycle.

Diagnosis and Evaluation of Data

With all of the data now available, the manager and consultant must work with the group to summarize the data—i.e., put the information into a priority listing. The summary categories should be listed as either: **A**—those issues we can work on

in this meeting; **B**—those issues that someone else must work (and identify who the others would be); or **C**—those issues that apparently are not open to change—things we must learn to accept or live with.

Category **A** items become the top agenda items for the rest of the team-building session. Category **B** items are those where strategies must be developed for involving others. And, for category **C** items, the group must plan coping mechanisms. If the manager is prepared, he or she can handle the summary and the category development process. If the manager feels uneasy about this, the consultant may function as a role model to show how this is done.

The next important step is to review all of the data and to try to identify underlying factors that may be related to several problems. A careful analysis of the data may show that certain procedures, rules, or job assignments are causing several disruptive conditions.

Problem Solving and Planning

After the agenda has been developed out of the data, the roles of the manager and consultant diverge. The manager should move directly into the customary managerial role of group leader. The issues identified should become problems to solve and plans for action should be developed.

While the manager is conducting the meeting, the consultant functions as a group observer and facilitator. Schein has referred to this activity as "process consulting," a function that others in the group can also learn to handle. In this role, the consultant helps the group look at its problem-solving and work processes. He or she may stop the group if certain task or maintenance group functions are missing or being poorly performed. If the group gets bogged down or "steamrollered" into uncommitted decisions, the consultant helps look at these processes, why they occur, and how they can be avoided in the future. In this role, the consultant is training the group to develop more group problem-solving and collaborative action-taking skills.

Implementation and Evaluation

If the actions planned at the team-building session are to make any difference, they must be put into practice. This has always been a major function of management—to see that plans are implemented. The manager must be committed to the team plans; without this commitment, it is unlikely that a manager can be effective in holding people responsible for assignments agreed on in the team-building meeting.

The consultant's role is to observe the degree of action during the implementation phase and to be particularly active during the evaluation period. Another data-gathering process now begins, for that is the basis of evaluation. It is important to see if the actions planned or the goals developed during the team-building time have been achieved. This again should ultimately be the responsibility of the manager, but the consultant can be a help in training the manager to carry out good program evaluation.

Reading 18

OPTIMIZING TEAM–BUILDING EFFORTS

Richard Beckhard

The Problem of Energy

A tremendous amount of human energy in organizations is expended by participation in groups. In addition to the time spent in meetings exchanging necessary operating information, most management groups and work teams also spend a significant amount of time on issues such as future planning or improvement planning.

In the truly effective organization, most of the energy of the work force is available for *doing* and *improving* the *work* of the organization, and a minimum amount of energy is needed to maintain the human organization.

In trying to achieve this state, organizations devote considerable effort to improving the effectiveness of work teams. For example, such efforts form one of the major foundations in the Blake and Mouton Grid Organization Development Program. The programs of laboratory training are designed to help people improve the effectiveness of their collaborative work in group settings. Many teambuilding efforts conducted by internal and external organization development consultants are aimed at improving the effectiveness and working relationships of work groups.

The Purpose of Team Building

In recent years I have observed a number of teamdevelopment efforts and have lately come to the

Source: Richard Beckhard. Reprinted with permission of the *Journal of Contemporary Business*, copyright, Summer 1972, pp. 23–27 and 30–32.

realization that there may be a discrepancy in priorities between those people in charge of teams engaging in such efforts and those people who are facilitating them. Team leaders often consider their objectives to be improving work, setting priorities, or solving problems. Consultants, trainers, and helpers often see the prime purpose of the effort to be improving the workings of the group and/or the relationships of its members.

To help understand this more fully, I have developed a classification, in order of importance, of the reasons why teams or groups meet other than for the sharing of information. These are:

1. To set goals and/or priorities.
2. To analyze or allocate the way work is performed.
3. To examine the way a group is working: its processes (such as norms, decision making, communications).
4. To examine relationships among the people doing the work.

These purposes are usually operating in any teamdevelopment effort; but unless *one* purpose is defined as *the* primary purpose, there tends to be considerable misuse of energy. People then operate from their own hierarchy of purposes and, predictably, these are not always the same for all members.

In looking at the disenchantment of some managers and leaders regarding the amount of time spent on team improvement activities in their organizations, I have noted that organization development consultants and trainers frequently are perceived by ''clients'' or team leaders as having a ''universal'' rank-order of the four purposes, as follows:

The relationships among people.

The way the group works together.

The work.

The goals and priorities.

This perception is too often correct because the ''orientation'' of the organizational development (OD) consultant—his value system and much of his competence—probably is built around helping people work together in groups and is probably less related to the specific goal of an organization. However, if the perception is there on the part of the team leader, there probably will be a discrepancy between *his* preferred rank-ordering of priorities and his perceptions regarding preferences of the consultant.

It has also become clear that team leaders often tend to be inexplicit about their own rank-ordering. Therefore, the rank-ordering of the consultant may well be the controlling factor in a team-development effort. This is reinforced by the ''client's'' perception that the OD specialist is the *expert*. In such cases, the team leader tends to lean on the consultant for expert guidance and, in some cases, to give up his own responsibility for the effort.

Some Conditions for Effective Team Building

From the observations, I have developed a set of guidelines for team development:

The primary goal of a team development meeting must be explicit and well articulated.

This primary goal must be *owned* by the leader of the group and understood (hopefully, agreed to) by the work group members.

The leader's goal should be the condition within which third parties (consultants) work (i.e., the primary purpose is defined by the leader who sets the agenda and activities of the meeting).

If the consultant is working with a team, he should help the leader be explicit in *defining* and sharing the primary purpose.

The four goal categories probably will be dealt with in a particular activity, but only as appropriate in relation to a primary purpose.

A Model for Team-Building Activities

The following model examines for each of the four primary purposes (setting goals or priorities, the work, the way the group works, relationships within the group) four dimensions which would be considered:

Leader behavior.

Member behavior.

Outcomes.

Third-party or consultant behavior.

I will describe each of these dimensions in relation to *each* of the primary purposes, and follow the description with a case illustration.

Primary Purpose—Setting Goals or Priorities

Leader Behavior Issues

Are the work goals ''given'' (the leader's), or are they to be decided by the group?

Are the priorities a ''given'' or are they to be decided by the group?

How much freedom does the leader *wish* others to have in determining the agenda?

To what organization conditions, other goals, policies, etc., must these goals or priorities be related?

What preparation is necessary to optimize use of the resources of the members at the activity?

What are the leader's specific hoped-for outcomes for the meeting?

Member Behavior Issues

What behavior around the task is expected from members—i.e., Understanding? Decision making? Agreement to implement? Action-plans?

What data are needed during the meeting—i.e., effects of alternative goals or priorities on members' work and the work of suborganizations?

Outcomes Possible

What is required from the meeting—i.e., A new statement of goals or priorities? Agreement to develop one?

What action plans and responsibilities for carrying out meeting outputs should be developed?

How will assignments of responsibilities be made?

What kind of feedback and checkpoints are or should be available?

Third-Party Behavior Issues

Some of the ''process'' questions that might be asked by a facilitator concern:

1. Clarity of the goal—i.e., agreement on priorities.
2. To what degree people are understanding each other.
3. Clarity of the ownership of the goals.
4. *Awareness* of consequences.
5. Commitment to action.

Case. In a large consumer organization there were a number of departments with computer and information systems capabilities. These departments were combined into a new Management Methods Department, which was to provide leadership in applying the various technologies to requirements of the organization. It also was to provide support and assistance to a variety of users with respect to methods and hardware. A third mission was to provide an educational effort to increase the internal market of users.

The membership of the management team of this group comprised a variety of bases—some had worked together before, others had not. Each member had headed a specialty or specialists' group and had had his own ''technological empire.'' The management group was asked to combine all these

resources and develop a new kind of service organization.

The leader of the group wanted to introduce some new technologies which he knew would provide significant savings to some parts of the organization. He also was concerned with centralizing some hardware installations; with communicating the new department's capabilities and services to the rest of the organization; with upgrading both the amounts and the quality of services provided; with developing some major new applications; and with creating a new image of *helpfulness* to the line managements of the business.

Having defined the primary purpose of the meeting as setting goal and mission priorities, the leader now needed to clarify his expectations around the first issue—were the priorities *given* or to be decided by the group? It became clear, by discussion, that the leader had preferences, but he really wanted *consensus* from this group on priorities and goals. He felt that all of his goals were interdependent; thus, it did not matter which one was worked first. Therefore, his first effort at the meeting was to convince the members that relative to *their* role expectations, *he expected* that this group would, as a group, determine the priorities of the various goals, set programs, and provide the resource management for carrying out the programs necessary to achieve the goals. The leader wanted a great deal of freedom to be shared among subordinates.

In the course of a couple of meetings, it became clear from discussions that there was also a need for exploration of the way the work was going to be done. Issues arose about how the group would handle decisions around priorities, how the information should flow between sections, and how the group norms regarding openness or leveling would be decided.

Some people were unclear about the leader's position on these issues but when his attitudes were shared, their confusion ended. He wanted all to have freedom to challenge goals and priorities.

Relationship problems surfaced which, after discussion, turned out to be goal problems. For example, one person in the group had held a job now held by another person in the group. Because they had different work priorities for that subsection, there was concern about the relationship between them. Discussion quickly cleared this up.

By treating the "how we work" and "relationship" questions as agenda matters to be dealt with as they got in the way of the *goal-setting* issues, the group was able to move quite rapidly toward actual setting of goals and priorities and to make action plans for following up.

Primary Purpose—Analyzing and Assigning Work

Leader Behavior Issues

Defining areas of work to be studied.

Defining the *current* situation—i.e., where work and responsibility are located.

Defining boundaries of his willingness to change.

Defining roles he wants others to take in the meeting—i.e., suggestions, decisions, actions.

Member Behavior Issues

An understanding of the areas of work to be allocated, the alternative possibilities, and the parameters of freedom to relocate work.

Clear role expectations—what behavior is expected of them in the decision making?

Awareness of implications and *costs* of changing work.

Payout for subordinates or members of changing allocations of work.

Outcomes Possible

New work distribution.

An action plan for communicating changes to others.

Answers on costs, effects on compensation and rewards, effects on roles, titles, etc.

Action plan for follow-up evaluation of the changes.

Third-Party Behavior Issues

Providing a method for working the issues—e.g., providing methods of analyzing work.

Helping to clarify work boundaries.

Getting the group to face action implications and to plan.

Helping people understand each other.

Raising issues of openness of communications within the group.

Case. The top management of a division of a large chemical organization is managed by a board composed of a chairman, two deputy chairmen, and ten members of the management board. The group functions as an executive board. Each member of the team except the chairman and deputy chairmen have functional responsibilities, such as manufacturing, engineering, personnel; they also are responsible at the division level for some business area; e.g., serving as chairman of a wholly owned subsidiary.

Officially, the power of decisions rests centrally with the chairman. The remainder of the group had been perceived by its members as being mostly advisory. Actual functioning of the upper management of the organization was somewhat unclear; there were questions about the responsibilities of management board members acting in their functional capacities as opposed to their responsibilities as board members. There was considerable dissatisfaction with this ambiguity.

The chairman suggested having a team meeting to analyze realistically the tasks that needed to be performed by the board as a board; the tasks that were not getting performed; and the possibilities of delegating some tasks below board level to operating managers.

The method used was a review of the board agendas for the previous six months and an analysis of these agendas. This analysis provided three lists:

1. Things that the group did which absolutely must be done by them as a group.

2. Work that was not being done that should be done by this group—e.g., long-range planning.
3. Work that was being done by this group that could be done as well or almost as well by the same members operating in other roles or by other people.

The analysis showed that between 25 and 30 percent of the work being done by this group could be done by others. There was a roughly similar amount of work that needed to be done that was not getting done.

The group examined its own *attitudes* and *commitment* toward turning over some major areas of work to other people. It explored the training, development, and changes of procedure that would be required for the transfer of work—it identified what this would mean in terms of rewards (who would be held accountable and responsible.) The discussion also identified areas of personal development that the board or executive committee members needed in order to take on some of the work that they were not doing. It also provided some clarification of what the chairman expected of them. This discussion produced the need for further examination of some of the relationships between roles, particularly the roles between the deputy chairman and the junior board members.

Outputs involved (1) a minor structural reorganization, (2) the delegation of a considerable amount of work, with full responsibility and accountability for its disposition, to the operating manager level, (3) the organization of a planning group within the board, and (4) a change of many of the practices of their board meetings.

Primary Purpose—How the Group Works

Leader Behavior Issues

Dissatisfaction with the status quo as a reason for wanting to change.

Willingness to look at all data, styles, attitudes, titles, rewards, and processes.

Willingness to be influenced.

Self-realization by the leader that he is probably part of the relevant data.

Methods for working the problem.

Member Behavior Issues

The need for clear ground rules on "voting"; how much openness is allowed and the punishments or consequences of deviant behavior.

The need to know what the boss's feelings are regarding present practices and possible changes.

The need for a set of parameters of possibilities for change.

The need for some readiness to work the problems.

Outcomes Possible

Some new norms are possible.

Action plans regarding change procedures can emerge.

Some changed "ownership" in the management of certain processes, such as agenda planning, structure, decision making, and leadership.

Third-Party Behavior Issues

Process interventions around issues are relevant, such as communication, decision making, norms, and leadership.

He can provide methods for working the problems.

He can help work issues such as those on listening, problem-solving, role distortion, and projection.

Case. In a large, diversified organization, the personnel function had previously been managed by a director and several department heads, each of whom heads a function, such as employment, compensation, salary administration, benefits, training and development, industrial relations, and employee relations.

The heads of these groups were specialists. Their departments functioned as relatively independent staffs handling the particular function for which they were responsible. For general information-sharing—updating company policies and priorities and providing liaison with top management—there were "cabinet" meetings of the heads of departments with the director. However, there was no shared responsibility for or commitment to total management of the personnel function by the heads of the specific functions.

A new director moved in who believed that the personnel organization should be reorganized and redirected to focus around *organization issues* and *human resources management issues* rather than along the strict functional lines previously followed. For example, relations with employees involved not only the head of industrial relations, but also the training and development people and the employment people. He also wanted to develop a management *team* in the personnel function that could *locate* the priority issues in the organization, and *mobilize* the *total resources* of the personnel staff and others in the organization to manage these priorities.

In his early weeks in the organization, he communicated these desires and priorities and received responses ranging from outright resistance to "lip service" approval. In most cases, people responded in a "subordinate" way to what they perceived to be commands.

The director really wanted to change the mode of working. He convened a meeting with the specific purpose of "taking a look at how we're working together"—what processes and procedures are used, what processes, procedures, and systems will be necessary to move toward the kind of management of human resources that he required and desired. At the meeting, his statement of wishes immediately led to a discussion of how these decisions *had been made* and how they were now being made by him, and how people hoped they would be made.

A second issue developed around communication and influence; a third issue was the director's leadership style and the differences between his style and that of the previous leadership. A fourth issue was what were the rewards and punishments for acting one way or another in this new situation?

As the group worked, it was able to examine thoroughly the various processes, procedures, roles, norms, etc., within which they worked, and to relate these to the defined goal of a coordinated management of the human resources function. This was a case where the goal was clearly to work on *how* we work, and specific plans for changing the way work was done in the organization became the *case material* and the validating point for the work on the primary purpose of the meeting.

Primary Purpose—Relationships among the Group Members

Leader Behavior Issues

An awareness of the interpersonal issues in the group.

A willingness to expose his own attitudes and biases.

A willingness to be nonpunitive.

Some assurance that group members see this activity as relevant.

A willingness to change or to be influenced.

Member Behavior Issues

Enough personal security to take some risks.

A knowledge and belief that the leader has real interests in the process.

Some confidence in the process and/or the third party.

Some feelings of relevance of the activity.

Some feelings of potency.

Some willingness to expose feelings.

Outcomes Possible

Increased understanding and acceptance of each other.

Better listening.

Some new norms—e.g., leveling, more information-based decisions.

More feelings of ownership.

More willingness to take risks.

More willingness to confront conflict and work to resolve it.

Third-Party Behavior Issues

Interventions in this mode are most helpful around process issues.

Intervention process—i.e., communications, decision making.

Protection of parameters of openness, confrontation, etc.

Modeling behavior—e.g., feedback.

Objectivity as applied to the group's work.

Nonjudgmental feedback.

Resolution of interpersonal difficulties.

Case. A management group in a division of an organization had developed norms of openness, problem solving, and goal direction. The organization climate was quite open and free. The division was a high-technology group with a number of extremely capable scientists whose whole background was entrepreneurial and professional. The management group was committed intellectually to building a participative, democratic organization. Obstacles toward achievement of this generally shared goal and value system were: (1) their own personal styles, and (2) the interaction among them. The group was able to be very open around technical problems, intergroup problems within the organization, and role problems. However, they were not able to deal with each other as people with different biases, interests, and styles. The norm of "nonconfronting" this kind of material was reinforced by the president, a brilliant executive, greatly admired by all the members of the team. He was a rational, sensible, analytically minded person who could keep the discussions rational and data-based. He managed, simultaneously, though inadver-

tently, to suppress much of the emotional data which were crucial and with which they needed to deal.

After a considerable amount of time working as a team—including outside developmental experiences by many individual members—a subgroup emerged which had a common goal of facing these relationship questions. It had enough potency to deal with both the president and colleagues. They suggested an extended meeting to have a thorough review of where they stood as *people* managing this business. The suggestion was accepted by all the members and the meeting was held.

At this meeting each individual received some feedback from all of his colleagues about his strengths and weaknesses as they perceived them, what bothered or pleased them about his behavior. Each individual could use this feedback any way he wished—there was no requirement for change. The feedback surfaced some historic issues that had been affecting the work of the group; for example, two people who had been competing throughout their careers maintained this competition in the group. They were perceived by all the others as sometimes robbing the group of their technical resource capability on the tasks because of their interpersonal relationship. It was agreed that the group would try to draw this to their attention whenever it arose in the future.

The feedback to the president by the team was accepted and generally understood by him. He acted on it to some degree; however, the main benefit of *this* feedback was that it freed the group to produce this kind of information in the future as needed. This became a norm of the group and was perhaps the single most significant result.

Here is a case in which interpersonal relationships of a group of responsible adults were impeding their doing what they all really wanted to do: effective work on goals and plans and effective management of their scientific capability in a humanized setting.

Summary

Work groups and teams spend a significant amount of man-hours, in addition to their administrative information meetings, on group activities aimed at one of the following goals:

1. Establishing goals or priorities.
2. Analyzing and distributing the work.
3. Examining how the group works (procedures, processes, norms).
4. Examining the relationships among the group members as they work.

There is a need for criteria for sorting out the rank-ordering of these purposes and for selecting *one* of them as a primary purpose.

The team leader must take responsibility for setting the specific core purpose of a meeting.

Third parties can make a major contribution in facilitating the work of such groups. Their help should be as process consultants within the core purpose defined by the client or team leader.

Managers can more or less systematically relate the primary purpose—goal setting, work planning, work relationships—to issues of leader behavior, member behavior, outcomes, and third party or consultant behavior.

These options can help group leaders determine the goal of an improvement activity, the information needed to work the activity, an understanding of the kind of facilitation which might be helpful by a third party, and a clear commitment to some appropriate outcomes.

Conscious management of such team-building efforts can do much to utilize the human energy in organizationally and personally profitable ways.

Reading 19

A GESTALT ORIENTATION TO
ORGANIZATION DEVELOPMENT

Stanley M. Herman

A few months ago a psychotherapist friend of mine asked me to join him in consulting with one of his patients. The patient, a highly successful general manager of a building supply company, had just been offered the presidency of a very large retail chain organization. Taking over the new assignment would, as he saw it, require drastic changes in the company's way of doing business, and likely the "reformation" or replacement of several high-level people. That was the dilemma. This energetic, talented and essentially tough-minded general manager had about a year or so before attended a sensitivity training laboratory, had been deeply touched by his experience of warmth, affection, and support in the group and had attempted subsequently to expand his knowledge by readings in organization development. Then, he had tried to apply the principles he had learned to his own and others' relationships in his organization. The results of his attempts had been mixed. Some subordinates had responded well to his openness and participative style. Others had used the greater leeway he gave them as an opportunity to become lax and ineffective. Nevertheless, the general manager stayed devotedly with his perceptions of what good human relations ought to be, and in fact his hesitancy about accepting the new job offer had to do with his doubt that his management approach would work with his new subordinates. And as he put it: "I would rather quit managing altogether than go back to my old authoritarian ways."

Source: Stanley M. Herman, reproduced by special permission from *Contemporary Organization Development: Conceptual Orientations and Interventions,* ed. W. Warner Burke. Copyright 1972 NTL Institute, Arlington, Virginia, pp. 69–89.

After some exploratory discussion it became clear that a certain amount of misinterpretation had occurred in this man's understanding of sound human relations practice (as most experienced OD people will have guessed). But in a larger sense a great deal of what was troubling this manager I recognized as a common theme among many people who have been influenced by the sensitivity-training–derived theories of OD. He had come to regard his own power—both his organizational position and his personal force—as something uncomfortable, even bad. And so he worked diligently to restrain that power for the sake of others whom he saw as less powerful. I believe that this discomfort with the overt exercise of directive authority is quite common among many people involved in OD theory and practice.[1]

For some time the main thrust of organization development efforts has been directed at changing

---

[1]To provide closure on the incident: the manager, my friend, and I discussed the issue he raised, and he did some "gestalt work" on his decision to accept or not accept the new job. I also later sent him an earlier draft of this paper and a related one and got the following response:

"Dear Stan:

I cannot thank you enough for taking an evening to help out a troubled person with some good, sound organizational development advice.

I read your two articles. Funny thing, it seemed as though these articles were written especially for me and it seems as though there is a common thread between the problem I am incurring when I attempt to fit myself into the mold of the prototype leader. I am quite sure I am much more effective just being myself. You point this out rather dramatically. This application of Gestalt techniques to organizations is an exciting idea. . . ."

organization environments in ways that will make them more supportive and facilitative to people. For example, we frequently speak of the requirement to change an organization culture in ways that will support such values as openness, participation, interdependence, etc. I believe that emphasis has been useful but not sufficient. In this paper I want to suggest an additional approach, one that is largely derived from the theory and practice of gestalt therapy.

In the following pages I intend to emphasize the "ungentle" aspects of organizational behavior, those that have generally received less attention and have frequently been regarded with less comfort by many OD theoreticians and practitioners.[2] My objective here is not to provide instruction on making the organization culture safer, more pleasant or easier for the individual, but rather to help the individual recognize, develop and experience his own potency and ability to cope with his organization world, whatever its present condition. Further, I would like to encourage him to discover for himself his own unique wants of that environment and his capacity to influence and shape it in ways that get him more of what he wants.

The most formidable barrier to the person and his free expression of himself in the organization setting is probably fear. Fear of others, and how they might affect him and his life, and even more importantly fear of himself and how he might make mistakes, do the wrong thing, and so imperil "his future" and/or his image of himself as a modern manager, specialist, or whatever.

One of the most crucial areas of study in examining organization behavior is the manager-subordinate relationship. In this relationship, probably more than any other, both managers and subordinates frequently constrict the potential range of their interaction (and their potential capacity to enjoy each other). In the sections below I will discuss currently prevalent patterns of relationships and some alternatives, first from the perspective of the manager and then the subordinate.

The Myth of Omnipotence

For many years an important focus for theories of management has been the area of power and control. Even before Douglas McGregor postulated his X and Y theories of management many other theorists advocated caution in the manager's use of power and control. Cases were made for participative permissive or otherwise moderated styles of supervision. By now it has become clear to almost every manager or supervisor who sees himself as "beyond the dark ages" that bosses are not supposed to be domineering and authoritarian, or, at least if they are, they are not supposed to seem that way to their subordinates. This was a heavy self-imposed requirement of the building supply company general manager in my earlier case example.

It is clearly true that a dictatorial or oppressive style of management is no longer generally acceptable in the United States. But I believe that the real basis for this truth is not found in philosophical images of theoretical democracy; rather, it stems from the high probability that most people who work in present-day organizations are unwilling to tolerate oppression. They will find a way of rising up against it, either overtly or covertly, through sabotage.

For many managers though, the image of "democratic leadership" has not served as a useful model. Their attempts to regulate their own behavior to make it "fit the image" have been strained and unnatural, and frequently received with discomfort and suspicion by their subordinates. A man is a man, and if his behavior is authentic it must reflect his own internal personal realities at any given point in time, not a prescribed external ideal. In the gestalt context, forced or deliberately planned "corrections" in behavior—even when they are ostensibly voluntary—produce exhibitionistic rather than genuine change. Such change is very difficult to sustain and the effort to sustain it is usually at great cost to the individual. *Genuine growth requires that a person first recognize and acknowl-*

---

[2] I do want to note that recently there has been increased attention to the power aspects of organization life by some OD people and I believe this is a hopeful sign.

edge his present qualities before he can proceed with his own natural development.

Withheld Thrust

In the practice of psychotherapy, therapists repeatedly encounter the guilt and anxiety-ridden patient who tortures himself with fantasies of how he has abused or injured others. In this way he brings himself to a state of such self-mistrust or self-hate that he becomes unable to encounter people around him and can only turn inward. His vitality and excitement are lost as he spends his energy in restraining and punishing himself.

In an organization culture where the exercise of direct authoritarian power is ostensibly disapproved by the established norms of the organization, many people in positions of authority may experience a comparable (though, of course, less extreme) pattern. They may become vaguely uncomfortable or even terribly concerned about the "awesome force" they have over other people. I call this syndrome the myth of omnipotence.

The myth of omnipotence is a specter that can paralyze potency. The manager who believes too much in his own power to harm begins to withhold or divert his energy, his spontaneity and his thrust in order to avoid hurting others. This withheld thrust has adverse affects both on the withholder and on those from whom he withholds. In the course of my organization consulting I have encountered many cases in which the manager of an organization struggles painfully within himself to try to force his behavior to conform to an image of managership in which he is continually benign, nonauthoritarian, encouraging, and facilitative toward his subordinates. And at the same time within himself he feels but holds back his own wants, convictions, and desires to move things ahead. He also experiences "negative" emotions toward his subordinates, such as irritation, criticism, impatience, and so on and yet withholds these because a "good manager" (like a "good parent") is not supposed to express such things to those who are below him (his children).

Believing the myth of his own omnipotence might have some consolation for a manager if he could, at least subjectively, feel himself stronger and more capable in comparison to his subordinates. But the typical manager seldom enjoys that feeling of superiority even at a subjective level, instead he struggles with intermittent ambivalence and lack of fulfillment.

Perhaps more important, his subordinates may also suffer from the ambiguity of the signals the manager sends out. On the one hand the manager's words are encouraging, patient, and reasonable, but on the other hand the expressions on his face, his tone, his body signs (e.g., fidgeting, tension, etc.) almost invariably also show through, and these too are perceived by his subordinates. The disparities, however, are seldom if ever dealt with.

Full Expression

It would be far healthier for the manager to fully express his feelings, negative as well as positive, and to allow himself fuller expression of his authoritarian-directive impulses as well. With their full expression his subordinates can more completely experience the totality of the manager's reality. Then they can accept or contest it (and him) as they see fit. From this interchange of full expression and full reaction both the manager and his subordinates can grow in a more meaningful way. Their growth follows at least two dimensions. First, in the interpersonal and intrapersonal sense they learn to really know each other more richly and authentically, and through a heightened awareness of their own feelings, they learn to know themselves better as well. Second, with repeated practice and greater familiarity between each other, the substance of their ideas can also be more adequately tested and new, more effective ways of working together developed.

In one organization I worked with the high-level manager of a large staff who had developed a strong, indeed passionate, commitment to "OD values." Included in these values, as he saw them, was the requirement for a manager to be fair, rational, and helpful to those who reported to him. Most of the time he conformed to these requirements quite easily and naturally. He was, however, an individual of great personal force, with strong emotions and subject to occasional moodiness. Those who reported to him recognized these qualities and had gradually grown accustomed to them, though as might be expected, comfort with his style differed among them.

Over a considerable period of time this strong, able manager grew increasingly discontent and unhappy in his relationships with several members of his staff, and staff members, in turn, were also troubled. The "problem" can best be illustrated by the patterns of interaction in the manager's staff meetings. These were generally conducted in a fairly free-flowing and participative style with the floor pretty much available to anyone who wanted it. Sometimes the meetings were quite businesslike and at other times they consisted mostly of a series of rambling discourses punctuated occasionally by concise irrelevancies.

For the most part the manager and his staff were fairly satisfied with both the focused and the "nonproductive" discussions. From time to time, however, and for no very apparent reason except his mood at the moment, the manager would suddenly jump into the discussion with all the force of a safe dropped from a ten-story window, usually landing on one of about three or four members of his staff. Frequently, though not always, his "attack" was logically sound, it was not so much the substance as the vehemence and unexpectedness that seemed to most affect those who were its targets.

The responses of those who were "attacked" by the boss varied, but few were completely unresponsive. This was clearly not an oppressive environment. Some replied by defending their position with counter-logic. One used humor, including self-depreciating comments, to "reduce the tension." Still another acted out and sometimes verbally expressed his feelings of being "punished" by the boss. Whatever the response though, what most frequently seemed to happen was that after a round or two of exchange the boss would cease to re-

spond, frequently settling into a glum, silent posture. When that happened the entire group would experience a long awkward pause, with no explicit resolution of the issue, if indeed an issue was even identifiable from the brief exchange.

After working with the group for some period of time, I found myself face-to-face with their classic syndrome. An important proposal for a change of policy had been made by one of the staff, and tentatively supported by two others. The manager's reaction was quick and strongly negative. He accused all the proponents of being panicky, unrealistic, and out of touch with the organization's needs. After the typical pattern of responses from these staff members and another round or two of exchange the manager lapsed into grim silence.

The alternatives for me as a consultant then were: (1) I could intervene in such a way as to focus even more sharply on the disruptive, inhibiting effects on his staff of the manager's outbursts, possibly I could analyze or encourage the group to analyze the reasons for and consequences of the interaction pattern or (2) I could intervene in a way that *encouraged the fight to continue* (without having any clear idea of what consequences might come out the other end). With some anxiety I made the latter choice, primarily by allowing my own emotions of resentment and antagonism to come out. I challenged the manager to follow through on his punishing behavior—in fact to really get into it more fully.

After some hesitation the manager began, at first with some awkwardness, but soon with great enthusiasm, to blast a number of his staff. At the same time the people he attacked were encouraged to respond, even counterattack if they felt like it. Soon other members of the staff also joined the fray, usually on the side of their colleague. This free-for-all style was allowed to develop into a room full of shouting people that more resembled a disorderly convention of longshoremen than a staff meeting of high-level managers of a major corporation. And the outcome was marvelous.

As the group reexamined its processes some time later, members recognized that this turbulent meeting (and a few others since) had produced for the entire group a greater sense of vitality, excitement and relatedness than they had felt for many months, and that this feeling had carried over into subsequent staff meetings as well. In addition, the manager reported that their fights had brought him a new sense of respect for the staff members who stood up to him. In subsequent encounters other staff members also began to stand their ground more readily.

What was the theoretical basis for my choice of intervention? First, I need to say that the choice was mostly intuitive rather than theoritical. It came out of my immediate feelings and my willingness to risk making a mistake. (Since I've mostly gotten over my own myth of omnipotence I'm less worried about making *catastrophic* mistakes. As a consultant, I'm just not that crucial to my clients.) Nevertheless, in looking back on the incident for an ex-post-facto theorization I recognize the following.

As I worked with the group over some period of time it became clear to me that the manager was quite aware of the effect of his "attacks" on his staff members, *perhaps too aware*. Why then did he, an enlightened, devoted, "Theory Y" manager, continue this behavior?

The answer is because the feelings behind his behavior were part of him—part of the whole of his humanness, power, and emotionality—those same qualities for which his staff and many others respected and trusted him. What then could be done? To preach self-control or even temperance to this manager hardly seemed worthwhile (whether the preaching was overt and direct or through the more subtle use of group "feedback.") Even if he resolved to stop his verbal interruptions his feelings would still be sensed by others and would float like a pervasive phantom among them all. No, the answer was not for this manager to back away from his impulsive behavior, but rather, again, in the gestalt framework, *to go further into it*. The point was not to cut himself off with his guilt feelings about abusing his subordinates after an exchange or two and then settle into melancholy self-blame.

Rather it was to stay engaged with them in "the battle" until it reached its natural conclusion—until he and they had the opportunity to fully experience and possibly to finish the unfinished business between them.

Over time some major positive effects came from this new style of engagement for the group: The entire staff became more comfortable with the boss and each other, and the manager began to *enjoy* his relations with his people more than he had before. I believe that the experience the manager had in allowing himself to follow through on his aggressive impulse rather than holding back was a significant one in his own growth. He discovered that, lo and behold, his "victims" did not perish from his onslaught, but rather seemed to grow stronger. Conversely, I suspect a similar positive effect in the subordinates' discovery that they were able to handle whatever the boss threw at them and to come back swinging.

I have seen several high-level managers, long inhibited by their images of the good "participative manager," finally able to fully and spontaneously release their pent-up feelings. When the breakthrough comes out in strong expressions of anger, affection, dislike, or whatever, there may well be an initial shock that is uncomfortable to everyone, including the consultant. But with time and courage to stay engaged, those involved work it through. They are able to deal with each other's strong emotions much better than they can handle the avoidance and phantom expressions, and eventually they may achieve a vital, robust and mutually satisfying relationship in which both manager and subordinates are far freer and energetic than in the past.

It is, of course possible that some managers, if encouraged to fully express themselves, would turn out to be intolerable tyrants. I believe there are few such people. In the context of gestalt theory the "intolerable tyrant" is likely to be an individual suffering the myth of his own personal total helplessness. Thus he defends himself by trying to control completely all those around him. In the therapy for such individuals, as they are able to confront their feelings of helplessness and come to recognize for themselves that they are not as totally helpless as they feel, the tyrannical behavior begins to disappear. At any rate I suspect that a straightforward undisguised tyrant is easier and better to deal with than a disguised one.

Consultant's Focus

In most organizations the interaction style just described would not be an easy one for people to initiate and pursue without help. Generally most organizations have too much of an overlay of historical norms and traditions of "appropriate behavior." Here, I believe, is where organization development and the third-party consultant can be of great help. The consultant can concentrate on assisting managers and subordinates to fully experience and express "where they are" both on issues and in relationships with each other. He can highlight their interpersonal process, help them to discover their own vitality and the satisfaction and excitement of full expression. He can help them to become aware of *how they stop themselves* from completing their experiences. He can help them become aware of their own predictive (and usually catastrophic) fantasies, i.e., the manager imagines: "If I really let myself go I would oppress, overpower, do terrible damage to my subordinates." The subordinate thinks, "I must be very careful because this is a very dangerous environment." And when these murky catastrophic expectations have been surfaced the consultant can help the people explore and test them against reality, and finally work out individual arrangements between people that will allow them greater self-expression and fulfillment.[3]

While many of the processes I am describing, I'm sure, seem quite similar to typical OD consultation theory, in practice there are important dif-

[3]In a later paper detailed approaches and techniques for these purposes as well as other gestalt-oriented OD applications will be outlined.

ferences of execution. "Confrontation" and "owning feelings" are, of course, common concepts in OD. In my experience, however, many OD consultants facilitate confrontation only to the point of emergence of an identifiable problem (e.g., manager A does not listen to subordinate B, or the manager of one organization repeatedly fails to solicit the advice and involvement of other managers with whom he "ought" to be interdependent, etc.). In some organizations the surfacing of such complaints—the fact that they have finally been brought out into the open and acknowledged—can be a major step, but frequently the consultant then moves too rapidly to the task of problem solving. Thus with the consultant's help, the manager acknowledges his fault and resolves to "listen more carefully" to his subordinate; or action items are prepared and task groups formed to develop new processes to assure better coordination between the various organization subunits, etc. The trouble is that this premature movement into problem solving may be addressing symptoms rather than causes and may produce solutions that are superficial and temporary at best.

The gestalt mode encourages stronger, deeper, and more concrete (as contrasted to abstract or generalized) interactions. Most importantly we emphasize *staying with* the transaction until both parties have *completed* their business with each other. The individual or contesting parties are encouraged to dramatize and even exaggerate their behavior—to become fully aware of what they are doing and how they are doing it (not why). The manager who does not listen is encouraged to go further into his nonlistening mode, to discover and be explicit about what he is doing instead of listening, how he keeps himself from listening, and to complete whatever it is he needs to complete before he can give his attention to listening. The subordinate who is not listened to may be encouraged to discover how he keeps himself from being heard (i.e., from talking louder or more forcefully—from *demanding* attention). The managers of the noninteracting organizations are encouraged to state clearly what each wants (or even demands) of the other, with emphasis on meeting his own selfish needs rather than because it would be good organizational practice. And each manager is encouraged to respond "yes" or "no" to each demand.[4] Interdependence is not an automatically presumed virtue in every case (though it may be a real operating requirement) and when consensual decisions cannot be reached within a reasonable time, power-based decisions are not considered disreputable.

The Tyranny of the Underdog

The other side of the myth of managerial omnipotence is the tyranny of the underdog. OD theory has for most of its relatively brief history stressed the support of "the underdog"—the subordinate, the reticent team member, etc.—and the solution of disagreement through rational processes. In the context of our national culture and traditions this is not surprising nor can I object to the general underlying philosophy. Unfortunately, however, some of our approaches have attempted to "help" the underdog by providing an easier world for him through advocating the restraint (usually by "self-control" and under the moral pressure of "human relations rightness") of the powerful manager or team member. I believe this approach is wrong. Not only does it foster the inhibiting omnipotence myth and guilt feelings of the manager discussed earlier, it can also be experienced as a *confirmation of his own inferiority or invalidism by the individual who is granted the so-called benefits of other people holding themselves for his sake.* Better by far to help the underdog to discover, use, and rejoice in his strength and ability to move forward for himself than to have others take turns pushing his wheelchair for him.

---

[4]The reaction to this "selfish," demand-oriented process is frequently quite remarkable. Paradoxically these heated exchanges generate more respect and positive feeling between the contesting parties than a raft of cool, rational, for-the-good-of-the-company sessions. The ultimate decisions also seem to be more viable.

Robert W. Resnick (1970), a gestalt-oriented psychotherapist, makes the point this way in his paper, "Chicken Soup Is Poison":

> Many therapists see themselves as members of the "helping professions" engaged in the helping relationship. Beware! Such people are dangerous. If successful they kill the humanness in their patients by preventing their growth. This insidious process is somehow worse realizing such therapists typically want the reverse. They want their patients to grow, to live, and to be, and they guarantee the antithesis with their "help." The distinction between true support and "help" is clear: To do for the other what he is capable of doing for himself insures his not becoming aware that he can stand on his own two feet. . . .

Polarities

An important part of gestalt therapy is the concept of polarities, the extremes within each of us; i.e., weakness-strength, activism-passivity, etc., that together comprise our full natures. One of the manifestations of polarity is the "top dog" versus "underdog." The top dog is that part of us that mostly serves the function of director and disciplinarian, that part of our personalities that tells us what we *should do*. The underdog is the resistive part of us, that part that balks at the bossiness of top dog and attempts to subvert or derail his directives.

Our underdog may work at his mission by pleading that we are unable to do what the top dog demands, or he may delay and promise to do it tomorrow, or he may divert the top dog's directions, and so on. Fritz Perls in his development of gestalt therapy believed that the underdog in each individual almost always triumphed in the long run over the top dog. This phenomenon, incidentally, may well explain why in organizations as well as elsewhere so many plans and vows to change seem to fare no better than most people's New Year's resolutions.

Great energy is frequently bottled up in the conflict between these two conflicting drives within an individual, energy that is therefore not available for other more satisfying purposes. Further, the conflict between the top dog and the underdog frequently produces unhappiness and a sense of lack of fulfillment for the person.

Relationships between some individuals within organizations have many of the same characteristics as this top dog/underdog conflict. The apparently powerful, assertive person makes demands on the ostensibly weaker underdog, but somehow, the demands are never quite met. And while the top dog's pressure may be great, the underdog's ability to divert, deflect. or delay is often greater. So-called weak parties in a variety of relationships may have very great, though not immediately apparent, advantages in their ability to resist without attacking and to use, like a judo expert, the strong person's own strength against him. I have worked with a number of teams in which one or two members, undoubtedly without conscious intent, skillfully manipulated the apparently stronger members of the group, including the boss into "helping" them. This helping takes many forms. It can be protecting the quiet member, taking his side in a competitive situation, being more sympathetic to his problems and inabilities to meet his commitments than would be the case for other members of the team, etc. One of the most harmful accommodations to the "weak party" involves others holding back their forcefulness and vitality in order to keep from offending or upsetting the underdog.

Ogre Building

A variation of the underdog game is ogre building. Almost all of us in organizations have the capacity to build ogres fearsome enough to scare ourselves half to death. The ogre may be a supervisor, especially one at a higher level than those we are accustomed to dealing with, another organization, or, perhaps most insidious of all, "the system." Ogres can be very useful sometimes in helping us to avoid doing what we don't really want to do anyway. I do not object to the use of the ogre for that purpose if indeed we are conscious of what we are doing and that we *want* to do it. More frequently, however, we are not aware of what we

are doing and our ogres are not so clearly useful. They are compounded of some degree of organizational reality plus our own projections and predictions of dire consequences. Organization development methodology is frequently useful in dealing with ogres, especially the mutual ogres dreamed up by internally competitive organizations for each other. I believe more can be done, especially in working with individuals in helping them to discover their courage and capacity to confront and deal with their own ogres.

In the therapeutic process that addresses top dog/underdog conflicts the first step involves heightening polarization. The patient increases his awareness of both forces within himself; especially, he becomes aware of *the power inherent in his underdog position.* With this new awareness grows a sense of excitement, pride and energy. Later, when he has well experienced his own extremes he may move naturally to an "integration," i.e., he is able to regain his access to those parts of himself he had submerged or renounced and so eventually he becomes able to utilize as the situation requires, a more complete spectrum of his behavioral potential.

Consultant's Focus

In the organization consulting process, especially when dealing with "complaining people"—those who see others and/or their environment as oppressive and preventing them from doing what they want to do—it is a good idea for the consultant to begin working with his client in a way that concentrates on identifying the client's strength. That may not be easy, the complainer's strength is not readily apparent. On the contrary he usually spends much of his time denying he has any strength at all. All power belongs to "the others"—his boss, his more influential, articulate, or aggressive coworkers, or most oppressive of all to "the company."

As a consultant I begin by being suspicious of these complaints. This is not to say that I think the complainer is intentionally deceptive, nor do I doubt that widespread inequalities of power and opportunity for certain classes of organization citizens do exist. Rather, I have found that most people do possess some form of power even if that power is passive, resistive, or a withholding kind that is used to manipulate others, often by triggering feelings of guilt among the more active and assertive people with whom they deal.

A case that illustrates the subtleties of power distribution involved a large government agency I worked with. We began with a team-building session between the top-management group (including the chief and his central staff) and about a dozen field supervisors, each of whom headed a local service office. The pattern of complaints, and there were many from each side, were clear and repeated. For the central staff it was that those in the field seldom seemed to be able to respond to the requests for new information that they were asked to provide, nor did they often try out proposed new methods developed by the central staff for use in the field. When they occasionally did try out the recommended procedures, it was in a most cursory way that practically assured the failure of the new approach. Finally, after repeated efforts, the central staff people had quietly abandoned their efforts to direct the field supervisors and adopted what they felt to be the more modern management approach of asking the field people to submit their own ideas for innovation and improvement. This approach fared no better.

What I noticed as I heard the presentation of this information from the central staff people was their almost complete lack of emotion. This pattern of relationships which had been going on for about a year must have produced frustration for the agency chief and his staff, yet in listening to the presenters I heard only careful neutrality, infinite patience, and dispassionate though devoted interest in objective "problem solving."

It took considerably longer for the case of the field supervisors to emerge. Their first responses to the complaints of the central staff were rather desultory and almost apologetic. They had very heavy work loads, many new people to train, spent a great deal of time on public relations, and so on. All of which limited their ability to concentrate on

new approaches. Besides, they felt it was quite likely that they could develop any new methods that would really satisfy the central staff, since the central staff people were obviously so much better informed about the latest trends in their specialized field. Similarly, the information emerged that in the past year a few of the field supervisors felt they had attempted to institute some of the recommended new approaches of the central staff but had not done well at it. And while they had not been overtly criticized by the staff they had "felt" disapproved of.

As a consultant here I again experienced myself at a decision point. I could try to help the field supervisors by encouraging the central staff to examine their olympian posture and how their cool paternalism put down the supervisors. They could then examine ways they might change this pattern into a more encouraging one. Second, I could pursue the problem-solving approach by helping the total group to recognize specific areas of weakness in the supervisor's skills and then to develop training programs for building those skills. Third, I could encourage the field supervisors to (in the gestalt sense) go even further into their complaints. I chose the third.

I requested that the supervisors (in a "fish-bowl" arrangement) elaborate further on their grievances against the staff. The result, after some initial hesitancy, was a veritable river of complaints, many of which went back for years. In essence, the field supervisors reported they felt like second-class citizens, without influence or power in their dealings with the staff. They didn't know what the staff meant by "innovation," and what's more they didn't much care. (They did, however, have some good ideas from time to time which they put into effect without fanfare, seldom telling the staff anything about them.)

When the venting had subsided I asked the field supervisors to talk about how they characteristically dealt with the staff. After a slow start the supervisors rolled out a substantial list of "passive resistance" and "playing stupid" techniques. In a little while they were enjoying their catalog immensely, as were the central staff people, who prior to this time had perceived themselves in the superior position, and so very much "responsible" for the oppressed feelings of the supervisors.

Sometime later, after the supervisors had become aware of the way in which they exerted their own resistive power in their dealings with the staff, we were able to turn successfully to the possibilities of developing different modes of interaction between the groups. Now, however, they were able to do so, not as impotent sufferers, but as equals. Interestingly, one of their demands was that the staff be more clearly demanding. Their experience in the past, they reported, had been confusing. Since the staff (in their efforts to be "understanding") had been so tactful in making requests, it was almost impossible to tell what was really important to them and what wasn't.

Many other aspects of this case emerged and were dealt with in this and subsequent meetings, including our attention to the operating styles of the agency chief and the central staff members, the identification of real developmental needs for both staff and field personnel, and so on. I believe we were able to deal with these other problems better, later on, because we started where we did.

Conclusion

In the model of the consultant's role I advocate the primary step is not to help people embark on self-improvement programs. Rather, it is to encourage them to recognize and appreciate where they are now. Then the consultant may help them find their own unique paths forward to change and growth. It is also important to recognize that this change and growth, at best, will occur naturally rather than being forced either by external pressure or internalized models. Paradoxically, natural change in an individual does not preclude his boss or others from exerting power or expressing their wants strongly and explicitly. *What is explicit and upfront is seldom harmful, though it may be difficult to deal with.* Covert, withheld, or truncated expression is harmful. In most circumstances the consultant will do best to encourage in both individuals and organizations the full recognition and completion of their negative feelings rather than a premature objectivity or problem-solving approach. The consultant will also do best in setting an example through his own clear and explicit statement of what *he* wants and how *he* feels.

We in the field of behavioral science have placed great emphasis on the negative consequences of authoritarian management for both organizations and individuals. In voices sometimes gentle and sometimes determined, we have addressed the power figures in organizations and called upon them to depart from old patterns, to risk a new approach and allow greater and more meaningful participation in the organization's affairs by those below them in the hierarchy. Many of us have made substantial contributions in helping managers to recognize and exercise their responsibilities toward their subordinates. This has in the main been good and worthwhile. The time has come though, I believe, for us to begin to address subordinates as well. We need to help manager and subordinate become aware of alienating and vitality-sapping consequences of both "playing helpless" and "playing helpful." We must question ourselves and encourage others to question unthinking acceptance of an adaptation to someone else's rules of good human relations, without regard to how those feel inside.

I believe it is worthwhile to urge ourselves and others to take new risks—risks of greater self-assertion, more spontaneity, and more willingness to experiment with power and aggression as well as trust and love. If we in OD do indeed believe in a wider distribution of power it would be well for us to stop trying to deny power's existence, muffle it, wish it away, or disguise it under velvet wrappings. Rather we can encourage as many people as possible at *all* levels of the organization from highest manager to lowest subordinate to discover his own power and use it.

Reading 20

STRATEGIC PLANNING: A MAJOR OD INTERVENTION

Thomas H. Rogers

The purpose of this presentation is to provide participants with a sense of strategic planning and to equip them with a complete strategic planning tool. The method is to give participants an opportunity to experience the process with step-by-step instruction and to offer convincing evidence of the usefulness of the approach. The range of application includes all levels of government, financial institutions and manufacturing firms.

Given OD's basic processes of data feedback interventions, confrontation/problem–resolution sessions and team building, the resulting information can be sorted into the following issues:

What we are doing and how we are doing it.

How varied activities interrelate.

How these activities move us toward our goals.

How structural planning precedes strategic planning.

The need to, as much as possible, turn our backs on the past and concentrate on effective future plans.

Sound implementation of strategic plans depends on having adequate performance management, career development and management succession systems in place. These help the strategic plan survive and support the structural planning that is initiated by others in the organization.

There are three persuasive reasons why strategic planning is an appropriate OD activity.

Source: Thomas H. Rogers, reprinted from *American Society for Training and Development Journal*, copyright 1981 American Society for Training and Development, pp. 50–55. Reprinted with permission. All rights reserved.

1. It requires the successful facilitation of a group process without becoming entrenched within one functional discipline (e.g., EDP, financial, or marketing).
2. It supports the core OD tenet that key executives' active participation in a process heightens client ownership of the plan and awareness of the discarded alternatives, thus reducing anxiety and resistance. Process *by* the organization, facilitated by the OD professional, improves commitment and the executives' ability to predict accurately and to develop useful scenarios, making planning the first step of implementation.
3. It is a natural offshoot of other OD assignments/ projects.

The OD consultant's contribution to strategic planning includes objectiveity, facilitation/process skills, experience from other organizations, systems analysis/organization diagnosis skills, change strategy design skills, interpersonal skills and energy. The client contributes historical perspective, overall awareness of the organization, technical product knowledge, product marketing knowledge, financial asset/forcasting information, perspective of the organizational needs, and perspective of feasibility. In short, the clients provide essential grounding— who, what, when, where, and why. The OD consultant is responsible for how.

Components of this "how" are the mission, identification of domains, domains analysis, action plan development (strategic statements of purpose), and management. Since strategic planning can be utilized in any system—corporate, division, function or individual—it is suggested that participants have the opportunity to apply or practice the principle immediately in their own life planning. The process recommendations are:

Who should participate: key executives, support personnel as needed, and consultants (internal and external).

Where? Sequestered off-site is far superior to in-house location.

How long will the process take: a minimum of two days with multiple sessions. If full benefit is to result, overnight accommodations are necessary, even if the site is near staff homes. Pre-workshop preparation will be needed to soak in data on the client organization: financial position, competition, social/economic or population trends, listening to what others write and say about "The Future."

How to start: move participants out of technical domains and into a cohesive, involved group that is focused on the total organization. Specific recommendations on openers include recording responses to questions like "What is success for your company/agency?" or "We have been managing this organization as if our objectives were to…" or "What are our strengths and weaknesses right now?" Brainstorming without editing or weighting is essential at this stage. Review of the data will include categorizing in positive and negative columns.

The ideas that are generated are the raw material of the organization's mission statement, the response to "What is my business?" The technique for extracting and refining this statement includes asking participants to write 25-word paragraphs utilizing the action verbs and nouns, reviewing the paragraphs to see the richness and differences, and selecting one paragraph to be edited and rewritten until it yields an inclusive and satisfactory assertion of the company's purpose. There is no "right" statement. Each organization's priorities and emphasis must be reflected in its mission statement.

Significant features of this approach to creating a mission statement are that it:

Is an easy first step.

Unifies the group.

Gives a sense of accomplishment.

Ends with a result that participants like—it is theirs.

Starts to erase doubts about the process (maybe we can agree/develop a plan).

Establishes a loose framework for the rest of the strategic planning process.

Given a group of 11 participants, a sound statement could be developed in an average of four hours. It is clearly a prerequisite to the other components of this process: identify and analyze domains, develop action plans and develop systems to manage plans.

A major premise about domains is that organizations do not exist independently, but in an interactive state with the various bodies they affect and are affected by. Four basic domains are suppliers, consumers, competition, and regulators, either professional or governmental. Participants can refine and supplement this list with such domains as agency board, families of staff, media, third parties. As with mission statements, identification of domains must reflect the real world and genuine values of the organization.

To analyze domains, it is the OD consultant's task to facilitate and the client participants' task to provide the technical data, marketing knowledge, history and perspectives. This analysis may be accomplished by eliciting responses to six questions:

1. What demands is this domain currently making on our organization? This identifies present realities.
2. How do we currently respond to these demands? (Current activities)
3. Given our perspective of the future, what demands will these domains be making in two years, five years, ten years? (Environmental scan)
4. Given our inertia, direction and present style, how will we probably respond in two years, five years, ten years? (Highlights any inconsistencies with the mission statement.)

5. What are the ideal demands we would like these domains to make upon us? (Opens up "wants" and interprets what we can be—proactive vs. reactive, then reduces itself to strategic objective statements.)

6. What must be done differently to get the domain to make the ideal demands? The ideal demand is actually the strategic objective statement and moves participants to analyze strategies by developing "what if" scenarios, to develop action plans, determine who has responsibility, what is the first step, and when we will face our first deadline. Finally, this question yields tangible planning output, written and systematic.

Once a strategic objective is selected, particpants can develop a statement of the objective. This statement must be clear and succinct. Then the OD consultant asks the clients to describe how the objective will be accomplished:

Identify the major resources needed, including initial staffing.

Identify the major activities needed (e.g., cost analysis, merger/acquisition studies).

Develop a schedule.

Determine who has responsibility for the objective. (It is recommended that a person be made responsible rather than a committee.)

A narrative report developed from the material recorded by the consultant provides:

A general discussion of each domain:
  Its present state (question 1).
  The organization's involvement (question 2).
  Its projected future (question 3).
  Its anticipated reactions (question 4).
Statements explaining strategic objectives (question 5).

Action plans to accomplish the objectives (question 6).

If there will be a time lag between the strategic planning session and distribution of the report, the chief executive officer should be responsible for monitoring the early action steps with individuals rather than having groups accountable to the CEO.

The final component in the strategic planning process is the development of systems to manage plans. A strategic objective is more likely to fail through inadequate implementation of the plan than through poor conception. Effective performance management systems will include clear strategic objective statements, measurement criteria, expected completion dates, and frequent review and follow-up. Accountability and clarity of purpose, then, are key indicators of good strategic planning.

The tools to utilize are those that will contribute to sound performance management. GANTT or PERT charts, SCHED-U-GRAPH, or M-5 forms, for example, can aid in identifying activities, preparing schedules, and establishing deadlines. Progress updates must be reviewed in committee meetings as well as one-on-one sessions.

In addition to performance management, the other major systems dependent on strategic planning are career development and management succession. For succession planning, the organization may find pool rather than sequence approaches more productive. Members of the pool are likely to be involved in implementation of the strategic plans and will therefore be able to demonstrate their ability to be accountable to the organization's mission and long-term plans.

Strategic planning must occur at the corporate level initially, then at division and unit levels. Broader mission statements can then test the legitimacy of division and unit planning.

Reading 21

OPERATION KPE: DEVELOPING A
NEW ORGANIZATION

Ishwar Dayal and John M. Thomas

It was . . . decided that analysis of each role in the organization might be facilitated if, as a group, we could strive for an atmosphere in these sessions where individuals could express disagreement with the manner in which a particular role was being defined or currently being performed by the focal role incumbent, particularly in terms of how this performance either failed to meet expectations from others or convey obligations to others. Analysis of the role system could best be accomplished alongside some critical analysis of current role performance, with a view toward helping individuals understand how they might alter their characteristic styles of working with others. Our hope here was to be able to assist the group in developing a climate where it could begin to undertake analysis of the interpersonal sphere in conjunction with analysis of its task interdependencies: in other words, how the group might begin to share and work together on these concerns about interpersonal needs discussed with us in individual counseling sessions. In addition to ideas of one's own role, it would be valuable for each other member of the group to think about the role under discussion in terms of its specific linkages with his role.

As a model for role analysis in the group we attempted to integrate the Glacier formulations of *prescribed* and *discretionary* components of roles (Brown, 1960) with that of Kahn, et al. (1964). This included discussion of the following:

Reproduced by special permission from *The Journal of Applied Behavioral Science*, ''Operation KPE: Developing a New Organization,'' by Ishwar Dayal and John M. Thomas. Volume 4, number 4, pp. 473–505. Copyright by NTL Institute for Applied Behavioral Science.

1. Analysis of why a particular role is needed and what purpose in the organization it would serve. This point has relevance to the expressed individual problem of identity.
2. The expectations and obligations of related roles in relation to a focal role (Kahn, et al., 1964).

Thus each role analysis consisted of three parts: discussion of purpose of the role, its prescribed and discretionary components, and its linkages with other roles.

Beginning with the GM as the first focal role, the phase aimed at developing what we have termed interdependence was launched. To date, each member of the management group has taken sessions in which he has been a focal role under discussion. The live format evolved for these discussions came to include the following steps:

The focal role individual initiates discussion and the group begins an analysis of the purpose of the role in the organization, how it fits into the overall objectives of the company, and its rationale.

The focal role individual lists on the blackboard the activities which he feels constitute his role; other members discuss this and ask for clarification; additions and subtractions are often made to this list. The group agrees upon the prescribed elements of the role and helps the role incumbent analyze its discretionary elements. Often this enables the individual to clarify the responsibility he must take on himself for decisions, the choices open to him for alternative courses of action, and new competencies he must develop in his assigned role. For example, during discussion of the role of the sales manager, he thought that the GM should initiate contact with major customers because he was more likely to influence them by virtue of his social contacts with top management in those companies. In contrast, the consultants suggested that the sales manager might, for various reasons, be taking "flight" from this responsibility and wondered whether he had any feelings about this matter that he could explore with the group. This led to an intensive, useful clarification of the relationship of the general manager with customers and with the sales manager. Similar issues came to center stage while discussing the roles of the purchasing and personnel officers. These discussions often led the group to examine the social customs prevailing in business firms which seem to require members of the group to establish social contacts with key people. These discussions also helped the GM and the members of the management team visualize what kind of support they would have to give to one another in this activity. For example, the sales and purchasing role incumbents discussed the development of a formal system for effective exchange of information about customers and suppliers.

The focal role individual then lists his expectations from each of those other roles in the group which he feels most directly affect his own role performance. Often a lively dialogue ensues at this point between the focal role incumbent and the role sender under discussion. They may disagree over expectations and obligations. Other group members enter in to help clarify by adding their own perceptions of that role relationship. In the end a workable formula is evolved describing mutual expectations and obligations.

Each role sender then presents his list of expectations from the focal role. This consists of their views of his obligations to them in role performance, and much the same process as in the previous step is repeated.

Upon concluding an individual role analysis, the focal role incumbent is held responsible for writing up the major points evolved during the group discussion. This consists of *(a)* a set of activities classified as to the prescribed and discretionary elements of the role, *(b)* the obligations of the role to each role in its set, and *(c)* the expectations of this role from others in its set. Viewed in toto, this provides a comprehensive understanding of each individu-

al's "role space." In addition, note is made of procedures and suggestions which may have been brought out as to how the role incumbent might more effectively implement his role activities. This write-up is done with the aid of the consultants and is circulated to all group members.

Briefly, at the next meeting, before another focal role is taken up, the previous role write-up is discussed and points are clarified. This statement is then accepted as a picture of the responsibilities and activities of that position in the organization. Unlike the traditional job description, however, this statement has been evolved live and entirely in the context of the *interaction* of that role with others. It expresses the group's views of how that role fits into the internal structure of the organization.

References

Argyris, C. *Interpersonal competence and organizational effectiveness.* Homewood, Ill.: Irwin-Dorsey, 1962.

Bamforth, K. Some experiences of the use of t-groups and structured groups within a company. *Working paper no. 3.* University of Leeds, U.K.: Industrial Management Division, 1963.

Benne, K. Deliberate changing as the facilitation of growth. In Bennis, W. G., Benne, K., & Chin, R., eds. *The planning of change.* New York: Holt, Rinehart & Winston, 1961.

Bennis, W. G. *Changing organizations.* New York: McGraw-Hill, 1966.

Brown, W. *Explorations in management.* London: Heinemann, 1960.

Burns, T., & Stalker, G. *The management of innovation.* London: Tavistock, 1961.

Dayal, I. Organization of work. In Baumgartel, H., Bennis, W., & De, N., eds. *Readings in group development for managers and trainers.* Bombay: Asia Publishing House, 1967.

Deutsch, M. Cooperation and trust: Some theoretical notes. In Bennis, W., Schein, E., Berlew, D., & Steele, F., eds. *Interpersonal dynamics.* Homewood, Ill.: Dorsey Press, 1964.

Jaques, E., & Brown, W. *The Glacier project papers.* London: Heinemann, 1965.

Kahn, R., & Rosenthal, R. *Organizational stress,* New York: Wiley & Sons, 1964.

Lorsch, J., & Lawrence, P. Organizing for product innovation. *Harvard Business Review,* 1965, *43* (1), 109–122.

Rogers, C., & Roethlisberger, F. J. Barriers and gateways to communication. *Harvard Business Review,* 1952, *30* (4), 46–52.

Schultz, W. *FIRO–B*. New York: Holt, Rinehart & Winston, 1958.

Selznick, P. *Leadership in administration*. New York: Harper & Row, 1957.

Shepard, H., & Blake, R. Changing behavior through cognitive change. *Human Organization,* 1962, *21*(2), 88–96.

Walker, C. *Modern civilization and technology*. New York: McGraw-Hill, 1958.

Reading 22

PLANNING PROCEDURES/MANAGING INTERFACES/CHARTING RESPONSIBILITY

Richard Beckhard and Reuben T. Harris

From new structures, multiple roles, and new reporting relationships emerge problems of job definitions, reporting lines, accountability, and performance review. In managing a change effort in a large system, the point of pressure for change will probably occur at some organizational interface. Significant changes occur when: (1) the task relationships between, say, market research and market development are reorganized; (2) it is necessary to superimpose programs on top of functional organizations; or (3) there are mergers of different organizations with different backgrounds or cultures. Such reorganizations tend to have some characteristics of a matrix organization—increased ambiguity, role confusion, problems with decision making, and communications problems.

The typical ways of resolving these dilemmas are to:

1. Try to get clearer job descriptions of each job or position involved;
2. Use a mediating mode, e.g., upper management defines the responsibilities of the various roles;
3. Utilize intergroup development activities designed to clarify responsibilities, authority, and rewards.

Most of these efforts do not succeed too well, however, because they are focused on improving the decision making *or* the communications *or* the power. They are not focused directly on *optimizing work,* although they may appear to.

Source: Richard Beckhard and Reuben T. Harris, *Organizational Transitions: Managing Complex Change,* (Reading, Mass.: Addison-Wesley Publishing, 1977), pp. 76–82. © 1977, Addison-Wesley. Reprinted with permission.

Responsibility Charting

In recent years a new technique has emerged which does focus on allocating work responsibilities; this technique is called *responsibility charting.* The first step is to construct a grid; the types of decisions and classes of actions that need to be taken in the total area of work under discussion are listed along the left-hand side of the grid, and the actors who might play some part in decision making on those issues are identified across the top of the grid (see Figure 1).

The process, then, is one of assigning a behavior to each of the actors opposite each of the issues. There are four classes of behavior:

1. *Responsibility (R)*—the responsibility to initiate action to ensure that the decision is carried out. For example, it would be a department head's responsibility (R) to initiate the departmental budget.
2. *Approval required, or the right to veto (A–V)*—the particular item must be reviewed by the particular role occupant, and this person has the option of either vetoing or approving it.
3. *Support (S)*—providing logistical support and resources for the particular item.
4. *Inform (I)*—*must be* informed and, by inference, cannot influence.

Each item is considered and responsibility (R) assigned. A very important aspect of the technique is that there can be only *one* R on any one horizontal line. Therefore, a consensus must be reached or an authoritarian decision made on who has the responsibility. If the group is unable to agree about where the R should go, there are three options:

FIGURE 1 Responsibility Chart

CODE: R– Responsibility (initiates)
A–V Approval (right to veto)
S– Support (put resources against)
I– Inform (to be informed)

Actors →
Decisions
↓

1. Break the problem out—always the most desirable alternative. For example, the R for a large capital expenditure might be different from the R for a small capital expenditure.
2. Move the R up one level in the organization hierarchy. For example, if the marketing manager and production manager cannot agree which one of them should have the R for defining monthly production targets, move the R up to their boss, the division general manager.
3. Move the *decision about assigning the* R up one level. In the previous example, the division general manager would assign the R for setting production targets rather than define the targets themselves.

Once the R has been assigned, the next step is to take a new item and assign a behavior for the various actors. In addition to R-A-S-I alternatives, it is possible that an actor has no assigned behavior opposite a particular type of activity, and this situation should be indicated by a dash (—).

Completion of the horizontal line gives one a de facto modus operandi for handling that particular class of task and its associated roles. Completion of a responsibility chart for all of the tasks relevant to the interfaces between departments or organizations and reading down a column vertically reveals the consensus role description of a particular actor on all those matters in which he or she is interdependent with other roles.

Some Further Guidelines in the Process

1. If an item has several As, e.g., one R, six As, one S, and one I, undoubtedly it will be very difficult to accomplish that task. For example, one organization decided to increase its benefits plan for management. The plan was agreed to by all levels of the organization; the board approved it, and the compensation people were told to install the plan. Nine months later, the plan was still not in. A responsibility-charting exercise indicated that each of the major profit centers had defined itself as having an A because it was an independent profit center with a budget commitment to the center. Because this new program required investment of funds not budgeted, each profit center's manager felt it was his or her choice to decide whether or not to institute the program this year or next year. It did not take long for the managing director to indicate, and for the profit center managers to see, that S rather than A was the appropriate symbol to describe the profit center's role. Then the program got instituted very quickly.

2. Depending on who is filling out the chart, one might find a skewing of A's under the senior executive. Subordinate managers tend to give their bosses more As than in fact the bosses want. It is desirable to try to minimize the number of As for any task if one wishes to facilitate the accomplishment of the task.

3. The decision about who can allocate a letter to a role can be tricky. In one situation, for example, the management group decided that first-line supervisors in the production organization should be held accountable for weekly scrap losses and various other things and should have timely information about their progress toward their objectives and organization standards. However, the controller's department, which was part of the general headquarters, refused to develop and introduce a new cost-accounting system. The department's requirements for accounting systems were focused primarily on the needs of the top of the organization, the tax people, etc., and another system would have to be added in order to provide this new type of information. The department felt that as the top financial resource, it should have responsibility for deciding whether or not such a system, with the attendant costs, would be introduced.

At a responsibility-charting session, it became clear that the department had defined itself as having an A, whereas others lower in the organization felt strongly that the department should have an S—that it should be required to produce the system. At the meeting, the general manager supported those who were arguing for the S on the basis that the task required it. This changed the basis for making decisions from hierarchy position to task accomplishment.

Some Applications

Illustration One: A Change in Structure. A large consumer company identified with a particular product orientation decided to "go to market" in a different way. Previously the company had sold its product, which was used in interior decorating, through specialty stores. Instead of being known as a single-product company, the company now wanted to be known as a decorating company. This meant changing the products in the stores, changing the relationship of the franchised stores to the corporation, differentiating the various types of buyers—housewives, contractors, etc.—and providing outlets for customers' different needs.

The prechange organization was a marketing-sales-functional organization. All selling was done in the geographic regions under the direction of division and, ultimately, regional salesmanagers. Plants made products on demand from the different regions. The technical-service organization made the special blends of products required by the sales organization.

The company's top management felt that given the new marketing plan and corporate image, a new organizational structure was needed. Accordingly, the sales organization was maintained, but purely as a selling organization. Product managers were created within the marketing organization and were given worldwide responsibility for sales in their particular product or market area. Also created were product-technical managers, who came from the technical organization but also had a product or business orientation. People in the new technical-service role would now receive all of their instructions from the product-technical director rather than from the sales organization.

Everyone in the organization, with the exception of the production and finance organizations, now had a new role, a new set of task responsibilities, and new relationships. Much confusion could be expected.

The strategy for dealing with the confusion was to conduct a series of *responsibility-charting conferences*. The first two-day conference focused on the new roles—the product managers from marketing, the technical-product managers, and the top of the organization, i.e., the directors of marketing, manufacturing, technical and finance, and the group vice-president. After opening remarks by the group vice-president, the participants proceeded to do a responsibility-charting exercise. They identified areas of decision and activities that needed to be done, made a list of the actors, and then assigned behaviors to these actors. Because the top of the organization was also present, the assigned behavior could be "reality-tested" right then. The output of the two days was a "map" of the general modus operandi as seen by the top management and the occupants of the new roles.

Next, the two sets of roles in marketing—sales and product management—and the two sets of technical roles—product management and technical service—met to work through responsibilities and to assign behaviors for their roles in the new setup. Difficulties arising with the earlier models and maps were resolved by the top-management group that had attended the first workshops. The results were then distributed to everybody and became the basis for work.

The change, a massive one involving several thousand managers, was in effect. People were operating in their new roles within six weeks of the announcement of the change. The process of having all of the key people sit down together and develop the new modus operandi was credited by most as having a significant effect on the efficiency of the change.

Reading 23

WHEN POWER CONFLICTS TRIGGER
TEAM SPIRIT

Roger Harrison

Getting people to work together in harmony is no easy task. Modern management techniques abound with new approaches to improving the working relationship between employees. In the United States, sensitivity training has had quite a vogue, and various techniques such as the T-group or the managerial grid have been brought forth to encourage managers to abandon their competitiveness and to create mutual trust and egalitarian approaches to decision making.

Or managers have been urged to change their motivations from reliance upon monetary reward or punishment to more internal motivation based on intrinsic interest in the job and personal commitment to meeting work objectives: for example, in Management by Objectives and programs of job enrichment. Still other practitioners have developed purely rational approaches to group problem solving (for example, Kepner Tregoe in the United States, and Coverdale in Britain).

Running through these approaches is the tendency to ignore or explain away competition, conflict and the struggle for power and influence. They assume people will be cooperative and productive if they are taught how, or if the barriers to their so being are removed. These approaches may be called *tender minded* in that they see power struggles as a symptom of a managerial *mistake* rather than a basic and ubiquitous process in organizations.

The problem of organizational change is seen as one of *releasing* human potential for collaboration and productivity, rather than as one of controlling or checking competition for advantage and position.

Source: Roger Harrison, *European Business*, Spring 1972, pp. 57–65.

However, consider the case of the production and engineering managers of a plant who had frequent disagreements over the work that was done by the latter for the former. The production manager complained that the engineering manager set maintenance priorities to meet his own convenience and reduce his own costs, rather than to make sure production targets were met. The engineering manager maintained that the production manager gave insufficient notice of jobs which could be anticipated, and the production operators caused unnecessary breakdowns by failure to carry out preventive maintenance procedures faithfully. The two men aired their dissatisfaction with one another's performance from time to time; but, according to both parties, no significant change has occurred.

Or take the case of the scientist in a development department who complains of overly close supervision by his section manager. According to the scientist, the manager intervenes to change the priorities he assigns to work, or to interfere with his development of promising lines of enquiry, and to check up with insulting frequency to see whether the scientist is carrying out the manager's instructions.

The scientist is actively trying to get a transfer to another section, because he feels he cannot do a proper job with so much hampering interference from above.

On the other hand, the section manager says the scientist does competent work but is secretive and unwilling to heed advice. He fails to let the manager know what he is doing and deviates without discussion from agreements the manager thought they had reached about how the work should be carried out. The manager feels he has to spend far too much time checking up on the scientist and is beginning to wonder whether his otherwise good work is worth the trouble required to manage him.

In both of these examples, the men are concerned with either gaining increased control over the actions of the other, reducing control by the other or both. And they know it. A consultant talking to them about communication problems or target setting would no doubt be listened to politely, but in their hearts, these men would still feel it was a question of who was going to have the final say, who was going to be boss.

And, in a way, they are more intuitively right than any outside consultant could be. They know where the power and influence lie, whether people are on their side or against them. They are aware of those with whom they can be open and honest and those who will use information against them. And these concerns are much more accurate and real than an outsider's suggestions for openness and collaboration.

Knowing Where the Power and Coercion Lie

Does this mean that most behavioral science approaches to business are too optimistic? What is certain is that they fail to take into account the forces of power, competitiveness, and coercion. In this article, I shall propose a method that does work directly with these issues, a method that gets tough with the team spirit.

This program is based on role negotiation. This technique describes the process that involves changing through *negotiation* with other interested parties the *role* that an individual or group performs in the organization. By an individual's or a group's *role,* I mean what activities he is supposed to perform, what decisions he can make, to whom he reports and about what and how often, who can legitimately tell him what to do and under what circumstances, and so on. Some people would say that a man's *job* is the same as what I have called his *role,* and I would partially agree with this. But what I mean by *role* includes not only the formal job description but also all the informal understandings, agreements, expectations, and arrangements with others which determine the way one person's or group's work affects or fits in with another's.

Role negotiation intervenes directly in the relationships of power, authority, and influence within the group. The change effort is directed at the work relationships among members. It avoids probing into the likes and dislikes of members for one another and their personal feelings about one another. In this it is more consonant with the task-oriented norms of business than are most other behavioral approaches.

The Fear of Touchy Emotional Confrontations

When I first developed the technique, I tried it out on a client group which was proving particularly hard to work with. They were suspicious and mistrustful of me and of each other, and said quite openly that talking about their relationships was both "irrelevant to our work problems" and "dangerous—it could split the group apart." When I introduced them to role negotiation, they saw ways they could deal with issues that were bothering them without getting into touchy emotional confrontations they could not handle. They dropped their resistance dramatically and turned to work with a will that surprised and delighted me.

I have used role negotiation successfully with top management groups, project teams, even between husbands and wives. The technique can be used with very small or quite large groups—although groups of over eight or ten should be broken down.

The technique makes one basic assumption: *most people prefer a fair negotiated settlement to a state of unresolved conflict,* and they are willing to invest some time and make some concessions in order to achieve a solution. To operate the program a modest but significant risk is called for from the participants: they must be open about the changes in behavior, authority, responsibility, etc., they wish to obtain from others in the situation.

If the participants are willing to specify concretely the changes they desire from others, then significant changes in work effectiveness can usually be obtained.

How does this program work in reality? First of all, the consultant must have the participants' sufficient confidence in his motives and competence so that they are willing at his behest to try something new and a bit strange. It also stands to reason that the consultant should know enough about the people, their work system and their relationship problems to satisfy himself that the members of the group are ready to make a real effort towards improvement. No technique will work if the clients don't trust the consultant enough to give it a fair try or if the members of the group (particularly the high-influence members) devote most of their effort to maintaining the status quo. In the description that follows I am assuming that this confidence and readiness to work have been established. Although this is a rather large assumption, these problems are universal in consulting and not peculiar to role negotiation. If anything, I have found that role negotiation requires somewhat less preparation than other team development techniques I have used.

Let us say we are working with a group of five to seven people, including a manager and his subordinates, two levels in the formal organization. Once basic assumptions of trust are established, I try to get at least a day with the group away from the job location to start the role negotiation process going. A two-day session with a commitment to follow up in three to four weeks is best. If the group is not felt to be quite prepared to undertake serious work, the session may be made longer with some trust building and diagnostic activities in the beginning, working into the role negotiation when and if the group is ready for it.

No Probing into People's Feelings

The first step in the actual role negotiation is *contract setting*. Its purpose is to make it clear between the group and the consultant what each may expect from the other. This is a critical step in the change process. It controls and channels everything that happens afterwards.

My contract is usually based on the following provisions, which should be written down, if only as a first practice step in the formal way of working which I try to establish.

It is not legitimate for the consultant to press or probe anyone's *feelings*. We are concerned about work: who does what, how and with whom. How people *feel* about their work or about others in the group is their own business, to be introduced or not according to their own judgment and desire. The expression or nonexpression of feelings is not part of the contract.

Openness and honesty about behavior are expected and essential for achieving results. The consultant will insist that people be specific and concrete in expressing their expectations and demands for the behavior of others. Each team member is expected to be open and specific about what he wants others to do *more* or *do better* or *do less* or *maintain unchanged*.

No expectation or demand is adequately communicated until it has been *written down* and is clearly understood by both sender and receiver, nor will any change process be engaged in until this has been done.

The full sharing of expectations and demands does not constitute a completed change process. It is only the precondition for change to be agreed through negotiation. It is unreasonable for anyone in the group, manager or subordinate, to expect that any change will take place merely as a result of communicating a demand or expectation. Unless a team member is willing to change his own behavior in order to get what he wants from the other(s), he is likely to waste his and the group's time talking about the issue. When a member makes a request or demand for changed behavior on the part of another, the consultant will always ask what quid pro quo (something for something) he is willing to give in order to get what he wants. This goes for the manager as well as for the subordinates. If the former can get what he wants simply by issuing orders or clarifying expectations from his position of authority, he probably does not need a consultant or a change process.

The change process is essentially one of bargaining and negotiation in which two or more members each agree to change behavior in exchange for some desired change on the part of the other. This process is not complete until the agreement can be *written down* in terms which include the agreed changes in behavior and make clear what each party is expected to give in return.

Threats and pressures are neither illegitimate nor excluded from the negotiation process. However, group members should realize that overreliance on threats and punishment usually results in defensiveness, concealment, decreased communication and retaliation, and may lead to breakdown of the negotiation. The consultant will do his best to help members accomplish their aims with positive incentives wherever possible.

The Secret Game of Influence Bargaining

Each member has power and influence in the group, both positively to reward and collaborate with others, and negatively to resist, block or punish. Each uses his power and influence to create a desirable and satisfying work situation for himself. Most of the time this process is gone about secretly. People use a lot of time and energy trying to figure out how to influence another person's behavior covertly, but since they rarely are aware of others' wants and needs, their attempts fail.

Although in stable organizations, employees can learn what works on others just through trial and error over long periods of time, nowadays the fast personnel turnover makes this primitive process obsolete.

Role negotiation tries to replace this old process with a more efficient one. If one person knows because it has been made public what another's wants or intentions are, he is bound to be more effective in trying to influence that person. In addition, when someone tries to influence him, the quid pro quo put forward is more likely to be one he really wants or needs. I try to show my clients that by sharing the information about desires and attempts, *role negotiation increases the total amount of influence group members have on one another.*

The next stage is *issue diagnosis.* Each member spends some time thinking about the way business

is conducted between himself and the others in the group. What would he change if he could? What would he like to keep as is? Who and what would have to change in order to improve things? I ask the participants to focus especially on the things which might be changed to improve their *own effectiveness,* since these are the items to be discussed and negotiated.

After he has spent 20 minutes or so thinking about these matters and perhaps making a few notes, each member fills out one Issue Diagnosis Form (like the one in Figure 1) for each other member, listing those things he would like to see the other person

1. Do more or do better.
2. Do less or stop doing.
3. Keep on doing, maintain unchanged.

All of these messages are based on the sender's increasing his own effectiveness in his job.

These lists are exchanged so that each person has all the lists pertaining to his work behavior. Each member makes a master list for himself on a large piece of paper itemizing the behavior which each other person desires him to do *more* or *better, less* or *continue unchanged* (Figure 2). These are posted so that the entire group can peruse and refer to each list. Each member is allowed to question the others who have sent messages about his behavior, querying the what, why, and how of their requests, *but no one is allowed a rebuttal, defense or even a yes or no reply to the messages he has received.* The consultant must assure that only clarification is taking place; argument, discussion and decision making about issues must be engaged in at a later stage.

Defensiveness Just to Save Face

The purpose of the consultant's rather rigid and formal control on communication is to prevent the group from having a negative problem-solving experience, and members from becoming polarized on issues or taking up extreme positions which they will feel impelled to defend just to save face. Communication is controlled to prevent escalation of

---

FIGURE 1   Issue Diagnosis Form

Messages from _Jim Farrell_

to _David Sills_

1. If you were to do the following
   things <u>more</u> or <u>better</u>, it would help
   me to increase my own effectiveness:

   - Being more receptive to
     improvement suggestions
     from the process engineers.
   - Give help on cost control
     (see 2).
   - Fight harder with the G.M.
     to get our plans improved.

2. If you were to do the following
   things <u>less,</u> or were to <u>stop</u> doing
   them, it would help me to increase
   my own effectiveness:

   - Acting as judge and jury
     on cost control.
   - Checking up frequently on
     small details of the work.
   - Asking for so many detailed
     progress reports.

3. The following things which you have
   been doing help to increase my own
   effectiveness, and I hope you will
   continue to do them:

   - Passing on full information
     in our weekly meetings.
   - Being available when I
     need to talk to you.

---

actual or potential conflicts. Channeling the energy released by the sharing of demands and expectations into successful problem solving and mutual influence is behind this strategy of control.

The consultant intervenes to inhibit hostile and destructive expression at this point and later to facilitate constructive bargaining and negotiation of mutually beneficial agreements.

This initial sharing of desires and change goals among group members leads to a point at which the team development process is most vulnerable. If sufficient anger and defensiveness are generated by the problem sharing, the consultant will not be able to hold the negative processes in check long enough for the development of the positive problem-solving spiral on which the process depends for its effectiveness. It is true that such an uncontrollable breakthrough of hostility has not yet occurred in my experience with the method. Nevertheless, concern over the negative possibilities is in part responsible for my slow, deliberate, and rather formal development of the confrontation of issues within the group.

The Influence Trade

After each member had had an opportunity to clarify the messages he has received, the group selects the issues for negotiation. The consultant begins this phase by reemphasizing that unless a quid pro quo can be offered in return for a desired behavior change, there is little point in having a discussion about it: *unless behavior changes on both sides the most likely prediction is that the status quo will continue.*

If behavior changes merely as the result of an exchange of views between men of good will, all the better. However, one cannot count on it.

Each participant is asked to choose one or more issues on which he particularly wants to get some changes on the part of another. He is also asked to select one or more issues on which he feels it may be possible for him to move in the direction desired by others. He does this by marking his own

---

FIGURE 2   Summary of Messages to James Farrell from Other Group Members

---

MORE OR BETTER:	LESS OR STOP:	CONTINUE AS NOW:
Give information on project progress (completion date slippage) Bill, Tony, David.	Let people go to other good job opportunities — stop hanging on to your good engineers — Tony, Bill.	Training operators on preventive maintenance — Henry.
Send progress reports on Sortair project — Bill.	Missing weekly planning meetings frequently — Jack, Henry, David.	Good suggestions in meetings — Tony, Henry.
Make engineers more readily available when help needed — Jack, Henry.	Ignoring memos and reports re cost control — David.	Asking the difficult and awkward questions — Tony, Jack.
Keep better informed re plans and activities — David.	Setting aside my priorities on engineering work — Henry, Jack.	Willingness to help on design problems — Bill, Jack.
Enforce safety rules on engineers when in production area — Henry.	Charging time on Sortair to other accounts — David.	Good quality project work — Bill, Henry, David, Jack.
Push harder on the Sensiter project — David, Henry, Tony, Jack.	Overrunning agreed project budget without discussing beforehand — David.	

---

flip chart and those of the other members. In effect, *each person indicates the issues upon which he most wants to exert influence and those on which he is most willing to accept influence.* With the help of the consultant the group then goes through the list to select the most negotiable issues, those where there is a combination of a high desire for change on the part of an initiator and a willingness to negotiate on the part of the person whose behavior is the target of the change attempt. The consultant asks for a group of two or more persons who are involved in one such issue to volunteer for a negotiation demonstration before the rest of the group.

The negotiation process consists of the parties making contingent offers to one another such as "If you do X, I will do Y." The negotiation ends when all parties are satisfied that they will receive a reasonable return for whatever they are agreeing to give. The consultant asks that the agreement be formalized by writing down specifically and concretely what each party is going to give and receive

in the bargain (Figure 3). He also asks the participants to discuss openly what sanctions can be applied in the case of nonfulfillment of the bargain by one or another party. Often this involves no more than reversion of the status quo, but it may involve the application of pressures and penalties as well.

After the negotiation demonstration, the members are asked to select other issues they wish to work on. A number of negotiations may go on simultaneously, the consultant being involved at the request of any party to any negotiation. All agreements are published to the entire group, however, and questioned by the consultant and the other members to test the good faith and reality orientation of the parties in making them. Where agreement proves impossible, the consultant and other group members try to help the parties find further incentives (positive or, less desirably, coercive) which they may bring to bear to encourage agreement.

FIGURE 3   Final Agreement between James Farrell and David Sills

Jim agrees to let David know as soon as
agreed completion dates and cost projections
look as though they won't be met, and also to
discuss each project's progress fully with
David on a bi-weekly basis.
    In return, David agrees not to raise questions
about cost details and completion dates, pending
a trial of this agreement to see if it provides
sufficient information soon enough to deal with
questions from above.

This process is, of course, not as simple as it sounds. All kinds of difficulties can occur, from bargaining in bad faith, to refusal to bargain at all, to escalation of conflict. In my experience, however, group members tend to be rather wise about the issues they can and cannot deal with, and I refrain from pushing them to negotiate issues they feel are unresolvable. My aim is to light the sparks of team development with a successful experience which group members can look on as a fruitful way of improving their effectiveness and satisfaction.

The Consultant Withers Away

The cycle ends here. Each group must then try living with their agreements. There is always, of course, the occasion to meet later with the consultant to work out new agreements or renegotiate old ones.

Ideally, the group should learn this process so thoroughly that the consultant's role withers away. To do this, though, they must be so fully aware of the dangers and pitfalls involved in the negotiation process that a third party's arbitration is no longer needed.

So far this has not occurred in my experience. The positive results are expressed mostly in terms of less backsliding between visits than has occurred in groups where I have applied more interpersonal

behavior-change methods. Role negotiation agreements have more teeth in them.

What are the advantages of role negotiation? First of all, participants seem more at home with problems of power and influence than other interpersonal issues. They feel more competent and less dependent on the consultant in dealing with the problems and so they are ready to work sooner and harder.

Furthermore, the consultant's or referee's amount of skill and professional training which is required to conduct role negotiation is less than for more sensitive approaches.

That does not mean that role negotiation poses no threat to organization members. The consultant asks participants to be open about matters that are often kept secret in everyday life. This requires more than the normal amount of trust and confidence. If not, these matters would have been talked about before the group ever got to the role negotiation.

There also seems to be some additional discomfort involved in *writing down* the changes one would like to see another make in his work behavior. Several times participants have questioned the necessity of doing this, because one feels so *exposed* when his concerns are written out for all to see, and there is the fear that others will think them silly, childish or odd (though this never seems to happen). If the matter comes up, I point out that one need not write down *all* the concerns he has, but only those he would like to work on with others at this time.

Of course, role negotiation, like any other process that changes relationships, does pose a threat to the participants. The members are never sure they will personally be better off after the change than before. In the case of role negotiation, most of these fears arise around losing power and influence, or losing freedom and becoming more controlled by others. Particular resistance to talking openly about issues occurs when someone is trying to manipulate another person to his own advantage, or when he feels that he might want to do this in the future. I think this is the main reason participants in role negotiation so often try to avoid the step of writing down their agreements. If things aren't down in black and white, they feel, it will be easier to ignore the agreement later on if it becomes inconvenient. Also, writing down agreements seems to dispel the aura of trust and good fellowship which some groups like to create on the surface and below which they engage in quite a lot of cutthroat competition.

Role negotiation is of course no panacea for power problems in groups and between people. People may bargain in bad faith; agreements once reached may be broken; circumstances and personnel may change so that the work done becomes irrelevant. Of course, these problems can exist in any group or organization. What role negotiation *does* is try to deal with the problems directly and to identify and use constructively those areas of *mutual* advantage where both sides can benefit from discussion and agreement. These areas are almost always larger than people think they are, and when they find that they can achieve something *for* themselves by open negotiation which they could not achieve by covert competition, then the more constructive process can begin to grow.

Avoiding the Consultant's High Fees

One other likely advantage of role negotiation is the ease and economy with which it can be introduced into the firm.

One disadvantage of most behavioral approaches to team development is that the consultant's level of skill and experience must be very high indeed. Managers themselves are not confident in dealing with these issues, and because they feel uneasy in this area they reasonably want to have as much safety and skill as money can buy. This demand for skilled consultants on interpersonal and group processes has created a shortage and a meteoric rise in consulting fees. It seems unlikely that the supply will soon catch up with the demand.

The shortage of highly skilled workers in team development argues for deskilling the requirements for effective consultant performance. I see role negotiation as a way of reducing the skill requirements for team development consultation. Preliminary results by internal consultants using the approach have been promising.

For example, one management development manager teamed up with a colleague to conduct a successful role negotiation with his own top management. He reported that his main problem was getting up enough confidence to take on the job. The team development session itself went smoothly. Although I cannot say whether this experience was typical (I suspect it was not), it does lead me to hope that role negotiation will prove to be practical for use by internal consultants without professional training in the behavioral sciences.

What then are the main points about role negotiation? Firstly, role negotiation focuses on work relationships: what people do, and how they facilitate and inhibit one another in the performance of their jobs. It encourages participants to work with problems using words and concepts they are used to using in business. It avoids probing to the deeper levels of their feelings about one another unless this comes out naturally in the process.

Second, it deals directly with problems of power and influence which may be neglected by other behavioral approaches. It does not attempt to dethrone the authority in the group, but other members are helped to explore realistically the sources of power and influence available to them.

Also, unlike some other behavioral approaches to team development, role negotiation is highly action-oriented. Its aim is not just the exposing and understanding of issues as such, but achieving changed ways of working through mutually negotiated agreements. Changes brought about through role negotiation thus tend to be more stable and lasting than where such negotiated commitments are lacking.

In addition, all the procedures of role negotiation are clear and simple if a bit mechanical, and can be described to participants in advance so they know what they are getting into. There is nothing mysterious about the technique, and this reduces participants' feelings of dependency upon the special skill of the consultant.

Furthermore, role negotiation actually requires less skill from the consultant than some other behavioral approaches. Internal consultants can suitably use the technique without lengthy special training in the behavioral sciences. It can therefore be a moderate cost approach to organization change.

It's important to understand that role negotiation does not necessarily replace other "soft" behavioral approaches to organization change. Work groups can be effective and achievement-oriented and at the same time allow open and deeply satisfying interpersonal relationships.

However, resolving conflict successfully at the interpersonal level can only be done by first attacking the ever-present issues of power and influence among members. Role negotiation does this and provides a sound and effective base upon which to build more satisfying relationships.

If role negotiation is an effective first or "basic" approach to team development, it goes without saying that employee growth means moving beyond this stage into a deeper exploration of intergrating work and relationships.

C. Third-Party, Intergroup, and Comprehensive Interventions

This section moves to the facilitator assisting with issues between two people, between two groups, and between two organizations.

The brief piece by Carl Rogers looks at the dynamics of two-person conflict. (These dynamics are comparable to the dynamics of intergroup conflict as described in the selection in Part 2 by Edgar Schein.) The selection by Walton is a case study of a facilitator working with two executives who are in conflict. The Blake, Shepard, and Mouton article describes the intergroup intervention technique which they developed, and which is based on their research and that of Sherif. The essay by Young was selected because it refers to the relations by objectives program (RBO) of the Federal Mediation and Conciliation Service, a program with clear parallels to OD approaches, and because it focuses on union-management relationships.

This section also includes an essay on survey-feedback by Bowers and Franklin. We selected it for the first edition and have returned to it for this edition because this essay is one of the clearest statements we have seen on the use of a measurement-guided approach to change. The essay also tells us some of the history of the approach, a number of the underlying assumptions of survey-feedback, and a description of the change agent's role. We consider survey-feedback a comprehensive intervention because it comprises an essentially complete OD effort when the data-gathering and team workshops unfold throughout the organization.

Reading 24

TWO–PERSON DISPUTES

Carl Rogers

When persons are in serious discord, whether we are speaking of a discordant marital relationship, friction between an employer and an employee, a formal and icy dispute between two diplomats, or tension growing out of some other base, we tend to find certain very common elements:

1. In such a dispute there is no doubt at all but that I am right and you are wrong. I am on the side of the angels, and you belong with the forces of darkness.
2. There is a breakdown of communication. You do not hear what I say, in any understanding way; and I am unwilling and unable to hear what you are really saying.
3. There are distortions in perception. The evidence which is taken in by my senses—your words, your actions, your responses to my words and actions—is trimmed and shaped by my needs to fit the views of you which I already hold.

Source: Carl Rogers, ''Dealing with Psychological Tensions,'' *The Journal of Applied Behavioral Science*, January–February–March 1965, pp. 12–14. Reproduced by special permission. Copyright 1965, NTL Institute.

Evidence which is clearly and openly contradictory to my rigidly held views is conveniently ignored or made acceptable by being grossly distorted. Thus, a real gesture toward reconciliation on your part can be perceived by me as only another deceitful trick.

4. Implicit in all this is the element of distrust. While whatever *I* do is obviously done with honorable intent, whatever *you* do is equally obviously done with an underlying evil intent, no matter how sweetly reasonable it may appear on the surface. Hence, from the perspective of each opponent, the whole relationship is shot through with suspicion and mistrust.

I believe I am correct in saying that in any serious two-person dispute, these four elements are invariably present and often make the situation appear hopeless. Yet there are knowledge and skill available which can be applied to such a situation. If there is to be progress in reducing this kind of tension, we have learned that the first necessity is a facilitative listener—a person who will listen empathically and will understand the attitudes of each disputant.

Reading 25

INTERPERSONAL CONFRONTATION AND BASIC THIRD–PARTY FUNCTIONS: A CASE STUDY

Richard E. Walton

The study describes an interpersonal conflict[1] and illustrates the role which a third party may play in helping two persons confront each other concerning their differences. In particular, it analyzes the role attributes of the third party and the other circumstances operating in this particular case to enhance the likelihood of a successful interpersonal confrontation. The threefold purposes of this paper are to contribute to an emerging theory of third-party interventions; to help improve the practice of consultation; and to stimulate client systems to consider how third parties can be useful in their daily functioning, especially in connection with other organizational development activities.

Background

The episode reported here occurred in January between two program directors in the administrative services component of a large government agency. The agency had an organization development program with goals and methods similar to those of TRW Systems described by Davis (1967). It em-

Source: Reproduced by special permission from *The Journal of Applied Behavioral Science*, ''Interpersonal Confrontation and Basic Third-Party Functions: A Case Study,'' by Richard Walton. Volume 4, number 3, pp. 327–43. Copyright 1968 by NTL Institute for Applied Behavioral Science.

---

[1]It would be more precise to continuously refer to this conflict as an intergroup-interpersonal conflict because issues at both levels of social relationships were involved. However, as the conflict episode developed, the former gave way perceptibly more to the latter than vice versa.

phasized openness of feelings in interpersonal relations, utilized sensitivity training and team-building experiences, and was staffed by both internal and external consultants. The recently established program had had limited impact on the organization as a whole, but had worked more intensively with the administrative services component.

One of the principals, Bill, was responsible for the development of a new organization systems procedure (OSP) to be considered for adoption by the line organization. He had been director of the Information Systems (IS) program for about five months. (See Figure 1.) During that period he had learned to cope with many frustrating conditions. There was uncertainty whether the system would ever be adopted and when that decision would be made. Moreover, he had to rely upon several layers of superiors above him to represent his interests with the high-level official who could make this decision. Communication downward from the top was equally unsettling; there was a continuous stream of reports reaching him and his group which were interpreted as alternatively encouraging and discouraging signs relative to the adoption of the system they were developing. The uncertainty of the program in turn resulted in a high turnover of the better members of his staff. Finally, he had to rely upon another group, Systems Research (SR), also within the administrative services component, to supply much of the professional talent required by the project. For several months these factors depressed morale within the professional staff and increased tensions between Bill and George, the section head of SR who was responsible for the group's efforts on OSP.

FIGURE 1   Administrative Services Component of Government Agency

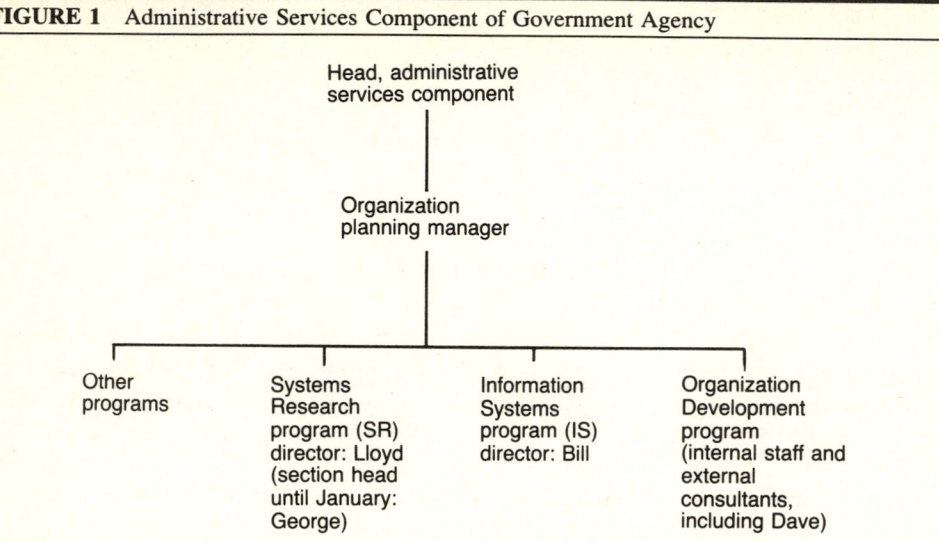

In October, four months before the episode described here, the combined staffs working on the OSP project, including both Bill and George, had met two days in an off-site location to "build a team" and accomplish some program task work. Several internal and external consultants on the organization development staff, including the third-party consultant in this case, participated in the meeting to facilitate the team-building process. The meeting helped increase the familiarity, respect, and trust among members of the total group; improve the integration of the two subgroups; and increase staff members' feelings that they were being utilized. Especially important for Bill was an increased if not perfect understanding between himself and George regarding their roles and personal styles. Also, Bill and the total group somehow resolved to prevent the uncertainties of the OSP program from continuing to interfere with their ability to work on the tasks at hand.

The operating style for the groups which emerged from the October meeting and stabilized over the next three months had characteristics along the general lines of Theory Y advocated by Douglas McGregor in *The Human Side of Enterprise* (1960). It involved low structure; i.e., roles were loosely defined and changed according to the changing task demands. There was greater mutual influence; for example, professionals had more opportunity to influence how their own resources would be used. In part because the fluid task structure and the mutual influence process required it, there was somewhat more time spent in group sessions. The meetings themselves moved in the direction of a mixture of direct task work and group maintenance work. Also, more social-emotional support was available for members who needed it both in the group and in interpersonal relationships. Apparently this group pattern was more appropriate to the triple problem of coping with the environmental stress factors, meeting the needs of a majority of the particular persons involved, and performing the task at hand, because internal operations did improve through November and December.

The other principal, Lloyd, became the SR liaison to IS early in January when George was transferred. During the previous year, Lloyd, too, had been coping with problems of uncertainty about the future of the whole program of his group. He was acutely aware of the need to clarify and improve the group's status and functions in the agency. He had not become personally involved in the work on OSP. He had allowed his subordinate, George, considerable autonomy in handling their personnel working on the OSP project. Lloyd had, however, heard from two members of his group that the OSP project still did not have the direction and rigor which they desired and that too much time was devoted to analysis of group process. When Lloyd assumed direct liaison responsibility early in January, he wanted to review the entire OSP project, including the role of his staff and his own role.

One event in particular played a part in precipitating the conflict reported here. The setting was a large meeting which included the combined staffs working on OSP and certain other persons. Lloyd made some statements, apparently in an outspoken manner, which were very disconcerting to Bill.

Early in January, a casual meeting occurred involving Bill; Bill's superior, who had responsibility for both IS and SR programs, as well as the organization development program; and Dave, a behavorial science consultant (see Figure 1). Dave was an external consultant available for working on organizational development projects as means and opportunities were identified. Bill mentioned his concern about Lloyd's participation in the combined staff meeting in particular, and about their relationship in general. Bill was urged to confront Lloyd with his own concerns, try to learn what prompted Lloyd to speak the way he did in the earlier meeting, and try to establish a better working relationship. Bill agreed to this and expressed a desire to have a consultant present. Dave offered to participate.

The following day, Bill first called Lloyd and set up a meeting in his office for later that morning, and then called Dave and asked whether he could attend. Dave agreed to attend if Bill would be responsible for explaining the former's presence to Lloyd, who had never met Dave. Dave further said

Bill and Lloyd together would have to determine whether and in what ways Dave could be helpful.

The Confrontation

Familiarization

Lloyd and Bill were present in Bill's office when Dave arrived. Bill introduced Dave as a consultant to the organization, explaining that this was part of a larger pattern of the OSP program which involved using behavioral science consultants whenever possible. He asked whether Lloyd approved; Lloyd said he was glad to have Dave present. Dave asked Lloyd whether he had attended one of the many sensitivity-training workshops which had been sponsored by the organizational development group. Lloyd indicated that he had, and Dave in turn identified himself as a member of the outside consulting organization (NTL) which had been staffing the agency's sensitivity training laboratories. Under the circumstances of this case, this brief interchange tended to go a long way in establishing Dave's identity in a way appropriate for his third-party role. Further analysis of this point will come in a later section.

Bill busied himself on other matters for several minutes, allowing Dave and Lloyd to get somewhat acquainted. During this time, Lloyd did almost all of the talking and Dave the listening. Lloyd discussed education, including his current problem of having a constructive influence on his children's choice in educational institutions. Dave's occasional participation on the topic was directed to the difficulties in the relationship between parents and children in their teens, rather than the relative merits of different educational institutions. As a result of this brief conversation, Dave mentally registered two tentative observations. First, Lloyd could be overpowering in his interpersonal style, with the result that the other person might experience frustration and either withdraw or attack. Second, Lloyd might generally tend to resist discussing the more personal aspects of issues, as he did with the question of his children's preference for colleges. Only the first hypothesis tended to be borne out by subsequent developments.

Bill concluded his discussion with his secretary, and the trio moved to sit opposite one another in three comfortable chairs. The first topic of discussion was not pertinent to the relationship, and Dave excused himself from the room for a few minutes. He hoped that the break might help them get down to work when he returned. Moreover, he wanted to allow Lloyd a greater opportunity to express to Bill any concerns he might have about the involvement of a third party.

Opening Charges

After Dave's return, Bill and Lloyd finally turned to what they both knew they had met to do, namely, to discuss their relationship and especially Lloyd's role in the OSP program. Lloyd led off with a set of statements in which he asserted that, in contrast to George, with whom Bill had been dealing, he was a different person, with different views and preferences. Lloyd also indicated that he saw some "real gaps in the OSP design" thus far and was anxious to remedy these if he were involved. His remarks about OSP included the following points:

Lloyd charged that his own staff had not been allowed to contribute to the "strategic, architectural, broad-design level" of the project; rather that they had been delegated merely the lower level technical-computer work. Lloyd continued: "If this is the type of resource talent you need for the OSP project, perhaps my staff should not be in the business of supplying the manpower."

Second, Lloyd observed that the role his staff had was defined as strictly advisory to the IS group. Yet it did not seem a viable arrangement for his staff to make important contributions of resources without a role in decision making, he continued.

Third, he objected to Bill's supervisory pattern, complaining, for example, that the manner in which professionals from the two groups were being assigned tasks allowed him little or no leadership role

with respect to his own professionals involved in the project.

To summarize, he was charging that his unit's resources were being used below their capacity on the OSP project, that his unit had too little decision influence, and that his leadership position was undermined by the operating style encouraged by Bill. Lloyd concluded that the status quo was unacceptable to him. But he went on to offer an alternative: to "break off" the SR professional manpower utilized by OSP and permanently reassign them to IS. This alternative, Lloyd noted, should be attractive to Bill; it also had the advantage of "freeing SR up to do something else, getting new customers." This proposal sounded to Dave more like a bargaining tactic than a seriously proposed solution.

Counterpoints

After several unsuccessful attempts to break into Lloyd's long presentation of his views, Bill dropped his tack of trying to respond to Lloyd's points. Instead he challenged Lloyd directly for not allowing him any opportunity to respond. Lloyd stopped abruptly, acknowledged the appropriateness of Bill's challenge, and resolved to listen.

Bill then recalled that he "had real trouble" with Lloyd's participation in the large meeting referred to earlier. He said he had not understood what Lloyd was trying to do. "In fact," he said, "I am having some of the same reactions to what you have just been saying."

Bill's subsequent statements could be arranged as responses to Lloyd's assertions as follows:

First, Bill said he disagreed with Lloyd's view that computer-technical-mechanical contributions were of a "lower level" than the strategic-architectural-conceptual. Moreover, in his view, Lloyd's staff *had* been allowed to contribute to the latter.

Second, Bill described his view of the client-consultant roles of the two groups: "SR should make resources and advice available to IS, who then has final decisions on design and the responsibility for working with the line organization." Thus he acknowledged open conflict with Lloyd on this point.

Third, Bill defended his working style, claiming that the pattern had not detracted from the leadership role of Lloyd's predecessor, George. Also, he denied that he had given work assignments to SR personnel before consultation with George. Bill assured Lloyd that he would respond to any concerns of this kind when they arose.

After both persons had had an opportunity to express themselves and make rebuttals, Bill turned to Dave and asked him for his observations. Before Dave could respond, Lloyd explained that first he wanted to make another statement. He asked Bill directly whether he would want several members of Lloyd's staff if their positions could be transferred. Bill objected that such a transfer would never be approved and therefore he saw no reason to give it further thought; besides, his need for the talent in question was temporary, which argued against any transfer.

Digging Deeper: From the Intergroup to the Interpersonal Level

When Dave did participate, he suggested that the interchange could be characterized as a negotiation. In effect, Lloyd was saying: "Here are my needs, or requests, which must be given due consideration if my staff is going to continue to contribute to OSP." Dave sharpened the three issues which Lloyd had put on the agenda, first citing Lloyd's concern and then describing what he heard as Bill's answer, in much the same terms as reported above. After some further discussion of these issues, they identified other areas of concern which were probably more basic to the conflict.

First, Lloyd did not feel comfortable with the operating style of the total OSP group under Bill's leadership: it was too loose, too unstructured, and too "groupy." He preferred more "crispness" and more structure. In contrast, Bill was quite pleased with the group's method of operating, which he

thought had been working well and which he found personally satisfying. Bill did not want Lloyd to try to change the method of operation. He did not respond to Lloyd's preferences. Therefore Lloyd indicated with increasing emphasis that he had preferences different from those of his predecessor and that Bill *was* going to have to take these into account. In effect, Lloyd wanted the operating methods reconsidered to take into account his own stylistic preferences.

Second, Lloyd had some general ideas on the OSP, but he had not yet been given enough information about the status of the project in order to test these ideas. Therefore, he wanted to get together soon for a review. Later in the discussion, he acknowledged that one of his underlying concerns was in "getting connected" with the project and also in being recognized as an experienced and competent person on the project team. This need to be seen as competent was underscored in a side conversation with Dave (when Bill was on the telephone) in which Lloyd enumerated many experiences in the past in which he had had full responsibility for developing such systems in other organizations. He noted, in contrast, that members of the OSP group did not have any really practical experience.

Bill, for his part, failed to communicate a direct interest in what Lloyd could contribute nor did he seem to become fully aware of Lloyd's needs to be recognized in this respect. On the other hand, he felt somewhat attacked by Lloyd's criticism of the group's efforts to date. It appeared to Dave that Bill's nonattention to Lloyd's need for recognition might be related to the latter's attacks on the performance of Bill's group, and vice versa. Dave tried to alert the two parties to these more subtle interpersonal issues which could serve to keep them apart.

The action outcome of the session was to schedule a meeting of both groups to review the work and to further explore how SR and IS could and should work together on OSP.

As the session concluded, Bill expressed satisfaction with the meeting, indicating that he felt there was more understanding. Dave asked to meet with each person later to discuss the meeting and to determine whether he could be of any further help. Both agreed that this was desirable.

Postconfrontation Reactions and Developments

Late that afternoon, Bill told Dave in convincing terms that the session with Lloyd had been quite productive. He believed that as a result of the confrontation they understood each other better and could maintain a dialogue on the outstanding issues between them. He said that, in his opinion, the presence of the consultant had made a great difference in encouraging a genuine confrontation; for example, without Dave's presence and support, he probably would not have challenged Lloyd "at the process level" for dominating the discussion.

Several days later, Dave telephoned Lloyd to learn his reactions to the confrontation meeting, to learn of subsequent developments, and to offer his further assistance if it should be desired. (The review meeting between the SR and IS groups had occurred in the meantime.) From Lloyd's report it was clear that some of the differences between Bill and himself remained, but that the two men had a better basis for managing these differences.

Lloyd's remarks indicated continued but reduced concerns about whether the resources of his staff were being used productively and whether his group was "too far in" or "too far out" of OSP. He showed increased understanding of the operating style of the combined groups by commenting on how this had been influenced by the great uncertainty under which this development work was being conducted. He continued to be critical of some aspects of the OSP as it stood currently and of the "cold, hard fact that Bill doesn't have anyone on his staff who has been through this." He added, however, that he did not think his own group "could make it in toto, either."

Now he also had reason for not pressing for an immediate resolution of certain of the intergroup issues involving the respective roles of the two groups. Apparently in talking with his own superior, he had gained a better appreciation of the provisional nature of the composition and leadership of the development effort. He seemed satisfied that if and when there was a decision to go ahead on the project, a definite structure would be created at that time and that the present structure would not prejudice the form that the eventual one would take.

Regarding the effect of the confrontation on his continuing relationship with Bill, he made these comments:

> I think we have made headway....I feel more relaxed about the way things are going....I came away from the meeting with a better understanding of Bill's position—as a matter of fact, I stressed him a little bit to get him to be explicit—...and I know Bill better understands my position. I know this because at the larger group meeting Bill made a summation of the discussion we had in his office and I was satisfied with it; he was able to accurately state my position....We have opennesss going for us....

Lloyd believed that Dave had been helpful and that it would be desirable to keep a consultant involved "who is familiar with the developing situation, but who can take a spectator position."

Several months later Bill read these comments and added,

> Against a longer time frame, the results were even better than the report conveys. As a human being Lloyd is accustomed to more structure than we had in the total group. Nevertheless, within a month we were operating very well, and he felt as much at home as anyone. Referring back to the personal needs he communicated during that session in January, his participation in the project became both visible and valued.

Dave also learned that Lloyd had developed high regard for Bill over the same time period.

Analysis of Factors in Succesful Confrontations

Differences between persons or groups in organizations can be handled in a variety of ways including avoidance, repression, and indirect conflict. A more direct approach to conflict involves confrontation, hopefully leading toward problem solving. Confrontation itself involves clarification and exploration of the issues in conflict, the nature and strength of the underlying needs or forces involved, and the types of current feelings generated by the conflict itself. It requires that a person be candid about his feelings as well as opinions. This act in itself often violates organizational norms prescribing rationality and proscribing emotionality (Argyris, 1962). Moreover, additional risks are incurred by owning up to the personal needs, concerns, and doubts as well as the antagonistic feelings often integrally involved in an organizational conflict. For example, if one does not resolve the relationship issue, one's statements may serve to add further fuel to the other's antagonisms. Moreover, one may feel even more vulnerable because of what the other knows about him.

The idea that organizations are more effective if they "confront and problem-solve conflicts" in contrast to "smoothing" or "forcing" them is supported by persuasive reasoning (Schmidt & Tannenbaum, 1960), plenty of anecdotal evidence (Blake, Shepard, & Mouton, 1964), and some systematic research (Lawrence & Lorsch, 1967).

What does this episode suggest about the factors which facilitate successful confrontations?

Creating Mutual Incentive

Here two persons found that there were important issues between them. Lloyd was dissatisfied with the role of his staff in OSP, with his role relationship with Bill, and with the operating style of the larger OSP project group. Bill obviously had been satisfied with these factors. Lloyd's approach was to create an incentive for Bill to review these conditions. The disturbance he caused for Bill in the first combined group meeting he attended had the effect of creating an incentive for Bill to work on their relationship, and perhaps, if necessary, to renegotiate it. In any event, by the time they met in Bill's office, both had decided it was in their respective interests to discuss their relationship; both were prepared for some form of interpersonal confrontation.

Lloyd continued to build pressure on Bill during the confrontation, presumably in order to create bargaining leverage and to convince Bill that he could not be taken for granted. In Lloyd's own words, he "stressed" Bill. It appeared that he threatened to break off the relationship in order to induce Bill to take a more flexible attitude.

Thus, the important condition developed that each person was being inconvenienced by the other, and both were aware of this interdependence. Lloyd was the prime mover on renegotiating the terms of the intergroup relationship; Bill felt the need to clarify and improve their interpersonal relationship. Lloyd's aversive behavior established a bargaining point from which he could accede to more accommodating behavior if he were more satisfied with other terms of the relationship.

Normative Support for Openness

In this particular situation many factors supported openness in interpersonal relationships. Within the past year, both Bill and Lloyd had participated in a one-week sensitivity training workshop which emphasized the value of openness about feelings and confrontation of interpersonal differences (Psathas & Hardert, 1966). These norms had become a part of the working process of the larger OSP group. Lloyd was aware that Bill and George had maintained an open relationship. Finally, the presence of a third-party consultant associated with sensitivity training further strengthened the normative support for openness.

Synchronization

Two persons who would like to reach a better understanding of their apparent differences frequently experience difficulty synchronizing their efforts to confront each other. One may choose a time and a place not suitable to the other, who then tries to avoid the open confrontation, which is taken as further rejection or an indication that the other prefers to play out the conflict by indirect means, and so on. If the second party later tries confrontation in a different situation, the first in the meantime may have resolved to handle the differences by avoidance or indirect means, and now the second party is offended, further aggrieved, and more resistant to an open confrontation.

In this particular case, both parties were prepared for the confrontation. Bill was encouraged by his superior and by Dave to arrange a session for that very reason. Bill needed to act quickly in order to avail himself of Dave's presence on the scene. He apparently communicated to Lloyd his reason for asking to meet. The participation of Dave added incentive for the parties to follow through in the time allotted for the meeting that morning. The few telephone interruptions to the meeting, which carried the risk of ''aborting'' the confrontation, did not break down communication.

Interpersonal Styles and Process Skills Available

The two principals had styles and skills that increased the likelihood of a successful confrontation. Although Lloyd was often dominating in interpersonal discussion and although he sometimes resisted more personal interpretations of his own behavior, he had a directness and a strength that were consistent with direct interpersonal confrontation. For Bill's part, his general skill at understanding interpersonal process not only made him better able to hear Lloyd out, but also to challenge the latter's occasional dominating manner.

The third-party consultant was perceived by the parties as decreasing the risk of an abortive confrontation. By being identified as a ''sensitivity trainer,'' he was presumed to possess substantial skills at facilitating such processes; therefore the parties perceived less risk that the confrontation would bog down, become repetitive, and result in more frustration and even bitterness.

The third party slightly increased the potential payoff for the confrontation in the sense that the participants believed that he could assist them in learning something of value in generalizing about their behavior in such situations.

Reassurance and Acceptance Available

One of the reasons for not confronting an issue is that exposing an underlying issue in a conflict means owning up to resentments, rejections, and other feelings that the person himself is reluctant to admit. Many of us have been brought up to regard these feelings as petty and silly and as ''being too sensitive.'' Also, as was stated earlier, one may know or believe that these feelings result from insecurities (about his competence or his acceptance or membership) that he is unwilling to acknowledge either to himself or to someone else.

A third-party consultant who is assumed to be nonevaluative of these feelings and who can provide acceptance and emotional support is reassuring to the participant in confrontation. He can assume that there is a greater likelihood that someone present will understand and accept his feelings.

Sharpening Issues and Regulating Process

In addition to contributing to the above factors encouraging confrontation, the third party performed a diagnostic function during and after the confrontation. He listened to each discuss his views and feelings and sharpened what he understood to be an issue, to which the participants responded in ways which tended to confirm or disconfirm this as a deeper, underlying issue. An effort was made to state these issues in ways which made each person's position understandable, legitimate, and acceptable. One apparent effect of this understanding, legitimating, and sharpening of issues was to encourage Lloyd then to identify the more personal concerns he had about not being involved and not being recognized as a competent person with experience relevant to OSP.

The third party chose to play what *he* regarded as a minor role in regulating the process. Essentially he let the parties run their own course. For example, he waited for Bill to deal with the way Lloyd was dominating the discussion. Thus he gave the two parties an opportunity to reveal or develop their own interaction equilibrium. Lloyd, however, perceived Dave to have played a relatively active role, a recollection he communicated after reading this report:

> I believe the report understates Dave's effect as a third party and casts him more outside the process than I experienced him. Both his presence and his active, constructive participation influenced the process. For example, he "turned me off" once when I was getting long-winded, reminding me of the need to listen. When you hear something from a third party who doesn't have an investment in the issues at stake, you are more likely to respond to that advice, especially if it is given to you in a timely way on the spot....In sum, for me, he was not only a catalytic agent, but also an ingredient in the situation.

Establishing Third-Party Neutrality

Differences in the third party's relationships to the two principals can influence his effectiveness. Three different types of third-party symmetry are important: (1) He is neutral with respect to outcome. (2) He is equally close to or distant from the parties in a sociometric sense. (3) He advances ground rules for handling differences which do not inadvertently operate to the advantage of one and the disadvantage of the other. Symmetry is not necessary but it is usually helpful. Actually, in some cases, asymmetrical third-party roles or interventions are more effective (e.g., when they offset a basic power or skill asymmetry between the parties themselves). The discussion here calls attention to the importance of this role attribute and analyzes this dimension of the episode.

First, it is usually important for a third-party consultant to be neutral regarding outcome (Walton, 1967). Was Dave neutral with respect to the positions of the parties in this conflict? Recall that he had participated in the team-building session which had helped to create the open, fluid pattern of group functioning which Bill wanted to preserve and Lloyd said he wanted to change. However, Dave himself felt as sympathetic to Lloyd as to Bill as the confrontation unfolded. For example, it

seemed perfectly appropriate to Dave that Bill agree to reconsider the operating pattern of the group and that he should take into account Lloyd's preferences. Also, Lloyd's demands at the intergroup level seemed to him to be legitimate and deserving of response.

Second, was Dave equally close to the principals? No; in fact, Dave's considerable prior consulting relationship with Bill made it impossible for him in a short period of time to become similarly related to Lloyd—in terms of warmth, personal respect, trust, and general familiarity. Nevertheless, it might have been advisable for Dave to seek a way to spend more time with Lloyd before the confrontation in order to reduce this type of asymmetry.

Third, did the model which the consultant held up to the principals to work on their differences favor either one? The norms of openness, acceptance, emotional support, and analysis of group process which the consultant passively (by his identity and presence) and actively (by his interventions) brought to the confrontation were those Bill favored. Considering Lloyd's relative concern about excessive "groupiness" in the OSP task group and also Dave's earlier hunch that Lloyd might tend to resist dealing with the more emotional aspects of issues, one might have expected him either to resent or resist the consultant's methodology. As it turned out, he participated fully, utilizing the process to get his own views and concerns out in a forceful way. Moreover, the process was general enough to allow him to utilize bargaining behavior—e.g., to hint at contingent actions if the two of them could not reach agreement. Inasmuch as the consultant's own methodological model also incorporated this form of interpersonal conflict resolution, he made no attempt to sanction Lloyd for those departures from a conciliatory problem-solving approach.

In sum, various aspects of the consultant's relationship to the two parties were asymmetrical, favoring Bill. However, Dave did not perceive himself—in his interventions—as favoring either person. Nor did Lloyd, who said:

Yes, I recognized that Dave was closer to Bill and the group, but I didn't assume he was therefore biased. This gets into professionalism. I assume that Dave, in his professional role, has his own built-in gyros, keeping him neutral. Sure, he confronted me about some of my behavior and made me uncomfortable, but he couldn't be a dishrag and still be effective, either.

Implications for Third-Party Roles

This was a successful interpersonal confrontation, and the third party had a constructive influence on the outcome. The third party's influence resulted in part from his more active contributions (some regulating of the interaction, sharpening issues, and diagnosing the relationship). More surprising were the basic functions he performed in a passive way— by his mere presence. His function in encouraging the confrontation in the first place derived from the participants' expectations about him (support, process skill, learning, and insight) and from the symbolic meaning attributed to him as a result of his identification with a class of persons, namely sensitivity trainers, with whom the two had shared an intensive and successful experience. In this case, the third party had very little "face work" or other work to do in establishing his role and competence and in communicating the attitudes which support a successful confrontation. In other situations, at least half of the third party's total job in assisting two parties in conflict may be concerned with this effort to establish the appropriate role identity and personal attributes. This is not to underestimate the general requirements of effective intervention into the ongoing process or follow-up work with the participants. These requirements just did not turn out to be demanding aspects of the third party role in this case.

References

Argyris, C. *Interpersonal competence and organizational effectiveness*. Homewood, Ill.: Irwin–Dorsey, 1962.

Blake, R. R., Shepard, H. A., & Mouton, Jane S. *Intergroup conflict in organizations*. Ann Arbor, Mich.: Foundation for Research on Human Behavior, 1964.

Davis, S. A. An organic problem-solving method of organizational change. *Journal of Applied Behavioral Science*, 1967, *3*(1), 3–21.

Lawrence, P. R., & Lorsch, J. W. *Organization and environment: Managing differentiation and integration*. Boston: Division of Research, Graduate School of Business Administration, Harvard University, 1967.

McGregor, D. *The human side of enterprise*. New York: McGraw-Hill, 1960.

Psathas, G., & Hardert, R. Trainer interventions and normative patterns in the t-group. *Journal of Applied Behavioral Science*, 1966, *2*(2), 149–169.

Schmidt, W., & Tannenbaum, R. The management of differences. *Harvard Business Review*, November–December 1960, *38*, 107–115.

Walton, R. E. Third-party roles in interdepartmental conflict. *Industrial Relations*, October 1967, *7*(1).

Reading 26

STRATEGIES FOR IMPROVING
HEADQUARTERS–FIELD RELATIONS

Robert Blake, Herbert A. Shepard, and Jane S. Mouton

Organizations whose operations extend over great distances encounter complex problems in maintaining effective integration between the headquarters facility and field installations.[1] Geographical distance makes communications difficult. Differences in regional experience are hard for the person at a distance to comprehend. Psychological distance develops to enhance the mechanical difficulties created by geography.

In all other parts of an organization, superordinate groups are joined to subordinate groups by a common member, i.e., the leader of a subordinate group is himself a subordinate in the group consisting of himself, his peers and his boss.[2] The linkpin between groups of unequal power, while more responsive to those above than below, nonetheless has a powerful mediating effect. He is placed in personal conflict and stress if the two groups in which he has membership are in conflict. The stresses on the foreman are so great that in many organizations he loses membership in both groups; that is, he has little influence up or down. Clearly, there is no linkpin between union and management, and through unionization and legislative supports, union and management are approximately equal in power.

Source: Robert Blake, Herbert A. Shepard, and Jane S. Mouton, *Managing Intergroup Conflict in Industry* (Houston: Gulf Publishing, 1964), pp. 114–21.

[1]R. R. Blake and J. S. Mouton, ''Headquarters-Field Team Training for Organizational Improvement.'' *ASTD J.* 16, no. 3 (1962), pp. 3–11.
[2]R. R. Blake and J. S. Mouton, *The Managerial Grid* (Houston: Gulf Publishing, 1964); and R. Likert, *New Patterns of Management* (New York: McGraw-Hill, 1961).

Most headquarter-field relationships lack this cement, and it is not uncommon for negative attitudes to develop between the parties. In formal theory, field units are subordinate to headquarters, but field units can acquire great informal power. This is particularly true if one field organization is very much larger than other field divisions and accounts for a majority, or at least a large portion, of the company's business. In such cases, the head of the field division may be given formal membership in the top corporate group, thus providing the missing cement. But if, as is more often the case, there are several large or many small field units, headquarters maintains its power by placing them in competition with one another. Building good relations and a good record with headquarters can lead to promotion for key executives in a field unit and to a favored position when headquarters contemplates new investment.

Field groups can develop resentment toward headquarters for many reasons. For example, each field unit is, in most companies, treated as a profit center. However, the profitability of the whole corporation may sometimes require that a given field unit do something which reduces its own profitability. Similarly, new investment by headquarters in one field unit can arouse feelings of injustice in others.

Such problems were causing severe deterioration of relationships between headquarters and a large division in the Tennex Corporation. The following pages describe the problem-solving procedures employed to bring about adequate working relationships. The design was, of course, adapted to the particular set of problems being experienced by Tennex. A different design would be used, for example, if the object were to build better team relations among several field units, and between them and headquarters.

The Scofield Case

The following example illustrates an approach to the improvement of working relationships between headquarters and field. The Scofield division is one of several subsidiaries of the Tennex Corporation. The Tennex Corporation is a highly diversified organization, moderately decentralized.

Since World War II, Tennex has grown quite rapidly, partly by acquisition. Corporate efforts to develop strategies in marketing and production which took advantage of its diverse resources brought many changes which affected Scofield, one of the divisions. Over a period of years, a number of points of friction had developed between the division's management and the top corporate management.

Headquarters personnel felt the division managers were "secretive" and "unresponsive." The division was looked upon as unwilling to provide information that headquarters felt it needed. In turn, Scofield division management saw the headquarters management as "prying" and "arbitrary." For example, headquarters was critical of the labor relations practices of the division. The division management resented the criticism, regarding it as prejudiced and ill-informed. Again, headquarters felt that Scofield managers had been "dragging their feet" in implementing corporate marketing policies. Scofield felt that headquarters' demands in the area were unrealistic and that the corporate marketing group was behaving "unilaterally," and so on.

The behavioral science consultants called in to help first acquainted themselves with key management in both locations and were exposed to the patterns of action and reaction, frustration and negative stereotypes, which characterize a deteriorating intergroup working relationship. Some of the headquarters executives were considering replacing certain Scofield managers. The latter, in their turn, were attempting to influence other top corporate officers in Scofield's behalf.

Gaining Perspective on Intergroup and Intragroup Dynamics

In separate three-day conferences with each group, the consultants provided intragroup (or "team") and intergroup training experiences and theory. The intergroup training had two effects. First, managers were able to see the headquarters-field problem in sufficient perspective to analyze the destructive consequences of the win-lose trap which had been dictating their actions. Second, an intergroup experiment and its analysis created a degree of openness within each group of managers that enabled them to review their own intragroup relationships and to develop greater mutual understanding and acceptance. This teamwork training is an important prelude to intergroup confrontation, because friction, "politics," or inability to level within each team clouds and confuses intergroup communication when the two groups are brought together.

The Headquarters-Field Laboratory

As a next step after the separate three-day conferences, the two teams met together, again for a three-day period. It will be convenient to describe their work as a sequence of phases.

Phase I: Listing Issues Requiring Joint Problem Solving. The laboratory opened with a joint session in which members discussed those issues they felt the group should debate. These were then listed in order of priority to provide an overview of the work to be accomplished over the three-day period.

Phase II: Preparation of Group Self-Images and Images of the Other Group. Each group met separately to prepare a description of itself as viewed by its members. The issues listed in Phase I provided a basis for elaborating and giving substance to the self-image descriptions.

Next, each group constructed a verbal image *of the other group.* Scofield's "secretiveness" as experienced by headquarters and headquarters' "prying" as experienced by Scofield could thus be bought into open communication.

Finally, each group built a description of the relationship between Tennex headquarters and the Scofield division.

These images were developed to provide a background statement of existing attitudes, feelings and difficulties which needed to be examined, understood and overcome.

Phase III: Exchange of Images. During this phase, each group in turn exposed its own image of itself, and in turn listened to the image as perceived by the other group. The process of bringing these images into the open created a background of understanding and brought a new atmosphere of mutual acceptance into the discussion.

Finally, a review was undertaken of relationship problems with respect to the issues that had been listed at the beginning of the conference. Since most of these were related to specific functions and activities, they provided the basis for moving to the subgroup meetings of Phase IV.

Phase IV: Subgroup Meetings Based on Similarity of Function in Field and Headquarters. During Phase IV, members from the headquarters staff with functional responsibilities at the corporate level met with Scofield managers who had responsibility for the corresponding function in the plant.

The purpose of these discussions was akin to the "team development" of the earlier three-day conferences: to explore relationship problems between individuals whose responsibilities make them interdependent. Once interpersonal relationship issues had been explored and sources of difficulty had been cleared out of the way, it was possible to discuss functional problems in a climate conducive to understanding and collaboration.

The latter part of Phase III and beginning of Phase IV brought out dramatically how confused and inadequate communication between Scofield and headquarters had been in many areas. The headquarters group seized on the relationship-image exchange as an excellent opportunity to "explain" to Scofield things that they believed Scofield did not understand. As the discussion proceeded, how-

ever, the tables were turned. When the field group presented its view of the relationship it began to "get through" to headquarters. By the end of Phase IV, headquarters staff members were *really* able to understand operational difficulties from a field point of view. They were also able to see more clearly how they might serve as consultants in the field, rather than as persons who attempt to "control" field operations.

Phase V: Review and Planning. In this phase the two groups met to prepare an overall summary of problems that had been identified and defined. This led to a joint discussion of the kinds of changes required to bring about improvements. Some of the problems implied changes in the behavior of only one of the groups, but most required joint implementation by functional subgroups.

The most significant product of this phase was that it provided a new concept of the way to bring about change and innovation. For instance, prior to the headquarters-field conference, it was accepted that "headquarters formulates policy; the field implements it." The inappropriateness of this concept for policies which had long been in force was evident to both parties. Reports from the field told headquarters whether the policy was being implemented adequately and enabled the headquarters to take special action where departures from policy were detected.

Conference discussions clearly disclosed that this control was woefully inadequate during a period of policy changing, policy making or during implementation of new or changed policies. Communication distortions and breakdowns, areas of mutual frustration with the accompanying charges of "foot-dragging" and "arbitrariness," were seen to be the result of those methods which had been used in developing and implementing new policies.

Both sides came to see clearly that making and implementing new or changed policy is a complex process requiring continuous feedback among those involved. Efforts to implement a change are experiments, the results of which need to be quickly available to the organization. They are reality tests which may lead to policy modification, and they are explorations to find sufficient methods of implementation. The policy-making-and-implementing process was thus seen as an innovation phase requiring open communication and collaboration among members of the leadership groups.

Phase VI: Followup. By the end of Phase V, much had been accomplished in the areas of mutual trust, respect, and understanding. Moreover, the groups had made a number of commitments to new ways of working, and had reached a number of agreements in defining certain problems and the courses of action to be taken in solving them.

Realizing that planning is insufficient to bring about desired results, the groups established some means for operational followup. The groups also agreed to reconvene for review and evaluation after a period of implementation. The purpose of this meeting would be to insure that they could find ways to handle possible difficulties in carrying out the plans of Phase V, and in "checking on the health" of the relationship. Thus, if new sources of friction were to arise for which no problem-solving procedure was available, they could be dealt with appropriately.

Summary

The normal day-by-day working arrangements between the headquarters facilities and field units often generate many problem areas. Some of the problems tend to become chronic. As a rule, formal communication and decision-making arrangements are insufficient for correcting these chronic difficulties.

Headquarters-field training situations as described in this chapter are useful devices for exploring and improving organizational interrelationships, including: headquarters interrelations and operations, field interrelations and operations, problems at the general level between headquarters and the field, and functional and concrete operational difficulties within those segments of the organization which are responsible for smooth working arrangements between headquarters and field.

Appendix: Postscript for "Strategies for Improving Headquarters-Field Relations"

This article represented one of the series of spinoff applications of the basic intergroup confrontation and resolution design that we pioneered in the mid-50s. We see no revisions, based on our experience with it over 25 years, that constitute fundamental improvements. However, consultants using this design implement it in short-cut ways that may fail to solve problems underlying headquarters-field tensions. Limitations such as this in using the design are most likely to derive from the consultant's failure to sense the depth of intergroup tensions, and therefore to prompt premature informality in a way that is not present in the design itself. This is likely to lead to mutual accusations and defensive retaliations rather than to constructive efforts to resolve the underlying problems.[3]

---

[3]Robert Blake and Jane Mouton, personal correspondence.

Reading 27

THE CAUSES OF INDUSTRIAL PEACE
RE–REVISITED: THE CASE FOR RBO

Harvey A. Young

There have been numerous attempts in this century to resolve the bitter conflicts that can be generated by union-management relations. Probably the most famous private attempts to achieve industrial stability was the "Protocols of Peace" developed by Louis Brandeis in 1910 for the garment industry. Although short-lived, the "Protocols" serve as the foundation of the present-day grievance procedure which has as its last step final and binding arbitration. Government action such as the Norris-LaGuardia Act, the Wagner Act, and the Taft-Hartley Act have effectively reduced the bitterness of past industrial conflict.[1]

Today conflict is less violent but it may still be disruptive. In 1948, a landmark project was initiated by the National Planning Association of Washington, D.C., to ascertain the major ingredients of good labor-management relationships. The study was known as the Causes of Industrial Peace Under Collective Bargaining. In 1968, the original study was re-examined and many of its findings were found wanting. The 1968 study raised the questions of what constitutes a good labor-management relationship and how the parties can achieve this goal.

As part of its mission for assisting good labor relations, the Federal Mediation and Conciliation Service (FMCS) has recently developed a procedure for changing union-management situations characterized by bitterness, strikes and antagonism between the parties. This method of achieving labor-management peace is known as "RBO-

Source: Harvey A. Young, *Human Resource Management* Copyright, Summer, Fall 1982. Reprinted with permission of John Wiley & Sons, Inc.

Relationships by Objectives." While this paper is primarily concerned with RBO, it will examine the 1948 NPA study and its 1968 counterpart to compare various prescriptions for achieving labor-management peace as compared to the RBO problem-solving-process approach. The paper will also touch briefly on alternative approaches to organization change, such as Management by Objective (MBO) and Organizational Development, which have some similarities to the RBO.

The NPA Study and Its Follow-up

After the great strike years of 1945 and 1946 and the controversy generated by passage of the Taft-Hartley Act in 1947, the National Planning Association (NPA) set out to demonstrate that if collective bargaining were grounded on sound principles, industrial peace would result. In its final report, the NPA committee listed nine key causes of industrial peace (see Table 1).[1] These causes range from management's acceptance of the union as an institution, to the settlement of grievances promptly, flexibly and informally. This committee believed that "each of these causes was found to be important in explaining the degree of industrial peace in the specific case." This report also noted that their contemporary scene (1948–1953) was not typical but, despite this, it generally reflected optimism that the basic causes of industrial peace had been isolated.

In the mid-1960's a research project of the Wharton School conducted a follow-up or longitudinal study of the original NPA study. In 1968, the results of this project were published.[2]

TABLE 1   Causes of Industrial Peace as Defined by the National Planning Association

1. There is a full acceptance by management of the collective bargaining process and of unionism as an institution. The company considers a strong union an asset to management.

2. The union fully accepts private ownership and operation of the industry; it recognizes that the welfare of its members depends upon the successful operation of the business.

3. The union is strong, responsible, and democratic.

4. The company stays out of the union's internal affairs; it does not seek to alienate the workers' allegiance to their union.

5. Mutual trust and confidence exist between the parties. There have been no serious ideological incompatibilities

6. Neither party to bargaining has adopted a legalistic approach to the solution of problems in the relationship.

7. Negotiations are ''problem-centered'' — more time is spent on day-to-day problems than on defining abstract principles.

8. There is widespread union-management consultation and highly developed information.

9. Grievances are settled promptly, in the local plant whenever possible. There is flexibility and informality within the procedure.

Brief Update of the Follow-up Study

The longitudinal study of the Wharton School stressed the fact that the economic environment sets the boundaries of the union-management relationship and that this was either not understood or ignored by the authors of the original study. The study also mentioned the fact that given the economic environment, managerial policies can set the tone of the relationship and a well-oriented and executed long-range managerial policy can be the driving force in a relationship even when the union has more economic power than the company. In concentrating on these themes, other significant findings were crowded out.

It is clear that the longitudinal study should have also stated that for an effective union-management relationship to be maintained, given the economic environment, the parties must actively and effectively strive through continuous effort to make the relationship work. Failure of either party to live up to this commitment (not just by management, as suggested in the longitudinal study) will provide the other with the kind of advantage that may negate an effective relationship. Although this was implicit in the follow-up study, it was not clearly enunciated.

Several elements of the NPA study not touched upon in the longitudinal study, deserve some mention. The first is the fact that the original NPA findings were limited even if the principles enunciated were found to be viable, which they were not. The NPA study did not attempt to show how other situations could adopt these enunciated principles. This is a serious defect because there was no method for transferring these prescriptions or formulas to other relationships. What good are a series of principles if there is no ''delivery system'' to implement them? (As will be shown below, the method of implementation is a critical element in any program designed to help correct poor labor relations). Another element not discussed in the Wharton study, and more suggestive of social change, is the fact that the term ''industrial peace'' is now somewhat limited because it does not include the more recent developments in public and federal sector bargaining.

New Approaches to Collective Bargaining

Since the follow-up study was completed in 1968, there have not been many new techniques introduced that have attempted to develop labor peace.[3] Probably the most important is the Experimental Bargaining Agreement in the basic steel industry. This program has as its major element the resolution of bargaining impasses through voluntary arbitration, an approach which is by no means new. This general approach has proven quite unacceptable to most bargaining situations.[4] Conflict resolution techniques such as binding arbitration, final offer selection, and various combinations of fact-finding and arbitration are now widespread in the public sector. These, however, are normally considered substitutions for the strike not normally permitted, where these procedures are practiced. The process of Med-Arb has also been given widespread attention, although it has not gained widespread acceptance.

Productivity programs such as those established in basic steel and those encompassed by the Scanlon Plan have also been given wide attention.[5] Another program which has been growing is a new variation of profit sharing known as the Employee Stock Ownership Plan.[6] Still another program which has received mixed results is expedited arbitration, first established in basic steel and now adopted in other bargaining situations. Nonetheless, most of these approaches are not really new with the possible exception of expedited arbitration and the conflict resolution techniques used in the public sector. Most were around in some form at the time of the original National Planning Association's study.

One of the more novel and innovative approaches for helping to create labor-management peace in a climate where there is a great antagonism between the parties is the technique developed by FMCS called "RBO—Relationships by Objectives"[7]. This approach is basically a process wherein the parties, with the assistance of federal mediators, attempt to change a poor labor-management relationship into an acceptable one. The balance of this paper is concerned with a discussion of this new and innovative approach to labor relations.

The RBO

RBOs were first introduced by the Service in 1975. Basically, RBO is a conflict resolution *process* which is found effective for changing poor intra-plant labor-management relations.[8] It is not a set of principles, as enunciated by the NPA, without means of implementation. The process itself is the key to the RBO program because it provides a vehicle for the parties to resolve differences in their own way.

In many respects the technique has similarities to the much discussed concept of "MBO—Management by Objectives"[9] and to change agent ingredients associated with Organization Development theory. MBO may be defined as an attempt to have managers themselves determine their future objectives or goals and then devise plans by which these objectives can be accomplished. The manager is then judged or rated by whether his performance lived up to the pre-established goals.

RBOs encompass much of the same procedures—the development of goals and plans of action to achieve these goals—but in a different setting and with different participants. A poorly-oriented labor-management situation, one characterized by bitterness, and severe antagonism between the parties is the normal setting—not the confines of a managerial hierarchy as in the case of the MBO. Union and management officials who are coping with these problems are the participants, not individual managers in a corporate setting. Another variance is the fact that the participants feel and accept the need to change the situation, they believe their work environment must be improved.

This approach then requires a joint undertaking by equals—not in the setting of the superior-subordinate relationship as in the case of the MBO. The desire of both parties to make these needed changes is an important prerequisite for the participation in the RBO. Basically, the parties jointly develop their own goals for labor peace and then by a variety of actions work together to achieve these goals in designated areas of responsibility— hence the term Relationships by Objectives. This all seems simple, but it is not. Like the MBO systems which are not easy to apply (currently there is much criticism of them[10]), there are potentially great hazards in implementing an RBO program.

The Development of the RBO Program

The "Preventive Mediation" program of the Service, which was developed to improve plant level labor-management relations, dates back to Cyrus Ching, first Director of FMCS.[11] (This program was reorganized and is now known as the Technical Assistance program.) One of the traditional methods used by this program and still in use by the Service today is the labor-management committee.[12] An attempt to improve the problem-solving capabilities of such committees eventually led to the development of the RBO program.

The first RBO program in its present form was implemented early in 1975 at the Georgia Pacific plant in Woodland, Maine. Its apparent success triggered the development of the RBO into a nationwide Service program. As of January 1980, 87 RBO programs have been implemented. Most have been quite successful in correcting bitter strike-prone union management relationships. There also have been some failures. Time here does not permit a description of the experience of individual case situations; nonetheless, success and failure have normally been based upon the depth of the parties' commitment to the program. (This will be discussed in more detail below.) Nor can a complete list of the union-management situations be given because this would violate the confidentiality that the Service has with its clients. However, the Service is at liberty to name a few such case situations.

The Techniques of RBO

The basic philosophy behind the RBO concept has already been discussed. RBOs provide a process by which the parties can modify their current relationship outside of contract negotiations. They do this by jointly defining what they perceive their relationship should be and by carefully prescribing areas of responsibility and goals to achieve this relationship. The RBO requires the active participation of trained FMCS mediators to help the parties achieve these objectives. In most situations, a minimum of four mediators are required. Parenthetically, FMCS is somewhat reluctant to initiate an RBO program because of the large commitment of its resources. As a consequence, a prerequisite for Service approval of such a program is a very strong commitment on the part of both parties—labor and management—to want to change their antagonistic, bitter relationship.

The management officials who normally take part consist of the plant manager, labor relations director, plant production personnel, and several key foremen. The union representatives consist of the local union officials, international representatives, and key shop stewards. Anywhere from 10 to 20 representatives of each party may participate. The relatively large group is necessary because it provides greater participation, hence great commitment for implementation. As a consequence, many individuals take the program into the shop floor to make it work. Normally the program is held in a "retreat" setting away from the distractions and tensions of the job site. The time frame for the sessions is from 3 to 5 days.[13]

Preliminary Step

A preliminary step in the RBO program is the showing of the FMCS produced film, "Barney and Clyde" or "You Can't Negotiate an Attitude" which dramatizes the inherent problems of poor union-management relations at the plant floor. The basic purpose for showing the film is to encourage the parties to compare their own relations with that seen in the film. First, the participants are divided into mixed teams consisting of an equal number of union and management participants (each team has a mediator as its chairman). The teams are asked to develop among their members a consensus of what each wishes to obtain from the RBO program. They are then asked to respond to the film in three ways: (1) analyze the attitudes of the supervisor and union steward; (2) list the problems in the union-management relationship; and (3) make recommendations for improving this relationship.

The respective reports for each team (the mediator assigned each team attempts to gain a consensus report) are discussed by the entire group of participants. This element in the RBO program is really an exercise in small group dynamics for the dual purpose of developing a team spirit among adversaries and, as stated above, of encouraging the parties to jointly compare their own relationship with that of "Barney and Clyde".

Step 1

The atmosphere is now developed for the first stage in the RBO. The parties are separated into their union-management components. In separate conferences, which are simultaneously held, the participants (all

Partial List of Union-Management Situations Which
Have Implemented RBO Programs

Company	Union	Location
Georgia Pacific Corporation	UPIU	Woodland, Maine
United Parcel Service, Inc.	IBT	New York City
Columbus Coated Fabrics, Inc.	TWUA	Columbus, Ohio
Olin Corporation	UPIU	Pigsah Forest, North Carolina
Whirlpool Corporation	IUE	Evansville, Indiana
Marion Power Shovel Company	USW	Marion, Ohio
National Airlines, Inc.	ALEA	System-Wide
Aluminum Company of America	UAW	Vernon, California
Ameron Steel Producing Company	USW	Etiwanda, California

UPIU —United Paperworkers International Union
IBT   —International Brotherhood of Teamsters
TWUA —Textile Workers Union of America now Amalgamated Clothing and Textile Workers Union
IUE   —International Union of Electrical Workers
USW —United Steelworkers of America
ALEA —Air Line Employees Association
UAW —United Auto Workers

management and all union) are asked to respond to the following questions: (1) What should the other party be doing to improve labor-management? (2) What should we be doing to improve labor-management relations? While one mediator guides a particular group (union or management), a second records the answers to each of the questions. After these sessions have reached a set of conclusions, they are adjourned temporarily. From the answers each team gives to the above questions, four lists of preliminary goals are developed by the mediators. These four lists are: (1) according to the company, the union should . . .; (2) according to the company, the company should . . .; (3) according to the union, the company should . . .; (4) according to the union, the union should . . . These lists of preliminary goals

serve as the starting point for the next step in the RBO program.

Step 2

This step attempts to develop general agreement by the participants on the goals needed to develop union-management stability. The participants are assembled (both union and management representatives together) and asked to review the four lists developed by the mediators in Step 1. In essence, this step may be considered a joint bargaining session in which the parties are asked to determine the objectives necessary for improving their current relationship. The difference between this and their normal contract negotiations may be considered as that between integrative and distributive negotiations (which typifies their normal bargaining).[14] Integrative bargaining occurs because both parties gain from the encounter since they are working to achieve their mutual objectives. Step 2 is an important element in the RBO program because failure of the parties to reach a consensus on these objectives would indicate a failure of commitment. (Commitment by the parties is essential for an RBO to be effective).

The participants attempt to develop a series of subgoals necessary to achieve their purpose of improving labor-management relations. These subgoals are derived from the four lists developed by the mediators in the previous step. In so doing, the parties usually see common elements on these lists. For example, there may be similar elements on the list (2) according to the company, the company should . . . and (3) according to the union, the company should . . .

As a result, the parties begin to see that they have numerous mutual objectives, and with the skilled guidance of the mediators are able to develop a series of goals that are necessary to effectuate a better relationship. The mediators then group these goals into common categories. Although not limited to the following, the categories generally touch on (1) labor-management communications, (2) attitudes and practices of the management, (3) attitudes and practices of the union, (4) training, and (5) foremen-steward relations.

Step 3

Step 2 normally provides the parties an opportunity to develop an awareness of their mutual objectives. In Step 3, the union and management participants jointly review the four lists of objectives developed in the previous step in an attempt to whittle down the four separate categories of objectives to one list. Both groups compare their respective lists and attempt to reach agreement on one common list of objectives from their respective lists. In essence, the list finally agreed upon is one which both sides have spent considerable time, individually and jointly, in reaching. The list thus becomes a set of common objectives that both feel, if implemented, will reverse their present poor internal environment.

Steps 4 Through 6

Once consensus is obtained on a common list of objectives, the mixed union-management teams (initially formed in the preliminary step) are reformed to develop action steps for implementing specific subsets of the agreed-upon objectives. This team approach facilitates a broad base of active participation to formulate ideas for correcting the poor labor relations situation. Because each team is working on a portion of the goals in Step 3, they act as expert resources (i.e., subcommittees) on behalf of their respective group.

In Step 5, the team members make reports to their respective group (union or management) on the proposals developed by the mixed team. Each group then reviews these reports and develops a set of action steps based upon them. The team reports tend to carry great weight in the formulation of the action steps agreed to by the group because group members actively participate in their development and can explain the reasons upon which they are based. In addition, the group is generally more willing to accept recommendations from its own members than from outsiders.

When each group has agreed internally to the action steps required to implement the RBO's objectives, they are brought together to reach final agreement (Step 6).

Steps 4 through 6 are the heart of the process because they enable the parties themselves to decide how they will go about implementing the objectives of the RBO program. This is significant because each labor-management situation tends to be unique even though the parties may experience problems considered similar to other situations. And since the parties know the nuances of their situation better than anyone else, they are in the best position to develop the action steps necessary to achieve their objectives.

Step 7

The final step in the RBO program involves assigning areas of responsibility and establishing a timetable for implementing action steps developed above. This is normally achieved in a joint union-management meeting.

Follow-Up

Chances for the RBO to succeed are quite high since the key personnel on both sides have agreed upon a series of objectives, a plan of action, assignment of responsibilities for the plan of action, and a time frame for implementation. And, because a relatively large number of individuals participate in these formulations, implementation may be easier because of the wide base of acceptability. The fact that the parties, faced with problems that are not really unique, are nonetheless able to develop their own methods of resolving them under the skilled guidance of Federal mediators is another factor in RBO's favor. Recommendations are not forced upon subordinates. (Subordinates have been known to undermine such attempts at change through a variety of passive resistance techniques which may be better described as passive aggressions!)

The Service monitors implementation of an RBO program by periodically contacting the parties to evaluate the progress of the program and offering additional advice and assistance if necessary. Normally such follow-up contacts are scheduled at 90 day intervals, but can be more frequent if necessary.

Role of the Federal Mediator

Another element in the RBO program which contributes to its effectiveness is the role played by the federal mediators, who become the agent for change in the process by skillfully leading the parties through one critical area of discussion after another. Failure on the part of the mediators to understand the depth of feelings of the parties may result in intensifying their respective animosity and creating a worse situation than before the program was initiated. Faulty guidance may also permit the parties to implement an unworkable plan of action which would fall of its own weight and set the parties even further back in their attitudes. There is, in fact, an endless array of ways in which the outside party can insure the program's failure. As a result, the individual who acts as the change agent must be thoroughly experienced, professional, and neutral in the process of union-management relations. And the Service feels that, for the present, only Federal mediators, because of their particular background, can properly conduct an RBO. (Mediators are given extensive training in the techniques of the RBO before they are permitted to participate in such programs.)

OD Theory and RBO

Time does not permit an extensive comparison between Organization Development theory and RBO. As in the above discussion of MBO, a comparison of OD theory and the RBO is really another topic unto itself. Nonetheless, some of the similarities in the role of the outside change agent should be noted. First, it has been stated that the role of the consultant in an OD program is to help "the client system (a community, a social work agency, an organization, etc.) to (1) assess existing patterns or attitudes, perceptions and behavior . . .; (2) set targets and goals for change or further learning; and (3) monitor (feedback) evidence related to progress toward these goals."[15] To a great extent, the mediator in the RBO programs does this, although in a union-management environment which is quite different from that normally envisioned by behavioralists. Secondly, each type of process needs

extremely well-qualified and skilled trainers. For example, OD practitioners usually use some variation of the T-group, a psychological technique which has been criticized because of poorly qualified trainers. This concern over trainer qualification is widely acknowledged and the profession has developed accrediting procedures.[16] Likewise, RBO can potentially cause great mischief, as discussed above, because of faulty techniques on the part of poorly qualified change agents. And as stated above, this is why only experienced, well qualified and professional mediators should attempt to effectuate the kind of change in attitudes and practices that are involved with an RBO program. It is not the kind of program that amateurs should attempt.

Concluding Remarks

RBO is a new and different method of achieving labor relations peace. Unlike the much heralded NPA study "The Causes of Industrial Peace" that enunciated a series of principles that later research found wanting, the RBO is basically a process which enables the parties to develop their own strategies for achieving labor peace. It is a special purpose tool developed by the FMCS to help correct a basically disruptive, antagonistic labor-management relationship. It is based on the commitment of the parties to want to change this relationship and is predicated on the technical expertise of Federal mediators to guide the parties into a better relationship. The action steps for this turnaround is nonetheless developed and planned by the parties themselves. The RBO process is only as good as the parties want to make it. It is not an end in itself and can only work with the full and continuing support and commitment of the parties.

Moreover, the current trend in collective bargaining is witness to the erosion of (top down) labor-management relations at the plant level. On the union side, decisions once made at the international level are increasingly being made at the local level instead, while on the management side new methods of supervision are taking hold. The RBO is one of the few recent innovations in labor

relations which is responsive to these trends because it embodies participation from the bottom-
up or floor level. Basically, the RBO permits decisions to be influenced from the plant floor—where
they are to be implemented and this is a major
reason for their apparent acceptance and success.

Notes

1. Committee on the Causes of Industrial Peace Under
   Collective Bargaining of the National Planning Association, *Fundamentals of Labor Peace: A Final
   Report* (Washington: National Planning Association,
   1953), Case Study No. 14.

2. The author was a member of the research team. For
   review of its findings, see Herbert R. Northrop and
   Harvey A. Young, ''The Causes of Industrial Peace
   Revisited,'' *Industrial and Labor Relations Review,*
   October 1968.

3. Not that there has not been a great variety of sug-
   gestions by various experts for such innovations.
   See for example, Jerome T. Barrett, ''Legislative
   Enforcement of Labor Peace,'' *Labor Law Journal,*
   September 1967 and ''Exploring Alternatives to the
   Strike'' in *Monthly Labor Review,* September 1973,
   articles by Theodore W. Kheel, David L. Cole, I.
   W. Abel, W. J. Usery, Sam Kagel, among others.

4. Economic considerations unique to basic steel were
   primarily responsible for adoption of voluntary arbitration. Both producers and employees were adversely affected by hedge buyings that preceded
   contract negotiations in anticipation of a strike. This
   hedge buying created peaks and troughs in both sales
   and employment which became unacceptable to the
   parties.

5. For a complete discussion on the workings of the
   Scanlon Plan, see Frederick G. Lesieur (ed.), *The
   Scanlon Plan: A Frontier in Labor-Management Co-
   operation* (Cambridge, Mass.: M.I.T. Press, 1958).
   Also see 'Scanlon Plans in Operation'' in *Recent In-
   itiatives in Labor-Management Cooperation* (Wash-
   ington, D.C: National Center for Production and
   Quality of Working Life, 1976), pp. 43–50; A *Plant-
   Wide Productivity Plan in Action: Three Years of Ex-
   perience with the Scanlon Plan* (Washington, D.C.:
   National Commission on Productivity and Work
   Quality), 1975, and Edgar Weinberg, ''Labor-Management Cooperation: A Report on Recent Initiatives,'' *Monthly Labor Review,* April 1976.

6. For a discussion of the ESOP, see David Robinson,
   ''Employee Stock Option Plans Under New Scrutiny'', *World of Work Report,* Vol. 1, No. 7, September 1976. An unpublished FMCS study has found
   300 such programs in existence, mainly in small
   companies.

7. See John J. Popular, ''U.S. Mediators Try to Build
   Common Objectives,'' *World of Work Report,* Vol.
   1, No. 7, September 1976; Abraham, Raskin, *New
   York Times,* September 20, 1976; *Business Week,*
   April 1975; and speech given by James F. Scearce,
   National Director, FMCS, to Automation House,
   New York City, October 20, 1976.

8. The definition of poor labor relations at the plant
   level is associated with great hostility where the
   antagonism of the parties does not permit the normal
   process of dispute resolution to operate effectively.
   This definition is not precise but is serves as a benchmark. The concept of good plant relations is more
   difficult to define. Theoretically, it is the opposite
   of bad labor relations but good relations may, as in
   the case of many of the NPA case studies, have as
   its base the over-giving of management.

9. This similarity has already been noted in the literature. See Thomas H. Patten, Sr., ''A Perspective
   on Management-by-Objectives for the Industrial Relations Scholar and Specialist.'' *Proceedings of the
   Twenty-Ninth Annual Winter Meetings of the Industrial Relations Research Association* (September
   16–18, 1976 at Atlantic City) Edited by James L.
   Stern and Barbara D. Dennis (Madison, Wisconsin:
   IRRA, 1977) Pg. 9

10. See Thomas H. Patten, Jr., op. cit, Jan P. Mucazyk,
    ''MBO in a Bank or a Railroad Company: Two Field
    Experiments Focusing on Performance Measures'',
    in *IRRA's Twenty-Ninth Annual Winter Meetings,*
    op. cit. Pg. 13, and Stephen J. Carroll and Henry
    L. Tosi, ''Relationship of Various Motivational
    Forces to the Effects of Participation in Goal Setting
    in MBO Programs in *IRRA's Twenty-Ninth Annual
    Winter Meeting,* op. cit. Pg. 20.

11. For a discussion of the Preventive Mediation Pro-
    gram, see William E. Simkin, *Mediation and the
    Dynamics of Collective Bargaining* (Washington,
    D.C.: BNA, 1971) and Cyrus Ching, *Review and
    Reflection* (New York: B. C. Forbes and Sons, 1953).

12. Passage of the Labor-Management Cooperation Act
    of 1978, which authorizes FMCS to provide funding
    for the establishment and operation of plant, area,

and industrywide labor and management committees may dramatically alter the Service's L-M committee activity. However, a discussion of this new assignment would be the subject of a separate paper. Suffice here to say the program is still in the formative stage.

13. For another review of the RBO procedure, see John J. Popular, op. cit.

14. For a full discussion of the differences between distributive and integrative bargaining, see Richard E. Walton and Robert B. McKersie, A Behavioral Theory of Labor Relations (New York City: McGraw-Hill, 1965).

15. Raymond E. Miles, "Organization Development," in Strauss, Miles, Snow and Tannenbaum, (editors), *Organization Behavior Research and Issues* (Madison, Wisconsin: Industrial Relations Research Association, 1973), Pg. 175.

16. Ibid., Pg. 177.

Reading 28

SURVEY-GUIDED DEVELOPMENT: USING HUMAN RESOURCES MEASUREMENT IN ORGANIZATIONAL CHANGE

David G. Bowers and Jerome L. Franklin

As it exists today, organizational development (OD) in various forms and practices includes many common values and goals. However, there is also a considerable degree of difference in the various concepts, procedures, and assumptions that are identified within this field. The common elements reflect to some extent the fact that those engaged in the field share some aspects of their backgrounds. The differences reflect different evolutionary streams from which the practice of OD has emerged. Much of what is currently considered within the realm of OD can be traced to the fields of adult education, personnel training, industrial consultation, and clinical psychology. Organizational development now represents a crystallization of the experiences of practitioners from these fields. Examples of the techniques and procedures that have evolved in this way include sensitivity training, human relations training, team development training, process consultation, and role-playing.

Some portion of what presently may be considered organizational development came into existence through a different route, which is perhaps best described as a concern for the utilization of scientific knowledge. This data-based type of development and, specifically, the survey feedback technique, originated not from the search by practitioners for more effective helping tools, but from the concern of organizational management researchers for better ways of moving new scientific

Source: David G. Bowers and Jerome L. Franklin. Reprinted with permission of the *Journal of Contemporary Business.* Copyright Summer 1972, vol. 1, no. 3, pp. 43–55.

findings from the producers (researchers) to the consumers (organizational managers.)

This view is clearly spelled out in the prospectus which launched the organizational behavior research program at the Institute for Social Research over 25 years ago:

> The general objective of this research program will be to discover the underlying principles applicable to the problems of organizing and managing human activity. *A second important objective of the project will be to discover how to train persons to understand and skillfully use these principles* [9, p. 2].

> The major emphasis during the last four years of the project will be on the experimental verification of the results and *especially on learning how to make effective use of them in everyday situations.* . . . Each experiment will be analyzed in terms of measures made before and after the experiment, and often a series of measures will be made during the experiment [9, p. 10].

> The entire progress of our society depends upon our skill in organizing our activity. Insofar as we can achieve efficiently through systematic research new understandings and skills instead of relying on trial and error behavior, we can speed the development of a society capable of using constructively the resources of an atomic age. Unless we achieve this understanding rapidly and intelligently, we may destroy ourselves in trial and error bungling. Understanding individual behavior is not enough, nor is an understanding of the principles governing the behavior of men in small groups. We need generalizations and principles which will point the way to organizing human activity on the scale now required [9, p. 12].

This same prospectus also stated that the basic measurement tool to be used in the proposed studies would be the sample survey, employing procedures that the proposers had developed during their years with the Program Surveys Division of the Department of Agriculture. It was also stated that the study design would be generally like that employed by Rensis Likert in the Agency Management Study [7].

Thus the stage was set for an organizational development emphasis that first engaged in scientific search for principles of organizational management, and then, once such principles were established, set forth to identify effective implementation strategies for them. This plan was provided impetus by real-life circumstances. Researchers rapidly discovered that the generation of sound findings regarding organizational management was one thing and their implementation quite another. Two factors seriously diminished the effective use of early findings. First, although survey items referred to work-world events, there was often no readily accepted "map" tying what was measured to operating realities in ways that were readily understood. Second, because there was a lack of implementation procedures geared to the data, presentation of findings normally involved a narrative report. As a result of both these factors, there was a great propensity either to file the report away, to pass it along to lower levels accompanied by vague directives to "use it," or simply to seize selectively upon bits which reinforced managers' existing biases [3].

The Nature of Survey Feedback

In an effort to solve this problem, Floyd Mann and his colleagues at the Institute for Social Research developed the *survey feedback* procedure as an implementation tool. No authoritative volume has as yet been written about this development tool. Partially as a result of this absence of detailed description, many persons mistakenly believe that survey feedback consists of a rather superficial handing back of tabulated numbers and percentages, but little else. On the contrary, where the survey feedback is employed with skill and expe-

rience, it becomes a sophisticated tool for using the data as a springboard to development. Data are typically tabulated for each and every work group in an organization, as well as for each combination of groups that represents an area of responsibility, including the total organization.

Each supervisor and manager receives a tabulation of this sort, containing data based on the responses of *his own* immediate subordinates, together with documents describing their interpretation and use. A resource person, sometimes from an outside (consulting) agency and at other times from the client system's own staff, usually counsels privately with the supervisor-recipient about the contents of the package and then arranges a suitable time when the supervisor can meet with his subordinates to discuss the findings and their implications. The resource person attends that meeting to provide help to the participants, both in the technical aspects of the tabulations and in the process aspects of the discussion.

Procedures by which the feedback process progresses through an organization may vary from site to site. In certain instances a "waterfall" pattern is adhered to, in which the process substantially is completed at high-level groups before moving down to subordinate groups. In other instances, feedback is more or less simultaneous to all groups and echelons.

By whichever route it takes, an effective survey feedback operation depicts the organization's groups as moving, by a discussion process, from the tabulated perceptions, through a cataloging of their implications, to commitment for solutions to the problems that the discussion has identified and defined.

The Necessity of Differential Diagnosis

From these general and specific concerns there has emerged a viewpoint, largely identified with persons associated with the Institute for Social Research, that constructive change is measurement-centered, beginning with a quantitative reading of the state of the organization and direction of movement. Even more than this, change is, throughout, a rational process that makes use of information, pilot demonstrations, and the persuasive power of evidence and hard fact.

A successful change effort begins with rigorous measurement of the way in which the organization presently is functioning. These measurements provide the material for a diagnosis, and the diagnosis forms the basis for the design of a program of change activities. Likert has stated this quite pointedly in an early publication:

> One approach that can be used to apply the findings of human relations research to your own operation can be described briefly. Your medical departments did not order all of your supervisors nor all of your employees to take penicillin when it became available, even though it is a very effective antibiotic. They have, however, administered it to many of your employees. But note the process of deciding when it should be administered. The individual was given certain tests and measurements obtained—temperature, blood analysis, etc. The results of these measurements were compared with known facts about diseases, infections, etc., and the penicillin was prescribed when the condition was one that was known or believed to be one that would respond to this antibiotic.
>
> We believe the same approach should be used in dealing with the human problems of any organization. This suggests that human relations supervisory training programs should not automatically be prescribed for all supervisory and management personnel. Nor should other good remedies or methods for improvement be applied on a blanket basis to an entire organization hoping it will yield improved results [5, p. 35].

One of the reasons for the importance of the diagnostic step early in the life of a change program is stated explicitly in the preceding quotation: it will increase the probability of focusing upon the right, not the wrong, problems, and it will add to the likelihood of the right, not the wrong, course of treatments being prescribed. A clear statement of the problems, courses of action, and change objectives, based upon sound measurements allied to the best possible conceptualization from research and theory, will maximize the likelihood that true

causal conditions, rather than mere symptoms, will be dealt with [2].

The Rationale For Survey-Guided Development

The preceding sections have pointed to the existence of two somewhat different approaches to organization development. One, growing out of applied practice, is identified more obviously with the laboratory approach to education. It uses the *immediate* behavior (verbal and nonverbal) of the participants as the source material around which development forms. It focuses much more upon the "here-and-now" than upon the "there-and-then" and emphasizes experience-based learnings. It focuses more sharply on issues related to interpersonal processes than those less observable issues of role and structure.

The other approach, which we propose to elaborate on in greater detail, is related more obviously to an information-systems approach to adaptation. This approach uses participants' summarized perceptions of behavior and situation as the source material around which development is focused. It focuses on the "there-and-then" at least as much as upon the "here-and-now," attaches considerably more importance to cognitive understanding than does the other approach, and is concerned with such issues as role and structure, at least as much as with those of interpersonal process.

These brief identifications are more descriptive than explanatory. A true understanding of the survey-guided approach requires that we look more closely at the assumptions which it appears to make and the operating propositions which it derives from those assumptions.

Like most organization development techniques, survey feedback is only one aspect of a measurement-guided approach to change. As a tool or procedure, it emerged as a response to a practical need to see research findings implemented. It did not emerge as the logical conclusion of a formal body of scientific thought, and it remains for us presently to search, after the fact, for a rationale about how and why it works.

In this vein, two bodies of scientific thought seem relevant. One comes from the research done in the area of perception and involves the fundamental concept that a difference between perceptions is motivating—an idea originally and most clearly stated by Peak [8]. This is perhaps illustrated by the following example: if I perceive, on the one hand, that I cannot complete a particular piece of work by the end of the normal workday and perceive, on the other hand, that that work must be complete by the start of office hours in the morning, I am motivated to work late or to take home a work-loaded briefcase.

According to this view, the perceptions must be associated; i.e., they must be seen as belonging to the same "domain." I may perceive that I do not play the piano as well as Arthur Rubenstein, but this discrepancy is hardly motivating, because I do not consider myself to be a professional concert pianist. Although associated, the perceptions must be different, yet not so different as to destroy their association. The perceptions may be related to emotion-laden or "feelings" issues, or they may consist of different perceptions of conditions in the external world. Peak illustrates the process by drawing an analogy:

> Think of a thermostat. Here there are two events. One is the temperature setting (an expected state if you will). The other event or term in the system is the height of the mercury in the tube, representing the present state of affairs (room temperature). These are analogous then to the two events in our motive construct, and disparity exists between them when there is a difference in the setting and in the temperature reading. Now, the second feature of our motive construct, which is called contact or association, is provided by the structure of the thermostat and is not modifiable in this system as it is in the motive system. In other words, the two terms (or events) remain in association. Only disparity can vary, and when there is disparity there is "motivation" and action; i.e., the furnace starts to run. The results of this action are fed back to produce change in one of the terms of the disparity relation (the mercury level). When the disparity disappears through rise in temperature or resetting

of the thermostat, action ceases. . . . But since the thermostat lacks the capacity to stop action through isolation, and in the simple design we have described, cannot select different actions, the model must be regarded merely as illustrative . . . [8, pp. 172–73].

Another closely related set of ideas comes from engineering psychology and begins with the observation that human behavior is goal-seeking or goal-oriented. As such, behavior is characterized by a search for processes by which the human being controls his environment; i.e., means by which he reshapes it toward more constructive or productive ends.

Oversimplifying the control process greatly, at least four elements are involved (1) a model, (2) a goal, (3) an activity, and (4) feedback. The *model* is a mental picture of the surrounding world, including not only structural properties, but cause-and-effect relations. It is built by the person(s) from past accumulations of information, stored in memory. From the workings of the model and from the modeling process which he employs, alternative possible future states are generated, of which one is selected as a *goal*. At this point what is called the "goal selection system" ends and that is known as the "control system" per se begins. *Activities* are initiated to attain the goal, and *feedback,* which comes by some route from the person's environment, is used to compare, confirm, adjust, and correct responses by signaling departures from what was expected.

The process as just described is beguilingly simple. However, in actual life it is often extremely complex. The thermostat example, although embodied in a marvelous and valuable piece of equipment, is basically a simple instance of an adaptive system. Others are much more complicated, such as that contained in the role of a Mississippi river boat pilot. The shifting character of currents and channels make this adaptive task quite complex. Therefore the difficulty in this as in other complex systems stems from not having learned how to predict system performance under various conditions. As one of the foremost human factors writers has described it, "The ability to predict system performance is in major respects the same as the ability to control the system" [4, p. 42]

The human organization reflects the same type of a complex, difficult control system, in part for these same reasons. Activity is only as good as the model which leads to it, yet human organizations are often managed according to grossly imperfect models (models which ignore much of what is known from research about organizational structure and functioning). Predictability is enhanced, in human systems as elsewhere, by quantification, yet many of the relationships are often not quantified, if, indeed, they are recognized at all.

In the absence of a sound model, what is expected varies with immediate experience. It is for this reason that objective feedback on organizational functioning is absolutely essential in organizational development. In its absence, true deviations are unknown because expectations constantly adjust to incurred performance.

From this very condensed discussion, it is apparent that, when organizational change is viewed as a problem in optimal control or adaptation (which it inherently is) several things are required:

1. An adequate model—one which is a valid representation of that external reality known as "the organization," including both structural properties, knowledge of cause-effect relations, and predictive capability.
2. A goal—a preferred potential future state, generated by the model.
3. An activity—selected as instrumental to attaining that goal.
4. Objective feedback—about deviations from what the model would lead us to expect.

These two sets of concepts—the one drawn from basic work in the area of perception, the other taken from the human factors work of engineering psychology—provide jointly a plausible rationale for survey-guided development. As in the human factors area, feedback of information about the actual state of functioning provides key input to selecting development goals and making mid-course corrections. It tells the developing system what needs to

be done. The power source, which in human factors descriptions is shown as an external input, is in survey-guided development provided by the sort of discrepancy described by Peak. Survey feedback, by pointing to the existence of differences between what is actually going on and what the model indicates one wants and needs, provides the energy (motivation) to undertake change activities.

In detail, as in general, organizational development (as the survey-guided approach envisions) may be seen as an analog of adaptation as described by human factors theorists. What they have termed the "goal selection system" is, in survey-based development, the *diagnostic* process. What they have referred to as the "control system" is the *therapeutic* process.

To serve its function within the diagnostic process, the work group draws inputs from the same sorts of areas drawn upon by all adaptive systems:

From higher level systems: from the larger organization, its top management, and from society in general in the form of performance trends, top management evaluations, labor relations trends, changes in laws or regulations, etc.

From its own information about the model which they have thus far accepted, as well as information concerning past experiences and results.

From a reading of how things actually are: from the survey; through what we have described as survey feedback, which deals largely with intragroup behavior, attitudes, and relationships; and from a more formal *diagnosis* (an analytic report prepared by persons skilled in the survey data area) which deals with intergroup and systemic properties.

From the environment: in many forms, but particularly from the "change agent," the organizational development scientist-consultant who helps to catalyze the overall change process.

Each of these input sources has potential impact by virtue of its presence or comparative absence, its kind, and its quality. For example, the higher level system inputs ordinarily create some degree of felt urgency. Often, discrepancy generated by this input motivates the initial search and culminates in serious consideration of organizational development as a possible course of action. The extent to which these inputs encourage the development efforts of the client entity is also critical. Many of the development failures occur in instances in which higher level system inputs are either lacking, which indicates acquiescence, or instead, are signaling outright disapproval of organizational development. A general example of such an instance might involve a supervisor who verbally acquiesces to an organizational development effort for his subordinates but behaves and rewards his subordinates for behaving in ways which are incongruent with the values, assumptions, and goals that are emphasized in organizational development. Efforts that proceed in the face of such higher level system inputs run a great risk of death by neglect.

From the group's own information storage comes the model of organizational functioning already held by group members. This includes information regarding past organizational practices (behaviors, interaction patterns, managerial styles) as well as outcomes at various levels of finality (absenteeism, turnover, profit, production efficiency, growth, etc.).

The survey provides a means by which multiple perceptions of behaviors and organizational conditions related to effectiveness can be gathered, compiled, and compared. As has been indicated above, one must consider not one, but two, separate input streams from the survey. One of these input streams consists of the survey feedback process itself, in which tabulations of the group's *own data,* especially concerning its internal functioning, is used as a springboard to the identification, understanding, and solving of problems. The other consists of a more formal diagnosis, prepared by persons skilled in multivariate analysis, and focuses on those problem streams which occur in the system as a whole and which can be seen only by careful comparison of the tabulated data of many groups.

The Change Agent's Role

The change agent, as an adjunct person, seems to have no exact counterpart in *manual* control problems. The reason for his presence in organizational development is that a model of organizational functioning and human behavior is not as simple or

programmable as that involved in manual control. Reading and digesting survey data are not the same as reading a gauge. Accomplishing an organizational "correction" is much more complicated than pushing a button or turning a wheel a certain number of degrees. In most instances the controller in organizational change—the client group—must be shown what the "gauge" says and how to read it, and must be guided through the operations of making the desired changes. The survey discrepancy, properly digested with the aid of the change agent, both builds the *motivation* to make the change and indicates *what* changes in functioning must occur. However, the change agent helps the client group learn *how* to make the necessary changes.

The primary role of the change agent in survey-guided development is that of a transducer (i.e., an energy link between scientific knowledge regarding principles of organizational functioning and the particular organization or group with which he is working). As such, the change agent enters into both the diagnostic and therapeutic phases of the development effort. During the diagnostic phase, the model that the change agent presents must be reasonably complete, predictive, and adequate to provide the client with useful information. If the model lacks any of these characteristics, the change agent will be supplying the system with little more than noise.

In addition to having these characteristics, the model must be presented to the members of the group or organization accurately and adequately. The issue of acceptance is critical: the best model loses its value unless it is understood in useful ways by members of the system. The model and evidence in its support must be presented in such a manner that acceptance is based upon rational evaluations of the evidence as well as the experiences and insights of those involved in the organization. During this activity, the change agent must have the model clearly in mind, must be able to present the model and its evidence clearly, and must also be able to call upon his group process and related skills to facilitate understanding and acceptance.

As in any other situation in which the talents and knowledge of one man are to be made available to assist another, the manner in which that occurs is, of course, important. In the area of human organizational development, of all places, it is important that the knowledge be made available in a supportive, not a demeaning, fashion; it is not to be "laid on," ordered into place, or delivered as some form of speech from a pretentious throne. Skill in patient explanation, in aiding understanding, and in helping the client entities themselves to come to grips with reality—in short, the whole array of interpersonal skills—are extremely important. But the change agent must have the knowledge of what must be explained, the grasp of what must be understood, and the comprehension of what that reality is.

In this vein, the change agent facilitates the understanding and digesting of diagnostically useful information. In the survey-guided approach, this role involves helping members of the system to understand better the survey feedback information. It also may involve a range of activities, from a detailed explanation of the meaning and relevance of certain content areas to helping group members understand information from the survey in terms of the here-and-now of the feedback meeting process. In addition, he aids the client group members in setting goals and formulating action plans for the development effort. In this activity, as in the others, the change agent may serve both as a source of information (e.g., suggesting potential actions to be undertaken or considered) and as a facilitator who focuses upon the group's processes.

The change agent also serves as a transducer in the therapeutic phase of survey-guided organizational development. Once a diagnosis has pointed to problem areas in organizational functioning, the change agent provides a link between scientific knowledge regarding effective methods of correcting specific problems and the problems exhibited in the immediate situation. A variety of activities may be undertaken during this phase. Each has, as its ultimate goal, movement toward the model of organizational functioning held (after its initial establishment) by both change agent and clients.

In part, the specific type of activity undertaken depends upon the stage in the therapeutic phase. In the early stages, the change agent is likely to be involved largely with supplying informational inputs regarding specific possible activities, helping organizational members cope with attitudinal shifts, and handling defensive reactions. The motivation to change created by a discrepancy between the ideal model and the actual state of the organization is alone not sufficient to produce change. Methods of actually accomplishing the change must also be evident to organizational members. In this respect, the change agent in part fulfills his transducer role by informing members of the client system of the available alternatives.

In later stages the change agent is often involved with skill acquisition and perfection by group members. The range and variety of potentially necessary skills is large. Problem solving, giving and receiving personal feedback, listening, general leadership, goal-setting, resolving conflict, and diagnosing group processes are but a few of those which might be cited. The change agent must not only know which skills are needed, but also must be competent in guiding their acquisition. It is as a result of this acquisition and perfection of skill that organizational members come to rely less on the change agent and more on themselves in movement toward the goal.

In addition to the emphasis on skills, the change agent provides and facilitates informal intermediate-phase feedback during the therapeutic phase. For example, he may provide the group with feedback in the form of process comments inserted during or after key intragroup interactions. He may also facilitate attempts by the members themselves to gather and understand information regarding their progress toward accepted goals.

A Recapitulation

As the preceding pages have indicated, the survey-guided approach suggests several general propositions regarding: (1) certain basic assumptions of organizational development; (2) change processes; and (3) the change agent's role.

Basic Assumptions of OD

There are systemic properties; i.e., characteristics of the organization as a total system, not definable by the simple sum of individual and/or group behaviors.

A *model* of organizational functioning which includes these systemic properties, reflecting available evidence and testable by quantifiable and scientific means, should be used as a basis for development efforts.

Systemic properties in particular can improve only as a result of *carefully sequenced planned interventions*.

Valid information about the state of group and organizational functioning (objectives and useful reflections of reality) is best obtained from summarized, quantified longtudinal perceptions. (There-and-then data are at least as useful as here-and-now data.)

A *diagnosis* based upon a quantitative comparison with the model and prepared by competent professionals should be used to evaluate the organization on both intragroup and systemic levels.

Prescription of intervention activities should be *diagnostically based*.

Change Processes

Motivation is created by the realization that the actual state differs from the accepted model (i.e., a discrepancy exists between that which is desired and that which exists).

The discrepancies exist in terms of both *intragroup* and *systemic* processes and properties.

Change involves a *sequence of events* including informational inputs; formation of a model; selection of a goal; assessment of the situation; formation of a diagnosis, feedback; adjustment; and reevaluation.

Change Agent's Role and Activities

The change agent acts as *transducer* between scientific knowledge regarding organizational functioning and change processes, on the one hand, and the particular situation, on the other.

He has a *model* of organizational functioning and *works toward* its realization.

Except in those rare instances which require a nondirective stance, the change agent is an *active advocate of goal-oriented behavior*. He evaluates and helps the client group to *evaluate progress toward the goals,* but he is not punitive.

He must have a *wide range of knowledge and skills* and not be bound to one or two particular techniques.

These general propositions of survey-guided development are illustrated as a flow of events in Figure 1.

Perspective and Prologue

We conclude by offering an apology to the reader who anticipated a less labored description. What has been written has been, in many ways, a rather technical document. It reflects our strong belief that organizational development rightfully is becoming more a science than an art. This view was expressed several years ago by one of the authors:

> By science I mean discernible in replicatable terms—objective, understandable (rather than "mystique"), verifiable, and predictive. Should these conditions for organizational develpment fail to be met, it will go the way of the Great Auk and the "Group Talking Technique." In short, organizational development will die, having been remembered as one more fad.
>
> Organizational development cannot survive on the goodwill of top management persons who are already sold on its potential and effectiveness. It can survive only if it proves its method and its contribution beyond reasonable doubt to the hard-headed skeptics. Organizational development must prove with hard, rigorous evidence that it can beneficially affect: *(a)* the volume of work done by the organization, *(b)* the cost per unit of doing the

FIGURE 1   Survey–Guided Development

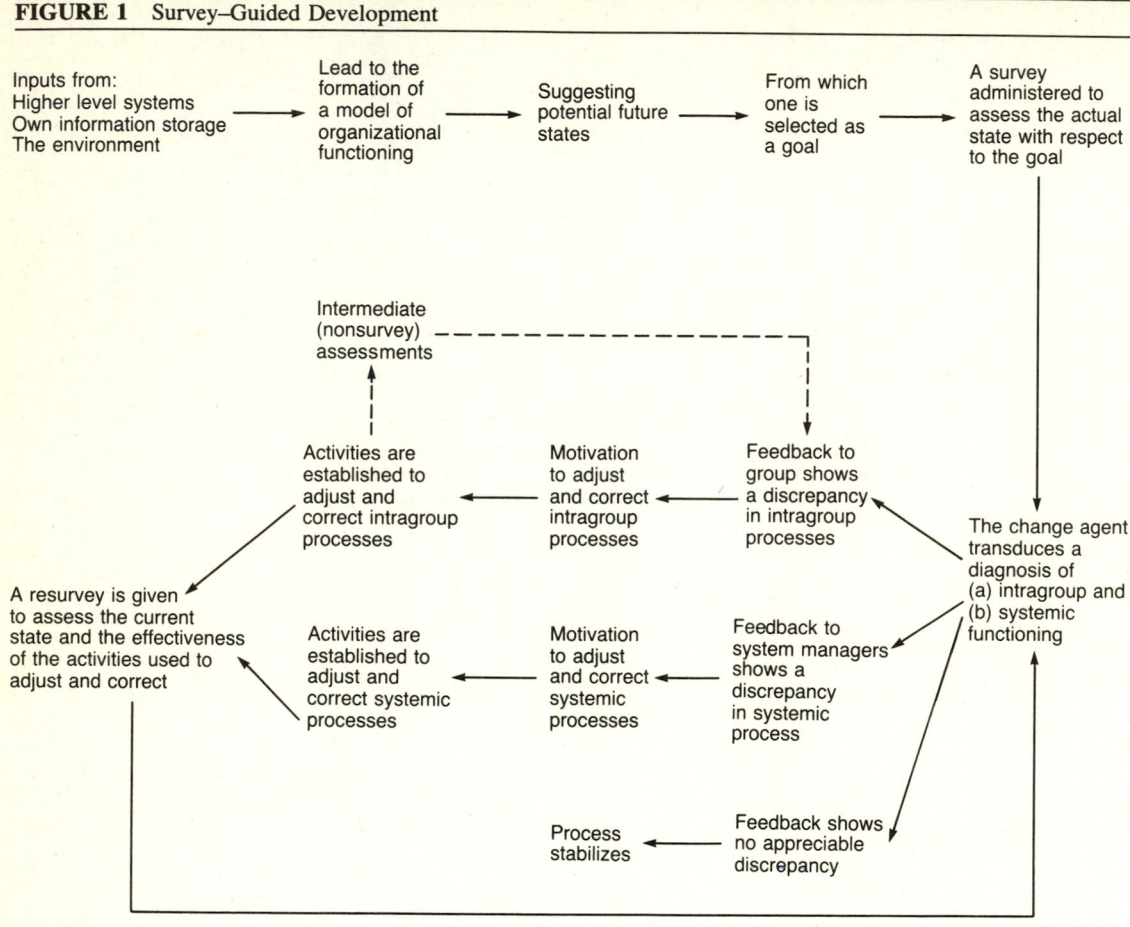

Inputs from: Higher level systems, Own information storage, The environment → Lead to the formation of a model of organizational functioning → Suggesting potential future states → From which one is selected as a goal → A survey administered to assess the actual state with respect to the goal

Intermediate (nonsurvey) assessments

Activities are established to adjust and correct intragroup processes ← Motivation to adjust and correct intragroup processes ← Feedback to group shows a discrepancy in intragroup processes

A resurvey is given to assess the current state and the effectiveness of the activities used to adjust and correct

Activities are established to adjust and correct systemic processes ← Motivation to adjust and correct systemic processes ← Feedback to system managers shows a discrepancy in systemic process

The change agent transduces a diagnosis of (a) intragroup and (b) systemic functioning

Process stabilizes ← Feedback shows no appreciable discrepancy

organization's work, and *(c)* the quality of work done [1, p. 62].

The same article described barriers which, up to that time, had impeded the progress of organizational development as a science:

The lack of a "critical mass" of knowledge in the field.

The tendency for organizational development to take the form of a single general practitioner, operating on an isolated island.

The absence of an adequate measuring instrument, geared to an adequate model of organizational functioning, for use in organizational development efforts.

Within the last decade, considerable progress has been made on each of these fronts. Books and articles, describing and integrating findings in this field, have appeared in increasing numbers and richness. This present journal issue is a case in point.

To the extent that our own experience is typical, opportunities for researchers and change agents to collaborate in multifaceted, large system development efforts have emerged.

Efforts have similarly been undertaken by a number of persons to develop procedures and instruments for rigorous description of change agent interventions and their immediate effects.

Finally, we feel that survey-guided development has pressed, from its own necessity, the construction of reliable, valid, standardized instruments for assessing organizational functioning.

The availability of such instruments, together with the accumulating critical mass of knowledge, leads us to considerable optimism concerning the future of organizational development in general and concerning the survey-guided approach, in particular.

References

1. Bowers, D. G. "The Scientific Data-Based Approach to Organization Development," Part 2, in A. L. Hite, ed. *Organizational Development: The State of the Art*. Ann Arbor, Mich.: Foundation for Research on Human Behavior, 1971.
2. Bowers, D. G. *System 4: The Ideas of Rensis Likert*. New York: Basic Books, 1972.
3. Katz, Daniel, and Kahn, Robert L. *The Social Psychology of Organizations*. New York: John Wiley & Sons, Inc., 1966.
4. Kelley, C. R. *Manual and Automatic Control*. New York: John Wiley & Sons, Inc., 1968.
5. Likert, R. "Findings of Research on Management and Leadership." *Proceedings, 43,* Pacific Coast Gas Assn., 1952.
6. Likert, R. *The Human Organization*. New York: McGraw-Hill, 1967.
7. Likert, R., and Willets, J. M. *Morale and Agency Management*. Hartford, Conn.: Life Insurance Agency Management Association, 1940. 4 vols.
8. Peak, H. "Attitude and Motivation," in M. R. Jones, ed., *Nebraska Symposium on Motivation*. Lincoln, Neb.: University of Nebraska Press, 1955.
9. Survey Research Center. *A Program of Research on the Fundamental Problems of Organizing Human Behavior*. Ann Arbor, Mich.: University of Michigan, 1947.
10. Taylor, J. C., and Bowers, D. G. *The Survey of Organizations: A Machine-Scored, Standardized Questionnaire Instrument*. Ann Arbor, Mich.: Institute for Social Research, 1972.

SUGGESTED ADDITIONAL READINGS FOR PART 3

Bennis, Warren G.; Kenneth D. Benne; Robert Chin; and Kenneth E. Corey. *The Planning of Change,* 3rd ed. New York: Holt, Rinehart & Winston, 1976, ch. 7.

Blake, R. R., and J. S. Mouton. *Corporate Excellence through Grid Organization Development.* Houston: Gulf Publishing, 1968.

Bowers, David G. *Systems of Organization.* Ann Arbor: University of Michigan Press, 1976.

Burke, W. Warner. "A Comparison of Management Development and Organization Development." *Journal of Applied Behavioral Science* 7, no. 5 (1971), pp. 569–79.

Burke, W. Warner, ed. *The Cutting Edge.* La Jolla, Calif.: University Associates, 1978.

Burke, W. Warner, and Richard Beckhard, eds. *Conference Planning,* 2nd ed. San Diego: University Associates, 1970.

Conlon, Edward J., and Lawrence O. Short. "Survey Feedback as a Large-Scale Change Device: An Empirical Examination." *Group & Organization Studies,* September 1984, pp. 399–416.

Delbecq, A. L.; A. H. Van de Ven; and D. H. Gustafson. *Group Techniques for Program Planning.* Glenview, Ill.: Scott, Foresman, 1975.

Dyer, William G. *Team Building.* Reading, Mass.: Addison-Wesley Publishing, 1977.

Eddy, William B. *The Manager and the Working Group.* New York: Praeger Publishing, 1985.

Eden, Dov. "Team Development: Quasi-Experimental Confirmation Among Combat Companies." *Group & Organization Studies,* September 1986, pp. 137–46.

Ferguson, Charles K. "Ten Case Studies From an OD Practitioner's Experience, Coping with Organization Conflict." *Organization Development Journal,* Winter 1986, pp. 20–30.

Fordyce, Jack K., and Raymond Weil. *Managing with People.* Reading, Mass.: Addison-Wesley Publishing, 1979, pp. 891–142.

Franklin, Jerome L. "Improving the Effectiveness of Survey Feedback." *Personnel,* May–June 1978, pp. 11–17.

French, Wendell, and Cecil H. Bell, Jr. *Organization Development: Behavioral Science Interventions for Organization Improvement,* 3rd ed. Englewood Cliffs, N.J.: Prentice-Hall, 1984.

Gavin, James F. "Survey Feedback: The Perspectives of Science and Practice." *Group & Organization Studies,* March 1984, pp. 29–70.

Goodstein, Leonard D. *Consulting with Human Service Systems.* Reading, Mass.: Addison-Wesley Publishing, 1978.

Guest, Robert H. *Work Teams and Team Building.* New York: Pergamon Press, Work in America Institute Studies in Productivity, 1986.

Harrison, R. "Choosing the Depth of Organizational Intervention." *Journal of Applied Behavioral Science* 6 (1970), pp. 181–202.

Herman, Stanley, and Michael Koronich, *Authentic Management: A Gestalt Orientation to Organizations and Their Development.* Reading, Mass.: Addison-Wesley Publishing, 1977.

Lindaman, E., and R. Lippitt. *Choosing the Future You Prefer.* Washington, D.C.: Development Publications, 1979.

Lundberg, C. C. "Zero-In: A Technique for Formulating Better Mission Statements." *Business Horizons,* September–October 1984, pp. 30–33.

McKinnon, D. Kim. "Reaping The Real Rewards of Employee Surveys." *Training,* November 1985, pp. 49–52.

Nadler, D. A. *Feedback and Organization Development: Using Data Based Methods.* Reading, Mass.: Addison-Wesley, 1977.

Patten, Thomas H., Jr. *Organizational Development through Team Building.* New York: John Wiley & Sons, 1981.

Schein, Edgar H. *Process Consultation: Its Role in Organization Development.* Reading, Mass.: Addison-Wesley Publishing, 1969.

Sherif, Muzafer. "Superordinate Goals in the Reduction of Intergroup Conflict. *American Journal of Sociology* 63 (1958), pp. 67–85.

Smith, M. *A Practical Guide to Value Clarifications.* San Diego, Calif.: University Associates, 1977.

Walton, R. W. *Interpersonal Peacemaking: Confrontation and Third-Party Consultation.* Reading, Mass.: Addison-Wesley Publishing, 1969.

Weisbord, Marvin. *Organizational Diagnosis: A Workbook of Theory and Practice.* Reading, Mass.: Addison-Wesley, 1978.

PART 4

Individual and Educational Interventions vis-à-vis OD

While the central "units" or instruments for anticipated organization improvement in OD are work teams comprised of interdependent individuals, in most training and management development the "units" for hoped-for organization improvement are noninterdependent individuals. In most OD interventions the team is present, and problems confronting the team are worked on; in most training and management development activities, intact work teams are not in attendance as a group, and immediate problems of the participants' workplaces may or may not be addressed.[1]

This is not in any way to suggest that the individual becomes submerged through the team focus of an effective OD effort. Individual tasks, individual initiative, individual judgment and decision making continue. Further, enhanced individual skills are now applied to interpersonal and group settings and to transactions between units. Paradoxically, we believe that through more effective team interaction, most individuals find a heightened sense of individuality and enhanced ability to influence others. No longer are individuals as much subject to the prevailing unit or organizational culture. They are now more active agents in shaping that culture.

So emphasis on individuals vis-à-vis emphasis on teams is not an either-or proposition in organization development. It is our opinion that OD enhances individuality in the context of heightened attention and skillbuilding relative to interpersonal, group and organizational processes. A good deal of this understanding and skillbuilding can be furthered through educational experiences aimed at individuals who are temporarily away from their team or organizational relationships.

This part of the book is about individual and educational interventions that can be congruent with and supportive of an OD effort but are not in themselves, strictly speaking, OD interventions. If, however, the techniques described in this part are used in a team

---

[1]For a comparison of management development and organization development, see W. Warner Burke and Warren H. Schmidt, "Management and Organization Development: What Is the Target of Change?" *Personnel Administration*, March–April 1971, pp. 44–57; and Larry E. Greiner, "Confessions of an Executive Educator," *New Management*, Winter 1987, pp. 34–38.

255

situation as vehicles for dealing with work-group problems, they might then be properly classified as OD interventions.

The interventions we will focus on here are T-groups (T for training), transactional analysis (TA), and life-career planning, all of which are of high interest to training and OD specialists and to many organizations nationally and internationally. Space will not permit us to include essays on instrumented techniques for developing insight into one's leadership and interpersonal styles, such as Grid® Phase 1.[2]

T-GROUPS

It is difficult to write about T-groups, sensitivity training, laboratory education, and encounter groups because the terms are frequently used interchangeably, and because actual practice under these labels varies a great deal. However, it appears to be generally accepted that the term *laboratory education* refers broadly to experience-based learning workshops and that the concept is, therefore, broader than the term *T-group*. The T-group, aimed largely at enhancing interpersonal skills, is typically a major component in some forms of laboratory training workshops but does not comprise the totality. Schein and Bennis illustrate the broad thrust of laboratory education by describing the major components of a two-week residential "laboratory" of the variety invented and developed by NTL Institute for Applied Behavioral Sciences:

1. *T-groups* or small groups (usually 10–15 members) that are essentially "unstructured" in the sense that the staff provides a minimum of agenda and formal leadership. The T-group is the basic learning group that meets regularly throughout the laboratory and is typically the central emotional focus for most participants.
2. *Information sessions* or theory sessions in the forms of a lecture or demonstration to present some concepts or research findings relevant to the laboratory goals.
3. *Verbal and Nonverbal exercises* designed to deepen or intensify sensory awareness.
4. *Focused exercises,* that is, specified or structured activities such as role-playing or group observation for either small or large groups.
5. *Other activities* such as seminars, two-person interview groups (dyads), informal "bull sessions," etc.[3]

Other versions of laboratory training might, for example, include instrumented exercises instead of the T-group. Sensitivity training is sometimes used synonymously with T-group methods, but is sometimes used as a broader term encompassing any intensive group experience, including encounter groups.[4] Again, while there is no standardization in terminology, the encounter group is usually seen as having more emphasis on personal growth than the T-group.[5]

---

[2]See Robert R. Blake and Jane S. Mouton, *The New Managerial Grid* (Houston: Gulf Publishing, 1978).

[3]E. H. Schein and W. G. Bennis, *Personal and Organizational Change through Group Methods: Laboratory Approach* (New York: John Wiley & Sons, 1967), pp 10–23.

[4]See Kurt W. Back, *Beyond Words: The Story of Sensitivity Training and the Encounter Movement* (New York: Russell Sage Foundation, 1972), p. 6

[5]See Carl Rogers, *On Encounter Groups* (New York: Harper & Row, 1970), pp. 2–6.

As discussed in a Part 1, Section A essay, we see the T-group and survey-feedback techniques as important in the emergence of contemporary OD. Organization development emerged partly as a recognition of the difficulty in transferring insights and skills from stranger T-groups to the work situation. What emerged, in rough sequence historically, were "cousin" T-groups (people from the same organization but not the same unit), the "family" T-group (an intact work team), and finally, two inventions: *(a)* team building, where the intact work team, with the help of a facilitator, worked on a broader range of issues including interpersonal issues and *(b)* intergroup team building, where problems in between-group relationships were addressed. We sense that over the last decade the pure T-group format is used less and less in working with intact work teams, and that the central OD mode at this juncture is to utilize interventions which are responsive to a wider range of unit and organizational problems being experienced by the participants. A pure T-group format, we believe, would only infrequently be on target in initial interventions with client groups. There are, however, applications of T-group trainer behavior such as process-consultation interventions (e.g., asking a group member to further describe his/her feelings about some matter) which might be appropriate early in a consultant-client relationship. As the OD process unfolds, and depending upon problems being experienced by the client group and upon the skills and attitudes within the client team, a more in-depth exploration of interpersonal and group dynamics problems may be warranted. In such circumstances, skills as a T-group trainer would be highly desirable for the OD consultant.

Generally, however, we do not see either the family T-group or the stranger T-group as central to OD. But we believe learnings from T-group experiences to be facilitative of the OD process when applied and reinforced in a supportive organizational culture. For example, some of the learning can be:

1. Increased awareness and ability to deal with one's feelings.
2. Increased competency in dealing with directly and indirectly expressed feelings and behavior of others.
3. Increased clarity in communications, in contrast to sending mixed messages.
4. Increased competency in more effectively giving and receiving feedback.
5. Increased insight into the impact of one's behavior on others.
6. Increased reliance on self rather than role or position.
7. Increased interpersonal and group competency, generally.

Many group-process workshops, from our experience, typically have a high T-group component and thus enhance the above kinds of learnings but have other outcomes as well. With more emphasis on the broader dynamics of group life, additional learnings about such matters as leadership, norms, and structure can occur. Another learning that can occur from T-group and group-process workshops, and which is perhaps more subtle than the ones above, is that it is possible to effectively and collaboratively manage the culture of a group. This insight can provide strong impetus and sustaining energy to an OD effort as it unfolds.

The first article in Part 4, by Elliot Aronson, is about what goes on in T-groups. It is also about what T-groups are *not,* i.e., therapy, the seminar, and the lecture mode of teaching. The concept of "the cultural island" is particularly important in explaining the power of the T-group mode of learning; this concept, we might add, is also of significance in explaining some of the difficulty in translating T-group learnings to the "back home" organizational setting.

TAVISTOCK CONFERENCES

Another form of laboratory training is the Tavistock Conference. As described in the brief selection by Clayton Alderfer, these conferences are more structured than the T-group, and the trainers stay more remote from participants than in the T-group setting. Particular attention is paid to authority relationships, to individual, subgroup, and group boundaries, and to relationships within the group. Tavistock conferences have been sponsored in the United States and abroad by the A. K. Rice Institute.

TRANSACTIONAL ANALYSIS

Another largely individual/educational approach, transactional analysis (TA), has caught the attention of many managers, training directors, and OD specialists. Publications and workshops on transactional analysis have been increasingly conspicuous in the past decade. The central professional association of this movement, the International Transactional Analysis Association, was formed in 1964 from a nucleus of the San Francisco Transactional Analysis Association,[6] and functions primarily "as an educational institute for people in the broad field of social psychology: psychiatrists, psychologists, psychiatric nurses and social workers, correctional officers, social scientists, educators, and the clergy." Its educational activities are largely oriented "toward group therapy, social dynamics, and personality theory based on transactional analysis."[7]

TA can be viewed as an interpersonal diagnostic tool, of use in more accurately assessing the nature of the many transactions including "games" that occur between people, toward the end of modifying one's own dysfunctional behaviors and/or responding more effectively to the behavior of others. As described by Eric Berne, a psychiatrist who did much of the pioneering work in the development of the concepts, the approach is based on the notion that each person has a repertoire of behavior associated with a system of three "ego states," the Parent, Adult, and Child. According to Berne, "all three aspects of the personality have a high survival and living value, and it is only when one or the other of them disturbs the healthy balance that analysis and reorganization are indicated." Implicit in this statement, in the context of Berne's work, is that psychotherapy is warranted in the case of major disturbances, but that normals can enhance their interpersonal relationships through better understanding of how each of the three ego states is being manipulated in a given situation. In particular, "crossed transactions" are likely to be dysfunctional, as when an employer gives an Adult direction to an employee but the Child in the employee responds as though dealing with a Parent. "Games" are essentially "ulterior transactions" in which two or more ego states come into play simultaneously.[8]

---

[6]John M. Dusay, "The President's Page," *Transactional Analysis Journal,* October 1975, p. 337.
[7]Ibid., p. 336.
[8]Eric Berne, "Structure Analysis" and "Transactional Analysis," from *Games People Play: The Psychology of Human Relationships* (New York: Grove Press, 1964), pp. 23–34.

It appears that the predominant application of TA in the organizational setting is to help people become more sensitive to the nature of their interactions with others—customers, for example—and to be more aware of optional behaviors they have at their disposal so that dysfunctional transactions can be minimized. TA can provide a commonly held framework for understanding organizational behaviors. A knowledge of TA could supplement other significant skills; for example, ability to check on meaning ("paraphrasing") or to display the effective group behaviors described in the essay by Benne and Sheats included in Part 2 of the book. Successful application would appear to be associated with the terminology which was designed to identify and minimize game playing, and with a widely shared commitment to enhance the quality of transactions within the organization and of external relationships such as with clients or customers.

The selection by Nykodym, Nielsen, and Christen describes the use of TA in an OD effort in the home office of a national company. Research on the outcomes suggests that, among other outcomes, TA increased listening, teamwork, information flow, and supervisory approachability.

LIFE-CAREER PLANNING

As it becomes less risky and more legitimate within the culture of an organization openly to discuss one's career concerns and aspirations, the techniques of Life-Career Planning can be a useful adjunct to an OD effort. Essentially invented and developed by Herbert Shepard, Life-Career Planning techniques have been widely used in recent years in workshops where the central objective has been to provide participants with an opportunity for reflection and self-assessment as to their careers and/or life patterns. These techniques—really assignments to individuals to answer certain questions and to discuss them in a supportive group setting—can be selectively used in short workshops of a few hours in length or in more comprehensive workshops of several days. Parts can be used in team-building sessions where getting better acquainted appears to be an important objective; for example, using the "Who am I?" exercise.

Life planning includes career planning in the conceptualization provided in the essay by Herbert Shepard. Before describing a series of life-planning exercises in the appendix to his essay, Shepard expresses his philosophy about fulfillment in terms of "autonomy," "resonance," and "tone." Life-career planning to him is a quest involving self-confrontation and the induction of both an identity crisis and a destination crisis.

Thus, to us it would seem that coercion in the use of these techniques would be exceedingly dysfunctional in terms of both resulting attitudes and in terms of benefits to participants. This argues for most use in stranger or "cousin" groups at the outset, and only in "family" work teams when the trust and support levels are sufficiently high. Successful application of these techniques depends upon voluntarism and a nonevaluative and supportive environment. This caveat is applicable, of course, to all of the deeper interventions—deeper in the sense of involving the more private kinds of data—utilized in OD or educational efforts.

Reading 29

COMMUNICATION IN SENSITIVITY-
TRAINING GROUPS . . .

Elliot Aronson

Broadly speaking, the term *T-group* refers to the more conservative, more traditional group, in which the primary emphasis is on verbal behavior and the group discussions are almost exclusively confined to the here and now. It is associated with East Coast centers, principally the National Training Laboratories in Bethel, Maine. The term *encounter group* is most often associated with the more radical wing of the human potential movement; the activities of such groups often include such nonverbal procedures as touching, body movement, dance, and massage. Although they tend to be associated with such West Coast centers as Esalen Institute, encounter groups may be found throughout the United States. In recent years, many of the more traditional T-groups have incorporated some of these nonverbal procedures, but they still remain relatively conservative. I will use the term *T-group* throughout this chapter; the groups that I will be describing are more toward the traditional end of the spectrum, although they may use some of the more recent innovations usually associated with the encounter group.

The first T-group was an accident. But, like most productive accidents, it occurred in the presence of a brilliant and creative person who was quick to appreciate the importance and potential utility of what he had stumbled upon. In 1946, Kurt Lewin, perhaps the greatest innovator and theorist in the brief history of social psychology, was asked to conduct a workshop to explore the use of small group discussions as a way of addressing some of the social problems of the day. The participants

Source: From Elliot Aronson, *The Social Animal*, 3rd ed., W. H. Freeman and Company, Copyright © 1976, 1980.

were educators, public officials, and social scientists. They met during the day in small groups. The small groups were observed by several of Lewin's graduate students, who met in the evenings to discuss their interpretation of the dynamics of the group discussions they had observed during the day.

One evening, a few of the participants asked if they could sit in and listen while the graduate students discussed their observations. Lewin was a little embarrassed by the request, but, much to the surprise of his graduate students, he allowed the visitors to sit in. As it happened, one of the educators joined the group just as the observers were discussing her behavior and interpreting an episode that she had participated in the preceding morning. She became very agitated and said that the observer's interpretation was all wrong. She then proceeded to give her version of the episode. The discussion proved very exciting. The next night, all 50 of the participants showed up and gleefully joined the discussion, frequently disagreeing with the observations and interpretations of the trained observers. The session was both lively and illuminating.

Lewin and his students were quick to grasp the significance of that event: A group engaged in a problem-solving discussion can benefit enormously by taking time out to discuss its own dynamics or "group process" without special training as observers. Indeed, the participants themselves are much better observers of their own process because each is privy to his or her own intentions—something that is not easily available to outside observers, no matter how astute and well trained they are. After a time, what evolved was the agendaless group: The group could meet with maximum benefit if it had no formal agenda and no problems to discuss other than its own dynamics.

Interest in T-groups has grown rapidly since 1946. They are conducted in all sections of the country, and their members include individuals from all walks of life. There have been specialized groups consisting solely of college students, high-school teachers, corporation presidents, police officers, members of the State Department, and delinquents; there have been groups for married couples, unmarried couples, and families; there have been confrontation groups of street people and police, blacks and whites, and managers and their employees. But most groups have been heterogeneous—the same group might contain a lawyer, a laborer, a nun, a housewife, a bank teller, a college student, and a smattering of male and female business executives, teachers, and drop-outs. T-groups have become a phenomenon of the 1960s and 1970s—they have received wide (and often sensational) publicity; they have been treated with an uncritical, cultish, almost religious zeal by some of their proponents; and they have been castigated by the right-wing as an instrument of the devil, as a subversive form of brainwashing that is eating away at the fabric and soul of the nation. In my judgment, sensitivity-training groups are neither the panacea nor the menace that they frequently are made out to be. When properly used, they can be enormously useful as a means of learning communication skills, increasing self-awareness, and enriching human relations. With this in mind, the distinguished psychotherapist Carl Rogers characterized the T-group as "the most significant social invention of the century," and the social historian William Thompson considered the T-group "a rehearsal for the complete transformation of human nature and civilization." When abused, they can be a waste of time—or, in extreme cases, they might even provide people with some very painful experiences, whose effects can persist long beyond the termination of the group.

The primary focus in this chapter will be on the sensitivity-training group as an instrument of communication. Although there are all kinds of groups, I will discuss only the traditional T-groups. I will attempt to describe them from within and from without and discuss what happens in a group, what gets learned, and what the inherent problems and dangers are.

The Content and Process of a T-group

A T-group experience is educational, but educational in a different way from what most of us have grown accustomed to. It is different both in the *content* of the material that is learned and in the *process* by which the learning takes place.

The Content: What Gets Learned. Generally, individuals in a T-group learn things about themselves and their relations with other people. It can be said that, in a college psychology course, I learn how people behave; in a T-group, I learn how *I* behave. But I learn much more than that: I also learn how others see me, how my behavior affects them, and how I am affected by other people.

The primary purpose of T-groups is to learn how to communicate effectively, to listen carefully, and to understand one's own feelings and those of other people. In addition, many people are motivated to participate in a T-group not only to learn to communicate but because they believe that there may be something missing in their lives. A person may feel alienated from other people; he may feel that life is going by too quickly; he may feel that he wants something more out of life than waking up in the morning, eating breakfast, going to work, coming home, watching television, and going to sleep. In short, many people are searching for greater self-awareness and greater enrichment of their lives through these groups. This does not mean that a person has to be in the middle of an existential crisis in order to join a group; many people join because they have specific confusions and are searching for specific answers: "Why do I have trouble getting along with my children (or my employees, or the opposite sex)" "Why do other people make friends easily, while I tend to be alone?" "Why do I have difficulty opening up to people?" "What is there about people that makes them so untrustworthy?" "How can I handle my anger?" "What do I do that turns people off?" "Why is it that, when I meet a guy, all he wants to do is take me to bed?''

Interacting with other people in a competently led T-group *can,* and frequently *does,* provide individuals with answers to specific questions like these. But, more generally, the T-group provides the first step toward the achievement of a number of goals and forms the basis for the clarification of a wide range of confusions. Among the major goals of a T-group are:

1. To develop ways of communicating that are clear, straight, and nonattributional.
2. To develop a spirit of inquiry and a willingness to examine one's own behavior and to experiment with one's role in the world.
3. To develop an awareness of more things about more people.
4. To develop greater authenticity in interpersonal relations; to feel freer to be oneself and not feel compelled to play a role.
5. To develop the ability to act in a collaborative and mutually dependent manner with peers, superiors, and subordinates rather than in an authoritarian or submissive manner.
6. To develop the ability to resolve conflicts and disputes through problem solving rather than through coercion or manipulation.

The Process: How Things Are Learned. The single most important distinguishing characteristic of a T-group is the method by which people learn. Again, a T-group is not a seminar or a lecture course. Although a great deal of learning *does* occur, it's not the kind of learning that can be easily transmitted verbally in a traditional teacher-student relationship. It is learning through doing, learning through experience. In a T-group, people learn by trying things out, by getting in touch with their feelings, and by expressing those feelings to other people, either verbally or nonverbally. ''Trying things out'' not only helps individuals understand their own feelings, it also allows them the opportunity of benefitting from learning about how their behavior affects other people. If I want to know whether or not people find me to be a cold, aloof,

unemotional person, I simply *behave*—and then others in the group will tell me how my behavior makes them feel.

An implicit assumption underlying these groups is that very little can be gained if someone tells us how we are *supposed* to feel, how we are *supposed* to behave, or what we are *supposed* to do with our lives. A parallel assumption is that a great deal can be gained if we understand *what* we're feeling, if we understand the kinds of interpersonal events that trigger various kinds of feelings, if we understand how our behavior is read and understood by other people, and if we understand the wide variety of options available to us. The role of the T-group leader is not to present us with answers but simply to help establish an atmosphere of trust and intensive inquiry in which we are willing to look closely at our own behavior and the behavior of others.

It is in this sense that a T-group is not a therapy group. The leader does not attempt to interpret our motives or probe into our experiences outside the group; in addition, he tends to discourage other group members from doing this. Instead, he simply encourages us to behave and to react to the behavior of others.

The Cultural Island. As we race through life, we are frequently distracted. Thoughts about the work we must do compete for our attention with the person we are supposedly listening to now; thoughts about the person we must see during the *next* hour distract us from the work we are trying to do now; as we stand at the cocktail party, balancing a drink in one hand and holding a cigarette in the other, ''listening'' to the pompous fellow in the flashy suit, we glance over his shoulder to see who else is at the party, and we begin to wonder why we didn't go to that other party instead. This kind of distraction is minimized in a T-group, because there is literally no alternative to paying attention. Here, we are in a room—on a ''cultural island''—with several other people for two weeks (or 10 days, or a weekend) with nothing to do and no agenda and no one directing us toward any specific action. We are meeting for 12 to 16 hours a day—there's nothing else happening. Initially, this can be somewhat frightening, as we realize how difficult it is to interact with people in the absence of conversational crutches (the weather, have you seen any good films lately, and so on). Then, as we learn to pay attention to others, to listen, to look, we begin to pick up nuances of speech and behavior that we didn't think we were capable of noticing. We also begin to listen to ourselves more—to pay attention to those rumblings in our gut and to try to make sense out of them in the context of what is going on in the room, *outside* our gut.

OK, but what happens? How do people get started? What is there to talk about? Typically, the group begins with the leader (trainer) outlining the "housekeeping" schedule—when meals will be served, how long each session will last before it breaks, and so on. She may or may not proceed to outline her philosophy of groups and the limits of her own participation. She may or may not discuss the "contract"—what the participants do *not* have to do. In any case, she soon falls into silence. Minutes pass. They seem like hours. The group members may look at each other or out the window. We are not accustomed to being left to our own devices by people in leader-teacher roles. Typically, the participants will look to the trainer for guidance or direction. None is forthcoming. After several minutes, someone might express his discomfort. This may or may not be responded to. Eventually, in a typical group, someone will express some annoyance at the leader: "I'm getting sick of this. This is a waste of time. How come you're not doing your job? What the hell are we paying you for? Why don't you tell us what we're supposed to do?" There may be a ripple of applause in the background. But someone else might jump in and ask the first person why he's so bothered by a lack of direction—does he need someone to tell him what to do? And the T-group is off and running.

Learning from Each Other

How does learning occur? How can we learn from people who are not experts? We learn through communicating. There are many ways for communi-

cations to become distorted. Occasionally, in our everyday lives, when we think we are communicating something to a person, that person is hearing something entirely different. Suppose, for example, that Fred has warm feelings for Jack, but, out of shyness or out of a fear of being rejected, he finds it difficult to express these feelings directly. He may choose to communicate those warm feelings by engaging in a teasing, sarcastic kind of banter. Jack may not understand this as warmth, however; indeed, the sarcasm might hurt him. As I indicated earlier, in our culture, it is difficult to communicate hurt feelings because it indicates weakness and vulnerability. So Jack keeps quiet. Thus, Fred, oblivious to the fact that his behavior is disturbing to Jack, continues to express his warmth via sarcastic jocularity—continuing to hurt the person he likes—until he succeeds in driving Jack away. Not only does Fred lose out on what could have been a warm friendship, but he may also fail to learn from this experience and may continue to alienate the very people toward whom he feels most warmly.

It may be useful to view the interaction between two people as a chain of events, as illustrated in Figure 1. The Person (P) has some feelings about

---

FIGURE 1

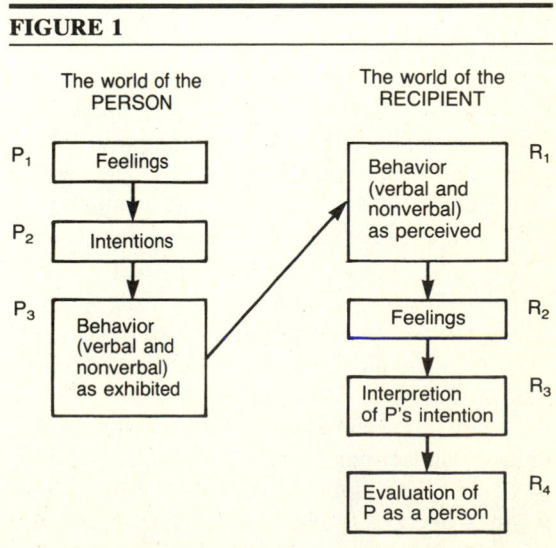

The world of the PERSON

The world of the RECIPIENT

P_1 Feelings

P_2 Intentions

P_3 Behavior (verbal and nonverbal) as exhibited

R_1 Behavior (verbal and nonverbal) as perceived

R_2 Feelings

R_3 Interpretion of P's intention

R_4 Evaluation of P as a person

the Recipient (R). He intends to communicate a particular feeling. This manifests itself in some kind of behavior—some words, a gesture, a smile, a look, or whatever. The Recipient perceives this behavior in his own way, based upon his own needs, feelings, past history, opinions about P, and so on. This perception of P's behavior evokes a feeling in R (warmth, anger, annoyance, love, fear, or whatever). This feeling is quickly translated into an interpretation of what P's intentions were, which in turn flows into an evaluation of what kind of a person P is.

There are possibilities for error or distortion along any point in the links of this chain. Thus, to return to our example, Fred (P) has some warm, loving feelings (P_1) toward Jack. He intends to communicate these (P_2), but he does it in an oblique, noncommittal, self-protective way: He teases Jack, makes fun of his clothes, is jocular and sarcastic (P_3). Jack perceives this sarcasm and teasing (R_1); it causes him pain (R_2); and he decides that Fred was trying to put him down (R_3). He concludes, therefore, that Fred is a cruel, aggressive, unfriendly person (R_4).

Error can occur in a different part of the chain. Imagine a totally new situation in which Fred is completely direct and honest, but Jack is suspicious. Suppose that Fred expresses his warmth directly—by putting his arm around Jack's shoulder, by telling Jack how much he likes him, and so on. But, in this case, such behavior may be too fast for Jack. Accordingly, Jack may feel uncomfortable, and, instead of simply admitting his discomfort, he may interpret Fred's behavior as manipulative in its intent. He may evaluate Fred as an insincere, political, manipulative person.

The process described above may be familiar to readers of this book. If we see a person behaving in a particular way, we have a strong tendency to attribute some motive or personality disposition to him on the basis of his behavior. If this process can be explored and examined, there is a great deal of potential learning in the encounter for both Fred and Jack. Is Fred too scared to display his warm feelings openly? Is Jack too suspicious to accept genuine warmth without vilifying Fred? These are important questions whose answers can produce a lot of insight, *but the opportunity for gaining this insight rarely occurs in the real world*. This learning can occur only if Fred and Jack share their feelings with each other. The T-group provides an atmosphere in which these feelings can be expressed and worked through. The group accomplishes this by encouraging the participants to stay with their feelings and to avoid "short-circuiting" the process by skipping from Fred's behavior (P_3) all the way to Jack's attribution (R_3) and ultimately to Jack's evaluation of Fred (R_4) without exploring the preceding and intervening events.

Openness and the Need for Privacy

Basically, then, a T-group is a setting in which people are provided with the opportunity to talk straight to each other—and to listen straight. The emphasis is on the *here and now,* rather than on past history. Thus, a participant is *not* encouraged, for example, to explain to everyone the kind of person she is, nor is she encouraged to reveal her childhood experiences, her job anxieties, or the intricacies of her sex life. She *may* talk about these things if she chooses, but she usually learns more if she simply allows events to happen, reacts to the events openly as she experiences them, and allows others to respond to her as she *is* rather than as she describes herself to be. "Openness" is the key aspect of behavior in a T-group. Many critics of T-groups have reacted against the emphasis on openness, because they believe that it violates the dignity of the individual and his need for privacy. But, in this context, openness does not mean detailed self-revelation; it simply means straight talk between two or more people. In a competently conducted T-group, a norm is established that provides each member with the right to as much physical and emotional privacy as that person desires. Participants are encouraged to resist any pressure to make them reveal things that they would rather hold private. But a member who wishes to express something in a group is helped to learn how to express it directly rather than obliquely. For example, if Bill is angry at Ralph, it is his right to keep that anger to himself, if he so chooses. But if he chooses to express his anger, it is much more useful (for Bill, for Ralph, and for everyone else concerned) if he expresses it directly by telling Ralph about his feelings than it is if he expresses it by any one of a number of indirect means—such as making snide remarks or sarcastic statements, grunting whenever Ralph talks, making fun of Ralph covertly, or lifting his eyes toward the ceiling, so that everyone can be made aware of his contempt for Ralph. If Bill makes a snide remark, someone in the group will almost invariably ask him if he has any feelings about Ralph that he wants to share with the group. He is not forced to share his feelings—but he's discouraged from talking in riddles and encouraged to translate the muddy language of sarcasm into straight talk.

This is not to deny that, in some groups, a great deal of coercion is used to make people reveal things that they might prefer not to reveal. Sigmund Koch, a vocal and erudite critic of group encounter, provides a graphic description of some of the more lurid and extreme examples of coercive groups. But he goes beyond that and asserts that *all* T-groups constitute a threat to human dignity and "a challenge to any conception of the person that would make life worth living." Koch has sounded a warning siren that is well worth heeding. Personally, I would choose not to participate in a group that invaded my privacy and pressured me to make self-revealing statements against my better judgment; but I believe that Koch's condemnation of all T-groups on these grounds is based upon a misunderstanding of the term *openness* and an overgeneralization of his limited exposure to the goings on in "far-out" groups. At the same time, I would agree with Koch to the extent of advising people to steer clear of encounter groups unless they are competently conducted and unless they practice the value that no one has to do anything that he doesn't want to do.

Reading 30

TAVISTOCK CONFERENCES

Clayton P. Alderfer

The self-study group has evolved from a tradition which traces its roots to modern psychoanalytic theory of object relations (Klein, 1959). During World War II, British psychoanalyst W. R. Bion discovered that groups were a useful way to treat psychiatric casualties from the war. His group work led to his writing of *Experiences in Groups* (1959), a book that has become a classic in the field and a key theoretical work for leaders of Tavistock study groups. Although Tavistock theories have evolved from the psychoanalytic tradition, the conferences are directed to learning, not therapeutic goals (Rice, 1965).

Authority relationships form a key element in the learning process of self-study groups. Tavistock staff members, who are called consultants, remain distant and remote in their relationships with group members. They think about their behavior in terms of "staying in role," with the intent of contributing to the group's exploration of relations within the group. In carrying out their roles, the consultants are very punctual in entering and leaving group meetings, dress in relatively formal attire, and intervene in group activity only when they believe it will promote learning. Their statements tend to be metaphorical and they consistently point out how members seem to be relating to them, often as surrogates for other key figures such as parents, siblings, lovers, and the like (Astrachan and Klein, 1961; Redlich and Astrachan, 1969).

Tavistock laboratories also focus on intergroup relations through the use of exercises which ask participants to negotiate among groups in order to make a decision or carry out a task. These activities serve to underline the impact of individual,

subgroup, and group boundaries. The analysis of boundaries plays a key role in Tavistock theory and methods. One of the key learnings is the types of fantasy and mythmaking that groups indulge in, with respect to each other, across group boundaries. A. K. Rice's work (1965, 1969) on laboratory design and on individual, group, and intergroup transactions as boundary crossings is the major conceptual work in this area.

Staff members direct their interventions to the group rather than to any individual. The latter's behavior or statements, however, are assumed to express group concerns unless contradicted by others. Thus, whenever a person speaks in the group he is viewed as speaking for the group and his statement is viewed as representing some element of the group opinion.

Little in the staff behavior allows one to determine the degree to which the interventions cause the study group behavior or merely reflect it. Consultants rarely discuss their own feelings with the group, although they do use their feelings as an important source of data for understanding group events (Rice, 1965). It might be expected that group members would focus much of their attention on the consultant when he intervenes in the group activity yet behaves in a relatively inaccessible manner. Important questions can be raised about the generality of the learning about leadership that participants achieve in study groups. It is one thing to learn that persons develop vivid and hostile fantasies about persons who appear to be leaders yet deny the role, who behave in distant ways and speak metaphorically about their perceptions of the group. It may be a mistake, however, to assume that reactions of this sort are representative of typical reaction to authority figures regardless of how they behave.

Source: Clayton P. Alderfer, "Understanding Laboratory Education: An Overview," reprinted from *Monthly Labor Review*, December 1970, pp. 21–22.

Tavistock consultants do not suggest that their behavior is a model for group members to follow. Yet a question can be raised as to whether modeling occurs nonetheless. There is research to support the notion that modeling or imitation is a general human learning process (Bandura and Walters, 1963). If modeling does occur in study groups, then it would appear that the Tavistock style of study group would teach participants to be leaders who do not share their feelings, remain personally distant from the group, talk in metaphors, focus attention on themselves by their mode of intervention, and hold quite strictly to the prescribed definition of their roles.

This writer has serious questions about whether these types of learning are very useful for small group effectiveness. However, there are times when learning of this kind is realistic. Leaders of large social systems cannot be seen regularly by more than a few members. They frequently serve as spokesmen for the group. To come to terms with leaders in this kind of role, group members have little choice but to rely on their fantasies and therefore to project and transfer their reactions from prior relationships. Learnings from study group and intergroup activities in a Tavistock laboratory can be very enlightening with regard to multiple group functioning in large scale social systems.

Reading 31

CAN ORGANIZATION DEVELOPMENT
USE TRANSACTIONAL ANALYSIS?

Nick Nykodym, Warren R. Nielsen, and Joseph C. Christen

In recent years both organization development (OD) and transactional analysis (TA) have been widely used as organizational change strategies. OD is used in a wide variety of settings and recent research has indicated its effectiveness in organizational application (Kimberly & Nielsen, 1975; Pate, Nielsen, & Bacon, 1976; French & Bell, 1978). TA has also been used in a large number of organizations. However, the data regarding its organizational impact is not as extensive, although support does exist for its effectiveness (Nykodym, 1978).

OD and TA have both been used to improve organizational effectiveness in both behavioral and performance terms. However, in spite of their overlap in philosophy and application, little discussion has occurred regarding their mutual roles. Randall has commented that, ''the transactional analysis conceptual system of human behavior has a potentially important role to play in the evolution of OD'' (1974, p. 143). French and Bell have observed that ''transactional analysis is best thought of as only one part of a larger OD program where it is used in conjunction with other interventions'' (1978, p. 146). In addition, the conceptual framework for TA has great similarities to that of OD (Fox, 1975, pp. 345–353).

While these sources may discuss the potential interface of OD and TA, little has been written outlining the specifics of this complementary interrelationship.

Organization development can be viewed as ''a complex, proactive strategy intended to improve organizational health and effectiveness through planned activities using knowledge from the behavioral sciences'' (Nielsen, Pate, & Wakefield, 1977, p. 1). Although every OD effort, to be effective, must be tailored to an organization's situation and problems, steps in a typical OD program are outlined in Figure 1. Extensive discussion of OD programs may be found in Kimberly & Nielsen (1975) and Christen & Nykodym (1980).

Briefly outlined, a typical OD project consists of the following steps:

Initial Diagnosis is accomplished through meetings with various levels of management in order to communicate the program's intended goals, obtain cooperation from various levels, and gain perspective on organizational goals and objectives. A steering committee and an internal consultant are often designated during this period. Both work with the outside consultants to tailor the OD program to their specific organizational needs.

Team Skills Training consists of a two- to three-day experiential based learning workshop to introduce teamwork concepts and to foster skills, knowledge, and capabilities in group dynamics, group influence and coordination, personal management style, self-assessment, and interpersonal awareness in individual and group relationships (Frame, Hess, & Nielsen, 1982, p. 139). Team Skills Training is used as an OD intervention when it is determined through the initial diagnosis that the organization is too closed or lacks the skills to adequately begin to identify and solve team organization problems.

An expected outcome of the training is also to improve employee perception of the work climate as measured by increased satisfaction with deci-

Source: Nick Nykodym, Warren R. Nielsen, and Joseph C. Christen, ''Can Organization Development Use Transactional Analysis?'' *Transactional Analysis Journal,*

FIGURE 1   Steps of a Typical OD Program

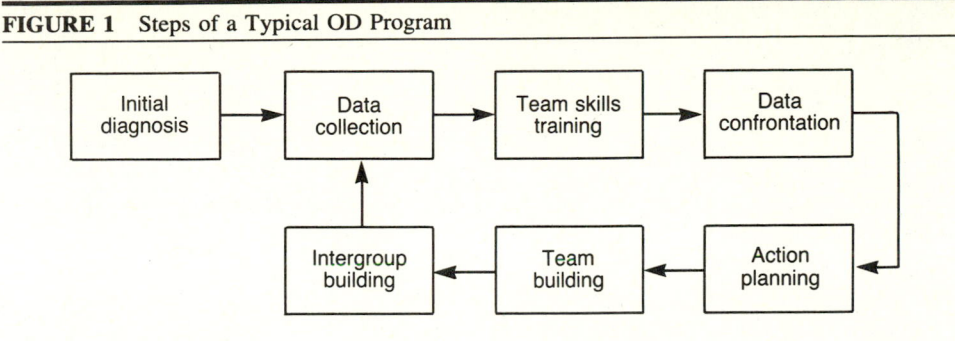

sions, coordination, and flow of job-relevant data. Team Skills Training workshops are generally held off-site to minimize interruptions and maximize concentration. Where used as an early OD intervention, a variety, if not all organizational levels are involved and the training receives top management participation and support.

Data Collection generally consists of a survey instrument or questionnaire developed by the consultants with input from the internal consultant and the steering committee. Some OD practitioners also use structured confidential interviews with the firm's top officers as well as a diagonal slice of employees. Usually ten to twenty questions are asked which give the participants an opportunity to voice their concerns and perceptions about such issues as: (1) company strengths and weaknesses, (2) communication effectiveness, (3) whether people, equipment, and time are being effectively utilized, and (4) conflict resolution. In a long term project these data are often supplemented by appropriate organizational performance indicators such as profit, performance to budget, absenteeism, turnover, waste, or scrap. Other appropriate indices may be used as well.

Data Confrontation is achieved by various work groups in the organization reviewing the data and determining problem areas and priorities in these areas, as well as some preliminary recommendations for change.

Action Planning is based on the problem analysis, priorities, and preliminary recommendations of the data confrontation stage. Specific plans de-

termine what should be changed, who should be responsible, and when the action should be completed. Action planning uses a diagonal slice of organizational members, several levels of organizational participants, or natural work groups.

Team Building is conducted with each intact (natural) work group in the entire system. This generally consists of a manager and his/her immediate subordinates. The primary focus is on how groups can specifically improve their productivity by identifying blocks to effectiveness and on developing strategies and plans for accomplishing group goals and objectives.

Intergroup Building consists of data-based meetings between interdependent work units. The groups work on shared goals, problems, cooperation, and increased mutual understanding. Specific joint action plans are developed to improve effectiveness and performance within given time periods.

Data Collection using the original instruments is generally repeated after an appropriate interval (usually twelve to eighteen months) to chart the progress of the organization as well as the effectiveness of the organizational change strategies.

While transactional analysis and organization development may have similar goals, most TA programs do not have the detailed phases just listed that are so typical of many OD programs. A notable exception to this is the Organizational Analysis with Results using Transactional Analysis (OARTA) outlined by Clary and Clary (1976, pp. 18–24).

The basic objective of Team Skills Training listed above was achieved by the use of a TA intervention researched by Nykodym (1978). He discovered that an organizational TA program improved perceived supervisory behavior. This was reflected by enhanced employee perception of manager listening, approachability to supervisors, teamwork, and information flow (Nykodym, 1978).

However, given the extensive use of OD and TA, additional data are needed. Often the groundwork of an OD project is laid by improving the organization climate, increasing decision-making information, improving the flow of job-relevant information, and improving both subordinate and managerial skills in problem identification, problem confrontation, and action planning.

Statement of the Problem

While TA is widely used, little data are available on its use and effectiveness as a tool in the OD process. The research question in this study is: What is the impact of TA as a strategy in Team Skills Training within an OD project? Specifically, can TA improve organizational climate through employee perception of increased decision making and flow of job-relevant information? In addition, could TA be used as an effective substitute for Team Skills Training in preparing organization participants for more in-depth and demanding OD interventions?

Generation of Hypothesis

The authors of this study were able to investigate the impact of an application of transactional analysis in an organizational environment. The home office of a national company had decided to use a TA program and the researchers were permitted to intervene and measure the program. Enthusiasm existed for measurement since organization members were quite interested in the impact and value of a TA program on employee perceptions and behavior.

The transactional analysis program was designed to encourage the development of a more flexible management style with employees. Performance appraisals and coaching of employees were emphasized as means of encouraging subordinates to move from Child behavior to Adult behavior (Cole-

man, 1974). The program attempted to achieve increased Adult-Adult transactions between supervisors and employees. Increased listening and approachability on the part of supervisors were the focus of attention. Performance standards were to be maintained by increased supervisor emphasis on information flow and team work. The program did not claim to improve performance; it only asserted that coaching and counseling could improve the existing climate for employee growth by improving the organizational climate as reflected by increased satisfaction with decisions and coordination as well as by increased job-relevant information. Changes in these items are consistent with those identified as first order change which, given other change interventions, could lead to second order change or change in system performance indicators (Kimberly & Nielsen, 1975).

The goals stated above form the research hypothesis:

H: A systematic program of transactional analysis in an organizational context will result in improvement of perceived organizational climate by organizational members.

Sample and Design

The work group which initially received the TA training and participated in the evaluation consisted of an intact work unit (family group) from a division of the home office of a national company (n = 17). This group was compared to another intact work unit in the same division (n = 28) which did not receive the TA training but completed the evaluation instrument. Thus, for research purposes within the change project, the authors were utilizing a simple pretest/posttest control group design as described by Campbell and Stanley (1963, pp. 13–24). The intact or family group was necessary to prevent contamination of the results. Transactional analysis stresses communication and interaction with fellow employees. If randomization were to occur by individuals, with some group members going through the training and others not, variation in the group not receiving the training could be credited to their contact with fellow employees who received the training. In addition, most Team Skills Training occurs in family groups; therefore, to determine the effectiveness of TA as a substitute for Team Skills Training, application of the two processes needed to be similar. The group not receiving the transactional analysis was established in a manner similar to that used by Ottemann and Luthans (1975) who closely matched a control group with a treatment group based on experience, age, education, highest grade, and mental scores. The two groups in this study were closely matched for age, experience, education (grade school = 1, high school = 2, college = 3, completed college = 4, graduate work = 5), and job point rating [see Table 1].

Job point rating consisted of a system established by the company to qualify: (1) amount of job know-how, (2) amount of problem-solving ability, and (3) accountability. The dimensions of accountability are freedom to act, job impact on end results, and magnitude as reflected by control of dollar resources.

Randomization occurred by intact work units. Each work unit had equal chances of receiving or not receiving the TA training. All work units of the division eventually received the training. Only random assignment determined which group received the training first.

The TA training consisted of six half-day sessions which included: (1) introduction to TA and the Parent ego state, (2) the Child ego state, (3) Adult ego state, (4) transactions, (5) management process, Part I, and (6) management process, Part II (Coleman, 1974).

The sessions emphasized the fundamentals of Parent, Child, and Adult ego states. Sessions on management application and transactions stressed the importance of recognizing the ego states of one's employees. Managers were instructed to use their own Adults to determine an appropriate approach to each transaction. Supervisors were encouraged to use Adult-Adult transactions where possible. The workshops illustrated the Parent-Child environments of many companies. Increased communication and listening were the main tools in increasing manager effectiveness (Coleman, 1974). Team effort could be achieved by increased information, job data, exchange of ideas, and feedback on performance. Employee satisfaction with decisions made could be improved by increased information sharing. The main goal of the TA program was to increase employee satisfaction with the work environment. A basic theme was increased manager awareness of the needs of employees to function in an Adult-Adult milieu (Coleman, 1974). Satisfaction with how differences and conflicts were resolved would increase in an Adult-Adult atmosphere. Managers were urged to create an environment that would encourage employees to communicate with them. Approachability on the part of managers was increased by their ability to listen to employees, to aid in the solution of work problems, and to emphasize team goals. The management application sections were held in the last

TABLE 1 Demographic Comparison of Trained and Untrained Groups

Characteristic	Average Group Receiving TA	Group not Receiving TA
Age	32.35	37.89
Time on present job	4.18	4.19
Time with company	7.08	10.6
Educational level	4.71	4.23
Job Point Rating	328.00	370.54

days of the program. It should be noted how similar the focus of this training was to that of the Team Skills Training portion of the OD study reported by Kimberly and Nielson (1975).

The training was conducted by the training and development staff of the company. Trainers had considerable background in transactional analysis. The program included video presentations, introspective exercises, role-plays, video interaction, and reading assignments (Coleman, 1974). Reading consisted of a participant manual prepared by the consulting firm. Eric Berne's *Games People Play* (1964) and Thomas Harris' *I'm OK — You're OK* (1967) were recommended but not required reading.

Measuring Instrument

A basic purpose of the transactional analysis program was to positively and significantly change employee perceptions of organizational climate.

To determine change in perception, the authors sought to utilize an instrument that had wide application, yet would measure the dimensions of organizational climate. The Survey of Organizations Questionnaire of the Institute for Social Research (ISR) was selected since it has been validated against thirty different organizations with widely different cultural settings and many different technologies. Over 24,000 individual respondents from all organizational levels completed the instrument during its development and refinement (Hain, 1972).

Validation analyses of the survey consisted of four time periods covering an eighteen-month time span. Validity is reported as follows:

> Fairly clear evidence exists that the *Survey of Organizations* measure relates approximately to both efficiency and attendance criteria. Relationships to efficiency extend across all four time periods and reach levels as high as .80. Relationships to attendance attain only slightly lower levels, and, where data are available, show every sign of extending across all time periods . . . In the Human cost area, organizational climate seems to have appropriate and significant relationships to all three measures available for analysis: minor injuries, physical health, and grievance rate (Taylor and Bowers, 1972).

Internal consistency reliability coefficients for organizational climate range from .70 to .80.

As indicated previously, the instrument was administered to the trained and untrained groups in a pretest/posttest control design. Administration of the instrument occurred both before and after training for the trained group. It was administered to the untrained group at the same time as the trained group, once before the other group was trained, and again after their training was complete. The posttest administration occurred six months after the training was completed.

Statistical Analysis

The trained and untrained groups were matched for age, experience, and educational level. The groups were also matched for amount of job know-how, amount of problem-solving ability required, freedom to act, job impact on end results, and magnitude through job rating. Nevertheless, differences existed between the trained and untrained groups on the measure of organizational climate.

Randomization occurred by intact group. Kirk recommends the use of analysis of covariance (1968). He states: "Analysis of covariance may be particularly appropriate for . . . *intact groups,* a situation that is common in educational and industrial research" (1968, p. 455).

Analysis of covariance was used to equalize initial differences between trained and untrained groups. Pretest scores were used as covariates and differences between posttest dependent measures were used to test significance of differences between trained and untrained groups. The alpha level was set at .05.

Results

The following data [see Table 2] were obtained for organizational climate. Initial differences between the two groups were controlled by the use of analysis of covariance. A significant difference was found between the group receiving the TA training and the group receiving no training on the measure of organizational climate. The research hypothesis was confirmed.

TABLE 2 Results of TA Training

Source of Variation	Sum of Squares	df	Mean Square	F	Significance of F
Covariates, pretest	2014.035	1	2014.035		
Main effects, posttest	135.721	1	135.721	5.706	.02
Residual	999.038	42	23.787		
Total	3148.795	44	71.864		

H: A systematic program of transactional analysis in an organizational context will result in improvement of perceived organizational climate by organizational members.

Discussion

A quick inspection of the results from a TA organizational renewal project and the typical phases of an OD intervention will reveal that the TA results and the OD Team Skills Training Phases objectives are very similar. The intentions of the Team Skills Training phase is to build communication skills and an improved environment for problem solving. Improvement in the climate for employee growth by enhanced supervisory behavior reflected increased employee perception of listening, approachability to supervisors, teamwork, and information flow (Nykodym, 1978).

The new data from this study of increased satisfaction with decisions and coordination, as well as flow of job-relevant information, strengthens the position of TA as an organizational intervention. The intentions of the Team Skills Training phase of OD is to build communication skills as well as to change attitudes and the environment to enhance an overall OD project.

The results of the previous data as well as the results of this TA study indicated increased listening, supervisory approachability, teamwork, information flow, decision making, and job-relevant data. Also, the data were very consistent with that reported on the Team Skills training portion of a major OD project. (Kimberly & Nelson, 1975). These data demonstrate that TA has a strong potential role to play in the OD process. The skills and perceptions cited above are vital to a successful Team Skills Training phase in any OD project. If communication channels are not opened at this phase, the entire OD intervention may be endangered. The success of the phases of data confrontation, action planning, team building, and intergroup team building and other OD interventions of any OD project may be determined by the success of the Team Skills Training introduction to OD. The results of this study would indicate that TA may be viable as the Team Skills Training phase of an organization development intervention.

Recommendations

Further research on the usefulness of TA as a substitute or possible addition to the Team Skills Training OD intervention might profitably focus on at least four areas. First, additional studies should be undertaken to measure the relative impact of TA and Team Skills Training utilizing identical measurement instruments. To date, evaluation of the two interventions had been measured using similar but not identical instruments and therefore potential information regarding real differences and change potential have not been obtained. Second, the two interventions must be tested in a variety of organizational settings to determine if they have similar impact in different settings. Third, similar studies to this should be undertaken to determine whether or not the results obtained in the two groups tested in this study are indicative of what could be expected on a continuing basis. Fourth, studies should be undertaken over a longer period of time utilizing multiple testing to determine if there are similarities or dissimilarities in the long run impact of TA training and Team Skills Training.

References

Berne, E. (1964). *Games people play.* New York: Grove Press.

Campbell, G. T., & Stanley, J. C. (1963). *Experimental and quasi-experimental designs for research.* Chicago, IL: Rand McNally.

Christen, J. C., & Nykodym, N. (1980). *Process consultation: A tool for organizational renewal and change.* Tulsa, OK: American Society for Training and Development.

Clary, T. C., & Clary, E. W. (1976). Organizational analysis with results using transactional analysis. *Training and Development Journal, 30,* 18–24.

Coleman, P. (1974). *Transactional analysis and successful management.* Elk Grove, IL: Advanced Systems.

Fox, E. M. (1975). Berne's theory of organizations. *Transactional Analysis Journal, 5,* 345–353.

Frame, R. M., Hess, R. K., & Nielsen, W. R. (1982). *The OD source book: A practitioner's guide.* San Diego, CA: University Associates.

French, W. L., & Bell, C. H. (1978). *Organization development.* Englewood Cliffs, NJ: Prentice-Hall.

Hain, T. (1972). *Organizational change patterns.* Flint, MI: General Motors Institute.

Harris, T. (1967). *I'm OK, You're OK.* New York: Harper & Row.

Kimberly, J. R., & Nielsen, W. R. (1975). Organization development and change in organizational perfor-

mance. *Administrative Science Quarterly, 20,* 191–206.

Kirk, P. (1968). *Experimental design: Procedures for the behavioral sciences.* Belmont, CA: Brooks/Cole.

Nielsen, W. R., Pate, L. E., & Wakefield, J. J. (1977). *An organization development approach to reducing crisis in management: Combining research and practice.* Paper presented at Michigan Academy of Science, Mount Pleasant, MI.

Nykodym, N. (1978). Transactional analysis: A strategy for the improvement of supervisory behavior. *Transactional Analysis Journal, 8,* 254–258.

Ottemann, R., & Luthans, F. (1975). An experimental analysis of the effectiveness of an organizational behavior modification program in industry. In A. Bedian, A. Armenakis, W. Holley, & H. Field (Eds.), *Proceedings of the Thirty-Fifth Annual Meeting of the Academy of Management* (pp. 140–42). New Orleans, LA.

Pate, L. E., Nielsen, W. R., & Bacon, P. C. (1976). Advances in research on organizational development: Toward a beginning. In R. L. Taylor, M. J. O'Connell, R. A. Zawacki, & D. D. Warrick (Eds.), *Proceedings of the Thirty-Sixth Annual Meeting of the Academy of Management* (pp. 389–394). Kansas City, MO.

Randall, L. (1971). Red, white, and blue TA at 600 mph. In D. Jongeward (Ed.) *Everybody Wins: Transactional Analysis Applied to Organizations* (pp. 43–85). Reading, MA: Addison-Wesley.

Taylor, J., & Bowers, D. (1972). *The survey of organizations: A machine-scored standardized questionnaire instrument.* Ann Arbor, MI: Institute for Social Research.

Reading 32

LIFE PLANNING

Herbert A. Shepard

Life planning is planning life-worth-living. The choices you make today create your future, as well as your here and now. And you have some freedom of choice, today, and tomorrow as well. We are only slowly emerging from an era of deterministic science, when it was assumed that today's choices are completely the product of yesterday's choices, and the very notion of choice a quaint illusion. The psychologists assured us that life after the age of five was merely an unfolding of a personality set in early childhood. And our culture demands of each of us so many promises and contracts that most of us seem to have signed away our future choices. We seal our fates.

Many people see their futures as fated in another way. They think of the future as something that happens to them. When they are asked to draw a line representing the way they think about their total lives—from the beginning in the past to the end in the future—they can portray certain aspects of their past, but are unable to map the future. The past can be reinterpreted, but it cannot be managed. Only the future is manageable, but these people have great difficulty in thinking about it that way.

Some people plan their careers and invest their energies in bringing about certain career achievements. Unfortunately, when people plan only their careers, the other aspects of their lives are unanticipated and sometimes unhappy consequences of their career choices. When these people draw their life lines, they draw only career lines.

Life planning is a self-confrontation. It is the induction of an identity crisis and a destination crisis for yourself. It requires the reexamination of basic values and assumptions. Many of us are enslaved to beliefs and fears that turn us into instruments used for some purpose outside outselves. One therapist greets new patients with the question: "Why haven't you committed suicide?" The answers often lie outside the person and his joy in life, or lack of it: responsibilities to family, God and country, or even to the life insurance company. And if a married couple is asked: "Why haven't you divorced?" the answers are often outside their joy in each other, or lack of it: family responsibilities or social embarrassment.

Yet Fritz Perls's Gestalt Prayer counsels:

I do my thing, and you do your thing.
I am not in this world to live up to your
   expectations
And you are not in this world to live up to mine.
You are you and I am I
And if by chance we find each other, it's beautiful.
If not, it can't be helped.[1]

Who am I and who are you? The first answers that come to mind are usually "marketing" answers. They describe what makes you or me a respectable commodity: title, profession, memberships, loyalties, skills, hobbies, roles as parent, spouse, or manager. The answers that come later take us beyond the boundaries of such socially prescribed selves, and precipitate an identity crisis.

Who *should* you be? Our culture provides us with many reasons for being that lie outside our-

Source: Herbert A. Shepard, *The Laboratory Method of Changing And Learning: Theory And Application*, ed. Kenneth D. Benne, Leland P. Bradford, Jack R. Gibb, and Ronald D. Lippitt (Palo Alto, Calif.: Science and Behavior Books, 1975), pp. 240–51.

[1]Frederick S. Perls, *Gestalt Therapy Verbatim* (Moab, Utah: Real People Press, 1969).

selves, with many images of what we should be. The self-confrontations of life planning involve the unravelling of deeply, often automatically, held assumptions about shoulds and oughts, goods and bads. A dictator concerned only with the maintenance of his own power would value such qualities in the citizenry as loyalty, respect for authority, law and order, unselfishness, humility, and competitiveness. When you perform well, whom are you trying to please? When you are winning, is it ever at the cost of something more important? Is having a fine reputation at all like being trapped? Is being independent ever lonely? Is the greatest risk not risking?

On the subject of what one ought to be, Kahlil Gibran had this story to tell.

> It was in the garden of a madhouse that I met a youth with a face pale and lovely and full of wonder.
>
> And I sat beside him upon the bench, and I said, "Why are you here?"
>
> And he looked at me in astonishment, and he said, "It is an unseemly question, yet I will answer you. My father would make of me a reproduction of himself; so also would my uncle. My mother would have me the image of her illustrious father. My sister would hold up her seafaring husband as the perfect example for me to follow. My brother thinks I should be like him, a fine athlete.
>
> "And my teachers also, the doctor of philosophy, and the music master, and the logician, they too were determined, and each would have me but a reflection of his own face in a mirror.
>
> "Therefore, I came to this place. I find it more sane here. At least I can be myself."
>
> Then of a sudden he turned to me and he said, "But tell me, were you also driven to this place by education and good counsel?"
>
> And I answered, "No, I am a visitor."
>
> And he said, "Oh, you are one of those who live in the madhouse on the other side of the wall."[2]

The location of the madhouse is less important than whether either the inmate or the visitor has learned to make his own life worth celebrating. What were those moments when you rejoiced in life, when you were fully alive, and living fully, and experiencing fulfillment? You're likely to find that many of them were quite "simple," and had little to do with the way you spend most of your time. If you can identify the conditions under which your life is fulfilling, you can set about creating those conditions.

Easier said than done. A basic fact of life—that it is to be lived fully—is difficult to grasp. Lyndon Johnson's widow, reflecting on their last years together, commented:

> To be close to death gives you a new awareness of the preciousness of life, and the extreme tenuousness of it. You must live every day to the fullest, as though you had a short supply—because you do. I said that glibly for years, but I didn't know how intensely one should live.[3]

Some people can apprehend the preciousness of life by writing their own obituaries, focusing on activities and feelings, and writing the obituary twice: once as an extrapolation of present life style, and again as one would wish it to be. But many others find this rather direct way of facing the question, "What shall I do with the time I have left?" too threatening to be taken seriously.

What are the conditions under which it is possible to rejoice in life? Perhaps one can learn from infants. An infant rejoices when it can affect its environment in ways that please it. It rejoices in loving and playful interaction with other beings. And it rejoices in the functioning of its own body. These three sources of fulfillment, translated into adult words, can be called autonomy, resonance, and tone.

As used here, autonomy refers to your ability to create a world worth living in for yourself. Typically, the autonomous person has many skills useful to himself and society, continually develops his physical, emotional, and intellectual capacities, can relate in many ways to others, is proactive and foresighted, imaginative and realistic, takes re-

---

[2]Kahlil Gibran, "The Madman," in *The Wanderer* (London: Heinemann; New York: Knopf, 1932).

[3]Ladybird Johnson, *Time,* May 21, 1973, p. 41.

sponsibility for his choices and their consequences, is open to new experience and learns from it. But the essence of autonomy is not in what one's resources are, but in how they are used, the purpose they serve: namely, the creation and maintenance of a world worth living in. Thus, autonomy differs from related terms like power, skill, achievement, independence, or wealth, which may become ends in themselves, or may be used to create a world for oneself that is not worth living in. The characteristics of such a world and of autonomy are not the same for every person. Robert Frost described the meaning of autonomy in the poet's world.

> The reason artists show so little interest
> In public freedom is because the freedom
> They've come to feel the need of is a kind
> No one can give them—they can scarce attain—
> The freedom of their own material:
> So, never at a loss in simile,
> They can command the exact affinity
> Of anything they are confronted with.
> This perfect moment of unbafflement,
> When no man's name and no noun's adjective
> But summons out of nowhere like a jinni.
> We know not what we owe this moment to.
> It may be wine, but much more likely love—
> Possibly just well-being in the body,
> Or respite from the thought of rivalry.
> It's what my father must mean by departure,
> Freedom to flash off into wild connections.
> Once having known it nothing else will do.
> Our days all pass awaiting its return.[4]

The second source of fulfillment is resonance, a relationship with other beings which is empathic, responsive, mutually stimulating, and expansive for all those involved. The term can describe a person's relationship with other environments as well. Resonance differs from the common meaning of love, which is usually understood to be an exchange relationship rather than a resonance relationship. Freya Stark describes the essence of resonance in the following passage.

For it must be remembered that silence can be dead or living, and the two kinds must be distinguished. And perhaps the poles of Being are in the distinction—the one an end and a downfall and a destruction, and the other a part of that which has neither beginning nor end; and even in the humblest instance there is a difference in the silence of these two.

There is, for instance, regrettably often a noticeable blank in the wedded silence, when a couple have been married a long time. One sees them in restaurants or on cruises—middle-aged, averted faces that turn toward each other with no light in their eyes and drop words of such astonishing triviality that one wonders how the air consents to carry them: surely the sort of conversation Sartre was thinking of when he described Hell as one prolonged domestic scene.

Yet if a young creature were to ask for advice whether to say yes or no to the man or woman she or he thought of marrying, one might do worse than ask: 'Are you happy to be silent together?' That companionship is the living silence—a relaxation that finds speech superfluous, an atmosphere of well-being where nothing needs to be explained, a part of that current which can make not only men but most living things happy to be together. It is, I like to imagine, the stream that flows beneath all differences of language and carries each one of us from those cindery beginnings toward our undiscovered end.[5]

The third source of fulfillment, tone, is an alertness of all the senses and organs. The meaning we attach to the term "muscle tone" captures the quality referred to as the tone of the whole organism—sensory, mental, emotional, muscular, etc. The concept of tone differs from the concept of health. Health is usually defined as the absence of disease, and mental health is usually regarded as something different from physical health. Tone is a psychophysiological concept: anxiety is as much its enemy as drugs. Lowen expresses this idea as follows:

A person experiences the reality of the world only through his body. . . . If the body is relatively

---

[4]Robert Frost, "How Hard It Is to Keep from Being King when It's in You and in the Situation," in *The Poetry of Robert Frost* (New York: Holt, Rinehart & Winston, 1969), p. 453.

[5]Freya Stark, "On Silence," *Holiday Magazine*. Reprinted with permission © 1965, The Curtis Publishing Company, also John Murray, Ltd., London.

unalive, a person's impressions and responses are diminished. The more alive the body is, the more vividly does he perceive reality and the more actively does he respond to it. We have all experienced the fact that when we feel particularly good and alive, we perceive the world more sharply. . . . The aliveness of the body denotes its capacity for feeling. In the absence of feeling, the body goes "dead" insofar as its ability to be impressed by or respond to situations is concerned. The emotionally dead person is turned inward: thoughts and fantasies replace feeling and action; images compensate for the loss of reality. . . . It is the body that melts with love, freezes with fear, trembles in anger, and reaches for warmth and contact. Apart from the body these words are poetic images. Experienced in the body, they have a reality that gives meaning to existence.[6]

When autonomy, resonance, and tone are all high, we rejoice in life. This is a peak experience, and as Frost says, "Once having known it, nothing else will do." The three are closely intertwined: if autonomy is used in ways that reduce resonance, it will not produce a world worth living in; low tone will adversely affect resonance and autonomy. Treating them as separate aspects of life-worth-living may have some value in the life-planning process for persons who have been spending all their energies on work and neglecting their relationships with others or their own bodies; or for persons who only feel strong when they are going against others and don't know that it is possible to be strong when going with others; or for persons who overeat at the expense of tone and resonance; or for persons with many resources, person who possess the elements making for autonomy, but have experienced little fulfillment.

How does the infant's delighting in its experience of autonomy become transformed into the adult's striving for status or winning over others? How does the infant's joy in resonance become transformed into the adult's view of love as a commodity and commodities as substitutes for love? How does the infant's joy in its own body become

transformed into emotional deadness? Perhaps it is because our socializing institutions demand that the child give up his search for autonomy in exchange for packages of pseudoromance. Whatever the telling events in the process of socialization are, many people "grow up" having learned "truths" that blind them to life. Such distorting values are reflected in the following excerpt from a paper examining the relevance of Taoist and Buddhist philosophy to modern man in modern organization.

The second piece of advice is: observe the cormorant in the fishing fleet. You know how cormorants are used for fishing. The technique involves a man in a rowboat with about half a dozen or so cormorants, each with a ring around the neck. As the bird spots a fish, it would dive into the water and unerringly come up with it. Because of the ring, the larger fish are not swallowed but held in the throat. The fisherman picks up the bird and squeezes out the fish through the mouth. The bird then dives for another and the cycle repeats itself.

To come back to the second piece of advice from the neo-Taoist to the American worker:

Observe the cormorant, he would say. Why is it that of all the different animals, the cormorant has been chosen to slave away day and night for the fisherman? Were the bird not greedy for fish, or not efficient in catching it, or not readily trained, would society have created an industry to exploit the bird? Would the ingenious device of a ring around its neck, and the simple procedure of squeezing the bird's neck to force it to regurgitate the fish have been devised? Of course not.

Greed, talent, and capacity for learning, then, are the basis of exploitation. The more you are able to moderate and/or hide them from society, the greater will be your chances of escaping the fate of the cormorant. . . . It is necessary to remember that the institutions of society are geared to make society prosper, not necessarily to minimizing suffering on your part. It is for this reason, among others, that the schools tend to drum into your mind the high desirability of those characteristics that tend to make society prosper—namely, ambition, progress, and success. These in turn are to be valued in terms of society's objectives. All of them gradually but

---

[6]Alexander Lowen, *The Betrayal of the Body* (New York: Macmillan, 1967), pp. 5–6.

surely increase your greed and make a cormorant out of you.[7]

One need not view the fate of the cormorant as gloomily as does Siu to recognize that he provides a novel perspective on some attributes—ambition, talent, and capacity for learning—which are prized in our culture. Life planning is essentially an invitation to explore new perspectives from which to view past experience, one's current life, and future alternatives. As Siu implies, the value system we inherited is not necessarily designed to make life worth living.

The discovery and creation of perspectives that deepen our appreciation of ourselves in the universe is the fourth aspect of life-worth-living. It is akin to resonance, as suggested by the terminology William O. Douglas used to describe what is meant here by perspective:

> Man is whole when he is in tune with the winds, the stars, and the hills as well as with his neighbors. Being in tune with the apartment or the community is part of the secret. Being in tune with the universe is the whole secret.[8]

In everyday experience, being in tune with the universe, or having an adequate perspective, means seeing problems from above rather than from underneath, means not getting locked in to one end or the other of a presumed polarization, means being free in your situation rather than dependent on it, means owning your behavior rather than claiming someone else's behavior "caused" yours.

Life planning is a quest, and it is also a continuous part of life-worth-living. And while the life-planning process and outlook described here may help you to live more fully, it will not protect you from pain. Developing toward higher levels of autonomy, resonance, tone, and perspective faces you with all the awkwardness, mistakes, and painful choices involved in any learning. Living more fully

means investing yourself more fully in the creation of your experience: and anything you invest yourself in to the point that it can bring you great joy can also bring you great grief by its loss.

An Appendix

If you ask a person why he is in his present job, he is quite likely to tell you how he got into it rather than how he is using it in the accomplishment of his purpose. Life planning is learning to see the environment through the eyes of your purpose, and the principal work of life planning is the creation of purpose. You become what you think. "A man defines himself by his project."[9]

Logically, career planning is a part of life planning. But psychologically and culturally, the two are often separated. For some, work or career or profession is the sole source of self esteem, the only justification for being permitted to exist. For others, it is not felt to be a part of life at all, and life planning refers to the time outside of work, when they can live a little.

Life planning is to make life more whole, to make living a good gestalt, so that the parts of one's life are mutually enriching. Work belongs in life, along with love, laughter, prayer, and all the other elements of human experience.

Life planning has several aspects: arousal of motivation, freeing of imagination, generation of data about oneself, identification of themes in the data, formulation of purpose, and development of action plans. Many vehicles are available for taking this trip, and the ones noted below are examples.

Draw Your Life Line. Draw a line that represents ways you have of thinking about your life. Maybe it will be a straight sloping line drawn between the coordinates of chronological age and maturity. Maybe it will be a chart of your educational and work life. Maybe it will be two lines, one representing your career, the other the rest of your life. Maybe it will be jagged, with lots of peaks and valleys. Maybe it won't be a line at all, but a string

---

[7]Ralph Gildi Siu, "Work and Serenity," *Journal of Occupational Mental Health 1*, no. 1 (1971), p. 5.

[8]Attributed to William O. Douglas, associate justice, U.S. Supreme Court.

[9]R. D. Laing and G. O. Cooper, *Reason and Violence* (London: Tavistock, 1964), p. 61.

of pictures, or something that looks like a tree, or a map. Maybe it will be several lines, each concerned with a different aspect of your life.

Make it a complete life line: beginning with your birth and ending with your death. Put a mark on it to show where you are right now. Let yourself play with the future part of the line. Be sure to bring the line to an end: the decisions on how long to live is best made by yourself, and you can change your mind about it tomorrow.

When you have completed your drawing, its meaning is apparent only to yourself. If you explain to some others what you tried to portray, their questions and comments may lead you to discover additional meanings, and you can also gain perspective on your own life by learning how others represent theirs.

Identity Search. The next steps are explorations of the space between the "now" mark on your line and the future end of the line, beginning with the now mark: your current identity. Find as many answers as you can to the question "Who am I?" The first answers that occur to you probably will be the roles you take: your occupation, your family roles, your memberships, etc. Then explore the many other sides of yourself: adjectives that describe some aspect of you and your life: personality traits, beliefs, skills, attitudes, habits; impulses and inhibitions; dreams, wishes, fears and regrets; the kinds of relationships you form with other people; the things you like about yourself and the things you don't; the things you're not; the other people who are a part of your life.

If you are in the company of someone who knows you, ask her or him to make a list of answers to the question "Who are you?" to provide you with additional data for your identity search. Now look over your list item by item, and spend some time assessing the importance of that item to your sense of yourself. Suppose it were suddenly removed, how would you feel? You may find that some are so important that if they were taken away you'd be lost and terrified; you may find some whose disappearance would be a relief.

Then review the list again, marking those aspects of your identity you want to maintain, and perhaps

enhance, in the future, and those aspects of which you want to rid yourself. Add any new identities you want to become.

The identity search is enriched by being shared with others; for example, some of the items on this lists probably belong on yours, too.

Write Your Obituary. After exploring the now mark on your life line in this way, move to the future end of the line and look back over your whole life, especially the part you haven't lived yet. Write your obituary, covering as many aspects of your life as you can, and concentrating on the part between the now mark and the future end of the line. Write about the way your life will probably turn out if you continue in your current life patterns and trends. If you don't make any major shift in life-style, priorities, values, etc., what will your obituary say? After you've written it and shared it with the others, you can think about any changes you want to make in it.

Newspaper Clippings. The next steps are explorations of the space between now and the future end of the line. Take the Sunday edition of a large metropolitan newspaper and clip out items that intrigue you. They may be news items of a political, educational, scientific, sports, or cultural nature; or travel advertisements and descriptions of other countries; or cartoons and pictures; or business and real estate opportunities; or jobs and occupations; things offered for sale; perhaps a portion of someone's obituary.

Paste the clippings on a large sheet of paper and share them with others. See what patterns you can find in the things that interested you.

Fantasy Day. Somewhere in the space between now and the end of the line, create a special day for yourself. Give your fantasy free rein: don't ask whether you can afford to do what you want to do in that day; don't ask whether all those things could be fitted into one day. Just plan a day that you would love to have.

After you've lived that day in fantasy, and shared what you dare about it with others, look at it more critically. Did you build into that day any wishes or dreams that you want to take seriously and turn into plans? Many people suppress and altogether forget youthful dreams and wishes when they become "responsible adults." Dreams that were unattainable when you were younger may no longer be out of reach. See if you can recapture some of your wishes. Are they still attractive? Are they realizable?

A Way of Life. Take a large segment of the line between now and the end, perhaps a year, and describe a life style you'd like to try. Again, don't be too "realistic." Take the segment from far enough in the future that you'd have time to do something about the obstacles that stand in the way of spending such a year. And after you've written and shared it, think about whether you mean any of it seriously enough to start planning.

A Review of Highs. What can you learn from your past that you can use in creating your future? If you can identify the conditions under which your life was fulfilling, you may be able to recreate those conditions.

Think back to the times when you felt best about yourself and your life. Some of them may have been brief moments; peak experiences. Some of them may have been projects that took years to accomplish. Some may have been work, some pure play. Some may have been solitary experiences, others full of people.

Write a paragraph about each one, describing it in as much detail as you can. Give yourself lots of time to recapture these highs: a whole evening, or a weekend. After you've described a number of them (try to find at least ten), go back over them in search of patterns. What strengths did you display or develop in each of these experiences? What did you contribute to the creation of the experience? What were the sources of your satisfaction in each experience? Ask others to help you with this analysis: they are likely to see strengths that were too obvious for you to see yourself.

Psychological Tests. Through the use of psychological tests, you can generate more data about your identity and your potentials. For example, the Thematic Apperception Test can give you a new perspective on your needs for achievement, influence, and intimacy. FIRO-B reflects your needs in the areas of control, affection, and inclusion.

The Strong Interest inventory tells you how your patterns of interests, likes, and dislikes match those of people who have been successful in various occupations.

Getting It All Together. By now you have amassed so much information about yourself that it will take some time and thought to assimilate it and comprehend it. As you look through it all, you will find the same set of messages, in different words and contexts, many times. You may also find some seeming contradictions and paradoxes. Some of these may be artifacts of the method used in generating the data: for example, the product of a particular mood you were in during one of the exercises. But often the paradoxes contain the possibility of discoveries about yourself that can be important to you in creating your future. A person with whom you have good rapport can be helpful to you in the process of sorting it all out and getting it all together.

Purpose and Themes. When you have identified some of the themes that you want to be central in your life, try to formulate a statement of mission or purpose that organizes the themes into a good gestalt, a wholeness that is satisfying to you. Your purpose may evolve logically and obviously from your study of the data; it may have emerged clearly in the process of generating the data; or it may continue to elude you and then appear as a flash of insight. It may also be that you cannot formulate a purpose until you have made some further explorations.

Your Partners in Life. If you have a partner or partners in life, you should probably have been together throughout the process described above. But partners do not build identical life plans, nor plan to do everything together. The partners are separate beings who have created a third being, the couple, and the welfare of the couple is not served by imprisoning the partners within it. The couple should reserve itself those areas of mutuality which are fulfilling for both partners, and the partners need to discover what those are and can be. Beyond that, the value of the gift of being or having a partner is in serving as resources to each other in creating the life that the other is seeking.

SUGGESTED ADDITIONAL READINGS FOR PART 4

Alderfer, Clayton P. "Understanding Laboratory Education: An Overview." *Monthly Labor Review,* December 1970, pp. 18–27.

Argyris, Chris. *Behind the Front Page.* San Francisco: Jossey-Bass, 1974.

Back, Kurt W. *Beyond Words: The Story of Sensitivity Training and the Encounter Movement.* New York: Russell Sage Foundation, 1972.

Benne, Kenneth D., et al. *The Laboratory Method of Changing and Learning.* Palo Alto: Science and Behavior Books, 1975.

Berne, Eric. *Games People Play.* New York: Grove Press, 1964.

Cooper, Gary L. "How Psychologically Dangerous Are T-Groups and Encounter Groups?" *Human Relations,* April 1975, pp. 249–60.

Dyer, William G. *The Sensitive Manipulator.* Provo, Utah: Brigham Young University Press, 1972.

Fordyce, Jack K., and Raymond Weil. *Managing with People.* Reading, Mass.: Addison-Wesley Publishing, 1979, pp. 101–42.

Greiner, Larry E. "Confessions of an Executive Educator." *New Management,* Winter 1987, pp. 34–38.

Harman, Robert L. "Techniques of Gestalt Therapy." *Professional Psychology,* August 1974, pp. 257–62.

Harris, Thomas A. *I'm OK—You're OK: A Practical Guide to Transactional Analysis.* New York: Harper & Row, 1969.

Hunsaker, Philip L. "T-Groups for MBA's: A State of the Art Survey." *Group and Organization Studies.* September 1978, pp. 356–64.

Jongeward, Dorothy. *Everybody Wins: Transactional Analysis Applied to Organizations.* Reading, Mass.: Addison Wesley Publishing, 1973.

Lieberman, Morton A. "Change Induction in Small Groups." In *Annual Review of Psychology* 27 (1976). Ed. Mark R. Rosenzweig and Lyman W. Porter, pp. 217–50.

Luft, Joseph. *Group Processes,* 3rd ed. Palo Alto, Calif.: Mayfield Publishing, 1984.

Maier, Norman R. F.; Allen R. Solem; and Ayasha A. Maier. *The Role-Play Technique.* San Diego, Calif.: University Associates, 1975.

Rogers, Carl R. *Carl Rogers on Encounter Groups.* New York: Harper & Row, 1970.

Schein, Edgar H. *Career Anchors: Discovering Your Real Values.* San Diego, Calif.: University Associates, 1985.

Schein, Edgar H., and Warren G. Bennis. *Personal and Organizational Change through Group Methods.* New York: John Wiley & Sons, 1965.

Smith, Peter B. *Group Processes and Personal Change.* New York: Harper & Row, 1980.

Walter, Gordon A., and Stephen E. Marks. *Experiential Learning and Change.* New York: John Wiley & Sons, 1981.

PART 5

Structural Interventions vis-à-vis OD

A number of contemporary organization improvement strategies or techniques can be subsumed under the label "structural interventions." These interventions are consulting activities aimed at improving organization effectiveness through changes in structure. Broadly defined, by structure we mean such aspects of organizations as how the overall work is divided among units, spatial arrangements of machines and people, work flow, operating procedures, who reports to whom, role definitions and expectations, and goal setting and compensation procedures. Thus, we view structure broadly as consisting of procedures or devices that channel, direct, or constrain activities.

Why deal with structural interventions in an OD book? The reasons are several. In the first place, OD practitioners and clients alike can profit by a broader understanding of the impact of structure on the "people" aspects of organization. Second, a broader understanding of the range of contemporary organization improvement strategies can give consultants and clients a broader range of options to exercise. For example, a preliminary organizational diagnosis might reveal strong interest and need for production-level job restructuring, and the initial consulting effort might start there. Third, a better understanding of structural approaches can enhance the ability of consultants and clients to make different strategies mutually reinforcing instead of instigating programs that are in opposition to each other, a condition we sometimes see. For example, we have seen or heard about a number of participative team-building efforts launched almost simultaneously with autocratic forms of management by objectives; the incongruency usually becomes apparent to organizational members but not before there had been considerable wasted effort. Fourth, some strategies may have features that would enhance the implementation of other strategies. For example, we suspect that many job enrichment efforts might be improved if there were better diagnosis, if the approach were more collaborative, and if the approach were more group centered. In short, many structural interventions might profit by having more OD-like features. There is some evidence for this. For example, Richard Hackman finds that one of the major deficiencies in many job enrichment programs is that the problems in the work system are not diagnosed before the jobs are redesigned.[1] And finally, there needs to be better agreement on what the language of these various improvement strategies means so that communication about these matters can be enhanced.

Some structural interventions currently very visible in the literature and in practice are quality of work life (QWL) projects, sociotechnical systems, work redesign, quality circles, management by objectives, and the use of task forces and collateral organizations. Quality of work life projects are frequently amalgamations of effective personnel practices, the use of semiautonomous work groups, and some aspects of OD, but we will let the essay by Walton and the essay by Lawler and Ledford define the area. Sociotechnical systems, as described in the essay by Cummings, are interventions designed to enhance the congruence between group attitudes and norms, the technology used, and organizational structure. Sociotechnical-systems approaches typically feature the concept of semiautonomous (or ''self-managed'') work teams.

Work redesign is essentially a vertical and horizontal restructuring of jobs to provide for more planning and control by the job incumbent. (Vertical restructuring is frequently called ''job enrichment.'') Quality circles are participative, problem-solving sessions usually utilized in production departments, but also found in such diverse settings as offices and hospitals. Management by objectives (MBO) establishes procedures for goal setting and performance review, and largely makes explicit what each job incumbent is to accomplish in a given period of time. (As we will see, there are many versions of MBO, and some are congruent with OD and some not.) Task forces and collateral organizations are temporary or parallel organization structures designed to augment the ongoing or permanent structure. Many of these approaches have common threads.

As the reader will note, a common dimension between QWL projects and sociotechnical systems is the concept of the semiautonomous or self-managed work team. This concept is also evident in some job enrichment approaches and in quality circles. Perhaps less evident from the literature is the fact that QWL projects have frequently used facilitators using OD approaches.

Are these structural interventions OD interventions per se? Generally not if organization development is defined as we have defined it in Part 1. Structural interventions might be intermediate outcomes of OD interventions, however. For example, a job enrichment program might emerge as one of many outcomes of a long-range OD effort. In such an instance, the form of the job enrichment effort is likely to be congruent with and complementary to the OD process. Most of the structural interventions dealt with in this part have the potential for being implemented in ways that are congruent with OD, or may be combinations of an OD approach with a structural approach, but in themselves are usually not organization development interventions as we have defined them. An exception may be the ''collateral organization,'' to be discussed later.

To emphasize a point of view that has been both implicit and explicit in this book: We believe that there is an organization improvement strategy that has some central characteristics that differentiate it from other improvement strategies, and that these characteristics include the use of a collaborative action research model, a focus on intact work

---

[1]J. Richard Hackman and Greg R. Oldham, *Work Redesign* (Reading, Mass.: Addison-Wesley Publishing 1980), pp. 99–130.

groups, a focus on collaborative management of group and organizational culture broadly conceived, the use of a consultant who establishes an essentially equal relationship with the client in contrast to the expert or ''purchase'' model of consultation,[2] and a view of the effort as a long-range process. This strategy we call ''organization development.'' If the latter term were preempted as a label for some other improvement strategy, it would then be important to have wide agreement on a new term for the particular improvement strategy we are dealing with in this book. We think the gestalt that we are labeling ''OD'' is a highly significant invention, and is a distinguishable improvement strategy. (Figure 1 depicts some of the variables that tend to characterize OD in contrast to non-OD. Improvement strategies that generally fulfill the conditions described in the middle column of the chart we see as OD; improvement strategies that generally fulfill the conditions on the right we see as non-OD; mixtures fall in between.)

FIGURE 1   Organizational Improvement Strategies

	Organization Development (OD)	*Non-OD (Examples)*
Target of intervention	Work-related groups.	Individuals, or noninterdependent persons in a group of audience setting.
Consultant model used	Collaborative equal power (change agent model)	Expert or ''purchase'' model.
Task or structure versus process orientation	Focuses largely on processes such as group interaction, norms, leadership, decision making; outcomes may be task/structural changes.	Focuses largely on changing tasks or structure.
Depth of culture managed	Attempt to manage culture in depth; both formal aspects and informal; e.g., cognizance of attitudes, perceptions, feelings.	Primary focus on one selected aspect of formal system—e.g., structure, technology, tasks, or goals
Time perspective	Two to three years and beyond.	Ad hoc, short-range orientation.
Systems perspective	High systems orientation; i.e., high cognizance of interdependencies.	Narrow attention to functional organizational subsystem or problem.

[2]For a discussion of the ''purchase'' model of consultation, see Edgar Schein, *Process Consultation: Its Role in Organization Development* (Reading, Mass.: Addison-Wesley Publishing, 1969), pp. 5–6.

A. Quality of Work Life Projects

The first selection in this section, by Richard Walton, provides criteria for quality of work life (QWL). Any of the criteria could be furthered by a properly conducted OD effort; some dimensions, such as "social integration in the work organization," might be uniquely furthered by OD approaches.

The second selection, by Edward Lawler III and Gerald Ledford, Jr., defines both quality of work life and productivity and then looks at the complex relationships between the two. The multiplicity of interventions subsumed under the QWL label becomes evident when we see that such interventions as gainsharing, problem-solving groups, job enrichment, and so on may be included. In addition to other features of their essay, Lawler and Ledford discuss some situational factors that can affect the success of such interventions.

Reading 33

QUALITY OF WORKING LIFE: WHAT IS IT?

Richard E. Walton

Introduction

In recent years the phrase "quality of life" has been used with increasing frequency to describe certain environmental and humanistic values neglected by industrialized societies in favor of technological advancement, industrial productivity, and economic growth. Within business organizations, attention has been focused on the "quality of human experience in the work place." At the same time many firms have questioned their viability in increasingly competitive world markets. These dual concerns have created a growing interest in the possibilities of redesigning the nature of work. Many current organizational experiments seek to improve both productivity for the organization and the quality of working life for its members.

Although the broad productivity criterion contains some dilemmas, such as short run versus long run effectiveness, this criterion is relatively straightforward when compared with the concept of the quality of working life. How should the quality of working life be conceptualized, and how can it be measured? What are the appropriate criteria, and how are they interrelated? How is each related to productivity? Are criteria uniformly salient for all employee groups? These questions are central to both research on the quality of the human experience in work organizations and action programs which seek to improve that experience.

The phrase "quality of working life" suggests comprehensiveness. The concept embraces, but is broader than, the aims of a long series of legislative acts that began in the early 20th century. These acts include child labor laws, the Fair Labor Standards Act which established the eight-hour day and the forty-hour work week, and workmen's compensation laws which have protected the job-injured employee and have eliminated many hazardous working conditions.

The concept is also broader than the aims of the unionization movement which made rapid progress in the 1930s and the 1940s, when emphasis was placed on job security, due process at the work place, and economic gains for the worker. It is broader than the notion proposed by psychologists in the 1950s that a positive relationship existed between moral and productivity and that improved human relations would lead to the enhancement of both. Finally the concept is broader than any of the attempts at reform in the 1960s, such as the drive for equal employment opportunity and the numerous job enrichment schemes.

The concept of the quality of working life in the 1970s nevertheless must include the values that were at the heart of these earlier reform movements. It also must include recently emphasized human needs and aspirations, such as the desire for a socially responsive employer.

Criteria for the Quality of Work Life

Eight major conceptual categories are now proposed, ranging from adequate and fair compensa-

Source: Richard E. Walton, *Sloan Management Review* Fall 1973, pp. 11–21. Reprinted by permission of the publisher. © 1973 by the Sloan Management Review Association. All rights reserved. An earlier draft of this paper was presented to the Conference on the Quality of Working Life, held at Arden House, Harriman, New York, on September 25–29, 1972. The proceedings of this conference were edited by Louis Davis. Research was supported by the Division of Research, Graduate School of Business Administration, Harvard University.

tion for work to the social relevance of work; they provide a framework for analyzing the salient features of the quality of working life.

1. Adequate and Fair Compensation

The typical impetus for employment is earning a living. How well that aim is achieved fundamentally affects the quality of working life. More than any of the other criteria, adequacy of compensation is a relative concept. There simply is no consensus on objective or subjective standards for judging the adequacy of compensation.

Fairness in compensation, on the other hand, has various operational meanings. Job evaluation specifies relationship between pay and factors such as training required, job responsibility, and noxiousness of working conditions. By other approaches, supply and demand for particular skills or community averages determine the fair level of compensation. Another standard of fairness relates to ability to pay; more profitable firms should pay more. A variant of this standard is that when changes in work rules increase productivity of employees, it is only fair that the economic fruits of productivity be shared with the employees involved. Occasionally the application of one standard of fairness produces a pattern of compensation that is judged unfair by another standard.

The adequacy and fairness of pay are partly ideological questions. For example a 20 to 1 ratio between the pay of the top executive and the hourly worker of a firm may have been accepted in the recent past, but it may be regarded as too large in the future.

Although accepted operational measures are not available to judge the adequacy and the fairness or work compensation, both factors are important determinants of the quality of working life.

Adequate income: Does the income from full-time work meet socially determined standards of sufficiency or the subjective standard of the recipient?

Fair compensation: Does the pay received for certain work bear an appropriate relationship to the pay received for other work?

2. Safe and Healthy Working Conditions

It is widely accepted in our society that workers should not be exposed to physical conditions or hourly arrangements that are unduly hazardous or detrimental to their health. Legislation, union action, and employer concern have resulted in continually rising standards of satisfactory working conditions. Aspects of these improvements include: reasonable hours enforced by a standardized normal work period beyond which premium pay is required; physical working conditions that minimize risk of illness and injury; age limits imposed when work is potentially destructive to the welfare of persons below (or above) a certain age.

It is possible that in the future, more stringent standards will be imposed where health is less the issue than comfort; the goal will be to minimize odors, noises, or visual annoyances. On the other hand, the general improvement in the quality of working conditions and the earlier maturation of youth may lead to a relaxation of age limits in some areas of work.

3. Immediate Opportunity to Use and Develop Human Capacities

The industrial revolution and a simplistic extension of its underlying logic have taken much of the meaning out of work. Work has tended to be fractionated, deskilled, and tightly controlled. The planning of work has been separated from its implementation. These tendencies have progressed in varying degrees from one job to the next; therefore jobs differ in how much they enable employees to use and develop their skills and knowledge. Some of the job qualities necessary for this development follow:

Autonomy: Does the work permit substantial autonomy and self-control relative to external controls?

Multiple skills: Does the work allow one to exercise a wide range of skills and abilities rather than merely repeat the same narrow skill?

Information and perspective: Is one allowed to obtain meaningful information about the total work process and the results of his own action, so that he can appreciate the relevance and consequences of his actions?

Whole tasks: Does one's work embrace a whole task or is it some fragment of a meaningful task?

Planning: Does one's work include planning as well as implementation of activities?

These aspects of the job affect the ego involvement, self-esteem, and challenge obtained from the work itself.

4. Future Opportunity for Continued Growth and Security

Here the focus shifts from the job to career opportunities. Although the opportunity for self-improvement through education and hard work has been considered an American birthright, the typical industrial job can now be completely learned within a few weeks or a few years, after which the blue-collar worker has reached nearly the peak of his earnings and can look forward to only minor improvements.

Promotion of blue-collar workers to supervisory and managerial positions is often foreclosed by formal educational prerequisites. Engineers and other professionals tend to peak somewhat later, but they often confront an additional source of discouragement, the obsolescence of their knowledge and skills. When these professionals reach their middle 30s, their earnings begin to level off. Frequently by this time their knowledge has been exploited and their specialties deepened, but no provision for continued education or broadened capabilities has been made. There is little prospect for advancement in salaries and promotions. This period coincides with a stage of life where professionals are likely to be reevaluating their commitments to careers, families, and avocations. The result is that many lose interest in their professional work, no longer invest in their career pursuits, and increase the sterility of their work lives. Thus attention needs to be given to the following aspects of working life:

Development: The extent to which one's current activities (work assignments and educational pursuits) contribute to maintaining and expanding one's capabilities rather than leading to obsolescence.

Prospective application: The expectation to use expanded or newly acquired knowledge and skills in future work assignments.

Advancement opportunities: The availability of opportunities to advance in organizational or career terms recognized by peers, family members, or associates.

Security: Employment or income security associated with one's work.

5. Social Integration in the Work Organization

The preceding categories relate to the worker's immediate and long-range opportunities of expressing and developing individual abilities. Since work and career are typically pursued within the framework of social organizations, the nature of personal relationships becomes another important dimension of the quality of working life. Whether the worker has a satisfying identity and experiences self-esteem will be influenced by the following attributes in the climate of his work place:

Freedom from prejudice: Acceptance of the worker for work-related traits, skills, abilities, and potential without regard to race, sex, creed, and national origin, or to life styles and physical appearance.

Egalitarianism: The absence of stratification in work organizations in terms of status symbols and/or steep hierarchical structures.

Mobility: The existence of upward mobility as reflected, for example, by the percentage of employees at any level who potentially could qualify for higher levels.

Supportive primary groups: Membership in face-to-face work groups marked by patterns of reciprocal help, socioemotional support, and affirmation of the uniqueness of each individual.

Community: The sense of community in work organizations that extends beyond face-to-face work groups.

Interpersonal openness: The way members of the work organization relate to one another their ideas and feelings.

6. Constitutionalism in the Work Organization

A member of a work organization is affected by many decisions that are made on his behalf or about his status in the organization. What rights does he have, and how can be protect his rights? The labor unions have brought constitutionalism to the work place to protect employees from arbitrary or capricious actions by employers. In a few unions workers now enjoy some of these same rights vis-à-vis the union authority structure itself; mechanisms exist whereby a member may appeal, ultimately to an impartial judge, certain union actions that affect the member. In unorganized employment, there are wide variations in the extent to which the organizational culture respects personal privacy, tolerates dissent, adheres to high standards of equity in distributing organizational rewards, and provides for due process in work-related matters. The following aspects of constitutionalism are key elements in providing higher quality to working life:

Privacy: The right to personal privacy; for example, withholding from the employer information about the worker's off-the-job behavior or about actions of members of his family.

Free speech: The right to dissent openly from the views of superiors in the organization without fear of reprisal.

Equity: The right to equitable treatment in all matters including the employee compensation scheme, symbolic rewards, and job security.

Due process: Governance by the "rule of law" rather than the rule of men in such matters as equal opportunity in all aspects of the job, privacy, and dissent, including procedures for due process and access to appeals.

7. Work and the Total Life Space

An individual's work experience can have positive or negative effects on other spheres of his life, such as his relations with his family. Prolonged periods of working overtime can have a serious effect on family life. If frequent transfers are required, there are psychological and social costs when families are uprooted from their networks of friends, acquaintances, and local affiliations. The relationship of work to the total life space is best expressed by the concept of balance. The balanced role of work is defined by work schedules, career demands, and travel requirements that do not take up leisure and family time on a regular basis. Likewise balance refers to advancement and promotion that do not require repeated geographical moves.

The application of this criterion is often debatable. When a person invests enormous time and energy in work at the expense of family, it is unclear whether this pattern is a cause or symptom of deficiencies in the family situation. Sometimes the employing organization is imposing demands that seriously affect the employee's ability to perform other life roles, such as spouse or parent. In other cases, however, these demands are largely self-imposed to escape the responsibilities and strains of family roles. If work did not absorb this time and energy, the person would shift his attention to other pursuits outside the family, such as hobbies or civic activities.

8. The Social Relevance of Work Life

The socially beneficial roles of the employing organization and the socially injurious effects of its activities increasingly have become salient issues for employees. Does the worker perceive the organization to be socially responsible in its products, waste disposal, marketing techniques, employment practices, relations to underdeveloped countries, participation in political campaigns, etc.? Organizations which are seen to be acting in a socially irresponsible manner will cause increasing numbers of employees to depreciate the value of their work and careers, which in turn affects worker self-esteem.

Perspectives on the "Quality of Working Life" Criteria

The scheme of eight conceptual categories outlined above invites several types of analyses, including how each quality-of-life attribute is related to the others in practice; how each relates to productivity; how some criteria currently are especially salient for one employee group but not for others; and why there are changes over time.

Interrelationships among Quality of Work Life Criteria

There are complex relationships among the eight conceptual categories. Several pairs tend to be positively correlated; for example, the quality of the immediate work challenge not only affects current job satisfaction but also offsets the tendency toward skill obsolescence. Other pairs contain apparent inconsistencies; for example, heavy emphasis on the rule of law in work organizations may promote impersonality and impede some forms of social integration. The elaborate rules governing job rights, which provide job security and prevent arbitrary treatment by superiors, have limited the flexibility to make work more challenging. The high involvement of employees which results from such job attributes as autonomy, whole task responsibility, and membership in a cohesive face-to-face group occasionally works against a balance between work and other life roles.

The question arises whether there are inherent trade-off relationships among some of these qualities of working life which necessitate a decline in one quality in order to improve another. Perhaps this is not the case, since these relationships are not immutably set. For example it may be that new mechanisms or changes in cultural attitudes can provide constitutionalism without encouraging impersonal relations and rigidity in roles and responsibilities.

Relationship of Criteria to Productivity

How do changes in each of these aspects of working life affect the productivity and long-run effectiveness of the employing organization? General positive or negative correlations between productivity and changes in the quality of a particular dimension of work life cannot be proposed; the relationship depends to some extent upon the particular employee's awareness of deficiencies. Productivity also seems to have a curvilinear relationship to most of the dimensions of work life. Two general criteria are examined below.

Considering the potential levels of productivity for any given class of work and group of employees, there is probably some optimal level of opportunity to use and develop capacities; this opportunity level is created by the autonomy, multiplicity of skills required, work information, and planning responsibility existing in the work situation. It is also recognized that increasing autonomy, multiplicity of skills, etc., does not have a linear effect on the quality of the work experience. Since employee satisfaction and self-esteem are derived from this aspect of work, there is some optimal amount of opportunity to use and develop one's capacities. Figure 1 illustrates these points, showing the quality of work experience continuing to rise with increases in opportunity after the maximum effects on productivity have been realized. The particular slopes of the curves and the relationship between the quality of work life and productivity curves would vary from one work setting to another. Current interest in redesigning work in order to increase the opportunity for employees to utilize and develop their capacities nevertheless indicates a widely held assumption that the employee groups involved are now somewhere to the left of the optimal point on both of these curves.

The curves portraying the direct effects of constitutionalism on productivity and on the quality of work life probably have a relatively small region of coincidence between them as shown in Figure 2. It can be hypothesized that situations characterized by only minimum rights depress productivity as well as quality of working life because of the consequences of insecurity, anxiety, and employee resentment on performance. Beyond some point, however, additional forms and degrees of consti-

FIGURE 1 Effect of Opportunity on the Quality of Work and on Productivity

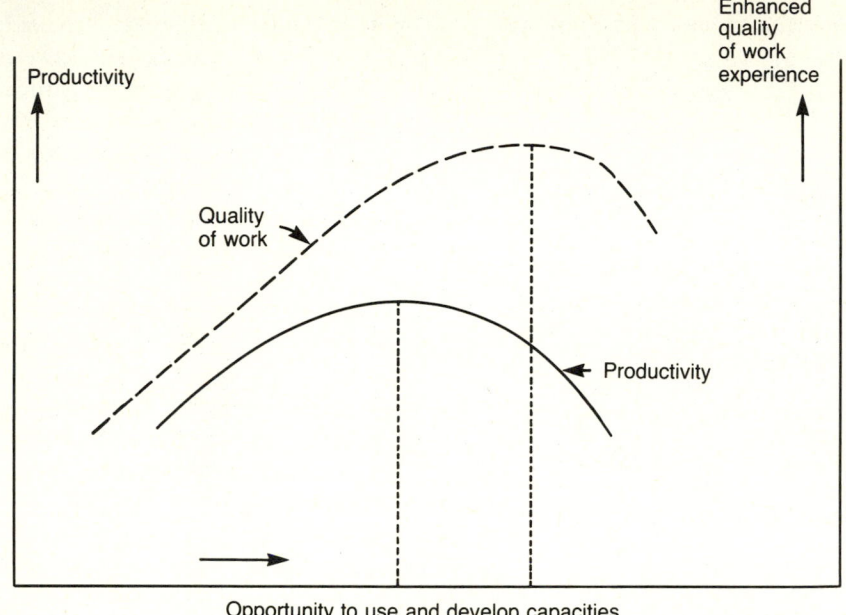

FIGURE 2 Effect of Constitutionalism on the Quality of Work and on Productivity

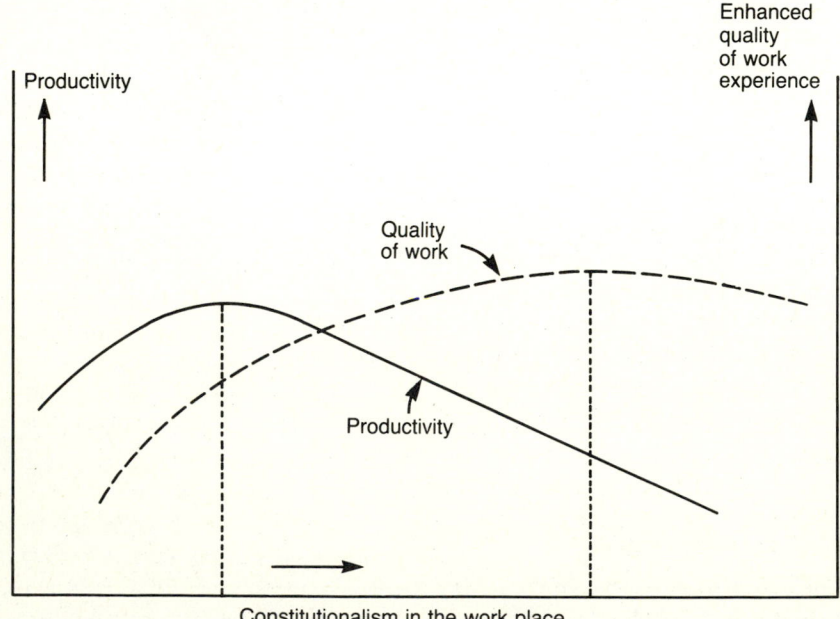

tutionalism continue to improve quality, but at a price to productivity. At a still higher level of constitutionalism, the marginal effect on quality is zero or negligible.

Deficiencies Affecting Different Employee Groups

Currently various employee groups experience different deficiencies in the quality of their work lives. The variety of existing problems is illustrated in the following situations.

Inadequate compensation is a major reason for unrest among agricultural workers and hospital employees.

A priority need has developed to provide blue- and white-collar factory workers with more autonomy, challenge, and satisfying social contact. Improvement along these dimensions of quality of work life requires innovative design in the content of work, sequence of work assignments, job hierarchies, and information and reward systems.

The lack of constitutionalism has suddenly become a recognized deficiency in the quality of work life for a number of groups of nonunionized professional employees. Engineers are laid off according to criteria different from those which they had understood determined their job security. Faculty members despair at the lack of due process in decisions affecting tenure. Primary teachers in nonunion school systems often have no recourse when they are fired for certain activities off the job. Recent growth in unionization among teachers and university professors probably results more from concerns about this aspect of work life than from concerns about the level of compensation.

A number of young doctors and lawyers have recently demanded that their employing organizations adopt policies and practices more responsive to certain acute social problems. Some engineers and scientists express similar opinions, while others become increasingly concerned about technical obsolescence. Even stockbrokers, advertising agency executives, and business managers whose work lives score high on most of the criteria listed make the news by dropping out of the career "rat race" to redress the imbalance which exists between work and other aspects of their lives.

The Diversity of Human Preferences. Regardless of how one approaches the issue of the quality of working life, one must acknowledge the diversity of human preferences—diversity in culture, social class, family rearing, education, and personality. Society is becoming more conscious of the quality of work life at a time when there is a growing heterogeneity in lifestyles in America. Differences in subcultures and lifestyles are accompanied by different definitions of what constitutes a high quality of working life. The young person with a college degree who elects to work as an auto mechanic, a taxi driver, or a mail carrier is saying something significant about his or her preferred pattern of working life. Of two employees equally skilled in performing basic elements of their work, one may prefer autonomy and the other detailed instruction. Similarly one may prefer to be closely integrated into a work team and the other relatively unencumbered by work relations.

How can these differing preferences be accommodated? Diversity within a single work unit may be realized by tailoring individual work assignments to fit individual preferences. Within an organization, diversity can be achieved by organizing work differently from one work unit to the next and allowing employees to select the pattern of work life they prefer. Finally diversity among organizations can be attained if each organization develops a unique and internally consistent pattern of work life while providing persons on the job market with information for choosing an organization that is suitable for them. Employees are thus encouraged to exercise a free and informed choice that takes into account some of the more subtle aspects of the quality of working life.

Forces Altering the Salience of Criteria over Time

Conditions of work are important because the employees involved have certain expectations about them. These conditions take on more meaning by assessing how different employees perceive their organizations along these dimensions. Each person has subjective standards of adequacy.

Why do changes occur in employees' expectations about organizational conditions? There are two different types of change and two corresponding causes for change. First, expectations are steadily changing for many of the quality criteria listed above. The evolving needs and desires reflect some basic, and not readily reversible, trends in American and Canadian societies: the rising level of education; the rising level of wealth and security; the decreased emphasis given by churches, schools, and families to obedience and authority; the decline in achievement motivation; and the shifting emphasis from individualism to social commitment.

Second, a sharp rise in expectations can be observed as a result of some focused stimuli. If change agents or the news media call attention to the plight of a certain group, its members are likely to become more aware of the oppressive conditions, more dissatisfied, and more likely to manifest negative feelings in aggressive behavioral symptoms. Examples of minor improvements then further raise expectations. This scenario of tendencies is illustrated by the blacks' expressions of dissatisfaction in the 1950s and women's discontent late in the 1960s.

Change in the Future

This examination of the causes of change suggests future developments which may occur as attitudes about the quality of working life change. There will be a period of one or two decades during which changes in organizational conditions will occur at a slower pace than that of rising employee expectations. This situation will create a trend toward more employee alienation. At the same time, the positive feedback cycle will occur more frequently, and publicized incidents of aggressively expressed alienation (for example, sit-ins) will raise the consciousness, expectations, and alienation of others. As a result, there will be rashes or epidemics of such incidents in work organizations.

These pessimistic trends are not inevitable. To deal with the problems of change, technologists, managers, union officials, and social scientists must be willing to give high priority to the redesign of work. Through such efforts, the quality of working life can be enhanced, and the expectations of workers on all levels can be understood and satisfied.

Reading 34

PRODUCTIVITY AND THE QUALITY OF WORK LIFE

Edward E. Lawler III and Gerald E. Ledford, Jr.

Quality of work life (QWL) has become a national concern. Until the 1980s, it seemed to be largely the province of a few researchers, companies, and academics. Suddenly the situation has changed. It is virtually impossible to pick up a national publication these days without finding some reference to QWL. Because of this widespread attention, many people have heard of General Motors' success with its QWL program and of some of the exciting new plants that have been built by General Foods, Procter and Gamble, and Cummins Engine.

A key issue in discussions about QWL concerns its relationship to productivity. Much of the current interest stems from the belief that QWL improvements will lead to productivity improvement. Despite the importance of understanding the impact of QWL improvements on productivity, little work has been done on the issue. This article analyzes the relationship between productivity and the quality of work life. It does not argue for a simple relationship between the two, nor does it argue that the two are unrelated. Rather, it argues that, by carefully specifying a number of factors, it is possible to predict what the relationship between productivity and QWL will be. In addition, practical implications for the design of QWL projects are examined and key types of projects are reviewed.

Basic Concepts

A variety of meanings, usages, and measures are attached to the terms "productivity" and "quality of work life." Hence, the first issue to be consid-

ered is their definition and measurement, an issue often not addressed when organizations undertake QWL projects.

Productivity

Productivity is typically defined as a ratio of *outputs* to *inputs*. Outputs are the goods and services produced by an organization. Inputs include labor, capital, materials and supplies, and energy. The most common productivity indicators are really measures of labor productivity. For example, the U.S. Department of Labor's Bureau of Labor Statistics publishes quarterly data on private-sector productivity, defined as the constant-dollar value of all goods and services produced in relation to total labor hours worked.

Managers prefer to think of productivity as a "hard" (i.e., valid, reliable, and quantifiable) measure of organizational performance, unlike "softer" measures of job satisfaction or employee morale. However, there are many problems with measuring inputs, outputs, or both (and thus productivity) in most organizations.

Problems in Measurement. In some organizations, output measures are difficult to obtain or may not be meaningful. This is especially true for government, many parts of the service sector, and the construction industry. For example, what is the proper measure of productivity for a hospital? The number of medical services performed in a given number of labor hours tells little about organizational performance; the quality of medical care (in itself difficult to measure) is much more important. In fact, maximizing the number of medical services administered to each patient would needlessly increase the

Source: Reprinted with permission from *National Productivity Review*, 1, no. 1, (Winter 1981–82). Copyright © 1982, Executive Enterprises, Inc., New York, N.Y.

cost of care and would probably be harmful to patients.

Even in industrial plants, where outputs usually are relatively easy to measure, meaningful productivity data may be difficult to collect. If the plant's output includes many different products, and if the relative contribution of inputs to outputs is different for each product, overall plant productivity may appear to rise or fall dramatically simply because of fluctuations in product mix. This problem arose in a southern bakery sponsoring a QWL project. The bakery made over thirty products, and productivity levels differed for the various products. Yet the company's productivity index did not take product mix into account. A management crisis was precipitated by a sharp drop in the bakery's "productivity," and the QWL project was blamed. However, close inspection of the data by an outside assessment team suggested that productivity had not really changed; instead, a change in product mix and other factors not considered in the company's formula was responsible for the apparent decline in productivity.

Adequate measurement of inputs also is often difficult. Clearly, the best productivity indicators take all major inputs into account. For instance, it is misleading to ignore the contributions of capital and energy inputs to productivity, especially in organizations that are not labor-intensive. However, conventional methods of accounting for capital expenditures are based primarily on financial and tax considerations, and such methods are typically not very useful for developing productivity measures. Methods of accounting for energy and materials are still fairly primitive.

A QWL project in a southern automobile parts plant illustrates the implications of these problems. A rise in labor productivity occurred during the course of the project, and the increase appeared to result largely from a new incentive plan designed by employees. However, the company also made some significant plant and equipment improvements during this period, and these probably also improved labor productivity. While the company had excellent measures of labor productivity, it had no measures of capital productivity. Hence, it was difficult to determine how much of the total increase in labor productivity was due to the QWL program's incentive plan (which led employees to work harder and "smarter"), compared to how much was due to capital improvements (which reduced the amount of labor input needed).

The problems of adequately measuring inputs are compounded if product mix is a factor. Properly allocating the relative contribution of a particular type of input—capital expenditures, for example—to each kind of product may be difficult or impossible.

Implications for QWL projects. For organizations with no productivity measures or misleading ones, it is difficult or impossible to know whether QWL projects (or any other innovations) have affected productivity. Indeed, adequate measures may need to be developed in order to have a successful QWL program. Quality of work life programs are hampered in organizations that lack sound productivity measures. Productivity data is needed as an important source of feedback on the effectiveness of experimental changes. Without this feedback, it is much more difficult to detect, correct, and learn from mistakes. It is also more difficult for a QWL program to focus the energy of people on productivity improvement and to prove itself by showing productivity benefits.

Quality of Work Life

There is wide agreement about the conceptual meaning of productivity; the major difficulties are in applying the concept to measure productivity in specific organizations. Quality of work life is a much newer concept, and there is much less agreement about its basic meaning. The definitions that have been offered so far fall into two broad categories.

The first definition equates QWL with the existence of a *certain set of organizational conditions or practices.* This definition frequently argues that a high quality of work life exists when democratic management practices are used, employees' jobs are enriched, employees are treated with dignity, and safe working conditions exist. The second approach to defining QWL equates it with *the impact of working conditions on employee well-being*. This definition emphasizes the degree to which individuals are accident-free, enjoy good health, express satisfaction, and are able to grow and develop as human beings. In short, it equates a good QWL with the work place in which the full range of human needs are met.

Measurement of QWL. A variety of measures may be used to assess the degree to which either type of QWL exists. Employee questionnaires and interviews are relevant to most aspects of either definition. For example, employees may be asked about the degree to which their jobs are enriched (i.e., the degree to which the jobs provide variety, autonomy, and so on); employees may also be asked about the degree to which they are satisfied with their jobs or find their jobs fulfilling. Other types of data may be relevant for specific purposes. For example, measures of accidents and employee illnesses often are available. There is no single best indicator of QWL, regardless of which definition is used. Rather, a variety of indicators must be pieced together to form a more complete picture of the state of QWL in a given organization.

In many cases, the differences between these two types of definitions are minimal, since working conditions that are equated with a good QWL often produce a positive impact on individuals. Thus, both approaches often lead to a common determination of whether a good QWL exists. There are enough differences among people, however, so that the two definitions can lead to varying conclusions about the relationship between QWL and productivity. Thus, we will first discuss the relationship between productivity and QWL measured as an outcome. Then we will discuss QWL measured as a set of working conditions and its relationship to productivity.

Quality of Work Life as an Outcome

The issue of how individual employee well-being and productivity are related is a traditional one in organizational psychology. Since the 1930s, psychologists have been concerned about the relationship between employee satisfaction and employee performance effectiveness. Rephrasing this idea slightly—that is, does QWL affect productivity?—does not change the basic question. The essential issue still is: Are satisfied employees more productive? The answer to this question seems fairly clear based on the research evidence. Overall, satisfied employees do perform slightly better. How much better depends on a number of factors, including which kind of satisfaction is considered—that is, satisfaction with pay, opportunities to influence decisions, social needs, security, etc. It also seems to depend on such conditions as the structure of the job and the type of pay system.

It is incorrect, however, to assume that the positive relationship between satisfaction and performance comes about because satisfaction causes performance. Satisfaction is not the same as motivation, even though some assume that increased satisfaction means higher motivation. Rather, the relationship seems to come about because performance leads to rewards which, in turn, cause satisfaction. In most settings, the rewards that accrue to a better performer are slightly more positive than are the rewards that accrue to a poor performer; as a result, better performers are more satisfied. Indeed, the same thing also seems to be true of organizations: organizations that perform better tend to accrue more rewards and, as a result, employees are more satisfied. Thus, because of the relationship between performance and rewards, we would expect that those organizations with higher QWL will also tend to be ones in which performance is slightly higher.

There is one other factor that may contribute to a positive relationship between QWL and performance when we look at organizational productivity as our measure of performance. When employees are more satisfied, there is typically less turnover in the organization and, to a degree, less absenteeism. In addition, there is evidence that more satisfied employees are less likely to go on strike, suffer psychosomatic illnesses, etc.—behaviors that tend to increase costs and decrease the effectiveness of the organization. Thus, in an organization where turnover, absenteeism, illness, labor strife, and so on, are reduced, the increased levels of satisfaction or QWL would be responsible for causing better productivity.

Putting the two arguments together, so far, we would expect a significant, but not strong, positive relationship between QWL and productivity in most situations. It would be wrong, however, to conclude that this is a simple, causal relationship in which productivity leads to a higher QWL or vice versa. Rather, we are arguing that the relationship is likely to exist because of multiple forces and, to a degree, is dependent on situational forces. Thus, when QWL is considered as an outcome state, we can make a general statement about its relationship to productivity; yet, for any particular situation we must be cautious in deciding whether QWL improvement will have any impact on productivity.

Implications for the Design of QWL Projects

Most QWL projects established during the last decade have focused on twin outcomes: improving employee quality of work life, and improving productivity and other aspects of organizational effectiveness. An important political reality underlies the twin goals of improved productivity and organizational effectiveness: organizations are unlikely to voluntarily make continual, long-term improvements in QWL if the improvements have no significant payoff to the organization. As a result, QWL project leaders have argued for projects that simultaneously meet both organizational goals and employee QWL goals.

The preceding discussion of the relationship between QWL outcomes and productivity helps explain why several major QWL projects have been abandoned: the projects did not result in increased productivity or other organizational benefits, even though they improved QWL. This is a very possible result, given the complex nature of the relationship between QWL and productivity. A common mistake of QWL projects is to attempt to directly improve employee satisfaction and well-being, while hoping that this will in turn improve organizational

productivity and effectiveness. Specifically, QWL projects are sometimes dominated by attempts to improve various aspects of the physical work environment, such as parking lots, cafeterias, restrooms, time clocks, and other possible sources of employee dissatisfaction.

There are usually two reasons why QWL projects take this direction. First, many managers, union leaders, and employees believe that satisfaction causes productivity (often translated as "a happy worker is a productive worker"); hence, project leaders try to find ways of making employees more satisfied with the work place. Second, it often seems easier to concentrate on creating a more pleasant work environment than on changing management style, job design, the reward system, or patterns of coordination and communication. Suggestions for improving physical working conditions are easy to generate, since making the suggestions requires no special expertise and since problems in the work environment are usually highly visible. Anyone can see the need for a bigger parking lot, for example, but problems in the way work is performed, rewarded, and managed are abstract, complex, and difficult to solve.

Thus, it is usually a mistake for QWL projects to concentrate primarily on improving amenities in the work place. This is not to say that organizations should callously ignore needed improvements in the work environment. On the contrary, improvements in working conditions are desirable ends in themselves; employees should be able to work in as much comfort as possible. The argument here, however, is that QWL programs are unlikely to survive for long if they focus mostly on improving the physical work environment. There are four reasons for this position.

First, as we have seen, the belief that satisfaction causes productivity is too simplistic and is sometimes wrong. Even if improvements in work-place amenities increase QWL, productivity and organizational effectiveness are unlikely to be affected significantly. A slight gain may be expected over the long run because of lower turnover, fewer strikes, and less absenteeism; but, as is often noted, the financial books are "balanced" in the short run.

Second, implementing changes in the work environment often takes longer than managers and employees expect. Major construction projects can take months or even years to be approved, designed, and completed. Delays are common because work environment changes generally have a lower priority than matters more central to organizational survival and effectiveness. In addition, work environment changes often require money approvals and end up making management look cumbersome and unsympathetic. During the long period of time usually needed to complete work environment improvements, employees and managers may come to view the QWL project as a failure because they see no progress.

Third, the costs of work environment improvements often far exceed the productivity benefits. Even if a better work environment does translate into higher productivity and other organizational benefits, the benefits are almost always small. The costs of building a new cafeteria or air-conditioning an old facility, for example, are rarely, if ever, recouped. Managers may come to see QWL as a costly giveaway program with no benefits for the organization, and thus withdraw support for the project.

Fourth, some of the very problems that QWL project leaders try to avoid by concentrating on the work environment and ignoring more complex organizational issues usually come back to haunt attempts to improve the work environment. Especially important are problems in coordination and communication. A major construction project can involve the purchasing, maintenance, and engineering departments, as well as other departments where work may be disrupted by the construction; top local management must approve the expenditure; in large organizations, management and staff above the local level usually must review and approve large expenditures; employees may be consulted about their views on the proposed changes; and there may be one or more outside contractors to deal with over a long period of time. With so many interdependent groups involved, it is not difficult to see how coordination and communication problems can block or delay the work.

There are, however, some conditions in which initially it may be desirable to focus QWL efforts on the work environment rather than on issues more directly related to organizational productivity.

It may be necessary to improve working conditions in order to win credibility for a new QWL program. If the work environment is dangerous or extremely uncomfortable, employees may not trust management's motivation for improving QWL. This was the case in one area of a western wood products plant that was poorly protected from cold winter weather. Employees in the area refused to participate in a new QWL program because every cold working day provided what seemed like evidence of management's lack of concern for their welfare. Fixing this problem could have been a way of giving the QWL program credibility; it was never corrected, however, because of "administrative problems," and the QWL project failed.

Some improvements in the work environment offer the potential for joint benefits to the organization and to employees. Improvements designed to reduce safety or health hazards are a good example. Employees benefit by the reduced health hazards or threats to their safety; employers benefit by the reduced medical and workers' compensation costs, and sometimes by increased productivity as well. In addition, safety and health hazards are more likely than parking lots and restrooms to be widely viewed as important, worthy QWL issues by both managers and employees.

In summary, changes that are directed only at better QWL outcomes, such as improvements in work-place amenities, ought to be pursued as ends in themselves rather than as a means to productivity improvements. Routine management decision making, collective bargaining in unionized settings, and, to some extent, government regulation of working conditions are among the means for directly pursuing QWL outcomes. Major, long-term QWL programs should be concerned with much more than the amenities of the working environment; truly meaningful QWL efforts must directly address both individual and organizational needs. The next section discusses in more detail the ways in which this can be done.

Quality of Work Life as a Process

Perhaps the most interesting question regarding the relationship between productivity and QWL is: What impact does introducing certain QWL practices into an organization have on productivity? Unfortunately, this question is also much more difficult to answer than the question of whether QWL outcomes and productivity are related. The correct answer requires a number of assumptions and varies widely, depending on which QWL intervention is being considered. To illustrate this point, two QWL interventions—*gain-sharing plans* and *employee problem-solving groups*—will be discussed. First, some background on how to think about the relationship between QWL practices and productivity is needed.

Figure 1 shows that there are three primary ways a QWL intervention or practice can improve productivity: it can improve communication/coordination, motivation, and employee performance capabilities. Not shown in the figure, but certainly relevant in determining whether a QWL intervention will improve these factors, are such characteristics as an individual's needs and abilities. Clearly, for motivation to improve, the practice must affect the important needs of the individual; the individ-

ual's level of ability affects both the degree to which individual motivation can be translated into improved performance, and the prospects for improved performance capabilities.

Also not shown in the figure is the important fact that for these three factors to lead to increased productivity, the situation and key technological elements must allow room for people to influence productivity. In certain situations, the intervention may improve motivation, for example, but may not lead to higher productivity if the technology does not allow higher productivity. Overall, however, it is possible to look at a QWL intervention in terms of whether it improves one or more of these three factors and, based on this, then make a reasonable estimate regarding whether the intervention will lead to improved productivity.

Figure 2 carries the thinking about the relationship between QWL interventions and productivity one step further. It shows that if a particular QWL intervention improves productivity directly, it also can influence productivity indirectly.

As Figure 2 shows, the intervention may directly improve employee satisfaction because it provides a better work environment for the individual; it may improve employee satisfaction because it leads to improved productivity which, in turn, leads to

---

FIGURE 1

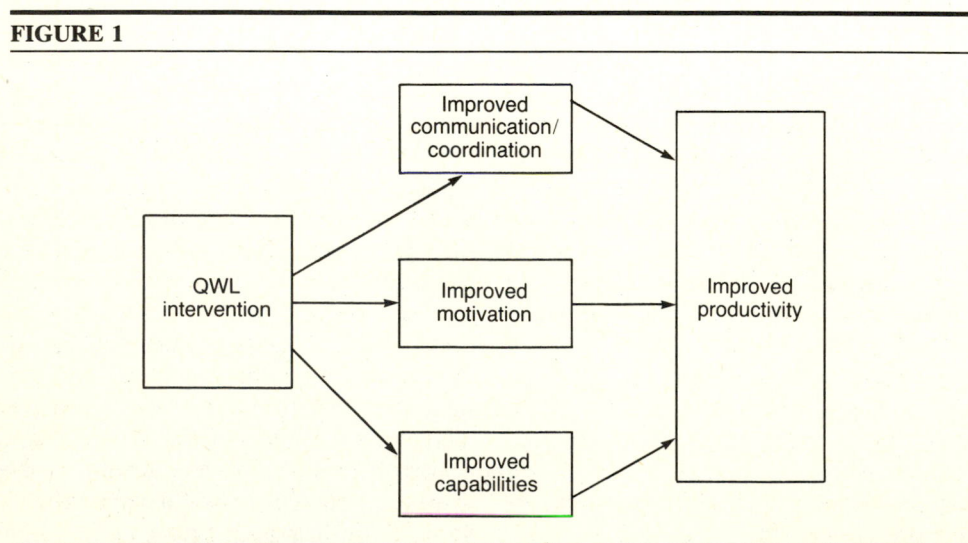

FIGURE 2

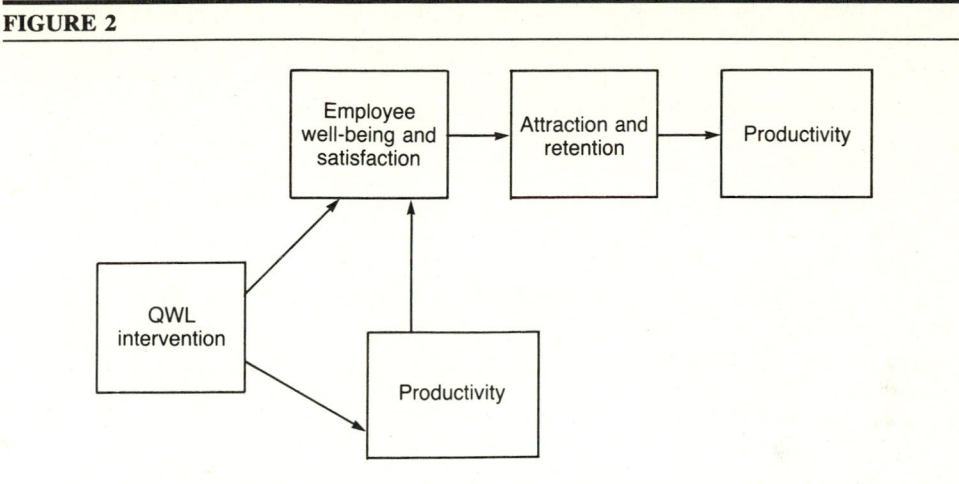

greater rewards. Where employee satisfaction increases, as a result of the intervention and improved productivity, this can ultimately have a positive influence on productivity by attracting good employees to work for the organization (attraction) and by reducing turnover (retention).

Overall, the argument here is that there are a number of ways that a QWL intervention can have a positive effect on productivity. However, improving productivity is dependent on the degree to which the intervention increases employee satisfaction, communication, motivation, and performance capability. Indeed, there is reason to believe that the intervention may have to influence motivation, communication, and capability in order to lead to improved productivity. This rationale is based on the view that for productivity to increase, motivation, performance capability, and coordination all need to be high in an organization. If any one of these is low or missing, the organization cannot be effective. However, since each one usually exists to some degree when the intervention is made, improvement in any one of them may lead to some improvement in productivity.

Gain-Sharing Plans

When fully and properly implemented, gain-sharing plans, like the Scanlon Plan, should lead to im-

proved productivity and also to employee well-being and satisfaction. The rationale for this is rather straightforward. Gain-sharing plans include organizational structures to improve communication and coordination; they relate pay to performance, therefore improving motivation; and, in most cases, they include a training component that improves performance capability.

There are three basic characteristics of the Scanlon Plan. First, a philosophy of management is developed. The philosophy stresses the importance of cooperation (including cooperation with the union in unionized settings), teamwork, open sharing of information between employees and management, management leadership, and employee participation in decision making. Second, a bonus formula is developed. A historical baseline is established for the level of labor productivity in the organization; sometimes, similar baselines are established for other forms of productivity as well, such as material and supply usage in relation to total output. Any improvement in productivity is reflected in cost savings, which go into a pool. After reserving a specified percentage of the pool (e.g., for months in which productivity may drop), the pool is divided between the company and employees each month. All employees (including managers) receive the same percentage of their wages as a monthly bonus for productivity levels above the baseline. The relevance of productivity measurement to this feature should be obvious: organizations that cannot accurately measure productivity cannot use the Scanlon Plan or any other gain-sharing plan based on organizational productivity.

The third feature of the Scanlon Plan is a set of structures for participation. Employees are urged to continually submit suggestions for productivity improvement to a committee in their department or area. The committee includes representatives of management, employees, and in organized settings, the union. When possible, this committee implements worthwhile suggestions. More complicated proposals are passed on to an organizationwide committee (which again represents all parties). The organizationwide committee monitors the plan and develops policies.

In the Scanlon Plan, productivity improvements are passed on to the employee; thus, the plan indirectly leads to employee well-being and satisfaction, which in turn leads to attraction and retention. In addition, work-place changes that lead to more comfortable and safer working conditions are often made. Thus, the prediction is that the Scanlon Plan should increase both employee well-being and productivity. Indeed, our research and that of others generally supports this prediction.

Two reviews of the published Scanlon Plan cases have concluded that it has about an 80 percent success rate in improving productivity. This estimate is undoubtedly high since many failures go unreported. Nevertheless, in our own installations, we have found well above a 50 percent success rate. Interestingly the plan seems to be particularly successful in already participative plants. The climate here is right and, as a result, the plans are easily installed and accepted. It seems to be most difficult to install plans in unionized settings and in service organizations. Some unions oppose them; in other cases, it is difficult to devise plans consistent with collective bargaining agreements. In service organizations the needed measures often are not present. Not surprisingly, gain-sharing plans typically have been installed only in manufacturing plants.

No discussion of gain-sharing is complete without noting that several companies have had gain-sharing plans for decades. Herman Miller, Lincoln Electric, and Donnelly Mirrors all attribute part of their considerable success to a long-term commitment to gain sharing. Each had a dominant position in its field and excellent records of year-to-year productivity improvement.

One important caveat: there are a number of situational factors that can limit the degree to which the Scanlon Plan can improve motivation and, therefore, productivity. Specifically, organization size, labor-management trust levels, managerial attitudes toward the plan, an inadequate basic pay system, and so on, can affect the degree to which people see pay as tied to performance (and, therefore, the degree to which the plan affects their motivation). In addition, there are situational factors that may lead to stronger employee motivation without enough productivity improvement to generate a bonus. A shrinking market for the organization's product and poor management are typical of such factors.

Employee Problem-Solving Groups

There are several kinds of employee problem-solving groups, including union-management QWL committees and quality control (QC) circles. The discussion here will focus on the design issues of union-management QWL committees. Similar design issues are relevant to other types of employee problem-solving groups.

Typically, a hierarchy of committees is created in the organization, parallel to the management and union hierarchies. In large organizations, a *national level* union-management committee is created to set overall QWL policy, create and support site level committees, and help solve problems that local committees do not have the authority to solve. A *site level* steering committee (for a plant or equivalent organizational unit) is created to set local QWL policies, develop specific interventions affecting the site as a whole, and manage the QWL effort. Finally, *department or work team* committees are established to develop changes in particular areas of the site and to suggest plantwide changes to the site level committee.

If properly designed, a hierarchy of union-management QWL committees can be a powerful vehicle for developing organizational changes. Such a committee structure is capable of generating a great deal of employee participation in designing specific changes that benefit employees, the organization, and the union. A great advantage of such QWL committees is that they link the activities of employee QWL groups with the centers of decision-making power in the organization and the union. This also is true of the Scanlon Plan committee structure, which is very similar to the QWL committee structure.

However, many QWL committees not only fail to reach their potential, they fail to survive longer than a few years. Our research suggests that QWL committees that experience difficulties usually have been poorly designed from the outset. We have identified several key issues in the design of union-management QWL committees.

First, properly determining the number of layers of committees and their location in the management and union hierarchies is a critical factor. Too many levels in the committee structure lead to a paralysis of decision making, while too few may overburden each committee and exclude important centers of decision-making power from the QWL process. Committees that are located at the wrong hierarchical level may have no real authority to make decisions, or may be too far away from day-to-day problems to be helpful.

A second and equally critical issue involves membership on the committees. Committees that are too large cannot function effectively. Optimally, no committee should have more than ten members; committees of more than fifteen members rarely function well. QWL committees also cannot function effectively unless at least some active members have decision-making powers. Hence, the committees should always include management and union representatives appropriate to the level of the committee (e.g., top local managers

and members of the local union bargaining committee should sit on the site level committee). The site and work team committees should also include representatives of as many major segments of the work force (race, sex, union-nonunion, age, and other groups) as possible. However, committees should not become too large or exclude important decision makers simply to become more representative of the work force.

There are other important issues, as well, in designing QWL committees. Committees frequently need various kinds of *training,* such as in group-process and problem-solving skills as well as in specific topics related to the desired changes. *Consulting assistance* is often needed to help union and management learn to work together, to conduct training, and to help with specific interventions. The *relationship between the QWL committees and other important groups* must evolve over time if the committee system is to continue receiving the support of management, the union, and others.

Finally, it is important that QWL committees develop a *clear set of objectives and goals,* as well as some *clear guidelines about what types of topics* they can deal with. Many committees get in trouble because they talk about contractual issues or because they fail to focus on productivity improvements.

Designing union-management QWL committees is a delicate and arduous task. The entire QWL project can be inadvertently sabotaged before it really begins if design errors are built into the committee structure. Moreover, initial errors often are not correctable, even if the mistakes are discovered early in the project's history. It is difficult, for example, to eliminate unnecessary or inappropriately constituted committees; committee members fight to preserve their group, even if objectively the group is ineffective or worse. The pitfalls in creating effective QWL committees make it imperative that the groups be carefully designed from the outset. Properly designing committees is often a slow process—it may take months. In addition, external consulting help from those experienced in QWL committee design and start-up may be crucial if no one inside the organization has the skills and experience needed to avoid basic mistakes.

Union-Management QWL Committees and Productivity

A union-management QWL committee structure by itself does nothing to improve productivity. Indeed, it may harm productivity because it takes time away from production. As indicated, productivity increases can be expected only if the committees adopt or cause the organization to adopt organizational changes that improve communication and coordination, motivation, or performance capabilities. What kinds of organizational changes can affect these factors? Various union-management QWL committees have considered a vast number of potentially powerful changes. Some of the more prominent include the following.

1. A *Scanlon Plan* can be adopted through the QWL committee structure. As indicated above, the Scanlon Plan can positively affect all three determinants of productivity.

2. Other *incentive systems* can increase motivation, and group-based incentives can increase communication and coordination. One innovative incentive plan was adopted in a QWL project in the southern auto parts factory mentioned earlier, and was later emulated by other QWL projects. The productivity incentive was for time off rather than money. In areas of the plant where plans were feasible, employee groups adopted their own variation of the time-off bonus. Some employees earned two hours or more in time off per day primarily by working extremely hard during their hours on the job.

3. *Other changes in the reward system,* including changes in performance appraisal, promotion, and employee recognition processes, can increase motivation by linking performance to valued rewards.

4. There are many kinds of *job design changes,* ranging from simple job rotation to individual job enrichment to team-based plans such as autonomous work groups. All these changes can improve employee performance capabilities; all except job rotation may increase the intrinsic motivation of

the work; and team-based approaches also can include provisions for improved communication and coordination.

5. *Open information sharing* is a common QWL strategy for improving communication about organizational performance.

6. *Skills training* can obviously improve individual performance capabilities, and it is frequently adopted through the committee structure.

7. *Participative decision making* is not only the process by which other changes may be implemented through the QWL committee structure—it can also become a broader management style. Participation often leads directly to increased motivation to implement decisions as well as to communication.

The changes listed here are some of the more common ones adopted through union-management QWL committees. The types of changes attempted in any particular organization are limited only by employee and management knowledge, experience, and imagination.

Case Studies

Some data are available to help us determine whether QWL processes are associated with higher productivity. The authors of this article, together with Stanley E. Seashore and Cortlandt Cammann of the University of Michigan's Institute for Social Research (ISR), are currently engaged in a study reviewing eight major union-management QWL projects conducted during the 1970s. The eight projects were intensively studied over a period of at least three years by independent assessment teams associated with the Institute for Social Research's Quality of Work Life Program. (The review study, funded by the U.S. Department of Labor, will be published by Wiley-Interscience as part of the Wiley-Interscience Series on Organizational Assessment and Change.)

Table 1 summarizes several aspects of the eight projects that are relevant to understanding the relationship between QWL processes and productivity. First, the table indicates whether productivity data from the organization were analyzed by the

TABLE 1 Productivity Effects of QWL Processes

Type of Organization	Was Productivity Data Analyzed?	Some Productivity-related Changes Attempted in Project	Productivity Outcomes
1. Coal mine	Yes	Autonomous work groups; job training; supervisor training; pay changes; intershift communication	Slight but statistically nonsignificant increase
2. Auto parts factory	Yes	Time-off bonus incentives; training; union-management cost reduction to retain business; safety program; plant newsletter	Significant positive increase
3. Wood products plants	No	Survey feedback and other communication activities	(No data available, but probably no change)
4. Bakery	Yes	Survey feedback; newsletter; new equipment; job training; interdepartmental coordination	No significant change
5. Federal utility co. (engineering div.)	No	Merit pay; performance appraisal; four-day workweek; survey feedback; other communication activities	?
6. Hospital	No	Survey feedback; staff meetings and training; management development; attempts to increase interdepartmental coordination	?
7. Municipal transit system	No	Survey feedback; management development; work team system; communication efforts	?
8. Municipal government	No	Better equipment; increased communication	?

independent assessment team. The general pattern is that productivity data were available for the industrial organizations, but that no data were available for the four organizations in government and service sectors. The only exception is the wood products plants project. In this case, data were available but were not analyzed because the project was terminated before the QWL project had an opportunity to affect productivity. The overall availability pattern of productivity data for assessment purposes is consistent with our earlier discussion of productivity measurement problems. The difficulties with outcome measurement in government and service organizations means that productivity data often are simply unavailable. We should note, however, that indirect evidence (e.g., duration of the project, attitude measures, and so on) suggests that productivity probably did not significantly improve in the service and government organizations.

The table also provides examples of productivity-related changes attempted in each project. These examples indicate a wide variety of changes attempted within particular organizations and across all eight sites. This reflects a basic tendency toward diversity in organizational change efforts using employee problem-solving groups. Involving many different employees, managers, and union leaders in the change effort encourages a "shotgun" approach as different individuals and groups pursue changes of interest to them.

Such an approach differs from the single-intervention "rifle" approach common in top-down, management-directed change efforts. The shotgun approach has both strengths and weaknesses. Since organizational problems are complex and interrelated, a variety of more or less simultaneous changes is usually needed to deal adequately with the problems. Thus, multifaceted interventions are more effective than single interventions in some circumstances. However, the shotgun approach can also be the sign of a poorly managed change process. Decision-making groups may be unable to devote enough attention to any one change, and the lack of consensus about overall strategy may lead to interventions that work at cross-purposes. For example, the popularity of survey feedback in most cases had nothing to do with a well-conceived strategy for using the data. Rather, QWL committees tended to invest a large amount of energy in survey feedback primarily because the data were made available to them by the independent assessment teams, and survey feedback "seemed like a good idea."

The column on productivity-related changes attempted is incomplete in two respects. First, there is no indication of how successfully the changes were implemented. Most projects experienced difficulty in implementing, supporting, and sustaining productivity-related changes. In general, the more complex (and powerful) the change, the less likely it was to be well implemented. For example, gain-sharing plans and job redesign are complex, and probably require specialized outside consulting skill and experience during implementation. Each of these changes was seriously considered or attempted by at least four of the eight organizations. Only in the case of the coal mine was a job redesign

intervention implemented, largely through the efforts of consultants with a great deal of experience in sociotechnical systems. Even in the coal mine, however, the job redesign effort was not sustained in the long run. Despite discussion and, in several cases, agreement that they should do it, none of the sites installed gain sharing.

A second way in which the column on changes attempted is incomplete is that it does not list attempts to improve work-place amenities. Except for the coal mine experiment, all the QWL projects devoted at least some attention to improving workplace amenities. Indeed, several projects were far more oriented toward creating a more pleasant work environment than anything else. As noted earlier, it is generally a mistake for QWL projects to become excessively absorbed in such issues.

The final column in Table 1 concerns productivity outcomes. It is apparent that the productivity outcomes of the eight projects are unimpressive. There was a significant increase in productivity in only one case—the auto parts factory. The factory's change in the reward system—namely, the time-off bonus plan—was clearly the QWL project's most important contribution to productivity. Before the intervention, employees received no reward for reaching the daily production standard. When 90 percent of the hourly work force began earning time off for meeting production standards early, productivity levels increased sharply. There was a slight, but statistically nonsignificant, increase in productivity in the coal mine. It is difficult to separate the effects of each aspect of the intervention, but job skills training and the autonomous work group were probably most important. It is worth pointing out that after the intervention, the miners still had no incentive for improved productivity.

No change in productivity took place in the bakery, even though one intervention permitted much better communication and cooperation between different departments. Interdepartmental conflict had been a barrier to improving productivity at the bakery, so it was logical to assume that the intervention might have a positive effect. In this case, however, the experimental change was carried out on only one of seven lines in the bakery, and the target line was by far the most automated of the seven. The degree of automation was such that the need for improved communication and coordination was low on the line. Hence, the same intervention might have led to improvements in the productivity if it had been used on other lines where the need for communication and coordination was greater. Unfortunately, the experiment did not spread to other lines until after the termination of the independent assessment activities, so this possibility was not tested. The example does, however, illustrate the importance of situational determinants of productivity.

In the eight case studies, union-management QWL committees were generally not associated with productivity improvements. However, these were pioneering projects and thus could be expected to make mistakes. Some more recent union-management QWL committees seem to be doing better. The newer projects tend to be much better linked to the management and union hierarchies, receive better assistance from a widening circle of experienced consultants, have more realistic goals, and use more sharply focused organizational change strategies.

Summary and Implications

Does productivity improvement result from an improved quality of work life? Clearly this question does not lend itself to a simple yes or no answer. Indeed, the analysis presented here suggests that a good place to start may be with definitions of QWL and productivity. If inadequate measures of productivity exist, their development should receive a high priority. The data suggest that those who start a QWL program with an eye toward productivity should be very careful to determine whether a particular program being installed is targeted toward factors that will improve productivity. They should be careful to determine that there are not individual factors or situational factors that would block the intervention from producing the processes in the organization which will in turn improve productivity. In many cases, this type of analysis is not done and, as a result, productivity improvement programs relying on QWL interventions fail to produce the desired results. This is not so much a failure of the QWL intervention as it is a failure of people to understand the relationship between QWL improvement and productivity improvement.

The role of employee problem-solving groups also requires examination: it is not practical to make an overall prediction regarding their impact on productivity. More information is needed before a specific prediction can be made. Generally, employee problem-solving groups can have a positive impact if they install practices and policies that are likely to influence the major determinants of productivity—skills, motivation, and communication and coordination. If the groups fail to accomplish this, then their mere existence will not lead to productivity improvement.

B. Sociotechnical Systems and Work Redesign

The differences between QWL projects and sociotechnical systems projects are sometimes indistinct. While QWL projects may sometimes address a broader range of variables and may not necessarily stress productivity issues, in practice the two approaches may frequently be almost identical.

SOCIOTECHNICAL SYSTEMS

The concept of "sociotechnical systems" has largely been associated with studies and consulting work done under the auspices of the Tavistock Institute in England. The essence of the emerging interventions is to try to develop a better fit between the technology, structure, and social interaction of the workplace so as to enhance desired organizational outcomes. One of the earliest Tavistock studies, in British coal mining, found that broadening job scope and reintroducing a team approach to coal production, supplemented by team pay incentives, significantly improved productivity, morale, and safety.[1] Another Tavistock project, this one in an Indian weaving mill, took the same direction in terms of task broadening and the creation of semiautonomous work groups, with salutary results.[2] To the extent that there was a focus on work groups and that workers were involved in restructuring their jobs, there are some parallels in these experiments to contemporary OD.

In later experiments in Norway and Sweden, the creation of relatively autonomous work groups, which produced the final product, coupled with some other conditions

---

[1]E. L. Trist, G. W. Higgin, H. Murray, and A. B. Pollock, *Organizational Choice* (London: Tavistock, 1965). See also Eric Trist, *The Evolution of Socio-Technical Systems,* Ontario Quality of Working Life Centre, occasional paper no. 2, June 1981.

[2]A. K. Rice, "Productivity and Social Organization in an Indian Weaving Shed: An Examination of Some Aspects of the Sociotechnical System of an Experimental Automatic Loom Shed," *Human Relations* 6 (1953), pp. 297–329.

resulted in more job satisfaction and higher productivity and earnings. As in other studies, it is important to note that several variables were altered, including training, procedures for the allocation of workers as production demands varied, and the role of the supervisor, who became more of a "boundary manager" than a coordinator of internal activities.[3]

A sociotechnical experiment at the Rushton Coal Mine clearly had a number of OD characteristics. This experiment featured an extensive preliminary collaborative diagnosis of organizational problems and frequent participative rediagnoses of the state of the system with the help of a consultant team.[4]

The essay on sociotechnical systems included here, by Thomas Cummings, is of particular interest because it focuses on the aspect of self-regulating groups and the conditions necessary for their introduction and continued effectiveness. The essay goes further, however, and gives us some of the history and underlying theory of self-managing or self-regulating groups.

JOB ENRICHMENT AND WORK REDESIGN

While the Tavistock sociotechnical and other autonomous work-group experiments have had a large job enrichment component, job enrichment programs per se tend to focus more on the design of each individual's job and are not necessarily aimed at enhancing a team approach to production. Basically, job enrichment aims at increasing the planning and controlling aspects of a job.[5] Some applications, however, such as those at Texas Instruments, do have a team thrust to them. For example, Myers has described programs at TI in which work teams decide who will perform the various tasks and frequently allocate the work so that each member of the team will have a mixture of challenging tasks along with the more repetitive ones. As another example, some job enrichment programs at AT&T have included a "job nesting" concept designed to enhance teamwork.[6]

Implicit in the above paragraph is that one form of job enrichment may be quite different from another. Four dimensions in particular, we see as differentiating job enrichment efforts: (1) the extent to which a thorough and participative organizational diagnosis preceeds the application of a job enrichment effort; (2) the degree to which the job enrichment program is aimed at enhancing team efforts (discussed above); (3) the degree of employee participation in implementing the job enrichment process, i.e., in the restructuring of jobs; and (4) the degree to which attention is paid to impinging systems, for example, compensation schemes and leadership style. We believe these dimensions to be both very important in successful job enrichment efforts and to be dimensions of potential congruency-incongruency with OD.

---

[3]Doc E. Thorsrud, "Sociotechnical Approach to Job Design and Organization Development," *Management International Review* 8, no. 4–5 (1968), pp. 120–31.

[4]Ted Mills, "Altering the Social Structure in Coal Mining: A Case Study," *Monthly Labor Review* October 1976, pp. 3–10.

[5]See M. Scott Myers, *Every Employee a Manager* (New York: McGraw-Hill, 1970).

[6]Robert N. Ford, "Job Enrichment Lessons from AT&T," *Harvard Business Review,* January–February 1973, pp. 96–106.

To illustrate, the Scott Myers TI approach has a strong participative component, particularly through worker and supervisor involvement in diagnosing the meaningfulness of jobs. Further, in a publication not reproduced here, Myers outlines the use of a "problem-solving, goal-setting approach" at TI in which a problem involving a customer is presented to a factory work group. Members of the group then analyze the problem, make suggestions for solution, participate in deciding what changes to make, establish new goals, and implement the changes on the job. Frequently, such factory groups invite in specialists such as industrial or mechanical engineers to help them.[7] This approach is very similar to the quality circle approach described in Section D below.

In contrast, Frederick Herzberg and his colleagues seem to deemphasize or downgrade the utility of employee participation in job enrichment programs. In one essay, for example, Herzberg and colleagues were clearly doubtful about the merits of participation. They stated:

> It seems that employees themselves are not in a good position to test out the validity of the boundaries of their jobs. So long as the aim is not to measure experimentally the effects of job enrichment alone, there is undoubtedly benefit in the sharing of ideas. Our experience merely suggests that it would be unwise to pin too many hopes to it—or to the wrong hopes.[8]

Who is right? Clearly the dimensions of participation and work design and the extent to which a team approach is used are important dimensions needing further conceptualization, research and experimentation.

In his essay included here, Randall Dunham provides us with some more of the history of different approaches to the design of jobs. In particular, he focuses on the core job theory used by Hackman and Oldham, who in recent works are paying particular attention to group aspects in the design of work.[9]

---

[7]Myers, *Every Employee a Manager,* pp. 81–87.

[8]William S. Paul, Jr., Keith B. Robertson, and Frederick Herzberg, "Job Enrichment Pays Off," *Harvard Business Review,* March–April 1969, p. 75.

[9]See J. Richard Hackman and Greg R. Oldham, *Work Redesign* (Reading, Mass.: Addison-Wesley Publishing, 1980), pp. 161–90.

Reading 35

SELF-REGULATING WORK GROUPS:
A SOCIO-TECHNICAL SYNTHESIS

Thomas G. Cummings

Since its conception about 25 years ago at the Tavistock Institute of Human Relations in London, England, socio-technical systems theory has emerged as a significant approach for designing organizations, especially at the people and technology interface (27, 28). This body of theoretical and empirical work seeks to improve productivity and human enrichment through a design process that focuses on the interdependencies between and among people, technology, and environment. A concrete outcome of this theoretical perspective is development of self-regulating work groups. Variously referred to as "autonomous" (12, 13, 17, 26), or "composite" (28), or "self-managing" (14) work groups, these work designs generally include: a relatively whole task; members who each possess a variety of skills relevant to the group task; worker discretion over such decisions as methods of work, task schedules, and assignment of members to different tasks; and compensation and feedback about performance for the group as a whole (14). These attributes are intended to provide the work group with the task boundary, autonomy, and feedback necessary to control variances from goal achievement within the unit rather than external to it. This self-regulating capacity is hypothesized to lead to greater productivity and worker satisfaction.

Existing evidence suggests that self-regulating work groups are productive and satisfying (7). Current knowledge about such applications is limited primarily to their overall effects, with relatively little practical understanding of how self-regulating groups operate or how they are implemented. This

Source: Thomas G. Cummings, *Academy of Management Review* 3, no. 3 (July 1978), pp. 625–34.

lack of comprehension frequently leads organizations to apply self-regulating designs inappropriately, resulting in confusion and other unintended consequences. Moreover, the literature in this area is somewhat fragmented, making it difficult to develop a coherent theory of self-regulating groups or to conduct research in a cumulative manner.

This article outlines the theory behind self-regulating work groups, their implementation strategy, and the kind of supervision appropriate to their management. Such knowledge is needed if self-regulating designs are to emerge from loose metaphors for worker autonomy to scientifically-sound and practical operational strategies for work design.

Theory of Self-Regulating Groups

Socio-Technical Design

Self-regulating work groups are a direct outgrowth of socio-technical systems theory and design. Briefly, this perspective views production systems as comprised of both technological and social parts. The former consists of the equipment and methods of operations used to transform raw materials into products or services; the latter includes the work structure that relates people to the technology and to each other. A traditional division-of-labor work design, for example, relates workers to limited and highly-prescribed parts of the production process and to a narrow set of physically-proximate employees performing similar jobs. The concept of a socio-technical system arises from the consideration that any production system requires both a technology and a work structure (22). Since the work structure ties people to the technology, its design has a major impact on both of these substantive dimensions of work.

Based on this simple, yet often neglected premise, socio-technical experimenters attempt to design work structures so that a "best match" is obtained between employees and technology (12). This may involve changes in the technology (i.e., equipment and process layout), the work structure (i.e., work roles and their interrelationships), or both. The primary aim is to design a work structure that is responsive to the task requirements of the technology and the social and psychological needs of employees: a structure that is both productive and humanly satisfying. A division-of-labor work design, for instance, may well meet the task demands of a mechanized assembly-line and the needs of individuals who prefer direction and social isolation; yet, it is questionable whether this work structure would satisfy the task requirements of a research team or the needs of employees who desire autonomy and social interaction.

Beyond matching the social and technical dimensions of work, socio-technical systems must also relate effectively to their task environment—those external elements that are relevant to the setting and achievement of system goals (9). For many work systems, such as lower-level production units, the task environment consists primarily of other organizational units internal to the total organization. Conversely, other work systems, such as higher-level staff groups, engage a task environment that is predominately external to the organization.

Given this system and environment interdependence, socio-technical designers attempt to structure work systems so that they can meet environmental demands while remaining relatively resilient to external disruptions. This may involve changes in the system or the task environment. A work group may be given discretion to alter its production methods to account for changes in the quality of its raw materials; similarly, it may pressure the purchasing department to tighten the quality standards for raw materials inventory. The essential design issue is to match the work system to its task environment.

Unit of Design and Locus of Control

Self-regulating work groups are an attempt to design effective relationships between the social and technical components of work systems and between the systems and their task environments. Although such designs have been employed in a variety of work settings, at least two issues underlie their use: the relevant unit of design (i.e., groups versus individual jobs) and the locus of control (i.e., internal versus external to the system).

Socio-technical designers typically use the work group rather than the individual job as the basic building block of work design. The tendency is to group employees who perform interdependent tasks into a common work unit that is relatively differentiated from other units. This grouping appears necessary when the technology is such that interdependence among workers is essential (14). Referred to as "technically required cooperation" (20), this dimension is present in production systems where workers must share, in addition to time, the same equipment or materials to achieve a productive outcome. Examples of this include: oil refineries, where employees are responsible for materials flowing through the plant; coal mines, where workers are sequentially dependent on the output of previous employees; and hospitals, where a combination of techniques are applied concurrently to the same material. Under these conditions, group designs that account for necessary task interdependencies seem more appropriate than individual job designs. The obverse appears to hold in those situations where technically required cooperation is low (e.g., key punching, telephone installation, and field sales).

An underlying objective in designing any work system is to reduce variance from goal attainment (5). This involves a choice between two fundamental forms of system control: elaborating external mechanisms of control (i.e., hierarchical supervision, scheduling, and standardization) or increasing the internal control of members of the system (i.e., giving employees the autonomy needed for self-regulation (11). Socio-technical designers tend to structure work so that variance is controlled within the work system rather than external to it. This seems necessary when external control mechanisms are unable to reduce the uncertainty facing work systems. Specifically, two major sources of uncertainty affect goal achievement: those concerned with transactions across the system's boundary (e.g., scheduling input and output exchanges with the task environment) and those involved with the conversion of raw materials into finished output (e.g., operating production technology) (26). Boundary-transaction uncertainty is likely to be high when the work system's task environment is relatively complex and changing. Since the parts of the environment are richly interconnected and fused with a change gradient, it is difficult to know what, where, and when inputs and outputs will enter or leave the work system (e.g., the number and characteristics of students enrolling in a particular university course may be difficult to predict and control). Similarly, conversion uncertainty is likely to be high when there is incomplete technical knowledge about how to produce a desired outcome (e.g., surgery, psychotherapy, education, etc.). When either boundary-transaction or conversion uncertainty is high, external controllers, such as supervisors and technical staff, find it difficult to program the flow of inputs and outputs or the conversion activities of the work system. Rather, these regulatory functions are more effectively performed by those employees who are closer to the sources of uncertainty.

Conditions for Self-Regulation

The design of self-regulating work groups depends on at least three conditions that enhance technically required cooperation and employees' capacity to control variance from goal attainment: task differentiation, boundary control, and task control (6). Task differentiation refers to the extent to which the group's task is itself autonomous forming a self-completing whole. The more autonomous the group's task, the more differentiated its task boundary from other organizational units. This task discontinuity facilitates technically required cooperation by bounding interdependent tasks into

a common unit and aids variance control by increasing the likelihood that technical variances will be contained within the work group's boundaries rather than exported across them (21). For example, an assembly line may be divided into relatively differentiated task groups through expedient placement of buffer stocks and inventories; this may in turn help to restrict technical variances to discrete segments of the line. The opportunity to form whole task groups may be limited by such technological constraints as equipment size and location and length of the production cycle.

Boundary control involves the extent to which employees can influence transactions with their task environment (e.g., the types and rate of inputs and outputs). The major factors contributing to boundary control include: a well-defined work area which individuals can identify as their own territory (22); competent members who possess an adequate repertoire of skills which frees them from having to rely on external resources of task performance (18); and group responsibility for boundary control decisions (e.g., quality assurance) which reduces dependence on external boundary regulators (e.g., inspectors). The combination of these characteristics helps group members protect their work boundaries from external intrusions and perform selective environmental transactions.

Task control refers to the extent to which employees can regulate their behavior to convert raw materials into finished products. This factor is enhanced when group members are given: freedom to choose work methods and to adjust work activities to match task and environmental demands (17); influence over production goals allowing employees to modify their output as emergent situations are encountered, such as unpredictable breakdowns and stressful working periods (10); and feedback of relevant measures of group performance which provides the knowledge of results necessary for goal directed behavior (10, 17).

The above mentioned conditions—task differentiation, boundary control, and task control—relate directly to a group's capacity for self-regulation. Since the extent to which these conditions must be met to consider a group self-regulating is currently unknown, they are probably most useful in determining the relevance of particular organizational variables for self-regulation. This is a pertinent point, for many attempts to implement self-regulating groups have involved a number of organizational changes (7). Given this variety of potentially relevant organizational variables, it is important to know which factors are necessary for self-regulation and which are redundant or extraneous. The conditions discussed here can serve as a guide for identifying relevant changes and for understanding them conceptually.

Conceptual clarity concerning the interrelationship of self-regulating conditions is especially needed. Task differentiation and boundary control probably are related curvilinearly. Groups that score low on the task dimension may have such highly diffuse task boundaries that members are unable to differentiate themselves clearly from other organizational units, making boundary control difficult, if not impossible. Conversely, groups that score high on the task variable may have such highly differentiated task boundaries that mutual relations with external units are severely restricted (1). This may impede environmental exchanges required for task performance (e.g., the attainment of needed raw materials). One would expect a similar relationship between task differentiation and task control. Highly diffuse task boundaries may make it so difficult to separate the group's task from the task of related units that members are unable to control task-related variables, such as production scheduling. Highly differentiated task boundaries may lead to such high group cohesion that members reduce their openness to task-related inputs, such as performance feedback and managerial support. Such rigidity may also cause external others, such as management, to retaliate by withholding resources, information, or freedom needed for task control. The final relationship, between boundary control and task control, is likely to be positive. The more members influence transactions with their task environment, the more they regulate their behavior toward task achievement. Presumably, increased boundary control enhances members' ability

to engage with external units, including management, to obtain relevant feedback and freedom to control task variables. This depends on whether such attempts at environmental influence are perceived and acted upon positively by external others. If boundary control is experienced positively by external others, it is likely to improve task control; otherwise, it may thwart it.

The above discussion suggests possible relationships among the self-regulating conditions. Further study is needed to clarify these interactions. Specific information about the shape, direction, and strength of the relationships would provide a more accurate account of how the different properties of self-regulating groups affect each other systemically. Moreover, research into this issue would likely uncover a variety of other variables that moderate these relationships, such as group size, organization climate, and type of technology. Such knowledge is a necessary step toward explaining the conditions needed for self-regulation and how these operate in organizational settings.

While the previous discussion was aimed at how self-regulating groups promote required cooperation and employees' competence to respond to technical and environmental variances, how such designs affect the social and psychological needs of employees is equally important. Hackman and Oldham's (15) theory of job design suggests a framework for understanding how self-regulating groups affect individuals motivationally. They identify three psychological conditions that lead to both work effectiveness and personal satisfaction: (1) personally meaningful work; (b) responsibility for work conditions; and (c) knowledge of results. These states are present when the work content is high on the following five core dimensions: (a) skill variety; (b) task identity (i.e., ability to complete a whole piece of work); (c) task significance (i.e., degree to which the job has a substantial impact on the lives or work of other people); (d) autonomy; and (e) feedback.

When the conditions for self-regulation are implemented effectively, they seem to score high on all these work characteristics. They provide group members with the opportunity to use different skills, to complete a meaningful piece of work, to perform tasks that affect other team members, to make important work-related decisions, and to learn how well they are doing. Therefore, the combination of these work elements is likely to satisfy employees' needs for responsible autonomy over a meaningful task, at least for those individuals who have such needs.

The similarity of Hackman and Oldham's (15) job design characteristics and the self-regulating conditions of work groups suggest a common ground for integrating these two streams of theory and research. The former perspective views work variables primarily from a concern for individual motivation and the latter from a need for required cooperation and control of technical and environmental variances. This contrast, relatively neglected in other attempts to integrate these approaches (14, 23), suggests that each work characteristic may have two distinct yet complementary facets: one related to motivation and the other to self-regulation. For example, skill variety, task identity, and task significance each contribute to the psychological condition of personally meaningful work. They also enhance self-regulation: skill variety provides the behavioral flexibility necessary to develop group strategies for coping with changing task and environmental conditions; task identity furnishes the differentiated task boundary needed for grouping interdependent tasks and containing technical variances within a common work unit; task significance provides the social interdependence needed to relate individual task contributions to those of other workers. This distinction between motivational and self-regulating views of work characteristics raises the issue of how the work variables affect individual performance and satisfaction. Do they affect work outcomes primarily through their impact on individual psychological needs, or on workers' ability to develop a work structure for coping with technical and environmental demands, or on some combination of both? Research into this complex issue is an important starting point for integrating these so far separate perspectives.

Implementation of Self-Regulating Groups

Developmental System Design

The formation of self-regulating work groups typically follows a design strategy that facilitates group development toward responsible autonomy. Referred to as "developmental system design" (18), this process recognizes that self-regulation cannot be created in a one-step mechanical manner. Rather, the conditions for self-regulation (i.e., task differentiation, boundary control, and task control) may require considerable time and diagnosis to implement fully. This is especially relevant for the social aspects of work groups, such as group decision-making, task interaction, and other internal dynamics that occur among group members. These social conditions are not created by design fiat, but through careful attention to the processes by which group members develop their own ways of working together and of adjusting their internal activities to changing task and environmental circumstances. Given the substantial evidence about the ways that groups can thwart work effectiveness and members' well-being (2, 19, 29), development of an effective social system needs to be an explicit part of the design process. Indeed, it is probably the most salient feature distinguishing the design of self-regulating groups from that of enriched jobs.

Developmental system design starts from diagnosis and specification of the structural properties needed to form self-regulating work groups. These include: a clearly differentiated group task, a well-defined work area, and relevant measures of performance. These provide the physical and task boundaries for the group and the standards against which variances are monitored and controlled. Training employees to perform the requisite tasks is also a preliminary design issue. Although it seems desirable that all members initially learn all the tasks for which the group is responsible, it is probably more realistic to assume that each worker will acquire the full complement of skills on the job.

The design properties outlined above are aimed primarily at structuring the technical component of the work group and providing employees with the skills necessary to operate it. The problem of forming an effective social system is a more process-oriented task. This requires an understanding of how groups develop from a loose aggregate of individuals into a well-integrated, problem-solving unit. Although this issue has not received adequate attention in the socio-technical literature (14), there is a substantial body of theory and research about group development. Heinen and Jacobson (16) have integrated much of this literature into a pragmatic framework that is particularly relevant to self-regulating groups, since it accounts for the different kinds of issues that such groups are likely to face at each stage of their development—i.e., from an initial forming stage to a more mature phase.

Although it is beyond the scope of this article to present the strategy more fully, it is important to note that such process interventions are best used to support and maintain a self-regulating group that is initially well-designed (14) (i.e., that has a clearly differentiated task boundary, that is staffed with competent members who possess requisite skills, that has relevant feedback of performance, etc.). Given these conditions, a group consultant or leader who is trained in group process skill (e.g., a process consultant (25)) can help members work through their interpersonal and procedural problems and devise performance strategies (14) appropriate to carrying out the group's conversion and boundary-transaction tasks.

Organizational Context

This discussion has concentrated on self-regulating groups in relative absence of their organizational context. The larger organization has a major impact on whether such structures can be implemented effectively. Foremost among these external conditions is the structure of the organization. This appears to affect both the internal dynamics of the group and its relationships with other organizational units. Since self-regulating groups tend to be organic in character (4), an organization structure with similar dimensions would likely support and enhance the group's internal development (14)

(i.e., a structure with flexibility among units, decentralized authority, few formal rules and procedures, etc.). Moreover, an organic form of organization where there is a network structure of control, authority, and communication would also tend to promote interdependence among parts of the organization. This would increase the likelihood that a self-regulating group's boundaries remain permeable to mutual relationships with other organizational units, such as plant maintenance, procurement, and technically-related groups. A more mechanistic form of organization (4) would tend to place severe constraints on self-regulation. A hierarchic structure of authority and control, a precise definition of rights and obligations, and functional specialization of tasks would likely thwart a group's autonomy and flexibility, reducing its capacity for self-regulation (14). Group members would also tend to withdraw from the organization and enact rigid boundaries to protect their autonomy, thus reducing their mutual contacts with other organizational units.

The climate of the organization also affects implementation of self-regulating groups (8). Since such work designs may involve changes in the organization's reward system, power relationships, communication flows, work flows, and status hierarchies, organizational members must be capable of dealing with these related issues if work is to be redesigned effectively. Argyris (3) suggests that an organizational climate that fosters interpersonal openness, experimentation, trust, and risk-taking behavior is conducive to such structural changes. A review of sixteen selected autonomous group experiments seems to support this premise (7). In most cases, successful implementation of self-regulating designs followed from an organizational change strategy where experimentation, trust, and collaboration among workers and managers were relatively high.

Beyond the structure and climate of the organization, a number of more pragmatic organizational practices are likely to enhance self-regulating groups. Specific organizational measures that tend to promote group (as opposed to individual) forms of work include: a group-based pay scheme; performance data relevant to the group as a whole; self-selection of group members; and low turnover of group personnel (26). Similarly, organizational practices that are likely to nurture learning and responsible autonomy are: protection of the group during its early growth stages (e.g., reduced pressures to perform); wage and job security (e.g., a formal agreement among workers and management guaranteeing that no reductions in wages or employment will result from experimenting with new ways to work); and alternative work opportunities for those group members who become disenchanted with group forms of work (8).

Supervision of Self-Regulating Groups

Self-regulating work groups are designed to take on many of the functions traditionally ascribed to management (e.g., assigning members to individual tasks, determining methods of work, controlling task variances, etc.), but this does not mean that external supervision is unnecessary. The supervisory role emerging under such conditions involves two major functions: developing group members and helping the group maintain its boundaries (8, 26).

Developing group members for a self-regulating system requires a consultative style of management. The supervisor helps members organize themselves into an effective team that is capable of responsible autonomy. The essential task is to provide the group with clear boundaries for the exercise of discretion and to assist members to acquire the skills and knowledge to carry out the work assigned. Since first-level management is the critical link between the wider organization and the group, the supervisor's behavior largely determines how much autonomy workers can experience and how much support and encouragement is received from the organization.

Helping the group maintain its boundaries is necessary if members are to sustain sufficient autonomy to control variances and relate to their task environment. Referred to as "boundary management" (8, 26), this supervisory function operates in two directions: outward to the group's task environment and inward to its conversion activities.

Since work groups have limited control over their task environment, supervision must help to reduce the environmental uncertainty facing the group. This may include a number of strategies for controlling the flow and acceptability of the group's inputs and outputs (e.g., maintaining alternative sources of raw material, scheduling inventories, negotiating delivery dates for finished products, etc.). It may also involve mediating relationships with other organizational units that affect the group's performance, such as higher-level management, plant maintenance, and related groups in other territories or on other work shifts. Research into the management of lateral and horizontal relationships with the task environment suggests that the former may be more difficult, more lengthy, and involve more negotiation contacts than the former (24).

Focusing on the group's conversion activities, management may assist group members to control those variances that are beyond their knowledge and skills (e.g., handling raw materials with unusual properties, deciding whether to scrap or rework an expensive product, etc.). Supervision may also help the group to formulate a task definition appropriate to the group's technology and acceptable to the larger organization (e.g., defining textile weaving in terms of a set of looms for a group of workers (22)). Finally, management may assist group members to plan for a desired future and to *problem-solve ways* to bring this about, which may result, in turn, in redefining the group's task or redesigning the group itself.

The above discussion suggests that the supervision of self-regulating work groups may require skills and expertise that are not familiar to traditional line managers (8, 14). Among these skills are: knowledge of group dynamics and socio-technical principles; understanding the group's technology and task environment; an ability to intervene in the group and develop members' capacity for responsible autonomy.

Conclusion

Self-regulating work groups are a valuable contribution from socio-technical systems theory and practice. Their growing use in organizations in a number of industrialized countries suggests that they are a unique and viable alternative to traditional forms of work design. Their popularity, however, may lead organizational members to overestimate the general applicability of self-regulating groups or to underestimate the conditions necessary for their implementation and continued effectiveness. This article has attempted to provide a clearer understanding of the conditions, implementation strategy, and supervision needed for effective self-regulation.

The discussion suggests some preliminary propositions that may lead to much-needed research in this area:

1. To the extent that technically required cooperation and boundary-transaction or conversion uncertainty are high, self-regulating work groups are more task effective than individual job designs.

2. Self-regulating groups are more task effective to the extent that members have: (a) a moderately differentiated task; (b) high boundary control; and (c) high task control.

3. Self-regulating groups are more personally satisfying to the extent that members have: (a) the conditions in Proposition 2; and (b) needs for responsible autonomy over a meaningful task.

4. Self-regulating groups are more effectively implemented to the extent that: (a) attention is given to the social processes by which members develop their own ways of working together and of adjusting their activities to task and environmental conditions; (b) their organizational context is organic; and (c) their organizational climate fosters experimentation, trust, and collaboration among workers and managers.

5. Management of self-regulating groups is more effective to the extent that supervisors: (a) provide clear boundaries to the exercise of discretion; (b) assist members to acquire the skills and knowledge to carry out the work assigned; and (c) manage group boundaries both outward to the task environment and inward to conversion activities.

References

1. Alderfer, C. P. "Change Processes in Organizations," in M. D. Dunnette (Ed.), *Handbook of Industrial and Organizational Psychology* (Chicago: Rand McNally, 1976), pp. 1591–1638.

2. Alderfer, C. P. "Group and Intergroup Relations," in J. R. Hackman and J. L. Suttle (Eds.), *Improving Life at Work: Behavioral Science Approaches to Organizational Change* (Santa Monica: Goodyear, 1977), pp. 227–296.

3. Argyris, C. *The Applicability of Organizational Sociology* (London: Cambridge University Press, 1972).

4. Burns, T., and G. M. Stalker. *The Management of Innovation* (London: Tavistock Publications, 1961).

5. Cooper, R., and M. Foster. "Sociotechnical Systems," *American Psychologist,* Vol. 26 (1971), 467–474.

6. Cummings, T. G., and W. Griggs. "Worker Reactions to Autonomous Work Groups: Conditions for Functioning, Differential Effects, and Individual Differences," *Organization and Administration Sciences,* Vol. 7 (Winter 1977), 87–100.

7. Cummings, T. G., and E. S. Molloy. *Improving Productivity and the Quality of Work Life* (New York: Praeger Publishers, Inc., 1977).

8. Cummings, T. G., and S. Srivastva. *Management of Work: A Socio-Technical Systems Approach* (Kent, Ohio: The Comparative Administration Research Institute of Kent State University, 1977).

9. Dill, W. R. "Environment as an Influence on Managerial Authority," *Administrative Science Quarterly,* Vol. 2 (1958), 409–443.

10. Emery, F. E. "Some Hypotheses About the Way Tasks May Be More Effectively Put Together to Make Jobs," Doc. 527 (Tavistock Institute of Human Relations, 1959).

11. Emery, F. E. "The Next Thirty Years: Concepts, Methods and Applications," *Human Relations,* Vol. 20 (1967), 199–237.

12. Emery, F. E., and E. L. Trist, "Socio-Technical Systems," in F. E. Emery (Ed.), *Systems Thinking* (London: Penguin Books, 1969), pp. 281–296.

13. Gulowsen, J. "A Measure of Work Group Autonomy," in L. E. Davis and J. C. Taylor (Eds.), *Design of Jobs* (Middlesex, England: Penguin Books, 1972), pp. 374–390.

14. Hackman, J. R. "The Design of Self-Managing Work Groups," *Technical Report No. 11* (New Haven,

Conn.: School of Organization and Management, Yale University, December 1976).

15. Hackman, J. R., and G. R. Oldham. "Motivation Through the Design of Work: Test of a Theory," *Organizational Behavior and Human Performance,* Vol. 16 (1976), 250–279.

16. Heinen, J. S., and E. Jacobson. "A Model of Task Group Development in Complex Organizations and a Strategy for Implementation," *The Academy of Management Review,* Vol. 1, No. 4 (1976), 98–111.

17. Herbst, P. G. *Autonomous Group Functioning* (London: Tavistock Publications, 1962).

18. Herbst, P. G. "Socio-Technical Unit Design," *Doc. 899* (Tavistock Institute of Human Relations, 1966).

19. Janis, I. L. *Victims of Groupthink: A Psychological Study of Foreign Policy Decisions and Fiascos* (New York: Houghton Miffin, 1972).

20. Meissner, M. *Technology and the Worker: Technical Demands and Social Processes in Industry* (San Francisco: Chandler, 1969).

21. Miller, E. J., and A. K. Rice. *Systems of Organization* (London: Tavistock Publications, 1967).

22. Rice, A. K. *Productivity and Social Organization: The Ahmedabad Experiments* (London: Tavistock Publications, 1958).

23. Rosseau, D. M. "Technical Differences in Job Characteristics, Employee Satisfaction, and Motivation: A Synthesis of Job Design Research and Sociotechnical Systems Theory," *Organizational Behavior and Human Performance,* Vol. 19 (1977), 18–42.

24. Sayles, L. *Managerial Behavior* (New York: McGraw-Hill, Inc., 1964).

25. Schein, E. H. *Process Consultation* (Reading, Mass.: Addison-Wesley, 1969).

26. Sussman, G. I. *Autonomy at Work* (New York: Praeger Publishers, Inc., 1976).

27. Trist, E. L. and K. W. Bamforth. "Some Social and Psychological Consequences of the Longwall Method of Coal Getting," *Human Relations,* Vol. 4 (1951), 3–38.

28. Trist, E. L., G. W. Higgin, H. Murray, and A. B. Pollock. *Organizational Choice* (London: Tavistock Publications, 1963).

29. Whyte, W. F. *Money and Motivation* (New York: Harper, 1955).

Reading 36

THE DESIGN OF JOBS

Randall B. Dunham

Although the roots of job design can be traced to the book of Exodus, the beginning of "modern" job design dates to the latter part of the 18th century when economist Adam Smith wrote his classic entitled *Wealth of Nations* (1776). The attention of early scholars such as Smith and engineer Charles Babbage (1832) was directed toward division of labor and task specialization for workers. Attention was focused directly on *job* needs and virtually ignored most needs of the workers. Each worker was to learn only a small number of tasks which could each be highly programmed and, presumably, efficiently performed. The focus of job design 200 years ago was oriented toward economic effectiveness and engineering simplicity.

Scientific Management

Frederick W. Taylor, the father of Scientific Management, has undoubtedly had more impact on the design of jobs in America than has any other person. Taylor's comprehensive strategy for the design of jobs, scientific management, was consistent with the earlier ideas of Smith and Babbage in its focus on the simplification of work (see Taylor, 1911). Taylor's strategy of job design dominated the first half of the 20th century. Many of the principles of scientific management are still taught to engineers and used by many organizations even today.

According to Taylor, jobs should be studied *scientifically* to allow simplification and standardization. Each job should be simplified by breaking it down into a set of the smallest possible elements

and standardized to achieve the highest possible efficiency. This approach was intended to minimize worker ability requirements and reduce the amount of training needed.

What does this strategy mean to the worker? It means that s/he will hold a job which is very simple. In most cases only a few skills will be required for successful job performance. Typically, a given worker will perform only a small portion of an entire job (for example, s/he may bolt the left front door to a car) and will repeat that act many times in a work day. At some auto assembly plants, the same task is performed over 100 times *every hour!* Job duties are spelled out by management in great detail including the exact method for performing each job duty and the exact amount of time permitted for each part of the work. According to Taylor, workers should be motivated to perform at high levels almost entirely by the offering of financial incentives—the primary outcome offered the worker would be money.

The primary intent of scientific management was to benefit the organization economically. The extreme specialization and standardization was expected to lead to maximum worker efficiency and, therefore, greater productivity and income. Because the jobs were so simple, relatively unskilled (and, therefore, inexpensive) workers were hired, thus decreasing labor costs. The cost of training was greatly reduced because jobs were so easy to learn.

In many ways, the scientific management approach to job design is excellent. There has been only one major problem with the technique. The problem is that these scientifically designed jobs carefully structured by engineers and their computers are performed by *people*. Robots could per-

Source: Prepared especially for this volume.

L. L. Cummings and Randall B. Dunham, *Introduction to Organizational Behavior* (Homewood, Ill.: Richard D. Irwin, 1980), pp. 387–404.

form these jobs quickly, repeatedly, and efficiently without difficulty or complaint. But people are not robots.

As more and more workers were placed in extremely simplified jobs, it became clear that most workers did not wish to be treated as machines. Highly simplified jobs were boring. This boredom, coupled with a lack of challenge and depersonalization led to job dissatisfaction. Bored, dissatisfied workers often did things which were not always in the best interest of the organization. Workers behaved in a manner which was consistent with their feelings: they came to work late, or not at all, formed unions, and quit their jobs. In many cases, productivity also suffered. In short, the unexpected dysfunctional reactions of workers often outweighed the benefits associated with the scientific management approach.

Job Enlargement Enrichment Movement

In the late 1940s and early 1950s, management began to pay more attention to the human needs of their employees, and the trend toward greater simplification of work was about to be slowed. The era of the job enlargement/job enrichment fad had begun. During this era, reports of successful job design changes abounded and a number of theorists and practitioners of the techniques began to appear. These scientists hoped to alleviate many of the human problems often associated with the design of jobs from the scientific management era. The early job enlargement/enrichment studies were important because they stimulated much interest in alternative methods of work design. Unfortunately, much of the early research was poorly designed, carelessly conducted, and inflated in its reporting. As a result, a number of organizations jumped on the bandwagon early without giving enough consideration to several important aspects of job design. Many of these organizations paid the price of poor planning while many others found that they had produced happy but unproductive workers.

Because the terms job enlargement and job enrichment have often been used interchangeably and sometimes differentially, I will offer definitions for these two terms. *Horizontal enlargement* increases the number and variety of operations that an individual performs on the job. *Vertical enlargement* (often called job enrichment) increases the degree to which the job holder controls the planning and execution of the job and participates in the setting for organizational policy (Lawler, 1969).

To support and develop the idea of job enlargement/enrichment, researchers first looked to Maslow's theory of motivation (1943, 1954) based on a hierarchy of needs. They argued that traditional motivators were directed toward lower order types of needs. For example, money was offered to satisfy physiological needs, job security was provided to meet safety needs, and physical working conditions were provided to deal with physiological and safety needs. It was argued that these lower order needs had been satisfied to a great extent for the work force of the day while higher order needs, associated with self-fulfillment, were being overlooked. Attention was thus centered on the use of job characteristics as motivational tools to deal with needs for self-fulfillment, achievement, responsibility, autonomy, personal growth, etc.

The work of Herzberg (1966; Herzberg, Mausner, & Snyderman 1959) also has contributed significantly to the progress of job enlargement/enrichment principles. Without rehashing the problem of support for Herzberg's research, consider what the well-known two-factor theory has suggested. According to Herzberg, insufficient amounts of wages or benefits, inadequate working conditions, poor security, or other related factors which are only peripheral to the work itself were considered to contribute to dissatisfaction but their presence was not believed to lead to satisfaction. On the other hand, the factors centered in the job itself were believed to contribute to satisfaction and, presumably, motivation. A job which provided opportunity for achievement, recognition, responsibility, advancement, and growth in competence was expected to increase employee motivation and satisfaction. Thus, attention was focused on the intrinsic characteristics of jobs.

Encouraged by these theoretical ideas, a number of practitioners/researchers launched programs of job redesign. They attempted to restructure jobs to make them more challenging, motivating, and satisfying to the individual. Typically, these early applications consisted of redesign for all job incumbents without consideration of individual differences (i.e., it was assumed that *all* workers would prefer to have enlarged/enriched jobs). The early reports were predominantly case studies which often lacked the strong controls or adequate analyses necessary to prove cause-effect relationships.

Several of the early studies focused on the effects of general job enlargement/enrichment treatments on the productivity and efficiency of workers. These studies reported very positive outcomes from job design interventions but had few controls and involved multiple job changes. It was not possible to separate the effects of the job design interventions from the simultaneous technological innovations. Due to these problems, many of the early studies were of very limited value to the person attempting to understand and refine the techniques of job enlargement/enrichment. Reports of this type, however, have proven attractive to many practitioners and encouraged further use of job enlargement/enrichment attempts. Several examples of early job redesign work will be described at this point.

Maher and Overbagh (1971) reported on the effects of a horizontal job enlargement for a set of product inspection jobs. Sufficient controls were lacking but a considerable amount of quantitative data were obtained. In this study a simple step-by-step inspection task was redesigned to provide a broader, "more interesting," and challenging job. Short-term results indicated improvements in job satisfaction as well as increases for a number of performance measures. It is important to note that these higher levels of job satisfaction and performance returned to their original lower levels after a year. At the end of the year, jobs were redesigned again and again job satisfaction and performance rose. Maher and Overbagh treated this as added evidence that the positive effects were actually due to the redesign efforts. Another view, however, might suggest that these findings were evidence that it was the change process itself (and all of the

accompanying attention given to workers) which led to positive worker reactions.

In *Motivation through the Work Itself* (1969), Ford works through a great number of job design interventions which for the most part were performed in various companies of the American Telephone and Telegraph System. Most of these were case studies which had few controls. Ford argued that positive effects could be expected from enlargement/enrichment interventions for many different jobs. He cites job satisfaction improvements as well as turnover reductions and improvements in productivity quantity and quality. Ford reported varying degrees of effectiveness for 19 attempts at enlargement/enrichment. He classified 9 of these attempts as being "outstandingly successful," 9 as "moderately successful," and only 1 as a "failure." Although these studies were considered successful for the most part, the results indicated an unexplained range of effectiveness from no effect through moderate effect to apparently large effect.

Characteristic of the attention-getting job redesign studies of this early era is a study by Weed (1974) entitled "Job Enrichment Cleans up at Texas Instruments." In this job redesign study, Texas Instruments took over responsibility for the cleaning and janitorial services of its manufacturing, office, and laboratory space from an outside contractor. Jobs were redesigned by Texas Instruments so that individuals and crews had a role in the planning and controlling of their own work. It was reported that measures of cleanliness improved, turnover decreased greatly, work force size was reduced, and a $100,000 cost savings was realized. These outcomes were attributed by Weed to the job redesign efforts as suggested by the title of the article. But a more careful examination of the product reveals that, simultaneous to the job design changes, other extensive changes were made in the technology of the job, the pay system, the selection system, and even the work force itself. Each of these changes provides equally viable explanations for the positive results of the study. Unfortunately, it was blindly accepted by many that Weed's claims were true despite the fact that it was impossible to make any cause-effect statements given the design of the study.

At about the same time that these early studies were being questioned on the basis of their lack of methodological rigor, other studies began to surface which reported that job design changes sometimes failed to succeed. Because of these findings, many people began seriously to question the value of job enlargement/enrichment. For a while, it appeared as though the study and practice of job enlargement/enrichment was near its end. Instead, however, the study of job design became more rigorous, theory was refined, and the boundary conditions under which job enlargement/enrichment should succeed began carefully to be explored. This marked a critical turning point. The resulting systematic, comprehensive, and scientific exploration of job design still in progress has provided many advances in an understanding of how, why, and when job enlargement/enrichment is likely to succeed.

Recent Work in Job Enlargement/Enrichment

During the early job design era it was noted that job enlargement/enrichment did not always "work." A major contribution of the more recent work has been the identification of a number of factors about the individual and the organization which may systematically explain why this is so.

A classic study by Turner and Lawrence (1965), presented a careful evaluation of the role of various specific job characteristics. Turner and Lawrence developed measures of six task characteristics: variety, autonomy, required interaction, optional interaction, knowledge and skill required, and responsibility. Interviews and field observations were made of these six attributes across 47 different jobs. A summary measure of the six attribute scores was formulated called the Requisite Task Attribute (RTA) Index and related to job satisfaction and attendance. It was found that the predicted effect of high RTA leading to high satisfaction and attendance held only for workers from factories located in small towns. Turner and Lawrence concluded that reactions to job characteristics were moderated by cultural background. Their explanation of these results was based on "anomie"—

a normlessness proposed to exist among workers from large cities.

In another landmark study, Blood and Hulin (1967) further examined the issue of individual differences in responses to task characteristics. These researchers indexed communities on the basis of the degree to which they were assumed to foster alienation from middle-class work norms. Evidence was presented to suggest that workers from communities in which middle-class work norms were accepted would respond favorably to job enlargement practices while workers from communities at the alienated end of the continuum would not respond or would respond negatively.

In the last few years a large number of studies have addressed the importance of individual differences in responses to job characteristics. After reviewing the literature, Pierce and Dunham (1976) concluded that the evidence indicates that there are differences in worker preferences for job characteristics and that these differences usually influence worker reactions to their jobs. It should be noted that some researchers (e.g., Stone, 1976, Stone, Mowday, & Porter, 1977) have failed to identify significant moderating effects. Although these findings signal the need for caution, Dunham (1977a) has suggested that some of these findings may be explained by reference to characteristics of the organizations involved in the studies.

Hackman and Oldham Job Characteristics Model

The most complete and best known theory for explaining worker responses to job characteristics is that presented by Hackman and Oldham (1975) (see Figure 1). This theory was based on the earlier work of Hackman and Lawler (1971). According to Hackman and Oldham, any job can be described in terms of five core job dimensions which are defined as follows:

1. *Skill variety*. The degree to which a job requires a variety of different activities in carrying out the work, which involves the use of a number of different skills and talents of the person.

FIGURE 1

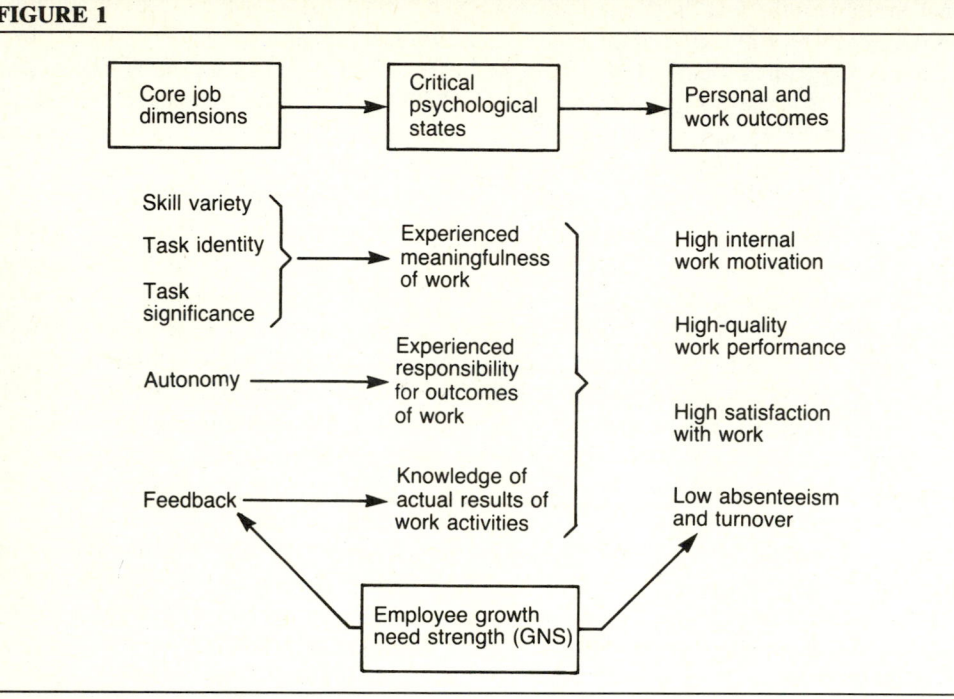

Source: J. R. Hackman and G. B. Oldham, "Motivation through the Design of Work: Test of a Theory," *Organizational Behavior and Human Performance* 16 (1976), pp. 250–79.

2. *Task identity.* The degree to which a job requires completion of a "whole" and identifiable piece of work—that is, doing a job from beginning to end with a visible outcome.

3. *Task significance.* The degree to which a job has a substantial impact on the lives or work of other people—whether in the immediate organization or in the external environment.

4. *Autonomy.* The degree to which a job provides substantial freedom, independence, and discretion to the individual in scheduling the work and in determining the procedures to be used in carrying it out.

5. *Feedback.* The degree to which carrying out the activities required by a job results in the individual obtaining direct and clear information about the effectiveness of his or her performance.

These core dimensions are said to influence three critical psychological states of workers. The ex-

perienced meaningfulness of work is theorized to be high when the job contains high skill variety, task identity, and significance. The experienced responsibility for work outcomes is said to be influenced primarily by the amount of autonomy in the job while knowledge of results of work activities is a function of feedback.

According to the theory, high levels of the critical psychological states will lead to favorable personal and work outcomes: high internal motivation, high work performance, high satisfaction, and low absenteeism and turnover. Hackman and Oldham originally proposed a noncompensatory model—they argued that positive outcomes were likely to result only if all three of the critical psychological states were present.

The remaining element of the Hackman and Oldham model is an individual difference variable called employee growth need strength (GNS). Hackman and Oldham reasoned that people with high needs for personal growth and development should respond more positively to jobs which are high on the core dimension, than would people with low GNS. The theorists suggested two ways in which GNS might be critical. The first of these is between the core job characteristics and the critical psychological states. It was hypothesized that high GNS workers would be more likely to experience the critical psychological states, given the appropriate job design, than would low GNS individuals. In other words, it was suggested that if a group of people were all placed on jobs with high levels of variety, autonomy, identity, significance, and feedback, only some (the high GNS people) would subsequently experience the critical psychological states. The second place where GNS was hypothesized to be important was between the critical psychological states and the personal and work outcomes. Here it was argued that, of the workers who do experience the critical psychological states, only some (the high GNS worker) would respond favorably to the experience.

Hackman and Oldham devised the following equation which they claimed would index the overall motivating potential of a job. Note that skill variety, task identity, and task significance were averaged because together they were believed to influence experienced meaningfulness of the work. On the other hand, autonomy alone was predicted to impact on experienced responsibility for work outcomes and feedback alone was predicted to influence knowledge of results.

According to this theory, the motivating potential of a job would be greatest when each of the major components of the formula is high. A low score on any of these major components, however, was predicted to have a major negative impact on the overall motivating potential of the job. In the extreme case, a zero score on any of the three major components would reduce the MPS to zero. Thus,

it would be difficult to compensate for a low score on one of the major components with a higher score on another. The only compensatory action allowed is in the component related to experienced meaningfulness of the work which involves skill variety, task identity, and task significance.

In 1976, Hackman and Oldham reported a test of their theory using data from 658 workers in 62 jobs and 7 organizations. This sample was quite varied and included blue-collar, white-collar, and professional workers from both industrial and service organizations from the East, Southeast, and Midwest. To test the theory, Hackman and Oldham obtained measures of each of the variables in the job characteristics model. Most of these measures were obtained using an instrument called the Job Diagnostic Survey (JDS) developed by the researchers. (The JDS has been the most widely used instrument for this purpose in recent years and will be discussed in more detail later in this reading.) The results of this study were moderately supportive of the theory:

1. It was found that the core job dimensions did relate to the critical psychological states: (*a*) skill variety, task identity, and task significance combined to predict the level of experienced meaningfulness of the work. Autonomy and feedback, however, also were related to this critical psychological state; (*b*) feedback was clearly the primary determinant of knowledge of results; (*c*) but autonomy was not strongly related to experienced responsibility for work outcomes as had been predicted. In fact, each of the other job dimensions was strongly related to this critical psychological state than was autonomy.

2. The critical psychological states related to most of the personal and work outcomes: (*a*) experienced meaningfulness and experienced responsibility had substantial relationships with internal motivation, general satisfaction, and growth sat-

$$\text{Motivating potential score (MPS)} = \left(\frac{\text{Skill variety} + \text{Task identity} + \text{Task significance}}{3} \right) \times \text{Autonomy} \times \text{Feedback}$$

isfaction; and knowledge of results had smaller but significant relationships with the same outcomes; (*b*) there was very little relation, however, between the experienced psychological states and either absenteeism or performance; (*c*) all three of the psychological states were needed to maximize the prediction of the outcomes.

3. It also was found that the job characteristics themselves were strongly related to the internal motivation, general and growth satisfaction measures. Relatively sophisticated analyses provided evidence that the experienced meaningfulness of work was a critical intervening variable between skill variety, task identity, task significance, and the personal and work outcomes. Similar analyses, however, suggested that the effects of autonomy and feedback may be more direct. Overall, the critical psychological state components of the Hackman and Oldham model received relatively weak support.

4. Individual differences in GNS were found to have a moderate impact of both types hypothesized by Hackman and Oldham: (*a*) Persons with high GNS scores were more likely to experience the critical psychological states as a function of high job dimension scores. (*b*) High GNS workers were more likely to have favorable personal and work outcomes after experiencing the critical psychological states. Finally, although GNS also moderated the direct link between the core job dimensions and the outcomes, this effect was significant only for the internal motivation outcome.

In summary, Hackman and Oldham found that jobs which are high on the core dimensions tend to be associated with high levels of both personal and work outcomes. It also was suggested that this effect may be strongest for persons with high growth need strength. The appropriateness or need for the intervening critical psychological states, however, was not well documented. In fact, most of the subsequent job design research of the type examined only the direct link between the job dimensions and outcomes.

Most of the job design research done subsequent to that of Hackman and Oldham has supported the link between the job dimensions and the personal and work outcomes (see the review of Pierce and Dunham, 1976). Most work on the effect of GNS also has been supportive of the moderating effect hypothesized by Hackman and Oldham. However, as noted earlier, there have been several studies which have contradicted this finding and the issue has not yet been resolved. It is important to note that the moderating effect of GNS, when identified, has suggested only that high GNS workers respond *more* favorably than do low GNS workers. In virtually all cases, even low GNS people respond more favorably to jobs which are high on the job dimensions than to jobs which are low along these dimensions.

Evaluation of the MPS Formula

The MPS formulation derives directly from the propositions of the job characteristics model and, therefore, should be valid to the extent that the model itself has validity. Yet it is important to compare the empirical performance of MPS with that of simpler alternative models because there is increasing evidence that in a wide variety of prediction situations simple, unweighted linear models outperform more complex and subtle formulations. Moreover, special concern about MPS may be warranted because the MPS formula includes two multiplicative terms. Given that multiplicative operations can compound the effects of measure unreliability (and are rarely warranted in any case by the scale properties of the data), there is cause for concern about how MPS predictions compare to those based on nonmultiplicative models. (Hackman and Oldham, 1976, p. 273).

Since the proposition of the Hackman and Oldham theory (1975), the effectiveness of the MPS formulation has been compared to several other formulas including a simple additive model. In one of the earlier comparisons of this type, Dunham (1976) found that an equally weighted linear model was at least as effective in explaining response variance as was the MPS formula. In fact, similar findings were obtained by Hackman and Oldham in their 1976 test of the theory. Other investigations of this type have produced similar results. Neither formulation has been shown to be clearly superior, but the implications of this issue are critical. As previously stated, the MPS model is predominantly a noncompensatory model. The additive model, however, is a fully compensatory one in which low scores on some job characteristics could be compensated for by higher scores on other characteristics. In a situation where one of the critical components was fixed at a low level, the Hackman and Oldham model would argue that raising the other components would have little or no effect on worker responses. The model suggested by Dunham, however, suggests that raising the other components could have a substantial effect on worker responses. A great number of studies have compared these two models in recent years, finding that the simple additive model adequately accounts for the effects of job characteristics.

The Role of the Nontask Environment

Research discussed to this point has strongly supported the argument that jobs which are high on the core dimensions tend to lead to more favorable worker responses. The research also has shown that certain characteristics of the person holding the job influence the degree of favorable reactions associated with such jobs. But neither jobs nor workers exist in a vacuum. Work of the last few years has focused on other factors in the work environment which may be important. For example, Oldham (1976) demonstrated that the relationship between task characteristics and internal motivation can be moderated by the worker's satisfaction with supervisors and co-workers and Dunham (1977a) found that functional specialty area influenced the relationship between task characteristics and job satisfaction.

Dunham (1977a) suggested that the nontask work environment may cause the worker to focus on or off the design of his job. Thus, although an employee's job may have an expanded job design, the worker might not be able to experience the favorable psychological aspects because of distracting environmental factors. The source of this distraction could be either positive or negative. With very

positive nontask environmental factors, the job itself may not be of great importance to the worker. Under certain negative environmental conditions, the worker might focus the majority of his attention on the job itself and, therefore, readily respond to high levels of the job characteristics. In fact, Dunham's study (1977a) suggested that those persons who perceived the organizational climate as least favorable were most likely to respond positively to such jobs. Although current research is exploring this hypothesis, it has not as yet been substantiated.

Porter, Lawler, and Hackman (1975) provided an important initial step toward the integration of the job, the person, and the organization when they presented a model containing predictions for various combinations of job design, individual differences, and organizational design. Porter et al. placed organization design on a continuum ranging from the classical Weberian bureaucratic (mechanistic) model to an organic social system design. Job design was placed on a continuum ranging from simple to complex. The third dimension in the conceptual paradigm was employee GNS ranging from low to high.

Porter et al. defined eight cells (a $2 \times 2 \times 2$ model) by dichotomizing and crossing the three constructs and predicted worker responses under each of the eight conditions. These predictions were based on a congruency concept in which job satisfaction and worker performance should vary as a function of the congruence between the organization, job design, and individual characteristics. Porter et al. predicted (see column 5 of Table 1) that the three "effects" will interact such that the highest levels of satisfaction and performance should be observed under the two completely congruent conditions: organic design, complex jobs, and high growth needs; and mechanistic design, simple jobs, and low growth needs. Expectations for performance and satisfaction were "somewhat higher" for the former congruent case. It also was predicted that the lowest levels of satisfaction and performance should be found for persons who experience both organizational and job designs which are incongruent with their growth needs, i.e., in situations where organic design, complex jobs, and low

TABLE 1   Predictions

Social System Structure	Job Design	Growth Need Level	Porter et al. Predicted Level of Satisfaction and Performance	Rank Order Predicted by Porter et al.	Rank Order Predicted by Pierce, Dunham, and Blackburn	Summary of Actual Rank Order
Organic	Complex	High	Highest	1.0	1	1
Mechanistic	Simple	Low	High	2.0	7	6
Organic	Simple	High	Intermediate	4.5	5	7
Mechanistic	Complex	High	Intermediate	4.5	2	3
Organic	Simple	Low	Intermediate	4.5	6	5
Mechanistic	Complex	Low	Intermediate	4.5	4	4
Organic	Complex	Low	Lowest	7.0	3	3
Mechanistic	Simple	High	Lowest	8.0	8	8

Reprinted (and revised) from J. L. Pierce, R. B. Dunham, and R. S. Blackburn, "Organization Structure, Job Design, and Growth Need Strength: A Test of a Congruency Model," *Academy of Management Journal* 22 (1979), pp. 223–40.

growth needs converge and/or where mechanistic design, simple jobs, and high growth needs converge. Finally, it was implied that the four remaining cells should produce intermediate levels of satisfaction and performance.

A reading of the current job design literature led Pierce, Dunham, and Blackburn (1979) to a set of predictions which are at variance with those of Porter et al. Pierce et al. were in agreement with Porter et al. in their predictions of the best and worst combinations of jobs, people, and organizations. It seems clear that the most positive worker response should be observed in the condition where persons with high growth need strength experience both a complex job and an organic social system structure. It also appears likely that the least favorable worker responses should be found when high growth need individuals experience both a job and a social system (simple/mechanistic) which are counter to their preference (i.e., incongruent with their needs). Several remaining predictions, however, were different from those of Porter et al.

There were two main reasons why the remaining predictions varied from those of Porter et al. The first of these was based on the empirical evidence concerning the role of growth need strength as a moderator of job designer-responses relationships.

This evidence clearly shows significant *positive* relationships between job design and worker responses for both high *and* low growth need persons. The moderating effects which have been identified simply suggest that there is a stronger positive relationship for high growth need persons. Thus, both high and low growth need workers should be expected to react more favorably when presented with either a complex job or an organic social system and most favorably when presented with both.

The second reason why the Pierce et al. predictions varied from those of Porter et al. concerned their feeling that the design of the job is of more importance to workers than the design of the social system. This is based on the fact that the job is "closer" to the worker and is experienced on a more regular and personal basis than the organizational or social system design. Thus, workers should be expected to react more favorably to a complex/mechanistic situation than to one which is simple/organic. The social system design was expected to be of secondary importance to job design as a determinant of worker responses.

Given these arguments, Pierce et al. predicted the rank orderings for worker responses as also shown in column 6 of Table 1. To evaluate the two sets of predictions, Pierce, Dunham, and Blackburn undertook an empirical evaluation of the two sets of predictions. Pierce et al. obtained data from 398 employees from 19 distinct work units of a large insurance company. Measures were obtained of job characteristics (complex versus simple) and GNS (high versus low) using the JDS. A variety of measures were used to classify each work unit as either mechanistic (low complexity, high centralization, high formalization, high stratification) or organic (complex, decentralized, informal, low stratification). Workers were placed into each of the eight conditions listed in Table 1. (Pierce et al. agreed with the statement made by Porter et al. that the types of jobs, people, and organizations presented in Table 1 are only "caricatures of the real world; pure types of any of the three simply do not exist. It is more useful and valid to think of the cells as end points on a continuum rather than as meaningful types in themselves" [Porter et al., 1975, p. 310]). The dependent variables studied included job satisfaction, motivation, effort, and performance.

The results of this study were strongly supportive of the need to consider the job, the person, and the organization in order to understand the impact of job design on worker responses.

1. Worker responses were more favorable on complex jobs than on simple jobs.
2. Worker responses were more positive in organic work units than in mechanistic work units.
3. The responses of high GNS workers were more favorable than those of low GNS workers.
4. There was a significant interaction between job design and GNS. High GNS employees reacted more favorably to complex jobs than did low GNS workers.
5. There also was a significant interaction between job design and work-unit design. Employees responded more favorably to complex jobs when they were located in organic work units than when they were located in mechanistic work units.
6. Finally, there was some evidence suggestive of a three-way interaction between job design, work-unit design, and GNS.

The predictions made by Pierce et al. received considerably more support than did those of Porter, et al. (see the last column of Table 1). An examination of the strongest findings from this study (primarily the effects on satisfaction) revealed a high degree of correspondence of the empirical rank order to that predicted by Pierce et al. In fact, predictions made independently for either high or low GNS groups were confirmed *exactly* as follows:

1. Complex/organic (most favorable).
2. Complex/mechanistic.
3. Simple/organic.
4. Simple/mechanistic (least favorable).

The results of this study suggested that the design of the job is more important to workers than is the design of social system. The findings also confirmed that both high and low GNS workers responded more favorably to complex jobs and organic social systems than to simple jobs and/or mechanistic social systems. If these findings are supported by future research, job design decisions will have to be made within a model which includes all three variables. In addition, if either person changes or social system structure changes are to be made in an organization, the potential impact on worker responses of the existing job design must be considered. These findings support the need for a systems congruency framework for understanding and predicting the responses of members of work organizations.

The Dimensionality and Measurement of Job Design

To apply effectively our knowledge of job design, we must be able to measure the various characteristics of jobs. It has been widely assumed in both theory and practice that job design is a multidimensional construct. Because of this, efforts to develop measures of job characteristics have attempted to discriminate between various job components. The measurements most commonly used today can be traced to the requisite task attribute index of Turner and Lawrence (1965). This index was first modified by Hackman and Lawler (1971) and then by Hackman and Oldham (1975), culminating in the development of the JDS. The JDS was intended to measure each of the five job characteristics included in the Hackman and Oldham theory (variety, autonomy, identity, significance, and feedback). It was assumed that the JDS provided a valid measure of each of these characteristics.

In 1976, however, Dunham conducted a study of the JDS with over 3,000 employees from more than 100 different jobs. The results indicated that the measures of variety and autonomy could not be adequately differentiated from one another and that a single dimension (job complexity) for describing job characteristics would clearly be most parsimonious. The results from this single study, however, were not adequate to determine if the JDS itself was perhaps "deficient." To evaluate these possibilities, Dunham, Aldag, and Brief (1977) administered the JDS to 20 samples of workers from 5 different organizations. Almost 6,000 workers in jobs ranging from unskilled materials handlers through top-level corporate executives were included. The results of this study indicated that either the JDS or its underlying theory might need revision.

At about this time, Sims, Szilagyi, and Keller (1976) developed another job design measure called the Job Characteristics Inventory (JCI), which was designed to overcome some of the problems associated with the JDS. Based on two large samples (a total of over 1,000 workers), Sims et al. successfully assessed the individual job characteristics (this instrument tapped six dimensions—four of which were also in the JDS).

To compare the JDS and the JCI, Pierce and Dunham (1978) administered both instruments to the employees of an insurance company. The results indicated that the proposed dimensionality was clearly defined by the JCI but not by the JDS. Reliability was also higher for the JCI than for the JDS. These findings suggested that the fluctuations of dimensionality of the JDS across samples was probably due to the measurement process rather than the underlying dimensionality of job design. Thus, it appears that the theory may be correct but the JDS measure problematic. The JCI appears to offer a viable alternative for the measurement of job characteristics.

Manpower and Compensation Implications

It is important that we be aware that changes in job design often change the staffing requirements of an organization. Workers must have the abilities and skills required by new job designs. Remember that the scientific management approach to job design attempted to minimize such requirements. Job enlargement/enrichment approaches tend to increase the very same requirements, but the increased requirements have been given very little attention. The organization must select workers who are able to perform the expanded jobs and train workers to acquire the new skills being demanded. As jobs place greater requirements upon workers, the compensation value of these jobs is also likely to increase. Unless equitable compensation is provided for these jobs, workers are likely to become dissatisfied and the positive effects of job design may be neutralized or reversed by these adverse consequences (see Locke, Sirota, and Wolfson, 1976).

Dunham (1977b) conducted a study of the relationships of perceived job design characteristics to job ability requirements and job value. Dunham obtained job design descriptions from 256 employees of a large metropolitan pharmaceutical plant. (As in most other studies, these measures were strongly related to worker satisfaction and motivation.) Dunham analyzed and evaluated each job using a standardized job analysis procedure. Based on the job analysis, estimates of job ability requirements were made for each job for each of the nine General Aptitude Test Battery tests (intelligence, verbal aptitude, numerical aptitude, spatial aptitude, form perception, clerical perception, motor coordination, finger dexterity, and manual dexterity). Using a job evaluation equation, Dunham also obtained an estimate of the compensation value of each job. The results identified moderately strong positive relations between the job design characteristics and the ability requirements.

The results also identified a moderate correlation of job design characteristics and job value ($r = .40$). It was clear that jobs perceived as being high in job complexity (variety, autonomy, identity, significance, and feedback) had both higher job ability requirements and compensation requirements. Dunham concluded that:

> These findings emphasize the importance of complete organizational planning in order to avoid dysfunctional consequences that might result from job redesign efforts that produce excessively high ability or compensation requirements (p. 762).

The Implementation of Job Design Concepts

The majority of research conducted on the effects of job design has been correlational in nature. Researchers have explored the impact of existing job differences on worker responses. Based on these findings, inferences have been drawn as to the expected effect of *changes* in the design of jobs. Much of the adequately designed research which has involved actual job design changes has failed to obtain as strong results as those suggested by the correlational studies (see Pierce and Dunham, 1976 for a review of this issue). Many of these disappointing findings can be attributed to inadequate diagnosis of jobs, people, and/or organizations. Other problems can be traced to factors such as a failure to train adequately workers and/or managers, lack of organizational commitment to the changes, limitations of the technology, or simply inadequate job design changes. Most of these problems can be traced to a lack of sufficient guidelines for implementation of job design changes. We know that increases in worker perceptions of variety, autonomy, identity, significance, and/or feedback are likely to lead to more favorable worker responses, but how do we produce changes in these perceptions? And what related factors must we consider to maximize the effectiveness of job design changes?

Hackman, Oldham, Janson, and Purdy (1975) have suggested a basic strategy for making job changes (see Figure 2). Although this model is actually quite rudimentary, it does provide some initial ideas for guiding the redesign of jobs. Unfortunately, the redesign of jobs today is as much of an art as it is a science.

Hackman et al. (1975) suggested that prior to redesigning jobs, a careful diagnosis should be done of the existing jobs and job incumbents. Each element of the model should be assessed. (Given the results of the study by Pierce et al. [1979], it also would be wise to diagnose the organization itself.) Once a diagnosis has been completed and it has been determined that job redesign is needed, Hackman et al. focus on techniques for increasing the job characteristics dimensions. Those characteristics which the diagnosis identified as most in need of change should be concentrated upon.

As seen in Figure 2, Hackman et al. suggest that the combining of tasks (task despecialization) should increase both the amount of skill variety and task identity of the job. The formation of natural work units (providing ''ownership'' of the job) is said to increase both task identity and task significance. Jobs can be changed to establish ''client'' relationships both within and outside the organization and, thus, increase the amount of skill variety, autonomy, and feedback in the job. Increases in vertical loading (providing the employee with greater latitude and job responsibility) is said to increase skill variety, task identity, task significance, and autonomy. Finally, changing the job so that feedback channels are opened (from performance of the work itself) should increase the amount of feedback actually experienced by the worker.

Hackman et al. reported an application of this strategy at the Travelers Insurance Company which led to quite dramatic results. In fact, compared to a control group, these changes led to significant improvements in employee attitudes and work quantity as well as decreases in error rates and absenteeism. The changes saved the company over $90,000 annually. Unfortunately, such thorough strategies have not been widely used and many job redesign efforts have suffered as a result.

The Hackman et al. model is, to some degree, overly restrictive. I agree with those scholars that changes in perceptions of job design are needed to

FIGURE 2

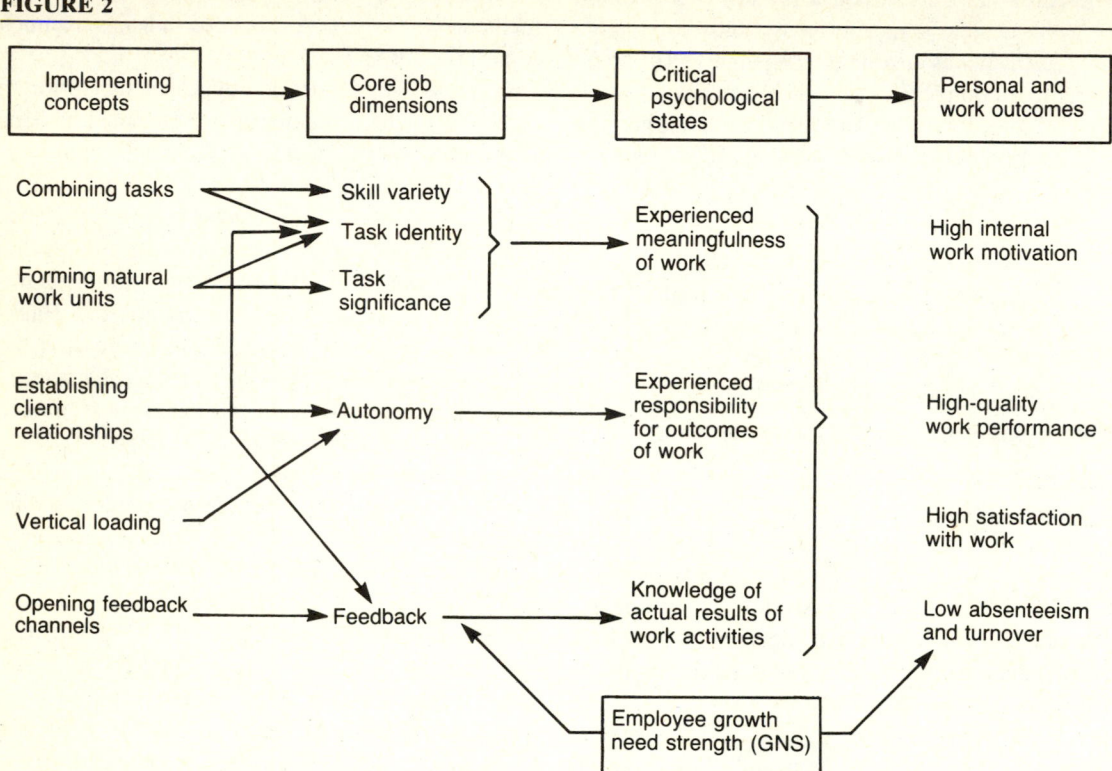

Source: J. R. Hackman, G. Oldham, R. Janson, and K. Purdy, ''A New Strategy for Job Enrichment.'' Copyright 1975 by the Regents of the University of California. Reprinted from *California Management Review,* vol. 18, no. 4, p. 62 by permission of the Regents.

influence worker responses. However, there are two broad categories of job changes which can successfully achieve this end. Basically, it is possible to change the total job which a person is doing or to change the method by which the ''old'' job is done. The latter is often much less disruptive to an organization. Changing the total job also requires changes in jobs which are adjacent to the focal job (and, consequently, the design of the organization). This would be the case, for example, when a worker takes over some of the tasks formerly assigned to another worker (e.g., instead of just handling orders, the worker also may handle billing). On the other hand, simply changing the method by which a job is done (e.g., assigning the worker only the handling of orders but allowing him to decide how to handle the orders), may have many of the pos-

itive effects for that worker without disrupting the rest of the organization. Dunham, Newman, and Blackburn (1978) provided evidence that this second type of job change is often performed by the worker on his/her own initiative and that such changes are often followed by more favorable worker responses. Obviously, these different approaches are likely to influence different job characteristics, but there is more than one way to succeed with job design changes.

Some Final Considerations

There are several final considerations which should be made. First, we must consider the effects which job design changes can have on others in the organization. For example, Lawler, Hackman, and

Kaufman (1973) cited a case in which job design changes led to problems for the supervisors of jobs which had been changed. Because subordinates had taken over many of their own former responsibilities, some supervisors reported lower satisfaction with interpersonal relations and perceived less job security. Hall, Goodale, Rabinowitz, and Morgan (1978) cited evidence which suggested that, when job change is forced upon workers by upper management, attitudes are much less positive toward the change than when change is introduced through participation or representation. Finally, Schwab and Cummings (1976) have argued that there may be a curvilinear relation between job design and worker responses. This suggests that jobs which are *too* high on the job characteristics dimensions could lead to unfavorable worker responses.

Summary and Conclusions

We are quite sure that jobs which are relatively high in the job characteristics of variety, autonomy, significance, identity, and feedback lead to higher levels of job satisfaction and worker motivation than do jobs which are low on these characteristics. We are also quite certain that some individuals respond more favorably to these complex jobs than do others. The evidence also suggests that certain nontask environmental factors influence worker responses to job design. Furthermore, the design of jobs can have a number of side effects for the organization (e.g., on manpower and compensation requirements). The theory and practice of job design is now well enough developed that we do not have to function blindly in the design or redesign of jobs.

Although it is obvious that we have considerable useful knowledge about job design and its effects, there are still some things for which we do not yet have the final answers. For example, we still don't understand with complete certainty the entire set of critical job characteristics dimensions. Nor are we sure of the optimal method for combining these various dimensions to maximize worker responses. More importantly, we do not yet know the specific *objective* job changes which must be made to improve the job. We know that individual differences are important but have not yet uncovered the complete set of critical personal characteristics. Although we now understand some of the nontask environmental factors which influence the effects of job design, we have not yet defined the entire set of these variables. Finally, although we are quite sure of the effects of job design on satisfaction and motivation, it is not yet clear if job design consistently affects worker performance and attendance.

After 200 years of study on the effects of job design, we only now understand the basics. The research of the last two decades has produced very large increments in our knowledge. The study of job design is currently one of the most popular in organizational behavior and the next few years should provide many exciting new answers.

References

Babbage, C. *On the economy of machinery and manufacturers.* London: Charles Knight, 1832.

Blood, M. R., & Hulin, C. L. Alienation, environmental characteristics and worker responses. *Journal of Applied Psychology,* 1967, *51*:284–290.

Dunham, R. B. Reactions to job characteristics: Moderating effects of the organization. *Academy of Management Journal,* 1977a, *20*:42–65.

Dunham, R. B. Relationships of perceived job design characteristics to job ability requirements and job value. *Journal of Applied Psychology,* 1977b, *62*:760–763.

Dunham, R. B. Measurement and dimensionality of job characteristics. *Journal of Applied Psychology,* 1976 *61*:404–409.

Dunham, R. B., Aldag, R. J., & Brief, A. P. Dimensionality of task design as measured by the Job Diagnostic Survey, *Academy of Management Journal,* 1977, *20*:209–223.

Dunham, R. B., Newman, J. E., & Blackburn, R. J. Employee reactions to technological and organizational changes: Two quasi-experimental job redesign field studies. Presented at Midwest Psychological Association Convention, Chicago, 1978.

Ford, R. N. *Motivation through the work itself.* New York: American Management Association, 1969.

Hackman, J. R., & Lawler, E. E., III. Employee reactions to job characteristics. *Journal of Applied Psychology Monograph,* 1971, *55*:259–286.

Hackman, J. R., & Oldham, G. R. Development of the job diagnostic survey. *Journal of Applied Psychology,* 1975, *60*:159–170.

Hackman, J. R., & Oldham, G. R. Motivation through the design of work: Test of a theory. *Organizational Behavior and Human Performance,* 1976, *16*:250–279.

Hackman, J. R., Oldham, G. R., Janson, R., & Purdy, K. A new strategy for job enrichment. *California Management Review,* 1975.

Hall, D. T., Goodale, J. G., Rabinowitz, S., & Morgan, M. A. Effects of top-down departmental and job change upon perceived employee behavior and attitudes: A natural field experiment. *Journal of Applied Psychology,* 1978, *63*:62–72.

Herzberg, F. *Work and the nature of man.* Cleveland: World Publishing, 1966.

Herzberg, F., Mausner, B., & Snyderman, B. *The motivation to work.* New York: John Wiley & Sons, 1959.

Lawler, E. E., III, Hackman, J. R., & Kaufman, S. Effects of job redesign: A field experiment. *Journal of Applied Social Psychology*, 1973, 3:49–62.

Lawler, E. E., III. Job design and employee motivation. *Personnel Psychology,* 1969, *22*:426–435.

Locke, E. A., Sirota, D., & Wolfson, A. D. An experimental case study of the successes and failure of job enrichment in a government agency. *Journal of Applied Psychology,* 1976, *61*:701–711.

Maslow, A. H. A theory of human motivation. *Psychological Review,* 1943, *50*:370–396.

Maslow, A. H. *Motivation and personality.* New York: Harper & Row, 1954.

Maher, J. R. Job enrichment, performance, and morale in a simulated factory, in J. R. Maher (ed.), *New perspectives in job enrichment.* New York: Van Nostrand Reinhold, 1971.

Maher, J. R. & Overbagh, W. B. Better inspection performance through job enrichment. In J. R. Maher (Ed.), *New perspectives in job enrichment.* New York: Van Nostrand Reinhold, 1971.

Oldham, G. R. Job characteristics and internal motivation: The moderating effect of interpersonal and individual variables. *Human Relations,* 1976, *29*:559–569.

Pierce, J. L., & Dunham, R. B. The measurement of perceived job characteristics: The Job Diagnostic Survey versus the Job Characteristics Inventory. *Academy of Management Journal,* 1978, *21*:123–128.

Pierce, J. L., & Dunham, R. B. Task design: A literature review. *Academy of Management Review,* 1976, *1*:83–97.

Pierce, J. L., Dunham, R. B. & Blackburn, R. S. Organization structure, job design, and growth need strength: A test of a congruency model. *Academy of Management Journal,* 1979, 22:223–240.

Porter, L. W., Lawler, E. E., III, & Hackman, J. R. *Behavior in organizations.* New York: McGraw-Hill, 1975.

Schwab, D. P., & Cummings, L. L. Impact of task scope on employee productivity: An evaluation using expectancy theory. *Academy of Management Review,* 1976, *1*:23–35.

Sims, H. P., Szilagyi, A. D. & Keller, R. T. The measurement of job characteristics. *Academy of Management Journal,* 1976, *19*:195–212.

Smith, A. *The wealth of nations.* New York: Modern Library, 1776.

Stone, E. F. The moderating effect of work related values on the job scope-job satisfaction relationship. *Organizational Behavior and Human Performance,* 1976, *15*:147–167.

Stone, E. F., Mowday, R. T., & Porter, L. W. Higher order need strengths as moderators of the job scope-job satisfaction relationship. *Journal of Applied Psychology,* 1977, 62:466–471.

Taylor, F. W. *The principles of scientific management.* New York: Harper & Row, 1911.

Turner, A. N., & Lawrence, P. R. *Industrial jobs and the worker: An investigation of response to task attributes.* Cambridge, Mass.: Harvard University Press, 1965.

Weed, E. D. Job enrichment "clean up" at Texas Instruments. In J. R. Maher (Ed.), *New perspectives in job enrichment.* New York: Van Nostrand Reinhold, 1971.

C. Management by Objectives and Compensation

This section includes one essay on management by objectives (MBO), and one on compensation. The Wendell French and Robert Hollmann article stresses the range of MBO efforts in different organizations, efforts which can vary greatly in terms of the leadership styles they implicitly reinforce. This article contrasts traditional MBO with OD and suggests that a team approach to MBO may have considerable merit. The article further discusses some of the skills needed to make such an approach effective.

An additional point about OD vis-à-vis MBO needs to be made. In the first place, simply because OD participants frequently identify goals and priorities as major areas of concern, most team-building workshops include a significant amount of time spent on goal clarification, prioritizing of goals, and developing action steps to attain goals. Team-building workshops also frequently include time devoted to following up to see if goals have been attained. Thus, a less formalized, team approach to goal setting is frequently a integral part of an OD effort.

We now turn to compensation. In the second essay, Lawler argues that starting a change effort in an organization by first focusing on the pay system "may be both meaningful and strategically desirable." He then deals with such issues as diagnosis, who is to be involved, and systems effects.

Reading 37

MANAGEMENT BY OBJECTIVES: THE TEAM APPROACH

Wendell L. French and Robert W. Hollmann

Study of the many books, articles, case studies, speeches, and discussions about management by objectives (MBO) indicates that most forms of this approach tend to reinforce a one-to-one leadership style. It is also apparent that MBO efforts vary from being highly autocratic to highly participative, among organizations and even within some organizations. In this article we present a case and strategy for *collaborative* management by objectives (CMBO), a participative team-centered approach. This approach has a number of unique features that will minimize some of the deficiencies in more traditional versions, but as we shall see, the skills involved and the organizational climate required for its optimal effectiveness may not come easily.

One-to-One MBO

Let us first compare the autocratic and participative characteristics of one-to-one versions of MBO. Examples 1a through 1d in Table 1 illustrate how this form can differ along the autocratic-participative continuum. In one contemporary version of MBO, the superior prepares a list of objectives and simply passes them down to the subordinate. In a second version, the superior prepares the subordinate's list of objectives and allows him or her ample opportunity for questions and clarification. In a third version, the subordinate prepares his own list of objectives and submits this list to his superior for discussion and subsequent editing and modification

by the superior. And in a fourth version, the superior and subordinate independently prepare lists of the subordinate's objectives and then meet to agree upon the final list. Similar degrees of subordinate participation also can occur at other steps in the MBO process (in determination of objective measures of performance and in the end-of-the-period evaluation, for example). Obviously many variations are possible, but the point is that the different versions of one-to-one MBO can fall anywhere along the traditional autocratic-participative continuum.

Deficiencies in One-to-One MBO

Disregarding the likely long-range inadequacies of any autocratic form of MBO, we believe that the one-to-one mode has a number of critical deficiencies. First, one-to-one MBO does not adequately account for the interdependent nature of most jobs, particularly at the managerial and supervisory levels. Second, it does not assure optimal coordination of objectives. And third, it does not always improve superior-subordinate relationships, as is widely claimed by MBO proponents. (We do not know whether a team approach always will improve relations either, but we are much more optimistic about the latter.) These deficiencies pertain to all versions of one-to-one MBO, regardless of how autocratic or participative, although we believe that the deficiencies would be more salient under autocratic supervisory behavior. Let us examine these limitations more closely.

Managerial Interdependence. A number of writers have pointed out that one-to-one, superior-

Source: Wendell L. French and Robert W. Hollmann, © (Spring 1975) by the Regents of the University of California. Reprinted from *California Management Review*, vol. 17, no. 3, pp. 13–22, by permission of the Regents.

TABLE 1   Objective Setting in Different Versions of MBO

Degree of Subordinate Influence on Objectives	*Very Little*	*Some*	*Moderate*	*Considerable*
Individual orientation . . .	*1a* Superior prepares list of subordinate's objectives and gives it to subordinate	*1b* Superior prepares list of subordinate's objectives; allows opportunity for clarification and suggestions.	*1c* Superior prepares list of his objectives; superior-subordinate discussion of tentative list is followed by editing, modification, and finalization by superior.	*1d* Superior and subordinate independently prepare list of subordinate's objectives; mutual agreement reached after extensive dialogue.
Team orientation . . .	*2a* Superior prepares individual lists of various subordinates' objectives; hands out lists in group meeting and explains objectives.	*2b* Superior prepares unit and individual objectives; allows opportunity for questions and suggestions in group meeting.	*2c* Superior prepares list of unit objectives which are discussed in group meeting; superior decides. Subordinates then prepare lists of their objectives, discuss with superior; individual's objectives discussed in team meeting with modifications made by superior after extensive dialogue.	*2d* Unit objectives, including team effectivenss goals, are developed among superior, subordinates, and peers in a group meeting, usually by consensus; superior and subordinates later independently prepare lists of subordinate's objectives, reach temporary agreement; subordinate's objectives finalized after extensive discussion in team meeting.

subordinate MBO does not recognize the interdependent or complementary nature of managerial jobs.[1] We concur with this criticism and believe

[1]See, for example, Gerard F. Carvalho, ''Installing Management by Objectives: A New Perspective on Organization Change,'' *Human Resource Management,* Spring 1972, pp. 23–30; Robert A. Howell, ''A Fresh Look at Management by Objectives,'' *Business Horizons,* Fall 1967, pp. 51–58; Charles L. Hughes, ''Assessing the Performance of Key Managers,'' *Personnel,* January–February 1968, pp. 38–43; Bruce D. Jamieson, ''Behavioral Problems with Management by Objectives,'' *Academy of Management Journal,* September 1973, pp. 496–505; Harold Koontz, ''Making Managerial Appraisal Effective,'' *California Management Review,* Winter 1972, pp. 46–55; and Harry Levinson, ''Management by Whose Objectives?'' *Harvard Business Review,* July–August 1970, pp. 125–34.

that effective implementation of MBO requires a "systems view" of the organization. Each manager functions in a complex network of vertical, horizontal, and diagonal relationships, and his success in achieving his objectives is often (if not always) dependent upon the communication, cooperation, and support of other managers in this network.

The relevance of managerial interdependence is particularly evident when MBO is used with staff managers. A number of authors have described the difficulties in applying MBO to staff positions.[2] We need not reiterate their ideas here, except to stress the point that the advisory and supportive nature of staff work dictates that a staff manager's objectives be highly interrelated with the activities and objectives of other managers, both line and staff. Furthermore, staff objectives are often more qualitative than quantitative, and therefore more difficult to set and measure. Asking the staff manager to set either qualitative or quantitative objectives in isolation from those upon whom his attainment of these objectives is largely dependent does not make good sense.

An indication of the lack of attention to the interdependent nature of managerial jobs can be found in two recent works, one including descriptions of MBO programs in four British firms,[3] the other including five American companies.[4] Eight of the nine companies require that forms be filled out in the MBO programs, but in only one company's form is there any space for the manager to specify the extent to which his objectives require involvement of other managers.

---

[2]See, for example, Thomas P. Kleber, "The Six Hardest Areas to Manage by Objectives," *Personnel Journal,* August 1972, pp. 571–75; Dale D. McConkey, "Staff Objectives Are Different," *Personnel Journal,* July 1972, p. 477ff.; and Burt K. Scanlan, "Quantifying the Qualifiable, or Can Results Management Be Applied to the Staff Man's Job?" *Personnel Journal,* March 1968, p. 162ff.

[3]John W. Humble, ed. *Management by Objectives in Action* (New York: McGraw-Hill, 1970).

[4]Walter S. Wikstrom, *Managing by and with Objectives* (New York: National Industrial Conference Board, 1968).

Coordination of Objectives. Another deficiency is associated with this interdependency. One of the highly touted advantages of MBO is that it results in effective coordination of objectives; that is, there is better integration (including minimization of gaps and duplication) of the objectives of all managers in the work unit. While this is certainly a desirable benefit, it must be recognized that one-to-one MBO places the responsibility for such coordination entirely upon the superior, since he is the only person in the MBO process to have formal contact with all subordinate managers. In effect, the superior is required to function as a "central processing center of objectives."

We believe that one-to-one MBO simply does not provide the opportunity for maximum coordination of objectives. The superior may be able to marginally, or even adequately, coordinate the objectives of his immediate subordinates on a one-to-one basis, but this procedure does not really do justice to the subtleties of interdependent relationships. Under such circumstances, except for information transmitted informally and sporadically between peers in on-the-job interaction, subordinate managers have little knowledge or understanding of each other's objectives. On the other hand, if these subordinates were provided with the opportunity for dynamic interactive processes in which their objectives are systematically communicated and adjusted, final objectives probably would be more effectively coordinated.

The deficiency in the coordination of objectives is magnified in cases of managers performing highly interrelated tasks but working in different departments. For example, a sales manager in a marketing division organized along product lines needs to coordinate his objectives with those of the appropriate production manager responsible for manufacturing the product. The sales manager may meet his objective of a 5 percent increase in the sales of product X, but the organization is likely to suffer a loss of future sales and customers if the manufacturing output of product X, which is based upon the production manager's objectives, is inadequate to meet these sales commitments. One-to-one MBO between the sales and production managers and their respective superiors provides no systematic method for integrating their objectives and, accordingly, these two managers must rely entirely upon their own initiative for the development of integrative mechanisms. Quite frankly, we doubt that this haphazard approach results in optimal coordination.

Improved Superior-Subordinate Relationships. The participative, or mutual involvement, form of one-to-one MBO is extolled largely for the improvement in superior-subordinate relationships it is expected to bring about. Not all research supports this claim, however. For example, Tosi and Carroll found that even after an intensive and carefully planned MBO program that stressed subordinate participation, subordinate managers did not feel that the superior-subordinate relationship had improved significantly in terms of helpfulness on the part of the superior.[5] While the researchers offered no specific empirical reasons for this finding, other authors have suggested factors that might provide some explanation.

Kerr believes that the typical organization hierarchy creates a superior-subordinate status differential that acts as a deterrent to the expected improvement in relationships.[6] For instance, when MBO is conducted in a somewhat autocratic manner the status differential inhibits the subordinate from challenging the decisions of his boss or the objectives he has established. Even in cases of greater subordinate involvement, status differences may hinder attainment of the desired ideal mutuality in the MBO process. A similar note is struck by Levinson, who believes that rivalry between a boss and his subordinate can easily impede the creation or maintenance of a positive relationship.[7] It is important to point out that Tosi and Carroll also found that the same MBO program stressing increased subordinate participation resulted in no significant increase in subordinates' perceived influence in the goal-setting process.[8] Perhaps superior-subordinate status differentials or rivalry were operating in this organization.

Incompatibility between the superior's role as a coach and his role as a judge may also hamper the superior-subordinate relationship. Researchers at the General Electric Company concluded that the two primary purposes of performance appraisal (performance improvement and salary adjustment) are in conflict.[9] They suggested that these two purposes could be better accomplished in two separate interviews—a proposal with which we agree. Yet even in this approach, it is easy to see the difficult position in which the superior is placed: prior to and during one interview he is expected to *constructively* evaluate the subordinate's performance and help him formulate plans for improvement, while in the second interview he is expected to *judiciously* evaluate the subordinate's performance in order to make crucial salary recommendations and to inform the subordinate of his decision. Only an exceptionally talented person could shift adroitly between these two roles (especially with the same subordinate), and it is our opinion that most managers have great difficulty doing so. Thus, an MBO program that requires the superior to have complete responsibility in performing these incompatible roles, even in separate interviews, could easily strain rather than improve superior-subordinate relationships.

[5]Henry Tosi and Stephen J. Carroll, Jr., "Improving Management by Objectives: A Diagnostic Change Program," *California Management Review,* Fall 1973, pp. 57–66.

[6]Steven Kerr, "Some Modifications in MBO as an OD Strategy," *Proceedings, 1972 Annual Meeting,* Academy of Management, 1973, pp. 39–42.

[7]Harry Levinson, "Management by Objectives: A Critique," *Training and Development Journal,* April 1972, pp. 3–8; see also Levinson, "Management by Whose Objectives?"

[8]Tosi and Carroll, "Improving Management by Objectives."

[9]Herbert H. Meyer, Emanuel Kay, and John R. P. French, Jr., "Split Roles in Performance Appraisal," *Harvard Business Review,* January–February 1965, pp. 123–29.

Team Collaboration in MBO

We believe that MBO could be strengthened considerably by increasing the opportunities for systematic collaboration among managers. Furthermore, MBO programs based on cooperative teamwork and group problem solving would represent a positive step toward rectifying some of the deficiencies found in one-to-one MBO. Ironically, in his original description of MBO, Drucker said, "Right from the start . . . emphasis should be on teamwork and team results,"[10] but it doesn't look to us as if the MBO movement has gone this way. A number of other authors have called for group or peer goal setting and evaluation in MBO[11] but, with few exceptions,[12] suggestions for a group approach to MBO generally have not been augmented with systematic guidelines or frameworks for implementation.

MBO programs described in the literature and in operation that *do* acknowledge the collaborative dimension can be classified in three categories. First, there are programs that superficially refer to the need for some sort of collaborative effort during the MBO process. For example, the MBO instruction manual may include a statement such as: "Each manager should exert maximum effort to ensure that his objectives are effectively coordinated with those of other managers in his work group." Under this unsystematic approach, then, collaboration is left entirely to each manager's own initiative.

Second, there are programs that provide some formal means for collaboration (see examples *2b* and *2c* in Table 1). For instance, Wikstrom describes one company program that includes "cross-checking meetings" in which managers present their tentative goals, check the impact of these goals on one another, and make adjustments before finalizing the goals.[13] In a similar vein, Raia suggests team reviews between the superior and his subordinates.[14] Based upon a joint problem-solving approach, these regular review sessions are intended to measure the team's progress toward its goals and to improve team relationships. Raia also encourages the use of a "responsibility matrix" to identify the degree to which various other management positions are related to the major activities a manager performs to accomplish his specific objectives.[15] In essence, then, programs in this second category include collaboration as a tangential aspect of an essentially one-to-one approach.

Third, there are MBO programs that include systematic collaboration as an integral part of the entire process (see example *2d* in Table 1). The three-day team-objectives meeting described by Reddin illustrates this approach.[16] In this program each team (superior and his immediate subordinates) concentrates on such matters as team-effectiveness areas, team-improvement objectives, team decision making, optimal team organization, team-meeting improvements, team-effectiveness evaluation, and team-member effectiveness. Such collaborative approaches appear to have many features congruent with contemporary organization development (OD) and are qualitatively quite different from one-to-one approaches.

MBO and OD Contrasted

One way to describe how CMBO differs qualitatively from a one-to-one approach is to contrast the one-to-one version with the emerging field of OD,

[10]Peter F. Drucker, *The Practice of Management* (New York: Harper & Row, 1954), p. 126.

[11]See, for example, Carvalho, "Installing Management by Objectives"; Wendell French, *The Personnel Management Process: Human Resources Administration,* 3d ed. (Boston: Houghton Mifflin, 1974); Howell, "A Fresh Look"; Charles L. Hughes, *Goal Setting* (New York: American Management Association, 1965), p. 123; Jamieson, "Behavioral Problems;" Kerr, "Some Modifications in MBO"; and Levinson, "Management by Whose Objectives?"

[12]A notable exception is W. J. Reddin, *Effective Management by Objectives: The 3–D Method of MBO* (New York: McGraw-Hill, 1971), chap. 14. Also see Wendell French and Cecil H. Bell, Jr., *Organization Development: Behavioral Science Interventions for Organization Improvement* (Englewood Cliffs, N.J.: Prentice-Hall, 1973), pp. 167–68; and Anthony P. Raia, *Managing by Objectives* (Glenview, Ill.: Scott, Foresman, 1974).

[13]Wikstrom, *Managing by and with Objectives,* pp. 22–23.
[14]Raia, *Managing by Objectives,* p. 110.
[15]Ibid., pp. 75–78.
[16]Reddin, *Effective Management by Objectives.*

which has a strong emphasis on team collaboration. Organization development, in the behavioral-science meaning of the term,[17] is a broader strategy for organizational improvement than is MBO, but it can include the collaborative version as we shall describe it. For instance, Blake and Mouton's six-phase grid OD program includes teamwork development (phase 2) and intergroup development (phase 3), both of which include collaborative goal setting.[18] In fact, they suggest that MBO can be "introduced as the culminating action of Teamwork Development."[19]

Some of the differences, as we see them, between the traditional one-to-one MBO and OD are shown in Table 2. Traditional MBO concentrates on the individual, on goal setting for the individual, on rationality, and on end results. In contrast, OD focuses on how individuals see the functioning of their teams and the organization, on nonrationality as well as rationality, and on means as well as ends. In addition, OD has a recurring component of system diagnosis that seems to be minimal or absent from the traditional forms of MBO. Further, OD efforts usually move toward legitimizing open discussion of individual career and life goals, which most MBO programs largely ignore.

A Strategy for Collaborative MBO

Contemporary organization-development efforts can provide insights and some of the technology for more widespread emergence of collaborative forms of MBO. We would like to propose a nine-phase strategy for Collaborative MBO. Basically, the essential process is one of overlapping work units interacting with "higher" and "lower" units on overall organizational goals and objectives, unit goals and objectives, and individuals interacting

with peers and superiors on role definition and individual goals and objectives.

Phase I. Diagnosis of Organizational Problems. A collaborative organizational diagnosis, by discussions or questionnaires involving a cross section of organization members, suggests the usefulness of a CMBO effort in solving *identified problems*. It appears to us that MBO, as frequently practiced, is a solution in search of a problem. For a variety of reasons, including the existence of a strong goal emphasis under some other name, overwork of many key people in the organization, or problems requiring other solutions, MBO may not be timely or appropriate.

Phase II. Information and Dialogue. Workshops on the basic purposes and techniques of CMBO are held with top management personnel, followed by workshops at the middle and lower management levels. These workshops can be conducted by qualified members of the personnel or training departments, by line managers trained in the approach, or if the organization prefers, by a qualified consultant. Having top-level managers conduct the workshops with middle and lower managers may speed up the process of shifting toward the more supportive climate necessary for CMBO.

Phase III. Diagnosis of Organizational Readiness. This diagnosis, based upon interviews and group meetings, must indicate an interest in and a willingness to use the process on the part of several organizational units, especially those at the top of the organization. Ideally, a number of overlapping units should express a desire to implement CMBO; for example, in addition to the president of a manufacturing firm and his immediate subordinates expressing interest, the manufacturing director and his immediate subordinates may want to be involved, and two of these subordinate managers may wish to start the process with their subordinate teams, and so forth. Favorable interest in CMBO from a few units randomly scattered throughout the organization would probably be inadequate to create enough interaction and momentum to give the

---

[17]French and Bell, *Organization Development,* p. 15.

[18]Robert R. Blake and Jane S. Mouton, *Corporate Excellence through Grid Organization Development* (Houston: Gulf Publishing, 1968); and Robert R. Blake and Jane S. Mouton, *Building a Dynamic Corporation through Grid Organization Development* (Reading, Mass.: Addison-Wesley Publishing, 1969).

[19]Blake and Mouton, *Corporate Excellence,* p. 110.

TABLE 2 Traditional MBO Compared with OD

What Traditional (one-to-one) MBO Seems to Do	*What OD Seems to Do*
1. Assumes there is a need for more goal emphasis and/or control.	1. Assumes there may be a variety of problems; a need for more goal emphasis and/or control may or may not be a central problem.
2. Has no broad diagnostic strategy.	2. Uses an "action-research" model in which system diagnosis and rediagnosis are major features.
3. Central target of change is the individual.	3. Central target of change is team functioning
4. Asks organization members to develop objectives for key aspects of their jobs in terms of quantitative and qualitative statements that can be measured.	4. Asks organization members to provide data regarding their perceptions of functional/ dysfunctional aspects of their units and/or the total organization.
5. Emphasizes avoidance of overlap and incongruity of goals. Assumes things will be better if people understand who has what territory.	5. Emphasizes mutual support and help. Assumes that some problems can stem from confusion about who has what responsibilities, but also looks at opportunities for mutual help in the many interdependent components across jobs.
6. Focuses on the "formal" aspects of the organization (goals, planning, control, appraisal).	6. Initially taps into "informal" aspects of the organization (attitudes, feelings, perceptions about both the formal and informal aspects, the total climate of the unit or organization).
7. Focuses on individual performance and emphasizes individual accountability.	7. Focuses on system dynamics that are facilitating or handicapping individual, team, and organizational performance; emphasizes joint accountability.
8. Stresses rationality ("logical" problem solving, man's economic motives).	8. Legitimizes for discussion nonrational aspects (feelings, attitudes, group phenomena) of organization life as well as rationality; frequently legitimizes open exploration of career and life goals.
9. Focuses on organizational end results of the human-social system (particularly as measured by "hard-data") such as sales figures, maintenance costs, and so forth.	9. Focuses on both ends and means of the human-social system (leadership style, peer relationships, and decision processes, as well as goals and "hard data").
10. Has little interpersonal-relations "technology" to assist superior and subordinate in the goal-setting and review processes.	10. Has extensive interpersonal relations, group dynamics, and intergroup "technology" for decision making, communications, and group task and maintenance processes.

approach a fair try. A good deal of diagnosis of organizational readiness will have already occurred in the information-and-dialogue phase. Similarly, diagnosis of organizational readiness may reveal the need for supplemental CMBO workshops for some units or for suspending the CMBO effort.

Phase IV. Goal Setting—Overall Organization Level.

Overall organization goals and specific objectives to be achieved within a given time period are defined in team meetings among top executives, largely on the basis of consensus. It is important that this phase be an interactive process with middle and lower levels of the organization: inputs about organization goals and objectives from subordinate managerial and supervisory levels must be obtained during (or before) this phase.

Phase V. Goal Setting—Unit Level.

Unit goals and objectives essential to achieving overall organization goals and objectives are defined in team situations, largely by consensus. Again, this is an interactive process between higher units and their respective subordinate units.

Phase VI. Goal Setting—Individual Level.

This phase begins with individual managers developing their specific objectives in terms of results to be achieved and appropriate time periods. Personal career and development goals are part of this "package." If desired, the manager's superior may simultaneously develop a list of objectives for the subordinate. The superior and subordinate discuss, modify, and tentatively agree on the subordinate's objectives. These discussions are followed by group meetings in which team members discuss each other's objectives, make suggestions for modification, and agree upon each manager's final list of objectives.

Phase VI assumes that there is agreement on the major responsibilities and parameters of the team members' roles. If major responsibilities need to be reviewed or redefined, the following sequence is used as the preliminary stage of phase VI: (1) individual team members list their major responsibilities; (2) individual team members meet with their superior to discuss, modify, and tentatively agree upon their major responsibilities; and (3) team members discuss and work toward consensus on their major responsibilities in group meetings.

Phase VII. Performance Review.

On a continuing basis, either the subordinate or the superior initiates discussion whenever progress toward objectives should be reviewed; matters of team concern are discussed in regularly scheduled team meetings. Particularly relevant at this stage are occasions when internal or external factors suggest the need for revision in the original set of goals and objectives; if appropriate, these revisions should be made in collaborative team meetings.

At the end of the agreed-upon time period, each manager prepares a report on the extent to which his objectives have been achieved and discusses this report in a preliminary meeting with his superior. These reports then are presented by each individual in a group meeting, with the discussion including an analysis of the forces helping and hindering attainment of objectives. This review process occurs at all levels (organization, unit, and individual) and ordinarily would start at the lower levels as a convenient way to collate information.

Phase VIII. Rediagnosis.

Diagnosis needs to reoccur, but at this phase it is the CMBO process itself that needs examining, as well as the readiness of additional units to use CMBO. Is the CMBO process helping? hindering? in what way? What is the process doing to the relationships between superiors and subordinates and within teams? Something has gone awry if goal setting and performance review are perfunctory or avoided, if the process seems unattached to the basic processes of getting the work of the organization done, or if relationships are becoming strained. On the other hand, if superiors and subordinates and teams find that the process is challenging and stretches and develops their capabilities, and if they feel good about it, the CMBO process is probably on the right track toward increased organizational effectiveness. Ideally such diagnosis should be ongoing as the CMBO process evolves.

Phase IX. Recycle. Assuming that rediagnosis has resulted in the decision to continue the CMBO effort, the cycle of phases IV through VIII is repeated, probably once a year at the overall organization level. Ongoing individual and team progress reviews may result in modification of unit- or individual-level goals more often than once a year. Through periodic problem sensing and rediagnosis, the details of the process will undoubtedly be modified to more adequately meet the needs of teams and individuals. The nine-phase strategy for implementing CMBO is presented in Figure 1.

Some Contingencies

CMBO is not likely to be an easy process for many organizations. Initial successes depend upon a strong desire on the part of the top-management team to cooperate with and help each other. In addition, the process requires some modicum of skill in interpersonal relations and group dynamics. Training in these skills can accompany the CMBO effort, or if an OD effort is under way, such skills will be emerging as part of this broader process.

Proper timing in the introduction of CMBO is also very important. CMBO is by no means a managerial panacea; it should be introduced only when diagnosis suggests its applicability and usefulness as well as organizational readiness. A CMBO effort can be time-consuming, and strong resistance can occur if the process is thoughtlessly superimposed at the wrong time—for example, during a period when people are preoccupied and harried with the annual budgeting process or faced with a major external threat to the organization. It is equally important to recognize that the utility of diagnosing organizational readiness is contingent upon the adequacy of information presented to managers in the CMBO workshops (phase II).

Successful expansion of the process to lower levels of the organization requires commitment to

and skills in participative management, as well as a willingness and ability to diagnose the impact of the goal-setting and review processes on organization members and organizational functioning. Such a diagnosis of how things are going might result, for instance, in temporarily postponing phase VI. Successful completion of phases I through V and the appropriate team aspects of phases VII through IX might in itself be a major achievement and a move forward in organizational effectiveness. Developing effective group dynamics takes time and an organization should proceed with caution in this area. A major shift to a collaborative mode cannot be made overnight.

The Merits of CMBO: Research and Practice Clues

There are a number of clues to the merits of a Collaborative MBO approach (that is, the kind that has a team emphasis, is truly collaborative, and exists in a climate of mutual support and help) in research reports and in practice. Likert cites a study of a sales organization in which salesmen held group meetings at regular intervals to set goals, discuss procedures, and identify results to be achieved before the next group meeting.[20] During these meetings the superior acted as a chairman; he stressed a constructive, problem-solving approach, encouraged high performance, and provided technical advice when necessary. The results of the study showed that salesmen using group meetings had more positive attitudes toward their jobs and sold more on the average than salesmen not using group meetings. According to Likert:

> Appreciably poorer results are achieved whenever the manager, himself, analyzes each man's performance and results, and sets goals for him. Such man-to-man interactions in the meetings, dominated by the manager, do not create group loyalty and have far less favorable impact upon the salesmen's motivation than do group interaction and decision meetings. Moreover, in the man-to-man

---

[20]Rensis Likert, *The Human Organization* (New York: McGraw-Hill, 1967), pp. 55–59.

FIGURE 1 A Strategy for Implementing Collaborative Management by Objectives

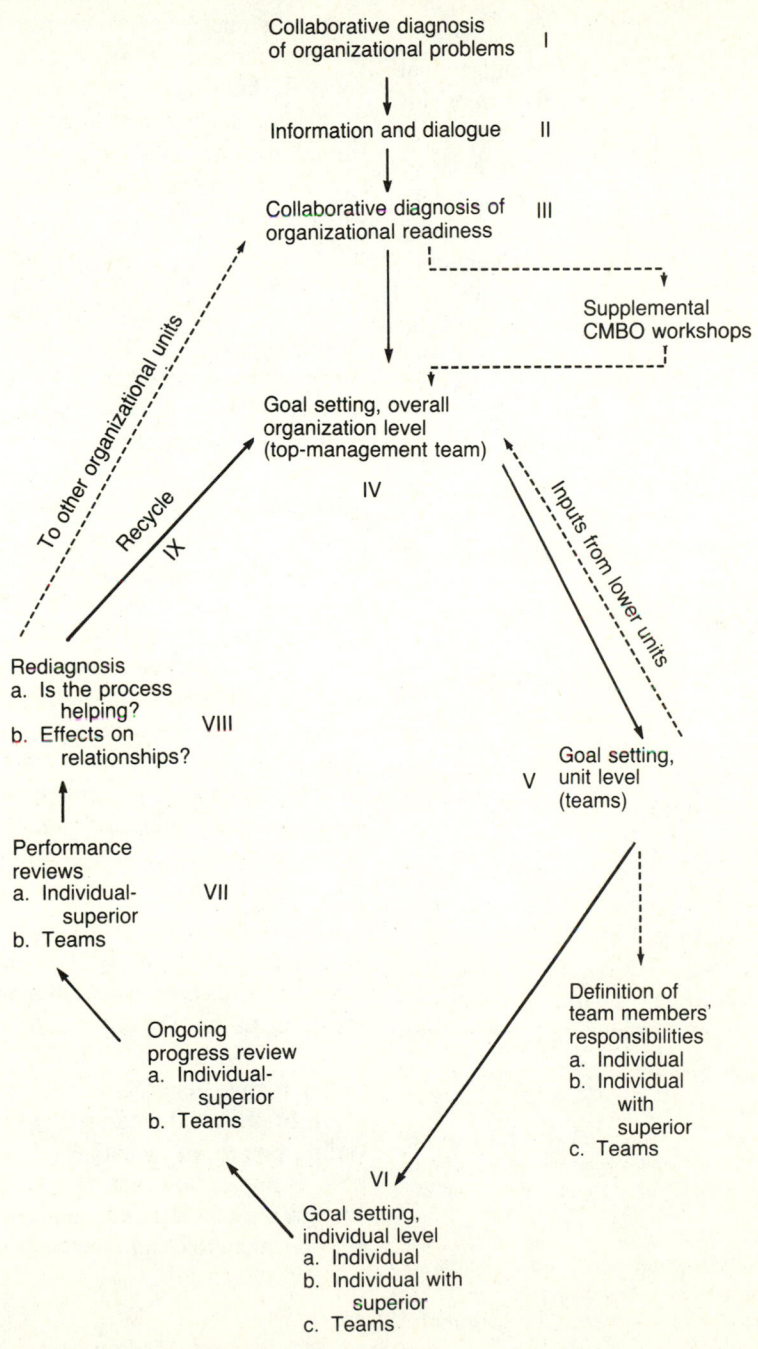

interaction little use is made of the sales knowledge and skills of the group.[21]

Another recent study found that managers' perceptions of the supportiveness of the organizational climate and their attitudes toward MBO were significantly related.[22] A supportive climate was viewed in terms of such features as high levels of trust and confidence between superiors and subordinates, multidirectional communication aimed at achieving objectives, cooperative teamwork, subordinate participation in decision making and goal setting, and control conducted close to the point of performance (self-control). Essentially, this climate was seen as comparable to Likert's Participative Group (System 4) management system.[23] The results of the study showed significant ($p > 0.01$) positive correlations between the supportiveness of the climate and how effective managers believed the MBO process to be. Managers' evaluations of MBO effectiveness were assessed in six areas: (1) planning and organizing work, (2) objective evaluation of performance, (3) motivation of the best job performance, (4) coordination of individual and work-group objectives, (5) superior-subordinate communication, and (6) superior-subordinate cooperation. Even more important was the significant ($p > 0.01$) positive correlation between supportiveness of the climate and managers' overall satisfaction with MBO as it related to their jobs.[24]

Holder describes how consensus decision making has been used at Yellow Freight System, Inc. since the early 1950s.[25] Work groups in the firm are organized according to the "linking-pin concept"[26] and decisions, including those dealing with managers' objectives, are made on a consensus basis within each work group. The writer's account is unclear as to whether consensus MBO operates throughout the management hierarchy; however, his description indicates that it extends to at least the regional-manager level. Although Holder provides no objective measure of effectiveness, he suggests that the length of time for which the program has been used attests to its success.

Finally, in explaining a job-enrichment program in a European chemical company, Myers reports: "In 1970, more than 40,000 additional employees conferred in work teams and functional groups to define criteria against which their performance could be measured and to set tangible goals."[27] According to Myers, the program has (*a*) moved decision making down to the levels where the work is performed, (*b*) resulted in better integration of individual and organizational goals, (*c*) required managers to rely upon interpersonal competence rather than official authority to get results, and (*d*) reduced the traditional barrier between management and nonmanagement. We think this experience is particularly significant; if operative work groups can effectively set objectives in a collaborative environment, it seems reasonable to expect that managers would also be able to do so.

Conclusions

The findings of these studies and organizational programs help confirm our belief that Collaborative Management by Objectives can work. We feel that CMBO, as we have described it, is congruent with a participative, team-leadership style and can avoid many of the dysfunctional spin-offs of the prevailing one-to-one versions of MBO. We do not wish to imply, however, that CMBO will work in all organizations and under any circumstances. Care must be taken to ensure that appropriate conditions

[21]Ibid., p. 57.

[22]Robert W. Hollmann, "A Study of the Relationships between Organizational Climate and Managerial Assessment of Management by Objectives" (Ph.D. dissertation, University of Washington, 1973).

[23]Likert, *The Human Organization;* and Rensis Likert, *New Patterns of Management* (New York: McGraw-Hill, 1961).

[24]Hollmann, "A Study of the Relationships."

[25]Jack J. Holder, Jr., "Decision Making by Consensus," *Business Horizons,* April 1972, pp. 47–54.

[26]Likert, *New Patterns of Management* and *The Human Organization.*

[27]M. Scott Myers, "Overcoming Union Opposition to Job Enrichment," *Harvard Business Review,* May–June, 1971, pp. 37–49.

are present before and that necessary skills emerge during the implementation of CMBO.

Successful application of CMBO requires that managers be motivated to shift the climate of the organization, or at least the climate of those units using CMBO, in the direction of more teamwork, more cooperation, more joint problem solving, and more support. While a team approach per se would tend to diminish the dysfunctional consequences of status differentials and could shift the locus of commitments among people away from the one-to-one arena toward the lateral or interdependent team arena, a team approach void of mutual support and group skills could create more problems than it would solve. Training of work teams in skills of communication, group processes, and joint problem solving is vital to this shift toward a more supportive climate.

Equally vital to the success of CMBO are skills in diagnosis—both the original diagnosis that identified the need and readiness of CMBO and the subsequent diagnoses that tune into managers' perceptions of the functional and dysfunctional aspects of the CMBO process and their assesssment of the emerging climate. Such continuous "tracking" will be hard work, but the resulting opportunities for modification and other corrective action should make the CMBO process that much more relevant to the needs of the organization and its members.

The nine-phase strategy we have proposed is one way of introducing more systematic collaboration into the MBO process. While it will undoubtedly take considerable effort and attention to make the CMBO strategy work well, this approach can help people, teams, and units become more goal-directed without undermining efforts to maintain or create a participative, responsive team climate in the organization.

Reading 38

CHANGING ORGANIZATIONS

Edward E. Lawler III

Surprisingly little has been written about the role of pay system change in organizational change efforts. With a few exceptions (e.g., Lawler and Bullock, 1978; Patten, 1977; Patten and Fraser, 1975), the issue has been ignored in both the organization development literature and the pay literature. Despite this, a considerable amount can and needs to be said about the important role that pay system change should play in change efforts. The pay system issues involved in changing established organizations are very different from those involved in starting new organizations. The differences stem primarily from two features of existing organizations: (1) the creation of timing issues due to the difficulty in changing all systems in an organization at the same time and (2) the existence of resistance to change. These factors will be examined in this chapter in order to point out how the many approaches to pay discussed so far can fit into organization development efforts in established organizations.

Sequencing System Change

The key issue in initiating a change effort is where to start. In most organizations, a number of systems offer potential leverage points for initiating change (e.g., jobs or organizational structure). In order for most change efforts to be successful, a number of systems must be changed; otherwise, congruence will not exist and the changes will not be institutionalized. One strategy is simply to try to change all systems simultaneously. In most cases, how-

Source: Edward E. Lawler III, *Pay and Organization Development*, (Reading, Mass.: Addison-Wesley Publishing, 1981), pp. 196–205. © 1981, Addison-Wesley. Reprinted with permission.

ever, this strategy is not practical because of the chaos it produces and because the resources to work on all systems simultaneously are usually not available in organizations. What typically happens is that one or more systems become lead systems in the change effort and others become lag systems. The pay system can be either a lag or a lead system. Let us first consider how it can operate as a lead system, then as a lag system. By doing this, we will be in a position to consider what determines which is the best strategy in a particular change effort.

Pay as a Lead System

There are a number of reasons why starting a change program with the pay system may be both meaningful and strategically desirable:

1. The pay system is important to employees and it impacts on all organization members. Many times, change programs are limited to an issue that is not important to most individuals or that does not affect everyone (e.g., the creation of several self-managing teams). As a result, change is slow and often not very significant in the eyes of many. Pay is an issue that can provide a firm base upon which to begin organizational change.

2. Beginning with the pay system can be an indication of an organization's commitment to meaningful change. A belief that serious commitment exists can lead to attacking serious problems. Many change programs have been stymied and discredited because they started with such insignificant changes as cafeteria painting or fixing the parking lot. The pay system provides a direct route to the core organizational systems and is substantial evidence of deep-seated commitment to improvement.

3. Most organizations have problems with their pay system. Perceptions of inequity, inadequate administration, and nonperformance-contingent rewards are all indicators of maladies in compensation that are common to most organizations. They lead to a felt need for pay system change, a basic precondition for change.

4. Dealing successfully with the pay system can lead to measurable differences in individual performance and organizational effectiveness. This, in turn, can produce a feeling of success and positive feedback. Successful interventions in pay systems can demonstrate clearly the possibility of obtaining improvements through planned changes and, as a result, can encourage further planned change.

5. Beginning with pay can provide a model for how other problems can be dealt with. Usually, organizations have little or no experience in using a systematic process for solving systemwide problems that affect the quality of work life and organizational effectiveness. These mechanisms and processes can be developed and made explicit through changing the compensation system, and organizational learning can thus take place. A good example of this can be found in some of my work in which task forces and surveys have been used to diagnose and solve pay system problems. Later these same approaches were then used to solve other important problems.

6. Beyond providing a specific model of change, beginning with the pay system can lead directly to identifying other problems in the organization since the pay system is so closely connected to the other systems (Patten and Fraser, 1975). Performance appraisal problems, dysfunctional management practices, poor supervision, control system errors, poor job designs, accounting inadequacies, and awkward communication networks are all examples of issues that may be highlighted by attempts to change the pay system because they are so closely tied to compensation issues. Commonly, the need for these other changes is made apparent by the initial diagnosis, but effort is only put into problem solving once the pay system change is made. Sometimes, the need for other changes is not even apparent until the pay system changes are in place because the pay change is needed to put them clearly out of tune with the other systems in the organization.

Despite the reasons for believing pay system changes can be a good place to start an organizational change effort, little research exists on how effective this approach is, and little is known about how to design and implement a change program that starts with the pay system. During the last five years, I have been involved in a number of studies which were designed to determine what happens when the pay system is used as the starting point for a change project. Included are studies of management and executive compensation, as well as studies of plant-wide gain sharing and base-pay systems. Most of these studies are still underway since they are attempting to look at the long-term effects of the change efforts. Thus definitive overall conclusions cannot be reached for several years. It is not too early, however, to report some of what has been learned.

Where to Begin?

The first strategic question to be addressed is: What aspect of the pay system represents the best place to begin? The choice is usually between starting with the base-pay system, a special performance-based bonus system, or the total pay system. The choice should be based on a careful diagnosis of the current state of the present pay system. As Patten and Fraser (1975) point out, an attitude survey can be very useful in this diagnosis, particularly when it is combined with an effective feedback process. (See Nadler (1977) for a discussion of survey feedback.) If the base-pay system is in reasonably good shape and improved performance is desired, it is advisable to start with consideration of a performance-based pay system. Consideration of performance-based pay seems to lead more quickly to consideration of such systemic issues as superior-subordinate communication, the trust level in the organization, and the overall effectiveness of the organization. Overall, it leads more quickly to widespread organizational change.

However, if the base-pay system is seriously out of line with people's perceptions of equity, there really is no choice but to begin with it. To do otherwise is to compromise the credibility of the entire effort. When the base-pay plan is the beginning point, it leads naturally to a consideration of performance-based pay. For example, in one plant where Jenkins and I did a change project, we were "forced" to deal with the base-pay system first, even though we had intended to start out with a participative gain-sharing plan (Lawler and Jenkins, 1976). The base-pay system was so out of line that the employees were unwilling to talk about a gain-sharing plan until the base pay was fair in their eyes. After a new base-pay plan was put into practice, a gain-sharing plan was developed and implemented.

Finally, it is worth noting that, in many unionized workplaces, there is no choice about where to start. The contract often prevents changes in base pay. As a result, the program must begin with consideration of a plant-wide or organization-wide gain-sharing plan, an approach that many unions will agree to consider outside of the contract.

Who Should Be Involved?

Once decisions have been made about where the change effort will start, the next question is: Who should be involved? Most approaches to changing pay systems are top-down—they assume that people above those on the pay plan should make the change decisions. However, there is evidence that people can design their own systems and that, in some cases, this has produced very positive results. Since there are risks involved in having lower-level employees involved in making pay system changes, a participative effort should only be undertaken when it is part of an overall change program designed to increase the communication and participation levels in the organization. An isolated attempt at participation may just raise expectations which are promptly disconfirmed. Participation also should only be undertaken after a careful mapping has been done of what decisions have to be made and a *clear* decision is made about who is going

to study, recommend, and reach a final decision on each.

In most of my change effort projects, small task forces (five to nine people) have been created, consisting of members who represent the groups that will be affected by the changes. Their first task is to diagnose the current situation. Because this diagnosis is a critical informational and educational base for future decisions, it must be accomplished effectively. The diagnosis consists of two questions: What is the objective situation? and What are the perceptions of the pay system in the eyes of the employees?

The objective diagnosis should be designed to firmly establish what compensation practices are currently in place in the organization. Once the objective definition of the compensation system has been established, it is important to determine the individuals' perceptions of the system. A well-designed survey can be instrumental in isolating various perceptions of the pay system and in educating task-force members on the issues involved in pay administration. In addition, a well-designed questionnaire can be instrumental in spreading participation throughout the organization by giving everyone a say in how the new plan will be structured. The results of the survey can also serve as a stimulus for change and as a base-line measure for monitoring improvement resulting from the pay system changes. The survey needs to look at such pay issues as internal equity (How fair is the distribution of pay within the organization?); external equity (How does pay in the organization compare to pay in the community?); the pay-performance relationship and personal equity (Is the pay fair considering the individual's investment of effort and responsibility?). The survey should also consider such nonpay issues as the climate of the organization, the nature of jobs, and superior-subordinate relationships. These nonpay issues are included for two reasons: (1) the pay system must take into account the characteristics of the organization of which it will be a part, and (2) exploring these issues may prepare the way for later changes in other systems.

Mediating Factors

Once the current situation and perceptions have been established, there is one last step that needs to be taken before recommendations for change are made. This step is the analysis of the organizational and situational factors which determine which type of pay system is appropriate. Because many of these factors have already been considered, only five of the more important ones will be reviewed here.

Organization Size. Most approaches to paying for performance vary in their effectiveness as a function of organization size. There are many levels at which performance can be assessed. Performance can be measured and rewarded at the individual, work-group, or organizational level. Organization size needs to be a major determinant of the level at which performance is measured. Size is also a major determinant in the complexity of the administration of the compensation system. As size increases, so does the difficulty of adequately explaining the system and any changes to it.

Interdependence. The extent of interdependence among tasks and individuals within the organization is another critical mediating component of changes to the pay system. High levels of interdependence require systems which reflect that interdependence. There must be a congruence between the pay system and the individual and group behaviors which are necessary for organizational effectiveness. This has some particularly important implications for the design of a performance-based pay plan. It means that when interdependence is high, it is crucial to use plans that reward overall group or plant performance, rather than individual performance. For example, in process production facilities (such as food processing plants, chemical plants, and many complex assembly plants), it does not make sense to try to measure and reward individual performance. It simply is not separable enough from the performance of others to be validly measurable for pay reward purposes.

Degree of interdependence also has some implications for base-pay programs. High interdependence increases the attractiveness of skill-based pay plans that reward individuals for having a broad knowledge of the work setting. With interdependence, this knowledge can have a very definite payoff. Skill-based pay systems are a good example of an approach which fits well in an interdependent situation but may not in an independent one.

Quality and Type of Information. For a pay system to be effective, employees must receive information about the things for which they are compensated, and the organization must produce reliable and face-valid measures to back up the system. This means that the information system has to provide appropriate information—both the type of information and the quality of information that is required to make pay decisions. This point has very important implications for the design of performance-based pay systems and base-pay systems. It means that if a type of performance, a job characteristic, or any other factor cannot be measured in a publicly discussible and defensible manner, it should not be considered as a basis for paying individuals. This rules out highly subjective and secret measures as a basis for pay and means that, in some situations, individuals should not be paid for their performance because individual performance is not and cannot be measured in a satisfactory manner. Not surprisingly, improvements in the information systems are often required if pay is to be based on performance at any level in the organization. This can lead to improvements in the information system that both solve the pay problem and give managers information that improves their ability to manage.

Value System of the Members. There are differences in the values and beliefs of organizational members that must be considered in designing changes in the pay system. For example, organizations often differ in the degree to which employees feel they should equally share in a companywide or plantwide bonus pool. In one situation I studied, the employees felt strongly that everyone should be treated equally; in another, they felt it would be unfair to treat good and poor performers the same. In another case mentioned earlier, I tried to install a base-pay system which tied the base-pay rate to the number of jobs a person could do (Lawler and Jenkins, 1976). It ended up being rejected by the employees because they wanted to concentrate on learning how to do their job better, not on learning other jobs.

Technological Change. The rate of technological change is important because of the limitations it places on the measurement and evaluation of performance and individual jobs. Stable technologies often permit relatively complex, sophisticated measures to be developed. Often, these same measures are not cost effective in rapidly changing technologies. Rapidly changing technologies often require excessive administration costs to properly measure and evaluate individual tasks and individual performance. In situations where change is rapid, it is therefore desirable to have a base-pay system that has very loose job descriptions and does not measure individual performance.

Design, Implementation, and Change

Once the important mediating factors have been assessed, it is time to design the new pay system. Rarely is this a simple process. Occasionally everything seems to fall into place, so that one particular pay approach is the clear, logical choice. Most situations, however, simply are not that straightforward. The state of the mediating factors is often such that no one approach is clearly indicated. Although this can cause frustration, it also can motivate a broad look at the condition of the organization, which may reveal that changes in other areas are needed if pay is to be administered in a way that will make the organization more effective and the quality of work life better. Eventually, if no pay system change can be agreed upon or other changes seem to have higher priority, then

it may be necessary to reexamine the decision to begin with a pay system change.

Regardless of what new approach to pay is chosen, it is crucial that a good change process be used in implementing it. As will be discussed later in this chapter, pay system change can be particularly difficult to manage. Since it is a highly important factor, it is particularly likely to produce distortion and resistance. This makes it extremely important that pay system change include those features which are known to reduce resistance: participation and open communication.

Systemic Effects

In most cases, pay system changes lead to an expressed need for other changes. A physicist once remarked that, "Every time we try to separate something to study it, we find it hitched to everything else in the universe." The same is true for organizations. The compensation system affects and is affected by virtually every other subsystem of the organization. The most important links are to performance appraisal, the information system, the design of jobs, and the managerial style. Not surprisingly, one or more of these usually needs to be changed when pay systems are changed. It is crucial that this be anticipated and prepared for before the pay system changes are made. If it is not, the pay system changes may only increase the frustration level in the organization. This point is clearly illustrated by what often happens when a gain-sharing plan is installed.

The motivation for changing other systems is often very high when a gain-sharing plan is installed. People want it to pay out and they realize that for it to pay a bonus, other changes are needed. At this point, the success of the plan depends on whether or not these other changes can be made. The following is a list of some of the things that often are asked for:

1. Better scheduling systems.
2. Better tools and equipment.
3. Supervisory training in technical skills.

4. Supervisory training in listening and dealing with suggestions.
5. Technical training for employees.
6. More information on the financial condition of the organization.
7. Fair base-pay rates.

As the reader can see, these issues cover a wide range of things. Not every one has to be or can be responded to immediately, but some of them must be. Otherwise, the gain-sharing plan is likely to fail because people develop the perception that "no one cares" and that "it is hopeless."

Conclusion

Although a great deal can be accomplished by using pay system change as a lead system in producing meaningful organizational change, it is important to conclude with two cautionary points.

First, it takes time. If an organization is serious about making meaningful changes, it will have to make a strong commitment of time and energy to understanding the current situation and developing successful changes. In my projects, it has usually taken at least six months for the new pay system to be designed and implemented. Change in other systems has taken much longer. Pay system change is no panacea. Typically it is only the beginning of a multiple system change effort.

Second, it is important to take a formative view of compensation system changes. It is not necessary to always be fiddling with the system, but it is vital to respond to problems and situational changes when they occur, as they occur. Because conditions change inside of and outside of organizations, pay systems need to change. This means that even the best conceived and implemented pay change program is not likely to be a permanent "fix" for either the pay problems or any other problems in the organization. The most that can be hoped for is that it will help the organization become more effective in adapting to changes in its environment and will make later changes in the pay system both possible and effective.

D. Collateral Organizations and Quality Circles

This section includes an essay on collateral organizations and an essay on quality circles. Both have implications for OD and vice versa.

The creation of collateral organizations and temporary task forces are not inherently OD interventions, but the way they are utilized in a selected portion of an article by Zand places them in these particular instances in the OD province. In general, however, these are clearly structural interventions in that they supplement and modify a present organizational structure.

A collateral organization as described by Dale Zand, "is a supplemental organization co-existing with the usual, formal organization" created to deal with "ill-structured" problems. He goes on to describe how OD specialists can help managers design and utilize such structures and what some of the operating problems are. In many ways, Zand's illustrations of the creation of collateral organizations are reminiscent of fairly task-oriented team-building sessions in that they involve a change agent, data gathering, data feedback, and process consultation. Further, one might argue that it is usually ill-structured problems that get dealt with in most team building, and therefore the use of collateral organizations and team building are the same thing. However, in the Zand illustrations, it appears that collateral organizations were used to deal with high-priority, systemwide problems involving more than one unit. In contrast, most team-building activities include just one unit, focus on its problems, and do not deal extensively with systemwide problems. In some ways, the use of collateral organizations as described by Zand could be the first phase of a comprehensive OD effort which could then move on to unit team building, intergroup workshops, and so on.

It should be emphasized that the collateral organization described by Zand is a task force but with a difference. In particular, the collateral organization features a different set of norms than the formal organization, including, as Zand states it, "careful questioning and analysis of goals, assumptions, methods, alternatives, and criteria for evaluation."

The second article, by Gregory Shea, on quality circles (QCs), deals with an approach that has received a great deal of attention in recent years. This approach, widely used in Japan, is seen as contributing to the competitive success of Japanese industry and is thus

354

seen as a potential method for American organizations to revitalize their quality control and productivity capabilities.

In this essay, Shea discusses the importance of thinking through the intended purposes of QCs before their introduction. He then develops a typology for examining various purposes of QCs for the short term and the long term. Shea concludes that different purposes can produce different benefits and risks about which managers should be aware. For example, one potential purpose, short-term improvement in working relationships, Shea sees as having high risk. Shea also contrasts Japanese and American use of QCs.

As a concluding note, we have discussed the potential relationship as well as potential incongruities between OD and a number of other improvement strategies, including socio-technical systems, MBO, job enrichment, and collateral organizations. How might OD impact on other fields, such as industrial engineering, and vice versa?

First of all, if an open, action-research model is used in OD, any other improvement strategy currently being carried forward in the particular organization is fair game for review and modification through the OD process. Second, one or more of a variety of other improvement strategies might be an outcome of an OD effort. Third, and more broadly, we know from personal experience that OD has made an impact on some practitioners in many nonbehavioral science fields such as architecture, industrial engineering, electronic data processing, and budgeting. We suspect (but have only fragmentary information through participating in "Introduction to OD" workshops, and in many team-building settings with people from a wide variety of disciplines) that many such practitioners begin to go about their tasks in substantially different ways after some exposure to OD. Our impression is that many of them begin to make better diagnoses, to involve more people in diagnosis and problem analysis, to have more of the systems view of problems, and so on.

An article by Sharon Lieder and John Zenger, not reproduced here, is illustrative of how an OD effort in one organization made an impact on industrial engineering practices and vice versa, to good effect. In this instance, an OD effort had started, and the OD people (from a "career development department") were asked to help launch a new industrial engineering department. The long-range consequences were innovative and effective, and it appears that congruence between the OD effort and industrial engineering practices—potentially quite disparate—was accomplished and maintained.[1]

---

[1] Sharon L. Lieder and John H. Zenger, "Industrial Engineers and Behavior Scientists: A Team Approach to Improving Productivity," *Personnel,* July–August 1967, pp. 68–75.

Reading 39

COLLATERAL ORGANIZATION: A NEW CHANGE STRATEGY

Dale E. Zand

Part One: Concepts

Many organization development specialists who emphasize behavioral rather than structural or technical change contend that free-form organizations, participative leadership, and humanistic values should—indeed, will—displace hierarchical organizations, directive leadership, and mechanistic values (Argyris, 1970; Bennis, 1965, 1966; Golembiewski, 1972; Likert, 1961, 1967; McGregor, 1960; Marguilies & Raia, 1972; Slater & Bennis, 1964; Tannenbaum & Davis, 1969). It is their view that knowledge rather than level of authority should (or will) determine decisions, and that environmental complexity and turbulence should (or will) cause one-man decision making to give way to group decision making.

These assertions have merit and are especially attractive to social scientists, but they are controversial to managers. Indeed, the idea of totally displacing existing systems may well have diverted managers into choosing sides, and thereby seriously interfered with their learning to improve their organization's adaptability and effectiveness. There is increasing evidence of a need for flexibility in structure and leadership style across different tasks and individuals; the superiority of any one approach above all others cannot be defended (Fiedler, 1967; Lawrence & Lorsch, 1967). The key issue is: How can OD specialists help managers design creative, problem-solving organizations and use them flexibly?

This article seeks to clarify and extend our concepts of organizational form and behavior by introducing the strategy of *collateral organization*[1] as a means of increasing flexibility. I shall present supporting theory and research; describe two field cases which illustrate methods of introducing collateral modes of organization; contrast collateral organizations with task forces, temporary systems, and matrix organizations; and finally, discuss their impact on the use of groups for solving problems and on the role of middle managers.

Collateral Mode Defined

Research into the relation between the structure of a problem and the effectiveness of different organizations suggests that a work group benefits from using more than one mode of organization. To state it simply: authority/production-centered organizations work best with "well-structured" problems; knowledge/problem-centered organizations work best with "ill-structured" problems. These organizational modes and problem structures will be described in greater detail later; the important point is that since problems vary in structure, managers can and should operate in more than one organizational mode.

Source: Reproduced by special permission from *The Journal of Applied Behavioral Science*, "Collateral Organization: A New Change Strategy," by Dale Zand, vol. 10, no. 1, pp. 63–89. Copyright 1974 by NTL Institute for Applied Behavioral Science.

[1] I shall use the word *organization* to mean the communication channels, relationships, and the inner workings of a group composed of a superior and his subordinates, and the working relationships between such groups—rather than the distinct major divisions of a company.

The concept of a secondary mode of working will be called a collateral organization. Hence a collateral organization is a supplemental organization coexisting with the usual, formal organization.[2] Of course a manager may develop more than one collateral organization, but to keep matters simple we will talk of only one collateral mode in the remainder of this article.

Typically, a group has a chain of command and a division or responsibilities designed primarily for coping with well-defined, repetitive problems. Continued changes in consumers' desires, competitors' tactics, and product technology introduce unforeseen, ill-defined problems and opportunities. The hierarchical organizational structure is not designed to discover and solve these "ill-structured" problems. Managers, regardless of organizational level, therefore need collateral modes.

But managers hesitate to depart from the formal hierarchy to use a collateral mode because they are rarely given concepts explaining and legitimizing such departures. Traditional organization theory, for example, offers only the vague concept of "informal organization" (Pfiffner & Sherwood, 1960). Moreover, managers are advised to avoid and suppress informal organization because it is unsanctioned, unplanned, and unpredictable (Delbecq, 1968).

The manager's confusion is sometimes compounded by laboratory-method organizational development programs. Sensitivity training, grid laboratories, and variations of group methods focus on improving the manager's skill in individual and group behavior, but rarely introduce relevant organization theory. When a manager applies his new knowledge to his formal organization, he usually encourages open questioning of goals and methods, which blurs formal boundaries between jobs. Other managers interpret his actions as undermining authority and disrupting the formal organization, so they resist and discard his changes. The manager

is in a theoretical limbo; without concepts, he cannot explain to other managers what he is doing in terms they can understand.

The concept of collateral organization is offered to aid managerial understanding and use of organizational development efforts. To explain and illustrate it, I shall first discuss the relationship between organizational problems and organizational structures, and the characteristics of a collateral organization.

Matching Problems and Modes. A problem is a dilemma and an organization is an instrument. It is useful to think of a problem and an organization as a set which is poorly or well matched. If the manager is to choose the right instrument for the job, it is important to understand when a problem and an organization are matched.

A problem can be classified as either well structured or ill structured. Some problems of course will have characteristics found in both categories, but analysis of the pure types will contribute most to understanding the matching process.

A well-structured problem—for example, preparing a customer's bill from a list of items and prices or putting values into a computer program which calculates the present worth of a capital investment—has the characteristics of physical or routine mental work.

In contrast, an ill-structured problem—for example, determining what new products should be added to a line over the next three years, preparing a schedule of prices for products that do not exist in any market, or projecting the long-range organizational, financial, and employment effects of a new marketing strategy—has the characteristics of complex, nonroutinized mental work. The elements of well- and ill-structured problems are outlined in Figure 1.

Usually a manager assumes that he has only one organization, which he must use for all problems. That is like a carpenter who uses a hammer for all jobs. A more effective manager first classifies a problem and then chooses an instrument best suited for it.

---

[2] *Collateral,* when used as a noun, denotes assets pledged as security for a loan. It is used here as an adjective, meaning to exist at the same time and level as, hence in association with, another organization.

FIGURE 1   Characteristics of Well-Structured and Ill-Structured Problems

Element	Well-Structured Problems	Ill-Structured Problems
Variation of output with hours of work	Known. Proportional.	Unknown. Nonproportional.
Variation of output with number of people	Known. Proportional.	Unknown. Nonproportional.
Characteristics of input and output	Countable. Quality accurately measurable. Errors detected quickly, precisely.	Not countable. Quality difficult to measure. Errors difficult to detect.
Information available	Relevant. Accurate. Complete.	Uncertain. Inaccurate. Incomplete.
Solutions	Few are feasible. All are known. Best one determined easily.	Many are feasible. Few are known. Best one difficult to determine.
Experts	Past solution of similar problems is a reliable indication of expertise.	Many claim to be expert, but past experience is an unreliable guide to expertise.
Methods of control	External standards such as output targets, hours allowed, cost goals can effectively control performance.	Extenal standards are inapplicable and misleading.
Feedback about results	Occurs shortly after action. Can be attributed to the action.	Occurs long after the action. Cannot be attributed only to the action.

An organization (work group) can be classified as *(a)* authority/production centered or *(b)* knowledge/problem centered. Of course, some organizations will cross both categories, but again we learn the most from studying the two pure types. The authority/production form is concerned with mobilizing people and equipment to maximize output of a finished product. The knowledge/problem form is concerned with processing or inventing knowledge to solve problems. Elements of the two organizational forms are compared in Figure 2.

Research Findings. Experimental research with small groups suggests that some combinations of organizations and problems are more productive than others. Communication network studies are especially relevant because they simulate many of the properties of the two types of organizations

described in Figure 2, and the problems used fit well into one or the other of the two classes of problems described above. Transfer of results from experimental settings to operating organizations requires caution; so the findings summarized here can be viewed only as suggestive. They are presented in condensed form for purposes of theory development, with some of the complex differences in morale and other factors set aside.

For well-structured problems, it appears that groups in the authority/production mode produce more output, more rapidly, than groups in the knowledge/problem mode (Bavelas, 1950; Christie, Luce, & May, Jr., 1952; Leavitt, 1951). And when groups organized in the knowledge/problem mode are given a series of well-structured problems and are allowed to reorganize, they shift toward the authority/production mode. They install a hi-

FIGURE 2   Types of Organizations

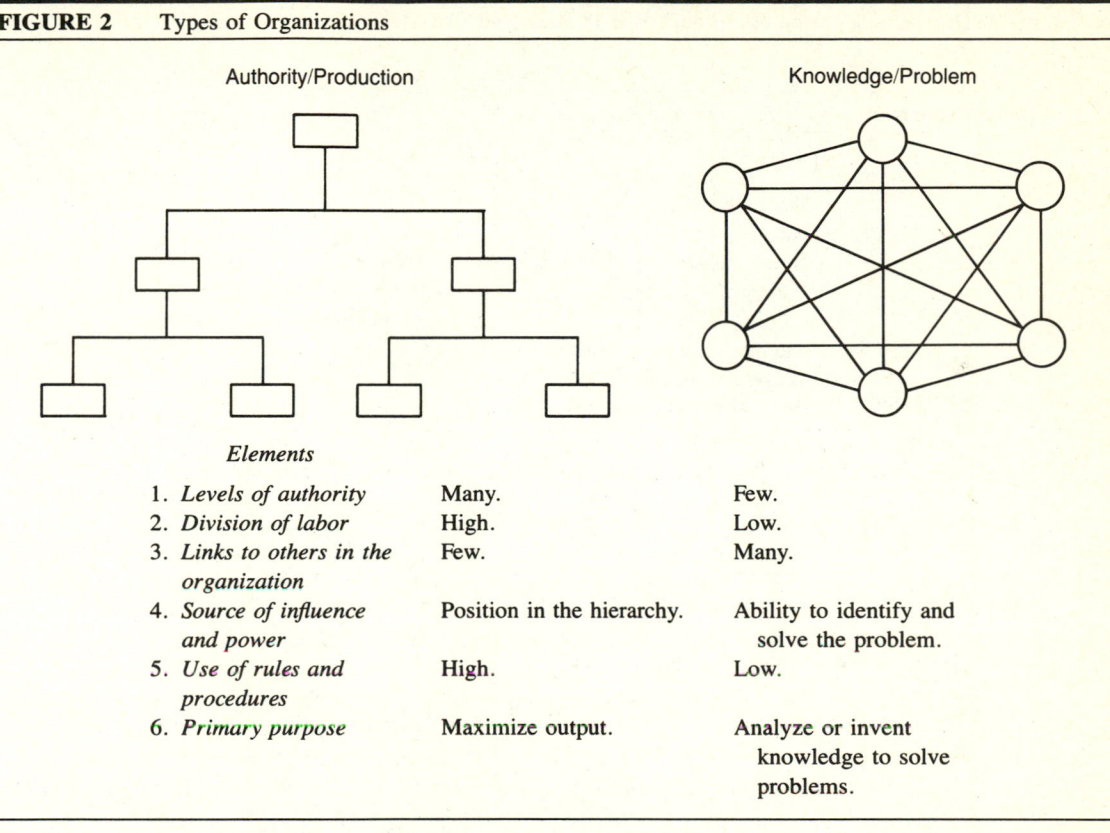

Authority/Production   Knowledge/Problem

Elements

	Authority/Production	Knowledge/Problem
1. *Levels of authority*	Many.	Few.
2. *Division of labor*	High.	Low.
3. *Links to others in the organization*	Few.	Many.
4. *Source of influence and power*	Position in the hierarchy.	Ability to identify and solve the problem.
5. *Use of rules and procedures*	High.	Low.
6. *Primary purpose*	Maximize output.	Analyze or invent knowledge to solve problems.

erarchy, divide labor, and cut unused communication links (Guetzkow & Dill, 1957; Guetzkow & Simon, 1955).

For ill-structured problems, however, groups in the knowledge/problem mode devise solutions of better quality, more rapidly, than do groups in the authority/production mode (Shaw, Rothchild, & Strickland, 1957). The hierarchy, the division of labor, and the rules that make the authority/production mode effective for well-structured problems seem to interfere with the group's ability to devise quality solutions to ill-structured problems.

Another characteristic of the authority production mode makes it unsuitable for ill-structured problems: it tends to reject unsolicited innovation. In this mode managers view an uninvited proposal for improvement as a distraction that will reduce output. In contrast, the knowledge/problem group tends to accept and use unsolicited innovations to improve productivity (Bavelas, 1950).

There are no experimental data on whether authority/production groups, given ill-structured problems, shift to a knowledge/problem mode. Observation of authority/production organizations suggests that when they are confronted with an ill-structured problem, such as entering a volatile market undergoing rapid technical change, managers do not shift to another mode but try to redefine the problem, forcing it to fit the existing hierarchy and division of labor. Burns and Stalker (1961) found that companies unable to shift to a knowledge/problem mode were unsuccessful in the new environment.

The most effective combinations (see Figure 3) are well-structured problems with authority/produc-

FIGURE 3   Relationship between Type of Problem and Type of Organization

	Type of Organization	
Type of Problem	*Authority/Production*	*Knowledge/Problem*
Well-Structured	**I** High Output Rapid processing Small number of errors in output Members low in authority report low satisfaction Tends to reject unsolicited innovations	**II** Lower output Slower processing More errors in output More satisfying Accepts unsolicited innovations
Ill-structured	**IV** Lower output Slower processing Low-quality solutions Low in creativity Orderly, but not functional	**III** High output Rapid processing High-quality solutions High creativity Appears disorderly but is functional

tion organization (Quadrant I), and ill-structured problems with knowledge/problem organization (Quadrant III). The other combinations (II and IV) are not so well matched.

Displacement Trap. Contrary to the "displacement belief," there is little likelihood that the authority/production mode, which is characteristic of most business organizations, will vanish. It works for well-structured problems and minimally disrupts the organization. There is, however, a limit to how far it can be stretched; and when a problem keeps recurring, that limit has by definition been exceeded. The challenge is: Can a manager and his group shift to a secondary mode before their primary mode becomes ineffective?

Many managers who make the shift to a new mode of organization are led to believe by poorly conceptualized OD efforts that they and their subordinates never again need directive behavior, specialized assignments, and limited communication. Such expectations prove unrealistic. Upon "regressing" to the authority/production mode, managers feel guilty and disappointed. Subordinates are frustrated and dissatisfied at relinquishing their newly found influence. Managers and subordinates frequently conclude that organizational development is a sham.

There may be a similar lack of realism about shifting even when the primary mode is knowledge/problem centered. For example, research units and educational institutions resist using the authority/production mode when it is needed, fearing that the primary, participative mode would not only be displaced but would be unrecoverable.

An understanding of collateral organization can help managers integrate needed changes while maintaining the primary organization.

Relation of Collateral Organization to Formal Organization

In the remainder of this paper, for discussion purposes, I shall assume that the formal organization is in the authority/production mode. The collateral organization will be the knowledge/problem mode. (This state of affairs may of course be reversed in some organizations; e.g., research units and educational organizations.)[3]

In Tandem. A collateral organization is distinguishable from and linked to the formal organization as follows:

1. The purpose of the collateral organization is to identify and solve problems not solved by the formal (primary) organization.
2. A collateral organization creatively complements the formal organization. It allows new combinations of people, new channels of communication, and new ways of seeing old ideas.
3. A collateral organization operates in parallel or in tandem with the formal organization. Both the collateral and the formal organizations are available; a manager chooses one or the other, depending on the problem. A collateral organization does not displace the formal organization.
4. A collateral organization consists of the same people who work in the formal organization. There are no new people.
5. The outputs of the collateral organization are inputs to the formal organization. The ultimate value of a collateral organization depends on successfully linking it to the formal organization, so its outputs are used.

6. A collateral organization operates with norms (that is, expectations of how people will behave) that are different from the norms in the formal organization. The different norms facilitate new ideas and new approaches to obstacles.

Characteristics. A collateral organization has the following characteristics:

1. All channels are open and connected. Managers and specialists are free to communicate without being restricted to formal channels in the hierarchy.
2. There is a rapid and complete exchange of relevant information.
3. Norms encourage careful questioning and analysis of goals, assumptions, methods, alternatives, and criteria for evaluation.
4. A manager can approach and enlist others in the organization to help solve a problem, without being restricted to his formal subordinates.

Part Two: Applications

The two cases that follow illustrate different social technologies for introducing collateral organization. They are brief descriptions of change efforts in the field. They do not have the benefit of control groups or the statistical data characteristic of rigorous experimental research, though information is presented about end results—ill-structured problems identified and solved, and productivity. The cases do not dwell on the interpersonal dynamics of group-based change efforts, which are described in other studies (e.g., Argyris, 1970; Golembiewski, 1972).

Silver City Bank

In August of 1968, Ralph Brady, vice president of Silver City Bank,[4] was concerned about future strategy for the international banking department. He wanted to improve the department's ability to

---

[3] When the knowledge/problem mode is primary, the organization requires and attracts individuals who value individual contribution, creativity, self-motivation, and low interdependence. Going from a knowledge/problem mode to an authority/production mode introduces complex problems of coordination, reduction of individual freedom, group operation, and conflicts with personal values. It is not simply the reverse of going from the authority/production mode to the knowledge/problem mode.

---

[4] Names in this case and the one that follows are fictitious.

compete with well-established competitors in a changing, worldwide market. At this stage in his thinking he felt the issues, problems, and opportunities were ill structured. He discussed his concern, in general terms, with his superiors, who encouraged him to recommend changes in strategy.

His work group functioned primarily in an authority/production mode. He and his subordinates were amiable and cooperative and deeply involved in getting work out. Although there was the glamour of international travel and negotiating loans of large dollar value, most of the situations were well structured.

Mr. Brady discussed strategy with several key subordinates but felt he and they were not able to dig into issues in any depth. Each could focus only on short-term obstacles close to his own group's productivity. The ill-structured problems of analyzing long-term strategy seemed to elude the problem-solving capability of his group. Finally, Mr. Brady consulted an OD specialist (the author) who had been working with another department in the bank.

Preparation for Introduction of Collateral Mode. The specialist interviewed Mr. Brady and his division managers. He observed that their daily work required many immediate decisions and was extremely demanding. They could not be away from a telephone. He concluded they would have great difficulty establishing the relationships needed to identify and solve the ill-structured issues of strategy. Although the managers were competent problem solvers with extensive knowledge of international banking, they could not direct their skills toward analyzing strategy. Somehow, they would have to depart from the norms of their intensive authority/production-centered work.

The OD specialist explained the need for a collateral organization to Mr. Brady and his group. He proposed an initial three-day meeting, at which strategy and operating issues would be discussed, analyzed, and if possible, resolved. (The men were so busy they insisted it be from Friday afternoon to Sunday evening.) Aware that collateral organizations frequently fail because managers may have

unrealistic expectations and cannot foresee the difficulties of a mode, the specialist stressed setting limited, attainable goals. He suggested that the group try to identify key issues but discuss only two or three priority issues in detail. Since there would be many unanswered questions after the meeting, they would also have to approve some structure which could be used to work on finding answers after they returned to work. Finally they should discuss how they could organize to solve ill-structured problems more effectively in the future.

Ten days before the meeting, the OD specialist interviewed each manager, gathering information for the meeting and answering questions about format. Each manager described the issues he most wanted discussed, the outcomes that would make him feel the meeting was worthwhile, and the difficulties that might interfere with managers' being reasonably open about important issues. The interview process itself stimulated managers to think about norms that departed from those of the primary mode.

Learning the Collateral Mode. At the start of the meeting, the specialist made the following statements to clarify the norms of the collateral mode and to assure its proper connection to the primary mode.

The power differences in the formal organization would still exist when the managers returned to work.

Mr. Brady, the vice president, was the group's superior, and this was his meeting, not the consultant's.

The group or its members could make recommendations, but Mr. Brady would have to approve any proposal before it could be implemented.

Regardless of formal position, managers usually have valuable insights and proposals that cut across many different areas. It would be the responsibility of the higher managers to facilitate expression and use of these views.

The OD specialist would suggest procedures and ask questions to help the group's problem solving.

The specialist then reported a summary of the issues managers wanted to discuss. At first, the group operated in an authority/production mode. Managers frequently proposed solutions before a problem had been clearly defined. The specialist made process observations to alter these norms. Discussion was brought back to managers whose views had not been heard adequately. There was regular testing to ensure that any problem was understood by all before solutions were discussed in depth. Regardless of status, managers began contributing important information and insights. This helped the senior managers see how the open channels of the collateral mode improved problem solving.

On the second day, the managers agreed to experiment with a collateral mode after they returned to work. They would set aside "unstructured" time (multichannels, free questioning, and so on) to study several ill-structured problems. Based on their new experience, they also adopted a special norm for their collateral mode: incomplete ideas, although not thoroughly reasoned and defendable, were welcomed. This was a deliberate and significant departure from behavior in their primary organization. It was intended to stimulate search and creativity. They reiterated, however, that in the hierarchical (primary) organization, a recommendation would still have to be supported by thorough reasoning and documentation. They had grasped the distinction between primary and collateral modes without falling into the trap of insisting that one had to displace the other.

Connecting to the Hierarchical Organization. After returning to work at the bank, Mr. Brady and his group used their collateral mode to analyze ill-structured problems one morning each week for the first six weeks. This helped stabilize the collateral mode and increase cohesion. They worked out a long-term agenda, which they used to enlarge their collateral organization with several task forces for specific problems. The daytime meetings were conflicting with work, so they reviewed their needs and shifted to one evening a month. They also convened three-day, off-site, collateral meetings at five-month intervals to review progress and react to task force reports. The task forces made proposals to Mr. Brady and the full group during the year; gradually a comprehensive international banking strategy was formulated.

There were differences of opinion within the task forces, and sometimes there were conflicting responses to reports from the task forces. The process had its difficulties, and in two instances Mr. Brady encouraged and arranged for the transfer of two individuals who were personally dissatisfied by and unable to contribute to the collateral mode. In general, the managers at this level were bright and aggressive and enjoyed the opportunity to do a better job of planning their department's future. At their daily work, the nature of their activities, however, impelled them toward an authority/production mode. (Incidentally, this did not mean that they were not caring, friendly, and thoughtful of one another and their subordinates.)

In any case, the primary and the collateral mode remained quite distinct. Managers were well aware of the distinct properties of the two modes and when one or the other was in use. The department was relatively autonomous and top management stayed out of its internal activities, so the use of the collateral mode caused no problems and raised no outside concerns.

Results. The original stimulus for the collateral organization was the need to develop a strategy for international banking. No before-after measures were taken of attitudes, perceptions, share in influence, or other intervening variables. At the time of the intervention, gathering data about casual variables was secondary to the change effort. Nevertheless, in terms of the criterion measure—quality of the strategy—the decisions made in 1969 are impressive, in view of the political and economic developments in Latin America, the Far East, and Europe in the early 1970s. The group decided to expand in Latin America and the Orient, where competition was thin, demand was growing, and the bank could effectively use its existing relationships to tap an expected increase in U.S. trade with countries in those areas. In Europe, where competition was heavy for the existing large market, a strategy of affiliating with strong foreign banks, and selectively establishing a few home office branches was instituted. To support the new strategy, relations between international banking officers and domestic banking officers who served U.S. companies with large overseas affiliates or subsidiaries were reviewed and significantly improved. Procedures in the bank's main European office were also substantially changed, facilitating more accurate and rapid responses to customers. The department's formal structure was changed to fit the new strategies. Several divisions were eliminated, others were combined. Finally, a manpower development plan which systematically rotated upcoming managers to selected world areas and headquarters assignments was instituted. Since 1968, top management has rated the international banking department's performance as outstanding each year. Mr. Brady was promoted to senior vice president and a subordinate moved into his job.

Of course, without control groups we cannot assert that an equally good strategy would not have developed without a collateral mode. Using Mr. Brady's group as its own control, however, we recall that it had repeatedly tried to formulate strategy while working in its primary mode but had been dissatisfied with the results.

Another interesting result is that the collateral organization concept spread during the three years following its initial use by Mr. Brady. Each of his five division managers developed collateral organizations with their own subordinates.

Ajax Corporation

Now we turn to the introduction of a complex multistage collateral organization. Again our purpose is to illustrate the usefulness of the collateral organization concept and to outline some social technology for introducing one. We do not intend to delve deeply into the interpersonal or social dynamics of the development process.

Fred Anderson, Manager of the Maintenance and Laboratory Service Division of Ajax Corporation, a large research and development company, was concerned about the cost effectiveness of his unit. His division had been performing more work with the same budget, and although objective standards were difficult to establish, he felt improvement was possible. Since the Service Division employed 300 of the 3,000 people in Ajax, it was a major expense.

The Service Division had been formed two years earlier by consolidating into one unit activities that had previously been performed by small groups in each of the major research and engineering divisions of Ajax. After consolidation, the foreman's job changed from supervising only craftsmen in one specialty (such as machinists or electricians) to supervising a team which could completely build and repair complex laboratory facilities. Thus, at the level of the foremen and below, the organization took on some properties of a *matrix*. Specialized craftsmen were assigned to different projects as needed, and they usually worked on several projects with groups of varying size and membership. In addition, for the first time, foremen and craftsmen were rotated between the company's two locations, 20 miles apart.

Middle managers advised Mr. Anderson that the foremen were at the crux of the division's difficulties and would be the key to any improvement effort. They described the foremen as unwilling to stress high output, reluctant to discipline workers, resistant to cost reduction and work changes, and tending to promise work dates that frequently were not met.

Mr. Anderson consulted organization development specialists, who observed that foremen were affected by the behavior and attitudes of their managers and that the problems Mr. Anderson was trying to solve were complex, ill defined, and substantially different from the well-structured routines of daily manager-foreman relations.[5] The

---

[5] I acknowledge my gratitude to Matthew B. Miles and William O. Lytle, Jr., who were the OD team with me. This case is based upon Enlarging Organization Choice through Use of a Temporary Problem-Solving System, by D. E. Zand, M. B. Miles, and W. O. Lytle, Jr. (mimeo, available from author).

consultants proposed, and management accepted, a sequence of collateral organizations involving both managers and foremen (Figure 4).

Collateral Phase 1. All 16 managers in the division met for three days away from the plant in order to (1) identify and solve work problems of concern to managers and foremen, and (2) learn a collateral mode of problem solving.

To help introduce the collateral mode, the OD specialists constrained the managers to work on one element of problem solving at a time, in a method called "staged problem solving." They also facilitated information flow, wider use of resources, and norms that encouraged questioning and creativity by placing managers in different groups with varying membership.

First, the managers developed an inventory of problems while working in three "diagonal slice" groups (no manager and immediate subordinate in the same group). Then, in a plenary meeting of all 16 managers, the groups discussed their problem inventories and consolidated them. At first the small groups were "stiff" and concerns were stated indirectly. However, with the aid of process observations by the OD specialists, role-playing, small-group exercises, and the discipline of discussing each group's product in plenary session, this stiffness disappeared.

Next each group diagnosed causes of a subset of problems. A written summary of each diagnosis was immediately duplicated and distributed to all the managers. The managers met again in plenary session and each group explained and discussed its diagnosis. By this time the managers were deeply involved in the effort. Highly relevant problems had been identified, and causes were being discussed without disguising names or incidents. The managers were stimulated by the open exchange of views and the increasing probability that several important problems might be solved.

On the second day of the meeting, the OD team arranged for the managers to meet in three peer groups. The groups were given the following tasks: (1) assign priorities to problems, (2) nominate managers to task forces that would recommend solu-

tions to Mr. Anderson at the meeting, and (3) nominate managers to a steering committee that would take control of the remainder of the meeting and also guide the collateral organization after returning to the plant and the hierarchical (primary) organization.

Linking to the Formal Organization.   To assure that the collateral organization would tie into the formal one, the managers were asked to use the following criteria for nominating candidates to a task force: *(a)* at least one manager should have formal authority to act on the problem; *(b)* several should be technical and procedural experts on the problem; *(c)* at least one should know and represent the views of people who would be affected by a solution.

The managers elected a five-man steering committee and asked the division manager to serve as chairman. Thus, they connected the collateral organization's steering committee to the highest authority in their formal organization.

The steering committee formed task forces for the high-priority problems and assigned every manager (including themselves) to a task force. The task forces rediagnosed their assigned problems and developed solutions.

Then, in plenary session, each task force presented and discussed its progress. All managers freely questioned, commented, and provided additional inputs. The task forces absorbed the new inputs and met again to refine their proposals. By this stage, involvement was intense. Groups worked late into the night to prepare their recommendations for the next day. The norms in these groups very closely followed the knowledge/problem-centered mode: A manager's position was secondary to his contribution.

During the last half day, each task force presented its recommendations in plenary session. To clarify that the organization was shifting back to its primary mode, the OD team explicitly stated that the division manager, Mr. Anderson, could respond in any of the following ways: (1) He could accept the task force recommendation, designate a manager to implement it, specify a completion date, and state how a report of progress would be given

FIGURE 4   Multiphase Collateral Organization

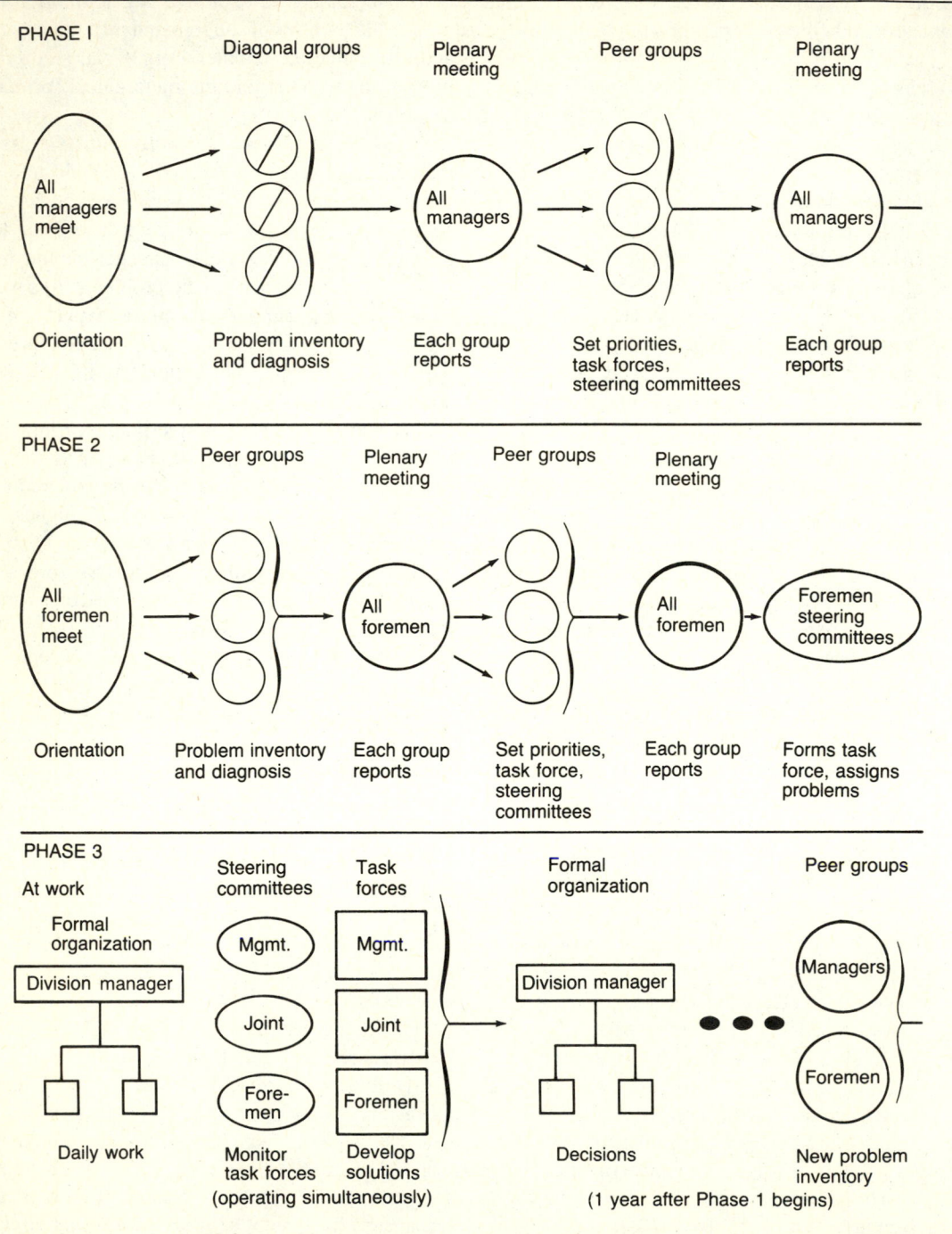

FIGURE 4   *(concluded)*

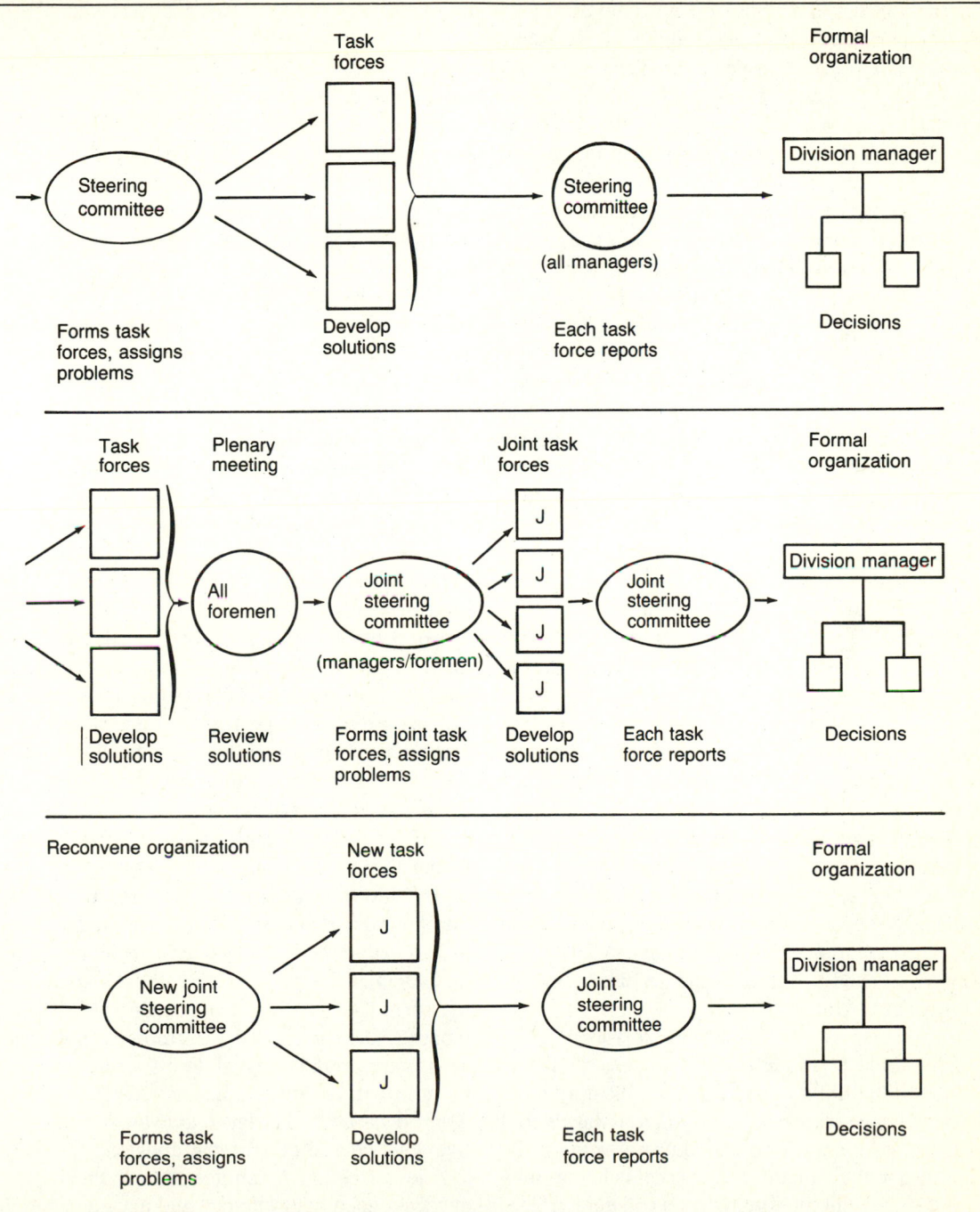

to all the managers. (2) He could suggest modifications, discuss them, and approve a modified recommendation. (3) He could withhold a decision, pending additional information or alternatives, and authorize the task force to continue its work back at the plant. (4) He could withhold a decision if in his judgment the proposal was not appropriate now but might be at a later date. (5) He could reject the recommendation and not give any reasons.

There was a good deal of excitement and joking as Mr. Anderson stood at the front of the room waiting to hear each group's statement of the problem, review of causes, and recommended solutions. During the presentations, managers freely called from the floor for clarification or elaborated a point when they felt it was misunderstood. The cohesiveness of the managers was noticeably higher than before the 3-day meeting.

By this time much information that had been known only in isolated pockets of the formal hierarchy had been exchanged across the organization. Managers had demonstrated their trust in one another through the openness of their discussions during the preceding two and one-half days. With this background, solutions that were not feasible or not integrative were readily discarded in the task forces. As a result, the final recommendations were appropriate and well thought out. Mr. Anderson neither rejected nor withheld a decision on any of the recommendations.

Results: Collateral Phase 1.   A new information system for managers was instituted. A new strategy for recruiting engineering and scientific specialists was approved. Middle managers were delegated additional decision powers. A task force was established to redesign the division's organizational structure.

The managers also made plans to follow up in the hierarchical organization problems they had identified but did not have time to solve during the three-day meeting. Finally, they agreed they would join the foremen in a collateral organization if the foremen invited them. They discussed how they might work with the foremen in a collateral mode.

Collateral Phase 2.   One week after the managers' collateral organization experience, all 18 foremen met for three days at the off-site location. The OD specialists had decided to separate managers from foremen to prevent tension and distorted communication between levels from interfering with learning to work in a collateral mode. The managers' collateral organization was developed first so they could decide from personal experience whether to approve a collateral organization for foremen.

The procedure and activities in the foremen's meeting were similar to the managers' meeting. Some mini-lectures and demonstration exercises were eliminated to save time, but in all other ways the foremen's collateral organization used the same "staged problem solving," small-group discussions, and plenary sessions.

The foremen, like the managers, developed their own inventory of problems, diagnosed causes, set priorities, and elected their own steering committee to take control of their meeting. The steering committee established foremen task forces, which began work at the meeting. At first, like the managers, the foremen were resistant and indirect. Again with the aid of process observations from the OD specialists, exercises, and the regimen of having to present their group's deliberations to all other foremen, the norms of the groups changed toward those in a knowledge/problem mode.

Linking Two Collateral Organizations.   Anticipating the need to link the managers' collateral organization to the foremen's collateral organization for work on common problems, management had agreed to the OD specialists' recommendation that foremen be permitted to invite managers to join them the last day and a half. The foremen (contrary to management's stereotype of foremen as insensitive) did not wish to offend any manager by not inviting him and negotiated with management to have all managers join them, except for five who were left to run the division.

A joint steering committee of foremen and managers assigned both foremen and managers to joint task forces. Comprehensive, ill-structured issues had been identified for work. Sample items which both managers and foremen agreed were adversely affecting the performance of foremen included: confusion about foremen's authority to work crews overtime, purchase inexpensive materials which were delaying completion of a job, or grant workers time off; misunderstandings about the scope of the foreman's job; need for a better system for screening and assigning priorities to incoming jobs; inadequate engineering services on complex, technical jobs; inadequate pay differentials between foremen and craftsmen; conflict about the merit pay system; need for a better manpower assignment system; conflict about training of foremen and craftsmen. There was tension within the joint task forces as managers and foremen who knew each other by name but had never worked closely together before prepared to discuss problems that had been suppressed, distorted, or circumvented in the formal organization. Some foremen became guarded when a manager tried to dominate, but the issues and the withheld information that had been constraining the organization were nevertheless introduced via the "impersonal" written task force reports.

During the last half day, the joint task forces presented their recommendations to Mr. Anderson (format as before), who immediately made several important decisions. Procedures for working on unsolved problems after returning to the plant were also established.

Results: Collateral Phase 2. The recommendations approved by Mr. Anderson included the following: Foremen were given wider latitude in authorizing overtime to complete a job without their supervisor's approval; they could authorize workers' time off without pay; they could purchase parts that were delaying job completion up to $200 per job without going through time-consuming, formal purchasing procedures. These measures cut costs and sped completion of jobs.

Mr. Anderson also decided that task forces concerned with the responsibilities of foremen, the training of foremen, the merit and performance review system, providing proper engineering support, and reviewing pay differentials between foremen and workers were to continue their investigation after they returned to the plant and the hierarchical organization.

Much misinformation about foremen attitudes and behavior had been dispelled, and managers had tested some of their stereotyped reactions to foremen and found them inappropriate. The outcome was a concerted effort on the part of both groups to provide the conditions that would enable foremen to be effective, rather than to blame them for inadequacies not under their control.

Thirty important problems had been identified, nine had been assigned to task forces, three had been resolved. Completion and review dates had been established for the others, and procedures had been developed for following through on the remaining problems. An attitude survey showed that managers and foremen felt they had learned much about one another and about problem solving. They were enthusiastic about the collateral organization.

Collateral Phase 3. After returning to the plant and the hierarchical organization, task forces of managers, foremen, and joint membership continued their work. Progress was slower than expected because of daily work pressures.

There also was testing of the authority/production mode. Some foremen task forces, impressed with their new influence potential, attempted to circumvent middle managers and moved directly to the joint steering committee or the division manager with short-term work issues. Senior foremen quickly sensed the resentment this was arousing among middle managers and redirected the foremen task forces to the issues they had been assigned. Managers of other divisions in the laboratory were skeptical about allowing foremen on task forces. They were also concerned that foremen might usurp higher management's authority. Mr. Anderson was able to reassure the other divisions that this dual mode of operation need not spread to other divisions unless they wanted it. He was also able to convince them on the basis of preliminary results that the performance of the Maintenance Division would improve over the long run.

Based on the measure of identifying and solving ill-structured problems, the collateral mode contributed to the organization's effectiveness. After nine months, six of the nine original high-priority and five secondary problems were solved. All but three task forces had completed their assignments and were dissolved. Work was to begin on 12 less critical problems.

The collateral organization was self-operating; no OD specialists were used. One year after the first meetings, a new division manager (promoted from within the division) continued the collateral organization with the aid of the joint steering committee. Using small groups, a new inventory of problems was developed, three new task forces were formed, and progress was reviewed with the steering committee until the new problems were solved.

To obtain information about attitudes toward the collateral mode, interviews were conducted 18 months after the start of the project. Five managers and five foremen representing all levels of management, every task force, and both steering committees were interviewed. Each respondent felt strongly that the collateral mode was extremely useful and strongly supported its continuation.

Additional Issues

These two cases, one relatively simple, the other more complexly structured, illustrate strategies for using collateral organization. Using the case material as reference, some additional issues deserve discussion: the distinction between collateral organization and related concepts such as "matrix organization" and "temporary systems," and some problems which may arise in the use of collateral organization.

Relation to Matrix Organization. Managers may sometime confuse a matrix organization with a collateral mode. A matrix organization is intended to provide a project manager with easier access to

functional specialists. Nevertheless it may operate primarily in an authority/production mode, as in the Ajax case. Internal competition for resources and conflicts among functional managers and project managers are heightened in a matrix organization (Galbraith, 1971). These conditions stimulate managers to overstate needs, to hoard resources, to withhold information, and to block others from access to needed manpower, in short, to behave in an authority/production mode with high conflict. Thus, a matrix organization may itself need a collateral problem-solving mode. Much of the organizational development activity at TRW Systems can be interpreted as an effort to build collateral modes to complement its matrix (primary) organization (Davis, 1967).

Relation to Task Forces. In both Silver City and Ajax, each collateral organization created task forces as part of its structure. This can be confusing, because a manager may assume he can install a collateral organization simply by forming a task force. The important question is: Does the task force operate with norms different from those in the hierarchical (primary) organization? Many task forces, spun off by conventional hierarchies, operate in the same authority/production mode as the primary organization. Individuals project their provincial interests and minimally question values, assumptions, methods, and criteria of evaluation. Such a task force contributes to restricted flow of information, legitimizes restricted use of resources, and adds little creativity to the hierarchical organization. The task forces in both Silver City Bank and Ajax worked in a collateral mode. They had learned the foundation for this mode in their initial off-site meeting. If they had not, it is doubtful that they would have contributed so creatively to the development of strategy. Indeed, a task force which operates under the authority/production norms prevailing in its primary organization will need a collateral mode for itself.

Relation to Temporary Systems. The relationship between collateral organization and a temporary system (Miles, 1964) also merits clarification. A temporary system is brought into existence with the understanding it will have limited duration. Its dissolution may be linked to (1) time (a two-day conference), (2) the occurrence of an event (the completion of a report), or (3) the attainment of a condition or level of functioning (a marketing unit solves its sales training problems without further aid from headquarters staff). A collateral organization is likely to terminate for one of two reasons. First, the ill-structured problems it is intended to solve are solved and there are no more. Second, the permanent, primary organization has internalized the norms and the competence of the collateral organization. In the second instance, the primary organization has attained a new level of functioning, thereby making the collateral mode redundant.

A collateral organization will be useful so long as it performs two functions: *(a)* it compensates for a deficiency in the primary system; *(b)* it is a vehicle for introducing needed changes in the primary system. In Silver City Bank, for example, the collateral mode was used intensively for strategy problems for about a year and a half. Then it was used to examine problems of implementation for about a year, but much less intensively. After that, it was used at semi-annual intervals to take stock of unresolved, ill-structured problems, with the understanding that its shift to more intensive use would be made if the problems warranted it.

Operating Problems. Collateral organization tends to increase the use of groups, at least initially, puts more stress on middle managers, and surfaces problems of individual tolerance and flexibility.

Need for Groups. A manager may be concerned that introducing a collateral organization will increase the number of problems going to groups for solution. This may happen initially for two reasons. First, there appears to be a temporary increase in the number of problems, because a collateral organization identifies problems that were previously diffused or unshared. Second, collateral organizations concentrate on high-priority, organizationwide problems, which are usually solved better by a group than by one person working alone.

After an initial surge, the need for groups rapidly decreases, because the collateral mode diligently separates problems that should go to one manager (or a pair of managers) from those that should go to a larger group.

Stress on Middle Managers. When a collateral organization permits lower and higher managers to interact directly, the stress on middle managers increases. Higher managers may discover that middle managers have been distorting and editing the upward flow of information. Lower managers may discover they can influence higher management decisions more easily than they thought possible. Both higher and lower managers discover they need less time to identify and solve complex problems. Management may be prompted to redesign the hierarchical organization and redefine the role of middle managers.

In the Silver City Bank, after working in a collateral mode, managers discovered they could expand operations more rapidly than planned because an anticipated shortage of managers could be met by freeing several middle managers for other assignments. In the Ajax case, managers in the collateral mode concluded that several middle management positions were redundant but should be kept for back-up purposes and for training.

Individual Flexibility. Some subordinates have a strong need for structure and a relationship with their superior that does not change. They are comfortable only when working in one mode all the time—either authority/production or knowledge/problem solving. The important element for them is stability and consistency (Adorno, Frenkel-Brunswick, Levinson, & Sanford, 1950; Vroom, 1959). Even though problems may change and require organizational versatility, they find shifting from one mode to another confusing. Most subordinates, however, can be productive in more than one organizational mode provided they understand the purposes of a collateral mode, know which mode they are in, and know when it will end.

Sometimes a superior may not have the flexibility to work in more than one mode. If this is the case, attempts to use a collateral organization will meet strong resistance. The majority of managers, however, seem to have enough flexibility to use collateral organizations. The achievements in the two cases described above were heavily dependent on the flexibility of Mr. Brady and Mr. Anderson.

Too often, a manager's skepticism toward attempts to displace one organizational mode with another have been misconstrued as a sign of deep-seated personal rigidity. This "rigidity" usually fades when the manager understands the concept of collateral organization. When he sees how it can productively complement the hierarchical organization without displacing or destroying it, he can be remarkably flexible. As a matter of fact, after a manager experiences his first successful collateral organization, the problem is usually not one of rigidity but of overoptimism. He feels he and his group have broken through to a new form of relationship and productivity, and he easily develops overly optimistic expectations of future accomplishment. The demands of daily work, however, quickly intrude, as they must, making continued use of the collateral mode an infrequent, disjointed activity. Some ill-structured problems are solved, but because of interruptions, solutions take longer to implement than he planned. New ill-structured problems that are identified take much greater effort to solve than he expected. He discovers that time for the collateral mode must be fought for and taken from the primary mode.

After using a collateral mode, the manager and his subordinates learn that the hierarchical organization can continue. Disorder does not take over. Directive behavior can still be used, but there is better understanding of how to integrate participation and group effort with the formal organization through use of a collateral mode. Perhaps most important, organization members learn concepts and methods which enable them to freely invent and use new modes for solving ill-structured problems.

References

Adorno, T. W., Frenkel-Brunswick, E., Levinson, D. J., and Sanford, R. N. *The authoritarian personality.* New York: Harper & Row, 1950.

Argyris, C. *Intervention theory and method.* Reading, Mass.: Addison-Wesley Publishing, 1970.

Bavelas, A. Communication patterns in task-oriented groups. *Journal of Acoustical Society of America,* 1950, 22, 725–730.

Bennis, W. G. Beyond bureaucracy. *Trans-Action,* July–August 1965.

Bennis, W. G. *Changing organizations.* New York: McGraw-Hill, 1966.

Burns, T., & Stalker, G. M. *Management of innovation.* London: Tavistock, 1961.

Christie, L. S., Luce, R. D., & May, J., Jr. Communications and learning in task-oriented groups. Cambridge, Mass.: Research Laboratory Electronics, 1952.

Davis, S. A. An organic problem-solving method of organizational change. *Journal of Applied Behavioral Science,* 1967, 3, 3–21.

Delbecq, A. L. How "informal" organization evolves: Interpersonal choice and subgroup formation. *Business Perspectives,* 1968, *IV* (3), 17–21.

Fiedler, F. E. *A theory of leadership effectiveness.* New York: McGraw-Hill, 1967.

Galbraith, J. R. Matrix organization designs. *Business Horizons,* February 1971, pp. 24–40.

Golembiewski, R. T. *Renewing organizations: The laboratory approach to planned change.* Itasca, Ill.: Peacock, 1972.

Guetzkow, H., & Dill, W. R. Factors in the organizational development of task-oriented groups. *Sociometry,* 1957, *20,* 175–204.

Guetzkow, H., & Simon, H. A. The impact of certain communication nets upon organization and performance in task-oriented groups. *Management Science,* 1955, *1,* 233–250.

Lawrence, P. R., & Lorsch, J. W. New management job: The integrator. *Harvard Business Review,* November–December 1967, 142.

Leavitt, H. J. Some effects of certain communication patterns on group performance. *Journal of Abnormal and Social Psychology,* 1951, *46,* 38–50.

Likert, R. *New patterns of management.* New York: McGraw-Hill, 1961.

Likert, R. *The human organization.* New York: McGraw-Hill, 1967.

McGregor, D., *The human side of enterprise*. New York: McGraw-Hill, 1960.

Margulies, N., & Raia, A. P. *Organizational development*. New York: McGraw-Hill, 1972.

Miles, M. B. On temporary systems. In M. B. Miles, Ed., *Innovation in education*. New York: Columbia University Press, 1964, 437–492.

Pfiffner, J. M., & Sherwood, F. P. *Administrative organization*. Englewood Cliffs, N.J.: Prentice-Hall, 1960, 16–32.

Shaw, M. E., Rothchild, G. H., & Strickland, J. F. Decision process in communication nets. *Journal of Abnormal and Social Psychology*, 1957, *54*, 323–330.

Slater, P. E., & Bennis, W. G. Democracy is inevitable. *Harvard Business Review*, March–April 1964, 51.

Tannenbaum, R., & Davis, S. A. Values, men, and organizations. *Industrial Management Review*, Winter 1969, *10*, 67–83.

Vroom, V. H. Some personality determinants of the effects of participation. *Journal of Abnormal and Social Psychology*, 1959, *59*, 322–327.

E. *Contextual Variables*

The two essays in this section provide insight into some of the contextual variables that can affect the viability of structural interventions. Some of these variables are matters of internal management planning and decision making, such as how the reward system relates to the change effort. Other variables, such as attitudes about collective responsibility, may have their roots in the societal culture.

In the first essay, "The Japanese Management Theory Jungle," J. Bernard Keys and Thomas R. Miller look at the various theories that have been advanced to explain the apparent effectiveness of management practices in Japan. One theory focuses on the widespread use of quality circles, another focuses on subtle aspect of consensus decision making, and so on. Keys and Miller extract what they see as the main underlying factors in the Japanese system that foster these theories, and then go on to describe the Japanese management practices that stem from these factors. For example, the notion of collective responsibility leads to such management practices as an emphasis on teamwork and cooperation, consensus decision making, the development of company unions rather than craft unions, and so on. At another level, this essay is about the multiplicity of variables that are operating simultaneously and how the Japanese manage these variables in a congruent, mutually reinforcing way.

In the second essay, "Why Productivity Efforts Fail," Paul S. Goodman and James W. Dean, Jr. look at the factors that affect the institutionalization of QWL-type change programs. They see five factors—or processes, as they call them—that affect the degree of institutionalization. They define an institutionalized act as "behavior that is performed by two or more individuals, persists over time, and exists as part of the daily functioning of the organization." The selection concludes with recommendations for making change programs last.

Reading 40

QUALITY CIRCLES: THE DANGER OF BOTTLED CHANGE

Gregory P. Shea

Quality circles were conceived by Americans and developed by the Japanese: they have returned to the United States amidst fanfare. Quality circles are often heralded as appropriate for treating any number of organizational ailments—in manufacturing or service sectors, among managers and nonmanagers—in any culture.[1] Such attention has increased awareness of quality circles as well as confusion about their use. This article evaluates quality circles and clarifies their uses and limitations.

Quality Control Circles and Japan

A typical Japanese quality control circle consists of members of a work group meeting regularly to identify and solve job-related problems. Member preparation includes considerable training in problem solving and statistical quality control. Approval or disapproval of circle recommendations rests with upper management. Quality control circles first appeared in Japan in 1962,[2] the result of efforts by U.S. consultants (dating back to at least 1950) and the Japanese government.[3] These efforts succeeded in part because of the following circumstances:[4]

1. Japanese managers sought to mobilize their organizations to combat foreign and domestic competition.
2. Japanese managers grew increasingly committed during the 1960s to decentralization as a strategy and to the small group as the respon-

Source: Reprinted from ''Quality Circles: The Danger of Bottled Change'' by Gregory P. Shea, *Sloan Management Review*, Spring 1986, pp. 33–46, by permission of the publisher. Copyright © 1986 by the Sloan Management Review Association. All rights reserved.

sible unit and vehicle for combining functions (e.g., maintenance and quality control).
3. Turbulence in Japanese society (and attendant concern about worker unrest and unionization) together with tightening of the labor market in the late 1960s and early 1970s fostered greater pressure on management to make work appealing (particularly to the better-educated).
4. Lifetime employment encouraged maximizing human resources, at least in larger firms.

By 1981, quality control circles had become a prominent yet far from universal part of Japanese organizational life. The Japanese Union of Scientists and Engineers had registered 125,000 quality control circles with a total membership of 1,132,000 and estimates of underregistration have led to speculation of two million or more members.[5] Cole states ''that a conservative estimate can be made that one out of every eight Japanese employees participates in quality control circles.''[6] Similarly, Wood, Hull, and Azumi note that ''the majority of Japanese firms do not use quality circles,'' and point out that quality control circles are more likely to appear in larger firms (''over three-fourths of establishments having 5,000 or more workers have QCs, compared to one-third for establishments having one hundred to two hundred workers'').[7]

The Role of Quality Control Circles

''In Japan there seems to be a greater 'belief in human potential'. . . It is more fundamental than fairness.''[8] Not surprisingly, the Japanese base quality control circles on the following beliefs:

- No one really knows the cause of quality problems.

- People need instruction in how to identify the true sources of those problems.
- People need help in securing remedies to quality problems.
- People need instruction in quality control methods in order to hold onto gains in quality.[9]

Japanese managers tend to assume that most quality problems exist not because of worker indifference, blundering, or sabotage, but because of poor technique. Consequently, the success of quality control circles in Japan "has, to an important degree, been due to the existence of a kit of tools which simplify greatly the attack on quality problems."[10] That is, a large part of the success of quality control circles in Japan is the success of a technique applied to technical problems.

Juran, for one, stresses that quality control circles in Japan are *not* a motivational program.[11] Even the name of the main registering body for quality control circles, the Japanese Union of Scientists and Engineers (JUSE), reflects the technical orientation of the Japanese toward quality control circle programs.[12] This perspective leads the Japanese to concentrate on circle work to solve *quality* problems, as opposed to, say, human relations problems. This perspective also leads Juran to caution that while some of the problem-solving techniques of quality control circles "are helpful in solving *any* problem . . . as applied to other subject matter, the kit is incomplete, and would need to be supplemented."[13]

Where they do exist, quality control circles comprise only a part of the fabric of organizational life, a fabric woven of material not generally present in American firms, differing because of:

1. "Strong emphasis on group work and collective responsibility and deliberate downplaying of the Western emphasis on individual effort and reward."
2. "Lifetime employment, which creates employee dependency and commitment to the firm, and an incentive to improve quality and efficiency."
3. "High-trust relations between managers and labor [that] fosters a labor relations system which

operates on the assumption that interests are shared and cooperation is easily achieved." (A condition fed no doubt by the fact that 20 percent of the presidents of Japanese firms formerly headed company unions [Simmons and Mares, 1985].)
4. "Job rotation and skill development within an internal market which means that Japanese employees often have a wider range of knowledge and resources than is found elsewhere."[14]

The fabric is intricate and reflects conscious workmanship. Many Japanese executives managed the culture of their organizations long before most American managers even became aware of the concept.[15] For example, Japanese managers and especially heads of personnel in major firms have long been aware of work on participatory structure by authors like Likert, McGregor, Maslow, Argyris, and Herzberg because of what Kobayashi and Burke describe as the rapid translation into Japanese of these writers' books and articles, the steady stream of Japanese students coming to the U.S., and lecture tours of American scholars.[16] Cole states that the ideas of American scholars were "combined with and adapted to indigenous values and practices [to form] the basis of the Japanese effort in the area of participatory work structures."[17] This combination formed a greater disposition in Japanese managers than in their American counterparts to use American behavioral sciences—the commitment by many Japanese managers beginning in the 1960s to establish "shoshudanshugi" or "small groupism"[18] and the development of quality control circles being but two cases in point.[19]

Quality Control Circles and Participative Management

Japanese managers did not initially establish quality control circles because they valued participation for its own sake or wished to democratize the workplace. On the contrary, Cole states that "participation was more a responsibility, an obligation, of each employee rather than an opportunity to express one's talents and take charge of one's own situation and environment."[20] Munchus states that "The idea behind the quality circle is that, armed with the proper training, the worker can discover previously unrecognized quality problems. However, the Japanese system does not rely on worker initiative in the absence of strong management control of the group program."[21]

Evidence of strong management control is readily apparent: membership in a quality circle is usually institutionalized (not voluntary) and a web of paternalism ". . . enables the work group supervisor to control apparently participative QC problem solving by selectively offering or withholding support . . . [and ensuring] that QC performance reflects directives of upper-level managers."[22]

As noted, quality control circles and other participatory schemes came to serve various purposes, but their primary purpose was technical: quality problem solving as part of a strategic plan of decentralization. Japanese managers wanted to change human interaction in the service of a structural imperative and quality control circles were but one tool employed. Japanese managers sought to manage culture and they consciously drew on American behavioral sciences to do so. That fact in and of itself distinguishes the Japanese from the American setting for quality circles.

Western Confusion about Quality Control Circles

Western observers[23] vary in what role they believe quality circles play in Japanese organizations: motivational scheme, technical program, or part of "a formidable process which focuses on one small organizational problem at a time and results in the gradual improvement of the total organization."[24] Westerners looking at quality control have seen any number of purposes and uses, not merely a problem-solving technology adopted in the service of a strategic objective. The confusion began because Westerners have tended to extract the technology of quality circles from its context and create a tool or solution in search of a problem.[25] Quality control circles came to America stripped of much of their original meaning and laden with additional ones.

Quality Circles and the U.S.

Quality circles began appearing in the United States in appreciable numbers during the mid–1970s and mushroomed in the 1980s. Reported large-scale success at Lockheed yielded publicity and consultants at a time when American business people were becoming painfully aware of the need to improve quality and increase productivity, when advocates of increased participation in management were growing more numerous and more vocal, and when Japanese business was succeeding dramatically. In 1980, researchers estimated that over 500 U.S. companies had initiated a total of more than 3,000 quality circles.[26] By 1982, 44 percent of U.S. companies with over 500 employees had quality circle programs, with 74 percent of these programs being at most two years old.[27] In 1985, Lawler and Mohrman estimated that over 90 percent of Fortune 500 companies had some quality circles.[28] As in Japan, quality circles (or at least their registration) and big organizations seemed to go together.

Confusion: The Danger of Loose Translation

Generally speaking, Americans regard quality circles as a formal program (complete with its own administrative structure or project organization) to solve workplace quality problems *and* to alter group process—a clear difference from the Japanese perception of QCs. Other modifications include meeting on company time (not after hours), voluntary membership, creation of a facilitator role (i.e., program promoter and implementer, trainer, and consultant as well as liaison between the circle and the organization), and a greater emphasis on "group dynamics, human relations, and interpersonal communications."[29] Thus, to equate Japanese quality control circles and American quality control circles is deceiving since their respective technologies and purposes differ, as does the diversity of the ends to which they are employed. One can argue the advisability of these changes, but the fact is that transplanting quality control circles from Japan to America led to altering their nature and their surroundings, both organizational and cultural. Quality circles can, in fact, easily end up running counter to basic tenets of American organizational life, especially norms of supervisor/worker relations.[30] Furthermore, whereas the use of quality control circles in Japan reflects a general orientation toward the design and operation of organizations as a whole, the orientation in America is more variable, fragmented, and unclear.

For example, Thompson attempts to help readers of his book better understand quality circles and the process of installing them by thoroughly discussing how to put them in place. Why an organization should install them remains decidedly less clear, as these two quotations indicate:

> Underlying and encompassing all of these misinterpretations is the notion that quality circles constitute a program. This usage has subtle implications. It makes quality circles an *encapsulated addition* to the organization. . . . To counteract these misconceptions, you should encourage managers to see the quality circle process for what it really is—a management practice or system. It changes the way managers manage by changing the very nature of the relationships among employees themselves and between employees and their supervisors and managers. . . .

> In short, how can you reform the system without losing control if it?. . . . First, management must have faith in its employees. . . . A quality circle program without sincere trust will not work. Second, management does not give away decision-making authority or responsibility in a quality circle process.[31]

These two quotations seem contradictory, if not mutually exclusive. Accomplishing fundamental, trust-based changes in all work relationships would seem to necessitate relinquishing at least some control—what else would make changes both fundamental and trust based? Quality circles may indeed be a multipurpose technology, one that can foster basic organizational change, improve workplace problem solving, alter work relations fundamentally, and not threaten managerial authority, but it cannot do all these things simultaneously in a single organization.

The premise that quality circles are a multipurpose technology has several noteworthy impli-cations. First, as just noted, some of the purposes may prove mutually exclusive *within* a single organization. Second, clearly, choosing reasons for having quality circles becomes more important given the variety and potential for conflicting purposes and expectations. Third, one potential use facing American managers is quality circles as "an encapsulated addition" to their organization, decidedly *not* the main use of quality control circles in Japan. Fourth, American managers encounter more confusion about why to have quality circles than do their Japanese counterparts.[32]

A Scenario for Failure

Confusion over the purpose of quality circles can easily produce tension during implementation, the following being one likely scenario. A top manager in search of "a way to fix" quality problems discovers quality circles and with them the claims that not only can they solve the quality problem but that they also can help improve employee morale, cooperation, and sense of true involvement in decision making without decreasing managerial control. Understandably impressed, the manager installs a quality circle program, completely packaged and ready to put in place. He asserts inside and outside the company that he is increasing employee participation even as he rests assured (a) that circles will only address those issues that management most wants addressed (i.e., those clearly identifiable as quality issues) and (b) that his involvement will not go beyond bankrolling circles, reviewing their recommendations, and providing ceremonial recognition of their cost-cutting achievements.

The manager's beliefs notwithstanding, the program sends markedly different cues to quality circles participants. The very structure of the program and training of participants signals to them that:

1. "This program is for real. Why else would management protect it with its own organization and commit company time and people to it?"
2. "This program is for us. Management is not only saying they want ideas, they're giving us air time. We get to change things around here."

3. "Part of what we get to change is how people get treated. Look at all that training we and the supervisors got about how to treat people!"

Thus, the manager seeking to use quality circles to solve quality problems, increase employees' sense of participation in decision making, and fundamentally alter work relations without relinquishing any control can sow the seeds of keen disappointment and failure. The confusion about what purpose quality circles actually serve moves to the American workplace because of varied perceptions about what Japanese circles are, American alterations, and mixed messages regarding the reasons for having quality circles. Therefore an approach to group problem solving developed in Japan and bottled in America is misused because of insufficient knowledge of the product and its side effects.

The Record to Date

Interestingly, Japanese managers tend not to quantify the costs and benefits of quality control circles. Rather, they utilize anecdotal data and intuition, an approach that makes sense given their use of quality control circles.[33] Cole states that the Japanese "were concerned with getting things done, getting on with their initiatives, experimenting with a wide range of techniques, and writing fairly sketchy reports to spread lessons."[34] The Japanese began quality control circles as part of a program of decentralization, hence that was their overall concern.[35] Furthermore, the technical nature of quality control circles and their heavy use of statistical analysis meant that quantifiable problems (e.g., defect rates) either were being solved or were not being solved (e.g., defect rates decreased or did not decrease). "Hard progress" in improving quality was easy enough to check if anyone wanted to do so, but the objective of improving quality, like the objective of decentralization, was what mattered, not the specific cost/benefit of one or more circles. The Japanese therefore have both a more purely technical, even mechanistic view of the purposes and nature of quality circles than do Americans and a less formal approach to their evaluation. The technical nature of the work and the

clarity of the reasons why Japanese organizations have quality control circles serve to free Japanese managers from the necessity of precise cost/benefit measures of their circles.[36]

Americans, on the other hand, tend to view quality circles as a stand-alone program which has to pay for itself. Cole (1982) reviews evidence that American managers often do not require detailed cost/benefit analysis when innovating, especially when innovating as part of a fad. He goes on to suggest that the attitude that quality circles have to justify themselves surfaces because of the threat to American management (namely participatory organizations) implicit in quality circles. Regardless of the appropriateness of this view, if American managers see quality circles as a program to solve specific, quantifiable problems, then numbers matter, and if American managers see quality circles as part of an effort to alter fundamentally an organization's work, then duration matters. And so we come to two criteria: (1) Is it cost effective? and (2) Does it last?

The first criterion is self-explanatory while the second merits further comment. A productivity program either yields savings or does not. However, full-fledged formal organizational change efforts often require at least three to five years to become established (a reality painfully apparent, for instance, in the quality of work life literature). Programs that expire in less time are less likely to have met their objectives and to have achieved enduring organizational change.

Applying these criteria returns us to the problem of confusion among American managers about quality circles. If, as has been argued, such confusion exists, then it would produce failures within organizations (e.g., the mixed-message scenario for failure sketched above). After all, the likelihood of success depends in large part on knowledge of what success looks like and what is required from all actors to achieve it. Furthermore, how can anyone measure something without knowing what it is? Mixed messages within an organization and markedly different uses of quality circles in different organizations should yield a track record of the following sort:

1. Few hard data about the cost effectiveness of quality circles.
2. Mixed indications that they are cost effective.
3. A sizable percentage of quality circle programs that fail to last as long as three years.

Cost Effectiveness

Limited data exists concerning the performance of quality circles.[37] Yager places the standard break-even point for American quality circles at three to five months after startup and a profit-to-cost return ratio of six to ten to one after a year of operation, while Simmons and Mares report claims of ratios from two to eight to one in years one and two of circle operation.[38] Mohrman and Novelli report a slight positive change in productivity in their case study as well as difficulty in determining the role of quality circles in the change. Platten presents findings from a survey of ninety-two quality circle members and eighty-three nonmembers in a manufacturing plant and his findings indicate that quality circles are an effective way of increasing the productivity and quality of work in remedial departments,[39] while Ferris and Wagner cite evidence indicating that even at Lockheed, the beachhead for quality circles in America, ". . . quality circles have languished since their initial promoters left the firm to consult elsewhere."[40] Wood, Hull, and Azumi offer these sobering comments:

1. Many success stories come from people who stand to benefit from news of the success (e.g., managers or consultants).
2. Two surveys of quality circle programs (total combined sample of seventy firms) each found that approximately 70 percent of the sample reported saving-to-cost ratio of less than one.
3. A change in management and capital investment (apart from quality circle recommendations) may have far more to do with reported successes than quality circles programs.
4. Anyone familiar with the Hawthorne effect (or the legacy of "productivity consultants") knows that paying more attention to people in and of

itself can produce temporary improvements in productivity and morale.[41]

Overall, Wood, Hull, and Azumi describe "The current state of information regarding the effectiveness of QCs . . . as a long list of claimed benefits, supported by anecdotal data and isolated cases which do not adequately establish the validity or generality of the benefits claimed."[42] Ferris and Wagner go even further: "Unfortunately, most of the literature appraising the effectiveness of American QCs has consisted of anecdotal case data presentations; little rigorous research exists. This lack of scholarship is especially alarming in light of recently reported failures of American QCs."[43] In other words, the available data is as hypothesized above: findings few in number and limited in quality.[44]

Duration of Quality Circles

Available data concerning the duration of quality circles is even scantier, a result of limited research, the recency of the explosion in the number of quality circles, and a probable reluctance to advertise failures. Wolff reports that within one year two of the three sites that he studied had started and ended formal quality circles.[45] Mohrman and Novelli report that two of the four quality circles they studied disbanded within about one year of forming.[46] And Lawler has stated that in his extensive research he found that quality circles rarely lasted more than nine months and has written that ". . . it is likely that few [quality circle] programs will be institutionalized and sustained over a long time period."[47] Causes of the demise of quality circles include:[48]

1. Running out of problems to solve.
2. Lack of support and/or disaffection (supervisory, managerial, and occasionally union).
3. Lack of change (connection to day-to-day operating style of workgroup and company) and/or failure to implement quality circle recommendations.
4. Development of a "what's in it for me?" attitude by circle members (often precipitated by

the failure of management to share gains precipitated by circle recommendations with circle members).

Summary

An explanation for the record of quality circles in the U.S. is the apparent general state of understanding (or misunderstanding) regarding the purpose, not the *technology,* of quality circles. Little hard data exists and what does tells, at best, a mixed tale: great and no financial success and little success in institutionalizing quality circles. A serious question exists as to whether quality circles generally survive long enough to affect organizational culture substantially.

Learning from the Past

The above indicates the need to clarify the purpose of quality circles and to recommend how best to use them. Below is an attempt to do so.

Quality circles can serve various purposes and serve them well, provided they are used in consonance with *a* selected purpose. Managers can choose to employ quality circles to solve problems and/or to change work relations. Furthermore, managers can use quality circles with a short-term or a long-term perspective. The purpose dictates how a manager should approach a quality circles program and, more important, how he or she should present the program to others, especially would-be participants. A typology appears in Figure 1 and, while the categories are not discrete or absolute, it limits the confusion (and the danger) surrounding quality circles.

Lessons Learned: The Short Term

Problem Solving/Short Term. The purpose here is participation of affected, involved, or knowledgeable parties in selecting and solving specific problems related to improving quality. Such problems might be high reject rates, rising warranty work, introduction of a new technology, consolidation/expansion of work areas, or merging of work units. These problems are not new; traditionally they are handled by managers, often working in *ad hoc* groups. Quality circles provide a way of involving, in a specifically structured and trained way, anyone affected or informed about a problem in the handling of that part of the problem that concerns his or her work. A quality circles program can provide both the opportunity to contribute as well as the skills and structure necessary for more people to work more effectively in groups. Managers and nonmanagers alike may learn considerable amounts about the problem (and its solution) while also learning about how to function better in groups.

Quality circles under such circumstances can mobilize parts of an organization to solve a quality problem. All involved should expect quality circles to be discontinued once the problem has been addressed. This self-contained, self-limited use of quality circles may have special appeal for American managers because it does not present the specter of large-scale change in organizational culture and operating style. Organizational benefits could include solving a problem, improving communication, creating a sense of teamwork, disseminating skills about group problem solving, and developing the ability to construct a quality circles program quickly.

The risks associated with this use of quality circles are:

1. Great expectations about the organization "going participative."
2. A sense of manipulation, particularly by workers. "We get to participate only when management wants and only on those problems they can't handle. We do their job and they get the profit."
3. Failure to own the problem. Mobilization requires a shared sense of immediacy which in turn requires that each group member understand the consequences of a problem for him or her *and* believe that he or she can contribute to a solution.

FIGURE 1   A Typology of Purposes for Using Quality Circle Programs

		Short-Term	Long-Term
Improved Problem Solving	*Purpose*	Mobilization of specific parts of the organization to solve specific problems.	Continued improvement in organizational problem-solving ability.
	Benefits	Problem solution; camaraderie; skill development; mobilization experience.	Problem solutions; dissemination of problem-solving skills and practice throughout the organization; experience in collaborative problem solving.
	Risks	Broader expectations/sense of manipulation; crisis management; burnout.	Misunderstanding (especially by top management) of nature of participative decision-making and change process; corresponding impact of large-scale failure.
	"To-do's"	Clarity of purpose; empower circle members; preemptive orientation.	Informed commitment by top management; inclusion of all organizational members.
Improved Work Relations	*Purpose*	Short-term improvement in general work relations.	Overall change in working relations throughout the organization.
	Benefits	Short-term improvement in problem solution; skill development.	More thoroughly based, hence more secure, SOP (including problem solving).
	Risks	Strong sense of manipulation; alienation; erosion of trust; anger.	Failure by management to appreciate enormity of cultural change; general negative impact on work relations.
	"To-do's"	Do not. Do not use quality circles for this end.	Education (including experiential) of top management and the rest of the organization; special importance of active, ongoing top management involvement in the process.

---

4. Mobilization and burnout. Crisis management develops and people burn or opt out.
5. A call throughout the organization to participate more in more decisions.

Minimizing these risks entails:

1. Clearly and repeatedly stating the purpose of the quality circles program, namely, "to solve quality problem X."
2. Clear, explicit identification of consequences of the problem needing solving and of the oppor-

tunities that circle members have to counter those consequences.
3. Provision of necessary skills and resources.
4. Anticipatory or proactive use of quality circles, i.e., using them to avoid and not to meet crises.

Improving Work Relations/Short Term. The purpose here is the short-term improvement of general work relations (not just problem-solving ability) by providing training in cooperative problem solving and the regular occasion to practice cooperation on actual workplace problems. Many quality circle programs may end up looking as if this were their purpose (namely, they do not last long and do not pay for themselves), however, this approach is fraught with dangers, including:

- A strong sense of manipulation.
- Alienation of lower and middle management (''So top management thinks *we're* the problem?!'').
- A corresponding erosion of trust and decreased likelihood of worker involvement in future improvement efforts.

The best way to avoid these dangers is *not* to employ quality circles for these ends. Short-term improvements in working relations are frustrating enough when unplanned. Add to that a sense that management actively manipulates people by pursuing *short*-term improvements and the frustration can easily become directed anger.

Lessons Learned: The Long Term

Organizational Change and Quality Circles. One choice facing anyone out to change organizational culture, to manage the norms of an organization, is whether to start at the top and work down or to start at the bottom and work up. The issue is how serious top management is about change and when it wishes to confront changing its own behavior (as distinct from concentrating on changing other people's behavior). Quality circles can generate organizational dynamics common to a bottom-up change strategy whether such dynamics are planned or not.

Managers who begin quality circles are, unquestionably, starting problem-solving groups. They are also choosing to create the potential for:

- A vehicle for employee involvement in traditionally managerial activities.
- An occasion for employees to become more involved in and more committed to their work.
- An opportunity for employees to learn more about their work and the work of the organization as a whole.

- The chance for employees to learn more about what it takes to make the organization function.
- A statement about a belief in the capacity of employees to contribute to organizational success in nontraditional ways.
- The possibility that employees will come to know more of what management knows, both information-wise and skill-wise, and that management as an activity will be demystified.
- Grounds for hopes about a more participative and open organization.

Why these creations? Because people want more say over their jobs and their working conditions: once people start having a say they want more. The truism holds—on the shop or office floors of America and in the shipyards of Gdansk. Consequently, quality circles are not experienced by their members as simply problem-solving groups. They are, undeniably, problem-solving groups, but humans form them and invest them with meaning—their meaning. Quality circle members therefore set about their work with items on their agenda other than solving quality problems. Participants can experience quality circles as a bottom-up change effort, or, more accurately, as a springboard for such an effort, regardless of the intention of upper management. Whereas the preceding section on short-term lessons dealt with managing quality circles in order to limit that experience, this section concerns managing in order to maximize it.[49]

Problem Solving/Long Term. The interest here is the continued long-term improvement in the ability of the organization to identify and resolve performance-related problems. Quality circles constitute a way to realize this goal by starting at the bottom of the organization. The orientation critical to this use of quality circles is: that these are tools to realizing an objective; that the objective is a process; that the process must envelop the organization; and that the process will occur/endure only with the conscious and continued involvement (as distinct from mere advocacy) of key organizational actors.

Quality circles can thereby serve these ends:

1. Dissemination of training and experience in co-operative problem solving.
2. Visible support for the notion of collaborative problem solving.
3. Expansion of the appreciation by organizational members of the effort involved in participative decision making.
4. A springboard to expanded participation and a testing ground for large-scale participation.

Recommendations consonant with these ends are as follows:

1. Management commitment to a long-term change in how the organization solves problems before asking others to do so. Personally trying out quality circles or other group problem-solving technologies first for an extended period (like three to six months) would greatly help management make an informed, responsible choice, as well as convince organization members of management's commitment.
2. Inclusion of all organizational members in the program, i.e., managerial and nonmanagerial quality circles.
3. Recognition that long-term change involves pressures for expansion *and* for elimination of the efforts.
4. Education about the process of change and explicit attention to expanding the nature and scope of change.

Improving Work Relations/Long Term. The focus in this case is on a broader range of processes than mere problem solving. The objective includes an overall pattern of relationships, encompassing, but not limited to, collaborative problem solving. How people communicate, handle conflict, and manage authority are as important as problem solving. The main argument in favor of this orientation is that without a general change in the organization, enduring change in group problem solving will not occur, and, therefore, overall organizational effectiveness will not improve.

Points made about long-term improvement in problem solving apply here too, only more so. To say that the objective is full scale, encompassing

cultural change, is to invite an explosion of expectations, hopes, and fears. Doing so raises the ante for everyone and demands even more expertise and involvement from key actors in key choices, expectation management, education, and the process of change.

Conclusion

Confusion has surrounded quality circles from the time that Americans "discovered" them in Japan. Westerners were confused about their purpose in Japan and then about their purpose in America. That confusion has manifested itself in the alteration of the quality circle technology (including considerably more emphasis on human relations skills), in the presentation (selling) of quality circles to American organizations as a multipurpose technology (often bordering on being a panacea), and in the data available (the amount and nature of it as well as the tale it tells).

Quality circles are a technology, a tool—one replete with potential. The technology is not the challenge: its use *is,* and that is what managers must clarify before they implement or evaluate quality circles. Managers must decide what they are trying to accomplish. Failure to do so sets up the program (and those associated with it) to fail and invites a string of casualties. Indeed, developing clarity about behavioral objectives, communicating such goals, and acting consistently with them could be the biggest, most difficult, and most noteworthy aspect of any quality circles program. It might also prove to be the most beneficial.

Figure 1 presents a typology that can help organize thinking about quality circles (and other kinds of technologies designed to change behavior in organizations). The discussion summarized in Figure 1 suggests these rules of thumb for managers considering the installation of quality circles:

1. *Decide why you want quality circles*. The reasons have everything to do with the success or failure of the program, in everyone's eyes, managers and employees.
2. *Try it yourself first*. This rule has special saliency the more the purpose of quality circles is

organizational change, but the point remains that being a participant will help you manage the program by helping you know what you are managing.

3. *Manage expectations, your own included.* Keep yourself and others informed about what is happening and why. Expectations, including your own, are like anything else that matters in organizations—they need managing.

4. *Make the quality circle option a universal one.* This will help to limit resistance based on feelings of being excluded and facilitate the dissemination of quality circles if it is desired.

5. *Mark the program boundaries clearly and walk the line yourself.* Just because you and others were clear once upon a time about what quality circles were and why they were installed does not mean that you or they still are. Check.

References

1. P. Gibson, "Quality Circles: An Approach to Productivity Improvement," *Work in America Institute Studies in Productivity* (New York: Pergamon, 1982); L. Pickler, "Quality Circles in the Systems Environment," *Journal of Systems Management,* November 1983, pp. 14–16; J. Simmons and W. Mares, *Working Together: Employee Participation in Action* (New York: New York University Press, 1985).

2. Gibson (1982).

3. K. Bradley and S. Hill, "After Japan: The Quality Circle Transplant and Productive Efficiency," *British Journal of Industrial Relations,* November 1983, pp. 291–311; J. M. Juran, "The QC Circle Phenomenon," *Industrial Quality Control,* January 1967, pp. 329–336; R. Wood, F. Hull, and K. Azumi, "Evaluating Quality Circles: The American Application," *California Management Review,* Fall 1983, pp. 37–53.

4. R. E. Cole, "Diffusion of Participatory Work Structures in Japan, Sweden, and the United States" in *Change in Organizations,* P. S. Goodman and Associates (San Francisco: Jossey-Bass, 1982). G. Munchus III, "Employer-Employee Based Quality Circles in Japan: Human Resource Policy Implications for American Firms," *Academy of Management Review* 8 (1983): 255–261.

5. Wood, Hull, and Azumi (1983); Bradley and Hill (1983); Registration figures unquestionably include inactive circles, there being little incentive for companies to deregister a circle (especially if it ceases to function because the firm goes out of business). Nonetheless, Cole (1982) believes that the number of unregistered circles (mainly in small- and medium-sized firms) easily amounts to five times the number of registered circles and includes approximately four million members.

6. Cole (1982).

7. Wood, Hull, and Azumi (1983); A phenomenon explainable in part because larger Japanese firms have lifetime employment (until age 55) while smaller firms, which employ 72 percent of the workforce, do not. Smaller firms do have the highest bankruptcy rate in the world, three times the American rate (Simmons and Mares, 1985).

8. Simmons and Mares (1985).

9. Juran (1967).

10. Ibid.

11. Ibid.

12. Cole (1982).

13. Juran (1967).

14. Bradley and Hill (1983).

15. W. F. Whyte, "Worker Participation: International and Historical Perspectives," *Journal of Applied and Behavioral Science* 19(1983):395–407.

16. M. K. Kobayashi and W. W. Burke, "Organization Development in Japan," *Columbia Journal of World Business,* Summer 1976, pp. 113–123.

17. Cole (1982).

18. Cole (1982) estimates that by the late 1970s over 50 percent of Japanese firms with more than thirty employees were using small groups of some sort to involve workers in decision making.

19. S. Takezawa, "The Quality of Working Life: Trends in Japan," *Labor and Society,* January 1976, pp. 29–48; This predisposition helps to explain why Japanese managers do not, as noted above, generally employ outside consultants to devise and implement their solutions—Japanese managers already have the orientation that many American consultants offer. Cole (1982) reports estimates that in 1973 500 to 1000 external Organizational Development consultants practiced in the United States while in 1976 there were *at most* 12 in Japan, and that the number of private U.S. firms consulting in quality circles rose from 3 in 1979 to over 30 in 1982.

20. Cole (1982).

21. Munchus (1983).

22. G. R. Ferris and J. A. Wagner III, "Quality Circles

in the United States: A Conceptual Reevaluation,'' *Journal of Applied Behavioral Science* 21(1985): 155–167.

23. Bradley and Hill (1983); R. E. Cole, *Work, Mobility and Participation* (Berkeley: University of California Press, 1979); Gibson (1982).

24. Gibson (1982).

25. This tendency is not unique to quality circles. Discussions of the garbage can approach to decision making appear in numerous places; among the most notable is J. March and J. Olsen, editors, *Ambiguity and Choice in Organizations* (Bergen, Norway: Universitetsforlaget, 1976).

26. K. D. Ramsing and J. D. Blair, ''An Expression of Concern about Quality Circles'' in *Academy of Management Proceedings,* edited by K. H. Chung (Wichita, KA: Academy of Management, 1982).

27. K. Ohmae, ''Quality Control Circles: They Work and They Don't Work,'' *The Wall Street Journal,* 29 March 1982.

28. E. Lawler and S. Mohrman, ''Quality Circles After the Fad,'' *Harvard Business Review,* January–February 1985, pp. 65–71.

29. Ferris and Wagner (1985); Wood, Hull, and Azumi (1983).

30. Ferris and Wagner (1985).

31. P. Thompson, *Quality Circles: How to Make Them Work in America* (New York: AMACON, 1982).

32. Cole (1982) believes that he can locate much of the responsibility for confusion about the purposes of quality circles and says that quality circles ''are being marketed by many consultants as a panacea to all problems management has or could have with its employees.''

33. Cole (1982).

34. Ibid.

35. Cole (1979) provides evidence supporting the success of decentralization: estimates of inspector/worker ratios at GM manufacturing and assembly plants (1:10 and 1:17) and Toyota (1:25 and 1:30).

36. Cole (1982) argues convincingly for the point of view presented here. Nissan, however, does have suggestion quotas for its circles (Public Television Networks, ''We Are Driven,'' *Frontline,* 1984) and Munchus (1983) reports the existence of mandatory suggestion rates at Toyota. Suggestion quotas or rates indicate that Japanese management does have short-term measures of quality control circle performance although not traditional cost/benefit.

37. Gibson (1982); S. Mohrman and L. Novelli, Jr., ''Beyond Testimonials: Learning from a Quality Circles Program,'' USC Graduate School of Business Administration, Center for Effective Organizations, G82-10(29), revised 1982; Wood, Hull, and Azumi (1983).

38. E. Yager, ''Examining the Quality Control Circle,'' *Personnel Journal,* October 1979, pp. 683–684 and ''Quality Circle: A Tool for the '80s,'' *Training and Development Journal,* August 1980, pp. 60–62; Simmons and Mares (1985). As for the cost of installation, the first circle runs from $8,000 to $15,000, given the use of an outside consultant (Yager, 1980). Subsequent circles cost less to install, given the development of internal training capacity, and start-up of the first circle may cost less if the organization has the capacity to train in-house.

39. P. Platten, *The Investigation of Organizational Commitment as a Source of Motivation in Quality Control Circles,* unpublished Ph.D. dissertation (New York University, 1983).

40. Ferris and Wagner (1985).

41. Wood, Hull, and Azumi (1983).

42. Ibid.

43. Ferris and Wagner (1985).

44. Gibson (1982) and Thompson (1982) suggest concrete measures of the impact of quality circles on individuals and organizations.

45. P. Wolff II, ''Quality Circles at King James County,'' paper presented at the 44th Annual Meeting of the Academy of Management, 1984.

46. Mohrman and Novelli (1982).

47. E. Lawler and S. Mohrman, ''Quality Circles: A Self-Destruct Approach?'' USC Graduate School of Business Administration, Center for Effective Organizations, G84-1 (49), 1984; E. Lawler, question-and-answer period following: ''A Report on Research Concerning the Problems and Failures of Some Employer–Employee Work Innovations,'' presentation at the Second National Labor-Management Conference, Washington, D.C., June, 1984.

48. Bradley and Hill (1983); Lawler and Mohrman (1984, 1985); Simmons and Mares (1985); Thompson (1982); Wolff (1984); Wood, Hull, and Azumi (1983).

49. A reader interested in more detailed discussion of how to link quality circles to larger change efforts should consult Lawler and Mohrman (1984, 1985) or E. Trist and C. Dwyer, ''The Limits of Laissez-faire as a Sociotechnical Change Strategy'' in R. Zaeger and M. Rosow, editors, *Innovative Organizations: Productivity Programs in Action* (New York: Pergamon, 1982).

Reading 41

THE JAPANESE MANAGEMENT
THEORY JUNGLE[1]

J. Bernard Keys and Thomas R. Miller

In response to Japan's impressive business performance over the last decade, the mystique of Japanese management has been addressed by a deluge of books and articles. The perceived superiority of management practices in Japan has been the subject of intensive inquiry by both the academic and the executive communities. Researchers' efforts to unlock this mystery have revealed a multitude of factors presumed to account for the excellence of Japanese management, but the most striking results perhaps are the diversity of factors cited and the disagreement over the causes of this success.

Competing hypotheses abound, ranging from the "Seven S" theory of Pascale and Athos (1981) about a unique Japanese management style to the "bottom line" explanation that stresses the Japanese focus on long term operating results. Some observers believe that excellence in Japanese management springs primarily from an emphasis on human resource development. Others maintain that the source of Japanese success is not found in social practices, but rather in the profound understanding of the intricacies of the decision making process. Several researchers laud the effective use of employee quality circles as the key element of Japanese success. Still others claim that Japanese expertise in technological developments and in manufacturing management is the basis of their

effectiveness. Yet another school of thought attributes Japanese achievement to their mastery of the use of statistical quality control applications.

To those attempting to comprehend the Japanese phenomenon, it appears that a dense jungle of confusion has grown up consisting of conflicting "theories" (using the term broadly), each of which offers hope as an explanation for the apparent superiority of the Japanese system of management. The jungle of Japanese theories is reminiscent of the "mental entanglement" that characterized American management theories in the 1950s, addressed in a classic article by Harold Koontz (1961). The purpose of this paper is to classify and to clarify the state of knowledge of Japanese management.

The Jungle of Theories

Manufacturing Management

Robert H. Hayes (1981) conducted his research by visiting and studying several plants of six Japanese companies. He finds the answer to Japanese superiority in their excellent manufacturing management: clean facilities, responsible employees, little or no inventories on the plant floor made possible by the absence of work stoppages, almost no rejected products, and "just-in-time" materials arrival. He discovered a remarkable absence of crisis management in the plant and excellent maintenance of equipment. Hayes captures the essence of Japanese manufacturing management in the old Japanese proverb: "pursuing the last grain of rice in the corner of the lunchbox." He points out that the Japanese are never satisfied with the quality of their products even when the defect rate is at an unbe-

Source: J. Bernard Keys and Thomas R. Miller, *Academy of Management Review* 9, no. 2, (1984), pp. 342–53.

[1]Portions of this paper were presented at the 42nd Annual Meeting of the Academy of Management, New York, 1982. The authors acknowledge Harold Koontz (1961), author of the classic paper, "The Management Theory Jungle."

lievable 1 percent, nor are they satisfied as long as any defect exists in the manufacturing operation. Hayes believes that technological advantages in Japan stem not from superior technology per se, but from the Japanese insistence on building their own process equipment in-house, which they in turn match with skilled employees trained in-house. They will not accept the compromise of a machine developed for several "users, and therefore several uses."

Further support for the manufacturing management theory is provided by Wheelwright (1981), who states that Japan's impressive accomplishments in manufacturing result chiefly from the effective integration of operations policy and manufacturing strategy. In marked contrast to the Japanese, the author cites the common American tendency to treat product quality and production planning as "swing factors" that can be traded off in order to meet the production output deadline. Thus, an American manager may deliver a product that, although functionally acceptable, does not meet the quality specifications. In reporting their impressions after visiting the plants of three Japanese companies—Tokyo Sanyo Electric, Toshita Tsurumi Works, and Yokogaua Electric Works, General Electric manufacturing executives agreed that the critical differences between Japanese and American manufacturing were not really cultural and environmental, but rather were related to basic manufacturing policy and practice. Observers reported a high degree of cleanliness and organization with orderly and timely flow of materials through the production system. They commented that although Americans have the necessary knowledge of effective manufacturing processes, they have lacked the discipline to implement them fully (Wheelwright, 1981). Wheelwright concludes that Japan's "truly impressive discipline and consistency in manufacturing operations" is the result of "a deliberate, thorough, and painstakingly developed way of thinking about the day-to-day management of production" (1981, p. 68). In other words, he holds that the Japanese have become so efficient chiefly because of excellent manufacturing practices. However, in interpreting these observations in order to isolate causes, an alternative hypothesis should be recognized: orderly production operations may be the *result* of the effective practice of management rather than the *cause* of manufacturing efficiency.

Quality Circle

A common theme in the literature on the effectiveness of Japanese management is their development and utilization of "quality control circles" or just "quality circles," as they are now commonly called (Cole, 1980; Rehder, 1981; Takeuchi, 1981; Yager, 1980). Although there are many variations of quality circles in practice, nearly all are structured as a relatively small group of employees who meet together to discuss and develop solutions for work problems relating to quality, productivity, or cost.

In many respects, quality circles are rooted in the work of the humanistic behavioral scientists such as Chris Argyris, Douglas McGregor, and Rensis Likert, who have long emphasized the significance of employee participation to effective management. Schooled in these behavioral techniques, the Japanese borrowed and adapted them to their organizations. However, it appears that the Japanese found their organizations more receptive to this form of participation than have American managers. Cole (1980) argues that Japanese managers have more fully accepted the fundamental premise of participative management—that employees are capable of contributing and desire to contribute to organizational requirements of a supportive supervisory climate and that the commitment of sufficient time for the participative process may be better satisfied in Japanese industry than in the United States.

Thus, the quality circle theory ascribes the effectiveness of Japanese management to an in-depth application of the participation concept, which apparently has resulted in improved productivity through higher levels of motivation, greater sharing of decision making, stronger employee commitment, and increased job satisfaction. In an extensive review of quality circles, Munchus (1983) concluded that they have been successful in widely diversified cultures, but that the results of their use in the United States are still open to question. Matsushita Electric, for example, uses them widely in Japan but does not consider the American worker suited to such activity.

Statistical Quality Control

In the 1950s the Japanese focused on upgrading the quality level of their manufactured products in an effort to reverse the notion that "made in Japan" signaled inferior merchandise. As with the development of quality circles, the expertise came largely from consultants in America—in particular from W. Edwards Deming and J. M. Juran, who lectured widely on the development and utilization of statistics and quality control techniques. The Japanese quickly embraced and effectively implemented the popular techniques developed in the United States, including zero defects and value engineering, and have become dedicated to the gospel of quality (Takeuchi, 1981). The Japanese appreciation for Deming's work is evidenced by his receipt of the Second Order Medal of the Sacred Treasure from Japan's Emperor Hirohito.

Of course, productivity is closely related to quality, and in Japan there is a fervent interest in "doing it right the first time." Deming argues that quality cannot be increased by inspection, and using men and machines to separate good products from bad is not the answer. The quality capability must be built into the production process. In comparing Japanese and American management, Deming (1980) argues that Americans learned the techniques too, but the Japanese took them seriously.

Long Term, Bottom Line

Peter Drucker suggests that the real reason for Japanese superiority springs from their focus on long term objectives. Large U.S. institutional investors, such as the pension funds, he laments, tend to reject firms that do not show strong performance in such short term measures as quarterly earnings per share. Thus, high technology companies are reluctant to "plow back money long term" for fear of adverse effects of their price earnings ratios. The market, he believes, has become far too sensitive to short term fluctuations (Flanigan, 1981).

A similar theme is echoed by William Anderson (1981), chairman and chief executive officer of National Cash Register Corporation. He cautions that American managers must look "beyond this month's sales report and this year's financial performance" and begin to evaluate both employee and organizational achievements from a long term prospective. The clear implication is that U.S. management should adopt criteria that look five years ahead, not just a month ahead.

Further evidence of the long planning horizon of Japanese management is the tradition of lifetime employment, resulting in a worker spending his entire career with one firm. For example, the average job tenure at Fujitsu is 13 years; the average job tenure in the United States is 3.6 years (Nakayama, 1980). While providing essentially a guaranteed job to the worker, the longevity of employment encourages extensive investment in employee training and development and promotes employee loyalty and esprit de corps, as evidenced by the company songs and exercise programs in many of the large plants. The nearly complete job security also reduces costs of turnover and subsequent recruitment. But, perhaps most important, the worker's assurance of economic security greatly reduces one's resistance to technological change that enables methods changes to be implemented more easily. Drucker maintains that this willingness to accept change and to embrace opportunities for productivity gains might be "the most important secret of the Japanese economy" (1971, p. 116). In sharp contrast, the typical American worker in a unionized firm has been conditioned to resist change, fearing both real and imagined threats to his/her economic security.

However, a key point in evaluating the unionization issue should be noted. In Japan, employees belong to company unions rather than craft unions; thus they could not readily change companies if they wished to do so. The strong company affiliation makes it easy to shift employees from plant to plant within the same company (Tanaka, 1981).

These employer advantages are enhanced by the strong feeling of security promoted by the Japanese lifetime employment concept. Drucker recently commented that lifetime employment, which restricts labor mobility and the threat of strikes, has rendered the union powerless in the private sector, almost an "organ of management" (1982, p. 26).

It should be recognized that the Japanese management focus on long term profitability is feasible, in part, because of the supportive role of the Japanese government. The comments of Reddy and Rao are revealing: "The Japanese government has been pursuing economic growth with a passion that American government has reserved for fighting communism" (1982, p. 5). The close relationship between business and government has been characterized as "Japan, Inc.," suggesting the behavior of a superconglomerate (Drucker, 1981). Indeed, some argue that Japan's economic success is related chiefly to the unique business-government relationship fostered by the Ministry of International Trade and Industry (MITI). As noted by Tsurumi (1981), government policies through tax incentives and other assistance programs are directed to rewarding the firms fulfilling the goals that support industrial growth and national stability. A related factor enabling business to focus its attention on the civilian product market is the low level of national resources committed to defense expenditures in Japan, a much publicized criticism by American producers.

Decision Making

At first glance, the consensus decision process of the Japanese appears to be simply an application of the American concept of participative management. Ouchi (1981) states that a consensus has been reached when there is agreement on a single alternative and when there is a mutual understanding of views of the participants and when there is support for the decision, whether one preferred it or not, because it was determined in an open and fair manner. However, Ouchi argues that even this degree of participation does not approach the Japanese concept of consensus decision making, in

which an important decision such as where to put a new plant or changing a production process would involve all who would likely be affected by it, perhaps 60 to 80 people. Ouchi further notes that two or three persons would have the task of discussing the decision with the affected employees and repeating this process when significant changes arise. Although this process is very time consuming, when the decision is finally determined, the support for it is nearly unanimous.

Howard and Teramoto (1981), professors in Great Britain and Tokyo, respectively, argue strongly that the most important difference in American and Japanese management involves the subtle differences in decision making. The word in the Japanese vocabulary that describes decision making is "nemawashi," which refers to the "political" processes by which an unofficial understanding is reached before any final decision is made on a particular matter. The literal meaning of nemawashi is "the process of planting a tree, i.e., implanting its roots into the soil so it can grow." The authors believe that it perfectly describes the appropriate process of practical decision making in any culture.

To the Western observer, the consensus decision making process may appear to be exceedingly inefficient, but this attitude fails to give proper consideration to the implementation of the decision. In defense of the Japanese decision making practice, it is advanced that a consensus decision, though mediocre, can yield better outcomes than an imposed decision, though brilliant, because of the support of employees, their knowledge of the decision parameters, and their commitment to successful execution of the decisions. Further, the considerable time that goes into defining the issue reduces the risk that a preconceived solution will prevent proper definition of the problem, a criterion of decision making practices of American managers (Kobayashi, 1970).

Attempts at Integrated Models of Japanese Management

Several students of the Japanese management process have gone beyond the search for the single-factor explanation in their efforts to develop more comprehensive theories. Three of these notable efforts will be reviewed briefly.

Seven S

Richard Pascale and Anthony Athos (1981) utilize in their model the framework of seven management variables developed by McKinsey & Company. The seven variables of S's are superordinate goals, strategy, structure, systems, staff, skills, and style. These are the ''levers'' of organizational and management functions with which executives can influence large complex organizations. Superordinate goals function as the unifying elements that tie together the various activities and interests of organizational members.

According to Pascale and Athos, the variables can be divided into ''hard S's'' and ''soft S's.'' The hard S's, presumably the more impersonal and institutional factors, are strategy, structure, and systems. In contrast, the soft S's, dealing more with human values and interpersonal issues, are staff (the concern for having the right sort of people to do the work), skills (training and developing people to do what is needed), and style (the manner in which management handles subordinates, peers, and superiors). The authors' chief research instrument included interviews and observations of the styles of chief executive officers in the United States and Japan—in particular, the Matsushita Corporation and ITT.

Pascale and Athos maintain that U.S. management is very similar to Japan on all the hard S's of strategy, structure, and system, but that Japan has advantages in the soft S's of staff, skills, and style. These advantages stem largely from the Japanese culture, which differs in its approach to ambiguity, uncertainty, imperfection, and interdependence. The authors discuss at length how the Japanese manager in communicating with others has learned to make the most of ambiguity, indirection, subtle cues, trust, interdependence, uncertainty, implicit messages, and management of process, as opposed to the U.S. managerial norm of striving for complete openness, explicitness, and directness in order to minimize ambiguity and uncertainty. Unfortunately, the authors support their theory only with broad generalizations drawn from comparisons of the chief executive officer of Matsushita Corporation and ITT's Geneen.

Organizational

William Ouchi (1981) summarizes his work in what has become the best selling book on Japanese management, *Theory Z*. Instead of emphasizing the differences in the styles of leaders of key organizations in the United States and Japan, Ouchi focused in his writing on the organizations themselves. He first describes the ideal Japanese organizational model, which he used as a ''foil'' against which to compare and understand the American model. The Japanese organization is characterized by lifetime employment, slow evaluation and promotion, nonspecialized career paths, implicit control mechanisms, collective decision making, collective responsibility, and holistic concern for employees. In sharp contrast, features of American organizations include short term employment, rapid evaluation and promotion, specialized career paths, explicit control mechanisms, individual decision making, individual responsibility, and segmented concern for workers.

Ouchi also argues that the characteristics of Japanese management have derived from their culture—a culture woven interdependently because of collective rice farming and crowded conditions causing Japan to be very ripe for industrialization. In contrast, the American culture has developed from the spirit of individualism of an expanding frontier, a culture less conducive to industrialization.

Ouchi and Jaeger (1978), like Pascale and Athos, point out that the Japanese style is not culture bound, however. Many Japanese firms, with little adaptation, have transported their successful operations to the United States. Theory Z, then, becomes the modified model, which includes the best of the Japanese and American models. Theory Z emphasizes long, but not lifetime, employment; consensual decision making, as in Japan; individual responsibility as opposed to the Japanese emphasis on collective responsibility; slow evaluation and promotion as in Japan; implicit control (Japanese) but with explicit measures (American); moderately specialized career paths (a compromise); and a holistic concern for employees, as in Japan (Ouchi & Jaeger, 1978).

Ouchi's theory has not been immune to criticism. In his review of *Theory Z,* for example, Gibney sharply challenges Ouchi's assertion that Japanese organizations can be so readily typified and understood from the few cases cited by Ouchi: "Ouchi has given us a chrome-plated collection of hasty generalizations, slogan-type writing, and dimestore business sociology, based on what one might call a modified dart-board technique of research" (1981, p. 17).

A thoughtful, incisive critique of Theory Z is provided by Sullivan (1983), who develops an antitheory Z "descriptive" conceptualization that contrasts sharply with Ouchi's "prescriptive" model. Anti-theory Z acknowledges the existence of life-time employment, nonspecialized careers, and automatic promotions, but suggests that these are cultural, historical factors rather than managerially initiated incentives. Further, Sullivan hypothesizes that these conditions produce some minimally competent managers who, when promoted automatically, must depend heavily on subordinates. The resultant consensus decisions and sharing of responsibility may stem more from necessity than from intimacy, involvement, and trust. Thus, consensus decisions and collective responsibility protect bureaucratic, hierarchical relationships, which, he proposes, exist in some Japanese firms. In addition, Sullivan argues that Theory Z does not, as Ouchi claims, emanate from humanistic management. Instead, Sullivan contends that Theory Z derives from the "industrial clan" values of Durkheim (1902/1933) that promote and sustain a regulated social order as opposed to the self-interest of individuals.

Human Resource

Hatvany and Pucik (1981) have conceptualized a model of Japanese management that focuses on the maximization of human resource development. Emphasizing the use of an integrated system of management, the authors' model rests on the implementation of three interrelated strategies: development of an internal labor market, articulation of a company philosophy stressing cooperation and teamwork, and utilization of a well-defined socialization process for hiring and integrating new employees into the company.

The unique element of Japanese management highlighted by Hatvany and Pucik is the internal labor market, which derives from the lifetime employment syndrome discussed earlier. Japanese firms hire males after graduation, with the expectation of retaining them for a lifetime. This security of male employment is assisted by using female and part time workers in order to adjust the size of the workforce to current economic conditions, by underpaying workers in the early stages of their careers in favor of compensation in later years, and by slow career path movement. The Japanese utilize an intensive socialization process designed to foster a "company man" identity.

Many specific techniques are utilized by the Japanese to promote and reinforce their management system. Broad knowledge of company operations is fostered by job rotation, slow promotion, and the lifetime employment. Company policies and assignments tend to build group cohesiveness and teamwork and emphasize the importance of the collective interests of the group, rather than the individual's own interests. Employee evaluation encompasses both performance factors and workers' attitudes and behaviors. Open communications are fostered by extensive face-to-face communications (the absence of private offices, even for high ranking managers) and by the frequency with which foremen and senior plant managers tend to visit workers on the plant floor. Use of consultative decision making practices is another supporting technique of Hatvany and Pucik's model. The final element in their model is management's expression of concern for employees enhanced by extensive company sponsored cultural, athletic, and recreational activities.

In contrast to the above model, Cole (1971) cautions that Western knowledge of the blue-collar worker in Japan is still shallow and laden with stereotypes of limited validity. He claims that the vision of the Japanese worker as always polite and unemotional differs sharply from the gregarious, spontaneous, openly expressive workers in the Tokyo plant he observed. The character of the Japanese worker is further explicated by Tsurumi (1981), who maintains that politeness, hard work, orientation toward group activity, and loyalty to management are no more inborn traits of the Japanese than of Canadians and Americans. Although a popular view of Japanese work groups touts their strong cohesiveness and the benefits of consensus decision making, Cole warns that this emphasis masks the strong competition within Japanese society. Such competition reveals itself in efforts to cultivate favor with superiors through flattery or politicking, which can result in conflicts within the work group. Further, Cole questions the authenticity of Japanese employee security through lifetime employment, noting that there are many devices employers can use to get employees to quit that fall short of actually firing them.

The transfer of strong family ties to industry has fostered several interesting phenomena. Tanaka (1981) reports that employees tend to hire "total persons," and employees tend to become totally immersed in the organization for which they work. Because the company becomes a surrogate for the family, work takes on the same ethos as a contribution to the family—loyalty, sincerity, and so on.

Yazaburo Mogi, first executive vice president of the Kikkoman soy sauce plant at Waleworth, Wisconsin, cautions that "the Japanese seniority system, while it offers security and creates a harmonious atmosphere conducive to good results, may also reduce incentives to do good work" ("How the Japanese Manage," 1981, p. 103). Rejecting the "myth" of the Japanese as "supermen" and the conclusion that Japan's industrial success is linked to the uniqueness of Japanese human factors or "the spirit of its workers," Blotnick argues that it would be as correct to link Japan's success to "the coercive, regimented side of its society," which Americans would "hardly want to emulate" (1981, p. 132).

The company's (family's) prosperity becomes more important than individual prosperity, and work for the company—not leisure—becomes the essence of life.

Sources of Entanglement in the Jungle

Many differences in the Japanese style of management and Western styles can be attributed to sharp differences in the respective cultures rather than to management practices (Schein, 1981). The common thread about which Japanese life has developed is "intimacy," which has evolved from the dictates of collective farming, little available land space, and the need to construct homes that offered little privacy. The family cultural forces are transferred to business firms, reinforcing compliance of behavior and promoting high performance (Cao, 1981). In strong opposition to this style, which promotes close social relations, American life has developed around rugged individualism and independence (Ouchi, 1981), which has grown out of the developing frontier and a land intense economy rather than a labor intense one. Thus, the cultural focus on the groups' interests, as opposed to the individual's, is strongly imbedded in Japanese workers in contrast to their American counterparts.

Several environmental and structural factors seem to offer Japanese management an advantage over the United States. Most Japanese employees who are union members belong to company unions. Of the directors of major corporations, 16 percent are former union officials (Janger & Berenkein, 1981). Unions and management tend to form a strong productive partnership, paving the way for easy introduction of labor-saving devices. The influence of such "macro" factors as MITI, extensive capital investment, modest defense expenditures, lower wage rates, and the relatively undervalued yen have been slighted as causal factors of Japan's economic success when compared to the much publicized managerial prowess of the Japanese. Further, Vogel has argued that the Japanese educational environment is the foundation of its economic achievement: "If any single factor explains the Japanese success, it is the group-directed quest for knowledge'' (1982 p. 65). Perhaps this quest arises in the very competitive school systems and is reinforced by the close relationships among academic performance, schools attended and job placement.

Nearly all of the confrontations faced by Japanese firms arise from consumer or environmental issues. Rarely does protest involve issues such as feminism, investment policy, wages, or living and working conditions. For protests that do arise, litigation is quite uncommon (Japan has half the population of the United States, but only 11,000 lawyers). Nor is shareholder pressure a viable alternative for special interest groups; 90 percent of all directors are ''inside'' directors employed by the company (Janger & Berenkein, 1981).

A further source of confusion is the tendency toward oversimplification in explaining the effectiveness of Japanese management. It is doubtful that a one-factor or two-factor theory of management such as ''decision making'' or ''quality control'' can account fully for a country's economic achievements. Surely a group of complex forces taken together delineate the dimensions of Japanese management experience. A related element of confusion is the difficulty of distinguishing causation from correlation. Sullivan (1983) bases his antitheory Z on such an argument.

Another caveat to the student of Japanese management concerns the tendency toward overgeneralization of the ''Japanese management'' mystique. Research on Japanese management practices has focused primarily on large, highly visible firms in the automotive and electronics industries. What of the experience of the smaller firms and businesses engaged in retailing, agriculture, chemicals, or in the service industries such as banking and finance? Can one characterize the management practices of an entire nation from such a small and nonrepresentative sample? Although Ouchi and Pascale and Athos have highlighted dramatic differences between Japanese and American management practices, it is doubtful that the few firms cited truly represent the norms of ''Japanese'' and ''American'' management. The excellent productivity and quality of Japanese manufacturing in such mass production industries as automobiles, household

appliances, and steel are well recognized, but one should not conclude that the Japanese enjoy superiority over international competitors in all industrial efforts. As noted by Tsurumi:

> Japanese industries do not outperform American, Canadian and other foreign counterparts . . . in agriculture, aircraft, nonferrous metals, and some advanced telecommunications equipment. In the fields of organic and non-organic chemicals, pharmaceuticals, large-scale computers and large earth-moving equipment, American firms lead the Japanese by a substantial margin (1981, p. 7).

The need for additional research to resolve inconsistencies and conflicts is clear. True, insights and understandings are developing, but much of the evidence is andecdotal or is so narrowly based that accurate conclusions must necessarily be tentative. Although these results are to be expected, given the youthful state of research on Japanese industrial sciences, some observers have been unable to resist drawing broad conclusions that are appealing in their simplicity but are unwarranted by the research data.

Common Factors in the Theories and Models—A Mental Factor Analysis

Although the positions of the writers above present different views and perspectives on Japanese management success that have contributed to the ''entanglement,'' there appear to be underlying factors at the heart of the Japanese system that foster the development of the various management theories and models. First, Japanese managers seem to be oriented to a longer planning horizon than their American counterparts. Second, Japanese firms are more inclined to accept a lifetime commitment and holistic concern for their employees. Finally, the Japanese appear more strongly committed to the concept of responsibility than individual accountability. These three factors are explored as integrating concepts in interrelating the streams of Japanese management throught presented above.

A suggested pattern of causality among the underlying factors of long run planning horizon, commitement to lifetime employment, and collective responsibility and a summary of outcomes characterizing Japanese management are shown in Figure 1. The authors contend that these underlying factors may be chiefly responsible for the development of the elements of the Japanese system of management and that these are rooted in the Japanese culture. Although a model of perfect causality is not claimed, the tentative pattern of causality in Figure 1 relates and summarizes much of the existing evidence.

Long Run Planning Horizon

Once management commits itself to planning for the long run rather than focusing on short run maximization, certain benefits are likely to follow. Management is allocated more time to develop objectives and implementation plans. The longer planning horizon is conducive to the generation of interpersonal relationships that foster mutual un-derstandings and implicit goals. Furthermore, the time frame of all plans—short run, intermediate, and long term—tends to lengthen, and immediate pressures tend to diminish. Deliberate planning and communication exhibits itself in orderliness and diligence of implementation of production operations and in the integration of manufacturing strategy and operations policy. There is time to produce customized in-house process equipment, and, perhaps more importantly, the long tenure of employees provides time to select employees whose skills match the equipment or to train those whose skills do not.

The impact of the long planning horizon on Japanese industry is further evidenced in the activities of the Ministry of Trade and Industry, which provide a supportive, stable environment for the industries that are responsive to expressed national economic goals. The predictability of public policy toward business and industry permits an easier or-

---

FIGURE 1   Fundamental Factors Underlying Japanese Management Practices: A Suggested Pattern of Causality*

Underlying Factors	Management Practices
Long-Run Planning Horizon	Commitment to sufficient time to manage Diligence in implementation of plans Discipline and order in work Sufficient time to implement concepts and systems Development of an integrated organizational philosophy Growth of implicit control systems
Commitment to Lifetime Employment	Articulation of company philosophy Executive investment in employee training and development Socialization process in hiring and integration Reduced turnover and high loyalty Nonspecialized career paths Development of internal labor markets
Collective Responsibility	Emphasis on soft S's—staff, skills, style Company unions rather than craft unions Emphasis on teamwork and cooperation Consensus decision making Participative management Trust and interdependence Quality circles

*Overlapping lines represent shadings of dual causality. The authors acknowledge that some of the resultant practices may, in turn, reinforce the underlying factors, suggesting two-way causality.

ganizational commitment to long term strategies rather than a penchant for short run expediencies.

The success in Japan of quality circles, statistical quality control, and consensus decision making also is facilitated by the long term focus. Often the lack of success with these approaches in the United States has not been because they are faulty in theory or concept, but rather because they have been implemented poorly. Poor implementation usually means too hastily introduced. However, given sufficient time for employers to become comfortable with these new approaches, and with co-workers, many implicit control systems and corrective adjustments arise to prevent the failure of these complex managerial concepts and systems.

Commitment to Lifetime Employment

The mutual commitment of Japanese management and the employee to lifetime employment appears to underlie a number of the celebrated Japanese management practices. The mutual awareness created by the investment of the two parties permits long term efforts in training and development. It also encourages rotational training programs outside one's specialized field and, perhaps most importantly, as cited by Drucker, promotes the acceptance of changes in work-methods and technology that enhance productivity. (This approach contrasts sharply with an American tendency to reap short term benefits from new employees with entry-level skills by retaining them in a job until they leave the organization.)

The recruitment and selection process is approached differently when one hires for a lifetime rather than the short term. More emphasis must be given to the socialization factors—the "fit" of the employee to the organization, one's satisfaction with the company philosophy, one's relationships with peer groups at work, the acceptance of management style, and so on. Indeed, hiring may be based more on social factors than on entry skills, because the latter will be utilized less.

The intensive socialization of the Japanese firm's efforts to inculcate the culture of the organization in employees—through such extensive ritualistic practices as employee calisthenics, singing the company songs, after-hours group activities, and company sponsored vacations—help develop and sustain long term commitment and loyalty to the organization. The holistic concern that is evidenced for employees and their families may be viewed as a sensible effort to safeguard the employer's substantial investment in human resources and further bond the employees to the organization.

The long term commitment and concern for employees and the consequent familial relationship promote trust and support of organizational leadership. Unlike the employee who is likely to remain with an employer (and a boss) for a short time, the Japanese system promotes accommodation and unity of interest. Knowing the extended nature of the employment practice, the worker is less inclined to engage in major confrontations or conflicts that would damage the long term superior-subordinate relationship. One would expect communications to be more gentle, subtle, implicit, and "family oriented."

Finally, a commitment to lifetime employment with holistic concern for employees is likely to produce a balanced, reciprocal psychological contract calling for a "company" type of identity. The employer's side of the contract is likely to include more participation of employees in the decision making process. When one has remained with a company long enough "to belong," the person also is more likely to be "consulted" on important matters affecting the company.

Emphasis on Collective Responsibility

According to most writers, Japanese management shuns individual accountability and credit in preference for collective or group responsibility and rewards. If true, organizations managed by such persons would place heavy emphasis on the values of teamwork and cooperation. Decisions more often would be made collectively or, more likely, nemawashi style. Participative management or consensus management would not be a style that most managers forced on themselves, but rather would be a natural way of engaging in the collective sharing of responsibility.

The present phenomena of quality circles and consensus decision making are rooted in the Japanese cultural traditions emphasizing interdependence, collaboration, and cooperation. The apparent subordination of the individual's needs and interests to those of the group has strong precedent in the Japanese culture. The willing acceptance of one's role in the organization reflects the traditional commitment to the priority of collective action. The emphasis on collective responsibility fosters a congruence of goals among employees and management, which is bolstered further by lifetime, two-way contracts between them.

The presence of a hard-working, orderly workforce can be related to the orientation to collective responsibility of the Japanese. When coupled with a high degree of goal congruence between employer and employee, the emergence of cohesive, productive, disciplined work groups is not surprising. The impressive performance of the Japanese work force, particularly their high productivity and exceptional quality levels, reasonably derives from those underlying conditions that support vigorous implementation of high output standards and superior quality control systems.

Clearing a Path through the Jungle

From a review of the research findings on Japanese managerial success, one is reminded of Porter's (1962) parable of the spindle, in which the proverbial specialists, called on to solve a problem, all found the answer deeply imbedded in their own particular expertise. On greater reflection, however, it is proposed that the writers probably are not biased in their analyses, but rather are unable to fully grasp the intricacies of the data to describe adequately Japan's industrial success. For, as noted, in addition to the host of management-based theories proposed as explanations for Japanese achievements, alternative theories built on government and environmental models, for example, "Japan Inc.," have been hypothesized. Thus, they are reacting not only as did the scientists in the parable of the spindle, but also as did the blind men in the fable in which they describe the elephant. You will

recall that one felt the knee of the elephant and described it as a tree-like creature; another felt the tusk and likened it to a spear; and a third felt the tail and insisted that it was small and round like a rope.

Perhaps all of the theorists are correct in attributing some Japanese excellence to the area of Japan's industry that they have examined. Maybe the Japanese, in their obsession to redeem the honor of their country after World War II and in their quest for world respect in industry, have produced excellence in many areas of the process of management. If so, it should not be surprising that existing research efforts have failed to capture adequately the essence of Japanese management effectiveness. Further, it seems unlikely that additional research seeking single-factor or dual-factor explanations of the Japanese success will be more successful; the panacea will continue to be elusive. Also, the jungle warfare among management theorists cited by Koontz in 1961 is not lacking among students of Japanese management today. For there exists a tendency to discount or discredit rival hypotheses or conceptualizations that are incompatible with one's own.

Of what value are the present theories in the jungle? It is argued that they are of considerable value as long as researchers and organization development implementors recognize that elements of Japanese management do not stand alone, but rather they require supporting cultural and environmental frameworks to be effective. As in most new systems of management, practice must precede research, and research must initially address small segments of the implementation. For the organization contemplating adoption of the Japanese system, Chung and Gray (1982) stress that extensive preparation and commitment is necessary, pointing out that an adoption will not work unless the organization is willing to change its whole philosophy of organizing people. In a similar vein, England (1982) presents evidence to suggest that the social and institutional framework of American industry is inimicable to the tenets of Ouchi's Theory Z, and this will limit its adoption by firms in the United States.

Perhaps the most fruitful approach for uncovering tracks in the Japanese management theory jungle will be to build models that reflect the "system" of Japanese management—the interdependencies of the political, economic, social, and religious variables with management practices. What appears to be most needed is the development of integrated, internally consistent models that encompass the evaluation and the context of Japanese management practices, rather than focusing on the techniques or concepts in isolation. Present understanding of Japanese management is limited by the narrow comprehension of the environment in which it exists—societal norms and values, educational and socialization processes, and the interfaces of business, government, and labor. Armed with a better understanding of the interrelationships of the elements of the Japanese management system, one will be better equipped to address the issues of emulation, adaptation, and implementation in American enterprises. When one attempts to traverse a jungle, a complete understanding of the terrain is helpful.

References

Anderson, W. S. Meeting the Japanese economic challenge. *Business Horizons,* 1981, 24(2), 56–62.

Blotnick, S. Supermen? *Forbes,* August 17, 1981, pp. 132–133.

Cao, A. D. The Japanese challenge in the 1980's: A sociocultural interpretation. *Mid-South Business Journal.* 1981, 2(1), 7–14.

Chung, K. H., & Gray, M. A. Can we adopt the Japanese methods of human resources management? *Personnel Administrator,* 1982, 28(5), 41–46, 80.

Cole, R. E. *Japanese blue collar: The changing tradition.* Berkeley, Cal.: University of California Press, 1971.

Cole, R. E. Learning from the Japanese: Prospects and pitfalls. *Management Review,* 1980, 69(9), 22–28, 38–42.

Deming, W. E. What can American manufacturers learn from the Japanese? *Iron Age,* October 6, 1980, p. 51.

Drucker, P. F. What we can learn from Japanese management. *Harvard Business Review,* 1971, 49(2), 110–122.

Drucker, P. F. Behind Japan's success. *Harvard Business Review,* 1981, 59(1), 83–90.

Drucker, P. Are unions becoming irrelevant? *Wall Street Journal,* September 22, 1982, p. 26.

Durkheim, E. Preface. In *The division of labor in society.* 2nd ed. New York: Macmillan Co., 1933, 1–31. (Originally published, 1902).

England, G. W. Japanese and American management: Theory Z and beyond. Unpublished paper, University of Oklahoma, 1982.

Flanigan, J. The wrong bottom line. *Forbes,* May 25, 1981, pp. 42, 46.

Gibney, F. B. Now it's time to imitate the Japanese. *Pacific Basin Quarterly,* 1981, 6, 17–18.

Hatvany, N., & Pucik, V. An integrated management system: Lessons from the Japanese experience. *Academy of Management Review,* 1981, 6, 469–480.

Hayes, R. H. Why Japanese factories work. *Harvard Business Review,* 1981, 59(4), 57–66.

How the Japanese manage in the U.S. *Fortune,* June 15, 1981, 97–98, 102–103.

Howard, N., & Teramoto, Y. The really important difference between Japanese and western management. *Management International Review,* 1981, 21, 19–30.

Janger, A. R. & Berenkein, R. E. *External challenges to management decisions: A growing international problem.* The Conference Board. Report no. 808, 1981, 48–68.

Kobayashi, S. The creative organization—A Japanese experiment. *Personnel,* 1970, 47(6), 8–17.

Koontz, H. The management theory jungle. *Journal of the Academy of Management,* 1961, 4(3), 174–188.

Munchus, G. Employer-employee based quality circles in Japan: Human resource policy implications for American firms. *Academy of Management Review,* 1983, 8, 255–261.

Nakayama, N. The United States and Japan: Some management contrasts. *Computers and People,* 1980, 29, 8–10.

Ouchi, W. C. Theory Z: How American business can meet the Japanese challenge. Reading, Mass.: Addison-Wesley, 1981.

Ouchi, W. C., & Jaeger, A. M. Type Z organization: Stability in the midst of mobility. *Academy of Management Review,* 1978, 3, 305–314.

Pascale, R. T., & Athos, A. G. *The art of Japanese management*. New York: Simon and Schuster, 1981.

Porter E. H. The parable of the spindle. *Harvard Business Review*, 1962, 40(3), 58–66.

Reddy, A. C., & Rao, C. P. Japanese marketing: Underlying reasons for its success. *Mid-South Business Journal*, 1982, 2(1), 3–6.

Rehder, R. R. What American and Japanese managers are learning from each other. *Business Horizons*, 1981, 24(2), 63–70.

Schein, E. H. Does Japanese management style have a message for American managers? *Sloan Management Review*, 1981, 23(1), 55–67.

Sullivan, J. J. A critique of theory Z. *Academy of Management Review*, 1983, 8, 132–142.

Takeuchi, H. Productivity: Learning from the Japanese. *California Management Review*, 1981, 23(4), 5–18.

Tanaka, F. J. Lifetime employment in Japan. *Challenge*, 1981, 24(4), 23–29.

Tsurumi, Y. Productivity: The Japanese approach. *Pacific Basin Quarterly*, 1981, 6, 7–11.

Vogel, E. F. *Japan as number one: Lessons for America*. New York: Harper & Row, 1979. Quoted in L. A. Bryan, Jr., The Japanese and the American first-line supervisor. *Training and Development Journal*, 1982, 36(1), 65.

Wheelwright, S. C. Japan—Where operations really are strategic. *Harvard Business Review*, 1981, 59(4), 67–74.

Yager, E. Quality circle: A tool for the 80's. *Training and Development Journal*, 1980, 34(8), 60–62.

Reading 42

WHY PRODUCTIVITY EFFORTS FAIL

Paul S. Goodman and James W. Dean, Jr.

In the 1970s we saw a proliferation of new forms of work organization projects conceived by labor and management. These projects were aimed at improving the quality of working life (QWL), the quality of union-management relationships, and organizational effectiveness. In many ways the new forms of work organization were revolutionary in the sense that they represented fundamental changes in how labor and management could work together, how work would be organized, and how organizations might be designed.

Autonomous work groups represent one type of new form of work organization project. Basically, these are self-governing groups organized by process, place, or product. There is a substantial shift in authority and decision making as the group takes over decision making on hiring, discipline, allocation of production tasks, etc. Matrix business teams represent another new form of work organization. Here line and staff managers are organized around business teams rather than functions. Attached to each team is a voluntary set of shop floor teams whose task is to improve productivity. Many other organizational changes such as QC circles, Scanlon plans, job enrichment activities, and labor-management problem-solving groups were introduced during this period. They all represent fundamental changes in the organization's communication, decision making, authority, and reward systems. They also create fundamental changes in the relationships among people within the organization.

Source: This paper was partially supported by the Organizational Effectiveness Research Program, Office of Naval Research, Contract N0014–79–C–0167. It was presented at American Psychological Association, August 1981, and Quality of Work Conference, Toronto, Canada, September 1981.

This paper is concerned with whether these programs last. That is, after some initial period of success, do these change programs persist and become institutionalized, or are they just temporary phenomena? Why do some projects decline while others do not? What factors shape whether these QWL projects have some long-term viability?

Significance

The importance of understanding more about the concept of persistence or institutionalization of change should be apparent. If one is interested in bringing about long-term changes in productivity and in the quality of working life, labor-management relationships, and organizational effectiveness, then we must know more about why some change programs remain viable while others decline.

There is some growing evidence (Mirvis & Berg, 1977; Goodman & Dean, 1981) that many of these new forms of work-organization projects do not last. Goodman and Dean recently examined the persistence of change in a heterogeneous sample of new forms of work-organization projects. They selected organizations in which the change program had been *successfully* introduced and where some *positive* benefits had been identified. Goodman and Dean interviewed participants in these organizations four to five years after the projects had been implemented. They wanted to know whether the change activities had persisted. Only *one third of the change programs* exhibited some reasonable level of persistence. The other change activities were either nonexistent or in decline. Given the huge amount of human and financial resources allocated to programs of change, such a low rate of persistence makes for a disturbing practical problem for managers and practitioners of organizational change.

Institutionalization—A Definition

Our approach is to study the persistence of organizational change via the concept of institutionalization. Institutionalization is examined in terms of specific behaviors or acts. We are assuming here that the persistence of QWL-type change programs can be studied by analyzing the persistence of the specific behaviors associated with each program. An institutionalized act is defined as a behavior that is *performed by two or more individuals, persists over time,* and *exists as a part of the daily functioning of the organization.* It should be clear from our definition of institutionalization that an act is not all-or-nothing. An act may vary in terms of its persistence, the number of people in the organization performing the act, and the degree to which it exists as part of the organization. Most of the organizational cases we have reviewed cannot be described by simple labels of *success* or *failure.* Rather, we find various degrees of institutionalization. The basic questions are, then: What do we mean by degrees of institutionalization? How do we measure these degrees?

We have identified five factors that contribute to the degree of institutionalization:

1. *Knowledge of the behaviors.* Remember that institutionalization is analyzed by looking at the behaviors required by the change program. Here we are interested merely in how many people know about these behaviors, and how much they know. Do they know how to perform the behaviors? Do they know the purposes of the behaviors? For example, team meetings are a part of many QWL programs. In some cases, people know that they are supposed to have team meetings, but don't know what they are supposed to do in the meetings. In other cases, people may not even know that they are supposed to have the meetings. In this type of situation, the change program is not very institutionalized. This is why knowledge of the behaviors is important.

2. *Performance.* Here we are interested in how many people perform the behaviors, and how often

they perform them. This is not quite as simple as it sounds, however. First, some behaviors are supposed to happen more often than others. A labor-management committee may be expected to meet occasionally, say about once a month, while team meetings are held weekly. We would not say that team meetings are more institutionalized than the labor-management committee just because they are more frequent. Second, some behaviors are supposed to be performed by more people than others. Most employees would be involved in team meetings, but only a few would take part in a labor-management committee. Again, we would not want to say that the team meetings were more institutionalized than the labor-management committee. The idea is not merely to count the number of persons or the frequency of behaviors, but rather to compare numbers and frequency to the levels required by the change program. Only then can reasonable comparisons be made.

3. *Preferences for the behaviors.* Here we are interested in how much people either like or dislike performing the behavior. In well-institutionalized change programs, most organizational members will like the critical program behaviors. In change programs on the decline, there generally are negative feelings expressed toward the critical program behaviors.

4. *Normative consensus.* This aspect of institutionalization measures two things: (1) how aware individuals are that other people in the organization are performing the behaviors and (2) how aware people are that other people feel they *should* perform the behaviors. Generally, when we see other people performing a behavior, we assume that they want to perform it, even though this may not be true.

5. *Value.* The final measure of institutionalization is the extent to which people have developed values concerning the behaviors in the change program. Values are general ideas about how people ought to behave. For example, many change programs include behaviors consistent with the values of freedom and responsibility, as in autonomous work groups. The more people have developed these values, and the more aware they are that others have developed these values, the greater the degree of institutionalization for the change program.

The five aspects above represent measures of the degree of institutionalization. But how do we combine them to get an overall measure? The answer is relatively simple, because the five aspects of institutionalization generally occur in the same order. This is the order in which we presented them. First, people develop beliefs about the behaviors (1), and then they begin to perform them (2). People start to develop feelings about the behaviors (3), and others come to be aware of these feelings (4). Finally values start to evolve concerning the behaviors (5). The further this sequence has progressed, the more the program has become institutionalized. Thus, in one program, people may know about the behaviors and perform them, but none of the other aspects may be present. In another program, the behaviors may be known, performed, liked, and supported by norms and values. The latter program is obviously more institutionalized.

Factors Which Affect Institutionalization

General Framework

Now that we have a way to represent the degree of institutionalization, we can try to explain how and why it happens. Why are some QWL programs more institutionalized than others? Our opinion is that there are *five processes which affect the degree of institutionalization*. We believe that these five processes are the major factors in predicting the degree of institutionalization a program will attain. There are, however, other important factors that affect these five processes. They are the *structure of the change* program and *organizational characteristics*. The structure of the change program means such things as the goals of the change, how general it is, the critical roles associated with the change (consultant, facilitator), etc. Organizational characteristics are arrangements existing in the organization prior to the change program. Organizational characteristics include such things as work force skill level, labor-management relations, and existing values and norms. It should be emphasized

that these factors are important only insofar as they affect the five processes (see figure 1). We will also briefly present in this section some empirical findings of the present authors, as well as others, about the processes and other organizational factors related to institutionalization.

A. Five Processes

1. Training. The first process to be discussed is training. Training is providing information to organizational members about the new work behaviors. There are three major situations in which training is important: training as the program is started, retraining after the program has been in place for a while, and training of new members of the organization. The importance of training in general has been demonstrated in studies by Golembiewski and Carrigan (1970) and by Ivancevich (1974) in manufacturing firms, and by Goodman (1979) in an underground coal mine. Most organizations do an extensive amount of initial training, but are less consistent in retraining and in the training of new members. Goodman and Dean (1981) found that programs in which attention was paid to these latter types of training were likely to be more institutionalized.

2. Commitment. Commitment refers to how motivated people are to continue to perform a behavior. Therefore, a high degree of commitment should increase the chances that behaviors in a QWL program would continue, or be institutionalized. Commitment toward a behavior is increased when people *voluntarily* select that behavior in some *public context*. A recent study by the present authors (Goodman & Dean, 1981) has demonstrated the importance of commitment for institutionalization. For example, an autonomous work-group program seemed to grow and develop when personal choices were carried out freely. Later in the program, when the organization required others to participate in the program, it began to decline. The same study also found that programs with more frequent commitment opportunities were more institutionalized than those with limited commitment opportunities.

FIGURE 1 A Simple Model of Variables Related to Institutionalization

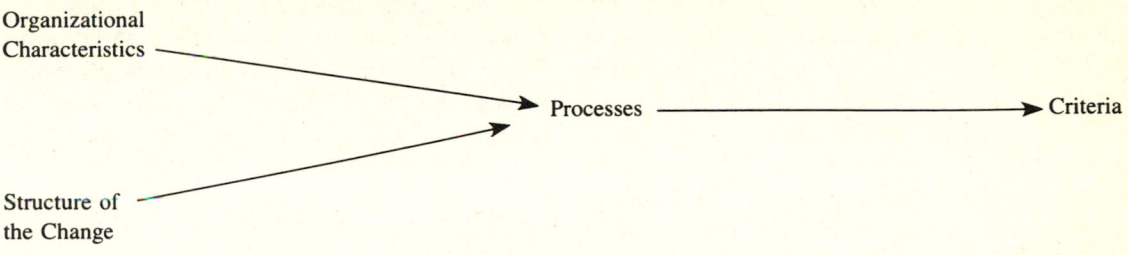

Organizational
Characteristics

Structure of
the Change

Processes

Criteria

Several other studies have noted the impact of commitment on institutionalization. For example, Ivancevich (1972) attributed the failure of a management by objectives (MBO) program to a lack of commitment by top management. Walton (1980), on the other hand, notes high levels of commitment in several successful programs of work innovation. Research on commitment by Kiesler (1971) and his associates suggests that institutionalization can be facilitated by withholding challenges to the new behaviors (e.g., new work group members) until the workers are firmly committed to the new behaviors.

3. Reward Allocation. This is the process by which rewards are distributed to employees in connection with the change program. Three aspects of the reward allocation process are important in understanding institutionalization: what types of rewards are available, the links between behaviors and rewards, and problems of inequity in the distribution of the rewards.

Many organizational change programs have been based on the assumption that intrinsic rewards (such as autonomy and responsibility) are sufficient for institutionalization. However, Goodman (1979) and Walton (1980) have questioned this assumption. In the recent study by the present authors, programs that combined both extrinsic (e.g., bonuses) and intrinsic rewards attained the highest degree of institutionalization, while programs with intrinsic rewards alone were less institutionalized.

The second issue in reward allocation concerns the link between the behaviors required by the change program and rewards. It is important that the rewards be linked to the *actual performance* of the behaviors, as opposed to mere participation in the program. We have found that there is a higher degree of institutionalization in programs where the link between performance and rewards is strong. This is consistent with statements by Vroom (1964) and Lawler (1971) concerning reward allocation.

A final issue concerning reward allocation is the potential for problems of inequity. Problems of inequity occur when an employee feels he is not being fairly compensated for the work he is doing. Results of studies have shown that new programs often became complicated by problems of inequity. For example, Goodman describes problems in a program to develop autonomous work groups in a coal mine. Part of the program involved job switching, whereby each new member would eventually learn all the jobs in the crew. The problem was that the entire crew was to be paid at the same (higher) rate, which originally was paid only to certain crew members. Since it had taken years for some of the men to attain this rate, they felt it inequitable that the other crew members should come upon it so easily. This contributed to the decline of the change program. Similar problems of inequity have been reported by Locke, Sirota, and Wolfson (1976) in their study of an attempt at job enrichment in a government agency.

4. Diffusion. Diffusion refers to the spread of the change program from one part of an organization to another. Diffusion is significant because the more the change program becomes diffused, the stronger the levels of institutionalization. As long as the program is restricted to one part of the organization, people may not feel compelled to take it seriously or they may object to it. But as diffusion starts to occur, people in other parts of the organization will begin to consider whether they should participate. As the program spreads, there also are chances for counterattacks on its validity.

The importance of diffusion for institutionalization has been noted by Goodman (1979) in the coal mine study mentioned above. In this study, when the intervention failed to diffuse beyond the original target group, it was perceived as inappropriate and failed to become institutionalized. Similar findings have been reported in a study of work teams in several plants of a large manufacturing company (personal correspondence, 1980). When the innovations continued to be limited to a few parts of the organization, they were not seen as appropriate, and failed to become institutionalized. However, the researchers in this study caution against diffusion that is too rapid, as widespread understanding, acceptance, and resources are necessary to support such an effort. Without these prerequisites, the program will collapse under its own weight. In general then, a medium course must be found between no diffusion and diffusion that is too ambitious for the resources supporting it.

5. Sensing and Recalibration. Sensing and recalibration are the processes by which the organization finds out how well the program is doing, and takes steps to correct problems that have emerged. One of the common findings in our study (Goodman and Dean, 1981) was that what was actually occurring in the programs was often different from what was intended. That is, the organizations seldom had any formal way of detecting whether the intended change was "in place." Only in the most institutionalized programs in our study did mechanisms exist for feedback and correction. Walton (1980), who has undertaken a number of case studies of organizational change, says that the lack of sensing and recalibration mechanisms is a major cause of the failure of institutionalization.

In another study, feedback mechanisms were in place, so that information about the progress of the program was available (personal correspondence). However, nothing was done about the problems that were detected. Both sensing and correction mechanisms are important in attaining a high degree of institutionalization.

B. Structure of the Change

Now that we have discussed the findings about the processes, we can discuss some of the factors that affect the processes. First we will discuss the structure of the change, which refers to the unique aspects of the change program. Specifically, we will talk about the goals of the programs, the formal mechanisms associated with the programs, the level of intervention in the programs, how consultants were used, and sponsorship for the programs.

1. Goals. Some programs have very specific and limited goals, whereas others have more general, diffuse goals. In our study (Goodman & Dean, 1981), we found that programs with specific goals became more institutionalized than those with diffuse goals.

2. Formal Mechanisms. Most change programs have some new organizational form and procedures associated with them. These include the hierarchy of groups found in the parallel organization, the self-governing decisions made by autonomous work groups, etc. Here we are interested in how formal these arrangements are. For example: Are meetings scheduled in advance? Are procedures written down? In general, we have found that programs with more formal mechanisms and procedures attain higher levels of institutionalization.

3. Level of Intervention. Here we are interested in whether the QWL program was introduced in a part of the organization, or in the whole organization. In our study, programs that were introduced throughout the whole organizational unit were more institutionalized than programs limited to a part of the organization. One of the problems with smaller-scale intervention is that people from other parts of the organization sometimes attempt to sabotage the program. This was true in four of the organizations that we studied (Goodman & Dean, 1981), none of which had programs which were very institutionalized.

4.   Consultants. Most organizations, when undertaking a change program, will employ a consultant to help them. This was true in the organizations we recently studied. Some organizations use consultants for longer periods of time than others. We found that firms that rely on consultants for a long time are less able to develop their own capacity for managing the program. Consequently, after the consultant leaves they are less able to institutionalize the program. The greater the dependence on the consultant, the less successful the program.

5. Sponsorship. Another factor that appears to affect the degree of institutionalization is the presence of a sponsor. The sponsor is an organizational member in a position of power who initiates the program, makes sure that resources are devoted to it, and defends it against attacks from others in the organization. If the sponsor leaves the organization, no one will perform these necessary functions, and processes such as commitment and reward allocation will be hampered, thus making it harder for institutionalization to occur. In our study, the initial sponsor was still present in organizations which had more institutionalized programs, but programs whose sponsors had left were low in institutionalization. Problems with withdrawal of sponsorship are well documented in the literature on organizational change, having been reported by Walton (1975, 1978), Miller (1975), Frank and Hackman (1975), Crockett (1977), and Levine (1980).

C. Organizational Characteristics

Organizational characteristics are those aspects of the organization which exist prior to the change program, which will have an effect on the degree of institutionalization which the program will attain. These characteristics are important to the extent that they affect the processes we have discussed (commitment, diffusion, etc.).

1. Congruence with Organizational Values and Structure. Whatever the nature of the change program, one important factor for institutionalization is the extent of congruence or incongruence between the change program and existing organizational properties. In general, the more congruence, the greater will be the likelihood of institutionalization. Various organizational characteristics may be important in understanding congruence. In the cases studied by the present authors, congruence between the change program and preexisting management philosophy led to higher degrees of institutionalization. Other authors have demonstrated the importance of congruence between the organizational change and corporate policies (Fadem, 1976), individual values and motives (Seashore & Bowers, 1978), the authority system (Mohrman et al., 1977), the skills of the employees (Walton, 1980), organizational norms and values (Levine, 1980; Warwick, 1975; Crockett, 1977), and cultural norms and values (Miller, 1975). Of course, if these are already in conflict with one another, it will be difficult for programs to be congruent with all of them.

2. Stability of the Environment. From the evidence reported so far, it should be clear that institutionalizing a change program in an organization is a difficult task, even in the best of situations. Adding instability to the situation only makes things worse. In our study, (Goodman & Dean, 1981) there were only two cases of instability in the environment. In these cases there was a major decline in demand for the organization's products, which led to curtailments in the work force. This in turn changed the composition of many of the groups that were an integral part of the change program. These groups became less effective, which lowered the degree of institutionalization. Similar results were found in another study (personal correspondence) as an economic recession led to layoffs and bumping. Environmental instabilities such as these represent a major obstacle to institutionalization.

3. Union. The role of the union can play a major role in determining the degree of institutionalization. Many of the new forms of work-organization changes run in parallel with other union-management activities related to the traditional collective bargaining process. If there are high levels of labor-management conflict in the collective bargaining area, we expect these to spill over to the productivity and "quality of working life" activities and negatively affect their viability.

Most local unions are part of larger institutional structures. In other studies (c.f., Goodman, 1979) there is evidence that the quality of the relationship between the local union and the international will have a critical impact on the viability of any change program in a given firm.

How To Make Programs Last

Our recommendations for how to make programs last should come as no surprise to the reader, as they are derived from the above findings and theory:

1. Be selective in implementing programs. Organizations or subunits which have labor-management problems or an unstable economic environment are not good locations.
2. Plan for institutionalization in the beginning. Many programs do not persist because all of the resources are directed at initiating the program, rather than maintaining it.
3. Be aware of congruence problems. Programs which are incongruent with organizational norms and values seldom persist. Gradual changes to reduce the incongruence are possible but they require much time and effort (see Goodman & Dean, 1981).
4. Structure of the change. The following characteristics of programs have been shown to facilitate persistence:
   a. specific, written-out statements on program goals.
   b. formal procedures to implement the program activities.
   c. total system intervention, with organizational resources to support it.
   d. limited, short-term use of consultants.
5. Training over time. Training should not be abandoned after a month or even a year, but must be redone periodically to reinforce the change.
6. Commitment. High commitment comes from (1) voluntary participation in program activities and (2) opportunities for recommitment over time.
7. Effective reward systems. Reward systems should:
   a. include both extrinsic and intrinsic rewards.
   b. link rewards to specific behaviors.
   c. introduce a mechanism to revise the reward system.
   d. minimize problems of inequity over compensation.
8. Diffusion. Programs which are linked to one organizational subunit often die in isolation. Attempts must be made to spread the program to other organizational areas.
9. Sensing and recalibration. A direct and accurate feedback mechanism which measures the performance of program activities is necessary if the change program is to adjust, grow, and remain viable over time.

Summary

Many programs of organizational change, while initially successful, do not persist. We have conceived of persistence of institutionalization as occurring by degrees, ranging from knowledge about the behaviors associated with the program to values supporting these behaviors. Five processes which affect the degree of institutionalization have been identified, and aspects of the structure of the change and organizational characteristics which affect the processes were also examined. Finally, recommendations, based on our findings, were enumerated as to what managers can do to facilitate persistence of change in their organization.

References

Crockett, W. Introducing change to a government agency. In P. Mirvis & D. Berg (Eds.), *Failures in organizational development: Cases and essays for learning.* New York: Wiley-Interscience, 1977.

Fadem, J. *Fitting computer-aided technology to workplace requirements: An example.* Paper presented at the 13th annual meeting and technical conference of the Numerical Control Society, Cincinnati, March 1976.

Frank, L. L., & Hackman, J. R., A failure of job enrichment: The case of the change that wasn't. *Journal of Applied Behavioral Science*, 1975, *11* (4), 413–436.

Golembiewski, R. T. & Carrigan, S. B., The persistence of laboratory-induced changes in organizational styles. *Administrative Science Quarterly*, 1970, *15*, 330–340.

Goodman, P. S. *Assessing organizational change: The Rushton quality of work experiment.* New York: Wiley-Interscience, 1979.

Goodman, P. S., & Dean, Jr., J. W. The process of institutionalization. Paper prepared for conference on organizational change, Carnegie-Mellon University, May 1981. To be published in a forthcoming volume on organizational change, P. S. Goodman (ed.)

Ivancevich, J. M., A longitudinal assessment of management by objectives. *Administrative Science Quarterly*, 1972, *17*, 126–138.

Ivancevich, J. M. Changes in performance in a management by objectives program. *Administrative Science Quarterly*, 1974, *19*, 563–574.

Kiesler, C. A. *The psychology of commitment: experiments linking behavior to belief.* New York: Academic Press, 1971.

Lawler, E. E. *Pay and organizational effectiveness.* New York: McGraw-Hill, 1971.

Levine, A. *Why innovation fails.* Albany: State University of New York Press, 1980.

Locke, E. A., Sirota, D., & Wolfson, A. D. An experimental case study of the successes and failures of job enrichment in a government agency. *Journal of Applied Psychology*, 1976, *61*, 701–711.

Miller, E. J. Sociotechnical systems in weaving, 1953–1970: A follow-up study. *Human Relations*, 1975, *28* (4), 349–386.

Mirvis, P. H., & Berg, D. N. (Eds.) *Failures in organization development and change.* New York: Wiley-Interscience, 1977.

Mohrman, S. A., Mohrman, A. M., Cooke, R. A., & Duncan, R. B. A survey feedback and problem-solving intervention in a school district: "We'll take the survey but you can keep the feedback." In P. Mirvis & D. Berg (Eds.), *Failures in organizational development: Cases and essays for learning.* New York: Wiley-Interscience, 1977.

Seashore, S. E., & Bowers, D. G. Durability of organizational change. In W. L. French, C. H. Bell, Jr., & R. A. Zawacki (Eds.), *Organization development: Theory, practice, and research.* Plano, Tex.: Business Publications, 1978.

Vroom, W. H. *Work and motivation.* New York: John Wiley & Sons, 1964.

Walton, R. E. The diffusion of new work structures: Explaining why success didn't take. *Organizational Dynamics*, Winter 1975, pp. 3–21.

Walton, R. E. Teaching an old dog food new tricks. *The Wharton Magazine*, Winter 1978, pp. 38–47.

Walton, R. E. Establishing and maintaining high commitment work systems, in J. R. Kimberly & R. H. Miles (Eds.), *The organizational life cycle,* San Francisco: Jossey-Bass, 1980.

Warwick, D. P. A theory of public bureaucracy. Cambridge, Mass.: Harvard University Press, 1975.

SUGGESTED ADDITIONAL READINGS FOR PART 5

Carrigan, Patricia M. "Up From the Ashes." *OD Practitioner,* March 1986, pp. 1–6.

Campion, Michael A., and Paul W. Thayer. "Job Design: Approaches, Outcomes, and Trade-Offs." *Organizational Dynamics,* Winter 1987, pp. 66–79.

Cass, Eugene L., and Frederick G. Zimmer, eds. *Man and Work in Society.* New York: Van Nostrand Reinhold, 1975, chap. IV and V.

Cole, Robert E., and Dennis S. Tachiki. "Forging Institutional Links: Making Quality Circles Work in the U.S." *National Productivity Review,* Autumn 1984, pp. 417–29.

Couger, J. Daniel, and Robert A. Zawacki, *Motivating and Managing Computer Personnel.* New York: Wiley-Interscience, 1980.

Dalton, Gene W.; Paul R. Lawrence; and Jay W. Lorsch. *Organizational Structure and Design.* Homewood, Ill.: Richard D. Irwin, 1970.

Davis, Louis E., and Albert B. Cherns. *The Quality of Working Life.* Vols. I and II. New York: Free Press, 1975.

Donovan, J. Michael. "Self-Managing Work Teams—Extending the Quality Circle Concept." *Quality Circles Journal,* September 1986, pp. 15–20.

Ferris, Gerald R., and John A. Wagner III. "Quality Circles in the United States: A Conceptual Reevaluation." *Journal of Applied Behavioral Science,* May 1985, pp. 155–67.

Frank, L. C., and J. Richard Hackman. "A Failure of Job Enrichment: The Case of the Change That Wasn't." *Journal of Applied Behavioral Science,"* October–November–December 1975. pp. 413–36.

French, Wendell, and John A. Drexler, Jr. "A Team Approach to MBO; History and Conditions for Success." *Leadership & Organization Development Journal* 5, no. 5 (1984), pp. 22–26.

Glaser, Edward M., and Paul A. Nelson. "A Quality of Worklife Improvement Effort at Five Mental Health Facilities." *OD Practioner,* March 1987, pp. 1–6.

Goldstein, S. G. "Organizational Dualism and Quality Circles." *Academy of Management Review,* July 1985, pp. 504–17.

Hackman, J. Richard, and J. Lloyd Suttle. *Improving Life at Work.* Santa Monica, Calif.: Goodyear Publishing, 1977.

Hackman, J. Richard, and Greg R. Oldham. *Work Redesign.* Reading, Mass.: Addison-Wesley Publishing, 1980.

Lawler, Edward E. III. *Pay and Organization Development.* Reading, Mass.: Addison-Wesley Publishing, 1981.

Lawler, Edward E., III, and Susan A. Mohrman. "Quality Circles: After the Honeymoon." *Organizational Dynamics,* Spring 1987, pp. 42–54.

Lawrence, Paul R., and Jay W. Lorsch. *Developing Organizations: Diagnosis and Action.* Reading, Mass.: Addison-Wesley Publishing, 1969, pp. 1–40.

Leavitt, H. "Applied Organizational Change In Industry: Structural, Technological, and Humanistic Approaches." In *Handbook of Organizations,* ed. James G. March. Skokie, Ill.: Rand McNally, 1965, pp. 1144–70.

London, Manuel. "Employee-Guided Management." *Leadership & Organization Development Journal* 6, no. 1 (1985), pp. 3–8.

Margulies, Newton, and Lora Colflesh. "A Socio-Technical Approach to Planning and Implementing New Technology." *Training and Development Journal,* December 1982, pp. 16–29.

Miller, Eric J. "Sociotechnical Systems in Weaving, 1953–1970: A Follow-Up Study." *Human Relations,* May 1975, pp. 349–86.

Pasmore, William A., and John J. Sherwood, eds. *Sociotechnical Systems: A Sourcebook.* LaJolla, Calif.: University Associates, 1978.

Pava, Calvin H. P. "Designing Managerial and Professional Work for High Performance: A Sociotechnical Approach." *National Productivity Review,* Spring 1983, pp. 126–35.

Reich, Robert B. "The Team as Hero." *Harvard Business Review,* May–June 1987, pp. 77–83.

Schoonhoven, Claudia Bird. "Sociotechnical Considerations for the Development of the Space Station: Autonomy and the Human Element in Space." *Journal of Applied Behavioral Science* 22, no. 3 (1986), pp. 271–86.

Steele, Fred I. *Physical Settings and Organization Development.* Reading, Mass.: Addison-Wesley Publishing, 1973.

Stymne, Bengt, and Peter Duchorty. "Office Worker Participation in Organizational Development: An Experiment in a Swedish Insurance Company." *Organization and Administrative Science,* Winter 1974–75, pp. 55–71.

Susman, Gerald I., and Richard B. Chase. "A Sociotechnical Analysis of the Integrated Factory." *Journal of Applied Behavioral Science* 22, no. 3 (1986), pp. 257–70.

Trist, E. L. *The Evolution of Socio-Technical Systems.* Toronto, Ontario: Quality of Working Life Centre, Occasional Paper No. 2, 1981.

Walton, Richard E. "A Vision-Led Approach to Management Restructuring." *Organizational Dynamics,* Spring 1986, pp. 4–16.

White, Donald D., and David A. Bednar. "Locating Problems with Quality Circles." *National Productivity Review,* Winter 1984–85, pp. 45–52.

Woodward, Joan. *Industrial Organization: Theory and Practice.* London: Oxford University Press, 1965.

PART 6

Power, Politics, and Organization Development

The selections in this section are on the important topics of power, politics, and organization development. Power is a fact of social life. Politics is a fact of organizational life. Organization development practitioners must be knowledgeable about power and politics, must know how to deal effectively with these phenomena, and must know how they impact on OD programs.

OD has been criticized in the past for not taking account of organizational politics and power. The criticism was essentially correct for many years; it is less valid today. Organizational power and politics have recently come under serious investigation by theorists and researchers in organizational psychology and organizational behavior.[1] Implications for the practice of OD have been quick to follow.[2] This section is intended to provide a better understanding of the concepts of power and politics to examine the implications of these concepts for the practice of organization development.

POWER DEFINED AND EXPLORED

Definitions

''Power is the intentional influence over the beliefs, emotions, and behaviors of people. Potential power is the capacity to do so, but kinetic power is the act of doing so. . . .

---

[1]Jeffrey Pfeffer, *Power in Organizations* (Marshfield, Mass.: Pitman Publishing, 1981); John P. Kotter, ''Power, Success, and Organizational Effectiveness,'' *Organizational Dynamics,* March–April 1976, pp. 27–40; David McClelland and David Burnham, ''Power Is the Great Motivator,'' *Harvard Business Review,* March–April 1976, pp. 100–110; Kenneth Thomas, ''Conflict and Conflict Management,'' in *Handbook of Industrial and Organizational Psychology,* ed. Marvin D. Dunnette (Skokie, Ill.: Rand McNally, 1976), pp. 889–935.

[2]See, for example, Virginia E. Schein, ''Political Strategies for Implementing Organizational Change,'' *Group and Organization Studies* 2 (1977), pp. 42–48; Michael Beer, *Organization Change and Development* (Santa Monica, Calif.: Goodyear Publishing, 1980); and the article in this section by Anthony T. Cobb and Newton Margulies.

One person exerts power over another to the degree that he is able to exact compliance as desired."[3]

Power is "the ability of those who possess power to bring about the outcomes they desire."[4]

"Most definitions of power include an element indicating that power is the capability of one social actor to overcome resistance in achieving a desired objective or result."[5]

From these definitions it can be seen that interpersonal power in a social situation is *the ability to get one's way.* Examples of social power are seen everywhere: influence, leadership, persuasion, selling, forcing, and coercing—all these acts are power in action. To have power or to exercise power is not, in itself, either good or bad. The phenomenon of power is ubiquitous. Problems with power stem from some of the aims (goals) of powerful persons and some of the means used by powerful persons. Without influence (power) there could be no cooperation and no society. Without leadership (power) in medical, political, technological, financial, spiritual, and organizational activities, humankind would not have the standard of living it does today. Without leadership (power) directed toward warfare, confiscation, repression, and the like, humankind would not have much of the misery it does today.

Two Faces of Power

According to David McClelland, there are "two faces of power"—negative and positive. The negative face of power is characterized by a primitive, unsocialized need to have dominance over submissive others. The positive face of power is characterized by a socialized form of leading and initiating that helps others reach their goals as well as helps the person exercising power to reach his or her goals. The negative face of power seeks to dominate others; the positive face of power seeks to empower others as well as the person exercising power.[6] These two faces of power are a useful distinction for understanding the nature of power. In most organizations the positive face of power is much more prevalent than the negative face of power.

Sources of Social Power

Power exists in virtually all social situations. It is especially salient in coordinated activities, such as those found in organizations. In fact, for organizations to function, the power (authority) dimension must be clarified and agreed upon in a more or less formal way. In organizations, some individuals are *given* power over others. In addition, some people *acquire* power over others.

---

[3]R. G. H. Siu, *The Craft of Power* (New York: John Wiley & Sons, 1979), p. 31.

[4]Gerald R. Salancik and Jeffrey Pfeffer, "Who Gets Power—And How They Hold On To It: A Strategic-Contingency Model of Power," *Organizational Dynamics* 5 (1977), p. 3.

[5]Pfeffer, *Power in Organizations,* p. 2.

[6]David C. McClelland, "The Two Faces of Power," *Journal of International Affairs,* 24, no. 1 (1970), pp. 29–47.

How is power acquired or given in organizations? John R. P. French and Bertram Raven[7] identified five sources, or bases, of social power as follows:

1. *Reward power*— defined as the power whose basis is the ability of the person with power to reward another, that is, to give something valued by the other.

2. *Coercive power*—defined as the power whose basis is the ability of the person with power to punish another, that is, to give something negatively valued by the other.

3. *Legitimate power*—defined as the power whose basis is internalized values in the power-receiver, that is, values stating that the person with power has a legitimate right to influence and the power-receiver has a legitimate obligation to accept influence.

4. *Referent power*—defined as the power whose basis is identification with (attraction to, or feeling of oneness with) another person, that is, when we identify with another, we give that person power over us.

5. *Expert power*—defined as the power whose basis is the fact that a person who has expert knowledge or expertise has power due to that knowledge. Another source of power is *informational power,* power based on possession of important facts or information. Informational power is related to expert power.

The French and Raven analysis is a useful framework for understanding who has what kind of power and why in organizations. The boss has legitimate power based on mutual expectations that the role carries with it the right to exercise power over others. Persons in legal, engineering, and data processing departments may possess expert power because of their specialized knowledge. Authorized representatives of management have reward and coercive power based on the right to reward and punish. The OD practitioner, whether external or internal, may have expert power, informational power, legitimate power (to do some things but not others), and perhaps referent power. The OD consultant wields considerable power as he or she guides events in an OD program. This power derives from multiple sources.

Another Source of Power—Dependence

According to Richard Emerson's "power-dependence" theory, power is inherent in any relationship in which one person is dependent upon another. Specifically, the theory states that being dependent upon another person gives that person power over us. Power does not exist without a relationship between two actors; and one person must be dependent on the other for power to be present. Power-dependence theory and French and Raven's bases of social power may both be viewed within the framework of *social exchange theory.* Exchange theory posits that what goes on between persons in interaction is an exchange of social commodities: love, hate, respect, power, influence, information, praise, blame, attraction, rejection, and so forth. We enter into and continue in exchange rela-

---

[7]John R. P. French, Jr., and Bertram Raven, "The Bases of Social Power," in *Studies in Social Power,* ed. Dorwin Cartwright (Ann Arbor: Institute for Social Research of the University of Michigan, 1959), pp. 150–67. These "exchange" ideas also underlie Richard M. Emerson's "Power-Dependence Relations," *American Sociological Review* 27 (1962), pp. 31–40.

tionships when what we receive from others is equivalent to or in excess of what we must give to others. When the net balance for us is positive, we will continue the exchange relationship; when the net balance for us is negative, we will terminate or alter the relationship. Power is only one of many social commodities exchanged between persons, albeit a very important commodity. We accept power and influence from others and others accept power and influence from us when the other things we exchange make that particular exchange worthwhile.

Summary

To summarize, power is the ability to get one's way. Power arises from many sources. Power is only one of many social commodities exchanged between people. Power has a negative side and a positive side. For the OD practitioner it is important to know who has power and from what sources that power comes. It is also important to know how to exercise power and how to resist other people's exercise of power, when appropriate.

POLITICS DEFINED AND EXPLORED

Definitions

Harold Lasswell defined politics as the study of who gets what, when, and how.[8]

"Organizational politics involves those activities taken within organizations to acquire, develop, and use power and other resources to obtain one's preferred outcomes in a situation in which there is uncertainty or dissensus about choices."[9]

"Organizational politics involve intentional acts of influence to enhance or protect the self-interest of individuals or groups."[10]

These definitions suggest that the concepts of power and politics are very similar. They both relate to effectance—getting one's way. They both relate to pursuing self interests. They both relate to overcoming resistance of others.

Two Faces of Politics

Like power, organizational politics can have a positive and a negative face. The negative face is characterized by *extreme* pursuit of self-interest; unsocialized needs to dominate others; a tendency to view most situations in win-lose terms—what I win, you must lose—rather than win-win terms; and predominant use of the tactics of fighting such as

---

[8]Harold Lasswell, *Politics: Who Gets What, When, How* (New York: McGraw-Hill, 1936).

[9]Pfeffer, *Power in Organizations*, p. 7.

[10]Robert W. Allen, Dan L. Madison, Lyman W. Porter, Patricia A. Renwick, and Bronston T. Mayes, "Organizational Politics: Tactics and Characteristics of Its Actors," *California Management Review* 22 (1979), p. 77.

secrecy, surprise, holding hidden agendas, withholding information, deceiving. The positive face of politics is characterized by a *balanced* pursuit of self-interest; viewing situations in win-win terms as much as possible; engaging in open problem solving and goal clarification and then moving to action and influencing; a relative absence of the tactics of fighting; and a socialized need to lead, initiate, and influence others.

Organizations can be arrayed along a continuum of how political they are and whether the organizational politics show a positive face or a negative face. (See Figure 1.)

It can be seen that the political side of the organization can range from minimal to maximal use of political behavior, that minimal and moderate uses of politics reflect the positive face of organizational politics, and that maximal or extensive uses of politics reflect the negative face of organizational politics. It is relatively easy to diagnose where an organization falls on the political continuum: look for the characteristics described in the positive and negative faces of politics; and look for these features in the organization's decision making, resource allocation, and conflict resolution processes. The presence or absence of these characteristics in key organizational processes shows the political nature of the organization.

We have seen organizations where the negative face of power prevails, where the modus vivendi seems to be a constant "war of all against all." We have seen other organizations where politics either play a minimal role in the way things get done, or where the face of politics is usually positive.

Our impression is that in extremely political organizations so much time, effort, and energy go into internecine warfare that the organization does not get its job done well; it consequently loses ground to its external competitors, and it loses many of its best people either through purges or self-initiated flight. Likewise, our impression is that in extremely apolitical organizations little productive and innovative work gets done; complacency is widespread, tough decisions do not get made, and the organization loses ground to its external competitors. We would speculate that a modest amount of organizational politics is necessary to produce optimal individual and organizational performance. See the highly tentative "⊗" in Figure 1 denoting "the right place" on the continuum for an organization to be, in our opinion.

FIGURE 1   The Nature of Organizational Decision Making, Resource Allocation, and Conflict Resolution

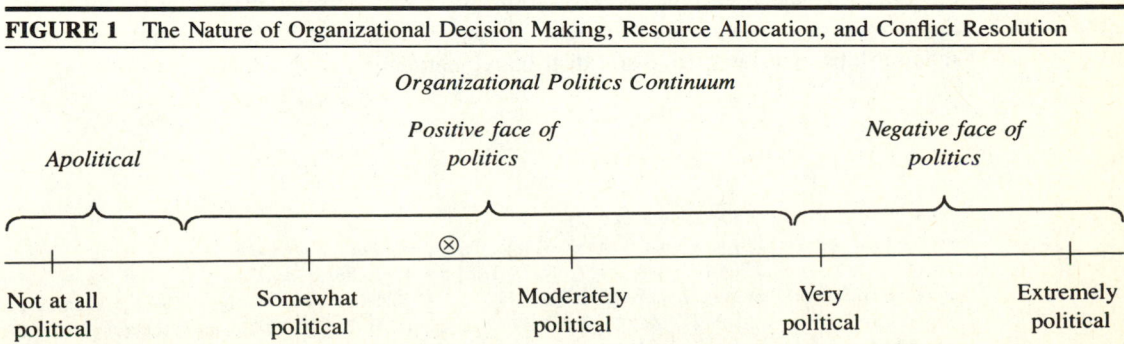

Modes of Operation in Organizations

Organizations sometimes display modal patterns in the way their decision-making, resource-allocation, and conflict-resolution processes operate. Patterns identified in the literature include bureaucratic, rational, and political.[11] In a bureaucratic mode, decisions are made on the basis of rules, procedures, traditions, and historical precedents. In a rational mode, decisions are made on the basis of rational problem solving: goals are identified and agreed upon; situations are analyzed objectively in relation to goals; alternative action plans are generated and evaluated; and certain alternatives are chosen and implemented. In a political mode decisions are made on the basis of perceived self-interest by coalitions jockeying for dominance, influence, or resource control.

Most organizations exhibit all these modes in the conduct of their business. Some organizations exhibit one predominant mode. It is important to realize that a predominantly political organization is only one of several possibilities.

Summary

To summarize, organizational politics is the act of acquiring and wielding power in the organization. It is the act of doing those things necessary to get one's way. There are positive and negative faces of politics. Organizations may be arrayed on a continuum in terms of the amount of political behavior exhibited by the major actors. Modal patterns of decision making, resource allocation, and conflict resolution exist in organizations, the most prevalent ones being bureaucratic, rational, and political, or a combination of these.

A FRAMEWORK FOR ANALYZING POWER AND POLITICS

A useful paradigm for analyzing and understanding power-oriented behavior in organizations comes from game theory and bargaining theory. Winning and losing, dominating and submitting, cooperating and competing, being powerful or powerless—all these phenomena have been studied extensively by game theorists.[12] And some critical concepts have been isolated that provide an ongoing framework for understanding power issues. Some of these concepts are: conflict, the payoff matrix, the nature of interdependent relationships, and integrative and distributive bargaining.

---

[11]Pfeffer, *Power in Organizations*, chap. 1.

[12]See, for example. J. Von Neumann and O. Morgenstern, *Theory of Games and Economic Behavior* (Princeton, N.J.: Princeton University Press, 1947); R. D. Luce and H. Raiffa, *Games and Decisions: Introduction and Critical Survey* (New York: John Wiley & Sons, 1957); T. C. Schelling, *The Strategy of Conflict* (Cambridge, Mass.: Harvard University Press, 1960); and J. W. Thibaut and H. H. Kelley, *The Social Psychology of Groups* (New York: John Wiley & Sons, 1959).

Conflict and the Payoff Matrix

A critical condition leading to political behavior in organizations is conflict—conflict of interest (different parties prefer different goals), and conflict or competition for scarce resources (different parties want the same resources but both cannot possess them). Although conflict gives rise to the use of power and politics, other modes of conflict resolution are available—bureaucratic and rational, for instance. But conflict is a powerful condition promoting political activities.

Conflict arises because of the real or perceived nature of the payoff matrix. The term *payoff matrix* refers to the way the goods and services sought by two or more parties are distributed. Understanding the nature of the payoff matrix is the key to understanding conflict, which in turn is the key to understanding most political behavior. The nature of the payoff matrix defines to a great extent the nature of the relationship between the two parties.

The Nature of Relationships

Two parties in interdependent interaction with each other can have one of three possible relationships (based on the payoff matrix that obtains): *purely competitive* (a win-lose or zero-sum situation in which what you win I lose and vice versa, and the payoffs always sum to zero); *purely cooperative* (we both have identical interests and the task is to coordinate our activities so we can both receive the payoffs); and *mixed* or *mixed motive* (our interests are in conflict to some extent so there is a push to compete, but our interests are also in concert so there is a push to cooperate to work together).[13] (An independent, ''nonrelationship'' is also possible in which the behavior of each party is irrelevant to the other; this situation is not germane to the present discussion since the parties are not in interdependent interaction.)

In the purely competitive, win-lose situation, power and politics will predominate; in fact, that is the most appropriate behavior pattern. In the purely cooperative, win-win situation, cooperation, coordination, and communication behaviors will predominate while power and politics should be absent. In the mixed-motive situation (a potentially win-win, win-lose, or lose-lose situation) cooperation or competition or both may occur. Here each party needs the other to transact an exchange, yet each party wants to maximize its own payoffs and minimize payoffs to the other party.

The mixed-motive situation is of paramount importance because many interpersonal and organizational relationships are mixed-motive in nature. Examples would be: we need to cooperate to get the job done, but only one of us will receive the next promotion; both production and maintenance rely on each other, yet each is trying to cut costs and stay within its own budget; I need to make a sale to this customer, yet our profits depend on striking a good price; all of us want our team to win, but only one of us can be voted most valuable player.

---

[13]Schelling, *The Strategy of Conflict.*

A mixed-motive or bargaining situation contains the potential for either cooperation or competition. *Cooperation usually requires problem-solving behavior; competition usually requires political or power-oriented behavior.*

Integrative and Distributive Bargaining

Richard Walton and Robert McKersie, in the course of studying labor-management negotiations, developed a behavioral theory of labor negotiations.[14] They introduced the extremely useful concepts of integrative and distributive bargaining as two separate stages of the bargaining process. They clarify these concepts as follows:

1. For a mixed-motive or bargaining decision situation to exist there must be two persons, party (P) and other (O), making joint decisions about the terms on which they will relate to each other.

2. Each of the parties must obtain positive value from the relationship; that is, both would experience losses or costs if the relationship were terminated. (This joint dependence places a limit on conflict.)

3. Both parties are aware of a possibility that there might be ways to increase the positive values produced by the relationship which have not occurred to them, or which they have not explored together. This dimension involves the process of problem solving and represents potential benefits from collaboration.

4. The outcomes available in the relationship will be allocated between the parties in different share ratios. This dimension represents the conflict element inherent in the relationship and involves the process of bargaining.[15]

Most mixed-motive theorists consider conditions 1, 2, and 4, but rarely take into account condition 3. The collaborative potential of condition 3, however, introduces an incentive toward a more positive and active form of cooperation. Attention to the problem-solving, collaborative aspects of the bargaining situation leads to *integrative* bargaining. Attention to the win-lose conflictual aspects of the bargaining situation leads to *distributive* bargaining.

These authors propose the critical idea that bargaining should be conceptualized as a two-phase process: The first phase would be the problem-solving, collaborative, integrative bargaining phase. The second phase would be the conflictual, bargaining-proper, or distributive phase.

Appropriate behaviors in the problem-solving phase are the following: identifying the areas of mutual concern, searching for alternative courses of action, and identifying the largest sum of values possible given the alternatives. (This last mentioned refers to maximizing or recognizing the preferred utility functions of both parties individually and then together.) The bargaining phase represents the conflict situation; here each tries to establish norms in which he maximizes his gains, but without going far enough to disrupt the interdependent relationship. In the problem-solving phase the parties collaborate in creating positive values which are to be divided in the bargaining phase. During the

---

[14]R. E. Walton and R. B. McKersie, *A Behavioral Theory of Labor Negotiations* (New York: McGraw-Hill. 1965).

[15]R. E. Walton and R. B. McKersie, "Behavioral Dilemmas in Mixed-Motive Decision Making," *Behavioral Science* 10 (1966), pp. 370–84.

problem-solving phase, open communication, honesty in dealing with the other party, and mutual exploration of all ideas are the desired behaviors for most beneficial results. During the bargaining phase, however, secrecy, suspicion, deception, and not accepting ideas of the other party are the functional behaviors. These two interaction modes are called integrative bargaining and distributive bargaining, respectively.

Integrative bargaining has several important benefits: better solutions are developed for problematic situations; total payoffs are increased; and affective relations between parties become more positive. The most compelling feature of distributive bargaining is that *it is necessary*—there are many situations where the only feasible way to resolve differences is through distributive bargaining. Distributive bargaining is a fact of life. However, prolonged distributive bargaining or win-lose interaction has several negative consequences: hostility and negative stereotyping occur between the parties; total payoffs decrease in size and amount; the quality of solutions to problems decreases; and the parties become more vulnerable to outside forces that may destroy them both. Many of the negative consequences of distributive bargaining can be overcome if both the integrative and distributive phases are present.

Summary

To summarize, power and politics constitute one of several modes of interparty behavior, with another prevalent mode being problem solving. It is the nature of the payoff matrix—how the goods will be divided among the ''wanting'' parties—that determines what mode is most appropriate in a given situation. Integrative bargaining, calling for problem solving, is appropriate in most mixed-motive situations found in organizations. Distributive bargaining, calling for political behavior, is appropriate for dividing and distributing scarce resources. Advantages are obtained by structuring bargaining situations into two phases, problem solving and dividing the goods.

THE ROLE OF POWER AND POLITICS IN OD, AND THE ROLE OF OD IN POWER AND POLITICS

Organization development is a strategy for organizational improvement that works within the broad frameworks of the normative-reeducative and empirical-rational strategies for planned change; the power-coercive strategy of change is generally absent in OD programs.[16] The normative-reeducative strategy of change focuses on norms, culture, processes, and prevailing attitudes and beliefs. Change occurs through examination of these norms and through education and reeducation in which dysfunctional beliefs are replaced with more functional ones. The empirical-rational strategy of change focuses on data, facts, and finding ''better'' ways to do things. Change occurs through discovering these better ways, coupled with the expectation that reasonable and prudent individuals will naturally choose to adopt them. The power-coercive strategy of change focuses on gaining

---

[16]See the article in Part 2 of this volume by Robert Chin and Kenneth D. Benne entitled ''General Strategies for Effecting Changes in Human Systems.''

and using power and developing enforcement methods. Change occurs through the people with power forcing their preferences on people with less power, and exacting compliance.

The role of power and politics in OD can be inferred from a number of sources. For one thing, we can look at the nature of OD interventions, almost all of which are designed to increase problem solving, collaboration, cooperation, fact-finding, and effective pursuit of goals, while at the same time managing conflict and the negative faces of power and politics. We can think of no OD interventions designed to increase coercion or unilateral power.

Further, the OD approach is founded on the belief that collaborative problem solving is more effective than politics and power for solving most organizational problems and for seizing organizational opportunities. This belief gave rise to the field of organization development and to the technologies used by the field. Note that this belief relates to the best way to do things *within* a particular social system or organization; it does not relate to the best way to do things *between* two or more systems.[17]

Likewise the values espoused in organization development—trust, openness, collaboration—are congruent with rational problem solving and incongruent with political modes of operating. OD interventions generate valid, public data about the organization's culture, processes, strengths, and weaknesses. Valid, public data are indispensable for problem solving but anathema for organizational politics.

"Power equalization" has been frequently described as one of the major tenets of organization development. That is essentially correct, we think. But the emphasis on power equalization stems from two beliefs: first, problem solving beats power coercion as a way to find solutions to problematic situations; second, power equalization, being one aspect of the positive face of power, *increases* the amount of power available to organization members, that is, it empowers many and by so doing adds power to the organization.

We conclude that not only is organization development not a power/political intervention strategy, it is instead a rational problem-solving approach that is incompatible with extreme power-oriented situations.

Indeed, OD programs in highly political organizations usually fail, are summarily terminated, or (most likely) are never initiated. The main reason for this is that those power holders, whose ascension to power has been based largely on win-lose tactics, stand to lose if the OD program succeeds. They will not let that happen. A major exception to the general rule that organization development programs will not be found in highly political organizations should be mentioned, however. Often an OD program can and will be implemented at the lower echelons of the organization in relatively insulated operations. Here the program is for the benefit of hourly employees and lower levels of management as they solve their everyday problems. But the "generals" and their silent armies continue with "business as usual" (organizational politics).

We further conclude that the OD practitioner is not a political activist or a power broker.[18] The practitioner is a facilitator, catalyst, problem solver, and educator. The

---

[17]It may be that *between* systems and organizations the most appropriate modes of behavior are power/political ones. The nature of the payoff matrix may enhance competition, such as the case between Democrats and Republicans, and between Ford, GM, Chrysler, and American Motors, etc.

[18]A growing number of authors assert that the OD practitioner should be a political activist and/or power

organization members are free to choose or reject what the OD practitioner has to offer—in terms of values, methods, and probable end results. Chris Argyris lists the three primary tasks of the interventionist as follows: (1) generate valid, useful information; (2) promote free, informed choice; and (3) help promote the client's internal commitment to the choices made.[19] These tasks comprise a facilitative role, not a political role.

We have explored the role of power and politics in OD. What about the role of OD in power and politics? As previously mentioned, politics is an organizational fact of life; politics and power are "social facts" of great importance. Not to understand political realities is not to understand a significant segment of organizational realities. The first thing, then, is to have knowledge about the understanding of power and political issues. This discussion and the readings in this section are designed toward that end.

Second, the continuum of organizational politics suggests that a moderate amount of political activity is desirable; hence, too little political activity or too much political activity would be treated in an OD program as a problem to be solved. Data would be generated about the functional and dysfunctional consequences of the current level of political activity, toward the objective of finding an optimal amount for the organization and its members. The problem-solving technologies of OD can be applied to political problems as well as other kinds of problems. A key educational activity of the OD practitioner might be to clarify both the positive and negative faces of power and politics for the client group.

Third, in situations where politics in moderation is a "normal" part of the organizational environment within which everyone operates, the OD practitioner is no more and no less political than everyone else. Successful performance in such an environment requires knowing and abiding by organizational norms concerning power, playing the game according to the rules, influencing others and being influenced by others, and providing something of value to individuals and the organization. The OD practitioner draws on several power bases—legitimate power, referent power, expert power, and informational power. The OD practitioner knows that the OD program is in competition with all other programs for scarce resources. This means that: the practitioner seeks support and sponsorship from top-level executives; the program is designed to be vital and useful—it meets genuine organizational needs; the program is designed to have early, visible successes; the OD practitioner sets high standards of excellence for self and others involved in the program; etc.

Finally, the positive faces of power and politics are as necessary for organizational functioning as the phenomena of planning, budgeting, communicating, and making decisions. The effective OD practitioner neither fears nor idolizes power.

---

broker. We disagree. For this other point of view see: R. G. Harrison and D. C. Pitt, "Organizational Development: A Missing Political Dimension?" (pp. 65–85) and P. Reason, "Is Organization Development Possible in Power Cultures?" (pp. 185–202) both from the book *Power, Politics, and Organizations,* eds. A. Kakabadse and C. Parker (Chichester: John Wiley and Sons, Ltd., 1984); W. R. Nord, "The Failure of Current Applied Behavioral Science—A Marxian Perspective," *Journal of Applied Behavioral Science* 10 (1974), pp. 557–78; A. M. Pettigrew, "Toward a Political Theory of Organizational Intervention," *Human Relations* 28 (1975), pp. 191–208; V. E. Schein, "Political Strategies for Implementing Organizational Change," *Group and Organization Studies* 2, (1977), pp. 42–48; and N. Margulies and A. P. Raia, "The Politics of Organization Development," *Training and Development Journal* 38 (1984), pp. 20–23.

[19]See the selection in Part 2 of this volume from Argyris's *Intervention Theory and Method.*

Reading in Power, Politics, and Organization Development

The first selection comes from an important recent book, *Power in Organizations,* by Jeffrey Pfeffer. The nature and structure of power situations are described. An overview of the concepts of power and politics is presented. Strategies for reducing the amount and use of power in organizations are explored. This reading provides an excellent foundation for understanding the variety of issues inherent in the concept of power.

Cobb and Margulies address the theme of this entire section in their article, "Organizational Development: A Political Perspective." The place of OD in politics and the place of politics in OD are framed in the wider context of the OD literature. These authors explore relevant issues and examine possible intended and unintended consequences of different levels of political activism in organization development. Their conclusions are cautious and, in our opinion, correct.

Some practical hints for the OD practitioner are contained in the selection by Michael Beer from his book, *Organization Changes and Development: A Systems View.* Specifically, this passage tells how an OD group can gain and maintain the necessary organizational power to conduct its programs by drawing on different sources of power. Political awareness and sophistication plus attention to political details spells success when operating in a political arena.

The final selection is from Henry Mintzberg's book, *Power in and around Organizations.* Mintzberg describes the bases of power, the importance of will and skill in wielding power, and the players of the power game—the influencers. There are internal and external sets of influencers in organizations. Mintzberg defines power as follows:

> *Power is defined in this book simply as the capacity to effect (or affect) organizational outcomes.* The French word *pouvoir* stands for both the noun "power" and the verb "to be able." To have power is to be able to get desired things done, to effect outcomes—actions and the decisions that precede them.[1]

He views politics as a subset of power, an informal power that is illegitimate in nature; and he views authority as formal power, the power vested in an office.

---

[1]Henry Mintzberg, *Power in and around Organizations* (Englewood Cliffs, N. J.: Prentice-Hall, 1983), p. 4.

Reading 43

CONDITIONS FOR THE USE OF POWER

Jeffrey Pfeffer

The following situation was used by Gerald Salancik to illustrate the conditions under which power is employed. Two wounded soldiers are lying in a tent on some distant battlefield. A medical corpsman is with them in the tent. Each man requires precisely one pint of blood to live; if each man does not receive the pint of blood, he will die. The pint of blood, then, is both a necessary and sufficient condition for the survival of each of the two wounded soldiers. In the tent, in addition to some medical supplies, is a single pint of blood. Because of the course of the battle going on around them and the associated logistical difficulties, it would be impossible to get any more supplies in time. A decision will have to be made: one man will live, the other will die. Splitting the blood between the two soldiers will cause them both to die, so compromise is out of the question.

One man is a captain, the other a corporal. Each implores the corpsman to save his life, and each musters arguments to support his position. The captain argues that he is entitled to the blood because of his superior hierarchical rank. If the arguments of rank and formal status are not convincing enough, he further argues that captains are important in the planning and organizational work of fighting. He has many men in his command, and the pint of blood given to him will make his unit a more effective fighting force because it will enable him to recover. While the captain has impact over many men, the corporal has much less influence on the war, being only a single soldier. The corporal, on the other hand, argues that captains

are, after all, part of the administrative overhead of the war; it is the corporals and the other front line troops that actually do the fighting. The corporal argues that he has killed many more enemy than the captain, and if he is allowed to live, is likely to have a more direct impact on the fighting in the future. Furthermore, the captain is older, and other things being equal, the corporal will have a longer life expectancy if he gets the blood. The pint of blood given to him, in other words, will probably result in more years of human life. Each then musters tales of his family—the captain has a wife and two young children back at home; the corporal tells about his poor, aged parents who are depending on him to take over the family business after the war.

How shall the corpsman decide? Each soldier has raised legitimate, relevant, and reasonable criteria which favor him over the other soldier. The captain has rank and organizational impact; the corporal has impact on the direct work of the organization; both have claims based on family and other reasons. The corpsman, who is attempting to provide the maximum benefit to the army, finds it difficult to determine which soldier will really have the greatest potential benefit to the service. After all, there are a lot of desk officers and fighting men are scarce; on the other hand, the ability to lead and organize is important, too.

The corporal reaches into a heap of his possessions, and pulls out a gun. Suddenly, the decision becomes clear. The captain dies and the corporal obtains the blood.

This apocryphal situation is a paradigm of a decision-making setting in which the use of power may be introduced. Furthermore, the situation il-

Source: Jeffrey Pfeffer, *Power in Organizations,* Marshfield, Mass.: Pitman Publishing, 1981, pp. 67–94.

lustrates well how the introduction of power is both a necessary and sufficient condition for making the choice. The elements that produce conflict and the use of power, or political activity, in organizations are diagrammed in Figure 1. A consideration of that figure along with the example indicates when and why power comes to be employed.

The first condition of the use of power is interdependence, a situation in which what happens to one organization actor affects what happens to others. In the present example, there is competitive interdependence, in the sense that blood which is given to one soldier will not be available to another. Other forms of interdependence exist in organizations, including the interdependence which arises from joint activity on some work product, so that what one unit does to the product affects and may be affected by what another unit does. Interdependence is an important condition because it ties the organizational participants together, in the sense that each is now concerned with what the other does and what the other obtains. In the absence of such interdependence, there would be no basis for conflict or for interaction among the participants.

The second condition of the use of power is heterogeneous goals, or goals which are inconsistent with each other. In the present case, the goal of the corporal to stay alive is inconsistent with the goal of the captain to live because of the interdependence. A related condition would be heterogeneous beliefs about technology, or the relationship between decisions and outcomes. In the present example, this was not a problem as there was agreement on the connections between actions and consequences; all parties understood that obtaining the pint of blood was both necessary and sufficient for survival. As we shall explore later, such agreement on technology is not inevitable within organizations.

The third condition producing the use of power is scarcity. If there were two pints of blood, there would be no decision problem. To the extent that resources are insufficient to meet the various demands of organizational participants, choices have to be made concerning the allocation of those resources. The greater the scarcity as compared to the demand, the greater the power and the effort that will be expended in resolving the decision.

FIGURE 1   A Model of the Conditions Producing the Use of Power and Politics in Organizational Decision Making

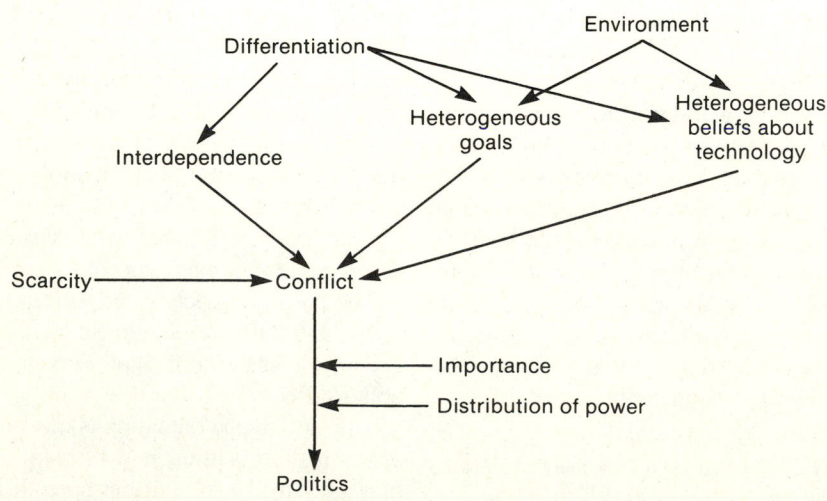

As indicated in Figure 1, together the conditions of scarcity, interdependence, and heterogeneous goals and beliefs about technology produce conflict. Whether that conflict eventuates in politics, the use of power in organizational settings depends upon two other conditions. The first condition is the importance of the decision issue or the resource. In the case of our example, the resource was very important—necessary for survival. In situations in which the decision may be perceived as less critical, power and politics may not be employed to resolve the decision because the issue is too trivial to merit the investment of political resources and effort. The second condition is the distribution of power. Political activity, bargaining, and coalition formation occur primarily when power is dispersed. When power is highly centralized, the centralized authority makes decisions using its own rules and values. The political contests that sometimes occur in organizations take place only because there is some dispersion of power and authority in the social system.

Before considering each of these conditions in additional detail, one final point should be made about the example. When the conditions which were specified in the figure and present in the example occur, the use of power is virtually inevitable and furthermore, it is the only way to arrive at a decision. Given conflicting and heterogeneous preferences and goals and beliefs about the relationship between actions and consequences, interdependence among the actors who possess conflicting preferences and beliefs, and a condition of scarcity so that not all participants can get their way, power is virtually the only way (except, perhaps, to use chance) to resolve the decision. There is no rational way to determine whose preferences are to prevail, or whose benefits about technology should guide the decision. There may be norms, social customs, or tradition which dictate the choice, but these may be all efforts to legitimate the use of power to make its appearance less obtrusive. In situations of conflict, power is the mechanism, the currency by which the conflict gets resolved. Social power almost inevitably accompanies conditions of conflict, for power is the way by which such conflicts becomes resolved. . . .

Some Causes of Goal and Technology Disagreements

As indicated in Figure 1, differentiation within the organization is one important source of disagreements on goals and beliefs about technology. Differentiation simply refers to the fact that in most large organizations, there is specialization of the participants and subunits by task—a division of labor which enables the organization to achieve certain economies but which also entails some costs. . . .

Disagreement, Conflict, and the Use of Power

The next part of the model argues that disagreements about cause-effect relations and preferences lead to conflict and, potentially, the use of power to resolve the choice. This position is well supported in the existing literature on the causes of conflict, in which the effects of disagreement are widely recognized. Dahrendorf (1959: 135) virtually defined conflict in terms of goal discrepancies:

> All relations between sets of individuals that involve an incompatible difference of objective—i.e., in its most general form, a desire on the part of both contestants to obtain what is available only to one, or only in part—are, in this sense relations of social conflict.

Schmidt and Kochan (1972: 361) noted that "perception of goal incompatibility is a necessary precondition for . . . conflict." Finally, examining the bases of conflict, Walker (1970: 18) noted:

> If two members hold divergent goals . . . and if these goals motivate their behavior, then one member will be motivated to behave in a way which is inconsistent with the goals of the other.

Because of the potential for goal disagreements to engender conflict and political activity in organizations, goal statements are made frequently at a very general level, so that all or at least most of the participants can agree with them. In attempting to explain organizational actions in terms of the stated goals, vaguely stated objectives can cause problems for the analyst. However, the very lack of clarify and specificity in these goal statements makes it possible for the various constituencies within the organization to accept them. This reduces conflict, at least at this level. Of course, as Etzioni (1964) recognized, the operative goals—the bases on which decisions and choices are actually made within the organization—are necessarily more specific. The fact that there may be agreement on general goals will not prevent conflict over the details of what the organization is to do when a specific action is to be taken. At the same time, such overall agreement can serve to potentially moderate the intensity of the conflict and provides some additional integration into the organization for the various participants.

The Role of Profit Maximization

If goal or value dissensus is an important condition leading to the use of power and politics and to a greater effect of power on decision outcomes, then it should be evident why business organizations are, for the most part, less overtly political than organizations in the nonprofit or public sectors such as governmental agencies, hospitals, and universities. The reason is not that businessmen are more rational, more analytical, or less political than administrators in the other organizations. Rather, business organizations have a reasonably agreed-upon goal of profit maximization, and this goal consensus negates much of the need for the use of power that might otherwise exist. In a debate, for instance, over the addition of a piece of medical equipment in a hospital, the decision turns not just on the return on investment as compared with the hospital's cost of funds. Rather, the hospital may have to go through a certificate-of-need application process, thus exposing itself to regulatory delays and political review. Concerns about cost and return on assets must be balanced against physicians' demands for equipment to improve the quality of patient care. The hospital may have a reputation and self-image as providing state-of-the-art care, and this may influence the decision. A similar type of decision, the addition of equipment, in a business firm is much more likely to turn primarily on

economic return considerations. Other issues are less legitimately raised, given the consensus that profit is what business firms are all about.

* * * * *

The objective of profit maximization can serve as an archetype of what a consensually shared goal can accomplish, in terms of legitimating and organizing collective action. Indeed, the development of language that facilitates this process of consensus building is an important administrative activity. It is important to remember, however, that profit is not the only possible objective that could fill such a role of legitimating and organizing behavior. Rather, it fills the role solely because it has come to be shared and believed within this country at a particular period of time.

Scarcity and Power and Conflict

Interdependence among subunits and differences in goals and in perceptions of technology are not sufficient, by themselves, to produce conflict and the resulting use of power and politics to reach decisions. It is only when the conditions are coupled with resource scarcity that conflict and power arise in organizational settings. Schmidt and Kochan (1972: 363) note that shared resources are one of the precursors to conflict. But unless these resources are in short supply, there will be little need or incentive for the various organizational actors to engage in a political struggle over them.

Decisions are contested, it is suggested, because choices must be made which will determine who will benefit and how much, from the organization's activities. When benefits and resources allocated within organizations are scarce, the funds allocated to one subunit may make another subunit unable to fulfill its objectives or maintain sufficient support to remain viable, due to its lack of funds. A promotion allocated to one individual forecloses the position to other potential contenders. If there are as many positions as contenders, it will matter much less than if many must contend for a very few promotional opportunities. It is because resources are scarce, because choices have to be made among courses of action, beneficiaries, and others interested in the organization and its activities, that conflict arises and power comes to be used in making decisions.

* * * * *

The fact that resource scarcity produces more power and influence attempts, as well as more conflict over the limited resources to be allocated, is one important reason that formal organizations have a strong preference for growth. As Katz and Kahn (1966), among others, have noted, growth in size provides the organization with more positions, and more budget resources, to allocate each successive year. These positive increments permit all participants to obtain more, to some degree, each year, and limit the intensity and amount of conflict engendered. When the organization faces a constant, or worse yet, shrinking pool of resources, conflict and power struggles become more intense. Because few participants enjoy the conflict and the requirement of making very difficult decisions among numerous worthy contenders for the limited resources, there is a strong preference for growth—a situation in which conflict is reduced and in which power and political activity are less prominent features in decision making. . . .

The Importance of Decisions

When resource scarcity is coupled with interdependent units and heterogeneous goals and beliefs about technology, conflict is produced within organizations. Two other conditions determine whether or not this conflict will become expressed in political activity organized around the development and use of power in order to obtain the preferred decision. One such condition is that the decision being made or the resource being allocated must be perceived as being important or critical. The use of power requires time and effort. Moreover, power typically is not inexhaustible. Votes or favors called in on one issue may not be available for use in other decisions. Thus, the use of the resources that provide power, and power itself, is husbanded. Just as there is no need to use power

in the absence of scarcity, there is no desire to use power to affect decisions that are not perceived as being important or critical to the organization's operations. . . .

Centralization and Political Activity

The second condition which determines whether or not political activity will be the method by which choices are made in conditions of conflict is the extent to which power is centralized within the organization. In this dimension, the present analysis departs from the Thompson and Tuden typology, in which the extent to which power was concentrated in the organization was not considered to be a feature which affected the form of decision process that was employed.

This condition is important in explaining why decision making in many organizations appears as it does. Many observers report that most organizational decision making seems to be orderly, systematic, and to employ bureaucratic or rationalistic decision procedures. Yet, it is agreed that few decision situations in complex organizations are characterized by consensus over both goals and technology. Using Thompson and Tuden's argument, one would be left with a paradox—the use of apparently computational decision-making procedures in settings which are not characterized by the requisite amounts of consensus and certainty.

The explanation of this paradox is straightforward. In many organizations, particularly in business organizations, power is relatively highly concentrated at the top of the organization. This concentration of control is sometimes accomplished through concentrated share ownership. In other circumstances the concentration of power may occur because of managerial control over the election of directors, the choosing of auditors, and the consequent release of information. In still other contexts, concentrated power may result from the tremendous rewards and sanctions that may be available to those at the highest executive levels. Furthermore, the socialization accomplished in schools produces an expectation of hierarchical power, so that power which is concentrated at the top of the organization is legitimate and acceptable. When the power is concentrated, potential conflicts in goals and in definitions of technology are resolved by the imposition of a set of preferences and a view of technology which reflects the position of the dominant coalition controlling the organization. The decisions which are made are enforced through various control procedures. The decision-making process appears to be orderly and rational only because technological uncertainty and goal disagreements have been submerged in the organization's choice processes through the use of concentrated power and influence.

Conversely, politics, the less rational-appearing interplay of power and political strategy, occurs when power and control are dispersed. The resolution of conflicting beliefs and goals then occurs on a more equal basis. An analogue can be drawn to make the argument clearer. There is more political activity in democratic countries with relatively equal political parties than there is in countries which are run by strong dictatorships. When power is centralized, decisions are made and imposed by the central authority. When power is dispersed, decisions become worked out through the interplay of various actors with more equal power in a political process. This argument does not mean that power is not critical in determining decision outcomes in either case; regardless of the degree to which power is dispersed, power still affects the extent to which a given social actor's preferences will prevail. The argument, rather, is that when power is highly concentrated, the other participants in the system have little ability or motivation to engage in a contest for control which provokes the visible conflict and political activity observed when power is more equally distributed. . . .

Making Decision Making Less Political

The identification of those factors that tend to lead to the use of power and political activity in decision making also indicates what might be done in organizations to reduce the use of power and politics. It is worth considering the costs of such strategies,

to clarify some of the advantages of retaining political decision processes.

Slack Resources

Slack, or excess resources, in the organization can reduce the use of power and politics in two ways. In the first place, as Galbraith (1973) has noted in his discussion of organization design, slack reduces the amount of interdependence among subunits. Interdependence is an important prerequisite for conflict (e.g., Schmidt and Kochan, 1972). By reducing the amount of interdependence among units in the organization, the potential for conflict is also reduced. Slack reduces interdependence by permitting the activities of the various units to be relatively uncoupled. To illustrate the point, consider one form of slack observed in most organizations: work-in-process inventories. We will consider the copy editing and production departments of a publishing company. If the organization permits large in-process inventories, the two subunits will have little contact and little cause for conflict. The copy editing department will do its work on the manuscript, and then add the book to the inventory of manuscripts ready for production. For its part, the production department will work on the manuscripts as it has time, according to whatever priority rules the organization has set. The existence of the inventory essentially uncouples the two departments. If there were no inventory, then the production department would be arguing with the copy editing department about manuscript preparation, or, the copy editing department would be fighting with the production department about producing finished books. By decoupling the process, interdependence is reduced and so is the potential for conflict.

Slack also reduces conflict by affecting the existence of scarcity of resources. The existence of slack or excess resources implies less scarcity, and less scarcity means that there will be less conflict. With plenty of resources, there is less need to contest for allocations since there will be enough for all subunits to get what they need.

The cost of slack, of course, is the cost of keeping excess resources on hand, a cost that may entail inventory costs and costs of excess capacity. These various costs of slack have led Galbraith (1973) to suggest that this strategy is not very useful in solving coordination problems. By the same token, it may be a rather costly way of reducing the incidence of power and politics in decision making. However, it is clear that slack, or excess resources, is one way of reducing the use of power in organizational choice. As we will argue throughout this book, one of the advantages of organizational growth is its ability to generate excess resources at least in the short run, and this reduces the use of power and the incidence of conflict within the organization.

One of the more prominent slack-creating tactics used in organizations is the creation of additional administrative positions and titles. Williamson (1975: 120) has argued, ''The expansionary biases of internal organization are partly attributable to its dispute-settling characteristics. . . . Persistent conflict . . . results frequently in role proliferation.'' Instead of choosing among subunits for a new-position incumbent, the vacant position is filled with a person from one subunit *and* additional positions are created to keep at least some of the other subunits moderately happy. If new positions are not created, then titles can be manufactured. In addition to chief executive officers, there can be presidents, chairmen of the board, chief operating officers, chief financial officers, vice chairmen, and so forth. If position creation is a means of producing slack in an attempt to reduce conflict and its consequences for the use of power, then one would expect to see more position creation in systems in which power and conflict might otherwise be endemic. For instance, if resource scarcity produces conflict over the allocation of some kinds of resources, then position creation may proceed apace in order to pay off the subunits that lose in the struggle over those resources. Certainly, the creation of administrative positions in universities has increased as these organizations began to face more and more resource scarcity. Position creation would

be expected to increase in situations where there is great interdependence between subunits and great heterogeneity in preferences and beliefs about technology among organizational participants.

Homogeneity and Agreement

In addition to slack, the use of power can be diminished through the production of a homogeneous set of organizational participants, homogeneous with respect to their goals and preferences and in their beliefs about cause-effect relations. Such homogeneity can be produced through selectively recruiting persons with very similar backgrounds and training, socialization of persons once they have been recruited into the organization, or the use of rewards and sanctions to produce at least outward conformity to the dominant set of beliefs.

The production of homogeneity has its own costs for organizational decision making. Davis (1969), in reviewing the literature on group decision making, noted that groups tended to make better decisions than individuals because of the different information and different points of view that were brought to bear on the situation by the various group members. Homogeneous groups, facing certain kinds of tasks, performed less effectively than more heterogeneous groups. Clearly, the advantages of different sources of information and different perspectives on issues can be lost in an organization in which homogeneity in goals and technological beliefs has been produced.

This problem is likely to be the most troublesome for those organizations that face a changing set of environmental conditions. If the organization faces a stable environment in terms of demands and constraints, then the solutions developed at one point in time will probably suffice long into the future. In this situation, there is less need for change or adaptation, and thus, less need for new and diverse informational inputs into decision making. By contrast, an organization facing a more rapidly changing environment may require frequent changes in strategy and direction; such change is less likely to emerge from a homogeneous group. Janis (1972) has illustrated the problems of conformity to a single point of view in his discussion of groupthink and the decision making that occurred in the Kennedy administration. Janis argued that even in the absence of homogeneity, a crisis situation tends to produce demands for loyalty and conformity within the group that cause the group to make faulty analyses and to miss obvious problems and other alternatives. These problems are certainly going to be worsened if the group is already homogeneous in preferences and outlook and has been chosen specifically to minimize the potential for conflict.

Reducing the Importance of Decisions

The final strategy to be considered in the reduction of the incidence of power and politics involves reducing the importance, or at least the perceived importance, of the decision being made. This can be accomplished in several ways. In some instances, a decision that is perceived as being critical and about which there is disagreement may simply be avoided. Although this may not seem to be an optimal way of running an organization, the avoidance of conflict is not at all uncommon, and does result at times in the refusal to make a decision. In a firm in California which manufactured and constructed large, highly engineered projects, a conflict arose as to whether or not something should be added to the product line which would involve the use of more standard parts and subassemblies, but which might open up new markets to the firm. The firm, dominated by engineering in the past, wrestled with the decision. Production and marketing favored the addition. Marketing would have more to sell and possibly an easier job in selling. Production would gain substantial power in the firm, because the manufacture of standardized parts and components would now become a more important activity within the firm. At the same time, engineering, which previously had power because of its control over the critical contingencies in the design of the projects, would lose some control. In this particular instance, the decision was simply put off—for additional market research, financial analysis, production facilities feasibility analysis,

and so forth. It was clear from observing the key executives that by putting off the decision they were able to avoid a severe conflict. Because of the generally favorable orientation toward analysis and data gathering, the postponements could be made to appear to be a reasonable part of a rational decision-making process.

A second strategy is somewhat more common. Critical decisions are labeled as being relatively unimportant in order to avoid the involvement and concern of organizational participants. This can be accomplished by stating that the decision is relatively unimportant. Relatively little formal analysis can be done and few people, or few people of importance, can be involved in the decision process. Attention can be kept away from the decision and on other matters occurring in the organization. This strategy is somewhat risky and not always successful, in that the criticality of the decision may be so widely known that it is impossible to make it appear otherwise. Nevertheless, power and political activity can be reduced substantially if the choice can be made to seem relatively unimportant.

A related strategy involves taking a decision and breaking it into smaller pieces, each one of which is likely to appear to be less important for the organization. Peters (1978), in describing techniques for implementing change, recommends precisely such a strategy. Its benefit is that change occurs slowly, and in pieces, as part of an ongoing process. Because few may realize the totality of what is occurring, it is less likely that power will organize to contest the decisions.

This strategy is frequently used to change the direction of an organization when the person in charge does not have the direct power to do so. The dean of a school of business which had been primarily research-oriented and firmly grounded in the basic social science disciplines was confronted with the task of changing the orientation and activities of the school. One way to proceed would have been to announce that a decision would be made about the future direction of the school. This would undoubtedly have been perceived as an important decision, and the various constituencies would have organized and mustered their power to affect the choice according to their preferences. There would have been a lot of conflict and a lot of political activity over what would be perceived as a crucial decision. The alternative, and what was done in fact, was not to make an announcement about a new direction, but rather, to make a series of small and relatively trivial decisions that, in their total effects, resulted in the accomplishment of much of the change that was desired. A decision was made to incorporate a placement center in the school for its master's graduates. This decision was treated as a relatively trivial matter of moving the facility from one part of the campus to the building where the business school was located. Certainly, no one could care much about that. In a similar fashion, alumni relations, corporate fund raising, and external affairs activities were added; the advisory board, comprised of business executives, was involved more heavily in the decision making in the school; and, some changes were made regarding the importance of teaching and in minor aspects of the curriculum. Treated individually, the changes were not worth even thinking about, much less fighting. Taken together, the changes had the effect of moving the school toward a new strategy. Most importantly, the course of action avoided the conflict and exercise of power that would undoubtedly have been engendered, had the total change been announced and effected at once. This strategy too has costs. In the case of avoiding important but contested choices, the costs involve failing to act when action may be required, and the possibility of missing opportunities or failing to act in time to avoid threats. In the case of trying to make an important decision appear unimportant, as well as in the strategy of breaking an important decision into a series of small, unimportant ones, the costs include the possibility of discovery, resulting in even more intense conflict. In addition, the disguising of the true consequences of decisions may fail to produce the kind of thorough analysis and discussion that such important actions warrant. Implementation may be achieved, but the wrong action may have been implemented.

In Table 1, we summarize the discussion of strategies for avoiding the use of power and politics and some of the costs of those strategies. It is clear that it is possible to avoid political decision making, but that the manager must strike a balance between the costs of doing so and the benefits to be obtained through the avoidance of conflict.

TABLE 1 Strategies for Avoiding the Use of Power and Politics in Decision Making, and Their Costs

Strategy	*Costs*
Slack or excess resources, including additional administrative positions or titles.	Inventory costs, costs of excess capacity, costs of extra personnel and extra salary.

Homogeneity in goals and beliefs about technology produced through:
    Recruitment practices
    Socialization.
    Use of rewards and sanctions.
	Fewer points of view, less diverse information represented in decision making; potentially lower quality decisions.

Make decisions appear less important.	Decision may be avoided; subterfuge may be discovered; analysis and information may not be uncovered.

Reading 44

ORGANIZATION DEVELOPMENT:
A POLITICAL PERSPECTIVE

Anthony T. Cobb and Newton Margulies

During the last several years the area of organizational politics (OP) has attracted the interest of social scientists and practitioners alike. In the field of organization development (OD), interest has focused on the use of OP in intervention programs. It is now generally recognized that such programs inevitably affect organizational politics and are affected by them (Bennis, 1969; Cobb, 1977; Pettigrew, 1975).

Despite this knowledge, the movement of OD into the study and use of OP has been cautious and conservative. At present, the interest OD displays in OP remains largely peripheral to what can be called its clinical or process orientation: one that relies on a relatively intimate client/consultant relationship to facilitate self-discovery, help, and renewal (Margulies & Raia, 1978, pp. 110–11). There are a number of views regarding this level of OP interest. One extreme holds that any political orientation will necessarily divert attention from OD's clinical mission and inevitably subvert it. Another extreme view holds that OD consultants ought to assume a political activist role to ensure that program objectives are implemented. Both views maintain that OD has been devoid of any political orientation. The former maintains that this is how it should be, the latter that it must no longer remain so.

Our purposes in this article are two: First, we assert that, while OD is not politically sophisticated, neither is it devoid of a political orientation. OD has developed an unrecognized political ori-

entation in many of its values and some aspects of its most frequently used technology. Although this political orientation is restricted in scope, it has proved useful in supporting OD's clinical objectives. We believe that the effectiveness of OD can be enhanced when professionals recognize, accept, and use this existing political orientation in the service of organizational change.

Our second purpose is to explore some of the ramifications of a greater level of political involvement in intervention programs. Although increased political involvement can aid the OD consultant and the host organization, so too can it do harm, particularly when it moves to the extreme of political activism.

To address these issues properly, a political perspective is developed first to view OD's past and its alternative political futures. This perspective provides focus for subsequent discussions.

A Political Perspective

A political perspective with sufficient range to deal with the issues raised here can be developed by briefly addressing two topics. First, a definition of the term *organizational politics* is provided and, second, what can be called the "political subsystem" is described.

The Meaning of Organizational Politics

The literature provides many definitions of OP developed from a variety of perspectives. Mayes and Allen (1977) provide an adequate survey of these. In terms relevant to OD, organizational politics can be defined as *the use of power to modify or protect an organization's exchange structure*. An ex-

Source: Anthony T. Cobb and Newton Margulies, reprinted from *Academy of Management Review*, January 1981, pp. 49–59.

change structure is composed of an organization's resource distribution system and those who have formal authority to decide to what purposes resources will be used. An exchange structure in equilibrium represents the status quo and is "legitimate." Efforts to change the status quo, then, involve political action both on the part of those who challenge and those who seek to maintain it.

As seen in this light, OP per se is neither good nor bad. Actually, OP can either help or hinder the organization, depending on the processes used and the objectives sought. Even though it is easy for the OD consultant to become involved in politics, it is entirely another matter to have the sophistication to manage the use of OP productively.

The Political Subsystem

For convenience, the notion of a social subsystem (Guest, Hersey, & Blanchard, 1977) is used here to denote the subsystem about which the OD consultant is expert and in which he or she operates. This subsystem coexists with many others, one of which can be labeled the political subsystem.

The political subsystem is composed of the sources, locations, and flow of power through the organization. The basic criterion of effectiveness within the subsystem is the extent to which sufficient power can be accumulated and transferred to those locations (i.e., individuals) in the organization to maintain productive operations, solve problems, and implement solutions. A political subsystem is efficient to the extent that power can be accumulated and transferred quickly and with precision.

A tenet of general systems theory is that subsystems interact with one another. Therefore, changes in either the social or political subsystem will produce changes in the other. The interactive relationship poses at least two basic problems to OD consultants concerned with organizational politics. The first is determining how support can be generated within the political subsystem to aid work within the social subsystem. The second is knowing what changes are necessary in the social subsystem to facilitate the development of an effective and efficient political subsystem.

Political Orientations in Organization Development

Because there is interaction between the social subsystem and the political subsystem, successful change in the former requires complementary and supportive changes in the latter. It is because OD is well aware of such subsystem interaction (Benne & Birnbaum, 1969; Leavitt, 1965) that there has been recent concern that OD consultants should become more politically sophisticated and active in order to increase intervention success (Burke, 1976; Pettigrew, 1975). Yet, historically speaking, OD interventions on the whole have enjoyed a great deal of success. Given that OD consultants have traditionally displayed, at most, a minimal interest in OP, the issue must be raised of how they are able to survive at all, much less be successful. One reason may be just good fortune. Another may be that clients themselves come to see that political cooperation is necessary to protect their own self-interests. We will argue that there is still a third reason: OD has developed a largely unrecognized political orientation in addition to its clinical one and this political orientation complements the clinical one in producing successful interventions.

Where in OD does this political orientation lie? Even now, organization development does not appear to be an easily defined field or profession. For the purposes here, OD can be viewed as a profession built on a foundation composed of three basic interactive elements: its values, its technology, and its knowledge of the human side of organizations. If there is a political orientation in OD that helps guide the political behavior of consultants, then, it should reside in one or more of these elements.

The knowledge base of OD incorporates clinical concepts relevant to power, models of power, and even sources of power available to consultants for work in interventions (Huse, 1980, pp. 143–148). Properly viewed, such concepts of power *can* form a foundation on which to build political theory and intervention strategy. Yet, even today the knowledge base of OD remains essentially lacking in political theory and models to help *guide* the consultant in terms of political intervention strategies

(Beer, 1976; Bennis, 1969). Therefore, if political assistance is given to the consultant, it must come from the value or technological base of the field. It is our view that it comes from both.

Political Support in the Value Base

For the purposes here, the value component of OD is viewed in structural terms. At its base lie fundamental philosophical or value orientations. These would include rationalism, pragmatism, existentialism (Friedlander, 1976), humanism, and democracy (Friedlander & Brown, 1974). These basic orientations, then, provide the context for the development of more specific values: values concerning intervention concepts, means, and end-states. Valued clinical *aims,* or end-states of intervention, include individual growth and increased organizational effectiveness with the capability of self-renewal (French, Bell, & Zawacki, 1978). Valued *means* for reaching this end-state include confrontation, honesty, open communications, the movement toward power equalization, and collaboration. Concepts that support these valued means include beliefs in the goodness of people, Theory Y assumptions, and the potential and desire for growth by organizational members. Such historically entrenched values of OD, then, provide the general context here for discussion.

The OD consultant is an expert in creating a social environment within which the client system can achieve full utilization of its own human resources to solve its problems (French et al., 1978). Basic to the full utilization of human resources are such necessary processes as collaboration and participation. Collaboration, however, requires that power be exchanged, shared, and pooled. Participation in decision making requires a "franchise" that comes only with the power to make inputs. Thus, if the consultant is to achieve collaboration and participation in the social subsystem, supportive changes must occur within the political subsystem to allow it. Some of these changes include the general reduction of power differentials between organizational members, the transfer of power to those who are to participate in decision making,

and the removal of structural obstacles to the flow of power in the organization generally and between levels of authority in particular. The consultant is guided in these tasks by many of the values OD has developed.

The belief that power equalization should be used in interventions is a central concept in OD (Leavitt, 1965). Strauss (1963, p. 41) stated, for example, that "the main thrust of the human relations movement over the last 20 years has been toward . . . 'power equalization'." In the nearly twenty years since Strauss's observation, this general orientation has become valued in its own right and is reflected in a number of other values that focus on more specific political problems. This can be demonstrated by examining specific values oriented to the individual, superior/subordinate relations, and organization structures paralleling the micro, intermediate, and macro perspectives of the organization.

The Individual's Political Position. Participation raises the basic political issue of who should be given the right, and thus the power, to participate in decision making. On the level of the nation or state, for example, the extent of citizen participation is justified and supported by the assumptions made regarding the capabilities and traits of the polity (i.e., citizens).

The political position of organizational members is justified and supported as well by basic assumptions regarding workers. McGregor (1960) has articulated some of these assumptions. Theory X assumptions support a political structure in which power is centralized and participation removed from the rank and file. Theory Y assumptions support a political structure in which power is decentralized, justifying a wide base of participation. The clinical side of Theory Y assumptions focuses on the individual as a potential resource in problem solving. Theory Y also justifies the political necessity of transferring some measure of participatory power to the worker. Thus, although OD consultants may not recognize it, when they promote a clinical value orientation, coinciding with Theory Y, they are establishing as well some of the political subsystem changes needed to support their clinical aims.

Superior/Subordinate Relations. Historically, one of OD's principal concerns has been with leadership style. In its clinical context, OD has tied leadership style to interactions among subordinates, satisfaction, and productivity (Lewin, Lippitt, & White, 1939). In terms of organizational change, OD has recognized that changes on one level require "complementary and reinforcing changes in organizational levels above and below that level" (Benne & Birnbaum, 1969, p. 331). It is not surprising, therefore, to see that OD has developed a value orientation to leader/subordinate relations that supports the power exchange required for collaboration and interlevel adjustments between subordinates and superiors. Authoritarian leadership removes power from subordinates, thereby suppressing participation, collaboration, and the upward flow of influence, whereas democratic leadership facilitates them. The fact that OD values democratic leadership produces changes not only in the social subsystem, but complementary and reinforcing changes in the political subsystem as well.

The Organization Structure. In accordance with general systems theory, the structural subsystem (Guest et al., 1977) will affect the political subsystem. Although they did not address the political subsystem specifically, Burns and Stalker (1961) recognized this interactive effect. They noted that the rigid power structure of mechanistic organizations tends to hamper the power flow necessary for broad organizational problem solving. Organic organizations, on the other hand, facilitate problem solving by allowing an easier flow of power through the political subsystem to wherever it is needed.

The behavioral administrative structures articulated by Likert (1961, 1967) are relevant to this discussion. System 1 tends to impede, but System 4 tends to facilitate the flow of power through the political subsystem. As a result, System 4 facilitates broad organizational collaboration, participation, and communication in the establishment of goals and resource distribution.

Organization development values an organic System 4 administrative structure for a number of clinical reasons. When such a structure is adopted by the client, however, it promotes changes within the political subsystem. These political changes, in turn, facilitate work within the social subsystem.

The Practical and Political Utility of Values. Fundamentally, OD values a democratic work place and the power equalization inherent in it. It was demonstrated above that this value orientation is manifest whether one takes a micro, intermediate, or macro perspective of the organization. Part of the reason OD may hold these values is that they are generally accepted in our society. Clinically speaking, they are valued because OD believes that they promote effective organizational performance and personal growth. One should not ignore, however, the political utility these values have in terms of the consultant's clinical objectives.

Consider the problems typically faced by the consultant and client system. They tend to be unstructured, complex, novel, and complicated. Evidence indicates that these types of problems are best solved by a broad-based participatory effort utilizing the resources of those best able to attend to them regardless of formal power position (Burns & Stalker, 1961; MacCrimmon & Taylor, 1976).

Such collaborative and participative efforts, however, require commensurate political subsystem support. Many OD values, some of which have been presented here, can be seen as helpful in promoting political support for clinical objectives.

Political Support in the Technological Base

The technological base of OD can be divided into two interdependent components. One includes the tools and techniques the consultant can use in intervention. The second includes the roles assumed by the consultant (e.g., facilitator, interviewer) and the operational know-how, expertise, or knowledge to use the tools, techniques, and roles available to the consultant. Political supports can be found in both components.

Tools and Techniques. The value OD gives to power equalization finds expression in some of its techniques as well. Laboratory training, for example, promotes a commitment to open and honest communications regarding interpersonal relations, organizational life, and diagnosis. But such a commitment "does inevitably imply some democratization [that] . . . may indeed undermine formal authority to a considerable degree" (E. Schein, 1972, p. 93). Intervention techniques that include such components as these, then, serve to operationalize the political as well as clinical side of the democratic values held by OD consultants.

Other techniques appear to play a political part in integrating vested interests by facilitating actual change in the exchange structure. Techniques oriented toward roles provide a case in point. Organizational roles prescribe occupant behavior, areas of decision making, character of reporting relationships, legitimate power, and the like. In short, roles contain many components of the status quo exchange structure. Many role techniques, therefore, have a political side in that they intervene "directly in the relationship of power, authority, and influence" of role occupants and reciprocals (Harrison, 1978, p. 159). When OD consultants facilitate change in such role components, then, they are working within both the social and political subsystems to accomplish their aims.

The political subsystem is also affected by a number of techniques oriented to "structural" or "work engineering." The negotiation of resource exchanges and integration of vested interests, for example, is a political subsystem change that occurs along with the institution of a management-by-objectives system. The clinical objectives of job enrichment include ownership of the task, increases in perceived task importance, and the like. To accomplish these objectives, however, "vertical loading" is required, whereby previous supervisory perogatives are given to the subordinate.

Consultant Roles and Operational Knowledge. Consultants are called on to play a variety of roles when using their knowledge and techniques. The literature describes many of these roles; our focus here is on a distinctly political role that cuts across many others and is often ignored: the diplomatic role. The purpose of this role is to communicate the vested interests of one party to another in a language that can be fully understood. The diplomat then seeks to integrate these vested interests when possible and, when not, to reduce the friction caused by competition by negotiations, trade-offs, and the like.

In order to support the clinical objectives of intervention, the consultant often assumes one of at least two diplomatic roles. One might be called the "enfranchiser" role. The socio-organizational distance between higher- and lower-level participants is often large. So, too, is the power differential within the political subsystem. In order to communicate and facilitate the integration of vested interests, the consultant often becomes a "communications channel" between the parties. For lower-level participants, consultants become surrogate participants in decision making; for higher-level decision makers they are representatives of the organizational citizenry.

The consultant often plays a diplomatic role horizontally in the organization as well. The consultant is frequently called on to mediate between organizational groups that are interdependent but have different vested interests, values, perceptions, and beliefs. Like Lawrence and Lorsch's integrator (1967), the consultant facilitates communication between parties by serving as a communications channel or by facilitating face-to-face interaction. By working with and between both groups, the consultant aids in the integration of their vested interests while focusing on their interaction process.

Whether moving vertically, horizontally, or obliquely in the organization, the OD consultant is in a unique position to carry the interests of one party to another. The parties can speak openly to the consultant, without fear of repercussions, and can be confident that the consultant is concerned about them as well as about the general welfare of the organization. This promotes the power generation and transfer necessary for effective political subsystem operation. Thus, the consultant plays the clinical role of communications channel and the political role of power channel at the same time for the same purpose: beneficial change in the social subsystem.

The Political Side of Organization Development

The more one explores OD, the more one can see its political side. It is true, however, that OD's clinical orientation remains paramount and that the political side plays a mostly unrecognized, supportive role. Evaluations made by Bennis (1969), Beer (1976), and Burke (1976) hold true today. Organization development has not come to fully appreciate the impact that OP has on change programs. Nor has OD developed the models, knowledge, and facts that represent a sophisticated political orientation.

Nevertheless, OD's brand of "political pacifism" should not be ignored. It needs to be further explored for at least three reasons. The first is to see if the direction it provides is appropriate for the various situations OD consultants encounter. Second, if OD is determined to become more politically active, a foundation for such growth may be found not only in the values and technology of OD but its knowledge base as well. Third, OD's present political orientation can serve as a reference point. As such, it is useful for exploring those issues involved in assuming a greater political role.

Political Involvement: Considerations for Organization Development

The OD profession has been urged to become more politically oriented and active (Bennis, 1969; Burke, 1976; Pettigrew, 1975). In this regard at least two questions need to be raised. First, what would be the utility of increased political intervention? Second, what would be the consequences in terms of OD's ethical/value base? Before these questions can be answered, just what is meant by "increased political involvement" needs to be explored.

A Continuum of Political Involvement

It is possible to describe the extent and character of OP involvement along a continuum. At the extremes lie "political pacifism" and "political activism." The midrange is represented by the "political moderate" position.

Political Pacifism. Political pacifism has been represented above. It includes a fundamental commitment to clinical rather than political intervention. While a political element does exist, it is minimal, generally unrecognized, and oriented to clinical support rather than being used as a means of change in its own right.

Political Moderation. The political moderate advocates the development of knowledge, models, and strategies to overcome political blindspots (Bennis, 1969; Harrison, 1978; Pettigrew, 1975). The use of these, however, remains subordinate to, and strictly supportive of, work within the social subsystem. The political role played by the consultant is at most one of a "political facilitator" who seeks to establish a political climate supportive of clinically oriented change. Honesty, truth, collaboration, participation, and the like are still pursued. Political facilitation works to overcome the political impediments to these components of change. The clients operating within this climate work toward the establishment of a new status quo, *one chosen by them.*

Political Activism. Political activism advocates deep involvement in the political subsystem—at least as much as, if not more than, in the social subsystem. Here the consultant adopts the role of "political activist," of someone who has some vision of what the client system's condition ought to be. This vision is realized by politically overcoming resistance to it. In this sense, then, the political activist maintains that "the ends justify the means" and advocates such strategies as limiting and channeling communication for political purposes, the use of covert or hidden agendas, and the political use of intervention research (V. Schein, 1977). Coercive politics may also be used. Damaging information gained in intervention, for example, might be used against those who stand in the way of the consultant (Pettigrew, 1975).

The Utility of Increased Political Involvement

It has been argued that increased political involvement will lead to greater chances of intervention success than that provided by the current approach of political pacifism. Because these arguments have been directly and indirectly stated in the literature (Bennis, 1969; Harrison, 1978; Pettigrew, 1975; V. Schein, 1977), they are only briefly reviewed here.

The moderate position takes due note of the evidence that supports the existence of OP and the political subsystem, and their effect on any change program (Bennis, 1969; Cyert & March, 1964; March, 1962; March & Simon, 1958; Thompson, 1967). Ignoring this evidence creates a significant gap in the operational knowledge of OD and its approach to change. Furthermore, this knowledge gap makes it impossible to develop appropriate reactive and proactive strategies to support the clinical aims of the intervention program. Evidence can be cited demonstrating that once this gap is filled, political tools, techniques, and strategies can be developed to serve the clinical ends of the OD consultant (Harrison, 1978, Selznick, 1949). Although individual studies are subject to criticism, the corpus of evidence represents a systematic approach with generally positive results across applications. As a whole, then, the evidence lends support to the moderate position.

Political activism builds on the arguments provided by the moderate position. Activists assume that not only are politics a fact of organizational life but that some powerful and sophisticated members of the client system use politics to protect and extend their own selfish interests. These are formidable "opponents." Political activism, say the activists, is the best way to deal with them, and they cite evidence indicating that activist techniques (e.g., political manipulation of communication, research information) have successfully overcome such opponents (Pettigrew, 1975; V. Schein, 1977). Unfortunately, most of this evidence is anecdotal and lacking in empirical validation. Much more empirical work needs to be done to support the activist position.

Some Caveats Regarding Increased Political Involvement

With all the arguments made for increased political involvement on the part of OD consultants, there is a surprising lack of attention given to some of the problems that may emerge. These potential problems deserve attention.

Political Success Requires Political Sophistication. Consultants in OD are probably more politically sophisticated than they realize or may be willing to admit. Nevertheless, OD consultants are clinicians, not politicians. Their training may have prepared them for political pacifism but not activism. To urge political pacifists to use techniques employed by activists can invite disaster. Recently, a broader base of political training and knowledge has been offered to OD consultants [Huse, 1980, pp. 143–148; NTL Institute, 1980]. Though consultants now have the opportunity to develop greater political sophistication, the cautious and conservative progress of OD into OP may well be justified on utilitarian grounds. Little, if any, sophistication is required to enter the political arena, but a great deal is required to work productively within it.

Political Reaction in the Client System. Largely ignored in arguments favoring political involvement are considerations of how the client system may react. Activists maintain, for example, that organizational "opponents" should be politically overcome. It must be remembered, however, that what is home ground to the opponent is foreign territory to the consultant. If opponents have any political sophistication, they will have identified and marshalled sources of power, formed long-standing alliances, and developed political strategies that have proven value in that particular system. One can expect such opponents to use their power and strategies when they perceive that their vested interests are attacked.

In addition, one needs to consider how the client system itself will react to political confrontation. It is one thing to be able to win a political confrontation; it is quite another to keep such confrontations from adversely affecting the political subsystem. Political pacifism seems to have evolved to minimize the danger of disruption. Political moderates, and activists in particular, need to carefully consider this aspect of political subsystem reactivity.

Reaction to the OD profession. Perhaps the biggest concern related to increased political activity, particularly political activism, is how clients will react to OD itself. Since its beginning, OD has developed an image of being close to what Charles Perrow (1977) called "the forces of light." This image derives from the emphasis on such fundamental values as honesty, openness, collaboration, and a steadfast concern for everyone in the client system. This image has utilitarian value. OD technology, for example, requires cooperation, trust, and client confidence in the consultant. The OD image supports these qualities, and the consultant depends on this image.

The success that political activists have enjoyed may be partly based on this image as well. Limiting and channeling communication for political purposes, the use of hidden or covert agendas, and the political manipulation of intervention research strategies may be successful partly because clients don't expect OD consultants to behave in this manner. Thus, using the element of surprise, the activist can catch opponents unprepared to effectively resist.

Images can change. As the reputation of the activist consultant grows, clients will no longer be caught by surprise. They can be expected, rather, to take the initiative and attack the consultant first. At the very least, the activist will no longer enjoy the trust and cooperation of clients who are preparing for political confrontation.

This would be a relatively minor concern for OD as a profession if clients could be counted on *not* to generalize their perceptions of activist consultants—an unrealistic hope. If the OD profession suffers an image change reflecting political activism, the chances of success even for political pacifists are reduced.

Consider the following example: A nationally known consultant company conducted management audits for a major governmental unit in the Pacific Southwest. Following the audit, high-ranking officials were fired, in light of evidence gained in some of the audits. Word quickly spread that these audits were political covers with the hidden agenda of marshalling evidence to do away with preselected officials. Whether or not this rumor was correct, from that point forward the audits created a great deal of political turmoil. Perhaps the activist is prepared for this type of reaction. The issue, however, is whether OD as a profession can accept this type of image change.

Facilitation versus Activism. Political moderates remain committed to the traditional clinical orientation of organization development. They argue that political facilitation of social change is not only compatible with this orientation but will increase chances of intervention success as well. They conclude, therefore, that OD ought to promote such political involvement on the part of its practitioners. Although there is evidence to support this position, a number of caveats must be kept in mind. First, OD must take care to see that consultants are properly prepared to assume the role of a political facilitator. Second, political facilitation must be exercised with due caution lest the client system overreact. Third, OD must recognize that it is all too easy to slip from the facilitator role into the activist role. The boundaries between them are often difficult to define, particularly in the hour-to-hour and day-to-day operation of an intervention program.

Political activists maintain that political facilitation is not enough to achieve intervention success in the face of determined political resistance. Greater rates of success can, however, be expected if the consultant uses whatever power politics are required to confront and remove such resistance. Political activism, however, carries with it not only the problems of negative client-system reaction, but also the problems of a negative image change for the OD profession as a whole.

On utilitarian grounds alone, OD is well advised to increase political involvement only with extreme caution and due deliberation. Beyond utilitarian considerations, OD consultants and the field as a whole should address as well the issue of how political involvement affects the value base of the profession.

Value Considerations

Political involvement, particularly as it approaches political activism, has consequences for the values of organization development. There has been a general lack of discussion regarding what these consequences may be, yet this is an important topic, because the distinctive character and practice of OD, as with any professional field, is based as much on its values as on its technology and knowledge (Margulies & Raia, 1978). The value base plays an important role in the image of OD, the use of its technology, and in providing the context and objectives for intervention itself. The value base reflects the nature of the relationship between client and consultant and what constitutes acceptable consultant behavior. Clients depend on the value base of OD just as they do in any professional relationship. It has been argued above that consultants depend on it as well.

Political activism provides a good context for discussion. The sharp contrast between the values inherent in political activism and the traditional values of OD produces issues more easily discerned than when lesser levels of political involvement are addressed. At the same time, the issues raised by these contrasts provide some points of departure for addressing the more subtle issues of lesser forms of political involvement. The assertion that the ends justify the means, whether explicitly advocated (V. Schein, 1977) or implicitly assumed, provides the focus for value considerations.

Can the Means and Ends Be Separated? In theory, it may be possible to separate one's objectives and the means used to achieve them. In practice, and particularly in OD, the means used appear more often than not to affect the ends attained. From a value perspective, an OD intervention program is successful if the organizational health of a client system is improved and if it has achieved or

expanded its capacity for self-renewal (French et al., 1978). These goals, in turn, are dependent on, and evolve from, the achievement of a host of other clinical objectives. Such objectives may well be displaced in an intervention program using the philosophy and techniques of political activism.

The displacement of clinical objectives can occur for a number of reasons. First, intense political activity often leads to the compromise of objectives for political expediency. One must consider the point at which such compromise becomes failure from a clinical perspective. Second, political activism, by its nature, fosters political activity in the client system of a similar character. Such activity can itself displace clinical goals. Moreover, the aftermath of political activism, with its tendency to produce win/lose conflict, can leave strains and tensions in the client system that drain energy from productive uses and future renewal. Finally, the capacity for self-renewal requires that the consultant teach those in the client system the concepts, methods, and values that will allow them to solve future as well as present problems (French et al., 1978). One must consider, then, whether political activism teaches the client methods of self-renewal, or suspicion, distrust, and the fine art of political warfare.

Presuming the Ends that Justify the Means. Political activism is literally presumptuous: the activist presumes to know the good ends that justify the means used to achieve them. Traditionally, however, the OD consultant leaves the configuration of the ends (i.e., desired condition) to the decision making of the clients. In fact, the end traditionally pursued by OD consultants is to help establish the means by which the client can effectively and efficiently pursue a new status quo. Thus, within OD the means and ends are often the same.

The political-moderate position recognizes this. It seeks to work within the political subsystem to help establish the climate necessary to support such traditional change elements as honesty, openness, collaboration, and participation. There is no doubt that these elements are value laden. To the extent that political activism replaces these traditional elements with a conscious restriction of openness and a limitation of both collaboration and participation, it is replacing the valued ends of OD for the means to reach some other set of objectives. Thus OD must consider, for example, if political resistance is a form of participation to be confronted and worked through or confronted and wiped out for some vision of what ought to be. In so considering, OD must consider as well whether it will still value the welfare of individuals, even those frightened enough to resist.

On the Value of Conserving OD Values. If OD itself is to remain dynamic, the profession must constantly undergo changes to meet the challenges it faces. To the extent that OD values have promoted political naiveté within the profession, they may need to change to guide action in the political arena. It should be recognized, however, that the value base has served OD well in the past. If some values are to change, perhaps this would be best accomplished conservatively with the objective of *guiding* political involvement to reach *clinical ends.* Certainly traditional values should not be casually tossed aside to allow for politically expedient behaviors.

Concluding Remarks

We have focused on an important aspect of the growing field of organization development—its movement into the study and use of organizational politics. The present political orientations in the field, largely operationalized by OD consultants themselves, have been generally ignored and in some cases rejected. One purpose of the foregoing discussion has been to establish, as clearly as possible, the existence of these orientations. Broader recognition of OD's political orientations and the further development of political knowledge and skills can aid both the OD consultant and the field.

Political involvement is not, however, without its problems, and our second purpose has been to explore some of the utilitarian and value problems that can arise from increased political intervention. By exploring OD's present political orientation and

its future political alternatives, we obtain a more complete understanding of the roles, skills, and strategies available to the OD consultant. This understanding, in turn, can only enhance the field.

References

Beer, M. On gaining influence and power for OD. *Journal of Applied Behavioral Science,* 1976, *12,* 45–51.

Benne, K., & Birnbaum, M. Principles of changing. In W. G. Bennis, K. Benne, & R. Chin (Eds.), *The planning of change.* New York: Holt, Rinehart & Winston, 1969.

Bennis, W. G. Unresolved problems facing organization development. *Business Quarterly,* 1969, *34*(4), 80–84.

Burke, W. W. Organization development in transition. *Journal of Applied Behavioral Science,* 1976, *12,* 22–43.

Burns, T., & Stalker, G. M. *The management of innovation.* London: Tavistock, 1961.

Cobb, A. T. *Political planning and organizational innovation.* Paper presented at the annual meeting of the Academy of Management, Orlando, Florida, August 1977.

Cyert, R. M., & March, J. G. *A behavioral theory of the firm.* Engelwood Cliffs, N.J.: Prentice-Hall, 1964.

French, W., Bell, C., & Zawacki, R. Mapping the territory. In W. French, C. Bell, & R. Zawacki (Eds.), *Organization development: Theory, practice, and research.* Plano, Tex.: Business Publications, 1978, 5–12.

Friedlander, F. OD reaches adolescence: An exploration of its underlying values. *Journal of Applied Behavioral Science,* 1976, *12,* 7–22.

Friedlander, F., & Brown, L. D. Organization development. In M. Rosenzweig & L. Porter (Eds.), *Annual review of psychology.* Palo Alto, Calif.,: Annual Reviews, 1974, 313–41.

Guest, R., Hersey, P., & Blanchard, D. *Organizational change through effective leadership.* Englewood Cliffs, N.J.: Prentice-Hall, 1977.

Harrison, R. When power conflicts trigger team spirit. In W. French, C. Bell, & R. Zawacki (Eds.), 1978, 158–64.

Huse, E. F. *Organization development and change.* New York: West, 1980.

Lawrence, P., & Lorsch, J. *Organization and environment.* Boston: Harvard University Graduate School of Business Administration, 1967.

Leavitt, H. J. Applied organizational change in industry: Structural, technological, and humanistic approaches. In J. G. March (Ed.), *Handbook of organizations.* Skokie, Ill.: Rand McNally, 1965, 1144–1170.

Lewin, K., Lippitt, R., & White, R. Patterns of aggressive behavior in experimentally created "social climates." *Journal of Social Psychology,* 1939, *10,* 271–99.

Likert, R. *New patterns of management.* New York: McGraw-Hill, 1961.

Likert, R. *The human organization: Its management and value.* New York: McGraw-Hill, 1967.

MacCrimmon, K., & Taylor, R. N. Decision making and problem solving. In M. Dunnette (Ed.), *Handbook of industrial and organizational psychology.* Skokie, Ill.: Rand McNally, 1976, 1397–453.

March, J. G. The business firm as a political coalition. *Journal of Politics,* 1962, *24,* 662–78.

March, J. G., & Simon, H. *Organizations.* New York: John Wiley & Sons, 1958.

Margulies, N., & Raia, A. P. *Conceptual foundations of organizational development.* New York: McGraw-Hill, 1978.

Mayes, B. T., & Allen, R. Toward a definition of organizational politics. *Academy of Management Review,* 1977, *2,* 672–78.

McGregor, D. *The human side of enterprise.* New York: McGraw-Hill, 1960.

National Training Laboratories Institute. *1980 programs.* Arlington, Va.: NTL Institute, 1980.

Perrow, C. The short and glorious history of organizational theory. In H. Tosi & W. C. Hamner (Eds.), *Organizational behavior and management.* Chicago: St. Clair, 1977, 8–19.

Pettigrew, A. M. Toward a political theory of organizational intervention. *Human Relations,* 1975, *28,* 191–208.

Schein, E. *Organizational psychology.* Englewood Cliffs, N.J.: Prentice-Hall, 1972.

Schein, V. Political strategies for implementing changes. *Group & Organization Studies,* 1977, *2,* 42–48.

Selznick, P. *TVA and the grass roots.* Berkeley: University of California Press, 1949.

Strauss, G. Some notes on power equalization. In H. J. Leavitt (Ed.), *The social science of organizations.* Englewood Cliffs, N.J.: Prentice-Hall, 1963.

Thompson, J. D. *Organizations in action.* New York: McGraw-Hill, 1967.

Reading 45

THE POLITICS OF OD

Michael Beer

Staff groups usually develop power in organizations by obtaining the support of top management. This usually means supporting them with services that they require and see as crucial. Often it means avoiding head-on confrontations with their core values and beliefs. The OD group cannot follow this model if it is to be trusted by multiple constituencies and maintain a systems perspective. The problem then is how to achieve neutrality and independence, even with respect to top management, while developing enough power to be effective and survive.

Since it cannot rely on top management or any other constituency for its only source of power, an OD group must develop additional sources of power. This can be done by developing credibility based on competence and ability to provide clients with help that *they* need and request. An OD group can do this by developing a reputation for serving system needs rather than being self-serving. Research by Pettigrew (1976) on how specialty staff groups gain influence and power suggests the following six sources of power an OD group can consciously develop:

1. *Competence*. The first and foremost source of influence for the OD group is their own competence and effectiveness. They must be seen by the line organization, the union, or any other group of employees as professionally capable. This means that they are acknowledged experts in organization behavior and in the process and techniques of change agentry. But it also means that they must be interpersonally competent, and model effective ways of managing conflict—ways which they often encourage in their clients. The OD unit must also demonstrate competence as a group, operating efficiently internally and operating effectively in their relations with various parts of the organization. This means meeting deadlines, achieving goals, following up, keeping people informed, and so on.

2. *Political Access and Sensitivity*. The OD group can increase power by developing multiple relationships in the organization with key power figures (not only management, but union leaders, heads of minority groups, etc.). These relationships are informal and informally developed. They allow the change agents access to key individuals who know what is going on in the organization. Relationships with key power figures allow the change agents to determine what is important to them and gear their services to meet felt needs. Relationships also allow the OD group access to information about their reputation so they can detect early on any political activity aimed at reducing the influence of the group or eliminating it.

3. *Sponsorship*. Substantial research literature supports the general proposition that innovations (technological or managerial) are adopted at least in part because there is a strong and powerful sponsor in the organization who supports the innovation. In the product development area, these people have been called product champions. Organization development groups will gain power to the extent that they have sponsorship, preferably multiple sponsorship, in powerful places. This means vice presidents, presidents, or union leaders, respected elder statesmen, etc. For example, it is likely that Irving Bluestone's sponsorship (he is vice president of the United Auto Workers) of the

Source: Michael Beer, *Organization Changes and Development: A Systems View* (Santa Monica, Calif.: Goodyear Publishing, 1980), pp. 258–61.

Quality of Work projects at General Motors is an important source of power for the OD group. Multiple sponsors can be obtained by successfully completing OD projects in support of powerful people. Thus, past clients who are powerful become sponsors and some may even get more powerful as they move up in the organization. The key is not to rely on a single sponsor or power center (e.g., management).

4. *Stature and Credibility.* Power accrues to people and groups who develop a reputation for success and effectiveness. For the OD group, this stature must come first and foremost from line management's view that OD efforts have paid off. If key line managers spread the word that OD helped their organization to increase profits, reduce turnover, or in some other way improve effectiveness, stature and credibility are assured. Assuming they are capable of providing and delivering successful OD projects, OD groups can help themselves by encouraging their clients to communicate and spread the word. Organization development groups can also enhance their stature by developing a positive reputation in their professional community so that feedback comes back into the organization from other sources. This secondary strategy must be carefully managed so that the group does not become viewed as so ''professionally'' oriented that they are seen as unconcerned with the organization's primary goals.

5. *Resource Management.* Power accrues to those who control resources. If OD groups can deliver services to clients when they need to solve problems, they enhance their influence and reinforce interest in OD. Flexibility in assignment of OD specialists is one way to achieve this. A second way is to develop a pool of line and staff people in the organization who are capable of doing OD work, thus freeing the corporate OD group to shift their focus as new requests are made. A third way is for the OD group to bill their services to line managers. In this way the availability of change-agent resources is geared to the demands of clients rather than to an arbitrary budget of dollars or people. Resources would be added when a client is ready. This stance is also consistent with the idea

that change resources are likely to be most effective when the managers are motivated to use them. It is important to recognize, however, that this market strategy has downside risks because it makes the OD group more independent than some managements would like.

6. *Group Support.* Groups that are cohesive are more powerful. OD units that are able to work out internal differences, agree on common goals and strategies, share a philosophy of OD, and support each other are more likely to be effective. OD work involves a lot of stress and risk-taking. It becomes easier when there is an internal atmosphere of supportiveness. Furthermore, internal strife takes up energy that could be spent in task-related activities and in determining future direction. For this reason OD groups, like other specialist groups, need to spend a substantial amount of time in team-building activities. For this they may need an external OD consultant of their own. But this must not be done at the cost of bringing an OD group into conflict with other staff groups whose missions overlap with OD (e.g., personnel). A frequent problem of OD in many corporations has been conflict with the personnel function generated in part by the cohesion and arrogance which OD groups develop.

An OD group that tries to have a systems perspective is constantly balancing two relationships. It must maintain influence with multiple constituencies through the means just described. Unless the OD group can maintain its credibility, its effectiveness in serving the organization as a total system is reduced. When this happens, its capacity to generate enough influence to prevent its own destruction at the hands of a threatened constituency is diminished. On the other hand, the OD group must not allow the process of developing an independent and credible position to become so threatening to the power structure that the group is reduced in size or eliminated. This is likely to happen when top management feels the group has become too independent and systems-oriented and not enough management oriented. Political access and sensitivity, sponsorship by key members of the power structure, and direct services for members of the power structure are important means of avoiding this outcome.

The essence of this complex political process is simultaneous maintenance of independence from the power structure and the development of dependence by the power structure on the OD group's services. This is a function of both political skill and luck. For example, hard financial times can occur just when the OD group is developing its power base but has not yet attained it. Or sponsorship can be withdrawn for reasons beyond the group's control. However, a combination of competence, political access, and multiple sponsorship can reduce the probability that the occurrence of these events will eliminate the OD group.

Reading 46

THE POWER GAME AND THE PLAYERS

Henry Mintzberg

The core of this book is devoted to the discussion of a theory of organizational power. It is built on the premise that organizational behavior is a power game in which various players, called *influencers,* seek to control the organization's decisions and actions. The organization first comes into being when an initial group of influencers join together to pursue a common mission. Other influencers are subsequently attracted to the organization as a vehicle for satisfying some of their needs. Since the needs of influencers vary, each tries to use his or her own levers of power—*means* or *systems of influence*—to control decisions and actions. How they succeed determines what configuration of organizational power emerges. Thus, to understand the behavior of the organization, it is necessary to understand which influencers are present, what needs each seeks to fulfill in the organization, and how each is able to exercise power to fulfill them.

Of course, much more than power determines what an organization does. But our perspective in this book is that power is what matters, and that, if you like, everyone exhibits a lust for power (an assumption, by the way, that I do not personally favor, but that proves useful for the purposes of this book). When our conclusions here are coupled with those of the first book in this series, *The Structuring of Organizations* (Mintzberg 1979 which will subsequently be referred to as the *Structuring* book), a more complete picture of the behavior of organizations emerges.

The Exercise of Power

Hirschman (1970) notes in a small but provocative book entitled *Exit, Voice, and Loyalty,* that the participant in any system has three basic options:

- To stay and contribute as expected, which Hirschman calls *loyalty* (in the vernacular, "Shut up and deal")
- To leave, which Hirschman calls *exit* ("Take my marbles and go")
- To stay and try to change the system, which Hirschman refers to as *voice* ("I'd rather fight than switch")

Should he or she choose voice, the participant becomes what we call an influencer.[1] Those who exit—such as the client who stops buying or the employee who seeks work elsewhere—cease to be influencers, while those who choose loyalty over voice—the client who buys without question at the going rate, the employees who do whatever they are told quietly—choose not to participate as active influencers (other than to support implicitly the existing power structure).

To resort to voice, rather than exit, is for the customer or member to make an attempt at changing the practices, policies, and outputs of the firm from which one buys or of the organization to which one belongs. Voice is here defined as any attempt at all to change, rather than to escape from,

---

[1]Some writers call the influencer a "stakeholder," since he or she maintains a stake in the organization the way a shareholder maintains shares. Others use the term "claimant," in that he or she has a claim on the organization's benefits. Both these terms, however, would include those who express loyalty as well as voice.

Source: Henry Mintzberg, *Power in and around Organizations,* (Englewood Cliffs, N.J.: Prentice-Hall), © 1983, pp. 22–30. Reprinted with permission of the publisher.

an objectionable state of affairs. . .(Hirschman 1970, p. 30)[2]

For those who stay and fight, what gives power to their voice? Essentially **the influencer requires (1) some source or basis of power, coupled with (2) the expenditure of energy in a (3) politically skillful way when necessary.** These are the three basic conditions for the exercise of power. In Allison's concise words, ''Power . . . is an elusive blend of . . . bargaining advantages, skill and will in using bargaining advantages. . .'' (1971, p. 168).

The General Bases of Power

In the most basic sense, the power of the individual in or over the organization reflects some *dependency* that it has—some gap in its own power as a system, in Crozier's view, an ''uncertainty'' that the organization faces (Crozier 1964; also Crozier and Friedberg 1977). This is especially true of three of the five bases of power we describe here.[3] **Three prime bases of power are control of (1) a resource, (2) a technical skill, or (3) a body of knowledge, any one critical to the organization.** For example, a monopolist may control the raw material supply to an organization, while an expert may control the repair of important and highly complex machinery. To serve as a basis of power, a resource, skill or body of knowledge must first of all be *essential* to the functioning of the organization. Second, it must be *concentrated,* in short supply or else in the hands of one person or a small number of people who cooperate to some extent. And third it must be *nonsubstitutable,* in other words irreplaceable. These three characteristics create the dependency— the organization needs something, and it can get it only from the few people who have it.

A fourth general basis of power stems from legal prerogatives—exclusive rights or privileges to impose choices. Society, through its governments and judicial system, creates a whole set of legal prerogatives which grant power—*formal* power—to various influencers. In the first place, governments reserve for themselves the power to authorize the creation of the organization and thereafter impose regulations of various sorts on it. They also vest owners and/or the directors of the organization with certain powers, usually including the right to hire and fire the top executives. And these executives, in turn, usually have the power to hire and perhaps fire the rest of the employees, and to issue orders to them, tempered by other legal prerogatives which grant power to employees and their associations.

The fifth general basis of power derives simply from access to those who can rely on the other four. That access may be personal. For example, the spouses and friends of government regulators and of chief executives have power by virtue of having the ear of those who exercise legal prerogatives. The control of an important constituency which itself has influence—the customers who buy or the accountants who control costs—can also be an important basis for power. Likewise power flows to those who can sway other influencers through the mass media—newspaper editors, TV commentators, and the like.

Sometimes access stems from favors traded: Friends and partners grant each other influence over their respective activities. In this case, power stems not from dependency but from *reciprocity*, the gaining of power in one sphere by the giving up of power in another. As we shall see in many examples in this

---

[2]There are some interesting linkages among these three options, as Hirschman points out. Exit is sometimes a last resort for frustrated voice, or in the case of a strike (temporary exit), a means to supplement voice. The effect of exit can be ''galvanizing'' when voice is the norm, or vice versa, as in the case of Ralph Nader who showed consumers how to use voice instead of exit against the automobile companies (p. 125). Of course, an inability to exit forces the disgruntled individual to turn to voice. Hirschman also makes the intriguing point that exit belongs to the study of economics, voice to that of political science. In economic theory, the customer or employee dissatisfied with one firm is supposed to shift to another: ''. . . one either exits or one does not; it is impersonal'' (p. 15). In contrast, voice is ''a far more 'messy' concept because it can be graduated, all the way from faint grumbling to violent protest . . . voice is political action par excellence'' (p. 16). But students of political science also have a ''blind spot'': ''. . . exit has often been branded as *criminal,* for it has been labelled desertion, defection, and treason'' (p. 17).

[3]Related discussions of bases of power can be found in Allison (1971), Crozier and Friedberg (1977), Jacobs (1974), Kipnis (1974), Mechanic (1962), and Pfeffer and Salancik (1978).

book, the organizational power game is characterized as much by reciprocal as by dependency—one-sided, or "asymmetrical"—relationships.[4]

Will and Skill

But having a basis for power is not enough. The individual must act in order to become an influencer, he or she must expend energy, use the basis for power. When the basis is formal, little effort would seem to be required to use it. But many a government has passed legislation that has never been respected, in many cases because it did not bother to establish an agency strong enough to enforce it. Likewise managers often find that their power to give orders means little when not backed up by the effort to ensure that these are in fact carried out. On the other hand, when the basis of power is informal, much effort would seem to be required to use it. If orders cannot be given, battles will have to be won. Yet here too, sometimes the reverse is true. In universities, for example, power often flows to those who take the trouble to serve on the committees. As two researchers noted in one study: "Since few people were involved and those who were involved wandered in and out, someone who was willing to spend time being present could often become influential" (March and Romelaer 1976, p. 272). In the game of power, it is often the squeaky wheel that gets the grease.

In effect, the requirement that energy be expended to achieve outcomes, and the fact that those with the important bases of power have only so much personal energy to expend, means that power gets distributed more widely than our discussion of the bases of power would suggest. Thus, one

article shows how the attendants in a mental hospital, at the bottom of the formal hierarchy, could block policy initiatives from the top because collectively they were willing and able to exert far more effort than could the administrators and doctors (Scheff 1961, discussed at greater length in Chapter 13). What this means is that influencers pick and choose their issues, concentrating their efforts on the ones most important to them, and, of course, those they think they can win. Thus Patchen (1974) finds that each influencer stakes out those areas that affect him or her most, deferring elsewhere to other influencers.

Finally, the influencer must not only have some basis for power and expend some energy, but often he or she must also do it in a clever manner, with political skill. Much informal and even formal power backed by great effort has come to naught because of political ineptness. Managers, by exploiting those over whom they have formal power, have often provoked resistance and even mutiny; experts regularly lose reasonable issues in meetings because they fail to marshall adequate support. Political skill means the ability to use the bases of power effectively—to convince those to whom one has access, to use one's resources, information, and technical skills to their fullest in bargaining, to exercise formal power with a sensitivity to the feelings of others, to know where to concentrate one's energies, to sense what is possible, to organize the necessary alliances.

Related to political skill is a set of intrinsic leadership characteristics—charm, physical strength, attractiveness, what Kipnis calls "personal resources" (1974, p. 88). *Charisma* is the label for that mystical quality that attracts followers to an individual. Some people become powerful simply because others support them; the followers pledge loyalty to a single voice.

Thus power derives from some basis for it coupled with the efforts and the abilities to use the basis. We shall assume this in the rest of the book, and look more concretely at the channels through which power is exercised, what we call the *means* and *the systems of influence*—the specific instruments influencers are able to use to effect outcomes.

---

[4]French and Raven's (1959) five categories of power, as perhaps the most widely quoted typology of power, should be related to these five bases of power. Their "reward" and "coercive" power are used formally by those with legal prerogatives and may be used informally by those who control critical resources, skills, or knowledge (for example, to coerce by holding these back). Their "legitimate" power corresponds most closely to our legal prerogatives and their "expert" power to our critical skills and knowledge. Their fifth category, "referent" power, is discussed below in our section on political skill.

The Cast of Players in Order of Appearance

Who are these influencers to whom we have referred? We can first distinguish *internal* from *external* influencers. **The internal influencers are the full-time employees who use voice, those people charged with making the decision and taking the actions on a permanent, regular basis; it is they who determine the outcomes, which express the goals pursued by the organization. The external influencers are nonemployees who use their bases of influence to try to affect the behavior of the employees.**[5] The first two sections of our theory, on the elements of power, describe respectively the *External Coalition,* formed by the external influencers, and the *Internal Coalition,* formed by the internal influencers.

(As the word *coalition* was retained in this book only after a good deal of consideration, it is worth explaining here why it was chosen. In general, an attempt was made to avoid jargon whenever it was felt to be possible—for example, employing "chief executive officer" instead of "peak coordinator." "Coalition" proved to be a necessary exception. Because there are no common labels—popular or otherwise—to distinguish the power in from that around the organization, one had to be selected. But why "coalition"? Because it seems to fit best, even though it may be misleading to the reader at first. The word coalition is normally used for a group of people who band together to win some issue. As the Hickson research team at the University of Bradford notes, it has the connotation of "engineered agreements and alliances" (Astley et al. 1980, p. 21). Ostensibly, we are not using the word in this sense, at least not at first. We use it more in the sense that Cyert and March (1963) introduced it, as a set of people who bargain among themselves to determine a certain distribution of organizational power. But as we proceed in our discussion, the reader will find the two meanings growing increasingly similar. For one thing, in the External or Internal Coalition, the various influencers band together around or within the same organization to satisfy their needs. They do form some sort of "coalition." As Hickson et al. note in an earlier publication, "it is their coalition of interests that sustains (or destroys) [the] organization" (1976, p. 9).[6] More importantly, we shall see that the external and internal influencers each typically form rather stable systems of power, usually focussed in nature. These become semipermanent means to distribute benefits, and so resemble coalitions in the usual meaning of the term.)

Our power play includes ten groups of possible influencers, listed below in order of appearance. The first four are found in the External Coalition:

- First are the *owners,* who hold legal title to the organization. Some of them perhaps conceived the idea of founding the organization in the first place and served as brokers to bring the initial influencers together.
- Second are the *associates,* the suppliers of the organization's input resources, the clients for its output products and services, as well as its trading partners and competitors. It should be noted that only those associates who resort to voice— for example, who engage in contacts of other than a purely economic nature—are counted as influencers in the External Coalition.
- Third are the *employee associations,* that is, unions and professional associations. Again these are included as influencers to the extent that they seek to influence the organization in other than purely

---

[5]As we shall soon see, there are some circumstances in which external influencers can impose decisions directly on the organization, and others in which full-time employees acting in concert through their associations behave as external influencers by trying to affect the behavior of the senior managers. As Pfeffer and Salancik (1978, p. 30) point out, actors can be part of the organization as well its environment. Nevertheless, the distinction between full-time employees—those individuals with an intensive and regular commitment to the organization—and others will prove to be a useful and important one in all that follows.

---

[6]It might be noted that the Hickson group in the 1980 publication cited earlier (as Astley et al.) decided to replace the word "coalition" by "constellation." That was tried in this book, but dropped as not having quite the right ring to it.

economic ways, that is, to use voice to affect decisions and actions directly. Such employee associations see themselves as representatives of more than simple suppliers of labor resources. Note that employee associations are themselves considered *external* influencers, even though they represent people who can be internal influencers. Acting collectively, through their representatives, the employees choose to exert their influence on the organization from outside of its regular decision-making and action-taking channels, much as do owners and clients. (Singly, or even collectively but in different ways, the employees can of course bring their influence to bear directly on these processes, as internal influencers. Later we shall in fact see that it is typically their impotence in the Internal Coalition that causes them to act collectively in the External Coalition.)

• A fourth category comprises the organization's various *publics,* groups representing special or general interests of the public at large. We can divide these into three: (1) such general groups as families, opinion leaders, and the like; (2) special interest groups such as conservation movements or local community institutions; and (3) government in all of its forms—national, regional, local, departments and ministries, regulatory agencies, and so on.

• Another group of influencers, which is really made up of representatives from among the other four, as well as from the internal influencers, are the *directors* of the organization. These constitute a kind of "formal coalition." This group stands at the interface of the External and Internal Coalitions, but because it meets only intermittently, and for other reasons we shall discuss in Chapter 6, it is treated as part of the External Coalition.

The Internal Coalition comprises six groups of influencers:

• First is the top or general management of the organization, Papandreou's peak coordinator. We shall refer to this by the single individual at the top of the hierarchy of authority, in standard American terminology, the *chief executive officer,* or CEO.[7]

• Second are the *operators,* those workers who actually produce the products and services, or who provide the direct support to them, such as the machine operators in the manufacturing plant or the doctors and nurses in the hospital.

• Third are the managers who stand in the hierarchy of line authority from the CEO down to the first-line supervisors to whom the operators formally report. We shall refer to these simply as the *line managers*.

• Fourth are the *analysts of the technostructure,* those staff specialists who concern themselves with the design and operation of the systems for planning and for formal control, people such as work study analysts, cost accountants, and long-range planners.

• Fifth is the *support staff,* comprising those staff specialists who provide indirect support to the operators and the rest of the organization, in a business firm, for example, the mailroom staff, the chef in the cafeteria, the researchers, the public relation officers, and the legal counsel.[8]

• Finally, there is an eleventh actor in the organizational power system, one that is technically inanimate but in fact shows every indication of having a life of its own, namely the *ideology* of the organization—the set of beliefs shared by its internal influencers that distinguishes it from other organizations.

Figure 1 shows the position of each of these eleven groups schematically. The Internal Coalition is shown in the center, with the Chief Executive Officer at the top, followed, according to the formal hierarchy of authority, by the line managers and then the operators. (In some parts of the discussion,

---

[7]An alternate term which appears frequently in the more recent literature is "dominant coalition." But we have no wish to prejudice the discussion of the power of one of our groups of influencers by the choice of its title.

[8]For a more elaborate description of each of these five groups as well as clarification of the differences between technocratic and support staff and of line and staff in general, see Chapter 2 of the *Structuring* book.

FIGURE 1   The Cast of Players

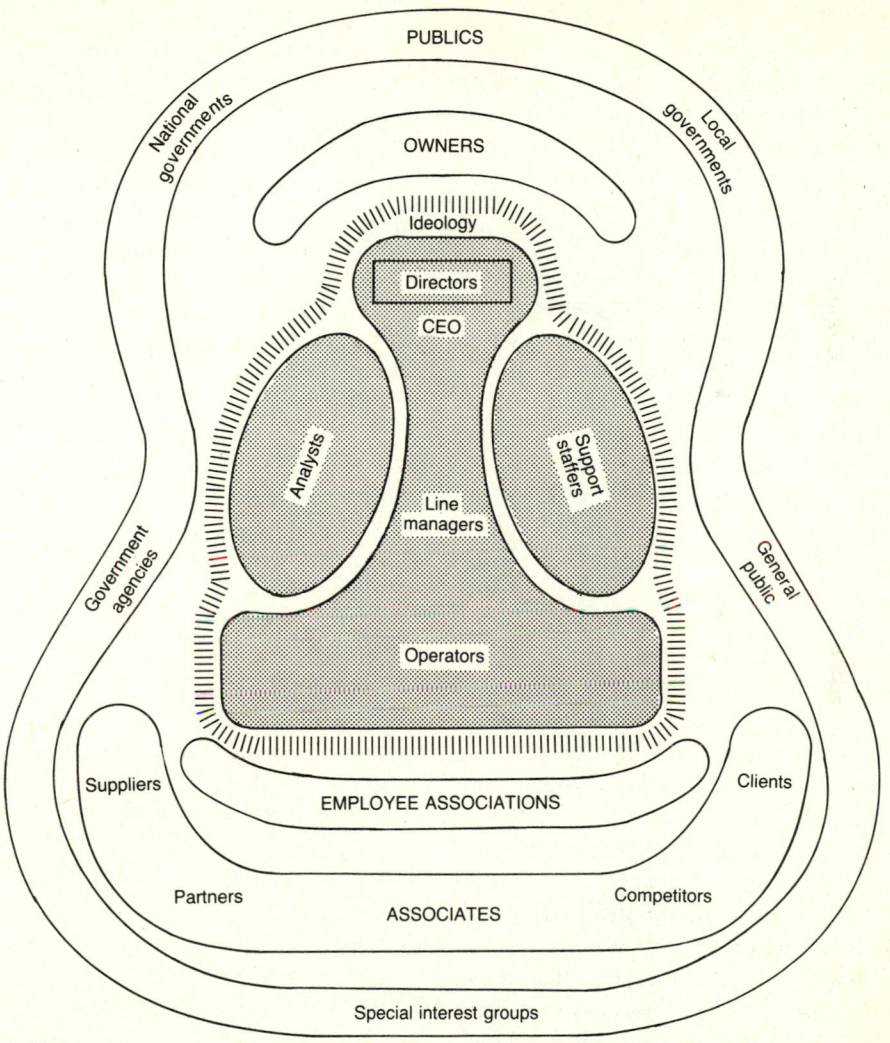

we shall accept these notions of formal authority, in others, we shall not. For now, we retain them.) Shown at either side to represent their roles as staff members are the analysts and the support staff. Above the CEO is shown the board of directors to which the CEO formally reports. And emanating from the organization is a kind of aura to represent its ideology. Surrounding all this are the various groups of the External Coalition. The owners are shown closest to the top of the hierarchy, and to the board of directors, where they are often inclined to exert their influence. The associates are shown surrounding the operating core where the operators work, the suppliers on the left (input) side and the clients on the right (output) side, with the partners and competitors in between. The employee associations are shown closest to the operators, whom they represent, while the various publics are shown to form a ring around the entire power system, in effect influencing every part of it. Thus the organization of Figure 1 can be seen to exist in a complex field of influencer forces.

Each of these eleven groups of players in the organizational power game will be discussed in turn, together with the means of influence they have at their disposal. We assume in this discussion that each is driven by the needs inherent in the roles they play. For example, owners will be described as owners, not as fathers, or Episcopalians, or power-hungry devils. People are of course driven by a variety of needs—by intrinsic values such as the need for control or autonomy, or in Maslow's (1954) needs hierarchy theory, by physiological, safety, love, esteem, and self-actualization needs; by the values instilled in them as children or developed later through socialization and various identifications; by the need to exploit fully whatever skills and abilities they happen to have; by their desire to avoid repetition of painful experiences or to repeat successful ones; by opportunism, the drive to exploit whatever opportunities happen to present themselves. All of these needs contribute to the makeup of each influencer and lead to an infinite variety of behaviors. All are, therefore, important to understand. But they are beyond the scope of this book. Here we focus on those behaviors that are dictated strictly by role. We assume throughout that each group discussed above is driven to gain power in or over the organization—in other words, is an influencer; our discussion then focusses on what ends each seeks to attain, what means or systems of influence each has at its disposal, and how much power each tends to end up with by virtue of the role it plays in the power coalition to which it happens to belong. This is the point of departure for the discussion of our theory.

References

Allison, G. T. *Essence of Decision: Explaining the Cuban Missile Crisis.* Boston: Little, Brown, 1971.

Astley, W. G.; R. Axelsson; R. J. Butler; D. J. Hickson; and D. C. Wilson. ''Decision Making: Theory III.'' Working Paper, University of Bradford Management Centre, 1980.

Crozier, M. *The Bureaucratic Phenomenon.* Chicago: University of Chicago Press, 1964.

Crozier, M., and E. Friedberg. *L'acteur et le Système.* Paris: Editions du Seuil, 1977.

Cyert, R. M., and J. G. March. *A Behavioral Theory of the Firm.* Englewood Cliffs, N. J.: Prentice-Hall, 1963.

French, J. R. P., Jr., and B. Raven. ''The Bases of Social Power.'' In *Studies in Social Power,* ed. D. Cartwright, pp. 150–67. Ann Arbor: Institute for Social Research, University of Michigan, 1959.

Hickson, D. J.; R. J. Butler; R. Axelsson; and D. Wilson. ''Decisive Coalitions.'' Paper presented to International Conference on Coordination and Control of Group and Organizational Performance, Munich, West Germany, 1976.

Hirschman, A. O. *Exit, Voice, and Loyalty: Responses to Decline in Firms, Organizations, and States.* Cambridge, Mass.: Harvard University Press, 1970.

Jacobs, D. ''Dependency and Vulnerability: An Exchange Approach to the Control of Organizations.'' *Administrative Science Quarterly,* 1974, pp. 45–59.

Kipnis, D. ''The Powerholder.'' In *Perspectives on Social Power,* ed. J. T. Tedeschi, pp. 82–122. Chicago: Aldine, 1974.

March, J. G., and P. J. Romelaer. ''Position and Presence in the Drift of Organizations.'' In *Ambiguity and Choice in Organizations,* eds. J. G. March and J. P. Olsen. Bergen, Norway: Universitetsforlaget, 1976.

Maslow, A. H. *Motivation and Personality.* New York: Harper & Row, 1954.

Mechanic, D. ''Sources of Power of Lower Participants in Complex Organizations,'' *Administrative Science Quarterly,* 1962, pp. 349–64.

Mintzberg, H. *The Structuring of Organizations: A Synthesis of the Research.* Englewood Cliffs, N. J.: Prentice-Hall, 1979.

Patchen, M. ''The Locus and Basis of Influences on Organizational Decisions.'' *Organizational Behavior and Human Performance,* 1974, pp. 195–221.

Pfeffer, J., and G. R. Salancik. ''Organizational Decision Making as a Political Process: The Case of a University Budget.'' *Administrative Science Quarterly,* 1974, pp. 135–51.

Scheff, T. J. ''Control over Policy by Attendants in a Mental Hospital.'' *Journal of Health and Human Behavior,* 1961, pp. 93–105.

Organization and Implementation of the OD Process

This section of seven essays plus a checklist focuses on the organization, implementation, and tracking of the OD process. Broadly, it looks at (*a*) effective consultant behavior, and (*b*) managing the OD process.

The dimensions covered in Part 7 are crucial to the effective implementation of an OD effort. OD techniques are important, but they are of no more importance than the kinds of behavior the consultant displays as a person, day in and day out, in contact with clients. Nor is a given technique more important than the context in which it occurs. Techniques, behavior, and context—all are important in an OD effort.

While effective consultant behavior needs to be managed in the sense that consultants who are effective need to be selected, and individual consultants must conscientiously practice the best they know how, the *context* or environment in which the consultant intervenes needs to be carefully shepherded. While the consultant facilitating a team-building session needs to have good group and interpersonal skills, the consultant who is advising (perhaps the same person) on the management of the overall OD effort also needs to have extensive insight into the management of change efforts in complex systems. He or she needs to be aware of the critical "make or break" dimensions involved; for example, the ability of the internal consultant to be a trusted "broker" in bringing together two people or two groups who are in conflict. Knowledge about such make-or-break dimensions is fragmentary, but is evolving. Critical aspects of the consultant's behavior and the context in which that behavior occurs, and suggestions for monitoring the unfolding OD process, are what this part of the book is about.

A. *Effective Consultant Behavior*

In this section, essay topics range from some practical guides for consultants to the question of how deep interventions should be in terms of the emotional involvement of the client participants to an analysis of what went wrong in an unsuccessful OD effort. All of the essays are written by consultants, each of whom has had many years of successful practice.

In the first essay, Walter Sikes presents seven practical principles of personal and organizational change. These are highly useful for consultants and managers.

The second essay, by Herbert Shepard, is an insightful, well-known selection that presents some "rules of thumb" for consultants. Issues of survival, initial entry, and building support are dealt with in this essay. Clearly, Shepard has in mind a model of organizational change which includes notions about complexity and interdependency in organizations; about the use of power; and about helping relationships, i.e., the need for empathy, participation and patience.

In the third essay, Marvin Weisbord provides some insights on the nature of the "contract" between consultant and client. He tells us the nature of the explicit agreements he attempts to develop with each client, and provides valuable information on how he handles the first meeting. He concludes the essay on when the contract should be ended.

In the fourth essay, Roger Harrison defines "depth of intervention" and provides some criteria for making professional judgments about this important matter. In the fifth and final essay, Wayne Boss and Mark McConkie present a case study of ineffective consultant behavior in a manufacturing organization. They present their case study on the assumption that OD theorists and practitioners can learn much—sometimes more—by studying OD failures as they can be studying their successes. After describing the intervention, they clearly state 15 contributing causes to the failure. They conclude their autopsy of an unsuccessful OD intervention with guidelines, or "object lessons," for the OD consultant. Their guidelines are both insightful and revealing.

Some of the themes pertaining to effective consultant behavior that we see in the essays in this section are as follows: (1) the need for self-awareness and self-understanding on the part of the consultant, (2) the need for the consultant to have cognitive maps (theories) for analyzing what is going on and what is functional and dysfunctional in the client system, and (3) the need to understand and conceptualize what the individuals in the client system are capable of learning from, in contrast to being hurt by or simply resisting.

But a great deal of what these authors are saying has to do with effective, almost intuitive behavior on the part of the consultant as he or she balances, mediates, or modifies any of a myriad of countervailing forces in the organization. And these forces can be political, intra- or interpersonal, intra- or intergroup, technological, economic, or having to do with subcultures within the organization.

One issue which is touched upon only lightly in the essays in this section, the issue of the degree to which a consultant should interpret resistance in a client group and press for working through the matter, warrants highlighting. Harrison states that the tendency to confront resistance emerged from individual psychoanalysis and psychotherapy, but that the conditions are usually so substantially different in the organizational context "that a good many potentially fruitful and mutually satisfying consulting relationships are terminated early because of the consultant's taking the role of overcomer of resistance to change rather than that of collaborator in the client's attempts at solving his problems." Jaques, on the other hand, in an essay not included here, takes the point of view—a point of view which has adherents in contemporary consulting practice—that interpretation of resistance is highly beneficial. He states: "Lewin has pointed out that participation in group decisions frequently overcomes individual resistances very rapidly. On the other hand, direct interpretation of the resistances, in terms of negative transference behavior toward the therapist, has probably more deep-rooted and lasting effects, if properly worked through."[1]

Who is right? The answer may lie in the areas of consultant preference, clinical expertise and training, and/or ego-strength of the practitioner. It may be that psychoanalytic training of the consultant is necessary for constructive use to be made of interpretation of resistances. Jaques, it should be noted, was a practicing psychoanalyst along with his industrial consulting and research practice.

---

[1]Elliot Jaques, "Social Therapy: Technocracy or Collaboration?" *Journal of Social Issues,* Spring 1947, pp. 64–66.

Reading 47

SOME PRINCIPLES OF PERSONAL AND ORGANIZATIONAL CHANGE

Walter Sikes

A few years ago, as I was flying to Memphis to lead a workshop on managing change, I decided to identify what I knew for sure about the principles of change. I could remember lots of research, theories, concepts, and provocative ideas, but they all seemed to be reducible to just four basic generalizations.

This disturbed me because I did not consider four points a sufficient output from a quarter of a century of work as a student and practitioner of change. I later shared my distress with Jack Linquist, who was presenting the workshop with me, and together we came up with three more generalizations—a thin, but possibly more respectable output.

This article presents these seven principles, which I consider the core of what is known about personal and organizational change. Although much more could be said about the various complex processes of change, I feel that the following points represent a good amalgam of the key concepts that persons dealing with change will find helpful.

1. *You Must Know What Something Is Before You Try to Change It.* Diagnosis is the key to effecting planned change. A change agent must have a sound, internalized understanding not only of the "facts," but also the feelings important to the change process. Thus, data collection and feedback are essential to initiating either personal or organizational change. A thorough understanding of the particular dynamics of a system that is to be

Source: Walter Sikes, reprinted from *Sunrise Seminars*.

changed will allow one to tailor the innovation to the specific situation—and greatly increase the chances for success. As Jack Linquist says, "plan for adaptation, not adoption."

2. *Because All Human Change Takes Place in Systems or Organic Units, You Cannot Change Just One Isolated Element.* Everything in a system is ultimately connected, so a change in one part affects the whole system. Therefore, one must understand the total impact of the proposed change on all parts of the system so as to reduce the chances of unwanted and unpredicted side effects.

Whether the system constitutes a large, complex organization or a single individual, the person(s) involved probably likes stability and predictability. Kurt Lewin's concept of a field of forces operating to maintain equilibrium presents an accurate image of the tendency of systems to oppose change. When people return from a T Group to their families or work groups, they typically encounter much resistance to their applying their brand-new skills and insights and much pressure to resume their old behaviors—even if those behaviors were dysfunctional. Partners in architectural firms find it almost impossible to change their functions without involving at least the entire group of partners—and often other members of the firm—in the change process. When designing change, assume that those involved will probably be reluctant to go along with the new ways of doing things.

3. *People Resist Punishment.* Change generally generates discomfort, requiring at the least that one use extra energy to adapt to a new situation. People tend to consider alterations in a system a form of punishment. Even changes that one considers desirable may entail some discomfort. For example, the families of alcoholics frequently become so programmed to deal with the problems of the addict that they resist making changes that would produce more functional behaviors.

We often have difficulty understanding why others consider change so punishing. A parent may wonder, ''What does my teenage son consider so painful about reading an additional half hour per day?'' Even the son may not be able to give a clear answer—but he knows it feels bad.

4. *People Are Reluctant to Undergo Temporary Discomfort for Long-Term Gain.* Learning a new skill, whether it is technical or behavioral, at the least causes one to undergo the pain of feeling incompetent for a time. We feel more comfortable using familiar behaviors and already-mastered skills, so we prefer to polish, refine, and rely on them rather than develop new, possibly better skills. Even people and organizations taking part in programs to facilitate change tend to depend on the skills developed beforehand and avoid moving into untried areas.

Typically, people will resist changing their lives even on the chance that they will be better off for doing so. When the prospect of future benefit is uncertain, one especially tends to hang onto the current way of doing things. Therefore, people entering a change effort must be provided with support and motivation during the ''painful'' early stages. They will also find it helpful to experience early rewards.

5. *Change Generates Stress.* Studies of the sources of stress have shown that any kind of change induces stress, which is a reaction of a system accommodating new conditions. Changes that we feel we cannot control are the most stressful. Therefore, to reduce the stress of the change process, those affected must, as much as possible, perceive that they can influence the process. They must also have access to devices like support groups that can help them manage their stress.

6. *Participation Reduces Resistance.* Probably no principle of social psychology has been studied or confirmed more fully than the concept that one may increase people's acceptance of an innovation by getting them involved in setting goals and devising strategies for achieving these goals.

Such participation, however, requires such preconditions as time in which to consult with those involved, a communications system that allows the parties to reach one another, and sufficient common purposes or values to allow potentially fruitful exchanges to occur. Moreover, those involved must be willing to invest time and energy in the participative process, and those with the most power must be willing to share at least some of that power. These conditions do not always prevail, but frequently they do, and they may often be generated in circumstances in which we assume they are absent. In any event, to the extent that those involved in a changing system can become involved in establishing where the system is going and how it will get there, the movement will occur less stressfully and will likely be more enduring.

7. *Behavioral Change Usually Comes in Small Steps.* Few individuals or organizations are willing or able to make dramatic, sweeping changes in a hurry. When we attempt to produce change in or by another—or ourselves—we usually seek to have it occur right away, especially if the one trying to induce the change has more power than the other. When a parent tells a child to stop bouncing on the bed, the parent means ''stop now.'' The child, however, will try to maintain its self-worth and take a few more bounces before stopping. When a boss tells an employee to change her or his way of doing things, the boss usually expects this to occur immediately—but the employee will need some time to make the adjustments requested. This expectation even prevails in T Groups. Despite all of the rules regarding feedback, when a group member expresses a negative reaction to another's behavior, it is usually said in the hope that the behavior will never occur again. Realistically, however, we must realize that abrupt changes in behavior are rare— and probably even unhealthy—and that we must allow adequate time for changes to take place.

These seven points do not represent everything one must know to be an effective change agent. But in my own efforts to bring about or support innovation, I have found that I am more likely to succeed if I can design the effort to take these principles into account.

Reading 48

RULES OF THUMB FOR CHANGE AGENTS

Herbert A. Shepard

The following aphorisms are not so much bits of advice (although they are stated that way) as things to think about when you are being a change agent, a consultant, an organization or community development practitioner—or when you are just being yourself trying to bring about something that involves other people.

Rule I: Stay Alive

This rule counsels against self-sacrifice on behalf of a cause that you do not wish to be your last.

Two exceptionally talented doctoral students came to the conclusion that the routines they had to go through to get their degrees were absurd, and decided they would be untrue to themselves to conform to an absurd system. That sort of reasoning is almost always self-destructive. Besides, their noble gesture in quitting would be unlikely to have any impact whatever on the system they were taking a stand against.

This is not to say that one should never take a stand, or a survival risk. But such risks should be taken as part of a purposeful strategy of change, and appropriately timed and targeted. When they are taken under such circumstances, one is very much alive.

But Rule I is much more than a survival rule. The rule means that you should let your whole being be involved in the undertaking. Since most of us have never been in touch with our whole beings, it means a lot of putting together of parts that have been divided, of using internal communications channels that have been closed or were never opened.

Staying alive means loving yourself. Self-disparagement leads to the suppression of potentials, to a win-lose formulation of the world, and to wasting life in defensive maneuvering.

Staying alive means staying in touch with your purpose. It means using your skills, your emotions, your labels and positions, rather than being used by them. It means not being trapped in other people's games. It means turning yourself on and off, rather than being dependent on the situation. It means choosing with a view to the consequences as well as the impulse. It means going with the flow even while swimming against it. It means living in several worlds without being swallowed up in any. It means seeing dilemmas as opportunities for creativity. It means greeting absurdity with laughter while trying to unscramble it. It means capturing the moment in the light of the future. It means seeing the environment through the eyes of your purpose.

Rule II: Start Where the System Is

This is such ancient wisdom that one might expect its meaning had been fully explored and apprehended. Yet in practice, the rule—and the system—are often violated.

The rule implies that one should begin by diagnosing the system. But systems do not necessarily *like* being diagnosed. Even the *term diagnosis*

Source: Herbert A. Shepard, ''Rules of Thumb for Change Agents,'' *Organization Development Practitioner*, November 1975, pp. 1–5. (Publication of the National OD Network 1011 Park Ave., Plainfield, N.J.)

may be offensive. And the system may be even less ready for someone who calls himself or herself a change agent. It is easy for the practitioner to forget that the use of jargon which prevents laymen from understanding the professional mysteries is a hostile act.

Starting where the system is can be called the Empathy Rule. To communicate effectively, to obtain a basis for building sound strategy, the change agent needs to understand how the client sees himself and his situation, and needs to understand the culture of the system. Establishing the required rapport does not mean that the change agent who wants to work in a traditional industrial setting should refrain from growing a beard. It does mean that, if he has a beard, the beard is likely to determine where the client is when they first meet, and the client's curiosity needs to be dealt with. Similarly, the rule does not mean that a female change agent in a male organization should try to act like one of the boys, or that a young change agent should try to act like a senior executive. One thing it does mean is that sometimes where the client is, is wondering where the change agent is.

Rarely is the client in any one place at any one time. That is, s/he may be ready to pursue any of several paths. The task is to walk together on the most promising path.

Even unwitting or accidental violations of that Empathy Rule can destroy the situation. I lost a client through two violations in one morning. The client group spent a consulting day at my home. They arrived early in the morning, before I had my empathy on. The senior member, seeing a picture of my son in the living room, said, "What do you do with boys with long hair?" I replied thoughtlessly, "I think he's handsome that way." The small chasm thus created between my client and me was widened and deepened later that morning when one of the family tortoises walked through the butter dish.

Sometimes starting where the client is, which sounds both ethically and technically virtuous, can lead to some ethically puzzling situations. Robert

Frost[1] described a situation in which a consultant was so empathic with a king who was unfit to rule that the king discovered his own unfitness and had himself shot, whereupon the consultant became king.

Empathy permits the development of a mutual attachment between client and consultant. The resulting relationship may be one in which their creativities are joined, a mutual growth relationship. But it can also become one in which the client becomes dependent and is manipulated by the consultant. The ethical issues are not associated with starting where the system is, but with how one moves with it.

Rule III: Never Work Uphill

This is a comprehensive rule, and a number of other rules are corollaries or examples of it. It is an appeal for an organic rather than a mechanistic approach to change, for a collaborative approach to change, for building strength and building on strength. It has a number of implications that bear on the choices the change agent makes about how to use him/herself, and it says something about life.

Corollary 1: Don't Build Hills as You Go

This corollary cautions against working in a way that builds resistance to movement in the direction you have chosen as desirable. For example, a program which has a favorable effect on one portion of a population may have the opposite effect on other portions of the population. Perhaps the commonest error of this kind has been in the employment of T-group training in organizations: turning on the participants and turning off the people who didn't attend, in one easy lesson.

---

[1]Robert Frost, "How Hard It Is to Keep from Being King When It's in You and in the Situation," *In The Clearing* (New York: Holt, Rinehart & Winston, 1962), pp. 74–84.

Corollary 2: Work in the Most Promising Arena

The physician-patient relationship is often regarded as analogous to the consultant-client relationship. The results for system change of this analogy can be unfortunate. For example, the organization development consultant is likely to be greeted with delight by executives who see in his specialty the solution to a hopeless situation in an outlying plant. Some organization development consultants have disappeared for years because of the irresistibility of such challenges. Others have whiled away their time trying to counteract the Peter Principle by shoring up incompetent managers.

Corollary 3: Build Resources

Don't do anything alone that could be accomplished more easily or more certainly by a team. Don Quixote is not the only change agent whose effectiveness was handicapped by ignoring this rule. The change agent's task is an heroic one, but the need to be a hero does not facilitate team building. As a result, many change agents lose effectiveness by becoming spread too thin. Effectiveness can be enhanced by investing in the development of partners.

Corollary 4: Don't Overorganize

The democratic ideology and theories of participative management that many change agents possess can sometimes interfere with common sense. A year or two ago I offered a course, to be taught by graduate students. The course was oversubscribed. It seemed that a data-based process for deciding whom to admit would be desirable, and that participation of the graduate students in the decision would also be desirable. So I sought data from the candidates about themselves, and xeroxed their responses for the graduate students. Then the graduate students and I held a series of meetings. Then the candidates were informed of the decision. In this way we wasted a great deal of time and everyone felt a little worse than if we had used an arbitrary decision rule.

Corollary 5: Don't Argue If You Can't Win

Win-lose strategies are to be avoided because they deepen conflict instead of resolving it. But the change agent should build her/his support constituency as large and deep and strong as possible so that s/he can continue to risk.

Corollary 6: Play God a Little

If the change agent doesn't make the critical value decisions, someone else will be happy to do so. Will a given situation contribute to your fulfillment? Are you creating a better world for yourself and others, or are you keeping a system in operation that should be allowed to die? For example, the public education system is a mess. Does that mean that the change agent is morally obligated to try to improve it, destroy it, or develop a substitute for it? No, not even if he or she knows how. But the change agent does need a value perspective for making choices like that.

Rule IV: Innovation Requires a Good Idea, Initiative, and a Few Friends

Little can be accomplished alone, and the effects of social and cultural forces on individual perception are so distorting that the change agent needs a partner, if only to maintain perspective and purpose.

The quality of the partner is as important as the quality of the idea. Like the change agent, partners must be relatively autonomous people. Persons who are authority-oriented—who need to rebel or need to submit—are not reliable partners: the rebels take the wrong risks and the good soldiers don't take any. And rarely do they command the respect and trust from others that is needed if an innovation is to be supported.

The partners need not be numerous. For example, the engineering staff of a chemical company designed a new process plant using edge-of-the-art technology. The design departed radically from the experience of top management, and they were about to reject it. The engineering chief suggested that the design be reviewed by a distinguished engineering professor. The principal designers were in fact former students of the professor. For this reason he accepted the assignment, charged the company a large fee for reviewing the design (which he did not trouble to examine), and told the management that it was brilliantly conceived and executed. By this means the engineers not only implemented their innovations, but also grew in the esteem of their management.

A change agent experienced in the Washington environment reports that he knows of only one case of successful interdepartmental collaboration in mutually designing, funding, and managing a joint project. It was accomplished through the collaboration of himself and three similarly-minded young men, one from each of four agencies. They were friends, and met weekly for lunch. They conceived the project, and planned strategies for implementing it. Each person undertook to interest and influence the relevant key people in his own agency. The four served one another as consultants and helpers in influencing opinion and bringing the decision makers together.

An alternative statement of Rule IV is as follows: Find the people who are ready and able to work, introduce them to one another, and work with them. Perhaps because many change agents have been trained in the helping professions, perhaps because we have all been trained to think bureaucratically, concepts like organization position, representativeness, or need are likely to guide the change agent's selection of those he or she works with.

A more powerful beginning can sometimes be made by finding those persons in the system whose values are congruent with those of the change agent, who possess vitality and imagination, who are willing to work overtime, and who are eager to learn. Such people are usually glad to have someone like the change agent join in getting something important accomplished, and a careful search is likely to turn up quite a few. In fact, there may be enough

of them to accomplish general system change, if they can team up in appropriate ways.

In building such teamwork the change agent's abilities will be fully challenged, as he joins them in establishing conditions for trust and creativity; dealing with their anxieties about being seen as subversive; enhancing their leadership, consulting, problem solving, diagnosing, and innovating skills; and developing appropriate group norms and policies.

Rule V: Load Experiments for Success

This sounds like counsel to avoid risk-taking. But the decision to experiment always entails risk. After that decision has been made, take all precautions.

The rule also sounds scientifically immoral. But whether an experiment produces the expected results depends upon the experimenter's depth of insight into the conditions and processes involved. Of course, what is experimental is what is new to the system; it may or may not be new to the change agent.

Build an umbrella over the experiment. A chemical process plant which was to be shut down because of the inefficiency of its operations undertook a union-management cooperation project to improve efficiency, which involved a modified form of profit sharing. Such plans were contrary to company policy, but the regional vice president was interested in the experiment, and successfully concealed it from his associates. The experiment was successful; the plant became profitable. But in this case, the umbrella turned out not to be big enough. The plant was shut down anyway.

Use the Hawthorne effect. Even poorly conceived experiments are often made to succeed when the participants feel ownership. And conversely, one of the obstacles to the spread of useful innovations is that the groups to which they are offered do not feel ownership of them.

For example, if the change agent hopes to use experience-based learning as part of his/her strategy, the first persons to be invited should be those who consistently turn all their experiences into constructive learning. Similarly, in introducing team development processes into a system, begin with the best-functioning team.

Maintain voluntarism. This is not easy to do in systems where invitations are understood to be commands, but nothing vital can be built on such motives as duty, obedience, security-seeking, or responsiveness to social pressure.

Rule VI: Light Many Fires

Not only does a large, monolithic development or change program have high visibility and other qualities of a good target, it also tends to prevent subsystems from feeling ownership of, and consequent commitment to the program.

The meaning of this rule is more orderly than the random prescription—light many fires—suggests. And part of a system is the way it is partly because of the way the rest of the system is. To work towards change in one subsystem is to become one more determinant of its performance. Not only is the change agent working uphill, but as soon as he turns his back, other forces in the system will press the subsystem back toward its previous performance mode.

If many interdependent subsystems are catalyzed and the change agent brings them together to facilitate one another's efforts, the entire system can begin to move.

Understanding patterns of interdependency among subsystems can lead to a strategy of fire-setting. For example, in public school systems it requires collaboration among politicians, administrators, teachers, parents, and students to bring about significant innovation, and active opposition on the part of only one of these groups to prevent it. In parochial school systems, on the other hand, collaboration between the administration and the church can provide a powerful impetus for change in the other groups.

Rule VII: Keep an Optimistic Bias

Our society grinds along with much polarization and cruelty, and even the helping professions compose their world of grim problems to be "worked through." The change agent is usually flooded with the destructive aspects of the situations he enters. People in most systems are impressed by one another's weaknesses, and stereotype each other with such incompetencies as they can discover.

This rule does not advise ignoring destructive forces. But its positive prescription is that the change agent be especially alert to the constructive forces which are often masked and suppressed in a problem-oriented, envious culture.

People have as great an innate capacity for joy as for resentment, but resentment causes them to overlook opportunities for joy. In a workshop for married couples, a husband and wife were discussing their sexual problem and how hard they were working to solve it. They were not making much progress, since they didn't realize that sex is not a problem, but an opportunity.

Individuals and groups locked in destructive kinds of conflict focus on their differences. The change agent's job is to help them discover and build on their commonalities, so that they will have a foundation of respect and trust which will permit them to use their differences as a source of creativity. The unhappy partners focus on past hurts and continue to destroy the present and future with them. The change agent's job is to help them change the present so that they will have a new past on which to create a better future.

Rule VIII: Capture the Moment

A good sense of relevance and timing is often treated as though it were a "gift" or "intuition" rather than something that can be learned, something spontaneous rather than something planned. The opposite is nearer the truth. One is more likely to "capture the moment" when everything one has learned is readily available.

Some years ago my wife and I were having a very destructive fight. Our nine-year-old daughter decided to intervene. She put her arms around her mother and asked: "What does Daddy do that bugs you?" She was an attentive audience for the next few minutes while my wife told her, ending in tears. She then put her arms around me: "What does Mommy do that bugs you?" and listed attentively to my response, which also ended in tears. She then went to the record player and put on a favorite love song ("If Ever I Should Leave You") and left us alone to make up.

The elements of my daughter's intervention had all been learned. They were available to her, and she combined them in a way that could make the moment better.

Perhaps it's our training in linear cause-and-effect thinking and the neglect of our capacities for imagery that makes us so often unable to see the multiple potential of the moment. Entering the sit-uation "blank" is not the answer. One needs to have as many frameworks for seeing and strategies for acting available as possible. But it's not enough to involve only one's head in the situation: one's heart has to get involved too. Cornelia Otis Skinner once said that the first law of the stage is to love your audience. You can love your audience only if you love yourself. If you have relatively full access to your organized experience, to yourself and to the situation, you will capture the moment more often.

Reading 49

THE ORGANIZATION DEVELOPMENT CONTRACT

Marvin Weisbord

In OD consulting, the contract is central to success or failure. Most other kinds of contracts—employment, service, research, etc.—focus heavily on content, that is, the nature of the work to be performed, the schedule, and the money to change hands. Generally, these issues are negotiated through a proposal, which one party writes and the other accepts or rejects. The consulting contract most people are familiar with takes two forms: (1) You hire me to study the problem and tell you what to do and (2) You hire me to solve the problem for you. I call these "expert" consulting contracts. In either case the quality of the advice and/or the solution is the focus, and the *consultant* is a central figure, whatever happens.

But in OD consulting, the *client* is the central figure. He hires me to consult with him while he is working on his problem, helping him to achieve a better diagnosis of what has happened and what steps he must take to improve things. This is a form of collaboration which, if successful, helps the client also to achieve better working relationships with others, for example peers, boss, and subordinates.

For that reason, in OD contracting, more so than other kinds, the *process* by which content issues are pinned down is critical. Unless this negotiation is a model of the consultant's values and problem-solving behavior, the contract, when it's tested, probably won't stand up. More about testing later.

Source: Marvin Weisbord, "The Organization Development Contract," *Organization Development Practitioner* 5, no. 2 (1973), pp. 1–4 (publication of the National OD Network, 1011 Park Ave., Plainfield, N.J.).

What do I mean by contract? I mean an explicit exchange of expectations, part dialogue, part written document, which clarifies for consultant and client three critical areas:

1. What each expects to get from the relationships.
2. How much time each will invest, when, and at what cost.
3. The ground rules under which the parties will operate.

What Each Expects

Clients expect, and have a right to expect, change for the better in a situation that is making their lives hard. This situation, as my clients experience it, has three main components:

1. Organizational crises: i.e., people leaving; excessive absenteeism; too high costs; too little budget; unmanageable environmental demands; pressure from above; conflict between individuals or work groups.

2. People problems; i.e., one or two or more "significant others" are singled out as particular sore spots.

3. Personal dilemma: i.e., whether this job, or this career, is what I really want.

The third component always grows in magnitude in direct proportion to the first two. Clients in a bind don't get much fun out of their work. They long for something simpler, better suited to their strengths, more consistent with their values. Above all, most clients long for outcomes. They want permanent "change" for the better, with no backsliding. I, on the other hand, see new outcomes as evidence the client is learning a better way of coping. From my point of view the *process*—gathering information, becoming aware of deeper meanings, making choices—is my most important product. While the client identifies three kinds of difficult situations he wants to work on, I keep in mind three levels of improvement he might achieve:

1. Solution of the immediate crisis—changing structures, policies, procedures, relationship.
2. Learning something about his own coping style—how he deals with crises, how he might do it better.
3. Learning a process for coping better, continually becoming aware and making choices, about whatever issue presents itself.

From my point of view, the existing problem is a vehicle for learning more about how to manage organizational life better. I have no preferences for the kinds of problems clients have. From my point of view, one issue will do as well as another.

However, clients rarely ask my direct help in cutting costs, reducing absenteeism, raising morale, or improving services. Instead, identifying me mainly with the ''people'' issue, they nearly always look for guidance in taking swift, painless, self-evidently correct actions toward the significant others who contribute to their misery. I always ask prospective clients to name what outcomes they hope to achieve by working with me.

> Want others to understand our goals better.
> Better communications, fewer misunderstandings.
> _____. will shape up or ship out.
> Better meetings—more excitement, more
> decisions made.

Notice that each of these statements is somewhat abstract, self-evidently ''good,'' and very hard to measure. I never accept such generalities as adequate statements of a client's expectations. Instead, I push hard on outcomes. What would you see happening that would tell you communications are improving? How will you know when goals are clearer, or morale has gone up? What will people

do? Will you be able to watch them do it? When I push at this level, I get more realistic statements:

> Pete will come to me with his gripes directly instead of going to Fred.
> Deadlines will be taken seriously and met more often.
> In meetings, decisions will be made, actions agreed upon, and names and dates put on them.
> I will understand how to set up the _____unit, and will have agreement on whatever way I decide.
> We will have a new procedure for handling customer complaints.
> I will make a decision whether to keep or fire
> _____.

These statements are good short-run indicators of change. They are realistic expectations. Are changes like these worth the client's investment of time and money? Is there enough in it for him to go ahead? It's important that he be clear he is choosing to do whatever we do together because it's worth it to him (and not because it's this year's panacea, or somebody else tried it and liked it, or because he thinks his problems will go away). What does he want personally out of this? Easier life? What does *that* mean? etc.

I expect some things too. Clients know I work mainly for money and want to be paid on time. However, I try also to indicate some of my secondary motives for working with them.

For example, I crave variety. I like learning about and using my skills in various ''content'' areas—manufacturing and service industries, medicine, law enforcement, public education. I like to try new technologies, to break new theoretical ground, to write and publish my experiences. The chance to do something new raises my incentive with any client. So does a client's ready acceptance of some responsibility for the crisis. If clients are well-motivated to work on their problems, so am I—and I tell them so. In doing this, I am trying to say that each of us has a right to some personal benefits from our relationship, apart from any benefits the organization may derive.

Structuring the Relationship: Time and Money

OD, like much of life, is carried forward by a sequence of meetings between people. The central decision in any contract discussion is which people should sit in what room for how long and for what purpose. At some point it is essential to name those people, pick dates, and set a budget. The client has a right to know how much time I will invest in interviewing, or survey sampling, or whatever, and how long our meetings will require. If I need time in between to organize data, I estimate how much. Often the initial contract is diagnostic, to be completed at a face-to-face meeting where the data will be examined, a common diagnosis arrived at, and next steps decided upon. Always, I work to clarify the costs, time and money, of each next step. Generally, this information will be written down.

In addition, there are some things I will and won't do, money aside. I know what these things are, and only mention them if the client does, on the premise that there's no point in solving a problem I don't have. For instance, I always turn down opportunities to work weekends. I'll work morning, noon, and night on any scheduled day if necessary. On weekends my contract is with my family. In addition, I have a strong value that *when* you work on your organization indicates how important you consider it. People get themselves into crises during the week. If they don't have time to get out during the week, they're never going to get out by working weekends. That makes me the wrong consultant for them. (Incidentally, I have never lost a client because of this policy.)

Ground Rules

Ground rules speak to the process of our relationship. Sometimes I write them down, sometimes not. In any case, I try to get an understanding that includes these explicit agreements:

1. I supply methods, techniques, theory, etc. to help you understand and work better on your problems. You supply energy, commitment, and share responsibility for success. I do *not* study your problems and recommend expert solutions.

2. Part of my job is to raise sticky issues and push you on them. You have a right to say no to anything you don't want to deal with. If you feel free to say no, I'll feel free to push.

3. Tell me if I do something puzzling or irritating, and give me permission to tell you the same.

4. I have no special preferences for how you deal with others. Part of my job is to make you aware of what you do, and what possible consequences your actions have for me and for the people around you. My job is also to preserve and encourage your freedom of choice about what, if anything, you should do.

5. My client is the whole organization. That means I intend not to be seen as an advocate for anybody's pet ideas, especially ones requiring your special expertise. However, I do advocate a certain process for problem solving, and recognize that some people oppose my process. I accept that risk.

6. Any information I collect and present will be anonymous. I will never attach names to anything people tell me. However, in certain situations (e.g., team building) I don't *want* confidential information, meaning anything which you are unwilling for other team members to know, even anonymously.

7. All data belongs to the people who supply it. I will never give or show it to anyone without their permission.

8. Either of us can terminate on 24 hours notice, regardless of contract length, so long as we have a face-to-face meeting first.

9. We evaluate all events together, face-to-face, and make explicit decisions about what to do next.

Contracting, like the seasons, is repetitive and continually renewable. If I have a long-term contract (e.g., four days a month for a year) I also have a separate contract for each meeting, which I present on a flipsheet and discuss at the outset. If I have a contract with a boss to help him build his team, I need to extend it to the team before we go to work. If I succeed with the team, and some members want to work with *their* teams, I need again to negotiate a new deal with the new people. Once, having worked with a team, I found the boss wanting to confront *his* boss. He wanted the whole team to do it with him, with me as consultant. I pointed out that that would require a temporary contract between me, him and his boss. He set up a dinner meeting—the night before the confrontation—and his boss and I made a one-day contract which stood up very well next morning.

In short, I'm never finished contracting. Each client meeting requires that I reexamine the contract. Does it cover everybody I'm working with? Is it clear what we're doing now? And why?

Moreover, contracting—while it deals ostensibly and mainly with content issues—has a process side crucial to its success. Consider, in some detail, where and how an OD contract is made.

OD contracts usually begin with a phone call or letter. Somebody has heard about what I did somewhere else. They wonder whether I can do it for (or with, or to) them. If I receive a letter, I respond with a phone call to the writer. If he calls first, I return his call at a time when I can spend 10 minutes or more discussing what he wants and whether or not it makes sense to meet. This initial contact is crucial to any contract. Each of us is trying—over the phone—to decide whether he likes the other well enough to proceed. I try not to prejudge the conversation. I want a face-to-face meeting *if* there's a chance of getting a solid contract. Here are some questions running through my mind:

1. How open is caller with me? Me with him?

2. Is the caller window-shopping, maybe calling several consultants to find the "best deal" (whatever that means)? Does he really want me? Perhaps—as is often the case—he doesn't know what he wants. If that's so, I have a good chance to consult with him on the phone, helping him clarify what he's after.

3. To which of his problems am I the solution? How does he name the issue?

4. What does he see as the solution? Is it a workshop? A meeting? A series of meetings? Magic?

5. Is his mind made up? Has he diagnosed his troubles and prescribed something already, which I'm to administer?

6. Does he have a budget? Is it adequate to his expectations? To mine? Is it likely to be worth my while to invest in a face-to-face meeting? I don't talk price on the phone, but do test whether a budget exists or could be got together. If the answer is no, I decide not to pursue it further.

7. Assume a budget, and willingness on his part and mine to go forward. We need a meeting. Should anybody else be there? Who? Is the caller in a position to enter into a contract? If not, who is? His boss? Can he make the meeting? Is there another consultant I want to involve? If so, I ask whether I can bring an associate.

I end the phone call by clarifying that each of us intends to explore further whether there is a fit between the kinds of things my potential client needs help on and the skills and experience I have. I am investing up to a day at no fee. (If there are travel expenses involved, I test whether he will pay those.) At the end of that day, each of us will know whether to go further.

First Meeting

I arrive, greet my prospective client, introduce myself and associate to him and his associates. We have coffee and exchange pleasantries. Each of us is deciding, silently, privately, and maybe unconsciously, how much we like the other. We look for cues. We give cues. Early on, we get down to business—or appear to. The content issues might include:

1. Our backgrounds—potential client needs to know enough about me to feel I can help, before he'll put out major problems.

2. Issues bothering client system—Are they symptomatic of other things, which are not being discussed. I always ask for examples in terms of observable behavior. "Communications" or "decision making" are not issues you can see, feel, or pin down. Who needs to talk to whom? Why?

What do they do now? What do people do when they disagree? What patterns of behavior do the people present see in the organization?

3. What changes would the people I'm talking to like to see? What things would they observe happening that would tell them they are getting desired outcomes? This step in naming outcomes is important in reducing the level of fantasy around OD and what it can do.

4. What first event would be appropriate to moving the system in the desired direction? Nearly always, this event should be diagnostic. It should be an activity which will heighten the awareness of the people I'm meeting with about how the issues they raise are seen by others in the system—colleagues, subordinates, customers, students, peers, etc. If the system is ready, the budget exists, and my reading of the willingness to proceed is good, I may propose a workshop activity, based on interviews. Sometimes I propose that the workshop start with interviews of each person as a first step in agenda building (okay if no more than 10 or 12 attend). Sometimes, it makes more sense to consult to a work group within the framework of their regular weekly or monthly meetings. Sometimes, a survey questionnaire provides a data base for a diagnostic meeting.

Whatever the event, we need a schedule, a place to meet, and a division of labor for organizing materials, sending out the agenda, etc. Sometimes these things can be decided in the first meeting. Sometimes I agree to write a formal proposal and proceed from there. Always I try to close on the next step—what I will do, what the client will do, and by what date.

The above considerations focus mainly on content. However, there are several process issues surrounding this meeting which I'm continually working on too:

1. First among these is, "Do I like this person?" If not a spark of fondness, or warmth, or empathy, then what *am* I feeling? Annoyance? Frustration? Wariness? Can I find *something* to like, respect, or admire about the other person? Usually, I can. Until

I do, however, and until the other person finds it in me, I think our work on issues, possible next steps, logistics, etc. is largely fictional. It is a way of using the task at hand to help us get greater clarity about our relationship. Any time I'm uncertain about a relationship I believe my contract is in jeopardy, no matter what fine words are spoken or written on paper. Each time the relationship question is resolved, a little spark jumps. I watch for it.

2. The client's depth of commitment is an issue for me. Does he really want to change things? Does he accept responsibility—at least a little bit—for the way things are? If he says, "I want you to change *them,*" and I say, "Okay, but how open are you to changing?", does he pull back, hem and haw? Or does he smile and admit the possibility? How open is he to understanding how what he does affects other people? My value about organizations improving themselves—that is, people learning to do things better with each other—is clear; I try to test how my client feels about that.

3. Part of client commitment is resources. Clients find money to do things they want to do. If money seems to be an insurmountable problem, I look to some other process issue—anxiety about failure, a boss who's negative about OD, fear of opening up "destructive issues," etc. Helping the client get in touch with these possibilities, if I can, is valuable for both of us, whether I work with him again or not. How to do it? By asking such questions as: What is the risk? What's the worst thing that could happen? How much exposure can you stand? I also ask what good things might happen, and whether the possible outcomes are worth the price.

In some ways OD is like playing the market. Every intervention is a calculated risk. There are no guarantees. The client will have problems no matter what he does. So will I. The question I continually confront is: Which problems would you *rather* have? The ones you have now? Or the ones you *will* have if you try to solve the ones you have now? Once in a while, potential clients decide they would rather live with what they've got. I support this insight. It's better that both of us know it sooner rather than later.

More often this process leads to greater clarity and commitment on both our parts to make an intervention successful. My value set goes something like this: I want to find out what's real, what the environment will support, what's possible in this relationship, and then learn how to live with it. Of course I want to sell my services. I want to try new interventions. More than that, I want to be successful. I am learning to spot conditions under which I fail. An unclear contract ranks high on the list.

I resist entering untenable contracts, for I know deep down that they are like airplanes without fuel. No matter how beautiful they look, they won't fly. The fuel for an OD contract is (1) client commitment, (2) a good relationship between us, and (3) a clear structure to that relationship, symbolized by our ability to agree on what services I will perform, when, and at what costs in time and money.

Structuring the Relationship

Item 3 brings us to the specific first intervention. It has several criteria:

1. It is responsive to the client's perceived problem. He must see it as helping him gain greater clarity, insight, and control over whatever issues are bugging *him*. It is not based on my need to use any particular trick in my bag.

2. It names the people who will come together, when, for how long, and why. "Why" is generally the client's to answer, in his own words, but I help him shape the language if he has trouble. I get clear that *the* boss will tell people why they are there, as he sees it, and *I* will tell them what I see as *my* contract with them. It is never my job to tell people why they are there.

3. It involves some form of diagnosis. That means some systematic information is collected which will heighten the clients' awareness and enlarge their freedom of choice. Sometimes this information fits some conceptual scheme, which I make explicit. Sometimes I help the client build a scheme from the information which will make sense

to him. Always, data collection, as I see it, must be done in such a way that the people who supply the information will recognize it as critical to their lives together when I collate it and hand it back. The more interpreting, or categorizing I do in advance, the less likely this is to happen.

I ensure confidentiality and anonymity. Interpretation, I try to make clear, will result when people who supplied the information meet face-to-face to assign meaning to it. I try always to specify how much time people must give, what kinds of questions will be asked, and what will become of the answers. This structuring reduces anxiety and sets up reasonable expectations.

4. I establish that part of the contract is mutual feedback. I expect clients to confront me openly on my behavior when it doesn't make sense, to question anything I do, and to point out to me words or behavior that violate their sense of what's appropriate. In return, I expect to be open with them.

It is around this clause, I think, that all contracts are tested sooner or later. In a workshop the test may come in the form of protest that the activities are irrelevant to the agenda and a waste of time. In a one-to-one relationship the test may be something I did or said that really irritated the client. It takes some risk to let me know. In opening the issue, he is checking to see whether I'm as good at handling deeds as I am at manipulating words.

I define testing the contract as an emotion-provoking exchange between me and the client in some risky situation. As a result our relationship will become more "real," more truly experimental, more like the action research model which I advocate as an appropriate way to live. I don't expect the burden for testing to rest entirely on the client. I test, too, whenever the time seems right, usually around something the client is doing which affects our relationship. Once, I noticed a client would continually express disappointment in others, and told him I was worried that one day—if not already— he was going to feel the same way about me. He owned up to the possibility, and assured me I would be the first to know, which, when the time came, I was. The confrontation deepened our relationship and strengthened the contract. It might have ended it, too.

I welcome ending a contract explicitly by having it tested and found wanting. Better a clean death than lingering agony. It is time to test (and maybe end) a contract when:

The client keeps putting things off.

Agreements are made and forgotten (by either side).

The consultant appears to have a higher emotional stake in the outcomes than the client does.

The consultant asks for events, or activities, which intensify the feeling of crisis and pressure without much prospect for eventual relief.

The client looks to the consultant to do things which he, as manager of his own organization, should be doing—i.e., arranging meetings, sending out agendas, carrying messages, and getting other people to do everything the client always wanted them to do but was afraid to ask.

The client is doing better and really doesn't need outside help.

For me, a crisp, clean ending remains desirable, but sometimes elusive. Going over 14 major contracts during the last four years, I find 9 ended cleanly with no "unfinished business," 3 ended because the boss lacked commitment to continue, and 2 because organizational changes left a leadership vacuum and me uncertain who the client was.

Where the boss lacked commitment, the intended follow-up meetings never took place, and I let things alone, feeling, I suppose, relatively little commitment myself. In the cases of organizational changes, it became plain the interim leadership lacked either incentive or authority to keep up the contract, and I had other fish to fry.

It seems to me contracts have a natural life. Organizations eventually outgrow or tire of or cease needing a particular consultant, and vice versa. It's better for me and my client that we recognize explicitly when it's time to part.

Reading 50

CHOOSING THE DEPTH OF
ORGANIZATIONAL INTERVENTION

Roger Harrison

Since World War II there has been a great proliferation of behavioral science-based methods by
which consultants seek to facilitate growth and
change in individuals, groups, and organizations.
The methods range from operations analysis and
manipulation of the organization chart, through the
use of Grid laboratories, T-groups, and nonverbal
techniques. As was true in the development of clinical psychology and psychotherapy, the early stages
of this developmental process tend to be accompanied by considerable competition, criticism, and
argument about the relative merits of various approaches. It is my conviction that controversy over
the relative goodness or badness, effectiveness or
ineffectiveness, of various change strategies really
accomplishes very little in the way of increased
knowledge or unification of behavioral science. As
long as we are arguing about what method is better
than another, we tend to learn very little about how
various approaches fit together or complement one
another, and we certainly make more difficult and
ambiguous the task of bringing these competing
points of view within one overarching system of
knowledge about human processes.

As our knowledge increases, it begins to be apparent that these competing change strategies are
not really different ways of doing the same thing—
some more effective and some less effective—but
rather that they are different ways of doing *different*
things. They touch the individual, the group, or

Source: Reproduced by special permission from *The Journal
of Applied Behavioral Science,* ''Choosing the Depth of Organizational Intervention,'' by Roger Harrison. Volume 6, No.
2, pp. 182–202. Copyright 1970 NTL Institute for Applied
Behavioral Science.

the organization in different aspects of their functioning. They require differing kinds and amounts
of commitment on the part of the client for them
to be successful, and they demand different varieties and levels of skills and abilities on the part
of the practitioner.

I believe that there is a real need for conceptual
models which differentiate intervention strategies
from one another in a way which permits rational
matching of strategies to organizational change
problems. The purpose of this paper is to present
a modest beginning which I have made toward a
conceptualization of strategies, and to derive from
this conceptualization some criteria for choosing
appropriate methods of intervention in particular
applications.

The point of view of this paper is that the depth
of individual emotional involvement in the change
process can be a central concept for differentiating
change strategies. In focusing on this dimension,
we are concerned with the extent to which core
areas of the personality or self are the focus of the
change attempt. Strategies which touch the more
deep, personal, private, and central aspects of the
individual or his relationships with others fall toward the deeper end of this continuum. Strategies
which deal with more external aspects of the individual and which focus upon the more formal
and public aspects of role behavior tend to fall
toward the surface end of the depth dimension. This
dimension has the advantage that it is relatively
easy to rank change strategies upon it and to get
fairly close consensus as to the ranking. It is a
widely discussed dimension of difference which
has meaning and relevance to practitioners and their
clients. I hope in this paper to promote greater

flexibility and rationality in choosing appropriate depths of intervention. I shall approach this task by examining the effects of interventions at various depths. I shall also explore the ways in which two important organizational processes tend to make demands and to set limits upon the depth of intervention which can produce effective change in organizational functioning. These two processes are the autonomy of organization members and their own perception of their needs for help.

Before illustrating the concept by ranking five common intervention strategies along the dimension of depth, I should like to define the dimension somewhat more precisely. We are concerned essentially with how private, individual, and hidden are the issues and processes about which the consultant attempts directly to obtain information and which he seeks to influence. If the consultant seeks information about relatively public and observable aspects of behavior and relationships and if he tries to influence directly only these relatively surface characteristics and processes, we would then categorize his intervention strategy as being closer to the surface. If, on the other hand, the consultant seeks information about very deep and private perceptions, attitudes, or feelings and if he intervenes in a way which directly affects these processes, then we would classify his intervention strategy as one of considerable depth. To illustrate the surface end of the dimension let us look first at operations research or operations analysis. This strategy is concerned with the roles and functions to be performed within the organization, generally with little regard to the individual characteristics of persons occupying the roles. The change strategy is to manipulate role relationships; in other words, to redistribute the tasks, the resources, and the relative power attached to various roles in the organization. This is essentially a process of rational analysis in which the tasks which need to be performed are determined and specified and then sliced up into role definitions for persons and groups in the organization. The operations analyst does not ordinarily need to know much about particular people. Indeed, his function is to design the organization in such a way that its successful operation does not depend too heavily upon any uniquely individual skills, abilities, values, or attitudes of persons in various roles. He may perform this function adequately without knowing in advance who the people are who will fill these slots. Persons are assumed to be moderately interchangeable, and in order to make this approach work it is necessary to design the organization so that the capacities, needs, and values of the individual which are relevant to role performance are relatively public and observable, and are possessed by a fairly large proportion of the population from which organization members are drawn. The approach is certainly one of very modest depth.

Somewhat deeper are those strategies which are based upon evaluating individual performance and attempting to manipulate it directly. Included in this approach is much of the industrial psychologist's work in selection, placement, appraisal, and counseling of employees. The intervener is concerned with what the individual is able and likely to do and achieve rather than with processes internal to the individual. Direct attempts to influence performance may be made through the application of rewards and punishments such as promotions, salary increases, or transfers within the organization. An excellent illustration of this focus on end results is the practice of management by objectives. The intervention process is focused on establishing mutually agreed-upon goals for performance between the individual and his supervisor. The practice is considered to be particularly advantageous because it permits the supervisor to avoid a focus on personal characteristics of the subordinate, particularly those deeper, more central characteristics which managers generally have difficulty in discussing with those who work under their supervision. The process is designed to limit information exchange to that which is public and observable, such as the setting of performance goals and the success or failure of the individual in attaining them.

Because of its focus on end results, rather than on the process by which those results are achieved, management by objectives must be considered less deep than the broad area of concern with work style which I shall term instrumental process analysis.

We are concerned here not only with performance but with the processes by which that performance is achieved. However, we are primarily concerned with styles and processes of work rather than with the processes of interpersonal relationships which I would classify as being deeper on the basic dimension.

In instrumental process analysis we are concerned with how a person likes to organize and conduct his work and with the impact which this style of work has on others in the organization. Principally, we are concerned with how a person perceives his role, what he values and disvalues in it, and what he works hard on and what he chooses to ignore. We are also interested in the instrumental acts which the individual directs toward others: delegating authority or reserving decisions to himself, communicating or withholding information, collaborating or competing with others on work-related issues. The focus on instrumentality means that we are interested in the person primarily as a doer of work or a performer of functions related to the goals of the organization. We are interested in what facilitates or inhibits his effective task performance.

We are not interested per se in whether his relationships with others are happy or unhappy, whether they perceive him as too warm or too cold, too authoritarian or too laissez-faire, or any other of the many interpersonal relationships which arise as people associate in organizations. However, I do not mean to imply that the line between instrumental relationships and interpersonal ones is an easy one to draw in action and practice, or even that it is desirable that this be done.

Depth Gauges: Level of Tasks and Feelings

What I am saying is that an intervention strategy can focus on instrumentality or it can focus on interpersonal relationships, and that there are important consequences of this difference in depth of intervention.

When we intervene at the level of instrumentality, it is to change work behavior and working relationships. Frequently this involves the process of bargaining or negotiation between groups and individuals. Diagnoses are made of the satisfactions or dissatisfactions of organization members with one another's work behavior. Reciprocal adjustments, bargains, and trade-offs can then be arranged in which each party gets some modification in the behavior of the other at the cost to him of some reciprocal accommodation. Much of the intervention strategy which has been developed around Blake's concept of the Managerial Grid is at this level and involves bargaining and negotiation of role behavior as an important change process.

At the deeper level of interpersonal relationships the focus is on feelings, attitudes, and perceptions which organization members have about others. At this level we are concerned with the quality of human relationships within the organization, with warmth and coldness of members to one another, and with the experiences of acceptance and rejection, love and hate, trust and suspicion among groups and individuals. At this level the consultant probes for normally hidden feelings, attitudes, and perceptions. He works to create relationships of openness about feelings and to help members to develop mutual understanding of one another as persons. Interventions are directed toward helping organization members to be more comfortable in being authentically themselves with one another, and the degree of mutual caring and concern is expected to increase. Sensitivity training using T-groups is a basic intervention strategy at this level. T-group educators emphasize increased personalization of relationships, the development of trust and openness, and the exchange of feelings. Interventions at this level deal directly and intensively with interpersonal emotionality. This is the first intervention strategy we have examined which is at a depth where the feelings of organization members about one another as persons are a direct focus of the intervention strategy. At the other levels, such feelings certainly exist and may be expressed, but they are not a direct concern of the intervention. The transition from the task orientation of instrumental process analysis to the feeling orientation of interpersonal process analysis seems, as I shall suggest later, to be a critical one for many organization members.

The deepest level of intervention which will be considered in this paper is that of intrapersonal analysis. Here the consultant uses a variety of methods to reveal the individual's deeper attitudes, values, and conflicts regarding his own functioning, identity, and existence. The focus is generally on increasing the range of experiences which the individual can bring into awareness and cope with. The material may be dealt with at the fantasy or symbolic level, and the intervention strategies include many which are noninterpersonal and nonverbal. Some examples of this approach are the use of marathon T-group sessions, the creative risk-taking laboratory approach of Byrd (1967), and some aspects of the task group therapy approach of Clark (1966). These approaches all tend to bring into focus very deep and intense feelings about one's own identity and one's relationships with significant others.

Although I have characterized deeper interventions as dealing increasingly with the individual's affective life, I do not imply that issues at less deep levels may not be emotionally charged. Issues of role differentiation, reward distribution, ability and performance evaluation, for example, are frequently invested with strong feelings. The concept of depth is concerned more with the *accessibility* and *individuality* of attitudes, values, and perceptions than it is with their strength. This narrowing of the common usage of the term *depth* is necessary to avoid the contradictions which occur when strength and inaccessibility are confused. For instance, passionate value confrontation and bitter conflict have frequently occurred between labor and management over economic issues which are surely toward the surface end of my concept of depth.

In order to understand the importance of the concept of depth for choosing interventions in organizations, let us consider the effects upon organization members of working at different levels.

The first of the important concomitants of depth is the degree of dependence of the client on the special competence of the change agent. At the surface end of the depth dimension, the methods of intervention are easily communicated and made public. The client may reasonably expect to learn something of the change agent's skills to improve his own practice. At the deeper levels, such as interpersonal and intrapersonal process analyses, it is more difficult for the client to understand the methods of intervention. The change agent is more likely to be seen as a person of special and unusual powers not found in ordinary men. Skills of intervention and change are less frequently learned by organization members, and the change process may tend to become personalized around the change agent as leader. Programs of change which are so dependent upon personal relationships and individual expertise are difficult to institutionalize. When the change agent leaves the system, he may not only take his expertise with him but the entire change process as well.

A second aspect of the change process which varies with depth is the extent to which the benefits of an intervention are transferable to members of the organization not originally participating in the change process. At surface levels of operations analysis and performance evaluation, the effects are institutionalized in the form of procedures, policies, and practices of the organization which may have considerable permanence beyond the tenure of individuals. At the level of instrumental behavior, the continuing effects of intervention are more likely to reside in the informal norms of groups within the organization regarding such matters as delegation, communication, decision making, competition and collaboration, and conflict resolution.

At the deepest levels of intervention, the target of change is the individual's inner life; and if the intervention is successful, the permanence of individual change should be greatest. There are indeed dramatic reports of cases in which persons have changed their careers and life goals as a result of such interventions, and the persistence of such change appears to be relatively high.

One consequence, then, of the level of intervention is that with greater depth of focus the individual increasingly becomes both the target and the carrier of change. In the light of this analysis, it is not surprising to observe that deeper levels of intervention are increasingly being used at higher organizational levels and in scientific and service organizations where the contribution of the individual has greatest impact.

An important concomitant of depth is that as the level of intervention becomes deeper, the information needed to intervene effectively becomes less available. At the less personal level of operations analysis, the information is often a matter of record. At the level of performance evaluation, it is a matter of observation. On the other hand, reactions of others to a person's work style are less likely to be discussed freely, and the more personal responses to his interpersonal style are even less likely to be readily given. At the deepest levels, important information may not be available to the individual himself. Thus, as we go deeper the consultant must use more of his time and skill uncovering information which is ordinarily private and hidden. This is one reason for the greater costs of interventions at deeper levels of focus.

Another aspect of the change process which varies with the depth of intervention is the personal risk and unpredictability of outcome for the individual. At deeper levels we deal with aspects of the individual's view of himself and his relationships with others which are relatively untested by exposure to the evaluations and emotional reactions of others. If in the change process the individual's self-perceptions are strongly disconfirmed, the resulting imbalance in internal forces may produce sudden changes in behavior, attitudes, and personality integration.

Because of the private and hidden nature of the processes into which we intervene at deeper levels, it is difficult to predict the individual impact of the change process in advance. The need for clinical sensitivity and skill on the part of the practitioner thus increases, since he must be prepared to diagnose and deal with developing situations involving considerable stress upon individuals.

The foregoing analysis suggests a criterion by which to match intervention strategies to particular organizational problems. It is *to intervene at a level no deeper than that required to produce enduring solutions to the problems at hand*. This criterion derives directly from the observations above. The cost, skill demands, client dependency, and variability of outcome all increase with depth of intervention. Further, as the depth of intervention increases, the effects tend to locate more in the individual and less in the organization. The danger of losing the organization's investment in the change with the departure of the individual becomes a significant consideration.

Autonomy Increases Depth of Intervention

While this general criterion is simple and straightforward, its application is not. In particular, although the criterion should operate in the direction of less depth of intervention, there is a general trend in modern organizational life which tends to push the intervention level ever deeper. This trend is toward increased self-direction of organization members and increased independence of external pressures and incentives. I believe that there is a direct relationship between the autonomy of individuals and the depth of intervention needed to effect organizational change.

Before going on to discuss this relationship, I shall acknowledge freely that I cannot prove the existence of a trend toward a general increase in freedom of individuals within organizations. I intend only to assert the great importance of the degree of individual autonomy in determining the level of intervention which will be effective.

In order to understand the relationship between autonomy and depth of intervention, it is necessary to conceptualize a dimension which parallels and is implied by the depth dimension we have been discussing. This is the dimension of predictability and variability among persons in their responses to the different kinds of incentives which may be used to influence behavior in the organization. The key assumption in this analysis is that the more unpredictable and unique is the individual's response to the particular kinds of controls and incentives one can bring to bear upon him, the more one must know about that person in order to influence his behavior.

Most predictable and least individual is the response of the person to economic and bureaucratic controls when his needs for economic income and security are high. It is not necessary to delve very deeply into a person's inner processes in order to influence his behavior if we know that he badly needs his income and his position and if we are in a position to control his access to these rewards. Responses to economic and bureaucratic controls tend to be relatively simple and on the surface.

Independence of Economic Incentive

If for any reason organization members become relatively uninfluenceable through the manipulation of their income and economic security, the management of performance becomes strikingly more complex; and the need for more personal information about the individual increases. Except very generally, we do not know automatically or in advance what styles of instrumental or interpersonal interaction will be responded to as negative or positive incentives by the individual. One person may appreciate close supervision and direction; another may value independence of direction. One may prefer to work alone; another may function best when he is in close communication with others. One may thrive in close, intimate, personal interaction; while others are made uncomfortable by any but cool and distant relationships with colleagues.

What I am saying is that when bureaucratic and economic incentives lose their force for whatever reason, the improvement of performance *must* involve linking organizational goals to the individual's attempts to meet his own needs for satisfying instrumental activities and interpersonal relationships. It is for this reason that I make the assertion that increases in personal autonomy dictate change interventions at deeper and more personal levels. In order to obtain the information necessary to link organizational needs to individual goals, one must probe fairly deeply into the attitudes, values, and emotions of the organization members.

If the need for deeper personal information becomes great when we intervene at the instrumental and interpersonal levels, it becomes even greater when one is dealing with organization members who are motivated less through their transactions with the environment and more in response to internal values and standards. An example is the researcher, engineer, or technical specialist whose work behavior may be influenced more by his own values and standards of creativity or professional excellence than by his relationships with others. The deepest organizational interventions at the intrapersonal level may be required in order to effect change when working with persons who are highly self-directed.

Let me summarize my position about the relationship among autonomy, influence, and level of intervention. As the individual becomes less subject to economic and bureaucratic pressures, he tends to seek more intangible rewards in the organization which come from both the instrumental and interpersonal aspects of the system. I view this as a shift from greater external to more internal control and as an increase in autonomy. Further shifts in this direction may involve increased independence of rewards and punishments mediated by others, in favor of operation in accordance with internal values and standards.

I view organizations as systems of reciprocal influence. Achievement of organization goals is facilitated when individuals can seek their own satisfactions through activity which promotes the goals of the organization. As the satisfactions which are of most value to the individual change, so must the reciprocal influence systems, if the organization goals are to continue to be met.

If the individual changes are in the direction of increased independence of external incentives, then the influence systems must change to provide opportunities for individuals to achieve more intangible, self-determined satisfactions in their work. However, people are more differentiated, complex, and unique in their intangible goals and values than in their economic needs. In order to create systems which offer a wide variety of intangible satisfactions, much more private information about individuals is needed than is required to create and maintain systems based chiefly on economic and bureaucratic controls. For this reason, deeper interventions are called for when the system which they would attempt to change contains a high proportion of relatively autonomous individuals.

There are a number of factors promoting autonomy, all tending to free the individual from dependence upon economic and bureaucratic controls, which I have observed in my work with organizations. Wherever a number of these factors obtain, it is probably an indication that deeper levels of intervention are required to effect lasting improvements in organizational functioning. I shall simply list these indicators briefly in categories to show what kinds of things might signify to the practitioner that deeper levels of intervention may be appropriate.

The first category includes anything which makes the evaluation of individual performance difficult:

A long time span between the individual's actions and the results by which effectiveness of performance is to be judged.

Nonrepetitive, unique tasks which cannot be evaluated by reference to the performance of others on similar tasks.

Specialized skills and abilities possessed by an individual which cannot be evaluated by a supervisor who does not possess the skills or knowledge himself.

The second category concerns economic conditions:

Arrangements which secure the job tenure and/or income to the individual.

A market permitting easy transfer from one organization to another (e.g., engineers in the United States aerospace industry).

Unique skills and knowledge of the individual which make him difficult to replace.

The third category includes characteristics of the system or its environment which lead to independence of the parts of the organization and decentralization of authority such as:

An organization which works on a project basis instead of producing a standard line of products.

An organization in which subparts must be given latitude to deal rapidly and flexibly with frequent environmental change.

I should like to conclude the discussion of this criterion for depth of intervention with a brief reference to the ethics of intervention, a problem which merits considerably more thorough treatment than I can give it here.

The Ethics of Delving Deeper

There is considerable concern in the United States about invasion of privacy by behavioral scientists. I would agree that such invasion of privacy is an actual as well as a fantasized concomitant of the use of organizational change strategies of greater depth. The recourse by organizations to such strategies has been widely viewed as an indication of greater organizational control over the most personal and private aspects of the lives of the members. The present analysis suggests, however, that recourse to these deeper interventions actually reflects the greater *freedom* of organization members from traditionally crude and impersonal means of organizational control. There is no reason to be concerned about man's attitudes or values or interpersonal relationships when his job performance can be controlled by brute force, by economic coercion, or by bureaucratic rules and regulations. The "invasion of privacy" becomes worth the cost, bother, and uncertainty of outcome only when the individual has achieved relative independence from control by other means. Put another way, it makes organizational sense to try to get a man to *want* to do something only if you cannot *make* him do it. And regardless of what intervention strategy is used, the individual still retains considerably greater control over his own behavior than he had when he could be manipulated more crudely. As long as we can maintain a high degree of voluntarism regarding the nature and extent of an individual's participation in the deeper organizational change strategies, these strategies can work toward adapting the organization to the individual quite as much as they work the other way around. Only when an individual's participation in one of the deeper change strategies is coerced by economic or bureaucratic pressures, do I feel that the ethics of the intervention clearly run counter to the values of a democratic society.

Role of Client Norms and Values in Determining Depth

So far our attention to the choice of level of intervention has focused upon locating the depth at which the information exists which must be exchanged to facilitate system improvement. Unfortunately, the choice of an intervention strategy cannot practically be made with reference to this criterion alone. Even if a correct diagnosis is made of the level at which the relevant information lies, we may not be able to work effectively at the desired depth because of client norms, values, resistances, and fears.

In an attempt to develop a second criterion for depth of intervention which takes such dispositions on the part of the client into account, I have considered two approaches which represent polarized orientations to the problem. One approach is based upon analyzing and overcoming client resistance; the other is based upon discovering and joining forces with the self-articulated wants or "felt needs" of the client.

There are several ways of characterizing these approaches. To me, the simplest is to point out that when the change agent is resistance-oriented he tends to lead or influence the client to work at a depth greater than that at which the latter feels comfortable. When resistance-oriented, the change agent tends to mistrust the client's statement of his problems and of the areas where he wants help. He suspects the client's presentation of being a smoke screen or defense against admission of his "real" problems and needs. The consultant works to expose the underlying processes and concerns and to influence the client to work at a deeper level.

The resistance-oriented approach grows out of the work of clinicians and psychotherapists, and it characterizes much of the work of organizational consultants who specialize in sensitivity training and deeper intervention strategies.

On the other hand, change agents may be oriented to the self-articulated needs of clients. When so oriented, the consultant tends more to follow and facilitate the client in working at whatever level the latter sets for himself. He may assist the client in defining problems and needs and in working on solutions, but he is inclined to try to anchor his work in the norms, values, and accepted standards of behavior of the organization.

I believe that there is a tendency for change agents working at the interpersonal and deeper levels to adopt a rather consistent resistance-oriented approach. Consultants so oriented seem to take a certain quixotic pride in dramatically and self-consciously violating organizational norms. Various techniques have been developed for pressuring or seducing organizations members into departing from organizational norms in the service of change. The "marathon" T-group is a case in point, where the increased irritability and fatigue of prolonged contact and lack of sleep move participants to deal with one another more emotionally, personally, and spontaneously than they would normally be willing to do.

I suspect that unless such norm-violating intervention efforts actually succeed in changing organizational norms, their effects are relatively short-lived, because the social structures and interpersonal linkages have not been created which can utilize for day-to-day problem solving the deeper information produced by the intervention. It is true that the consultant may succeed in producing information, but he is less likely to succeed in creating social structures which can continue to work in his absence. The problem is directly analogous to that of the community developer who succeeds by virtue of his personal influence in getting villagers to build a school or a community center which falls into disuse as soon as he leaves because of the lack of any integration of these achievements into the social structure and day-to-day needs and desires of the community. Community developers have had to learn through bitter failure and frustration that ignoring or subverting the standards and norms of a social system often results in temporary success followed by a reactionary increase in resistance to the influence of the change agent. On the other hand, felt needs embody those problems, issues, and difficulties which have a high conscious priority on the part of community or organization members. We can expect individuals and groups to be ready to invest time, energy, and resources in dealing with their felt needs, while they will be relatively passive or even resistant toward those who attempt to help them with externally defined needs. Community developers have found that attempts to help with felt needs are met with greater receptivity, support, and integration within the structure and life of the community than are intervention attempts which rely primarily upon the developer's value system for setting need priorities.

The emphasis of many organizational change agents on confronting and working through resistances was developed originally in the practice of individual psychoanalysis and psychotherapy, and it is also a central concept in the conduct of therapy groups and sensitivity training laboratories. In all of these situations, the change agent has a high degree of environmental control and is at least temporarily in a high status position with respect to the client. To a degree that is frequently underestimated by practitioners, we manage to create a situation in which it is more unpleasant for the client to leave than it is to stay and submit to the pressure to confront and work through resistances. I believe that the tendency is for behavioral scientists to overplay their hands when they move from the clinical and training situations where they have environmental control to the organizational consulting situation, where their control is sharply attenuated.

This attenuation derives only partially from the relative ease with which the client can terminate the relationship. Even if this most drastic step is not taken, the consultant can be tolerated, misled, and deceived in ways which are relatively difficult in the therapeutic or human relations training situations. He can also be openly defied and blocked if he runs afoul of strongly shared group norms; whereas when the consultant is dealing with a group of strangers, he can often utilize differences among the members to overcome this kind of resistance. I suspect that, in general, behavioral scientists underestimate their power in working with individuals and groups of strangers, and overestimate it when working with individuals and groups in organizations. I emphasize this point because I believe that a good many potentially fruitful and mutually satisfying consulting relationships are terminated early because of the consultant's taking the role of overcomer of resistance to change rather than that of collaborator in the client's attempts at solving his problems. It is these considerations which lead me to suggest my second criterion for the choice of organization intervention strategy: *to intervene at a level no deeper than that at which the energy and resources of the client can be committed to problem solving and to change.* These energies and resources can be mobilized through obtaining legitimation for the intervention in the forms of the organization and through devising intervention strategies which have clear relevance to consciously felt needs on the part of the organization members.

The Consultant's Dilemma: Felt Needs versus Deeper Levels

Unfortunately, it is doubtless true that the forces which influence the conditions we desire to change often exist at deeper levels than can be dealt with by adhering to the criterion of working within organization norms and meeting felt needs. The level at which an individual or group is willing and ready to invest energy and resources is probably always determined partly by a realistic assessment of the problems and partly by a defensive need to avoid confrontation and significant change. It is thus not likely that our two criteria for selection of intervention depth will result in the same decisions when practically applied. It is not the same to intervene at the level where behavior-determining forces are most potent as it is to work on felt needs as they are articulated by the client. This, it seems to me, is the consultant's dilemma. It always has been. We are continually faced with the choice between leading the client into areas which are threatening, unfamiliar, and dependency-provoking for him (and where our own expertise shows up to best advantage) or, on the other hand, being guided by the client's own understanding of his problems and his willingness to invest resources in particular kinds of relatively familiar and nonthreatening strategies.

When time permits, this dilemma is ideally dealt with by intervening first at a level where there is good support from the norms, power structure, and felt needs of organizational members. The consultant can then, over a period of time, develop trust, sophistication, and support within the organization to explore deeper levels at which particularly important forces may be operating. This would probably be agreed to, at least in principle, by most organizational consultants. The point at which I feel I differ from a significant number of workers in this field is that I would advocate that interventions should *always* be limited to the depth of the client's felt needs and readiness to legitimize intervention. I believe we should always avoid moving deeper at a pace which outstrips a client system's willingness to subject itself to exposure, dependency, and threat. What I am saying is that if the dominant response of organization members indicates that an intervention violates system norms regarding exposure, privacy, and confrontation, then one has intervened too deeply and should pull back to a level at which organization members are more ready to invest their own energy in the change process. This point of view is thus in opposition to that which sees negative reactions primarily as indications of resistances which are to be brought out into the open, confronted, and worked through as a central part of the intervention process. I believe that behavioral scientists acting as organizational consultants have tended to place overmuch emphasis on the overcoming of resistance to change and have underemphasized the importance of enlisting in the service of change the energies and resources which the client can consciously direct and willingly devote to problem solving.

What is advocated here is that we in general accept the client's felt needs or the problems he presents as real and that we work on them at a level at which he can serve as a competent and willing collaborator. This position is in opposition to one which sees the presenting problem as more or less a smoke screen or barrier. I am not advocating this point of view because I value the right to privacy of organization members more highly than I value their growth and development or the solution of organizational problems. (This is an issue which concerns me, but it is enormously more complex than the ones with which I am dealing in this paper.) Rather, I place first priority on collaboration with the client, because I do not think we are frequently successful consultants without it.

In my own practice I have observed that the change in client response is frequently quite striking when I move from a resistance-oriented approach to an acceptance of the client's norms and definitions of his own needs. With quite a few organizational clients in the United States, the line of legitimacy seems to lie somewhere between interventions at the instrumental level and those focused on interpersonal relationships. Members who exhibit hostility, passivity, and dependence when I initiate intervention at the interpersonal level may become dramatically more active, collaborative, and involved when I shift the focus to the instrumental level.

If I intervene directly at the level of interpersonal relationships, I can be sure that at least some members, and often the whole group, will react with anxiety, passive resistance, and low or negative commitment to the change process. Furthermore, they express their resistance in terms of norms and values regarding the appropriateness or legitimacy of dealing at this level. They say things like, "It isn't right to force people's feelings about one another out into the open"; "I don't see what this has to do with improving organizational effectiveness"; "People are being encouraged to say things which are better left unsaid."

If I then switch to a strategy which focuses on decision making, delegation of authority, information exchange, and other instrumental questions, these complaints about illegitimacy and the inappropriateness of the intervention are usually sharply reduced. This does not mean that the clients are necessarily comfortable or free from anxiety in the discussions, nor does it mean that strong feelings may not be expressed about one another's behavior. What is different is that the clients are more likely to *work with* instead of *against* me, to feel and express some sense of ownership in the change process, and to see many more possibilities for carrying it on among themselves in the absence of the consultant.

What I have found is that when I am resistance-oriented in my approach to the client, I am apt to feel rather uncomfortable in "letting sleeping dogs lie." When, on the other hand, I orient myself to the client's own assessment of his needs, I am uncomfortable when I feel I am leading or pushing the client to operate very far outside the shared norms of the organization. I have tried to indicate why I believe the latter orientation is more appropriate. I realize of course that many highly sophisticated and talented practitioners will not agree with me.

In summary, I have tried to show in this paper that the dimension of depth should be central to the conceptualization of intervention strategies. I have presented what I believe are the major consequences of intervening at greater or lesser depths, and from these consequences I have suggested two criteria for choosing the appropriate depth of intervention: first, *to intervene at a level no deeper than that required to produce enduring solutions to the problems at hand;* and second, *to intervene at a level no deeper than that at which the energy and resources of the client can be committed to problem solving and to change.*

I have analyzed the tendency for increases in individual autonomy in organizations to push the appropriate level of intervention deeper when the first criterion is followed. Opposed to this is the countervailing influence of the second criterion to work closer to the surface in order to enlist the energy and support of organization members in the change process. Arguments have been presented for resolving this dilemma in favor of the second, more conservative, criterion. The dilemma remains, of course; the continuing tension under which the change agent works is between the desire to lead and push, or to collaborate and follow. The middle ground is never very stable, and I suspect we show our values and preferences by which criterion we choose to maximize when we are under the stress of difficult and ambiguous client-consultant relationships.

References

Byrd, R. E. Training in a nongroup. *Journal of Humanistic Psychology,* 1967, *7,* (1), 18–27.

Clark, J. V. Task group therapy. Unpublished manuscript, University of California, Los Angeles, 1966.

Reading 51

AN AUTOPSY OF AN INTENDED OD PROJECT

R. Wayne Boss and Mark L. McConkie

Our purpose in this report is to review some ineffective intervention activities that had the effect of contributing to, rather than decreasing, the frustrations of personnel in a large private-sector manufacturing firm, known here only as Kingston. The short case study presented here, like similar examinations of OD failures (Mirvis & Berg, 1977), rests on the assumption that we often learn as much—and sometimes more—by studying our failures as we do by studying our successes. Admittedly, many of the mistakes reported here are errors that could have been avoided had the consultants been more cautious and perceptive. They are reported here in the hope that others may also profit by these mistakes and become more effective in their consultation.

We have deliberately disguised the actual identity of Kingston to protect both the integrity and confidentiality of those involved. We have not, however, distorted the facts, either by adding to or taking from the events that transpired. Exaggerated though it may appear, it is a "real" case study. Moreover, we believe that both the organizational climate and structure at Kingston are similar to those frequently found in correctional institutions, mental health programs, halfway houses (and similar community-based programs), alcohol and drug rehabilitation efforts, group foster homes, youth detention centers, and even hospitals and psychiatric therapy wards, as well as to those found in the manufacturing world. Thus, the concepts and

Source: R. Wayne Boss and Mark L. McConkie, "An Autopsy of an Intended OD Project," *Group and Organization Studies,* June 1974, pp. 183–200. Copyright © 1974 University Associates, Inc., with permission of Sage Publications, Inc. and the authors.

conclusions drawn from this case study seem to us to be in some ways generalizable to public and quasi-public organizations, as well as to some other private sector organizations.

By combining the experiences at Kingston with the empirical and theoretical literature of the behavioral sciences, we have drawn some "object lessons" that we believe are helpful guides to both consultants and clients. We propose no panaceas nor do we pretend that each "object lesson" is defensible to the nth degree; rather, each represents significant findings illustrated by the Kingston effort, and each, we believe, merits the serious consideration of those associated with the consultation process.

The Setting

Before discussing the people, events, and processes at Kingston, a medium-size (700 employees) manufacturing organization, we must visualize the environment in which the project took place. In the early 1970s this environment was turbulent, filled with pressures, and frustrating to employees. Nearly thirty years of stern, tight-fisted leadership had guided Kingston to a respected competitive position. The former president, who resigned four months before the OD intervention, left behind a climate of authoritarianism. All top-level policies and many lesser and inconsequential ones flowed from his desk. Only one or two besides himself were privy to "his" budget, and almost none knew of its substantial size. He controlled and often conducted employee selection and recruitment interviews and committee work, program design and training formats, and much of the public relations work with the surrounding community. The organizational climate was one in which employees understood they were to do as they were told—not more, not less.

Subordinates at every organizational level mirrored the president's authoritarian attitude and behavior. Sanctions and controls were externally applied: "big tough dudes" were co-opted and paid handsomely to maintain order among their peers; punishment was common; and the mail was uniformly censored. At the same time, the staff employed no uniform or universal application of Kingston policies and procedures. Consequently, staff privileges frequently went to the least deserving but most politically or interpersonally astute employees. In this atmosphere, many administrative personnel either ignored and/or concealed such rule violations as alcoholism, drug abuse, embezzlement, and outright theft.

Additional factors compounded Kingston's problems. Trust levels were low, and the staff seldom worked harmoniously. Individual brilliance was encouraged at the expense of team accomplishment. Employee morale, already declining, sank to new depths when the public media first exposed and later ridiculed Kingston's policies. As time passed, negative community sentiment toward Kingston grew. The resultant pressures left Kingston with a tense, anxiety-ridden atmosphere.

In the wake of these pressures and because of a felt need for change, the president resigned. His replacement arrived in September, bringing a reputation as an effective, democratically styled leader. His welcome was warm and sincere.

The new president immediately set out to heal Kingston of its many ills. He devoted himself diligently to administration and quickly won the respect of Kingston personnel. In January he hired a new vice president, a man of prodigious talent with more than twenty years of managerial experience. The vice president chose his two immediate aides from among his former work companions in another state. They arrived with ideas of mental health models for organizational rehabilitation that they were certain could be applied at Kingston. A third top-level staff member, who served as an equal to the other two, was added by the president.

From the beginning the new president and vice president worked together as a team. Although their reasoning often differed, they shared many common goals and values, one of the most important of which was the belief that by utilizing the findings of the behavioral sciences, many of Kingston's personnel problems could be eradicated. This common faith in the potential of the behavioral sciences motivated Kingston's top management to hire a team of organization development (OD) consultants. In February two consultants were retained; in early March they joined the vice president and his assistants in a three-day off-site team-building session. The session was so well received that the personnel involved insisted that employees at all organizational levels become involved. In late April and early May the rest of the staff participated in similar three-day team-building sessions. The employees considered the team building highly successful. People who had refused to work together for years were now cooperating; employee morale had rarely been so high.

Suddenly, however, things changed. By mid-July the consultants had been fired, the vice president had resigned, the new employees had been fired, and Kingston was clearly and deliberately returning to its authoritarian past. The OD effort was dead before it ever really started.

The Autopsy

Our purpose is to examine, in chronological order, some of the more apparent causal factors in the death of this particular consultative intervention. We intend, in effect, to conduct an autopsy of an intended OD project. Just as several factors often combine to cause death in humans, several major things contributed to the death of this particular OD effort. Some of these factors are outgrowths of an entangled organizational climate; others represent clear consultative errors. Together they illustrate how poor administrative practices can undermine consultative efforts, just as improper consultative behaviors can compound administrative problems.

Our aim is fourfold: to further knowledge of disease—in this case consultative and organizational disease; to discover and describe deviations from normal operating behaviors; to explain, on the basis of post-mortem findings, abnormal functionings manifested during life; and, finally, to confirm or invalidate the clinical diagnosis made during life.

In analyzing why the OD effort died, we have noted 15 major contributing causes, most of which are interrelated. In sum, we have noted the importance of (1) establishing, understanding, and maintaining clear budget and financial responsibilities in the client organization, (2) creating professional rather than personal consulting relationships, (3) doing preentry consultative diagnosis of the organization, (4) having a clear psychological contract, (5) using consultative double entry, (6) understanding the values of the client organization, (7) having the support and involvement of the chief executive officer, (8) ignoring the organizational critics, (9) avoiding destructive change strategies, (10) developing internal change agents, (11) assuring accessibility of consultants, (12) working through organizational "linkingpins," (13) knowing the implications of mandatory training, (14) creating realistic client expectations, and (15) collecting data.

No Clear Budget or Financial Responsibility

"Whoever controls the purse strings," we are told in our introductory management courses, "controls!" So it was at Kingston. The former president had concentrated the budgeting functions in his own office. Division heads and other staff who would normally have access to budget information were ignorant of budget content and were always required to request needed monies for training, office supplies and equipment, travel, and research support. Frustrated personnel, unable to get what they wanted and needed, ultimately developed methods of beating the system. Taking advantage of Kingston's archaic and ineffectual system of financial accountability, thousands of dollars were

drained annually from Kingston accounts, false payments were common, and a spirit of suspicion and imminent corruption grew. The former president had known of some of these financial irresponsibilities and had responded with a tightened fist. This seemed to force personnel needing funds to become still more devious. Thus, the vicious cycle continued, and tension grew.

When the new president was hired, he immediately began cleaning house. Some personnel were fired, others were reassigned. Nevertheless, financial information still remained a mystery to most, and the new president, like his predecessor, kept complete control for both personal and institutional reasons. On the one hand, he felt responsible for spending Kingston monies wisely; on the other hand, even though the former president was frequently viewed with animosity, many of his strong—and vocal—supporters still remained in the organization and supported the former budget procedures. The new president found it convenient to retain the previous budgeting structure but, in so doing, he perpetuated many of the financial problems of his predecessor.

When the vice president was hired, he assumed that he would have access to budget information. He soon discovered that he, like all other personnel, had to request funds personally—an awkward arrangement considering that he supervised more than 300 personnel. He immediately felt the weakness of his own position; everything he did was subject to the examination and approval of the president, whose constant assurances that money was no problem sounded empty to the vice president.

The consultants' ignorance of this financial morass gave birth to a host of problems. First, it increased the consultants' vulnerability to manipulation by Kingston personnel, who were largely aware of the existence, though not the extent, of Kingston's financial problems. Because the staff knew of these problems, they learned to distrust the new president (who continued the previous practices) and those associated with him or those perceived to be associated with him. In Kingston's authoritarian environment, the consultants were seen by many as the president's "eyes and ears," so the financial problems contributed to the spirit of distrust and suspicion.

Second, the tight financial control tended to reinforce a suspicion-ridden, authoritarian climate and values that were at odds with the democratic, power-sharing values of organization development.

Third, the situation not only permitted, but frequently encouraged, illegal and unethical financial practices and gave rise to unnecessary paperwork and bureaucracy.

Finally, although financial support for the OD project was assured by the Kingston administrative staff, the assurances were false and the monies were committed only on a tentative basis—dependent on the perceived success of the initial OD intervention. Although under most circumstances this is a desirable condition, the qualifications of what constituted a successful project were not clearly understood by the client, and a discussion of those expectations between the client and the consultant never took place.

All of these factors provided clues that the consultants missed about the degree of cultural preparedness and how much personnel were willing to deal honestly with one another. In the absence of such willingness, the consultants should have anticipated problems for the forthcoming team-building and OD efforts.

> Object Lesson 1: Consultants must pay attention to organizational financial operations. Organizations with financial and budgeting problems are likely to develop serious and financially related people problems.

The Consultant-Client Relationship Was Personal, Not Professional

Prior to coming to Kingston, the vice president had done graduate work at one of the prestige universities in the United States and been introduced to a good deal of behavioral science research. He was an enthusiastic OD supporter, confident that OD could untangle such problems as Kingston's. Consequently, when he was hired he contacted a long-time friend who was a practicing OD consultant

and suggested that he come to Kingston to conduct some team building. The consultant contacted a close colleague and suggested that the two work together. Thus, both consultants' decisions to enter the organization were based on personal association and friendship rather than on a clear understanding of Kingston's problems and a belief that those problems could be resolved. It is not surprising then that the consultants were initially perceived by the Kingston administration to be "ringers" whom the vice president had brought in as allies to make himself look good and to undermine the president and members of the informal power structure. The personal relationship between the vice president and the consultants seriously hampered the consultants' objective.

> Object Lesson 2: Consultant-client relationships must be built on mutually shared professional expectations, which should be agreed on prior to work with the client system itself. Consultant-client relationships based solely or primarily on personal or "friendship" reasons may breed problems destructive to effective OD interventions.

No Preentry Diagnosis of the Organization

Because both the consultant and managerial allegiance were personal, the consultants accepted the vice president's determination that team building was the appropriate intervention strategy. On the strength of that decision, the consultants conducted no preentry diagnostic activities to determine the accuracy of the vice president's diagnosis or the cultural preparedness at Kingston.

Because they had no data-based diagnosis of actual organizational needs, the resulting design, although it had some organizational utility, was not specifically tailored to Kingston's needs. Resembling a "packaged program," the design lost the potency that preassessment allows. Moreover, there were no data to instruct the second consultant on the attitudes and needs of the client system; he was not party to the very limited preentry conversations with the vice president so was left totally to his own devices. Consequently, there were no data to tie the consultant team to a single goal or course of action and the consultants were free to drift apart.

> Object Lesson 3: Without a data-based diagnosis of organizational needs, consultants are left to instinct, previous experience, or available packaged programs and are therefore unable to tailor intervention activities to the unique needs of the organization.

No Clear Psychological Contract

Because their relationship with the vice president was highly personal, the consultants felt little need to negotiate a clear psychological contract regarding the problems at Kingston, the vice president's expectations of the project, or the consultants' expectations of the vice president and the client system. Both parties assumed that things could be worked out and problems could be resolved when they arose. However, when such problems did arise, their resolution proved much more difficult than anticipated. For example, the failure to specify the need to collect survey data created tensions in later stages when the consultants sought to collect such data and were refused permission.

Because no contract existed, and because they were friends anyway, the consultants and the client overlooked the need for a specific and systematic format for monitoring, reviewing, and reporting on either consultant or organizational progress. The informal reporting arrangement was soon drowned in the flood of activities, and interim checkups were not done. Consequently, both the consultants and the client fought considerable ignorance—and sometimes each other.

> Object Lesson 4: Consultants and clients must share, emotionally and perceptually, the same expectations of their relationship. Unless these expectations are established and shared, it is extremely difficult to establish accountability, ensure goal accomplishment, monitor progress, or intervene in organizational processes without fear of violating organizational purposes.

The Need for Consultative Double Entry

The initial entry point for the consultants was at the vice presidential level. Shortly after the first team-building session, the consultants requested a meeting with the president but were informed that he was "extremely busy," since he was out of town a great deal, and that it was virtually impossible to see him. The president was said to have "complete confidence" in the vice president and to support his decisions. It thus was impossible for the consultants to inform the president of the status of the OD project, the nature of the problems in the organization, and the steps that were being taken to resolve those problems. The president not only lacked ownership of the project, but as exaggerated and often inaccurate reports of off-site meetings filtered back to him, he became increasingly suspicious. His suspicions climaxed in his own informal investigation into the proceedings of the off-site sessions. Not until the conclusion of the project were the consultants allowed a 15-minute meeting with the president. By this time, the perceptions of the president had been biased to a point at which neither the consultants nor the vice president had credibility.

> Object Lesson 5: The consultant(s) should insist on double entry into the client system. That is, he or she should be allowed full access to both the primary client and to that person's immediate superior.

Consultant Naiveté Regarding the Values of the System

The Kingston experience illustrates how important it is for external consultants to become immediately familiar with the prevailing value structures and attitudes of organization members. For example, Kingston was significantly influenced by a prominent local church. The former president and the new president were both deeply committed to this religion, as were several other administrative officers. Local clergy were often called on for counseling, weekly devotional services were conducted, and local prelates were among the most influential members of the board of directors. Because of this, some voiced the suspicion that church members were given preferential treatment in hiring practices, although substantive data were difficult to uncover.

Problems arose not only because of the basically authoritarian and religious climate, but because of the consultants' ignorance of the impact these religious values had on organizational operations. Because top-echelon personnel shared the same philosophy and made the same basic assumptions about what was best for Kingston, questions of right and wrong rarely surfaced. Consequently, some problems that would have been unlikely in more heterogeneous organizations aggravated the already ailing Kingston. Notably, the press raised serious ethical questions about the misuse of some of Kingston's funds, and the common belief structure facilitated a number of secret "brotherhood" pacts, some of which had a negative impact on Kingston's operations.

Had the consultants been more sensitive to the impact of these religious feelings, they might have avoided later problems. Shortly before the consultants were dismissed, the tensions and frustrations began to intensify, largely because managers and subordinates were taking risks and modifying behaviors while top management, and particularly the new president, were not. Perhaps the most common source of support for top management was the church. Local clergy informally reported to the president about what the consultants and others in the organization were doing.

At Kingston if the consultants had made deliberate efforts to understand the climate and value structure, they might have designed specific skill training aimed at altering or changing negative and damaging behaviors or at improving church member and nonmember working relationships. Some of the problems might have been avoided by including someone committed to these religious sentiments on the consultative team. Although religious values alone would not have toppled the consultative effort, when added to Kingston's other problems they became potent.

Object Lesson 6: When consultants are working with an organization that has values noticeably different from their own, ways of understanding and communicating must be devised. Typically, it is wise to include someone in the consulting team who shares the prevailing opinions, perspectives, feelings, prejudices, or "causes" of the organization members under consideration.

Lack of CEO Support

As mentioned earlier, the consultants sought to meet with the new president to explain what would be taking place, hoping thereby to avoid any surprises. The president, however, chose to minimize interactions with the consultants. He was "very busy," had "complete confidence" in the vice president, and promised to support the vice president in whatever he wanted to do. The unhappy result of this arrangement was that the vice president was filled with hope and enthusiasm while the president was ignorant of what OD really is—except that, as the consultants learned later, he knew it had something to do with "sensitivity training and nude therapy."

The lesson is a powerful one. If consultants do not have the active support of the chief executive officer (CEO), program failure is virtually inevitable (Argyris, 1973; Boss, 1978). This is true for at least two reasons. First, as outlined in the literature (Campbell, Dunnette, Lawler, & Weick, 1970), people generally behave as they do because they expect their behavior to lead to a desired end. Many examples of leader or manager expectations affecting subordinate behaviors (Berlew & Hall, 1964, 1966; Cooper, 1970; Dunbar, 1975; Neeley & Fielder, 1968) make it appear plausible that the president's noninvolvement had an undermining effect on the OD effort. Second, subordinates knew that pleasing the "boss" was perhaps the best way of increasing the possibility of favorable rewards. If the president did not support the OD effort, it would logically have been in the interest of personnel to become uninterested in, and even opposed to, the project.

Object Lesson 7: Consultants' efforts that lack the active support of the chief executive officer are almost inevitably doomed to failure.

Ignoring the Organization Critics

Early in the change process, the consultants learned of a small group of personnel who were highly critical of Kingston in general, and of the vice president in particular. The consultants were cautioned to be highly selective about any information they might obtain from these people. Although the consultants did not intentionally ignore these critics, they did not actively seek them out. This proved to be a major tactical error. Late in the consultation process, it was learned that persons in this group had information that could have helped prevent many of the problems.

A second viewpoint is always helpful to consultants, who face the possibility of becoming victimized by the "company line." For this reason it is wise to seek out persons with viewpoints and opinions known to be different from those held by top management in order to avoid being victimized.

Object Lesson 8: When possible, the consultant should seek out the perceptions of those who have viewpoints different from the prevailing norms.

Change for the Sake of Change: A Destructive Change Strategy

When the vice president accepted his position at Kingston, he simultaneously accepted the charge to "clean things up" and "straighten the place out." He was quick to announce that many changes were needed and forthcoming. Among his first actions was hiring two administrative assistants and one line supervisor. The two administrative assistants were good friends of his and had worked with him previously. The line supervisor, responsible for 250 of 300 employees who reported to the vice president, was hired as a result of pressure from the president.

Because these assistants were not known to the Kingston personnel, their initial response was

guarded optimism. However, the assistants' backgrounds soon became common conversation prices: one was a former policeman and the other an ex-convict. Stereotypic images of "cop" and "con" complicated their relationships with other employees. The line supervisor, a member of the local lay clergy, was similarly type cast, although not as negatively.

The vice president was required to travel a great deal. In his absence he customarily appointed one of the three new people to act in his stead. They received specific instructions to "get out in the organization and keep things stirred up to keep people off guard." The ex-convict was particularly adept in this function. Typically, he would confront employees in their work settings with remarks such as "What do you think you're doing?" or "Who told you to do that?" After short and often biting interrogation, he left people frustrated, bewildered, and frequently angered. This strategy, coupled with its often brusk implementation, contributed to the low trust levels and the degenerative environment. Resentment was soon directed at the assistants. Aware of this criticism, the vice president deliberately and consistently declared unyielding support of his assistants, declaring "When they leave, I leave." As a result of this unrealistic support of his assistants, he found it easy to ignore criticism of them, which heightened the growing suspicion and distrust of him.

Object Lesson 9: The newness that comes with planned change is sufficiently frustrating without compounding it. Successful consultative efforts do not "stir things up" but focus on funneling organizational energies—both physical and psychological—in the desired direction.

The Development of Internal Change Agents

The growing suspicion and distrust of the vice president and his assistants had additional by-products. For example, the consultants requested that some personnel be identified as internal change agents, with the expectation that they could fulfill a number of functions, i.e., they could provide on-the-spot contact with the organization and be a resource for making administrative arrangements, as they would have knowledge of both the norms of the organization and the behavior of critical people in the change process. Thus, they could provide information to the organization and to the consultants that would not otherwise be available. They also could function as resources in training other internal change agents and subsequently decrease the dependence on the external consultants. In addition, they could reinforce, over time, the values and changes introduced by the consultants.

Because suspicion and distrust of the vice president and his assistants extended in some measure to the consultants, their credibility was also weakened. As a result of guilt by association, some personnel were hesitant to serve as internal consultants. In addition, Kingston's top management refused to permit anyone to take on any additional responsibilities, particularly those associated with the change process.

> Object Lesson 10: Unless a consulting contract specifies a joint approach to problem diagnosis and resolution, it is almost impossible to train and utilize an internal OD consultant effectively, although his or her knowledge of the organization would be a valuable aid in facilitating change.

Inaccessibility of the Consultants

The distance between Kingston and the consultants' home office further dramatized the need for internal OD consulting both during the consulting period and later. The consultants flew in for training and team-building sessions. Therefore, it was extremely difficult for them to gain either a thorough "feel" for the organization or a sense of what was currently happening. Occasional telephone conversations with the vice president revealed only scanty and selective information, and the degree of turmoil and conflict was hidden.

Long-distance consulting has definite disadvantages. Short-term or "we'll be there once in a while" consulting styles seem unlikely to have the power to introduce a sustained change. Lasting changes are slow in coming and require long-term interactions between the client and consultant. Whether deliberate or not, the consultant who does not agree to a long-term consultative arrangement may do more damage than good, simply because client expectations are raised and then frustrated by the fact that it takes a long time and a great deal of work to introduce lasting change.

> Object Lesson 11: Consultants should arrange their consulting interactions so that they can be with the client over substantial periods of time. When geography or any other factor prevents consultants from maintaining constant and long-term relationships with the client, the likelihood of introducing sustained and lasting change is reduced.

The Linking-Pin Was Skipped

Rensis Likert (1961) identified people who simultaneously belong to two groups in an organization as "linking pins." The notion illustrates the upward, as well as the traditionally recognized downward, flow of influence in an organization. Because a linking-pin manager is not only a connector of two groups but also a *member* of those groups, he or she reflects the values, biases, and opinions of each group when interacting with the other. The perceptions and behaviors of a linking-pin manager are important components of the attitudinal and behavioral makeup of the groups; therefore, he or she becomes a key facilitator of accurate communication and the chief guarantor that the attitudes of one level of management are passed up or down to the next level.

It is imperative for a consultant to ensure linking-pin participation in the activities of *both* groups to which the linking-pin belongs. Failure to do so seriously disrupts the organization-wide influence the consultant(s) can have, because the organization's chain of command exerts much influence.

At Kingston, the vice-president and his immediate subordinates participated in an off-site team-building session. Their experience was so positive that they were convinced that their subordinates, particularly the line supervisor's immediate subordinates, should experience the same design. They thought it would obviously be good for the rest of the organization. However, negative feelings toward the vice president and his assistants were nearly universal at this point. Time constraints complicated the issue, making it difficult for the line supervisor to meet with his division heads, who by this time were near revolt.

Thus, the decision was made that the division heads should experience the training with their own subordinates. This proved to be a serious mistake. Although the consultants felt uncomfortable about proceeding without being sure that issues were resolved between the line supervisor and the division heads, they nonetheless acquiesced to the wishes of the vice president.

> Object Lesson 12: Generally speaking, team building with natural teams should not proceed until issues with the linking-pin and his or her peers and superiors are resolved satisfactorily.

Mandatory Training

The most effective training—and learning—occur when participants choose to participate of their own volition. At Kingston, the reverse occurred. The division heads and their subordinates received notice of the team-building sessions in a memo that said: "You are hereby directed to attend a management-training seminar to be held at the local YMCA during the following three-day period . . ." Even though the training was held in Kingston's hometown, personnel were required to stay at the YMCA during the three-day period. After appropriate sleeping arrangements had been made for the training population, several personnel asked the line supervisor if they had a choice of whether to attend. His reported response was, "If you don't go, you'll lose your job."

This loss of free agency resulted in a bitter and hostile training population. It was not surprising that the consultants spent the first day and a half defusing the explosive attitudes of the participants. Although the training was considered beneficial in terms of personal growth and resolving issues among the individual team members, nothing was done to resolve the tremendous difficulties that existed between the vice president, his assistants, and the line supervisor on the one hand and the lower level employees in the organization on the other.

> Object Lesson 13: The potential of effective training or team building is drastically reduced under coercive conditions. Participants must be invited or encouraged to participate, but should never be compelled or coerced under threat of termination.

Unrealistic Expectations

A major problem facing the OD effort was unrealistic expectations of the president and the other vice presidents about what would result. They had thought that OD was the answer to all organizational problems and that everything would be resolved in a few months with minimal investment by the president and those in the informal power structure. When this did not happen, extreme frustration resulted.

> Object Lesson 14: To protect both clients and themselves from the frustrations of false expectations, in the early stages of psychological contracting, consultants must clearly define with the client what roles each will assume and what kinds of expectations are realistic.

Consultants Not Permitted to Collect Data

When the president ordered the consultants to leave the organization, the vice president protested, arguing that conditions had in fact improved substantially. The president, feeling certain that few, if any, of the so-called changes were the result of the intervention activities, demanded proof. Because the initial request to collect questionnaire data had been denied (on the grounds that such an examination of organizational climate might ultimately be detrimental to the organization), no data were available. All that could be offered were hollow testimonials. In addition, the consultants were left without any before-after comparison data with which to assess the effectiveness of their efforts.

In short, the consultants were handcuffed by client fears of data collection and the vice president found that what he had originally intended as a protection was the variable that sealed his fate.

> Object Lesson 15: Wherever possible it is wise to collect data formally so that (1) the consultants can monitor their progress and specifically tailor their design to organizational needs; (2) the client can see and know what changes have in fact occurred; and (3) reliable before-after comparisons can be made.

The Patient Dies

A by-product of the training session with the division heads and their subordinates was a commitment from the vice president and the line supervisor to meet with the division heads in a confrontation/team-building meeting to resolve problems. That session proved to be hostile and explosive. Many issues were raised, and both administrators received a great deal of criticism. However, issues were worked through, the problems were resolved, and the division heads left the meeting apparently committed to support attempts to facilitate change and resolve problems that had plagued Kingston for years.

The line supervisor's emotional stability and personal commitment, however, were not as strong as his verbal commitment. Although he was the object of intense personal attack during the confrontation/team-building session, all involved, including a group of his committed followers, felt that the issues had been resolved. The next day, however, he went to the president and complained that he had been "crucified" by the vice president and the division heads. With a "tyranny known only in groups," he felt they had "mercilessly attacked everything" he believed in while trying to reduce him to "a state of emotional helplessness."

Although the relationship between the line supervisor and the president was not based on actual kinship, their shared fraternal, religious, educational, and moral values made their loyalty and commitment to one another very binding. The president believed him without question. Thus, he effectively neutralized the vice president's influence with the president and caused the president to seriously question the vice president's integrity. When information the line supervisor supplied to the president was not the same as that which the vice president publicly supplied in open forum, the president believed the former.

Thus, based on misinformation and unrealized and wholly unrealistic expectations about the change effort, the president decreed that the OD effort was over.

Many forces joined to kill the OD effort at Kingston before it ever really began. None of the factors alone was enough by itself. Taken as a whole, however, it appears as if the human autopsy had revealed that the patient was simultaneously suffering from cancer, cirrhosis of the liver, congestive heart failure, tuberculosis, rickets, and chronic halitosis. In addition, the operating physicians seem to have added occasional blows with a blunt instrument. It is our hope that this case analysis will serve as a reminder of the danger of ignoring some basic principles of effective consultation and, in turn, help save some OD projects from such an examination.

References

Abramovitz, A. B. Methods and techniques of consulation. *American Journal of Orthopsychiatry,* 1958, *28,* 78–90.

Argyris, C. *Intervention theory and method.* Reading, Mass.: Addison-Wesley Publishing, 1970.

Argyris, C. *Management and organization development.* New York: McGraw-Hill, 1971.

Argyris, C. The CEO's behavior: Key to organizational development. *Harvard Business Review,* 1973, *51,* 55–64.

Berlew, E., & Hall, D. T. The management of tension in organizations: Some preliminary findings. *Industrial Management Review,* 1964, *6,* 31–40.

Berlew, E., & Hall, D. T. The socialization of managers: Effects of expectations on performance. *Administrative Science Quarterly,* 1966, *11,* 207–222.

Boss, R. W. The effects of leader absence on a confrontation–team-building design. *Journal of Applied Behavioral Science,* 1978, *14*(4), 469–478.

Bowman, P. H. The role of the consultant as a motivator of action. *Mental Hygiene,* 1959, *63,* 105–110.

Campbell, J. P., Dunnette, M. D., Lawler, E. E., III, & Weick, K. E., Jr. Expectancy theory. In D. R. Hampton, C. E. Summer, & R. A. Webber, *Organizational behavior and the practice of management.* Glenview, Ill.: Scott, Foresman, 1970.

Cooper, R. Task-oriented leadership and subordinate response. In B. M. Bass, R. Cooper, & J. A. Haas (Eds.), *Managing for accomplishment.* Lexington, Mass.: D. C. Heath, 1970.

Dunbar, R. L. M. Manager's influence on subordinates' thinking about safety. *Academy of Management Journal,* 1975, *18,* 364–369.

Ferguson, C. K. Concerning the nature of human systems and the consultant's role. *Journal of Applied Behavioral Science,* 1968, *4*(2), 179–194.

Frank, L. L., & Hackman, J. R. A failure of job enrichment. *Journal of Applied Behavioral Science,* 1975, *11,* 413–436.

Gibb, J. R. The role of the consultant. *Journal of Social Issues,* 1959, *15,* 1–4.

Gilbert, R. Functions of the consultant. *Teachers College Record,* 1960, *61,* 177–187.

Gouldner, A. Explorations in applied social science. *Social Problems,* 1956, *3,* 26–40.

Jacques, E. Social therapy: Technocracy or collaboration. *Journals of Social Issues,* Spring 1947, 59–66.

Koch, W. H., Jr. A stance toward helping: Reflections on the role of a consultant. *Adult Leadership,* 1967, *16,* 202–204, 235–236, 239.

Likert, R. *New patterns of management.* New York: McGraw-Hill, 1961.

Lippitt, R. Dimensions of a consultant's job. *Journal of Social Issues,* 1959, *15,* 15–33.

Long, M. A. Action versus advice: Conflict in consulting. *American Library Association Bulletin,* 1966, *60,* 12–27.

Margulies, N., & Raia, A. Action research and the consultative process. *Business Perspective,* 1968, *5,* 26–30.

Marrow, A. J. *Making waves in foggy bottom.* Washington, D.C.: National Training Laboratory, 1974.

McMillan, C. B. Organizational change in schools: Bedford-Stuyvesant. *Journal of Applied Behavioral Science,* 1975, *11,* 437–453.

Mirvis, P. H., & Berg, D. N. *Failures in organization development and change.* New York: John Wiley & Sons, 1977.

Nealey, S., & Fiedler, F. E. Leadership functions of middle managers. *Psychological Bulletin,* 1968, *70,* 313–329.

Rogers, C. The characteristics of a helping relationship. *Personnel and Guidance Journal,* 1958, 12, 6–16.

Seashore, C., & Van Egmond, E. The consultant-trainer role in working with a total staff. *Journal of Social Issues,* 1959, *15*(2), 36–42.

Schein, E. *Process consultation: Its role in organization development.* Reading, Mass.: Addison-Wesley Publishing, 1969.

Tilles, S. Understanding the consultant's role. *Harvard Business Review,* 1961, *39,* 87–99.

B. Managing the OD Process

The first essay in this section, by David Nadler, presents a general systems model of organizations and looks at three major problems in organizational change: resistance, control, and power. The essay concludes with specific action steps that can be taken to manage these problems and with an illustrative case.

In the next essay, Jerry Porras, Joan Harkness, and Coeleen Kiebert present a framework for analyzing the OD process. In particular, they focus on the four factors they see as being "altered by any complex OD intervention," namely, the organization's structure, technology, human processes, and internal physical environment. The method of diagramming planned and actual changes in the unfolding OD process, the authors assert, has multiple uses in tracking and managing the change process.

Finally, this section includes a "strategy checklist" by Wendell French. This checklist lists many of the dimensions or variables that the author believes must be managed effectively if the OD process is to be successful. Suggestions for the management of each variable are included.

The checklist grew out of one of French's experiences as a consultant in a long-range OD effort in a city government situation. This checklist may be particularly useful in highlighting some of the system variables which may "make or break" an OD effort in many settings.

The reader will note that participation by the chief executive officer (CEO) is emphasized in this checklist.[1] This person might be the president of a company, a school superintendent, a city manager, the dean of a relatively autonomous school within a university, or the administrator or chief medical officer of a hospital. It is unrealistic to expect OD efforts to "start at the top" in all instances but, as a general rule, OD efforts do not flourish unless the CEO of a major unit is involved. Ultimately, even the head of a relatively autonomous unit will at least need support from higher in the organization if the OD effort is to be sustained.

---

[1]Chris Argyris, "The CEO's Behavior: Key to OD," *Harvard Business Review,* April–May 1973, pp. 55–64.

Reading 52

MANAGING ORGANIZATIONAL CHANGE: AN INTEGRATIVE PERSPECTIVE

David A. Nadler

Introduction

Bringing about major change in a large and complex organization is a difficult and problematic task. Individuals and groups must be motivated to continue to perform in the face of major turbulence. People must be told that the "old ways" which include familiar tasks, jobs, procedures, and structures are no longer applicable. Political behavior frequently becomes more active and more intense. It is not surprising, therefore, that the effective implementation of organizational change has long been a topic pondered by both managers and researchers. While there is still much that is not understood about change in complex organizations, the experiences and research of recent years do provide some guidance to those concerned with implementing major changes in organizations.

This paper presents a framework to aid in understanding the dynamics of change and in planning and managing major organizational changes. First will be a brief discussion of a model of organizational behavior. Some notion of why organizations work the way they do in the first place is essential before thinking about changing them. The second section of this paper will define what is meant by "organizational change" and identify criteria for effective management of change. Third, some of the basic problems of implementing change will be discussed. In the last section, specific guidelines for effective implementation of organizational

changes will be presented. In general, the goal of this paper is to integrate existing findings, theories, and models of change rather than to develop new ones. The question to be investigated is whether existing knowledge can be synthesized to create a valid, yet pragmatic, conceptual framework for the management of organizational change.

A View of Organizations

There are many different ways of thinking about organizations and the patterns of behavior that occur within them. During the past two decades, however, there has been an emerging view of organizations as complex, open, social systems (Katz & Kahn, 1966). Organizations are seen as mechanisms which take input from the larger environment and subject that input to various transformations which result in output.

As systems, organizations are seen as composed of interdependent parts. Change in one element of the system will result in changes in other parts of the system. Similarly, organizations have the property of equilibrium: the system will generate energy to move toward a state of balance. Finally, as open systems, organizations need to maintain favorable transactions of input and output with the environment in order to survive over time.

While the systems perspective is useful, systems theory by itself may be too abstract a concept to be a tool of managers. Thus, a number of organizational theorists have attempted to develop more pragmatic theories or models based on the general systems paradigm. There are a number of such models in use, one of which will be employed here.

Source: Reprinted with permission from NTL Institute, "Managing Organizational Change: An Integrative Perspective" by David A. Nadler, pp. 191–211, *The Journal of Applied Behavioral Science* 17, no. 2. Copyright 1981.

The particular approach, called a *Congruence Model of Organizational Behavior* (Nadler & Tushman, 1977, 1980), is based on the general systems model. The model is structured around input, transformation, and output. The major types of input to the system of organizational behavior are seen as the *environment* which presents constraints, demands, and opportunities; the *resources* available to the organization; and the *history* of the organization, including key events, decisions, crises, norms, etc., which influence current behavior. A fourth input, and perhaps the most crucial, is the organization's *strategy*. Strategy is the set of key decisions about the match of the organization's resources to the opportunities, constraints, and demands in the environment within the context of history.

The output of the system includes the patterns of activity and performance at different levels of analysis. Specifically, the output includes *organizational performance,* as well as *group performance,* and *individual behavior and affect* which, of course, contribute to organizational performance.

The basic framework thus views the organization as the mechanism that takes input (strategy and resources in the context of history and environment) and transforms it into output (patterns of individual, group, and organizational behavior). This view is portrayed in Figure 1.

The major focus of organizational analysis is, therefore, this transformation process. The model conceives of the organization as comprising four major components:

1. the *task* of the organization, or the work to be done and its inherent critical characteristics;
2. the *individuals* who are to perform organizational tasks;
3. the *formal organizational arrangements*, including various structures, processes, systems, etc., which are designed to motivate and facilitate individuals in the performance of organizational tasks; and
4. a set of *informal organizational arrangements* which are usually neither planned nor written, but which tend to emerge over time. These include patterns of communication, power, and influence, values, and norms, etc., which characterize how an organization actually functions.

How do these four components (task, individuals, organizational arrangements, and the informal organization) relate to each other? The relationship among components is the basic dynamic of the model. Each component can be thought of as having a relationship with every other component. Between each pair, then, we can think of a relative degree of consistency, congruence, or

FIGURE 1   The Systems Model Applied to Organizational Behavior

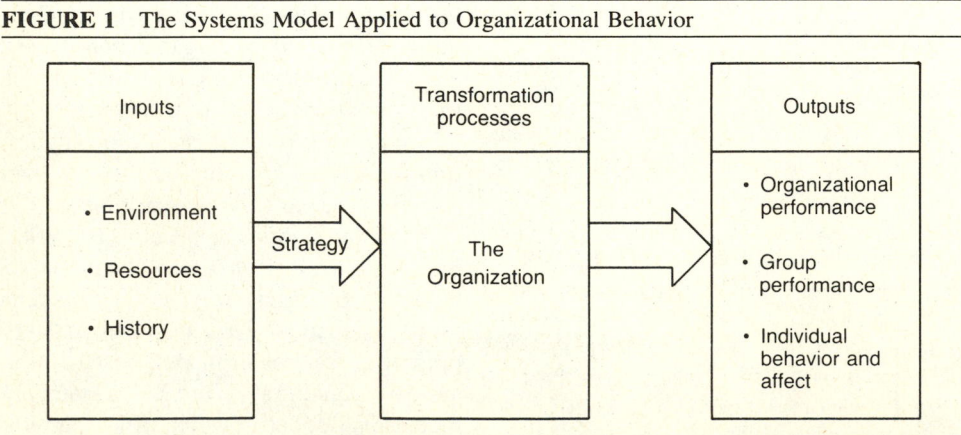

FIGURE 2   A Congruence Model of Organizational Behavior*

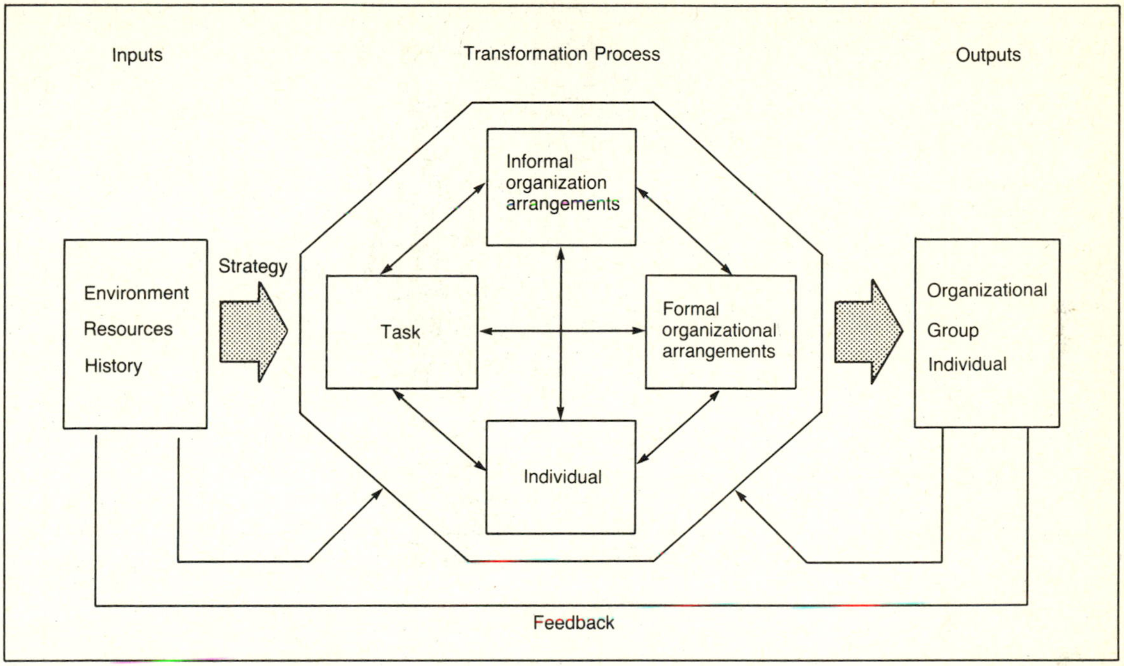

*From Nadler and Tushman, 1980.

''fit.'' As a simple example, we could look at the type of work to be done (task) and the nature of the people available to do the work (individuals), and we could make a statement about the congruence between the two by seeing whether the demands of the work are consistent with the skills of the individuals. At the same time we could compare the rewards that the work provides vs. the needs and desires of the individuals. By looking at these factors, we would be able to assess how congruent the nature of the task was with the nature of the individuals in the system.

In fact, we could look at the question of congruence between all the components, or in terms of all six of the possible relationships among them (see Figure 2). The basic hypothesis of the model is that *organizations will be most effective when their major components are congruent with each other.* To the extent that organizations face problems of effectiveness resulting from management

and organizational factors, these problems will stem from poor fit, or lack of congruence, among organizational components.

The concept of fit or congruence is not a new one in organizational theory. Homans (1950), in his pioneering work on social processes in organizations, emphasized the critical role of the interaction and consistency among key elements of organizational behavior. The concepts of consistency and/or relationships among organizational components have been used by a variety of theorists during the last two decades (e.g., Leavitt, 1965; Seiler, 1967; Lawrence & Lorsch, 1969; Lorsch & Sheldon, 1969; Galbraith, 1977). At the core of this systems-based perspective is the assumption that the interaction among the organizational components is perhaps more critical than the characteristics of the components themselves, and that as systems, organizations fundamentally work better when the pieces fit together.

This perspective on organizations is thus a contingency approach. There is not one best organization design, or style of management, or method of working. Rather, different patterns of organization and management will be most appropriate in different situations. The model recognizes the fact that individuals, tasks, strategies, and environments may differ greatly from organization to organization.

The Task of Implementing Change

Changes may be prompted by environmental variations, strategic shifts, the introduction of new technologies, changing worker characteristics, etc. In most cases, major changes require not only changes in strategy and the nature of the work to be done, but also alterations in structures, people, processes, etc.

Beckhard and Harris (1977), in their discussion of change management, provide a simple but powerful vocabulary for talking about the different kinds of significant changes that occur in organizations. They argue that almost any major change, no matter what the content, can be thought of as a transition (see Figure 3).

A change begins with the organization existing in a *current state* (A). The *future state* (B) is how the organization is planned or envisioned. It is the expected state that would ideally exist after the change. The period between A and B can be thought of as the *transition state* (C). Beckhard and Harris argue that the transition state is critical because it greatly determines the quality of the future state,

yet it has characteristics that make it uniquely different from either the current or future state.

What constitutes effective management of change? Using the transition management language presented above, organization change has been effectively managed when:

1. The organization is moved from the current state to the future state (obviously a necessary but not sufficient criterion).
2. The functioning of the organization in the future state meets expectations—i.e., it works as planned.
3. The transition is accomplished without undue cost to the organization.
4. The transition is accomplished without undue cost to individual organizational members.

Of course, not every organizational change can be expected to meet these criteria, but such standards provide a target for planning change. The question is how to manage the implementation of change so that the change will be most effective.

Problems in Implementing Change

Using the organizational model presented above, we can envision how organizations, as systems, are resistant to change. The forces of equilibrium tend to work to cancel out many changes. Changing one component of an organization may reduce its congruence with other components. As this happens, energy develops in the organization to limit, encapsulate, or revise the change.

FIGURE 3   Organizational Change as a Transition State*

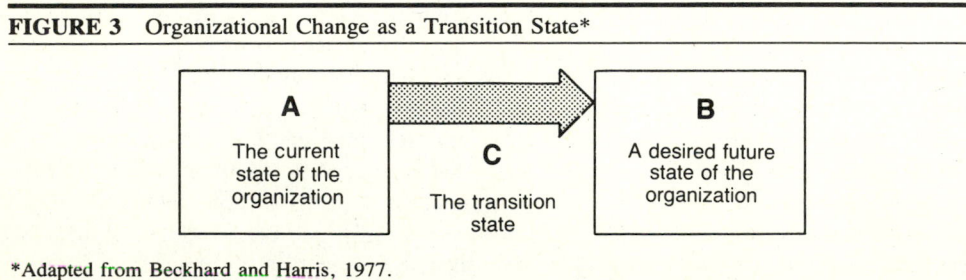

*Adapted from Beckhard and Harris, 1977.

It is therefore critical to take a holistic or systemic perspective when thinking about a major organizational change. At the most general level, effective management of change requires three steps. First, there is a need to assess or diagnose the current state. In terms of the Congruence Model, this involves an analysis of input, output, and the nature of the consistency among organizational components as a way to identify problems or opportunities. Second, there is a need to design the future state. Typically, this involves a determination of desired output, the development of strategy to achieve that output, and the design of the task, individual, formal organization, and informal organization component configuration needed to execute that strategy. The third step is implementing the movement or modification of those components, and it is here that a special set of problems are encountered.

First is the problem of *resistance* to change (Watson, 1969; Zaltman & Duncan, 1977). Any individual faced with a change in the organization in which he or she works may be resistant for a variety of reasons. People need a certain degree of stability or security, and change presents unknowns which cause anxiety. In addition, a change that is imposed on individuals reduces their sense of autonomy or self-control. People typically develop patterns for coping with or managing the current structure and situation. Change means that they will have to find new ways of managing their own environments— ways that might not be as successful as those currently used. In addition, people who have power have a vested interest in the status quo and may resist change because it threatens that power. Finally, individuals may resist change for ideological reasons; they may truly believe that the way things are done is better than the proposed change. Whatever the source, individual resistance to change must be overcome for successful implementation.

The second problem is organizational *control*. Change disrupts the normal course of events within an organization. It thus disrupts and undermines existing systems of management control, particularly those developed as part of the formal organizational arrangements. Change may make those systems irrelevant and/or inappropriate. As a result, during a change the organization may lose the capacity to effectively coordinate the work being done. As goals, structures, and people shift, it becomes difficult to monitor performance and make corrections as in normal control processes.

The problem of diminished control is exacerbated by the fact that most formal organizational arrangements are designed for stable states, not transition states. Managers become fixated with the future state (B) and concentrate their energies on designing the most effective organizational arrangements for the future, while thinking of change from A to B as simply a mechanical or procedural detail. The problems created by lack of concern for the transition state are compounded by its unique character. In most situations, the management systems and structures developed to manage their A or B are simply not appropriate or adequate for the management of C. They are steady-state management systems, designed to run organizations already in place rather than to manage transitions.

The third problem is *power*. Any organization is a political system made up of different individuals, groups, and coalitions competing for power (Tushman, 1977; Salancik & Pfeffer, 1977). Political behavior is thus a natural and expected feature of organizations in both A and B states. In state C (transition), however, these dynamics become even more intense as the old order is dismantled and a new order emerges. This happens because any significant change poses the possibility of upsetting or modifying the balance of power among groups. The uncertainty created by change creates ambiguity, which in turn tends to increase the probability of political activity (Thompson & Tuden, 1959). Individuals and groups may take action based on their perception of how the change will affect their relative power position in the organization. They will try to influence where they will sit in the organization that emerges from the transition and will be concerned about how the conflict of the transition period will affect the balance of power in the future state. Finally, individuals and groups may engage in political action because of their ideological position on the change—

it may be inconsistent with their shared values, culture, or image of the organization (Pettigrew, 1972).

In some sense, each of these problems is related primarily (but not exclusively) to one of the components of the organization (see Figure 4). Resistance relates to the individual component, getting people to change their behavior. Control concerns the design of appropriate organizational arrangements for the transition period. Power relates to the reactions of the informal organization to change. The implication is that if a change is to be effective, all three problems—resistance, control, and power—must be addressed.

Guidelines for Implementing Change

The three basic problems that are inherent in change each lead to a general implication for the management of change (see Figure 5).

The implication of the resistance problem is the need to *motivate* changes in behavior by individuals. This involves overcoming the natural resistance to change that emerges and getting individuals to behave in ways consistent with both the short-run goals of change and long-run organizational strategy.

The implication of the control problem is the need to *manage the transition period*. Organizational arrangements need to be designed and used to ensure that control is maintained during and after the transition. These devices and approaches need to be ones specifically appropriate to the transition period rather than the current or future state.

Finally, the implication of the power issue is the need to *shape the political dynamics of change* so that power centers develop that support the change rather than block it (Pettigrew, 1975).

Each of these general implications suggests specific actions that can be taken to improve the prob-

---

FIGURE 4   Problems of Change in Relation to the Components of the Organizational Model

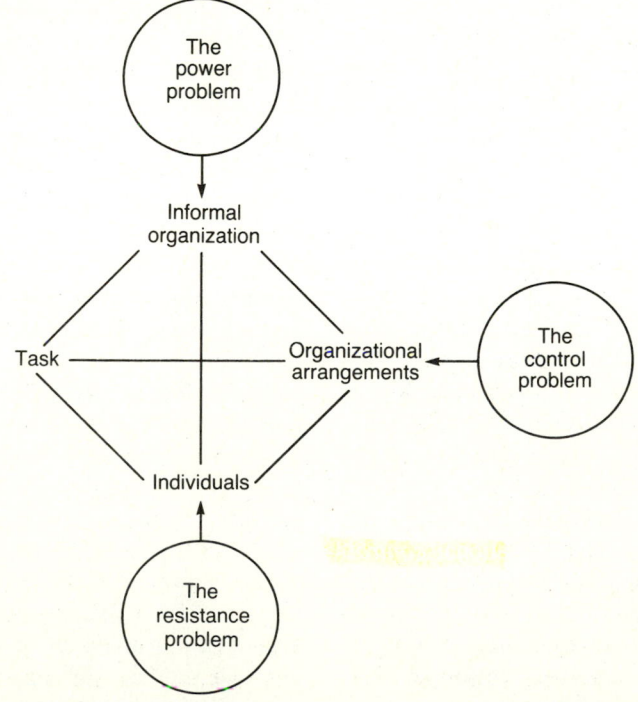

FIGURE 5 Problems of Change and Implications for Change Management

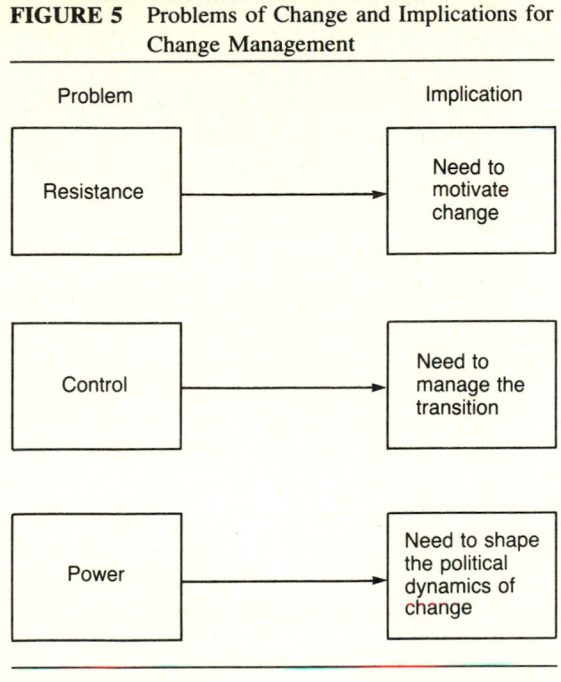

abilities of achieving an effective change. A number of those action steps can be identified for each of the three implications.

Action Steps to Motivate Change

The first action step is to *identify and surface dissatisfaction with the current state*. As long as people are satisfied with the current state, they will not be motivated to change; people need to be "unfrozen" out of their inertia in order to be receptive to change (Lewin, 1947; Bennis, Berlew, Schein & Steele, 1973). The greater the pain and dissatisfaction with the current state, then the greater the motivation to change and the less the resistance to change. As a consequence, the management of change may require the creation of pain and dissatisfaction with the status quo. Dissatisfaction most commonly results from information concerning some aspect of organizational performance which is different from either desired or expected performance. Discrepanices can therefore be used to cre-

ate dissatisfaction. As a result, data can be an important tool to initiate change (Nadler, 1977).

The second action step is to build in *participation* in the change. One of the most consistent findings in the research on change is that participation in the change tends to reduce resistance, builds ownership of the change, and thus motivates people to make the change work (Coch & French, 1948; Vroom, 1964; Kotter & Schlesinger, 1979). Participation also facilitates the communication of information about what the change will be and why it has come about. Participation may also lead to obtaining new information from those participating, information that may enhance the effectiveness of the change or the future state.

On the other hand, participation has costs since it involves relinquishing control, takes time, and may create conflict. For each situation, different degrees of participation may be most effective (Vroom & Yetton, 1973). Participation may involve work on diagnosing the present situation, in planning change, in implementing change, or in combinations of the above. Participation may also vary in the specific devices that are used, ranging from large-scale data collection to sensing groups, to questionnaires, to cross-unit committees, and so on.

A third step is to build in *rewards* for the behavior that is desired both during the transition state and in the future state. Our understanding of motivation and behavior in organizations suggests that people will tend to be motivated to behave in ways that they perceive as leading to desired outcomes (Vroom, 1964; Lawler, 1973). The implication is that both formal and informal rewards need to be identified and tied to the behavior that is needed, both for the transition and for the future state. The most frequent problem is that organizations expect individuals to behave in certain ways (particularly in a transition) while rewarding them for other conflicting behaviors (Kerr, 1975). In particular, rewards such as bonuses, pay systems, promotion, recognition, job assignment, and status symbols all need to be carefully examined during major organizational changes and restructured to support the direction of the transition.

Finally, people need to be provided with the *time and opportunity to disengage from the present state*. Change frequently creates feelings of loss, not unlike a death. People need to mourn for the old system or familiar way of doing things. This frequently is manifested in the emergence of stories about the "good old days," even when those days were not so good. The process of accepting a loss and going through mourning takes time, and those managing change need to take this into account. This factor underscores the need to provide information about the problems of the status quo and also to plan for enough time in advance of a change to allow people to recognize the loss and prepare for it.

Action Steps to Manage the Transition

An early and critical step for managing the transition state should be to *develop and communicate a clear image of the future* (Beckhard & Harris, 1977). Resistance and confusion frequently develop during an organizational change because people are uncertain about what the future state will look like. Thus, the goals and purposes of the change become blurred, and individual expectancies are formed on the basis of information that is often erroneous. In the absence of a clear image of the future, rumors develop, people create their own fantasies, and they act on them. The clearest image possible of the future state needs to be developed to serve as a guideline, target, or goal. In particular, a written statement or description of the future state may be of value in clarifying the image, particularly when articulated by formal and/or informal leaders. Specifically, it is important to communicate information to those involved in the change, including what the future state will look like, how the transition will come about, why the change is being implemented, and how individuals will be affected by the change.

A second action step for managing the transition involves the use of *multiple and consistent leverage points*. If, building on the model presented above, an organization is made up of components which are interdependent, then the successful alteration of organizational behavior patterns must utilize multiple leverage points. Structural change, task change, change in the social environment, as well as changes in individuals themselves are all needed to bring about significant and lasting changes in the patterns of organizational behavior. This observation flows directly from systems theory and the Congruence Model. If the organization is in some kind of balance or state of fit, then major alterations in one component will tend to disrupt the balance. Forces of equilibrium, however, tend to move the organization back into balance or fit, with the result of stamping out or nullifying single-component changes. Changes that are targeted at individuals and social relations (such as training, group interventions, etc.) tend to fade out quickly with few lasting effects when done in isolation (Porter, Lawler & Hackman, 1975). On the other hand, task and structural changes alone, while powerful and enduring, frequently produce unintended and dysfunctional consequences (see, for example, literature on control systems—e.g., Lawler & Rhode, 1976).

Change which is in the direction intended and which is lasting therefore requires the use of multiple leverage points or modifications in the larger set of components which shape the behavior of the organization and the people in it (Nadler & Tichy, 1981). Similarly, the changes have to be sequenced and structured with regard for consistency; the training of individuals, for example, should dovetail with new job descriptions, rewards systems, or reporting relationships. In the absence of consistency, changes run the risk of creating new "poor fits" between organizational components. The result is either an abortive change or decreases in organizational performance.

The third action step involves a number of different activities. The implication is that *organizational arrangements for the transition* need to be explicitly considered, designed, and used. As mentioned earlier, the organizational arrangements that function in either the present or future state are typically steady-state designs, rather than designs for use in managing the transition state. The whole issue of developing structures to manage the transition has been discussed in depth elsewhere (see Beckhard & Harris, 1977), but a number of the most important elements should be mentioned here. In particular, the following organizational arrangements are important for managing the change:

a. *A transition manager.* Someone should be designated as the manager of the organization for the transition state. This person may be a member of management, a chief executive, or someone else, but frequently it is difficult for one person to manage the current state, prepare to manage the future state, and simultaneously manage the transition. This person should have the power and authority needed to make the transition happen and should be appropriately linked to the steady-state managers, particularly the future-state manager.

b. *Resources for the transition.* Major transitions involve potentially large risks for organizations. Therefore, they are worth doing well, and it is worth providing the needed resources to make them happen effectively. Resources such as personnel, money, training, consultation, and so on, need to be provided for the transition manager.

c. *Transition plan.* To manage an effective movement from one state to another, and to measure and control performance, a plan is needed with benchmarks, standards of performance, and similar features. Implicit in such a plan is a specification of the responsibilities of key individuals and groups.

d. *Transition management structures.* Frequently, it is difficult for a hierarchy to manage the process of changing itself. As a result, it may be necessary to develop other structures or use other devices outside the regular organizational structure during the transition-management period. Special task forces, pilot projects, experimental units, etc., need to be designed and employed for this period (see again, Beckhard & Harris, 1977, for a discussion of these different devices).

The final action implication for transition management involves developing *feedback mechanisms* to provide transition managers with information on the effectiveness of the transition and provide data on areas which require additional attention or action. There is a huge amount of anecdotal data about senior managers ordering changes and as-

suming those changes were made, only to find out to their horror that the changes never occurred. Such a situation develops because managers lack feedback devices to tell them whether actions have been effective or not. During stable periods, effective managers develop various ways of eliciting feedback. During the transition state, however, these mechanisms often break down because of the turbulence of the change or because of the natural avoidance of providing "bad news." Thus, it becomes important for transition managers to develop multiple, redundant, and sensitive mechanisms for generating feedback about the transition. Devices such as surveys, sensing groups, and consultant interviews as well as informal communication channels need to be developed and used during this period.

Action Steps for Shaping the Political Dynamics of Change

If an organization is a political system composed of different groups each competing for power, then the most obvious action step is *assuring or developing the support of key power groups.* For a change to occur successfully, a critical mass of power groups needs to be assembled and mobilized in support of the change. Those groups that may oppose the change have to in some way be compensated for or have their effects neutralized. Not all power groups have to be intimately involved in the change. Some may support the change on ideological grounds while others may support the change because it enhances their own power. With other groups, they will have to be included in the planning of the change so that their participation will motivate them, or coopt them (Selznick, 1949). Yet others may have to be dealt with by bargaining or negotiation. The key point is that the important groups who may be affected by the change need to be identified, and strategies for building support among a necessary portion of those groups need to be developed and carried out (Sayles, 1979).

A major factor affecting the political terrain of an organization is the behavior of its powerful leaders. Thus, a second major action step involves *us-*

ing leader behavior to generate energy in support of the change. Leaders can mobilize groups, generate energy, provide models, manipulate major rewards, and do many other things which can affect the dynamics of the informal organization. Sets of leaders working in a coordinated manner can have a tremendously powerful impact on the informal organization. Thus, leaders need to think about using their own behavior to generate energy (see House, 1976, on charismatic leadership) as well as building on the support and behavior of other leaders (both formal and informal) within the organization. Specifically, leaders can enhance change efforts in various ways, including emphasizing the need to change, articulating the future state, modeling behavior consistent with the future state, rewarding those who aid the transition, and by expressing support of the organization's ability to successfully make the transition.

The third action implication in this area is related to the question of leadership. Energy is also created by the use of *symbols and language* (Peters, 1978; Pfeffer, 1980). By providing a language to describe the change and symbols that have emotional impact, it is possible to create new power centers or to bring together power centers under a common banner. Language is also important in defining an ambiguous reality. If a change, for example, is declared a success, then it may become a success in the perceptions of others. This implication is closely related to the previous point about leaders since they are frequently the major symbol creators or manipulators in organizations. Symbolic acts such as recognizing contributions in public and giving projects or positions particular names are examples of these. The senior manager's calendar is another example; how a senior manager's time is spent sends important messages to the organization.

Finally, there is the need to *build in stability.* Organizations and individuals can only stand so much uncertainty and turbulence. An overload of uncertainty may create dysfunctional effects: people may begin to panic, engage in extreme defensive behavior, and become irrationally resistant to any new change proposed. The increase of anxiety

created by constant change thus has its costs. One way of offsetting this reaction is to provide some sources of stability (structures, people, physical locations, that stay the same) to serve as "anchors" for people to hold onto and to provide a means for definition of the self in the midst of turbulence. For example, timetables for transition might help define the periods of stability or movement. Similarly, announcements about what pieces of the organization will not be modified can help to reduce anxiety. Thus, those aspects of the organization that will not change during a transition period need to be identified and communicated to organization members.

A Case Example

Introduction and Background

One way of illustrating the concepts of change management presented here is to describe a case in which a manager attempted to follow the guidelines and was successful in bringing about relatively effective change.

The unit was a staff department in a major corporation. With an operating budget of more than $50 million, the department was known for high technical expertise but was perceived as poorly managed, plagued by duplication of effort, and not being responsive to line-manager needs. Three previous department heads had attempted to "shake up" the department, but with little success. Somehow the same patterns of behavior persisted.

The change began when a new manager was assigned as department head. A successful line manager with a good track record, he analyzed the problems of the department and began to make changes. Soon, however, he became frustrated because of the lack of results. Several times he identified changes to be made, his staff agreed to them, but somehow the changes never occurred. There was always some plausible reason (budgets, new demands from the line, etc.), but nothing changed.

At this point the manager began talking with an external consultant (the author) about his problems.

The consultant presented the framework discussed above to the manager, and they decided to work together to use this approach to managing the change.

Preliminary Analysis

The work started with identifying the various "stakeholders" related to the change—those who might have a stake in the change succeeding or failing. The manager began having regular meetings with key stakeholders outside the department. Having identified the key stakeholders inside the department, the manager named them to a *planning team* and asked them to join him with the consultant for a five-day, off-site planning meeting. Before the meeting the consultant conducted general diagnostic interviews with each of the planning team members.

The Off-Site Meeting

The meeting began with an opening statement by the manager about the objectives and structure of the week. He followed this with a strong statement that the department was not performing as well as it could, and that if it did not perform better, it would face serious funding cuts in the future. Next, the consultant presented the summarized interview data which indicated that dissatisfaction with the department performance was widely shared.

During the week, the group (about 14 people) worked on analyzing their environment, resources, and history, and developing a basic strategy including a core mission statement, supporting strategies, and objectives. They then worked to design a new structure (three new units within the department) to implement their strategy.

On the last day, the group was presented with the change management concepts described in this paper. In small groups they generated lists of issues to be considered relating to each of the three major areas (motivating change, managing the transition, shaping the political dynamics). The manager announced his intention to appoint a transition manager and name a transition team.

Organizing the Transition

The day the planning team returned from the off-site, the manager distributed a memo to all department employees summarizing the results of the meeting, announcing the formation of the transition team, and setting a date for department-wide meetings on the new structure.

The transition team first finalized the design (writing a detailed statement of the strategy and new structure) and planned meetings so that each employee would have a presentation on the new organization in a large meeting, and would get a chance in a small-group meeting to ask questions and make comments or suggestions.

The transition team then developed a detailed transition plan outlining a sequence for changes, methods, and criteria for movement of functions, etc. The transition team met with the planning team (the original off-site group of stakeholders) for several off-site, one-day meetings to review and get approval on the transition plan.

Senior Management Support

During this time, the department manager continued to play a visible role. He attended joint planning/transition team meetings and started each with an opening statement reconfirming the importance of the activity. At times, in private, he confronted several of his staff who were resisting. Several promotions became possible, and those who were promoted were enthusiastic supporters of the transition. Finally, the performance appraisals and pay increases of his direct subordinates, which were all reviewed during this time, reflected the role that these managers played in the transition. Once the plan had been finalized, a large chart of the new organization and a flow chart of the transition plan were posted outside the manager's office.

Executing the Plan

The transition team got its plan approved and began executing it over a period of four months. During this time it used a short questionnaire at different points to collect data on employee perceptions of the transition. Based on these data, alterations in the transition plan were made and implemented. At the end of the time, the new structure was in place and all indicators were that it was functioning well and had occurred without major costs to the department or the people in it. In general, department members were positive about the new structure, their new roles, and the new sense of competence and effectiveness in the department.

Reflection

Despite the brevity of the case, a number of factors which contributed to the effective change are clear. First the manager motivated change by surfacing the common concerns about the current state, by building in participation, and by the use of rewards. Second, he managed the transition by developing and communicating a clear image of the future and by using explicit transition management structures (a transition manager, team, and plan; feedback devices; etc.). Third, he shaped the political dynamics by his own actions with stakeholders, through the creative use of the planning team, and through his own actions, both substantive and symbolic.

Summary

This paper has attempted to identify some of the problems, issues, and issues bringing about changes in complex organizations. At the same time, a number of general and specific action steps have been suggested. To understand how to change organizational behavior, we need a tool to understand how it occurs in the first place. The model used here (Nadler & Tushman, 1977, 1980) suggests that any change will encounter three general problems: resistance, control, and power. The general implication is the need to motivate change, manage the transition, and shape the political dynamics of change. For each of these three general implications, a number of specific action steps have been identified (see Table 1).

Obviously, each of these action steps will be more or less critical (and more or less feasible) in different situations. Thus, students of organization and managers alike need to use a diagnostic approach to the problems of managing change. Each situation, while reflecting general patterns, has its own unique characteristics, based on its own differences of individuals, history, and circumstances. Thus, specific variants of the action steps need to be developed for specific situations. To do this, managers need diagnostic models to understand problems, as well as guidelines for implementing changes, as presented here. Together, these two types of tools can be powerful aids in building and maintaining effective organizations.

References

Beckhard, R., & Harris, R. *Organizational transitions.* Reading, Mass.: Addison-Wesley, 1977.

Bennis, W. G., Berlew, D. E., Schein, E. H., & Steele, F. I. *Interpersonal dynamics: Essays and readings on human interaction.* Homewood, Ill.: Dorsey Press, 1973.

Coch, L., & French, J. R. P., Jr. Overcoming resistance to change. *Human Relations,* 1948, 11, 512–532.

Galbraith, J. R. *Organization design.* Reading, Mass.: Addison-Wesley, 1977.

Homans, G. C. *The human group.* New York: Harcourt, Brace & Co., 1950.

Katz, D., & Kahn, R. L. *The social psychology of organizations.* New York: John Wiley & Sons, 1966.

Kerr, S. On the folly of rewarding A while hoping for B. *Academy of Management Journal,* 1975, Dec., 769–783.

Kotter, J. P., & Schlesinger, L. A. Choosing strategies for change. *Harvard Business Review,* 1979, Mar.-April, 106–114.

Lawler, E. E. *Motivation in work organizations.* Belmont, Calif.: Wadsworth Publishing Co., 1973.

Lawler, E. E., & Rhode, J. G. *Information and control in organizations.* Santa Monica, Calif.: Goodyear, 1976.

Lawrence, P. R., & Lorsch, J. W. *Developing organizations: Diagnosis and action.* Reading, Mass.: Addison-Wesley, 1969.

Leavitt, H. J. Applied organizational change in industry. In J. G. March (Ed.), *Handbook of organizations.* Chicago: Rand McNally, 1965. Pp. 1144–1170.

TABLE 1 Implications for Change Management and Related Action Steps

Implication	*Action Steps*
Need to motivate change	1. Identify and surface dissatisfaction with the present state
	2. Participation in change
	3. Rewards for behavior in support of change
	4. Time and opportunity to disengage from the present state
Need to manage the transition	5. Develop and communicate a clear image of the future
	6. Use multiple and consistent leverage points
	7. Develop organizational arrangements for the transition
	8. Build in feedback mechanisms
Need to shape the political dynamics of change	9. Assure the support of key power groups
	10. Use leader behavior to generate energy in support of change
	11. Use symbols and language
	12. Build in stability

Lewin, K. Frontiers in group dynamics. *Human Relations*, 1947, 1, 5–41.

Lorsch, J. W., & Sheldon, A. The individual in the organization: A systems view. In J. W. Lorsch & P. R. Lawrence (Eds.), *Managing group and intergroup relations*. Homewood, Ill.: Irwin-Dorsey, 1972.

Nadler, D. A. *Feedback and organization development: Using data based methods*. Reading, Mass.: Addison-Wesley, 1977.

Nadler, D. A., & Tushman, M. L. A diagnostic model for organizational behavior. In J. R. Hackman, E. E. Lawler, & L. W. Porter (Eds.), *Perspectives on behavior in organizations*. New York: McGraw-Hill, 1977.

Nadler, D. A., & Tushman, M. L. A model for orga-

nizational diagnosis. *Organizational Dynamics*, 1980, Autumn.

Nadler, D. A., & Tichy, N. M. The limitations of traditional intervention technology in health care organizations. In N. Margulies & J. Adams (Eds.), *Organization development in health care organizations*. Reading, Mass.: Addison-Wesley, 1981.

Peters, T. J. Symbols, patterns, and settings: An optimistic case for getting things done. *Organizational Dynamics*, 1978, Autumn, 3–23.

Pettigrew, A. *The politics of organizational decision-making*. London: Tavistock Press, 1972.

Pettigrew, A. Towards a political theory of organizational intervention. *Human Relations*, 1978, 28, 191–208.

Pfeffer, J. Management as symbolic action: The creation and maintenance of organizational paradigms. In L. L. Cummings & B. M. Staw (Eds.), *Research in organizational behavior, Vol 3*. Greenwich, Conn.: JAI Press, 1980.

Porter, L. W., Lawler, E. E., & Hackman, J. R. *Behavior in organizations*. New York: McGraw-Hill, 1975.

Salancik, G. R., & Pfeffer, J. Who gets power and how they hold on to it: A strategic-contingency model of power. *Organizational Dynamics*, 1977, Winter, 3–21.

Sayles, L. R. *Leadership: What effective managers really do and how they do it*. New York: McGraw-Hill, 1979.

Seiler, J. A. *Systems analysis in organizational behavior*. Homewood, Ill.: Irwin-Dorsey, 1967.

Selznick, P. *TVA and the grass roots*. Berkeley, Calif.: University of California Press, 1949.

Thompson, J. D., & Tuden, A. Strategies, structures and processes of organizational decision. In J. D. Thompson, P. B. Hammond, R. W. Hawkes, B. H. Junker, & A. Tuden (Eds.), *Comparative studies in administration*. Pittsburgh: University of Pittsburgh Press, 1959, pp. 195–216.

Tushman, M. L. A political approach to organizations: A review and rationale. *Academy of Management Review*, 1977, 2, 206–216.

Vroom, V. H. *Work and motivation*. New York: John Wiley & Sons, 1964.

Vroom, V. H., & Yetton, P. W. Leadership and decision making. Pittsburgh: University of Pittsburgh Press, 1973.

Watson, G. Resistance to change. In W. G. Bennis, K. F. Benne, & R. Chin (Eds.), *The planning of change*. New York: Holt, Rinehart & Winston, 1969.

Zaltman, G., & Duncan, R. *Strategies for planned change*. New York: John Wiley & Sons, 1977.

Reading 53

UNDERSTANDING ORGANIZATION DEVELOPMENT: A STREAM APPROACH

Jerry I. Porras, Joan Harkness, and Coeleen Kiebert

Organizations, as complex, constantly evolving systems, present a substantial challenge to those who try to understand and improve their performance. It is seldom easy to determine the true nature of organizational phenomena. Consequently, trying to consciously change an organization to improve its effectiveness is difficult and time-consuming. Yet, in today's world, planned improvement of organizational functioning is a constant and necessary task of many executives and managers.

Organization development has evolved as one response to the need for strategies and approaches to planned change. The last two decades have produced numerous perspectives on how to accomplish OD and how organizational change takes place. No widely accepted view exists, however, and few methods for understanding the planned change process currently exist. Nevertheless, OD professionals need to decide which change model to use, what the most appropriate next step might be and how to better understand the effects of past actions to improve the impact of future interventions.

Tools for analysis and planning of change activities are few, but urgently needed. This article describes an approach, "stream analysis," which can be used to understand and plan the change process. During an intervention, it can facilitate clearer insights into the current state of the change process, and after the intervention it can improve understanding of what actually occurred.

Source: Jerry I. Porras, Joan Harkness, and Coeleen Kiebert, *Training and Development Journal* 37, no. 4 (April 1983). Copyright 1983, *Training and Development Journal*, American Society for Training and Development. Reprinted with permission. All rights reserved.

The stream approach is based on first identifying the key organizational factors altered by any complex OD intervention. Given the current state of OD technology, the organizational factors typically affected fall into one of four general categories: the organization's structure, technology, human processes and internal physical environment. In other words, any change activity would probably affect one or more of these aspects of the organization. Team building, for example, would primarily affect the human processes of the organization. Introducing a new machine would affect the technology; redesigning the organization's reporting relationships would alter the structure; and constructing a new building would influence the physical environment.

As change technologies evolve, new factors may be affected. When this happens, they can easily be added to the stream framework.

Stream Analysis Framework

The stream framework stems from the premise that all change activities in an organization development program can be conceptualized as a stream of actions occurring over time. In an OD process, the key dimension is time.

Figure 1 shows an example of how a change program might be represented using this stream notion. In the figure, Activity 1, the first intervention activity, would be shown first in the stream. It would be followed by Activities 2, 3 and so on. Note that each activity block is drawn to begin and end at points in time corresponding to the actual beginning and ending of the intervention activity it represents.

FIGURE 1 Stream Representation of a
Change Process

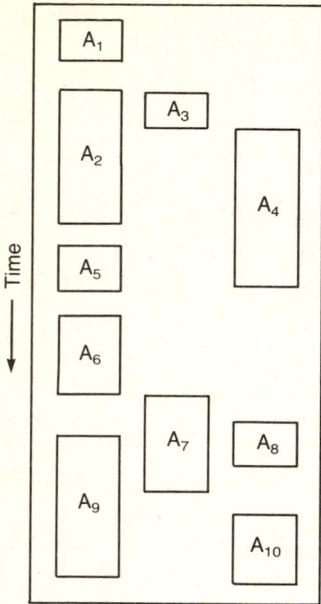

A_n = A UNIQUE INTERVENTION ACTIVITY

Several other characteristics of this representation are important. For example, two different activities might start at the same time (e.g., A_2 and A_3), yet end at different times; one activity might start and continue for a time, with a second activity starting somewhat later and continuing after the first is ended (A_2 and A_4). There may be periods of time when no change activities occur (between A_5 and A_6); several activities may occur at once, each having begun at a different point in time (A_7, A_8 and A_9); and so on. The result of this perspective is a pictorial representation, in correct temporal sequence, of all the activities conducted as part of a complex change program.

Although a useful analogy, this representation is not sufficient because it doesn't significantly add to current methods for understanding OD. By conceptualizing several parallel streams of activities flowing over time, the analysis becomes more complex. In the case of the OD stream, each set of

parallel streams may contain all of the change activities directed at altering one of the key change factors described earlier (human process, technology, structure or physical environment).

Figure 2 shows four parallel streams flowing together across time, each containing all the activities aimed at altering one of the key organizational factors. The activities in this figure are the same as in Figure 1, except now they belong to one particular intervention stream or another. By identifying the particular focus of each change activity and placing it in its proper temporal position, we begin to decompose a complex organization development intervention into its main parts and, as a result, gain a better understanding of what happened and when.

Once activities have been organized into streams, a final step is to make the appropriate links between activities. Organization development interventions typically are organic processes in which one activity builds on the results of a previous activity, or in which a specific activity precipitates a need for a follow-on activity.

For example, consider a structural change which creates new work teams. This type of change might trigger the need for a human process intervention such as team building or process consultation. Probably neither of these human process interventions would have been necessary without the change in organizational structure. With the formulation of new teams, however, some intervention geared to developing more effective work relationships would probably be appropriate.

Figure 3 shows some possible interconnections between intervention activities in the four different streams. In general, one can follow a single path through the intervention by proceeding down the four streams as indicated by the interconnecting arrows. Occasionally, however, two or more actions may have been precipitated by an intervention in one stream.

For example, action H_2 followed S_1, as did T_1 and T_2. In other words, the action taken in S_1 may have required supportive actions (H_2), or may have made consequent actions of T_1 and T_2 feasible. Actions either lead to new actions (i.e., make new actions possible) or facilitate new actions (i.e., make

FIGURE 2   Decomposition of an OD Intervention into its Principal Streams of
Change Activity

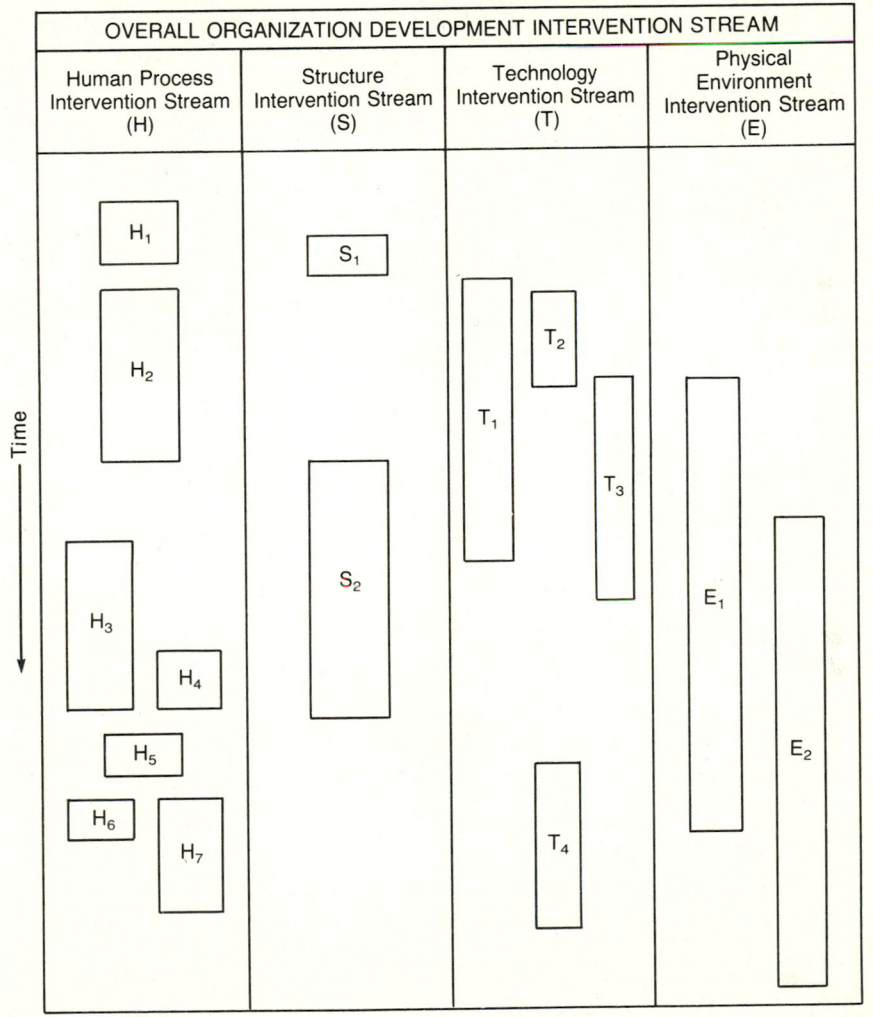

new actions necessary in order to bring the overall
system into balance or make it consistent across its
four domains). Both of these processes are called
triggering actions or triggers.

   Conceptualizing a complex organization development intervention as consisting of four parallel
streams of action provides a way of looking at
change processes. This can be useful not only from
the point of view of the professional OD consultant

who is attempting to facilitate change, but also for
the manager who is trying to keep the organization
operating as effectively as possible.

Applying the Framework

The stream framework was used to analyze a complex 22-month change project conducted in the operating room of a large suburban community
hospital. During the 20 years since its inception,

FIGURE 3   Interconnection of Change Activities Conducted in Different Intervention Streams

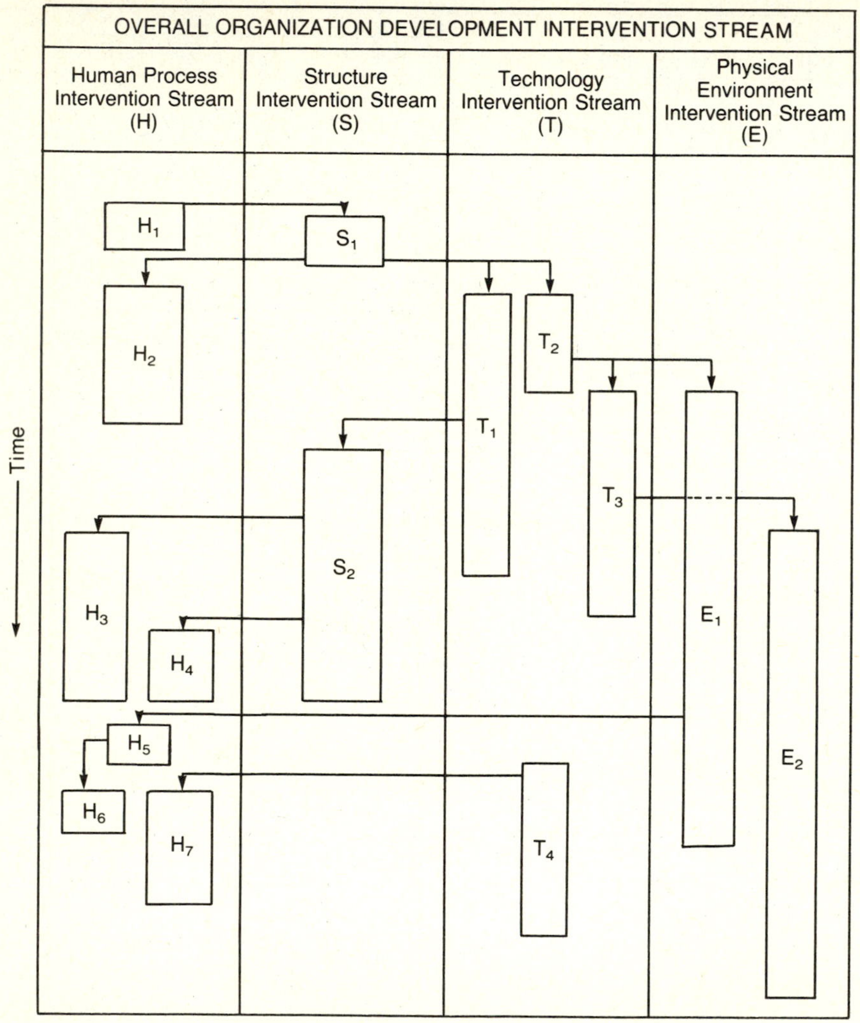

the hospital has grown into a sophisticated medical complex serving a community diverse in age, economic level and race. In recent years, federal and state government regulations had significantly affected hospital operations with increasing demands for cost accountability, altered facilities and equipment standards and regulation of services.

The operating room department (OR) plays a key role in the functioning of the entire hospital, with 60 percent of all hospital patients originally entering for surgery. At the beginning of this research, the OR occupied a space of approximately 13,500 square feet and each day handled 50 patients in 10 operating rooms, with a team of 35 nurses, 20 to 30 doctors and 13 nursing assistants. These 50 patients fell into any of nine different categories of surgical specialty. Since 80 percent of the patients were under general anesthesia during surgery, the OR team assumed complete responsibility for the physical well-being of almost all their patients. The OR team was required to provide rapid, efficient, specialty care for each patient, responding quickly to surgical needs, minimizing the anesthesia time and maintaining sterile techniques.

To maintain a sterile environment, the OR is isolated from the rest of the hospital, but its impact is significant. The scheduling of a surgical procedure puts into motion a succession of activities that encompasses many other hospital departments. The admitting department reserves a bed, the food service schedules a diet, the pharmacy prepares medication, nursing service schedules staffing, housekeeping prepares the bed, laboratory and x-ray provide diagnostic tests, and business office tracks costs and billings and central service, purchasing and engineering provide supplies and equipment.

The OR is reserved for an appropriate amount of time and fitted out for the particular type of surgery scheduled. The proper supplies are then ordered, wrapped, sterilized and gathered together into a "picked case." A head nurse coordinates equipment, sutures, instruments and nurses. An anesthesiologist checks and prepares his or her equipment. Other departments are notified: blood bank; x-ray; recovery room; and/or the intensive care unit. Finally, the patient's name is entered into a daily surgery schedule, which is distributed throughout the hospital. Once surgery is completed and the patient sufficiently recovered, he or she becomes the responsibility of the hospital staff.

The Change Process

During the 15 years prior to this study, no significant improvements in the organization or management of the OR department had taken place. Organizational structure and methods of scheduling, billing, supply handling and personnel assignment had not changed substantially.

The change project was preceded by an increasing number of complaints from nurses and physicians about their own inter-relationships, as well as the work environment and managerial systems. New technology was continuously introduced into surgical procedures, and physicians were demanding that nurses have expertise in its use. As a consequence, systems for training nurses in new procedures and equipment were critically needed.

To compound the situation, a heavy workload overwhelmed the whole department. Supply management, instrument processing and the physical plant could not deal with growing demands. A shortage of nurses added to the burden of the unhappy and overworked staff.

A first attempt at systematic change occurred with the institution of a planning procedure aimed at expanding the physical facilities of the operating room. An assistant OR director position was created and an external organization development consultant brought in to help identify problem areas and facilitate the actions needed to resolve them.

The consultant's initial diagnostic process led to team-building activities with the management group, improvements in the care and processing of instruments, minor reorganization of the management structure and one-to-one counseling sessions with managers. These activities eventually led to the development and implementation of a new organizational structure.

Facilities planning continued, but became more integrated with other parts of the planned change process. Since the plans called for tripling the floor space, it became clear that existing systems for delivery and processing of supplies and equipment were inadequate. Thus, the development of new systems began.

The influx of new surgical technology continued to affect the functioning of the operating room. Fiber optics, nitrogen-driven power tools and laser beam tools were only a few examples of the new equipment demanded by surgeons. Anesthesiologists needed proper equipment to deliver new anesthetic gases. New, sophisticated monitoring devices were introduced. Plans were developed and implemented to care for this new equipment and to train nurses in its use. Because the new equipment required special storage, the remodeling plans were altered.

In the seventh month of the project, further refinement of the organizational structure occurred. Nine surgical specialties were divided into four groups called "pods," with an acting nurse manager heading each one. Each pod included nurses, focused on a group of specialties, who were trained to deal with the ever expanding technology of those specialties.

Between the fourth and eleventh months of the organization development intervention, changes were made in the business systems and the billing and scheduling procedures. The need for a new system to deliver sterile supplies became apparent. An anesthesia department was created to support the anesthesiologists and their expanding technology.

In the twelfth month of the project, the operation room director resigned and was replaced by the assistant director, who immediately redistributed the managerial functions. Activities focused on clarifying new managerial roles and the managerial philosophy of the new director. Psychological tests such as the Myers-Briggs and the FIRO-B were used by the consultant to heighten managerial self-awareness and facilitate the formation of a new managerial work culture.

Ancillary areas such as the recovery room and outpatient surgery, both a part of the total department, were severely affected by the change in director. Turmoil in both areas resulted in the need for extensive conflict resolution efforts during the thirteenth month of the project.

Approximately 15 months after the beginning of intervention, renovation of the facilities began. Construction plans called for three phases over a two-year period, during which time the entire operating room suite would be torn down and rebuilt a section at a time.

By the eighteenth month, the pod organizational structure was firmly in place. The scheduling office had partially completed a system to interact with the four pods, and new nursing record forms had been developed to provide a better method for billing. The billing system was also designed to be consistent with the pod organizational structure.

The middle management team was formalized in the eighteenth month, with the promotion of four staff nurses to the head nurse position for each pod. Team building, among head nurses and within pods,

further strengthened the organizational structure. For the head nurses, one-to-one counseling and psychological testing again helped develop interpersonal relations skills. Head nurses also participated in training on inventory control, budgeting and staffing.

Although the change project continued past the twenty-second month, for purposes of this research our analysis terminated here. The overall project covered an extensive array of change activities focusing on all four of the organizational factors described earlier.

A Stream View

Figure 4 shows the operating room interventions laid out in a stream format. The blocks reflect beginning and end points by their position in relation to the temporal scale on the left axis. The lines connecting activity blocks indicate that any two activities were related in the same manner, either because the first activity made the second one necessary or the first one allowed the second one to occur. Where appropriate, key reasons for the linkage are briefly indicated next to the connecting line. The chart starts the month before the OD consultant entered the system. This is shown as month O.

Laying out the intervention in this manner gives a more systematic view of the process and when and how activities related. It was developed after the 22-month period it describes, but a stream chart could be laid out before or during a planning process. As a retrospective document, a stream chart lays out the history of an intervention so that it can be analyzed from the perspective of one who wants to learn more about the OD process.

Intensity of intervention. A visual analysis of the stream chart shows that activity within each stream was not constant across the entire time period. For example, during the first three months of the project, many human process interventions took place and, although the management planning process (H_5) continued until month 8, essentially very little additional human process work was done until months 12 and 13 when H_6, H_7 and H_8 occurred.

This was followed by a gap of seven months. The same ebb and flow is true of the structural and technological streams. Overall, therefore, although an OD intervention may appear relatively full of action across time, activity within the streams is not constant.

Triggers. The pattern of triggers (i.e., one intervention precipitating another) presents a second interesting insight into the dynamics of this change process. Prior to the beginning of the formal change project (month O), technological interventions triggered most of the other activities. During months 1–3, human process and structure streams became the most common sources of both activity and triggers. A second phase, in which physical environment and technology dominated, occurred over months 4–6, followed by a third phase (months 7–12) emphasizing structure and human process again. The final phase (months 13–22) predominantly contained actions in the technological and structural streams.

Analysis of this result implies a pattern in which human process and structure interventions cycle in and out of the change process. Pre-intervention concerns primarily in the technological area were followed by human process and structure activity. After a period of time, physical environment and technology began to dominate, but structure and human process returned. Finally, these interventions were no longer necessary, and technology (with some structure) took over as the dominant activity. One would expect, then, that if this cyclical pattern of human process and structure intervention exists, then these two streams would return to dominance after technological change activity had run its course.

This phenomenon might be explained in one of two ways. First, it could be that the human process/ structure activities are a precondition for other interventions.

A second way of looking at this pattern is to conceive of human process/structure activities as a process of "putting the world back together again." In this view, the technological and physical environment changes create such a turmoil that in order

for the organization to continue operating effectively, it needs to be restabilized.

Holes. A third insight derived from this method of mapping OD processes concerns inaction. We use the term *hole* to indicate those places in the life of the project when things should have been done but weren't. The stream chart provides some interesting examples of holes.

The planning for operating room construction (E_1) did not include input from the employees who would be working in the new environment. This resulted in some oversights in design which did not become apparent until the new facilities were completed and in use. The staff rightfully saw any problems with construction as a managerial or administrative mistake and tended to be more critical than supportive of efforts to deal with any difficulties.

Another hole in the process occurred in the method used to select new managers (S_2 and S_3). The staff was not included in the selection process in any way. Lack of data about managerial candidates resulted in some mismatches between those selected and the job to be done. This eventually required replacing some managers—a painful and expensive process.

A third hole occurred in the technological stream. There was no provision for potential managers to learn skills. Furthermore, there was no organizational structure created to allow them to demonstrate their effectiveness in using such skills. One important consequence of not dealing with this developmental issue was that the replacement of managers became a high-risk process. New managers would be selected without knowing how technologically proficient they would eventually become. Since expertise in surgical technology is a key component of the manager's job in the operating room, the risks involved in selecting blindly in this area were great.

A fourth hole also involved the technological stream. Not enough energy and emphasis were given to meeting the technological needs of the staff. Although much was being done in the structural stream to create an organization that could support

FIGURE 4   Stream Representation of an Organization Development Intervention

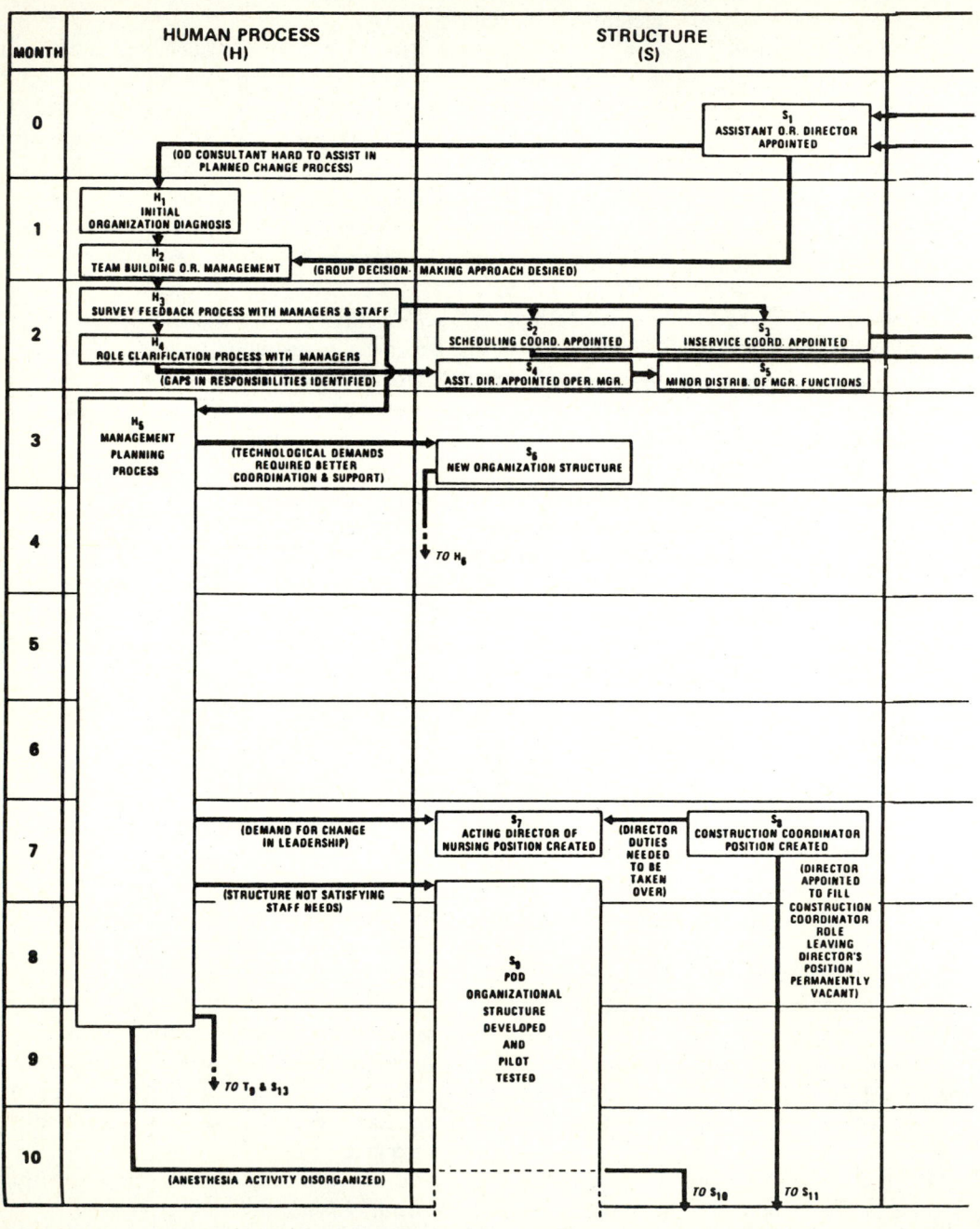

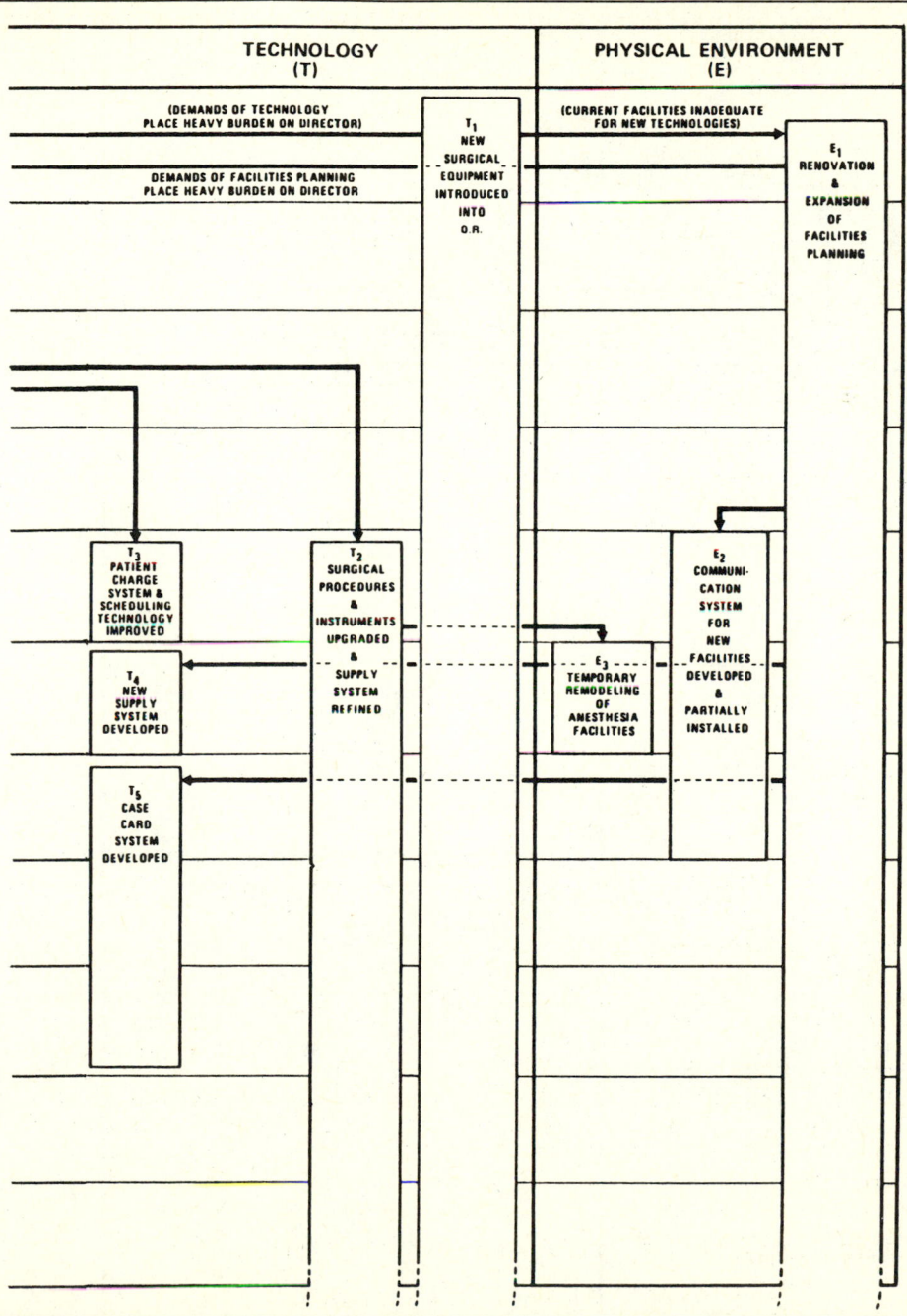

TECHNOLOGY
(T)

PHYSICAL ENVIRONMENT
(E)

(DEMANDS OF TECHNOLOGY
PLACE HEAVY BURDEN ON DIRECTOR)

DEMANDS OF FACILITIES PLANNING
PLACE HEAVY BURDEN ON DIRECTOR

(CURRENT FACILITIES INADEQUATE
FOR NEW TECHNOLOGIES)

T_1
NEW
SURGICAL
EQUIPMENT
INTRODUCED
INTO
O.R.

E_1
RENOVATION
&
EXPANSION
OF
FACILITIES
PLANNING

T_3
PATIENT
CHARGE
SYSTEM &
SCHEDULING
TECHNOLOGY
IMPROVED

T_2
SURGICAL
PROCEDURES
&
INSTRUMENTS
UPGRADED
&
SUPPLY
SYSTEM
REFINED

E_2
COMMUNI-
CATION
SYSTEM
FOR
NEW
FACILITIES
DEVELOPED
&
PARTIALLY
INSTALLED

T_4
NEW
SUPPLY
SYSTEM
DEVELOPED

E_3
TEMPORARY
REMODELING
OF
ANESTHESIA
FACILITIES

T_5
CASE
CARD
SYSTEM
DEVELOPED

FIGURE 4 *(concluded)*

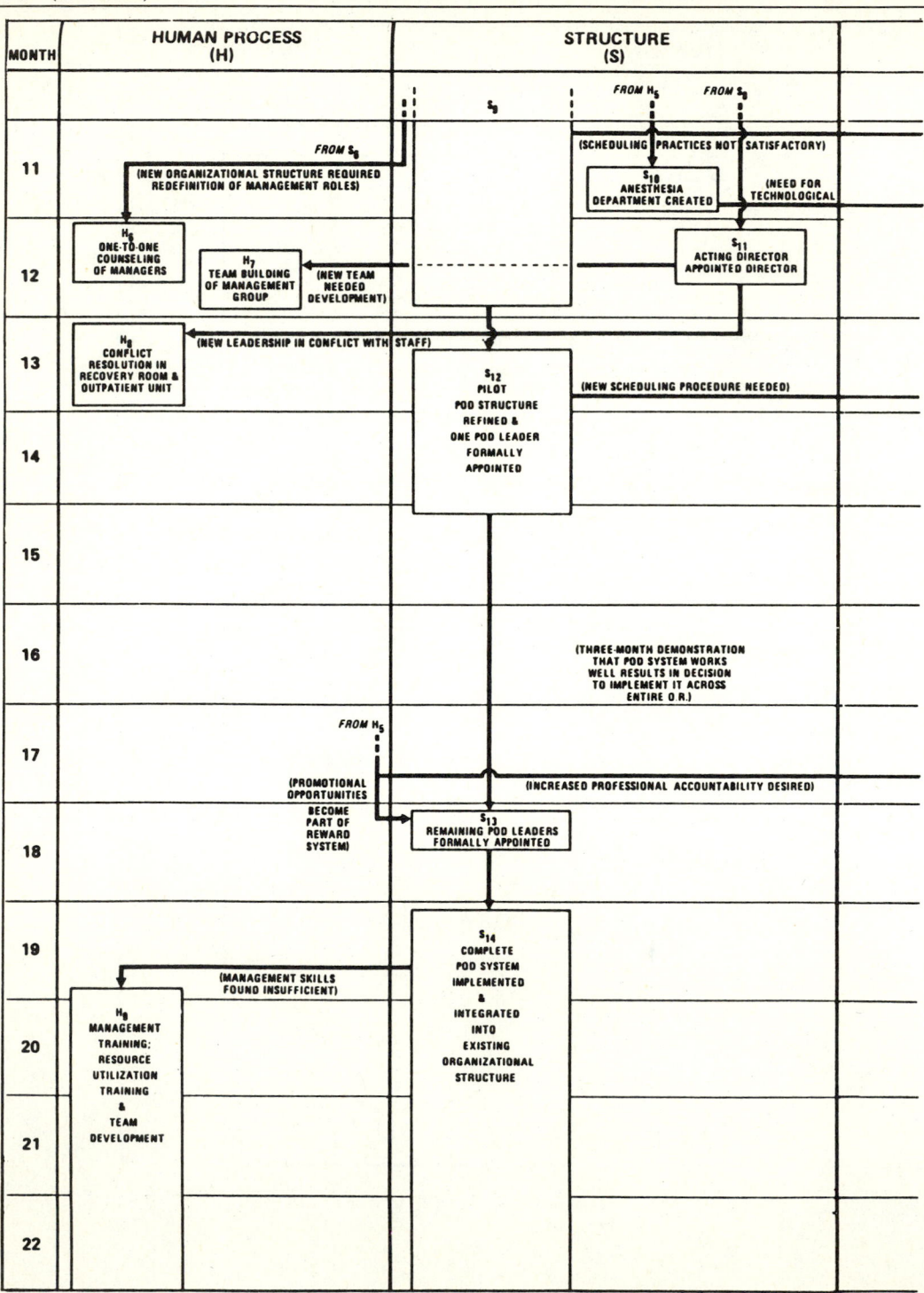

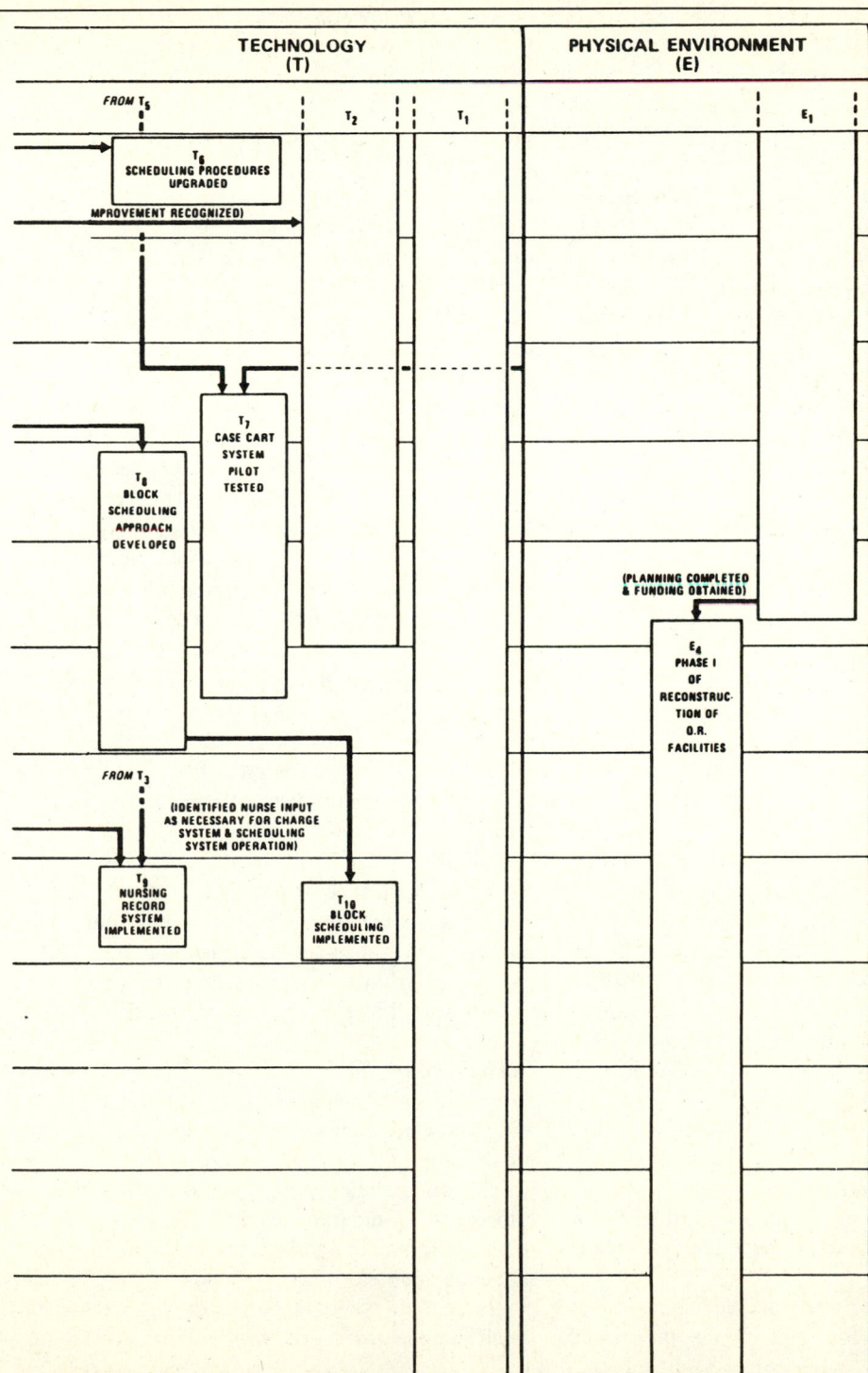

the expanding technology, more could have been done to alleviate the pressures on the staff by providing active, hands-on training and more back up. Lack of attention to this aspect of technical support created a gap between management and staff that was slow to mend. It also inhibited the overall training and development process at the staff level.

One of the most important learnings derived from the use of the stream approach was the demonstration that most changes affect all four streams in varying degrees. Retrospective analysis of holes in any process can help practitioners develop greater expertise in avoiding past mistakes.

Intensity of intervention, triggers and holes are but a few of the potential insights that can be gained from application of the stream approach. We believe that many additional uses of this technique are possible.

Using the Stream Approach

Three groups interested in planned organizational change are: managers who lead organizations targeted for change; practitioners who help systems to change; and research scholars who are interested in codifying the existing knowledge of change processes. The stream framework carries great potential for application by each of these three groups.

Applications for managers. Managers would use stream analysis to diagnose the problems they face in their organizations. By classifying problems in each of the stream areas, then determining the interconnections between problem areas, it becomes possible to identify the underlying dynamics of organizational malfunctioning. Doing so can then point toward more effective actions for dealing with fundamental problems.

Once diagnosis has been achieved, the stream framework can be used for planning actions. Mapping the existing diagnosis into potential actions can yield plans that are more directly tied to organizational realities and which have a greater chance of success.

Finally, once actions are planned, stream diagrams can be used for tracking the process of change. Control of the change process can be enhanced if the manager has a clear sense of where things are in relation to where they were planned to be. Later, the tracking document can be used as historical support for justifying or validating the process to outside entities who could influence the continuation of activity. It can also be used internally to show organizational members "where we've been," a process which often provides additional motivation for change.

Applications for practitioners. Practitioners can certainly use the stream approach in the three ways prescribed above for managers. But, in addition, there are several other applications particularly appropriate for the change professional. First, if stream diagrams are kept for several independent change projects, they can be used by the change agent to build learning across cases. Initially, creating a stream diagram for one project can be useful in thinking about and intervening in a follow-on project. The first two can build knowledge for the third, and so on.

Eventually, practitioners can begin to develop their own models of change based on the findings that evolve from repeated application of this framework. Theories in use can grow from these models with consequent improvements in the practice of OD.

A third potential application for practitioners includes using this approach to educate clients. A clear, easy-to-understand method for communicating diagnostic information, for helping in planning and for clarifying current states can prove extremely useful to practitioners of change.

Applications for researchers. Those who study the processes of change for the purpose of generating knowledge about change dynamics can also use this approach in their work. Codifying the trigger patterns and relating them to outcomes of change efforts could yield information on the effectiveness of one pattern over another. Taking the trigger codifications and determining if repeatable cycles occur is another potential output of this method of specifying the process of change. Finally, using the stream diagram as the basis for assessing the impact of an OD process could be a third way of helping research scholars to better understand organization development.

Conclusions

The stream analysis approach has the potential for helping managers, practitioners and researchers improve their understanding and practice of OD. The basic framework is quite flexible and can be expanded to include greater numbers of change factors as the need arises. By its structure, it yields a more easily interpretable view of complex change processes and, as a consequence, enhances the possibilities of improving the quality of our activity in the field of planned change.

Reading 54

A CHECKLIST FOR ORGANIZING AND IMPLEMENTING AN OD EFFORT

Wendell L. French

We are presenting here a checklist of variables to be considered in the management of an OD effort. We believe that the key factors in such an effort must, over time, pay attention to these dimensions if the process is to be optimally effective.

These dimensions are an outgrowth of the author's experience as an external consultant in an OD effort in a city government situation. In that effort, a checklist similar to the one reported here, but without the comment portions, was used several times by the OD steering committee over the first three years. The "Comment" column is an

amalgamation of experiences across OD efforts in several different kinds of organizations of both the public and private nature.

The various dimensions are listed only very roughly in terms of the sequence with which concerted attention needs to be paid to them. Ideally, team building ordinarily needs to precede attempts at intergroup problem solving for optimum results, and life career planning is not likely to emerge as a high priority area until other things are under way. We say "very roughly" in sequence, however, because most if not all of these dimensions need to be planned and managed in a simultaneous, congruent manner.

Source: Written especially for this volume.

Strategy Checklist

Dimensions	Imme-diate	3 Months	6 Months	1 Year	18 Months	2 Years	3 Years	Etc.	Comment
Preliminary diagnosis									Some form of preliminary diagnosis needs to occur before the launching of OD efforts, even if it's to be a very tentative start. Shared perceptions of a number of people that things could be substantially better, of some specific deficiencies, and that OD might make a significant contribution to the solution of problems is probably adequate as a starter.
Selection of external consultants									One or more consultants might be interviewed after obtaining recommendations from other clients with whom the consultants have worked, or from Certified Consultants International (CCI), NTL Institute for Applied Behavioral Science, university contacts, or other sources. Not infrequently, laboratory (sensitivity) trainers who are experienced in OD are contacted by managers who have had a positive laboratory training experience. However, while group facilitator skills are necessary for OD consulting practice, such skills are not sufficient. The OD practitioner needs a repertoire of skills and a perspective which is systemwide.
OD information and knowledge Briefing sessions									A cognitive understanding of the essential aspects of the process is vital to cooperation and support on an OD effort and to the avoidance of confusion about OD vis-à-vis other strategies. Many organizational participants may cast a baleful eye at any new intervention, having been expected to cooperate with one change program or study after the other over the years. Training workshops are thus important for both diagnostic purposes and ventilating irritations about previously imposed programs. The external
Union involvement									

Strategy Checklist (continued)

Dimensions	Immediate	3 Months	6 Months	1 Year	18 Months	2 Years	3 Years	Etc.	Comment
Special seminars									consultants should be prepared to recommend not going forward if the people are not receptive. Union involvement in the early information phase is vital in the unionized situation. Above and beyond these important/discussion sessions for everyone, intensive, specialized seminars in OD for a few selected line managers can be very helpful to the OD effort.
Team-building and team problem-solving work-shops									These activities are at the heart of the OD process, and are likely to constitute the main expenditure of consultant time and off-site workshop time. By CEO we mean the top person in the particular organizational pyramid that is moving in the direction of a comprehensive OD effort.
CEO's office and department heads									
CEO's immediate office									We include the CEO's immediate office because the culture of the chief's immediate office is frequently overlooked, but the people in it—assistants and secretaries, for example—are significant actors in the system. Incongruency between this subculture and others can be highly dysfunctional. Further, we see the top part of the organization modeling behavior for the rest, thus requiring efforts at this level even more intensive and demanding than elsewhere in the organization.
OD steering committee									
Department heads and key people									
Department A									
Department B									
Department C, etc.									
Task forces									
Follow-up									Follow-up is so important to organizational improvement that this item could well be listed relative to each major OD intervention such as team-building workshops. Follow-up on action plans needs to occur in regular meetings, in special meetings called to review progress, and in subsequent workshops.

OD steering committee	
Membership	Our experience suggests that a broad-based steering committee is needed to give overall direction to an OD effort. Ideally, membership might look something like this: the CEO, one or two key staff people such as the personnel director, one major line department head, a representative of first-line supervision, a rank-and-file employee
Role in policy, budget, priorities, etc.	
Frequency of meeting	(or a union officer in the unionized setting if the union is willing to participate in such discussions), the internal OD coordinator, the key external consultant; and one or more internal consultants. Some membership slots might be rotated. Meetings probably ought to occur once a month and should focus on budget, policy, and priorities.
	We believe that team building for this group is essential and that the group should make a major effort to create a committee culture congruent with the one being fostered through the OD effort.
Internal coordinator	
Job definition	The percentages of time the person designated as an internal coordinator spends as the coordinator, as consultant, and on other activities, can be a source of tension for that person, for his or her superior, for peers, and for clients. Conflicting demands will inevitably arise and need to be faced openly, sometimes in the steering committee. In addition, unless it is clear what the coordinator's authority is in determining direction, assigning consultants and scheduling off-site sessions, tensions will arise between that person, members of that committee, the consultants, and others. This is an issue that needs to be "worked" periodically in many OD efforts.
Role in policy, budget, priorities, etc.	
Role as a consultant	
Relationship to external and internal consultants	Further, multiple roles will create a number of dilemmas for the internal coordinator. For

Strategy Checklist (continued)

Dimensions	Imme-diate	3 Months	6 Months	1 Year	18 Months	2 Years	3 Years	Etc.	Comment
									example, should that person use insights in a team-building session that were derived from some other capacity such as administrative assistant to the CEO? (Probably not.) Should the coordinator report details of a team-building session in X department to the CEO? (Emphatically no.)
Selection and development of internal consultants									This is a particularly sensitive area. Internal consultants need to be selected for demonstrated potential and interest, but the system needs to be open enough so that it is neither a closed system nor has the appearance of one. Basic competence and continuously enhanced competence in facilitation skills need to be the criteria for membership. Those facilitators recognized as having the highest competence need to assume leadership in establishing standards of performance. Competence development also requires that the organization allocates resources for specialized OD training, apprenticeship situations, and interaction with the external consultants.
Selection									
External education									
Internal progress and development									
Process consultation and group effectiveness									This is a function in which, hopefully, client groups will have high interest and will develop skills. At the outset, consultants can be helpful in modeling this activity and in coaching group members. Ultimately, the client group can routinely rotate this function among group members, and debriefing how things went in a meeting can become a way of life. We see this activity becoming pervasive in the meeting life of the organization, but, of course, in balance with the tasks to be accomplished. However, we
CEO–department head meetings									
Department meetings									
Other									

	see complacency leading to ignoring this activity to be more likely than overdoing it.
Individual counseling	We suspect that this is insufficiently utilized in most OD efforts, and probably for reasons similar to the following: (1) lack of counseling training for internal consultants, and/or (2) lack of stated validation of the worthwhileness of this function by the CEO and other key figures. Counseling, whether by an internal or external consultant, ultimately is a cost item in terms of someone's time. (The costs of not engaging in effective counseling need to be weighed, of course.)
Two-party conflict resolution Sessions with clients	The consultant, whether internal or external, needs high skill and acceptance to be effective in this area. Availability is also critical—he or she needs to be around enough to be in a position to suggest a private meeting between the parties when the moment is right. The consultant and the two clients also need to be available to meet
Follow-up	in a subsequent session or sessions to check progress or work on issues still unresolved.
Intergroup team building and problem solving Workshops with client groups	Assertiveness by the OD coordinator or other consultants will frequently make the difference as to whether or not this actually occurs. People need to know the nature of the process, that top management supports resources being allocated to this function; and consultants need to act in a delicate ''broker'' role when it becomes evident that two units are expressing difficulty with each
Follow-up	other. Follow-up with clients on workshop outcomes is vital.
Human resources management vis-à-vis OD Human resources department role in OD	The human resources department needs to be actively involved in the OD process for at least two reasons: (1) unfortunate territorial and status issues have developed in some organizations when personnel people were not involved, and

Strategy Checklist (continued)

Dimensions	Imme-diate	3 Months	6 Months	1 Year	18 Months	2 Years	3 Years	Etc.	Comment
MBO and perform-ance appraisal									(2) many, if not all, personnel practices are potentially critical areas for congruency or incongruency with an OD effort. An autocratic
Job enrichment									MBO program, for example, occurring simultaneously with an OD effort, which by
Management and employee training and development									definition is participative, can have a deleterious effect on either or both processes. The curricula of training and development programs also need to be managed in concert with an OD effort.
OD applications to and implications for other person-nel systems									We are not suggesting a "party line," but we are suggesting that incongruencies between training and OD be surfaced and worked, including the way training needs are assessed. Frequently, many personnel practices become modified as an OD effort proceeds. For example internal posting of job vacancies tends to occur; employees are consulted about fringe benefits; group methods may be used in orientation; etc.
Facilitator team (internal plus external consul-tants)									If a team of consultants is working with a client, clinical review of interventions is obviously best conducted while topics are "hot," and time needs to be allocated for this activity. It also can
Review of interven-tions									be highly productive in terms of consultant development to schedule periodic clinics during which the total consulting staff focuses on their
Team maintenance									consulting practices and their own relationships. The spin-off of unworked interpersonal and group issues can severely handicap the ability of the facilitator group to help others because of clients seeing the incongruency between doing and saying, and more substantively, because of the resulting lack of personal growth.

CEO and line management	The team effectiveness and interpersonal effectiveness of the CEO and the top management group has a profound impact on the climate in the organization and on interpersonal, group, and intergroup effectiveness throughout the organization. We have seen unresolved problems between a CEO and a deputy perpetuating serious problems lower in the organization. Sometimes the spin-off is obvious, sometimes very subtle. Therefore, we are strong advocates of the top-management team working longer and harder than anyone else in the organization to get its own house in order.
Depth of involvement	
Internationalization of skills	
Development of external and internal consultants	
Management of the OD process	Ongoing, real involvement by the top team of the organization involved in an OD effort is vital to the success of the OD effort. This includes significant internalization of group dynamics skills. We also see the CEO and top managers playing a vital role in supporting ongoing professional development of the consultants (e.g., supporting regular consultant clinics) and in seeing to it that the overall OD process is managed effectively.
Laboratory (sensitivity) training	The relevance or irrelevance of sensitivity training to an optimally successful OD effort needs to be faced. Our opinion is that positive experience in stranger sensitivity or group dynamics labs may enhance a depth of insight and skill development that will "grease the wheels" of an OD effort. If key people are not attending such experiences, we believe the issue should be raised.
Life/career planning	Life/career planning can be a logical offshoot of an OD effort. As the climate becomes more open and trusting, candid discussions between superiors and subordinates and between colleagues about careers becomes natural, and intensive workshops focusing on career

Dimensions	Imme-diate	3 Months	6 Months	1 Year	18 Months	2 Years	3 Years	Etc.	Comment
									development can be very useful. A number of organizations have found that the potential risk in life/career planning workshops of key people gaining so much insight that they leave is far outweighed by the vitality that is unleashed, particularly when the individual attention and concern evidenced in the workshops becomes part of the broader organizational culture.
Key system relationships									In addition to the union, the support and understanding of the board of directors—whether called by that label, or whether called "school board," "city council," or whatever—is necessary for an OD effort to flourish. Ultimately, the board will approve the budget and will set the pattern for what is desirable in the organization. Frequently, boards see the efficacy of the OD effort to their own operation, and with the help of a facilitator, get involved in the process by looking at their own way of doing things and at their key interfaces with the operating organization and/or their constituents. Separate workshops on the nature of the OD process for governing boards—and for union officials in the case of unionized situations, and for members of the press in the case of public agencies under open-meeting laws—can be extremely useful in the early phases of an OD effort to provide a common base of understanding and to avoid the gross distortions which lack of direct information can create. Such workshops can also increase the odds of these groups utilizing OD.

Evaluation of OD effort Progress evaluation by department heads and others	A periodic review of the entire OD effort by the steering committee and others is necessary for revitalization of the OD effort and modification in practices and direction. In short, OD needs to be applied to the OD effort routinely to assess climate and progress. In particular, department heads and a cross section of employees at all levels need to be interviewed to tap their perceptions of the functional and dysfunctional consequences of the OD effort. For example, problems like the formation of in-groups and out-groups sometimes emerge. And, if the OD effort is largely successful, people need to know it.
Assessment of dysfunctional aspects of emerging culture	
Review of basic assumptions and purposes	While more painstaking and thorough research would be desirable, including the use of outside researchers, the collection of anecdotal data would seem to be the minimum research needed, both for improvement purposes and for interpreting the effort to the various interested parties. A step closer to more thorough research would be the collection of attitudinal data and "hard" data such as productivity measures, with an attempt to draw cause and effect conclusions about the impact of various phases of the OD effort.
Review of relationship with external consultants	A review of the relationship between the external consultants and the client system needs to occur periodically. Is there too much dependency on outside help on the part of the client system? Are the consultants being used so infrequently that they are losing interest, feeling alienated? Have internal resources/skills developed to the point that use of external consultants can be reduced greatly or eliminated? What would be the consequences? We are convinced of the efficacy of at least some minimum of external consultant involvement to provide an additional avenue of innovation and to help keep the OD effort "honest" in the sense of helping avoid emerging dysfunctional norms.

Strategy Checklist (concluded)

Dimensions	Imme-diate	3 Months	6 Months	1 Year	18 Months	2 Years	3 Years	Etc.	Comment
Managerial succession									Positive changes in organization culture due to an OD effort can be set back due to turnover in the executive and supervisory ranks. It is important that the board of directors understands this. This has implications relative to the qualifications of replacements, the way they are selected, and the way they are brought aboard. If the momentum of an OD effort is to be sustained, it would seem wise to look for leadership skills and attitudes congruent with the OD effort, and it may be productive to have some subordinate participation in the selection. Further, internal or external consultant help in team assimilation of the new member may be desirable.
Selection									
Orientation									

532

SUGGESTED ADDITIONAL READINGS FOR PART 7

Beckhard, Richard, and Reuben T. Harris. *Organizational Transitions*. Reading, Mass.: Addison-Wesley, 1977.

Bennis, W. G.; K. K. Benne; R. Chin; and K. Corey, eds. *The Planning of Change*. 3rd ed. New York: Holt, Rinehart & Winston, 1976.

Burke, W. Warner, and Richard Beckhard, eds. *Conference Planning*. 2nd ed. LaJolla, Calif.: University Associates, 1970.

Couger, J. Daniel, and Robert A. Zawacki. *Motivating and Managing Computer Personnel*. New York: Wiley-Interscience, 1980.

Ferguson, Charles K. "Concerning the Nature of Human Systems and the Consultant's Role." *The Journal of Applied Behavioral Science* 4 (1968), pp. 186–93.

Filley, Alan C. *Interpersonal Conflict Resolution*. Glenview, Ill.: Scott, Foresman, 1976.

French, Wendell L., and Cecil H. Bell, Jr. *Organization Development: Behavioral Science Interventions for Organization Improvement*. 3rd ed. Englewood Cliffs, N.J.: Prentice-Hall, 1984.

Goodman, Paul S. and associates. *Change in Organizations*. San Francisco: Jossey-Bass, 1982.

Goodstein, Leonard D. *Consulting with Human Science Systems*. Reading, Mass.: Addison-Wesley, 1978.

Kellogg, Diane M. "Contrasting Successful and Unsuccessful Consultation Relationships." *Group & Organization Studies*, June 1984, pp. 151–76.

Kilmann, Ralph. *Beyond the Quick Fix*. San Francisco: Jossey-Bass, 1984.

Larwood, Laurie, and Urs E. Gattiker. "Client and Consultant Management Problem-Solving-Values." *Group & Organization Studies*, December 1986, pp. 374–86.

Leitko, Thomas A., and David Szczerbacki. "Why Traditional OD Strategies Fail in Professional Bureaucracies." *Organizational Dynamics*, Winter 1987, pp. 52–65.

Likert, Rensis. *The Human Organization*. New York: McGraw-Hill, 1967.

Lippitt, Gordon, *Organization Renewal*. 2nd ed. Englewood Cliffs, N.J.: Prentice-Hall, 1982.

Lubin, B.; Leonard Goodstein; and Alice Lubin, eds. *Organizational Change Sourcebook I: Cases in Organization Development*. LaJolla, Calif.: University Associates, 1979.

Lubin, B.; Leonard Goodstein, and Alice Lubin, eds. *Organizational Change Sourcebook II: Cases in Conflict Management*. LaJolla, Calif.: University Associates, 1979.

Mirvis, Phillip H., and David N. Berg, eds. *Failures in Organization Development and Change*. New York: John Wiley & Sons, 1977.

Pfeffer, Jeffrey, et al. "Managing Organizational Change." *The Academy of Management Executive*, February 1987, pp. 31–55.

Porras, Jerry I., and Joan Harkness. "Managing Planned Change: A Stream Approach." In Robert Tannenbaum et al. *Human Systems Development*. San Francisco: Jossey-Bass, 1985, pp. 224–45.

Reznick, Herman, and Reno J. Patti, eds. *Change from Within*. Philadelphia: Temple University, 1980.

Tichy, Noel M. *Managing Strategy Change*. New York: John Wiley & Sons, 1983.

Walton, Richard E. *Interpersonal Peacemaking*. Reading, Mass.: Addison-Wesley Publishing, 1969.

Warrick, D. D., ed. *Contemporary Organization Development: Current Thinking and Applications*. Glenview, Ill.: Scott, Foresman, 1985.

PART 8

Application in the Public and Service Sectors

As economy of the United States and the world economy changes from a manufacturing to a knowledge-based economy, we believe that organization development consultants will be used more and more to adjust to this shift. Over half the new jobs being created in America are in the service sector and that sector has some unique constraints that require special knowledge by the OD practitioner. The first article by Robert Golembiewski is presented to the reader as a classical statement of the constraints that are unique to the public sector.

Throughout the 1980s President Reagan increased the Department of Defense budget and his critics asked for increased effectiveness from the military. The military turned to OD as a practical response to these problems. The article by Denis D. Umstot summarizes the results of OD efforts in the United States military and he states that "OD appears to be thriving in a military environment."[1] Since he wrote this article, our research indicates that OD activities in the U.S. military have waxed and waned, partly depending upon top command interest and support. Further, new military commanders have a need to implement their programs and generally become impatient with slow but steady progress. They want quick fixes!

OD in the public sector has not been limited to the military. OD programs have been initiated with the State Department, health care systems, religious institutions, local municipal governments, police departments, and/or various educational institutions at both the secondary and college level. Although OD continues to be practiced more in the business–industrial (private) sector, the size of the OD effort in the public sector has been increasing. Evidence to support this conclusion comes from the 1,600-plus members of the OD Network (formally associated with NTL–Institute), an organization of practitioners who are affiliated for professional purposes. As we have stated, much of what we have learned about OD from applications in the private sector can be transferred to the public sector; however, we believe there are important contingencies in the public that tend to limit this transferability. Some of these contingencies are:

---

[1]Denis D. Umstot, "Organization Development Technology and the Military: A Surprising Merger," *Academy of Management Review* 5, no. 2 (1980), p. 189.

1. Public and Private Organizations Have Different Measures of Organizational Effectiveness.   Although relating outcome variables (such as profitability, cost reduction, turnover, and the like) to improvement efforts is difficult in the private sector, the problem is even more substantial in the public sector. Without profit measures in the public sector, the external change agent must learn to adapt to different measures of effectiveness. Organizations such as government agencies and schools do not have clear-cut, verifiable outputs that lend themselves to objective measurement.[2] Most public sector organizations are producing a product, largely intangible services, that is not only hard to measure but also restricts quantitative feedback to the clients. It is simply difficult to demonstrate to the public that a large expenditure for an OD effort is positively related to better public service. Further, without this specific feedback from objective measurement, it may be harder for the OD consultant to facilitate adaptive behavior by the organizational participants.

Thus, a major challenge to improvement efforts in the public sector is to develop and refine ''hard'' measures of organizational effectiveness. The essay by Rosenbach, Gregory, and Taylor explains the use of survey feedback in a public school district. This study demonstrates a successful application of OD in the public sector with multiple positive outcomes.

2. The Greater Importance of Regulatory Constraints and a Diffusion of Power within the Public Sector.   In the private sector, the chief executives tend to be the focus of power in the organization and the external change agent can better evaluate their need awareness and commitment to the objectives of the OD program. Although coordination and management of the OD program is difficult in the private sector, there is often even greater difficulty in the public sector because chief executives, in many cases, have limited power due to a complex system of checks and balances which make it more difficult to make commitments on long-range programs. ''This difference is the traditions and/or law that require governments to define their organization structure in detail by statute. Thus, when a major change is desired, it must be done through the political process. . . .''[3] And effecting change through the legislative and political processes requires strategies that are different from the private sector. For example, the Civil Service Commission, Energy Research and Development Agency, General Accounting Office, and county boards of commissioners are regulatory agencies unique to the public sector.

We are aware of one county system of government where the three commissioners are elected, and of the nine department heads reporting to the commissioners, two are elected and seven are appointed. All nine departments have career civil service people. Therefore, in this system there are units with different rates of turnover at the executive ranks, executives with differing commitments to organizational versus personal objectives, and units which probably differ in terms of cohesiveness. Further, the turnover rate is higher among political appointees than among career civil service managers. This results in an organizational posture where the political appointees are initially learning about their respective agencies. About the time they have mastered the learning curve, they may return to their previous private

---

[2]For a short essay on effectiveness measures in schools, see Richard A. Schmuck and Matthew B. Miles, eds., *Organization Development in Schools* (Palo Alto, Calif.: National Press Books, 1971), pp. 235–36.

[3]William F. Glueck, ''Organization Change in Business and Government,'' *Academy of Management Journal*, December 1969, p. 448.

positions. This produces a strategy of waiting by career officers, if they cannot get support from political appointees for their ideas or change efforts.

In another example, Argyris reported that the majority of the career officers in the State Department described norms of the following kinds:

> A tendency to withdraw from interpersonal difficulties and conflict. Not being open about interpersonal problems or substantive issues that could be threatening to others, especially superiors and peers. Distrust of aggressive or openly competitive behavior in others.[4]
>
> The dysfunctional consequences of this mass-conditioning process are attitudes by top executives that may be incongruent with the OD objectives of increasing the level of self and group responsibility in the decision-making process.[5]

Inflexible and cumbersome budgeting processes in the public sector may restrict the options of chief executives. How money is budgeted and appropriated is determined by legislative action. An OD proposal may require up to two years for coordination, staffing, and approval through designated budget channels. By the time the review process is complete the original need awareness, by key officials of the organization, for an OD program may have changed and/or there may have been major turnover in the executive ranks.

3. Conditioning of Executives in the Public Sector.   Chief executives in the public sector are conditioned during their careers to favor management styles that maximize sources of downward control and minimize the control owned by subordinates. Public executives are conditioned, by the time they become middle or top managers, to follow the smallest detail of legislation, policies, rules, and procedures.[6] In addition, to progress upward in a public institution, the executives must indicate a molding of attitudes to fit the particular agency affiliation.[7] While this phenomenon is not unique to the public sector, the problem is intensified there. President Harry S Truman was very direct on this point when he projected the problems General Eisenhower would experience as President Eisenhower, without the defined career patterns and strong authority he was conditioned to expect in the U.S. Army. "He'll sit here," Truman predicted, "and he'll say, 'Do this!' 'Do that!' and nothing will happen. Poor Ike—it won't be a bit like the Army."[8]

4. Greater Visibility of the Decision-Making Process in the Public Sector.   Woodrow Wilson asserted that "corruption thrives in secret places and avoids public places . . . there is no air so wholesome as the air of utter publicity."[9] Vietnam and Watergate provided evidence to support his statement and many states such as Colorado have passed

---

[4]Alfred J. Marrow, *Making Waves in Foggy Bottom* (Washington, D.C.: NTL–Institute, 1974), pp. 53–54.

[5]For a discussion of conflicting values between OD and bureaucracy, see Daniel L. Kegan, "Organizational Development: Descriptions, Issues, and Some Research Results," *Academy of Management Journal,* December 1971, pp. 453–64. Also see *Psychology Today,* August 1975, pp. 26–28, for a discussion of the fear of innovation in a public agency.

[6]For an interesting personal observation of this phenomenon, see Merle Miller, *Plain Speaking: An Oral Biography of Harry S. Truman* (New York: Berkley Publishing, 1974), pp. 343–74.

[7]Bob L. Wynia, "Federal Bureaucrats' Attitudes toward a Democratic Ideology," *Public Administration Review,* March–April 1974, pp. 156–62.

[8]Richard E. Neustadt, *Presidential Power* (New York: John Wiley & Sons, 1960), p. 9.

[9]Woodrow Wilson, *The New Freedom* (Englewood Cliffs, N.J.: Prentice-Hall, 1961, pp. 76–85.

legislation which opens state meetings to the public and the mass media. For example, the administration of Kansas City, Missouri, and its biggest public employee union hailed their contract talks which were held in public to support the city's open-meeting policy.[10] Also, in response to bureaucratic secrecy, there is the federal Freedom of Information Act which, although it contains nine exemptions, is broad in its applicability.[11] One of the exemptions is "purely internal management matters," which we would interpret as exempting most OD activities and which, as we discuss below, we see as wise.

Because of open meeting laws, particularly at the state level, and because the ultimate measure of government effectiveness is determined by the public vote at the polls, public executives increasingly operate in a fishbowl observed through the eyes of the mass media. This fishbowl atmosphere is not always congruent with the objectives and values of OD. For example, admitting to problems in an organization may be interpreted by the press and the public as a sign of weak management. We are aware of an OD program where data obtained from the diagnosis of the organization were publicized by the press, then subpoenaed by a grand jury, and ultimately contributed to the director of the agency being asked to resign. The mass media simply did not understand or refused to accept the value system of OD which encourages the client group to surface and deal with problems rather than sweeping them under the rug.

Nor did the media and grand jury understand the importance of anonymity for respondents in early phases of an OD effort. It would seem to us that diagnostic procedures aimed at assisting an organization to improve its internal processes, and the data gathered through such procedures, should be immune from public and court scrutiny. The consultant and the emerging data should be accorded the same protection as the psychologist-client relationship.[12]

In another OD effort in a city government situation, two reporters from different newspapers sat in on seminars during which the city council and city manager worked on problems relating to role clarification, meeting effectiveness, and so on. The published articles of one reporter, in our opinion, reflected considerable understanding of the OD process, while the articles of the other equated OD with sensitivity training and group therapy. It was also quite apparent that the presence of reporters affected the candidness of the participants and the consultants.

While we do not advocate closed organizations, the mass media's presence can in certain situations be dysfunctional toward implementing change in public agencies. One of the authors (Zawacki) was involved in an OD effort with a school district where the press would attend OD problem-solving sessions and then publish articles that further

---

[10]*The Wall Street Journal,* August 19, 1975, p. 1.

[11]For a detailed discussion of the act and exemptions, see Robert L. Saloschin, "The Freedom of Information Act: A Governmental Perspective," *Public Administration Review,* January–February 1975, pp. 10–14.

[12]In a case which may have parallel implications for the protection of the consultant-client relationship, U.S. District Court Judge Charles Renfrew, of the Northern District of California, issued a Memorandum of Opinion in which he denied the attempt of a plaintiff to compel a professor from the Harvard School of Public Health and the Kennedy School of Public Administration to divulge the contents of notes made during confidential interviews held with employees of Pacific Gas & Electric Company. The interviews were part of a research project focusing on the way in which utilities make environmental decision. *Richards of Rockford* v. *Gas & Electric Company,* United States District Court, San Francisco, May 20, 1976.

intensified the conflict and tensions on both sides. After two dysfunctional newspaper articles, the newspaper reporter was briefed by the consultant on the values and objectives of OD. After that briefing, the reporter became a positive influence in the community through his active participation in OD efforts and by writing more positive articles. It appears that the openness of organizations must always be qualified by the interests of private individuals, of the community welfare, and organizational effectiveness. There is a need to strike a balance—the location of that balancing point must be based upon careful analysis rather than an emotional plea. For example, we believe open-meeting laws should permit closed seminars for agendas which include dealing with organizational processes including interpersonal relations, group skills, leadership style, and structural and procedural matters.

The final selection in Part 8, by Paul and Gross, is an attempt to increase productivity and morale in a municipality. This OD field experiment indicates that OD can be successful in city government.

Finally, we believe that the three main issues in the public and service sectors for the remainder of the 80s will be productivity, marketing, and commitment to service. If OD is to make a meaningful contribution in this growing arena, it must incorporate these issues into its programs.

Reading 55

ORGANIZATION DEVELOPMENT IN PUBLIC AGENCIES: PERSPECTIVES ON THEORY AND PRACTICE

Robert T. Golembiewski

The special genius of each age is reflected in distinctive ways of organizing work. If the preceding age stressed stability and consistency, roughly, the emphasis today is on organizing for change and variability. The specific implications are diverse and still obscure, but the general point is overwhelming. John W. Gardner reflects both the certainty and the caution. "What may be most in need of innovation is the corporation itself," he notes. "Perhaps what every corporation (and every other organization) needs is a department of continuous renewal that could view the whole organization as a system in need of continuing innovation."[1]

The major recent response to the need for planned organizational change is the burgeoning emphasis on organization development, or OD. Three themes constitute the core of typical OD concepts. As Winn explains:

> The term *organizational development* . . . implies a normative, reeducation strategy intended to affect systems of beliefs, values, and attitudes within the organization so that it can adapt better to the accelerated rate of change in technology, in our industrial environment and society in general. It also includes formal organizational restructuring which is frequently initiated, facilitated, and reinforced by the normative and behavioral changes.[2]

Changing attitudes or values, modifying behavior and inducing change in structure and policies, then, are the three core objectives of OD programs. In contrast, the reorganization literature in political science is concept oriented and gives little attention to changes in attitudes and behavior necessary to implement its guiding concept.

This article provides a variety of perspectives on the characteristics of OD programs and also summarizes experience from a number of OD efforts in public agencies at federal and local levels. Not all these agencies can be identified here, unfortunately, but the data base consists of seven cases. No attempt will be made to evaluate the effectiveness of any particular OD application; and even less is the purpose here to assess the specific technology of OD programs such as the use of sensitivity training.[3]

The motivation of this piece derives from the following propositions. First, government agencies have begun experimenting with various OD approaches, if less bullishly so than business and service organizations. Second, the public sector has a variety of distinctive features that provide special challenges to achieving typical OD objectives.

[1]John W. Gardner, *Self-Renewal* (New York: Harper & Row, 1965).

[2]Alexander Winn, "The Laboratory Approach to Organization Development: A Tentative Model of Planned Change" a paper read at the Annual Conference, British Psychological Society, Oxford, September 1968, p. 1. More broadly, see Edgar H. Schein and Warren G. Bennis, *Personal and Organization Change through Group Methods: The Laboratory Method* (New York: John Wiley & Sons, 1965); and Warren G. Bennis, *Changing Organizations* (New York: McGraw-Hill, 1966).

[3]For an overview of the technique, see Robert T. Golembiewski, "The Laboratory Approach to Organization Development: The Schema of a Method," *Public Administration Review,* September 1967, pp. 211–20.

Third, these distinctive features have received inadequate attention in the literature and in the design of OD programs in public agencies. Fourth, applications of OD programs in public agencies probably will become more common. The need to tailor OD programs in public agencies more closely to the distinctive constraints of their environment should consequently increase sharply. Finally, students of public administration can play useful and distinct roles in such OD programs, providing they develop appropriate competencies.

* * * * *

Character of the Institutional Environment: Constraints on Approaching OD Objectives

Public agencies present some distinctive challenges to OD programs, as compared with business organizations where most experience with OD programs has been accumulated. Four properties of the public institutional environment particularly complicate achieving the common goals of OD programs.

1. Multiple Access

As compared to even the largest of international businesses, the public environment in this country is characterized by what might be called, following David Truman, unusual opportunities for *multiple access to multiple authoritative decision makers*. Multiple access is, in intention if not always in effect, a major way of helping to assure that public business gets looked at from a variety of perspectives. Hence the purpose here is to look at the effects of multiple access rather than to deprecate it. Figure 1 details some major points of multiple access relevant to OD programs in four interacting "systems": the executive, legislative, "special interests," and mass media systems.

FIGURE 1   Some Critical Publics Relevant to Federal OD Programs

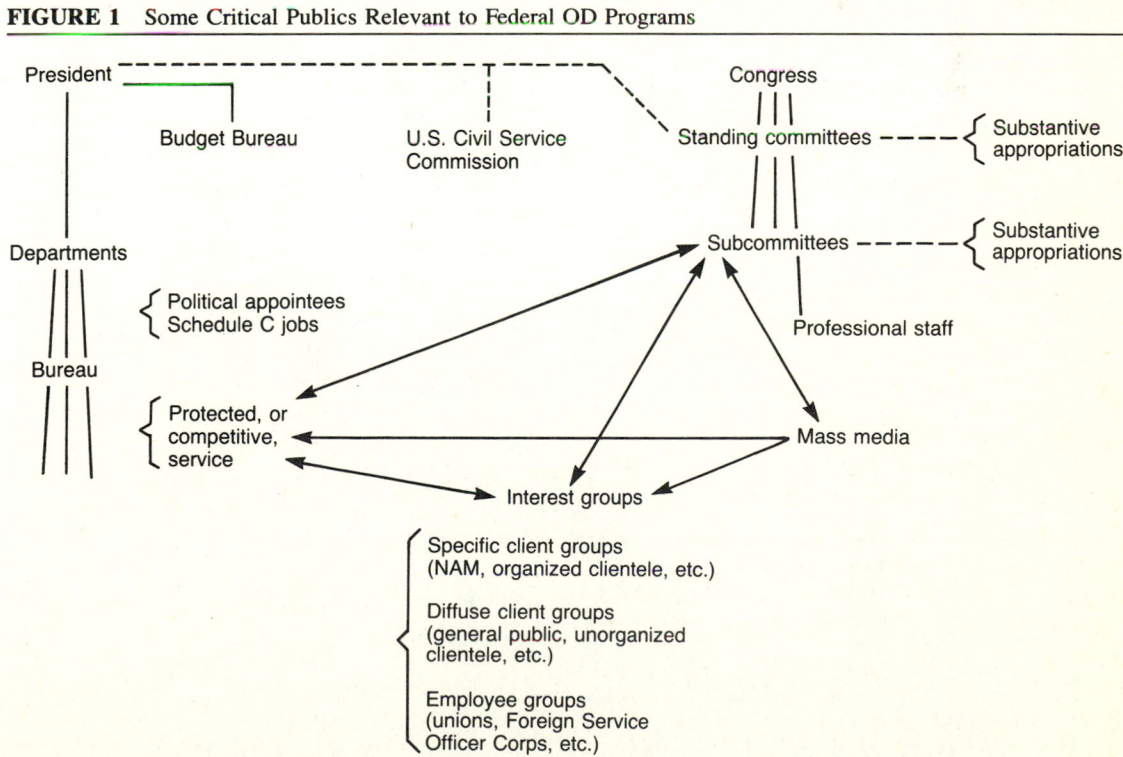

Multiple access has its attractive features in beginning OD programs in public agencies. For example, one large OD program was inaugurated in an economical way: a top departmental career official sponsoring an OD program had developed a relation of deep trust with the chairman and the professional staff of a congressional appropriations subcommittee, and that relation quickly, even mercurially, triumphed over lukewarm support or even opposition from the department head, the Bureau of the Budget, and the U.S. Civil Service Commission.

But multiple access can cut two ways. Funds for that very OD program ''became unavailable'' after its inception, despite strong support from both career and political officers at the top levels. In short, the successful counterattack was launched by agency personnel in the protected/competitive service, an interest group representing these employees, members of a concerned substantive committee of Congress, and the media. The two themes of the counterattack were common to several reactions against OD programs of which I know. First, ordinary decency required allowing the dedicated civil servants affected to complete their careers in peace and in the traditional ways, rather than being subjected to an unwanted program that was seen as having problematic value.[4] Second, the use of sensitivity training in the OD program was disparaged as violating the privacy of organizational members, or worse.[5]

Viewed from the perspective of top-level political and career officials intent on inaugurating a public OD program, the ''iron quadrangle'' in Figure 1 inspires substantial pessimism about a fair trial, in the general case. Specific conditions may raise or lower the odds, since the several links in the counterattacking forces above can be variously strong or weak. For example, a public agency may have a very positive constitutional image, which gives its top officials an important edge in presenting their case to congressional committees, the mass media, or the general public. Similarly, top political and career officials can induce—or capitalize on—organized clientele opposition to policies and procedures and use it to force changes at the protected levels. Or political resources and professional skills may provide agency executives with substantial power to control their environment.[6]

Whether the iron quadrangle is more or less integral, the design and implementation of OD programs in public agencies has give that constellation short shrift. Perhaps this is because most experience with OD programs has been gained in business organizations, where nothing even remotely like the iron quadrangle exists at managerial levels.

2. Greater Variety

Again as compared to business organizations, the public arena involves in all OD programs a greater variety of individuals and groups with *different and often mutually exclusive sets of interests, reward structures, and values*. In the case outlined above, for example, the appropriations subcommittee was interested in improved operations and reduced costs. But the substantive subcommittee was concerned more with safeguarding program and personnel with which they had developed a strong identification. And never the twain did meet. Role conflicts between legislators and administrators also seem to have been significant. For example, one congressman explained his opposition to an OD program in these terms: ''Improvement of efficiency is O.K., but messing with people's attitudes sounds subversive to my constituents.'' The agency's top administrators felt no such constituency pressure, and their view was that attitudes toward work had to be changed.

---

[4]The theme also appeared in mass-circulation news stories and editorials which argued against Project ACORD in the U.S. Department of State, for example. Stewart Alsop, ''Let the Poor Old Foreign Service Alone,'' *Saturday Evening Post,* June 1966, p. 14.

[5]For example, sensitivity training has been criticized as ''amateur group therapy.'' For an incisive distinction between training and therapy, see Chris Argyris, ''Conditions for Competence Acquisition and Therapy,'' *Journal of Applied Behavioral Science,* June 1968, pp. 147–78.

[6]See Francis E. Rourke, *Bureaucracy, Politics, and Public Policy* (Boston: Little, Brown, 1969).

Such incongruencies of expectations, rewards, and values also occur in business organizations, of course, as in labor-management issues. In my experience, however, they occur there in less intense and exotic forms.

A conclusion need not be forced. All OD programs have to stress the development of viable "interfaces," that is, relations between individuals or groups with different values and interests. This problem is enormously complicated in public agencies undertaking OD programs and has received little explicit attention in concept or in practice. For example, in no case that I know of has the development of an explicit interface between legislative and administrative interests been attempted as part of an OD program, apparently in part because of the constitutional separation of powers.

The failure to build such interfaces was a major contributor to the death of a major recent urban OD program. Departmental officers rejected the idea of attempting to build an explicit interface between a substantive subcommittee, an appropriations subcommittee, and the agency as part of an OD program. Tradition, jealousy over prerogatives, and separation of powers were blamed, and with good reason. But it also seemed that departmental officials preferred things as they were. The lack of integration between subcommittees, perhaps, provided alternative routes of access and gave departmental officials some room to operate.

3. Command Linkages

The "line of command" within public agencies, as compared to business and service organizations, is more likely to be characterized by *competing identifications and affiliations*. Again the difference is one of degree, but it approaches one of a kind. Consider only one aspect of the integrity of command linkages common in business organizations. In them, typically, "management" is separated from "labor" only very far down the hierarchy, at or near the level of the first-line supervisor. Moreover, the common identification of all levels of management often is stressed. "Management," moreover, commonly does not enjoy the

kind of job security that can come from union contracts. One of the effects of such carrots and sticks, without question, is the more facile implementation of policy changes at all levels of organization.

Hierarchy has its effects in public agencies as well as businesses, but the line of command seems less integral in the former. Thus a unique family of identifications alternative to the hierarchy exists at levels both low and high in public agencies, the apparent underlying motivation being to maximize the probability that evil will not occur, or at least will be found out. That is, the chain of command at the federal level is subject to strong fragmenting forces even up to the highest levels, where political and career strata blend into one another. For example, the ideal of a wall-to-wall civil service is approached closely in practice, and it provides a strong countervailing identification to the executive chain of command. Career officials are "out of politics," but their commitments to programs may be so strong as to inhibit or even thwart executive direction.[7]

That the public institutional environment permits (indeed encourages) a fragmenting of the management hierarchy at points well up in the higher levels may be illustrated in three ways. First, the "neutrality" of civil servants has been a major defensive issue in at least two federal OD programs in which I have participated, the OD efforts having been painted by many career people as sophisticated but lustful raids on a chaste, protected service. Second, Congress is an old hand at creating similar countervailing identifications so as to enhance its control over administration,[8] for which the Constitution and tradition provide a solid rationale. Third, the executive has also played the game, sometimes unwittingly. Consider the presidential-inspired federal executive boards. Basically, these boards were intended to be a horizontal link between field units of federal agencies and vertically between the pres-

---

[7]For a sensitive summary of the programatic commitments of career personnel, see John J. Corson and R. Shale Paul, *Men Near the Top* (Baltimore, Md.: Johns Hopkins Press, 1966), pp. 23–51.

[8]Joseph P. Harris, *Congressional Control of Administration* (Washington, D.C.: Brookings Institution, 1964).

idency and top career field officialdom. The FEBs provide career field managers with a potential way to supplement or even bypass departmental reporting relations, both career employees and political appointees. Indeed, President Kennedy may have intended them as just such a bypass around "the feudal barons of the permanent government" whom he saw as obstacles to change.[9]

A conclusion flows easily. Congress often encourages slack in the executive chain of command to facilitate its oversight of the president and his major appointees; and the executive as well as the protected service itself often uses the same strategy. The integrity of the executive chain of command suffers. Although the consequences are mixed, public executives are limited in initiating (for example) OD programs.[10] Witness the furor over the mere handful of Schedule C jobs removed from the protected service during Eisenhower's first term to permit greater executive leverage. Any corporation president would have an immensely broader field to act upon. The motivation to avoid "spoils politics" is recognized, but managerial rigidity is the other side of the coin. Herbert Kaufman concludes that although extensions of the civil service were intended to provide upper-level political administrators with capable help, the latter have often been driven to "pray for deliverance from their guardians."[11]

4. Weak Linkages

Exacerbating the point above, the *linkages between political and career levels* are weak as a conse-

quence of a variety of features of the public institutional environment.[12] This slippage between managerial levels significantly complicates beginning and implementing OD programs, and severely challenges the linkage of executive management with operating management.

The generalization concerning weak linkages in the managerial chain of command is meant to apply in four distinct senses. First, political and career-levels often are weakly linked due to the brief tenure of the former. Second, the job of linking the political leadership and the permanent bureaucracy must be handled by a tiny group of executives—political appointees and occupants of Schedule C jobs—who owe diverse allegiance to the chief executive. Third, there is reason to suspect significant slippage between the top-career officialdom and lower levels. For example, what lower-level careerists see as necessary protections of tenure, top-career officials perceive as cumbersome limitations on managerial flexibility. Fourth, the executive often weakens its own managerial linkages, as it seeks sometimes-unreconcilable political and administrative goals. Thus the unionization of public employees which has been encouraged by presidential executive order hardly discourages labor unions looking for new fields to conquer. But one of the groups of federal employees to organize were inspectors in the U.S. Civil Service Commission who, if anybody, would be seen as "management" in most business organizations.

OD programs consequently must face the issue of somehow interfacing political and career linkages which powerful forces—constitutional, political, and historic—tend to pull apart. Consider only one dilemma facing OD programs. The general rule of thumb is that OD programs should begin "at the top" of organizational hierarchies, or as close to the top as possible. The rationale is obvious: that is where the power usually is in business organizations. Respecting this rule of thumb in public agencies raises a multidimensional dilemma. Ba-

---

[9]Arthur Schlesinger, *A Thousand Days* (Boston: Houghton Mifflin, 1965), p. 681.

[10]President Truman expressed the point directly in contemplating the problems that General Eisenhower would experience as President Eisenhower, without the discipline and definite career patterns and established ways of doing things he knew in the military. "He'll sit here," Truman predicted, "and he'll say, 'Do this!' 'Do that!' *And nothing will happen*. Poor Ike—it won't be a bit like the Army. He'll find it very frustrating." Richard E. Neustadt, *Presidential Power* (New York: John Wiley & Sons, 1960), p. 9. His emphases.

[11]Herbert Kaufman, "The Rise of a New Politics," in *The Federal Government Service*, ed. Wallace S. Sayre (Englewood Cliffs, N.J.: Prentice-Hall, 1965), p. 58.

[12]Dean E. Mann, "The Selection of Federal Political Executives," *American Political Science Review*, March 1964, pp. 81–99.

sically, "the top" in public agencies is more complex than in most businesses. Initiating an OD program at the level of the political leadership maximizes formal executive support, but it may also raise complex problems. Support of the OD program is problematic because of frequent personnel changes at that level,[13] because of possible well-entrenched resistance from the permanent service, because legislators may fear that any strengthening of the executive chain of command would only mean fewer points of access and sources of information, and because employee associations may resist executive direction. Relying more on support from those in the competitive/protected service maximizes the chances of permanent support, and it may raise congressional and CSC trust in the program. But this approach may encourage executive resistance from such vantage points as the Bureau of the Budget.

The OD specialist faces real dilemmas, then, in choosing the "top" of the hierarchy at which to direct his interventions. I have participated in change programs that have taken both approaches to seeking a power base, and they show only that avoiding Scylla seems to imply meeting Charybdis. The ideal is to appeal to both the political officialdom and to the permanent service, of course, but that is a demanding ideal indeed.

In summary, four properties of the institutional environment of public agencies complicate attaining the objectives of typical OD programs. Consider the objective of building trust among individuals and groups throughout the organization. Technically, viable interfaces should be created between political officials, the permanent bureaucracy, congressional committees and their staffs, and so on and on. Practically, this is a very tall order, especially because the critical publics tend to have mutually exclusive interests, values, and reward systems. Indeed, although it is easy to caricature the point, Congress has a definite interest in cultivating a certain level of distrust within and between government agencies so as to encourage a flow of information. This may seem a primitive approach, but in the absence of valid and reliable measures of performance, it may be a necessary approach. No OD program in a business organization will face such an array of hurdles; that much is certain.

Character of the Habit Background: Constraints on Approaching OD Objectives

The "habit background" of public agencies also implies serious obstacles to approaching OD objectives. Five aspects of this habit background are considered below by way of illustrating their impact on OD objectives. These five aspects do not comprise an exclusive list, and they are conceived of only as general patterns and behaviors which give a definite flavor to the broad institutional environment sketched above.

Patterns of Delegation

"Habit background" is perhaps better illustrated than defined. First, in my experience, public officials tend to favor patterns of delegation that maximize their sources of information and minimize the control exercised by subordinates. Specifically, the goal is to have decisions brought to their level for action or review. The most common concrete concomitants of the tendency are functional specialization and a narrow span of control, one of whose major consequences is a large number of replicative levels of review.[14]

---

[13]One ambitious OD program, for example, was unable to overcome the rumor that several political appointees were negotiating terms of private employment. Agency personnel were encouraged to inaction, since these officials would "soon be riding their OD hobbyhorse" someplace else. These officials did leave. But all claim that the stories were seeded by career personnel who opposed the OD program, and that it was only the intensity of such "dirty fighting" that encouraged the political appointees to seek private employ after the rumors began.

[14]Before a reorganization inspired by an OD program in the Department of State, some review layers were so numerous that "it could take as long as six months for an important problem to reach the deputy under secretary. Now it takes an average of two days." Alfred J. Marrow, "Managerial Revolution in the State Department," *Personnel,* December 1966, p. 13.

"Layering" of multiple levels of review is not unique to public administration; indeed it inheres in generally accepted organization theory. But it is supported by forces more or less unique to public agencies that have been powerful enough to substantially curtail innovation of ways to centralize policy and to decentralize operations.[15] The protection of the "public interest" is one such unique factor, for example. The rationale is familiar. Political officials of short tenure often cannot rely on established relations of confidence with personnel at lower levels, nor do they exercise as much control over career rewards and punishments as is common in business organizations or in the military. However, the legislature will hold the political officials responsible. Consequently, political officials seek to maximize information sources and minimize the control exercisable by subordinates. This tendency is reinforced by law and tradition so that it permeates down the hierarchy throughout the permanent bureaucracy. The tendency is often referred to as "keeping short lines of command."

Keeping chains of command short implies constraints on approaching OD objectives in public organizations, based on my experience as well as the logic of the situation. Consider only two of the OD objectives:

To locate decision making and problem-solving responsibilities as close to the information sources as possible.

To increase self-control and self-direction for people within the organization.

To the degree that the rough distinction above is accurate, public agencies will experience difficulties in approaching both objectives. The prevailing

habit pattern in public agencies patently constitutes a tide to swim against in these two particulars, although there are outstanding exceptions to this generalization.

Legal Habit

Second, and again only as a description of what exists, legal patterns make approaching OD objectives severely more difficult in public agencies than in business organizations.[16] The point applies in two major senses. Thus patterns of administrative delegation are often specified in minute detail in legislation, basically so as to facilitate oversight by the legislature. To be sure, we are a considerable distance beyond the first Morgan case, which seemed to argue that only administrative actions personally taken by, or under the direct supervision of, a department head were constitutionally defensible. But flexibility in delegation is still a major problem. Perhaps more important, a corpus of law and standard practice exists which also makes it difficult to achieve OD objectives. For example, considering only those employees on the General Schedule, salary and duties are tied to a position classification system whose underlying model emphasizes transdepartmental uniformity and compensation for individual work.[17]

This legal habit background complicates approaching OD values. Thus efforts to achieve OD objective three may run afoul of the possibility that relocating responsibilities in one agency is considered to have systemwide implications, with consequences that complicate the making of local adjustments. As one official noted of an OD effort in such straits: "I feel like I have to raise the whole civil service by my bootstraps." Relatedly, OD objective two seeks:

---

[15]Such innovation has been the major trend in large businesses over the last three or four decades. See Robert T. Golembiewski, *Men, Management, and Morality* (New York: McGraw-Hill, 1965); and *Organizing Men and Power* (Chicago: Rand McNally, 1967). Strong pressures for just such innovations are now being widely felt in public administration. Aaron Wildavsky provides a case in point in his "Black Rebellion and White Reaction," *The Public Interest,* Spring 1968, especially pp. 9–12.

[16]A very useful discussion of the antimanagerial thrust of much legislation is provided by Harris, *Congressional Oversight of Administration.*

[17]Robert T. Golembiewski, "Civil Service and Managing Work," *American Political Science Review,* December 1962, pp. 961–74.

To supplement the authority associated with role or status with the authority of knowledge and competence.

This is hard to do to the degree that a pattern of delegation is specified by law. The same point applies to any rigidities due to the duties classification common in public agencies in the United States, and especially to the concepts for assigning authority and for organizing work underlying the duties classification. Job enlargement begun as part of OD programs has run afoul of such concepts, for example.

At the bread-and-butter level, existing legal patterns also inhibit approaching OD objectives. Consider objective six, which proposes:

To develop a reward system which recognizes both the achievement of the organization's mission and organization development.

Existing law and practice severely limit the search for such a reward system. Thus rewards for exceptional performance—in money payments or in higher-than-normal GS levels for personnel in the civil service—are now possible, but they still are exceptional in practice. Equal pay for equal work, in sum, still practically means that exceptional work is not rewarded exceptionally. Management in business organizations typically has far greater control over reward systems, and especially at managerial levels. More of a problem, neither existing law nor practice promise much in the way of support for various group compensation plans. Experiments in industry with some such plans have yielded attractive results.

Need for Security

Third, the need for security or even secrecy in public agencies as against business organizations is more likely to be strong enough to present obstacles to approaching OD objectives. Military and defense agencies come to mind first, but they hardly exhaust the list. The "need for security" as used here can concern national security, it can be induced by a general anxiety born of a need to make

significant decisions whose results will not be manifest for a very long time, or it can derive from felt needs for protection from such outside forces as a congressman with fire in his eye.[18] The need can also be real, exaggerated, or even imagined in various combinations.

Consider one case which seemed to reflect some of all of these components. Agency personnel were exposed to sensitivity training, one of whose major purposes is to increase skills in being open about both positive and negative emotions or reactions. The training staff provided several settings in which these intentions might be approached, one of which was a "park bench." During one week of sensitivity training some time was set aside each evening for a meeting of all participants in a large room which was the locus of the "park bench." But agency personnel seldom used the arena, although there was a good deal of nervous laughter from the periphery of the "park." After some three abortive tries of an hour each, one participant approached me. "I see the point of the thing," he said, "but a park bench is all wrong." Suddenly, the dawn came. "Park benches," were seen as stereotypic sites for sexual assignations and/or for exchanging secrets with enemy agents. Without doubt, some participants, thought the "park bench" a silly notion and hence did not participate. For most participants, however, the symbolism was so compelling that they could not use the "park bench." Moreover, many agency personnel were so closed, distrustful, and fearful of taking a risk that they could not talk about their guiding symbolism, even if they were aware of it.

This greater need for security cannot be established completely, to be sure, and all that may be said definitely is that to the degree this need exists

---

[18]Great needs for "security" as here broadly defined can rigidify an organization and curb the effectiveness of its members. To the point, see Chris Argyris, "Some Causes of Organizational Ineffectiveness within the Department of State," Center for International System Research, *Occasional Papers* 2 (1967).

so are OD objectives more difficult to reach. Consider only OD objective one:

> To create an open, problem-solving climate throughout the organization.

An open climate and a great need for security or for secrecy do not mix well.

Procedural Regularity and Caution

Fourth, for a variety of reasons, government personnel are rather more likely to stress procedural regularity and caution. Perhaps better said, even if agency personnel are convinced that certain heuristics provide solutions that are "good enough," this conviction may conflict with other (and especially congressional) needs for external control. For example, sample checking of vouchers was widely accepted as an efficient enough administrative approach long before relevant publics in Congress and the General Accounting Office recognized it as appropriate for their control purposes.

Good reasons support this bias toward procedural regularity and caution in public agencies, of course, and so much the worse for OD objectives. For example, the bias patently runs against the grain of OD objective eight, which seeks:

> To help managers to manage according to relevant objectives rather than according to "past practices" or according to objectives that do not make sense for one's area of responsibility.

> The underlying rub, of course, is that a "past practice" making little or no sense administratively may seem an utter necessity from the legislative point of view. To be sure, the dictum "where you sit determines what you see" applies to all organizations. But the needs and identifications of administrators and legislators are likely to differ more than is the case for (let us say) the executives and middle managers of a business organization.

"Professional Manager"

Fifth, the concept "professional manager" is less developed in the public versus the business arena,

in rough but useful contrast. The relative incidence of business schools and schools of public administration suggests the conclusion,[19] as do the Jacksonian notions deep at the roots of our basic public personnel policies. For example, the "career system" notion has been a difficult one to develop in this country at the federal level. No small part of the difficulty derives from the value we place on an "open service" with lateral entry. Hence the tendency of our public personnel policies to emphasize hiring for a specific position rather than for long-run potential.

Derivations from these taproots have had profound impact. For example, to simplify a little, massive federal attention to training was long delayed by the wrigglesworthian legislative notion that, since the federal service was hiring people who already had the abilities to do the specific job for which they were hired, there was little need to spend money on training.[20] The relative attractiveness of public employment at the federal level at least through World War II provided the proverbial finger in the dike, but conditions changed much faster than did public policy. Instructively, also, the system of regional executive development centers manned by the U.S. Civil Service Commission began as late as 1964, and then only with a miniscule budget and against substantial congressional opposition. Roughly, business has a 10–20-year lead over government in acting on the need for training. Not very long ago, in contrast, the federal government was considered *the* model employer.

The relatively lesser stress on the "public professional manager" implies significant problems for approaching OD objectives. Thus OD objective seven proposes:

> To increase the sense of "ownership" of organization objectives throughout the work force.

---

[19]Revealingly, it was not until 1946 that Cornell developed the first two-year Master of Public Administration program comparable to the MBA long given by schools of commerce or business administration.

[20]Paul P. Van Riper, *History of the United States Civil Service* (Evanston, Ill.: Row, Peterson, 1958), pp. 429–34.

No sharp contrast is appropriate. But a definite bias of public personnel policy limits such a sense of identification with, and commitment to, public agencies. If there is one thing most civil services reformers did not want, it was a public work force who "owned" the objectives of their agency. The only "owner" was the public; the model employee was a politically neutral technician who repressed his own values in return for guaranteed tenure. Only thus could an elite and unresponsive bureaucracy be avoided, goes a major theme shot through our public personnel policies and institutions.

Conclusion

The body of this paper can be summarized tersely. Organization development programs are appearing with increasing frequency in both business and public agencies. Moreover, applications of OD programs in government agencies face some unique problems. However, these unique problems tend to go unrecognized or underrecognized by OD teams, in part because students of public administration have tended to be underrepresented on such teams. Hence this paper.

Some derivative implications seem appropriate, in addition. First, "poaching" in the public sector by OD teams composed basically of psychologists and sociologists will continue to grow, if only because (as William F. Whyte noted in another connection) such poaching is necessary. Second, students of public administration can play a useful and partially distinct role in such OD programs. But, third, students of public administration are likely to play such a role only as substantial numbers of them develop competencies that complement their special interests in public administration. Such competency enlargement for "change agents" or organization consultants in provided by the NTL Institute of Applied Behavioral Science and by such university-based programs as those at UCLA and Boston University.

Reading 56

ORGANIZATION DEVELOPMENT
TECHNOLOGY AND THE MILITARY:
A SURPRISING MERGER?

Denis D. Umstot

The theory and practice of organization development (OD) have been linked to values since the early development of the OD approach. Friedlander and Brown (1974) noted that the future of OD seems to rest on the congruence between practice, theory and research, and OD values. It has been assumed that for OD to succeed, it must be conducted in organizations that encourage such values as power sharing, decentralization of decision making, openness, and trust (French & Bell, 1978). These values seem counter to those of mechanistic, bureaucratic organizations. Schein and Greiner (1977) may echo the feelings of many OD practitioners when they assert that many current OD practices are not suitable for mechanistic, bureaucratic organizations. They hypothesize that because the behavioral problems emanating from bureaucratic structures are different from those emanating from organic structures, different OD techniques are needed to deal with mechanistic structures. Students of public–sector OD (Golembiewski, 1972; Giblin, 1976) also see basic problems and conflicts between public–sector bureaucracies and OD technology.

For many, the military is perceived to be the epitome of an authoritarian, mechanistic organization. If the values of the military are incongruent with those of OD, it would appear that OD tech-

nologies and military organizations are basically incompatible. Surprisingly, this is not the case—OD appears to be thriving in the military environment. There are several plausible explanations for this apparent paradox. First, values may not be as important to OD practice as previously supposed. Bowen (1977) suggests this view when he argues that OD should be more concerned with a theory of consultancy, based on Argyris's (1970) model of concern for valid information, free choice about how to proceed, and internal commitment to the decision made. A second explanation might be that the OD technologies being used in the military are more appropriate for bureaucratic organizations and less linked with traditional OD values. Schein and Greiner might support this view. The final explanation might be that managers who are involved with OD in the military do, in fact, adhere to traditional OD values. Although this review of military OD efforts does not provide conclusive support for any of these views, it does provide some insights into this controversial topic.

The primary purpose of this article is to describe, analyze, and evaluate the results of military OD efforts. It is also concerned with the issues that seem to make OD more or less successful in the military environment.

Defining OD

Before the detailed analysis begins it would be helpful to resolve some definitional issues. OD is defined as a long–range effort to improve organizational effectiveness, using the theory and technology of applied behavioral science, including action research. There are other elements of the

Source: Reprinted from *Academy of Management Review* 5, no. 2 (1980), pp 189–201.

I wish to thank the numerous colleagues who commented on earlier versions of this paper; William Rosenbach, Raymond Forbes, James Rosenzweig, and Robert A. Zawacki were particularly helpful. The views expressed are mine and are not necessarily shared by the Department of Defense.

OD process that may or may not be present such as the assistance of a change agent, concentration on intact work groups, focus on organizational culture, problem–solving orientation, or process emphasis (French & Bell). Although the above elements are often present in OD, they are not considered to be essential for defining OD. For me, the essence of OD is using the action research model (French & Bell; Froham, Sashkin, & Kavanagh, 1976; Margulies & Raia, 1978) to apply behavioral science and management techniques aimed at organizational improvement, including both institutional effectiveness and the quality of life of the members of the system (Alderfer, 1977).

The Military Stereotype

One possible barrier to understanding OD in the military is that many of us have a strong stereotype of military organizations. We see highly structured, authoritarian, controlled organizations. Although this stereotype is true in many military organizations (just as it is true in many private–sector organizations), there are other organizations that are participative, decentralized, and relatively autonomous. There are great differences in organizational climate between and within the services. And, because of frequent rotation of personnel, there are often differences in the same organization over time. In addition, military organizations probably have some unique characteristics such as the rank structure, the total-immersion environment, and restrictions on individual freedom that make them fundamentally different from most other organizations (see Turney & Cohen [1978] for further discussion of these issues).

OD in Olive Drab: The Decentralized Process Approach of the U.S. Army

During the late 1960s and early 1970s, the army experienced the same turmoil that had plagued private-sector institutions: dissent, racial unrest, drug abuse, and a general disrespect for traditional values and institutions. On top of these problems came the end of the draft, forcing the army to rely solely on volunteers. This combination of events created a readiness and perhaps even an imperative for improving their human resource management processes. In 1972 they established a three-year testing program to try out new management approaches. Projects included job enrichment, human relations training, assessment centers, survey feedback (quarterly surveys with feedback to the battalion commander), and OD. Although all of these programs met with some degree of success, OD was selected for armywide implementation.

Organizational Effectiveness (OE) Program

The army's first step was to give the program a new name: Organizational Effectiveness (OE). They define OE as the military application of a technology that is derived from successful leadership and command practices and the applied behavioral and management sciences, using consulting services and the direct involvement of the chain of command (Nadal, Duey, Ray, & Schaum, 1977).

Using a nucleus of people who had participated in one of the pilot OD projects, the army expanded their OE program by setting up a training center at Ft. Ord, where it trains its internal consultants in a 16-week course. The consultants selected for training are line officers (captains and majors) who, in most cases, have advanced degrees in behavioral science or management. Consultants are taught process consultation, team building, survey feedback, conflict resolution, group problem solving, and other similar OD techniques. Over 400 consultants have been trained during the first three years of operation.

Consultants are assigned in pairs to major army units and installations (such as an airborne division). Since they are permanently assigned to a specific installation, they are an integral part of the organization. This has its benefits and drawbacks. Being part of the organization probably means the consultant has more long-term ownership in the OD effort and is more readily available if problems arise. However, the consultant is subject to the reward and control systems of the organization, which may make it difficult to maintain proper consultant behavior. The army has attempted to overcome the problems of using installation-level consultants by carefully defining the roles and responsibilities of the consultant. So far, they seem to have been fairly successful with their internal consultant approach (Cahn, 1978).

Consultants have to sell their services to interested units because participation is voluntary. Ordinarily the client will be a relatively autonomous subunit such as a battalion. The consultants work with the client to assess what OE strategy, if any, would be appropriate. An intervention may begin with information gathering through interviews, questionnaires, or sensing sessions. Once the client makes the diagnosis (with the assistance of the consultant), they jointly agree on plans for workshops or other interventions that may be appropriate. The OE interventions are tailored to the needs of the client. Consultants have a wide variety of interventions at their disposal and they are encouraged to fit the intervention to the situation and the client. Some of the techniques employed are team building, survey feedback, leadership transition, and process consultation (see Umstot, 1979, for more details). Actually, almost all common OD interventions are used except for those with a deep interpersonal focus, such as sensitivity training. As in the private sector, most OE interventions focus at the managerial level.

With over 350 trained full-time consultants in the field and more expected, the army's OE program is becoming truly pervasive. Team building, goal setting, survey-guided development, and transition models are widely employed. For example, the whole division staff of an airborne division (lieutenant colonel and above) goes off site for three days every six months for a problem-solving and action-planning conference. With the help of an OE consultant, they examine what they are doing right, what they are doing wrong, and what they should be doing. Almost all army installations now have at least two OE consultants.

OE Results

As of 1979, the chief of staff of the army, General Bernard Rogers, seemed satisfied with the results of OE and continued to provide strong support and involvement. A statement he made in 1977 illustrates this support: "My goal is to institutionalize OE and to integrate it fully with our leadership and management processes so that after a few years people will say, 'Didn't we always do it this way?'" (Nadal et al., p. A2).

This strong support is based primarily on anecdotal reports from OE clients (Cahn). Empirical studies of OE are almost nonexistent. Although numerous opportunities seem to be present for carefully controlled experiments, or at least longitudinal designs based on existing data sources, few such studies have been attempted. The reason for this lack of research may be due in part to their decentralized approach to OE. The goal is to have the effort be "owned" by the client, not by army headquarters. This approach may be congruent with Argyris's (1968) view that rigorous research may run counter to the goals of OD. If outside researchers are involved in measuring the OE effort, the ownership, confidentiality, and trust in the process might be compromised. In addition, the OE consultants are not trained in rigorous research methods. Another barrier to systematic research is the nonstandard nature of the OE intervention. A centralized measurement approach with standard criteria is very difficult in view of the variety of interventions being used. The Army Research Institute has recently instituted several studies that may result in a more definitive picture of the effectiveness of OE.

Other Army OD Efforts

Although no empirical research has been reported on the effects of OE, several isolated studies of other army OD efforts (those not conducted by people trained under the OE program) have been conducted.

OD with Enlisted Personnel. Cohen and Turney (1978) evaluated the effects of survey feedback, team building, and job enrichment on 154 enlisted members (working-level personnel) of an army communications processing facility. Results showed no effects due to survey feedback or team building. Job enrichment, which involved forming 16-member teams to handle unique communication tasks, resulted in several positive outcomes. Goals were clearer, evaluation standards were better understood, supervision improved, and productivity indices showed gains. However, job responsibility decreased, thus making it more likely the jobs had been more efficiently designed rather than enriched.

Team-Building Seminars. A nonempirical study by Patton and Dorey (1977) evaluated the longitudinal effects of team-building seminars on groups of middle-level executives (mostly GS-15s and lieutenant colonels) who participated. Interviews conducted 6 to 22 months later showed the participants perceived substantial benefits in terms of trust and team-work, improved managerial skills, interpersonal conflict resolution, and time management. The testimonial-type evidence from the interviews provides some support for the usefulness of team-building seminars. However, without some type of comparison groups and measures of the changes in skills, attitudes, and performance, little reliance can be placed on a single study of this type.

Conclusions about OE

The army's program appears to have strong top-management support, participation, and understanding. The army chief of staff has approved a plan to fully institutionalize OE by 1987. The army staff responsible for the program wants OE to grow because line managers understand the process and see how it will benefit them. The goal is for OE to be an institutionalized management approach. The army appears to have done a credible job of training a large number of OE consultants in a rather flexible, process-oriented approach to OD. This decentralized, flexible approach may be the most effective one; unfortunately, it also hampers efforts to systematically evaluate the OD effort. Thus, in spite of the appeal of the army's OD process, more detailed studies are needed to assess its net effects on attitudes and performance.

Although the army's OD effort seems to be progressing, problems do exist. Selection of competent, motivated, and skillful consultants is a problem that is growing with the significant increase in the number of OE consultants. The initial successes of OE may be due to having exceptionally well-qualified consultants but, in the future, less-qualified people may be taking their place. The strong top-management support listed as an advantage earlier may also become a disadvantage now that General Rogers has left. Will current and future chiefs of staff continue this strong support? Another problem that is particularly acute for army consultants is the potential for role conflict between their role as an OD consultant and the role of a good, conforming, loyal army officer. The potential exists for an installation commander to put considerable pressure, either perceived or real, on a consultant to violate the OD process or disclose client confidences.

OD in the U.S. Navy: A Survey Feedback Approach

Although the navy was not so dependent on the draft, it too has felt the need to improve its human resource management. In November 1970, Admiral Zumwalt, chief of naval operations, established a pilot program to develop and evaluate new ideas and techniques in the human relations area (Forbes, 1976). A pilot group of 24 people spent a year exploring a wide range of applied behavioral science techniques and finally settled on OD.

Based in part on the OD model of Kolb and Frohman (1970) (scouting, entry, diagnosis, planning, action, evaluation, termination), the navy adopted an OD process called command development and conducted a series of pilot projects. Although commanders were generally favorable toward the OD pilot projects, several major criticisms emerged. The process took too much time and was too rigid. The nonmilitary appearance of the consultants clashed with the conservative naval culture. For example, early consultants wore civilian clothes and were perceived to be outsiders by their clients. In addition, there was little ownership or involvement by senior line managers.

In spite of the less-than-spectacular results of the pilot program, the navy decided in early 1973 to streamline, refine, and institutionalize the OD process. Their first step was to rename the program Human Resource Management or HRM. They established five human-resource management centers with detachments throughout the world. These consulting centers work directly for the fleet commander (whose organizational relationship is roughly equivalent to a manager of a major autonomous division of a large corporation). Thus, navy consultants are more aloof from organizational politics and rewards than the army consultant. The pilot test, which resulted in a cultural clash between consultants and clients, convinced the navy that the credibility of the consultants was crucial. Thus, the centers are staffed with experienced line officers (usually lieutenant through commander) and senior noncommissioned officers with outstanding records and recent operational experience. The consultants are trained in a formal 12-week school and then placed on an internship with an experienced consulting team.

A typical HRM center might have six six-person teams plus administrative personnel. The centers are normally co-located with the home ports of the fleet so that HRM programs can be conducted while the ships are in port. The navy has approximately 700 people involved full time in the HRM program. Almost all navy operational units have now received HRM at least once. Some shore activities have received HRM interventions, but so far efforts have been concentrated on the fleet.

The Human Resource Management Process

The navy's approach is based heavily on *survey-guided development* (Bowers & Franklin, 1975) using an instrument similar to the Survey of Organizations (Taylor & Bowers, 1972. The survey, which has been revised a number of times, currently contains 88 Likert-scaled items. The major OD-related dimensions covered by the survey are *command climate* (communications flow, decision making, motivation, and human resource emphasis), *supervisory leadership* (support, team coordination, team emphasis, goal emphasis, and work facilitation), *peer leadership* (support, team co-

ordination, team emphasis, goal emphasis, and work facilitation), *work group processes* (coordination, readiness, discipline), and *outcome measures* (satisfaction, integration of meeting individual and organizational goals, and lower-level influence). A complete description of the instrument along with detailed item analysis may be found in Drexler (1974).

Conducting HRM

The Navy's HRM program is mandatory and quite standardized. The detailed steps involved in the process are summarized in Table 1. Although participation in the HRM program, taking the survey, and preparation of a Command Human Resource Management Action Plan are required, all the other steps in the process are optional. In other words a CO (commanding officer) could, in effect, decline to participate by ignoring all the optional workshops and planning sessions. In actuality COs do participate in most of the activities. However, many of them do not make full use of the survey feedback process in Step 6. Often the data are fed back only to the CO, or to the CO and the immediate staff. A full survey feedback model where the data are fed back to all work groups is not the norm (although this varies somewhat between centers).The workshops in Step 8 offer an unusual opportunity for data-based, problem-solving sessions because the units usually stand down for a full five workdays for human resource activities. Unfortunately, the workshops are often focused more on human relations training than on action research and problem solving.

Although it may appear the navy model is quite lockstep, there is perhaps more flexibility than first appears. Because each center and detachment works as a relatively autonomous consulting center, it can tailor its interventions to the needs and readiness of its clients or perhaps to its own preferences. In fact, this seems to be happening. Although some consulting teams take the easy way out by concentrating on a standard training package, others are engaged in a full range of OD techniques, including sensing sessions, survey feedback, team building, and transition models.

TABLE 1   The Navy's Human Resource Management Cycle

Time Phasing	Time to conduct		Step Activity
Weeks 1 and 2	1½ days	1.	Initial meetings between commanding officer (CO) and consultants.
Week 2	½ day	2.	Data-gathering planning meetings. • Will interview be conducted? What questions? • Are additional survey questions desired? • Schedule the survey administration.
Week 3	1 hour per person	3.	Survey administration (mandatory). • To all hands.
Week 4	As required	4.	Conduct interviews (optional).
Week 5	1 day	5.	Return survey results to CO. • Brief printout format, terms. • Study and analysis.
Weeks 6–7	½ day per working group	6.	Survey feedback to work groups (optional). • Familiarization with data. • Source of perceptions? • Supervisory self-knowledge. • Possible solutions/recommendations for action.
Weeks 8–9	½ day	7.	Action-planning meeting (optional). • Develop plans for human resource availability week: OD, equal opportunity, alcohol, drug abuse, and overseas diplomacy.
Week 10	1–3 days per group	8.	Human resource workshops (optional). • Vertical slice of ship or intact work group. • Modular training packages (standardized series of lectures, films, and exercises on such topics as motivation, communications, MBO, leadership, and race relations).
	2 days	9.	Command action-planning workshop (optional). • Selected members of crew normally (CO participates part-time). • CO approves plan (a command action-plan is mandatory).
Week 11	Indefinite	10.	Action phase. • Implement action-plans.
Weeks 25–30	½ day	11.	Follow-up by consultant. • Determine effect of human resource activities through interviews and discussions. • Meet with CO.
Weeks 11–104	As negotiated	12.	Follow-on activities (optional). • Survey readministered. • Conduct additional workshops or training activities.

Results of HRM

Most COs who have participated in HRM are positive toward it. One recent estimate made by the consultants is 75 percent. Others do not like the survey, think the survey is irrelevant, or the process too time consuming. The COs who encounter HRM for the second time appear to be much more favorable toward it; they now understand the process and can zero in on problems they are interested in. Turning to the empirical side of evaluation, the evidence points to a relationship between the indices contained in the HRM survey and organizational effectiveness. However, there is little evidence that the HRM process results in changes that the survey measures. A brief review of the empirical evidence follows.

Reenlistment Rates and the Survey. In a sample of 20 ships and 2 carrier air groups, Drexler and Bowers (1973) found reenlistment rates were positively related to all survey indices. Data were analyzed on an aggregate basis using 22 groups. Each of five indices accounted for 25 percent or more of the variance in enlistment rates: peer interaction facilitation ($r = .51$), peer goal emphasis ($r = .53$), communication flow ($r = .52$), lower-level influence ($r = .55$), and group processes ($r = .50$). They concluded that organizational climate, peer leadership, and group processes were all positively related to reenlistment rates.

An experimental comparison of first-term reenlistment rates were recently completed by Crawford and Thomas (1978). A sample of 60 units from the Pacific fleet (30 experimental and 30 controls) included a mix of matched pairs of ships and air squadrons. During the six-month period in which HRM occurred, reenlistment rates improved 5.8 percent. This difference was significant ($t(20) = 2.61, p<.01$). However, when the data were examined for periods of six months or more after the HRM occurred, the improved reenlistment rates were not sustained, although the trends were still in the correct direction. Based on these results, it appears participation in the HRM process may have short-term effects on retention of younger personnel, but that the effects may not last.

Disciplinary Rates and the HRM Survey. Crawford and Thomas (1977) related disciplinary rates aboard 41 ships to the HRM survey. All of the correlations were in the predicted direction—they were negatively correlated with nonjudicial punishments. Five HRM indices accounted for 20 percent or more of the variance in disciplinary rates: communications flow ($r = .47$), supervisory support ($r = .50$), supervisory teamwork ($r = .46$),

peer teamwork ($r = .47$), and work-group coordination ($r = .45$). The authors conclude that punishments are related to the type of organizational climate within a ship: the more effective the management, the lower the rates of disciplinary offenses.

An experimental examination of the link between HRM and disciplinary rates was performed by Crawford (1977), based on the assumption that OD activities should improve management of human resources and that concomitant improvements in nonjudicial punishments should result. Crawford examined 46 experimental ships and 46 control ships. The results showed no significant differences between experimental and control ships. One confounding factor may have been turnover of top management. Over 50 percent of the ships changed *both* commanding officers and executive officers during the experimental period. With turnover of key leadership like this, it is not surprising rigorous experiments are difficult.

Operational Readiness and the HRM Survey. Mumford (1976) performed a post hoc correlational analysis of operational readiness (as measured by refresher training exercises) on six ships. She found all the rank-order correlations were in the predicted direction and 56 percent of them were significant at the .01 level. Correlations ranged from .25 (satisfaction) to .75 (peer teamwork). It should be noted that all data on operational readiness were collected prior to administering the HRM survey. Thus we cannot attribute the relationship between the survey results and readiness to the effects of HRM.

Another study compared 103 ships (experimental) that had participated in HRM with 103 matched ships (control) that had not (Ellermeier & Curtis, 1978). Although the full results of this study are not yet available, it appears the experimental ships had significantly higher scores on their status-of-forces ratings for overall readiness and for equipment readiness than did the control ships. There were no differences for personnel, supply, or training readiness. This research indicates a small, but significant, effect of the HRM cycle on overall ship readiness ratings.

A Research Critique. Although there is some fairly good support for the link between the HRM survey indices and organizational outcomes, there is an almost complete lack of published empirical evidence that the HRM program actually changes the organizations that receive the intervention. Before-after comparisons of survey scores with control groups are needed. Survey-guided development by its very nature lends itself to this type of research. If HRM changes the dimensions that correlation studies have shown to be related to organizational effectiveness, then the usefulness of HRM would be on much sounder ground. A study of intervention effects would also provide data concerning the effectiveness of various HRM strategies. For example, do the team-emphasis, goal-emphasis, or work-facilitation indices actually change? Once the treatment effects have been determined, an experimental examination of the outcomes of HRM is the next step. If the HRM program is successful in significantly changing the lower-level influence or job-satisfaction indices, then significant improvements in reenlistment rates would be predicted, because correlational studies indicate these factors are related. In short, more carefully controlled experimental evidence is needed to establish the validity of the HRM effort.

Conclusions about HRM

The navy effort appears to be one of the largest OD programs, in terms of resources invested, ever attempted. Its survey-feedback conceptual basis appears fairly solid; however, the actual implementation of the process of OD is uneven. The mandatory nature of the program casts doubt about whether OD is meeting the needs of the client or simply conforming to system requirements. The relatively low-level involvement of some commanding officers in the process also causes problems—HRM may be seen as just another program to give the illusion of participation. Another weakness in practice is the weak emphasis on the action-research model. Sometimes there is no real problem solving or action planning taken to resolve

problems. When survey data are collected and not acted on, expectations may be raised and dashed.

In spite of these weaknesses, perhaps a more optimistic view is warranted. The navy has an institutionalized, standardized approach to OD that is concerned with those variables (contained in the HRM survey) shown to be related to organizational effectiveness. The potential exists for really major gains on a large scale since almost all navy units are exposed to HRM.

OD in the U.S. Air Force: A Potpourri

Although the air force does not have a centralized effort, human-resource management programs with an OD flavor abound. Conventional OD has been conducted in air force research laboratories, team building was attempted with Air Force Academy cadets, a major industrial depot tried OD at the shop level, survey-guided OD has been researched, and several small internal OD programs have flourished. In addition, OD efforts focused on the technostructural system—primarily job enrichment—have been conducted.

OD in Air Force Research Laboratories

In 1971, as a result of declining funding for research and development and a desire to establish a strong team of senior management personnel, the director of one of the air force research laboratories initiated an OD program under the guidance of two external consultants, George Lehner and Herbert Shepard. The goals of the OD effort were to reduce dysfunctional competition, improve communications, increase the use of goals and objectives, maximize decision-making decentralization, and facilitate the development of laboratory personnel (McNichols & Manley, 1976). The initial OD activities centered on executive team building, intergroup development, third-party peace-making, life and career planning, secretarial effectiveness workshops, and individual counseling. In addition, an effective interdisciplinary planning process was created and problem-solving processes were emphasized. As a result of the success of the initial effort, OD gradually spread to all the laboratories.

Results of the Laboratory OD Program. In 1973, McNichols and Manley researched the effects of OD at the laboratory where OD began. Because the baseline data did not exist, respondents were asked to answer each question in two modes: the pre-OD condition and the present condition. The analysis was based on 183 responses. Results indicated decision making, communications, goals and objectives, personnel development, and dysfunctional competition were all perceived to be significantly ($p < .001$) improved after the OD program.

In 1975, another research study was conducted by McNichols and Manley with 201 respondents from the same laboratory. This time slight improvements (when compared to the 1973 levels) appeared in leadership and communications but substantial decreases occurred in decision making, goal setting, and interaction influence. Thus, the overall results of the program were mixed. The changes in perceptions between 1973 and 1975 were probably caused more by environmental influences than by the OD program. There was a reorganization with changes in budgeting and tighter controls that was generally counter to the OD program. Of course the entire research design was not optimal. Since no pre-OD measures existed, the validity of the research in terms of measuring effects of OD is questionable. Subjective evaluations by members of the organization generally indicate OD has been successful. One of the internal consultants reported that OD fostered the development of organizational goals, facilitated program integration, enabled the resolution of some tough people-problems, reduced defensiveness, and improved internal mobility and career planning (Gregory, 1977).

OD on the Shop Floor

The Fuel Control Shop. In 1974 one of the air force logistics centers in the southwestern United States decided to try an OD project in one of their maintenance shops. Approximately 100 blue-collar, unionized employees participated in the OD effort, which was directed by psychologists from the regional Civil Service Commission. Questionnaires and interviews were used to generate data.

Then a diagnosis was made primarily by the consultants. Weekly meetings were held by an OD planning committee to identify problems and generate possible solutions. Examples of the focal issues included: parts problems; trust issues between supervisors, workers, and the union; class training; and working conditions. The success of this project has been limited. The OD effort seems to have been more like a suggestion committee than an OD workshop. Top-level management support and involvement were quite limited. The OD planning meetings were of relatively short duration (a few hours at most), thus limiting the time needed to get into meaty problems. In short, this project seemed to be a half-hearted experiment with OD that yielded marginally postitive benefits.

Team Building for Matrix Teams. Another logistics center located in the far West decided better coordination and integration were needed to improve logistics support. They decided to get together all the people who supported a particular component (such as a radar set) and build them into a cohesive group. Teams included concerned people from item management, engineering, scheduling, quality control, distribution, planning, and the like. Once formed, the matrix teams went through a series of team-building and management-development workshops conducted by internal consultants and aimed at improving team effectiveness. The matrix-team OD project was judged by the consultants and managers to be generally successful.

Survey Feedback OD. Another shop-floor effort was a research-oriented survey feedback OD effort at a midwestern logistics center. The original consultant for this project proposed an elaborate research design to test the effects of various survey feedback strategies (Van Gundy, 1976). When the project was partially completed, the original consultant moved to another state and the intervention was redesigned and taken over by a new consultant/researcher (Lloyd, 1977). The new design called for testing two intervention styles: first, merely giving the data back to the supervisors for analysis and dissemination (Model I) and second, providing extensive training on the analysis of the data and feedback techniques (Model II). It was expected that Model II would be superior to Model I. This hypothesis was partially supported when a significant increase in perceived productivity was found; however, no positive changes in organizational climate occurred. In fact, there were adverse effects from the use of co-located experimental and control groups and there was some resistance from supervisors who did not wish to participate in the research. Overall, it is difficult to conclude that this OD project was a success; however, the combination of rigorous research with OD may inherently limit the effectiveness of such endeavors (Argyris, 1968).

Will Shop-Floor OD Survive? It seems unlikely that shop-floor OD will survive. When the high cost of OD is considered, success appears to be quite limited. A shortage of skilled OD consultants is also a problem—only a handful of qualified internal people exist. Another major problem is the conflict between OD and the bureaucratic system. When OD starts at the top, this is a minor problem. When it starts at the bottom, it is a major problem because system sanctions of OD-type changes may be difficult, if not impossible, to obtain.

Technostructural OD Approaches: Job Enrichment

Orthodox Job Enrichment. By far the largest air force behavioral-science intervention has been Herzberg's "Orthodox Job Enrichment" or OJE (1974) efforts in Air Force Logistics Command (AFLC). Although there is some disagreement whether job enrichment is an OD technique or not, I agree with Friedlander and Brown (1974) that it is a major technostructural approach to OD. Although a limited action research model is generally used for OJE, one element that is conspicuously absent is the participation of the workers whose jobs are being redesigned. This need not preclude the intervention from being called OD because many OD efforts may be focused on redesigning the or-

ganization or setting goals that involve lower-level employees who are not present. It is beyond the scope of this paper to provide a detailed report on OJE (see Herzberg & Rafalko, 1975). Generally, OJE has been successful. As of late 1978, 376 job-enrichment projects were underway with reports of major cost savings and improved job satisfaction (Herzberg & Zautra, 1976).

A Different Approach to Job Enrichment. Herzberg's projects have all been conducted in relatively stable industrial organizations with mostly civilian workers. In the combat support forces, a somewhat different job enrichment approach has been used (Umstot, 1979; Umstot & Rosenbach, in press). Pilot projects have been conducted with security police (Rosenbach, 1977), vehicle maintenance and operations, air freight, word-processing centers, aircraft maintenance, supply, personnel administration, and other types of activities. Results of these experiments, while not complete, are encouraging. The consulting approach being used in the combat support forces is much closer to an OD model. A joint diagnosis, based on survey results from a Job Diagnostic Survey (Hackman & Oldham, 1975), is used as the basis for action-planning workshops. The workshops are a joint management-worker effort to generate ideas, evaluate their worth, develop action steps, and pinpoint responsibilities. This approach to job enrichment is still evolving but the experiences to date are promising.

Conclusions Issues, and Implications

With over 1,000 people involved full-time in OD, the military probably has the largest OD program in existence. The size, scope, and possibly even the survival of military OD might be interpreted as an indirect measure of the success of the programs. Without considerable funding and manpower support, OD could not have existed for almost a decade. However, this review has made it clear that the perception of success is based largely on anecdotal reports, testimonials, and personal involvement of the decision makers. Since hard data and rigorous empirical research are lacking, the successes could be illusionary or an artifact of a compliant system. Thus, the following conclusions based on the "success" of military OD must be taken with caution and are certainly open to alternate explanations.

The conclusions address both theoretical and practical issues. From the theoretical perspective, two controversial topics are examined: the necessity of value congruence and the notion that traditional OD technology applies only to certain types of organizations (i.e., non-bureaucracies). From the practical perspective, issues and problems faced by large-scale OD efforts are addressed.

Value Congruence Issues

Although this review does not provide definitive answers to the apparent incongruence between OD values and military values, it does raise an interesting question. If value congruence is necessary, then why does OD seem to enjoy popularity among widely divergent types of military units, from technical labs (where OD might be expected to be more appropriate) to infantry battalions (where OD would seem to be inappropriate)? There is no evidence that those managers who have participated in OD efforts hold different values from those who have not. In fact, the widespread application of OD in the army and navy almost precludes this from happening. Of course, one might realistically argue that since empirical evidence of OD success is lacking, a more rigorous evaluation might show OD to be successful only with managers who hold values that are congruent with those of OD.

Perhaps the perspective of Argyris (1970) and Bowen (1977) are more cogent in explaining the military OD experience. Since most military OD processes concentrate on developing valid information, allowing participants free choice about how to proceed, and developing internal commitment to the decision made, it may be that the consulting process itself is more important to OD success than is value congruence.

Do Bureaucracies Require Different OD Technologies?

Schein and Greiner (1977) have argued for a contingency approach to OD because "the behavioral diseases emanating from bureaucratic structures are uniquely different from those of organic structures" (p. 52) and because current OD practices ("team building, encounter sessions, survey feedback, third-party consultation, interface labs, and confrontation meetings," p. 49) are more effective in organic situations. Their contingency view suggests "the differential utility of certain OD techniques depending upon the structure of the organization" (p. 59). They go on to suggest that a critical issue facing the OD field today is whether OD can be made relevant to bureaucratic structures. Some of the interventions they predict will be more appropriate for bureaucracies are team building (especially for top management), job rotation, assessment centers, job posting, collateral organizations, MBO, and job enrichment.

The military experience provides support for a contingency view, although it does not seem to provide much support for the assumption that the major contingency variable is the type of organizational structure, bureaucratic or organic. All of the interventions (except perhaps encounter sessions) that Schein and Greiner argue are more suitable to organic structures have been successfully employed in bureaucratic, military organizations. In addition, several of the interventions they recommend for bureaucracies have indeed been successfully employed in the military. What is striking about this review and my earlier comparison of military OD interventions (Umstot, 1979) is that a full repertoire of OD interventions seems to work in a wide variety of organizational structures. This tends to indicate OD is not contingent on structural variables. Perhaps other variables are more relevant, such as the leadership style of the client (task or relationship), the problems or felt needs that are salient within the particular system, and the skills and capabilities of the consultant. A more rigorous evaluation and comparison of military OD intervention strategies in light of various contingency variables might help resolve this cloudy issue.

Issues and Problems with Military OD

Although military OD has grown rapidly and currently enjoys substantial management support, there are a number of issues that affect consulting relationships and threaten the long-term viability of the program. These issues are discussed in the following paragraphs.

Needs for Empirical Data. Military OD exists in a political environment where resources and funds are scarce and managers have less control over resources. So far, there is little hard data to show that these 1,000-plus OD people are cost effective. Most of the OD expansion is based on anecdotal evidence or an intuitive feeling that the program is inherently worthwhile. It is very likely that Congressional reviews of the defense budget will sooner or later force strong emphasis on the cost savings, or demonstratable benefits of OD. Unless there is evidence, it is possible the programs could be cancelled. Thus, the challenge is to develop an empirical research program that will produce measurable results without adverse side effects (e.g., breach of confidentiality, feelings of being manipulated, distorted reporting, and false expectations).

Need for More Top Management Involvement. Except for a few instances, OD has been seen as something that is good for the rank and file, but not needed by the generals and admirals. Although OD does seem to work in relatively autonomous subunits of large organizations, the most powerful leverage and payoff potential are from OD at the top (Beckhard, 1969).

Consultant Selection and Training. Most military OD programs rely on internal consultants without academic or practical consulting credentials. Can effective OD consultants be trained in three or four months? Most practitioners would say no; however, the services seem to be fairly successful with this approach. Since many military OD interventions are more task focused than interpersonally focused, less training may be required. But what happens when serious interpersonal conflicts occur? Is the consultant trained well enough to handle these situations? Perhaps each service should have a small cadre of master consultants (both internal and external) that could be called on as specialists, much like a medical specialist, to handle difficult OD problems. (The army is exploring this concept.)

Managerial Turnover. Since the military, like many large civilian organizations, rotates its managers to different locations and jobs, there is always a certain amount of change and turmoil in the system. A crucial issue for OD viability may be developing a systematic way of dealing with the succession problem. If OD gets started in an organization and the climate and processes improve, what happens if a new manager comes in and scraps the program? Is the organization worse off than it would have been without OD? One might expect that perceptions of the difference between "what is" and "what should be" would be greater after a terminated OD program. A good example of this problem is the OD experience in the air force laboratories discussed earlier. Perhaps more attention to transition models and more education about the effect of changing OD programs would help alleviate this problem.

How to Institutionalize without Bureaucratizing? As in all large organizations there is a tendency for a function, such as OD, to become bureaucratized. Closed-mindedness and rigidity may develop; standardization is encouraged; productivity at the expense of quality is emphasized. "Square filling" seems to increase. For OD to succeed, it must meet the needs of the client. If OD is to be voluntary, then the client must own the program and the data. OD must not deteriorate into oneupmanship. It must be tailored to the needs of managers and employees. If OD does indeed need to meet the above criteria, then the decentralized, flexible approach of the army seems to offer the most potential for successfully institutionalizing OD.

Implications of Military OD

The applicability of OD technology may be much wider than previously supposed. A wide variety of OD technologies can succeed in authoritarian, bureaucratic organizations. By emphasizing organization improvement, client ownership, and action research, many military managers see the value of OD and are prepared to use it. However, this optimistic conclusion must be taken with some caution because empirical research to back up the claims of OD successes is weak. Without such evidence, it seems quite improbable that OD will survive in the long run.

Another implication of the military experience is that relatively quickly trained, internal OD consultants appear to be doing a credible job. Perhaps the stereotype that an OD consultant is a person with a PhD and several years' experience in a wide variety of organizations is fallacious. If so, a major stumbling block to OD diffusion may be removed—that of too few qualified consultants to make major changes in organizational systems.

In conclusion, the widespread application of OD in the military may be an indication that OD technology is quite robust. Perhaps it should not be all that surprising that OD works in a military environment. If the OD *process* is a valid model for organization improvement, then it should be generalizable to a wide variety of organizational settings.

References

Alderfer, C. P. Organization development. *Annual Review of Psychology*, 1977, *28*, 197–223.

Argyris, C. Some unintended consequences of rigorous research. *Psychological Bulletin*, 1968, *70*, 185–197.

Argyris, C. *Intervention theory and method*. Reading, Mass.: Addison-Wesley Publishing, 1970.

Beckhard, R. *Organization development: Strategies and models*. Reading, Mass.: Addison-Wesley Publishing, 1969.

Bowers, D. G., & Franklin, J. L. *Survey-guided development: Data-based organizational change*. Ann Arbor, Mich.: Institute for Social Research, 1975.

Bowen, D. Value dilemmas in organization development. *Journal of Applied Behavioral Science*, 1977, *13*, 543–556.

Cahn, M. C. Organization development in the United States Army: An interview with Lt. Col. Ramon A. Nadal. *Journal of Applied Behavioral Science*, 1978, *14*, 523–536.

Cohen, S. L., & Turney, J. P. Intervening at the bottom: Organizational development with enlisted personnel in an Army work setting. *Personnel Psychology*, 1978, *31*, 715–730.

Crawford, K. S. *Organization development in the navy: A strategy for addressing disciplinary problems* (Report No. NPRDC TR 7738). San Diego, Calif.: Navy Personnel Research and Development Center, July 1977.

Crawford, K. & Thomas, E. Organizational climate and disciplinary rates on navy ships. *Armed Forces and Society*, 1977, *3*, 165–182.

Crawford, K. S., & Thomas, E. D. *Rates of first-term enlistment*. Unpublished paper, San Diego: Navy Personnel Research and Development Center, 1978.

Curra, W. S., & Hallen, J. F. *Organization development pilot test for Army Personnel Center; Technical Report No. 4: Understanding the process of change* (Defense Documentation Center, Report No. AD 786670). Santa Monica, Calif.: System Development Corporation, August 10, 1974.

Drexler, J. A. *The human resource management survey: An item analysis* (Defense Documentation Center, Report No. AD 784458). Ann Arbor, Mich,.: Institute for Social Research, Technical Report, July 1974.

Drexler, J. A., & Bowers, D. G. *Navy retention rates and human resource management* (Defense Documentation Center, Report No. AD 761656). Ann Arbor, Much.: Institute for Social Research, 1974.

Ellermeier, J. D., & Curtis, E. W. *Readiness status of navy ships before and after the human resource management cycle*. Unpublished paper. San Diego, Calif.: U.S. Navy Personnel Research and Development Center, 1978.

Forbes, R. L. *A cause celebre: Organization development in the United States Navy*. Paper presented at the joint meeting of the Inter-University Seminar and the

American Psychological Association, Washington, D.C., September 1976.

French, W. L., & Bell, C. H., Jr. *Organization development: Behavioral science interventions for organization improvement* (2nd ed.). Englewood Cliffs, N.J.: Prentice-Hall, 1978.

Friedlander, F., & Brown, L. D. Organization development. In M. R. Rosenzweig & L. W. Porter (Eds.), *Annual Review of Psychology,* Vol. 25. Palo Alto, Calif., 1974.

Frohman, M. A.; Sashkin, J.; & Kavanagh, M. J. Action research as applied to organization development. *Organization and Administrative Sciences,* 1976, *7,* 129–142.

Giblin, E. J. Organization development: Public sector theory and practice. *Purpose Personnel Management,* March–April 1976, 108–119.

Golembiewski, R. T. Organization development in public agencies: Perspectives on theory and practice. In W. W. Burke & H. A. Hornstein (Eds.), *Social technology of organization development.* Fairfax, Va.: National Training Laboratories, 1972.

Gregory, R. A. *Organization development (OD) efforts in the United States Air Force.* Paper presented at the annual meeting of the American Psychological Association, San Francisco, September 1977.

Hackman, J. R., & Oldham, G. R. Development of the job diagnostic survey. *Journal of Applied Psychology,* 1975, *60,* 159–70.

Herzberg, F. The wise old turk, *Harvard Business Review,* 1974, *52*(5), 70–80.

Herzberg, F. I., & Rafalko, E. A. Efficiency in the military: Cutting costs with orthodox job enrichment. *Personnel,* 1975, *52*(5), 38–48.

Herzberg, F., & Zautra, A. Orthodox job enrichment: Measuring true quality in job satisfaction. *Personnel,* 1976, *53*(5), 54–68.

Kolb, D. A., & Frohman, A. L. An organization development approach to consulting. *Sloan Management Review,* Fall 1970, 51–65.

Lloyd, R. F, *Introducing model II survey feedback: A longitudinal investigation of the effect of traditional survey feedback and a proposed organizational performance measure.* Unpublished doctoral dissertation, Purdue University, 1977.

Margulies, N., & Raia, A. P. *Conceptual foundations of organizational development.* New York: McGraw-Hill, 1978.

McNichols, C. W., & Manley, T. R. Organizational development at a major government research laboratory. *Proceedings of the American Society of Public Administrators,* Washington, D.C., April 1976.

Mumford, S. J. *Human resource management and operational readiness as measured by refresher training on navy ships.* (Defense Documentation Center Report No. AD A0223372). San Diego: Navy Personnel Research and Development Center, 1976.

Nadal, R. A.; Duey, W. E.; Ray, R.; & Schaum, F. W. *Organizational effectiveness in the U.S. Army* (Defense Documentation Center Report No. AD A043500). Washington, D.C.: Department of the Army, DACSDMOE, April 1977.

Patten, T. H., & Dorey, L. E. Long-range results of a team-building OD effort. *Public Personnel Management,* January–February 1977, 31–50.

Rosenbach, W. E. *An evaluation of participative work redesign: A longitudinal field experiment.* Unpublished doctoral dissertation, University of Colorado, 1977.

Schein, V. E., & Greiner, L. E. Can organization development be fine-tuned to bureaucracies? *Organizational Dynamics,* 1977, *5*(3), 48–61.

Taylor, J. C., & Bowers, D. G. *Survey of organizations: A machine-scored standardized questionnaire instrument.* Ann Arbor, Mich.: Institute for Social Research, 1972.

Turney, J. R., & Cohen, S. L. Organizational implications for practicing OD in the army. *Personnel Psychology,* 1978, *31,* 731–738.

Umstot, D. D. Organization development intervention strategies in the U.S. military. *Group and Organizatinal Studies,* 1979, *4,* 135–142.

Umstot, D. D., & Rosenbach, W. E. From theory to action: Implementing job enrichment in the air force. *Air University Review,* in press.

Van Gundy, A. B. *Integration of technostructural and human processual approaches in a field-based organization development program.* Unpublished paper, University of Oklahoma, 1976.

Zawacki, R. A. Personal communication, March 1978.

Reading 57

SURVEY FEEDBACK AS AN ORGANIZATION DEVELOPMENT STRATEGY IN A PUBLIC SCHOOL DISTRICT

William E. Rosenbach, Robert A. Gregory, and Robert L. Taylor

Derr (1976) suggests that Organization Development (OD) will not work in public school systems because public schools are reactive institutions as opposed to proactive and because they lack an environmental force supportive of change. Fullan and Miles (1978), however, report that OD in schools is as old as OD itself. They analyze and report on 76 sustained OD programs in public schools ("sustained" being defined as ". . . self-study and improvement over a period of at least 18 months, focusing on change in organizational procedures, norms, or structures using behavioral science concepts" (p. 150.)) Fullan and Miles report data acquired from a survey of 357 OD students who were working at least part-time in educational settings.

Derr's report that "OD won't work in schools" makes a quite strong point that schools are subject to close public scrutiny and that administrators react to community crises by retrenching and defending rather than by the more creative, proactive problem solving techniques which might be said to characterize OD. Though many such differences might be found when comparing schools to other organizations, perhaps a more constructive approach than saying "OD won't work in schools" would be to examine the goals of particular OD efforts and to describe the conditions under which a particular OD technique might be successfully employed to attain those goals.

While Fullan and Miles (1978) report that OD techniques are fairly widespread in school systems,

they also note that proportionately fewer schools than other types of organizations seem to be using OD; this is the case in spite of the fact that schools are subject to the same ills as other organizations for which OD offers potential benefits. They go on to describe the special properties of school systems (goal diffuseness, sub-optimal technical capability, poor coordination, problems with boundary management, non-competitive nature, and constrained, decentralized systems) and suggest that these characteristics may directly influence a school system's choice to seek or avoid OD. The median length of the OD programs in school systems reported by Fullan and Miles was three years; thus it seems that OD has been seen as effective in many of the school systems where it has been used.

Miles (1976) also disagrees with Derr's thesis that OD will not work in school systems, referring to several conditions that may explain why the use of OD is not more prevalent. OD may well be less prevalent because not enough administrators are exposed to OD interventions, financial and organizational incentives are not vigorous enough, the absence of a critical mass of practitioner advocates, and coherent documentation and evaluation data being unavailable.

Overall, it seems that OD is seen as effective in public school systems, and the report of Fullan and Miles (1978) is convincing enough that the use of OD is widespread. A more recent, comprehensive study by Fullan, Miles, and Taylor (1980) leaves little doubt that OD can be of great value in improving public schools, given proper matching of goals, strategies and evaluation schemes. There is a need to obtain more data on what type of OD

Source: William E. Rosenbach, Robert A. Gregory, and Robert L. Taylor, reprinted from *Education,* Summer 1983, pp. 316–25.

interventions are most effective and under what circumstances. The present study is an example of the uses to which one OD intervention, survey feedback, can be employed in a typical public school system.

Survey feedback has been variously defined and described. Bowers and Franklin (1972) discuss the theoretical rationale for the use of survey feedback as an OD tool. Huse (1980) describes survey feedback as gathering and analyzing data from a work group or larger unit by questionnaires, interviews, and/or observations and then feeding the data back to the group for their use in diagnosis, action planning, and problem solving. Not all cases exactly fit this description, but it describes the model used by the present researchers. Multiple data sources are generally used, though the model prescribed by a particular survey will often dictate the nature and form of the data feedback.

In a popular OD text, Huse (1980) devotes about seven pages to OD in school systems, yet barely touches survey feedback as a useful OD technique. He reports that interventions typically consist of training sessions and exercises related to communications, leadership, and problem analysis; groups included are teachers, administrators, and other school staff members. "Collegial problem solving" is the recurrent theme in most OD programs in schools. Survey feedback is mentioned only once in this section and, ironically, one of the two references to survey feedback reports on failures of OD (Mohrman, Mohrman, Cooke, and Duncan, 1977). Where Huse discusses survey feedback and development in another section of his text, he mentions schools as one type of public sector institution in which survey feedback has been used frequently. However, he emphasizes the previously mentioned survey feedback failure as an example of how the technique was detrimental in the school situation. From the coverage by Huse, one is left with the feeling that while survey feedback may be a useful and very popular technique, perhaps something unique about school systems causes it to fail as an intervention.

Other research indicates that survey feedback is a popular OD technique in schools. In their extensive study, Fullan and Miles (1978) report that data feedback was among the most popular techniques used by educational institutions. After undoubtedly the most extensive review of research on OD in schools to date, Fullan, Miles, and Taylor (1980) cite several studies which generally conclude that survey feedback in schools can have a significant impact on numerous indices of organizational health. Their evidence suggests that OD is a useful strategy for school improvement and that survey feedback is one of the more successfull, proven OD strategies. These authors lament the poor quality of much of the OD research that has been accomplished in school systems, and call for more intelligent and illuminating research to be carried out. First in their list of ". . . research topics which seem potentially most valuable" is the need for "case studies of OD programs, and their coping strategies over time." The current study is one step toward the fulfillment of that need.

The Study

The present study was initiated by the superintendent of a public school district. His overall interest was in developing more systematic ways of getting information upon which to base decisions. He saw the job of managing the school system as similar to managing a business and felt that he could make better decisions in a variety of areas if they were based upon valid data rather than on intuition alone. After consultation with the authors, the superintendent specifically requested we help him better understand the dynamic interactions and impacts of climate, supervision and change in the organizational setting of the school district.

The Setting

The school district is located adjacent to a medium-sized city in the Rocky Mountain area. There are six elementary schools, a junior high school and a high school serving some 5,200 students.

Generally, the administrators were confident that the school district was a great place to work. Students scored higher than national norms on achievement tests, and the high school graduates won a proportionally larger share of scholarships and awards than most of the adjacent districts. Growth and a transient community provided nearly ten applicants for every job opening, and salaries were in line with the other districts. There were 225 teachers and 16 administrators. The school board took an intense interest in the administration of the district and details of everyday school management. This put greater pressure on the superintendent to understand that elusive concept, effectiveness. With an expanded organization and increased staff, the superintendent found that he no longer really knew all of his people. The faculty was too big; what he had was a large, unwieldy bureaucratic organization that he needed to understand.

The goals of the superintendent included:

1. Obtaining systematic, reliable data regarding the school system employees and their perceptions of the ''health'' of the system (climate, leadership, etc.). From this data more sound decisions could be made and the system managed more efficiently.

2. Giving his staff administrators and principals information on the school system and on particular areas of interest in order that they be able to improve their decision making.

3. Increasing the communication, both vertical and horizontal, within the school district.

4. Focusing attention of the school district employees, particularly those in supervisory positions, on the variables of leadership, climate, work group relations, performance feedback, and other such variables that could lead to more effective operation of the district and improved employee attitudes and behavior.

A survey feedback approach was selected as the most appropriate and effective strategy to use to accomplish these goals. If other OD techniques were called for (team building, for example), the data from the survey would be invaluable as a starting place for further OD efforts.

Description of the Survey Instrument

An organizational climate survey developed by Umstot and Rosenbach (1978) was adapted for the school district setting. Five categories of information were solicited:

Demographics. Sex, age, marital status, education, certification, school assignment, experience, tenure, extra duties, intentions to remain, and attitude towards year-around school were collected.

Factors Influenced Most by District Administrators. These factors reflected policies and management style of the central administration. The following variables were measured: Commitment to district, communication climate and structural climate.

Factors Influenced Most by Individual School Administrators. Here, we focused on the basic organizational unit, the school. Policy and styles are set by the principal. The variables measured were: communication climate, structural climate, psychological climate, feedback from supervisors, group norms, social satisfaction, satisfaction with supervision, and commitment to the school.

Factors Influenced by the Job Itself. These job dimensions were developed by Hackman and Oldham (1980) and measure the potential of the work itself to motivate the people performing the job. The specific variables measured were: Skill variety, task identity, task significance, autonomy and feedback from the job itself. The scores for these five variables (which may range from 1 to 7) can be combined into a single index, the motivating potential score (MPS) which reflects the overall potential of a job to foster internal work motivation on the part of job incumbents. This is expressed mathematically as:

$$\text{MPS} = \frac{\text{Skill Variety} + \text{Task Identity} + \text{Task Significance}}{3} \times \text{Autonomy} \times \text{Feedback}$$

The resultant MPS score may vary from a low of 1 to a high of 343. For all jobs, the national average is 128. The national average for professionals—physicians, lawyers, engineers, accountants, teachers, etc.,—is 154 (Hackman and Oldham, 1980). The higher the MPS, the more potential the job itself has for providing motivation to the individuals performing the job.

Individual and organizational outcomes. These effectiveness measures are influenced by district and school administrators as well as the work itself; they were general job satisfaction and perceived group productivity.

Administration of Survey

Initially, the questionnaire was administered to district administrators and building principals. We were introduced to the group by the superintendent; we then explained the intent of the survey, what kinds of data it would produce, timing, how we would assure participant anonymity and promised to feedback the results. Then, the survey was administered in each of the buildings. Faculty, secretarial and custodial staff, librarians, cooks and bus drivers were all invited to participate. Principals dedicated normal meeting times for the effort; all of the data were collected in less than a week. A total of 290 responses were received. Most of those not participating were part-time personnel—secretaries, librarians, cooks and bus drivers. The response rate for administrators was 100 percent; for faculty it was 89 percent.

After the data were analyzed and a summary briefing prepared for the district and for each school, we were prepared to begin the feedback process. The first presentation was to the central office administrators and principals. Summary of district findings was followed by a school-by-school analysis. This session lasted for nearly two hours since there were many questions and requests for interpretation. Then, a district summary was given to a closed session of the school board. One of us then went to each of the schools to provide feedback to participants on the results from their school, providing comparisons with district data and, where possible, national norms. Some of the school sessions were voluntary; others had required attendance. In every case, there was a lot of discussion and interest.

The final step in this series of sessions was a meeting with the superintendent to discuss action recommendations. In a few cases, specific management initiatives were suggested, and the superintendent wanted to try them out. For example, certain teachers thrive with a great deal of autonomy while others like a lot of structure. Aligning teacher needs with supervising style should improve productivity and satisfaction. With three new schools opening, staff assignments could be made using data from the survey. Thus, not only was this a study of attitudes and behaviors, but decisions were made based on the information received. Most findings were already "felt" by the administrators although there were also a few surprises.

Results and Discussion

Some of the results are presented here, along with examples of the type of feedback presented to various groups of members of the school district. Survey data were analyzed and descriptive statistics reported for each of the relevant variables.

District Administration. Descriptive statistics for factors most influenced by district administration are presented in Table 1. These statistics are for those factors of primary interest to the superintendent and his staff since they deal with the school system as a whole.

The mean score for commitment to the district was about what other groups of public sector employees in similar situations in the local area had scored. The high mean for communications climate was important and supported a conscious emphasis the superintendent had placed on communications as his theme for the year. The mean score for structural climate was higher than normally found in public sector organizations, indicating that respondents viewed district rules and regulations as not being a hinderance to accomplishing their jobs. The

TABLE 1   Descriptive Statistics for Factors
              Influenced by District Administrators

Factor	M	SD
Commitment to District	4.9	1.1
Communications Climate	5.7	1.3
Structural Climate	4.1	1.1

Note: Scores can range as low as 1 to as high as 7.

greatest value of these results will be in subsequent studies where variations from their scores can be studied to determine if changes occur due to the feedback process and changes implemented as a result of it.

School Administration. A post hoc analysis of variance (ANOVA) was performed to determine significant differences between schools, particularly for those variables that are most affected by school administrators. As expected a great deal of variance was found between schools on these variables since the factors studied are those influenced directly by the principal and his or her staff. Results are presented in Table 2. The six elementary schools and two secondary schools are compared with the district. Grade School E was significantly lower on five of the eight variables studied. Two grade schools, C and F, were significantly higher than the other schools on a number of factors

Grade School E results were not surprising. Problems had plagued the school for several years, and a new principal had just been appointed. Having a strong personality, the new principal had increased discipline for the faculty and instituted several work changes, including arbitrary revised work standards. Teachers, for example, were required to sign in and out of the school each day, and weekly administrative meetings were held 45 minutes before classes started. Requests for late arrivals or early departures were routinely disapproved. Thus, the low means for structural climate, psychological climate, feedback from supervisor, satisfaction with supervisor and commitment to the school reflect a continuing conflict between faculty

and principal. When we reported these results to school personnel, they told us that they had anticipated the low scores. Further, they admitted that a general dissatisfaction with the principal's autocratic leadership style was the reason for the scores.

As a contrast, Grade School F was the smallest of the six elementary schools in the district. Faculty and staff described themselves as a family. There was great respect for the principal and her concern for students and faculty. The highest scores for feedback from supervisor, group norms, social satisfaction and satisfaction with supervision are easily attributed to the principal's leadership. For some time Grade School C has been regarded as the "best" elementary school in the district—in terms of academic excellence and strong leadership. Results of feedback from supervisor, satisfaction with supervision and commitment to the school support the general feeling.

In each of the school feedback sessions, we discussed differences from district means and asked those participating in the survey feedback sessions to provide a rationale for those differences. The catharsis of talking through strengths and shortcomings led, in each case, to school groups conducting several sessions on the survey results and coming up with recommendations for improvement. The survey feedback was simply a starting point for meaningful dialogue and, most importantly, for planned change.

Factors Influenced by the Job Itself. Table 3 presents the descriptive statistics and ANOVA for the five job characteristics that comprise the MPS. Once again, we see statistically significant differences between the schools.

Autonomy and feedback from the job itself are powerful job characteristics in the MPS equation. However, autonomy is probably more important in this study because of the direct influence from the principal—he or she sets the tone in allowing faculty the discretion to make their own decisions concerning the job and how it is accomplished.

Note that Grade Schools C and F have significantly higher means on three of the job character-

TABLE 2 Descriptive Statistics and ANOVA for Factors Influenced by School Administrators

Factor	District		A		B		C		D		E		F		Junior High		High School		F	SIG
	M	SD	M	SD	M	SD	M	SD	M	SD	M	SD	M	SD	M	SD	M	SD		
Communications Climate	5.7	1.3	5.7	1.6	6.3	.9	5.9	1.3	6.0	.7	4.5	1.6	6.4*	.8	5.7	1.1	5.5	1.3	4.9	.00
Structural Climate	4.1	1.1	4.4	1.1	4.5	1.1	4.5	1.0	4.5	.7	3.8	1.1	4.4	1.0	4.2	1.0	4.0	1.3	1.8	.08
Psychological Climate	4.9	1.2	4.7	1.6	5.1	1.0	5.3	1.1	5.3	1.0	3.8*	1.4	5.7*	.8	5.3	.9	4.5	1.2	8.0	.00
Feedback from Supervisor	4.6	1.6	5.1	1.7	4.7	1.5	5.5*	1.4	4.3	1.2	3.9*	1.6	6.0*	.8	4.9	1.4	4.1	1.6	5.7	.00
Group Norms	5.6	1.0	5.9	.9	5.2	1.1	5.9	.9	5.7	.9	5.1	1.2	6.2*	.6	5.7	.8	5.6	1.1	2.5	.01
Social Satisfaction	5.7	1.0	5.8	1.0	5.9	.9	6.0	.8	6.0	.6	5.3	1.2	6.3*	.6	5.6	1.1	5.6	1.0	2.0	.07
Satisfaction with Supervision	5.5	1.4	5.2	2.0	5.9	.8	6.1	.9	6.0	.7	4.4*	1.9	6.3*	.8	5.6	1.1	5.1	1.6	5.5	.00
Commitment to School	5.2	1.1	5.3	1.0	5.1	1.0	5.9	1.1*	5.1	1.1	4.6	1.2*	5.5	.8	5.4	1.2	5.1	1.1	2.8	.00

Note: Scores can range as low as 1 to as high as 7.
*Statistically significant higher or lower mean score.

TABLE 3 Descriptive Statistics and ANOVA for Job Characteristics and Motivating Potential Scores

Job Characteristics	District		A		B		Grade School C		D		E		F		Junior High		High School		F	SIG
	M	SD	M	SD	M	SD	M	SD	M	SD	M	SD	M	SD	M	SD	M	SD		
Skill Variety	5.5	1.3	5.5	1.4	5.4	1.7	6.1*	1.1	5.5	1.3	5.7	1.0	6.2*	.9	5.5	1.0	5.3	1.3	1.5	.17
Task Identity	5.0	1.4	4.8	1.4	5.0	1.3	5.2	1.6	5.3	.9	4.1*	1.5	5.6*	1.1	5.0	1.4	5.1	1.4	2.1	.04
Task Significance	5.9	1.1	6.1	.9	6.0	1.3	6.6*	.7	5.5	1.3	5.7	1.0	6.7*	.4	5.8	1.0	5.7	1.1	3.6	.00
Autonomy	6.0	1.0	5.8	1.2	6.3	.7	6.1	1.0	5.8	.8	5.1*	1.6	5.9	1.1	6.1	.9	6.0	1.0	3.0	.00
Feedback from Job	5.4	1.2	5.4	1.3	5.4	1.3	6.1*	.8	5.5	1.0	5.3	1.3	5.9	.8	5.3	1.1	5.3	1.2	2.0	.05
MPS	184.6	69.7	178.1	75.0	195.1	74.6	227.1*	72.5	179.1	61.0	150.3	70.6	222.3*	67.6	178.3	60.4	180.1	70.2	2.9	.00

Note: With the exception of the MPS, scores can range as low as 1 to as high as 7. The MPS can range as low as 1 to as high as 343.
*Statistically significant higher or lower mean score.

istics. In other words, the teachers are intrinsically motivated by their jobs, and the MPS scores of the two groups are among the higher values ever computed.

On the other hand, Grade School E scored significantly lower on task identity and autonomy. The low MPS suggests that the teachers at that school are less motivated by their job than teachers at other schools who identify more with meaningful work and have more discretion in doing their work. This school was also significantly less satisfied with their school administration; whether one causes the other is not known.

The national average MPS for professions is 154. District personnel scored almost 30 points higher. In perspective, even the lowest mean scores (Grade School E) was near the national average. These results indicate that, as far as the job itself is concerned, the jobs in the district are intrinsically motivating and satisfying to the people performing them.

Individual and Organizational Outcomes

With the exception of Grade School E, the level of job satisfaction by district respondents is high. Perceived quality of performance—respondent feelings that they are performing their job well is unusually high for all schools in the district. Perceived overall productivity, the perception that, overall, the respondents are accomplishing a lot was highest in Grade School F—the school that scored significantly higher in previous measures. The complete results are shown in Table 4.

Other Findings

Generally, there were no significant differences with respect to the demographic variables. We did find a statistical difference in the MPS for females and males. Further examination showed that the difference was due not to sex but to job. We found the higher MPS was for K-6 teachers; those teachers tended to be female. This K-6 finding was not surprising. Elementary teachers are likely to be responsible for the "start-to-finish" education of their charges. Secondary teachers have a frag-

mented effort, teaching one subject to a variety of different students. With less variety, autonomy and feedback from the job itself, the MPS for secondary teachers would be expected to be less than that for elementary teachers.

Finally, we discovered significant differences between teachers who planned to remain in the district only until something better came along and those who planned to stay indefinitely. Those planning to leave tended to score lower on all items except the job characteristics. What we don't know is whether the climate caused them to want to leave or whether their frustrations led to lower climate scores.

Implications

Information *is* available to school administrators on factors like organizational climate, supervision and perceptions about the job and its outcomes. The same techniques employed by other managers can be useful to public school administrators and their public overseers. However, careful collection and rational interpretation through a process like survey feedback are necessary. Objective and subjective data must be evaluated and compared as meaningful inputs to the decision-making process.

The project described was not a research project. It was designed to help administrators make decisions. Some of the results and actions taken included such things as reassignment of teachers, appointment of a new principal, placement of principals to newly built schools, different forms of information exchanges, greater emphasis by principals on frequent and accurate feedback, and more encouragement and rewarding of autonomy and feedback.

Conclusion

OD can work in schools. It is clear from this study, that using the technique most suited to the goals of a project can lead to results worthy of the effort. Fullan and Miles (1978) conclude with ". . . it seems that OD programs [in schools] are more successful if they are of moderate size, focused on educational issues, and characterized by task-ori-

TABLE 4 Descriptive Statistics and ANOVA for Individual and Organization Outcomes

Outcome Measures	District		Grade School													Junior High		High School		F	SIG
			A		B		C		D		E		F									
	M	SD	M	SD	M	SD	M	SD	M	SD	M	SD	M	SD			M	SD	M	SD	F	SIG
Job Satisfaction	5.9	1.1	5.8	1.3	6.2	.8	6.4	.6	6.3	.6	5.1	1.4	6.2	1.0			5.9	1.0	5.8	1.2	3.1	.00
Perceived Quality of Performance	6.0	1.2	6.4	1.1	5.7	1.0	6.4	.9	6.2	.9	5.9	1.1	6.9	.5			6.0	1.2	5.9	1.2	3.8	.00
Perceived Overall Productivity	5.9	1.1	6.2	.8	5.6	1.0	6.3	.9	5.9	.9	5.7	1.1	6.6*	.5			5.9	1.1	5.6	1.1	3.5	.00

Note: Scores can range as low as 1 to as high as 7.
*Statistically significant higher or lower mean score.

ented, structural, system changing approach. . . .''
Much of the research pointing up failure in schools
(as in other settings where OD is tried) points toward vague external causes such as the nature of
school systems; it might be more appropriate to
examine internal causes such as definition of the
problem, specificity of goals, selection of the most
appropriate OD technique, follow through—and
overriding all of these is the competency of the
consultant.

Perhaps one of the major results of this effort
was the use of data collected to make strategic
decisions. It is clear, from these results, that the
goals of the effort were met. Decisions in the public
sector are always difficult; yet school administrators cannot afford to work on intuition alone. We've
shown that a carefully constructed study of attitudes can provide useful information relative to the
organizational climate, leadership and job satisfaction in a public school setting.

References

Bowes, D. OD Techniques and Their Results in 23 Organizations: The Michigan ICL Study. *Journal of Applied Behavioral Science,* 1973, 9 (1,) 21–43.

———, and Franklin, J. Survey-Guided Development:
Using Human Resources Measurement in Organiza-

tional Child. *Journal of Contemporary Business,* 1972,
1, 43–55.

Derr, C. B. OD Won't Work in Schools. *Education and
Urban Society,* 1976, 8 (2), 227–241.

Fullan, M., and Miles, M. OD in Schools: The State of
the Art. From Burke, W. W. (Ed.) *Current Theory
and Practice in Organizational Development.* La Jolla,
California: University Associates, Inc., 1978

———, Miles, M. B., and Taylor, G. Organization Development in Schools: The State of the Art, *Review
of Educational Research,* 1980, 50 (1), 121–183.

Hackman, J. R., and Oldham, G. R. *Work Redesign.*
Addison-Wesley: Reading, Massachusetts, 1980.

Huse, E. F. *Organizational Development and Change
(Second Ed.).* St. Paul, Minnesota: West Publishing
Co., 1980.

Miles, M. B. Diffusing OD in Schools: A Critique.
Education and Urban Society, 1976, 8 (2), 242–254.

Mohrman, S. A., Mohrman, M. A., Cooke, R. A, and
Duncan, R. B. A Survey Feedback and Problem-
Solving Intervention in School District. *Failures in
Organizational Development and Change* P. H. Mirvis
and D. N. Berg (Eds.). New York: Wiley-Intersci-
ence, 1977.

Umstot, D. D., and Rosenbach, W. E. *Job Attitude
Survey.* United States Air Force Academy, Colorado
Springs, Colorado, 1978.

Reading 58

INCREASING PRODUCTIVITY AND MORALE IN A MUNICIPALITY: EFFECTS OF ORGANIZATION DEVELOPMENT

Christian F. Paul and Albert C. Gross*

This paper reports the outcome of a year-long organization development (OD) project conducted in the City of San Diego, California.[1] During fiscal year 1978 (FY 78), the OD and Training Section of the City's General Services Department conducted and evaluated an intervention in the Communications and Electrical (C&E) Division. Consistent with their values, the management of C&E and the OD consultants who conducted the project established the following goals: *to increase productivity, to improve morale, and to maintain or improve customer satisfaction.* While such projects are not particularly rare, adequate evaluation of them is quite uncommon.

Porras and Berg (1978) reviewed the OD evaluation research for the period 1959 to 1975. While Porras and Berg disconfirmed the notion that OD projects have not been scientifically evaluated, their article nevertheless suggests how difficult it is to find rigorous quantitative evaluations of OD proj-

ects. By exhaustively searching journals, bibliographies, and abstracts, Porras and Berg found 160 articles that reported evaluation of OD interventions. Approximately 130 of those articles (Porras, personal communication, May 14, 1979) met two criteria: *(a) that the intervention be concerned with people and processes rather than with technology and organization structure, and (b) that the projects involve real-life organizations.* Only 35 of the 130 articles (Porras, personal communication, May 14, 1979) met two additional criteria: *(c) that the evaluation measure at least organizational (as opposed to solely project or output) variables, and (d) that the research use quantitative evaluation techniques.* Only 27 of the 35 studies used methods that Campbell and Stanley (1963) classified as quasi-experimental in nature, rather than pre-experimental. That is, of the 160 articles initially identified by Porras and Berg, only 27 (16.9%) employed a design adequate for investigating the effects of the intervention with some degree of scientific precision.

Apparently, effective evaluation of OD projects is rare. Even rarer still, however, is rigorous evaluation of public sector OD interventions, although many municipalities have conducted OD projects. Of the 35 articles that met all four criteria of Porras and Berg, none reported an intervention in a municipal government setting. There were eight projects in public organizations (six were school districts or groups of administrators and teachers; one was a hospital; one was a group of religious communities), and the remaining 27 articles evaluated interventions in such private sector organizations as businesses, sales groups, and restaurants.

[1]We do not wish to add to the already large number of definitions of OD (see Friedlander & Brown, 1974; French & Bell, 1973; Porras & Berg, 1978), but for the benefit of the reader unfamiliar with OD, we will venture what we see as the common element in such definitions. OD intervention is an intentional effort to improve some dimension of an organization by using applied behavioral science techniques. Often, as in the present case, the "action research" model (see Method section) is followed in the OD project.

Although Porras and Berg demonstrated that OD projects can be scientifically evaluated, the myth persists, especially among OD practitioners themselves, that the efficacy of the process has not been (and perhaps cannot be) adequately demonstrated. Katzell and Yankelovich (1975) reported, on the basis of surveys, that managers and labor leaders generally believe that job satisfaction and work performance are positively correlated; hence the myth must not be the product of "hard boiled" resistance of line personnel to humanistic approaches to organization improvement. A statement typical of the strange self-doubt of OD practitioners was made by Farkash (1979) in a paper investigating the beliefs of OD consultants:

> Research has yet to prove that there is a positive relationship between OD activities and objective organizational outcomes like: productivity, profits and decreased turnover and absenteeism. (Farkash, 1979, n. p.)

Of course, research results never prove causal relationships; rather, they provide evidence concerning one or more hypotheses (Crano & Brewer, 1973). We believe that the results of the San Diego OD project reported here support the hypothesis that both productivity and morale can be improved simultaneously by OD intervention. We attempted to avoid the pitfalls for which similar research efforts have been justly criticized (Porras & Berg, 1978). We employed a quasi-experimental design; took care to obtain high-quality comparison groups; made frequent measurements; used eclectic data-collection methods; and sought appropriate statistical methods for analyzing the data. The evaluation of this project was decided in advance of the intervention. Whereas many similar projects employ *post hoc* evaluation procedures, in the present study all dependent measures were chosen before the project had commenced.

Method

Overview

We applied the OD treatment to the experimental group and gathered data from that group and from a variety of other (comparison) groups. Not all forms of data were available from all the comparison groups, so the design of the present study is in reality several designs, each one applicable to a few dependent measures. Therefore, the study may be most easily understood by considering in turn the nature of the treatment, the character of the comparison groups, and the measures taken.

Experimental Group

The experimental group was the Communications and Electrical Division of the City of San Diego. The C&E Division is primarily a service organization that maintains several electronic systems that directly or indirectly benefit the public. Briefly, the C&E Division is responsible for the following:

1. Maintenance of all city radio systems and communication equipment used by the Police, Fire, Lifeguard, General Services, Transportation, and Utilities departments. This equipment includes mobile and fixed radios, pocket pagers, intercoms, speaker systems, and so on.

2. Maintenance of a radio communications center for all radio-equipped vehicles except Police, Fire, and Lifeguard vehicles. The center operated 24 hours a day during the OD intervention.

3. Maintenance and operation of all traffic-signal equipment and systems in the city. This includes handling customer service calls, relamping, repair, routine maintenance, and so on. There are approximately 12,500 lights in service.

4. Maintenance of all outside lighting of city-owned grounds—playgrounds, recreation centers, and the like—and all city street lights.

5. Maintenance and coin collection of all parking meters (approximately 5,200).

This division ordinarily employs about 90 people. Its budget for FY 77 totaled $3.95 million, 43% of which was spent on power for exterior lighting and traffic signals.

OD Treatment

The OD treatment given to the C&E Division consisted of a rigorous application of the action research model (Chein, Cook & Harding, 1948).

Briefly, the action research model progresses through stages of gathering data, feeding information back to the organization's personnel, planning and implementing change, and evaluating the results of the entire intervention with a view toward repetition of the process in order to deal with new and unresolved issues. The OD intervention team[2] and the C&E Division management used the findings of the data gathering to jointly plan a series of specific project activities. The activities included interviewing, team-building workshops, counseling, process consultancy, and classroom training in management skills; all activities occurred during FY 78.

Interviews. Members of the intervention team individually interviewed each employee of the C&E Division, including the superintendent, to discover employee perceptions of the organization's climate. Both open-ended questions (e.g., "What makes cooperation between work groups difficult?") and Likert-scale questions (e.g., "On a scale of 1 to 5, how satisfied are you with your job?") were included. These one-on-one interviews required approximately 30 to 45 minutes each. While the interviews were conducted informally and in a style intended to establish rapport between the interviewer and the employee, an interview question guide was used to impose a measure of standardization. In order to encourage candor, employees were assured that their individual reponses would be treated confidentially. No tape recorders were used, but the interviewers noted answers and other relevant information on a data-collection form. Subjective and objective data from the interviews were used in planning later project activities.

Team-Building Workshops. The top management group of the C&E Division participated in a three-day, team-building workshop. This group consisted of the Division Superintendent and his immediate subordinates. Diagnostic data obtained from the interviews, employee attitude surveys, and the organization's management information system guided the design of the workshop. At the workshop, the participants:

a. received training in communication and management skills;
b. were briefed on the overall results of the earlier data gathering, employee attitude surveys, and interviews;
c. went through a role-clarification exercise in which each person had an opportunity to enumerate the duties of his or her position and to verify that role perception with the Division Superintendent; and
d. engaged in formal exercises designed to identify specific organizational problems and to plan solutions for them.

In this initial workshop, the Division Superintendent served as the focus for the role clarification and problem identification. In subsequent, two-day workshops, each of the Superintendent's direct subordinates also served as the leader/focal point for his/her immediate subordinates. Those subordinates in turn served as hosts in workshops attended by their work groups. Substantially the same workshop was repeated for each immediately subordinate work group until each employee had participated in a workshop with his or her supervisor. Likert (1961, 1967) has called this process "linking down the organization."

The most important result of the team-building workshops was the identification of organization problems and the formulation of plans to solve them. During the remainder of the project, managers, supervisors, and other employees of the division were assigned individual and group responsibility for solving specific problems.

Counseling. Throughout the intervention, the OD team provided C&E's top managers with individual advice and counseling on how to implement the OD program and solve problems identified in the workshops. A major purpose of the counseling was to provide objective insight on the division's functioning—an outsider can often provide

---

[2]The intervention team included Albert C. Gross, Haywood H. Martin, and C. Greg Wright, assisted by consultant Peter Gregg.

a fresh perspective on problems. Another major purpose of the counseling was to allow the OD specialists to expand available alternatives by describing problem solutions that had worked in other settings. The counseling was designed to facilitate the organization's solution of its own problems by providing support without usurping any of the power of the division's managers.

Process Consultancy. OD specialists attended numerous meetings of division personnel in order to act as process consultants. The role of OD process consultants is to provide meeting participants with insights and feedback concerning decision making, problem solving, and communication within the group. The consultants are supposed to focus on group processes, making only minor contributions to the content of a conference. Process consultants are not required to be devoid of personal opinions, but their role in meetings is to subordinate expression of their own attitudes to the task of facilitating the expression of ideas and attitudes by the meeting's other participants. Their role is to make the conference more effective.

Management-Skills Training. C&E's managers identified a need to train division supervisors on several management skills and City of San Diego administrative procedures. The intervention team agreed to present a series of two-hour training events on topics which the supervisors had identified. Specifically, the division received training on the City Manager's expectations of supervisors, methods for conducting effective meetings, stress reduction, effective discipline, leadership style, employee motivation, performance evaluation, solving organizational problems, effective time management, and the city's Memorandum of Understanding with employee labor unions.

The assistance requested was traditional skill training. However, the manner in which the needs had been assessed and the manner in which the skill building had been incorporated into the project make this traditional training an integral part of the OD treatment. Many of the skills taught in the training sessions were related to resolving specific

issues from the workshops. The desired result of the training was more than cognitive knowledge; the meetings were designed to lead to organizational improvement. To keep the training from becoming ''just a supervisory skills course,'' we varied the time of the meetings, set an informal participative tone, and encouraged supervisors to use the meetings to solve real-life organizational problems.

Comparison Groups[3]

Pains were taken to secure data from comparison groups wherever possible. Since random assignment of groups was impossible, it was important to find the most similar comparison groups available. While each group had some attributes to recommend it as a good comparison group, it was unfortunately not possible to obtain data on all measures from all groups. For example, productivity data from the Long Beach comparison group was simply not available, and job satisfaction data could not be collected from CALTRANS employees.

Buildings Division. We chose the Buildings Division of the City of San Diego as a comparison group because its employees work at crafts and trades similar to those practiced by C&E personnel and because the division works under administrative regulations and political conditions virtually identical to those in the C&E Division. The Buildings Division thus was the best available comparison group within the City of San Diego. This group received both administrations of the three surveys discussed below.

Long Beach Communications and Electrical Workers. The personnel in the City of Long Beach, California, who provide the same services as San Diego's C&E Division, constituted a second comparison group. This group was chosen for comparison because the people perform the same tasks as

[3]We appreciate the assistance of Bob West (Buildings Division), Robert Kennedy (Long Beach), and Dean Burns (CALTRANS), who facilitated the data collection from the comparison groups.

the C&E employees but under slightly different institutional policies and procedures. While the Long Beach group was not identical to C&E on administrative procedures, it was in a city strikingly similar to San Diego in demographic, geographic, climatic, political, and economic characteristics; and its employees performed the same tasks as C&E's employees. This group, like the Buildings Division, received both administrations of the surveys but experienced no OD treatment.

Similarity of Buildings, Long Beach, and C&E Groups. The Survey of Organizations contained several demographic questions. Respondents were asked to give their sex, age, tenure on the job, level of education, and type of community where reared. Chi-square analysis of the demographic variables suggests that C&E, Buildings, and Long Beach differed on only sex ($X^2(2) = 8.46$, $p < .02$) and job tenure ($X^2(10) = 20.22$, $p < .03$). The significant difference in the proportion of male and female workers can be attributed to the fact that there were no women in the Buildings Division sample, while C&E included 12% women and Long Beach included 7% women. The significant tenure difference was caused by the fact that 69% of the Long Beach sample had been on the job for less than 10 years, while approximately 47% of the Buildings and C&E samples had less than 10 years of tenure. It should be noted that the shorter job tenure at Long Beach was not reflected in a difference in age. In short, this analysis means that these groups were not appreciably different from one another on most demographic variables.

CALTRANS District 11. The traffic-signals and street-lamps crews of District 11, California State Department of Transportation (CALTRANS), constituted a third comparison group. District 11, which encompasses the City of San Diego, had a crew that maintained street lamps and traffic signals. That crew was used as a comparison group for the productivity-index measurements compiled on the sections in C&E which performed the same functions.

Other City of San Diego Groups. Six groups of city employees were used as comparison groups for the absenteeism and turnover measures. These groups were Buildings Division, General Services Department, Fire Department, Police Department, Park and Recreation Department, and total of all city groups.

Dependent Measures

Productivity. Productivity was measured by simple tabulation of the number of specific tasks completed by two sections of the C&E Division during both the year preceding and the year of intervention. The tasks performed by the street-lamping section were number of street lights relamped, number of outages repaired, and total amount of preventive maintenance performed. The tasks performed by the traffic-signals section were number of emergency repairs begun within an hour and number of nonemergency repairs begun within one day. No similar data were available from any of the comparison groups.

Efficiency Measures. The ratio of productive work hours to available work hours was obtained for the C&E traffic-signals and street-lamps sections combined. A total count of specific tasks completed by employees in these sections was taken in biweekly periods coinciding with pay periods. This information was available on individuals' daily work cards and so was a relatively unobtrusive measure of efficiency.

For each task, the total volume of work done by all employees in the section was multiplied by the task's "time guideline," a fair-work time standard in minutes generated by time-and-motion studies that had been completed just prior to the OD project. For example, wiring a traffic signal takes 76.8 minutes. If the traffic-signals section repaired the wiring on four signals in one pay period, the total productive time for that task during that period would be 307.2 minutes. The productive times for all tasks were totaled to arrive at a grand total of productive time achieved during the pay period. This total was adjusted for unavoidable process losses as determined by the time-and-motion studies (e.g., clean-up time, transportation time) and converted to total hours earned. When divided by total work hours available, this figure yielded an efficiency index totaled for two sections.

The California State Department of Transportation compiles records of work output for crews performing the same tasks as the two sections in the C&E Division. Because District 11 includes the City of San Diego, that district's lighting crew often works under conditions identical to those encountered by the C&E Division's street-lamps and traffic-signals sections. For that reason, we also compiled efficiency indices for the CALTRANS lighting crew to use for comparison.

Differences in the two reporting systems necessitated computing the CALTRANS efficiency index in a manner slightly different from that of the C&E group. Mileage records and correction factors for unavoidable delays differed somewhat between the two groups, but otherwise the computations were identical. Therefore, while it is legitimate to compare trends in productivity between C&E and CAL-TRANS, it would be misleading to directly compare actual efficiency ratios.

Job Satisfaction: Surveys. Three widely used and previously validated surveys were administered to the C&E personnel, to employees of Buildings Division, and to Long Beach communications/electrical workers. These surveys all have job satisfaction scales; there were seven such scales in all.

1. The Survey of Organizations (SO) includes 124 questions eliciting reactions to organizational climate, leadership, peer influence, group dynamics, and satisfaction. Development of the SO began in 1966, and the instrument has been submitted to several validity and reliability studies (see Taylor & Bowers, 1972). The survey provides a profile of an organization. Many of the 32 subscales which the instrument yields are more useful for guiding the actual intervention than for evaluating the intervention's effect on morale, organizational climate, and job satisfaction. Consequently, here we report results only from the satisfaction scale of

the SO. (See Hausser, Pecorella, and Wissler, 1975, for a complete description of the SO and its subscales.)

2. In the short form of the Minnesota Satisfaction Questionnaire (MSQ), Weiss, Dawis, England, and Lofquist (1967) diagnose morale by eliciting respondents' satisfaction with 20 aspects of their jobs (e.g., chances for advancement, feelings of accomplishment, pay, and workload). The questions are clustered into three scales: intrinsic satisfaction, extrinsic satisfaction, and general satisfaction. Factor analysis of the long form of the MSQ had revealed two factors—intrinsic and extrinsic satisfaction—and general satisfaction is the sum of the two. All three scales were used in the present study.

3. The Job Diagnostic Survey (JDS) (Hackman & Oldham, 1974) was designed both to diagnose jobs and to assess effects of job redesign. The 20 scales of the instrument are divided into three classes:

a. those that assess objective job attributes (e.g., amount of skill required to perform the job;

b. those that assess affective reactions to the performance of the job (essentially satisfaction and motivation); and

c. those that assess "critical psychological states" thought to be necessary for positive affective reactions to occur.

Since some of the scales are used primarily for job redesign, only the scales most relevant to measuring job satisfaction and employee morale are presented in this report. The relevant scales are the satisfaction, pay satisfaction, and supervisor satisfaction scales.

Job Satisfaction: Unobtrusive Measures. The City of San Diego Civil Service Commission routinely compiles data on all city departments and divisions. These data are known simply as "Personnel Statistics." Released quarterly, these data are basically tabulations of the number of persons employed, total number of days of sick leave taken, and number of employees separated per quarter per division or department. We computed mean number of days of sick leave taken and percent of employees resigning for the seven city work groups for the six quarters prior to and the six quarters after the onset of the intervention. These data constituted unobtrusive measures of absenteeism and turnover. C&E records of employee grievances filed during FY 77 and FY 78 were also available.

Customer Satisfaction. In order to assess the changes in the ability of the C&E Division to serve the public effectively, both private citizens and institutional customers were asked to evaluate the service. The general public's opinion of C&E Division was found by conducting a telephone survey of a random sample ($n = 20$) of private citizens who had previously reported malfunctioning traffic signals or street lamps. The institutional users of C&E's services were surveyed by mail. Both the telephone survey and the mail survey questioned the respective customers at two times, once at the beginning of the intervention and once at the end. Comparison group data were not available on this dependent measure.

Summary

A standard OD intervention, made up of interviews, workshops, counseling, process consul-

tancy, and classroom training, was applied to the C&E Division of the City of San Diego. Data were unobtrusively collected to assess changes in productivity, job satisfaction, and customer satisfaction attributable to the intervention. Unobtrusively collected efficiency data were also available for both the experimental group and the CALTRANS District 11 comparison group for the entire period of the intervention. Finally, pre- and postintervention survey results assessing job satisfaction were collected from the experimental group and two appropriate comparison groups, Long Beach and Buildings Division. Table 1 summarizes the dependent variables.

Results

Productivity

Productivity in the C&E Division generally increased from FY 77 to FY 78. The increase in amount of work done by the street-lamping section is reflected in the number of lights re-lamped (2,767 in FY 78 vs. 2,422 in FY 77) and in the number of outages repaired (494 vs. 431) as well as in the total amount of preventive maintenance re-lamping/re-cleaning accomplished (11,291 vs. 9,494). Similarly, the traffic-signals section showed an increase

TABLE 1   Summary of Dependent Measures Available from the C&E Group and from Various Comparison Groups

Variable	Measure	Frequency of Measure	Comparison Groups
Job Satisfaction	SO	Before/After	Long Beach, Buildings
	JDS	Before/After	Long Beach, Buildings
	MSQ	Before/After	Long Beach, Buildings
	Absenteeism	Quarterly	Six City groups
	Turnover	Quarterly	Six City groups
	Grievances	FY 77/FY 78	None
Production Efficiency	Five Tasks	FY 77/FY 78	None
	Time	FY 77/FY 78	None
	Cost	FY 77/FY 78	None
	Efficiency Index	Monthly	CALTRANS
Customer Satisfaction	Telephone Survey	Before/After	None
	Mail Survey	Before/After	None

in the number of emergency repairs begun within one hour (1,422 in FY 78 vs. 1,070 in FY 77), although there was a drop in the number of non-emergency repairs begun within one day of notice (3,198 vs. 3,740). Clearly, more work was done by the C&E Division during the year of OD intervention than during the previous year, but lack of any comparison group data for this particular measure prevents us from venturing beyond that simple observation.

Efficiency

Work Hours. Data on the number of work hours required for the completion of specific tasks in the C&E Division support the expectation that the employees' efficiency rose during the intervention period. Fewer hours were required for repair of both stationary FM components (5.31 vs. 5.43) and mobile FM components (2.67 vs. 4.47). Similarly, less time was needed to complete 100 communications (1.00 vs. 2.08 hours) and slightly less time was spent per 100 parking meter collections (.99 vs. 1.03 hours). On the other hand, repair of parking meters required more time both in the field (.21 vs. .16 hours) and in the shop (1.17 vs. .62), and so did repair of microwave components (7.38 vs. 5.94 hours). However, even though group re-lamping of street lamps, a time-saving practice, was suspended during FY 78, mean work hours for that task increased only from .06 to .07 during the intervention period. On balance, then, it would seem that efficiency, as measured by time spent per task, did improve during the period of intervention.

Cost. The cost per unit per year to repair and maintain streetlights increased by 5% in FY 78, from $23.26 to $24.42. At the same time, the repair and maintenance of a signal intersection fell from $829.00 in FY 77 to $723.24 in FY 78, a decline of 13%. This is a substantial saving.

Efficiency Index. A plot of the efficiency index data over time for the C&E group shows a slow decline in efficiency prior to intervention followed

by an increase during the intervention period (see Figure 1). This picture is supported by the slopes of the regression lines: the pre-intervention slope is indeed negative ($b = -.0003$), while the slope during the intervention is positive ($b = .0002$). However, 95% confidence intervals indicate that these gradients do not differ significantly from zero or from each other. Nevertheless, analysis of variance applied to the means suggests that efficiency did increase dramatically in the C&E Division during the period of intervention. The pre-intervention mean of .728 rose by 29% to .939 during the intervention, $F(1, 35) = 36.35$, $p < .001$. Hence we may safely conclude that efficiency did increase during the intervention period.

Data from the CALTRANS comparison group, plotted the same as the C&E data, show just the opposite trends; but again the trends were not statistically significant (see Figure 2). The pre-intervention slope of .0002 did not differ from zero or from the postintervention slope of $-.0007$. The means (.727 and .721, respectively) did not differ from one another either, $F(1,22) < 1$.

These results lend support to the belief that efficiency improved in the C&E Division as a result of OD intervention. Savings in both time and money were made during the intervention period, and efficiency (as measured by the efficiency index) increased substantially for the C&E group but not at all for the similar CALTRANs comparison group.

Job Satisfaction: Surveys

Survey responses[4] for the seven job-satisfaction scales were submitted to nonorthogonal, repeated-measures analyses of variance (Woodward & Overall, 1976) with group (C&E, Long Beach, and

---

[4]Scores on these seven scales consist of the mean of the responses to the questions constituting the scales. No scale score was computed for any subject who answered fewer than half the questions for that scale. Naturally, since there were repeated measures, no subject is represented on a given scale who did not have both a pre-intervention score and a postintervention score. The scores had the following possible ranges: SO, 1–5; MSQ, 1–5; JDS, 1–7.

FIGURE 1   Efficiency in Communications and Electrical Division (Intervention Group)

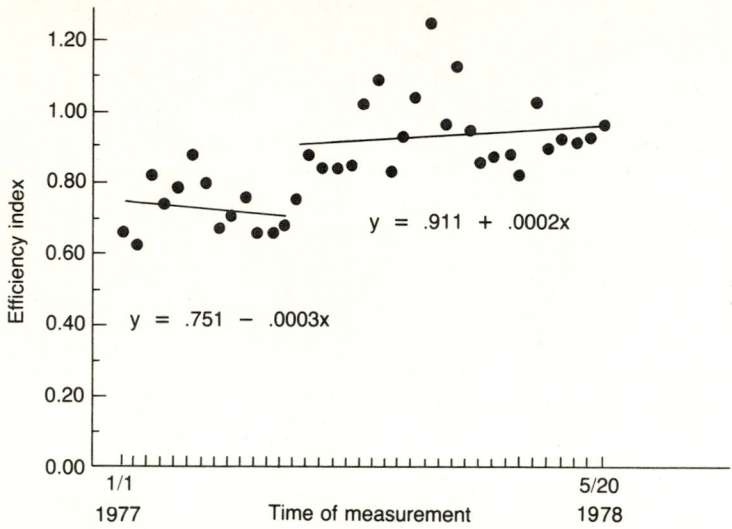

The increments on the horizontal axis are the biweekly pay periods mentioned in the text.

Buildings) and time (pre-intervention, postintervention) as factors, and repeated measures on the time factor. Only four of the 21 F values proved reliable: two were associated with the main effect of group, and two were associated with the two-way interaction effect.

The main effect of group was significant for both the JDS general satisfaction scale and the JDS pay satisfaction scale, Fs$(2, 110) = 5.52$ and 6.54, respectively, ps $< .01$. The order of means for the JDS general-satisfaction scale was C&E ($M = 5.10$), Long Beach ($M = 4.91$), Buildings ($M = 4.43$), but these means were not reliably different from one another by Newman-Keuls test. The order of means for the JDS pay satisfaction scale was Long Beach ($M = 4.68$), C&E ($M = 3.86$), Buildings ($M = 3.12$); the Newman-Keuls test indicated that Long Beach and Buildings were reliably different from each other, with C&E intermediate.

The significant interaction effects appeared in the MSQ extrinsic satisfaction scale, $F(2, 107) = 3.90$, $p < .05$, and the JDS supervisor satisfaction scale, $F(2, 107) = 3.30$, $p < .05$. The means appear in Table 2, where it can be seen that, for the former scale, the C&E group experienced an increase in extrinsic satisfaction over time, while the comparison groups reported less satisfaction. For the latter scale, the error term was too high for the multiple-comparison test to detect any differences.

These survey results are not overly impressive evidence for the efficacy of the OD intervention, although they are not by any means damaging. The repeated-measures analysis of variance is an excellent statistical test for this kind of data, but in the present case there is good reason to inspect the data in other ways as well. The main problem with the present analysis is that only those individuals who answered a sufficient number of questions on both administrations of the surveys (see Footnote 4) and

FIGURE 2 Efficiency in CALTRANS District 11 (Comparison Group)

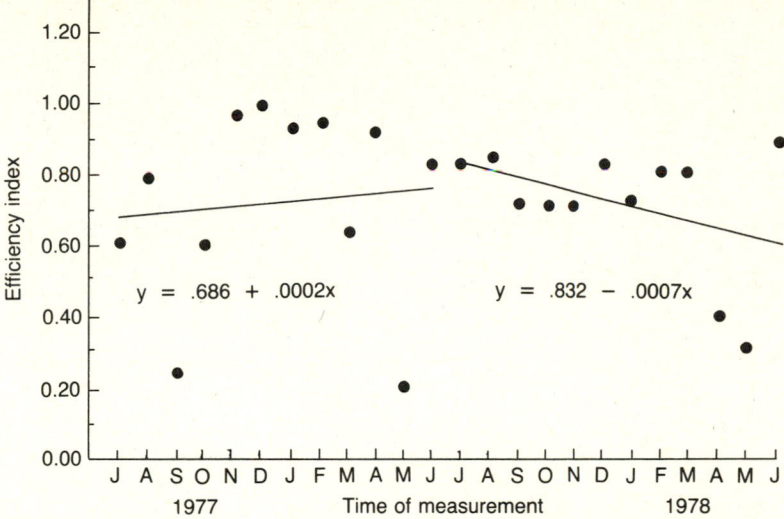

The increments on the horizontal axis are months of the year, beginning with July. The horizontal axis is on the same scale as that of Figure 1.

identified themselves the same way both times are represented in the repeated-measures analysis. Therefore, these results may represent only the least disgruntled, most compulsive, least distrustful, most consistent employees.

To compensate for these shortcomings, we re-analyzed these survey data, submitting them to one-way, unweighted-means analyses of variance.[5] The group means and particulars about the tests appear as Table 3. We note that job satisfaction was fairly high in the C&E group to begin with, falling even with or below the Long Beach group on all seven

---

[5] For these analyses, all data were transformed to a 0–4 scale.

TABLE 2 Satisfaction Scale Means from Three Groups Taken Before and During the OD Intervention

Scale	Time	Buildings	Group Long Beach	C&E
MSQ Extrinsic	Pre-intervention	2.76	3.19	2.93
Satisfaction	Postintervention	2.72_a	2.96_b	3.13_{ab}
		$(28)_a$	$(22)_{ab}$	$(60)_b$
JDS Supervisor	Pre-intervention	4.87	5.11	4.85
Satisfaction	Postintervention	5.05	4.52	5.01
		(29)	(22)	(59)

Note: Means sharing no subscript differ at the .05 level by Newman-Keuls test. The JDS means did not differ from each other by that test. Cell *ns* appear in parentheses.

TABLE 3   Job Satisfaction Data from Three Groups Collected Before and During the OD Intervention

Scale	Time	Buildings	Group Long Beach	C&E	F value	df	p
SO	1	1.87_a	2.40_b	2.22_b	7.04	2,200	.002
Satisfaction	2	1.97_a	2.18_{ab}	2.38_b	3.50	2,182	.04
MSQ	1	2.26_a	2.56_b	2.59_b	5.48	2,197	.005
General	2	2.52_b	2.22_a	2.68_b	7.62	2,167	.001
MSQ	1	1.65_a	2.15_b	1.93_{ab}	6.13	2,201	.005
Extrinsic	2	1.89	1.79	2.13	2.58	2,173	.08
MSQ	1	2.62_a	2.82_{ab}	2.95_b	4.36	2,202	.02
Intrinsic	2	3.86_b	3.47_a	3.92_b	8.14	2,170	.001
JDS General	1	2.12_a	2.62_b	2.69_b	10.86	2,195	.001
Satisfaction	2	2.26_a	2.43_{ab}	2.69_b	4.51	2,180	.02
JDS Pay	1	1.52_a	2.58_c	1.96_b	15.75	2,197	.001
Satisfaction	2	1.25_a	2.14_b	1.86_b	8.91	2,179	.001
JDS Supervisor	1	2.29_a	2.75_b	2.55_{ab}	3.31	2,196	.04
Satisfaction	2	2.54_{ab}	2.18_a	2.69_b	3.56	2,178	.04

Note: All means scaled to 0-4. Within rows, means with no common subscript differ at the .05 level by Newman-Keuls test. Time 1 refers to measurement prior to intervention; Time 2, to measurement during intervention.

scales prior to intervention. By the second administration of the surveys, the C&E group means exceeded the comparison group means in absolute value on every scale but one.

These results lend credence to the notion that the intervention program helped to improve satisfaction with a variety of aspects of the job for C&E employees.

Job Satisfaction: Unobtrusive Measures

Absenteeism. A two-way analysis of variance, with time (pre-intervention, postintervention) and group (the seven city comparison groups) as factors failed to yield an significant effects. The grand mean number of days of sick leave taken per employee was 2.16. The mean for C&E was 1.92.

Turnover. The analysis of variance on the turnover data produced significant main effects of time, $F(1,70) = 18.53$, $p < .001$, and group,

$F(6,70) = 3.69, p < .01$, but no significant interaction, $F(6,70) = 1.55$. This analysis was therefore rather uninformative. The grand mean probability of quitting was .0131; that for C&E was .0146. The range for the seven groups was .0036 (Fire Department) to .0212 (Buildings Division).

Grievances. C&E employees filed seven grievances in FY 77 and seven in FY 78. Whereas in FY 77 one complaint was resolved at the first level, one at the second, and the remainder at the fifth level, in FY 78 the grievances were resolved much earlier: three at the first level, three at the second level, and one at the third level. These data point to an increased responsiveness to employees' complaints.

Customer Satisfaction

Telephone Survey. Responses to the three questions, scaled from 1 to 5, were submitted to *t* tests.

None of the test results were significant (all *t*s < 1), indicating no change in customer satisfaction during the nine-month interval. Responses to these questions were positive. Customers reported that they had been treated courteously (*M* = 3.54) and had had little trouble locating the right person to help them (*M* = 4.28).

Mail Survey. As with the telephone survey, highly favorable responses characterized both preintervention and postintervention data from the mail survey. The only significant finding indicated a more favorable attitude on the second administration than on the first. Asked to indicate the amount of influence that the C&E Division had on the way the respondent's agency does its work, these customers' replies moved from a mean of 2.85 to 3.04, where 2 = *too much influence* and 3 = *about the right amount,* paired *t*(26) = 2.00, *p* < .05. A summary of the results appears as Table 4.

Discussion

The present study supports the notion that OD intervention can produce both increased productivity and increased job satisfaction in municipal government employees. With respect to productivity, the C&E groups seems to have benefited by the treatment. The amount of work done increased for four of five specific tasks, and less time was required to complete four of eight tasks that could be assessed. Of two cost measures, one—streetlamp maintenance—increased at less than the rate of inflation, whereas the other—traffic-signal maintenance—fell by some $100 per intersection. Furthermore, a dramatic increase in rated efficiency, from 73% to 94%, occurred for the intervention group but not for a comparison group, whose efficiency was rated on a highly similar scale at 73% and 72% during the same periods.

These important increases in productivity were by no means accompanied by any decrease in morale or service rendered to the customers of the intervention group. To the contrary, both verbal responses and unobtrusive measures of job satisfaction indicate improvement in morale for a group that already had relatively well-satisfied employees. The survey results for seven self-report scales show that the C&E employees' job satisfaction rose after the onset of the intervention period, to exceed that of two comparison groups. The unobtrusive measures of satisfaction (absenteeism, turnover, and grievances) showed no reliable changes. Finally, both private citizens and agency representatives remained highly satisfied with the service they received from the C&E Division.

TABLE 4 Summary of the Impact of the OD Treatment on C&E Morale and Efficiency

Variable	Measure	Outcome
Job Satisfaction	SO	Increased satisfaction
	JDS	Increased satisfaction
	MSQ	Increased satisfaction
	Absenteeism	No difference over time
	Turnover	Mixed result
	Grievances	Earlier resolution of grievances
Production Efficiency	Five Tasks	More work done
	Time	Less time needed for four tasks
	Cost	Substantial savings
	Efficiency Index	Significant increase
Customer Satisfaction	Telephone Survey	No decrease over time
	Mail Survey	No decrease over time

These results illustrate the efficacy of OD intervention precisely because there was comparatively little room for upward movement on the measures we employed. At the beginning of the OD project, the C&E Division employees were already well satisfied with their jobs, and they already performed at adequate levels of efficiency. Nevertheless, on a variety of measures, we found substantial improvements that may reasonably be attributed to the intervention treatment.

The present study shows that it is feasible to assess the effects of OD intervention projects that are conducted in municipal government settings. Even though there is no product or service sold to a specific market, as is the case in many private sector organizations that undergo OD treatment, organizations within municipalities do produce both goods and services for their customers, including other governmental agencies, private organizations, and the general public. As mentioned earlier, such projects in municipal governments, although frequent, seem rarely to be adequately assessed. We see this oversight as unfortunate and increasingly difficult to justify. It is unfortunate in that those who invest time, energy, and money to accomplish certain goals via an OD project can never know whether those goals have been reached unless they make some effort to evaluate the project. In a time of increasing demand for accountability to a cost-conscious public, government agencies that conduct OD projects will very likely find it harder and harder to gain approval for those projects that lack adequate evaluation.

References

Campbell, D. T., & Stanley, J. D. *Experimental and quasi-experimental designs for research.* Chicago: Rand McNally, 1963.

Chein, I., Cook, S., & Harding, J. The field of action research. *American Psychologist,* 1948, 3, 43–50.

Crano, W. D., & Brewer, M. B. *Principles of research in social psychology.* Reading, Mass.: Addison-Wesley, 1973.

Farkash, A. *An empirical investigation of organization development beliefs, activities and outcomes.* Selected Paper No. 8, American Society for Training and Development. Madison, Wisc., March 1979.

French, W. L., & Bell, C. H. *Organization development: Behavioral science interventions for organization improvement.* Englewood Cliffs, N.J.: Prentice-Hall, 1973.

Friedlander, F., & Brown, D. Organization development. *Annual Review of Psychology,* 1974, 25, 313–341.

Hackman, J. R., & Oldham, G. R. *The job diagnostic survey: An instrument for the diagnosis of jobs and the evaluation of job redesign projects.* Technical Report No. 4, Yale University Department of Administrative Sciences, May 1974.

Hausser, D. L., Pecorella, P. A., & Wissler, A. L. *Survey-guided development: A manual for consultants.* Ann Arbor, Mich.: University of Michigan Institute for Social Research, 1975.

Katzell, R. A., Yankelovich, D., and others. *Work productivity and job satisfaction: An evaluation of policy-related research.* New York: The Psychological Corporation, 1975.

Likert, R. *New patterns of management.* New York: McGraw-Hill, 1961.

Likert, R. *The human organization.* New York: McGraw-Hill, 1967.

Porras, J. I., & Berg, P. O. Evaluation methodology in organization development: An analysis and critique. *Journal of Applied Behavioral Science,* 1978, 14, 151–173.

Taylor, J., & Bowers, D. *The survey of organizations: A machine-scored standardized questionnaire instrument.* Ann Arbor, Mich.: Institute for Social Research, 1972.

Weiss, D. J., Dawis, R. V., England, G. W., & Lofquist, L. H. *Manual for the Minnesota Satisfaction Questionnaire.* University of Minnesota: Industrial Relations Center Work Adjustment Project, 1967.

Woodward, A. J., & Overall, J. E. Nonorthogonal analysis of variance in repeated measures experimental designs. *Educational and Psychological Measurement,* 1976, 36, 855–859.

PART 9

Research on Organization Development

In this section we examine some of the problems inherent in evaluating the effects of organization development programs and give an overview of research results. Research is the means of discovering if and how things work. Research verification of organization development's efficacy is necessary for the field to become a mature discipline. Katz, Kahn, and Adams state the case well: "Social studies become social sciences when their substantive core derives from research investigations rather than from untested theory and uncontrolled observation. . . . Research is especially important in organizational psychology because it links the world of knowledge to the world of practice. We can check the validity of our generalizations if we put them into practice and test the results."[1]

Considerable research activity is devoted to organization improvement strategies in general and to organization development in particular.[2] These studies confirm that OD works. OD programs have led to positive changes in attitudes and morale as well as productivity and profitability. Critiques of research on OD correctly identify several problem areas, such as the need for stronger research designs, more longitudinal studies, more control over competing explanations that may have caused the results, and better theory about OD and the change process.[3] Although assessing the effects of OD programs is difficult, substantial progress has been made in recent years.

---

[1]Daniel Katz, Robert L. Kahn, and J. Stacy Adams, eds., *The Study of Organizations* (San Franscisco: Jossey-Bass, 1980), p. ix.

[2]See, for example, Sam E. White and Terence R. Mitchell, "Organization Development: A Review of Research Content and Research Design, " *Academy of Management Review,* (April 1976), pp. 57–73; E.F. Huse and T.G. Cummings, *Organization Development and Change,* 3d. ed. (St. Paul, Minn.: West, 1985); and J. I. Porras and P. O. Berg, "The Impact of Organization Development," *Academy of Management Review,* (April 1978), pp. 249–66.

[3]See Larry E. Pate, Warren R. Nielsen, and Paula C. Bacon, "Advances in Research on Organization Development: Towards a Beginning," in *Academy of Mangement Proceedings '76,* eds. R. L. Taylor, M. J. O'Connell, R. A. Zawacki, and D. D. Warrick, Proceedings of the 36th Annual Meeting of the Academy of Management, Kansas City, Missouri, August 11–14, pp. 389–94; and John M. Nicholas and Marsha Katz, "Research Methods and Reporting Practices in Organization Development: A Review and Some Guidelines," *Academy of Management Review* 10, (1985) pp. 737–49.

To demonstrate the general trends in OD research, let us examine several literature reviews. Margulies, Wright, and Scholl[4] analyzed 30 research reports on OD programs and found positive results in over 70 percent of them. Dunn and Swierczek[5] reviewed 67 studies and found positive results in about 70 percent of them. A review by John Nicholas[6] focused on the effects of OD programs on such "hard criteria" as costs, profits, and quantity and quality of production. Positive gains were found in about half of the 65 studies he analyzed. Golembiewski, Proehl, and Sink[7] reviewed 574 cases of OD applications occurring from 1945 to the mid-1980's and found that "highly positive" or "a definite balance of positive outcomes" were obtained about 80 percent of the time.

In a comprehensive review, Porras and Berg[8] screened 160 studies and reduced them to a set of 35 studies that met two criteria: they were clearly OD interventions; and they had been evaluated by rigorous research standards. In these cases the researchers had measured the effects of the OD treatments on a wide variety of indicators that were classified by Porras and Berg into "process" variables and "outcome" variables. Process variables are such indicators as trust, motivation, conflict resolution, goal emphasis, and leader-follower relations. Outcome variables are such things as task accomplishment, satisfaction, productivity, and turnover. Outcome variables showed positive change in 51 percent of the cases where they were measured; process variables showed positive changes in 46 percent of the cases where they were measured. Additional analyses revealed new insights about the organization development process. For example, different interventions produced different results, with the Managerial Grid having the greatest impact on outcome variables, followed by task-oriented laboratory training and survey feedback. Multiple interventions produced more positive changes than single interventions. And finally, either relatively short (4 to 6 months) or relatively long (25 or more months) programs were associated with the greatest amount of change.

Several conclusions may be drawn from the research and the research reviews. First, a large majority of OD programs produce positive results. Second, some OD interventions are more effective than others. And third, although the nature of the OD process is becoming better understood, the actual causal mechanisms involved are not yet well known.

Some "Restraining Forces" Affecting Research on OD

There are no doubt many reasons why research on OD is difficult. Several of them will be identified and discussed as "restraining forces" operating in the total field of forces.

---

[4]Newton Margulies, Penny L. Wright, and Richard W. Scholl, "Organization Development Techniques: Their Impact on Change," *Group and Organization Studies* (December 1977), p.449.

[5]William N. Dunn and Frederic W. Swierczek, "Planned Organizational Change: Toward Grounded Theory," *Journal of Applied Behavioral Science* 13, no. 2 (1977), pp. 135–57.

[6]John M. Nicholas, "The Comparative Impact of Organization Development Interventions on Hard Criteria Measures," *Academy of Management Review* 7, no. 4 (October 1982), pp. 531–41.

[7]Robert T. Golembiewski, Carl W. Proehl, Jr., and David Sink, "Estimating the Success of OD Applications," *Training and Development Journal* 36, no. 4 (April 1982), pp. 86–95.

[8]Jerry I. Porras and P. O. Berg, "The Impact of Organization Development," *The Academy of Management Review* 3, no. 2 (April 1978), pp. 249–66.

1. Competent research on the effectiveness of OD is hard to do. Research on OD is perhaps best described as ''evaluation research''—research using social science research methods to *find out how well action programs work*. Evaluation research is inherently difficult. It is complicated by a number of characteristics such as the fact that the action program takes place in a real-life, complex social situation; the fact that the goals, interventions, and measurements may change over time; the fact that the evaluators may also be program sponsors or advocates; the fact that the program may extend over a long time period, having ups and downs during that time; and the likelihood (almost certainty) that events occurring simultaneously with the treatment, the OD program, may also be having profound effects on the outcomes being measured. Coupled with these difficulties are the mundane but almost insurmountable problems of finding adequate control groups, random (!) assignment of subjects (organizations, units within organizations, or individuals) to experimental and control groups, collecting both hard data (objective information such as return on investment, productivity, efficiency, turnover, and waste) and soft data (subjective information such as people's attitudes, opinions, perceptions, and feelings about things), and finding organizations that will permit themselves to be ''experimented on.'' The obstacles to conducting competent evaluation research are enormous.

Carol Weiss describes the evaluation research process as consisting of five stages:

1. Finding out the goals of the program.
2. Translating the goals into measurable indicators of goal achievement.
3. Collecting data on the indicators for those who have been exposed to the program.
4. Collecting similar data on an equivalent group that has not been exposed to the program (control group).
5. Comparing the data on program participants and controls in terms of goal criteria.[9]

But she goes on to note that it is much easier to describe the process than to carry it out, and she calls attention to many of the problems that have been discussed here.[10]

Another factor that is related to the difficulty of conducting research on the effectiveness of OD is that the methods and tools for such research are still being developed, and competence to use the new tools is not widespread. The important essay on experimental and quasi-experimental designs for social science research by Donald Campbell and Julian Stanley played a significant role in improving research designs and overcoming some of the sources of invalidity in social research.[11] We now see quasi-experimental designs in research on OD.[12] Ability to tease out causal relations between variables in complex situations requires advanced analytic techniques. Sociologists such as Hubert Blalock[13] and Herbert Costner[14] have worked on drawing causal inferences from nonexperimental

---

[9]Carol Weiss, ed., *Evaluating Action Programs* (Boston: Allyn & Bacon, 1972), p. 6.

[10]Ibid., chap. 1.

[11]Donald T. Campbell and Julian C. Stanley, *Experimental and Quasi-Experimental Designs for Research* (Skokie, Ill.: Rand McNally, 1963).

[12]See the methodological article on this point by Norman H. Berkowitz, ''Audiences and Their Implications for Evaluation Research,'' *Journal of Applied Behavioral Science* 5 (1969), pp. 411–28.

[13]Hubert Blalock, *Causal Modes in the Social Sciences* (Hawthorne, N.J.: Aldine Publishing, 1971).

[14]Herbert Costner, ''Theory, Deduction, and Rules of Correspondence,'' *American Journal of Sociology,* September 1969, pp. 245–63.

data. Economists have developed sophisticated techniques for analyzing data that have applicability to behavioral research. For example, a study by economists at the Federal Reserve Bank of Philadelphia attempted to discern the impact on learning (achievement) of various factors such as class size, teacher experience, and ethnic mixture of the school, in the public schools in Philadelphia[15] And, unlike past research that generally concluded that nothing in the educational process had any effect on anything or anybody, this research, through regression analyses, found several critical factors that impacted significantly on learning. The secrets to success were to be found in the research design and, especially, in the data analysis techiniques—techniques that allowed for the analysis of relationships between variables that were nonlinear, complex, contingent, conditional, and confounded. Research such as this can be used as a model for research on the effects of OD programs.

   2. Another major reason why research on OD is difficult is that the independent and dependent variables have not been conceptualized well enough so that meaningful research can be done on them. The term *independent variable* (IV) refers to the treatment, intervention, or "cause"; the term *dependent variable* (DV) refers to the outcome of the treatment or intervention, or the "effect" of the treatment. But generally speaking, the IVs we find in the literature are not comparable—OD program A at company A is quite different from OD program B at company B—the activities are different, the actors are different, the climates of the organizations are different, and so forth. Is it possible to treat the global intervention, say, a two–year OD program as a meaningful independent variable? Is it more desirable to treat parts of the OD program, say an organization mirror exercise with a key staff department, as the independent variable?

   A further confounding problem is that we would expect different effects to the same treatment at different times (stages) in the OD effort. Hence the OD program is a changing, shifting "cause." For example, the first team-building session with a work group is not the same thing as the tenth team-building session, even though we call them both by the same name, and some similar activities may occur.

   Likewise the results (effects) both expected and unexpected, of organization development activities are quite underconceptualized. Global criterion measures such as productivity and satisfaction really represent complex mixtures of variables such as—for productivity—quantity, quality, defective products, rejected products, costs per unit—daily/annually, and so on. And the dependent variable organizational effectiveness is more elusive still. These DVs have not been conceptualized very rigorously, and are usually not comparable across studies, since they have been operationalized in different ways.

   An important aspect of this issue is determining whether or not there are other, more relevant and tractable dependent measures. Number of meetings held in a specified time period, number of complaints concerning department X's service, turnover rates analyzed by departments—measures such as these might be more helpful in building a theory of what is going on in OD at this stage of development than more global measures.

   3. There is not a strong push to conduct research on OD, either from clients or consultants. Many subtle forces mitigating against research on OD arise from both clients

---

[15]A. Summers and B. L. Wolfe, "Which School Resources Help Learning? Efficiency and Equity in Philadelphia Public Schools," *Business Review,* February 1975, published by the Federal Reserve Bank of Philadelphia.

and consultants. For instance, a client system may be hurting, and want immediate help. In such a case, they would probably not want to be experimented on but would want to get on with the treatment. We know that client pressures to ''get on with it'' often jeopardize adequate diagnosis; these pressures are doubly deadly for research projects.

Clients and consultants are not waiting for research evidence to tell them that OD works or does not work. Case studies, anecdotal evidence, and their own sense data often provide all the information really needed or wanted to make a ''go-no go'' decision. OD practitioners probably have pretty good ideas about whether or not they are being effective and so do clients; they generally have little doubt that it is an effective organization improvement strategy, perhaps better than any others they have seen. Although it would be good to do research on OD, it is not necessary for it to be done for them to believe in the value of what they are doing.

4. Research on OD is costly—in terms of time, money, and effort. Clients and consultants (or researchers) must be willing to pay a great cost for competent research. These costs may be too great for the benefits derived by any one consultant/researcher/ client system; perhaps multisystem research programs could share some of the costs. One potentially very important research program that may serve as a model for research on organizational change projects is that of the Institute for Social Research (ISR) of the University of Michigan and its affiliate, the National Quality of Work Center (NQWC) in Washington, D.C. Basically, this is a program in which the National Quality of Work Center sponsors various organizational change implementation projects around the United States and researchers from ISR evaluate the projects in terms of both processes and outcomes.

5. Finally, it is likely that research on OD is to a great extent a thankless task. People who don't believe in OD are not likely to change their minds or behaviors if the research shows that it works; people who advocate the benefits of OD are not likely to change their minds or behaviors if the research shows that OD doesn't work. These people are believing or not believing for a lot of reasons other than rational ones; confirming or disconfirming evidence probably will not lead many people to change their positions on the subject.

In spite of these problems, research on organization development continues to be conducted with the result that managers and OD practitioners alike learn more about the underlying processes of organizational change.

Research Results, Examples, and Issues

These readings address research on OD from several perspectives. The first selection, by Robert Golembiewski, Carl Proehl, and David Sink, is a thorough and comprehensive review of the OD research literature. The authors analyzed 574 studies conducted over a 35-year period to determine the types of OD programs in use and the effects of those programs. Their results are promising: a wide variety of programs are in use; OD efforts have been directed toward both public sector and private sector organizations; and positive results were found in the vast majority of programs with very few negative effects reported. Reviews such as this are very useful for taking stock of where OD is as a field and pointing the way toward needed future research efforts.

The second article reports on the results of an OD program in one plant of a large multiplant, multidivisional corporation. John Kimberly and Warren Nielsen tackle a difficult research task and show how to overcome some of the problems and pitfalls inherent in assessing OD programs. Note some of the features of this article:

Conceptualization. Models of planned change and causal linkages are used to formulate both the appropriate intervention strategy and the research questions and measures.

Design. The concepts are translated into a plan of action; the plan follows from the model. This is theory-guided research and theory-guided action taking.

Execution. Do it. The concepts (model) suggest a design that translates into a set of actions that are executed. The overall flow of events is known in advance; timing, sequencing of activities, when to do what—all these are played out against an overall game plan. Execution activities are established for both the intervention and the research.

Proactive pragmatism. The authors take the constraints of field research in stride, but find ways to make the most of what they have. Methods to test alternative explanations for the results are devised; threats to internal validity are removed by design features; multiple measures and multiple analyses are used to extract all possible information.

This is an excellent research effort.

The article by Jerry Porras and Susan Hoffer addresses a different question: What behaviors can be expected to change as a result of successful organization development interventions? This is very important for building theory in OD, and their results make a valuable contribution to the literature. Better collaboration, participation, open communication, problem solving effectiveness, and a shared vision of the goals are among the expected outcomes of successful OD programs.

The article by R.J. Bullock and Daniel Svyantek directs attention to a debate currently surrounding research on OD. At issue is whether the methods of "normal science" are relevant or appropriate for research on organization development. Bullock and Svyantek assert that research on the OD process itself can not be subjected to the standards of behavioral science research that call for random selection of subject groups and random assignment of groups to treatment conditions. Further support for this side of the debate can be found in the article by Beer and Walton in Part One. They argue that the methods of traditional science are not appropriate to research on OD. They state: "Rather than attempt to find the perfect quantitative methodology and 'scientifically' prove its value, OD should attempt to build a different model of knowledge." However this debate eventually turns out, the dialogue will be good for the field of organization development.

Reading 59

ESTIMATING THE SUCCESS OF OD APPLICATIONS

by Robert T. Golembiewski, Carl W. Proehl, Jr., and David Sink

One of the better topics over the years for inspiring argument has involved assessing the state of organization development (OD). In more recent days, however, a curious agreement has developed. Friend and foe alike tend to have real doubts about OD's future. Critics point to a range of problems—theoretical, methodological and ethical.[1] Many historic supporters see OD at a critical life-stage—as an adolescent, with quite definite signs of lacking those qualities associated with "most likely to succeed."[2] Other supporters see a kind of academic and applied aging, with the memories of early hopes still alive but with a growing sense that the "heydays" are all over.[3] I have in mind a recent academic symposium of OD "afficionados," who had for several hours zestfully played "can you top this" with pronouncements concerning the deficiencies and all-but-inevitable doom facing OD— poor research, inadequate underlying theory, etc.

Three Base-Line Minima

This article seeks to provide needed perspective for ardent supporters, convinced critics and zestful flagellants alike, specifically by rooting this argument in three base-line minima about which broad and even universal consensus exists.

First, without doubt, OD still shows many of the signs of a burgeoning area of activity. We will be selective only, but illustrations suffice to make the case. Thus, OD texts[4] and books of readings[5]

Source: Robert T. Golembiewski, Carl W. Proehl, Jr., and David Sink, *Training and Development Journal* 36, no. 4 (April 1982), pp. 86–95. Copyright 1982, *Training and Development Journal*, American Society for Training and Development.

find a ready market. Professional associations with thousands of members have developed in the last decade.[6] The catalog of public or business organizations having had at least a flirtation with OD is very long and growing. Degree programs in OD have proliferated. It is certainly noteworthy that the largest employers of OD perspectives, designs and personnel include the U.S. military services,[7] whose base-values provide a very difficult target for penetration by OD perspectives and technologies.

Second, both major interpretations of this business rest on similar bases tht are palpably inadequate and may be wrong as well. That is, the business implies to some that OD "works." Others see a kind of "market high" just before an inevitable and formidable sell-off. Commonly, however, neither conclusion rests on satisfactory *and* comprehensive documentation of OD's efficacy, or lack thereof.

Note that this second base-line conclusion refers to satisfactory *and* comprehensive documentation, rather than to the absence of documentation. Documentation exists. Indeed, several comparative studies[8] suggest an appreciable success rate for various OD applications, but such work has two major limitations for present purposes. The data-bases for such summary studies tend to be small, on the order of scores of cases. For example, the study by Porras deals with 35 cases.[9] Morrison's methodological overview involves 26 cases.[10] In addition, only a small fraction of such data-bases refers to public sector applications, which are widely regarded as posing unusually difficult problems for OD and, by implication at least, as having low success rates. Perhaps 10-15 percent represents the usual proportion of public applications in available data-bases, and one-tenth of a small data-base does not provide a very solid foundation for generalizations.

Third, these information gaps have not often deterred enthusiasts or critics. They seem to *know*, absent the required documentation. Artfully, for example, some observers see the OD intervener as a kind of contemporary shaman,[11] while (at least to these authors) also conveying the distinct impression that more rattle-shaking than technology and theory are involved in OD applications. Generally, in addition, the state of affairs is presented as being worse in the public sector. Drawing on his experience as both a designer and a student of OD interventions, for example, Giblin concludes that the "unique constraints imposed on public organizations appear to render them almost immune from conventional OD interventions."[12] Others conclude that public sector OD—if defined as something more than "tinkering with the system"—will be very difficult, if not palpably impossible, for a broad range of reasons.

Burke concludes that: "Most OD consultants find working with bureaucracies, especially public ones, to be difficult at best....Apparently, most OD consultants either become more pragmatic and realistic or they have given up when it comes to working with large, bureaucratic organizations."[13]

The Present Date-Base

What do the data imply about OD applications? Specifically, this article reports an effort to transcend the all-but-universal limitations of the literature, based on a very intensive search for OD applications in both business and government contexts. Five basic sources are used to develop a database of OD applicatons that could support useful conclusions about effects:[14]

- Seven specialized bibliographies;
- Searches of the several relevant computerized listings (e.g., ERIC) of publications in social science journals over the past 20 years;
- A review of the last 20 years of studies reported in 88 journals, including 10 from overseas;
- More than 100 books surveyed for bibliographic items as well as for reports of interventions;
- Personal letters sent to 50 well known change agents, especially soliciting unpublished materials such as internal memos, dissertations or theses and so on.

Appropriate citations occurred as early as 1945, and the search extended into mid-1980 when it was closed to analyze data. This search-process has two gaps, neither of which is seen as damning, but which all may wish did not exist. First, journals unavailable in English were searched only selectively, but 17 percent of the total batch of interventions were accomplished in non-American settings. This leaves our data-base with a dominant locus and a distinct cosmopolitan flavor.

Second, the search did not encompass the twice-yearly meetings of the Organization Development Network or of the OD Division of ASTD. Until recently, neither interest group published proceedings. Many interventions reported at these meetings, however, got into our data-base, either after being published or because they were forwarded by our 50 personal contacts. Through mid-1980, these two gaps notwithstanding, our search uncovered a substantial number of OD applications—574 cases, to be exact.[15]

We make only two claims about this set of cases. First, there seems almost no question that public sector applications get adequate representation. Indeed, the very number of such applications—270—may itself constitute a major finding, since most sources emphasize the paucity of public sector applications.[16] In contrast, public sector cases constitute over 47 percent of the present batch of OD studies.

Second, we propose, a little more tentatively, that the 574 cases provide a reasonable replica of all OD activity. Early published work has some bias toward "successful" applications, but we include a broad range of unpublished sources. Moreover, the 35-year collection period and the large number of cases should substantially compensate for any early but artifactual hopes. Hence we propose that the 574 cases provide a credible source for seeking answers to two major questions concerning OD:

- What is the range and diversity of interventions or applications?
- What is the probability that an intervention will be successful?

Range and Diversity

The range of the 574 interventions is broad, with major representation from all the major classes of interventions associated with OD. Let us build toward this conclusion by providing useful detail.

Most observers see OD as one of the major derivatives of the "laboratory approach"—a major way of learning to learn. Globally, the laboratory approach to OD has at least six distinguishing features:[17]

- Rootedness in a definite set of values, which emphasize openness, trust and collaborative effort;
- Seeking to simultaneously meet individual needs and the needs of several levels of systems—small groups, large organizations and so on;
- Grounding in immediate experiences as they occur: this often gets expressed as a here-and-now orientation and is reflected in "process analysis" of the panoply of personal and institutional forces acting on individuals and groups;
- Emphasis on feelings and emotions, as well as ideas and concepts;
- Preeminence of the individual's involvement and participation—as subject and object, as generator of data as well as responder to those data—in an "action-research" sense;
- Heavy reliance on group contexts for choice and change; to validate data, to develop and enforce norms and to provide emotional support and identification.

The laboratory approach had its first major technological expression in the T-group or sensitivity training group. The T-group was typically composed of strangers, meeting on a "cultural island" and focused on learning from each other about (for example) "how we are seen by others and how we see them."[18] Such work sparked major attention to interaction-centered OD designs.

In a decade or so, OD became the major extension of such early work. It commonly came to encompass not only interaction-centered designs but those focused on structure and policies/procedures. Basically, the core values and central dynamics of the laboratory approach were built into several classes of learning designs, appropriate for choice or change in large aggregates. Each OD application will be unique to an extent and typically will combine several basic designs. As a first-cut, however, these alternative designs can be classified in terms of eight "activities." The classes are listed here, roughly in order of their complexity and subtlety:

- *Process analysis activities,* or applications of behavioral science perspectives to understand complex and dynamic situations. These perspectives can be simple—e.g., as in routine retrospection among task-group members who ask: How do we feel about what we just did? The perspectives also can be complex, as in seeking to understand interpersonal conflict as an expression of differing predispositions.
- *Skill-building activities,* or various designs for gaining facility with behaviors consistent with OD values, as in giving/receiving feedback, listening, resolving conflict, etc.
- *Diagnostic activities,* which often include process analysis, but which also may employ interviews, psychological instruments or opinion surveys to generate data from and for members of some social systems. These data get fed back into that system, to serve as the raw material for action-research sequences: diagnosis, prescription of changes, implementation and evaluation.
- *Coaching/counseling activities,* which seek to apply OD values in intimate situations, as between a pair-in-conflict in an organization via "third-party consultation."

- *Team building activities,* or efforts to increase the efficiency and effectiveness of intact task-groups. Variants may use T-group or sensitivity training modes, as well as one or more of the activities listed here.
- *Intergroup activities,* which seek to build effective and satisfying linkages between two or more task-groups, such as departments in a large organization.
- *Technostructural activities,* which seek to build need-satisfying roles, jobs and structures. Typically, these activities rest on a "growth psychology," such as that of Maslow, Argyris or Herzberg. These structural or policy approaches—job enlargement, flexi-time and so on—often are coupled with other OD activities.
- *System-building or system-renewal activities,* which seek comprehensive changes in a large organization's climate and values, using complex combinations of the seven activities sketched above, and having time spans in the three to five year range.

These eight activities fit with varying precision into three basic OD modes: interaction-centered, structure and policies or procedures. Process analysis, skill-building and coaching/counseling are basically interaction-centered. Technostructural and system-building emphasize structure, although not to the exclusion of the other two modes. Team-building and intergroup activities often have dominant interaction emphases, but also deal with structure and especially policies or procedures.

What is the distribution of our 574 cases among these classes of activities? Table 1 implies that our population covers the field of interventions. The most narrow designs—diagnostic activities and process analysis—constitute the dominant intervention mode in *less* than five percent of the cases. OD interventions tend to hunt bigger game. To illustrate, nearly 40 percent of the private sector cases can be categorized as emphasizing the most complex intervention modes—system-building or renewal and technostructural activities. Reading the individual case reports in the public sector also reinforces this impression. The applications there seem to give substantial attention to the tough cases, on balance. Hence, the common emphases on: racial tension; conflict between individuals, specialties and organization units; community conflict between police and minorities; and basic reorganization. OD applications seem to respect this difficult prescription: *Intervene where the pain is felt!*

The 574 cases imply similar reliance on dominant OD modes in both public and business settings. In most cases, the probabilities of using the

TABLE 1 Incidence of Eight Classes of OD Activities in Public and Private Sectors.

	Individual Applications Classified by Dominant Design			
	Public Sector		Private Sector	
Class of OD Design	No.	%	No.	%
Process analysis activities	10	4	6	2
Skill-building activities	65	24	57	19
Diagnostic activities	14	5	18	6
Coaching/counseling activities	19	7	30	10
Team-building activities	51	19	56	18
Intergroup activities	38	14	18	6
System-building or system-renewal activities	29	11	35	11
Technostructural activities	44	16	84	28
	N = 270	100	N = 304	100

eight classes of activities vary in a very narrow range only. Technostructural activities constitute the most prominent exception, perhaps because public structures/policies/procedures are more likely to be set by distal authorities, especially legislatures. Therefore, these activities would more often be out of convenient reach. Even so, technostructural activities constitute the dominant OD mode in nearly one of every five public sector cases.

In sum, the 574 cases do not constitute a collection of easy pieces, and the data-base suggests no huge differences between the reliance on specific modes of OD interventions in public and business sectors. Consequently, the data-base should provide a real test of the efficacy of OD techniques and perspectives, of how often and to what degree they tend to ''work,'' within and between the private and public sectors.

The classification of the 574 published OD reports by dominant mode of intervention has a high reliability. Two independent observers classified all cases and had a very high degree of agreement. A 10 percent sample (approximately) places that agreement at nearly 98 percent of the cases. These few differences were reconciled before summation in Table 1.

High interobserver reliability was not crucial in this case. The efficacy of OD interventions was uniform over the full range of dominant modes.

Two Estimates of Success

How can we estimate specifically the efficacy of OD interventions? Do public-sector interventions have a lower success rate than their counterparts in business organizations? Two approaches to answers will be sketched here and tested against business and government OD applications. The approaches may be labeled ''global'' and ''multiple indicators.''

Global Estimate of Efficacy

A few details provide needed perspective on the ''global'' evaluation of OD interventions. Two independent readers reviewed each of the 574 interventions and assigned each set of effects to one of four categories whose content the observers had discussed and illustrated in detail. The evaluative categories include:

- *Highly positive and intended effects* on the efficacy and effectiveness of some relatively discrete system, as in improving the ability of individuals to hear one another without distortion, or in reducing the degree of hostility between conflicting actors or units.
- *Definite balance of positive and intended effects,* defined in terms of mixed but generally favorable effects; e.g., most but not all intended effects were achieved on a number of variables; or major positive effects occurred in one system, while some negative but not counterbalancing effects occurred in another system.
- *No appreciable effect.*
- *Negative effects,* or a case in which substantial reductions occurred in the efficiency and effectiveness of some subsystem or of some broader system of which it was a part.

What did this laborious rating and cross-checking reveal? Four points summarize the major findings. First, by and large, the observers saw the same effects. Specifically, the observers' ratings correlated .78, which indicates substantial agreement between raters. Almost all cases of disagreement involved the first two rating categories. Some differences were reconciled after this reliability check, but in all cases, the ratings of one observer are reflected in Table 2. One can then conclude with some confidence that *in this population of studies* more than 80 percent of the interventions had at least a definite balance of positive and intended effects.

Third, global estimates of the efficacy of OD interventions do not vary much between the public and business sectors. Table 2 implies that major point.

Fourth, global estimates of success vary somewhat by dominant mode of intervention. Table 3 summarizes the experience for private sector interventions, which do not differ markedly from public sector experience. Except for two classes of

TABLE 2   Global Estimate of the Success of 574 OD Applications

| | Individual Applications Classified by Degree of Effects | | | |
| | Public Sector | | Private Sector | |
Rating Categories	No.	%	No.	%
Highly positive and intended effects	110	41	122	40
Definite balance of positive and intended effects	116	43	148	49
No appreciable effect	18	7	14	5
Negative effects	26	9	20	6
	N = 270	100	N = 304	100

OD activities—process analysis and diagnostic—the efficacy estimates are all 83 percent or greater for at least a definite balance of positive and intended effects.

Multiple Indicators Estimate Efficacy

Another approach to estimating the efficacy of OD interventions relies on numerous multiple indicators which comprise 308 variables. Proehl[19] coded each of the 574 cases in the present batch of studies, in terms of the comprehensive set of indicators developed by Porras and Berg.[20] Proehl describes his procedure in these terms:

". . . each of the . . . studies in this research's data-base was searched for the 308 variables developed by Porras and Berg. When one of the variables was found, it was coded according to whether

TABLE 3   Global Estimates of Efficacy, Private Sector Cases Only, N = 304

| | Estimated Effects in Percent* | | | |
Class of OD Design	Highly Positive and Intended Effects	Definite Balance of Positive and Intended Effects	No Appreciable Effects	Negative Effects
Process analyis activities	16.7%	50.0%	16.7%	16.7%
Skill-building activities	40.4%	52.6%	3.5%	3.5%
Diagnostic activities	33.3%	44.4%	5.6%	16.7%
Coaching/counseling activities	40.0%	46.7%	6.7%	6.7%
Team-building activities	39.3%	51.8%	3.6%	5.4%
Intergroup activities	44.4%	39.0%	5.6%	11.1%
System-building or system-renewal activities	45.7%	40.0%	5.7%	8.7%
Technostructural activities	40.5%	51.2%	3.6%	4.8%

*Due to rounding, totals may accumulate to > 100%.

it had improved (0) or not improved (1) during the course of the change project. Once all of the variables present in each study were identified and coded, the *'percentage of positive reported change'* was calculated for each organizational level (individual, leader, group or organization) or study. This was accomplished by dividing the number of positive variables by the total number of variables in whch change was desired in each organizational level of each study. For example, a change effort which sought to change five individual-level variables and reported three of them as having changed positively was given a score of 60 percent. Scores ranged from zero percent in a change effort which failed to produce any positive change in process and outcome variables to 100 percent for a case in which positive change was reported in all variables for which change was desired.''

The reliability of these assignments was estimated by a limited, if random, process. Three independent observers each rated two randomly selected variables, and agreement existed on 228 of 240 cases. This interobserver reliability of 95 percent is taken to be representative of the record on the other variables, and seems an acceptable level of reliability of assignments on which to base analysis.

The ''percentage of positive reported change'' was 70.5 percent, overall, when the 574 cases were scored for all of the 308 Porras/Berg variables applicable in each case. The efficacy of the 574 applications also can be arrayed according to levels of analysis, four of which were distinguished by Porras and Berg. The specific percentages of positive reported change are:

- Individual: 78.1 percent for 243 cases;
- Leader: 68.1 percent for 173 cases;
- Group: 77.9 percent for 161 cases;
- Organization: 72.4 percent for 206 cases.

We conclude that, as the best-informed possible estimate from the standpoint of multiple indicators, at least 7 of 10 variables show a balance of positive effects resulting from OD applications. Because not all of the same variables are considered in the two comparisons above, the success rate at the four

levels of analysis surpasses 70 percent by a noticeable margin. In addition, no major differences distinguish public vs. business applications.

Five Perspectives on Success

These results confirm a substantial success rate for a large batch of OD interventions. To be conservative, the two approaches to an estimate imply a success ratio of at least 7 in 10 cases. The more ebullient might choose to give credence to the global bottom-line estimate of efficacy, which approximates an 85 percent success rate.

These data powerfully imply that both critics and previously pessimistic supporters of OD must ''sing a different tune'' in the future, or at least a more complicated one. Such adaptation must take cognizance of at least five factors. First, these results are reinforced in other studies, although with databases that are small fractions of the size of the present batch. To sample only:

- Eight percent of Morrison's 26 cases deal with ''failures'';[21]
- In Dunn and Swierczek's 67 cases, 65-70 percent were considered ''effective'';[22]
- In Porras' 35 cases selected for high degrees of methodological rigor, variables changed in the predicted directions in about 50 percent of the cases;[23]
- Margulies and his associates rated 73 percent of 30 applications as ''positive,'' with 10 percent ''mixed,'' 24 percent ''no change'' and 3 percent as ''negative.''[24]

Second, these favorable success rates do not mean that all OD problems have been recognized, let alone solved to such a degree that designs and perspectives can be applied following a cookbook approach. Positively, these results imply that whatever exists in the organizational world can be accommodated, most of the time, by the kind of OD interveners who research and write up their experiences. Diagnosis is critical.

Third, the results do not imply that public sector OD is easier than ''in business,'' more difficult or the same. To restate the previous point, the results here only imply that the unique constraints existing in various organizations, whether governmental or business, can be accommodated by the written experiences of appropriate OD interventions.

This is no cute conclusion. In fact, we know quite a bit about how to develop such accommodations to the specific characteristics of agencies in the public sector. This is not the place, however, to detail that experience and theory, which has been accomplished elsewhere.[25]

Fourth, greater specificity will be required for finer-tuned analyses than the one attempted here. To illustrate, future comparative analysis will require a more precise typology of interventions, as well as a more complex differentiation of hosts or targets for such interventions. This consciousness has been raised recently,[26] but much remains to be done. In the present case, for example, interventions are distinguished only in gross terms. Targets/hosts are differentiated only as "public" and "business." A more satisfactory typology of OD systems will eventually take into explicit account the full range of differences/similarities usually encapsulated in the short-hand "public vs. private"; and it seems just as clear that this typology also will encompass those equally significant differences/similarities *within* "public" and "business" sectors.

Fifth, and finally, this analysis may be faulted by a major contaminant. As some observers emphasize,[27] published materials may be biased toward reporting "positive results." If this bias characterizes the present data-base, that would obviously account for some part of the high success rate. Our procedures provide only partial protection against such a bias. Note the effort to solicit unpublished materials—consultant reports, in-house memos, theses and dissertations; this implies a counter-balance to any bias toward "positive results" in published work. Presumably, unpublished materials would be less contaminated in this regard.

These five concluding points encompass the present analysis rather than nullify it. The present results may be considered the best available comprehensive estimate of the efficacy of OD efforts.

References

1. Warner Woodworth, Gordon Meyer and N. Smallwood, "A Critical Assessment of Organization Development Theory and Practice," unpublished MS, Department of Organizational Behavior, Brigham Young University, 1980.

2. Frank Friedlander, "OD Reaches Adolescence," *Journal of Applied Behavioral Science,* **12,** 7 (January 1976).

3 W. Warner Burke, "Organization Development in Transition," *Journal of Applied Behavioral Science,* **12,** 24 (January 1976); W. Warner Burke, "Organization Development and Bureaucracies in the 1980s," *Journal of Applied Behavioral Science,* **16,** 423 (July 1980).

4. Wendell F. French and Cecil H. Bell, Jr., *Organization Development,* Prentice-Hall, Englewood Cliffs, N.J., 1978; Robert T. Golembiewski, *Approaches to Planned Change,* 2 vols., Marcel Dekker, New York, 1979; Edgar F. Huse, *Organization Development and Change,* West Publishing, St. Paul, Minn., 1980.

5. Wendell F. French, Cecil H . Bell, Jr. and Robert A. Zawacki, eds., *Organization Development: Theory, Practice and Research,* Business Publications, Inc., Dallas, Texas, 1975; and Robert T. Golembiewski and William Eddy, eds., 2 vols., *Organization Development in Public Administration,* Marcel Dekker, New York, 1978.

6. The Organization Development Network is the most prominent professional association, achieving nearly 5,000 members in less than two decades of existence. Its energy level is reflected in its two yearly meetings, each lasting nearly a week.

7. *Southern Review of Public Administration,* **1,** 406 (March 1978).

8. Peggy Morrison, "Evalution in OD: A Review and An Assessment," *Group and Organization Studies,* **3,** 42 (March 1978); Jerry Porras, "The Comparative Impact of Different OD Techniques and Intervention Intensities," *Journal of Applied Behavioral Science,* **15,** 156 (April 1979).

9. Porras, *op. cit.*

10. Morrison, *op. cit.*

11. Warner Woodworth and Reed Nelson, "Witch Doctors, Messianics, Sorcerers and OD Consultants: Parallels and Paradigms," *Organizational Dynamics,* **8,** 16, (Autumn 1979).

12. Edward J. Giblin, "Organization Development: Public Sector Theory and Practice," *Public Personnel Management,* **5,** 108, (March 1, 1976).

13. Burke, "Organization Development and Bureaucracies in the 1980s," p. 429.

14. Carl W. Proehl, Jr., *Planned Organizational Change,* unpublished doctoral dissertation, Appendix A, University of Georgia, 1980.

15. The full bibliography of 574 cases is reported in *ibid.,* and those interested can obtain copies from the senior author.

16. As an exception, Miller isolates 138 applications that are included in the present batch. See Garald J. Miller, *The Laboratory Approach to Planned Change in the Public Sector,* unpublished doctoral dissertation, University of Georgia, 1979.

17. Arthur Blumberg and Robert T. Golembiewski, *Learning and Change in Groups,* Penguin, London, 1976, pp. 22–35.

18. *Ibid.,* esp. pp. 57–61.

19. Proehl, *op. cit.*

20. Jerry I. Porras and Per-Olof Berg, "Evaluation Methodology in Organization Development," *Journal of Applied Behavioral Science,* **14,** 151, (April 1978).

21. Morrison, *op. cit.*

22. William N. Dunn and Frederick W. Swierczek, "Planned Organizational Change," *Journal of Applied Behavioral Science,* **13,** 135, (April 1977).

23. Porras, *op. cit.*

24. Newton Margulies, Penny L. Wright and Richard W. Scholl, "Organization Development Techniques: Their Impact on Change," *Group and Organization Studies,* **2,** 449, (December 1977).

25. A developmental version of guidelines for public sector applications appears in Robert T. Golembiewski, "Managing the Tension Between OD Principles and Political Dynamics," pp. 27–46, in W. Warner Burke, ed., *The Cutting Edge: Current Theory and Practice in Organization Development,* University Associates, La Jolla, Calif., 1978. An expanded version will appear in Golembiewski's *Humanizing Public Organizations* (in preparation).

26. David G. Bowers, Jerome L. Franklin and Patricia A. Pecorella, "Matching Problems, Precursors and Interventions in OD: A Systematic Approach," *Journal of Applied Behavioral Science,* **11,** 391 (December 1975).

27. Philip H. Mirvis and David N. Berg, eds., *Failures in Organization Development and Change,* Wiley, New York, 1977.

Reading 60

ORGANIZATION DEVELOPMENT AND CHANGE IN ORGANIZATIONAL PERFORMANCE

John R. Kimberly and Warren R. Nielsen

This study examined the impact of an OD effort on organizational performance using a model of causal linkages in planned change which appears to underlie the OD approach to organizational intervention. Significant positive changes in target-group attitudes and perceptions were found, as was significant positive change in quality of output and in profit. No change in the levels of productivity was found, and a strong positive correlation between those levels and levels for the industry as a whole was interpreted as indicating that this particular index of performance was outside the direct control of plant management and more a function of corporate policy and market conditions.[1]

Organization development (OD), a philosophy of and technology for producing organizational change, has been implemented in a variety of organizations. Growing out of the human relations tradition in the 40s and 50s, it is actually a pastiche of techniques developed in the behavioral sciences which focus on problems of organizational learning, motivation, problem solving, communications, and interpersonal relations. While it is misleading to speak of OD as a clearly defined and integrated approach to producing change (Kegan, 1971), its proponents (Blake & Mouton, 1968;

Source: John R. Kimberly and Warren R. Nielsen, *Administrative Science Quarterly*, June 1975, pp. 191–206.

[1] This research was supported, in part, by the Institute of Labor and Industrial Relations at the University of Illinois, Champaign. The authors would like to acknowledge the comments of an anonymous reviewer and those of George Graen, Michael Moch, and Louis Pondy on previous drafts of this paper.

Beckhard, 1969; Bennis, 1969; Schein, 1969; Dalton, Lawrence, & Greiner, 1970; and French & Bell, 1973) argue that it can lead to improved organizational effectiveness and health.

Given the importance of change in the literature on organizations and the prevalence of OD in management circles, there is a surprising lack of systematic evidence regarding its efficacy, particularly in terms of its impact on organizational performance. With certain exceptions (Trist, Higgin, Murray & Pollock, 1963; Marrow, Bowers, & Seashore, 1967; Blumberg & Golembiewski, 1967; Zand, Steele, & Zalkind, 1969; Seashore & Bowers, 1970; Hill, 1971; and Bowers, 1973), most of the evidence to date consists of testimonials, anecdotes and impressions, or research focused on changes in attitudes toward and perceptions of organizational reality. This evidence is generally favorable, that is, it attests to the success of OD interventions in producing change in positive directions. Less numerous, however, are studies of change in measures of organizational performance, as Friedlander and Brown (1974) in their extensive review of the literature have pointed out. The purpose of this article is to begin to fill that gap.

Research Setting

The study on which this article is based involved the implementation of a planned change program in an automotive division of a large multiplant, multidivisional corporation. The plant employed approximately 2,600 hourly and 200 salaried employees; work was organized on an assembly-line basis. Parts were furnished by other plants of the parent corporation, with the employees assembling the final product. The plant operated with three separate shifts. Shifts one and two were responsible for building the product and the third shift repaired those units that were unacceptable upon final inspection. There were five basic hierarchical levels in the organization made up of hourly employees, foremen, general foremen, assistant superintendents, and superintendents. A plant manager oversaw the total plant operation.

There were a number of factors which influenced the management of the plant to embark on an OD program. First, the plant was a major unit in a division which had been considered very successful in the past, but which in recent years was experiencing decreases in production, quality, and profits and increases in absenteeism, turnover, and grievance rates. Second, there was a general feeling in the plant that supervisors and managers were not working together and that the level of teamwork had decreased. Third, many managers believed that the first-line supervisors did not see themselves as a part of the team and some effort was needed to rectify this situation. Finally, the plant manager appeared to have a genuine concern for improving the performance of the organization.

Although members of plant management did not think that their values were in conflict with those underlying OD, they did not enter into the change project because of a particular commitment to OD values. Rather, they felt that OD and its accompanying methods and techniques might be a vehicle for improving organizational effectiveness and they agreed to try it on that basis.

The plant manager, production superintendents, and the change agents decided that the OD effort should be concentrated on the production group since this group's performance was most directly related to the performance of the organization as a whole. All production supervisors—foremen and general foremen—and managers—assistant superintendents and superintendents—as well as the plant manager therefore participated in various phases of the OD program, which began in January 1970 and continued formally, with the use of outside assistance, through March 1971.

Change Program

A brief summary of the OD program used in the organization includes the following six phases.[2]

1. *Initial Diagnosis.* The diagnosis consisted of three stages. First a series of interviews was held with a sample of 15 supervisory and managerial personnel including the plant manager and his immediate staff; second, group meetings were held with those interviewed to examine the results and to determine problem areas and priorities; and finally, the plant manager, his immediate staff, and the external consultants met to finalize the change design.

2. *Team Skills Training.* Foremen, general foremen, assistant superintendents, and superintendents participated with their peers in groups of approximately 25 individuals in a series of experience-based exercises during a two-and-a-half-day workshop.

3. *Data Collection.* Immediately following the team skills training, all foremen completed two questionnaires. The first concentrated on organizational health and effectiveness and the second asked them to describe the behavior of their immediate supervisors—general foremen or assistant superintendents.

4. *Data Confrontation.* In this phase, various work groups were asked to review the data described above and determine problem areas, establish priorities in these areas, and develop some preliminary recommendations for change.

5. *Action Planning.* Based on the data and conversation during the data confrontation, each group developed some recommendations for change and plans for the changes to be implemented. The plans included what should be changed, who should be responsible, and when the action should be completed.

6. *Team Building.* Each natural work group in the entire system, including the plant manager and his immediate staff of superintendents, then met

---

[2] For a more complete description of these methods and techniques, see Fordyce and Weil (1971); Margulies and Raia (1972); and French and Bell (1973).

for two days. The agenda consisted of identifying blocks to effectiveness for the specific group and the development of change goals and plans to accomplish the desired changes.

7. *Intergroup Building.* This phase consisted of two-day meetings between groups that were interdependent in the plant. The groups met for the purpose of establishing mutual understanding and cooperation and to enhance collaboration on shared goals or problems.

The sequence in which the interventions occurred is outlined in Table 1.

Research Design

One criterion for judging the utility of any research design is its ability to rule out the possibility of alternative explanations. From an experimental point of view, it would be highly desirable to design the research using controls that would make it possible to isolate the effects of treatment conditions—the OD interventions—on the dependent variables—changes in perceptions of organizational climate and supervisory behavior and change in productivity, quality, and performance to budget. In this case, however, as in most field research, ideal procedures specified by formal canons of experimental design had to be modified to meet situational constraints. Three particular constraints were present. First, the change program had been initiated and was well along before this phase of research was developed. Second, the fact that the interventions were plantwide precluded the estab-

lishment of internal controls, although such control would have had to occur after the program. Finally, the plant itself was structurally different from other plants in the parent corporation, which made the use of another plant in the system as a control for the organizational performance data questionable. Hence, what emerged was a post hoc design combining elements of what Campbell and Stanley (1966) have called a One Group Pretest Posttest Design and a Time Series Experiment. This quasi-experimental design, used in conjunction with industrywide data for the time period in question, enables one to begin to deal with the issue of alternative explanations, albeit on less than ideal terms.

Data were collected from the management subsystem or target group of the organization regarding perceptions of organizational climate and supervisory behavior just before and immediately after the involvement of the outside consultants in the OD program. These data, collected anonymously at two times, were used to measure extent of change in the managerial subsystem as a whole. Two questionnaires were employed. One was developed by Douglas McGregor for use in team building and asked the respondents to rate such factors as trust, support, communication, understanding of objectives, commitment to objectives, handling of conflict, utilization of resources, control methods, and organizational environment. The second, developed by Ed Nevis for use in OD projects and modified for this study, asked employees to describe the behavior of their immediate supervisors relative to listening, expressing ideas to others, influence style, decision making, relations with others, task orientation, handling of conflict, willingness to change, problem solving, and self-development.

Indices of organizational performance, namely, production rate, quality levels, and performance to budget, were compiled on a daily basis for the 15 months before, the 14 months during, and the 12 months after the interventions. These data meet the criteria for a modified time-series experiment design. Within the limitations of this design, therefore, the impact of the OD interventions on the

---

TABLE 1 Change Program Sequence

Intervention	Initiated	Completed
Initial diagnosis	12– 1–69	12–31–69
Team skills training	1– 9–70	2–28–70
Data collection	1–10–70	3– 1–70
Data confrontation	5– 9–70	8–19–70
Action planning	9– 1–70	12–31–70
Team building	1– 1–71	2– 1–71
Intergroup building	2– 2–71	2–28–71
Data collection	3–15–71	3–15–71

organization which is the setting for the study could be considered. Longitudinal data on hard measures of organizational performance are generally absent in the literature on organizational development; by contrast with what is in the literature, the approach used here, though developed after the change program had been initiated, has a variety of advantages, both theoretical and empirical.

Hypotheses

The model used to generate testable hypotheses about the impact of the interventions was based on an assumption about causal linkages in an organization that is central to the OD approach to organizational change. Since the interventions were explicitly designed to produce change in the attitudes, perceptions, and behaviors of the individuals who were participants in the change program, this change was called first-order change. Change of this sort may produce changes in the attitudes, perceptions, and behaviors of other individuals in other parts of the organization, for instance reducing absenteeism among hourly employees, as a consequence of the interdependencies that exist or are created between subsystems in the organization. This was called second-order change. Finally, change in indices of the performance of the organization as a whole, indices which reflect aggregated individual behaviors, may occur as a consequence of first-order change alone or the combination of first- and second-order change. At the start of any planned change program of this type, therefore, it is posited that first-order change should be temporally antecedent to other kinds of change. Thus, it is argued that change in the attitudes, perceptions, and behaviors within the OD target subsystem is a necessary condition for the attribution of changes in other organizational indices to the interventions. Over time, however, because of the nature of the interdependencies among organizational variables and feedback mechanisms inherent in the change program itself, there will be reciprocal causation.

The model developed, therefore, was based on what was perceived to be a major assumption about

causal linkages that is inherent in the technology of OD in general and that is reflected in, among others, the work of Argyris (1962, 1971), Likert (1967), and Blake and Mouton (1968). The merits of the model itself are not argued here; alternative models, in fact, may capture more effectively the complexity of causal relations. It is argued, however, that this model is a reasonable approximation of that used explicitly or intuitively by most OD change agents and for that reason its tenability should be examined empirically.

Schematically, the model is outlined in Figure 1. It is assumed that the impact of the OD interventions on attitudes, perceptions, and behaviors within the target subsystem can be directly tested. If change in the predicted direction occurs, the impact of the interventions on other organizational variables can be indirectly tested. A finding of no change in the target subsystem would mean that *(a)* any changes observed in other organizational variables could not reasonably be attributed to the interventions or *(b)* that if changes in performance were observed in the absence of change in the target subsystem, the causal assumption should be seriously questioned. If change in the predicted direction occurred, the attribution of change in other variables to the interventions would become more plausible.

Using this approach, the following hypotheses were tested.

Direct Test

As a consequence of the OD change program, (1A) significant positive change will be produced in perceptions of organizational climate within the target subsystem, and (1B) significant positive change will be produced in perceptions of supervisory behavior within the target subsystem.

Indirect Test

As a consequence of the OD change program, (2A) significant increases in units produced will be observed, (2B) significant decreases in the variance in units produced will be observed, (3A) significant increases in the level of the quality index will be observed, (3B) significant decreases in the variance

FIGURE 1   Causal Linkages in Planned Change

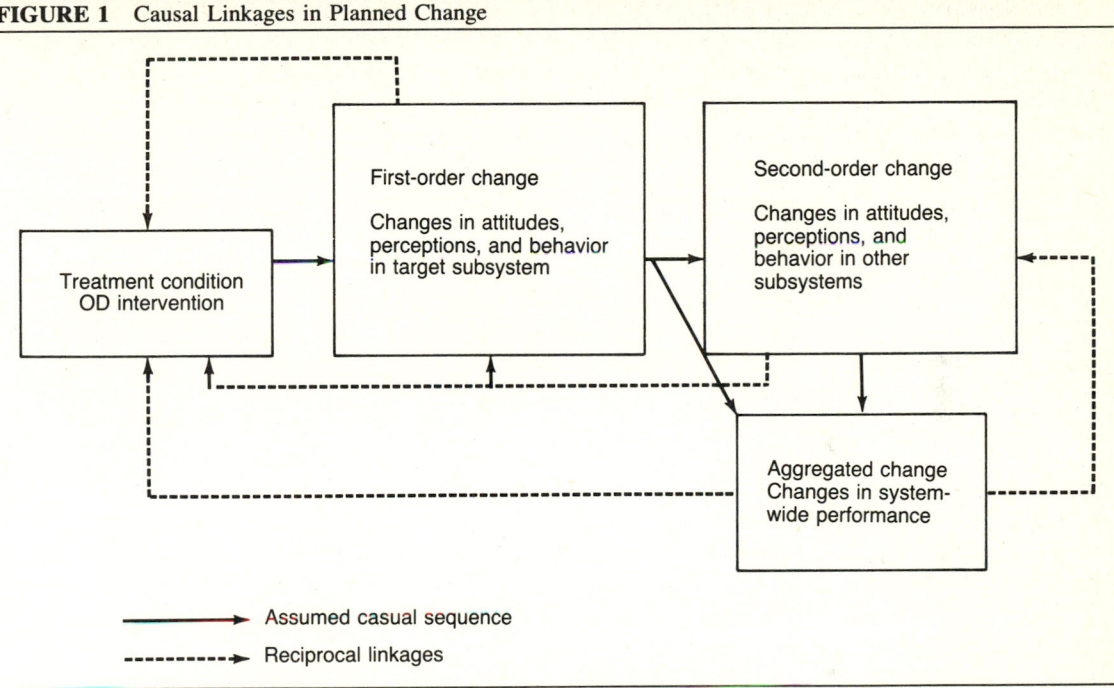

in the quality index will be observed, and (4) significant increases in the profit index will be observed.

There is a great deal of literature (Beer and Kleisath, 1967; Friedlander, 1967), which constitutes the theoretical basis for which hypotheses 1A and 1B are generated. The hypotheses about changes in production and quality rates need some further discussion, however. Changes in both the absolute level and in the variance around that level are hypothesized. Based on the kinds of impacts OD interventions are designed to produce, changes in both measures logically could be expected. Positive changes in organizational climate and supervisory behavior could be expected to lead to better planning, more cooperation, and improved problem solving and to the discussion and adoption of new ideas which would, in turn, lead to an increase in the total volume of organizational outputs, as well as increases in the predictability of the flow of outputs from period to period.

Results

The approach used to conceptualize the process of change requires that analysis of change in perceptions within the target subsystem precede analysis of change in organizational performance. To determine whether significant perceptual change took place between pre-1970, and post-1971, measurement, separate t-tests were computed for each item on the two questionnaires regarding organizational climate and supervisory behavior. In each case, one-tail tests of significance were used since the direction of change was hypothesized. The sample consisted of responses from approximately 90 production foremen. The results of these tests are presented in Tables 2 and 3.[3]

---

[3] It would have been desirable to have control group scores on these items to serve as a benchmark and to help with the potentially confounding influences of regression, history, and maturation effects. In the absence of a control group, however,

---

TABLE 2 Organizational Climate

Item	January 1970 (N = 90)		March 1971 (N = 87)		
	$\overline{X}$	SD	$\overline{X}$	SD	t-Value
Trust	3.73	1.48	4.78	1.14	5.09*
Support	3.76	1.74	4.36	1.48	2.37†
Open communications	3.04	1.61	4.64	1.38	6.83*
Understanding of objectives	4.52	1.42	5.29	1.27	3.64*
Commitment to objectives	4.40	1.49	5.17	1.26	3.58*
Handling of conflict	3.79	1.54	4.91	1.36	4.88*
Utilization of member resources	3.80	1.67	4.78	1.35	4.14*
Self-direction, autonomy	3.20	1.85	4.77	1.51	5.88*
Supportive environment	3.24	1.76	4.56	1.36	5.28*

*$p < .0005$.
†$p < .01$.

The analysis performed on the data pertaininig to organizational climate indicates that the pre-1970 and post-1971 period means for all items differed more than might be expected by chance—the items showing the least change were significant at the .01 level. In addition, the change for all items was in the predicted direction. The data relative to organizational climate suggested that after the OD program, the organizational participants perceived greater levels of trust and support in the target subsystem, conflicts were handled more openly, and the skills and resources of the participants were more fully utilized. In addition, they saw greater opportunities for autonomy and self-direction.

The supervisory behavior data is consistent with the data on organizational climate in that the pre- and post-means for all items comprising this variable differed more than might be expected by chance, and changed in the predicted direction. After the initiation of the OD program, the first-line supervisors perceived their managers as encouraging more subordinate involvement in such activities as planning, decision making, and direction of group activities. The managers were also perceived as making a greater effort to hear and understand the subordinate's position on problems and work goals as well as making increased use of subordinates' skills in problem solving.

The results provided strong support for the hypothesis that significant positive change would be observed in perceptions of organizational climate and supervisory behavior within the target subsystem. As Campbell and Dunnette (1968) have pointed out, there is a variety of problems associated with data of this sort, particularly in an N = 1 design.

---

the results of a study by Hribal (1973) in the same corporation provide insight into the nature of the movement on the team effectiveness questionnaire. He found that (1) there was significant positive movement over time on all items in the questionnaire in his experimental group, (2) with one exception, there were no significant differences between the means on the items in the experimental group at time 2 and the control group, measured at only one point in time, and (3) the means for the control group were lower than those for the experimental group at time 2 on seven out of nine items. Had the reverse been true, the regression argument would have been more persuasive. Thus, in the absence of formal controls, these results, combined with the fact that performance in the plant under study was in a downward trend in the period before initiation of the change program, suggest that the effects noted above are likely to account for only a small portion of the observed variability.

TABLE 3   Supervisory Behavior

Item	January 1970 (N = 90)		March 1971 (N = 87)		t-Value
	$\overline{X}$	SD	$\overline{X}$	SD	
Listening	3.45	1.73	4.48	1.56	3.90*
Expressing ideas to others	4.14	1.78	5.07	1.35	3.60*
Influence	2.85	1.50	4.05	1.80	4.55*
Decision making	3.43	1.55	4.40	1.63	3.82*
Relations with others	2.85	1.61	3.86	1.66	3.82*
Task orientation	4.20	1.46	4.85	1.45	2.76†
Handling of conflict	3.71	1.76	4.33	1.85	2.14‡
Willingness to change	4.28	1.40	5.00	1.36	3.26†
Problem solving	3.30	1.80	4.25	1.93	3.06†
Self-development	3.24	1.90	4.01	1.62	2.71†

*$p < .0005$.
†$p < .005$.
‡$p < .025$.

Clearly, all of them have not been solved here. The results however, suggested that it would be appropriate to analyze the hard performance data and examine indirectly the impact of the OD interventions on organizational outcomes. Had change in the target subsystem not occurred, it would not have been reasonable to attribute changes in organizational performance to the change program, at least in terms of the theoretical rationale of OD.

Data regarding the rate of production were collected on a daily basis and then averaged across the 41 months and the three time periods. The analysis is based on separate t-tests for this index that were performed on the period data—before, during, and after—to determine if significant change had taken place. In each case, one-tail tests of significance were used. A separate analysis of the data was performed for both the day and night shifts of the organization. Table 4 presents the results of these tests.

The results suggest two conclusions. First, the production rate for both shifts declined from the period before the OD program and then recovered in the period after it. The monthly production rates data (see Figure 2) indicate that the decline had begun in late 1968 and continued for seven months

into the change program. At this point, the production rates began to improve and continued improving throughout the period following the program. Second, there are significant differences between the periods before and during and those during and after the intervention, but not between the periods before and after. The production rate had not increased; it had only recovered to previous levels.

These results provide no support for hypothesis 2A. In an attempt to understand the lack of support, a secondary analysis was undertaken. The analysis was stimulated by the notion that rates of production might be outside the control of the plant studied and more a function of market conditions and corporate policy. If this were the case, the OD interventions and the kinds of change they produce could not be expected to be related to change in this particular variable. Accordingly, rates of production in the plant—number of units produced per month—were compared with rates of production for the same period measured in the same way for the industry as a whole. It was hypothesized that, if the preceding were in fact the case, the two rates would be highly correlated. The results of this analysis are presented in Table 5.

TABLE 4   Production Rates by Periods

Period	$\bar{X}$	SD	t-Value
Day shift			
Before versus during	14,039–11,649	2,639–3,234	2.19*
During versus after	11,649–13,442	3,234–1,394	1.77*
Before versus after	14,039–13,442	2,639–1,394	.71 NS
Night shift			
Before versus during	13,076–11,446	2,718–3,080	2.09*
During versus after	11,446–13,371	3,080–1,563	1.94†
Before versus after	13,706–13,371	2,718–1,563	.38 NS

Note: $\bar{X}$ = Average number of units produced per month.
*$p < .025$.
†$p < .05$.

TABLE 5   Plant–Industry Correlation Analysis

Period	Plant $\bar{X}$	SD	Industry $\bar{X}$	SD	Correlation*	
Before	52,524.4	10,337.6	660,714.1	138,531.6	.93	($N = 16$)
During	42,996.9	15,685.4	582,263.1	143,043.6	.93	($N = 13$)
After	45,700.5	8,256.3	644,293.1	104,129.8	.90	($N = 12$)
Total time	47,896.5	12,431.8	631,033.2	132,268.9	.90	($N = 41$)

*Sample size is the number of months in each time period.

The results of the correlation analysis indicate that the level of production in the plant is closely related to that of the industry. The recovery made by the plant while engaged in the OD program almost duplicates that made in the industry as a whole, apparently as a result of market conditions.

The second hypothesis about organizational performance advanced was that if the OD program improved planning, decision making, problem solving, and use of internal resources, there would be a reduction in the amount of variance in levels of production. To test the hypothesis, an analysis of the variance in the production rate was performed. The variance for the index was computed and 95 percent confidence intervals were established. Following the procedure outlined in Hays (1964, pp. 344–47), the confidence intervals were then used as a basis for determining whether there was reason to believe that the variance in the production index for the periods before and after the program were drawn from the same population. Table 6 presents the confidence intervals for the variance for the periods before intervention by shift and the variance in production levels in the period after.

For both the day and the night shifts, the lower limits of the 95-percent confidence interval for the period before are higher than the variance in the period after. It is unlikely, therefore, that the variance in the period after would fall within the boundaries of the period before. This in turn, would indicate that there is reason to believe that the variances before and after are not drawn from the same population. In addition, the F-ratios for both shifts

TABLE 6   Changes in the Variance in the Production Index

| | 95 Percent Confidence Intervals | | |
| | Before | | After |
	Upper Limit	Lower Limit	Variance
Day shift	16,678,003	3,797,901	1,945,467
Night shift	17,865,355	4,395,611	2,442,969

were significant at the .05 level. This being the case, the results are consistent with the hypothesis that the variance in production would decrease as a consequence of the OD interventions. The reduction in the variance in production levels began during the OD program and continued after its completion.

Data regarding the level of quality were collected on a daily basis and then averaged across the 41 months and the three time periods. The analysis is based on separate *t*-tests for this index—average number of units produced per month which did not require repair or rework—which were performed on the period data—before, during, and after—to determine if significant change had taken place. In each case, one-tail tests of significance were used. A separate analysis of the data was performed for both the day and night shifts of the organization. Table 7 presents the results of these tests.

The data outlined in Table 7 indicate several things. First, the number of quality units that were produced on both shifts declined significantly from the period before the OD program and then increased significantly in the period after. Second, as might be expected, the decrease in quality units parallels the decrease in total units produced that is shown in Table 4. Third, whereas the production rate had only recovered to previous levels, the number of quality units produced in the period after increased significantly—.01 for the day and .005 for the night shift—relative to the period before. The quality-quantity ratio increased from 71/100 to 92/100 for the day shift and from 60/100 to 92/100 for the night shift. The interventions, therefore, appear to have had a positive and measurable effect on levels of quality in the plant.

A more graphic representation of the relation between the time series data—production and qual-

TABLE 7   Quality Units by Periods

Shift	Period	$\overline{X}$	SD	t-Value
	Before versus during	10,133– 7,984	2,673–3,413	1.90*
Day	During versus after	7,894–12,494	3,413–1,696	4.13†
	Before versus after	10,133–12,494	2,673–1,696	2.68‡
	Before versus during	9,539– 8,070	2,657–2,823	1.44§
Night	During versus after	8,070–12,362	2,823–1,642	5.59†
	Before versus after	9,539–12,362	2,657–1,642	3.24

Note: $\overline{X}$ = Average number of units produced per month not requiring repair or rework.
*$p < .05$.
†$p < .0005$.
‡$p < .01$.
§$p < .10$.
  $p < .005$.

ity levels—and the interventions used is found in Figure 2. In this graph, only data for the day shift are presented, since there were no appreciable differences between shifts. The relatively dramatic dips in production levels in the month of August are a consequence of annual model changeovers. The strike referred to on the graph took place in another part of the corporation, but closed down the plant under investigation for the time period indicated.

To test the hypothesis that as a result of the OD change effort significant decreases in the variance in the quality levels would occur, the variance for the index was computed and confidence intervals were established—95 percent. The confidence intervals were then used as a basis for determining whether there was reason to believe that the variances in the quality index for the period before and

after were drawn from the same population. Table 8 presents the confidence intervals for the variance for the period before by shift and the variance in quality levels in the period after.

For both the day and night shifts, the lower limits of the 95-percent confidence interval for the period before are higher than the variance in the period after. Therefore, on the basis of this test, it would appear unlikely that the variance in the period after would fall within the boundaries of the period before. In other words, the variance in the period after appears to be significantly lower than in the period before. The F-ratios for both shifts were significant at the .07 level.

The final hypothesis tested focused on the relation between the change program and profit. It was hypothesized that if the OD program led to improved managerial and supervisory skills, these

FIGURE 2   Production Rates and Quality Levels (average daily rate and level per month)

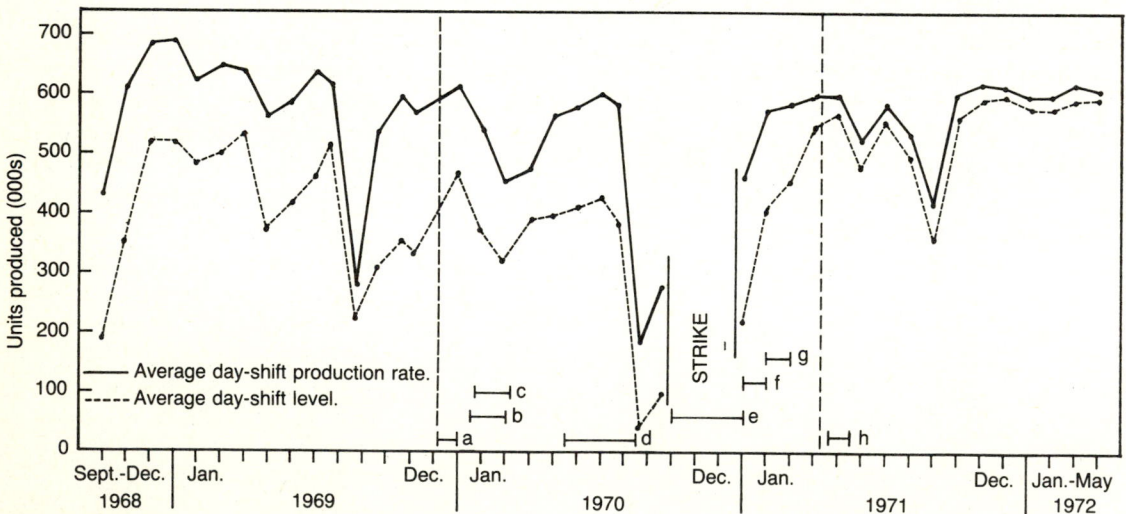

[a]Initial diagnosis.
[b]Team skills training.
[c]Data collection.
[d]Data confrontation.
[e]Action planning.
[f]Team building.
[g]Intergroup building.
[h]Data collection.

TABLE 8 Changes in the Variance in the Quality Index

| | 95 Percent Confidence Intervals | | |
| | Before | | After |
	Upper Limit	Lower Limit	Variance
Day shift	17,124,280	3,899,163	2,876,077
Night shift	16,909,725	3,850,669	2,695,506

changes would ultimately be reflected in changes in the profit index of the organization. To test this hypothesis, monthly profit or loss data for this index were averaged across the three time periods and separate *t*-tests were performed to determine if significant change had taken place. Table 9 presents the results of these tests.

These results indicate that the profit index, which was already in a negative position declined from the period before the OD program and then moved to a positive position in the period after. As Figure 3 indicates, the monthly profit level had begun to decline in late 1968 and continued until approximately the mid-point of the change effort. At this stage, the index began to improve and continued to improve throughout the period after. This trend is reflected in the fact that there are significant differences between the means for the periods during and after the program and those before and after, but not between those for the periods before and during.

Given these results, the major issue in the analysis was the extent to which change in the profit index within the organization was related to trends in the industry as a whole. This issue was critical, since the rate of production was found to be highly correlated with that of the industry. To explore it, a secondary analysis was undertaken. Monthly profit or loss data for the plant were standarized and were correlated with the rate of profit for the same period for the industry as a whole. It was hypothesized that if profit was a function of external market conditions and/or corporate policy, the two rates would be highly correlated. The correlation for the 41-month period was .48, as contrasted with the correlation of .90 for the production data. This correlation explains 24 percent of the variance in profit, which means that most of the variance, therefore, cannot be attributed to changes in market conditions or policy. Thus, it becomes more plausible to attribute change in the profit level to internal changes within the plant. Significant change did occur in the production variance, quality variance, and quality levels, and it appears highly probable that the changes in these indices contributed to the change in the profit index. This being the case, it can be concluded that the OD program did contribute to an improved profit position.

TABLE 9 Profit or Loss by Period

Period	$\overline{X}$	SD	t-Value
Before versus during	−116,995 to −133,700	165,089 − 185,514	.25 NS
During versus after	−133,700 to + 19,983	185,514 − 84,649	2.63*
Before versus after	−116,995 to + 19,983	165,089 − 84,649	2.62*

Note: $\overline{X}$ = Average monthly profit or loss. NS = not significant.
*$p < .01$.

FIGURE 3 Profit and Loss (performance to budget)

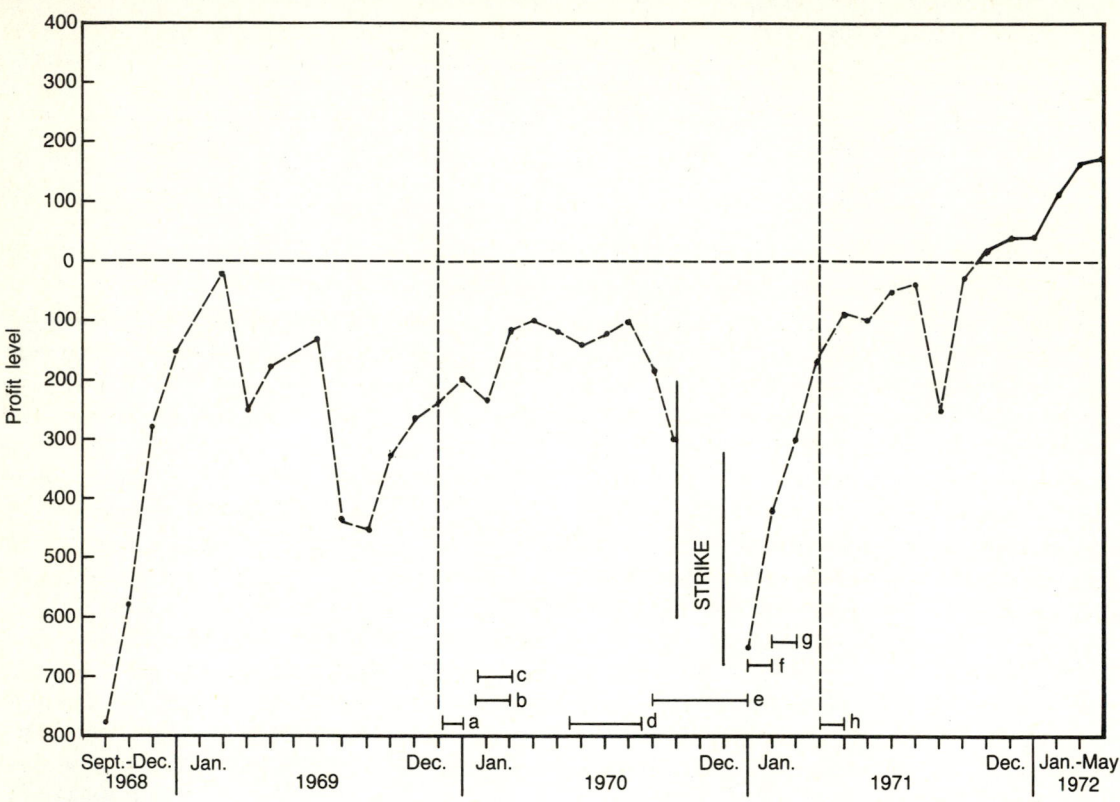

aInitial diagnosis.
bTeam skills training.
cData collection.
dData confrontation.
eAction planning.
fTeam building.
gIntergroup building.
hData collection.

Discussion

The results presented suggest two important conclusions about organization development as an organizational change modality. First, they indicate, given the limitations of the design, that the particular change program analyzed here did result in improved organizational performance, as well as positive change in attitudes and perceptions within the target subsystem. Changes in attitudes and perception of individuals were accompanied by changes in behavior, which were reflected, in turn, in changes in organizational performance. Thus, it can be concluded that OD can indeed result in directed change.

While comparative assessment of the two classes of indicators is problematic, it does appear that the extent of the impact of the program was more modest on the system performance indices than on the attitudes and perceptions of the employees. The difference in impact may be accounted for by *(a)* the fact that the OD program was not an attempt to manipulate the performance indices directly and *(b)* by expectation effects (King, 1974). The prime focus was on the attitudes, behavior, and skills of supervisory and managerial personnel and the program was designed on the explicit assumption that changes in them would ultimately lead to positive change in systemwide performance. At this point, it is impossible to determine how much of the change in the target system might be accounted for by learning or expectation effects or whether this trend would continue over an extended period of time.

Second, the results suggest some parameters within which OD may be expected to be effective and outside of which such expectations may be unwarranted. These conclusions go beyond the data at this point and the interpretation is speculative, but the assumptions are reasonable. The data indicate that perceptions of organizationally anchored phenomena—organizational climate and supervisory behavior—improved. Further, they indicate that production variance decreased, rates of quality increased, variance in quality decreased, and profits increased. Finally, there was no change in rates of production. While this latter finding was unexpected, the fact that the plant production figures were highly correlated with industry production figures for the same period led to the conclusion that rates of production are likely to be largely determined externally, by corporate policy and market conditions. Since neither of these is within the direct control of the group most directly affected by the OD program, there is no reason to expect that these rates should be affected by the interventions. Later discussion with the plant manager and his immediate staff suggested that this interpretation corresponded closely to their perception of reality.

What emerges from this combination of hypothesis testing and post hoc interpretation is the importance of target group control over variables used to assess the impact of OD interventions. Use of inappropriate indices of impact can create unrealistic expectations, both on the part of the researcher and, more important, on the part of the participants in the change program itself. The decision about what can realistically be expected must come from

the participants and evaluation must be made, at least in part, in terms of the kinds of results which they determine are significant. The notion of control is important, therefore, from the dual perspective of participants and observers. It is reasonable to expect that the managerial group in the study could influence quality levels within the plant; it is much less reasonable to expect that they could directly influence rates of production in the context in which they were operating. This finding may also have implications beyond the area of organization development. For example, managerial control may be a critical variable in the failure or success of other organizational change strategies. It may also be that the internal characteristics of an organization are more important in achieving organizational change than the particular strategy employed to produce that change. In any case the finding strongly suggests that performance in human systems is affected by a complex interplay of external as well as internal factors and that performance models which exclude either set of constraints or which are based on oversimplified causal assumptions about the directness of links between interventions and outcomes are inadequate. Much of the activity that is currently under way under the rubric of organization development is based on a closed-system approach, that is, an approach which focuses almost exclusively on internal dynamics. Because the model developed here was designed to reflect assumptions about causal linkages that are prevalent in the field, it is, in a very real sense, a closed-system model. There is an increasing awareness on the part of organizational analysts of the importance of the external environment, however, and those involved in developing planned change strategies undoubtedly will begin to make wider use of open-systems approaches in their work. As these shifts from the use of closed- to open-systems strategies occur, the model used here will have to be modified to take this movement into account.

The findings and interpretations presented here are based on one series of interventions in one industrial plant and on a research design which has both advantages and limitations. Thus, some questions remain which are discussed in detail elsewhere (Kimberly and Nielsen, 1973). Also, the approach to the analysis and interpretation of the data presented in this article was determined by a particular model that approximates the one used either explicitly or intuitively by many in the field of OD. The results of the analyses do provide some support for the tenability of the model as an abstract representation of the causal linkages involved in planned organizational change. Further support or contradictory evidence must await the results of similar studies in other organizational settings. In considering its utility, however, it is not suggested that it serve as a general model of organizational change. If, for example, one were interested in examining the relation between changes in what Hall (1973) has called the general environment and changes in organizational structure, a different model would be appropriate.

Further research on the relative efficacy of planned change efforts might profitably focus on at least two fronts. First, additional studies should be undertaken to explore more rigorously the tenability of the present model. For example, this study would have been stronger if it had been deliberately planned from the very start and it was possible to deal more effectively with the problems of control groups and soft measure instrumentation. Second, alternative models must be developed and tested in a variety of organizational settings. Only through increased efforts in careful monitoring of change processes over time can there be an understanding of the nature of planned change efforts and how to enhance their effectiveness.

References

Argyris, Chris. *Interpersonal Competence and Organizational Effectiveness*. Homewood, Ill.: Irwin-Dorsey, 1962.

Argyris, Chris. *Management and Organization Development: The Path from Xa to Yb*. New York: McGraw-Hill, 1971.

Beckhard, Richard. "An Organization Improvement Program in a Decentralized Organization." *Journal of Applied Behavioral Science* 2 (1966), pp. 3–25.

Beckhard, Richard. *Strategies of Organizational Development*. Reading, Mass.: Addison-Wesley Publishing, 1969.

Beer, Michael, and S. W. Kleisath. "The Effects of the Managerial Grid Lab on Organizational Leadership Dimensions." In *Research on the Impact of Using Different Laboratory Methods for Interpersonal and Organizational Change,* ed. S. S. Zalkind. Symposium presented at the American Psychological Association, 1967.

Bennis, Warren G. *The Nature of Organization Development*. Reading, Mass.: Addison-Wesley Publishing, 1969.

Blake, Robert R., and Jane S. Mouton. *Corporate Excellence through Grid Organizational Development*. Houston: Gulf Publishing, 1968.

Blumberg, A., and Robert T. Golembiewski. "Confrontation as a Training Design in Complex Organizations." *Journal of Applied Behavioral Science* 3 (1967), pp. 525–47.

Bowers, David G. "OD Techniques and their Results in 23 Organizations: The Michigan ICL Study." *Journal of Applied Behavioral Science* 9 (1973), pp. 21–43.

Campbell, Donald T., and J. C. Stanley. *Experimental and Quasi-Experimental Designs for Research*. Skokie, Ill.: Rand McNally, 1966.

Campbell, J. P., and Marvin D. Dunnette. "Effectiveness of T-group Experiences in Managerial Training and Development." *Psychological Bulletin* 70 (1968), pp. 73–104.

Dalton, Gene W.; Paul R. Lawrence; and Larry E. Greiner. *Organizational Change and Development*. Homewood, Ill.: Irwin-Dorsey, 1970.

Fordyce, J. K., and R. Weil. *Managing with People*. Reading, Mass.: Addison-Wesley Publishing, 1971.

French, Wendell L., and C. H. Bell. *Organization Development*. Englewood Cliffs, N.J.: Prentice-Hall, 1973.

Friedlander, Frank. "The Impact of Organizational Training Laboratories upon the Effectiveness and Interaction of Ongoing Work Groups." *Personal Psychology* 20 (1967), pp. 289–307.

Friedlander, Frank, and L. Dave Brown. "Organization Development," *Annual Review of Psychology* 25 (1974), pp. 313–40.

Hall Richard H. *Organizations: Structure and Process*. Englewood Cliffs, N.J.: Prentice-Hall, 1973.

Hays, W. L. *Statistics for Psychologists*. New York: Holt, Rinehart & Winston, 1963.

Hill, P. *Towards a New Philosophy of Management*. New York: Barnes & Noble, 1971.

Hribal, James F. "An Investigation of the Impact of an Organization Development Program in a Production Control Organization: A Post-intervention Measurement and Analysis Approach." Master's thesis, University of Illinois, Urbana, 1973.

Kegan, Daniel L. "Organization Development Description, Issues, and Some Research Results." *Academy of Management Journal* 14 (1971), pp. 453–64.

Kimberly, John R., and Warren R. Neilsen. "The Impact of Organizational Development on Organizational Productivity: An Empirical Analysis." *Proceedings: Midwest Academy of Management*, Chicago, 1973.

King, Albert S. "Expectation Effects in Organizational Change." *Administrative Science Quarterly* 19 (1974), pp. 221–30.

Likert, Rensis. *The Human Organization: Its Management and Value*. New York: McGraw-Hill, 1967.

Margulies, N., and A. P. Raia. *Organization Development: Values, Process, and Technology*. New York: McGraw-Hill, 1972.

Marrow, Alfred I.: David G. Bowers; and Stanley Seashore. *Management by Participation*. New York: Harper & Row, 1967.

Schein, Edgar H. *Process Consultation: Its Role in Organizational Development*. Reading, Mass.: Addison-Wesley Publishing, 1969.

Seashore, Stanley E., and David G. Bowers. "Durability of Organizational Change." *American Psychologist* 25 (1970), pp. 227–39.

Trist, Eric L.; G. W. Higgin; H. Murray; and A. B. Pollock. *Organizational Choice*. London: Tavistock, 1963.

Zand, D. E.; F. T. Steele; and S. S. Zalkind. "The Impact of an Organizational Development Program on Perceptions of Interpersonal, Group and Organization Function." *Journal of Applied Behavioral Science* 5 (1969), pp. 393–10.

Reading 61

COMMON BEHAVIOR CHANGES IN SUCCESSFUL ORGANIZATION DEVELOPMENT EFFORTS*

Jerry I. Porras and Susan J. Hoffer

Introduction

Observers of organization development (OD) have long noted that both research and practice in the field suffer from the lack of a unifying theory of planned change (Bennis, 1966; Burke, 1982; Golembiewski, 1979; Lundberg, 1978; Porras & Robertson, in press). This scarcity of theory can partly be explained by the field's relative youth, but more importantly by its complexity. Organizations are enormously complicated entities, interdependent with their environments and inextricably connected with the human beings making them function. Any theory of planned change must consider innumerable factors and relationships, and, to date, little agreement exists about the important variables to study or the key relationships to test. Although the body of OD theory and research is expanding, its diverse perspectives and findings are not becoming more integrated. This lack of integration is a central block to the growth of both theory and practice in the field.

At the macro level, broad agreement exists about the intended end results of planned organizational

Source: Jerry I. Porras and Susan J. Hoffer, *The Journal of Applied Behavioral Science* 22, no. 4, pp. 477–94. Copyright © 1986 by NTL Institute. All rights of reproduction in any form reserved.

* The authors thank Peter Robertson and Gary Dexter for their comments on earlier drafts of this article, and Zehava Rosenblatt for her contribution to the literature review. They also express their appreciation to the 42 OD scholars and practitioners who gave their valuable time to discuss their views on behavior change in organization development.

change efforts. Most, if not all, writers on this subject concur that OD's principal aim is to improve organizational performance (e.g., Beckhard, 1969; Beer, 1980; French & Bell, 1978; Lippitt, 1969). Others also include as a dual goal the personal development of organization members (Friedlander & Brown, 1974; Harvey & Brown, 1982; Huse & Cummings, 1985). These outcomes, however, are too global to give the field its needed focus; more operationally specific variables are required.

In searching for appropriate variables to analyze, the broad variety of models and practices for achieving OD's end results quickly becomes apparent. Theorists and practitioners differ widely in their emphases on the "action levers"—or independent variables—to be manipulated in an OD process,[1] on the interventions to use for changing the action levers,[2] and on the organization level to which change efforts are to be directed.[3]

Those in the field have also failed to agree on the relevant set of **intervening** variables in a change process. In 1967, Likert attempted to specify such a set, naming and describing the following two major categories of intervening variables: (1) attitudinal, motivational, and perceptual variables; and (2) behavioral variables (Likert, 1967). Efforts to develop Likert's set of intervening variables into an integrated theory of change have not yet succeeded, however, and the variables measured in OD research have remained diffuse and unintegrated (Porras & Berg, 1978).

This article attempts to take a first step toward an integrating focus for the field of OD. We first propose a model of organizational change in which **on-the-job behaviors of organization members** act as the important mediating variables. If behavior change can indeed serve as the needed "common denominator" for integrating diverse perspectives and focusing future theory and research, then we consider it valuable to learn whether any behavior changes are common to successful change efforts, and, if so, what those behavior changes are.[4] We next describe an investigation that sought to determine this by surveying 42 of the leading theoreticians and practitioners in the field of planned organizational change.

A Skeletal Organizational Framework and a Change Perspective

Any theory of planned change processes should begin with a model of organizations. Because a broadly accepted theory of organizations does not presently exist, however, we confront the task of developing a change theory for a phenomenon that is not yet clearly conceptualized. We therefore propose a partial model of organizations, one from which an integrated perspective of the change process might be developed. We emphasize that this is only a skeletal model, one lacking the complexity of a comprehensive theory of organizations. The model consists only of those elements we consider basic to an elemental theory of planned change.

Organizations consist of various elements constituting the overall environment of each organization member. These "system elements" can be clustered into four broad categories: (1) the organizing arrangements of a system, (2) the social factors of a system, (3) the technology of a system, and (4) the physical setting of a system (see Table 1 for definitions of each category).

TABLE 1   System Elements: Definitions and Categories

Category	Definition
Organizing arrangements	Those parts of an organization that are formally defined to provide the coordination and control necessary for organized activity. The formal organizational structure, administrative policies and procedures, formal goals and strategies, administrative systems such as the budget system, cost control and management information systems, and formal reward systems—including the evaluation and pay systems—are all examples of the organizing arrangements of an organization.
Social factors	The "human side" of an organization and all the characteristics and processes of the social system. Central to this category is the organization's culture, including the system's values, norms, stories, rituals, myths, history, symbols, and the like. Other social factors include informal networks of communication, decision making, and status; interpersonal, group, and intergroup interaction processes: and such attributes of individuals as attitudes, beliefs, and behavioral skills.
Technology	All of the factors associated with the transformation process through which a system's "inputs" are converted to "outputs." These include more traditional tools, equipment, and machinery, as well as job design, work flow design, technical procedures and systems, and the technical expertise of individual employees.
Physical setting	The configuration of the work space, its size and shape, and the relative location of work areas. This also includes architectural design, physical ambience, and interior decor.

These system elements, taken together, send organization members cues on how to behave on the job, which affect individuals' expectations about the consequences of performing various behaviors and about their own abilities to behave in ways the organization desires. Environmental cues and constraints interact with the internal needs, desires, and abilities of individuals, who end up behaving in various ways in the work setting.[5] The collective behavior of all organization members influences two primary outcomes: organization performance and individual development, which in turn influence each other (see Figure 1).

Clearly, this perspective on organizations is abbreviated and incomplete. It excludes several key factors, such as an organization's external environment and the environment's reciprocal interaction with the system elements and individuals'

behavior. These factors unquestionably affect an organization's outputs, but are often beyond its control and thus less often the targets of organizational change efforts. The model also excludes the reverse flow of effects—that is, the impact of improved organizational performance on individuals' behavior and the impact of changed behavior on the system elements—and the role of organizational purpose as an integrator of the four categories of system elements. For the purposes of this article, however, the model provides a basic framework from which to begin developing a perspective on the dynamics of planned change.

If behavior is influenced by characteristics of an organization's internal environment—that is, its system elements—then altering the system elements should lead to altered behavior on the job. This, we propose, is the function of OD interven-

---

FIGURE 1   A Skeletal Model of Organizations

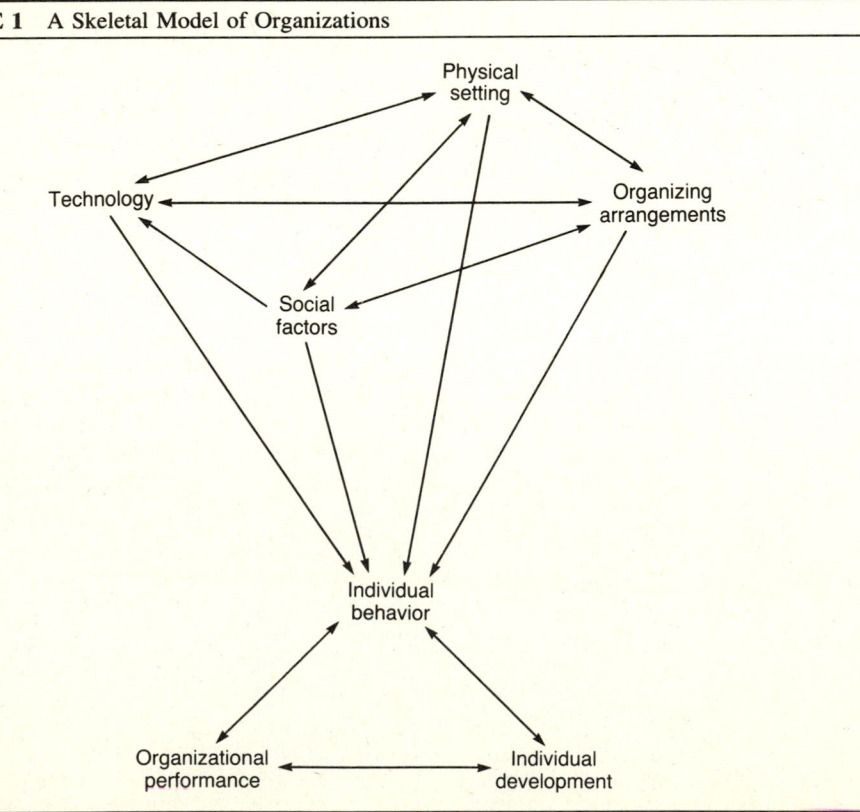

tions. Organization interventions change system elements so that they send organization members new messages about which behaviors are desired and will be rewarded. The more the pattern of the new messages is consistent and related to behaviors contributing to the desired end goals of improved organization performance and personal development, the more likely organization members are to behave in the desired ways, and the more likely the desired outcomes are to be achieved.

We provide a hypothetical example of an OD change to help clarify this perspective. Assume that an organization's present problems have been traced to ineffective communication. Persons with interdependent responsibilities are failing to share necessary information in a timely manner. The client and consultant might undertake numerous interventions aimed at the system elements implicated by the diagnosis. In the category of organizing arrangements, for example, the interventions might seek to change the organization's structure to bring interdependent units under a single manager or to alter incentive systems to reward employees who share information. Changing work area locations so that persons needing to share information work closer together would be a possible physical-setting intervention. A technological intervention might introduce a new computer system with terminals at key locations that can provide ready access to important data. With respect to social factors, team and cross-team activities might be instituted to erase interpersonal difficulties impeding communication. The common intention of these diverse actions would be to encourage organization members to share more information relevant to their jobs. Although individuals would respond to each change somewhat differently based on their own personal dynamics, one should expect an overall shift in collective information-sharing behavior. With necessary information finally reaching the right persons, heightened efficiency, fewer mistakes, and reduced levels of frustration—all factors affecting organization performance and individual development and well-being—should result.

Numerous alterations in an organization's internal environment are often required to deliver a con-

sistent message about desired behaviors. A plausible explanation for the failure of some OD efforts is that they may have failed to address enough of the system elements of an organization. This explanation is supported by evaluation research showing that large-scale, multiple-approach efforts are more successful at increasing productivity than are more limited programs focusing on only one or a few elements (Katzell & Yankelovitch, 1975).

We present a framework in which individual behavior serves as the link between organizational interventions and their subsequent outcomes. In this perspective, the role of individual behavior should serve as a central focus of any unifying theory of organizational change.[6]

Individual Behavior Change and Organization Development

Although much has been written about the need for a change process to affect behaviors (Liebowitz & De Meuse, 1982; McLean, Sims, Mangham, & Tuffield, 1982; Nadler, Cammann, & Mirvis, 1980), relatively few studies have actually measured behavioral change. Most often, reports of large-scale change projects do not even mention behaviors (Boje, Fedor, & Rowland, 1982; Patterson, 1981; Paul & Cross, 1981). Even when behaviors are mentioned, they are typically outcome behaviors such as turnover, absenteeism, or grievances (Nicholas, 1982). More frequently, OD study reports describe changes in the attitudes or awareness of individual employees (Nicholas, 1979; Porras & Berg, 1978; White & Mitchell, 1976).

Of the small number of studies dealing specifically with behavior, some examples include (1) studies counting the frequency of certain actions (Boss & McConkie, 1981; Harvey & Boettger, 1971; Moorhead, 1982; Porras, Hargis, Patterson, Maxfield, Roberts, & Bies, 1982) and (2) studies counting certain verbal statements (Greenbaum, Holden, & Spataro, 1984; Keys & Bartunek, 1979; Manz & Sims, 1982; Rasmussen, 1982; Waldie, 1981). None of the researchers, however, assert that their studies of the behaviors investigated stem from a theory that certain behaviors are generally instrumental in improving organization performance. Typically, they selected the behaviors studied because of the specific intervention employed.

In sum, OD theory and research have not examined the focal nature of behaviors in organizational change processes. Behaviors have not been identified or measured in a consistent or integrated manner, and their relationships with system elements and organizational outcomes have not been examined systematically. Identifying and operationally specifying behaviors common to successful change processes would be an initial step in this process, and could benefit the field for the following reasons.

- By providing a common denominator for linking diverse theories and approaches, developing a set of behaviors could help focus and integrate OD theory, research, and practice.
- A common set of behaviors could provide the basis for measurement instruments that could be used across organizations, thus facilitating the comparison of change efforts.
- Greater specification of desired behavioral changes would allow more rigorous evaluation of techniques for promoting change.
- Interventions could be designed and/or selected with more clarity of purpose, thus improving their chances for success.
- The behavioral specification of OD's professed goals—that is, openness and trust—would allow more focused investigation of their relationship with the ultimate organizational goals of productivity and personal development.
- An agreed-upon set of behavorial changes could lead to further investigation and understanding of the linkages among changes in the work environment and subsequent shifts in behavior.

The research reported in this article began the process of specifying behavior by asking the leaders in the OD field to identify behavioral changes common to their successful interventions.

Method

Sample

We identified 47 leaders in the field of planned organizational change, defining leaders as those who, by writing about their theoretical models, research, or interventions, had made a significant and sustained contribution to the field for at least 10 years.[7] We chose subjects to represent an approximate proportional balance along two dimensions, primary affiliation and primary approach. With respect to primary affiliation, 27 of the leaders (57%) were full-time academics who did consulting secondarily, and 20 (43%) were primarily consulting practitioners, some of whom had affiliations with universities, but not as full-time faculty members. With respect to primary approach, 30 of the leaders (64%) primarily used a human processual approach (Friedlander & Brown, 1974) and 17 (36%) primarily used a technostructural approach to change.[8]

The 47 potential participants for our study were contacted first by mail, then by telephone. Two declined to participate in the study, and we were unable to reach three, despite repeated attempts. Thus, 42 of the originally identified 47 leaders agreed to be interviewed. Two of these leaders asked to be interviewed together, since they do virtually all of their consulting as a team. Therefore, we conducted a total of 41 interviews. The five leaders who did not participate were evenly distributed across the categories of primary affiliation and primary approach. Table 2 shows the distribution of the 41 participants along these dimensions.[9]

Data

Data were gathered through telephone interviews. We developed two open-ended interview questions and pretested them with five persons who perform planned change consulting with organizations, but who were not included in the study. Letters describing our study and its intent were sent to the

TABLE 2   Distribution of Participants by Primary Affiliation and Primary Approach

	Primary Approach			
	Human Processual	Technostructural	Total	
Primary affiliation				
Academic	15 (37%)	9 (22%)	24 (59%)	
Practitioner	11 (27%)	6 (15%)	17 (41%)	
Total	26 (63%)	15 (37%)	41 (100%)	

47 potential participants. The two interview questions were provided to participants in advance so that they could think about them and make notes if they desired. The questions were the following:

QUESTION 1: In thinking about your work in planned organizational change, are there any behaviors that, in nearly all instances, you would target for change or improvement in **individuals at all levels of the organization?** If so, what are the individual behaviors that you would try to influence or change?

QUESTION 2: In thinking about your work in planned organizational change, are there any behaviors **specifically relevant** to **managers** that, in nearly all instances, you would target for change or improvement? If so, what are the managerial behaviors that you would try to influence or change?

Because some pretest subjects had initially tended to describe their models and techniques for diagnosing and intervening in organizations, the letter stressed the study's purpose of identifying the behaviors commonly occurring in systems that have undergone successful OD processes—that is, the behaviors that typically **result** from the applications of their models and techniques. Participants were asked to keep the following guidelines in mind when answering two questions:

1. Please describe the behaviors in the positive sense whenever possible. In other words, describe the behaviors you hope to achieve rather than those you wish to discourage.

2. Please be as behaviorally specific as possible. In other words, describe the behaviors you hope to achieve in terms of their observable characteristics.

Permission to record the interviews on audiotape was requested and anonymity assured, both in the letter and at the beginning of each subsequent interview.

During the interviews, the 41 participants were allowed to talk as long as they wished. The interviewer would prompt them only with open-ended, "nonleading" questions, usually to get the person interviewed to be more specific as to the behavior discussed. For example, a participant mentioning "openness" might be asked. "What would you be seeing or hearing that would tell you there was more openness in the organization?" The interviews would end when the participants were satisfied that they had listed all the behaviors thought to be common to their successful attempts at planned change.

The interviews ranged from 10 to 75 minutes in length, with the majority lasting for 20 to 40 minutes. The taped interviews were transcribed verbatim, yielding a total of 340 single-spaced pages of transcripts. To prevent any loss of a participant's meaning, care was taken to transcribe the tapes exactly and notations were made of emphatic speech, laughter, and significant pauses. A second researcher listened to the tapes, compared them to the transcripts, and made any necessary corrections.

We coded the written transcripts according to categories derived in the following manner. First, using a randomly drawn selection of approximately one-half (20) of the interviews, all behaviors mentioned were listed in the participants' own words, with remarks kept in context so that they would not lose their intended meaning. Categories of behaviors were then created by grouping all the similar behaviors listed. Once these categories were created, the remaining 21 transcripts were coded according to the presence or absence of behaviors in those categories. In some cases, data from the second set of transcripts provided information causing us to add new categories or redraw category boundaries. In such cases, transcripts that had been coded earlier were recoded according to the revised guidelines. A second rater independently coded a stratified (by interview length) random sample of six transcripts, and obtained an interrater reliability of .82.

Results

Five participants expressed some concern about the interview questions as worded, particularly with the word "target," which they thought suggested that the consultant, prior even to entering an organization, unilaterally determined the changes an intervention was to bring about. These five participants objected to this wording because they felt intervention targets should arise from entry discussions between the consultants and clients and from organizational diagnosis. Whenever this issue was raised, we clarified that we did not intend to suggest that the consultant unilaterally selected change targets a priori, but rather wanted to learn whether any behavior changes were common to successful planned change efforts, and, if so, what these behavior changes were. With this clarification, the participants who had voiced concern proceeded with the interviews.

Of the 41 participants interviewed, 40 reported that they did see behavior changes as common indicators of the success of their work with organizations.[10] Two of these 40, however, refused to elaborate on what these behaviors were. One of them said that the behavior dimensions along which individuals in different organizations commonly

improve number in the hundreds, with none more salient than the others. For this reason, and also because he thought that these dimensions had been well documented in the literature, this participant felt that listing any dimensions would be a waste of time. The second participant was worried that naming the common behaviors resulting from his successful interventions would result in their being listed out of context and made meaningless. He declined to state the behaviors for fear of their being misinterpreted. The remaining 38 participants stated that there were behavior changes to their successful interventions and specified them as well.

Common Behavior Changes: Answers to Questions 1 and 2

We identified a total of 13 categories of behavior based on the responses to Question 1, which sought common behavior changes for individuals at all levels of an organization. The responses to Question 2, which sought common behavior changes for managers, yielded nine categories. Only those categories mentioned by at least 25% of the sample (nine for Question 1 and five for Question 2) are reported. Table 3 presents the categories and their definitions. Table 4 presents specific examples of the behaviors as reported by the participants. The first two columns of Table 5 present the frequency and percentages of the responses, with the percentages based on the responses of the 38 participants who specified behaviors.

Chi square tests were conducted to determine if the participants' primary affiliations (academic versus practitioner) or primary approaches (human-processual versus technostructural) were related to the likelihood of their providing a response in a particular behavior category. No significant differences at the $p < .05$ level were found for any of the variables.

Overall Common Behavior Changes: "Boosted" Categories

One should note that three of the managerial-level behavior categories (in response to Question 2) strongly resemble three of the categories for behav-

TABLE 3 Common Behavioral Changes in Successful Organization Development Efforts: Category Definitions

Behavior Category	Description
All organization levels	
Communicating openly	Behaviors promoting or reflecting the direct giving and receiving of information relevant to getting the job done
Collaborating	Behavior promoting or reflecting the involvement of relevant persons in the processes of identifying and solving problems
Taking responsibility	Behaviors reflecting acceptance of responsibility and taking initiative in carrying out organizational tasks
Maintaining a shared vision	Behaviors reflecting a clear formulation, understanding, and commitment to organizational philosophy, values, and purposes and a commitment to high standards
Solving problems effectively	Behaviors reflecting a problem-solving orientation to difficult organizational issues
Respecting/supporting	Behaviors demonstrating respect and support for others as worthwhile individuals
Processing/facilitating interactions	Behaviors reflecting attention to and use of human process issues in one-on-one, group, and intergroup situations
Inquiring	Behaviors reflecting a probing, inquiring, diagnostic orientation to the organization and its environment
Experimenting	Behaviors promoting or reflecting an openness to trying new things
Managerial level	
Generating participation	Behaviors involving relevant persons in important organization decisions
Leading by vision	Behaviors shaping, communicating, modeling, and reinforcing organizational goals, values, purposes, and high work standards
Functioning strategically	Behaviors reflecting a systemic and long-range perspective on organizational matters
Promoting information flow	Behaviors increasing the overall amount of information in the organization
Developing others	Behaviors that develop the knowledge, skills and competency of subordinates and others in the organization

ior of individuals at all organizational levels (in response to Question 1). The category of "generating participation" resembles the category of "collaboration," and comprises managerial behaviors that encourage a collaborative work environment. Similarly, the category of "promoting information flow" resembles the managerial category of "communi-

cating openly," and "leading by vision" parallels "maintaining a shared vision" (see Table 5).

Some participants mentioned behaviors falling into the managerial side of these category pairs without mentioning the parallel behaviors of others at all organization levels. We find it difficult to imagine an organization in which promoting the

---

TABLE 4   Common Behavior Changes in Successful Organization Development Efforts as Reported by
Participants

Question 1: Common Behavior Changes for Individuals At All Organizational Levels

Communicating openly. Sharing intentions, motives, needs, feelings, and cognitions relevant to the work situation. Giving feedback that is descriptive rather than evaluative, and specific rather than general. Asking for and accepting feedback. Listening— including paraphrasing, summarizing, restating, asking for clarification, and checking out impressions. Directly confronting differences when they arise. Acting to produce structural and normative changes that lead to increased information sharing, such as loosening implicit or explicit guidelines as to who should talk to whom, and circulating minutes of meetings.

Collaborating. Solving problems as close to where they occur as possible. Discussing, planning, and readjusting organizational actions jointly and cooperatively. Holding more group and intergroup discussions and meetings. Involving critical outsiders to the organization in decisions that pertain to them. Making all the serious and creative decisions— particularly decisions where there are multiple stakeholders—in teams. Expanding influence skill beyond bargaining and authoritative commands to include softer means of influence such as seeding ideas, cajoling, and nudging. Moving away from ''oneupmanship'' and competition, and toward agreement and cooperation.

Taking responsibility. Figuring out for oneself what is necessary to be effective in one's job and taking initiative for getting whatever information, cooperation, services, or materials are needed from other relevant parties inside or outside of the organization. Asking for and taking responsibility and authority. Persisting in the struggle to make needed changes, especially in the face of frustration and ambiguity. Forming and offering more suggestions. Stating one's own contribution to a problematic situation rather than blaming others. Exhibiting behaviors that demonstrate movement along a continuum from monitoring one's own work to managing and prioritizing it to affecting the design of it to affecting its organizational context (e.g., policies and procedures) to affecting the goals and directions of the organization itself. Taking responsibility is also

reflected in expressions of interest and excitement in the work and in *decreased* approval seeking, face saving, indifference, burnout, or ''coasting.''

Inquiring. Taking multiple and numerous measures of the discrepancies between the organization's goals and its current state. Taking baselines and using surveys, audits, unobtrusive measures and control groups where possible to gain information about how the organization is functioning. Experimenting with changes in such a way that the outcome will allow causal inference and useful conclusions, soliciting information from customers, regulators, and competitors. Looking for new ideas in books, articles, technical studies, speeches, and from one another. Frequently examining and questioning structure, practices, and policies to be sure they maximize achievement of the organization's goals.

Maintaining a shared vision. Developing and communicating written statements of philosophy. Holding meetings to develop clarity of values, purpose, and the means by which the purpose will be achieved. Talking about how organization values translate into daily work behavior. Changing organizational structure, policies, and practices to reflect stated values. Having and telling a ''story,'' a shared history that gives meaning to the organization's activities. Creating rituals and ceremonies to reestablish and remember values. Setting, discussing, and reinforcing high standards.

Solving problems effectively. Defining problems from a win/win perspective, with an open-minded search for solutions that are mutually acceptable instead of pressing for one's own ''right'' answer. Taking problems out of a personal context and instead working on them vis à vis an agreed-upon superordinate goal. Keeping problem definition separate from solution seeking. Generating and simultaneously entertaining multiple explanations for a phenomenon. Generating and discussing multiple alternatives for resolving problems.

Respecting/supporting. Providing recognition for a job well done. Talking about what's going well versus what's deficient. Making use of an individual's assets

---

TABLE 4   (*continued*)

Question 1 (*continued*)

versus trying to "correct" their shortcomings. Acknowledging people. Encouraging and rewarding people for taking time for themselves and their families. Equalizing status symbols. Helping; standing in for one another. Treating people equitably. Suspending judgment when things go wrong; allowing for goodness in others and not automatically attributing negative motives. An *absence* of disrespectful and nonsupportive behaviors such as racial, ethnic, and sexist jokes, "scapegoating," and stereotyping. An *absence* of discrimination based on race, sex, or ethnicity. An *absence* of aggressive or punitive behavior.

Processing/facilitating interactions. Stopping meetings or one-on-one discussions to examine the process when things are not going well. Assigning (and rotating) the task of observing group process. Reserving time at the end of meetings to critique what was done well/poorly, what facilitated making the decision and/or doing the task, and so on. Clarifying meeting goals and purposes. Rotating the chairperson role. Making group-facilitating rather than group-

hindering interventions. Group members changing their roles in the group depending on what is needed for the group to function well. Effectively managing the process of meetings by consensually establishing relevant agendas, holding to them, and recording what is going on so people can understand and follow.

Experimenting. Taking risks. Having a "bias for action" and not waiting for the perfect design or plan before trying things out. Allowing time to meet, talk, and try new behaviors. Accepting mistakes. Rewarding good tries. Having fewer restrictions on how things get done. Eliminating symbols of conformity (e.g., three-piece suits) and structures/ policies that demand conformity (e.g., timeclocks). Deemphasizing action plans, milestones, and measurable objectives. Acting as umbrellas over experimental programs. Backing/sheltering risk takers, especially when they fail. Defending against intrusions from higher levels. Working with those who are experimenting to demonstrate that experimentation is valued and represents an investment in the organization's future.

Question 2: Common Behavior Changes for Managers

Generating participation. Linking planning and implementation in terms of time and who does it. Involving people when they have the necessary expertise, when the decision must be high quality, and when implementation depends on them. Using meetings, workshops, or a consultant to solicit input from people on proposed changes. *Not* dictating the exact way to accomplish a delegated task. Structuring the work in a way that opens possibilities for self-management by the job incumbent. Providing task and job designs that provide meaningful work, real responsibility for work outcomes, and reliable knowledge of results. Relaxing traditional authoritarian forms of control (e.g., over budgets and allocations of resources and people) and allowing workers to do more. Changing behavior *away from* unilateral edicts and imposing one's will as the basis for power and toward softer influence techniques. Facilitating more than directing.

Leading by vision. Continually articulating the organization's purpose, goals, values, and standards

and the means by which they are to be carried out operationally. Setting up feedback mechanisms to find out if the vision is being implemented. Structuring the organization and devising policies to be consistent with stated purpose, values, and goals. Reinforcing behaviors that reflect organizational values. Creating ceremonial occasions to reinforce values and goals. Scheduling their own activities to reflect commitment to values and goals. "Rolemodeling" behaviors that exemplify the organization's priorities and values.

Functioning strategically. Talking about underlying causes, interdependencies, and long-range consequences and acting accordingly. *Not* acting based on a single-function view of the organization. Having long time horizons. Resisting giving in to short term pressures for quick results in order to allow people to learn new behaviors. Deliberately and thoughtfully planning the markets and businesses in which the organization is engaged. Fitting the organizational structure to the organization's key objectives and to the nature of its businesses and markets. Planning for

TABLE 4   (*concluded*)

Question 2 (*concluded*)

the skills and knowledge required for meeting future objectives. Creating a well thought out and well understood strategic design to guide operating plans and activities.

Promoting information flow. Clearly communicating the elements of the job that need to be accomplished in order to succeed (e.g., communicating standards, goals, tolerances to be worked within, and limits of authority). Being clear about feelings, needs, expectations, commitment, and loyalty issues. Establishing multiple channels for upward, sideways, and downward communication that complement the core chain of command lines (e.g., use of task forces, advisory groups, and unions). Enhancing mechanisms and influencing social norms to promote direct cross-unit communication.

Developing others. Teaching needed skills. Helping subordinates identify needs, interests, skills, aspirations, and talents. Rewarding desired behaviors with "strokes" or whatever rewards the manager controls. Delegating tasks based on subordinates' competencies and according to a developmental plan. *Not* doing subordinates' jobs for them. Relating subordinates to a larger context. Giving people accurate information regarding their performance. Providing personal growth experiences for subordinates. Judging subordinates by their end outputs, not the methods used to produce them. Processing successes and failures with subordinates to help them learn. Helping subordinates take advantage of opportunities and resources offered by the organization.

TABLE 5   Distribution of Responses

Behavior Category	Original		Boosted	
	f	*%*	*f*	*%*
All organizational levels				
Communicating openly	26	68	30	79
Collaborating	18	47	28	74
Taking responsibility	22	58	22	58
Maintaining a shared vision	10	26	21	55
Solving problems effectively	20	53	20	53
Respecting/supporting	19	50	19	50
Processing/facilitating interactions	13	34	19	50
Inquiring	16	42	16	42
Experimenting	12	32	14	37
Managerial level				
Generating participation	22	58	—	—
Leading by vision	18	47	—	—
Functioning strategically	16	42	18	47
Promoting information flow	14	37	—	—
Developing others	11	29	11	29

flow of information would be a desired behavior for a manager, but in which communicating openly would not be desired for individuals at all levels— and indeed the goal and logical consequence of a manager's promoting the flow of information. The failure to mention these behaviors for the overall level while mentioning them for the managerial level can most reasonably be explained by the open-ended nature of the interviews, not by the purposeful intention of omitting mention of the behaviors for persons at all levels. Therefore, to generate a more inclusive list, the original data were "boosted" to reflect the total number of participants citing the behavior category in response to either Question 1 or Question 2. For example, 4 of the 14 participants who mentioned "promoting information flow" as a managerial behavior did not mention "communicating openly" in response to Question 1. Therefore, we boosted the "communicating openly" total to 30 participants (adding four to the original 26 who had previously mentioned it as a behavioral change commonly occurring in successful OD efforts).

The boosted frequencies appear in the last two columns of Table 5. Scores for "experimenting" and "processing/facilitating interaction" have been boosted in a similar manner from their parallel categories for the managerial level, "encouraging experimentation" and "running effective meetings," managerial behaviors not included in the original list because fewer than 25% of the respondents mentioned them. "Functioning strategically" is the only "reverse-boosted" category—that is, a category in response to Question 2 whose score was enhanced because of responses to Question 1—and two participants cited it as a desirable change for persons at all organizational levels, not only managers.

Discussion

Implications of the Findings

Certainly, the dimensions identified in this study are not new, for they reflect much of what has been written and practiced in OD. This is not surprising,

for the data were provided by the same persons who have shaped and guided the field. The strong humanistic flavor to the categories of behaviors is also not surprising, for humanistic values have provided the underpinnings of OD since its inception (e.g., Gellerman, 1985; Schein & Bennis, 1965; Tannenbaum & Davis, 1969). What is new about these findings is that the dimensions (1) appear together in one set, (2) are derived empirically from experts across the range of OD perspectives, and (3) are specified in behavioral terms, allowing for more agreement as to their operational meanings.

Our research was intended to coalesce thinking about the processes of planned change interventions around the common denominator of observable behavior. We believe the results provide a useful step in this direction, as discussed in our three main points below.

Leaders Agree nearly Unanimously that Common Behaviors Exist. The intellectual leaders of the field do perceive behavioral changes common to the intervention efforts: 40 of 41 persons interviewed agreed that common behavioral changes exist. Even those respondents who said they were more accustomed to thinking about their work in terms of changed values or beliefs had little trouble naming the behaviors from which they inferred these changed understandings.

Consensus Regarding the Behavior Categories Is at Least Moderate. The leaders showed a reasonable amount of consensus as to the behavior categories. Given the well-known disparity in theoretical perspectives in OD, the high level of agreement for the two most frequently mentioned categories, "communicating openly" and "collaborating" (mentioned by 79% and 74% of the respondents, respectively) is notable. The frequency of response rates for the other categories is lower; most are about 50%, making interpretation of the findings in this range more difficult. We see two possible explanations for these more moderate levels of agreement. First, the open-ended nature of the data collection procedure might have resulted in some respondents omitting to mention behaviors they would have endorsed had they been prompted with a list of specific behaviors (i.e., they may simply have forgotten to name certain behaviors). Other participants, unaccustomed to thinking in terms of behavior changes, may have been less adept at generating examples of behaviors, thus also omitting to mention behaviors they would have included had they been specifically prompted. Second, perhaps only moderate levels of consensus actually exist. In other words, even if respondents had been prompted with a list of behavior categories, their frequencies of endorsing categories might not have been much different from those obtained in our study.

A flawless argument for interpreting the midlevel frequencies as high or low cannot be made. Although both factors probably play a part, we suggest that the methodological and situational factors noted account for lower levels of agreement than actually exist, and that the frequencies obtained are at least high enough to warrant further investigation of these behaviors as potentially useful for integrating thinking and research on OD.

Theoretical Orientation and Professional Affiliation Do Not Cause Perceptions of Behaviors to Vary. This may be the most important finding—that the likelihood of mentioning a particular behavior category was independent both of a respondent's theoretical orientation (human processual versus technostructural) or professional affiliation (academic versus practitioner). This suggests that different models and approaches for changing organizations might converge to produce common behavioral changes. That is, a state of equifinality may exist in which numerous paths lead to the same changes in behavior. The potential exists, therefore, for behavior change to provide a point of focus for OD by specifying a common set of constructs upon which to anchor future theory, research, and practice.

Caveats

Although the field has much to gain from a clarification of its intervening processes and a focusing of attention on fewer, better-understood variables, some potential dangers exist. Problems could result if one takes the findings of our study too literally, without considering their context and the underlying values they reflect. Taken to the extreme, attempts could be made to achieve the identified behaviors by manipulating individuals, using means that usurp their freedom of choice. Such a practice would arrest individual growth and, in the long run at least, harm organizational performance as well. In general, if the emphasis on behavior becomes too great, the processes of OD may become so distorted that the broader meaning and purpose of the change effort will be lost. Care must be taken not to lift individual behaviors out of context. The consistency of patterns of behaviors must be observed over time to deduce the underlying system of values and beliefs manifested in the behaviors.

Another potential danger is that a focus on the behavior changes commonly occurring in OD interventions will create the mistaken impression that these are the only effects sought, or that OD efforts focus solely on facilitating interpersonal interactions and pursuing humanistic ends purely for their own sake—in the words of one participant, making the field look like "second-generation sensitivity training." For the past two decades, the field has grown and developed beyond its T Group roots. OD practitioners are applying their knowledge to implement complex technological systems and other changes vital to organizational functioning. Any move to block or ignore this healthy broadening of the field would do it a disservice. A balance of emphasis on the common and unique behavioral targets of any organizational change effort is needed.

Readers should keep these dangers in mind and make efforts to avoid them. We think, however, that the potential dangers should not deter attempts to specify the behavioral changes brought about by OD interventions. As one participant noted,

> . . . this whole OD effort is to help people be more effective in their behavior with each other. Behind that behavior may be all kinds of things that need to be looked at, but immediately it is the behavior .
> . . . One of the challenges I throw out to groups

is if when we're finished there is no behavior change, then I think you've wasted your money spending [time] here, or even having me come to talk to you . . . because what is the purpose of it all if there's no behavior change?

Future Research

We reemphasize that this study only begins the process of identifying behavior changes common to successful OD efforts by finding commonalities in the perceptions of the leaders of the field. More research is needed to determine whether the behavior changes identified here do, in fact, improve in change programs judged successful.

Empirical evidence of the relationship between changes in the behaviors and improvement in various indices of organizational performance and individual development would provide further support for finding these behaviors instrumental in achieving the end goals of organizational change efforts.[11] With empirical validation that these behaviors are (1) related to organizational performance and individual development and (2) common to successful organizational change efforts, exploration of the organizational dynamics that precipitate positive change in these behaviors could begin.

Conclusion

By identifying and specifying a set of behavioral variables fundamental to all successful organizational change processes, this study has attempted a first step toward integrating the field of organization development. The identified group of core behaviors has promise for benefiting OD theory, research, and practice. The set of behaviors might serve as a "common denominator" around which various models and research studies could be integrated and compared, providing the basis for future theory building and research. The behaviors might also provide a focus for intervention activity and suggest potential intervention "levers" by highlighting the organizational factors promoting or inhibiting desired behavior.

Notes

[1] Typical targets of change include an organization's formal structure (Davis & Lawrence, 1977; Galbraith, 1977; Lawrence & Lorsch, 1969), culture (Davis, 1984), incentive systems (Lawler, 1981), job design (Hackman & Oldham, 1980), sociotechnical "interfaces" (Cummings & Srivastva, 1977), physical settings (Steele, 1971), group processes (Dyer, 1977; Schein, 1969), interpersonal processes (Argyris, 1962; Walton, 1969), and intergroup relationships (Black, Shepard, & Mouton, 1964; Burke, 1974).

[2] Intervention technologies for changing group process, for example, include team building (Dyer, 1977), process consultation (Schein, 1969), group goal setting (Likert & Fisher, 1977), role analysis (Dayal & Thomas, 1969), and responsibility charting (Beckhard & Harris, 1977).

[3] Burke (1982) has categorized OD theory, research, and practice according to three major levels of organization: the system, the group, and the individual.

[4] Identifying such a set of behaviors does not imply that every behavior in the set is equally important for every organization or situation. Rather, the behaviors could be considered dimensions for which, in general, a higher ranking is linked to greater effectiveness and development. The emphasis on each dimension would vary across different change projects and different organizations.

[5] One should note that both the external environment of an organization and the internal psychological dynamics of each organization member also influence individual behavior. An organization cannot, however, significantly influence these factors, which thus are sources of additional variation one should consider when trying systematically to understand individual behavior on the job.

[6] Early OD perspectives have viewed the individual as the source rather than the mediator of change. Traditionally, change has been aimed toward feelings, perceptions, attitudes, awareness, ways of framing problems, and so forth. We argue that, although these intrapersonal changes may be important and necessary precursors of behavior change, unless they result in different actions—that is, different behaviors—they will not make the organization different.

[7] We doubt that the sample excluded anyone generally considered to be a "pioneer" in the field of planned change.

[8] We estimated that the ratio of OD professionals with human processual orientations to those with technostructural orientations to be about two to one. Our sample of leaders was chosen to reflect this estimate.

[9] We treat the two participants interviewed jointly as one participant.

[10] The dissenting participant said that our hypothesis was simply wrong, that there are no behavioral changes common to successful organizational interventions. For this participant, organizational change is fundamentally a nonlogical process, and therefore one that cannot be demonstrated by objective means.

The participant uses feelings, intuition, and subjective perceptions of her or his clients and her- or himself to ascertain the success or failure of a project.

[11] Effort has begun in this direction. Hoffer (1986) developed a questionnaire for measuring the identified behaviors and used it to investigate their relationship to financial performance, turnover, and other indices of effectiveness in a large, multi-unit organization. She found significant relationships between a composite index of the behaviors and financial performance and job satisfaction, but no relationship between the behavior index and employee turnover.

References

Argyis, C. (1962). *Interpersonal competence and organizational effectiveness*. Homewood, IL: Irwin.

Beckhard, R. (1969). *Organization development: Strategies and models*. Reading, MA: Addison-Wesley.

Beckhard, R., & Harris, R. (1977). *Organizational transitions: Managing complex change*. Reading, MA: Addison-Wesley.

Beer, M. (1980). *Organization change and development: A systems view*. Santa Monica, CA: Goodyear.

Bennis, W. (1966). *Changing organizations: Essays on the development and evolution of human organization*. New York: McGraw-Hill.

Blake, R., Shepard, H., & Mouton, J. (1964) *Managing intergroup conflict in industry*. Houston, TX: Gulf.

Boje, M., Fedor, D.B., & Rowland, K.M. (1982). Myth making: A qualitative step in OD interventions. *The Journal of Applied Behavioral Science, 18*(1), 17–28.

Boss, R.W., & McConkie, M.L. (1981, March). The destructive impact of a positive team-building intervention. *Group & Organization Studies,* pp. 45–56.

Burke, W.W. (1974). Managing conflict between groups. In J. D. Adams (Ed.), *New technologies in organization development,* (pp. 255–268). San Diego, CA: University Associates.

Burke, W.W. (1982). *Organization development: Principles and practices*. Boston: Little, Brown.

Cummings, T., & Srivastva, S. (1977). *Management of work: A socio-technical systems approach*. San Diego, CA: University Associates.

Davis, S. (1984). *Managing corporate culture*. Cambridge, MA: Ballinger.

Davis, S., & Lawrence, P. (1977). *Matrix*. Reading, MA: Addison-Wesley.

Dayal, I., & Thomas, J.M. (1968). Operation KPE: Developing a new organization. *The Journal of Applied Behavioral Science, 4,* 473–506.

Dyer, W.G. (1977). *Team building: Issues and alternatives*. Reading, MA: Addison-Wesley.

French, W.L., & Bell, C.H. (1978). *Organization development: Behavioral science interventions for organization improvement* (2nd ed.). Englewood Cliffs, NJ: Prentice-Hall.

Friedlander, F., & Brown, L.D. (1974). Organizational development. *Annual Review of Psychology, 25,* 313–316, 320–331, 336–341.

Galbraith, J. (1977). *Designing complex organizations*. Reading, MA: Addison-Wesley.

Gellerman, W. (1985). Values and ethical issues for human system development practitioners. In R. Tannenbaum, N. Margulies, F. Massarik, & Associates (Eds.). *Systems development*. San Francisco: Jossey-Bass.

Golembiewski, R. (1979). *Approaches to planned change*. New York: Marcel Dekker.

Greenbaum, H.H., Holden, E.J., Jr., & Spataro, L. (1984, March). Organization structure and communication processes: A study of change. *Group & Organization Studies, 8*(1), 61–82.

Hackman, J.R., & Oldham, G.R. (1980). *Work redesign*. Reading, MA: Addison-Wesley.

Harvey, D.F., & Brown, D.R. (1982). *An experiential approach to organization development* (2nd ed.). Englewood Cliffs, NJ: Prentice-Hall.

Harvey, J.B., & Boettger, C.R. (1971). Improving communication within a managerial work-group. *The Journal of Applied Behavioral Science, 7,* 164–179.

Hoffer, S.J. (1986). *Behavior and organizational performance: An empirical study*. Unpublished doctoral dissertation. School of Education. Stanford University.

Huse, E.F., & Cummings, T.G. (1985). *Organization development and change* (3rd ed.). St. Paul, MN: West.

Katzell, R.R., & Yankelovitch, D. (1975). *Work, productivity, and job satisfaction: An evaluation of policy-related research*. Princeton, NJ: The Psychological Corporation.

Keys, C.B., & Bartunek, J.M. (1979). Organization development in schools: Goal agreement, process skills, and diffusion of change. *The Journal of Applied Behavioral Science, 15*(1), 61–78.

Lawler, E.E. (1981). *Pay and organization development.* Reading, MA: Addison-Wesley.

Lawrence, P.R., & Lorsch, J.W. (1969). *Developing organizations: Diagnosis and action.* Reading, MA: Addison-Wesley.

Liebowitz, S.J., & De Meuse, K.P. (1982). The application of team building. *Human Relations, 35*(1), 1–18.

Likert, R. (1967). *The human organization: Its management and value.* New York: McGraw-Hill.

Likert, R., & Fisher, S.M. (1977, January–February). MBGO: Putting some spirit into MBO. *Personnel, 54*(1), 40–47.

Lippitt, G. (1969). *Organization renewal.* New York: Appleton-Century-Crofts.

Lundberg, C. (1978). *Organization development theory: A strategic and conceptual appraisal.* Unpublished manuscript. Oregon State University.

Manz, C.C., & Sims, H.P. (1982). The potential for "groupthink" in autonomous work groups. *Human Relations, 35*(9), 773–784.

McLean, A.J., Sims, D., Mangham, I., & Tuffield, D. (1982). *Organization development in transition.* New York: Wiley.

Moorhead, G. (1982, October). Groupthink: Hypothesis in need of testing. *Group & Organization Studies,* pp. 429–444.

Nadler, D.A., Cammann, C., & Mirvis, P.H. (1980). Developing a feedback system for work units: A field experiment in structural change. *The Journal of Applied Behavioral Science, 16*(1), 41–62.

Nicholas, J.M. (1979). Evaluation research in organizational change interventions: Considerations and some suggestions. *The Journal of Applied Behavioral Science, 15*(1), 23–40.

Nicholas, J.M. (1982). The comparative impact of organization development interventions on hard criteria measures. *Academy of Management Review, 7*(4), 531–541.

Patterson, K.J. (1981, March). The failure of OD success. *Group & Organization Studies,* pp. 5–15.

Paul, C.F., & Cross, A.C. (1981). Increasing productivity and morale in a municipality: Effects of organizational development. *The Journal of Applied Behavioral Science, 17*(1), 59–78.

Porras, J.I., & Berg, P.O. (1978, April). The impact of organization development. *Academy of Management Review,* pp. 249–266.

Porras, J.I., & Robertson, P.J. (In press.). A typology of organization development theory: A description and evaluation. In R.W. Woodman & W.A. Pasmore (Eds.). *Research in organizational change and development.* Greenwich, CT: JAI Press.

Porras, J.I., Hargis, K., Patterson, K.J., Maxfield, D., Roberts, N., & Bies, R.J. (1982). Modeling-based organizational development: A longitudinal assessment. *The Journal of Applied Behavioral Science, 18*(4), 433–446.

Rasmussen, R.V. (1982, March). Team training: A behavior modification approach. *Group & Organization Studies,* pp. 51–66.

Schein, E.H. (1969). *Process consultation: Its role in organization development.* Reading, MA: Addison-Wesley.

Schein, E.H., & Bennis, W.G. (1965). *Personal and organizational change through group methods: The laboratory approach.* New York: Wiley.

Steele, F. (1971). *Physical settings and organization development.* Reading, MA: Addison-Wesley.

Tannenbaum, R., & Davis, S.A. (1969). Values, man, and organizations. *Industrial Management Review, 10*(2), 67–83.

Waldie, K.F. (1981, December). The learning potential of the dominant personality within small intensive-training groups. *Group & Organization Studies,* pp. 456–463.

Walton, R.E. (1969). *Interpersonal peacemaking: Confrontations and third party consultation.* Reading, MA: Addison-Wesley.

White, S., & Mitchell, T. (1976). Organization development: A review of research content and research design. *Academy of Management Review, 1,* 57–73.

Reading 62

THE IMPOSSIBILITY OF USING RANDOM STRATEGIES TO STUDY THE ORGANIZATION DEVELOPMENT PROCESS*

R. J. Bullock and Daniel J. Svyantek

Introduction

Reviewers of organization development (OD) research have consistently concluded that "most OD research uses poor designs" (White & Mitchell, 1976, p. 70), that "the quality of OD research methodology is spotty" (Porras & Berg, 1978, p. 151), and that most OD research does not use "designs rigorous enough to adequately determine the outcomes of the OD process" (Morrison, 1978, p. 42). Particularly noteworthy has been the lack of true experiments in OD research. After searching all published bibliographies, 14 reviews of the literature, 3 computerized bibliographies plus standard computer indices, and 23 research journals, Porras and Berg (1978) report: "No study used a true experimental design" (p. 156). Similarly, Margulies, Wright, and Scholl (1977) found no true experiments of the six interventions they studied, and White and Mitchell (1976) found no true experiments in their facet analysis of OD research; nor were any true experiments of team building found by Woodman and Sherwood (1980) or by DeMeuse and Leibowitz (1981).

The lack of true experimental designs in OD research can be attributed to many things, including the newness of the field of OD (Margulies et al., 1977, p. 431), the difficulties of field research (Porras & Berg, 1978, p. 157), the lack of resources available to OD practitioners (Morrison, 1978, p. 65), bias by OD evaluators (Terpstra, 1981), and simply a "lack of motivation" to do the job correctly (DeMeuse & Leibowitz, 1981, p. 373). Given that much effort has been applied to OD research, and given that all of the possible explanations are potentially solvable problems, the persistent absence of true experiments in OD research suggests that a more fundamental problem may be involved.

To explore this possibility, this article examines the compatibility of the OD process with the random processes required for rigorous, true experiments. The sections below consider the nature of OD and random strategies separately and together, discussing an experimental OD field study to support the argument that random methods do not fit the OD process. The final section of this article considers the implications of the fundamental incompatibility of the OD process with random processes.

Nature of the OD Process

The nature of organization development has been widely discussed in the literature (see French, Bell, & Zawacki, 1983, pp. 5–60, for a review). For the analysis presented in this article, two fundamental characteristics of the OD process are particularly relevant. First, OD seeks collaboratively planned change, using joint decision making among members of the organization to introduce and man-

Source: R.J. Bullock and Daniel J. Svyantek, *The Journal of Applied Behavioral Science* 23, no. 2, pp. 255–262. Copyright © 1987 by NTL Institute. All rights of reproduction in any form reserved.

*The authors are grateful to Bob Pritchard, Chuck DeBettignies, John Nicholas, Jerry Franklin, Newt Margulies, Bob Golembiewski, and the *JABS* reviewers for their helpful comments and suggestions on earlier drafts of this article.

age the change process. This collaboration is often facilitated by internal or external OD practitioners, who foster informed choice among intervention alternatives and commitment to those choices (Argyris, 1970).

Second, the diagnosis characteristic of OD is relevant, as the selection of OD techniques is based on a system diagnosis—also collaborative— of the organization and its environment (see French, Bell, & Zawacki, 1983, pp. 123–145, for a review). Writing and research in OD has consistently emphasized the need for diagnosis, whose role has become more important as the field develops (see Seashore, Lawler, Mirvis, & Cammann, 1983).

Nature of Random Processes

In experimental terms, random means that each element of a set has an equal chance of being chosen for some purpose. Two random strategies are used in experimental design. First, random selection is used to develop a sample from some defined population of interest. By choosing the sample randomly, the researcher has a basis for claiming external validity of the findings of the study—that is, that the findings for the sample can be generalized to the entire population. Experimental design experts have emphasized the importance of random selection in rigorous research, even though it is often impossible to obtain (Campbell & Stanley, 1963, p. 19; Keppel, 1982, p. 18; Myers, 1972).

Second, once a sample has been determined, members of the sample can be randomly assigned to either the experimental or the control conditions used in the research. This random strategy, crucial for internal validity, serves as the basis for eliminating alternative hypotheses that the findings of the experiment resulted from factors other than those dictated by the experiment (Campbell & Stanley, 1963, p. 2).

Random assignment is so important that any nonrandom process occurring naturally needs to be "undone" in the experiment. Keppel (1982, p. 17) explains:

> Any factor which does not vary randomly in its "natural state" must be subjected to a process of neutralization consisting in essence of the superimposition of a random process upon the assignment of testing sessions and subjects to the treatment conditions. That is, variables that fluctuate in a systematic fashion during the course of the experiment must be transformed into variables that now fluctuate *unsystematically* with respect to their association with the treatment condition. (emphasis in original)

Random selection and random assignment are important elements of traditional experimental design. Indeed, random strategies are necessary conditions for a true experiment. Failure to use random selection and random assignment produces pre-experimental designs, or at best quasi-experimental designs, which are considered less rigorous than true experiments.

The OD-Random Strategies Fit

Random selection and random assignment to interventions require that the decision to participate in an intervention not be based on information that might increase or decrease the possibility that an intervention be used for a given organization. Random strategies, such as tossing a coin or using a table of random numbers, require that all "nonrandom information" be ignored so as to rule out the alternative hypothesis that effects of the research were determined by some factor other than that dictated by the experiment. Thus, the use of random strategies requires unilateral control of the situation by someone or some group concerned with statistical efficiency, such as a researcher (e.g. in a laboratory study), top management (e.g., in an autocratic organization), or those capable of physical force (e.g., in a military organization).

OD interventions, however, are based on participant commitment to choices based on valid information (Argyris, 1970). OD interventions emphasize the collection of diagnostic information, decisions based on that information, and commitment to these decisions. Indeed, the essence of OD is this collaborative, diagnosis-based process (see Burke & Hornstein, 1972; French & Bell, 1978, French et al., 1983, p. 1), not standard techniques, as some suggest (DeMeuse & Leibowitz, 1981, p. 372).

OD processes are the opposite of random processes: OD requires collaborative, diagnosis-based processes, whereas random processes require unilateral control. The goal of the OD process is to give people control over their lives at work and the diagnostic problem-solving skills necessary to use that influence more effectively. Because random strategies require total control by the researcher, their use prevents the OD process from occurring. If an OD process were already in effect, forcing random processes onto the study to neutralize the nonrandom diagnostic effects would change the process to something other than OD.

One must understand that we reject random strategies for research on the OD process on logical grounds, not logistical grounds. A common perspective among researchers is that random assignment is important in laboratory studies, but less important in field studies because random strategies are difficult to use in real organizations. Cook and Campbell (1979), for example, assert that "the desirability of randomized experiments is less in question than their feasibility" (p. 385), devoting an entire chapter to circumventing the practical difficulties of random strategies. The OD literature has also paid attention to solving logistical problems of random strategies. Porras and Berg (1978) suggest that experimental OD research be conducted in organizations with many comparable subsystems (e. g., Porras & Wilkins, 1980), such as the branches of a large bank (see Nadler, Mirvis, & Cammann, 1976), and note that one of the major benefits of using comparable units of a large system is that "Random selection of organizational units for inclusion in a research/OD project is also more plausible" (Porras & Berg, 1978, p. 17). We argue that even if researchers had enough control of the situation to use random strategies effectively, they could not use them to study the OD process.

To randomly assign persons to OD *techniques* is both logically and practically possible, but to assign them to the OD *process* is not. A laboratory study could, for example, randomly assign two different versions of team building to groups of students. This would differ, however, from studying the OD team-building process of involving an interdependent work group in deciding whether a task-based or an interpersonal, process-based team-building approach would better suit its situation, or whether the group's assessment of its situation would lead it to have any interest in or commitment to pursuing a team-building approach at all. As Golembiewski has pointed out, dictators can and have used OD techniques, but by no means have they used the OD process. Unfortunately, the myth that the technique *is* the process continues to be pervasive among non-OD professionals and researchers.

Consider, for example, the design of a study using a sample of organizations with the same needs and requiring the same intervention, with half of the organization randomly assigned to receive the intervention and the other half randomly assigned to not receive the intervention, or to receive it later. In this design, the random strategy would be applied *after* the important process of involving people in diagnostic problem solving about their situation. Thus, one could not use this design to understand the important initial phases of exploration or diagnostic planning (see Bullock & Batten, 1985, for a review), although one could use the design to study the effects of implementing the OD technique.

To study the entire OD process, one would have to use random strategies prior to entry, because even the initial psychological contract process is designed to be part of the OD process. An alternative design might use an expert to diagnose the situation and plan the intervention so that it minimized the effects of these phases, but this design would also fail to capture the OD process. This latter approach is similar to designs used in medical research, in which persons with a particular ailment are randomly assigned to receive either the medicine or a placebo so as to answer the question: What are the effects of this treatment for those who need it? Kaplan (1979), for example, suggests that process consultation techniques would not generally improve the performance of groups (e.g., as used in laboratory studies) unless the groups were experiencing significant process difficulties prior to the intervention. The essence of the OD process, then, is not a pill or a technique, even when applied as necessary, but rather a process of organizational learning. Even if a specific technique has initially negative results, the OD process has succeeded if the organization has learned the self-corrective process of collaborative, diagnosis-based intervention.

Some data are available to answer the empirical question of what happens when persons are randomly assigned to OD techniques. Based on psychological reactance theory predictions that negative consequences result when persons' choices are threatened or removed, Bullock (1986) hypothesizes that randomly assigning employees to OD techniques would have a negative effect on their attitudes, even if the OD technique itself had positive effects. This hypothesis was tentatively supported by the three relevant studies in the literature. Similar data are reported by Bullock and Svyantek (1985), who found random assignment to be the only indicator of methodological rigor that significantly correlated with the outcomes of success or failure for 90 intervention studies: Studies using random assignment showed more *negative* results. Thus, some evidence suggests that the random processes themselves produce negative results when applied to OD techniques, although answering this empirical question is not directly relevant to the issue of attempting to use random strategies to study the OD process.

Illustrative Example

We illustrate the logic of this analysis with an empirical study from the OD literature. Adams and Sherwood (1979) found a clear example of the incompatibility of OD and random processes in their study of the effects of survey feedback on four Army companies, all engineering units in the same battalion. Although random selection from the universe of possible Army units was not feasible, assignment to experimental and control conditions within the chosen units was random (Adams, 1977, pp. 38–39). Two companies were "randomly selected to participate" (Adams & Sherwood, 1979,

p. 172) in the feedback intervention, another was given a placebo—a training program—and a fourth, undergoing no intervention, served as a control group. The researchers identified commitment as a key factor in the negative results they obtained:

> Permission was granted by the top leaders of the battalion. However, no such permission was sought from the company commanders nor from the platoon leaders, although the senior author did discuss the purpose of the research with each company commander. In these meetings, the company commanders were merely informed. . . . Permission, then was guaranteed by the top authority; commitment on the part of a company platoon, and squad leaders was never secured. Herein lies a critical problem. The nature of survey feedback requires that there be commitment on the part of the participants. (pp. 176–178)

This example illustrates that attempting to use random strategies in OD research changes the process of survey feedback (see Bullock & Bullock, 1984) to something other than an OD process.

Summary and Implications

The OD process by definition seeks collaborative, diagnosis-based organizational change. The use of random strategies to study this process is inappropriate because such use fundamentally changes the nature of the OD process to something other than OD. It is never appropriate to attempt to use random selection or random assignment to study the OD process. We base this conclusion not on the argument that random strategies are too difficult for field research, but rather on the idea that using OD and random processes simultaneously is logically impossible. This conclusion is consistent with the literature describing attempts to use random strategies to study the OD process and with literature reviews that consistently report a lack of true experiments in OD. Given this primary conclusion, three implications follow.

First, a true experiment involving the OD process can never take place. True experiments require random strategies, and since these cannot be used with OD, a true experiment involving the OD process is logically impossible. Research that uses random strategies can study the effects of random assignment on OD techniques, but such research cannot truly study the OD process per se.

Second, OD research rigor will not improve in the future if random strategies are used as criteria of research quality. Some observers (Margulies et al., 1977, p. 431; White & Mitchell, 1976, p. 70) have suggested that because OD is a relatively new field, the rigor of experimental design may improve as the field matures. DeMeuse and Leibowitz (1981, p. 372) report, however, that this has not occurred, at least not for team building: ". . . research in team-building does not appear to be gaining in rigor, despite claims that it should." In this article, we suggest that greater rigor through random strategies will not be obtained for team building, or any other area of OD, because random strategies will not be any more relevant in the future than they are today.

Finally, our analysis suggests that the conclusions of past evaluations of OD research must be revised. Research methods and standards have become the foundation of the social sciences, and the subject matter is often force-fitted to the method. Previous evaluators of OD have accepted these methods and standards as given and concluded that OD has not been studied rigorously. We suggest instead that the theoretical domain of OD be accepted as given and that methods and standards be closely examined for relevance. The method of random strategies, a crucial component of standard experimental design, is simply not appropriate. Conclusions about OD research based on the uncritical acceptance of traditional social science research criteria may be inaccurate and deserve reconsideration and revision. No one has ever suggested that a rigorous OD researcher randomly select organizations from across the country—including, for example, volunteer organizations, work organizations, political organizations, health service organizations—then randomly assign them to OD interventions (the local Boy Scout troop to management by objectives, General Motors to team building, the Ku Klux Klan to T groups, the nursing home to career planning) designed to fundamentally change the organizations as social systems,

and with that change to alter the lives and careers of individuals. Yet we continue to evaluate OD research as if such an action were reasonable.

Conclusion

The time has come for a long, serious look at the limits and relevance of traditional research methods and standards for OD. DeMeuse and Leibowitz (1981) echo other OD reviewers in concluding: "The challenge for future research remains in more rigorous methodology" (p. 373). With respect to our analysis, the most significant challenge is not to increase rigor by following traditional standards, but to develop new research methods and standards that are relevant to OD (see Argyris, 1968).

Examining alternatives to meet this challenge is beyond the scope of this article, but we briefly mention two possibilities for future work. The first is to develop more rigorous qualitative methods. Techniques such as participant observation and the content analysis of meetings and minutes are imminently applicable to studies of planned change processes in organizations, but to date these methods have not gained a foothold according to the empirical organizational literature. Van Maanen, Dabbs, and Faulkner (1979) conclude that even after years of calls for more qualitative research, "virtually any qualitative method applied to the analysis of organizational matters is an innovation" (p. 12). The ground is fertile.

A second possibility is to use the meta-analysis method adapted to OD case studies. Bullock and Tubbs (1987) have developed a detailed methodology for aggregating results across case studies and estimating the sizes of effects, not only for an OD effort as a whole, but also for particular components of the intervention and intervention-situation interactions.

Regardless of the approach used, much attention is needed to establish research methods that are relevant to OD yet rigorous by social science standards. As a field, OD has the potential for achieving social progress simultaneously with scientific progress, but current research methods have promoted a schism rather than a bridge between the scientist and the practitioner. By closely examining current research methods, the ground can be broken and the road paved for developing new, rigorous, and relevant methods for OD research.

References

Adams, J. J. (1977). *An evaluation of organization effectiveness: A longitudinal investigation of the effects of survey feedback as an action research intervention on unit efficiency, employee affective response, intergroup relations and supervisory consideration in the U.S. Army.* Doctoral dissertation, Purdue University. (University Microfilms No. 78–13.016)

Adams, J. J., & Sherwood, J. J. (1979). An evaluation of organizational effectiveness: An appraisal of how Army internal consultants use survey feedback in a military setting. *Group & Organization Studies, 4,* 170–182.

Argyris, C. (1968). Some unintended consequences of rigorous research. *Psychological Bulletin, 70,* 185–197.

Argyris, C. (1970). *Intervention theory and method: A behavioral science view.* Reading, MA: Addison-Wesley.

Bullock, R. J. (1986). The effects of attitudes on random assignment to OD interventions. *Public Administration Quarterly, 10,* 310–324.

Bullock, R. J., & Batten, D. (1985). It's just a phase we're going through: A review and synthesis of OD phase analysis. *Group & Organization Studies, 10,* 383–412.

Bullock, R. J., & Bullock, P. F. (1984). Pure science vs. science-action models of data feedback: A field experiment. *Group & Organization Studies, 9,* 7–27.

Bullock, R. J., & Svyantek, D. (1985). Analyzing meta-analysis: Potential problems, an unsuccessful replication, and evaluation criteria. *Journal of Applied Psychology, 70,* 108–115.

Bullock, R. J., & Tubbs, M. E. (1987). The case meta-analysis method for OD. In R. W. Woodman & W. A. Pasmore (Eds.) *Research in organizational change and development.* Greenwich, CT:JAI Press.

Burke, W., & Hornstein, H. A. (1972). *The social technology of organization development.* Fairfax, VA: Learning Resources.

Campbell, D. T., & Stanley, J. C. (1963). *Experimental and quasi-experimental designs for research.* Chicago: Rand-McNally.

Cook, T. D., & Campbell, D. T. (1979). *Quasi-experimentation: Design and analysis issues for field settings.* Chicago: Rand McNally.

DeMeuse, K. P., & Leibowitz, S. J.(1981). An empirical analysis of team-building research. *Group & Organization Studies, 6,* 357–378.

French, W. L., & Bell, C. H. (1978). *Organization development.* Englewood Cliffs, NJ: Prentice-Hall.

French, W. L., Bell, C. H., & Zawacki, R. A. (1983). *Organization development: Theory, practice, and research.* Dallas, TX: Business Publications, Inc.

Kaplan, R. E. (1979). The conspicuous absence of evidence that process consultation enhances task performance. *Journal of Applied Behavioral Science, 15,* 346–360.

Keppel, G. (1982). *Design and analysis: A researcher's handbook.* Englewood Cliffs, NJ: Prentice-Hall.

Margulies, N., Wright, P. L., & Scholl, R. W. (1977). Organization development techniques: their impact on change. *Group & Organization Studies, 2,* 428–448.

Morrison, P. (1978). Evaluation in OD: A review and an assessment. *Group & Organization Studies, 3,* 42–70.

Myers, J. L. (1972). *Fundamentals of experimental design.* Boston: Allyn & Bacon.

Nadler, D. A., Mirvis, P. H., & Cammann, C. (1976). Developing a feedback system for work units: A field experiment in structural change. *Journal of Applied Behavioral Science, 16,* 41–62.

Porras, J. I., & Berg, P. O. (1978). Evaluation methodology in organization development: Analysis and critique. *Journal of Applied Behavioral Science, 14,* 151–174.

Porras, J. I., & Wilkins, A. (1980). Organization development in a large system: An empirical assessment. *Journal of Applied Behavioral Science, 16,* 506–534.

Seashore, S. E., Lawler, E. E., Mirvis, P. H., & Cammann, C. (1983). *Assessing organizational change: A guide to methods, measures, and practices.* New York: Wiley-Interscience.

Terpstra, D. E. (1981). Relationship between methodological rigor and reported outcomes in organization development evaluation research. *Journal of Applied Psychology, 66,* 541–543.

Van Maanen, J., Dabbs, J. M., & Faulkner, R. R. (1982). *Varieties of qualitative research*. Beverly Hills: Sage.

White, S. E., & Mitchell, T. R. (1976). Organization development: A review of research content and research design. *Academy of Management Review, 1,* 57–73.

Woodman, R. W., & Sherwood, J. J. (1980). Effects of team development intervention: A field experiment. *Journal of Applied Behavioral Science, 16,* 211–227.

PART 10

Problems and Prospects in Organization Development

Contemporary organization development is beset with issues and dilemmas that will greatly challenge practitioners and scholars in the years ahead. This is partly because it is a young field only now approaching maturity, and undoubtedly partly because of its eclectic nature. Contemporary OD practice borrows from social psychology, counseling psychology, organization theory, family group therapy, human resources management, group dynamics, management and administration, and other disciplines. Any attempt at an amalgamation of insights from such a spectrum of fields to develop effective interventions for ongoing organizations is bound to create many challenges. For example, how non-directive can the OD consultant afford to be if the client is talking about establishing benefits or privileges in one group without being cognizant of potential perceived inequities by other groups? Counseling psychology has something to say about the utility of a supportive nondirective consultation style, but human resources management and social psychology have something to say about cognitive dissonance and inequity. Reconciling the two conflicting action implications may be difficult in such a situation. What is the optimal mix of the source of authority in a given organization in terms of authority based on expertise, authority based on position, and authority based on group consensus? Organization theory, "principles of management," and group dynamics may have insights about such matters that are not easily reconciled. How does OD relate to various movements or contemporary areas of emphasis like "quality of work life" or behavior modification? Is OD the same thing? Different? How can one articulate the differences or similarities? What are the dangers in not doing so?

But OD practice is also beset with many problems and issues because it inevitably affects people's lives, and sometimes deeply. We would like to think that people are usually affected positively, and we believe this to be so, but questions of ethics, of values, of what is helpful and what is hurtful, must and do arise. How much manipulation is there in the particular OD intervention in the particular context; that is, to what extent is there a hidden agenda in the use of the intervention, or to what extent is the nature of the technique or its consequences kept from the participants? What should be the depth of an intervention in order to be both efficacious and at the same time not harmful? Should the consultant attempt to interpret and surface resistances? Under what circumstances is feedback constructive? How much can, or should, the OD consultant be aligned with the exercise of power in the organization? What should the OD consultant's training be? And how does one know when a consultant is qualified to practice? These are not simple matters.

Other issues have to do with the relationship of OD to culture. For example, what forms of OD bring about a deep change in the culture of an organization and what forms result in only modest changes in organizational functioning? To what extent does OD, as practiced in the United States, need to be modified when applied in other countries?

Some of these issues have been discussed earlier in the book; for example, issues centering on the depth of intervention and the interpretation of resistances. In this section of the book we conclude our overview of OD by presenting four essays that examine a number of additional key issues about the present and future state of OD.

William G. Dyer and W. Gibb Dyer, Jr., in their essay, "Organization Development: System Change or Culture Change?" assert that most OD efforts result in changes in an organization's system, not its culture. They define the two types of change, and present two case studies to illustrate their points. In "Ethical Dilemmas in Various Stages of Organizational Development," Louis White and Kevin Wooten present 5 categories of ethical dilemmas in OD and then 31 specific ethical dilemmas that tend to occur at various stages in the OD process.

Differences in national culture are the focus of the third essay. In "Organization Development and National Culture: Where's the Fit?" Alfred Jaeger compares the underlying values of OD with the cultural characteristics of 40 countries. Jaeger uses the dimensions developed by Hofstede[1] in this comparison. In this essay, Jaeger provides guidelines for adapting OD to different cultures. Finally, W. Warner Burke looks at the past and future of OD and concludes that the field is alive and well and that the future is full of opportunity. He provides the reader with a "knowledge assessment questionnaire" about OD and weaves a discussion of his answers into his text.

---

[1]G. Hofstede, *Culture's Consequences* (Beverly Hills, Calif.: Sage, 1980).

Reading 63

ORGANIZATION DEVELOPMENT: SYSTEM CHANGE OR CULTURE CHANGE?

William G. Dyer and W. Gibb Dyer, Jr.

The latest fashion in organization development (OD) is to view the organization as a cultural entity or a subculture of a larger culture. As a result, many analysts define organization change as an alteration of the organization's culture. However, some key questions are left unanswered: What is the organization's culture? When something is changed, does that alter the culture or has something other than culture undergone modification? We believe that most OD changes change an organization's system, not its culture. Culture change is much deeper and more pervasive than system change and more difficult to achieve through planning.

What Is System Analysis?

An organization is a complete functioning unit made up of integrated systems that allow it to operate to accomplish its purposes or goals. The separate subsystems of an organization include the social system, the technical or operational system, and the administrative system. Additionally, all organizations are open—that is, they continually interact with the external environment. Certain inputs (people, materials, controls, demands) must be processed by the subsystems, and ultimately certain outputs (products or services) must be produced.

The Social System

Every organization has its social component, made up of people in different positions interacting with each other—talking, arguing, helping, deciding,

Source: William G. Dyer and W. Gibb Dyer, Jr., reprinted from *Personnel Journal*, 1986, pp. 14–22.

solving problems—to achieve some of the goals of the organization and to satisfy some of their personal needs. Every social system has some basic features:

1. Climate: This is the prevailing emotional state shared by members in the system. The climate may be formal, relaxed, defensive, cautious, accepting, trusting, and so on.

2. Communication network: These are the formal and informal patterns of who talks with whom, when, how often, and about what.

3. Status/role structure: This involves the division of labor. Some people, because of their function or position, have higher status than others and, hence, more power and more influence.

4. Pattern of management: Some people in the organization work in superordinate positions with the assignment of helping subordinates to do their work. The way superordination is handled (e.g., in an authoritarian or a participative way) is decided at the top in an organization. This style becomes the prevailing condition throughout.

5. Decision-making method: This refers to the basic method for handling problem solving and decision making. It is closely linked to the pattern of management; but it also includes the number of people who make each decision, the degree to which all relevant resources are used, the degree of creativity of decisions, and the degree of commitment to implement the decisions.

6. Individuals: A social system is shaped by the kinds of people who make up the system. It might be expected, for example, that a group of older workers would behave differently than a group of younger people.

The Technical or Operational System

Every organization develops its method for getting work done—its unique arrangement of equipment, material, people, and processes. A common industrial operational system is the assembly line: Workers are arranged along a conveyor belt with the product moving along the belt, and each worker performs a specific task. The operational system can be altered by changing equipment, using different basic or raw materials, arranging people differently, or changing work assignments.

The operational system is integrally connected with the social system, for the arrangements of people will affect their ability to communicate with each other. Also, work assignments and work flow will influence the pattern of management used and perhaps the way decisions are made.

However, some unique elements in the operational system can be altered separately, although some concomitant effects in the social system may result. In a common university system, the professor stands at a podium in front of a large hall, lecturing to a whole class. If the class is broken up into small groups and students and the professor are arranged in a circle, a different learning process is likely to occur. However, if the professor is preoccupied with notions of status, he may continue to dominate this situation by lecturing and controlling the social-system factors. For real change to take place, some modification is necessary in both the operational and the social systems. But without changes in the operational system, the professor will find it almost impossible to change the basic nature of instruction.

The Administrative System

Interlocking the social and operational systems are certain formalized procedures for setting down the standards, rules, and regulations that influence what happens in the other two systems. The important elements in the administrative system are:

1. Wage and salary administration: Organizations establish procedures by which pay levels are set, salary increases are obtained, and bonuses or special benefits are awarded.

2. Hiring/firing/promotions: Each organization has prescribed methods for these three actions.

3. Report making/auditing: Many organizations collect data on use of materials, finances, work output, and quality control. This usually involves writing reports or conducting audits to determine what is happening to resources.

4. Fringe benefits: Organizations establish criteria for allocating such fringe benefits as vacations, sick leave, retirement, and insurance.

5. Budgets: Budgets are critical in determining the priorities and activities of every unit in the organization.

System analysis and change come into play when production, quality, profits, or service are down. Then, managers want to know what is wrong in the three systems and what action can be taken. The system approach to organization change emphasizes the inputs, the transformation processes, and the outputs that transverse the organization and focuses in particular on deficiencies in outputs. When something adverse occurs, the diagnosis focuses on which subsystems are malfunctioning and identifies the areas where corrective action is needed.

For example, in the classic study by W. F. Whyte of the restaurant industry, waitresses were frequently observed leaving their work to go into the restroom to get feelings of distress under control. Whyte observed that the cause of the problem was a work-flow system that required lower-status waitresses to hand orders directly to the higher-status chef. This led to interface problems and created conflicts within the social system. Whyte's solution was to alter the work flow by putting in a spindle to which waitresses attached orders. This eliminated a sensitive interface. The system was altered; the problem solved; but the culture of the restaurant had not changed.

What Is Culture Analysis?

Early anthropologists quickly distinguished between material and nonmaterial culture—the physical artifacts and the basic beliefs that directed the thinking, feelings, perceptions, and behaviors of the people of a culture. To know why some people got into trouble—were rejected or punished—you had to look at the belief system and the attendant mores and norms that guided behavior. These early distinctions led to the identification of the following elements of an organization's culture: (1) artifacts, (2) perspectives, (3) values, and (4) assumptions.

Artifacts are the more tangible aspects of an organization's culture. There are physical artifacts (office layout, company logo, employee dress), behavioral artifacts (rituals, ceremonies), and verbal artifacts (language, stories, and myths shared by members of an organization). These artifacts are the surface manifestations of the shared perspectives, values, and assumptions that form the belief system.

Perspectives are those shared ideas and actions that help people act appropriately in a given situation. For example, perspectives often develop around rules for correctly handling performance reviews or promotions. In one organization, the common perspective was that people had to be innovative and aggressive and take on as much responsibility as possible in order to get ahead. In another organization, however, innovation was not as important as conformity to group norms. Such differences in perspectives represent two very different cultures.

Values are broader, transituational principles that apply to a range of situations. They include the general ideals, standards, and sins of the organization. Values such as career employment, promote from within, protect the environment, and be honest with customers, are often articulated in a formal statement of the organization's management philosophy.

Basic assumptions are at the core of culture. They are the taken-for-granted beliefs group members hold about themselves, others, and the world. Since assumptions are considered a given, they are rarely, if ever, questioned; and the set of tacit assumptions forms a unique culture.

In a study of a large high-tech firm, the GEM Corporation, three core assumptions were discovered: (1) Truth and knowledge are discovered through conflict; (2) people are basically good and capable of governing themselves; and (3) relationships in an organization are collateral in nature—like those in a family.

Given this set of assumptions, the artifacts, perspectives, and values of this organization reflected a highly combative, independent work force that was also highly supportive of each member.

Those interested in managing culture change typically set out to uncover the set of core assumptions of the culture and then to discover the problems such assumptions may pose for the organization. Culture change takes place when there is a shift in the organization's basic assumptions. Changes at other levels are often only cosmetic in nature since the underlying pattern of assumptions remains the same. The culture of the GEM Corporation would be changed if relationships become hierarchical, or if truth was assumed to be learned from authority figures, or if people were deemed untrustworthy and in need of close supervision.

Fundamental changes in even one core assumption often change the culture completely, and such changes are essential if the culture is to change. This type of change is significantly different from the incremental changes used to make improvements under a systems approach.

Recent History of Organization Change

Douglas McGregor, writing at the end of the 1950s, identified some negative ways managers in some organizations viewed people (Theory X) and contrasted these to a significantly positive view of human nature found in other organizations (Theory Y). He proposed that organizations should find ways to change their outlooks from Theory X to Theory Y. McGregor was advocating a change in the organization's culture, and the T-group (a laboratory group for examining interpersonal and group process) was popularly in use at the time as the method for getting management to alter basic assumptions.

Because of evidence that the T-group was not the most effective means of altering the basic assumptions of an organization, however, a whole new set of technologies for dealing with problems in organizations developed. These included team building, confrontation meetings, role-analysis techniques, job enrichment, management by objectives, job redesign, flex-time, job sharing, quality control circles, process consulting, matrix organizations, open system mapping, sensing meetings, role negotiations, altered pay and promotion systems, human resources planning, succession planning, intergroup negotiations, and others.

Most of the practitioners who used these methods were problem-focused rather than culture-focused—that is, they were faced with a problem (low productivity, high numbers of grievances, high turnover, low morale, time wasted in conflicts or defensive actions), and they looked for some solution to the problem. All of this came under the heading of organization development, and the OD practitioner was a person adept in diagnosing the causes of organizational problems and then implementing solutions to these problems.

The OD practitioner, however, generally accepted the prevailing culture of the organization and worked within it, rather than challenging the basic belief system. In some cases the actions taken did hit at the deep-rooted assumptions held by people in the organization. But generally the practitioner made adjustments in one or another part of the subsystems of the organization, and the problem was solved. The basic values and core beliefs of the culture did not change.

Culture Change vs. System Change

Does is make any difference to anyone but the theorist whether a change attempt is aimed at the system or the culture? The answer is *yes*. If a new CEO feels that some basic things are apparently amiss in the organization—people are not loyal, there is a low concern about quality, people manipulate each other to gain personal or departmental advantage, lies or semitruths are released through the media to help maintain a positive public image—and if the CEO wants to turn these beliefs and values around, the tough issue of culture change has to be addressed.

That is a very different situation from a CEO faced with an expanding market who needs to find ways to identify new leaders quickly and to train an expanding sales force overnight. The basic problem for this CEO is to determine what personnel needs will arise in the next three years and how the organization will meet those needs. The solution involves human resources planning, personnel selection, and training. This can be done without changing anything in the basic culture.

Culture and System Overlap

Do the concepts of culture and system overlap? Of course they do; the two conceptual models are not so well defined as to make neat distinctions all of the time. Many aspects of an organization's social, technical, and administrative systems reflect the deeper assumptions of the culture. For example, one could claim that putting in a spindle in the Whyte restaurant case is adding an artifact to the organization's culture. While that is true, adding the artifact only makes sense if the nature of the problem in the system is understood. Moreover, this introduction of one artifact did not change the basic cultural assumptions of the restaurant.

As another example, if a manager makes mostly authoritarian decisions or one-to-one decisions with subordinates but through a gain in insight learns how to conduct effective meetings and involve subordinates in planning and decision making, has the social system or the culture been changed? Perhaps both. It may be that the manager held a belief about the value of people and the need for their involvement but did not know how to translate the belief into action. Training in meeting management or team building in this case would then allow the manager to change the social system. It is also possible that the manager changed a core belief about people and then changed his meeting practices. In this case, culture change would have led to a social system change.

Changing Cultures and Systems

Most current OD is system—not culture—change because most OD interventions stem out of problems that arise from some malfunctioning in the system. Exhibit 1 represents the OD system-change

EXHIBIT 1   OD Cycle: System Change

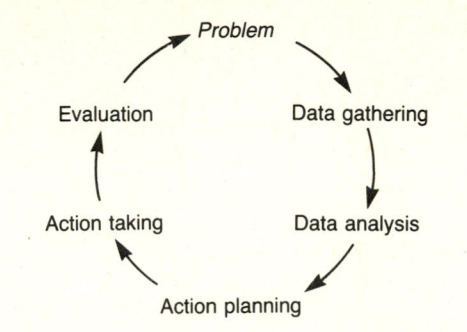

model. Data gathering and analysis allow the manager to identify what subsystems are malfunctioning and what actions need to be taken.

Culture change is far different than system change: It means engaging in some action that gets at basic beliefs, values, and perspectives. In a recent study of culture change, the six stages of culture change were identified. (See Exhibit 2.) This model suggests the culture of an organization changes in concert with the undermining of the organization's leadership. New leadership arises to resolve the crisis; and after a period of conflict, these leaders become the new cultural elite. The old guard is frequently purged in the process. Fi-

nally, the new leaders must reinforce their new culture with symbols, beliefs, and structures.

While the system-change cycle outlines a series of steps that can be followed to initiate change, the steps in the culture-change cycle are not easily controlled, for the process is often one of revolution and conflict—not of incremental change. It is not clear if culture change can be effected, by starting with some artifact change and slowly moving toward the core. There is clear evidence, however, that if the core beliefs are changed, the other outward aspects will also change.

Exhibit 3 outlines some of the differences between culture change and system change.

Two Case Studies

It may be instructive to look in some detail at two famous studies—one representing system change and the other culture change.

The Coch-French Case

This famous work was first published in 1948 by L. Coch and J.R.P. French, Jr., in an article entitled "Overcoming Resistance to Change." The recurring problem at the Harwood pajama plant was low production and morale when workers were asked to change from one kind of job to another.

EXHIBIT 2   OD Cycle: Culture Change

1. A crisis calls into question the leader's assumptions.

2. There is a breakdown of symbols, beliefs, and structure.

6. The new leadership establishes new symbols, beliefs, and structure to sustain the new culture.

3. New leadership emerges with a new set of assumptions.

5. If the crisis is solved and new leadership are given credit for the improvement, they become the new cultural elite.

4. Conflict occurs between the old and new cultures.

EXHIBIT 3   Differences Between System Change and Culture Change

System change	*Culture change*
1. Problem-oriented	1. Value-oriented
2. More easily controlled	2. Largely uncontrollable
3. Involves making incremental changes in systems	3. Involves transforming basic assumptions
4. Focuses on improving organization output/measurable outcomes	4. Focuses on the quality of life in an organization
5. Diagnosis involves discovering nonalignments between subsystems	5. Diagnosis involves examining dysfunctional effects of core assumptions
6. Leadership change is not essential	6. Leadership change is crucial

---

The authors described the culture of the company as follows:

> The policies. . . in regard to labor regulations are liberal and progressive. A high value has been placed on fair and open dealings with the employees, and they are encouraged to take up any problem or grievance with management at any time. Every effort is made to help foremen find effective solutions to their problems in human relations using conferences and role-playing methods.

The problems were these: When operators were required to change over to new work, turnover jumped from 4.5% to 12%. Additionally, among those workers who had to change, 62% either became chronically substandard operators or quit during the relearning period. Interviews with the operators showed feelings of resentment against management for changing them, feelings of frustration, loss of hope of regaining their former level of productivity and status, feelings of failure, and low levels of aspiration.

The OD intervention consisted of three different degrees of employee participation in the change—no participation, participation through representation, and total participation.

The results are widely known: The no-participation group continued its pattern of high turnover, low performance, and negative feelings. In the representation group, morale was good and relearning was high—reaching the old level in 14 days. The total-participation group recovered fast-est—returning to prechange levels after the first day and then showing a 14% increase in output.

Clearly, the action follows the OD cycle illustrated in Exhibit 1. There was a problem; data were gathered concerning why the problem existed; intervention was planned and implemented; and the problem was solved. A change was made in the social/administrative systems. There is no evidence that the culture was changed. In fact, one could argue that the OD intervention was more consistent with the culture than the old, nonparticipatory process of changeover.

The Guest Case

The famous case of culture change, written up by Robert Guest, occurred in an automobile assembly plant between 1953 and 1956. Guest began his case this way: "This is a study of a patient who was acutely ill and who became extremely healthy." Of the six plants in the same division, Plant Y was lowest in efficiency, quality, and safety, and highest in grievances, costs, absenteeism, and turnover. Plant Y was a place of high pressure; there was slavish obedience to division directives, blaming of subordinates, and uses of threats and verbal abuse—no one talked back. Additional characteristics included crisis meetings, no planning, fear, no listening to people, suspicion, confusion, inconsistent orders and treatment, and bottlenecks. The data supplied by Guest indicated that these conditions were present at all levels of the plant, in all units. It was the cultural condition of the plant; and the basic assumptions of the organization included these: obey division management at all costs; production is gained through pressure; people are expendable; and people should obey—not question.

At Plant Y a crisis occurred that called into question the old leaders' assumptions, and a new leader emerged with a new set of assumptions. The new plant manager was introduced to people in the plant, and he explained his new approach. As one worker said, "He was inviting us personally to see him any time about ways to make the plant better. He said he welcomed any suggestions. This was a completely new approach to [us]; and although some of the boys were skeptical, most of us felt that this man meant what he said."

Importantly, the new manager followed up his declaration of beliefs about people with a set of prescriptions and actions (perspectives and artifacts) consistent with his new assumptions. Meetings were held to get data and make decisions, and people were involved in planning. The people who did not adapt to the new values were shifted to other places; people committed to the new values

were moved into supervisory positions. Later changes were made in the technical system, but these came after the new culture had been introduced. The technical changes were all consistent with the new assumptions and values.

Guest says this about the reformed plant: "The reaction of supervisors to the improved situation was entirely favorable: it may even be described as 'euphoric.' Members not only felt different about their 'new life' at Plant Y; they behaved in a different manner." The Guest case is clearly one of culture change.

Conclusion

The processes of system change and culture change represent two different lenses through which to view an organization and take steps for improvement. The approach that one uses should be contingent on the type of problem being considered since the system and culture approaches employ different change strategies and technologies. Those interested in managing change in organizations often need both lenses to diagnose problems in organizations and select appropriate change strategies most effectively.

Reading 64

ETHICAL DILEMMAS IN VARIOUS STAGES OF ORGANIZATIONAL DEVELOPMENT

Louis P. White and Kevin C. Wooten

Increasingly, organizational change efforts are being utilized to solve many human, structural, and technological problems in contemporary organizations. This increased attention to the uses of organizational development (OD) has been accompanied by growth in the number of OD consultants as well as those who have long term needs for OD efforts. Practitioners in the field have increased in number and many organizations have sought OD programs and practitioners, but the professionalization of OD has not kept pace structurally and scientifically. Reviews of the OD literature (Alderfer, 1976, 1977; French & Bell, 1978; Friedlander & Brown, 1974; White & Mitchell, 1976) provide ample evidence of the tremendous growth in sophisticated techniques to conduct effective OD. At the same time, rapid increases in the use of OD to solve a myriad of organizational problems have caused some to ponder whether it is a religious movement (Harvey, 1974) or a new social technology (Havelock, 1972).

Within the last decade many efforts have been made to codify the evidence that OD efforts are effective, an indication that OD is developing as a science. With justification, however, the interdisciplinary approach to this developing science has given rise to scholarly critiques of what OD is as a discipline (Jones & Pfeiffer, 1977; Weisbord, 1977) and where OD is as a profession (Bowers, 1976; Burke, 1976). Simultaneously, a growing concern about professional ethics in the field has begun to emerge. The problem of ethical dilemmas

in OD practice has been written about, but never really examined in terms of where in the OD process they occur. This may be due in part to lack of a systematic approach to the study and analysis of the ethical dilemmas faced by the interventionist and client systems.

Ethical problems and dilemmas faced by OD practitioners may leave OD's scientific and professional progression in a disadvantageous position unless agreement can be reached as to the types of ethical dilemmas and the points at which they are likely to be encountered. It is not the purpose or scope of this paper to prescribe behaviors to resolve ethical dilemmas or to discuss the ethical principles that surround various dilemmas. As used herein, ''ethical dilemmas'' are the result of behaviors and inappropriate actions or roles on the part of both change agents and client systems. Therefore, this paper approaches ethical problems and dilemmas as a mutual responsibility of change agents and client systems, dependent largely on the nature of their specific relationship.

Ethical dilemmas, as approached from the perspective that such problems are caused largely by the nature of the relationship between the change agent and the client system, is a term that requires fuller elaboration. Previous approaches to the definition of an ethical dilemma (Benne, 1959; Walton & Warwick, 1973) have centered around the various values held by change agents, and how these values have influenced their actions. Operationally, then, an ethical dilemma can be defined as any choice situation encountered by a change agent or client system that has the potential to result in a breach of acceptable behavior. A dilemma therefore

Source: Louis P. White and Kevin C. Wooten, reprinted with permission of the *Academy of Management Review.* Copyright 1983, vol. 8, no. 4, pp. 690–97.

is different from a breach of ethics. A breach of ethics is a verifiable act or conduct on the part of a professional that breaches a law, role, standard, or established norm.

Major Categories of Ethical Dilemmas

Although a number of authors have addressed the area of professional ethics in organizational development, the literature is sparse concerning the specification of types of ethical dilemmas that occur. However, a review of the available literature from works in organizational development, management consulting, and training and development does yield some consistency in thought and form. Although ranging considerably in terminology, the dilemma categories described coincide remarkably. Generally, five types of ethical dilemmas in organizational development practice tend to be observed and described by practitioners and scholars alike. They are:

1. Misrepresentation and collusion
2. Misuse of data
3. Manipulation and coercion
4. Value and goal conflict
5. Technical ineptness

Misrepresentation and collusion is a pervasive and widely occurring dilemma in organizational development practice. This dilemma, or choice situation, requires the change agent or client system to decide between options of fully representing all available information and including or excluding various parties involved in the change effort. Works by Shay (1965), Pfeiffer and Jones (1977), French and Bell (1978), and Maidment and Losito (1980) have investigated its nature. This dilemma may occur for a variety of reasons. First, misrepresentation and collusion can occur when the change agent misrepresents his/her skill base, education, experience, certification, or specialized training, or when the client system misrepresents the organization's interest, need, or goal.

Another instance of misrepresentation and collusion occurs when the change agent or the client system attempts to exclude outside parties, such as other change agents or other parts of the client system, for personal gain or protection that negatively affects the OD effort. Collusion also may occur by inappropriately structuring the relationship between the change agent and the client systems. For example, lack of clarity concerning goals, values, needs, and change methods can result in poorly defined roles and subsequently a poorly defined change effort. Additionally, a lack of clarity or an agreement to collude among parties may result in an avoidance of unresolved issues. Moreover, collusion may occur through loss of objectivity by assimilating the change agent into the organizational culture.

The second major category of ethical dilemmas in organizational change is misuse of data (Pfeiffer & Jones, 1977; Shay, 1965; Walton & Warwick, 1973; Zaltman & Duncan, 1976). This dilemma or choice situation requires the change agent or client system to decide what information is used and how it is used. Misuse of data in organizational development occurs when the voluntary consent or confidentiality of the client system is violated or abridged. Misuse of data as a breach of ethics in organizational development also may occur in two other ways. It may occur when data are distorted, deleted, or not reported by either the client system or the change agent, or when the data are used to assess persons or groups punitively, resulting in personal, professional, or organizational harm. Data concerning personality traits, career interest, and market information are frequent examples.

Manipulation and coercion constitute the third major category of ethical dilemmas in organizational development (Huse, 1975; Lippitt & Lippitt, 1978; Pfeiffer & Jones, 1977; Walton & Warwick, 1973; Warwick & Kelman, 1973; Zaltman & Duncan, 1976). The dilemma presents itself in the form of a decision concerning the exercise of the "free will" of organizational participants. Basically, manipulation and coercion occur when the organizational development effort requires organizational members to abridge their personal values or needs against their will. Forced participation in a change effort, such as sensitivity training, is exemplary.

Closely related are examples involving changes in personal attributes or the structure of organizational members affected.

The fourth major category of ethical dilemmas in organizational development is value and goal conflict (Benne, 1959; Lippitt & Lippitt, 1978; Pfeiffer & Jones, 1977; Warwick & Kelman, 1973; Zaltman & Duncan, 1976). The dilemma in this situation involves a decision concerning the appropriate mix of change agent and client system values and goals as they relate to the overall change effort. Value and goal conflict occurs when there is ambiguity or conflict concerning whose values will be maximized by the change effort or whose needs will be fulfilled by meeting such goals. Value and goal conflict also occurs when there is ambiguity in defining change goals or choosing an intervention target. Another form of this type of dilemma occurs when conflict or ambiguity results in the reluctance on the part of the change agent or client system to alter change strategies or when the change agent or client system withholds services or needed resources.

The fifth major type of ethical dilemma in organizational development is technical ineptness. Technical ineptness is the most widely written about type of ethical dilemma (Benne, 1959; French & Bell, 1978; Lippitt & Lippitt, 1978; Pfeiffer & Jones, 1977; Shay, 1965; Walton & Warwick, 1973; Warwick & Kelman, 1973; Zaltman & Duncan, 1976). The dilemma of technical ineptness involves decisions by change agents and client systems whether to diagnose and divulge their deficiencies in required skills or whether to provide options for overcoming these deficiencies. This breach of ethics may occur when there is a lack of knowledge or skill in the use of techniques and procedures to diagnose social systems problems effectively, formulate change targets, choose and utilize the proper change technology and strategy, or intervene in the social system at the appropriate depth and scope. Technical ineptness also may occur when there is an inability to evaluate effectively an intervention or terminate an organizational development relationship. This dilemma also may result from the inability or reluctance to reduce client dependency or to transfer monitoring of the change effort to internal parties.

An Alternative View of the OD Process

Isolation of ethical dilemmas at various stages of the OD process requires examination not only of the relationship between the change agent and the client system but also of how this relationship changes as OD progresses. Role theory has been used to explain a broad range of organizational behaviors (House & Rizzo, 1972; Tracy & Johnson, 1981) and may be extended to include behavioral exchanges occurring in the OD process.

Role theory as proposed by Katz and Kahn (1966) bridges both personal and social behavior by illustrating their interaction. This is accomplished by viewing the conduct of individuals in a behavioral or organizational context as a number of role systems. This method allows the investigator to analyze the behavior not only of the individuals but also of the social system.

Although many authors have generally discussed the various roles of the change agent or the role of the client (Argyris, 1970; Havelock, 1973; Lippitt, 1975; Steele, 1969) there have been recent efforts toward expanding and incorporating the idea into the notion of role systems. Mirvis and Seashore (1979), in discussing the ethical dilemmas of organizational research used role theory to isolate clearly, for the first time, both a conceptual scheme and a pragmatic tool for investigating professional ethics. This argument can be broadened to include developing relationships between change agents and client systems. The role episode is illustrated in Figure 1. As shown, the role episode includes both a role sender and a role receiver, or a focal person. This role episode represents a continuous cycle of sending, receiving, responding, and the sending of new expectations. Related to organizational development, role sending and role receiving can be seen as a continuous cycle of role episodes on the part of change agents and client systems. Figure 1 further shows that the role episode is comprised of four concepts: role expectations, sent role, received role, and role behavior. These concepts are described by Katz and Kahn as follows:

FIGURE 1   A Model of the Role Episode[a]

Role Senders		Focal Person	
Expectations	Sent Role	Received Role	Role Behavior
Perception of focal person's behavior: evaluation	Information attempts at influence	Perception of role and perception of role sending	Compliance; resistence; "side effects"
I	II	III	IV

[a]From Katz and Kahn (1966)

Role expectations, which are evaluative standards applied to the behavior of any person who occupies a given organizational office or position; sent role, which consists of communications stemming from role expectations and sent by members of the role set as attempts to influence the focal person; received role, which is the focal person's perception of the role-sendings addressed to him, including those he sends himself; and role behavior, which is the response of the focal person to the complexity of information he has received (1966, p. 182).

A variety of authors (Blake & Mouton, 1976; Ford, 1974; Kaplan, 1978; Milstein & Smith, 1979; Schein, 1969) have dealt with the dynamic nature of the relationship between the change agent and the client system. Issues such as the nature of a change contract, depth of the intervention, and dependency and indentification of the real client are well documented in the OD literature. These factors influence not only the relationship between the change agent and the client system but the change process as well. However, few change models elaborate fully on how the relationship between the change agent and the client system can and should change as the OD intervention progresses from start to finish. It is through a fuller analysis and illustration of how stages of an intervention and change relationship evolve that their mutuality may be appreciated fully. Figure 2 is an attempt to illustrate globally the role episode that should occur between

---

FIGURE 2   A Process Relational Model of Organizational Development

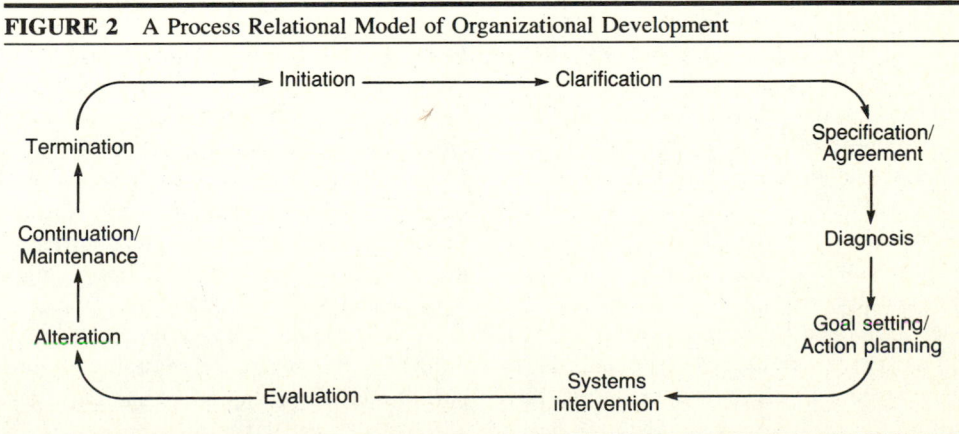

the change agent and the client system at various stages of an OD effort.

Role theory provides a vehicle to illustrate the interaction process occurring between the change agent and client system. The model in Figure 1, when used in conjunction with the process relational model (Figure 2), can demonstrate that the actors in each of the 10 stages of the OD process confront specific questions of ethicality. The roles that each actor assumes are inextricably linked to the resolution of these choice behaviors congruent with the underlying ethical principle.

The process relational model illustrates 10 stages of OD that deal with the conceptual framework of most organizational change methodologies (i.e., diagnosis, intervention, evaluation, etc.). Moreover, it focuses more fully on the role relationship between the parties involved (i.e., initiation, clarification, termination, etc.).

Although this model is shown to be sequential— that is, the relationship between the client system and the interventionist progresses from one stage to the next—its sequential presentation is offered only to illustrate what should occur in the ideal form. Many organizational change techniques, methodologies, and practices, by their very structure and content, do not deal systematically with one or several of these important stages. Implicit in this model is that these stages typically occur between the client system and the change agent, either consciously or unconsciously. On the conscious level, if each of these 10 stages is dealt with and worked through successfully between the client system and the change agent, there is a lower probability that ethical dilemmas will occur.

Also implicit in the process relational model is the change agent-client system relationship in any organizational change effort—a relationship that represents a collection of continuous interrelated activities in which both the change agent and the client system play their part or role in order to reach a predetermined outcome. Using the role system model developed by Katz and Kahn (1966), presented earlier, the behavior or role behavior of the change agent and client system during each

stage of an organizational change effort can be studied as a role episode or series of role episodes.

Ethical Dilemmas at Various Stages of Change

Of specific concern to most OD interventionists is the stage in the OD process at which specified dilemmas occur. Building on the notion that certain ethical dilemmas do tend to occur at various stages of OD, practitioners and consumers alike could deal with them more effectively by modifying and clarifying their role relationships. Although each organizational intervention and role relationship is situation specific, the OD literature and the experience of practitioners tend to indicate commonality of experience.

Table 1 depicts 10 stages of change, the appropriate role behaviors for change agents and client systems, and the possible ethical dilemmas that can occur at these various stages. Each of the 31 ethical dilemmas shown is a specific illustration of the five major categories of ethical dilemmas previously discussed. Implicit in the various dilemmas is the notion that ethical dilemmas are produced not only by change agents but by client systems as well. Also implicit in Table 1 is the notion that several of the dilemmas mentioned are closely related to other dilemmas at the various stages of change. The utility of Table 1, therefore, is to isolate the occurence of these dilemmas at specific stages of change, as the nature of the relationship between the client system and the change agent changes.

As shown, the stage of initiation often is impaired by various types of misrepresentation. Here, inaccurate information may be provided by either the change agent or the client system, resulting in either misrepresentation of the consultant's background or skill base or misrepresentation of organizational interest. As the role relationship moves into the stage of clarification, three different dilemmas may arise. Problems in determining who the real client is and the inappropriate determination of value orientations are of frequent mention. Additionally, the avoidance of reality testing on the part of both the change agent and the client system

TABLE 1 Organizational Development Change Stages, Appropriate Role Behaviors, and Possible Ethical Dilemmas

Stage	Purpose	Role of Change Agent	Role of Client System	Dilemmas
Initiation	First information sharing	To provide information on background, expertise, and experience	To provide information on possible needs, relevant problems, interest of management and representative groups	Misrepresentation of the consultant's skill base and background Misrepresentation of organizational interest
Clarification	Further elaboration of initiation stage	To provide details of education, licensure, operative values, optimum working conditions	To provide a detailed history of special problems, personnel, marketplace, internal culture, and organizational politics	Inappropriate determination of who the client is Avoidance of reality testing Inappropriate determination of value orientation
Specification/ agreement	Sufficient elaboration of needs, interest, fees, services, working conditions, arrangements	To specify actual services, fees to be charged, time frame, actual work conditions	To specify whose needs are to be addressed, goals, objectives, and possible evaluative criteria or end-state outcomes	Inappropriate structuring of the relationship Inappropriate definition of change problem Collusion to exclude outside parties
Diagnosis	To obtain an unfiltered and undistorted view of the organization's problems and processes pinpointing change targets and criterion	To collect data concerning organizational problems and processes, and to provide feedback	To assist change agent in data collection	Avoidance of problems Misuse of data Distortion and deletion of data Ownership of data Voluntary consent Confidentiality
Goal setting/ action planning	To establish the specific goals and strategies to be used	To agree mutually with the client system on the goals and strategies to be used	To agree mutually with the change agent on the goals and strategies to be used	Inappropriate choice of intervention goal and targets Inappropriate choice of operative means Inappropriate scope of intervention

TABLE 1 *(concluded)*

Systems intervention	The intervention into ongoing behaviors, structures, and processes	To intervene at specific targets, at a specific depth	To invest the energy and resources required by planned intervention	Assimilation into culture Inappropriate depth of intervention Coercion vs. choice, freedom, and consent to participate Environmental manipulation
Evaluation	To determine the effectiveness of the intervention strategies, energy, and resources used, as well as the change agent-client system relationship	To gather data on specified targets and report findings to the client system	To analyze the evaluation data and determine effectiveness of the intervention	Misuse of data Deletion and distortion of data
Alteration	To modify change strategies, depth, level, goals, targets, or resources utilized if necessary	To make alteration to meet original goals, or to develop new mutual goals and strategies with client system	To make known needs and expectations, and to provide the context for a modification of the original agreement, if necessary	Failure to change and lack of flexibility Adoption of inappropriate strategy
Continuation/maintenance	To monitor and maintain ongoing strategies, provide periodic checks, and continue intervention based on original or altered plans and strategies	To specify the parameters of the continuation of the maintenance of the relationship	To provide or allocate the resources required to maintain or continue the intervention	Inappropriate reduction of dependency Redundancy of effort Withholding of services
Termination	To have the change agent disenfranchise self from the client system and establish a long term monitoring system	To fulfill the role agreed on in previous stages and evaluate overall effectiveness from feedback from the client system	To determine the organization's state of health, and whether it has developed the adaptive change process	Inappropriate transition of change effort to internal sources Premature exit Failure to monitor change

may occur if there is difficulty or a lack of effort in raising issues that might hamper the change effort.

In the specification/agreement stage the finite structuring of the relationship occurs. At this point the ethical dilemma involves the degree of specificity concerning the range of services to be offered, the fee structure, a tenable time frame, resources to be used, and accountability for services and resources. Similarly, inappropriate definition of the change problem may result in ambiguity concerning the problems to be addressed—whose problems they are and by what means they are to be dealt with. Collusion of parties also may occur in the specification/agreement state, with change agents and client systems excluding outside competitions and influences.

As shown in Table 1, a wide variety of ethical dilemmas may occur in the diagnosis stage. Avoidance of diagnosing known problems occurs when the change agent and client system perceptually defend against their own inability or unwillingness to solve a problem. Of greater frequency in the diagnosis stage is the misuse, as well as the distortion and deletion, of data. Here misuse of data could result in personal, professional, and organizational harm. Deletion and distortion of data also may result in a misleading diagnosis, thereby rendering the intervention ineffective. Ownership of the data is a frequent dilemma as well, wherein survey feedback or process observation is not shared with all contributing members. Similarly, the question of voluntary consent of organizational members and insured confidentiality appears to be a frequent problem that has received much attention.

In the stage of goal setting/action planning, ethical problems include the choice of a change goal and targets, the choice of operative means, and the scope of the intervention. Here the major categories of collusion of parties, technical ineptness, and value and goal conflict are apparent. These dilemmas result in inappropriately choosing goals, targets, depth, and change method because of lack of skill, lack of objectivity, or differing needs and orientations.

In systems intervention, the assimiliation into the organization's culture presents a range of ethical considerations for the change agent. These dilemmas result in the change agent's losing the objectivity of a third party position by incorporation of inappropriate values, adherence to inappropriate norms, or development of a psychological state incongruent with the activities to be addressed by the change effort. Table 1 also shows the dilemma of inappropriate depth. This dilemma results in change efforts that cannot provide for adequate or effective change.

Frequently mentioned in the OD literature is the notion of free will and consent to participate in OD activities. Table 1 shows the dilemma for coercion to participate in OD activities. Here resides the potential for involuntary change or psychological or professional harm to organizational members. There also exists the possibility of environmental manipulation through the involuntary change in personal attributes, structure, or organizational process, without awareness or participation of organizational members.

As in the stage of diagnosis, the misuse, deletion, or distortion of data may occur in the evaluation stage. Here, evaluation data are distorted or deleted in a manner that results in personal, professional, or organizational harm. The misuse of evaluation data is frequent in cases in which the major motivation for collecting and reporting evaluation data is to advance the personal interest of change agents on internal parts of the client system.

Table 1 also illustrates the stage of alteration as beset by two dilemmas. These dilemmas are failure to change (or lack of flexibility) and the adoption of an inappropriate new strategy. Each can be seen to occur typically in an intervention in which alteration is necessary for full effectiveness of the intervention effort. Failure to change and a lack of flexibility can be caused by overadherence to the specifications of a contract, the lack of skill or expertise, or the lack of resources. Further, the adoption of an inappropriate new strategy may result from pressure to produce change in light of nonsupportive evaluation data.

As a change effort progresses into the latter stages, a variety of ethical dilemmas can be observed in the continuation/maintenance stage. Table 1 illustrates three specific ethical dilemmas for this stage. Reducing dependency is a difficult issue for most change agents to encounter. The reduction of effort and withholding of change agent services from the client system also are difficult. Of specific ethical interest is the change agent's continued intense helping relationship or service.

In the termination stage of change, a variety of dilemmas may occur. Value and goal conflict, as well as technical ineptness, may result in the transition of change to inadequately prepared or unskilled internal parties, premature exit, or the failure to monitor change longitudinally. Of specific difficulty is the determination of (1) when internal sources are capable of responsibly carrying through the long term aspects of a change effort and (2) whether the internal parties have developed the necessary processes to diagnose and solve problems. Improper assessment of a client system can lead to premature exit on the part of the change agent, which may result in the broader issue of responsibility to the client. Moreover, a failure to monitor change is an issue that has long term implications not only for the effectiveness of the organization but also for the long run viability of the change method.

Discussion

Through the use of role theory and an accompanying process relational model of OD, OD has been shown to be a highly integrative process. It involves an integration of technology, human interactions, and the ethical questions that arise as a result of these variables. A result of this analysis yields many more yet to be explored issues. Yet unanswered are questions such as "What are the underlying ethical principles that should serve the OD process?" and "What are the various ethical principles that apply to OD practice?" The models proposed may provide the necessary vehicles to address these types of substantive questions.

It can be said that a major distinguishing characteristic of OD as a profession is the high degree of heterogeneity of the change agent's education, training, and experience. Indeed, OD practitioners are drawn from fields ranging from business education to anthropology. The conceptualization presented herein provides a basis from which a systemic study of OD ethics can take place. For example, the ethical dilemmas shown in Table 1 can be analyzed and discussed in a way that would lead to the statement of the ethical principle underlying choice behaviors faced by the change agent and client system.

With the demand for the acceptance of OD programs and practitioners increasing rapidly, the ethical issues surrounding OD's practice should now receive increased attention. Its popularity in educational curriculum for practitioners serves as evidence for increased exposure by investigation and research. Because of the interdisciplinary values and backgrounds comprised in the OD field, ethical consonance among practitioners and consumers alike will require diligent effort. If OD is ever to be accepted as a legitimate science as well as a profession, then principles guiding the actions of those providing OD services must no longer be ignored.

References

Alderfer, C. P. Change processes in organizations. In M. D. Dunnette (Ed.), Handbook of industrial and organizational psychology. Chicago, Ill.: Rand McNally, 1976, 1591–1638.

Alderfer, C. P. Organizational development. *Annual Review of Psychology,* 1977, 28, 197–233.

Argyris, C. *Intervention theory and method: A behavioral science view.* Reading, Mass.: Addison-Wesley, 1970.

Benne, K. D. Some ethical problems in group and organizational consultation. *Journal of Social Issues,* 1959, 15, 60–67.

Blake, R. R., & Mouton, J. S. *Consultation.* Reading, Mass.: Addison-Wesley, 1976.

Bowers, D. G. Organizational development: Promises, performance, possibilities. *Organizational Dynamics,* 1976, 4 (4), 50–62.

Burke, W. W. Organizational development in transition. *Journal of Applied Behavioral Science,* 1976, 12, 22–43.

Ford, C. H. Developing a successful client-consultant relationship. *Human Resource Management, 1974, 13* (2), 2–11.

French, W. L., & Bell, C. H., Jr. *Organizational development.* Englewood Cliffs, N.J.: Prentice-Hall, Inc., 1978.

Friedlander, F., & Brown, L. D. Organizational development. *Annual Review of Psychology, 1974, 25,* 313–341.

Harvey, J. B. Organizational development as a religious movement. *Training and Development Journal, 1974, 28* (3), 24–27.

Havelock, R. G. A critique: Has OD become a social technology? *Educational Technology, 1972, 10* (2), 61–62.

Havelock, R. G. *The change agents guide to innovation in education.* Englewood Cliffs, N.J.: Educational Technology Publications, 1973.

House, R. J., & Rizzo, R. J. Role conflict and ambiguity as critical variables in a model of organizational behavior. *Organizational Behavior and Human Performance, 1972, 7,* 467–505.

Huse, E. *Organizational development and change.* St. Paul, Minn.: West Publishing, 1975.

Jones, J. E., & Pfeiffer, J. W. On the obsolescence of the term organizational development. *Group and Organizational Studies, 1977, 2,* 263–264.

Kaplan, R. E. Stages in developing a consulting relationship: A case study of a long beginning. *Journal of Applied Behavioral Science, 1978, 14,* 43–48.

Katz, D., & Kahn, R. L. The social psychology of organizations. New York: John Wiley and Sons, Inc., 1966.

Lippitt, G. L. The trainer's role as an internal consultant. *Journal of European Training, 1975, 4* (5), 14–23.

Lippitt, G. L., & Lippitt, R. *The consultant process in action.* LaJolla, Cal.: University Associates, 1978.

Maidment, R., & Losito, W. *Ethics and the consultant/trainer.* Madison, Wis.: American Society for Training and Development, Selected Paper No. 11, 1980.

Milstein, M. M., & Smith, D. The shifting nature of OD contracts: A case study. *Journal of Applied Behavioral Science, 1979, 15,* 179–191.

Mirvis, P. H., & Seashore, S. F. Being ethical in organizational research. *American Psychologist, 1979, 34* (5), 44–48.

Pfeiffer, J. W., & Jones, J. E. Ethical considerations in consulting. In J. E. Jones, and J. W. Pfeiffer (Eds.), *The 1977 annual handbook for group facilitators.* La Jolla, Cal.: University Associates, 1977, 217–225.

Schein, E. H. *Process consultation: Its role in organization development.* Reading, Mass.: Addison-Wesley, 1969.

Shay, P. W. Ethics and professional practices in management consulting. *Advanced Management Journal, 1965, 30* (1), 13–20.

Steele, F. Consultants and detectives. *Journal of Applied Behavioral Science, 1969, 5,* 187–202.

Tracy, L., & Johnson, T. W. What do the role conflict and role ambiguity scales measure? *Journal of Applied Psychology, 1981, 66,* 464–469.

Walton, R. E., & Warwick, D. P. The ethics of organizational development. *Journal of Applied Behavioral Science, 1973, 9,* 681–699.

Warwick, D. P., & Kelman, H. C. Ethics in social intervention. In G. Zaltman (Ed.), *Processes and phenomena of social change.* New York: Wiley Interscience, 1973, 377–449.

Weisbord, M. R. How do you know if it works if you don't know what it is? *O. D. Practitioner, 1977, 9,* 1–3.

White, S. E., & Mitchell, T. R. Organizational development: A review of research content and research design. *Academy of Management Review, 1976, 1* (2), 57–73.

Zaltman, G., & Duncan, R. Ethics in social change. In G. Zaltman & R. Duncan (Eds.), *Strategies for planned change.* New York: John Wiley and Sons, 1976, 323–377.

Reading 65

ORGANIZATION DEVELOPMENT AND NATIONAL CULTURE: WHERE'S THE FIT?

Alfred M. Jaeger

The appropriateness of management techniques of American origin in different cultural settings has been a problem perennially addressed by management theorists with relatively little practical success (Adler, 1983). This paper examines the cross-cultural applicability of one prominent American management tool, namely organization development (OD). The purpose of this paper is not to do a complete review of the area of OD and culture but to sensitize OD practitioners and others interested in OD to the culture-boundedness of OD and to provide them with an approach that allows the selection and design of appropriate OD interventions for specific cultural configurations.

Definitions of OD and Culture

OD has been defined in a number of ways. French and Bell define OD as:

> a long range effort to improve an organization's problem-solving and renewal processes, particularly through a more effective and collaborative management of organizational culture—with special emphasis on the culture of formal work teams—with the assistance of a change agent, or catalyst, and the use of the theory and technology of applied behavioral science, including action research (1978, p. 14).

Others focus less on the specific target of the intervention. Beckhard (1969) defines OD as an effort that is planned, organization-wide, managed

Source: Alfred M. Jaeger, reprinted with permission of the *Academy of Management Review*. Copyright 1986, vol. 11, no. 1, pp. 178–90.

from the top, and designed to increase organization effectiveness and health through planned intervention in the organization's processes using behavioral science knowledge. Huse points out that many of the popular definitions are:

> broad enough to include almost any technique, policy or managerial practice used in a deliberate attempt to change the individuals in an organization or the organization itself to accomplish organizational objectives (1980, p. 23).

A somewhat more focused definition is put forth by Huse:

> Organization Development is concerned with the deliberate, reasoned, introduction, establishment, reinforcement, and spread of change for the purpose of improving an organization's effectiveness and health. Effectiveness refers to setting and attaining appropriate goals in a changing environment. Health refers to the motivation, utilization, and integration of human resources within the organization (1980, p. 23).

A definition of OD gives one a sense of underlying raison d'être for OD and an inkling of how it is carried out. What OD is in practice, however, is defined solely by what practitioners do in the field. According to French and Bell, most OD practice in the United States has grown out of two "stems": laboratory training (i.e., T-group) and survey feedback. Thus, most OD interventions are based on some form of either of these two technologies.

To understand what is meant by cultural groups, one must understand what is meant by culture. Most management researchers subscribe to an ideational view of culture: that is, they conceptualize culture as a set of ideas shared by members of a group. A useful definition of culture from this perspective is that of anthropologist Roger Keesing (1974). He defines culture as an individual's theory of what his fellows know, believe and mean, his theory of the code being followed, the game being played. Thus, culture is not an individual characteristic but rather denotes a set of common theories of behavior or mental programs that are shared by a group of individuals.

Looking at culture from a broader perspective, Schein (1981) has described its three levels: basic assumptions and premises; values and ideology; and artifacts and creations. The first level includes such things as the relationship of man to nature, time orientation, beliefs about human nature, the nature of man's relationship to man, and man's concept of space and his place in it. These are usually taken for granted and are "preconscious." The middle level contains values and ideology, indicating ideals and goals as well as paths for "getting there." The third level includes such things as language, technology, and social organization.

Each successive level is, to an extent, a manifestation of the one before it, and all the levels thus are interrelated. One can see that the culture of a society is a fairly complex and deep-rooted phenomenon that in most management situations must be taken as a given, at least in the short run.

An Empirical Model of Culture

To connect culture to management and subsequently to OD, a recent and much heralded empirical model of culture developed by Hofstede (1980a) is helpful. Hofstede carried out an empirical analysis that resulted in a concise framework of dimensions for differentiating national cultures. Although it has some limitations, most likely it will "stand as one of the major landmarks of cross-cultural research for many years to come" (Triandis, 1982, p. 90).

Hofstede's work is unique in that it uses an empirical survey to build a model of cultures. He used a 40-country questionnaire survey of employees of one multinational organization; 116,000 question-

naires were administered in two waves (1968 and 1972). From these data, four principal factors were extracted.

Four Dimensions of Culture

The four dimensions found to differentiate national culture groups were: power distance, uncertainty avoidance, individualism (collectivism), and masculinity (femininity). These were succinctly described by Hofstede as follows:

Power distance is:

> the extent to which a society accepts the fact that power in institutions and organizations is distributed unequally (1980b, p. 45).

Uncertainty avoidance is:

> the extent to which a society feels threatened by uncertain and ambiguous situations by providing career stability, establishing more formal rules, not tolerating deviant ideas and behaviors, and believing in absolute truths and the attainment of expertise (1980b, p. 46).

Individualism:

> implies a loosely knit social framework in which people are supposed to take care of themselves and their immediate families only, while collectivism is characterized by a tight social framework in which people distinguish between in-groups and out-groups; they expect their in-group (relatives, clan, organizations) to look after them, and in exchange for that they feel they owe absolute loyalty to it (1980b, p. 45).

Masculinity expresses:

> the extent to which the dominant values in society are "masculine" that is, assertiveness, the acquisition of money and things, and not caring for others, the quality of life, or people (1980b, p. 46).

The opposite of masculine is of course feminine.

Associated with high masculinity is a performance orientation. Low uncertainty avoidance means a willingness to take risks and accept organizational change. An individualist believes that involvement with organizations is calculative, whereas a collectivist believes involvement with organizations has a moral basis. If power distance is low, subordinates consider superiors to be "people like me" and vice versa.

It is clear, then, that Hofstede subscribes to the ideational view of culture, that is, that persons in every society carry around "mental programs" that guide their behavior. He feels that these programs are conditioned into members of a given cultural group or society by their common socialization and life experience. Furthermore, although Hofstede's dimensions appear to fall into Schein's second level (values and ideology), they are substantively such that one can expect to find them to fit with and be manifest in the other two levels as well.

Critiques of the Model

Two related issues should be raised in regard to the validity and generalizability of Hofstede's work: (a) The representativeness of the sample, and (b) the validity of the dimensions.

As Hunt (1981) and others have pointed out, one can doubt the generalizability of findings based on a sample drawn from one large multinational firm, namely, IBM. Potential for several biases exists here. One is that IBM may tend to hire similar persons worldwide, reducing national differences. In addition, a firm with a strong organizational culture tends to have a homogenizing influence on the values of employees (Jaeger, 1983). If, indeed, these influences are present, then one would expect national differences within that multinational firm (IBM) to be reduced. Hofstede's results can be interpreted as Haire, Ghiselli, and Porter (1966) interpreted those of their 1960s study: there are great similarities in value patterns worldwide, supporting the notion of a global managerial culture. Nevertheless, national differences persist, in line with what one might expect given a knowledge of the cultures involved. This is consistent with Laurent's (1983) finding in a multicompany study that multinational corporations do not reduce national value differences among their members.

With respect to the dimensions at which Hofstede has arrived, most critics concede that although a more comprehensive study might be carried out to arrive at more methodologically valid dimensions of culture, the ones described in the 1980 book "make sense" (Triandis, 1982) and provide a "good framework" (Hunt, 1981). Triandis notes that the results give him a sense of "déjà vu" and that he has seen the dimensions elsewhere (e.g., individualism—Kluckhohn and Strodtbeck, 1961; uncertainty avoidance—Pelto, 1968). Furthermore, Triandis observes that although Hofstede's dimensions may be too narrow, they are included in the 20 dimensions that Triandis uses in his thinking about culture.

One other potential problem in using Hofstede's work stems from the assumptions it makes that cultures follow national boundaries. A number of countries in the sample such as Belgium, Canada, and even the United States are clearly multicultural. Unfortunately, within country differences have not been sorted out in Hofstede's data. This reduces the meaningfulness of his placement of multicultural countries on the map of cultural configurations. Fortunately for the ensuing analysis, however, even though the term national culture and country names are used for purposes of exposition, the actual analysis is based on the four dimensions of culture and configurations thereof. The reader who wishes to utilize the results of this analysis should bear in mind that the country names are actually being used as a shorthand for cultural configurations. Therefore, before actually applying the results, one should verify as best as possible the rankings on Hofstede's dimensions of the particular locale in question.

OD Values and National Cultures

Tannenbaum and Davis' OD Values

OD values have been concisely expressed by Tannenbaum and Davis (1969) in their well known paper "Values, Man, and Organizations." In this paper the authors list a set of 13 value scales along which one can define the value orientation of OD practitioners (Table 1). The position Tannenbaum and Davis take on these value scales is consistent

TABLE 1 Tannenbaum and Davis' Value Scales

Moving away from	*Moving toward*
A view of man as essentially bad	A view of man as essentially good
Avoidance or negative evaluation of individuals	Confirming individuals as human beings
A view of individuals as fixed	Seeing individuals as being in process
Resisting and fearing individual differences	Accepting and utilizing individual differences
Utilizing an individual primarily with reference to his/her job description	Viewing an individual as a whole person
Walling off the expression of feelings	Making possible both appropriate expression and effective use of feelings
Maskmanship and game playing	Authentic behavior
The use of status for maintaining power and personal prestige	The use of status for organizationally relevant purposes
Distrusting people	Trusting people
Avoiding facing others with relevant data	Making appropriate confrontation
Avoidance of risk taking	Willingness to risk
A view of process work as being unproductive effort	Seeing process work as being essential to effective task accomplishment
A primary emphasis on competition	A much greater emphasis on collaboration

Note. Adapted from Tannenbaum and Davis (1969).

with the values expressed by McGregor (1960) in his Theory Y assumptions.

The level of analysis is important here. Tannenbaum and Davis' OD values are operationalized at the individual (or group) level; Hofstede's dimensions grew out of an aggregate analysis at the organizational or even societal level. Although this, at first, would appear to pose a problem for the comparison of the two, in practice it does not.

The stated objective of OD interventions in general, according to Tannenbaum and Davis, is to institutionalize OD values in a group or organization. The greater the initial acceptance of these values by the individuals in the target group or organization, the easier the OD process will be and the greater the probability of ultimately institutionalizing these values, all other things being equal. Conversely, the lower the initial acceptance of these values by the target individuals, the greater will be the resistance to an OD effort and the lower the probability of its ultimate success.

Hofstede's dimensions were derived at the organization level and seem to have a reasonable representative validity of societal values and differences, as has been noted earlier. They therefore are indicators of the aggregate values of a society rather than direct measures of individually held values. Nevertheless, they are based on individual measures, and national scores reflect the aggregate orientations of a given national group. The underlying individual scores are generally assumed to be relatively homogeneous, and thus would be generally in line with the aggregate scores, except in the case of multicultural countries, such as those mentioned earlier. In any case, it should be reiterated here that the country names are being used for purposes of exposition so that before applying the results of this analysis in the field, one must verify the rankings on Hofstede's dimensions for the particular target group in question. Once this has been done, one then can proceed on the assumption that the greater the match between OD values and the score on Hofstede's dimensions for a specific cultural grouping, the greater the potential for acceptance and success of OD.

Although some of Tannenbaum and Davis' OD values cannot be related to one of Hofstede's dimensions, most can be. Overall, the present author would rate these values as follows on Hofstede's dimensions:

Power distance: Low
Uncertainty avoidance: Low
Masculinity: Low
Individualism: Medium

Low power distance is consistent with a number of key values expressed by Tannenbaum and Davis: "away from utilizing an individual primarily with reference to his job description toward viewing him as a whole person" (1969, p. 73); and "away from the use of status for maintaining power and prestige toward the use of status for organizationally relevant purposes" (1969, p. 75). A low or medium power distance often is necessary for persons at differing hierarchical levels to interact openly in order for problems to be resolved.

Low uncertainty avoidance also is very consistent with some of the values expressd by Tannenbaum and Davis: "away from avoiding facing others with relevant data toward making appropriate confrontation" (1969, p. 77) and "away from avoidance of risk taking toward willingness to risk" (1969, p. 78). A low uncertainty avoidance is necessary if problems are to be brought into the open and discussed. In common OD practice this is done even when a solution is far from certain.

Low masculinity is consistent with "making possible both appropriate expression and effective use" (1969, p. 73) of feelings. This is necessary for the OD practice of bringing feelings out to deal with them in the open in the solution of problems. Organizational problems often are associated with behaviors driven by the feelings of organization members.

Individualism is the only dimension in which a "nonextreme" (i.e., neither high nor low) ranking is consistent with OD values. High individualism would be inconsistent with an emphasis on collab-

oration. The high collectivism associated with traditional societies would be inconsistent with the acceptance of individual differences as espoused by OD practitioners. In OD practice, a balance must be struck so that organizational members can work together on the solution of problems but maintain their individuality so that their inputs are respected and can be utilized in the solution process.

OD Values and National Ratings

Hofstede found values in the United States as follows:

Power distance: Medium
Uncertainty avoidance: Low
Masculinity: High
Individualism: High

Somewhat surprisingly, these rankings hardly agree with those of general OD values. Absolute agreement is found only on the dimension of uncertainty avoidance. There is a large difference in masculinity, and there are somewhat smaller differences on the remaining two dimensions, individualism and power distance. With this perspective, one gains a heightened awareness of why OD may have had problems of acceptance and success, even in the United States (Porras & Berg, 1978).

A comparison of OD values and country rankings is presented in Table 2. Countries whose scores on all four of Hofstede's dimensions are in line with those just derived for OD values (i.e., near the median for individualism and on the low side of the median for all of the other dimensions) are classified as "hardly different." Countries whose scores on three of the dimensions are like OD values are classified "somewhat different." Within this classification, these countries are grouped by the one dimension on which the difference exists. In addition, if the difference is narrow, i.e., within 10 percent of the scale from the "border" which separates the particular ranking from the other half of the scale, this is indicated as being close, abbreviated "c" (e.g., the ranking for Finland on uncertainty avoidance is just above the median for all countries). Countries whose scores on Hof-

TABLE 2 Degree of Difference between OD Values and Country Rankings on Hofstede's Dimensions

Very different	*Somewhat different*	*Hardly different*
	on 1 dimension:	
On 3 or more dimensions:		
	Main difference	Denmark
Argentina (c-PD#, UA, MF)	on uncertainty	Norway
Belgium (PD, UA, MF, c-IC)	avoidance (UA):	
Brazil (PD, UA, c-MF)		
Chile (PD, UA, IC)	Finland (c-UA)	
Colombia (PD, UA, MF, IC)	Israel	
Greece (PD, UA, c-MF)		
Hong Kong (PD, MF, IC)		
Italy (c-PD, UA, MF, IC)		
Japan (PD, UA, MF)		
Mexico (PD, UA, MF, c-IC)	Main difference	
Pakistan (PD, UA, c-MF, IC)	on masculinity/	
Peru (PD, UA, IC)	femininity (MF):	
Philippines (PD, MF, c-IC)		
Portugal (PD, UA, c-IC)	Ireland	
Taiwan (PD, UA, IC)		
Thailand (PD, c-UA, IC)		
Venezuela (PD, UA, MF, IC)		
Yugoslavia (PD, UA, c-IC)	Main difference	
	on individualism/	
On 2 dimensions	collectivism (IC):	
Australia (MF, IC)	Netherlands (c-IC)	
Austria (UA, MF)		
Canada (c-MF, c-IC)		
France (PD, UA)		
Germany (UA, MF)		
Great Britain (MF, IC)		
India (PD, MF)		
Iran (PD, c-UA)		
New Zealand (MF, c-IC)		
Singapore (PD, IC)		
South Africa (c-PD, MF)		
Spain (PD, UA)		
Switzerland (c-UA, MF)		
Turkey (PD, UA)		
United States (MF, IC)		

Note. Difference means being on the other side of the median from the ranking of OD values on the specified dimension.
PD = power distance; UA = uncertainty avoidance; MF = masculinity/femininity; IC = individualism/collectivism.
# Means being close to the OD ranking on the dimension indicated after the letter ''c.''

stede's dimensions differ on two or more dimensions from those of OD values are classified as "very different." Within this category, countries are grouped as being different on two or different on three dimensions. Following each country name are the abbreviations of the dimensions on which the differences exist. Here again, "closeness" is indicated by a "c" where appropriate. Thus, for example, Italy is above the median for uncertainty avoidance (UA), masculinity (MF), power distance (PD), and individualism (IC), thus making it different from OD values on all four dimensions. Nevertheless, it is labeled as "close" on power distance (i.e., c-PD); its ranking is just above the median.

In reviewing all of the countries surveyed, one finds that few score exactly in line with OD values. Closest are the Scandinavian countries, Denmark, Norway, and Sweden, which are low (below the median) on power distance, uncertainty avoidance, and masculinity and medium (just above the median) on individualism. Thus, one might expect OD generally to be better accepted here than in the other countries studied.

Conversely, for a number of countries the scores on Hofstede's dimensions are polar opposites to those of OD values. In these countries, power distance, uncertainty avoidance, and masculinity would all be high and individualism would be extreme, either high or low (not medium). On the low individualism side, such countries are Colombia, Mexico, Pakistan, and Venezuela; and with high individualism they are Italy and Belgium. One would expect that OD would be most difficult to implement in these countries.

Examples of Cultural Barriers to OD

Some practical examples of cultural problems in the acceptance of OD are illustrated in a volume on OD failures (Mirvis & Berg, 1977). Steele (1977), drawing on his generally disappointing experiences with OD in the United Kingdom, concludes that some of the key assumptions underlying OD clash with British culture. The cultural factors in the UK that Steele found to undermine OD ef-

forts included a norm of avoidance of "unsuitable topics," a norm favoring security and stability versus the unknown resulting from "rocking the boat," a sense of fatalism, and a deeply rooted class structure that goes against the value of ownership of one's own personal space.

In Switzerland, Bennis (1977) was involved in an "autopsy" of the termination of a group development program at large international Swiss firm. Although many of the participants were sympathetic to the values of the training program, even though they were not "typically Swiss," the program was terminated by the company president after he sat in on one of the sessions. Bennis felt that the main reason for the cancellation of the program was its conflict with the president's values derived from his compulsory Swiss army training: "every organization has its hierarchy. . . . and authority needs enforcement" (1977, p. 204). In Japan, a North American consulting firm with which the author is familiar reports that it never does assertiveness training, even though it is carried out successfully elsewhere. The consultant feels that even though theoretically it could be carried out, it would make the Japanese individual a "deviant in his own society" and would thus be counterproductive. Indeed, assertive behavior would be in direct conflict with the combination of large power distance, strong uncertainty avoidance, high masculinity and low individualism found in Japan. Closer to the origins of OD, Crockett (1977) noted that McGregor's Theory Y assumptions were "not natural" at the U.S. State Department, and Steele (1977) found that OD was more readily accepted in Southern California than in New England, highlighting the role cultural differences play in determining OD's success or failure even in the United States.

Specific Interventions and Cultural Dimensions

An alternative and ultimately more practical approach to evaluating the applicability of OD in a particular culture, especially because OD's espoused general values hardly match those of its "birthplace," the United States, is to look at the individual interventions themselves. A starting point has been suggested by Hofstede (1980b) himself, who analyzed the values underlying management by objectives (MBO). Although sometimes not thought of as an OD intervention and not really growing out of the two original OD stems, MBO is included in most OD textbooks (French & Bell, 1978; Huse, 1980) as it fits with the general conception of OD as "planned organizational change."

Hofstede describes MBO as "perhaps the single most popular management technique 'made in the U.S.A.' "(1980b, p. 58), thus characterizing it as fitting the U.S. culture. Hofstede suggests that MBO presupposes the following underlying value orientations:

> That subordinates are sufficiently independent to negotiate meaningfully with the boss (not-too-large power distance).
> That both are willing to take risks (weak uncertainty avoidance).
> That performance is seen as important by both (high masculinity) (1980b, p. 58).

Thus, in Germany, which scores quite a bit higher on uncertainty avoidance, MBO has become management by joint goal setting, mitigating some of the risk and emphasizing the team approach, which is in line also with the lower individualism present in the German culture.

In France, MBO has generally run into problems (Trepo, 1973). The original DPO (Direction par Objectifs) became DPPO (Direction Participative par Objectifs) after the 1968 student revolts: "anything that fostered participation and decentralization was welcomed" (Trepo, 1973, p. 71). Nevertheless, the high power distance to which the French are accustomed from childhood ultimately has thwarted the successful utilization of MBO as a truly participative process. Trepo notes that the problem is not necessarily with MBO per se but its implementation by French managers. He describes examples of managers who are unaware that they are trying to exert control through the implementation of the objectives of MBO almost by fiat.

Another area directly addressed by Hofstede is what he calls the "humanization of work." This also is not one of the original stems of OD, but again is included in most OD textbooks. Hofstede contrasts the notion of job enrichment—the restructuring of individual jobs—which arose in the United States with the European, mainly Scandinavian, approach of restructuring tasks into group activities, as was done at Volvo. Hofstede attributes these differing approaches to the differences between the United States and Scandinavia on the masculinity/feminity dimension. In the more "masculine" United States, jobs are "masculinized," allowing for individual performance. In the more "feminine" Scandinavian countries, jobs are "feminized," allowing for the development of interpersonal relationships.

Most prominent among interventions growing out of the laboratory training stem of OD, is, of course, sensitivity training or T-groups. Although identified as one of the historical stems of OD by French and Bell, these groups were rapidly replaced in the United States by more focused "development groups," which were less interpersonally and more task-oriented (Blake, 1978). The interpersonal nature of the T-group is in line with a "feminine" orientation of allowing men to assume nurturing roles. One would expect T-groups to be successful only in cultures that are low on masculinity, have weak uncertainty avoidance, and are low on power distance. As has been pointed out, this is a relatively uncommon combination, found only in Scandinavia. In the United States, shifting the focus of groups to the task is more in accord with the masculine performance orientation.

An intervention with a broader target is the confrontation meeting (Beckhard, 1967). The confrontation meeting is a "classic" OD intervention in which the management of an organization meets for one day with an OD consultant to take a reading of organizational health and develop plans to deal with the problems that are discovered. Although the confrontation meeting is classified by French and Bell as a comprehensive intervention (i.e., targeting the whole organization), it still is based on group technology as it consists of a series of group meetings. These follow six steps: climate setting, information collecting, information sharing, priority setting and group action planning, immediate follow-up by top team, and progress review. For this intervention to succeed, it requires, above all, a low uncertainty avoidance, because a lot of unforseen data will be generated. Depending on the persons present, low power distance also may be necessary. Thus the confrontation meeting would be inappropriate in countries with a high uncertainty avoidance and high power distance, such as the Latin American and Mediterranean countries, as well as Belgium, Japan, Iran, Thailand, and Taiwan. The confrontation meeting is more likely to be successful in countries with low uncertainty avoidance and low power distance, such as the United States and Canada, the Scandinavian countries, the Netherlands, Great Britain and Ireland, and Australia and New Zealand.

The other "stem" of OD interventions, survey feedback, uses questionnaire data collected about employee attitudes and perceptions. These data are fed back to the employees and ultimately are discussed in a group situaiton. Survey feedback generates data that at first may be looked at in a dispassionate way without generating uncertainty or raising questions that overstep the boundaries of hierarchy. Thus, an evaluation of the data can proceed slowly and not reach sensitive issues very quickly, if at all. With survey feedback, one also has some control over the type of data generated— the consultant can decide which questions are asked. Therefore, depending on the degree of masculinity, the questions can be more or less task oriented. A culturally sensitive consultant can put together a questionnaire that generates data in such a way that a problem can be defined and discussed without upsetting the power relationships present. Thus, survey feedback can be an appropriate intervention even in those countries mentioned earlier with high uncertainty avoidance and high power distance.

Interventions for Problem Situations

It is possible for some dimensions to diverge greatly from OD values (i.e., uncertainty avoidance, power distance, and masculinity) and therefore become potentially threats to the successful practice of OD.

A high uncertainty avoidance among organization members can have a number of potential effects on the process of intervention for organizational change. Organization members, for example, will be reluctant to undertake any procedure whose outcome appears to be unpredictable. They will be hesitant to accept any intervention that cannot somehow be described in a straightforward fashion. They will tend to be unwilling to participate in any undertaking that might unleash conflict and aggression. Thus, the existence of high uncertainty avoidance suggests that OD interventions that unfold in a structured and controlled manner should be used.

The concept of depth intervention is a useful aid for the description of how interventions might successfully proceed when high uncertainty avoidance exists. Harrison (1970) defines depth as increasing to the extent that an intervention's target of change moves from the formal (organizational) system, to the informal (intra- and intergroup) system, to the self. The greater the depth of intervention, the more threatening, difficult, and costly it is to bring about changes successfully. High uncertainty avoidance would compound these problems.

Harrison as well as French and Bell (1978) have classified a number of interventions according to their depth, that is, target of change (see Table 3). These interventions range from job enrichment and MBO to T-groups and group psychotherapy. If uncertainty avoidance is high, the difficulty of achieving a particular depth of intervention is correspondingly high. In other words, the actual depth that can be successfully achieved is limited. Thus, for practical reasons (and all other things being equal), interventions at the top of Table 3 would be favored. In addition, the speed at which the depth is reached must be slowed, that is, the speed with which one moves from the top to the bottom in Table 3. Therefore one must be careful with respect to both the choice of interventions and the time one takes to carry it out.

The implications of a high power distance for OD interventions are fairly straightforward. Basically, the existence of a high power distance precludes a direct confrontation by organization

---

TABLE 3 Depth of Various Group and Organizational Interventions

Sample interventions (in order of increasing depth)	Intervention target(s)
Job enrichment	Formal system
Management by objectives	Formal system and informal system (role expectations)
Managerial grid (grid OD)	Formal system and informal system (intra- and intergroup interactions)
Survey feedback	Formal system and informal system (attitudes & feelings)
Team building	Informal system and formal system
T-groups	Informal system and self
Group psychotherapy	Self and informal system

Note. Based on Harrison (1970) and French and Bell (1978).

---

members across hierarchical levels. Thus, in such a situation it would be difficult to utilize interventions successfully if persons from different hierarchical levels must interact face to face in a group situation. Furthermore, whatever change that might occur would have to be viewed as one of two extremes, as originating from the top or as being a type of revolution in which those in power are "dethroned." (One of the correlates of high power distance is: "The way to change a social system is to dethrone those in power" Hofstede, 1980b, p. 46.) This severely limits the number of existing interventions that can be utilized.

High masculinity precludes the use of interventions in which participants must assume feminine nurturing roles and share their feelings openly. This rules out interventions that might be called "touchy feely," such as traditional T-groups, and favors interventions that are strictly task oriented and in which the logical link between the process and a successful outcome is apparent from the start.

Are there any existing OD interventions that could be utilized if a high uncertainty avoidance, a high power distance, and a high masculinity exist? This is the combination radically different from basic OD values and one found in several Latin and Asian countries. In such cases, it is best to use interventions in which direct confrontations can be avoided and data can be dealt with at arm's length, at least at first. Furthermore, the process should be relatively task oriented. Two types of interventions, if

employed in a culturally sensitive manner, come to mind here. The first, survey feedback, has been discussed. The other is the third party peacemaking intervention (Walton, 1969).

Third party peacemaking is essentially a form of the "shuttle diplomacy" that has been used with some success in the mediation of international disputes. It generally is employed when a crisis is at hand and great pressures exist for its resolution, and the parties involved generally are of equal status. In this case, although an attempt to resolve a conflict would create uncertainty, a great deal of uncertainty already exists and would actually be reduced with the introduction of a peacemaking effort. In addition, a high masculinity would contribute to pressure for a successful solution. Although it is not ideal to wait for conflict to break out before dealing with problems, it may be the only approach possible, given a situation of high uncertainty avoidance.

In an organizational setting, a skillful third party peacemaker can manage the uncertainty and keep the interaction "on track." If the consultant can become accepted by all parties as a legitimate go-between and carrier of information, then issues can be dealt with in such a way as to "save face." Furthermore, the consultant is the only one privy to both sides' information and therefore could manage the transfer of information in a manner minimizing the creation of uncertainty and keeping the emotional content down. Although these types of roles may run counter to the traditional OD consultant's value of openness as the ultimate goal, it may be a necessary cultural adjustment in certain societies.

Discussion and Conclusions

The foregoing analysis and discussion have illustrated the usefulness of looking at the values specific to a particular OD intervention when examining the applicability of OD for a given cultural configuration or national culture. This contingency approach has identified cultural areas in which most OD interventions would appear to be appropriate as well as other areas in which few existing OD interventions would seem to have a likelihood of success (Table 2). Furthermore, the framework presented allows an evaluation of the particular situation at hand as well as of individual OD interventions for an appropriate fit. It also provides some guidance as to the directions that appropriate modifications of existing interventions might take.

Nevertheless, there are a large number of cultural configurations, particularly in the developing world, that conflict with OD in general and with the values underlying most interventions in particular. Given this state of affairs, there is a need for a broader repertoire of interventions or approaches that can bring about necessary planned organizational change without running counter to accepted values in these areas. These new approaches to OD could either be skillful adaptations of existing interventions or new techniques that may be in partial conflict with traditional OD values.

Examples of Successful Adaptation of OD Overseas

One example of a unique application of an existing approach is provided by a consulting firm with which the author is familiar. This firm utilizes transactional analysis as the basis for its OD work. Its approach has been particularly successful in problem solving in family-owned firms in Latin America. Transactional analysis also has been reported to be successful by the aforementioned firm

in a variety of countries outside North America including Japan, India, Nigeria and Pakistan.

This experience in Latin America is not inconsistent with the findings of Bourgeois and Boltvinik (1981) in their analysis of the applicability of OD to that region. They pointed out that Latin Americans traditionally deal with conflict by "smoothing" or "pleasing" one's opposite number, rather than bringing a conflict into the open to deal with it, as would be suggested by traditional OD. This smoothing is in line with the high uncertainty avoidance and high power distance found in Latin America. To get around this problem, group interventions can focus on making members aware of the pleasing process and then getting them to understand and believe that one can also please or lend support to someone by bringing out negative facts about a situation so that problems can be resolved. This goal would be consistent with Latin America's relatively high masculinity and its associated performance orientation.

Indian experiences in the use of OD have been reported in several recent papers (Chattopadhyay & Pareek, 1984; Khandwalla, 1984). In summarizing the accumulated evidence, Khandwalla notes that despite the "alleged authoritarian and dependency prone managerial culture of India" (1984, p. 10) OD has found success there. He feels it perhaps is because of the "dysfunctionality of the traditional culture for contemporary Indian organizations" (1984, p. 10). This culture creates crises that result in situations more receptive to intervention. This experience fits with Indian scores on Hofstede's dimensions, particularly the weak uncertainty avoidance. On the other dimensions, India ranked as follows: large power distance, above the median on masculinity, and near the median on individualism/collectivism.

In the area of leadership and leadership training, an alternative and apparently effective model for India has been proposed by Sinha: the nurturant-task leader. A nurturant leader "cares for his subordinates, shows affection, takes personal interest in their well-being and above all is committed to their growth" (1980, p. 55). The effective leader, however, makes nurturance contingent on the subordinate's task accomplishment. Sinha (1984) contrasts this model to that underlying grid OD (Blake & Mouton, 1964): the "9,9" leader with a high concern for both task and people. Although the models are similar, the nurturant-task leader model allows for India's high power distance. Thus the concern for the subordinate expressed by the manager maintains the power distance by creating more of a dependent relationship as opposed to a participative or equal one. Sinha (1984) reports that this model has been applied with a great degree of success in India. Furthermore, in some cases it is used effectively as a transitional tool for moving towards a truly participative or "9,9" leadership style.

Guidelines for Adapting OD

If the underlying values of the societal culture and a particular OD intervention are in harmony, it does not mean, however, that an intervention can be applied without modification by someone who has little knowledge of that culture. The success of any intervention depends to a great extent on the skill of the OD practitioner. This means that the intervenor must have good general OD skills, in addition to being knowledgeable about the host culture.

Therefore, as part of the action planning process of any OD intervention, the following explicit steps are strongly recommended:

1. Evaluate the rankings of the dimensions of culture in the given situation.
2. Make a judgment as to which values are the most deeply held and unlikely to change.
3. Evaluate the "problem-appropriate" interventions' rankings on the dimensions of culture.
4. Choose the intervention that would clash least with the most rigidly held values.
5. Incorporate process modifications in the proposed intervention to fit with the given cultural situation.

It should be pointed out here that this procedure and the preceding discussion assume that national culture is something profoundly rooted in the individual and collective consciousness and is thus most difficult to change. This is in line with the view held by most anthropologists and is clear when one takes another look at Schein's (1981) three levels of culture. Therefore, although OD is often defined as a process of change in an organizaton's culture, one should not presume that an OD intervention can easily have a real and lasting impact on widely held nationl cultural values.

Practitioners of OD are exhorted to be thoroughly familiar with the culture in which they are operating, and to evaluate interventions to guard against fundamental conflicts between the intervention technology and its underlying values, and a societal culture. In doing this, in addition to the analysis of problem/process fit, they must introduce a new step in the OD process: namely, the analysis of process/culture fit. Within this context, practitioners are encouraged, on the one hand, to take great care in the analysis and selection of intervention techniques and, on the other hand, to be bold and innovative in the search for new intervention technologies appropriate to the culture in which they will be operating.

References

Adler, N. J. (1983) Cross-cultural management research: The ostrich and the trend. *Academy of Management Review,* 8, 226–232.

Beckhard, R. (1967) The confrontation meeting. *Harvard Business Review,* 45(2), 149–155.

Beckhard, R. (1969) *Organization development: Strategies and models.* Reading, MA: Addison-Wesley.

Bennis, W. (1977) Bureaucracy and social change: An anatomy of a training failure. In P. H. Mirvis & D. N. Berg (Eds.), *Failures in organization development and change: Cases and essays for learning* (pp. 191–215). New York: Wiley.

Blake, R. (1978) Personal correspondence with W. L. French and C. H. Bell, Jr. Cited in W. H. French & C. H. Bell, Jr., *Organization development: Behavioral science interventions for organization improvement* (2nd ed., p. 28). Englewood Cliffs, NJ: Prentice Hall.

Blake, R. R., & Mouton, J. S. (1964) *The managerial grid.* Houston, TX: Gulf Publishing.

Bourgeois, L. J. III, & Boltvinik, M. (1981) OD in cross-cultural settings: Latin America. *California Management Review, 23*(3), 75–81.

Chattopadhyay, S., & Pareek, U. (1984) Organization development in a voluntary organization. *International Studies of Management and Organization, 14*(2-3), 46–85.

Crockett, W. (1977) Introducing change to a government agency. In P. H. Mirvis & D. N. Berg (Eds.), *Failures in organization development and change: Cases and essays for learning* (pp. 117–147). New York: Wiley.

French, W. L., & Bell, C. H., Jr. (1978) *Organization development: Behavioral science interventions for organization improvement* (2nd ed.). Englewood Cliffs, NJ: Prentice Hall.

Haire, M., Ghiselli, E. E., & Porter, L. W. (1966) *Managerial thinking: An international study.* New York: Wiley.

Harrison, R. (1970) Choosing the depth of organizational intervention. *Journal of Applied Behavioral Science, 6,* 181–202.

Hofstede, G. (1980a) *Culture's consequences.* Beverly Hills, CA: Sage.

Hofstede, G. (1980b) Motivation, leadership, and organization: Do American theories apply abroad? *Organizational Dynamics, 9*(1), 42–62.

Hunt, J. W. (1981) Applying American behavioral science: Some cross-cultural implications. *Organizational Dynamics, 10*(1), 55-62.

Huse, E. F. (1980) *Organization development and change* (2nd ed.). St. Paul, MN: West.

Jaeger, A. M. (1983) The transfer of organizational culture overseas: An approach to control in the multinational corporation. *Journal of International Business Studies, 14*(2), 91–114.

Keesing, R. (1974) Theories of culture. *Annual Review of Anthropology, 3,* 73–97.

Khandwalla, P. N. (1984) Preface, Indian studies on organizational effectiveness. *International Studies of Management and Organizations, 14*(2-3), 3–29.

Kluckhohn, F., & Strodtbeck, F. (1961) *Variations in value orientations.* New York: Harper & Row.

Laurent, A. (1983) The cultural diversity of western conceptions of management. *International Studies of Management and Organization, 13*(1-2), 75–96.

McGregor, D. (1960) *The human side of enterprise.* New York: McGraw-Hill.

Mirvis, P. H., & Berg, D. N. (1977) *Failures in organization development and changes: Cases and essays for learning.* New York: Wiley.

Pelto, P. J. (1968) The difference between tight and loose societies. *Transaction, 5*(5), 37–40.

Porras, J. I., & Berg, P. O. (1978) The impact of organization development. *Academy of Management Review, 3,* 249–266.

Schein, E. H. (1981) SMR forum: Does Japanese management style have a message for American managers? *Sloan Management Review, 23*(1), 55–68.

Sinha, J. B. P. (1980) *The nurturant task leader.* New Delhi: Concept Publishing House.

Sinha, J. B. P. (1984) A model of effective leadership styles in India. *International Studies of Management and Organization, 14*(2-3), 86–98.

Steele, F. (1977) Is culture hostile to organization development? The UK example. In P. H. Mirvis & D. N. Berg (Eds.), *Failures in organizaton development and change: Cases and essays for learning* (pp. 23–31). New York: Wiley.

Tannenbaum, R., & Davis, S. A (1969) Values, man and organizations. *Industrial Management Review, 10*(2), 67–83.

Trepo, G. (1973, Autumn) Management style á la francaise. *European Business, 39,* 71–79.

Triandis, H. C. (1982) Review of culture's consequences: International differences in work-related values. *Human Organization, 41,* 86–90.

Walton, R. (1969) Interpersonal peacemaking: Confrontations and third-party consultation. Reading, MA: Addison-Wesley.

Reading 66

ORGANIZATION DEVELOPMENT, YOU, AND THE FUTURE

W. Warner Burke

The following article is an edited version of the keynote address by Warner Burke at the OD Network Conference in Washington, D.C. on November 2, 1985. In celebration of the 20th anniversary of the OD Network, Warner reflects on the past and present states of organization development and reports on what his personal crystal ball has to say about the future of our practice. We have attempted to edit the presentation in a manner that provides an understandable reading and yet retains some of Warner's spontaneity on that joyous occasion.

Before reading the article, it is recommended that you complete the knowledge assessment questionnaire on the following page.

This instrument is an excerpt from a larger 50-item questionnaire that I constructed as an assessment tool for practitioners to determine where they are with respect to the knowledge and skill base of organization development. As explained in a recent issue of the *Organization Development Journal*, this particular questionnaire was validated by selecting a number of highly experienced and competent people in our field and asking them to give me what they thought were the correct answers to the questions.

What I have to say today is organized into three parts: past, present, and future. Each of these categories is further subdivided into two subcategories: good news and bad news. This "uncommonly creative" format is my way of practicing the "KISS" principle, which is no reflection on you. It is simply my way of trying to keep up with what I want to say.

Source: W. Warner Burke, reprinted with permission of the *OD Practitioner*, March 1985, pp. 1–7.

As a way of involving you along the way with me, I would appreciate your completing the 12-item questionnaire.

The Past

Let's start now with the past, but I'd like to hold off for just a minute with the good news/bad news portion. Instead, I want to begin by talking about the OD Network for just a moment since we are involved in a 20-year celebration here.

The Birth of the ODN

One summer in Bethel, Maine, over 20 years ago, a small group which included people such as Herb Shepard, Shel Davis, and Sy Levy got together and decided to form an organization to be called the "Industrial Trainers Network." That was the original name of the OD Network. Jerry Harvey, who was then with the National Training Laboratories (NTL), was asked to be the coordinator/secretary. The first meeting of the group was in Estes Park, Colorado. I joined NTL in 1966, and the first meeting that I attended was in Midland, Michigan—of all places! There were about 40 people at that meeting, including the top management of Dow Chemical. The Dow Chemical group was participating in a panel discussion, and I was impressed with what was going on at the time. Little did I know that particular organization was manufacturing napalm—which shook me up a bit later on as the events of history unfolded. Anyway, while at that meeting, Jerry asked me to assume responsibility for coordinating the group's activities. At the next meeting, which was held at Punderson State Park outside Cleveland, Ohio, I told the group that I wanted to become Executive Director so I could provide more leadership and not just be a coordinator. That was done with their consent, as well as the changing of the group's name to the "OD Network." I had no idea at that time that the ODN would become what it is today.

Good News/Bad News

Now about the field of OD itself. I'll start with the bad news. As I look back at the changes (or lack thereof) over the years, three items are worthy of note. First, as the field has progressed, practitioners have tended to become more and more specialized. That is not necessarily bad news since specialization is a trend that is natural for any kind of field or discipline or profession. My concern is that we not lose generalists in our field, people who have a broad understanding of what this field is all about. It happens all the time, but we ought to know better and not let it happen to the degree that the group becomes segmented.

Second, despite this degree of specialization over the years, there has not been a great deal of new things to specialize in. We still do a lot of team building—and there's nothing wrong with that in itself. It's just that there have been very few advances in our social technology. We need more creativity in this area.

In terms of lack of change over the years, reward systems are the third point I consider as bad news. Reward systems to me are probably the key leverage for change in organizations. And yet, they are about the same today as they have been for the past 20 years. That's not good news. This situation persists despite the fact that Ed Lawler has written a super book on the subject, *Pay and Organization Development*. This book leads the way, but the field and our client organizations have not adapted very much. Rewards and power are two essential levers for change, and we clearly need to know more about how to change reward systems.

Now for the good news with respect to the past. *First,* this is no longer a man's field. The change began approximately ten years ago at an ODN meeting in Chicago. We had this panel of men up on the stage, and all were delivering their words of expertise and wisdom to close out the meeting. All of a sudden a woman jumped up and said that she didn't like what was happening, and didn't like the fact that the meeting was designed, conducted, etc. all by men, along with a few other words for us. Well, a few of us went to the men's room and stayed there and tried to figure out what in the hell was going on. That was the beginning of a major change; the OD Network has never been the same since. We're now well on the way toward women being an integral part of our field in a very significant way. Equal in all respects.

A *second* good news change is that quality control circles have taken hold and grown. This kind of technology is our bailiwick, and growth in such areas is certainly good news. An article to appear soon in *Organizational Dynamics* traces that technology in terms of plusses and minuses.

A *third* significant change emanating from our past is that participative forms of management are more accepted now and are proliferating. I'll have more to say on that in a moment.

A *fourth* change that represents good news from our past is that we're better now at organizational diagnosis than we used to be. The cry and hue of years ago was that we would enter an organization and try to change things without understanding what we were trying to change. Our technology in this area, and our understanding of it, are much better today. At the same time we are also beginning to face up to power and politics. That's not to say that we're totally proficient in these areas, but at least now we recognize their significance and have begun to face up to them in a useful way.

Now for the questionnaire. I have classified four items as most closely associated with our history:

- Item 1: Although organization development means many things to different people, it is most closely identified with (c) change. And that's how it has been defined by Dick Beckhard (1969), for example: planned change managed from the top.
- Item 3: Of the many values associated with organization development, (b) humanistic

Assessment Questionnaire for Knowledge and Understanding of Organization Development

By W. Warner Burke

1. While organization development may mean any of the following, it is most closely identified with:

   a) Management improvement.
   b) Growth.
   c) Change.
   d) Decentralization.

2. Which of the following depicts best a fundamental principle of human behavior on which OD is based?

   a) Organizational performance improves as individual employee autonomy increases.
   b) Involvement in decision making leads to commitment.
   c) Humanization of work increases productivity.
   d) Decentralization relates positively with organizational performance.

3. Which of the following values is most closely associated with organization development?

   a) Power decentralization.
   b) Humanistic treatment of organizational members.
   c) Racial and sexual equality in the workplace.
   d) Career development is a right of employment.

4. The concept which describes best the OD consultant's approach is:

   a) Systems analysis.
   b) Social change.
   c) Socio-technical.
   d) Action research.

5. While a variety of methods for collecting information are used by OD practitioners, the most popular one is:

   a) Questionnaire.
   b) Interview.
   c) Survey.
   d) The annual report.

6. Which of the following aspects of an organization is the OD practitioner likely to consider most?

   a) Organizational chart.
   b) Human resource development system.
   c) Informal organization.
   d) Intergroup relations.

7. In diagnosing organizations, OD consultants usually pay close attention to norms, those standards of conduct to which organizational members conform or from which they deviate to some degree. The primary reason for such close attention to norms is that they:

   a) Represent very clearly formal organizational patterns.
   b) Provide significant leverage for change.
   c) Reveal most clearly deviant behavior in the organization.
   d) Reflect the managerial hierarchy.

8. Which of the following sets of skills most clearly distinguishes OD consultants from other (e.g., management) consultants?

   a) Organizational diagnosis.
   b) Interviewing.
   c) Process consultation.
   d) Analytical.

9. From an ethical perspective, a risk of OD consultation is that:

a) Workers will control the organization more than the managers.
b) Issues and problems will surface and be discussed; that is, catharsis will have occurred, and then management will do what they intended in the first place, or will not do anything.
c) Productivity is likely, at least temporarily, to take a dip before it increases.
d) The client may feel that the cost-benefit ratio for the amount of energy and effort required is too imbalanced, i.e., too costly.

10. In working with a client, you have jointly concluded from your organizational diagnosis of a computer programming department that some form of job redesign or job enrichment would be a beneficial intervention. You realize, however, that even though you are an experienced consultant, you have had practically no experience in the area of job redesign. The best action for you to take under the circumstances is to:

a) Delay the intevention slightly to give yourself a chance to study and prepare more adequately.

b) Rely on the client to implement the intervention.
c) Suggest that another more experienced consultant be brought in to help with this phase of the change effort.
d) Tell the client to replace you with another consultant.

11. Highly successful organizations in the private sector are likely to be those that:

a) Have complex organizational structures.
b) Are value-driven.
c) Consistently compensate their employees in the top quartile of their respective industry groups.
d) Have highly efficient sub-systems (departments, division, etc.).

12. One clear indication that an OD effort is progressing according to principles that underlie the field is that:

a) The reward system becomes more individualized.
b) Managers hold more group meetings.
c) Organizational members express their feelings more often.
d) Organizational members feel more in control of their destiny.

---

treatment of organizational members is what most experts in OD view as the most relevant.

- Item 12: The answer to this one is (d). When organizational members begin to feel more in control of their destiny, it is a clear indication that an OD effort is progressing according to principles that underlie the field. (This item relates quite obviously with Item 2. This is a value from the past. It concerns the empowerment of people by giving them more control. Are we still true believers about this value from the past?)

- Item 5: The final item dealing with the past— While a variety of methods for collecting in-

formation are used by OD practitioners, the most popular one is (b) interview. I suspect, however, that in the future this answer may change because questionnaires are being used more and more as the primary mode of collecting data.

The Present

Bad News

As I think about the present, four things are disturbing me. *One* is that there seems to me to be a strong preoccupation with one's career in organization development with comparatively less concern with the field or with the changing of an organization over a time frame required for significant change to occur.

The *second* is a continuing trend from the past. There is an apparent increase in specialization, but we must also have *generalists*. Also, I am concerned about the potential divisiveness of other kinds of segmentation that can occur besides specialization. An example is the growth of OT, or organization transformation. On the plus side, it represents energy. On the other hand, I worry about its potential divisive effect on the OD Network. OT and OD—I really don't see the difference. To me, organization development has always been a process of cultural change, which really means transforming the organization.

Number *three,* I think we're long on facilitation, and short on prescription and implementation. Strategic management consulting firms are in trouble nowadays. Why? Because top-level managers in major corporations are finding that the consulting firms do a good job of diagnosing what is wrong with their strategy and perhaps suggesting new markets to enter, etc., but then fail to help them *implement* those strategies. We have an opportunity to fill that implementation gap by helping them to manage change. But filling that gap means more than just facilitation. It is time for us to be something beyond facilitators. Although facilitation is still our *raison d'etre,* we must begin to move more into the area of prescription. Increasingly, we must begin telling managers from an authoritative base what we think is the right way to do things, especially in the areas of change management, reward systems, etc. It is time for us to use our expertise in *content* as well as *process.*

The *fourth* bit of bad news is that we, like managers in America, are too short-term oriented. We rely too heavily on *events* to make a difference, when in reality the organizational flow is overwhelming, too powerful. It's like believing that a top management off-site meeting or a major structural change, or turnover at the top is really going to make a difference. These kinds of events sometimes, but rarely, make a *significant* difference. It

is far more important, however, for us to understand and attempt to change the flow, the pattern of activities, the routine that occurs in *between* these events. We must concentrate on such things as the organization's reward systems and performance appraisal systems—those flowing parts of the organization that are routinized and demotivating. That's where our work is.

The first bit of good news about the present is that we're alive and well! Our services are still in demand . . . and even paid for. Twenty years is *not* a very long time, but there just may be a trend here!

Next is that Peters and Waterman (from a McKinsey base, of all places) have opened up new doors for us. Clients now use the term "culture" even before I do. Further, it's not only okay, it's even accepted and legitimate to talk about values. Which brings us to Item 11 on the questionnaire. Hopefully you answered that highly successful organizations in the private sector are likely to be those that are (b) value driven.

The third good news item is that quality control circles have caught on, and participative management is finally in vogue. The following is a quote from a recent study (Report No. 849) conducted by the Conference Board which does research for mainstream, traditional American corporations:

A rising number of major American companies are dramatically changing the way they manage both work and workers in an attempt to make their firms more competitive. . . . Focusing on 52 "pace-setting" companies, the study finds virtually all these programs aimed at increasing productivity and boosting product quality by enabling workers to participate more directly in the management of their work and the overall goals of their companies. The report sees this movement as led by "change agents" who are typically human resources and organizational development types as well as engineers and managers of quality control. Techniques include: job redesign, problem-solving groups, autonomous work teams and productivity-sharing programs. Many firms use labor-management cooperative efforts. Some use "greenfield plants" which involve the building of facilities outside urban areas and carefully selecting workers for their ability to function as team members. (ASTD National Report, Oct. 19, 1984)

These words indicate that we're participating in a trend, and that's good news as far as I'm concerned.

Now let's see how well you did on the remaining questionnaire items pertaining to the present:

- Item 4: If you ever read the first textbook on OD written by French and Bell, you probably knew that the concept which describes best the OD consultant's approach is (d) action research.
- Item 6: Which of the following aspects of an organization is the OD practitioner likely to consider most? The experts say (c) informal organization. Why is the "informal" important? It's the primary reflection of power and politics in an organization.
- Item 7: Closely related to the last item is the one which asks for the primary reason for close attention to norms. The answer is (b) because they provide significant leverage for change—especially around the power and politics dimensions.

The Future

I see no bad news in the future—only opportunities!

More Politicizing of Organizations

One opportunity is that organizations will probably become even more political than they are now as a function of three variables highlighted by Jeffrey Pfeffer: (a) scarcity of resources, (b) work-force heterogeneity, and (c) the erosion of organizational authority—at least in its strict top-down hierarchical form.

Should the further politicization of organizations become a reality in the future, I believe that it will have several implications for our field. Certainly it will require that we become even more sophisticated with respect to diagnosis such as placing a greater emphasis on models, cognitive maps, conceptual frameworks, etc.

Another implication is that we will have to become more rigorous in our methodology, especially

data analysis. We now have at our disposal highly sophisticated, computer-based methods of statistical analysis. Those of us that want to stay on the leading edge of OD are going to have to learn how to use these tools.

Finally, a more politicized environment will require that we become as polished as possible in our presentation of self. Other kinds of things—meaning wearing tennis shoes (to reinforce our independence) to a presentation for top management—must not be allowed to get in the way of what we're trying to do.

The Nature of Work

Future . . . No doubt you've noticed that the nature of work is changing. I have two important points to make. The *first* is that we are now more concerned than ever with productivity and quality, and that will be even more true in the future. Bear in mind that you do NOT increase productivity or improve quality by *trying* to increase productivity and by *trying* to improve quality. Why? Because productivity and quality are outcomes, effects, consequences—i.e., something *causes* them to happen. This point is important because it is our job to find and to work on the causes, the mitigating factors. That is how improvements in outcomes such as productivity and quality are brought about.

The *second* point about the nature of work in the future is that work will become even more mental and less physical. Not long ago I heard a sixty year old man comment that it was hard for him to comprehend how young people coming off an eight-hour job could then go play squash. He remarked that "When I used to work fulltime, I'd come home at the end of the day totally exhausted." The difference, of course, is that now work is much more mental. A related area of interests is the effect of computers and computer-driven machines on people. There is much to learn yet about high technology and its effect on behavior.

Now for the remaining items on the questionnaire. The first two items are not necessarily future or past or present. They're timeless.

- Item 2: This is concerned with what is perhaps our basic premise of human behavior, at least for purposes of organization development—that (b) involvement in decision-making leads to commitment.
- Item 8: And this one addresses our most important product and perhaps our only unique skill, which is (c) process consultation.
- Item 10: Although many people are attracted to response (a)—i.e., "give me a little time to learn this stuff so I don't lose the contract"—over 80% of the experts agreed that when the appropriate intervention called for is one with which you have had no experience, one should (c) suggest that another more experienced consultant be brought in to help with this phase of the change effort.

Issues and Dilemmas

Items 9 and 12 will lead us to the final point I want to make:

- Item 9: This item is concerned with the ethical risk of OD consultation: that (b) issues and problems will be surfaced and discussed, that is, catharsis will have occurred, and then management will do what they intended in the first place, or will not do anything.
- Item 12: As already mentioned, the answer to this item is (d)—i.e., a clear indication that the OD effort is progressing according to principles that underlie the field is that organizational members feel more in control of their destiny.

With these two items as a backdrop, consider some of the following issues pertinent to our profession. The first is that organizations are incredibly difficult to change. For purposes of OD, it is not enough for people to *feel* better. Some things must be *different* than before; different with respect to goals, to responsibilities and roles, to ways of doing things, or to ways that organizational members relate. Something must *change*.

The second is that organizations are by their very nature highly political. Despite my lengthy involvement in this field, I still continue to be surprised (in my naive way) at what self-interest will cause people to do in organizations.

The third issue is that organizations are absurd. They're irrational. They're overcontrolling. Some people may not agree, but here's a recent example. I have a colleague and good friend whose wife assumed the traditional role of housewife and mother for many years. The children finally left the nest, and she went back to school and earned a law degree. About a month ago she took a job as a lawyer in a large bureaucratic organization. On several occasions since, she has come home at night and said, "You wouldn't believe what happened today!" and then went on to recount the crazy things that occurred that day. My friend's consistent response: "Sounds normal to me." He's not belittling her. It's just that he's had a lot of experience in our field, and he's come to understand that organizations are for the most part crazy. They aren't rational at all.

So these are some of the issues. While still on that subject, maybe a comment or two about us as persons would be appropriate. Most OD consultants have greater needs for power than other people do. If you don't believe that, ask your closest friends how they see you. And then when they tell you, watch your reaction: you will first deny it, then get angry, then reject it, and then *maybe* you will finally accept that your needs for power are higher than most.

Yet, we are also value-driven regarding the humane treatment of people in organizations. We espouse and believe strongly in individual growth and development. This is evidenced by the responses that OD practitioners select on the questionnaire. Of the eight theories that form the basis for the questionnaire the one theory set that is still the most popular for OD practitioners after all these years is Herzberg/Maslow. Skinner is rising in popularity, but has not yet overtaken the leader. Therein lies the dilemma. We're interested in power, we like to influence, and yet we cherish those humane kinds of values.

So, we want to influence, to change, to transform organizations, society and even international relations. There seems to be no end to our fantasy of how we can use our power. Still, in the face of Indira Ghandi's assassination, growing world terrorism, and the absurdity and the difficulty of changing organizations, we may feel despair, powerless and futile. I know I do at times.

Yet, the power and the values we hold are our strengths. Organizational change is the exercise of power, and our values say that exercise of power should be primarily by way of empowering others. Therein is a kind of paradox, a kind of dilemma— but therein also lies the answer. If we make every effort to empower people, which in turn empowers the organization and makes it more effective, then we're doing our job. Empowering people . . . certainly we have the skills. What we need to do now is to go forth and make it happen.

SUGGESTED ADDITIONAL READINGS FOR PART 10

Ackerman, Linda S. "Development, Transition or Transformation: The Question of Change in Organizations." *OD Practitioner,* December 1986, pp. 1–8.

Adams, John D., ed. *Transforming Work*. Alexandria, Va.: Miles River Press, 1984.

Argyris, Chris. *Strategy, Change, and Defensive Routines*. Boston: Pitman, 1985.

Benne, Kenneth D. "Some Ethical Problems in Group and Organizational Consultation." *Journal of Social Issues* 15, 1959, pp. 60–67.

Burke, W. Warner. "Who is the Client? A Different Perspective." *OD Practitioner,* June 1982, pp. 1–6.

Burke, W. Warner, and Leonard D. Goodstein, eds. *Trends and Issues in OD*. LaJolla: University Associates, 1980.

Desreumaux, A. "OD Practices in France: Part II." *Leadership & Organization Development Journal* 7, no. 1 (1986), pp. 10–14.

Gellerman, William, "Values and Ethical Issues for Human Systems Development Practitioners." In Robert Tannenbaum et al., *Human Systems Development*. San Francisco: Jossey-Bass, 1985, pp. 393–418.

Janis, Irving L. *Victims of Group Think*. Boston: Houghton Mifflin, 1972.

Kanter, Rossabeth Moss. *The Change Masters*. New York: Simon & Schuster, 1983.

Kilmann, Ralph. *Beyond the Quick Fix*. San Francisco: Jossey-Bass, 1984.

Mirvis, Phillip H., and David N. Berg, eds. *Failures in Organization Development and Change*. New York: John Wiley & Sons, 1977.

Schein, Edgar. *Organizational Culture and Leadership*. San Francisco: Jossey-Bass, 1985.

Neilson, E. *Becoming an OD Practitioner*. Englewood Cliffs, N. J.: Prentice-Hall, 1984.

Raia, Anthony P., and Newton Margulies. "Organizational Development: Issues, Trends, and Prospects." In Robert Tannenbaum et al., *Human Systems Development*. San Franciso: Jossey-Bass, 1985.

Rogers, Carl R., and B. F. Skinner. "Some Issues Concerning the Control of Human Behavior: A Symposium." *Science* 124, no. 3231 (1956), pp. 1057–66.

Sashkin, Marshall. "Organization Development Practices." *Professional Psychology*. 4 (1973), pp. 187–94.

Sashkin, Marshall. "Participative Management Remains and Ethical Imperative." *Organizational Dynamics*. Spring 1986, pp. 62–75.

Tannenbaum, Robert, and Sheldon Davis. "Values, Man, and Organizations," *Industrial Management Review* 10 (1969), pp. 67–83.

Tannenbaum, Robert; Newton Margulies; and Fred Massarick and associates, *Human Systems Development*. San Francisco: Jossey-Bass, 1985.

Tichy, N. M. "Agents of Planned Social Change: Congruence of Values, Cognitions, and Actions." *Administrative Science Quarterly,* June 1974, pp. 164–82.

Warrick, D. D., ed. *Contemporary Organization Development: Current Thinking and Applications*. Glenview, Ill.: Scott, Foresman & Co., 1985.